Lecture Notes in Computer Science   11132

Commenced Publication in 1973
Founding and Former Series Editors:
Gerhard Goos, Juris Hartmanis, and Jan van Leeuwen

More information about this series at http://www.springer.com/series/7412

Laura Leal-Taixé · Stefan Roth (Eds.)

Computer Vision – ECCV 2018 Workshops

Munich, Germany, September 8–14, 2018
Proceedings, Part IV

Springer

Editors
Laura Leal-Taixé
Technical University of Munich
Garching, Germany

Stefan Roth 🆔
Technische Universität Darmstadt
Darmstadt, Germany

ISSN 0302-9743   ISSN 1611-3349   (electronic)
Lecture Notes in Computer Science
ISBN 978-3-030-11017-8   ISBN 978-3-030-11018-5   (eBook)
https://doi.org/10.1007/978-3-030-11018-5

Library of Congress Control Number: 2018966826

LNCS Sublibrary: SL6 – Image Processing, Computer Vision, Pattern Recognition, and Graphics

This Springer imprint is published by the registered company Springer Nature Switzerland AG
The registered company address is: Gewerbestrasse 11, 6330 Cham, Switzerland

Foreword

It was our great pleasure to host the European Conference on Computer Vision 2018 in Munich, Germany. This constituted by far the largest ECCV event ever. With close to 2,900 registered participants and another 600 on the waiting list one month before the conference, participation more than doubled since the last ECCV in Amsterdam. We believe that this is due to a dramatic growth of the computer vision community combined with the popularity of Munich as a major European hub of culture, science, and industry. The conference took place in the heart of Munich in the concert hall Gasteig with workshops and tutorials held on the downtown campus of the Technical University of Munich.

One of the major innovations for ECCV 2018 was the free perpetual availability of all conference and workshop papers, which is often referred to as open access. We note that this is not precisely the same use of the term as in the Budapest declaration. Since 2013, CVPR and ICCV have had their papers hosted by the Computer Vision Foundation (CVF), in parallel with the IEEE Xplore version. This has proved highly beneficial to the computer vision community.

We are delighted to announce that for ECCV 2018 a very similar arrangement was put in place with the cooperation of Springer. In particular, the author's final version will be freely available in perpetuity on a CVF page, while SpringerLink will continue to host a version with further improvements, such as activating reference links and including video. We believe that this will give readers the best of both worlds; researchers who are focused on the technical content will have a freely available version in an easily accessible place, while subscribers to SpringerLink will continue to have the additional benefits that this provides. We thank Alfred Hofmann from Springer for helping to negotiate this agreement, which we expect will continue for future versions of ECCV.

September 2018

Horst Bischof
Daniel Cremers
Bernt Schiele
Ramin Zabih

Preface

It is our great pleasure to present these workshop proceedings of the 15th European Conference on Computer Vision, which was held during September 8–14, 2018, in Munich, Germany. We are delighted that the main conference of ECCV 2018 was accompanied by 43 scientific workshops. The ECCV workshop proceedings contain contributions of 36 workshops.

We received 74 workshop proposals on a broad set of topics related to computer vision. The very high quality and the large number of proposals made the selection process rather challenging. Owing to space restrictions, only 46 proposals were accepted, among which six proposals were merged into three workshops because of overlapping themes.

The final set of 43 workshops complemented the main conference program well. The workshop topics presented a good orchestration of new trends and traditional issues, built bridges into neighboring fields, as well as discussed fundamental technologies and novel applications. We would like to thank all the workshop organizers for their unreserved efforts to make the workshop sessions a great success.

September 2018

Stefan Roth
Laura Leal-Taixé

Organization

General Chairs

Horst Bischof — Graz University of Technology, Austria
Daniel Cremers — Technical University of Munich, Germany
Bernt Schiele — Saarland University, Max Planck Institute for Informatics, Germany
Ramin Zabih — CornellNYCTech, USA

Program Chairs

Vittorio Ferrari — University of Edinburgh, UK
Martial Hebert — Carnegie Mellon University, USA
Cristian Sminchisescu — Lund University, Sweden
Yair Weiss — Hebrew University, Israel

Local Arrangement Chairs

Björn Menze — Technical University of Munich, Germany
Matthias Niessner — Technical University of Munich, Germany

Workshop Chairs

Stefan Roth — Technische Universität Darmstadt, Germany
Laura Leal-Taixé — Technical University of Munich, Germany

Tutorial Chairs

Michael Bronstein — Università della Svizzera Italiana, Switzerland
Laura Leal-Taixé — Technical University of Munich, Germany

Website Chair

Friedrich Fraundorfer — Graz University of Technology, Austria

Demo Chairs

Federico Tombari — Technical University of Munich, Germany
Joerg Stueckler — Technical University of Munich, Germany

Publicity Chair

Giovanni Maria   University of Catania, Italy
  Farinella

Industrial Liaison Chairs

Florent Perronnin   Naver Labs, France
Yunchao Gong   Snap, USA
Helmut Grabner   Logitech, Switzerland

Finance Chair

Gerard Medioni   Amazon, University of Southern California, USA

Publication Chairs

Albert Ali Salah   Boğaziçi University, Turkey
Hamdi Dibeklioğlu   Bilkent University, Turkey
Anton Milan   Amazon, Germany

Workshop Organizers

W01 – The Visual Object Tracking Challenge Workshop

Matej Kristan   University of Ljubljana, Slovenia
Aleš Leonardis   University of Birmingham, UK
Jiří Matas   Czech Technical University in Prague, Czechia
Michael Felsberg   Linköping University, Sweden
Roman Pflugfelder   Austrian Institute of Technology, Austria

W02 – 6th Workshop on Computer Vision for Road Scene Understanding and Autonomous Driving

Mathieu Salzmann   EPFL, Switzerland
José Alvarez   NVIDIA, USA
Lars Petersson   Data61 CSIRO, Australia
Fredrik Kahl   Chalmers University of Technology, Sweden
Bart Nabbe   Aurora, USA

W03 – 3D Reconstruction in the Wild

Akihiro Sugimoto   The National Institute of Informatics (NII), Japan
Tomas Pajdla   Czech Technical University in Prague, Czechia
Takeshi Masuda   The National Institute of Advanced Industrial Science
                          and Technology (AIST), Japan
Shohei Nobuhara   Kyoto University, Japan
Hiroshi Kawasaki   Kyushu University, Japan

W04 – Workshop on Visual Learning and Embodied Agents in Simulation Environments

Peter Anderson	Georgia Institute of Technology, USA
Manolis Savva	Facebook AI Research and Simon Fraser University, USA
Angel X. Chang	Eloquent Labs and Simon Fraser University, USA
Saurabh Gupta	University of California, Berkeley, USA
Amir R. Zamir	Stanford University and University of California, Berkeley, USA
Stefan Lee	Georgia Institute of Technology, USA
Samyak Datta	Georgia Institute of Technology, USA
Li Yi	Stanford University, USA
Hao Su	University of California, San Diego, USA
Qixing Huang	The University of Texas at Austin, USA
Cewu Lu	Shanghai Jiao Tong University, China
Leonidas Guibas	Stanford University, USA

W05 – Bias Estimation in Face Analytics

Rama Chellappa	University of Maryland, USA
Nalini Ratha	IBM Watson Research Center, USA
Rogerio Feris	IBM Watson Research Center, USA
Michele Merler	IBM Watson Research Center, USA
Vishal Patel	Johns Hopkins University, USA

W06 – 4th International Workshop on Recovering 6D Object Pose

Tomas Hodan	Czech Technical University in Prague, Czechia
Rigas Kouskouridas	Scape Technologies, UK
Krzysztof Walas	Poznan University of Technology, Poland
Tae-Kyun Kim	Imperial College London, UK
Jiří Matas	Czech Technical University in Prague, Czechia
Carsten Rother	Heidelberg University, Germany
Frank Michel	Technical University Dresden, Germany
Vincent Lepetit	University of Bordeaux, France
Ales Leonardis	University of Birmingham, UK
Carsten Steger	Technical University of Munich, MVTec, Germany
Caner Sahin	Imperial College London, UK

W07 – Second International Workshop on Computer Vision for UAVs

Kristof Van Beeck	KU Leuven, Belgium
Tinne Tuytelaars	KU Leuven, Belgium
Davide Scaramuzza	ETH Zurich, Switzerland
Toon Goedemé	KU Leuven, Belgium

W08 – 5th Transferring and Adapting Source Knowledge in Computer Vision and Second VisDA Challenge

Tatiana Tommasi	Italian Institute of Technology, Italy
David Vázquez	Element AI, Canada
Kate Saenko	Boston University, USA
Ben Usman	Boston University, USA
Xingchao Peng	Boston University, USA
Judy Hoffman	Facebook AI Research, USA
Neela Kaushik	Boston University, USA
Antonio M. López	Universitat Autònoma de Barcelona and Computer Vision Center, Spain
Wen Li	ETH Zurich, Switzerland
Francesco Orabona	Boston University, USA

W09 – PoseTrack Challenge: Articulated People Tracking in the Wild

Mykhaylo Andriluka	Google Research, Switzerland
Umar Iqbal	University of Bonn, Germany
Anton Milan	Amazon, Germany
Leonid Pishchulin	Max Planck Institute for Informatics, Germany
Christoph Lassner	Amazon, Germany
Eldar Insafutdinov	Max Planck Institute for Informatics, Germany
Siyu Tang	Max Planck Institute for Intelligent Systems, Germany
Juergen Gall	University of Bonn, Germany
Bernt Schiele	Max Planck Institute for Informatics, Germany

W10 – Workshop on Objectionable Content and Misinformation

Cristian Canton Ferrer	Facebook, USA
Matthias Niessner	Technical University of Munich, Germany
Paul Natsev	Google, USA
Marius Vlad	Google, Switzerland

W11 – 9th International Workshop on Human Behavior Understanding

Xavier Alameda-Pineda	Inria Grenoble, France
Elisa Ricci	Fondazione Bruno Kessler and University of Trento, Italy
Albert Ali Salah	Boğaziçi University, Turkey
Nicu Sebe	University of Trento, Italy
Shuicheng Yan	National University of Singapore, Singapore

W12 – First Person in Context Workshop and Challenge

Si Liu	Beihang University, China
Jiashi Feng	National University of Singapore, Singapore
Jizhong Han	Institute of Information Engineering, China
Shuicheng Yan	National University of Singapore, Singapore
Yao Sun	Institute of Information Engineering, China

Yue Liao   Institute of Information Engineering, China
Lejian Ren   Institute of Information Engineering, China
Guanghui Ren   Institute of Information Engineering, China

W13 – 4th Workshop on Computer Vision for Art Analysis

Stuart James   Istituto Italiano di Tecnologia, Italy and University College
                           London, UK
Leonardo Impett   EPFL, Switzerland and Biblioteca Hertziana, Max Planck
                           Institute for Art History, Italy
Peter Hall   University of Bath, UK
João Paulo Costeira   Instituto Superior Tecnico, Portugal
Peter Bell   Friedrich-Alexander-University Nürnberg, Germany
Alessio Del Bue   Istituto Italiano di Tecnologia, Italy

W14 – First Workshop on Fashion, Art, and Design

Hui Wu   IBM Research AI, USA
Negar Rostamzadeh   Element AI, Canada
Leonidas Lefakis   Zalando Research, Germany
Joy Tang   Markable, USA
Rogerio Feris   IBM Research AI, USA
Tamara Berg   UNC Chapel Hill/Shopagon Inc., USA
Luba Elliott   Independent Curator/Researcher/Producer
Aaron Courville   MILA/University of Montreal, Canada
Chris Pal   MILA/PolyMTL, Canada
Sanja Fidler   University of Toronto, Canada
Xavier Snelgrove   Element AI, Canada
David Vazquez   Element AI, Canada
Julia Lasserre   Zalando Research, Germany
Thomas Boquet   Element AI, Canada
Nana Yamazaki   Zalando SE, Germany

W15 – Anticipating Human Behavior

Juergen Gall   University of Bonn, Germany
Jan van Gemert   Delft University of Technology, The Netherlands
Kris Kitani   Carnegie Mellon University, USA

W16 – Third Workshop on Geometry Meets Deep Learning

Xiaowei Zhou   Zhejiang University, China
Emanuele Rodolà   Sapienza University of Rome, Italy
Jonathan Masci   NNAISENSE, Switzerland
Kosta Derpanis   Ryerson University, Canada

W17 – First Workshop on Brain-Driven Computer Vision

Simone Palazzo	University of Catania, Italy
Isaak Kavasidis	University of Catania, Italy
Dimitris Kastaniotis	University of Patras, Greece
Stavros Dimitriadis	Cardiff University, UK

W18 – Second Workshop on 3D Reconstruction Meets Semantics

Radim Tylecek	University of Edinburgh, UK
Torsten Sattler	ETH Zurich, Switzerland
Thomas Brox	University of Freiburg, Germany
Marc Pollefeys	ETH Zurich/Microsoft, Switzerland
Robert B. Fisher	University of Edinburgh, UK
Theo Gevers	University of Amsterdam, Netherlands

W19 – Third International Workshop on Video Segmentation

Pablo Arbelaez	Universidad de los Andes, Columbia
Thomas Brox	University of Freiburg, Germany
Fabio Galasso	OSRAM GmbH, Germany
Iasonas Kokkinos	University College London, UK
Fuxin Li	Oregon State University, USA

W20 – PeopleCap 2018: Capturing and Modeling Human Bodies, Faces, and Hands

Gerard Pons-Moll	MPI for Informatics and Saarland Informatics Campus, Germany
Jonathan Taylor	Google, USA

W21 – Workshop on Shortcomings in Vision and Language

Dhruv Batra	Georgia Institute of Technology and Facebook AI Research, USA
Raffaella Bernardi	University of Trento, Italy
Raquel Fernández	University of Amsterdam, The Netherlands
Spandana Gella	University of Edinburgh, UK
Kushal Kafle	Rochester Institute of Technology, USA
Moin Nabi	SAP SE, Germany
Stefan Lee	Georgia Institute of Technology, USA

W22 – Second YouTube-8M Large-Scale Video Understanding Workshop

Apostol (Paul) Natsev	Google Research, USA
Rahul Sukthankar	Google Research, USA
Joonseok Lee	Google Research, USA
George Toderici	Google Research, USA

W23 – Second International Workshop on Compact and Efficient Feature Representation and Learning in Computer Vision

Jie Qin	ETH Zurich, Switzerland
Li Liu	National University of Defense Technology, China and University of Oulu, Finland
Li Liu	Inception Institute of Artificial Intelligence, UAE
Fan Zhu	Inception Institute of Artificial Intelligence, UAE
Matti Pietikäinen	University of Oulu, Finland
Luc Van Gool	ETH Zurich, Switzerland

W24 – 5th Women in Computer Vision Workshop

Zeynep Akata	University of Amsterdam, The Netherlands
Dena Bazazian	Computer Vision Center, Spain
Yana Hasson	Inria, France
Angjoo Kanazawa	UC Berkeley, USA
Hildegard Kuehne	University of Bonn, Germany
Gül Varol	Inria, France

W25 – Perceptual Image Restoration and Manipulation Workshop and Challenge

Yochai Blau	Technion – Israel Institute of Technology, Israel
Roey Mechrez	Technion – Israel Institute of Technology, Israel
Radu Timofte	ETH Zurich, Switzerland
Tomer Michaeli	Technion – Israel Institute of Technology, Israel
Lihi Zelnik-Manor	Technion – Israel Institute of Technology, Israel

W26 – Egocentric Perception, Interaction, and Computing

Dima Damen	University of Bristol, UK
Giuseppe Serra	University of Udine, Italy
David Crandall	Indiana University, USA
Giovanni Maria Farinella	University of Catania, Italy
Antonino Furnari	University of Catania, Italy

W27 – Vision Meets Drone: A Challenge

Pengfei Zhu	Tianjin University, China
Longyin Wen	JD Finance, USA
Xiao Bian	GE Global Research, USA
Haibin Ling	Temple University, USA

W28 – 11th Perceptual Organization in Computer Vision Workshop on Action, Perception, and Organization

Deepak Pathak	UC Berkeley, USA
Bharath Hariharan	Cornell University, USA

W29 – AutoNUE: Autonomous Navigation in Unconstrained Environments

Manmohan Chandraker   University of California San Diego, USA
C. V. Jawahar   IIIT Hyderabad, India
Anoop M. Namboodiri   IIIT Hyderabad, India
Srikumar Ramalingam   University of Utah, USA
Anbumani Subramanian   Intel, Bangalore, India

W30 – ApolloScape: Vision-Based Navigation for Autonomous Driving

Peng Wang   Baidu Research, USA
Ruigang Yang   Baidu Research, China
Andreas Geiger   ETH Zurich, Switzerland
Hongdong Li   Australian National University, Australia
Alan Yuille   The Johns Hopkins University, USA

W31 – 6th International Workshop on Assistive Computer Vision and Robotics

Giovanni Maria   University of Catania, Italy
  Farinella
Marco Leo   National Research Council of Italy, Italy
Gerard G. Medioni   University of Southern California, USA
Mohan Trivedi   University of California, USA

W32 – 4th International Workshop on Observing and Understanding Hands in Action

Iason Oikonomidis   Foundation for Research and Technology, Greece
Guillermo   Imperial College London, UK
  Garcia-Hernando
Angela Yao   National University of Singapore, Singapore
Antonis Argyros   University of Crete/Foundation for Research
                        and Technology, Greece
Vincent Lepetit   University of Bordeaux, France
Tae-Kyun Kim   Imperial College London, UK

W33 – Bioimage Computing

Jens Rittscher   University of Oxford, UK
Anna Kreshuk   University of Heidelberg, Germany
Florian Jug   Max Planck Institute CBG, Germany

W34 – First Workshop on Interactive and Adaptive Learning in an Open World

Erik Rodner   Carl Zeiss AG, Germany
Alexander Freytag   Carl Zeiss AG, Germany
Vittorio Ferrari   Google, Switzerland/University of Edinburgh, UK
Mario Fritz   CISPA Helmholtz Center i.G., Germany
Uwe Franke   Daimler AG, Germany
Terrence Boult   University of Colorado, Colorado Springs, USA

Juergen Gall	University of Bonn, Germany
Walter Scheirer	University of Notre Dame, USA
Angela Yao	University of Bonn, Germany

W35 – First Multimodal Learning and Applications Workshop

Paolo Rota	University of Trento, Italy
Vittorio Murino	Istituto Italiano di Tecnologia, Italy
Michael Yang	University of Twente, The Netherlands
Bodo Rosenhahn	Leibniz-Universität Hannover, Germany

W36 – What Is Optical Flow for?

Fatma Güney	Oxford University, UK
Laura Sevilla-Lara	Facebook Research, USA
Deqing Sun	NVIDIA, USA
Jonas Wulff	Massachusetts Institute of Technology, USA

W37 – Vision for XR

Richard Newcombe	Facebook Reality Labs, USA
Chris Sweeney	Facebook Reality Labs, USA
Julian Straub	Facebook Reality Labs, USA
Jakob Engel	Facebook Reality Labs, USA
Michael Goesele	Technische Universität Darmstadt, Germany

W38 – Open Images Challenge Workshop

Vittorio Ferrari	Google AI, Switzerland
Alina Kuznetsova	Google AI, Switzerland
Jordi Pont-Tuset	Google AI, Switzerland
Matteo Malloci	Google AI, Switzerland
Jasper Uijlings	Google AI, Switzerland
Jake Walker	Google AI, Switzerland
Rodrigo Benenson	Google AI, Switzerland

W39 – VizWiz Grand Challenge: Answering Visual Questions from Blind People

Danna Gurari	University of Texas at Austin, USA
Kristen Grauman	University of Texas at Austin, USA
Jeffrey P. Bigham	Carnegie Mellon University, USA

W40 – 360° Perception and Interaction

Min Sun	National Tsing Hua University, Taiwan
Yu-Chuan Su	University of Texas at Austin, USA
Wei-Sheng Lai	University of California, Merced, USA
Liwei Chan	National Chiao Tung University, USA
Hou-Ning Hu	National Tsing Hua University, Taiwan
Silvio Savarese	Stanford University, USA

Kristen Grauman   University of Texas at Austin, USA
Ming-Hsuan Yang   University of California, Merced, USA

W41 – Joint COCO and Mapillary Recognition Challenge Workshop

Tsung-Yi Lin   Google Brain, USA
Genevieve Patterson   Microsoft Research, USA
Matteo R. Ronchi   Caltech, USA
Yin Cui   Cornell, USA
Piotr Dollár   Facebook AI Research, USA
Michael Maire   TTI-Chicago, USA
Serge Belongie   Cornell, USA
Lubomir Bourdev   WaveOne, Inc., USA
Ross Girshick   Facebook AI Research, USA
James Hays   Georgia Tech, USA
Pietro Perona   Caltech, USA
Deva Ramanan   CMU, USA
Larry Zitnick   Facebook AI Research, USA
Riza Alp Guler   Inria, France
Natalia Neverova   Facebook AI Research, France
Vasil Khalidov   Facebook AI Research, France
Iasonas Kokkinos   Facebook AI Research, France
Samuel Rota Bulò   Mapillary Research, Austria
Lorenzo Porzi   Mapillary Research, Austria
Peter Kontschieder   Mapillary Research, Austria
Alexander Kirillov   Heidelberg University, Germany
Holger Caesar   University of Edinburgh, UK
Jasper Uijlings   Google Research, UK
Vittorio Ferrari   University of Edinburgh and Google Research, UK

W42 – First Large-Scale Video Object Segmentation Challenge

Ning Xu   Adobe Research, USA
Linjie Yang   SNAP Research, USA
Yuchen Fan   University of Illinois at Urbana-Champaign, USA
Jianchao Yang   SNAP Research, USA
Weiyao Lin   Shanghai Jiao Tong University, China
Michael Ying Yang   University of Twente, The Netherlands
Brian Price   Adobe Research, USA
Jiebo Luo   University of Rochester, USA
Thomas Huang   University of Illinois at Urbana-Champaign, USA

W43 – WIDER Face and Pedestrian Challenge

Chen Change Loy	Nanyang Technological University, Singapore
Dahua Lin	The Chinese University of Hong Kong, SAR China
Wanli Ouyang	University of Sydney, Australia
Yuanjun Xiong	Amazon Rekognition, USA
Shuo Yang	Amazon Rekognition, USA
Qingqiu Huang	The Chinese University of Hong Kong, SAR China
Dongzhan Zhou	SenseTime, China
Wei Xia	Amazon Rekognition, USA
Quanquan Li	SenseTime, China
Ping Luo	The Chinese University of Hong Kong, SAR China
Junjie Yan	SenseTime, China

Contents – Part IV

W22 – 2nd YouTube-8M Large-Scale Video Understanding Workshop

W23 – 2nd International Workshop on Compact and Efficient Feature Representation and Learning in Computer Vision

W19 – Third International Workshop on Video Segmentation

W19 – Third International Workshop on Video Segmentation

The Third International Workshop on Video Segmentation (IWVS) was held in Munich, Germany on September 14th, 2018, in conjunction with the European Conference on Computer Vision (ECCV). This is the third edition of the workshop, followed after the successful first and second IWVS in 2014 in Zürich, and 2016 in Amsterdam, respectively. Video segmentation could be of crucial importance for building 3D object models from video, understanding dynamic scenes, robot-object interaction and a number of high-level vision tasks. The theme of this workshop is *Video representation and segmentation in the deep learning* era which focuses on the conjunction between video segmentation and recent advances in deep learning for recognition, especially the learning of representations from video segmentation. This workshop is co-located with the workshop YouTube-VOS: A Large-Scale Benchmark for Video Object Segmentation which includes a fascinating challenge on video segmentation with 4000+ videos.

The workshop consisted of 4 invited talks, 1 invited short talk, and 2 talks from submitted work, and a panel discussion. Talks from the submissions are present in this conference proceedings. The workshop had received 4 valid submissions. The submissions were of very high quality. These submissions were reviewed by at least 2 separate organizers and discussed to decide on their acceptance. We would like to thank all the authors who submitted to the workshop.

The 2 papers in this proceedings covered using referring expressions as supervision for video segmentation, as well as a fast semantic segmentation approach in video using motion.

The invited talks were presented by Dr. Cordelia Schmid from INRIA, Dr. Daniel Cremers from Technical University of Munich, Dr. Bernt Schiele from Max Planck Institute for Informatics, and Dr. Vladlen Koltun from Intel Research. These invited speakers have also attended the panel discussion. Dr. Jordi Pont-Tuset from Google Research presented the invited short talk.

We would like to thank the ECCV 2018 workshop chairs (Stefan Roth and Laura Leal-Taixe) for their support and feedback. We would also like to thank all the invited speakers, authors who presented at the workshop and the attendees, as well as the organizers of the workshop YouTube-VOS: A Large-Scale Benchmark for Video Object Segmentation.

September 2018

Pablo Arbelaez
Thomas Brox
Fabio Galasso
Iasonas Kokkinos
Fuxin Li

Fast Semantic Segmentation on Video Using Block Motion-Based Feature Interpolation

Samvit Jain[(⊠)] and Joseph E. Gonzalez

University of California, Berkeley, CA 94704, USA
{samvit,jegonzal}@eecs.berkeley.edu

Abstract. Convolutional networks optimized for accuracy on challenging, dense prediction tasks are often prohibitively slow to run on each
frame in a video. The spatial similarity of nearby video frames, however,
suggests opportunity to reuse computation. Existing work has explored
basic feature reuse and feature warping based on optical flow, but has
encountered limits to the speedup attainable with these techniques. In
this paper, we present a new, two part approach to accelerating inference
on video. First, we propose a fast feature propagation technique that utilizes the block motion vectors present in compressed video (e.g. H.264
codecs) to cheaply propagate features from frame to frame. Second, we
develop a novel feature estimation scheme, termed feature interpolation,
that fuses features propagated from enclosing keyframes to render accurate feature estimates, even at sparse keyframe frequencies. We evaluate
our system on the Cityscapes and CamVid datasets, comparing to both
a frame-by-frame baseline and related work. We find that we are able to
substantially accelerate semantic segmentation on video, achieving twice
the average inference speed as prior work at any target accuracy level.

Keywords: Semantic segmentation · Efficient inference
Video segmentation · Video compression · H.264 video

Semantic segmentation, the task of assigning each pixel in an image to a semantic
object class, is a problem of long-standing interest in computer vision. Since the
first paper to suggest the use of fully convolutional networks to segment images
[7], increasingly sophisticated architectures have been proposed, with the goal of
segmenting more complex images, from larger, more realistic datasets, at higher
accuracy [1–3,6,9,10]. The result has been a ballooning in both model size and
inference times, as the core feature networks, borrowed from image classification
models, have grown in layer depth and parameter count, and as the cost of a
forward pass through the widest convolutional layers, a function of the size and
detail of the input images, has risen in step. As a result, state-of-the-art networks
today require between 0.5 to 3.0 s to segment a *single*, high-resolution image (e.g.
2048 × 1024 pixels) at competitive accuracy [5,11].

© Springer Nature Switzerland AG 2019
L. Leal-Taixé and S. Roth (Eds.): ECCV 2018 Workshops, LNCS 11132, pp. 3–6, 2019.
https://doi.org/10.1007/978-3-030-11018-5_1

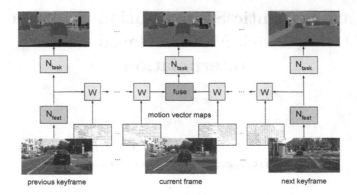

Fig. 1. Feature interpolation warps (W) and fuses the features of enclosing keyframes to generate accurate feature estimates for intermediate frames, using the block motion vectors in compressed (e.g. H.264) video.

At the same time, a new target data format for semantic segmentation has emerged: video. The motivating use cases include both batch settings, where video is segmented in bulk to generate training data for other models (e.g. autonomous control systems), and streaming settings, where high-throughput video segmentation enables interactive analysis of live footage (e.g. at surveillance sites). Video here consists of long sequences of images, shot at high frame rates (e.g. 30 frames per second) in complex environments (e.g. urban cityscapes) on modern, high-definition cameras (i.e. multi-megapixel). Segmenting individual frames at high accuracy still calls for the use of competitive image segmentation models, but the inference cost of these networks precludes their naïve deployment on every frame in a multi-hour raw video stream.

A defining characteristic of realistic video is its high level of temporal continuity. Consecutive frames demonstrate significant spatial similarity, which suggests the potential to reuse computation across frames. Building on prior work, we exploit two observations: (1) higher-level features evolve more slowly than raw pixel content in video, and (2) feature computation tends to be much more expensive than task computation across a range of vision tasks (e.g. object detection, semantic segmentation) [8,11]. Accordingly, we divide our semantic segmentation model into a deep feature network and a cheap, shallow task network [11]. We compute features only on designated keyframes, and propagate them to intermediate frames, by warping the feature maps with a frame-to-frame motion estimate. The task network is executed on all frames. Given that feature warping and task computation is much cheaper than feature extraction, a key parameter we aim to optimize is the interval between designated keyframes.

Here we make two key contributions to the effort to accelerate semantic segmentation on video. First, noting the high level of data redundancy in video, we successfully utilize an artifact of compressed video, block motion vectors, to cheaply propagate features from frame to frame. Unlike other motion estimation techniques, which introduce extra computation on intermediate frames, block motion vectors are freely available in modern video formats, making for a simple, fast design. Second, we propose a novel feature estimation scheme that enables the features for a large fraction of the frames in a video to be inferred accurately and efficiently (see Fig. 1). The approach works as follows: when computing the segmentation for a keyframe, we also precompute the features for the *next* designated keyframe. Features for all subsequent intermediate frames are then computed as a *fusion* of features warped forward from the last visited keyframe, and features warped backward from the incoming keyframe. This procedure thus implements an *interpolation* of the features of the two closest keyframes.

We evaluate our framework on the Cityscapes and CamVid datasets. Our baseline consists of running a state-of-the-art segmentation network, DeepLab [3], on every frame, a setup that achieves published accuracy [4], and a throughput of 1.3 frames per second (fps) on Cityscapes and 3.6 fps on CamVid. Our improvements come in two phases. Firstly, our use of block motion vectors for feature propagation allow us to cut inference time on intermediate frames by 53%, compared to approaches based on optical-flow, such as [11]. Second, our bi-directional feature warping and fusion scheme enables substantial accuracy improvements, especially at high keyframe intervals. Together, the two techniques allow us to operate at *twice the average inference speed* as the fastest prior work, at any target level of accuracy (see Fig. 2). For example, if we are willing to tolerate *no worse* than 65 mIoU on our CamVid video stream, we are able to operate at a throughput of 20.1 fps, compared to the 8.0 fps achieved by the forward flow-based propagation from [11] (see Table 1). Overall, even when operating in high accuracy regimes (e.g. within 3% mIoU of the baseline), we are able to accelerate segmentation on video by a factor of 2–6×.

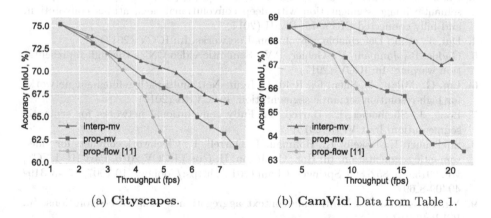

(a) **Cityscapes**.   (b) **CamVid**. Data from Table 1.

Fig. 2. Accuracy (**avg.**) vs. throughput on Cityscapes and CamVid for three schemes: (1) optical-flow based feature propagation [11] (**prop-flow**), (2) motion vector-based feature propagation (**prop-mv**), and (3) motion vector-based feature interpolation (**interp-mv**).

Table 1. Accuracy and throughput on **CamVid** for three schemes: (1) optical-flow based feature propagation [11] (**prop-flow**), (2) motion vector-based feature propagation (**prop-mv**), and (3) motion vector-based feature interpolation (**interp-mv**). Average accuracy refers to mean accuracy across all labeled frames in the test set. Minimum accuracy refers to accuracy on frames farthest away from keyframes.

Metric	Scheme	Keyframe interval									
		1	2	3	4	5	6	7	8	9	10
mIoU (**avg.**) (%)	prop-flow	68.6	67.8	67.4	66.3	66.0	65.8	64.2	63.6	64.0	63.1
	prop-mv	68.6	67.8	67.3	66.2	65.9	65.7	64.2	63.7	63.8	63.4
	interp-mv	**68.6**	**68.7**	**68.7**	**68.4**	**68.4**	**68.2**	**68.0**	**67.5**	**67.0**	**67.3**
mIoU (**min.**) (%)	prop-flow	68.5	67.0	66.2	64.9	63.6	62.7	61.3	60.5	59.7	58.7
	prop-mv	68.5	67.0	65.9	64.7	63.4	62.7	61.4	60.8	60.0	59.3
	interp-mv	**68.5**	**68.6**	**68.4**	**68.2**	**67.9**	**67.4**	**67.0**	**66.4**	**66.1**	**65.7**
Throughput (fps)	prop-flow	3.6	6.2	8.0	9.4	10.5	11.0	11.7	12.0	13.3	13.7
	prop-mv	3.6	6.7	9.3	11.6	13.6	15.3	17.0	18.2	20.2	21.3
	interp-mv	3.6	6.6	9.1	11.3	13.1	14.7	16.2	17.3	19.1	20.1

References

1. Badrinarayanan, V., Kendall, A., Cipolla, R.: SegNet: a deep convolutional encoder-decoder architecture for image segmentation. In: PAMI (2017)
2. Chen, L.C., Papandreou, G., Kokkinos, I., Murphy, K., Yuille, A.L.: Semantic image segmentation with deep convolutional nets and fully connected CRFs. In: ICLR (2016)
3. Chen, L.C., Papandreou, G., Kokkinos, I., Murphy, K., Yuille, A.L.: DeepLab: semantic image segmentation with deep convolutional nets, atrous convolution, and fully connected CRFs. In: PAMI (2017)
4. Dai, J., et al.: Deformable convolutional networks. In: ICCV (2017)
5. Gadde, R., Jampani, V., Gehler, P.V.: Semantic video CNNs through representation warping. In: ICCV (2017)
6. Lin, G., Milan, A., Shen, C., Reid, I.: RefineNet: multi-path refinement networks for high-resolution semantic segmentation. In: CVPR (2017)
7. Long, J., Shelhamer, E., Darrell, T.: Fully convolutional networks for semantic segmentation. In: CVPR (2015)
8. Shelhamer, E., Rakelly, K., Hoffman, J., Darrell, T.: Clockwork convnets for video semantic segmentation. In: Hua, G., Jégou, H. (eds.) ECCV 2016, Part III. LNCS, vol. 9915, pp. 852–868. Springer, Cham (2016). https://doi.org/10.1007/978-3-319-49409-8_69
9. Yu, F., Koltun, V.: Multi-scale context aggregation by dilated convolutions. In: ICLR (2016)
10. Zhao, H., Shi, J., Qi, X., Wang, X., Jia, J.: Pyramid scene parsing network. In: CVPR (2017)
11. Zhu, X., Xiong, Y., Dai, J., Yuan, L., Wei, Y.: Deep feature flow for video recognition. In: CVPR (2017)

Video Object Segmentation
with Referring Expressions

Anna Khoreva[1(✉)], Anna Rohrbach[2], and Bernt Schiele[1]

[1] Max Planck Institute for Informatics, Saarbrücken, Germany
khoreva@mpi-inf.mpg.de
[2] University of California, Berkeley, USA

Abstract. Most semi-supervised video object segmentation methods rely on a pixel-accurate mask of a target object provided for the first video frame. However, obtaining a detailed mask is expensive and time-consuming. In this work we explore a more practical and natural way of identifying a target object by employing language referring expressions. Leveraging recent advances of language grounding models designed for images, we propose an approach to extend them to video data, ensuring temporally coherent predictions. To evaluate our approach we augment the popular video object segmentation benchmarks, DAVIS$_{16}$ and DAVIS$_{17}$, with language descriptions of target objects. We show that our approach performs on par with the methods which have access to the object mask on DAVIS$_{16}$ and is competitive to methods using scribbles on challenging DAVIS$_{17}$.

1 Introduction

Segmenting objects at pixel level provides a finer understanding of video and is relevant for many applications, e.g. augmented reality, video editing, roto-scoping, and summarisation. Ideally, one would like to obtain a pixel-accurate segmentation of objects in video with no human input during test time. However, the current state-of-the-art unsupervised video object segmentation methods [9] have troubles segmenting the target objects in videos containing multiple instances and cluttered backgrounds without any guidance from the user. Hence, many recent works [1,10] employ a semi-supervised approach, where a mask of the target object is manually annotated in the first frame and the task is to accurately segment the object in successive frames. Although this setting has proven to be successful, it can be prohibitive for many applications. It is tedious and time-consuming for the user to provide a pixel-accurate segmentation and usually takes more than a minute to annotate a single instance. To make video object segmentation more applicable in practice, instead of costly pixel-level masks [6,8] propose to employ point clicks or scribbles to specify the target object in the first frame. However, on small touchscreen devices, such as tablets or phones, providing precise clicks or drawing scribbles using fingers could be cumbersome and inconvenient for the user.

L. Leal-Taixé and S. Roth (Eds.): ECCV 2018 Workshops, LNCS 11132, pp. 7–12, 2019.
https://doi.org/10.1007/978-3-030-11018-5_2

Fig. 1. Example result of the proposed approach.

To overcome these limitations, in this work we propose a novel task - segmenting objects in video using language referring expressions - which is a more natural way of human-computer interaction. It is much easier for the user to say: "I want the man in a red sweatshirt performing breakdance to be segmented" (see Fig. 1), than to provide a tedious pixel-level mask or struggle with drawing a scribble which does not straddle the object boundary. Moreover, employing language specifications can make the system more robust to background clutter, help to avoid drift and better adapt to the complex dynamics inherent to videos while not over-fitting to a particular view in the first frame.

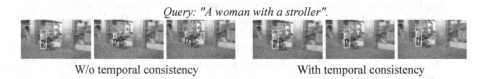

Fig. 2. Qualitative results of language grounding with and w/o temporal consistency.

We aim to investigate how far one can go while leveraging the advances in image-level language grounding and pixel-level segmentation in videos. We propose a convnet-based framework that allows to utilize referring expressions for video object segmentation, where the output of the grounding model (bounding box) is used as a guidance for segmentation of the target object in each video frame. To the best of our knowledge, this is the first approach to address video object segmentation via language specifications. For the extended version of this work we refer the reader to [5], collected language descriptions are available at https://www.mpi-inf.mpg.de/vos-language.

2   Method

Given a video $V = \{f_1, ..., f_N\}$ with N frames and a textual query of the target object Q, our aim is to obtain a pixel-level mask of the target object in every frame that it appears. Our method consists of two steps. Using as input the query Q, we first generate target object box proposals for every video frame by exploiting language grounding models, designed for images only. Applying these models off-the-shelf results in temporally inconsistent and jittery box predictions (see Fig. 2). To mitigate this issue we next employ temporal consistency, which enforces boxes to be coherent across frames. As a second step, using as guidance the obtained box predictions of the target object on every frame we apply a segmentation convnet to recover detailed object masks.

Grounding Objects in Video. The task of language grounding is to localize a region described by a given language expression. It is typically formulated as measuring the compatibility between a set of object proposals $O = \{o_i\}_{i=1}^M$ and a given query Q. The grounding model provides as output a set of matching scores $S = \{s_i\}_{i=1}^M$ between a proposal and a query. The highest scoring proposal is selected as the predicted region.

We employ the state-of-the-art language grounding model – MattNet [11], to localize the object in each frame. However, using the grounding model designed for images and picking the highest scoring proposal for each frame lead to temporally incoherent results. Even with simple queries for adjacent frames that look very much alike, the model often outputs inconsistent predictions. To resolve this issue we propose to re-rank proposals by exploiting temporal structure along with the original matching scores. Since objects tend to move smoothly through space and in time, there should be little changes from frame to frame and the box proposals should have high overlap between neighboring frames. By finding temporally coherent tracks that are spread-out in time, we can focus on the predictions consistent throughout the video and give less emphasis to objects that appear for only a short period of time. The grounding model provides the likeliness of each box proposal to be the target object by outputting a matching score s_i. Then each box proposal is re-ranked based on its overlap with the proposals in other frames, the original objectness score and its matching score from the grounding model. Specifically, for each proposal we compute a new score: $\hat{s}_i = s_i * (\sum_{j=1, j \neq i}^M r_{ij} * d_j * s_j / t_{ij})$, where r_{ij} measures an IoU ratio between box proposals i and j, t_{ij} denotes the temporal distance between two proposals ($t_{ij} = |f_i - f_j|$) and d_j is the original objectness score. Then, in each frame we select the proposal with the highest new score. The new scoring rewards temporally coherent predictions which likely belong to the target object and form a spatio-temporal tube.

Pixel-Level Segmentation. We exploit bounding boxes from grounding as a guidance for the segmentation network. The bounding box is transformed into a binary image and concatenated with the RGB channels of the input image and optical flow magnitude, forming a 5-channel input for the network. Thus we ask the network to learn to refine the provided boxes into accurate masks. As our architecture we build upon [2].

We train the network on static images, employing the saliency segmentation dataset [3] with a diverse set of objects. The bounding box is obtained from the ground truth masks. To make the system robust during test time to sloppy boxes from the grounding model, we augment the ground truth box by randomly jittering its coordinates (uniformly, ±20% of the original box width and height).

ID 1: "A girl with blonde hair dressed in blue".

ID 1: "A black scooter ridden by a man". ID 2: "A man in a suit riding a scooter".

Fig. 3. Qualitative results using only referring expressions as supervision.

We synthesize optical flow from static images by applying affine transformations for both background and foreground object to simulate the camera and object motion in the neighboring frames. This simple strategy allows us to train on diverse set of static images, while exploiting motion information during test time. We train the network on many triplets of RGB images, synthesized flow magnitude images and loose boxes in order for the model generalize well to different localization quality of grounding boxes and different dynamics of the object. During inference we estimate optical flow with Flow-Net2.0 [4].

We make one single pass over the video, applying the model per-frame. The network does not keep a notion of the specific appearance of the object in contrast to [1], where the model is fine-tuned during the test time. Neither do we do an online adaptation as in [10], where the model is updated on its previous predictions. This makes the system more efficient during the inference and more suitable for real-world applications (Fig. 3).

3   Experimental Results

Here we present video object segmentation results using language referring expressions. To validate our approach we employ two popular datasets, DAVIS$_{16}$ [7] and DAVIS$_{17}$ [8], which we augmented with non-ambiguous referring expressions. We ask the annotator to provide a description of the object, which has a mask annotation, by looking only at the first video frame. For evaluation on DAVIS$_{16}$ we use the mIoU measure and on DAVIS$_{17}$ we employ $J\&F$ metric [8].

Table 1 compares our results to previous work. On DAVIS$_{16}$ our method, while only exploiting language supervision, shows competitive performance, on par with techniques which use a pixel-level mask on the first frame (82.8 vs. 81.7 for OnAVOS [10]). Compared to [6] which uses click supervision, our method shows superior performance

Table 1. Results on DAVIS$_{16/17}$ validation sets.

Supervision	Method	DAVIS$_{16}$ mIoU	DAVIS$_{17}$ $J\&F$
1st frame mask	OSVOS [1]	80.2	57.0
	OnAVOS[a] [10]	81.7	59.4
Clicks	DEXTR [6]	80.9	-
Scribbles	Scribble-OSVOS [8]	-	39.9
Language	Our	82.8	39.3

[a]OnAVOS reports 86.1/67.8 on DAVIS$_{16/17}$ with online adaptation on successive frames.

(82.8 vs. 80.9). This shows that high quality results can be obtained via a more natural way of human-computer interaction – referring to an object via language, making video object segmentation more applicable in practice.

Lower numbers on DAVIS$_{17}$ indicate that this dataset is much more difficult than DAVIS$_{16}$. Compared to mask supervision using language descriptions significantly under-performs. We believe that one of the main problems is a relatively unstable behavior of the underlying grounding model. There are a lot of identity switches, that are heavily penalized by the evaluation metric as every pixel should be assigned to one instance. The underlying choice of proposals for grounding could also have its effect. If the object is not detected, the grounding model has no chances to recover the correct instance. The method which exploits scribble supervision [8] performs on par with our approach. Note that even for scribble supervision the task remains difficult.

4 Conclusion

In this work we propose the task of video object segmentation using language referring expressions. We present an approach to address this new task as well as extend two well-known video object segmentation benchmarks with textual descriptions. Our experiments indicate that language alone can be successfully exploited to obtain high quality segmentations of objects in videos. We hope our results encourage further research on the proposed task and foster discovery of new techniques applicable in realistic settings, discarding tedious mask annotations.

References

1. Caelles, S., Maninis, K.K., Pont-Tuset, J., Leal-Taixe, L., Cremers, D., Gool, L.V.: One-shot video object segmentation. In: CVPR (2017)
2. Chen, L., Papandreou, G., Schroff, F., Adam, H.: Rethinking atrous convolution for semantic image segmentation (2017). arXiv:1706.05587
3. Cheng, M.M., Mitra, N.J., Huang, X., Torr, P.H.S., Hu, S.M.: Global contrast based salient region detection. PAMI **37**, 569–582 (2015)
4. Ilg, E., Mayer, N., Saikia, T., Keuper, M., Dosovitskiy, A., Brox, T.: Flownet 2.0: evolution of optical flow estimation with deep networks. In: CVPR (2017)
5. Khoreva, A., Rohrbach, A., Schiele, B.: Video object segmentation with language referring expressions (2018). arXiv:1803.08006
6. Maninis, K., Caelles, S., Pont-Tuset, J., Gool, L.V.: Deep extreme cut: from extreme points to object segmentation. In: CVPR (2018)
7. Perazzi, F., Pont-Tuset, J., McWilliams, B., Gool, L.V., Gross, M., Sorkine-Hornung, A.: A benchmark dataset and evaluation methodology for video object segmentation. In: CVPR (2016)

8. Pont-Tuset, J., et al.: The 2018 Davis challenge on video object segmentation (2018). arXiv:1803.00557
9. Tokmakov, P., Alahari, K., Schmid, C.: Learning video object segmentation with visual memory. In: ICCV (2017)
10. Voigtlaender, P., Leibe, B.: Online adaptation of convolutional neural networks for video object segmentation. In: BMVC (2017)
11. Yu, L., et al.: Mattnet: modular attention network for referring expression comprehension. In: CVPR (2018)

W20 – PeopleCap 2018: Capturing and Modeling Human Bodies, Faces and Hands

W20 – PeopleCap 2018: Capturing and Modeling Human Bodies, Faces and Hands

The second edition of PeopleCap brought together expert researchers in the field of capturing and modeling humans from sensor data. This time, PeopleCap took place in conjunction with ECCV, in Munich on the last day of the conference. After five days of exciting papers and events at ECCV, the PeopleCap workshop was very well attended. The workshop consisted of excellent talks given by the invited speakers and stimulating discussions throughout the poster session.

Lourdes Agapito started the workshop with an exciting talk, first describing a deep learning method for inferring 3D pose followed by an optimization based technique to reconstruct 3D face geometry from monocular images. Adrian Hilton presented high end performance capture methods that leverage multiple cameras for both indoor and outdoor settings, some of which are already being used to render novel views during broadcasts of sport events. Franziska Mueller then demonstrated state of the art hand tracking results, showing how to learn to infer 3D hand pose from images of hands synthetically generated using a GAN.

The workshop continued with a poster session that included a selection of invited posters from other portions of the conference, along with posters for the five papers accepted to the workshop, each of which was peer reviewed by three expert reviewers in the field. The session featured a good mix of papers tackling 3D human pose estimation, reconstruction from single images and modeling of cloth, faces and hands.

After the poster session, Yaser Sheikh described methods to model and capture human, emphasiznig the need to capture as much detail as possible because "every detail carries a social signal" that will enable us to study the semantic intentions of body language. Stefanie Wührer finished with an encompassing talk describing methods to learn multilinear models of faces, factoring expression and shape, from noisy 3D face registrations with missing data.

The workshop concluded with the announcement of the best paper award. The award was given to the paper "Can 3D Pose be Learned from 2D Projections Alone?", a paper that demonstrated an interesting weakly supervised approach to estimate 3D pose points, given only 2D pose landmarks.

In summary, the workshop was a great success, allowing researchers in the field to meet and exchange ideas and thoughts, reflecting on the importance of integrating 3D geometry and reasoning in computer vision.

September 2018

Gerard Pons-Moll
Jonathan Taylor

MobileFace: 3D Face Reconstruction with Efficient CNN Regression

Nikolai Chinaev[1]([✉]), Alexander Chigorin[1], and Ivan Laptev[1,2]

[1] VisionLabs, Amsterdam, The Netherlands
{n.chinaev,a.chigorin}@visionlabs.ru
[2] Inria, WILLOW, Departement d'Informatique de l'Ecole Normale Superieure,
PSL Research University, ENS/INRIA/CNRS UMR 8548, Paris, France
ivan.laptev@inria.fr

Abstract. Estimation of facial shapes plays a central role for face transfer and animation. Accurate 3D face reconstruction, however, often deploys iterative and costly methods preventing real-time applications. In this work we design a compact and fast CNN model enabling real-time face reconstruction on mobile devices. For this purpose, we first study more traditional but slow morphable face models and use them to automatically annotate a large set of images for CNN training. We then investigate a class of efficient MobileNet CNNs and adapt such models for the task of shape regression. Our evaluation on three datasets demonstrates significant improvements in the speed and the size of our model while maintaining state-of-the-art reconstruction accuracy.

Keywords: 3D face reconstruction · Morphable model · CNN

1 Introduction

3D face reconstruction from monocular images is a long-standing goal in computer vision with applications in face recognition, film industry, animation and other areas. Earlier efforts date back to late nineties and introduce morphable face models [1]. Traditional methods address this task with optimization-based techniques and analysis-through-synthesis methods [2–6]. More recently, regression-based methods started to emerge [7–10]. In particular, the task has seen an increasing interest from the CNN community over the past few years [9–13]. However, the applicability of neural networks remains difficult due to the lack of large-scale training data. Possible solutions include the use of synthetic data [8,12], incorporation of unsupervised training criteria [10], or combination of both [14]. Another option is to produce semi-synthetic data by applying an optimization-based algorithm with proven accuracy to a database of faces [9,11,13].

Optimization-based methods for morphable model fitting vary in many respects. Some design choices include image formation model, regularization and optimization strategy. Another source of variation is the kind of face attributes

© Springer Nature Switzerland AG 2019
L. Leal-Taixé and S. Roth (Eds.): ECCV 2018 Workshops, LNCS 11132, pp. 15–30, 2019.
https://doi.org/10.1007/978-3-030-11018-5_3

being used. Traditional formulation employs face texture [1]. It uses morphable model to generate a synthetic face image and optimizes for parameters that would minimize the difference between the synthetic image and the target. However, this formulation also relies on a sparse set of facial landmarks used for initialization. Earlier methods used manually annotated landmarks [4]. The user was required to annotate a few facial points by hand. Recent explosion of facial landmarking methods [15–18] made this process automatic and the set of landmarks became richer. This posed the question if morphable model fitting could be done based purely on landmarks [19]. It is especially desirable because algorithms based on landmarks are much faster and suitable for real-time performance while texture-based algorithms are quite slow (on the order of 1 min per image).

Unfortunately existing literature reports only few quantitative evaluations of optimization-based fitting algorithms. Some works assume that landmark-based fitting provides satisfactory accuracy [20, 21] while others demonstrate its limitations [19, 22]. Some use texture-based algorithms at the cost of higher computational demands, but the advantage in accuracy is not quantified [5, 6, 23]. The situation is further complicated by the lack of standard benchmarks with reliable ground truth and well-defined evaluation procedures.

We implement a morphable model fitting algorithm and tune its parameters in two scenarios: relying solely on landmarks and using landmarks in combination with the texture. We test this algorithm on images from BU4DFE dataset [24] and demonstrate that incorporation of texture significantly improves the accuracy.

It is desirable to enjoy both the accuracy of texture-based reconstruction algorithms and the high processing speed enabled by network-based methods. To this end, we use the fitting algorithm to process 300W database of faces [25] and train a neural network to predict facial geometry on the resulting semi-synthetic dataset. It is important to keep in mind that the applicability of the fitting algorithm is limited by the expressive power of the morphable model. In particular, it doesn't handle large occlusions and extreme lighting conditions very well. To rule the failures out, we visually inspect the processed dataset and delete failed examples. We compare our dataset with a similarly produced 300W-3D [9] and show that our dataset allows to learn more accurate models. We make our dataset publicly available[1].

An important consideration for CNN training is the loss function. Standard losses become problematic when predicting parameters of morphable face models due to the different nature and scales of individual parameters. To resolve this issue, the MSE loss needs to be reweighted and some ad-hoc weighting schemes have been used in the past [9]. We present a loss function that accounts for individual contributions of morphable model parameters in a clear and intuitive manner by constructing a 3D model and directly comparing it to the ground truth in the 3D space and in the 2D projected space.

---

[1] https://github.com/nchinaev/MobileFace.

This work provides the following contributions: (i) we evaluate variants of the fitting algorithm on a database of facial scans providing quantitative evidence of texture-based algorithms superiority; (ii) we train a MobileNet-based neural network that allows for fast facial shape reconstruction even on mobile devices; (iii) we propose an intuitive loss function for CNN training; (iv) we make our evaluation code and datasets publicly available.

1.1 Related Work

Algorithms for monocular 3d face shape reconstruction may be broadly classified into two following categories: optimization-based and regression-based. Optimization-based approaches make assumptions about the nature of image formation and express them in the form of energy functions. This is possible because faces represent a set of objects that one can collect some strong priors about. One popular form of such prior is a morphable model. Another way to model image formation is shape from shading technique [26–28]. This class of algorithms has a drawback of high computational complexity. Regression-based methods learn from data. The absence of large datasets for this task is a limitation that can be addressed in several ways outlined below.

Learning From Synthetic Data. Synthetic data may be produced by rendering facial scans [8] or by rendering images from a morphable model [12]. Corresponding ground truth 3d models are readily available in this case because they were used for rendering. These approaches have two limitations: first, the variability in facial shapes is only limited to the subjects participating in acquisition, and second, the image formation is limited by the exact illumination model used for rendering.

Unsupervised Learning. Tewari et al. [10] incorporate rendering process into their learning framework. This rendering layer is implemented in a way that it can be back-propagated through. This allows to circumvent the necessity of having ground truth 3d models for images and makes it possible to learn from datasets containing face images alone. In the follow up work Tewari et al. [29] go further and learn corrections to the morphable model. Richardson et al. [14] incorporate shape from shading into learning process to learn finer details.

Fitting + Learning. Most closely related to our work are works of Zhu et al. [9] and Tran et al. [13]. They both use fitting algorithms to generate datasets for neural network training. However, accuracies of the respective fitting algorithms [2,3] in the context of evaluation on datasets of facial scans are not reported by their authors. This raises two questions: what is the maximum accuracy attainable by learning from the results of these fitting methods and what are the gaps between the fitting methods and the respective learned networks? We evaluate accuracies of our fitting methods and networks on images from BU4DFE dataset in our work.

2   MobileFace

Our main objective is to create fast and compact face shape predictor suitable for real-time inference on mobile devices. To achieve this goal we train a network to predict morphable model parameters (to be introduced in Sect. 2.2). Those include parameters related to 3d shape $\boldsymbol{\alpha}_{id}$ and $\boldsymbol{\alpha}_{exp}$, as well as those related to projection of the model from 3d space to the image plane: translation $\boldsymbol{t}$, three angles ϕ, γ, θ and projection f, P_x, P_y. Vector $\boldsymbol{p} \in \mathbb{R}^{118}$ is a concatenation of all the morphable model parameters predicted by the network:

$$\boldsymbol{p} = \begin{pmatrix} \boldsymbol{\alpha}_{id}^T & \boldsymbol{\alpha}_{exp}^T & \boldsymbol{t}^T & \phi & \gamma & \theta & f & Px & Py \end{pmatrix}^T \tag{1}$$

2.1   Loss Functions

We experiment with two losses in this work. The first MSE loss can be defined as

$$\text{Loss}_{\text{MSE}} = \sum_i ||\boldsymbol{p}^i - \boldsymbol{p}^i{}_{gt}||_2^2. \tag{2}$$

Such a loss, however, is likely to be sub-optimal as it treats parameters $\boldsymbol{p}$ of different nature and scales equally. They impact the $3d$ reconstruction accuracy and the projection accuracy differently. One way to overcome this is to use the outputs of the network to construct 3d meshes $\boldsymbol{S}(\boldsymbol{p}^i)$ and compare them with ground truth $\boldsymbol{S}_{gt}$ during training [30]. However, such a loss alone would only allow to learn parameters related to the 3d shape: $\boldsymbol{\alpha}_{id}$ and $\boldsymbol{\alpha}_{exp}$. To allow the network to learn other parameters, we propose to augment this loss by an additional term on model projections $P(\boldsymbol{p}^i)$:

$$\text{Loss}_{\text{2d + 3d, } l_2} = \sum_i \left(||\boldsymbol{S}(\boldsymbol{p}^i) - \boldsymbol{S}_{gt}||_2^2 + ||P(\boldsymbol{p}^i) - P_{gt}||_2^2 \right) \tag{3}$$

Subscript l_2 indicates that this loss uses l_2 norm for individual vertices. Likewise, we define

$$\text{Loss}_{\text{2d + 3d, } l_1} = \sum_i \left(||\boldsymbol{S}(\boldsymbol{p}^i) - \boldsymbol{S}_{gt}||_1 + ||P(\boldsymbol{p}^i) - P_{gt}||_1 \right) \tag{4}$$

We provide details of $\boldsymbol{S}(\boldsymbol{p}^i)$ construction and $P(\boldsymbol{p}^i)$ projection in the next subsection.

2.2   Morphable Model

Geometry Model. Facial geometries are represented as meshes. Morphable models allow to generate variability in both face identity and expression. This is done by adding parametrized displacements to a template face model called the mean shape. We use the mean shape and 80 modes from Basel Face Model

[1] to generate identities and 29 modes obtained from Face Warehouse dataset [31] to generate expressions. The meshes are controlled by two parameter vectors $\alpha_{id} \in \mathbb{R}^{80}$ and $\alpha_{exp} \in \mathbb{R}^{29}$:

$$S = M + A_{id} \cdot \alpha_{id} + A_{exp} \cdot \alpha_{exp}. \tag{5}$$

Vector $S \in \mathbb{R}^{3 \cdot N}$ stores the coordinates of N mesh vertices. M is the mean shape. Matrices $A_{id} \in \mathbb{R}^{3 \cdot N \times 80}$, $A_{exp} \in \mathbb{R}^{3 \cdot N \times 29}$ are the modes of variation.

Projection Model. Projection model translates face mesh from the 3d space to a 2d plane. Rotation matrix R and translation vector t apply a rigid transformation to the mesh. Projection matrix with three parameters f, Px, Py transforms mesh coordinates to the homogeneous space. For a vertex $v = (x_m, y_m, z_m)^T$ the transformation is defined as:

$$\begin{pmatrix} x_t \\ y_t \\ z_t \end{pmatrix} = \Pi \cdot \begin{pmatrix} R & t \end{pmatrix} \cdot \begin{pmatrix} x_m \\ y_m \\ z_m \\ 1 \end{pmatrix}, \quad \Pi = \begin{pmatrix} f & 0 & P_x \\ 0 & f & P_y \\ 0 & 0 & 1 \end{pmatrix}, \tag{6}$$

and the final projection of a vertex to the image plane is defined by u and v as:

$$u = \frac{x_t}{z_t}, \quad v = \frac{y_t}{z_t}. \tag{7}$$

The projection is defined by 9 parameters including three rotation angles, three translations and three parameters of the projection matrix Π. We denote projected coordinates by:

$$P(\Pi, R, t, S) = \begin{pmatrix} u_1 & u_2 & \cdots & u_N \\ v_1 & v_2 & \cdots & v_N \end{pmatrix}^T \tag{8}$$

2.3   Data Preparation

Our objective here is to produce a dataset of image-model pairs for neural network training. We use the fitting algorithm detailed in Sect. 3.3 to process the 300 W database of annotated face images [25]. Despite its accuracy reported in Sect. 4.3 this algorithm has two limitations. First, the expressive power of the morphable model is inherently limited due to laboratory conditions in which the model was obtained and due to the lighting model being used. Hence, the model can't generate occlusions and extreme lighting conditions. Second, the hyperparameters of the algorithm have been tuned for a dataset taken under controlled conditions. Due to these limitations, the algorithm inevitably fails on some of the in-the-wild photos. To overcome this shortcoming, we visually inspect the results and delete failed photos. Note that we do not use any specific criteria and this deletion is guided by the visual appeal of the models, hence it may be performed by an untrained individual. This leaves us with an even smaller amount of images than has initially been in the 300 W dataset, namely 2300 images.

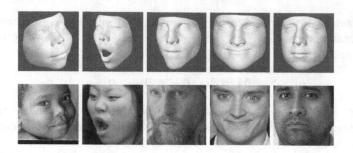

Fig. 1. Example images and corresponding curated ground truth from our training set.

This necessitates data augmentation. We randomly add blur and noise in both RGB and HSV spaces. Since some of the images with large occlusions have been deleted during visual inspection, we compensate for this and randomly occlude images with black rectangles of varied sizes [32]. Figure 1 shows some examples of our training images.

2.4   Network Architecture

Architecture of our network is based on MobileNet [33]. It consists of interleaving convolution and depth-wise convolution [34] layers followed by average pooling and one fully connected layer. Each convolution layer is followed by a batch normalization step [35] and a ReLU activation. Input images are resized to 96×96. The final fully-connected layer generates the outputs vector $\boldsymbol{p}$ Eq. (1). Main changes compared to the original architecture in [33] include the decreased input image size $96 \times 96 \times 3$, the first convolution filter is resized to $3 \times 3 \times 3 \times 10$, the following filters are scaled accordingly, global average pooling is performed over 2×2 region, and the shape of the FC layer is 320×118.

3   Morphable Model Fitting

We use morphable model fitting to generate 3d models of real-world faces to be used for neural network training. Our implementation follows standard practices [5,6]. Geometry and projection models have been defined in (Sect. 2.2). Texture model and lighting allow to generate face images. Morphable model fitting aims to revert the process of image formation by finding the combination of parameters that will result in a synthetic image resembling the target image as closely as possible.

3.1   Image Formation

Texture Model. Face texture is modeled similarly to Eq. (5). Each vertex of the mesh is assigned three RGB values generated from a linear model controlled by a parameter vector β:

$$T = T_0 + B \cdot \beta. \tag{9}$$

We use texture mean and modes from BFM [1].

Lighting Model. We use the Spherical Harmonics basis [36,37] for light computation. The illumination of a vertex having albedo ρ and normal n is computed as

$$I = \rho \cdot \left(n^T \ 1 \right) \cdot M \cdot \begin{pmatrix} n \\ 1 \end{pmatrix}, \tag{10}$$

M is as in [37] having 9 controllable parameters per channel. RGB intensities are computed separately thus giving overall $9 \cdot 3 = 27$ lighting parameters, $l \in \mathbb{R}^{27}$ is the parameter vector. Albedo ρ is dependent on β and computed as in Eq. (9).

3.2   Energy Function

Energy function expresses the discrepancy between the original attributes of an image and the ones generated from the morphable model:

$$E = E_{\text{tex}} + c_{\text{lands}} \cdot E_{\text{lands}} + r_{beta,2} \cdot E_{\text{reg,tex}} + r_{exp,2} \cdot E_{\text{reg,exp}}. \tag{11}$$

We describe individual terms of this energy function below.

Texture. The texture term E_{tex} measures the difference between the target image and the one rendered from the model. We translate both rendered and target images to a standardized UV frame as in [2] to unify all the image resolutions. Visibility mask $\mathcal{M}$ cancels out the invisible pixels.

$$E_{\text{tex}} = \frac{\| \mathcal{M} \cdot (I_{\text{target}} - I_{\text{rendered}}) \|}{|\mathcal{M}|}. \tag{12}$$

We produce I_{rendered} by applying Eq. (10) and I_{target} by sampling from the target image at the positions of projected vertices P Eq. (8). Visibility mask $\mathcal{M}$ is computed based on the orientations of vertex normals. We test three alternative norms in place of $\| \cdot \|$: l_1, l_2 and $l_{2,1}$ norm [5] that sums $l2$ norms computed for individual pixels.

Landmarks. We use the landmark detector of [15]. Row indices $\mathcal{L} = \{k_i\}_{i=1}^{68}$ for matrix P Eq. (8) correspond to the 68 landmarks. Detected landmarks are $L \in \mathbb{R}^{68 \times 2}$. The landmark term is defined as:

$$E_{\text{lands}} = \| L - P_{\mathcal{L},:} \|_2^2. \tag{13}$$

One problem with this term is that indices $\mathscr{L}$ are view-dependent due to the landmark marching. We adopt a solution similar to that of [20] and annotate parallel lines of vertices for the landmarks on the border.

Regularization. We assume multivariate Gaussian priors on morphable model parameters as defined below and use σ_{id} and σ_{tex} provided by [1].

$$E_{\mathrm{reg,id}} = \sum_{i=1}^{80} \frac{\alpha_{id,i}^2}{\sigma_{id,i}^2}, \quad E_{\mathrm{reg,exp}} = \sum_{i=1}^{29} \frac{\alpha_{exp,i}^2}{\sigma_{exp,i}^2}, \quad E_{\mathrm{reg,tex}} = \sum_{i=1}^{80} \frac{\beta_i^2}{\sigma_{tex,i}^2} \tag{14}$$

We regularize neither lighting nor projection parameters.

3.3 Optimization

Optimization process is divided into two major steps: First, we minimize the landmark term:

$$E_1 = E_{\mathrm{lands}} + r_{id,1} \cdot E_{\mathrm{reg,id}} + r_{exp,1} \cdot E_{\mathrm{reg,exp}}. \tag{15}$$

We then minimize the full energy function Eq. (11). These two steps are also divided into sub-steps minimizing the energy function with respect to specific parameters similarly to [6]. We minimize the energy function with respect to only one type of parameters at any moment. We do not include identity regularization into Eq. (11) because it did not improve accuracy in our experiments.

4 Experiments

We carry out three sets of experiments. First, we study the effect of different settings for the fitting of the morphable model used in this paper. Second, we experiment with different losses and datasets for neural network training. Finally, we present a comparison of our method with other recent approaches.

Unfortunately current research in 3d face reconstruction is lacking standardized benchmarks and evaluation protocols. As a result, evaluations presented in research papers vary in the type of error metrics and datasets used (see Table 1). This makes the results from many works difficult to compare. We hope to contribute towards filling this gap by providing the standard evaluation code and a testing set of images[2].

BU4DFE Selection. Tulyakov et al. [38] provide annotations for a total of 3000 selected scans from BU4DFE. We divide this selection into two equally sized subsets BU4DFE-test and BU4DFE-val. We report final results on the former and experiment with hyperparameters on the latter. For the purpose of evaluation we use annotations to initialize the ICP alignment.

---

[2] https://github.com/nchinaev/MobileFace.

4.1   Implementation Details

We trained networks for the total of $3 \cdot 10^5$ iterations with the batches of size 128. We added l_2 weight decay with coefficient of 10^{-4} for regularization. We used Adam optimizer [39] with learning rate of 10^{-4} for iterations before $2 \cdot 10^5$-th and 10^{-5} after. Other settings for the optimizer are standard. Coefficients for morphable model fitting are $r_{id,1} = 0.001$, $r_{exp,1} = 0.1$, $r_{beta,2} = 0.001$, $c_{lands} = 10$, $r_{exp,2} = 10$.

4.2   Accuracy Evaluation

Accuracy of 3D reconstruction is estimated by comparing the resulting 3D model to the ground truth facial scan. To compare the models, we first perform ICP alignment. Having reconstructed facial mesh S and the ground truth scan S_{gt}, we project vertices of S on S_{gt} and Procrustes-align S to the projections. These two steps are iterated until convergence.

Error Measure. To account for variations in scan sizes, we use a normalization term

$$C(S_{gt}) = ||S_{gt}^0||_2^2, \tag{16}$$

where S_{gt}^0 is S_{gt} with the mean of each x, y, z coordinate subtracted. The dissimilarity measure between S and S_{gt} is

$$d(S, S_{gt}) = c_s \cdot \frac{||S - S_{gt}||_2^2}{C(S_{gt})} \tag{17}$$

The scaling factor $c_s = 100$ is included for convenience.

Table 1. Methods and their corresponding testsets.

Work	Testset
Jackson et al. [11]	AFLW2000-3D, renders from BU4DFE and MICC
Tran et al. [13]	MICC video frames
Tewari et al. [10]	Synthetic data; Face Warehouse
Dou et al. [30]	UHDB31, FRGC2, BU-3DFE
Roth et al. [28]	Renders from BU4DFE

4.3   Morphable Model Fitting

We compare the accuracy of the fitting algorithm in two major settings: using only landmarks and using landmarks in combination with texture. To put the numbers in a context, we establish two baselines. First baseline is attained by computing the reconstruction error for the mean shape. This demonstrates the performance of a hypothetical dummy algorithm that always outputs the mean

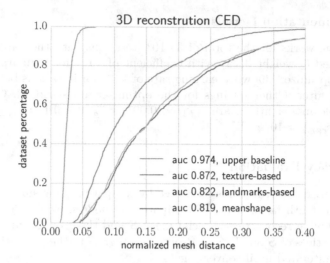

Fig. 2. Evaluation of fitting methods on BU4DFE-test. Areas under curve are computed for normalized mesh distances ranging from 0 to 1. Shorter span of x-axis is used for visual clarity.

shape for any input. Second baseline is computed by registering the morphable model to the scans in 3d. It demonstrates the performance of a hypothetical best method that is only bounded by the descriptive power of the morphable model. Landmark-based fitting is done by optimizing Eq. (15) from Sect. 3.3. Texture-based fitting is done by optimizing both Eqs. (15) and (11). Figure 2 shows cumulative error distributions. It is clear from the graph that texture-based fitting significantly outperforms landmark-based fitting which is only as accurate as the meanshape baseline. However, there is still a wide gap between the performance of the texture-based fitting and the theoretical limit. Figures 3a, b show the performance of texture-based fitting algorithm with different settings. The settings differ in the type of norm being used for texture term computation and the amount of regularization. In particular, Fig. 3a demonstrates that the choice of the norm plays an important role with $l_{2,1}$ and l_1 norms outperforming l_2. Figure 3b shows that the algorithm is quite sensitive to the regularization, hence the regularization coefficients need to be carefully tuned.

4.4 Neural Network

We train the network on our dataset of image-model pairs. For the sake of comparison, we also train it on 300W-3D [9]. The training is performed in different settings: using different loss functions and using manually cleaned version of the dataset versus non-cleaned. The tests are performed on BU4DFE-val. Figures 4a and b show cumulative error distributions. These experiments support following claims:

- Learning from our dataset gives better results than learning from 300W-3D,
- Our loss function improves results compared to baseline MSE loss function,
- Manual deletion of failed photos by an untrained individual improves results.

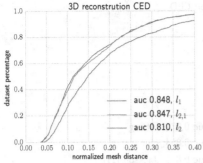
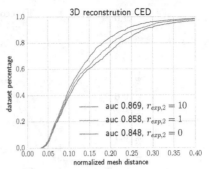

(a) Evaluations for different norms. $r_{exp,2} = 0$

(b) Evaluations with different regularizations. $l_{2,1}$ norm is used in all cases.

Fig. 3. Evaluation of texture-based fitting algorithm on BU4DFE-val with different settings.

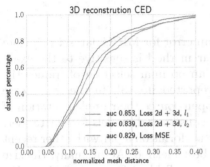
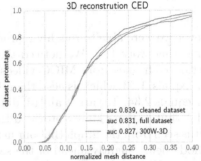

(a) Comparison of networks trained on our cleaned dataset with different losses.

(b) Comparison of networks trained with $\mathbf{Loss}_{2d+3d}$, l_2 on different datasets.

Fig. 4. Evaluation on BU4DFE-val for networks trained with different losses on different datasets.

4.5 Comparison with the State of the Art

Quantitative Results. Figure 5 presents evaluations of our network and a few recent methods on BU4DFE-test. Error metric is as in Eq. (17). The work of Tran et al. [40] is based on [13] and their code allows to produce non-neutral models, therefore we present an evaluation of [40] and not [13]. We do not present an evaluation of 3DDFA [9] because Jackson et al. [11] have already demonstrated that 3DDFA is inferior to their method. We do not include the work of Sela et al. [41] into comparison because we were not able to reproduce their results. For Jackson et al. [11] we were able to reproduce their error on AFLW2000-3D. We used MATLAB implementation of isosurface algorithm to transform their volumes into meshes. Tran et al. [40] do not present an evaluation on 3d scans,

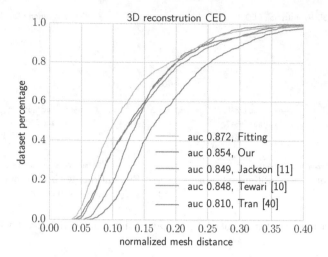

Fig. 5. Comparison of methods on BU4DFE-test.

however we were able to roughly reproduce an error for MICC dataset [42] from their earlier work [13]. We noticed that their method is sensitive to the exact selection of frames from MICC videos. For an optimal selection of frames the error equals 1.43 which is less than 1.57 reported in [13]. In the worst case error equals 2.34. Tewari et al. [10] did not open-source their implementation of MOFA, but authors kindly provided their reconstructed models for our testset.

It is seen from the graph that our network performs on a par with other recent methods being slightly ahead of the second-best method. Additionally, the size of our model is orders of magnitude smaller, see Table 4 for a comparison. We used Intel Core i5-4460 for CPU experiments, NVIDIA GeForce GTX 1080 for GPU experiments (except for Tewari [10], they used NVIDIA Titan X Pascal) and Samsung Galaxy S7 for ARM experiments.

Table 2. Comparison with Tran et al. [13] on MICC dataset [42]. All numbers are in mm.

Method	w.o. scale	w. scale
Tran [13]	1.83 ± 0.04	1.46 ± 0.03
Our	$\mathbf{1.70 \pm 0.02}$	$\mathbf{1.33 \pm 0.02}$

Table 3. Comparisons on a selection from Face Warehouse dataset. All numbers are in mm.

Method	Our	Tewari [10]	Garrido [6]
Error	1.8 ± 0.07	1.7	1.4

Table 4. Model size and running time comparison.

Method	Model size	GPU	CPU	ARM	AUC
Jackson [11]	1.4 GB	-	2.7 s	-	0.849
Tewari [10]	0.27 GB	4 ms	-	-	0.848
Tran [40]	0.35 GB	40 ms	-	-	0.810
Our	**1.5 MB**	**1 ms**	**1.8 ms**	**3.6 ms**	**0.854**

Original   Fitting   Our   Jackson [11] Tewari [10]   Tran [40]   GT

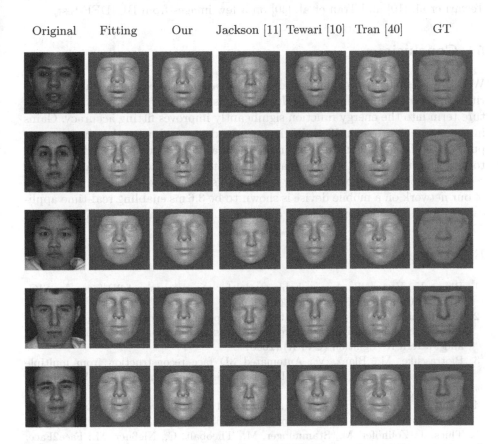

Fig. 6. Qualitative results. Images are from BU4DFE-test. Our implementation of fitting was used for the second column.

Table 2 presents a comparison with Tran et al. [13] on MICC dataset [42]. This is a dataset of 53 subjects. For each of the subjects it provides three videos and a neutral facial scan. It is therefore crucial that a method being evaluated on this dataset should output neutral models for any input. Method of Tran et al. [13] is specifically designed for this purpose. We adapt our method to this scenario by setting α_{exp} to zero. We randomly select 23 frames per individual and form 23 corresponding testsets. We compute errors over these testsets and average those. One important aspect affecting the errors is the use of scaling during ICP alignment: Tran et al. [13] did not allow models to scale during the alignment. We present evaluations in both settings.

Table 3 presents a comparison with Tewari et al. [10] and Garrido et al. [6] on a selection of 9 subjects from Face Warehouse [31] dataset. Version of Tewari et al. network with surrogate loss has been used for this and previous evaluations.

Qualitative Results. Figure 6 shows a comparison with Jackson et al. [11], Tewari er al. [10] and Tran et al. [40] on a few images from BU4DFE-test.

5 Conclusions

We have presented an evaluation of monocular morphable model fitting algorithms and a learning framework. It is demonstrated that incorporation of texture term into the energy function significantly improves fitting accuracy. Gains in the accuracy are quantified. We have trained a neural network using the outputs of the fitting algorithms as training data. Our trained network is shown to perform on a par with existing approaches for the task of monocular 3d face reconstruction while showing faster speed and smaller model size. Running time of our network on a mobile devise is shown to be 3.6 ms enabling real-time applications. Our datasets and code for evaluation are made publicly available.

References

1. Blanz, V., Vetter, T.: A morphable model for the synthesis of 3D faces. In: SIG-GRAPH Conference Proceedings (1999)
2. Romdhani, S., Vetter, T.: Estimating 3D shape and texture using pixel intensity, edges, specular highlights, texture constraints and a prior. In: Computer Vision and Pattern Recognition (CVPR) (2005)
3. Piotraschke, M., Blanz, V.: Automated 3D face reconstruction from multiple images using quality measures. In: Computer Vision and Pattern Recognition (CVPR) (2016)
4. Blanz, V., Vetter, T.: Face recognition based on fitting a 3D morphable model. IEEE Trans. Patt. Anal. Mach. Intell. **25**, 1063–1074 (2003)
5. Thies, J., Zollhöfer, M., Stamminger, M., Theobalt, C., Nießner, M.: Face2Face: real-time face capture and reenactment of RGB videos. In: Computer Vision and Pattern Recognition (CVPR) (2016)
6. Garrido, P., et al.: Reconstruction of personalized 3D face rigs from monocular video. ACM Trans. Graph. (Presented at SIGGRAPH 2016) (2016)
7. Zhu, X., Yan, J., Yi, D., Lei, Z., Li, S.Z.: Discriminative 3D morphable model fitting. In: Automatic Face and Gesture Recognition (FG) (2015)
8. Jeni, L.A., Cohn, J.F., Kanade, T.: Dense 3D face alignment from 2D videos in real-time. In: Automatic Face and Gesture Recognition (FG) (2015)
9. Zhu, X., Lei, Z., Liu, X., Shi, H., Li, S.Z.: Face alignment across large poses: a 3D solution. In: Computer Vision and Pattern Recognition (CVPR) (2016)

10. Tewari, A., et al.: MoFA: model-based deep convolutional face autoencoder for unsupervised monocular reconstruction. In: International Conference on Computer Vision (ICCV) (2017)
11. Jackson, A., Bulat, A., Argyriou, V., Tzimiropoulos, G.: Large pose 3D face reconstruction from a single image via direct volumetric CNN regression. In: International Conference on Computer Vision (ICCV) (2017)
12. Richardson, E., Sela, M., Kimmel, R.: 3D face reconstruction by learning from synthetic data. In: Fourth International Conference on 3D Vision (3DV) (2016)
13. Tran, A., Hassner, T., Masi, I., Medioni, G.: Regressing robust and discriminative 3D morphable models with a very deep neural network. In: Computer Vision and Pattern Recognition (CVPR) (2017)
14. Richardson, E., Sela, M., Or-El, R., Kimmel, R.: Learning detailed face reconstruction from a single image. In: Computer Vision and Pattern Recognition (CVPR) (2017)
15. Kazemi, V., Sullivan, J.: One millisecond face alignment with an ensemble of regression trees. In: Computer Vision and Pattern Recognition (CVPR) (2014)
16. Xiong, X., De la Torre, F.: Supervised descent method and its applications to face alignment. In: Computer Vision and Pattern Recognition (CVPR) (2013)
17. Bulat, A., Tzimiropoulos, G.: How far are we from solving the 2D & 3D face alignment problem? (and a dataset of 230,000 3D facial landmarks). In: International Conference on Computer Vision (ICCV) (2017)
18. Trigeorgis, G., Snape, P., Nicolaou, M.A., Antonakos, E., Zafeiriou, S.: Mnemonic descent method: a recurrent process applied for end-to-end face alignment. In: Computer Vision and Pattern Recognition (CVPR) (2016)
19. Bas, A., Smith, W.A.P.: What does 2D geometric information really tell us about 3D face shape? Arxiv preprint (2017)
20. Zhu, X., Lei, Z., Yan, J., Yi, D., Li, S.Z.: High-fidelity pose and expression normalization for face recognition in the wild. In: Computer Vision and Pattern Recognition (CVPR) (2015)
21. Fried, O., Shechtman, E., Goldman, D.B., Finkelstein, A.: Perspective-aware manipulation of portrait photos. ACM Trans. Graph. (Proc. SIGGRAPH) (2016)
22. Keller, M., Knothe, R., Vetter, T.: 3D reconstruction of human faces from occluding contours. In: Computer Vision/Computer Graphics Collaboration Techniques (2007)
23. Saito, S., Wei, L., Hu, L., Nagano, K., Li, H.: Photorealistic facial texture inference using deep neural networks. In: Computer Vision and Pattern Recognition (CVPR) (2017)
24. Yin, L., Wei, X., Sun, Y., Wang, J., Rosato, M.: A 3D facial expression database for facial behavior research. In: Automatic Face and Gesture Recognition (FG) (2006)
25. Sagonas, C., Tzimiropoulos, G., Zafeiriou, S., Pantic, M.: 300 faces in-the-wild challenge: the first facial landmark localization challenge. In: International Conference on Computer Vision (ICCV) (2013)
26. Kemelmacher-Shlizerman, I., Basri, R.: 3D face reconstruction from a single image using a single reference face shape. IEEE Trans. Patt. Anal. Mach. Intell. **33**, 394–405 (2011)
27. Suwajanakorn, S., Kemelmacher Shlizerman, I., Seitz, S.M.: Total moving face reconstruction. In: Fleet, D., Pajdla, T., Schiele, B., Tuytelaars, T. (eds.) ECCV 2014. LNCS, vol. 8692, pp. 796–812. Springer, Cham (2014). https://doi.org/10.1007/978-3-319-10593-2_52

28. Roth, J., Tong, Y., Liu, X.: Adaptive 3D face reconstruction from unconstrained photo collections. In: Computer Vision and Pattern Recognition (CVPR) (2016)
29. Tewari, A., et al.: Self-supervised multi-level face model learning for monocular reconstruction at over 250 Hz. arxiv preprint (2017)
30. Dou, P., Shah, S.K., Kakadiaris, I.A.: End-to-end 3D face reconstruction with deep neural networks. In: Computer Vision and Pattern Recognition (CVPR), vol. 5 (2017)
31. Cao, C., Weng, Y., Zhou, S., Tong, Y., Zhou, K.: FaceWarehouse: a 3D facial expression database for visual computing. IEEE Trans. Vis. Comput. Graph. **20**, 413–425 (2014)
32. DeVries, T., Taylor, G.W.: Improved regularization of convolutional neural networks with cutout. arXiv preprint arXiv:1708.04552 (2017)
33. Howard, A.G., et al.: MobileNets: efficient convolutional neural networks for mobile vision applications (2017)
34. Chollet, F.: Xception: deep learning with depthwise separable convolutions. In: Computer Vision and Pattern Recognition (CVPR) (2017)
35. Ioffe, S., Szegedy, C.: Batch normalization: accelerating deep network training by reducing internal covariate shift. In: International Conference on Machine Learning (ICML) (2015)
36. Ramamoorthi, R., Hanrahan, P.: A signal-processing framework for inverse rendering. In: SIGGRAPH (2001)
37. Ramamoorthi, R., Hanrahan, P.: An efficient representation for irradiance environment maps. In: 28th Annual Conference on Computer Graphics and Interactive Techniques (2001)
38. Tulyakov, S., Sebe, N.: Regressing a 3D face shape from a single image. In: International Conference on Computer Vision (ICCV) (2015)
39. Kingma, D.P., Ba, J.: Adam: a method for stochastic optimization. arXiv preprint arXiv:1412.6980 (2014)
40. Tran, A.T., Hassner, T., Iacopo, M., Paz, E., Nirkin, Y., Medioni, G.: Extreme 3D face reconstruction: looking past occlusions. arxiv preprint (2017)
41. Sela, M., Richardson, E., Kimmel, R.: Unrestricted facial geometry reconstruction using image-to-image translation. In: International Conference on Computer Vision (ICCV) (2017)
42. Bagdanov, A.D., Del Bimbo, A., Masi, I.: The florence 2D/3D hybrid face dataset. In: Proceedings of the 2011 Joint ACM Workshop on Human Gesture and Behavior Understanding (2011)

A Kinematic Chain Space for Monocular Motion Capture

Bastian Wandt[(✉)], Hanno Ackermann, and Bodo Rosenhahn

Institut für Informationsverarbeitung, Leibniz Universität Hannover,
Hanover, Germany
wandt@tnt.uni-hannover.de

Abstract. This paper deals with motion capture of kinematic chains
(e.g. human skeletons) from monocular image sequences taken by uncalibrated cameras. We present a method based on projecting an observation onto a kinematic chain space (KCS). An optimization of the nuclear
norm is proposed that implicitly enforces structural properties of the
kinematic chain. Unlike other approaches our method is not relying on
training data or previously determined constraints such as particular
body lengths. The proposed algorithm is able to reconstruct scenes with
little or no camera motion and previously unseen motions. It is not only
applicable to human skeletons but also to other kinematic chains for
instance animals or industrial robots. We achieve state-of-the-art results
on different benchmark databases and real world scenes.

1 Introduction

Monocular human motion capture is an important and large part of recent
research. Its applications range from surveillance, animation, robotics to medical research. While there exists a large number of commercial motion capture
systems, monocular 3D reconstruction of human motion plays an important role
where complex hardware arrangements are not feasible or too costly.

Recent approaches to the non-rigid structure from motion problem [1–4]
achieve good results for laboratory settings. They are designed to work with
tracked 2D points from arbitrary 3D point clouds. To resolve the duality of
camera and point motion they require sufficient camera motion in the observed
sequence. On the other hand, in many applications (e.g. human motion capture,
animal tracking or robotics) properties of the tracked objects are known. Exploiting known structural properties for non-rigid structure from motion problems is
rarely considered e.g. by using example based modeling as in [5] or constancy
of bone lengths in [6]. Recently, linear subspace training approaches have been
proposed [6–11]. They can efficiently represent human motion, even for 3D reconstruction from single images. However, they require extensive training on known

Electronic supplementary material The online version of this chapter (https://
doi.org/10.1007/978-3-030-11018-5_4) contains supplementary material, which is available to authorized users.

L. Leal-Taixé and S. Roth (Eds.): ECCV 2018 Workshops, LNCS 11132, pp. 31–47, 2019.
https://doi.org/10.1007/978-3-030-11018-5_4

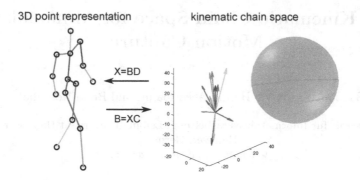

Fig. 1. Mapping from a 3D point representation to the kinematic chain space. The vectors in the KCS equal to directional vectors in the 3D point representation. The sphere shows the trajectories of left and right lower arm in KCS. Since both bones have the same length their trajectories lie on the same sphere.

motions which restricts them to reconstructions of the same motion category. Further, training based approaches cannot recover individual subtleties in the motion (e.g. limping instead of walking) sufficiently well.

This paper closes the gap between non-rigid structure from motion and subspace-based human modeling. Similar to other approaches which depend on the work of Bregler et al. [12], we decompose an observation matrix in three matrices corresponding to camera motion, transformation and basis shapes. Unlike other works that find a transformation which enforces properties of the camera matrices, we develop an algorithm that optimizes the transformation with respect to structural properties of the observed object. This reduces the amount of camera motion necessary for a good reconstruction. We experimentally found that even sequences without camera motion can be reconstructed. Unlike other works in the field of human modeling we propose to first project the observations in a *kinematic chain space (KCS)* before optimizing a reprojection error with respect to our kinematic model. Figure 1 shows the mapping between the KCS and the representation based on 2D or 3D feature points. It is done by multiplication with matrices which implicitly encode a kinematic chain (cf. Sect. 3.1). This representation enables us to derive a nuclear norm optimization problem which can be solved efficiently. Imposing a low rank constraint on a Gram matrix has shown to improve 3D reconstructions [3]. However, the method of [3] is only based on constraining the camera motion. Therefore, it requires sufficient camera motion. The KCS allows to use a geometric constraint which is based on the topology of the underlying kinematic chain. Thus, the required amount of camera motion is much lower.

We evaluate our method on different standard databases (CMU MoCap [13], KTH [14], HumanEva [15], Human3.6M [16]) as well as on our own databases qualitatively and quantitatively. The proposed algorithm achieves state-of-the-art results and can handle problems like motion transfers and unseen motion. Due to the noise robustness of our method we can apply a CNN-based joint labeling algorithm [17,18] for RGB images as input data which allows us to directly reconstruct human poses from unlabeled videos. Although this method is developed for human motion capture it is applicable to other kinematic chains such as animals or industrial robots as shown in the experiments in Sect. 4.3.

Summarizing, our contributions are:

- We propose a method for 3D reconstruction of kinematic chains from monocular image sequences.
- An objective function based on structural properties of kinematic chains is derived that not only imposes a low-rank assumption on the shape basis but also has a physical interpretation.
- We propose using a nuclear norm optimization in a *kinematic chain space*.
- In contrast to other works our method is not limited to previously learned motion patterns and does not use strong anthropometric constraints such a-priorly determined bone lengths.

2 Related Work

The idea of decomposing a set of 2D points tracked over a sequence into matrices whose entries are identified with the parameters of shape and motion was first proposed by Tomasi and Kanade [19]. A generalization of this algorithm to deforming shapes was proposed by Bregler et al. [12]. They assume that the observation matrix can be factorized into two matrices representing camera motion and multiple basis shapes. After an initial decomposition is found by singular value decomposition (SVD) of the observation matrix they compute a transformation matrix by enforcing camera constraints. Xiao et al. [20] showed that the basis shapes of [12] are ambiguous. They solved this ambiguity by employing basis constraints on them. As shown by Akther et al. [1] these basis constraints are still not sufficient to resolve the ambiguity. Therefore, they proposed to use an object independent trajectory basis. Torresani et al. [21–23] proposed to use different priors on the transformation matrix such as additional rank constraints and Gaussian priors. Gotardo and Martinez [24] built on the idea of [1] by applying the DCT representation to enforce a smooth 3D shape trajectory. Parallel to this work they proposed a solution that uses the kernel trick to also model nonlinear deformations [25] which cannot be represented by a linear combination of basis shapes. Hamsici et al. [2] also assume a smooth shape trajectory and apply the kernel trick to learn a mapping between the 3D shape and the 2D input data. Park et al. [26] introduced activity-independent spatial and temporal constraints. Inspired by [1] and [26] Valmadre et al. [27] proposed a dynamic programming approach combined with temporal filtering. Dai et al. [3] minimize the trace norm of the transformation matrix to impose a sparsity constraint. Different to [3] Lee et al. [28] define additional constraints on motion parameters to avoid the sparsity constraint. Since all these methods assume to work for arbitrary non-rigid 3D objects, none of them utilizes knowledge about the underlying kinematic structure. Rehan et al. [4] were the first to define a temporary rigidity of reconstructed structures by factorizing a small

number of consecutive frames. Thereby, they can reconstruct kinematic chains if
the object does not deform much. Due to their sliding window assumption, the
method is even more restricted to scenes with sufficient camera motion.

Several works consider the special case of 3D reconstruction of human motion
from monocular images. A common approach is to previously learn base poses
of the same motion category. These are then linearly combined for the estimation of 3D poses. To avoid implausible poses, most authors utilize properties of
human skeletons to constrain a reprojection error based optimization problem.
However, anthropometric priors such as the sum of squared bone lengths [7],
known limb proportions [8], known skeleton parameters [5], previously trained
joint angle constraints [9] or strong physical constraints [29] all suffer from the
fact that parameters have to be known a-priorly. Zhou et al. [10] propose a convex relaxation of the commonly used reprojection error formulation to avoid the
alternating optimization of camera and object pose. While many approaches try
to reconstruct human poses from a single image [30–35] using anthropometric
priors, such constraints have rarely been used for 3D reconstruction from image
sequences. Wandt et al. [6] constrain the temporal change of bone length without using a predefined skeleton. Zhou et al. [36] combined a deep neural network
that estimates 2D landmarks with 3D reconstruction of the human pose. A different approach is to include sensors as additional information source [37–39].
Other works use a trained mesh model for instance SMPL [40] and project it to
the image plane [41,42]. The restriction to a trained subset of possible human
motions is the major downside of these approaches.

In this paper we combine NR-SfM and human pose modeling without requiring previously learned motions. By using a representation that implicitly models
the kinematic chain of a human skeleton our algorithm is capable to reconstruct
unknown motion from labeled image sequences.

3   Estimating Camera and Shape

The i-th joint of a kinematic chain is defined by a vector $\boldsymbol{x}_i \in \mathbb{R}^3$ containing the
x, y, z-coordinates of the location of this joint. By concatenating j joint vectors
we build a matrix representing the pose $\boldsymbol{X}$ of the kinematic chain

$$\boldsymbol{X} = (\boldsymbol{x}_1, \boldsymbol{x}_2, \cdots, \boldsymbol{x}_j). \tag{1}$$

The pose $\boldsymbol{X}_k$ in frame k can be projected into the image plane by

$$\boldsymbol{X}'_k = \boldsymbol{P}_k \boldsymbol{X}_k, \tag{2}$$

where $\boldsymbol{P}_k$ is the projection matrix corresponding to a weak perspective camera. For a sequence of f frames, the pose matrices are stacked such that
$\boldsymbol{W} = (\boldsymbol{X}'_1, \boldsymbol{X}'_2, \ldots, \boldsymbol{X}'_f)^T$ and $\hat{\boldsymbol{X}} = (\boldsymbol{X}_1, \boldsymbol{X}_2, \ldots, \boldsymbol{X}_f)^T$. This implies

$$\boldsymbol{W} = \boldsymbol{P}\hat{\boldsymbol{X}}, \tag{3}$$

where $\boldsymbol{P}$ is a block diagonal matrix containing the camera matrices $\boldsymbol{P}_{1,\ldots,f}$ for
the corresponding frame. After an initial camera estimation we subtract a matrix
$\boldsymbol{X}_0$ from the measurement matrix by

$$\hat{W} = W - P\hat{X}_0, \tag{4}$$

where $\hat{X}_0$ is obtained by stacking X_0 multiple times to obtain the same size as W. Here, we take X_0 to be a mean pose. We will provide experimental evidence that the algorithm proposed in the following is insensitive w.r.t. the choice of X_0 as long as it represents a reasonable configuration of the kinematic chain. In all the experiments dealing with kinematic chains of humans, we take X_0 to be the average of all poses in the CMU data set.

Following the approach of Bregler et al. [12] we decompose $\hat{W}$ by Singular Value Decomposition to obtain a rank-$3K$ pose basis $Q \in \mathbb{R}^{3K \times j}$. While [12] and similar works then optimize a transformation matrix with respect to orthogonality constraints of camera matrices, we optimize the transformation matrix with respect to constraints based on a physical interpretation of the underlying structure. With A as transformation matrix for the pose basis we may write

$$W = P(\hat{X}_0 + AQ). \tag{5}$$

In the following sections we will present how poses can be projected into the kinematic chain space (Sect. 3.1) and how we derive an optimization problem from it (Sect. 3.2). Combined with the camera estimation (Sect. 3.3) an alternating algorithm is presented in Sect. 3.4.

3.1   Kinematic Chain Space

To define a bone b_k, a vector between the r-th and t-th joint is computed by

$$b_k = p_r - p_t = Xc, \tag{6}$$

where

$$c = (0, \ldots, 0, 1, 0, \ldots, 0, -1, 0, \ldots, 0)^T, \tag{7}$$

with 1 at position r and -1 at position t. The vector b_k has the same direction and length as the corresponding bone. Similarly to Eq. (1), a matrix $B \in \mathbb{R}^{3 \times b}$ can be defined containing all b bones

$$B = (b_1, b_2, \ldots, b_b). \tag{8}$$

The matrix B is calculated by

$$B = XC, \tag{9}$$

where $C \in \mathbb{R}^{j \times b}$ is built by concatenating multiple vectors c. Analogously to C, a matrix $D \in \mathbb{R}^{b \times j}$ can be defined that maps B back to X:

$$X = BD. \tag{10}$$

D is constructed similar to C. Each column adds vectors in B to reconstruct the corresponding point coordinates. Note that C and D are a direct result of the underlying kinematic chain. Therefore, the matrices C and D perform the mapping from point representation into the *kinematic chain space* and vice versa.

3.2   Trace Norm Constraint

One of the main properties of human skeletons is the fact that bone lengths do not change over time.

Let

$$\boldsymbol{\Psi} = \boldsymbol{B}^T \boldsymbol{B} = \begin{pmatrix} l_1^2 & \cdot & \cdot & \cdot \\ \cdot & l_2^2 & \cdot & \cdot \\ \cdot & \cdot & \ddots & \cdot \\ \cdot & \cdot & \cdot & l_b^2 \end{pmatrix}. \tag{11}$$

be a matrix with the squared bone lengths on its diagonal. From $\boldsymbol{B} \in \mathbb{R}^{3 \times b}$ follows $rank(\boldsymbol{B}) = 3$. Thus, $\boldsymbol{\Psi}$ has rank 3. Note that if $\boldsymbol{\Psi}$ is computed for every frame we can define a stronger constraint on $\boldsymbol{\Psi}$. Namely, as bone lengths do not change for the same person the diagonal of $\boldsymbol{\Psi}$ remains constant.

Proposition 1. *The nuclear norm of* $\boldsymbol{B}$ *is invariant for any bone configuration of the same person.*

Proof. The trace of $\boldsymbol{\Psi}$ equals the sum of squared bone lengths (Eq. (11))

$$trace(\boldsymbol{\Psi}) = \sum_{i=1}^{b} l_i^2. \tag{12}$$

From the assumption that bone lengths of humans are invariant during a captured image sequence the trace of $\boldsymbol{\Psi}$ is constant. The same argument holds for $trace(\sqrt{\boldsymbol{\Psi}})$. Therefore, we have

$$\|\boldsymbol{B}\|_* = trace(\sqrt{\boldsymbol{\Psi}}) = const. \tag{13}$$

Since this constancy constraint is non-convex we will relax it to derive an easy to solve optimization problem. Using Eq. (9) we project Eq. (5) into the KCS which gives

$$\boldsymbol{W}\boldsymbol{C} = \boldsymbol{P}(\hat{\boldsymbol{X}}_0 \boldsymbol{C} + \boldsymbol{A}\boldsymbol{Q}\boldsymbol{C}) \tag{14}$$

The unknown is the transformation matrix $\boldsymbol{A}$. For better readability we define $\boldsymbol{B}_0 = \boldsymbol{X}_0 \boldsymbol{C}$ and $\boldsymbol{S} = \boldsymbol{Q}\boldsymbol{C}$.

Proposition 2. *The nuclear norm of the transformation matrix* $\boldsymbol{A}$ *for each frame has to be greater than some scalar* c, *which is constant for each frame.*

Proof. Let $\boldsymbol{B} = \boldsymbol{B}_1 + \boldsymbol{B}_0$ be a decomposition of $\boldsymbol{B}$ into the initial bone configuration $\boldsymbol{B}_0$ and a difference to the observed pose $\boldsymbol{B}_1$. It follows that

$$\|\boldsymbol{B}\|_* = \|\boldsymbol{B}_1 + \boldsymbol{B}_0\|_* = c_1, \tag{15}$$

where c_1 is a constant. The triangle inequality for matrix norms gives

$$\|\boldsymbol{B}_1\|_* + \|\boldsymbol{B}_0\|_* \geq \|\boldsymbol{B}_1 + \boldsymbol{B}_0\|_* = c_1. \tag{16}$$

Since B_0 is known, it follows

$$\|B_1\|_* \geq c_1 - \|B_0\|_* = c, \tag{17}$$

where c is constant. B_1 can be represented in the shape basis S (cf. Sect. 3) by multiplying it with the transformation matrix A

$$B_1 = AS. \tag{18}$$

Since the shape base matrix S is a unitary matrix the nuclear norm of B_1 equals

$$\|B_1\|_* = \|A\|_*. \tag{19}$$

By Eq. (17) follows that

$$\|A\|_* \geq c. \tag{20}$$

Proposition 2 also holds for a sequence of frames. Let $\hat{A}$ be a matrix built by stacking A for each frame and $\hat{B}_0$ be defined similarly, we relax Eq. (20) and obtain the final formulation for our optimization problem

$$\min_{\hat{A}} \quad \|\hat{A}\|_* \\ \text{s.t.} \quad \|WC - P(\hat{A}S + \hat{B}_0)\|_F = 0. \tag{21}$$

Equation (21) does not only define a low rank assumption on the transformation matrix. By the derivation above, we showed that the nuclear norm is reasonable because it has a concise physical interpretation. More intuitively, the minimization of the nuclear norm will give solutions close to a mean configuration B_0 of the bones in terms of rotation of the bones. The constraint in Eq. (21) which represents the reprojection error prevents the optimization from converging to the trivial solution $\|A\|_* = 0$. This allows for a reconstruction of arbitrary poses and skeletons.

Moreover, Eq. (21) is a well studied problem which can be efficiently solved by common optimization methods such as Singular Value Thresholding (SVT) [43].

3.3   Camera

The objective function in Eq. (21) can also be optimized for the camera matrix P. Since P is a block diagonal matrix, Eq. (21) can be solved block-wise for each frame. With X_i' and P_i corresponding to the observation and camera at frame i the optimization problem can be written as

$$\min_{P_i} \|X_i'C - P_i(AS + B_0)\|_F. \tag{22}$$

Considering the entries in

$$P_i = \begin{pmatrix} p_{11} & p_{12} & p_{13} \\ p_{21} & p_{22} & p_{23} \end{pmatrix} \tag{23}$$

we can enforce a weak perspective camera by the constraints

$$p_{11}^2 + p_{12}^2 + p_{13}^2 - (p_{21}^2 + p_{22}^2 + p_{23}^2) = 0 \qquad (24)$$

and

$$p_{11}p_{21} + p_{12}p_{22} + p_{13}p_{23} = 0. \qquad (25)$$

3.4 Algorithm

In the previous sections we derived an optimization problem that can be solved for the camera matrix P and transformation matrix A respectively. As both are unknown we propose Algorithm 1 which alternatingly solves for both matrices. Initialization is done by setting all entries in the transformation matrix A to zero. Additionally, an initial bone configuration B_0 is required. It has to roughly model a human skeleton but does not need to be the mean of the sequence.

Algorithm 1. Factorization algorithm for kinematic chains

% **Input:**
$B_0 \leftarrow$ initial bone configuration
$C \leftarrow$ kinematic chain matrix
$W \leftarrow$ observation
$f \leftarrow$ number of frames
$A \leftarrow 0$

while no convergence **do**
    for $t = 1 \rightarrow f$ **do**
        optimize $\|X_t C - P_t(AS + B_0)\|_F$
        insert P_t in P
    end for
    perform SVT on
        $\min \|\hat{A}\|_*$ s.t. $\|WC - P(\hat{A}S + \hat{B}_0)\|_F = 0$
end while

% **Output:**
P: camera matrices
$(\hat{A}S + \hat{B}_0)D$: 3D poses

---

4 Experiments

For the evaluation of our algorithm different benchmark data sets (CMU MoCap [13], HumanEva [15], KTH [14], Human3.6M [16]) were used. As measure for the quality of the 3D reconstructions we calculate the *Mean Per Joint Position Error (MPJPE)* [16] which is defined by

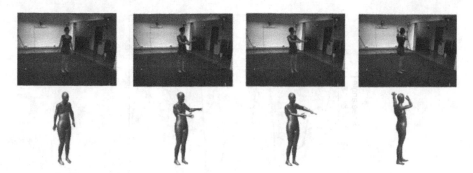

Fig. 2. Reconstruction of the highly articulated *directions* sequence from the Human3.6M data set subject 1.

$$e = \frac{1}{j} \sum_{i=1}^{j} \|\boldsymbol{x}_i - \hat{\boldsymbol{x}}_i\|, \tag{26}$$

where $\boldsymbol{x}_i$ and $\hat{\boldsymbol{x}}_i$ correspond to the ground truth and estimated positions of the i-th joint respectively. By rigidly aligning the 3D reconstruction to the ground truth we obtain the *3D positioning error (3DPE)* as introduced by [44]. To compare sequences of different lengths the mean of the 3DPE over all frames is used. In the following it is referred to as *3D error*.

Additional to this quantitative evaluation we perform reconstructions of different kinematic chains in Sect. 4.3 and on unlabeled image sequences in Sect. 4.4. All animated meshes in this section are created using SMPL [40]. The SMPL model is fitted to the reconstructed skeleton and is used solely for visualization.

4.1   Evaluation on Benchmark Databases

To qualitatively show the drawbacks of learning-based approaches we reconstructed a sequence of a limping person. We use the method of [6] trained on walking patterns to reconstruct the 3D scene. Although the motions are very

Fig. 3. Reconstruction of a running motion from the CMU database subject 35/17.

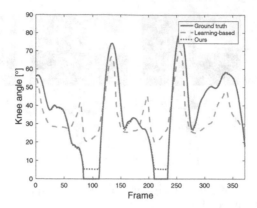

Fig. 4. Knee angle of reconstructions of a limping motion. The learning-based method [6] struggles to reconstruct minor differences from the motion patterns used for training whereas our learning-free approach recovers the knee angle in more detail.

similar, the algorithm of [6] is not able to reconstruct the subtle motions of the limping leg. Figure 4 shows the knee angle of the respective leg. The learning-based method reconstructs a periodic walking motion and cannot recover the unknown asymmetric motion which makes it unusable for gait analysis applications. The proposed algorithm is able to recover the motion in more detail.

We compare our method with the unsupervised works [1,2] and the learning-based approach of [6]. The codes of [1] and [2] are freely available. Although there are slightly newer works, these two approaches show the inherent problem of these unsupervised methods (as also shown in [4]). We are not aware of any works that are able to reconstruct scenes with very limited or no camera motion without a model of the underlying structure. Rehan et al. [4] assume a local rigidity that allows for defining a kinematic chain model. This reduced the amount of necessary camera motion to 2 degrees per frame. However, due to their assumption that the observed object is approximately rigid in a small time window they are limited to a constantly moving camera.

For each sequence we created 20 random camera paths with little or no camera motion and compared our 3D reconstruction results with the other methods. Table 1 shows the 3D error in *mm* for different sequences and data sets. For the entry *walk35* we calculated the mean overall 3D errors of all 23 walking sequences from subject 35 in the CMU database. The columns *jump* and *limp* show the 3D error of a single jumping and limping sequence. *KTH* means the football sequence of the KTH data set [14] and *HE* the walking sequence of the HumanEva data set [15]. The last four columns are average errors over all subjects performing the respective motions of the Human3.6M data set [16]. Note that the highly articulated motions from Human3.6M data set vary a lot in the same category and therefore are hard to learn by approaches like [6]. All these sequences are captured with little or no camera motion. The unsupervised methods of [1] and [2] require more camera motion and completely fail in these scenarios. The learning-based approach of [6] reconstructs plausible poses for all sequences. They even achieve a better result for the walking motions. However, motions with larger variations between persons and sequences (e.g. jumping and limping) are harder to reconstruct from the learned pose basis. Although the results look like plausible human motions, they lack the ability to reconstruct subtle motion variations. In contrast, the proposed method is able to reconstruct these variations and achieves a better result. Some of our reconstructions are shown in Figs. 2 and 3 for sequences of the Human3.6M and CMU data set, respectively.

Table 1. 3D error in *mm* for different sequences and data sets. The column *walk35* shows the mean 3D error of all sequences containing walking motion from subject 35 in the CMU database. *jump* refers to the jumping motion of subject 13/11 of the CMU database and *limp* to the limping motion of subject 91/16. *KTH* means the football sequence of the KTH data set [14]. The column *HE* shows the 3D error for the HumanEva walking sequence [15]. The last four columns are average errors over all subjects performing the respective motions of the Human3.6M data set [16].

	walk35	jump	limp	KTH	HE	3.6M walk	3.6M dir.	3.6M pose	3.6M photo
[1]	228.68	210.14	99.37	108.91	106.92	86.76	130.43	121.33	145.44
[2]	264.75	186.70	112.92	114.03	102.99	**66.70**	121.40	120.56	136.30
[6]	**11.22**	45.49	64.46	68.88	58.62	71.54	110.36	135.87	124.52
Ours	18.94	**36.50**	**19.24**	**53.10**	**44.36**	74.44	**80.83**	**109.28**	**101.76**

4.2   Convergence

We alternatingly optimize the camera matrices (Eq. (21)) and transformation matrix (Eq. (22)). Since convergence of the algorithm cannot be guaranteed we show it by experiment. Figure 5 shows the convergence of the reprojection error in pixel for a sequence from the CMU MoCap database. However, the reprojection error only shows the convergence of the proposed algorithm but cannot prove that the 3D reconstructions will improve every iteration. We additionally estimated the convergence of the 3D error in Fig. 5. In most cases our algorithm converges to a good minimum in less than 3 iterations. Further iterations do not improve the visual quality and only deform the 3D reconstruction less than 1 mm. The 3D error remains constant during camera estimation which causes the *steps* in the error plot.

Figure 6 shows the computation time over the number of frames for three different sequences. The computation time mostly depends on the number frames and less on the observed motion. We use unoptimized Matlab code on a desktop PC for all computations.

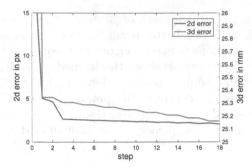

Fig. 5. Reprojection error and 3D error with respect to number of iterations for subject35/sequence1 from the CMU MoCap data set. Even steps refer to camera estimation while odd steps correspond to shape estimation.

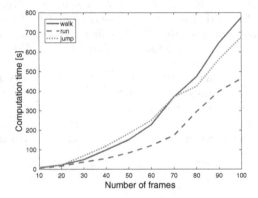

Fig. 6. Computation time for walking, running and jumping sequences of the CMU data set using unoptimized Matlab code. It mostly depends on the number of frames and less on the observed motion.

4.3   Other Kinematic Chains

Although our method was developed for the reconstruction of human motion, it generalizes to all kinematic chains that do not include translational joints. In this section we show reconstructions of other kinematic chains such as people holding objects, animals and industrial robots.

In situations where people hold objects with both hands the kinematic chain of the body can be extended by another rigid connection between the two hands. Figure 7 shows the reconstruction of the sword fighting sequence of the CMU data set. By simply adding another column to the kinematic chain space matrix C (cf. Sect. 3.1) the distance between the two hands is enforced to remain constant. The exact distance does not need to be known, however.

Fig. 7. Reconstruction of the sword play sequence of the CMU database. The kinematic chain is extended such that the hands are rigidly connected.

Fig. 8. Reconstruction of a sequence of an industrial robot moving along a path. The reconstruction is shown as an augmented overlay over the images.

Fig. 9. Reconstruction of a horse riding sequence. Although we use a very rough model for the skeleton of the horse we obtain plausible reconstructions. The complete reconstruction including more views can be seen in the supplemental video.

Figure 8 shows a robot used for precision milling and the reconstructed 3D model as overlay. The proposed method is able to correctly reconstruct the robots motion. In Fig. 9 we reconstructed a more complex motion of a horse during show jumping. We used a simplified model of the bone structure of a horse. Also in reality the shoulder joint is not completely rigid. Despite these limitations the algorithm achieves plausible results.

4.4 Image Sequences

The proposed method is designed to reconstruct a 3D object from labeled feature points. In the former sections this was done by setting and tracking them semi-interactively. In this section we will show that our method is also able to use the noisy output of a human joint detector. We use *deeperCut* [17,18] to estimate the joints in the outdoor run and jump sequence from [45]. Figure 10 shows the joints estimated by *deeperCut* and our 3D reconstruction. As can be seen in Fig. 10 we achieve plausible 3D reconstructions even with automatically labeled noisy input data.

Fig. 10. Reconstruction of a running and jumping sequence from [45] automatically labeled by *deeperCut* [17,18].

5   Conclusion

We developed a method for the 3D reconstruction of kinematic chains from monocular image sequences. By projecting into the kinematic chain space a constraint is derived that is based on the assumption that bone lengths are constant. This results in the formulation of an easy to solve nuclear norm optimization problem. It allows for reconstruction of scenes with little camera motion where other non-rigid structure from motion methods fail. Our method does not rely on previous training or predefined body measures such as known limb lengths. The proposed algorithm generalizes to the reconstruction of other kinematic chains and achieves state-of-the-art results on benchmark data sets.

References

1. Akhter, I., Sheikh, Y., Khan, S., Kanade, T.: Trajectory space: a dual representation for nonrigid structure from motion. IEEE Trans. Pattern Anal. Mach. Intell. **33**(7), 1442–1456 (2011)
2. Hamsici, O.C., Gotardo, P.F.U., Martinez, A.M.: Learning spatially-smooth mappings in non-rigid structure from motion. In: Fitzgibbon, A., Lazebnik, S., Perona, P., Sato, Y., Schmid, C. (eds.) ECCV 2012, Part IV. LNCS, vol. 7575, pp. 260–273. Springer, Heidelberg (2012). https://doi.org/10.1007/978-3-642-33765-9_19
3. Dai, Y., Li, H.: A simple prior-free method for non-rigid structure-from-motion factorization. In: Conference on Computer Vision and Pattern Recognition (CVPR 2012), Washington, DC, USA, pp. 2018–2025. IEEE Computer Society (2012)
4. Rehan, A., et al.: NRSfM using local rigidity. In: Proceedings Winter Conference on Applications of Computer Vision, Steamboat Springs, CO, USA, pp. 69–74. IEEE, March 2014
5. Chen, Y.-L., Chai, J.: 3D reconstruction of human motion and skeleton from uncalibrated monocular video. In: Zha, H., Taniguchi, R., Maybank, S. (eds.) ACCV 2009, Part I. LNCS, vol. 5994, pp. 71–82. Springer, Heidelberg (2010). https://doi.org/10.1007/978-3-642-12307-8_7
6. Wandt, B., Ackermann, H., Rosenhahn, B.: 3D reconstruction of human motion from monocular image sequences. IEEE Trans. Pattern Anal. Mach. Intell. **38**(8), 1505–1516 (2016)
7. Ramakrishna, V., Kanade, T., Sheikh, Y.: Reconstructing 3D human pose from 2D image landmarks. In: Fitzgibbon, A., Lazebnik, S., Perona, P., Sato, Y., Schmid, C. (eds.) ECCV 2012, Part IV. LNCS, vol. 7575, pp. 573–586. Springer, Heidelberg (2012). https://doi.org/10.1007/978-3-642-33765-9_41
8. Wang, C., Wang, Y., Lin, Z., Yuille, A., Gao, W.: Robust estimation of 3D human poses from a single image. In: Conference on Computer Vision and Pattern Recognition (CVPR) (2014)
9. Akhter, I., Black, M.J.: Pose-conditioned joint angle limits for 3D human pose reconstruction. In: IEEE Conference on Computer Vision and Pattern Recognition (CVPR 2015), pp. 1446–1455, June 2015
10. Zhou, X., Leonardos, S., Hu, X., Daniilidis, K.: 3D shape estimation from 2D landmarks: a convex relaxation approach. In: CVPR, pp. 4447–4455. IEEE Computer Society (2015)
11. Wandt, B., Ackermann, H., Rosenhahn, B.: 3D human motion capture from monocular image sequences. In: IEEE Conference on Computer Vision and Pattern Recognition Workshops, June 2015
12. Bregler, C., Hertzmann, A., Biermann, H.: Recovering non-rigid 3D shape from image streams. In: Conference on Computer Vision and Pattern Recognition (CVPR), pp. 690–696 (2000)
13. CMU: Human motion capture database (2014)
14. Kazemi, V., Burenius, M., Azizpour, H., Sullivan, J.: Multi-view body part recognition with random forests. In: British Machine Vision Conference (BMVC) (2013)
15. Sigal, L., Balan, A.O., Black, M.J.: Humaneva: synchronized video and motion capture dataset and baseline algorithm for evaluation of articulated human motion. Int. J. Comput. Vis. **87**(1–2), 4–27 (2010)
16. Ionescu, C., Papava, D., Olaru, V., Sminchisescu, C.: Human3.6M: large scale datasets and predictive methods for 3D human sensing in natural environments. IEEE Trans. Pattern Anal. Mach. Intell. **36**(7), 1325–1339 (2014)

17. Pishchulin, L., et al.: Deepcut: joint subset partition and labeling for multi person pose estimation. In: IEEE Conference on Computer Vision and Pattern Recognition (CVPR) (2016)
18. Insafutdinov, E., Pishchulin, L., Andres, B., Andriluka, M., Schiele, B.: DeeperCut: a deeper, stronger, and faster multi-person pose estimation model. In: Leibe, B., Matas, J., Sebe, N., Welling, M. (eds.) ECCV 2016, Part VI. LNCS, vol. 9910, pp. 34–50. Springer, Cham (2016). https://doi.org/10.1007/978-3-319-46466-4_3
19. Tomasi, C., Kanade, T.: Shape and motion from image streams under orthography: a factorization method. Int. J. Comput. Vis. 9, 137–154 (1992)
20. Xiao, J., Chai, J., Kanade, T.: A closed-form solution to non-rigid shape and motion recovery. In: Pajdla, T., Matas, J. (eds.) ECCV 2004, Part IV. LNCS, vol. 3024, pp. 573–587. Springer, Heidelberg (2004). https://doi.org/10.1007/978-3-540-24673-2_46
21. Torresani, L., Hertzmann, A., Bregler, C.: Learning non-rigid 3D shape from 2D motion. In: Thrun, S., Saul, L.K., Schölkopf, B. (eds.) Neural Information Processing Systems (NIPS). MIT Press, Cambridge (2003)
22. Torresani, L., Hertzmann, A., Bregler, C.: Nonrigid structure-from-motion: estimating shape and motion with hierarchical priors. IEEE Trans. Pattern Anal. Mach. Intell. 30, 878–892 (2008). https://ieeexplore.ieee.org/document/4359359
23. Torresani, L., Yang, D.B., Alexander, E.J., Bregler, C.: Tracking and modeling non-rigid objects with rank constraints. In: Conference on Computer Vision and Pattern Recognition (CVPR), pp. 493–500 (2001)
24. Gotardo, P., Martinez, A.: Non-rigid structure from motion with complementary rank-3 spaces. In: Conference on Computer Vision and Pattern Recognition (CVPR) (2011)
25. Gotardo, P., Martinez, A.: Kernel non-rigid structure from motion. In: International Conference on Computer Vision (ICCV). IEEE (2011)
26. Park, H.S., Sheikh, Y.: 3D reconstruction of a smooth articulated trajectory from a monocular image sequence. In: Metaxas, D.N., Quan, L., Sanfeliu, A., Gool, L.J.V. (eds.) ICCV, pp. 201–208. IEEE Computer Society (2011)
27. Valmadre, J., Zhu, Y., Sridharan, S., Lucey, S.: Efficient articulated trajectory reconstruction using dynamic programming and filters. In: Fitzgibbon, A., Lazebnik, S., Perona, P., Sato, Y., Schmid, C. (eds.) ECCV 2012, Part I. LNCS, vol. 7572, pp. 72–85. Springer, Heidelberg (2012). https://doi.org/10.1007/978-3-642-33718-5_6
28. Lee, M., Cho, J., Choi, C.H., Oh, S.: Procrustean normal distribution for non-rigid structure from motion. In: Proceedings of the IEEE Conference on Computer Vision and Pattern Recognition, pp. 1280–1287 (2013)
29. Zell, P., Wandt, B., Rosenhahn, B.: Joint 3D human motion capture and physical analysis from monocular videos. In: The IEEE Conference on Computer Vision and Pattern Recognition (CVPR) Workshops, July 2017
30. Martinez, J., Hossain, R., Romero, J., Little, J.J.: A simple yet effective baseline for 3D human pose estimation. In: Proceedings of the IEEE International Conference on Computer Vision (ICCV), Piscataway, NJ, USA. IEEE, October 2017
31. Lassner, C., Romero, J., Kiefel, M., Bogo, F., Black, M.J., Gehler, P.V.: Unite the people: closing the loop between 3D and 2D human representations. In: IEEE Conference on Computer Vision and Pattern Recognition (CVPR), July 2017
32. Pavlakos, G., Zhou, X., Derpanis, K.G., Daniilidis, K.: Coarse-to-fine volumetric prediction for single-image 3D human pose. In: Proceedings of the IEEE Conference on Computer Vision and Pattern Recognition (2017)

33. Rogez, G., Weinzaepfel, P., Schmid, C.: LCR-Net: localization-classification-regression for human pose. In: IEEE Conference on Computer Vision and Pattern Recognition, CVPR 2017, Honolulu, United States, pp. 1216–1224. IEEE, July 2017

34. Zhou, X., Huang, Q., Sun, X., Xue, X., Wei, Y.: Towards 3D human pose estimation in the wild: a weakly-supervised approach. In: The IEEE International Conference on Computer Vision (ICCV), October 2017

35. Kanazawa, A., Black, M.J., Jacobs, D.W., Malik, J.: End-to-end recovery of human shape and pose. In: Computer Vision and Pattern Recognition (CVPR) (2018)

36. Zhou, X., Zhu, M., Leonardos, S., Derpanis, K.G., Daniilidis, K.: Sparseness meets deepness: 3D human pose estimation from monocular video. In: The IEEE Conference on Computer Vision and Pattern Recognition (CVPR), June 2016

37. von Marcard, T., Pons-Moll, G., Rosenhahn, B.: Human pose estimation from video and imus. Trans. Pattern Anal. Mach. Intell. **38**(8), 1533–1547 (2016)

38. von Marcard, T., Rosenhahn, B., Black, M., Pons-Moll, G.: Sparse inertial poser: automatic 3D human pose estimation from sparse IMUs. In: Proceedings of the 38th Annual Conference of the European Association for Computer Graphics (Eurographics). Computer Graphics Forum, vol. 36(2) (2017)

39. von Marcard, T., Henschel, R., Black, M.J., Rosenhahn, B., Pons-Moll, G.: Recovering accurate 3D human pose in the wild using IMUs and a moving camera. In: Ferrari, V., Hebert, M., Sminchisescu, C., Weiss, Y. (eds.) ECCV 2018, Part X. LNCS, vol. 11214, pp. 614–631. Springer, Cham (2018). https://doi.org/10.1007/978-3-030-01249-6_37

40. Loper, M., Mahmood, N., Romero, J., Pons-Moll, G., Black, M.J.: SMPL: a skinned multi-person linear model. ACM Trans. Graphics (Proc. SIGGRAPH Asia) **34**(6), 248:1–248:16 (2015)

41. Bogo, F., Kanazawa, A., Lassner, C., Gehler, P., Romero, J., Black, M.J.: Keep it SMPL: automatic estimation of 3D human pose and shape from a single image. In: Leibe, B., Matas, J., Sebe, N., Welling, M. (eds.) ECCV 2016, Part V. LNCS, vol. 9909, pp. 561–578. Springer, Cham (2016). https://doi.org/10.1007/978-3-319-46454-1_34

42. Alldieck, T., Kassubeck, M., Wandt, B., Rosenhahn, B., Magnor, M.: Optical flow-based 3D human motion estimation from monocular video. In: German Conference on Pattern Recognition (GCPR), September 2017

43. Cai, J.F., Candès, E.J., Shen, Z.: A singular value thresholding algorithm for matrix completion. SIAM J. Optim. **20**(4), 1956–1982 (2010)

44. Simo-Serra, E., Ramisa, A., Alenyà, G., Torras, C., Moreno-Noguer, F.: Single image 3D human pose estimation from noisy observations. In: Conference on Computer Vision and Pattern Recognition (CVPR), pp. 2673–2680. IEEE (2012)

45. Hasler, N., Rosenhahn, B., Thormählen, T., Wand, M., Seidel, H.P.: Markerless motion capture with unsynchronized moving cameras. In: IEEE Conference on Computer Vision and Pattern Recognition (CVPR) (2009)

Non-rigid 3D Shape Registration Using an Adaptive Template

Hang Dai[(⊠)], Nick Pears[(⊠)], and William Smith[(⊠)]

Department of Computer Science, University of York, York, UK
{hd816,nick.pears,william.smith}@york.ac.uk

Abstract. We present a new fully-automatic non-rigid 3D shape registration (morphing) framework comprising (1) a new 3D landmarking and pose normalisation method; (2) an adaptive shape template method to improve the convergence of registration algorithms and achieve a better final shape correspondence and (3) a new iterative registration method that combines Iterative Closest Points with Coherent Point Drift (CPD) to achieve a more stable and accurate correspondence establishment than standard CPD. We call this new morphing approach *Iterative Coherent Point Drift* (ICPD). Our proposed framework is evaluated qualitatively and quantitatively on three datasets: Headspace, BU3D and a synthetic LSFM dataset, and is compared with several other methods. The proposed framework is shown to give state-of-the-art performance.

Keywords: 3D registration · 3D shape morphing
3D morphable models

1 Introduction

The goal of non-rigid shape registration is to align and morph a *source* point set to a *target* point set. By using some form of template shape as the source, morphing is able to reparametrise a collection of raw 3D scans of some object class into a consistent form. This facilitates full dataset alignment and subsequent 3D Morphable Model (3DMM) construction. In turn, the 3DMM constitutes a useful shape prior in many computer vision tasks, such as recognition and missing parts reconstruction.

Currently, methods that deform a 3D template to all members of a specific 3D object class in a dataset use the same template shape. However, datasets representative of global object classes often have a wide variation in terms of the spatial distribution of their constituent parts. Our object class in this paper is that of the human face/head, where the relative positions of key parts, such as the ears, mouth, and nose are highly varied, particularly when trying to build 3DMMs across a wide demographic range of age, gender and ethnicity. Using a single template shape means that often key parts of the template are not at the

© Springer Nature Switzerland AG 2019
L. Leal-Taixé and S. Roth (Eds.): ECCV 2018 Workshops, LNCS 11132, pp. 48–63, 2019.
https://doi.org/10.1007/978-3-030-11018-5_5

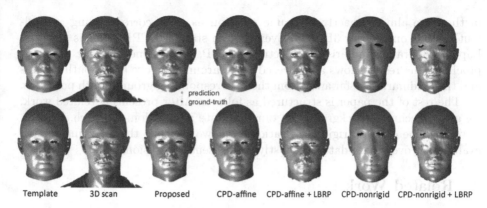

Template   3D scan   Proposed   CPD-affine   CPD-affine + LBRP   CPD-nonrigid   CPD-nonrigid + LBRP

Fig. 1. Proposed method compared with standard CPD. Ground truth points on target raw 3D data shown in red, corresponding template points shown in cyan. (Color figure online)

same relative positions as those of the raw 3D scan. This causes slow convergence of shape morphing and, worse still, leads to end results that have visible residual errors and inaccurate correspondences in salient local parts.

To counter this, we propose an adaptive template approach that provides an automatically tailored template for each raw 3D scan in the dataset. The adaptive template is obtained from the original template using *sparse* shape information (typically point landmarks), thereby locally matching the raw 3D scan very specifically. Although this is a pre-process that involves template shape adaptation, we do not consider it as part of the main template morphing process, which operates over *dense* shape information.

We present a new pipeline in fully-automatic non-rigid 3D shape registration by integrating several powerful ideas from the computer vision and graphics. These include Mixture-of-Trees 2D landmarking [1], Iterative Closest Points (ICP) [2], Coherent Point Drift (CPD) [3], and mesh editing using the Laplace-Beltrami (LB) operator [4]. We also provide comparisons of the latter approach with the use of Gaussian Processes (GPs) [5]. Our contributions include: (1) a new 3D landmarking and pose normalisation method; (2) an adaptive shape template method to accelerate the convergence of registration algorithms and achieve a better final shape correspondence; (3) a new iterative registration method that combines ICP with CPD to achieve a more stable and accurate correspondence establishment than standard CPD. We call this approach *Iterative Coherent Point Drift* (ICPD).

Our proposed pipeline is evaluated qualitatively and quantitatively on three human face/head datasets: Headspace [6–8], BU3D [9] and LSFM-synthetic [10], and is compared with several other methods. Note that this latter dataset are 100 faces generated randomly from the Large Scale Face Model [10] where samples lie within ±3SDs. The pipeline achieves state-of-the-art performance. Figure 1 is a qualitative illustration of a typical result where our method achieves a more accurate correspondence than standard CPD. Note that the landmarks on our method are almost exactly the same position as their corresponding ground-truth points on the raw 3D scan. Even though standard CPD-affine is aided by Laplace-Beltrami regularised projection (LBRP, a component of our proposed pipeline), the result shows a "squeezed" face around the eye and mouth regions and the landmarks are far away from their corresponding ground-truth positions.

The rest of the paper is structured as follows. After presenting related work, we give a technical background on our template adaptation approach. In Sect. 3 we describe our non-rigid registration framework, while the following section evaluates it over three datasets. Lastly we present conclusions.

2   Related Work

Here we provide background literature to our pipeline, in the order in which the processes are required.

2.1   Data to Template Alignment

All template morphing methods need to align the raw data to be sufficiently close to the template, which is in some canonical position (e.g. frontal for a human face/head). Thus the template is brought within the convergence basin of the global minimum of alignment and morphing. To this end, we use a 2D landmarker and project the detected landmarks to 3D. In particular, Zhu and Ramanan [1] use a *Mixture of Trees* model of the face, which both detects faces and locates facial landmarks. One of the major advantages of their approach is that it can handle extreme head poses even at relatively low image resolutions.

2.2   Template Adaptation

By template adaptation, we mean the ability to adapt the shape of a template using *sparse* shape information before applying *dense* morphing. Here we overview the two methods evaluated in our pipeline: (i) Laplace-Beltrami mesh manipulation and (ii) the posterior model (PM) of a Gaussian Process Morphable Model (GPMM).

Laplace-Beltrami Mesh Manipulation: The Laplace-Beltrami (LB) operator is widely used in 3D mesh manipulation. The LB term regularises the landmark-guided template adaptation in two ways: (1) the landmarks on the template are manipulated towards their corresponding landmarks on the raw 3D scan; (2) all other points in original template are moved *As Rigidly As Possible* (ARAP [11]) regarding the landmarks' movement, according to an optimised cost function, described later. Following Sorkine et al. [11], the idea for measuring the rigidity of a deformation of the whole mesh is to sum up over the deviations from rigidity. Thus, the energy functional can be formed as:

$$\mathbf{E}(\mathbf{S}') = \sum_{i=1}^{n} \mathbf{w}_i \sum_{j \in N(i)} \mathbf{w}_{ij} \|(\mathbf{p}'_i - \mathbf{p}'_j) - \mathbf{R}_i(\mathbf{p}_i - \mathbf{p}_j)\|, \qquad (1)$$

where we denote a mesh by $\mathbf{S}$, with $\mathbf{S}'$ its deformed mesh and $\mathbf{R}$ is a rotation. Mesh topology is determined by n vertices and m triangles. Also $N(i)$ is the set of vertices connected to vertex i; these are the one-ring neighbours. The parameters $\mathbf{w}_i$, $\mathbf{w}_{ij}$ are fixed cell and edge weights. Note that $\mathbf{E}(\mathbf{S}')$ depends solely on the geometries of $\mathbf{S}$, $\mathbf{S}'$, i.e., on the vertex positions $\mathbf{p}$, $\mathbf{p}'$. In particular, since the reference mesh (our input shape) is fixed, the only variables in $\mathbf{E}(\mathbf{S}')$ are the deformed vertex positions $\mathbf{p}'_i$. The gradient of $\mathbf{E}(\mathbf{S}')$ is computed with respect to the positions $\mathbf{p}'$. The partial derivatives w.r.t. $\mathbf{p}'_i$ can be computed as:

$$\frac{d\mathbf{E}(\mathbf{S}')}{d\mathbf{p}'_i} = \sum_{j \in N(i)} 4\mathbf{w}_{ij} \left((\mathbf{p}'_i - \mathbf{p}'_j) - \frac{1}{2}(\mathbf{R}_i + \mathbf{R}_j)(\mathbf{p}_i - \mathbf{p}_j) \right) \qquad (2)$$

Setting the partial derivatives to zero w.r.t. each $\mathbf{p}'_i$ gives the following sparse linear system of equations:

$$\sum_{j \in N(i)} \mathbf{w}_{ij}(\mathbf{p}'_i - \mathbf{p}'_j) = \sum_{j \in N(i)} \frac{\mathbf{w}_{ij}}{2}(\mathbf{R}_i + \mathbf{R}_j)(\mathbf{p}_i - \mathbf{p}_j) \qquad (3)$$

The linear combination on the left-hand side is the discrete Laplace-Beltrami operator applied to $\mathbf{p}'$, hence the system of equations can be written as:

$$\mathbf{L}\mathbf{p}' = \mathbf{b}, \qquad (4)$$

where $\mathbf{b}$ is an n-vector whose i-th row contains the right-hand side expression from (3). We also need to incorporate the modeling constraints into this system. In the simplest form, those can be expressed by some fixed positions

$$\mathbf{p}'_j = \mathbf{c}_k, k \in \mathcal{F}, \qquad (5)$$

where $\mathcal{F}$ is the set of indices of the constrained vertices. In our case, these are the landmark positions, automatically detected on the raw 3D data, with the corresponding points known *a priori* on the template. Incorporating such constraints into (4) requires substituting the corresponding variables, erasing respective rows and columns from $\mathbf{L}$ and updating the right-hand side with the values $\mathbf{c}_k$.

Gaussian Process Morphable Model: A Gaussian Process Morphable Model (GPMM) uses manually defined arbitrary kernel functions to describe the deformation's covariance matrix. This enables a GPMM to aid the construction of a 3DMM, without the need for training data. The posterior models (PMs) of GPMMs are regression models of the shape deformation field. Given partial observations, such posterior models are able to determine what is the potential complete shape. A posterior model is able to estimate other points' movements when some set of landmarks and their target positions are given.

Instead of modelling absolute vertex positions using PCA, GPMMs model a shape as a deformation vector field $\mathbf{u}$ from a reference shape $\mathbf{X} \in \mathbb{R}^{p \times 3}$, i.e. a shape $\mathbf{X}'$ can be represented as

$$\mathbf{X}' = \mathbf{X} + \mathbf{u}(\mathbf{X}) \qquad (6)$$

for some deformation vector field $\mathbf{u} \in \mathbb{R}^{p \times 3}$. We model the deformation as a Gaussian process $\mathbf{u} \sim GP(\mu, \mathbf{k})$ where $\mu \in \mathbb{R}^{p \times 3}$ is a mean deformation and $\mathbf{k} \in \mathbb{R}^{3 \times 3}$ a covariance function or kernel.

The biggest advantage of GPMMs compared to statistical shape models (e.g. 3DMMs) is that we have much more freedom in defining the covariance function. GPMMs allow expressive prior models for registration to be derived, by leveraging the modeling power of Gaussian processes. By estimating the covariances from example data GPMMs becomes a continuous version of a statistical shape model.

2.3 Dense Shape Registration

The Iterative Closest Points (ICP) algorithm [2,12] is the standard rigid-motion registration method. Several extensions of ICP for the nonrigid case were proposed [10,13–17]. Often these have good performance in shape difference elimination but have problems in over fitting and point sliding. Another approach is based on modelling the transformation with thin plate splines (TPS) [18] followed by robust point matching (RPM) and is known as TPS-RPM [19]. However, it is slow in large-scale point set registration [20–23]. Amberg et al. [13] defined the optimal-step *Nonrigid Iterative Closest Points* (NICP) framework. Recently Booth et al. [10] built a Large Scale Facial Model (LSFM), using the same NICP template morphing approach with error pruning, followed by Generalised Procrustes Analysis (GPA) for alignment, and Principal Component Analysis (PCA) for the model construction. Li et al. [24] show that using proximity heuristics to determine correspondences is less reliable when large deformations are present. Their Global Correspondence Optimization approach solves simultaneously for both the deformation parameters and correspondences [24].

Myronenko et al. consider the alignment of two point sets as a probability density estimation [3] and they call the method Coherent Point Drift (CPD). There is no closed-form solution for this optimisation, so it employs an EM algorithm to optimize the Gaussian Mixture Model (GMM) fitting. Algorithms are provided to solve for several shape deformation models such a affine (CPD-affine) and generally non-rigid (CPD-nonrigid). Their *'non-rigid'* motion model employs an $M \times M$ Gaussian kernel $\mathbf{G}$ for motion field smoothing, and the M-step requires solving for an $M \times 3$ matrix $\mathbf{W}$ that generates the template deformation (GMM motion field) as $\mathbf{GW}$. Such motion regularisation is related to motion coherence, and inspired the algorithm's name. The CPD method was has been extended by various groups [25–28]. Compared to TPS-RPM, CPD offers superior accuracy and stability with respect to non-rigid deformations in presence of outliers. A modified version of CPD imposed a *Local Linear Embedding* topological constraint to cope with highly articulated non-rigid deformations [29]. However, this extension is more sensitive to noise than CPD. A non-rigid registration method used Student's Mixture Model (SMM) to do probability density estimation [30]. The results are more robust and accurate on noisy data than CPD. Dai et al. [8] proposed a hierarchical parts-based CPD-LB morphing framework to avoid under-fitting and over-fitting. It overcomes the sliding problem to some extent, but the end result still has a small tangential error.

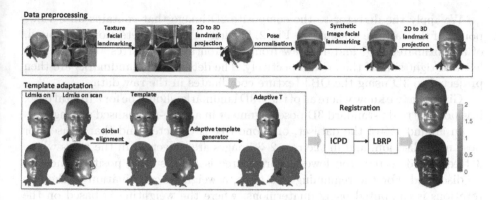

Fig. 2. Adaptive template registration framework, using ICPD based morphing.

Lüthi et al. [31] model shape variations with a Gaussian process (GP), which they represent using the leading components of its Karhunen-Loeve expansion. Such Gaussian Process Morphable Models (GPMMs) unify a variety of non-rigid deformation models. Gerig et al. [5] present a novel pipeline for morphable face model construction based on Gaussian processes. GPMMs separate problem specific requirements from the registration algorithm by incorporating domain-specific adaptions as a prior model.

3   Non-rigid Shape Registration Framework

The proposed registration framework is shown in Fig. 2 and includes four high-level stages: (1) data preprocessing of raw 3D image: landmarking and pose normalisation; (2) template adaptation: global alignment and adapting the template shape; (3) template morphing using Iterative Coherent Point Drift (ICPD); (4) point projection regularised by the Laplace-Beltrami operator (LBRP). These are detailed in the following four subsections.

3.1   Data Preprocessing

Data preprocessing of the raw 3D scan serves to place the data in a frontal pose, which allows us to get a complete and accurate set of automatic 3D landmark positions, for every 3D image, that correspond to a set of manually-placed (once) landmarks on the template. This preprocessing comprises five sub-stages: (i) 2D landmarking, (ii) projection to 3D landmarks, (iii) pose normalisation (iv) synthetic frontal 2D image landmarking and (v) projection to 3D landmarks.

We use the 'Mixture of Trees' method of Zhu and Ramanan [1] to localise 2D facial landmarks. In particular, the mixture we use has 13 landmark tree models for 13 different yaw angles of the head.

We apply the detector to the composite 2D image that contains all 5 viewpoints of the capture system, see Fig. 2, top left. Two face detections are found, of approximately 15° and 45° yaw from the frontal pose, corresponding to the left and right side of the face respectively. The detected 2D landmarks are then projected to 3D using the OBJ texture coordinates in the raw data.

Given that we know where all of these 3D landmarks should be for a frontal pose, it is possible to do standard 3D pose alignment in a scale-normalised setting [8].

In around 1% of the dataset, only one tree is detected and that is used for pose normalisation, and in the rest 2–3 images are detected. In the cases where 3 trees are detected, the lowest scoring tree is always false positive and can be discarded. For the remaining two trees, a weighted combination of the two rotations is computed using quaternions, where the weighting is based on the mean Euclidean error to the mean tree, in the appropriate tree component.

After we have rotated the 3D image to canonical frontal view, we wish to generate a set of landmarks that are accurate and correspond to the set marked up on the template. This is the set related to the central tree (0° yaw) in the mixture. After these 2D landmarks are extracted, they are again projected to 3D using the raw OBJ texture coordinates.

3.2   Template Adaptation

As shown in Fig. 2, template adaptation consists of two sub-stages: (i) global alignment followed by (ii) dynamically adapting the template shape to the data. For global alignment, we manually select the same landmarks on the template as we automatically extract on the raw data (i.e. using the zero yaw angle tree component from [1]). Note that this needs to be done *once only* for some object class and so doesn't impact on the autonomy of the *online* operation of the framework. Then we align rigidly (without scaling) from the 3D landmarks on raw 3D data to the same landmarks on the template. The rigid transformation matrix is used for the raw data alignment to the template.

The template is then *adapted* to better align with the raw scan. A better template helps the later registration converge faster and gives more accurate correspondence at the beginning and end of registration. A good template has the same size and position of local facial parts (e.g. eyes, nose, mouth and ears) as the raw scan. This cannot be achieved by mesh alignment alone. We propose two method to give a better template that is adapted to the raw 3D scan: (1) Laplace-Beltrami mesh editing; (2) Template estimation via posterior GPMMs. For both methods, three ingredients are needed: landmarks on 3D raw data, the corresponding landmarks on template, and the original template.

Laplace-Beltrami Mesh Manipulation: We decompose the template into several facial parts: eyes, nose, mouth, left ear and right ear. We rigidly align landmarks on each part separately to their corresponding landmarks on 3D raw data. These rigid transformation matrices are used for aligning the decomposed parts to 3D raw data. The rigidly transformed facial parts tell the original template where it should be. We treat this as a mesh manipulation problem.

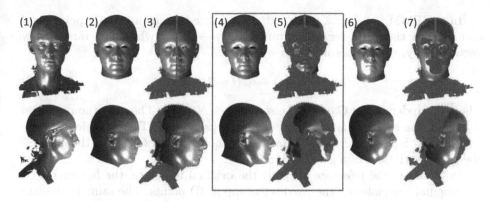

Fig. 3. Template comparison with raw data: (1) raw scan; (2) template with global rigid alignment; (3) 2 compared with the raw scan; (4) adaptive template via LB mesh editing; (5) 4 compared with the raw scan; (6) the mean template estimation via posterior models; (7) 6 compared with the raw scan in (7)

We use Laplace-Beltrami mesh editing to manipulate the original template towards the rigidly transformed facial parts, as follows: (1) the *facial parts* (fp) of the original template are manipulated towards their target positions - these are rigidly transformed facial parts; (2) all other parts of the original template are moved *as rigidly as possible* [11].

Given the vertices of a template stored in the matrix $\mathbf{X}_T \in \mathbb{R}^{p \times 3}$ and a better template obtained whose vertices are stored in the matrix $\mathbf{X}_{bT} \in \mathbb{R}^{p \times 3}$, we define the selection matrices $\mathbf{S}_{fp} \in [0,1]^{l \times p}$ as those that select the l vertices (facial parts in $\mathbf{X}_T$ and $\mathbf{X}_{bT}$) from the raw template and a better template respectively. This linear system can be written as:

$$\begin{pmatrix} \lambda \mathbf{L} \\ \mathbf{S}_{fp} \end{pmatrix} \mathbf{X}_{bT} = \begin{pmatrix} \lambda \mathbf{L} \mathbf{X}_T \\ \mathbf{X}_{fp} \end{pmatrix} \tag{7}$$

where $\mathbf{L} \in \mathbb{R}^{p \times p}$ is the cotangent Laplacian approximation to the LB operator and $\mathbf{X}_{bT}$ is the better template that we wish to solve for. The parameter λ weights the relative influence of the position and regularisation constraints, effectively determining the 'stiffness' of the mesh manipulation. As $\lambda \to 0$, the facial parts of the original template are manipulated exactly to the rigidly transformed facial parts. As $\lambda \to \infty$, the adaptive template will only be at the same position as the original template $\mathbf{X}_T$.

Template Estimation via Posterior Models: A common task in shape modelling is to infer the full shape from a set of measurements of the shape. This task can be formalised as a regression problem. The posterior models of Gaussian Process Morphable Models (GPMMs) are regression models of the deformation field. Given partial observations, posterior models are able to answer what is the potential full shape. Posterior models show the points' potential movements when the landmarks are fixed to their target position.

In a GPMM, let $\{x_1, ..., x_l\} \in \mathbb{R}^{l \times 3}$ be a fixed set of input 3D points and assume that there is a regression function $f_0 \to \mathbb{R}^{p \times 3}$, which generates a new vector field $\mathbf{y_i} \in \mathbb{R}^{p \times 3}$ according to

$$\mathbf{y_i} = f_0(\mathbf{x_i}) + \epsilon_i, (i = 1, ..., n). \tag{8}$$

where ϵ_i is independent Gaussian noise, i.e. $\epsilon_i \sim N(0, \delta^2)$. The regression problem is to infer the function f_0 at the input points $\{x_1, ..., x_l\}$. The possible deformation field $\mathbf{y_i}$ is modelled using a Gaussian process model $GP(\mu, k)$ that models the shape variations of a given shape family.

In our case, the reference shape is the original template, the landmarks on the original template are the fixed set of input 3D points. The same landmarks on 3D raw data are the target position of the fixed set of input 3D points. Given a GPMM $GP(\mu, k)$ that models the shape variations of a shape family, the adaptive template is

$$\mathbf{X}_{bT}^i = \mathbf{X}_T + \mathbf{y_i}, (i = 1, ..., n). \tag{9}$$

The mean of $\mathbf{X}_{bT}^i$ is shown in Fig. 3(6) and (7).

3.3 Iterative Coherent Point Drift

The task of non-rigid 3D registration (shape morphing) is to deform and align the template to the target raw 3D scan. Non-rigid Coherent Point Drift (CPD) [3] has better deformation results when partial correspondences are given and we have found that it is more stable and converges better when the template and the raw data have approximately the same number of points. However, the correspondence is often not known before registration. Thus, following an Iterative Closest Points (ICP) scheme [2], we supply CPD registration with coarse correspondences using 'closest points'. We refine such correspondences throughout iterations of the *Iterative Coherent Point Drift* (ICPD) approach described here.

We use the original code package of CPD available online as library calls for ICPD. Other option parameters can be found in the CPD author's release code. The global affine transformation is used as a small adjustment of correspondence computation. A better correspondence (idx2 in the pseudocode) is used as the priors for CPD non-rigid registration. The qualitative output of ICPD is very smooth, a feature inherited from standard CPD. A subsequent regularised point projection process is required to capture the target shape detail, and this is described next.

3.4 Laplace-Beltrami Regularised Projection

When ICPD has deformed the template close to the scan, point projection is required to eliminate any (normal) shape distance error. Again, we overcome this by treating the projection operation as a mesh editing problem with two ingredients. First, position constraints are provided by those vertices with mutual nearest neighbours between the deformed template and raw scan. Using mutual nearest neighbours reduces sensitivity to missing data. Second, regularisation constraints are provided by the LB operator which acts to retain the local structure of the mesh. We call this process *Laplace-Beltrami regularised projection* (LBRP), as shown in the registration framework in Fig. 2.

We write the point projection problem as a linear system of equations. Given the vertices of a scan stored in the matrix $\mathbf{X}_{scan} \in \mathbb{R}^{n \times 3}$ and the deformed template obtained by CPD whose vertices are stored in the matrix $\mathbf{X}_{deformed} \in \mathbb{R}^{p \times 3}$, we define the selection matrices $\mathbf{S}_1 \in [0,1]^{m \times p}$ and $\mathbf{S}_2 \in [0,1]^{m \times n}$ as those that select the m vertices with mutual nearest neighbours from deformed template and scan respectively. This linear system can be written as:

$$\begin{pmatrix} \lambda \mathbf{L} \\ \mathbf{S}_1 \end{pmatrix} \mathbf{X}_{proj} = \begin{pmatrix} \lambda \mathbf{L} \mathbf{X}_{deformed} \\ \mathbf{S}_2 \mathbf{X}_{scan} \end{pmatrix} \tag{10}$$

where $\mathbf{L} \in \mathbb{R}^{p \times p}$ is the cotangent Laplacian approximation to the LB operator and $\mathbf{X}_{proj} \in \mathbb{R}^{p \times 3}$ are the projected vertex positions that we wish to solve for. The parameter λ weights the relative influence of the position and regularisation constraints, effectively determining the 'stiffness' of the projection. As $\lambda \to 0$, the projection tends towards nearest neighbour projection. As $\lambda \to \infty$, the deformed template will only be allowed to rigidly transform.

4 Evaluation

We evaluated the proposed registration framework using three datasets: Headspace [6–8], BU3D (neutral expression) [9] and LSFM-synthetic. The latter two have ground-truth information. We use error to manually-defined landmark and the average nearest point distance error for evaluation on the Headspace dataset. Recently, two registration frameworks have become publicly available for comparison: Basel's Open Framework (OF) [31] and the LSFM pipeline [10].

For reproducibility of our results, parameters used are as follows: (1) when doing the 3D automatic face landmarking, we manually select the same landmarks on template mesh only for once across the whole dataset; (2) λ is set to 0.1; (3) the iteration limitation of CPD-affine is 200 and CPD-non-rigid is 300. (4) the Gaussian kernels in GPMM are defined as the same as that in [5].

4.1 Internal Comparison of Approaches

We validate the effectiveness of each step in the proposed registration pipeline qualitatively and quantitatively. The results of registration over children data in Headspace are shown in Fig. 4. After pure rigid alignment without template adaptation, the nose of template is still bigger than the target. As can be seen in Fig. 4(3), the nose ends up with a bad deformation result. The same problem happened in the ear. Without LB regularised projection shown in Fig. 4(4), it fails in capturing the shape detail compared with the proposed method.

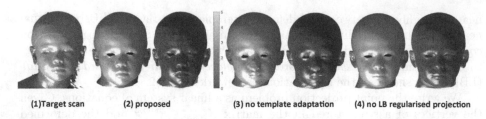

(1)Target scan   (2) proposed   (3) no template adaptation   (4) no LB regularised projection

Fig. 4. (1) Target scan; (2) proposed method (3) remove template adaptation; (4) remove LB regularised projection. Error map (mm).

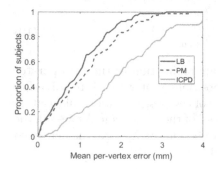

Table. Convergence of ICPD

	ICPD	LB	PM
ICP loops	6.47	3.52	3.74
Time (s)	831.35	426.13	434.53

Fig. 5. Improvement in correspondence and convergence performance when using adaptive templates: (1) ICPD without an adaptive template (cyan); (2) ICPD with LB-based adaptive template (blue); (3) ICPD with adaptive PM-based template (blue dashed). (Color figure online)

Using the BU3D dataset for quantitative validation, we compared the performance of (i) the proposed ICPD registration, (ii) ICPD with an adaptive template using LB mesh manipulation and (iii) ICPD with an adaptive template, using a posterior model (PM). The mean per-vertex error is computed between the registration results and their ground-truth. The number of ICPD iterations and computation time is recorded, when using the same computation platform. The per-vertex error plot in Fig. 5 illustrates that the adaptive template improves the correspondence accuracy of ICPD. The number of ICPD iterations and computation time is significantly decreased by the adaptive template method. In particular adaptive template using LB mesh manipulation has better performance than adaptive template using a posterior model. Thus, we employ an adaptive template approach using LB mesh manipulation for later experiments.

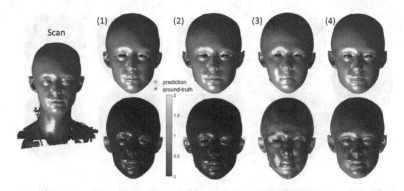

Fig. 6. First row - correspondence results and their landmarks compared with ground-truth on raw scan; Second row - the color map of per-vertex nearest point error. (1) proposed method with LB template adaptation; (2) proposed method without adaptive template; (3) Open Framework morphing [31]; (4) LSFM morphing [10].

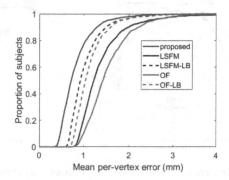

Fig. 7. Mean per-vertex in morphed template nearest point distance error, higher is better.

4.2 Correspondence Comparison

Headspace: We evaluate correspondence accuracy both qualitatively and quantitatively. 1212 scans from Headspace are used for evaluation. A typical registration result is shown in Fig. 6. Apart from the proposed method, there are clearly significant errors around the ear region, the eye region, or even multiple regions. We use per-vertex nearest point error for quantitative shape registration evaluation. The per-vertex nearest point error is computed by measuring the nearest point distance from the morphed template to raw scan and averaging over all vertices. As can be seen in Fig. 7, the proposed method has the best performance, when compared to Basel's Open Framework (OF) [31] and the LSFM [10] registration approach. The OF method has a smoothed output without much shape detail. The LSFM method captures shape detail, but it has greater landmark error and per vertex nearest point error. The quantitative evaluation in Fig. 7 validates that the proposed method outperforms the other two contemporary methods.

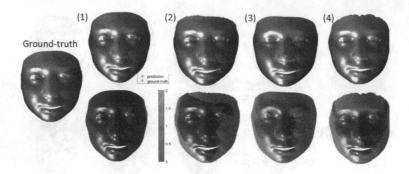

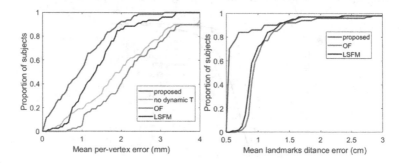

Fig. 8. First row - correspondence results and their landmarks; Second row - the color map of per-vertex error against ground-truth. (1) proposed method; (2) proposed method without adaptive template; (3) OF registration; (4) LSFM registration.

Fig. 9. Mean per-vertex error: (1) left - BU3D dataset, (2) right - LSFM dataset

BU3D: For the BU3D dataset, 100 scans with neutral expression are used for evaluation. We use 12 landmarks to perform adaptive template generation. Qualitatively from Fig. 8(1) and (2), the adaptive template can be seen to improve the registration performance. As shown in Fig. 9(1), compared with the ground-truth data, over 90% of the registration results have less than 2 mm per-vertex error. The proposed method has the best performance in face shape registration.

LSFM: The synthetic LSFM dataset are 100 faces generated randomly from the Large Scale Face Model [10] where samples lie within ±3SDs. The pipeline achieves state-of-the-art performance. we use the same 14 landmarks in [32] for the adaptive template generation. Since the synthetic data is already in correspondence, the 14 landmarks have the same indices across the dataset. As shown in Fig. 9(2), compared with the ground-truth data, over 83% of the registration results have less than 1 mm per-vertex error. The proposed method has the best performance in synthetic data registration.

5 Conclusions

We proposed a new fully-automatic shape registration framework with an adaptive template initialisation. Although there is a prior one-shot manual markup of landmarks on a generic template, this does not prevent our online process being fully-automatic. The adaptive template accelerated the convergence of registration algorithms and achieved a more accurate correspondence. We provided two methods: LB mesh manipulation and the posterior model of the GPMM to achieve template adaptation. In particular, an adaptive template using LB mesh manipulation has a better performance than an adaptive template using a GP posterior model. We proposed a new morphing method that combined the ICP and CPD algorithms that is both more stable and accurate in correspondence establishment. We evaluated the proposed framework on three datasets: Headspace, BU3D and LSFM-synthetic. The proposed framework has better performance than other methods across all datasets.

References

1. Zhu, X., Ramanan, D.: Face detection, pose estimation, and landmark localization in the wild. In: Proceedings of CVPR, pp. 2879–2886 (2012)
2. Besl, P.J., McKay, N.D.: Method for registration of 3-D shapes. In: Sensor Fusion IV: Control Paradigms and Data Structures, vol. 1611, pp. 586–607. International Society for Optics and Photonics (1992)
3. Myronenko, A., Song, X.: Point set registration: coherent point drift. IEEE Trans. Pattern Anal. Mach. Intell. 32(12), 2262–2275 (2010)
4. Sorkine, O., Cohen-Or, D., Lipman, Y., Alexa, M., Rössl, C., Seidel, H.P.: Laplacian surface editing. In: Proceedings of the 2004 Eurographics/ACM SIG-GRAPH Symposium on Geometry Processing, pp. 175–184 (2004)
5. Gerig, T., et al.: Morphable face models - an open framework. CoRR abs/1709.08398 (2017)
6. Duncan, C., Armstrong, R.: Alder hey headspace project (2016)
7. Robertson, B., Dai, H., Pears, N., Duncan, C.: A morphable model of the human head validating the outcomes of an age-dependent scaphocephaly correction. Int. J. Oral Maxillofac. Surg. 46, 68 (2017)
8. Dai, H., Pears, N., Smith, W.A.P., Duncan, C.: A 3D morphable model of craniofacial shape and texture variation. In: The IEEE International Conference on Computer Vision (ICCV), October 2017
9. Yin, L., Chen, X., Sun, Y., Worm, T., Reale, M.: A high-resolution 3D dynamic facial expression database. In: 2008 8th IEEE International Conference on Automatic Face & Gesture Recognition, FG 2008, pp. 1–6. IEEE (2008)
10. Booth, J., Roussos, A., Ponniah, A., Dunaway, D., Zafeiriou, S.: Large scale 3d morphable models. Int. J. Comput. Vis. 126(2–4), 233–254 (2018)
11. Sorkine, O., Alexa, M.: As-rigid-as-possible surface modeling. In: Proceedings of the Fifth Eurographics Symposium on Geometry Processing, pp. 109–116 (2007)
12. Arun, K.S., Huang, T.S., Blostein, S.D.: Least-squares fitting of two 3-D point sets. IEEE Trans. Pattern Anal. Mach. Intell. 5, 698–700 (1987)

13. Amberg, B., Romdhani, S., Vetter, T.: Optimal step nonrigid ICP algorithms for surface registration. In: Proceedings of CVPR, pp. 1–8 (2007)
14. Hontani, H., Matsuno, T., Sawada, Y.: Robust nonrigid ICP using outlier-sparsity regularization. In: 2012 IEEE Conference on Computer Vision and Pattern Recognition (CVPR), pp. 174–181. IEEE (2012)
15. Cheng, S., Marras, I., Zafeiriou, S., Pantic, M.: Active nonrigid ICP algorithm. In: 2015 11th IEEE International Conference and Workshops on Automatic Face and Gesture Recognition (FG), vol. 1, pp. 1–8. IEEE (2015)
16. Cheng, S., Marras, I., Zafeiriou, S., Pantic, M.: Statistical non-rigid ICP algorithm and its application to 3D face alignment. Image Vis. Comput. **58**, 3–12 (2017)
17. Kou, Q., Yang, Y., Du, S., Luo, S., Cai, D.: A modified non-rigid ICP algorithm for registration of chromosome images. In: Huang, D.-S., Jo, K.-H. (eds.) ICIC 2016, Part II. LNCS, vol. 9772, pp. 503–513. Springer, Cham (2016). https://doi.org/10.1007/978-3-319-42294-7_45
18. Bookstein, F.L.: Principal warps: thin-plate splines and the decomposition of deformations. IEEE Trans. Pattern Anal. Mach. Intell. **11**(6), 567–585 (1989)
19. Chui, H., Rangarajan, A.: A new algorithm for non-rigid point matching. In: 2000 Proceedings of IEEE Conference on Computer Vision and Pattern Recognition, vol. 2, pp. 44–51 IEEE (2000)
20. Yang, J.: The thin plate spline robust point matching (TPS-RPM) algorithm: a revisit. Pattern Recogn. Lett. **32**(7), 910–918 (2011)
21. Lee, J.H., Won, C.H.: Topology preserving relaxation labeling for nonrigid point matching. IEEE Trans. Pattern Anal. Mach. Intell. **33**(2), 427–432 (2011)
22. Lee, A.X., Goldstein, M.A., Barratt, S.T., Abbeel, P.: A non-rigid point and normal registration algorithm with applications to learning from demonstrations. In: 2015 IEEE International Conference on Robotics and Automation (ICRA), pp. 935–942. IEEE (2015)
23. Ma, J., Zhao, J., Jiang, J., Zhou, H.: Non-rigid point set registration with robust transformation estimation under manifold regularization. In: AAAI, pp. 4218–4224 (2017)
24. Li, H., Sumner, R.W., Pauly, M.: Global correspondence optimization for non-rigid registration of depth scans. In: Computer Graphics Forum, vol. 27, pp. 1421–1430. Wiley, Hoboken (2008)
25. Wang, P., Wang, P., Qu, Z., Gao, Y., Shen, Z.: A refined coherent point drift (CPD) algorithm for point set registration. Sci. China Inf. Sci. **54**(12), 2639–2646 (2011)
26. Golyanik, V., Taetz, B., Reis, G., Stricker, D.: Extended coherent point drift algorithm with correspondence priors and optimal subsampling. In: 2016 IEEE Winter Conference on Applications of Computer Vision (WACV), pp. 1–9. IEEE (2016)
27. Hu, Y., Rijkhorst, E.-J., Manber, R., Hawkes, D., Barratt, D.: Deformable vessel-based registration using landmark-guided coherent point drift. In: Liao, H., Edwards, P.J.E., Pan, X., Fan, Y., Yang, G.-Z. (eds.) MIAR 2010. LNCS, vol. 6326, pp. 60–69. Springer, Heidelberg (2010). https://doi.org/10.1007/978-3-642-15699-1_7
28. Trimech, I.H., Maalej, A., Amara, N.E.B.: 3D facial expression recognition using nonrigid CPD registration method. In: 2017 International Conference on Information and Digital Technologies (IDT), pp. 478–481. IEEE (2017)

29. Ge, S., Fan, G., Ding, M.: Non-rigid point set registration with global-local topology preservation. In: 2014 IEEE Conference on Computer Vision and Pattern Recognition Workshops (CVPRW), pp. 245–251. IEEE (2014)
30. Zhou, Z., Zheng, J., Dai, Y., Zhou, Z., Chen, S.: Robust non-rigid point set registration using student's-t mixture model. PloS one **9**(3), e91381 (2014)
31. Lüthi, M., Gerig, T., Jud, C., Vetter, T.: Gaussian process morphable models. IEEE Trans. Pattern Anal. Mach. Intell. **40**, 1860–1873 (2017)
32. Creusot, C., Pears, N.E., Austin, J.: A machine-learning approach to keypoint detection and landmarking on 3D meshes. Int. J. Comput. Vis. **1**, 146–179 (2013)

3D Human Body Reconstruction from a Single Image via Volumetric Regression

Aaron S. Jackson[1(✉)], Chris Manafas[2], and Georgios Tzimiropoulos[1]

[1] School of Computer Science, The University of Nottingham, Nottingham, UK
{aaron.jackson,yorgos.tzimiropoulos}@nottingham.ac.uk
[2] 2B3D, Athens, Greece
chris.manafas@2b3dglobal.com

Abstract. This paper proposes the use of an end-to-end Convolutional Neural Network for direct reconstruction of the 3D geometry of humans via volumetric regression. The proposed method does not require the fitting of a shape model and can be trained to work from a variety of input types, whether it be landmarks, images or segmentation masks. Additionally, non-visible parts, either self-occluded or otherwise, are still reconstructed, which is not the case with depth map regression. We present results that show that our method can handle both pose variation and detailed reconstruction given appropriate datasets for training.

Keywords: 3D reconstruction · Human body reconstruction
Volumetric regression · VRN · Single image reconstruction

1 Introduction

3D reconstruction is the process of estimating the 3D geometry from one or more 2D images. In this work, we focus on reconstruction of the human body from a single image, including the non-visible parts which have been self-occluded. Our method builds upon that of [1] where a 3D face is directly regressed from a single image, using what they refer to as a "Volumetric Regression Network" (VRN). In this paper, we show that the same idea can be applied to other deformable objects, in particular, the human body. This poses an array of challenges which are not present when reconstructing the face. While we are still only reconstructing an object of a single class, the body has many more axes of rotation compared to a face. As such, human body reconstruction is often considered to be a very difficult problem (Fig. 1).

Motivation. The pipelines required for 3D human reconstruction (and 3D reconstruction in general) are typically based on solving difficult non-convex optimisation problems. Perhaps the most common approach to 3D human body reconstruction is to fit a shape model. For example, the recent method of [2], uses optimisation to fit a 3D shape model to 2D body joints. However, optimisation methods are sensitive to initialization and are easily trapped to local minima, both of which are exacerbated by occlusions and potential scale changes.

© Springer Nature Switzerland AG 2019
L. Leal-Taixé and S. Roth (Eds.): ECCV 2018 Workshops, LNCS 11132, pp. 64–77, 2019.
https://doi.org/10.1007/978-3-030-11018-5_6

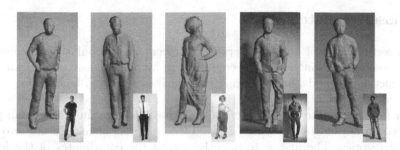

Fig. 1. Some example results using our method when trained with a high quality detailed training set.

In this work, we aim to significantly reduce the complexity of standard 3D human reconstruction techniques - to the point where it could just as easily be treated as a segmentation task. We do this by directly regressing a volumetric representation of the 3D geometry using a standard, spatial, CNN architecture, where the regressed volumetric structure is spatially aligned with the input. Notably, we do **not** regress a depth map; the 3D structure is regressed as slices and recovered from its volumetric representation using a standard surface extraction algorithm, such as Marching Cubes [3]. In summary, our main contributions in this work are as follows:

1. We are the first to apply volumetric regression networks [1] to the problem to human body reconstruction, not just human faces.
2. We propose several improvements to the network architecture described in [1], which show significant performance improvements. These include introducing intermediate supervision, using more advanced residual modules and altering the network structure by increasing the number of hourglass modules by reducing the number of residual modules.
3. We show that VRN is capable of reconstructing complex poses when trained on a suitable dataset.
4. Finally, we show that given high quality training data, our method can learn to produce previously unseen, highly detailed, full 3D reconstructions from only a single image. To the best of our knowledge, there is no other method capable of obtaining results with such high fidelity and reliability as ours.

The remainder of the paper is structured as follows: First, a review of closely related work on 3D human body reconstruction and human pose estimation is given. We then describe our method, including the volumetric representation we have already mentioned briefly, followed by the datasets and the training procedure. Next we will discuss several architectural variants of VRN, followed by results from a network trained with pose-variant data, but little detail. Finally, we will show results which have been generated by training a model with highly detailed data.

2   Closely Related Work

In this section we will give an overview of recent and popular approaches to human pose estimation (often a prerequisite to human reconstruction) and 3D reconstruction methods, both working from images and from landmarks.

Human Pose Estimation. All modern approaches to estimating the human pose are based on methods employing CNNs. These methods generally fall into one of two categories. The first is to directly regress the coordinates of the joints using an L2 (or similar) loss [4–10]. In particular, [5] estimate the 3D pose by combining the 2D predictions with image features. An autoencoder is employed in [6] to constrain the pose to something plausible. Similarly, [8] have the same goal but achieve this by using a kinematic model. Synthetic data is used for the full training procedure in [9], to ensure that the network is trained with accurate data. However, in [10], they only augment their existing training set with synthetic data. The second approach to CNN based human pose estimation is to regress a heatmap [11–14]. In [11] they do this from video. In [12] they regress a 3D heatmap, which is a similar idea to our own work. Another temporal based approach is described in [13], where the 2D landmarks are first refined also as a heatmap. A part based heatmap regression approach is shown in [14].

In this work, we do not aim to estimate the human pose as a set of coordinates. Instead, we aim to reconstruct the full 3D geometry of the human, from just a single image. This includes any parts of the body which are self occluded. However, in doing so, we optionally make use of information from a human pose estimation step, which is provided to the network as 16 channels, each with a Guassian centred above the respective landmark.

Reconstruction from Image. Many human reconstruction methods estimate the geometry from one or more images. For example, [15–17] fit a model based on a single RGB or grey scale images. In particular, [16] fit a skeleton model to the image by estimating the scale and pose of each body part separately. In [17], they fit a shape model initialised by a user clicking on separate body parts, assisted by a segmentation mask. Another shape model based approach is proposed in [15], using the SCRAPE model [18], which is fitted with a stochastic optimisation step. A general shape fitting method for reconstruction is proposed in [19], where two Gaussian models are used - one for shape and one for pose, by solving non-linear optimisation problems. The authors demonstrate this method on human bodies and sharks. In [20], a single image and corresponding landmarks are used to lookup a similar human pose using a kd-tree, containing about 4 million examples. A method intended for multi-instance model fitting from a single image is described in [21].

Several methods aim to estimate the 3D geometry using only the landmarks extracted via human pose estimation [2,22]. Particularly, SMPLify [2] (which uses the SMPL model [23]), was extended to also include further guidance from an segmentation mask in [24]. However, such an approach will never be able to capable of regressing finer details, unless information from the image is also captured.

Aside from SCRAPE [18] and SMPL [23], mentioned earlier, Dyna, the shape model capable of capturing large variations in body shape is presented in [25], but without an accompanying fitting method from a single image. A very recent shape model called Total Capture [26] captures many aspects of the body which are typically ignored by other shape models, including the face and hands.

Our work is different from all of the aforementioned methods in that we do not regress parameters for a shape model, nor do we regress the vertices directly. Further more, our method skips the model generation step entirely, which avoids the need to find dense correspondence between all training examples. Instead, we constrain the problem to the spatial domain, and directly regress the 3D structure using spatial convolutions in a CNN, via a volumetric representation from which the full 3D geometry can be recovered.

3   Method

This section describes our proposed method, including the voxelisation and alignment procedures.

3.1   Volumetric Regression

In this work, our goal is to reconstruct the full geometry of a human body from just a single image. There are several ways of estimating the geometry using deep learning. The first is to directly regress the vertices using a top-down network such as VGG [27] or ResNet [28] trained with an L2 loss. This has at least two disadvantages: firstly it requires the training data to be resampled to have a fixed number of vertices, which implies finding correspondence between all vertices of all meshes. Secondly, and more importantly, training a network to directly regress a very large number of vertices is hard. A common, and more efficient alternative is to regress the parameters of a 3D shape model. However, as these parameters are not scaled equally, it is necessary to employ normalisation methods, such as weighting the outputs using the Mahalanobis distance which has been also proven challenging to get it working well [1]. Additionally, 3D shape model based approach are known to be good at capturing the coarse shape but less able at capturing fine details (in the case of detailed 3D reconstruction).

To eliminate the aforementioned learning challenges, we reformulate the problem of 3D reconstruction by constraining it to the spatial domain, using a standard convolutional neural network. Our approach can be thought of as a type of image segmentation where the output is a set of slices capturing the 3D geometry. Hence architecturally one can use standard architectures for (say, semantic) segmentation. Following the work of [1] on human faces, we do this by encoding the geometry of the body in a volumetric representation. In this representation, the 3D space has been discretised with a fixed dimensionality. Space which is *inside* the object is encoded as a voxel with value equal to one. All other space (i.e. background or unknown object classes) are encoded with a voxel with a value equal to zero. For this particular application, the dimensionality of our volumes are $128 \times 128 \times 128$, which given the level of detail in our training set, is more than adequate (although we show in Sect. 6 results with much greater detail, and only a slightly larger volume). One of the main advantages of this representation is that it allows the non-visible (self-occluded or otherwise) parts of the geometry to also be reconstructed. This is not the case in methods attempting to reconstruct the body using depth map regression.

One of the most important aspects to note in the case of training a volumetric regression network is that the input and output must be spatially aligned. Put simply, the 2D projection of the target object should do a reasonable, if not very good, job at segmenting the input. Through experimentation, we have found that it is possible to ignore spatial alignment, as long as the pose is fixed (i.e. always frontal). However, ignoring spatial alignment will severely impact the performance of the method.

When trained to receive guidance from human pose estimation, landmarks are passed to the network as separate channels, each containing a Gaussian centred over the landmark's location. The Guassians have a diameter of approximately 6 pixels.

3.2   Dataset and Voxelisation

While Human3.6M [29,30] does include its own 3D scans, they are not in correspondence with the video frames. As such, we produced our training data by running SMPLify [2] on the Human3.6M dataset. The landmarks required by SMPLify were generated using the code made available with [14]. The fitted meshes were voxelised at a resolution of $128 \times 128 \times 128$. In terms of depth, the meshes are first aligned by the mean of the Z component. However, through experimentation, we found that as long as the Z alignment is performed in a seemingly sensible way, and remains stable across all images, the network will learn to regress the 3D structure without issue. Random scale augmentation was performed in advance of the training procedure, as doing this on-the-fly (for 3D volumes) can be quite demanding in terms of CPU usage.

An unfortunate side effect of using SMPLify to generate our training data is that it is not possible to regress features such as fingers or facial expressions. SMPLify does not model these, and as such, their pose remains fixed across all images. It also becomes a bottleneck in terms of performance. We show in Sect. 6, using a different dataset, that very high quality reconstruction is also possible with our proposed method.

3.3   Training

Our end-to-end network was trained using RMSProp [31] optimisation with a learning rate of 10^{-4}, which was reduced after approximately 20 epochs to 10^{-5} for 40 epochs. We did not observe any performance improvement by reducing this learning rate further. A batch size of 6 was used across 2 NVIDIA 1080 Ti graphics cards. During the voxelisation, random scale augmentation was applied.

Applying scale augmentation to a 3D volume on the fly, is very CPU intensive and slows down the training procedure too much. During training, augmentation to the input image was applied. This on-the-fly augmentation included colour channel scaling, random translation and random horizontal flipping.

4 Architecture

In the following subsections, we introduce the several architectural options we have explored as extensions to [1]. Our first network is the same as the one used in [1], referred to as *VRN - Guided*, which establishes our baseline. This network employs two Encoder-Decoder ("hourglass") networks in a stack. We follow a similar design, aside for the changes described in this section. All of our architectures were trained with the same loss function as in [1]:

$$l_1 = \sum_{w=1}^{W} \sum_{h=1}^{H} \sum_{d=1}^{D} [V_{whd} \log \widehat{V}_{whd} + (1 - V_{whd}) \log(1 - \widehat{V}_{whd})], \qquad (1)$$

where $\widehat{V}_{whd}$ is the corresponding sigmoid output at voxel $\{w, h, d\}$.

4.1 Ours - Multistack

This network makes the following changes to the *VRN - Guided* baseline network. We half the number of residual modules from four to two. In doing so, we also halved the memory requirements, allowing us to increase the number of hourglass modules in the stack, from two to four. Next, we replace the original residual module used in *VRN - Guided* with the multi-scale residual module proposed in [32]. We also show the performance improvement from introducing just this component in the results section. Finally, we introduce supervision after each hourglass module. We therefore have four losses. Each hourglass module forks to provide features for the next hourglass, and to regress the volumetric representation. The performance after each hourglass improves. We found that there was no benefit to adding more than four hourglass networks as the performance just fluctuates as more are added. This network is depicted in Fig. 2.

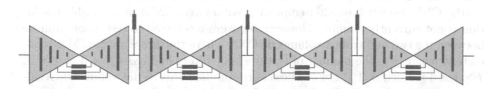

Fig. 2. The *Ours - Multistack* network. Dark blue boxes represent residual modules. Each Encoder-Decoder module has its own loss, while still passing features to the next module. (Color figure online)

4.2   Ours - Image Only

Our standard network (*Ours - Multistack*) is trained to receive guidance from the landmarks, while also using useful information from the images. With this network, we try to measure the impact of training with just images, while keeping the architecture identical. We call this network *Ours - Image Only*. We expect that the performance of this network be significantly lower than when guidance from the human pose is also provided.

4.3   Ours - Landmarks Only

Many methods, such as [2,22], use only the landmarks as input during training and inference. Hence, it is an interesting investigation to measure the performance of our method when only landmarks are provided, without the image. As such, we trained *Ours - Landmarks Only*. However, using only landmarks to fit a shape model results in generic appearing fittings. Provided high quality training data is available, our method can regress these fine details and match the body shape when also provided with the image.

4.4   Ours - Mask Only

Our method does not rely on a segmentation mask, as is the case in [33]. However, there is no reason why our method cannot reconstruct 3D geometry from a single segmentation mask, or silhouette. To show this, we train another network, *Ours - Segmentation Mask* which accepts only a single channel, containing the mask of the target object. From this, the network reconstructs the 3D geometry in the same way. Once again, this network has an identical configuration to *Ours - Multistack*, apart from the first layer receiving a different number of inputs. We expect this network to perform quite well since the segmentation mask we are providing to the network is the projection of the target volume.

4.5   Ours - 3D Convolution

While volumetric CNNs can likely outdo a spatial network in terms of performance, on this task, the memory requirements are much higher than that of a spatial CNN. So much so, that employing volumetric CNNs at a suitable resolution is not currently possible. However, we were interested to test a compromise between the two and train a volumetric CNN where the filters are flat. More concretely, where f is the number of features, our filters had sizes $f \times 3 \times 1 \times 1$, $f \times 1 \times 3 \times 1$ or $f \times 1 \times 1 \times 3$. These were combined into a flat volumetric residual module, as shown in Fig. 3, heavily inspired by [34]. This network also takes as input the image with corresponding landmarks. To provide a fair comparison with the other methods, we match the number of floating point operations of this network to *Ours - Multistack* by reducing the number of parameters (which also allows the network to fit into memory).

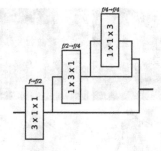

Fig. 3. A "flat" volumetric residual block

5 Results

In this section we will give an overview of the performance of the architectures we have described above. For each network, we give our results as an Intersection over Union (IoU) score, which is defined as the number of intersecting set voxels over the number voxels set in either volume. These numeric results may be found in Table 1. We will discuss these results in more detail in the proceeding paragraphs.

We show visual results for *Ours - Multistack* in Fig. 4. The quantitative results suggest that the changes we made to the baseline network *VRN - Guided* helped quite significantly, offering a performance increase of over 4% in terms of IoU. From this performance improvement, more than 2% was due to using the residual module proposed in [32], this can be seen from the results for *Ours - Old Residual*. As our data is generated by SMPlify [2], we are unable to provide a quantitative comparison with this method.

As expected, removing either the landmarks *or* the image reduces performance. The best performance is attainable by providing the network with both the image and landmarks, as seen quantitatively between *Ours - Multistack*, *Ours - Landmarks Only* and *Ours - Image Only*. Also unsurprisingly, landmarks alone offers better performance than the image alone. This is true at least in this case, as the groundtruth model has no detail. We also show performance where only the segmentation mask is provided to the network (this is not provided in the case of *Ours - Multistack*). These results are labelled *Ours - Mask Only*. We expected this network to perform better than the landmarks or image only networks, as the mask we provided was a direct 2D projection of the target volume.

Notes on Performance. A single forward pass through our network takes approximately 200 ms on an NVIDIA 1080 Ti GPU. This produces the volumetric representation. Surface extraction introduces 200–600 ms overhead depending on the implementation used. Significantly higher performance may be achieved with smaller volumes, but this will result in a lower level of detail. Training typically takes about two days.

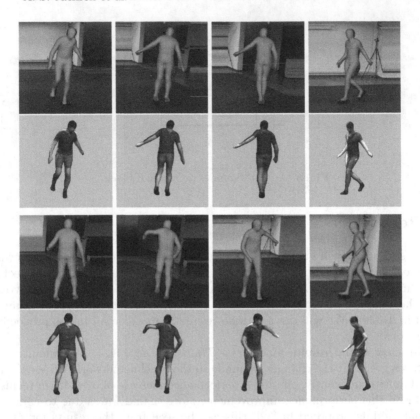

Fig. 4. Visual results from our main network, *Ours - Multistack*, on a test split of Human3.6m [30]. These results demonstrate VRN's ability to deal with large and complex pose. We also show the reconstructions with the texture projected onto them.

Table 1. Numerical performances of our proposed method and additional architectural experiments, all on data generated using SMPLify.

Method	IoU @ epoch 30	IoU @ epoch 60
VRN - Guided (Baseline)	61.6%	63.9%
Ours - Multistack	61.1%	**68.3%**
Ours - Old Residual	60.5%	66.1%
Ours - Landmarks Only	58.6%	61.0%
Ours - Image Only	46.8%	48.3%
Ours - Mask Only	52.8%	53.0%
Ours - 3D Convolution	57.3%	61.6%

6 High Quality Training Data

In the previous section, we showed that our method can reconstruct bodies of very large pose. However, due to the dataset we trained on, we are only able to regress the coarse geometry without any detail. Detailed 3D reconstruction was also not demonstrated in the case of faces in [1], which was also due to the lack of a detailed dataset. Hence, in this section, we demonstrate that VRN *is* capable of regressing details when a high quality dataset is provided. For this experiment, we use our best performing network *Ours - Multistack*.

Our dataset consists of highly detailed 3D scans from 40 participants, 4 of which were reserved for quantitative testing, but all of which are quite restricted in terms of pose. Only one scan per participant was available. These models do not have a corresponding image which is aligned with the model. As such, we rendered and voxelised these models under a large variety of different lighting conditions, scales and views to create our training set consisting of approximately 20,000 samples which are spatially aligned. The voxelisation was performed at a resolution of $128 \times 256 \times 96$, which efficiently encapsulates the poses found in the dataset. As in our previous experiment, the Z alignment was performed by the mean Z component. Unfortunately we are not able to publicly release this dataset.

6.1 Performance

The four models which we reserved for testing were also rendered and voxelised in the same way as above, to produce 60 testing images. Our method reconstructs these with an IoU of 78%. This is significantly higher than the reconstructions in our previous experiment. This is likely due to the better spatial alignment between the training images and target. Additionally, we show qualitative results on real-world images taken from the web[1]. These reconstructions can be found in Fig. 5. We show the backsides of these reconstructions, which demonstrate the networks ability to reconstruct the self-occluded body parts. Finer details can be seen in the wrinkles of clothing. As our method was trained on synthetic data, we believe there may be some performance degradation on real-world images. Additionally, several of the poses found in the reconstructions in Fig. 5 are not found in the 36 training samples. This suggests that VRN is somewhat tolerant to previously unseen poses.

---

[1] These images are licensed under Creative Commons. Attribution, where required, will be provided on our website.

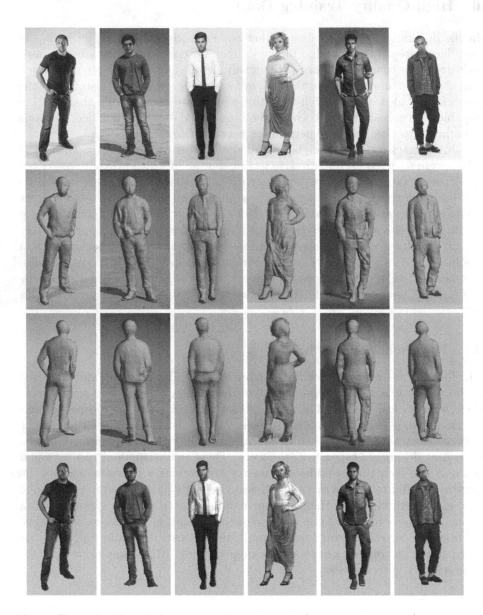

Fig. 5. Example 3D reconstructions from the web (Creative Commons) using our method trained with high quality training data. The first row shows the input image, the second shows the 3D reconstruction from the front, and the third row shows the 3D reconstruction when views from behind (i.e. the hallucinated side, in the case of these images). The final row shows the frontal reconstruction with the projected texture. These results show that VRN is capable of regressing finer details.

7   Conclusion

In this work we have shown that using Volumetric Regression Networks, as described in [1], for the task of 3D reconstruction, is not restricted to the simpler task of face reconstruction. Nor is it a limiting factor in terms of detail, despite the small size of the volumes we are working with. We have proposed several improvements to the original VRN which improve the performance quite substantially. Finally, we have shown, by using two different datasets, that VRN can regress both unusual poses (in networks trained on Human3.6m), and high levels of detail (in the case of our private but detailed dataset). We believe that given a large enough dataset containing many pose variations, and high levels of detail, the network will be capable of large pose 3D human reconstruction, while also capturing fine details, from a single image.

Acknowledgements. Aaron Jackson is funded by a PhD scholarship from the University of Nottingham. Thank you to Chris Manafas and his team at 2B3D for providing data for the experiments. We are grateful for access to the University of Nottingham High Performance Computing Facility, which was used for data voxelisation.

References

1. Jackson, A.S., Bulat, A., Argyriou, V., Tzimiropoulos, G.: Large pose 3D face reconstruction from a single image via direct volumetric CNN regression. In: 2017 IEEE International Conference on Computer Vision (ICCV), pp. 1031–1039. IEEE (2017)
2. Bogo, F., Kanazawa, A., Lassner, C., Gehler, P., Romero, J., Black, M.J.: Keep It SMPL: automatic estimation of 3D human pose and shape from a single image. In: Leibe, B., Matas, J., Sebe, N., Welling, M. (eds.) ECCV 2016, Part V. LNCS, vol. 9909, pp. 561–578. Springer, Cham (2016). https://doi.org/10.1007/978-3-319-46454-1_34
3. Lorensen, W.E., Cline, H.E.: Marching cubes: a high resolution 3D surface construction algorithm. In: ACM SIGGRAPH Computer Graphics, vol. 21, pp. 163–169. ACM (1987)
4. Li, S., Chan, A.B.: 3D human pose estimation from monocular images with deep convolutional neural network. In: Cremers, D., Reid, I., Saito, H., Yang, M.-H. (eds.) ACCV 2014. LNCS, vol. 9004, pp. 332–347. Springer, Cham (2015). https://doi.org/10.1007/978-3-319-16808-1_23
5. Park, S., Hwang, J., Kwak, N.: 3D human pose estimation using convolutional neural networks with 2D pose information. In: Hua, G., Jégou, H. (eds.) ECCV 2016, Part III. LNCS, vol. 9915, pp. 156–169. Springer, Cham (2016). https://doi.org/10.1007/978-3-319-49409-8_15
6. Tekin, B., Katircioglu, I., Salzmann, M., Lepetit, V., Fua, P.: Structured prediction of 3D human pose with deep neural networks. arXiv preprint arXiv:1605.05180 (2016)
7. Tekin, B., Rozantsev, A., Lepetit, V., Fua, P.: Direct prediction of 3D body poses from motion compensated sequences. In: Proceedings of the IEEE Conference on Computer Vision and Pattern Recognition, pp. 991–1000 (2016)

8. Zhou, X., Sun, X., Zhang, W., Liang, S., Wei, Y.: Deep kinematic pose regression. In: Hua, G., Jégou, H. (eds.) ECCV 2016, Part III. LNCS, vol. 9915, pp. 186–201. Springer, Cham (2016). https://doi.org/10.1007/978-3-319-49409-8_17

9. Chen, W., et al.: Synthesizing training images for boosting human 3D pose estimation. In: 2016 Fourth International Conference on 3D Vision (3DV), pp. 479–488. IEEE (2016)

10. Ghezelghieh, M.F., Kasturi, R., Sarkar, S.: Learning camera viewpoint using CNN to improve 3D body pose estimation. In: 2016 Fourth International Conference on 3D Vision (3DV), pp. 685–693. IEEE (2016)

11. Zhou, X., Zhu, M., Leonardos, S., Derpanis, K.G., Daniilidis, K.: Sparseness meets deepness: 3D human pose estimation from monocular video. In: Proceedings of the IEEE conference on computer vision and pattern recognition, pp. 4966–4975 (2016)

12. Pavlakos, G., Zhou, X., Derpanis, K.G., Daniilidis, K.: Coarse-to-fine volumetric prediction for single-image 3D human pose. In: 2017 IEEE Conference on Computer Vision and Pattern Recognition (CVPR), pp. 1263–1272. IEEE (2017)

13. Mehta, D.: Vnect: Real-time 3D human pose estimation with a single RGB camera. ACM Trans. Graph. (TOG) 36(4), 44 (2017)

14. Bulat, A., Tzimiropoulos, G.: Human pose estimation via convolutional part heatmap regression. In: Leibe, B., Matas, J., Sebe, N., Welling, M. (eds.) ECCV 2016, Part VII. LNCS, vol. 9911, pp. 717–732. Springer, Cham (2016). https://doi.org/10.1007/978-3-319-46478-7_44

15. Balan, A.O., Sigal, L., Black, M.J., Davis, J.E., Haussecker, H.W.: Detailed human shape and pose from images. In: 2007 IEEE Conference on Computer Vision and Pattern Recognition, pp. 1–8. IEEE (2007)

16. Grest, D., Herzog, D., Koch, R.: Human model fitting from monocular posture images

17. Guan, P., Weiss, A., Balan, A.O., Black, M.J.: Estimating human shape and pose from a single image. In: 2009 IEEE 12th International Conference on Computer Vision, pp. 1381–1388. IEEE (2009)

18. Anguelov, D., Srinivasan, P., Koller, D., Thrun, S., Rodgers, J., Davis, J.: Scape: shape completion and animation of people. In: ACM Transactions on Graphics (TOG), vol. 24, pp. 408–416. ACM (2005)

19. Chen, Y., Kim, T.-K., Cipolla, R.: Inferring 3D shapes and deformations from single views. In: Daniilidis, K., Maragos, P., Paragios, N. (eds.) ECCV 2010, Part III. LNCS, vol. 6313, pp. 300–313. Springer, Heidelberg (2010). https://doi.org/10.1007/978-3-642-15558-1_22

20. Jiang, H.: 3D human pose reconstruction using millions of exemplars. In: 2010 20th International Conference on Pattern Recognition (ICPR), pp. 1674–1677. IEEE (2010)

21. Zanfir, A., Marinoiu, E., Sminchisescu, C.: Monocular 3D pose and shape estimation of multiple people in natural scenes - the importance of multiple scene constraints. In: The IEEE Conference on Computer Vision and Pattern Recognition (CVPR), June 2018

22. Ramakrishna, V., Kanade, T., Sheikh, Y.: Reconstructing 3D human pose from 2D image landmarks. In: Fitzgibbon, A., Lazebnik, S., Perona, P., Sato, Y., Schmid, C. (eds.) ECCV 2012, Part IV. LNCS, vol. 7575, pp. 573–586. Springer, Heidelberg (2012). https://doi.org/10.1007/978-3-642-33765-9_41

23. Loper, M., Mahmood, N., Romero, J., Pons-Moll, G., Black, M.J.: SMPL: a skinned multi-person linear model. ACM Trans. Graph. 34(6), 248 (2015)

24. Varol, G., et al.: Learning from synthetic humans. In: 2017 IEEE Conference on Computer Vision and Pattern Recognition (CVPR 2017), pp. 4627–4635. IEEE (2017)
25. Pons-Moll, G., Romero, J., Mahmood, N., Black, M.J.: Dyna: a model of dynamic human shape in motion. ACM Trans. Graph. **34**(4), 120:1–120:14 (2015)
26. Joo, H., Simon, T., Sheikh, Y.: Total capture: a 3D deformation model for tracking faces, hands, and bodies. In: The IEEE Conference on Computer Vision and Pattern Recognition (CVPR), June 2018
27. Simonyan, K., Zisserman, A.: Very deep convolutional networks for large-scale image recognition. arXiv preprint arXiv:1409.1556 (2014)
28. He, K., Zhang, X., Ren, S., Sun, J.: Deep residual learning for image recognition. In: Proceedings of the IEEE Conference on Computer Vision and Pattern Recognition, pp. 770–778 (2016)
29. Ionescu, C., Li, F., Sminchisescu, C.: Latent structured models for human pose estimation. In: International Conference on Computer Vision (2011)
30. Ionescu, C., Papava, D., Olaru, V., Sminchisescu, C.: Human3.6m: large scale datasets and predictive methods for 3D human sensing in natural environments. IEEE Trans. Pattern Anal. Mach. Intell. **36**(7), 1325–1339 (2014)
31. Hinton, G., Srivastava, N., Swersky, K.: Neural networks for machine learning lecture 6a overview of mini-batch gradient descent
32. Bulat, A., Tzimiropoulos, G.: Binarized convolutional landmark localizers for human pose estimation and face alignment with limited resources. In: International Conference on Computer Vision (2017)
33. Sigal, L., Balan, A., Black, M.J.: Combined discriminative and generative articulated pose and non-rigid shape estimation. In: Advances in Neural Information Processing Systems, pp. 1337–1344 (2008)
34. Qiu, Z., Yao, T., Mei, T.: Learning spatio-temporal representation with pseudo-3D residual networks. In: 2017 IEEE International Conference on Computer Vision (ICCV), pp. 5534–5542. IEEE (2017)

Can 3D Pose Be Learned from 2D Projections Alone?

Dylan Drover[✉], Rohith M. V[✉], Ching-Hang Chen[✉], Amit Agrawal[✉], Ambrish Tyagi[✉], and Cong Phuoc Huynh[✉]

Amazon Lab126 Inc., Sunnyvale, CA, USA
{droverd,kurohith,chinghc,aaagrawa,ambrisht,conghuyn}@amazon.com

Abstract. 3D pose estimation from a single image is a challenging task in computer vision. We present a weakly supervised approach to estimate 3D pose points, given only 2D pose landmarks. Our method does not require correspondences between 2D and 3D points to build explicit 3D priors. We utilize an adversarial framework to impose a prior on the 3D structure, learned solely from their random 2D projections. Given a set of 2D pose landmarks, the generator network hypothesizes their depths to obtain a 3D skeleton. We propose a novel Random Projection layer, which randomly projects the generated 3D skeleton and sends the resulting 2D pose to the discriminator. The discriminator improves by discriminating between the generated poses and pose samples from a real distribution of 2D poses. Training does not require correspondence between the 2D inputs to either the generator or the discriminator. We apply our approach to the task of 3D human pose estimation. Results on Human3.6M dataset demonstrates that our approach outperforms many previous supervised and weakly supervised approaches.

Keywords: Weakly supervised learning
Generative Adversarial Networks · 3D pose estimation
Projective geometry

1 Introduction

Inferring 3D human poses from images and videos (automatic motion-capture) has garnered particular attention in the field [11,15,29,32] due to its numerous applications related to tracking, action understanding, human-robot-interaction and gaming, among others. Estimating 3D pose of articulated objects from 2D views is one of the long-standing ill-posed inverse problems in computer vision. We have access to, and continue to generate, large amounts of image and video data at an unprecedented rate. This begs the question: Can we build a system that can estimate the 3D joint locations/skeleton of humans by leveraging this abundant 2D image and video data?

The problem of training end-to-end, image to 3D, pose estimation models is challenging due to variations in background, illumination, appearance, camera characteristics, *etc*. Recent approaches [26,30] have decomposed the 3D pose

© Springer Nature Switzerland AG 2019
L. Leal-Taixé and S. Roth (Eds.): ECCV 2018 Workshops, LNCS 11132, pp. 78–94, 2019.
https://doi.org/10.1007/978-3-030-11018-5_7

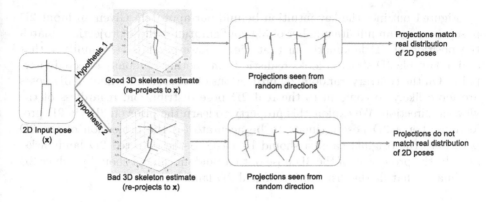

Fig. 1. Key intuition behind our approach: A generator can hypothesize multiple 3D skeletons for a given input 2D pose. However, only plausible 3D skeletons will project to realistic looking 2D poses after random projections. The discriminator evaluates the "realness" of the projected 2D poses and provides appropriate feedback to the generator to learn to produce realistic 3D skeletons

estimation problem into (i) estimating 2D landmark locations (corresponding to skeleton joints) and (ii) estimating 3D pose from them (lifting 2D points to 3D). Following such a scheme, suitable 2D pose estimators can be chosen based on the application domain [6,13,31,42] to estimate 2D poses, which can then be fed to a common 2D-3D lifting algorithm for recovering 3D pose.

A single 2D observation of landmarks admits infinite 3D skeletons as solution; not all these are physically plausible. The restriction of solution space to realistic poses is typically achieved by regularizing the 3D structure using priors such as symmetry, ratio of length of various skeleton elements, and kinematic constraints. These priors are often learned from ground truth 3D data, which is limited due to the complexity of capture systems. We believe that leveraging unsupervised algorithms such as generative adversarial networks for 3D pose estimation will help address the limitations of capturing such 3D data. Our work addresses the fundamental problem of lifting 2D image coordinates to 3D space without the use of any additional cues such as video [40,47], multi-view cameras [2,14], or depth images [35,38,46].

We present a weakly supervised learning algorithm to estimate 3D human skeleton from 2D pose landmarks. Unlike previous approaches we do not learn priors explicitly through 3D data or utilize explicit 2D-3D correspondence. Our system can generate 3D skeletons by only observing 2D poses. Our paper makes the following contributions:

- We present and demonstrate that a latent 3D pose distribution can be learned solely by observing 2D poses, without requiring any regression from 3D data.
- We propose a novel Random Projection layer and utilize it along with adversarial training to enforce a prior on 3D structure from 2D projections.

Figure 1 outlines the key intuition behind our approach. Given an input 2D pose, there are an infinite number of 3D configurations whose projections match the position of 2D landmarks in that view. However, it is very unlikely that an implausible 3D skeleton looks realistic from another randomly selected viewpoint. On the contrary, random 2D projections of accurately estimated 3D poses are more likely to conform to the real 2D pose distribution, regardless of the viewing direction. We exploit this property to learn the prior on 3D via 2D projections. For a 3D pose estimate to be accurate (a) the projection of the 3D pose onto the original camera should be close to the detected 2D landmarks, and (b) the projection of the 3D pose onto a random camera should produce 2D landmarks that fit the distribution of real 2D landmarks.

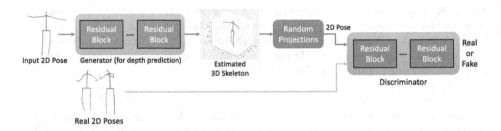

Fig. 2. Adversarial training architecture for learning 3D pose

Generative Adversarial Networks (GAN) [12] provide a natural framework to learn distributions without explicit supervision. Our approach learns a latent distribution (3D pose priors) indirectly via 2D poses. Given a 2D pose, the generator hypothesizes the relative depth of joint locations to obtain a 3D human skeleton. Random 2D projections of the generated 3D skeleton are fed to the discriminator, along with actual 2D pose samples (see Fig. 2). The 2D poses fed to the generator and discriminator do not require any correspondence during training. The discriminator learns a prior from 2D projections and enables the generator to eventually produce realistic 3D skeletons.

We demonstrate the effectiveness of our approach by evaluating 3D pose estimation on the Human3.6M dataset [17]. Our method shows an improvement over other weakly supervised methods which use 2D pose as input [10, 43]. Interestingly we also outperform a number of supervised methods that use explicit 2D-3D correspondences.

The remainder of this paper is organized as follows. We discuss related work in Sect. 2. Section 3 provides details of the proposed method and the training methodology. Our experimental evaluation results are presented in Sect. 4. Finally, we close with concluding remarks in Sect. 5.

2   Related Work

2D Pose Estimation: Significant progress has been made recently in 2D pose estimation using deep learning techniques [6,13,31,42]. Newell *et al.* [31] proposed a stacked hourglass architecture for predicting heatmap of each 2D joint location. Convolutional Pose Machines (CPM) [42] employ a sequential architecture by combining the prediction of previous stages with the input image to produce increasingly refined estimates of part locations. Cao *et al.* [6] also estimate a part affinity field along with landmark probabilities and uses a fast, greedy search for real-time multi-person 2D pose estimation. Kaiming *et al.* [13] accomplish this by performing fine-grained detection on top of an object detector. Our proposed method will continue to benefit from the ongoing improvement of 2D pose estimation algorithms.

3D Pose Estimation: Several approaches try to directly estimate 3D joint locations from images [28,33,34,37,49] in an end-to-end learning framework. However, in this paper we focus on benchmarking against methods which estimate 3D pose from 2D landmark positions, known as lifting from 2D to 3D [7,10,26]. Since the input to the methods is only 2D landmark locations, it is easy to augment training of these methods using synthetic data. Like other methods in this category, our method could be combined with a variety of 2D pose estimators based on the application without retraining. To better distinguish our work from previous approaches on lifting 2D pose landmarks to 3D, we define the following categories:

Fully Supervised: These include approaches such as [23,26,44] that use paired 2D-3D data comprised of ground truth 2D locations of joint landmarks and corresponding 3D ground truth for learning. For example, Martinez *et al.* [26] learn a regression network from 2D joints to 3D joints, whereas Moreno-Noguer [30] learns a regression from a 2D distance matrix to a 3D distance matrix using 2D-3D correspondences. Exemplar based methods [7,18,45] use a database/dictionary of 3D skeletons for nearest-neighbor look-up. Lin *et al.* [24] learn an end-to-end Recurrent Pose Sequence Machine whereas our approach does not use any video information. Mehta *et al.* [28] combine a regression network which estimates 2D and 3D poses with, temporal smoothing and a parameterized, kinematic skeleton fitting method to produce stable 3D skeletons across time. Tekin *et al.* [39] fuse 2D and 3D image cues relying on 2D-3D correspondences. Since these methods model 3D mapping from a given dataset, they implicitly incorporate dataset-specific parameters such as camera projection matrices, distance of skeleton from camera, and scale of skeletons. This enables such models to predict metric position of joints in 3D on similar datasets, but requires paired 2D-3D correspondences which are difficult to obtain.

Weakly Supervised: Approaches such as [5,9,41,47] use *unpaired* 3D data to learn a prior, typically as a 3D basis or articulation priors, but do not explicitly use paired 2D-3D correspondences. For example, Tome *et al.* [41] pre-train a low-rank Gaussian model from 3D annotations as a prior for plausible 3D poses. Wu *et al.* [43] proposed a 3D interpreter network that also estimates the weights of a 3D basis, which are learned separately for each object class using 3D data. Similarly Tung *et al.* [10] build a 3D shape basis using PCA by aligning 3D skeletons and predicting basis coefficients. Though this method accepts 2D landmark locations as input, this information is represented as an image within the network. On the other hand, we directly operate on the vectors of 2D landmark pixel locations, with the advantage of working in lower dimensions and avoiding convolution layers in our network. Zhou *et al.* [47] also use a 3D pose dictionary to learn pose priors. Brau *et al.* [5] employ an independently trained network that learns a prior distribution over 3D poses (kinematic and self-intersection priors) to impose constraints. Zhou *et al.* [49] combine the 2D pose estimation task with a constraint on the bone length ratio in each skeleton group for image-to-3D pose estimation.

Learning Using Adversarial Loss: Recently, Generative Adversarial Networks (GAN) [12] have emerged as a powerful framework for learning generative models for complex data distributions. In a GAN framework, a generator is trained to synthesize samples from a latent distribution and a discriminator network is used to distinguish between synthetic and real samples. The generator's goal is to fool the discriminator by producing samples that match the distribution of real data. Previous approaches have used adversarial loss for human pose estimation by using a discriminator to differentiate real/fake 2D poses [8] and real/fake 3D poses [10,20]. To estimate 3D, these techniques still require 3D data or use prior 3D pose model. Kanazawa *et al.* [20] trained an end-to-end system to estimate a skinned multi-person linear model (SMPL) [25] 3D mesh from RGB images by minimizing the re-projection error between 3D and 2D landmarks. However, they impose a prior on 3D skeletons using an adversarial loss with a large database of 3D human meshes. In contrast, our approach applies an adversarial loss over randomly projected 2D poses of the hypothesized 3D poses.

3   Weakly Supervised Lifting of 2D Pose to 3D Skeleton

In this section we describe our weakly supervised learning approach to lift 2D human pose points to a 3D skeleton. Adversarial networks are notoriously difficult to train and we discuss design choices that lead to stable training. For consistency with generative adversarial network naming conventions, we will refer to the 3D pose estimation network as a generator. For simplicity, we work in the camera coordinate system, where the camera with unit focal length is centered at the origin $(0, 0, 0)$ of the world coordinate system. Let $\mathbf{x}_i = (x_i, y_i), i = 1 \ldots N$, denote N 2D pose landmarks with the root joint (midpoint between hip joints) located at the origin. The 2D input pose is hence denoted by $\mathbf{x} = [\mathbf{x}_1 \ldots \mathbf{x}_N]$. For numerical stability, we aim to generate 3D skeletons such that the distance from the top of the head to the root joint is approximately 1 unit.

Generator: The generator G is defined as a neural network that outputs a *depth offset* o_i for each point $\mathbf{x}_i$

$$G_{\theta_G}(\mathbf{x}_i) = o_i, \tag{1}$$

where θ_G are parameters of the generator learned during training. The depth of each point is defined as

$$z_i = \max\left(0, d + o_i\right) + 1, \tag{2}$$

where d denotes the distance between the camera and the 3D skeleton. Note that the choice of d is arbitrary provided that $d > 1$. Constraining z_i to be greater than 1 ensures that the points are projected in front of the camera. In practice we use $d = 10$ units.

Next, we define the back projection and the random projection layers responsible for generating the 3D skeleton and projecting it to other random views.

Back Projection Layer: The back projection layer takes the input 2D points $\mathbf{x}_i$ and the predicted z_i to compute a 3D point $\mathbf{X}_i = [z_i x_i, z_i y_i, z_i]$. Note that we use exact perspective projection instead of approximations such as orthographic or paraperspective projection.

Random Projection Layer: The hypothesized (generated) 3D skeleton is projected to 2D poses using randomly generated camera orientations, to be fed to the discriminator. For simplicity, we randomly rotate the 3D points (in-place) and apply perspective projection to obtain *fake* 2D projections. Let $\mathbf{R}$ be a random rotation matrix and $\mathbf{T} = [0, 0, d]$. Let $\mathbf{P}_i = [P_i^x, P_i^y, P_i^z] = \mathbf{R}(\mathbf{X}_i - \mathbf{T}) + \mathbf{T}$ denote the 3D points after applying the random rotation. These points are re-projected to obtain fake 2D points $\mathbf{p}_i = [p_i^x, p_i^y] = [P_i^x/P_i^z, P_i^y/P_i^z]$. The rotated points $\mathbf{P}_i$ should also be in front of the camera. To ensure that, we also force $P_i^z \geq 1$. Let $\mathbf{p} = [\mathbf{p}_1 \ldots \mathbf{p}_N]$ denote the 2D projected pose.

Note that there is an inherent ambiguity in perspective projection; doubling the size of the 3D skeleton and the distance from the camera will result in the same 2D projection. Thus a generator that predicts absolute 3D coordinates has an additional degree of freedom between the predicted size and distance for each training sample in a batch. This could potentially result in large variance in the generator output and gradient magnitudes within a batch and cause convergence issues in training. We remove this ambiguity by predicting depth offsets with respect to a constant depth d and rotating around it, resulting in stable training. In Sect. 4, we define a *trivial baseline* for our approach which assumes a constant depth for all points (depth offsets equals zero, *flat* human skeleton output) and show that our approach can predict meaningful depths offsets.

Discriminator: The discriminator D is defined as a neural network that consumes either the fake 2D pose $\mathbf{p}$ (randomly projected from generated 3D skeleton) or a real 2D pose $\mathbf{r}$ (some projection, via camera or synthetic view, of a real 3D skeleton) and classifies them as either fake (target probability of 0) or real (target probability of 1), respectively.

$$D_{\theta_D}(\mathbf{u}) \rightarrow [0, 1] \tag{3}$$

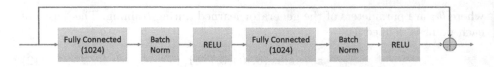

Fig. 3. Residual block used in our generator and discriminator architecture

where θ_D are parameters of the discriminator learned during training and $\mathbf{u}$ denotes a 2D pose. Note that for any training sample $\mathbf{x}$, we do not require $\mathbf{r}$ to be same as $\mathbf{x}$ or any of its multi-view correspondences. During learning we utilize a standard GAN loss [12] defined as

$$\min_G \max_D V(D,G) = \mathbb{E}(\log(D(\mathbf{r}))) + \mathbb{E}(\log(1 - D(\mathbf{p}))) \tag{4}$$

Priors on 3D skeletons such as the ratio of limb lengths and joint angles are implicitly learned using only random 2D projections.

3.1 Training

For training we normalize the 2D pose landmarks by centering them using the root joint and scaling the pixel coordinates so that the average head-root distance on training data is $1/d$ units in 2D. Although we can fit the entire data in GPU memory, we use a batch size of 32,768. We use the Adam optimizer [21] with a starting learning rate of 0.0002 for both generator and discriminator networks. We varied the batch size between 8,192 and 65,536 in experiments but it did not have any significant effect on the performance. Training time on 8 TitanX GPUs is 0.4 s per batch.

Generator Architecture: The generator accepts a 28 dimensional input representing 14 2D joint locations. Inputs are connected to a fully connected layer to expand the dimensionality to 1024 and then fed into subsequent residual blocks. Similar to [26], a residual block is composed of a pair of fully connected layers, each with 1024 neurons followed by batch normalization [16] and RELU (see Fig. 3). The final output is reduced through a fully connected layer to produce 14 dimensional depth offsets (one for each pose joint). A total of 4 residual blocks are employed in the generator.

Discriminator Architecture: Similar to the generator, the discriminator also takes 28 inputs representing 14 2D joint locations, either from the real 2D pose dataset or the fake 2D pose projected from the hypothesized 3D skeleton. This goes through a fully connected layer of size 1024 to feed the subsequent 3 residual blocks as defined above. Finally, the output of the discriminator is a 2-class softmax layer denoting the probability of the input being real or fake.

Random Rotations: The random projection layer creates a random rotation by sampling an elevation angle ϕ randomly from [0,20] degrees and an azimuth angle θ from [0,360] degrees. These angles were chosen as a heuristic to roughly emulate probable viewpoints that most "in then wild" images would have.

4   Experimental Results

We present quantitative and qualitative results on the widely used Human3.6M [17] for benchmarking. We also show qualitative visualization of reconstructed 3D skeleton from 2D pose landmarks on MPII [3] and Leeds Sports Pose [19] datasets, for which the ground truth 3D data is not available.

4.1   Dataset and Evaluation Metrics

The Human3.6M dataset is one of the largest Human Pose datasets, consisting of 3.6 million 3D human poses. The dataset contains video and MoCap data from 5 female and 6 male subjects. Data is captured from 4 different viewpoints, while subjects perform typical activities such as talking on phone, walking, eating, *etc.*

We found multiple variations of the evaluation protocols in recent literature. We report results on the two most popular protocols. Our **Protocol 1** reports test results only on subject S11 to allow comparison with [7,45]. **Protocol 2** reports results for both S9 and S11 as adopted by [10,22,26,40,47]. In both cases, we report the Mean Per Joint Position Error (MPJPE) in millimeters after scaling and rigid alignment to the ground truth skeleton. As discussed, our approach generates 3D skeleton up to a scale factor, since it is impossible to estimate the global scale of a human from a monocular image without additional information. Our results are based on 14-joints per skeleton. We do not train class specific models or leverage any motion information to improve our results. The reported metrics are taken from the respective papers for comparisons.

Similar to previous works [10,22,45], we generate synthetic 2D training data by projecting randomly rotated versions of 3D skeletons. These 2D poses are used to augment the 4 camera data already available in Human3.6M. We use additional camera positions to augment data from each 3D skeleton (we use 8 cameras compared to 144 in [45]). The rotation angles for the cameras are sampled randomly in azimuth between 0 to 360° and in elevation between 0 to 20°. We only use data from subjects S1, S5, S6, S7, and S8 for training.

Trivial baseline: We define a trivial baseline with a naive algorithm that predicts a *constant* depth for each 2D pose point. This is equivalent to a generator that outputs constant depth offsets. The MPJPE of such a method is 127.3 mm for **Protocol 2** using ground truth 2D points. We achieve much lower error rates in practice, reinforcing the fact that our generator is able to learn realistic 3D poses as expected.

4.2   Quantitative Results: Protocol 1

We first compare our approach to methods that adopt Protocol 1 in their evaluation. Table 1 compares the per class and weighted average MPJPE of our method with recent supervised learning methods [7,45], using ground truth 2D points for test subject S11. Our results are superior in each category and reduces the previous error by 40% (34.2 mm vs. 57.5 mm). Table 2 compares with the same

Table 1. Comparison of our weakly supervised approach to supervised approaches that adopt **Protocol 1**. Inputs are 2D ground truth pose points

Method	Direct.	Discuss	Eat	Greet	Phone	Pose	Purchase	Sit
Yasin et al. [45]	60.0	54.7	71.6	67.5	63.8	61.9	55.7	73.9
Chen et al. [7]	53.3	46.8	58.6	61.2	56.0	58.1	48.9	55.6
Ours	**34.3**	**36.4**	**28.4**	**33.7**	**30.0**	**43.8**	**31.7**	**32.5**
Method	SitDown	Smoke	Photo	Wait	Walk	WalkD	WalkP	Avg.
Yasin et al. [45]	110.8	78.9	96.9	67.9	47.5	89.3	53.4	70.5
Chen et al. [7]	73.4	60.3	76.1	62.2	35.8	61.9	51.1	57.5
Ours	**48.9**	**32.1**	**43.8**	**36.0**	**25.1**	**34.1**	**30.3**	**34.2**

Table 2. Comparison of our weakly supervised approach to supervised approaches that adopt **Protocol 1**. Inputs are 2D detected pose points. SH denotes stacked hourglass pose detector

Method	Direct.	Discuss	Eat	Greet	Phone	Pose	Purchase	Sit
Yasin et al. [45]	88.4	72.5	108.5	110.2	97.1	81.6	107.2	119.0
Chen et al. [7]	71.6	66.6	74.7	79.1	70.1	67.6	89.3	90.7
Ours (SH)	**58.4**	**59.4**	**58.7**	**64.5**	**59.0**	**60.9**	**57.0**	**61.6**
Method	SitDown	Smoke	Photo	Wait	Walk	WalkD	WalkP	Avg.
Yasin et al. [45]	170.8	108.2	142.5	86.9	92.1	165.7	102.0	108.3
Chen et al. [7]	195.6	83.5	93.3	71.2	**55.7**	85.9	62.5	82.7
Ours (SH)	**85.8**	**60.4**	**64.7**	**57.4**	63.0	**65.5**	**62.1**	**62.3**

methods using 2D points obtained from stacked hourglass(SH) [31] pose detector. We similarly reduce the best reported error by 25% (62.3 mm vs. 82.7 mm). Our method outperforms these supervised approaches in all activities, except *Walking*.

4.3   Quantitative Results: Protocol 2

Next, we compare against weakly supervised approaches such as [10,48] that exploit 3D cues indirectly, without requiring direct 2D-3D correspondences. Table 3 compares the MPJPE for the previous weakly supervised approaches using **Protocol 2** on ground truth 2D pose inputs. Our approach reduces the error reported in [10] by more than 50% (38.2 mm vs. 79.0 mm). A similar comparison is shown in Table 4 using 2D key points detected using the stacked hourglass [31] pose estimator. Our approach outperforms other methods in all activity classes and reduces the previously reported error by 33% (64.6 mm vs. 97.2 mm).

It is well known that supervised approaches broadly perform better than weakly supervised approaches in classification and regression tasks. For human 3D pose estimation, we do not expect our method to outperform the state of

Table 3. Comparison of our approach to other weakly supervised approaches that adopt **Protocol 2**. Inputs are 2D ground truth pose points. Results marked as * are taken from [10]

Method	Direct.	Discuss	Eat	Greet	Phone	Photo	Pose	Purchase
3DInterpreter [43]*	56.3	77.5	96.2	71.6	96.3	106.7	59.1	109.2
Monocap [48]*	78.0	78.9	88.1	93.9	102.1	115.7	71.0	90.6
AIGN [10]	53.7	71.5	82.3	58.6	86.9	98.4	57.6	104.2
Ours	**33.5**	**39.3**	**32.9**	**37.0**	**35.8**	**42.7**	**39.0**	**38.2**

Method	Sit	SitDown	Smoke	Wait	Walk	WalkD	WalkP	Avg.
3DInterpreter [43]*	111.9	111.9	124.2	93.3	58.0	-	-	88.6
Monocap [48]*	121.0	118.2	102.5	82.6	75.62	–	–	92.3
AIGN [10]	100.0	112.5	83.3	68.9	57.0	–	–	79.0
Ours	**42.1**	**52.3**	**36.9**	**39.4**	**36.8**	**33.2**	**34.9**	**38.2**

Table 4. Comparison of our approach to other weakly supervised approaches that adopt **Protocol 2**. Inputs are 2D detected pose points. SH denotes stacked hourglass. Results marked as * are taken from [10]

Method	Direct.	Discuss	Eat	Greet	Phone	Photo	Pose	Purchase
3DInterpreter [43]*	78.6	90.8	92.5	89.4	108.9	112.4	77.1	106.7
AIGN [10]	77.6	91.4	89.9	88	107.3	110.1	75.9	107.5
Ours (SH)	**60.2**	**60.7**	**59.2**	**65.1**	**65.5**	**63.8**	**59.4**	**59.4**

Method	Sit	SitDown	Smoke	Wait	Walk	WalkD	WalkP	Avg.
3DInterpreter [43]*	127.4	139.0	103.4	91.4	79.1	-	-	98.4
AIGN [10]	124.2	137.8	102.2	90.3	78.6	-	-	97.2
Ours (SH)	**69.1**	**88.0**	**64.8**	**60.8**	**64.9**	**63.9**	**65.2**	**64.6**

the art supervised approach [26]. However, our results are better than several previous published works that use 3D supervision as shown in Table 5. We have demonstrated the effectiveness of a relatively simple adversarial training framework using only 2D pose landmarks as input.

While the focus of this work is on weakly supervised learning from 2D poses alone, we are very encouraged by the fact that our results are competitive with the state of the art supervised approaches. In fact, our approach comes to within 1.1 mm of the error reported by [26] on the ground truth 2D input as shown in Table 6. We also experimented with a naïve ensemble algorithm where we combined 11 of our top performing models on the validation data and averaged the 3D skeleton for each input. This simple algorithm reduced the error to 36.3 mm, surpassing the state-of-the-art results of 37.1 mm (Table 6).

Table 5. Comparison of our approach to other supervised methods on Human3.6M under **Protocol 2** using detected 2D keypoints. The results of all approaches are obtained from [26]. Our approach outperforms most supervised methods that use explicit 2D-3D correspondences

Method	Direct.	Discuss	Eat	Greet	Phone	Photo	Pose	Purchase
Akhter and Black [1]	199.2	177.6	161.8	197.8	176.2	186.5	195.4	167.3
Ramakrishna et al. [36]	137.4	149.3	141.6	154.3	157.7	158.9	141.8	158.1
Zhou et al. (2016) [47]	99.7	95.8	87.9	116.8	108.3	107.3	93.5	95.3
Bogo et al. [4]	62.0	60.2	67.8	76.5	92.1	77.0	73.0	75.3
Moreno-Noguer [30]	66.1	61.7	84.5	73.7	65.2	67.2	60.9	67.3
Martinez et al. [26]	44.8	52.0	44.4	50.5	61.7	59.4	45.1	41.9
Ours (Weakly Supervised)	*60.2*	*60.7*	*59.2*	*65.1*	*65.5*	*63.8*	*59.4*	*59.4*
Method	Sit	SitD	Smoke	Wait	Walk	WalkD	WalkP	Avg.
Akhter and Black [1]	160.7	173.7	177.8	181.9	176.2	198.6	192.7	181.1
Ramakrishna et al. [36]	168.6	175.6	160.4	161.7	150.0	174.8	150.2	157.3
Zhou et al. (2016) [47]	109.1	137.5	106.0	102.2	106.5	110.4	115.2	106.7
Bogo et al. [4]	100.3	137.3	83.4	77.3	86.8	79.7	87.7	82.3
Moreno-Noguer [30]	103.5	74.6	92.6	69.6	71.5	78.0	73.2	74.0
Martinez et al. [26]	66.3	77.6	54.0	58.8	49.0	35.9	40.7	52.1
Ours (Weakly supervised)	*69.1*	*88.0*	*64.8*	*60.8*	*64.9*	*63.9*	*65.2*	*64.6*

Table 6. Comparison of our results to the state of the art fully supervised approaches under Protocol 2 using ground truth 2D inputs. Our model has error within 1.1 mm of the best supervised approach, and surpasses it with a naïve ensemble approach

Moreno-Noguer [30]	Martinez et al. [26]	Ours (Weakly supervised)	
		(Single Model)	(Ensemble)
62.2	<u>37.1</u>	38.2	**36.3**

4.4 Qualitative Results

Figure 4 shows a few 3D pose reconstruction results on Human3.6M using our approach. The ground truth 3D skeleton is shown in gray. We see that our approach can successfully recover the 3D pose. Figure 5 shows some failure cases of our approach. Our typical failures are due to odd or challenging poses containing severe occlusions or plausible alternate hypothesis such as mirror flips in the direction of viewing. Since the training was performed on images containing all 14 joints, we are currently unable to lift 2D poses with fewer joints to 3D skeletons.

To test the generalization performance of our method on images in the wild, we applied our method to MPII [3] and the Leeds Sports Pose (LSP) [19] datasets. MPII consists of images from short Youtube videos and has been used as a standard dataset for 2D human pose estimation. Similarly LSP dataset contains images from Flickr containing people performing sport activities.

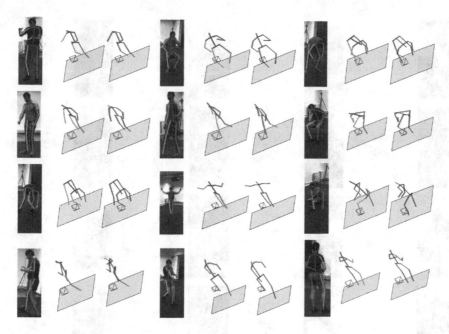

Fig. 4. Examples of 3D pose reconstruction on Human3.6M dataset. For each image we overlay 2D pose points, followed by the predicted 3D skeleton in color. Corresponding ground truth 3D shown in gray

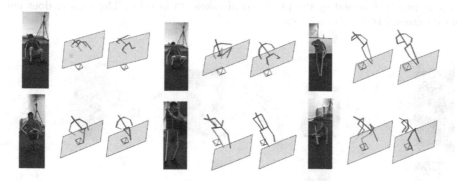

Fig. 5. Some failure cases for our approach on Human3.6m dataset. Ground truth 3D skeleton is shown in gray

Figures 6 and 7 show some representative examples from these datasets containing humans in natural and difficult poses. Despite the change in domain, our weakly supervised method successfully recovers 3D poses. Note, our model is not trained on 2D poses from MPII or LSP datasets. This demonstrates the ability of our method to generalize over characteristics such as object distance, camera parameters, and unseen poses.

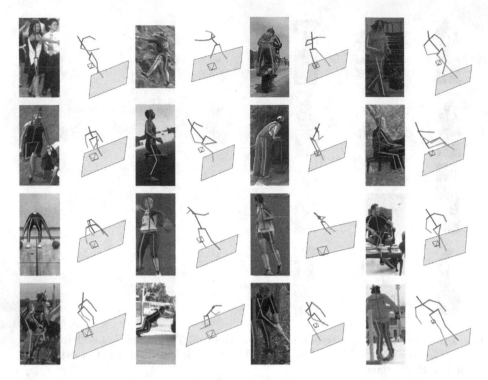

Fig. 6. Examples of 3D pose reconstruction on MPII dataset. For each image we overlay 2D pose points, followed by the predicted 3D skeleton in color. The dataset does not contain ground truth 3D skeletons

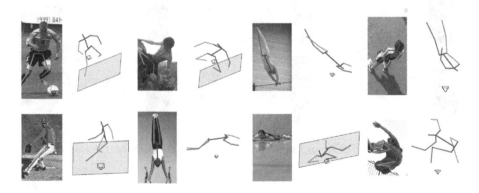

Fig. 7. Examples of 3D pose reconstruction on Leeds dataset. For each image we overlay 2D pose points, followed by the predicted 3D skeleton in color. The dataset does not contain ground truth 3D skeletons

4.5   Discussion

As a general observation, we noticed that the results for the *SitDown* class were the worst across the board for all methods on Human3.6M dataset. In addition to the obvious explanation of fewer available examples in this class, sit down poses lead to significant occlusion of the MoCap markers on legs or ankles (see for example Fig. 5). This phenomenon leads to some of the high errors for this class.

Overall our qualitative and quantitative results have substantiated the effectiveness of using adversarial training paradigm for learning 3D priors in a weakly supervised way. Not only do we outperform the majority of similar 2D-3D lifting methods in benchmarks, we have also shown robust performance on "images in the wild" datasets. Even though we do not leverage any temporal information when available, we found the results from our approach to be stable when applied on per frame basis to video sequences.

In summary, we believe that we have pushed the state of art in 3D pose estimation using weakly supervised learning. This paves way for new research directions that can extend this work by combining supervised, weakly-supervised, and unsupervised frameworks (*i.e.*, semi-supervised) for lifting 2D poses to 3D skeletons.

5   Conclusions

While most of the recent progress in deep learning is fueled by labeled data, it is difficult to obtain high quality annotations for most computer vision problems. For 3D human pose estimation, acquiring 3D MoCap data remains an expensive and challenging endeavor. Our paper demonstrates that an effective prior on 3D structure and pose can be learned from random 2D projections using an adversarial training framework.

We believe that our paper presents a unique insight into learning 3D priors via projective geometry and opens up numerous interesting applications, beyond human pose estimation. Applications such as sparse 3D reconstruction for indoor scenes as well as outdoor navigation typically requires a 3D sensor or multi-view images with a structure from motion pipeline. We envision that our approach can be applied for learning sparse 3D reconstructions from edges or keypoints extracted from a single image, using a collection of 2D images. Since the inference only requires running a small neural network, our approach can also be used for interactive graphics for rendering 3D models from line drawings, where the 3D prior is learned from a collection of such line drawings. We anticipate that our paper will spark further interest in applications combining learning techniques with projective geometry.

Finally, inspired by the results presented in this paper, we expect future work to explore the use of solely images "in the wild" for training the system. This could be achieved through an end to end, image to 3D adversarial pipeline or the use of a large annotated 2D pose dataset. Additional research could include analysis of difficult poses not generally seen (hand-stands, gymnast or yoga poses) as well as the use of additional datasets such as the MPI-INF-3DHP [27]. Improving the robustness of the system by incorporating compensation for noisy or imperfect 2D pose inputs or predicting a distribution of joint locations is another future research opportunity. There is also promise for our method to improve the state of the art by combining with fully supervised approaches.

References

1. Akhter, I., Black, M.J.: Pose-conditioned joint angle limits for 3D human pose reconstruction. In: Proceedings of the IEEE Conference on Computer Vision and Pattern Recognition, pp. 1446–1455 (2015)
2. Amin, S., Andriluka, M., Rohrbach, M., Schiele, B.: Multi-view pictorial structures for 3d human pose estimation. In: BMVC (2013)
3. Andriluka, M., Pishchulin, L., Gehler, P., Schiele, B.: 2d human pose estimation: New benchmark and state of the art analysis. In: CVPR (2014)
4. Bogo, F., Kanazawa, A., Lassner, C., Gehler, P., Romero, J., Black, M.J.: Keep it SMPL: Automatic estimation of 3D human pose and shape from a single image. In: Leibe, B., Matas, J., Sebe, N., Welling, M. (eds.) ECCV 2016, Part V. LNCS, vol. 9909, pp. 561–578. Springer, Cham (2016). https://doi.org/10.1007/978-3-319-46454-1_34
5. Brau, E., Jiang, H.: 3D human pose estimation via deep learning from 2D annotations. In: Fourth International Conference on 3D Vision, pp. 582–591 (2016)
6. Cao, Z., Simon, T., Wei, S.E., Sheikh, Y.: Realtime multi-person 2D pose estimation using part affinity fields. In: CVPR (2017)
7. Chen, C.H., Ramanan, D.: 3D human pose estimation = 2D pose estimation + matching. In: CVPR (2017)
8. Chen, Y., Shen, C., Wei, X.S., Liu, L., Yang, J.: Adversarial posenet: a structure-aware convolutional network for human pose estimation. In: IEEE International Conference on Computer Vision (ICCV), October 2017
9. Fang, H.S., Xu, Y., Wang, W., Liu, X., Zhu, S.C.: Learning pose grammar to encode human body configuration for 3D pose estimation. In: AAAI Conference on Artificial Intelligence (2018)
10. Tung, H.Y.F., Harley, A.W., Seto, W., Fragkiadaki, K.: Adversarial inverse graphics networks: Learning 2d-to-3d lifting and image-to-image translation from unpaired supervision. In: IEEE International Conference on Computer Vision (ICCV), October 2017
11. Forsyth, D.A., Arikan, O., Ikemoto, L.: Computational Studies of Human Motion: Tracking and Motion Synthesis. Now Publishers Inc., Breda (2006)
12. Goodfellow, I., Pouget-Abadie, J., Mirza, M., Xu, B., Warde-Farley, D., Ozair, S.: Generative adversarial nets. In: NIPS, pp. 2672–2680 (2014)
13. He, K., Gkioxari, G., Dollár, P., Girshick, R.: Mask r-cnn: In: IEEE International Conference on Computer Vision (ICCV), pp. 2980–2988. IEEE (2017)
14. Hofmann, M., Gavrila, D.M.: Multi-view 3d human pose estimation in complex environment. In: IJCV (2012)
15. Hogg, D.: Model-based vision: a program to see a walking person. Image Vis. Comput. 1, 5–20 (1983)
16. Ioffe, S., Szegedy, C.: Batch normalization: accelerating deep network training by reducing internal covariate shift. In: ICML, pp. 448–456 (2015)

17. Ionescu, C., Papava, D., Olaru, V., Sminchisescu, C.: Human3.6m: large scale datasets and predictive methods for 3d human sensing in natural environments. IEEE Trans Pattern Anal. Mach. Intell. **36**(7), 1325–1339 (2014)
18. Jiang, H.: 3d human pose reconstruction using millions of exemplars. In: Pattern Recognition (ICPR), 2010 20th International Conference on (2010)
19. Johnson, S., Everingham, M.: Clustered pose and nonlinear appearance models for human pose estimation (2010)
20. Kanazawa, A., Black, M., Jacobs, D., Malik, J.: End-to-end recovery of human shape and pose. In: TBD (2018)
21. Kingma, D.P., Ba, J.: Adam: a method for stochastic optimization. ICLR (2015). http://arxiv.org/abs/1412.6980
22. Li, S., Chan, A.B.: 3D human pose estimation from monocular images with deep convolutional neural network. In: Cremers, D., Reid, I., Saito, H., Yang, M.-H. (eds.) ACCV 2014, Part II. LNCS, vol. 9004, pp. 332–347. Springer, Cham (2015). https://doi.org/10.1007/978-3-319-16808-1_23
23. Li, S., Zhang, W., Chan, A.B.: Maximum-margin structured learning with deep networks for 3d human pose estimation. In: IEEE International Conference on Computer Vision (ICCV), December 2015
24. Lin, M., Lin, L., Liang, X., Wang, K., Cheng, H.: Recurrent 3d pose sequence machines. In: IEEE Conference on Computer Vision and Pattern Recognition (CVPR), July 2017
25. Loper, M., Mahmood, N., Romero, J., Pons-Moll, G., Black, M.J.: SMPL: a skinned multi-person linear model. ACM Trans. Graph. (TOG) **34**(6), 248 (2015)
26. Martinez, J., Hossain, R., Romero, J., Little, J.: A simple yet effective baseline for 3d human pose estimation. In: ICCV (2017)
27. Mehta, D., et al.: Monocular 3d human pose estimation in the wild using improved cnn supervision. In: International Conference on 3D Vision (3DV), pp. 506–516. IEEE (2017)
28. Mehta, D., et al.: Vnect: real-time 3d human pose estimation with a single rgb camera. ACM Trans. Graph. (TOG) **36**(4), 44 (2017)
29. Moeslund, T.B., Granum, E.: A survey of computer vision-based human motion capture. Comput. Vis. Image Underst. **81**(3), 231–268 (2001)
30. Moreno-Noguer, F.: 3d human pose estimation from a single image via distance matrix regression. In: IEEE Conference on Computer Vision and Pattern Recognition (CVPR), July 2017
31. Newell, A., Yang, K., Deng, J.: Stacked hourglass networks for human pose estimation. In: Leibe, B., Matas, J., Sebe, N., Welling, M. (eds.) ECCV 2016, Part VIII. LNCS, vol. 9912, pp. 483–499. Springer, Cham (2016). https://doi.org/10.1007/978-3-319-46484-8_29
32. O'Rourke, J., Badler, N.I.: Model-based image analysis of human motion using constraint propagation. IEEE Trans. Pattern Anal. Mach. Intell. **6**, 522–536 (1980)
33. Park, S., Hwang, J., Kwak, N.: 3D human pose estimation using convolutional neural networks with 2D pose information. In: Hua, G., Jégou, H. (eds.) ECCV 2016, Part III. LNCS, vol. 9915, pp. 156–169. Springer, Cham (2016). https://doi.org/10.1007/978-3-319-49409-8_15
34. Pavlakos, G., Zhou, X., Derpanis, K.G., Daniilidis, K.: Coarse-to-fine volumetric prediction for single-image 3d human pose. In: CVPR, July 2017
35. Rafi, U., Gall, J., Leibe, B.: A semantic occlusion model for human pose estimation from a single depth image. In: Proceedings of the IEEE Conference on CVPR Workshops (2015)

36. Ramakrishna, V., Kanade, T., Sheikh, Y.: Reconstructing 3D human pose from 2D image landmarks. In: Fitzgibbon, A., Lazebnik, S., Perona, P., Sato, Y., Schmid, C. (eds.) ECCV 2012, Part IV. LNCS, vol. 7575, pp. 573–586. Springer, Heidelberg (2012). https://doi.org/10.1007/978-3-642-33765-9_41
37. Rogez, G., Weinzaepfel, P., Schmid, C.: Lcr-net: localization-classification-regression for human pose. In: IEEE Conference on Computer Vision and Pattern Recognition (CVPR), July 2017
38. Shotton, J., et al.: Real-time human pose recognition in parts from single depth images. Commun. ACM **56**(1), 116–124 (2013)
39. Tekin, B., Marquez-Neila, P., Salzmann, M., Fua, P.: Learning to fuse 2d and 3d image cues for monocular body pose estimation. In: IEEE International Conference on Computer Vision (ICCV), October 2017
40. Tekin, B., Rozantsev, A., Lepetit, V., Fua, P.: Direct prediction of 3d body poses from motion compensated sequences. In: Proceedings of the IEEE Conference on Computer Vision and Pattern Recognition, pp. 991–1000 (2016)
41. Tome, D., Russell, C., Agapito, L.: Lifting from the deep: Convolutional 3d pose estimation from a single image. In: IEEE Conference on Computer Vision and Pattern Recognition (CVPR), July 2017
42. Wei, S.E., Ramakrishna, V., Kanade, T., Sheikh, Y.: Convolutional pose machines. In: CVPR, pp. 4724–4732 (2016)
43. Wu, J., et al.: Single image 3d interpreter network. In: ECCV, pp. 365–382 (2016)
44. Xiaohan Nie, B., Wei, P., Zhu, S.C.: Monocular 3d human pose estimation by predicting depth on joints. In: IEEE International Conference on Computer Vision (ICCV), October 2017
45. Yasin, H., Iqbal, U., Kruger, B., Weber, A., Gall, J.: A dual-source approach for 3d pose estimation from a single image. In: IEEE Conference on Computer Vision and Pattern Recognition (CVPR), June 2016
46. Yub Jung, H., Lee, S., Seok Heo, Y., Dong Yun, I.: Random tree walk toward instantaneous 3d human pose estimation. In: CVPR (2015)
47. Zhou, X., Zhu, M., Leonardos, S., Derpanis, K.G., Daniilidis, K.: Sparseness meets deepness: 3d human pose estimation from monocular video. In: CVPR (2016)
48. Zhou, X., Zhu, M., Pavlakos, G., Leonardos, S., Derpanis, K.G., Daniilidis, K.: Monocap: monocular human motion capture using a CNN coupled with a geometric prior. In: TBD (2017)
49. Zhou, X., Huang, Q., Sun, X., Xue, X., Wei, Y.: Towards 3d human pose estimation in the wild: a weakly-supervised approach. In: IEEE International Conference on Computer Vision (2017)

W21 – Shortcomings in Vision and Language

W21 – Shortcomings in Vision and Language

Shortcomings in Vision and Language (SiVL) was held on the 8th of September at ECCV in Munich. The workshop brought together experts at the intersection of vision and language to discuss modern approaches, tasks, datasets, and evaluation metrics for significant problems on the integration of these two modalities. The aim of the workshop was to facilitate discussion of novel research directions and to steer the community towards high-level challenges affecting the vision and language community broadly.

Inspiring talks were given by the invited speakers. Not surprisingly, Neural Networks dominated the scene, but interestingly the popular end-to-end one-big-black-box architecture has, in many cases, been replaced by a more modular one. On the one hand, traditional Computational Linguistics components – such as Part-of-Speech tags, question type detection etc. – have found their role in the NN architecture, and the importance to carry out qualitative analysis instead of only quantitative comparison of models' performance has been highlighted (Aishwarya Agrawal). On the other hand, traditional Computer Vision components – such as object localization – have been put back at work into end-to-end structures, showing the need for vision and language systems to focus on entities (Lucia Specia). Other interesting issues that emerged are the need to develop models that are not task specific and furthermore are able to deal with dataset bias (Vicente Ordóñez Román.) An example of the social impact of this research line has been shown by Danna Gurari, who presented her project to develop models to assist blind people. The workshop received 21 valid full-paper submissions. They were subjected to double-blind peer-review by at least two experts in vision and language. We also received 22 abstract submissions, which were selected by the workshop organizers based on topical relevance. In total, 10 full-papers and 19 abstracts were accepted to appear at the workshop. The workshop featured three poster sessions and one spotlight session where the authors of the accepted full-papers were given a chance to showcase their work in 4-minute spotlight talks.

The workshop also hosted the organizers of the 1st Visual Dialog Challenge (visualdialog.org/challenge/2018), who introduced a new robust evaluation metric for Visual Dialog and gave a detailed quantitative and qualitative overview of the systems that participated in the competition. Complete slides about the challenge are available at: https://goo.gl/SRkBEk. The workshop was sponsored by SAP (Moin Nabi) and was organized in collaboration with researchers from University of Amsterdam (Raquel Fernández), University of Edinburgh (Spandana Gella), University of Trento (Raffaella Bernardi), Georgia Institute of Technology (Dhruv Batra and Stefan Lee) and Rochester Institute of Technology (Kushal Kafle). Organizers in alphabetical order.

Dhruv Batra
Raffaella Bernardi
Raquel Fernández
Spandana Gella
Kushal Kafle
Stefan Lee
Moin Nabi

Towards a Fair Evaluation of Zero-Shot Action Recognition Using External Data

Alina Roitberg$^{(\boxtimes)}$, Manuel Martinez, Monica Haurilet, and Rainer Stiefelhagen

Karlsruhe Institute of Technology, Karlsruhe, Germany
{Alina.Roitberg,Manuel.Martinez,Monica.Haurilet,
Rainer.Stiefelhagen}@kit.edu

Abstract. Zero-shot action recognition aims to classify actions not previously seen during training. This is achieved by learning a visual model for the seen *source* classes and establishing a semantic relationship to the unseen *target* classes *e.g.* through the action labels. In order to draw a clear line between *zero-shot* and conventional *supervised* classification, the *source* and *target* categories must be disjoint. Ensuring this premise is not trivial, especially when the source dataset is external. In this work, we propose an evaluation procedure that enables fair use of external data for zero-shot action recognition. We empirically show that external sources tend to have actions excessively similar to the target classes, strongly influencing the performance and violating the zero-shot premise. To address this, we propose a corrective method to automatically filter out too similar categories by exploiting the pairwise intra-dataset similarity of the labels. Our experiments on the HMDB-51 dataset demonstrate that the zero-shot models consistently benefit from the external sources even under our realistic evaluation, especially when the source categories of internal and external domains are combined.

Keywords: Action recognition · Zero-Shot Learning

1 Introduction

Human activity recognition has a long list of potential applications, ranging from autonomous driving and robotics to security surveillance [7,8,12]. Knowledge transfer from external sources is crucial for using such models in practice, as they are especially sensitive to the amount of training data due to the 3-D convolution kernels leading to a higher number of parameters [2].

Intersection of vision and language allows us to generalize to new actions without any visual training data through Zero-Shot Learning (ZSL) [15]. ZSL connects a visual model trained on a dataset of known (*source*) classes to the unknown (*target*) classes through the high-level semantic descriptions of an action, e.g., the action label. The description is often represented by a word embedding model (e.g. *word2vec* [4,5]), previously trained on web data.

© Springer Nature Switzerland AG 2019
L. Leal-Taixé and S. Roth (Eds.): ECCV 2018 Workshops, LNCS 11132, pp. 97–105, 2019.
https://doi.org/10.1007/978-3-030-11018-5_8

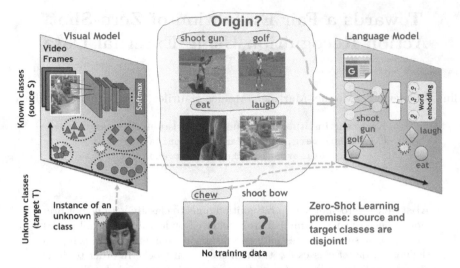

Fig. 1. Zero-shot action recognition paradigm: instances of the new *target* classes are recognized without any training data by linking visual features learned from the known *source* categories with a language-based representation of the action labels. Our work demonstrates, that the zero-shot premise of disjoint *source* and *target* categories may be violated when using external datasets for training.

Such ZSL methods would first compute the word vector by mapping a visual representation of a new instance to the common semantic space and then assign it to one of the previously unseen categories by selecting the category with the closest semantic representation Fig. (1).

ZSL for action recognition gained popularity over the past few years, usually dividing the dataset into *seen* categories for training and *unseen* categories for evaluation [9, 11, 14, 16, 17]. Recent emergence of large-scale action recognition datasets has led to an increasing interest in the field of domain adaptation, where the model trained on a high amount of external data is classifying instances from a smaller, potentially application-specific dataset [18]. At the first glance, one would assume, that classifying data from a foreign source would be a harder problem because of the existing domain shift. However, recent works using data from origins other then the evaluation dataset for training of the visual recognition model, report extraordinary results in zero-shot action recognition, doubling the performance of the previous models focused on the inner-dataset split [18]. A single dataset would not contain the same activity twice. Action labels of an external dataset, on the other hand, possibly intersect with the test categories, violating the ZSL premise of assigning action classes **not** seen during training and turning the problem into supervised classification. We argue, that in order to draw the line between *zero-shot* and standard *supervised* recognition across different datasets, it is crucial to take a closer look at the similarity of action categories of source and target data and create a standardized evaluation procedure which eliminates the influence of such overlapping activities.

Contributions and Summary. This work aims to highlight the fact that cross-dataset evaluation of zero-shot action recognition is greatly influenced by the presence of overlapping activity classes in the source and target datasets. We quantitatively analyze the similarities of labels used for training (*source*) and testing (*target*) in the inner-dataset and cross-dataset setup and demonstrate, that *external* labels tend to have categories excessively similar to the unseen *target* classes, therefore violating the ZSL assumption of disjoint source and target categories. We propose a novel procedure that enables the use of *external* data for zero-shot action recognition settings in a fair way, by using the maximum *internal* semantic similarity within the *target* dataset to restrict the *external* classes. We evaluate our method on the HMDB-51 dataset, and show how using external data improves the performance of ZSL approaches, even in our more fair evaluation setting. Finally, we propose a novel *hybrid* ZSL regime, where the model is allowed to use all the internal labels and additional large-scale external data, consistently improving the zero-shot action recognition accuracy.

2 Fair Transfer of External Categories

Problem Definition. We define the zero-shot learning task as follows. Let $A = \{a_k\}_{k=1}^K$ be a set of K previously seen *source* categories. Given the set of previously unseen *target* categories $T = \{t_m\}_{m=1}^M$ and a new data sample X, our goal is to predict the correct action category $t \in T$ without having any training data (*i.e.* labeled samples) for this class. Since the core idea of ZSL is to recognize previously unseen visual categories, source labels and target labels are set to be strictly disjoint. This is known as the *zero-shot premise* and is formalized as: $A \cap T = \emptyset$.

2.1 Evaluation Protocols for ZSL

Intra-dataset Protocol. A common way to evaluate zero-shot learning approaches is to divide a dataset into seen and unseen categories. That is, while a subset of unseen categories is held out during training, both the source and target labels belong to the same dataset: $A = A_{intra}$. In this setting, source and target categories do not overlap, since well designed datasets contain no category duplicates.

Cross-dataset Protocol. The main goal of zero-shot learning, however, is to apply knowledge from available data to tasks from a different domain where labeled data is difficult to obtain. This setting is evaluated by training and evaluating on a different datasets: $A = A_{cross}$. In that case, however, the zero-shot premise is not given by default. In the most extreme case, if $T \subset A$, no semantic transfer is needed.

Intra- and Cross- dataset protocol. Recently, several approaches in other computer vision areas have been presented that investigate ways of increasing the performance by mixing the available domain-specific datasets with large amounts of training data from external sources [10]. We transfer this paradigm to the zero-shot action recognition and formalize this *hybrid* evaluation regime as: $A = A_{\text{intra}} \cup A_{\text{cross}}$. Similarly to the previous setting, the zero-shot premise is not ensured.

2.2 Proposed Protocol to Incorporate External Datasets

In the intra-class protocol, compliance of the zero-shot premise is given for granted, and generally well accepted by researchers [9,14,16]. However, when external datasets are involved, one has to ensure that the terms of ZSL are still met and the *source* and *target* categories are disjoint. For example, Zhu *et al.* [18] excludes classes from the training dataset whose category label overlaps with a tested label. This procedure would remove the action *brushing hair*, present in both ActivityNet [1] and Kinetics [2], since the label *brush hair* is present in the target classes from the HMDB-51 [3] dataset.

However, it is not trivial to determine if a source class should be excluded and eliminating direct category matches may not be enough. External datasets often contain slightly diverging variants or specializations of the target actions (*e.g.*, *drinking beer* and *drink*), leading to a much closer relation of source and target actions compared to the inner dataset protocol, even if the direct matches are excluded. We argue, that taking into account the similarity of source and target labels is a key element for evaluation of zero-shot action recognition when external sources datasets are used.

We propose a standardized procedure to decide whether an external class should be used or discarded when training the visual model. Our corrective method is based on the fact that zero-shot learning is well-defined for the intra-class protocol, *i.e.* thus all *source* categories of the intra-dataset split can always be used to train our model. We will remove a source category if its label is semantically too similar to any of the target categories by leveraging the maximum similarity observed inside the same dataset as a rejection threshold for categories of foreign origin. Formally, an external category $a_k \in A$ is allowed if and only if following condition is satisfied:

$$\forall t_m \in T, \; s(\omega(a_k), \omega(t_m)) \leqslant s_{th}. \tag{1}$$

The similarity threshold s_{th} corresponds to the maximum pairwise similarity between the source and target labels in the intra-class setting:

$$s_{th} = \max_{a_k \in A_{\text{intra}}, t_m \in T} s(\omega(a_k), \omega(t_m)). \tag{2}$$

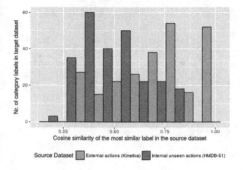
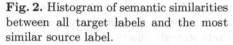

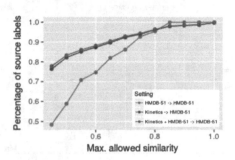

Fig. 2. Histogram of semantic similarities between all target labels and the most similar source label.

Fig. 3. Proportion of source labels allowed depending on the semantic similarity threshold s_{th}.

3 Experiments

Experimental Setup. To evaluate our idea, we adapt an off-the shelf ZSL approach Convex Combination of Semantic Embeddings (ConSE) [6]. While ConSE has been used for zero-shot action recognition before [17], where in the underlying visual model was based on dense trajectory features [13] encoded as Fisher Vector, we employ a model based on CNNs.

We denote the model for mapping an action label to the word vector representation as $\omega(\cdot)$ and the cosine similarity of the two word vectors as $s(\omega(a_i), \omega(a_j))$. In the next step, a word vector embedding for X is synthesized by taking a linear combination of the predicted probabilities and the semantic representation of source classes: $w^*(X) = \sum_{k=1}^{K} p(a_k|X)\omega(a_k)$. X will be classified to the target category whose semantic representation is most similar to the synthesized word embedding:

$$t_X^* = \operatorname*{argmax}_{t_m \in T} s(\omega(t_m), w^*(X)).$$

As our visual recognition model, we use I3D [2], which is the current state-of-the-art method for action recognition. The model is trained using SGD with momentum of 0.9, and an initial learning rate of 0.005 for 100 epochs. To compute the word vectors embeddings of the action categories, we use the publicly available *word2vec* model trained on 100 billion words from Google News articles, which maps the input into a 300 dimensional semantic space [5].

We use HMDB-51 [3] as our target dataset, and we follow the zero-shot learning setup of Wang *et al.* [14]: we generate 10 random splits with 26 seen and 25 unseen categories each. As a foreign data source we use the Kinetics dataset [2], which covers 400 activity categories.

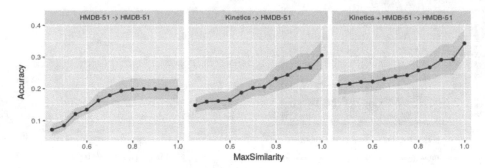

Fig. 4. Influence of source-target label similarity on ZSL performance. X-Axis denotes the semantic similarity threshold s_{th} above which source categories are excluded. Having similar classes in the seen and unseen sets strongly affects accuracy, an effect that is more pronounced when using external datasets.

Intra- and Cross-dataset Class Similarity. First, we re-assure our assumption that labels of seen actions tend to be significantly closer to the unseen categories if they originate from an external dataset. Figure 2 shows the distribution of the maximum pairwise source-target similarity for each source label. We observe that actions from external dataset are far closer, often even identical, to the target classes dataset in comparison to the same dataset case. We explain this distribution by the nature of datasets design, as a single dataset does not contain duplicates or activities that are too close to each other.

Effect of the Similar Activities on the Classification Accuracy. Our next area of investigation is the influence of such analogue activities and external data on the classification results. We report the average and standard deviation of the recognition accuracy over the splits for different similarity thresholds s_{th} for restricting the target categories (Fig. 4 and Table 1). Extending the model trained on the native data (intra-dataset) with external datasets (intra- and cross-dataset regimes) increases the accuracy by almost 15%, with 10% improvement observed when an external source is used alone (cross-dataset regime). Excluding direct matches (s_{th} of 0.95) leads to a performance decline of 4% for cross-dataset scenario, although only around 1% of external action categories are excluded (Fig. 3). In other words, only 1% of external action labels (which are extremely similar to the target) account for almost half of the cross-dataset performance boost.

The accuracy saturates at a similarity threshold of around 0.8 in the inner-dataset regime, as no duplicate activities are present (Fig. 3). Our evaluation procedure leverages this maximum inner-dataset similarity to effectively eliminate synonyms from external sources, while not influencing the inner-dataset performance. In our framework, the majority of the external dataset is kept 384.7 of 400. However, the influence of analogue activities is clearly tamed, leading to a performance drop from 34.77% to 25.67% for the inner- and cross-dataset protocol.

Table 1. ZSL on HMDB-51 for different evaluation regimes with and without our corrective approach. Naively using external sources may not honor the ZSL premise.

Exclusion protocol	Source	# Source labels	Accuracy	ZSL premise
n. a.	HMDB-51	26	19.92 (±3.3)	✓
Use all source labels	Kinetics	400	30.72 (±4.4)	–
	Kinetics+ HMDB-51	426	**34.77 (±4.5)**	–
Exclude exact labels	Kinetics	≈394.8	26.6 (±4.6)	–
	Kinetics+ HMDB-51	≈420.8	**29.22 (±4.9)**	–
Exclude similar labels (ours)	Kinetics	≈384.7	23.1 (±3.9)	✓
	Kinetics+ HMDB-51	≈410.7	**25.67 (±3.5)**	✓

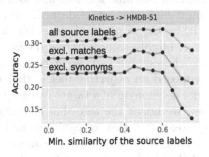

Fig. 5. Effect of eliminating unfamiliar concepts: source categories with similarity to the target labels below 0.4 hinder the performance

Still, using external data is very beneficial for the recognition results and using both internal and external data sources consistently outperforms single-source models. A clear standardized protocol for defining allowed external source classes without violating the ZSL rules, is a crucial step towards a more adequate model evaluation.

Context of Previous Work. In this work, our goal is to highlight the ambiguities which arise when external datasets come into play in zero-shot action recognition and we do not aim at state-of the art performance. The vast majority of evaluated methods has used the inner-dataset split, *e.g.* a similar ConSE model employed by [17] which reaches 15.0%, while our model with underlying deep showes an improvement of 19.92%. The state-of-the-art approach using inner-dataset evaluation achieves 22.6% [9], while the recent work of Zhu *et al.* [18] reports highly impressive results of 51.8% employing an external data source (ActivityNet). We want to note, that our model also consistently outperforms state-of-the-art which uses inner-dataset split only. However, we find that systematic elimination of synonyms is crucial for a fair comparison, as we do not know, which actions were allowed in the setting of [18] and we show, that few analogue actions might lead to a clear performance boost.

Eliminating too Unfamiliar Concepts for Better Domain Adaptation. As a side observation, we have found that using an additional **lower bound** on the similarity of the external and target categories leads to a performance increase of around 2% for every evaluation setting (Fig. 5). In other words, unfamiliar concepts act as a distractor for the purposes of ZSL.

4   Conclusions

Current machine learning methods based on CNNs benefit immensely from having a high amount of data. Hence, it is sensible to integrate external datasets within the context of zero-shot learning to improve its performance. However, blindly using external datasets may break the zero-shot learning premise, *i.e.* that source and target categories should not overlap. In this work, we have proposed an objective metric that defines which source categories may constitute a synonym of a target category. By pruning these categories from the source set, we honor the zero-shot learning premise. We evaluate this approach in the context of action recognition, and show that adding external data still helps considerably to improve the accuracy of zero-shot learning, even after removing all the similar categories from the source datasets.

Acknowledgements. The research leading to this results has been partially funded by the German Federal Ministry of Education and Research (BMBF) within the PAKoS project.

References

1. Caba Heilbron, F., Escorcia, V., Ghanem, B., Carlos Niebles, J.: Activitynet: a large-scale video benchmark for human activity understanding. In: Conference on Computer Vision and Pattern Recognition (2015)
2. Carreira, J., Zisserman, A.: Quo vadis, action recognition? a new model and the kinetics dataset. In: Conference on Computer Vision and Pattern Recognition (2017)
3. Kuehne, H., Jhuang, H., Stiefelhagen, R., Serre, T.: Hmdb51: a large video database for human motion recognition. In: Nagel, W., Kröner, D., Resch, M. (eds.) High Performance Computing in Science and Engineering, pp. 571–582. Springer, Heidelberg (2013)
4. Mikolov, T., Chen, K., Corrado, G., Dean, J.: Efficient estimation of word representations in vector space. arXiv preprint arXiv:1301.3781 (2013)
5. Mikolov, T., Sutskever, I., Chen, K., Corrado, G.S., Dean, J.: Distributed representations of words and phrases and their compositionality. In: Advances in Neural Information Processing Systems (2013)
6. Norouzi, M., et al.: Zero-shot learning by convex combination of semantic embeddings. arXiv preprint arXiv:1312.5650 (2013)
7. Ohn-Bar, E., Trivedi, M.M.: Looking at humans in the age of self-driving and highly automated vehicles. IEEE Trans. Intell. Veh. **1**(1), 90–104 (2016)
8. Poppe, R.: A survey on vision-based human action recognition. Image Vis. Comput. **28**(6), 976–990 (2010)
9. Qin, J., et al.: Zero-shot action recognition with error-correcting output codes. In: Conference on Computer Vision and Pattern Recognition (2017)
10. Radosavovic, I., Dollár, P., Girshick, R., Gkioxari, G., He, K.: Data distillation: towards omni-supervised learning. arXiv preprint arXiv:1712.04440 (2017)
11. Roitberg, A., Al-Halah, Z., Stiefelhagen, R.: Informed democracy: voting-based novelty detection for action recognition. In: British Machine Vision Conference (BMVC). Newcastle upon Tyne, UK, September 2018

12. Roitberg, A., Somani, N., Perzylo, A., Rickert, M., Knoll, A.: Multimodal human activity recognition for industrial manufacturing processes in robotic workcells. In: Proceedings of the 2015 ACM on International Conference on Multimodal Interaction, pp. 259–266. ACM (2015)
13. Wang, H., Schmid, C.: Action recognition with improved trajectories. In: International Conference on Computer Vision (2013)
14. Wang, Q., Chen, K.: Zero-shot visual recognition via bidirectional latent embedding. Int. J. Comput. Vis. **124**(3), 356–383 (2017)
15. Xian, Y., Schiele, B., Akata, Z.: Zero-shot learning-the good, the bad and the ugly. arXiv preprint arXiv:1703.04394 (2017)
16. Xu, X., Hospedales, T., Gong, S.: Semantic embedding space for zero-shot action recognition. In: International Conference on Image Processing (2015)
17. Xu, X., Hospedales, T., Gong, S.: Transductive zero-shot action recognition by word-vector embedding. Int. J. Comput. Vis. **123**, 1–25 (2017)
18. Zhu, Y., Long, Y., Guan, Y., Newsam, S., Shao, L.: Towards universal representation for unseen action recognition. In: Conference on Computer Vision and Pattern Recognition (2018)

MoQA – A Multi-modal Question Answering Architecture

Monica Haurilet[✉], Ziad Al-Halah, and Rainer Stiefelhagen

Karlsruhe Institute of Technology, 76131 Karlsruhe, Germany
{haurilet,ziad.al-halah,rainer.stiefelhagen}@kit.edu

Abstract. Multi-Modal Machine Comprehension (M3C) deals with extracting knowledge from multiple modalities such as figures, diagrams and text. Particularly, Textbook Question Answering (TQA) focuses on questions based on the school curricula, where the text and diagrams are extracted from textbooks. A subset of questions cannot be answered solely based on diagrams, but requires external knowledge of the surrounding text. In this work, we propose a novel deep model that is able to handle different knowledge modalities in the context of the question answering task. We compare three different information representations encountered in TQA: a visual representation learned from images, a graph representation of diagrams and a language-based representation learned from accompanying text. We evaluate our model on the TQA dataset that contains text and diagrams from the sixth grade material. Even though our model obtains competing results compared to state-of-the-art, we still witness a significant gap in performance compared to humans. We discuss in this work the shortcomings of the model and show the reason behind the large gap to human performance, by exploring the distribution of the multiple classes of mistakes that the model makes.

1   Introduction

Answering questions based on natural images has received growing attention in the Computer Vision community for several years [14,15,18,20]. While at a very early age humans can answer basic question about their environment, we start to analyze and understand graphics at later time. In school years, children learn to analyze and understand complex illustrations, and are capable to extract important information and answer difficult questions about them.

The type and style of these illustrations have many different forms in terms of colors, structure types and complexity. While some illustrations in textbooks are easy, like simple drawings, we see in later school years more difficult types of figures like diagrams, plots and tables. Diagrams are especially challenging since we have different type of nodes like drawings, text, natural images etc.

Electronic supplementary material The online version of this chapter (https://doi.org/10.1007/978-3-030-11018-5_9) contains supplementary material, which is available to authorized users.

L. Leal-Taixé and S. Roth (Eds.): ECCV 2018 Workshops, LNCS 11132, pp. 106–113, 2019.
https://doi.org/10.1007/978-3-030-11018-5_9

Furthermore, we have various relationship types between nodes, e.g. textual description and nodes, and textual description and edges. We also have directed relations, usually represented with edges marked with an arrow sign, while some relations are not explicitly marked (see an example in Fig. 1).

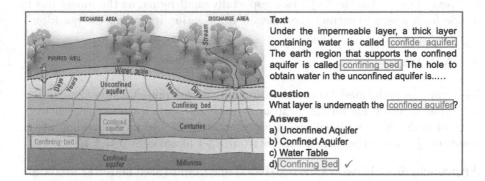

Fig. 1. Example diagram with corresponding question from the TQA dataset.

In this work, we compare different knowledge representations for our model: (1) the text-based model, where we use the surrounding text for answering the questions, (2) the image-based model uses the surrounding image by extracting the features of a pre-trained CNN and (3) the graph-based representation embeds the diagram as a graph where the nodes consist of the detected text and its location. We investigate the predictions of our model to find the reasons for the large gap to human performance, by analyzing a subset of incorrectly answered questions.

2 Related Work

VQA. Various topics join language with natural images like image captioning [19] and text-based image retrieval [5]. Visual Question Answering (VQA) obtains both an image and a question and produces an answer. In spite of a multitude of available datasets [1,11,17,21] and published models [14,15,18,20], VQA remains a hard task and the recognition rate remains far from human performance. Most VQA models do not consider the structure of the object instances in natural images, as most questions target single objects.

Textbook QA. In comparison to VQA, the Textbook Question Answering (TQA) task deals with different types of images: textbook illustrations like tables [4], plots [6,16] and diagrams [7,8,13]. Such figures are more structured than natural images, as the relations between the components have a higher importance for answering the questions. While tables are structural elements combining and ordering their entries - mostly text - in a specific way, diagrams can have much more types of relations (e.g. location-based, 'eating' relation between animals). Furthermore, the nodes have various types like text, natural objects and drawings (as in Fig. 1). This makes the task of diagram question answering difficult to solve, as we see in the diagram QA models presented in [7,13]. Finally, the TQA dataset [8] contains questions about both diagrams and text. This makes the VQA task especially challenging, as the model has to decide from where to extract the relevant information to answer the question.

3   Method

We define the multi-modal comprehension task in the context of question answering. That is, given knowledge K from a textbook lesson (a set of sentences S, a set of nodes N or a global image representation I) and an embedding of the question Q, choose the correct answer from a set of answers $A = \{A_i\}$.

Approach. Since in case of the text-based and graph-based networks we receive a large amount of data, we filter out unrelated sentences and nodes. Our approach relies on the basic intuition that for each question Q, there is a set of supporting sentences/nodes $K^Q = \{K_j\}$ in K that would help in verifying the correctness of each (Q, A_i) pair. The text-based approach consists of two main steps: (1) Selecting k supporting sentences/nodes from K for a given question Q. (2) Based on (Q, K^Q), verify the correctness of each answer $A_i \in A$.

Supporting Nodes and Supporting Sentences. To select the set of supporting knowledge for a certain question Q, we measure the similarity of all K_j in the provided text and diagram to the question in an embedding space. That is, for each $K_j \in K$ we calculate $f_s(f_v(Q), f_v(K_j))$, where f_v is a sentence encoding function (e.g. recurrent neural network) and f_s is a similarity metric (e.g. cosine similarity). Then, the top k most similar knowledge information are selected to be in K^Q. Given the supporting sentences/nodes and the question, we use the deep neural network presented in Fig. 2 to verify each of the available answers.

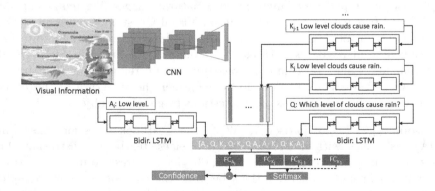

Fig. 2. Architecture of the image+text deep neural model

Neural Network. We start by encoding the triplet $(fc(Q), fc(K_j), fc(A_i))$ separately using fully connected layers fc. Then, the new embeddings are concatenated with the pairwise and triple-wise similarity of embeddings using element-wise multiplication, for each answer and knowledge: $mapping(A_i, K_j) = [K_j, Q, A_i, K_j \cdot Q, K_j \cdot A_i, Q \cdot A_i, Q \cdot A_i \cdot K_j]$.

Next, we split the output of this layer into two streams. The first stream captures the confidence of the answer A_i to be the correct one, while the second stream weights the model confidence in the knowledge subset K_j for being suitable to verify (Q, A_i). We calculate this confidence using an attention module using a softmax layer. The input of the softmax layer is the output of the fc_s layer for each of $K_j \in K^Q$ encoded by the same neural model. Finally, the two streams are fused using element-wise multiplication. In testing, the answer with highest confidence is selected as the correct one.

Text-Based Network. Our text-only model uses solely the surrounding text to generate the answers to the question $(K = T)$. In case of the Text+Image Network, we include the visual information as another vector in the supporting sentences set: $K = T \cup I$ (see Fig. 2).

Graph-Based Network. In a similar manner, as we have a high number of nodes in the diagrams, we select a set of supporting nodes based on the question. In this case, k nodes are selected that have the highest similarity to the question, where the similarity is $f_s(f_v(Q), f_v(N_i))$. However, the difference to the text-based model lies in the representation of the nodes for the neural network, as instead of using the representation of the supporting nodes, we use an edge representation. For each node N_j in the set of k supporting nodes, we use the source node N_j concatenated with the nearest node, i.e. $[N_j, N_{nearest_j}]$, as the knowledge representation K_j.

Graph Baseline. In the first step in the baseline model, we take the top-1 supporting node and calculate its nearest neighbor. The answer is chosen based on the similarity of the nearest node and the answers.

Image-Based Network. The image-based network receives in addition to the question and answer pair, solely a global representation of the diagram I using features extracted from a pre-trained CNN.

4 Evaluation

Dataset. TQA [8] is a dataset for multi-modal machine comprehension, which contains lessons and exercises from the sixth grade curricula. In total, the dataset contains 1 K lessons from Life Science, Earth Science and Physical Science textbooks with 26 K corresponding multi-modal questions. Around half of the questions have corresponding text (*text questions*), while the other ones also have an accompanying diagram (*diagram questions*). The text questions are further split into true/false questions, where the only possible answers are true and false, and multiple-choice, where we can have different answers.

Parameters. As a similarity metric (f_s) for selecting the supporting sentences we use the cosine similarity. We empirically set $k = 4$ for the multiple choice model and $k = 2$ for the true/false model. A sentence embedding (f_v), if not otherwise specified we use the SkipThought [10] encoding, however we also provide results for InferSent [2]. We represent the images using a Residual Network [3] trained on ImageNet [12]. Our model is trained using Adam [9] for stochastic optimization with an initial learning rate of 0.01.

Comparison to State-of-the-Art. We are able to outperform state-of-the-art in the true/false questions and obtain competitive results in the entire text-only task (see Table 1). In the case of diagrams, our model has a lower performance, but is able to outperform complex models such as BiDAF and Memory Networks. We notice that InferSent obtains a higher accuracy in the true/false questions than SkipThought. InferSent was trained in a supervised setting in a similar scenario as the true/false task, namely, to find the relation between a pair of sentences (i.e. no relation, contradiction and entailment).

Table 1. Validation accuracy of our model compared to state-of-the-art (left) and comparison of different variations of our model (right).

	T/F	MC	Text	Diag.
Random	50.1	22.9	33.6	25.0
MemN + VQA [8]	50.5	31.1	38.7	31.8
MemN + VQA + HT [13]	50.3	28.1	36.9	29.8
MemN + DPG [8]	50.5	30.1	38.7	32.8
BiDAF + DPG [8]	50.4	30.5	38.7	32.7
Challenge	–	–	45.6	35.9
IGMN [13]	**57.4**	**40.0**	**46.9**	**36.4**
Ours [InferSent]	61.9	36.2	46.4	33.4
Ours [SkipThought]	60.2	36.4	45.6	34.0

Modality	#S	#N	Diag.
Image-only	–	–	33.2
	3	–	33.8
Text-only	4	–	33.9
	5	–	33.4
	–	1	29.2
Graph-baseline	–	2	28.3
	–	4	25.8
Graph-only	–	4	33.3
Text+Image	4	–	34.0

Different Knowledge Representations. In Table 1 (right) we show the performance of the model for the three different knowledge modalities and varying number of supporting sentences S and nodes N. The image-only model obtained the worst accuracy, which however, can be explained with the use of a CNN pretrained on natural images and not diagrams. Furthermore, we note that the text may play a significant role for many questions, which is not taken into account in this approach.

5   In-Depth Analysis

In this section we explore the properties of our model and attempt to find the cause behind the existing gap between the model and human performance.

Text-Based Task. To have a better overview of the common problems, we categorize them into the following groups: (1) necessity of external knowledge to answer the question (*ext.*), (2) the required information spreads over more than one sentence (*mult.-Sent.*), (3) the supporting sentences selected by our model do not contain the correct one (*Supp.-Sent.*), (4) the attention module failed to attend to the correct sentence (*Attention*), and finally (5) the prediction module was not able to provide the correct answer, even though all other modules were correct (*Prediction*).

We show in Fig. 3, the distribution of the problem types for true/false and multiple choice questions for 100 randomly selected questions in the dataset. For the true/false case, most of our mistakes are due to the prediction module, followed by the supporting sentence and the attention module. Deciding if two sentences are contradictory or have the same statement is a hard task, especially when a sentence consists of multiple statements. Furthermore, finding the correct supporting sentence is the reason for around 30% of the mistakes of our T/F model, which is less than in the case of multiple choice. This is surprising as the the true/false models have two supporting sentences and thus the probability of the sentence being in the set is lower compared to multiple-choice case.

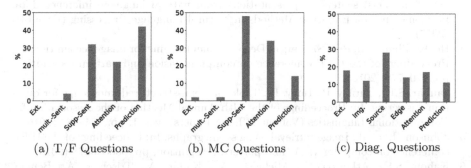

(a) T/F Questions   (b) MC Questions   (c) Diag. Questions

Fig. 3. Distribution of the problems of the model in the TQA task.

Diagram-Based Task. For the diagram questions, we additionally include the image information *Img.* that shows if visual information is necessary to answer the question. Furthermore, the *Source* shows if the supporting source nodes were correctly selected and the *Edge* shows if the target node is not the one that should be used to answer the question. We see that the model has the most difficulties selecting the source nodes, similar to the text-based questions where selecting the supporting sentences causes many mistakes. Extending the model with more nodes may be beneficial for this problem but leads to overfitting (see Table 1). Including visual information (Img.) has the potential to increase performance, however to attend to parts of the image without supervision and without a higher amount of data would probably lead also to overfitting. Overall, our text-based model has shown very strong performance on the Diagram Task. As 20% of the mistakes are caused by the absence of external knowledge (e.g. surrounding text), we believe that including this information as a further knowledge source would lead to a significant improvement.

6   Conclusion

In this work we introduced a novel neural architecture for multi-modal question answering in the multiple choice setup. We compare the network for different knowledge modalities: text-, image- and graph-based, and show that the text-based model has the best performance in all tasks. Furthermore, we analyze the mistakes our model makes and show the difficulties that our model encountered.

References

1. Antol, S., et al.: Vqa: Visual question answering. In: Proceedings of the IEEE International Conference on Computer Vision, pp. 2425–2433 (2015)
2. Conneau, A., Kiela, D., Schwenk, H., Barrault, L., Bordes, A.: Supervised learning of universal sentence representations from natural language inference data. In: Conference on Empirical Methods in Natural Language Processing (EMNLP) (2017)
3. He, K., Zhang, X., Ren, S., Sun, J.: Deep residual learning for image recognition. In: Proceedings of the IEEE conference on computer vision and pattern recognition, pp. 770–778 (2016)
4. Jauhar, S.K., Turney, P., Hovy, E.: Tables as semi-structured knowledge for question answering. In: Proceedings of the 54th Annual Meeting of the Association for Computational Linguistics (Volume 1: Long Papers), vol. 1, pp. 474–483 (2016)
5. Johnson, J., et al.: Image retrieval using scene graphs. In: Proceedings of the IEEE conference on computer vision and pattern recognition, pp. 3668–3678 (2015)
6. Kahou, S.E., Atkinson, A., Michalski, V., Kádár, Á., Trischler, A., Bengio, Y.: Figureqa: an annotated figure dataset for visual reasoning. arXiv preprint arXiv:1710.07300 (2017)
7. Kembhavi, A., Salvato, M., Kolve, E., Seo, M., Hajishirzi, H., Farhadi, A.: A diagram is worth a dozen images. In: Leibe, B., Matas, J., Sebe, N., Welling, M. (eds.) ECCV 2016, Part IV. LNCS, vol. 9908, pp. 235–251. Springer, Cham (2016). https://doi.org/10.1007/978-3-319-46493-0_15
8. Kembhavi, A., Seo, M., Schwenk, D., Choi, J., Farhadi, A., Hajishirzi, H.: Are you smarter than a sixth grader? textbook question answering for multimodal machine comprehension. In: Conference on Computer Vision and Pattern Recognition (CVPR) (2017)
9. Kingma, D.P., Ba, J.: Adam: a method for stochastic optimization. In: International Conference for Learning Representations (2014)
10. Kiros, R., et al.: Skip-thought vectors. In: Advances in Neural Information Processing Systems, pp. 3294–3302 (2015)
11. Krishna, R., et al.: Visual genome: connecting language and vision using crowdsourced dense image annotations. Int. J. Comput. Vis. **123**(1), 32–73 (2017)

12. Krizhevsky, A., Sutskever, I., Hinton, G.E.: Imagenet classification with deep convolutional neural networks. In: Advances in neural information processing systems, pp. 1097–1105 (2012)
13. Li, J., Su, H., Zhu, J., Wang, S., Zhang, B.: Textbook question answering under instructor guidance with memory networks. In: Proceedings of the IEEE Conference on Computer Vision and Pattern Recognition, pp. 3655–3663 (2018)
14. Lu, J., Yang, J., Batra, D., Parikh, D.: Hierarchical question-image co-attention for visual question answering. In: Advances In Neural Information Processing Systems, pp. 289–297 (2016)
15. Malinowski, M., Rohrbach, M., Fritz, M.: Ask your neurons: a neural-based approach to answering questions about images. In: Proceedings of the 2015 IEEE International Conference on Computer Vision (ICCV), pp. 1–9. IEEE Computer Society (2015)
16. Reddy, R., Ramesh, R., Deshpande, A., Khapra, M.M.: A question-answering framework for plots using deep learning. arXiv preprint arXiv:1806.04655 (2018)
17. Ren, M., Kiros, R., Zemel, R.: Exploring models and data for image question answering. In: Advances in Neural Information Processing Systems, pp. 2953–2961 (2015)
18. Xu, H., Saenko, K.: Ask, attend and answer: exploring question-guided spatial attention for visual question answering. In: Leibe, B., Matas, J., Sebe, N., Welling, M. (eds.) ECCV 2016, Part VII. LNCS, vol. 9911, pp. 451–466. Springer, Cham (2016). https://doi.org/10.1007/978-3-319-46478-7_28
19. Xu, K., et al.: Show, attend and tell: neural image caption generation with visual attention. In: International Conference on Machine Learning, pp. 2048–2057 (2015)
20. Yang, Z., He, X., Gao, J., Deng, L., Smola, A.: Stacked attention networks for image question answering. In: Proceedings of the IEEE Conference on Computer Vision and Pattern Recognition, pp. 21–29 (2016)
21. Zhu, Y., Groth, O., Bernstein, M., Fei-Fei, L.: Visual7w: grounded question answering in images. In: Proceedings of the IEEE Conference on Computer Vision and Pattern Recognition, pp. 4995–5004 (2016)

Pre-gen Metrics: Predicting Caption Quality Metrics Without Generating Captions

Marc Tanti$^{(\boxtimes)}$, Albert Gatt, and Adrian Muscat

University of Malta, Msida 2080, MSD, Malta
{marc.tanti.06,albert.gatt,adrian.muscat}@um.edu.mt

Abstract. Image caption generation systems are typically evaluated against reference outputs. We show that it is possible to predict output quality without generating the captions, based on the probability assigned by the neural model to the reference captions. Such pre-gen metrics are strongly correlated to standard evaluation metrics.

Keywords: Image captioning · Neural architectures
Evaluation metrics

1 Introduction

Automatic metrics for image description generation (IDG) compare c, a generated caption, to a set of reference sentences, $R_1...R_n$. We therefore refer to these as **post-gen**(eration) metrics. In most neural IDG architectures generation is performed by an algorithm such as beam search that samples the vocabulary at every timestep, selecting a likely next word after a given sentence prefix (according to the neural network) and attaching it to the end of the prefix, and repeating this procedure until the entire caption is produced. Given that the output thus generated is evaluated against a gold standard, post-gen metrics actually evaluate the neural network's ability to predict the words in the reference captions given an image. Unfortunately, generating sentences is a time consuming process due to the fact that every word in a sentence requires its own forward pass through the neural network. This means that generating a 20-word sentence requires calling the neural network 20 times. As an indicative example, it takes 20.8 min to generate captions for every image in the MSCOCO test set on a standard hardware setup (GeForce GTX 760) using a beam width of just 1.

Our question is whether a system's performance can be assessed *prior* to the generation step, by exploiting the fact that the output is ultimately based on this core sampling mechanism. We envisage a scenario in which a neural caption generator is evaluated based on the extent to which its estimated softmax probabilities over the vocabulary maximise the probability of the words in the reference sentences $R_1...R_n$. We refer to this as a **pre-gen**(eration) evaluation metric, as it can be computed prior to generating any captions. A well-known

© Springer Nature Switzerland AG 2019
L. Leal-Taixé and S. Roth (Eds.): ECCV 2018 Workshops, LNCS 11132, pp. 114–123, 2019.
https://doi.org/10.1007/978-3-030-11018-5_10

example of a pre-gen metric is language model perplexity although, as we show below, this metric is not the best pre-gen candidate in terms of its correlation to standard evaluation measures for IDG systems.

From a development perspective, the advantage of a pre-gen metric lies in that all the word probabilities in a sentence are immediately available to the network in one forward pass, whereas a post-gen metric can only be computed following a relatively expensive process of word-by-word generation requiring repeated calls to a neural network. To return to the earlier example, on the same hardware setup it only takes 28 sec to compute model perplexity.

Thus, if pre-gen metrics can be shown to correlate strongly with established post-gen metrics, they could serve as a proxy for such metrics. This would speed up processes requiring repeated caption quality measurement such as during hyperparameter tuning.

Finally, from a theoretical and empirical perspective, if caption quality, as measured by one or more post-gen metric(s), can be predicted prior to generation, this would shed further light on the underlying reasons for the observed correlations of such metrics [14].

All code used in these experiments is publicly available.[1]

The rest of this paper is organised as follows; background on metrics is covered in Sect. 2, the methodology and experimental setup in Sect. 3, and the results are given in Sect. 4; the paper is concluded in Sect. 5.

2   Background: *Post-gen* Metrics for Image Captioning

In IDG, automatic metrics originally developed for Machine Translation or Summarisation, such as BLEU [21], ROUGE [18], and METEOR [2], were initially adopted, followed by metrics specifically designed for image description, notably CIDEr [24] and SPICE [1]. Lately, Word Mover's Distance (WMD) [17], originally from the document similarity community, has also been suggested for IDG [14]. Like BLEU, ROUGE and METEOR, CIDEr makes use of n-gram similarities, while WMD measures the semantic distance between texts on the basis of word2vec [20] embeddings. All of these metrics are purely linguistically informed. By contrast, SPICE computes similarity between sentences from scene graphs [13], obtained by parsing reference sentences. This method is also linguistically informed; however the intuition behind it is that the human authored sentences should be an accurate reflection of image content.

A typical IDG experiment reports several post-gen metrics. One reason is that the metrics correlate differently with human judgments, depending on task and dataset [3], echoing similar findings in other areas of NLP [4–7,10,11,22,26]. Thus, BLEU, METEOR, and ROUGE correlate weakly [12,15,16] and yield different system rankings compared to human judgments [25]. METEOR has a reportedly higher correlation than BLEU/ROUGE [8,9], with stronger relationships reported for CIDEr [24] and SPICE [1]. Meta-evaluation of the ability of metrics to discriminate between captions have also been somewhat inconsistent [14,24].

---

[1] See: https://github.com/mtanti/pregen-metrics.

The extent to which post-gen metrics correlate with each other also varies, with stronger relationships among those based on n-grams on the one hand, and more semantically-oriented ones on the other [14], suggesting that these groups assess complementary aspects of quality, and partially explaining their variable relationship to human judgments in addition to variations due to dataset.

For neural IDG architectures, post-gen metrics have one fundamental property in common: they compare reference outputs to generated sentences which are based on sampling at each time-step from a probability distribution. Our hypothesis is that it is possible to exploit this, using the probability distribution itself to directly estimate the quality of captions, prior to generation.

3   Pre-gen Metrics

Given a prefix, a neural caption generator predicts the next word by sampling from the softmax's probabilities estimated over the vocabulary. Let R be a reference caption of length m. Given a prefix $R^{0...k}$ (where R^0 is the start token), $k \leq m$, a neural caption generator can be used to estimate the probability of the next word (or the end token) in the reference caption, R^{k+1}. The intuition underlying pre-gen metrics is that the higher the estimated probability of R^{k+1}, for all $k \leq m$, the more likely it is that the generator will approximate the reference caption. Note that the idea is to estimate the probability of *reference* captions based on a trained IDG model.

Pre-gen metrics produce a score by aggregating the word probabilities predicted by the generator for all reference captions (combined with their respective image) over prefixes of different lengths. To find the best way to do this, we define a search space by setting options at four different algorithmic steps which we call 'tiers'. Each tier represents a function and the composition of all four tiers together constitutes a pre-gen function. We try several different options for each tier in order to find the best pre-gen function. Figure 1 shows an example of how tiers form a pre-gen function.

Given a set of images with their corresponding reference captions, the process starts by computing each reference caption's individual words probabilities (given the image) according to the model. Note that the model may not predict every word in a reference caption as the most likely in the vocabulary.

The first tier is a filter that selects which predicted word probabilities should be considered in the next tier. We consider three possible filters: (a) the filter *none* passes all probabilities; (b) *filter0* filters out the word probabilities that are not ranked as most probable in the vocabulary by the model, i.e are not predicted to be maximally probable continuations of the current prefix; and (c) *prefix0* selects the longest prefix of the caption such that the model predicts all words in the prefix as being the most likely in the vocabulary.

At the second tier, we aggregate the selected word probabilities in each reference sentence into a single score for each sentence. We define four possible functions: (a) *prob* multiplies all probabilities; (b) *pplx* computes the perplexity; (c) *count* counts the number of word probabilities that were selected in the first

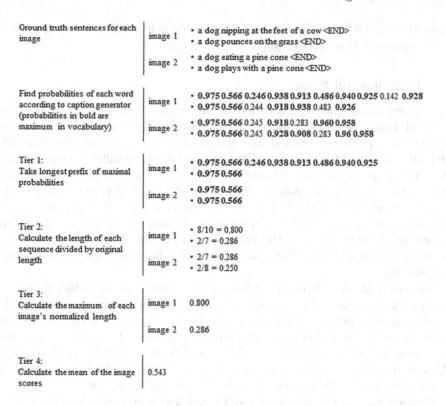

Fig. 1. An example illustrating how tiers work. This illustration shows the best pre-gen metric found: *mean_max_normcount_prefix0*.

tier; and (d) *normcount* normalises *count* by the total number of words in the reference sentence.

The third tier aggregates the scores obtained for all reference sentences into a single score for each image. We explore six possibilities: (a) *sum*; (b) *mean*; (c) *median*; (d) *geomean*, the geometric mean; (e) *max*; and (f) *min*. We also consider (g) *join*, whereby all the image-sentence scores are joined into a single list without aggregation so that they are all aggregated together in the next tier.

The fourth tier aggregates the image scores into a single dataset score, which is the final pre-gen score of the caption generator. For this aggregation, we use the same six functions as in the previous tier (excluding *join*).

The above possibilities result in 504 unique combinations. In what follows, we adopt the convention of denoting a pre-gen metric by the sequence of function names that compose it, starting from tier four e.g. *mean_max_normcount_prefix0*. In our experiments, we compute all of these different combinations and compare their predictions to standard post-gen metrics, namely METEOR, CIDEr, SPICE, and WMD. All metrics except WMD were computed using the MSCOCO

Evaluation toolkit[2]. Since the toolkit does not include WMD, we created a fork of the repository that includes it.[3]

3.1 Experimental Setup

For our experiments, we used a variety of pre-trained neural caption generators (36 in all) from [23].[4] These models are based on four different caption generator architectures. Each was trained and tested over three runs on Flickr8k [12], Flickr30k [27], and MSCOCO [19]. The four architectures differ in terms of how the CNN image encoder is combined with the RNN: `init` architectures use the image vector as the initial hidden state of the RNN decoder; `pre` architectures treat the image vector as the first word of a caption; `par` architectures are trained on captions where each word is coupled with an image vector at each time-step; and `merge` architectures keep the image out of the the RNN entirely, merging the image vector with the RNN hidden state in a final feedforward layer, prior to prediction.

Since only the final trained versions of the models are available, there is a bias towards good quality post-gen metric results. This renders the values of the post-gen metrics rather similar and concentrated in a small range. A pre-gen metric is useful if it makes good predictions on models of any quality not just good ones. Rather than re-training all the models and saving the parameters at different intervals during training, we opted to stratify the dataset on the basis of how well each individual image is rated by the CIDEr metric.

We grouped images into the best and worst halves on the basis of the CIDEr score (since CIDEr is the post-gen metric that best correlates with the other post-gen metrics [14]) of their sentences as generated by a model. This creates two datasets, one where the model performs well and one where the model performs badly. We stratified the dataset into different numbers of equal parts and not just two, namely: 1 (whole), 2, 3, 4 and 5, resulting in a 15-fold increase over the original 36 averaged results and more importantly, over a wide dynamic range in CIDEr scores, which we required to study the correlation in between pre- and post-gen metrics.

4 Results

We evaluate the correlation between pre- and post-gen metrics using the Coefficient of Determination, or R^2, defined as the square of the Pearson correlation coefficient. The reason for this is twofold. First, R^2 reflects the magnitude of a correlation, irrespective of whether it is positive or negative (the pre-gen metrics based on perplexity would be expected to be negatively correlated with post-gen

---

[2] See: https://github.com/tylin/coco-caption.
[3] See: https://github.com/mtanti/coco-caption.
[4] See: https://github.com/mtanti/where-image2.

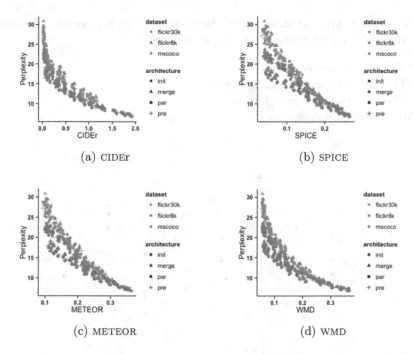

(a) CIDEr

(b) SPICE

(c) METEOR

(d) WMD

Fig. 2. Relationship between perplexity and post-gen metrics by dataset and architecture. The overall correlation has an R^2 of 0.76. (Best viewed in colour.) (Color figure online)

metrics). Second, given a linear model in which a pre-gen metric is used to predict the value on a post-gen metric, R^2 indicates the proportion of the variance in the latter that the pre-gen metric predicts.

As a baseline, we show the scatter plot for the relationship between language model perplexity and the post-gen metrics in Fig. 2. In terms of the description in the previous section, perplexity is defined as *geomean_join_pplx_none*. As can be seen, perplexity performs somewhat poorly on low scoring captions. Our question is whether a better pre-gen metric can be found.

For each of the 4 post-gen metrics, we identified the top 5 best correlated pre-gen metrics, based on the R^2 value computed over all the data (i.e. aggregating scores across architectures and datasets). The top 4 pre-gen metrics were the same for all post-gen metrics, namely:

1. *mean_max_normcount_prefix0*;
2. *mean_mean_normcount_prefix0*;
3. *mean_join_normcount_prefix0*;
4. *mean_sum_normcount_prefix0*

Note that all the best performing metrics are based on the variable *prefix0*. This is not surprising since when generating a sentence, it is probably the word with the maximum probability in the vocabulary which gets selected as a next word in a prefix. On the other hand, the fifth most highly correlated pre-gen metric differed for each post-gen metric, as follows:

– CIDER: *mean_min_count_filter0*;
– METEOR: *mean_mean_count_prefix0*;
– SPICE: *geomean_min_pplx_filter0*;
– WMD: *mean_join_count_prefix0*

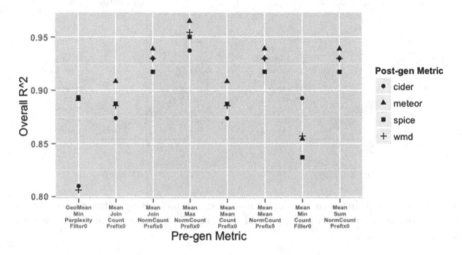

Fig. 3. Overall R^2 between the 4 post-gen metrics and their 5 most highly correlated pre-gen metrics. Scores average over architectures and datasets.

Figure 3 displays the relationship between these pre-gen metrics and the post-gen scores. Note that all R^2 scores are above 0.8, indicating a very strong correlation.[5] The top 4 scores have $R^2 \geq 0.9$.

To investigate the relationship between pre- and post-gen metrics more closely, we focus on the best pre-gen metric (that is, *mean_max_normcount_prefix0*) and consider its relationship to each post-gen metric individually. This is shown in Fig. 4. Irrespective of architecture and/or dataset, we observe a broadly linear relationship, despite some evidence of non-linearity at the lower ends of the scale, especially for CIDEr and WMD. This supports the hypothesis made at the outset, namely, that it is possible to predict the quality of captions, as measured by a standard metric, by considering the probability of the reference captions in the test set, without the need to generate the captions themselves.

---

[5] All correlations are significant at $p < 0.001$.

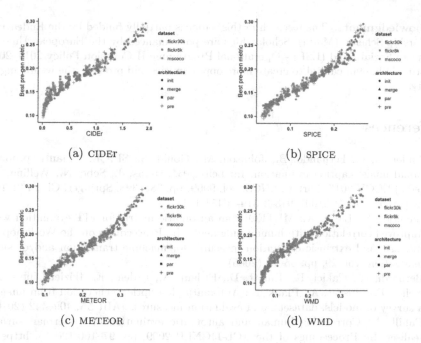

(a) CIDEr

(b) SPICE

(c) METEOR

(d) WMD

Fig. 4. Best pre-gen metric (*mean_max_normcount_prefix0*) vs post-gen metrics. The overall correlation has an R^2 of 0.94. (Best viewed in colour.) (Color figure online)

5 Discusison and Conclusion

We have introduced and defined the concept of pre-gen metrics and described a methodology to search for useful variants of these metrics. Our results show that pre-gen metrics closely approximate a variety of standard evaluation measures.

These results can be attributed to the fact that neural captioning models share core assumptions about the sampling mechanisms that underlie generation, and that standard evaluation metrics ultimately assess the output of this sampling process. Thus, it is possible to predict the quality of the output, as measured by a post-gen metric, using the probability distribution that a trained model predicts over prefixes of varying length in the reference captions. The practical implication is that pre-gen metrics can act as quick and efficient evaluation proxies during development. The theoretical implication is that the correlations among standard evaluation metrics reported in the literature are due, at least in part, to core sampling mechanisms shared by most neural generation architectures.

In future work, we plan to experiment with tuning captioning models using pre-gen metrics. We also wish to compare pre-gen metrics directly to human judgments.

Acknowledgments. The research in this paper is partially funded by the Endeavour Scholarship Scheme (Malta). Scholarships are part-financed by the European Union - European Social Fund (ESF) - Operational Programme II Cohesion Policy 2014–2020 Investing in human capital to create more opportunities and promote the well-being of society.

References

1. Anderson, P., Fernando, B., Johnson, M., Gould, S.: SPICE: semantic propositional image caption evaluation. In: Leibe, B., Matas, J., Sebe, N., Welling, M. (eds.) ECCV 2016, Part V. LNCS, vol. 9909, pp. 382–398. Springer, Cham (2016). https://doi.org/10.1007/978-3-319-46454-1_24
2. Banerjee, S., Lavie, A.: METEOR: an automatic metric for MT evaluation with improved correlation with human judgments. In: Proceedings on the Workshop on Intrinsic and extrinsic evaluation measures for machine translation and/or summarization, vol. 29, pp. 65–72 (2005)
3. Bernardi, R., Cakici, R., Elliott, D., Erdem, A., Erdem, E., Ikizler-Cinbis, N., Keller, F., Muscat, A., Plank, B.: Automatic description generation from images: a survey of models, datasets, and evaluation measures. JAIR **55**, 409–442 (2016)
4. Cahill, A.: Correlating human and automatic evaluation of a German surface realiser. In: Proceedings of the ACL-IJCNLP 2009, pp. 97–100 (2009). https://doi.org/10.3115/1667583.1667615, http://dl.acm.org/citation.cfm?id=1667583.1667615, http://www.aclweb.org/anthology-new/P/P09/P09-2025.pdf
5. Callison-Burch, C., Osborne, M., Koehn, P.: Re-evaluating the role of BLEU in machine translation research. In: Proceedings of the EACL 2006, pp. 249–256 (2006)
6. Caporaso, J.G., Deshpande, N., Fink, J.L., Bourne, P.E., Bretonnel Cohen, K., Hunter, L.: Intrinsic evaluation of text mining tools may not predict performance on realistic tasks. Pac. Symp. Biocomput. **13**, 640–651 (2008). http://www.ncbi.nlm.nih.gov/pmc/articles/PMC2517250/
7. Dorr, B., Monz, C., Oard, D., President, S., Zajic, D., Schwartz, R.: Extrinsic evaluation of automatic metrics. Technical report, Institute for Advanced Computer Studies, University of Maryland, College Park, College Park, MD (2004)
8. Elliott, D., Keller, F.: Image description using visual dependency representations. In: Proceedings of the 2013 Conference on Empirical Methods in Natural Language Processing, pp. 1292–1302. Association for Computational Linguistics, Seattle, Washington, October 2013. http://www.aclweb.org/anthology/D13-1128
9. Elliott, D., Keller, F.: Comparing automatic evaluation measures for image description. In: Proceedings of the ACL 2014, pp. 452–457 (2014)
10. Espinosa, D., Rajkumar, R., White, M., Berleant, S.: Further Meta-evaluation of broad-coverage surface realization. In: Proceedings of the EMNLP 2010, pp. 564–574 (2010). http://www.aclweb.org/anthology/D10-1055
11. Gatt, A., Belz, A.: Introducing shared tasks to NLG: the TUNA shared task evaluation challenges. In: Krahmer, E., Theune, M. (eds.) EACL/ENLG -2009. LNCS (LNAI), vol. 5790, pp. 264–293. Springer, Heidelberg (2010). https://doi.org/10.1007/978-3-642-15573-4_14
12. Hodosh, M., Young, P., Hockenmaier, J.: Framing image description as a ranking task: data, models and evaluation metrics. JAIR **47**(1), 853–899 (2013). https://doi.org/10.1109/cvprw.2013.51

13. Johnson, J., et al.: Image retrieval using scene graphs. In: IEEE Conference on Computer Vision and Pattern Recognition (CVPR). IEEE, June 2015. https://doi.org/10.1109/cvpr.2015.7298990

14. Kilickaya, M., Erdem, A., Ikizler-Cinbis, N., Erdem, E.: Re-evaluating automatic metrics for image captioning. In: Proceedings of the 15th Conference of the European Chapter of the Association for Computational Linguistics: Volume 1, Long Papers. Association for Computational Linguistics (2017). https://doi.org/10.18653/v1/e17-1019

15. Kiros, R., Salakhutdinov, R., Zemel, R.S.: Unifying visual-semantic embeddings with multimodal neural language models. CoRR 1411.2539 (2014)

16. Kulkarni, G., et al.: Baby talk: understanding and generating simple image descriptions. In: CVPR 2011. IEEE, June 2011. https://doi.org/10.1109/cvpr.2011.5995466

17. Kusner, M., Sun, Y., Kolkin, N., Weinberger, K.: From word embeddings to document distances. In: Bach, F., Blei, D. (eds.) Proceedings of the 32nd International Conference on Machine Learning. Proceedings of Machine Learning Research, vol. 37, pp. 957–966. PMLR, Lille (2015). http://proceedings.mlr.press/v37/kusnerb15.html

18. Lin, C.Y., Och, F.J.: Automatic evaluation of machine translation quality using longest common subsequence and skip-bigram statistics. In: Proceedings of the ACL 2004 (2004)

19. Lin, T.Y., et al.: Microsoft COCO: common objects in context. In: Proceedings of the ECCV 2014, pp. 740–755 (2014). https://doi.org/10.1007/978-3-319-10602-1_48

20. Mikolov, T., Chen, K., Corrado, G., Dean, J.: Efficient Estimation of Word Representations in Vector Space. CoRR 1301.3781 (2013)

21. Papineni, K., Roukos, S., Ward, T., Zhu, W.J.: BLEU: a method for automatic evaluation of machine translation. In: Proceedings of the ACL 2002, pp. 311–318 (2002)

22. Reiter, E., Belz, A.: An investigation into the validity of some metrics for automatically evaluating natural language generation systems. Comput. Linguist. 35(4), 529–558 (2009)

23. Tanti, M., Gatt, A., Camilleri, K.P.: Where to put the image in an image caption generator. Nat. Lang. Eng. 24(3), 467–489 (2018). https://doi.org/10.1017/S1351324918000098. https://www.cambridge.org/core/journals/natural-language-engineering/article/where-to-put-the-image-in-an-image-caption-generator/A5B0ACFFE8E4AEAA5840DC61F93153F3#fndtn-information

24. Vedantam, R., Zitnick, C.L., Parikh, D.: CIDEr: consensus-based image description evaluation. In: Proceedings of the CVPR 2015 (2015)

25. Vinyals, O., Toshev, A., Bengio, S., Erhan, D.: Show and tell: lessons learned from the 2015 MSCOCO image captioning challenge. IEEE Trans. Pattern Anal. Mach. Intell. 39(4), 652–663 (2017). https://doi.org/10.1109/tpami.2016.2587640

26. Wubben, S., van den Bosch, A., Krahmer, E.: Sentence simplification by monolingual machine translation. In: Proceedings of the ACL 2012, pp. 1015–1024 (2012). http://www.aclweb.org/anthology/P12-1107

27. Young, P., Lai, A., Hodosh, M., Hockenmaier, J.: From image descriptions to visual denotations: new similarity metrics for semantic inference over event descriptions. TACL 2, 67–78 (2014)

Quantifying the Amount of Visual Information Used by Neural Caption Generators

Marc Tanti[✉], Albert Gatt, and Kenneth P. Camilleri

University of Malta, Msida 2080, MSD, Malta
{marc.tanti.06,albert.gatt,kenneth.camilleri}@um.edu.mt

Abstract. This paper addresses the sensitivity of neural image caption generators to their visual input. A sensitivity analysis and omission analysis based on image foils is reported, showing that the extent to which image captioning architectures retain and are sensitive to visual information varies depending on the type of word being generated and the position in the caption as a whole. We motivate this work in the context of broader goals in the field to achieve more explainability in AI.

Keywords: Image captioning · Sensitivity analysis · Explainable AI

1 Introduction

The goal of explainable AI is to move beyond an exclusive focus on the outputs of neural networks, an approach which risks treating such networks as 'black boxes' which, though reasonably well-understood at the level of their macro-architecture, are hard to explain because of their complex, non-linear structure [5].

The broad goal of the present paper is to seek a better explanation of the behaviour of neural image caption generators [1]. Such generators typically consist of a neural language model that is conditioned on the features extracted from an image using a convolutional neural network, with several possibilities available on how to do the conditioning [8].

The main question we address is how sensitive such generators actually are to the visual input, that is, to what extent the string generated by these models varies as a function of variation in the visual features extracted by the image. We address this using a sensitivity analysis [5] and an analysis based on foils [6]. In addressing this question, we hope to achieve a better understanding of the extent to which caption generation architectures succeed in grounding linguistic symbols in visual features[1].

---

[1] Code is available on https://github.com/mtanti/quantifing-visual-information.

© Springer Nature Switzerland AG 2019
L. Leal-Taixé and S. Roth (Eds.): ECCV 2018 Workshops, LNCS 11132, pp. 124–132, 2019.
https://doi.org/10.1007/978-3-030-11018-5_11

2   Background

It is known that not all words in a sentence are given equal importance by a neural language model of the kind image captioning systems use [2]. Rather than measuring the importance of words, as was done in [2], we would like to measure how important the image is at conditioning the language model to emit the different words of a caption during the generation process. This can shed light on the extent to which the generator is grounded in visual data and help to explain some of the model's output decisions.

One way of making neural architectures more explainable is to examine their sensitivity with respect to their inputs [5]. Such sensitivity analysis can be done by measuring the gradient of the output with respect to different parts of the input. In this paper, we conduct such an analysis, measuring the gradient of the output with respect to the input image feature vectors.

A related approach is to compare the outcomes produced by a network when parts of the input are altered, or replaced by foils. This has been done in the image captioning domain, and has yielded datasets such as FOIL-COCO [6]. In [6], the visual sensitivity of images was tested by replacing words in captions with foils and checking if models are able to detect whether a caption contains an incorrect word. The results showed that this is a hard task for many vision-language models, despite being trivial for humans. However, this task does not directly quantify the visual sensitivity of such models with respect to different parts of a caption. This is what we attempt to do in the second part of our analysis.

3   Data and Methods

Our goal is to measure how much visual information is used in order to predict a particular word in a caption generator. To do this we make use of the data and models from [8]^2, which examines four different neural caption generator architectures which are often found in the literature. These are illustrated in Fig. 1. They differ mainly in the way the language model is conditioned on image features, as follows:

- *init-inject*: the image features are used as an initial hidden state vector of the RNN;
- *pre-inject*: the image features are used as the first input to the RNN;
- *par-inject*: the image features are included together with every word input to the RNN; and
- *merge*: the image features are concatenated with the RNN hidden state vector and fed to the softmax layer.

---

^{2} See: https://github.com/mtanti/where-image2.

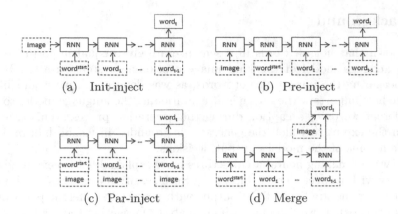

(a) Init-inject   (b) Pre-inject

(c) Par-inject   (d) Merge

Fig. 1. Different neural image captioning architectures.

In our experiments, each architecture uses a GRU as an RNN. The architectures were trained on MSCOCO [4] which was obtained from the distribution provided by [3][3]. The distributed datasets come with the images already converted into feature vectors using the penultimate layer of the VGG-16 CNN [7]. The vocabulary consists of all words that occur at least five times in the training set. We run two sets of experiments to see how much visual information is retained by each architecture: sensitivity analysis and omission scoring; both of which are explained in detail below.

3.1   Sensitivity Analysis

Sensitivity analysis involves measuring the gradient of a model's output with respect to its input in order to see how sensitive the current output is to different parts of the input [5]. The more sensitive, the more important that part of the input is to produce the output. We use this technique to measure how sensitive the softmax layer of the caption generator is to the image at different time steps in the generation process. We do this by computing the partial derivative of the softmax output with respect to the input image vector. It is important to note that even though the image might only be input once as an initial state to the RNN, its influence on the output will not be the same at every time step.

As we implemented our neural networks in Tensorflow, which does not currently allow for computing full Jaccard matrices efficiently, instead of finding the gradient of the whole softmax we only take the gradient of the probability of the next word in the caption. Measuring the gradient of this word allows us to infer what contribution the image made to the selection of this word during generation. Although the gradient is a single number, it is computed with respect to every element in the image feature vector. We aggregate these partial gradients by taking the mean of the absolute values.

---

[3] See: http://cs.stanford.edu/people/karpathy/deepimagesent/.

We take captions that were already generated by the same caption generator being analyzed. Each caption is fed back to the caption generator that generated them to re-predict the probability of the next word for every prefix of increasing length in the caption. We report the mean gradient for each time step aggregated over all corresponding time steps in captions of the same length.

We also compare these gradients to the gradient with respect to the last word in the prefix (i.e. with respect to the preceding word, but not the image) in order to compare a model's sensitivity to linguistic context, as compared to visual features.

3.2   Omission Scoring

Omission scoring [2] measures changes in the model's output or hidden layers as some part of an input is removed. The more similar the hidden layer representation, the less important the removed input is. We use a similar technique to measure how important the image is to the representation. Of course, the image cannot be omitted from a caption generator, but it can be replaced by a different image, known as a foil. In image caption generators, excluding the merge architecture, the RNN hidden state vector at each time-step consists of a mixture of visual information and the preceding caption prefix. In the case of merge architectures, the same mixture is found in the layer that concatenates the image vector to the RNN hidden state vector. We call these mixed image-prefix vectors 'multimodal vectors'.

We take the multimodal vector of a caption generator and measure by how much it changes when a caption prefix is input together with a distractor (foil) image, as opposed to when the correct image is used with that same prefix. This is done after each time step in order to measure whether the distractor image affects the representation less and less over time.

We take captions that were already generated by the caption generator. Each caption is fed back to the caption generator that generated it to re-predict the probability of the next word at every time-step. This is repeated with a distractor image in place of the correct one. We then compute the cosine distance between the multimodal vectors resulting from the correct and the distractor images. We report the mean cosine distance for each time step aggregated over all corresponding time steps in captions of the same length.

In addition to multimodal vectors, we also compare the softmax layers at each time step with the test image and the foil, to assess the impact of the image change on the output probabilities. Comparison of the softmax layer is done using both cosine distance and Jensen-Shannon divergence.

To identify distractor images, we compare each image in the test set to the others, finding the one whose feature vector is furthest (in terms of cosine) from the correct one.

Table 1. Part of speech tags found at different positions in all 9-word captions. Since different architectures generate different captions, the percentages are averaged over all the architectures. Maximum probability per word position is in bold.

word	ADJ	ADP	ADV	CONJ	DET	NOUN	NUM	PRON	PRT	VERB
0					**99.8%**		0.4%			
1	22.8%		0.2%			**77.1%**				0.1%
2	1.5%	**34.1%**	0.1%	7.3%	0.7%	26.2%				30.4%
3	7.5%	**30.6%**	0.1%	0.5%	9.9%	27.5%	0.1%	0.1%	1.3%	22.6%
4	3.8%	13.6%	0.1%	1.3%	**33.6%**	23.0%	0.1%	0.2%	1.1%	23.3%
5	11.8%	16.1%	0.1%	0.5%	6.7%	**52.0%**	0.1%		2.2%	10.5%
6	0.5%	**51.4%**		4.5%	17.0%	9.3%	0.1%	0.1%	13.7%	3.5%
7	5.7%	7.1%		1.0%	**68.8%**	13.3%		2.4%	0.1%	1.7%
8	8.5%	0.1%	0.1%			**88.7%**		2.5%		0.2%

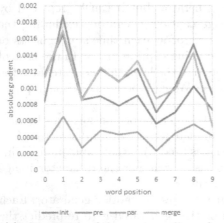
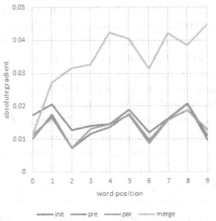

(a) Sensitivity of the next word's probability with respect to the image.

(b) Sensitivity of the next word's probability with respect to the previous word.

Fig. 2. Sensitivity analysis of 9-word captions (plus END token). Note that the previous word for position 0 is the START token and position 9 is the END token.

4   Results

The lengths of generated captions vary between 6 and 15 words. For the sake of brevity, we only report the results on captions of length 9, which is the most common length. The results follow the same pattern for captions of other lengths as well. Table 1 shows the distribution of parts of speech at each of the 9 word positions in the captions; this sheds light on which words cause spikes in visual information usage.

The results for the sensitivity analysis are shown in Fig. 2. It is clear that certain word positions are more sensitive to the image than others. Irrespective of architecture, there are substantial peaks in Fig. 2a at positions 1 and 8, both of which are predominantly nouns. It could be argued that the gradient can be used to detect visual words in captions, that is, nouns referring to objects in the pictures. Par-inject has a consistently low gradient throughout the caption, which is probably reflecting the tendency of the network to avoid retaining excessive visual information, since the same image is input at every time step.

Turning to Fig. 2b, the output is much more sensitive to the previous word than to the image, by an order of magnitude. The merge architecture has an upward trend in sensitivity to the previous word as the caption prefix gets longer whilst the other architectures are somewhat more stable. This could be because in the merge architecture, which does not mix visual features directly in the RNN, there is more memory allocated in the RNN to focus on the previous word.

Although nouns are more frequent at position 8 compared to 1, there is less sensitivity to the image, across all architectures. This happens even in the merge architecture, which doesn't include image features in the RNN hidden state. Hence, this downward trend in gradient is likely due to the caption prefix becoming more predictive as it gets longer, progressively reducing the image importance. Although more sensitive than par-inject, init-inject has a much steeper decline than merge and pre-inject, suggesting that something else is at play apart from prefix information content. One possibility is that image information is being lost by the RNN as the prefix gets longer. To investigate this, we can look at the results for the omission scores which are shown in Fig. 3.

Again, we see peaks at word positions predominately occupied by 'visual' words (nouns). The multimodal vector of the merge architecture seems to be an exception. This is because merge's multimodal vector concatenates separate image and prefix vectors, meaning that the image representation is unaffected by the prefix. The other architectures mix the image and prefix together in the RNN's hidden state vector, requiring the RNN to use memory for both image and prefix, thereby causing visual information to be degraded. Note that greater distance between multimodal vectors is unexpected in merge: since image features are concatenated with the RNN hidden state, the RNN part of the multimodal vector is identical in both foil and correct multimodal vectors, which should make the two vectors more similar, not less.

The softmax on the other hand changes very similarly for all architectures and this is reflected both in cosine distance and Jensen-Shannon divergence (compare Fig. 3b and c). Merge is slightly more influenced by the image when determining the last noun in the caption and par-inject being the least influenced throughout. The fact that the merge architecture has a very different multimodal vector distance from the other architectures but then ends up with a similar output distance merits further investigation.

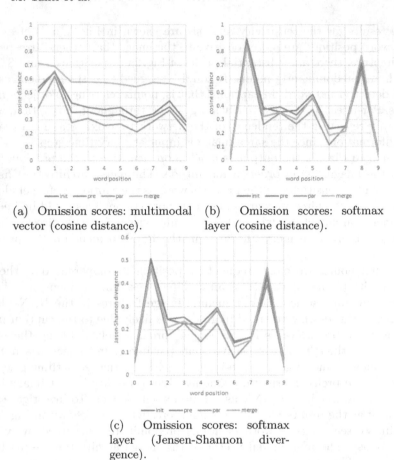

(a) Omission scores: multimodal vector (cosine distance).

(b) Omission scores: softmax layer (cosine distance).

(c) Omission scores: softmax layer (Jensen-Shannon divergence).

Fig. 3. Results for omission scoring of all 9-word long captions (plus the END token). Note that the previous word for position 0 is the START token and position 9 is the END token.

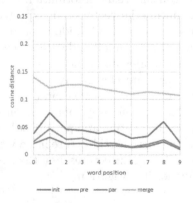

Fig. 4. Omission scores: logits (output layer without softmax)

We investigate the discrepancy in the results for the merge architecture – a relatively flat curve for the multimodal vector versus peaks at the output layer – by repeating the analysis for the logits vector, that is, the output layer prior to applying the softmax activation function. As shown in Fig. 4, this results in curves that are similar to those shown in Fig. 3a.

The logits vectors resulting from the original and foil images are much more similar to each other than the multimodal vector for all architectures (peaking at around 0.15 instead of 0.7), but the merge architecture still evinces higher distance between test and foil conditions, and greater stability. The fact that logits are similarly affected by the test-foil discrepancy as the multimodal vectors (compare Figs. 3a and 4) suggests that the peaks observed at the output layer (Fig. 3b and c) arise from the softmax function itself. One drastic change that the softmax function performs on the logits vector is the replacement of negative numbers with very small positive numbers. In fact we have found that merge uses fewer negative numbers in the logits vector than other architectures (about 94% rather than 97%[4]) which means that the extra cosine distance between the logits vectors resulting from the original and foil images is probably due to a larger number of elements with opposite signs which, after softmax is applied, become positive and hence more similar. This, coupled with the fact that the output probabilities of any trained caption generator should be similar (otherwise they would not be describing the same image similarly) gives at least a partial explanation for why the outputs in all architectures change similarly when a test image is replaced with the same foil image.

5 Conclusion

Caption generators use visual information less and less as the caption is generated, although the amount of visual sensitivity is highly dependent on the part of speech of the word to generate and on the length of the prefix generated so far. This has two implications.

First, as a caption gets longer, linguistic context becomes increasingly predictive of the next word in the caption, and the image is less crucial. An additional factor, in the case of inject architectures, is that the RNN hidden state stores both visual and linguistic features, making it harder to remember visual features as captions get longer. The evidence for this is that the multimodal vector and logits of the merge architecture change more when the original image to a caption is replaced with a different image, compared to inject architectures.

Second, the peaks observed with nouns in the sensitivity analysis show that image features as currently used in standard captioning models are highly tuned to objects, but far less so to relational predicates such as prepositions or verbs.

---

[4] Most logits will be negative since most words will have small probabilities in the softmax.

For future work we would like to attempt to extract visual words from captions based on how sensitive to the image a trained caption generator is at different word positions in the caption. We would also like to use these techniques to analyze state of the art caption generators, including those with attention, in an effort to deepen our explanation of what makes a good caption generator.

Acknowledgments. The research in this paper is partially funded by the Endeavour Scholarship Scheme (Malta). Scholarships are part-financed by the European Union - European Social Fund (ESF) - Operational Programme II Cohesion Policy 2014–2020 Investing in human capital to create more opportunities and promote the well-being of society.

References

1. Bernardi, R., et al.: Automatic description generation from images: a survey of models, datasets, and evaluation measures. JAIR **55**, 409–442 (2016)
2. Kádár, Á., Chrupała, G., Alishahi, A.: Representation of linguistic form and function in recurrent neural networks. Comput. Linguist. **43**(4), 761–780 (2017). https://doi.org/10.1162/coli_a_00300
3. Karpathy, A., Fei-Fei, L.: Deep visual-semantic alignments for generating image descriptions. In: Proceedings of the CVPR 2015 (2015). https://doi.org/10.1109/cvpr.2015.7298932
4. Lin, T.-Y., et al.: Microsoft COCO: common objects in context. In: Fleet, D., Pajdla, T., Schiele, B., Tuytelaars, T. (eds.) ECCV 2014, Part V. LNCS, vol. 8693, pp. 740–755. Springer, Cham (2014). https://doi.org/10.1007/978-3-319-10602-1_48
5. Samek, W., Wiegand, T., Müller, K.R.: Explainable artificial intelligence: understanding, visualizing and interpreting deep learning models. ITU Journal: ICT Discoveries - Special Issue 1 - Impact Artif. Intell. (AI) Commun. Netw. Serv. **1**(1), 39–48 (2018). https://www.itu.int/en/journal/001/Pages/05.aspx
6. Shekhar, R., et al.: Foil it! find one mismatch between image and language caption. In: Proceedings of the 55th Annual Meeting of the Association for Computational Linguistics (Volume 1: Long Papers), pp. 255–265. Association for Computational Linguistics, Vancouver, Canada, July 2017. http://aclweb.org/anthology/P17-1024
7. Simonyan, K., Zisserman, A.: Very Deep Convolutional Networks for Large-Scale Image Recognition. CoRR 1409.1556 (2014)
8. Tanti, M., Gatt, A., Camilleri, K.P.: Where to put the image in an image caption generator. Natural Language Engineering **24**(3), 467–489 (2018). https://doi.org/10.1017/S1351324918000098. https://www.cambridge.org/core/journals/natural-language-engineering/article/where-to-put-the-image-in-an-image-caption-generator/A5B0ACFFE8E4AEAA5840DC61F93153F3#fndtn-information

Distinctive-Attribute Extraction
for Image Captioning

Boeun Kim, Young Han Lee, Hyedong Jung, and Choongsang Cho[✉]

AI Research Center, Korea Electronics Technology Institute, Seongnam, Korea
{kbe36,yhlee,hudson,ideafisher}@keti.re.kr

Abstract. Image captioning has evolved with the progress of deep neural networks. However, generating qualitatively detailed and distinctive captions is still an open issue. In previous works, a caption involving semantic description can be generated by applying additional information into the RNNs. In this approach, we propose a distinctive-attribute extraction (DaE) method that extracts attributes which explicitly encourage RNNs to generate an accurate caption. We evaluate the proposed method with a challenge data and verify that this method improves the performance, describing images in more detail. The method can be plugged into various models to improve their performance.

Keywords: Image captioning · Semantic information
Distinctive-attribute
Term frequency-inverse document frequency (TF-IDF)

1   Introduction

Image captioning is a potent and useful tool for automatically describing or explaining the overall situation of an image [5,22,24]. However, generate qualitatively detailed and distinctive captions is still an open issue. Although in most cases captions with unique expressions are more useful than those with only safe ones, the current evaluation metrics do not adequately reflect this aspect. After the numerical performance of the previous researches increased to some extent, some works are studying how to generate detailed and accurate captions [4].

In this paper, we propose a Distinctive-attribute Extraction (DaE) method that extracts attributes which explicitly encourages RNNs to generate a caption that describes a significant meaning of an image. The main contributions of this paper are as follows: (i) We propose a semantics extraction method by using the TF-IDF caption analysis. (ii) We propose a scheme to infer distinctive-attribute by the model trained with semantic information. (iii) We perform quantitative and qualitative evaluations, demonstrating that the proposed method improves the performance of a base caption generation model by a substantial margin while describing images more distinctively.

© Springer Nature Switzerland AG 2019
L. Leal-Taixé and S. Roth (Eds.): ECCV 2018 Workshops, LNCS 11132, pp. 133–144, 2019.
https://doi.org/10.1007/978-3-030-11018-5_12

2   Related Work

Combinations of CNNs and RNNs are widely used for the image captioning networks [5,6,8,22–24]. The CNN was used as an image encoder, and an output of its last hidden layer is fed into the RNN decoder that generates sentences. Recent approaches can be grouped into two paradigms. Top-down includes attention-based mechanisms, and many of the bottom-up methods used semantic concepts. For the latter, Fang *et al.* [6] used multiple instance learning (MIL) to train word detectors with words that commonly occur in captions. The word detector outputs guided a language model to generate descriptions to include the detected words. Wu *et al.* [23] predicted attributes by treating the problem as a multi-label classification. The CNN framework was used and outputs from different proposal sub-regions are aggregated. Gan *et al.* [8] proposed Semantic Concept Network (SCN) integrating semantic concepts to the LSTM network. SCN factorized each weight matrix of the attribute integrated the LSTM model to reduce the number of parameters.

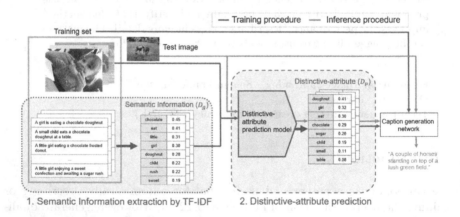

Fig. 1. An overview of the proposed framework including a semantic information extraction procedure and a distinctive-attribute prediction model

More recently, Dai *et al.* [4] proposed Contrastive Learning(CL) method which encourages the distinctiveness of captions. In addition to true image-caption pairs, this method used mismatched pairs which include captions describing other images for learning.

3   Distinctive-Attribute Extraction

In this paper, we describe a semantic information processing and extraction method, which affects the quality of generated captions. We propose a method to generate captions that can represent the unique situation of the image. Different from CL [4] that improved target method by additional pairs on a training set, our method lies on the bottom-up approaches using semantic attributes. We assign more weights to the attributes that are more informative and distinctive to describe the image. As illustrated in Fig. 1, there are two main steps, one is semantic information extraction, and the other is the distinctive-attribute prediction. First, we extract meaningful information from reference captions. Next, we learn the distinctive-attribute prediction model with image-information (D_g) pairs. After getting distinctive-attribute (D_p) from images, we apply these attributes to a caption generation network to verify their effect. For the network, we used SCN-LSTM [8] which is a tag integrated network.

3.1   Semantic Information Extraction by TF-IDF

Most of the previous methods constituted semantic information that was a ground truth attribute, as a binary form [6,8,23,25]. They first determined vocabulary using K most common words in the training captions. The vocabulary included nouns, verbs, and adjectives. If the word in the vocabulary existed in reference captions, the corresponding element of an attribute vector became 1. Different from previous methods, we weight semantic information according to their significance. Informative and distinctive words are weighted more, and the weight scores are estimated from reference captions by TF-IDF scheme which was widely used in text mining tasks.

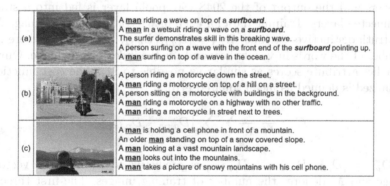

Fig. 2. Examples of images and their reference captions brought from MS COCO datasets [2,15]

Figure 2 represents samples of COCO datasets. In Fig. 2(a), there is a common word "surfboard" in 3 out of 5 captions, which is a key-word that characterizes the image. Intuitively, this kind of words should get high scores. To implement this concept, we apply average term frequency $TF_{av}(w, d)$, the number of times word w occurs in document d divided by the number of captions for an image. Another common word "man" appears a lot in other images. Therefore, that is a less meaningful word for distinguishing one image from another. To reflect this, we apply inverse document frequency term weighting $IDF(w) = \log\{(N_d + 1)/(DF(w) + 1)\} + 1$, where N_d is the total number of documents, and $DF(w)$ is the number of documents that contain the word w. "1" is added in denominator and numerator to prevent zero-divisions [19]. Then a semantic information vector is derived by multiplying two metrics as $TF - IDF(w, d) = TF_{av}(w, d) \times IDF(w)$. We apply L2 normalization to TF-IDF vectors of each image for training performance. The normalized value is the ground truth distinctive-attribute vector D_g. We apply stemming using Porter Stemmer [20] before extracting TF-IDF.

The next step is to construct vocabulary with the words in the reference captions. The vocabulary should contain enough characteristic words to represent each image. At the same time, the semantic information should be trained well for prediction accuracy. We determine the words to be included in the vocabulary based on the IDF scores which indicates the uniqueness of the word. The vocabulary contains the words whose IDF is higher than the IDF threshold (th_{IDF}) regardless of the part of speech. We observe the performance of the attribute prediction model and overall captioning model while changing the IDF value threshold in Sect. 4.3.

3.2   Distinctive-Attribute Prediction Model

For the Distinctive-attribute prediction model, convolutional layers are followed by four fully-connected layers (FCs). We use ResNet-152 [10] architecture for CNN layers and the output of the 2048-way pool5 layer is fed into a stack of fully connected layers. Training data for each image consist of input image I and ground truth distinctive-attribute $\mathbf{D}_{g,i} = [D_{g,i1}, D_{g,i2}, \dots, D_{g,iN_w}]$, where N_w is the number of the words in vocabulary and i is the index of the image. Our goal is to predict attribute scores as similar as possible to D_g. The cost function to be minimized is defined as mean squared error:

$$C = \frac{1}{M} \frac{1}{N_w} \sum_i \sum_w [D_{g,iw} - D_{p,iw}]^2 \tag{1}$$

where $\mathbf{D}_{p,i} = [D_{p,i1}, D_{p,i2}, \dots, D_{p,iN_w}]$ is predictive attribute score vector for ith image and M denotes the number of training images. The first three FCs have 2048 channels each, the fourth contains N_w channels. We use ReLU [17] as nonlinear activation function for all FCs. We adopt batch normalization [11] right after each FC and before activation. The training is regularized by dropout with ratio 0.3 for the first three FCs. Each FC is initialized with a Xavier initialization [9]. We note that our network does not contain softmax as a final layer, different from other attribute predictors described in previous papers [8,23]. Hence, we use the output of an activation function of the fourth FC layer as the final predictive score $\mathbf{D}_{p,i}$.

4   Results

4.1   Experiment Settings

Our results are evaluated on the popular MS COCO dataset [2,15]. The dataset contains 82,783 images for training, 40,504 and 40,775 images for validation and testing. The model described in Sect. 3.2 is implemented in Keras [3] and we used scikit-learn toolkit [19] to implement TF-IDF scheme. We set IDF threshold value to 7 in this experiment. The mini-batch size is fixed at 128 and Adam's optimization [13] with learning rate 3×10^{-3} is used and stopped after 100 epochs. For the prediction model, we train 5 identical models with different initializations, and then ensemble by averaging their outcomes. SCN-LSTM training procedure follows [8] and we use the public implementation [7] of this method opened by Gan who is the author of the published paper [8].

4.2   Evaluation

Firstly, we compared our method with SCN [7]. We evaluate both results on the online COCO testing server [2] and list them in Table 1. For SCN, we use the pre-trained weights provided by the author. The vocabulary size of the proposed scheme is 938, which is smaller than that of SCN [7] with 999. Results of both methods are derived from ensembling 5 models, respectively. The widely used metrics, BLEU-1,2,3,4 [18], METEOR [1], ROUGL-L [14], CIDEr [21] are selected to evaluate overall captioning performance. DaE improves the performance of SCN-LSTM by significant margins across all metrics. Specifically, DaE improves CIDEr from 0.967 to 0.981 in 5-refs and from 0.971 to 0.990 in 40-refs. The increase is greater at 40-refs which have relatively various expressions. The results for other published models tested on the COCO evaluation server are summarized in Table 2. In 40-refs, our method surpasses the performance of *AdaptiveAttention + CL* [4] which is the state-of-the-art in terms of four BLEU scores. The qualitative evaluation is shown in Table 6. We listed the top eight attributes. For DaE, words after stemming with Porter Stemmer [20] are

Table 1. COCO evaluation server results using 5 references and 40 references captions. DaE improves the performance by significant margins across all metrics

	B-1	B-2	B-3	B-4	M	R	CIDEr
5-refs							
SCN	0.729	0.563	0.426	**0.324**	0.253	0.537	0.967
DaE + SCN-LSTM	**0.734**	**0.568**	**0.429**	**0.324**	**0.255**	**0.538**	**0.981**
40-refs							
SCN	0.910	0.829	0.727	0.619	0.344	0.690	0.971
DaE + SCN-LSTM	**0.916**	**0.836**	**0.734**	**0.625**	**0.348**	**0.694**	**0.990**

Table 2. Results of published image captioning models tested on the COCO evaluation server

	B-1	B-2	B-3	B-4	M	R	CIDEr
5-refs							
Hard-Attention [24]	0.705	0.528	0.383	0.277	0.241	0.516	0.865
Google NIC [22]	0.713	0.542	0.407	0.309	0.254	0.530	0.943
ATT-FCN [25]	0.731	0.565	0.424	0.316	0.250	0.535	0.943
Adaptive Attention [16]	0.735	0.569	0.429	0.323	0.258	0.541	1.001
Adaptive Attention + CL [4]	0.742	0.577	0.436	0.326	0.260	0.544	1.010
DaE + SCN-LSTM	0.734	0.568	0.429	0.324	0.255	0.538	0.981
40-refs							
Hard-Attention [24]	0.881	0.779	0.658	0.537	0.322	0.654	0.893
Google NIC [22]	0.895	0.802	0.694	0.587	0.346	0.682	0.946
ATT-FCN [25]	0.900	0.815	0.709	0.599	0.335	0.682	0.958
Adaptive Attention [16]	0.906	0.823	0.717	0.607	0.347	0.689	1.004
Adaptive Attention + CL [4]	0.910	0.831	0.728	0.617	**0.350**	**0.695**	**1.029**
DaE + SCN-LSTM	**0.916**	**0.836**	**0.734**	**0.625**	0.348	0.694	0.990

Table 3. This table illustrates several images with extracted attributes and captions. The captions generated by using DaE+SCN-LSTM are explained more in detail with more distinctive and accurate attributes

	(a)	(b)	(c)
SCN	Generated captions: A woman standing in a kitchen preparing food Tags: person (0.99), food (0.91), indoor (0.85), table (0.58), woman (0.51), preparing (0.50), kitchen (0.42), small (0.35)	Generated captions: A group of people sitting at a table Tags: person (1.00), table (0.99), indoor (0.90), sitting (0.80), woman (0.76), man (0.57), front (0.46), group (0.36)	Generated captions: A group of people standing in front of a table Tags: indoor (0.83), table (0.63), standing (0.51), photo (0.49), computer (0.34), front (0.31), man (0.31), next (0.26)
DaE + SCN-LSTM	Generated captions: A woman cutting a piece of fruit with a knife Distinctive-attribute: cut (0.41), woman (0.28), knife (0.27), cake (0.18), fruit (0.14), food (0.13), kitchen (0.42), appl (0.11)	Generated captions: A group of people sitting at a table drinking wine Distinctive-attribute: wine (0.41), peopl (0.16), drink (0.13), tabl (0.12), woman (0.09), man (0.07), girl (0.07), group (0.06)	Generated captions: A room filled with lots of colorful decorations Distinctive-attribute: color (0.15), room (0.12), decor (0.11), hang (0.10), display (0.10), of (0.09), with (0.08), and (0.07)

displayed as they are. Scores in the right parentheses of the tags and distinctive-attributes have different meanings, the former is probabilities, and the latter is distinctiveness values of the words. The attributes extracted using DaE include important words to represent the situation in an image; as a result, the caption generated by using them are represented more in detail compared with those of SCN. The result of the proposed method in (a), "A woman cutting a piece of fruit with a knife" explains what the main character does exactly. In the SCN, the general word "food" get a high probability, on the other hand, DaE extracts more distinctive words such as "fruit" and "apple." For verbs, "cut", which is the most specific action that viewers would be interested in, gets high distinctiveness score. In the case of (b), "wine" and "drink" are chosen as the words with the first and the third highest distinctiveness through DaE. Therefore, the characteristic phrase "drinking wine" is added. More examples are in Appendix A.

4.3 Vocabulary Construction

To analyze DaE in more detail, we conduct experiments with differently constructed vocabularies. We set seven different IDF threshold values, th_{IDF}, from 5 to 11.

$$Vocab_i = \{w \mid IDF(w) > i, i = th_{IDF}\}. \tag{2}$$

The vocabulary contains only the words whose IDF is bigger than th_{IDF}. The number of vocabulary words is shown in the second row of Table 4(a) and (b). Semantic information of the images are extracted corresponding to this vocabulary, and we use them to learn the proposed prediction model. Widely used splits [12] of COCO datasets are applied for the evaluation. We evaluate the prediction considering it as a multi-label and multi-class classification problem. The distinctiveness score between 0 and 1 are divided into four classes; $(0.0, 0.25]$, $(0.25, 0.5]$, $(0.5, 0.75]$, and $(0.75, 1.0]$ and the macro-averaged F1 score is computed globally. The performance, of the prediction model is shown in the third row. Each extracted distinctive-attribute is fed into SCN-LSTM to generate a caption, and the evaluation result, CIDEr, is shown in the fourth row. The CIDErs increase from $Vocab_5$ to $Vocab_7$, and then monotonically decrease in the rest. In other words, the maximum performance is derived from $Vocab_7$ to 0.996. The vocabulary size and the prediction performance are in a trade-off in this experiment. With the high th_{IDF} value, captions can be generated with various vocabularies, but the captioning performance is not maximized because the performance of distinctive-attribute prediction is relatively low. $Vocab_6$ and $Vocab_9$ have almost the same CIDEr. In this case, If the vocabulary contains more words, it is possible to represent the captions more diversely and accurately for some images. Table 5 shows examples corresponding to this case. For the case of (a), the $Vocab_6$ does not include the stemmed word "carriag", but the $Vocab_9$ contains the word and is extracted as the word having the seventh highest value through DaE. The word led the phrase "pulling a carriage" to be included the caption, well describing the situation. "Tamac" in (b), and "microwav" in (c) plays a similar role.

Table 4(b) presents experimental results without stemming. The maximum value was 0.911, which is lower than the maximum value of the experiments applying stemming. When stemming is applied, the distinctiveness and significance of a word can be better expressed because it is mapped to the same word even if the tense and form are different. In addition, the size of vocabulary required to achieve the same performance is less when stemming is applied.

Table 4. Results of experiments with differently constructed vocabularies

	Vocab$_5$	Vocab$_6$	Vocab$_7$	Vocab$_8$	Vocab$_9$	Vocab$_{10}$	Vocab$_{11}$
(a) With stemming							
# of vocabulary	276	546	938	1660	2656	4009	**5530**
F1(DaE)	**0.432**	0.401	0.389	0.379	0.378	0.373	0.374
CIDEr(caption)	0.978	0.991	**0.996**	0.994	0.991	0.984	0.981
(b) Without stemming							
# of vocabulary	241	582	1121	2039	3572	5900	**8609**
F1(DaE)	**0.437**	0.399	0.383	0.374	0.366	0.362	0.358
CIDEr(caption)	0.955	0.989	**0.991**	0.986	0.990	0.988	0.979

Table 5. Several cases that more diverse and accurate captions are generated using $Vocab_9$ than using $Vocab_6$, although their CIDErs are similar

	(a)	(b)	(c)
Vocab$_6$	Generated captions: **A couple of people standing next to a horse** Distinctive-attribute: hors (0.58), pull (0.11), peopl (0.10), two (0.10), stand (0.07), field (0.07), of (0.07), in (0.06)	Generated captions: **A large air plane on a run way** Distinctive-attribute: airport (0.28), plane (0.26), air-plan (0.25), jet (0.22), park (0.13), runway (0.12), an (0.12), on (0.09)	Generated captions: **A toaster oven sitting on top of a counter** Distinctive-attribute: oven (0.51), counter (0.18), kitchen (0.13), on (0.06), of (0.06), top (0.06), an (0.05), in (0.05)
Vocab$_9$	Generated captions: **A couple of horses pulling a carriage in a field** Distinctive-attribute: horse (0.58), pull (0.17), peopl (0.10), two (0.08), of (0.07), in (0.07), **carriag** (0.06), stand (0.06)	Generated captions: **A large jetliner sitting on top of an airport tarmac** Distinctive-attribute: airport (0.30), airplan (0.28), plane (0.25), jet (0.18), runway (0.16), an (0.12), **tarmac** (0.12), park (0.09)	Generated captions: **A microwave oven sitting on top of a counter** Distinctive-attribute: oven (0.46), **microwav** (0.40), counter (0.14), kitchen (0.07), on (0.06), of (0.06), top (0.06), an (0.05)

5   Conclusion

In this study, we propose a Distinctive-attribute Extraction (DaE) method for image captioning. In particular, the TF-IDF scheme is used to extract meaningful information from the reference captions. Then the attribute prediction model is trained by the extracted information and used to infer the semantic-attribute for generating a description. DaE improves the performance of SCN-LSTM scheme by significant margins across all metrics; moreover, detailed and unique captions are generated. The proposed method can be plugged into various models to improve their performance.

Acknowledgement. This work was supported by IITP/MSIT [2017-0-00255, Autonomous digital companion framework and application].

A   Qualitative Evaluation of DaE

Table 6. This figure is an expansion in Table 3 which is the qualitative evaluation of the proposed method

	(a)	(b)	(c)
SCN	Generated captions: **A close up of a bowl of food** Tags: food (1.00), table (0.97), indoor (0.92), container (0.71), sitting (0.67), wooden (0.61), sauce (0.53), plate (0.53)	Generated captions: **A baseball player swinging a bat at a ball** Tags: grass (1.00), baseball (1.00), player (0.99), bat (0.97), person (0.95), game (0.95), sport (0.95), swinging (0.93)	Generated captions: **A close up of a plate of food on a table** Tags: food (1.00), plate (0.99), table (0.98), hot (0.43), sitting (0.35), small (0.29), fruit (0.24), filled (0.23)
DaE + SCN-LSTM	Generated captions: **Two plastic containers filled with different types of food** Distinctive-attribute: contain (0.34), food (0.22), **veget** (0.16), **and** (0.12), **broccoli** (0.11), dish (0.09), **meat** (0.08), of (0.09)	Generated captions: **A batter catcher and umpire during a baseball game** Distinctive-attribute: basebal (0.49), bat (0.32), player (0.18), **swing** (0.18), **catcher** (0.11), **umpir** (0.11), ball (0.10), **batter** (0.10)	Generated captions: **A white plate topped with a variety of vegetables** Distinctive-attribute: plate (0.48), **veget** (0.33), **carrot** (0.16), **salad** (0.16), **and** (0.13), food (0.10), on (0.09), with (0.09)
	(d)	(e)	(f)
SCN	Generated captions: **A dog is looking out of a fence** Tags: person (0.99), fence (0.87), building (0.65), window (0.61), looking (0.52), dog (0.47), standing (0.45), small (0.35)	Generated captions: **A fire hydrant spraying water from a fire hydrant** Tags: outdoor (0.99), orange (0.97), fire (0.83), water (0.76), hydrant (0.55), car (0.52), yellow (0.46), truck (0.44)	Generated captions: **A little boy is playing with a frisbee'** Tags: outdoor (1.00), grass (1.00), person (0.99), child (0.98), little (0.97), young (0.94), boy (0.93), small (0.85)
DaE + SCN-LSTM	Generated captions: **A person feeding a giraffe through a fence** Distinctive-attribute: **giraff** (0.40), **fenc** (0.25), **feed** (0.12), dog (0.10), out (0.07), look (0.06), in (0.05), is (0.05)	Generated captions: **A red truck driving down a snow covered road** Distinctive-attribute: truck (0.40), **snow** (0.19), orang (0.12), **drive** (0.11), car (0.09), the (0.09), toy (0.08), **red** (0.07)	Generated captions: **A small child sitting on the ground holding a banana** Distinctive-attribute: **banana** (0.35), boy (0.22), child (0.18), little (0.15), **hold** (0.12), young (0.11), skateboard (0.09), on (0.08)

(*continued*)

Table 6. (*continued*)

	(g)	(h)	(i)
SCN	Generated captions: **A man holding a nintendo wii game controller** Tags: person (1.0), indoor (0.99), holding (0.99), man (0.96), controller (0.91), remote (0.89), video (0.87)	Generated captions: **A close up of a sandwich on a plate** Tags: food (1.00), sandwich (1.00), cup (0.98), plate (0.94), dish (0.90), indoor (0.87), sitting (0.84), coffee (0.80)	Generated captions: **A close up of a cow in a field** Tags: outdoor (1.00), grass (0.97), cow (0.97), animal (0.95), mammal (0.93), standing (0.87), hay (0.79), brown (0.64)
DaE + SCN-LSTM	Generated captions: **A man is taking a picture of himself** Distinctive-attribute: **take** (0.35), man (0.27), **phone** (0.24), hold (0.20), hi (0.19), pictur (0.17), **camera** (0.15), cell (0.14)	Generated captions: **A sandwich cut in half on a plate** Distinctive-attribute: sandwich (0.70), plate (0.28), **cut** (0.16), **half** (0.13), and (0.11), on (0.10), with (0.09), fri (0.09)	Generated captions: **A bull is standing next to a tree** Distinctive-attribute: cow (0.27), stand (0.19), tree (0.13), in (0.09), **bull** (0.08), brown (0.08), the (0.06), field (0.06)
	(j)	(k)	(l)
SCN	Generated captions: **A large clock on the side of a building** Tags: building (0.99), outdoor (0.93), clock (0.85), front (0.70), sign (0.49), large (0.44), sitting (0.27), next (0.24)	Generated captions: **A man in a blue shirt is holding a sign** Tags: person (1.00), outdoor (1.00), man (0.99), sign (0.65), front (0.61), eating (0.55), holding (0.55), food (0.45)	Generated captions: **A close up of a cake on a plate** Tags: cake (1.00), food (0.96), plate (0.92), table (0.91), chocolate (0.86), indoor (0.86), decorated (0.85), top (0.83)
DaE + SCN-LSTM	Generated captions: **A store window with a clock on display** Distinctive-attribute: **store** (0.33), **window** (0.32), clock (0.31), **display** (0.30), **shop** (0.16), sign (0.10), of (0.09), front (0.07)	Generated captions: **A man wearing sunglasses standing next to a stop sign** Distinctive-attribute: sign (0.39), **stop** (0.23), man (0.21), wear (0.13), **sunglass** (0.12), stand (0.09), smile (0.08), in (0.06)	Generated captions: **A chocolate cake with white frosting on top** Distinctive-attribute: cake (0.42), chocol (0.41), plate (0.12), decor (0.12), on (0.11), **frost** (0.10), with (0.08), top (0.08)
	(m)	(n)	(o)
SCN	Generated captions: **A kitchen with green walls and green walls** Tags: green (1.00), indoor (1.00), window (0.89), sitting (0.70), small (0.69), room (0.43), table (0.42), painted (0.41)	Generated captions: **A man holding a cell phone in his hand** Tags: person (1.00), man (0.99), indoor (0.85), front (0.66), looking (0.58), photo (0.38), standing (0.35), holding (0.31)	Generated captions: **A cell phone sitting on top of a book** Tags: indoor (0.94), sitting (0.53), small (0.39), book (0.27), case (0.27), next (0.25), table (0.20), top (0.20)
DaE + SCN-LSTM	Generated captions: **A kitchen with a sink and a microwave** Distinctive-attribute: **microwav** (0.44), **kitchen** (0.43), counter (0.23), and (0.11), green (0.09), with (0.09), **sink** (0.09), oven (0.09)	Generated captions: **A man sitting in front of a computer monitor** Distinctive-attribute: **comput** (0.36), man (0.24), phone (0.17), desk (0.13), hi (0.12), at (0.12), **laptop** (0.09), sit (0.08)	Generated captions: **A close up of a pair of scissors** Distinctive-attribute: **scissor** (0.32), **pair** (0.13), phone (0.10), of (0.10), cell (0.07), and (0.06), on (0.06), book (0.05)

References

1. Banerjee, S., Lavie, A.: METEOR: an automatic metric for MT evaluation with improved correlation with human judgments. In: Proceedings of the ACL Workshop on Intrinsic and Extrinsic Evaluation Measures for Machine Translation and/or Summarization, pp. 65–72 (2005)
2. Chen, X., et al.: Microsoft COCO captions: data collection and evaluation server. arXiv preprint arXiv:1504.00325 (2015)
3. Chollet, F., et al.: Keras (2015). https://github.com/keras-team/keras
4. Dai, B., Lin, D.: Contrastive learning for image captioning. In: Advances in Neural Information Processing Systems, pp. 898–907 (2017)
5. Donahue, J., et al.: Long-term recurrent convolutional networks for visual recognition and description. In: Proceedings of IEEE Conference on Computer Vision and Pattern Recognition (CVPR), pp. 2625–2634 (2015)
6. Fang, H., et al.: From captions to visual concepts and back (2015)
7. Gan, Z.: Semantic compositional nets (2017). https://github.com/zhegan27/Semantic_Compositional_Nets
8. Gan, Z., et al.: Semantic compositional networks for visual captioning. In: Proceedings of IEEE Conference on Computer Vision and Pattern Recognition (CVPR), vol. 2 (2017)
9. Glorot, X., Bengio, Y.: Understanding the difficulty of training deep feedforward neural networks. In: Proceedings of 13th International Conference on Artificial Intelligence and Statistics, pp. 249–256 (2010)
10. He, K., Zhang, X., Ren, S., Sun, J.: Deep residual learning for image recognition. In: Proceedings of IEEE conference on Computer Vision and Pattern Recognition (CVPR), pp. 770–778 (2016)
11. Ioffe, S., Szegedy, C.: Batch normalization: accelerating deep network training by reducing internal covariate shift. In: International Conference on Machine Learning, pp. 448–456 (2015)
12. Karpathy, A., Fei-Fei, L.: Deep visual-semantic alignments for generating image descriptions. In: Proceedings of IEEE Conference on Computer Vision and Pattern Recognition (CVPR), pp. 3128–3137 (2015)
13. Kingma, D.P., Ba, J.: Adam: a method for stochastic optimization. arXiv preprint arXiv:1412.6980 (2014)
14. Lin, C.Y.: ROUGE: a package for automatic evaluation of summaries. Text Summarization Branches Out (2004)
15. Lin, T.Y., et al.: Microsoft COCO: common objects in context. In: Fleet, D., Pajdla, T., Schiele, B., Tuytelaars, T. (eds.) ECCV 2014. LNCS, vol. 8693, pp. 740–755. Springer, Cham (2014). https://doi.org/10.1007/978-3-319-10602-1_48
16. Lu, J., Xiong, C., Parikh, D., Socher, R.: Knowing when to look: adaptive attention via a visual sentinel for image captioning. In: Proceedings of the IEEE Conference on Computer Vision and Pattern Recognition (CVPR), vol. 6 (2017)
17. Nair, V., Hinton, G.E.: Rectified linear units improve restricted Boltzmann machines. In: Proceedings of 27th International Conference on Machine Learning (ICML), pp. 807–814 (2010)
18. Papineni, K., Roukos, S., Ward, T., Zhu, W.J.: BLEU: a method for automatic evaluation of machine translation. In: Proceedings of the 40th Annual Meeting on Association for Computational Linguistics, pp. 311–318. Association for Computational Linguistics (2002)

19. Pedregosa, F., et al.: Scikit-learn: machine learning in Python. J. Mach. Learn. Res. **12**(Oct), 2825–2830 (2011)
20. Porter, M.F.: An algorithm for suffix stripping. Program **14**(3), 130–137 (1980)
21. Vedantam, R., Lawrence Zitnick, C., Parikh, D.: CIDEr: consensus-based image description evaluation. In: Proceedings of IEEE Conference on Computer Vision and Pattern Recognition (CVPR), pp. 4566–4575 (2015)
22. Vinyals, O., Toshev, A., Bengio, S., Erhan, D.: Show and tell: a neural image caption generator. In: Proceedings of IEEE Conference on Computer Vision and Pattern Recognition (CVPR), pp. 3156–3164. IEEE (2015)
23. Wu, Q., Shen, C., Liu, L., Dick, A., van den Hengel, A.: What value do explicit high level concepts have in vision to language problems? In: Proceedings of IEEE Conference on Computer Vision and Pattern Recognition (CVPR), pp. 203–212 (2016)
24. Xu, K., et al.: Show, attend and tell: neural image caption generation with visual attention. In: International Conference on Machine Learning, pp. 2048–2057 (2015)
25. You, Q., Jin, H., Wang, Z., Fang, C., Luo, J.: Image captioning with semantic attention. In: Proceedings of IEEE Conference on Computer Vision and Pattern Recognition (CVPR), pp. 4651–4659 (2016)

Knowing Where to Look? Analysis on Attention of Visual Question Answering System

Wei Li[1,2], Zehuan Yuan[2(✉)], Xiangzhong Fang[1], and Changhu Wang[2]

[1] Shanghai Jiao Tong University, Shanghai, China
{liweihfyz,xzfang}@sjtu.edu.cn
[2] ByteDance AI Lab, Beijing, China
{levi.li,yuanzehuan,wangchanghu}@bytedance.com

Abstract. Attention mechanisms have been widely used in Visual Question Answering (VQA) solutions due to their capacity to model deep cross-domain interactions. Analyzing attention maps offers us a perspective to find out limitations of current VQA systems and an opportunity to further improve them. In this paper, we select two state-of-the-art VQA approaches with attention mechanisms to study their robustness and disadvantages by visualizing and analyzing their estimated attention maps. We find that both methods are sensitive to features, and simultaneously, they perform badly for counting and multi-object related questions. We believe that the findings and analytical method will help researchers identify crucial challenges on the way to improve their own VQA systems.

Keywords: Attention · Visual question answering

1 Introduction

Visual question answering (VQA) attracts increasing attentions in both computer vision and natural language processing community. The goal of VQA is to answer questions based on the information of any given image. As deep learning witnessed a series of remarkable success in artificial intelligence, VQA also made tremendous progress [1,6,15] over past few years such as several benchmark datasets, e.g., VQA 2.0 [2], CLEVR [4] and Visual Genome [7], and tons of approaches, e.g., MFB [15] and BAN [5].

VQA is usually formulated as a classification task with different answers as candidate categories. The current mainstream pipeline is to firstly extract image and question representations with Convolutional Neural Network and Recurrent Neural Network, respectively. Then, a lot of fusion methods such as early fusion [18] and bilinear pooling [1,5,6,15] are adopted to combine two-stream features.

W. Li—This work was done while the author was a research intern in ByteDance AI Lab.

L. Leal-Taixé and S. Roth (Eds.): ECCV 2018 Workshops, LNCS 11132, pp. 145–152, 2019.
https://doi.org/10.1007/978-3-030-11018-5_13

In addition, attention is playing an increasingly important role as the mechanism encourages deep cross-domain interactions without introducing substantial parameters. There are two main branches to add attention to VQA system: *uni-attention* and *co-attention*. *Uni-attention* merely considers question-guided visual attentions. In contrast, *co-attention* additionally takes image-guided question attentions into account to jointly model the multimodal correlations [5,9,10].

Although much progress has been made, few works lie on deep analysis on the influence of different attention mechanisms. In this paper, we dive into two state-of-the-art methods: multi-model factorized pooling (MFB) [15] and bilinear attention network (BAN) [5] to discover their inherent limitations. Both methods adopt the popular bilinear pooling to perform multimodal fusion. However, MFB only performs question-guided visual attention (*uni-attention*) while BAN extends *co-attention* into bilinear attention to enable more image and language interactions. We conduct all our experiments on VQA 2.0 dataset with a more balanced answer distribution than VQA 1.0 [16] and Visual Genome dataset. In addition, it covers more relations of real-world objects compared with CLEVR dataset full of synthetic images. In order to make a deeper understanding of both methods, we propose to directly delve into their attention maps. Observing whether estimated attentions relate to real answers could reflect the robustness and limitations of corresponding approaches.

To summarize, we present three key observations after thorough experiments on both approaches:

- The performance is sensitive to selected features. Representations based on object proposals are better than image-level features.
- Attention distribution becomes much more inaccurate for questions related to multiple objects.
- Counting problem is not well solved by soft attention mechanism.

In terms of each observation, we also analyze main reasons behind these phenomenons and claim that similar limitations probably exist in most of methods with attention mechanisms. We believe that these findings will inspire researchers to design more effective methods. Furthermore, our analytical method is hopeful to offer researchers an opportunity to identify potential roadblocks when debugging their VQA systems.

2   Multimodal Factorized Bilinear Pooling Revisited

Since bilinear pooling [12] allows abundant multimodal cross-channel interactions, the fusion method has been widely used in VQA systems compared to simple summation and concatenation operators. To further reduce the number of parameters in bilinear pooling, multimodal factorized bilinear Pooling (MFB) [15] decomposes the weight matrix as two low-rank matrices.

Specifically, given a question vector $x \in \mathbb{R}^m$ and an image feature vector $y \in \mathbb{R}^n$, each output channel of MFB pooling is formulated as:

$$\text{pool}(x, y)_i = x^T \mathbf{W}_i y + b_i = x^T \mathbf{U}_i \mathbf{V}_i^T y + b_i = \mathbb{I}(\mathbf{U}_i^T x \circ \mathbf{V}_i^T y) + b_i \qquad (1)$$

where $\mathbb{I} \in \mathbb{R}^k$ is a vector of all elements ones, $\mathbf{W}_i \in \mathbb{R}^{m \times n}$ is the weight matrix and $\mathbf{U}_i \in \mathbb{R}^{m \times k}$ and $V_i \in \mathbb{R}^{n \times k}$ are two factorized matrices.

The whole pipeline of MFB for VQA can be summarized as follows. First, an overall question representation $\hat{x} \in \mathbb{R}^m$ is obtained by a *self-attention* manner with weights α^x. Then, the weighted question feature guilds the visual attention on the image as follows:

$$\alpha^y = softmax(\{\mathbf{W}_p^T \text{pool}(\hat{x}, y_j)\}), \hat{y} = \sum_j \alpha_j^y y_j \qquad (2)$$

where y_j is an image feature vector and $\mathbf{W}_p \in \mathbb{R}^{m \times 1}$. Finally, attention weighted language feature $\hat{x}$ and visual feature $\hat{y}$ are fused together as $f = \text{pool}(\hat{x}, \hat{y})$ for further prediction.

3 Bilinear Attention Revisited

Co-attention based model jointly integrates question-guided visual attention and visual-guided question attention together. To further consider every pair of multimodal features, BAN [5] extends co-attention into bilinear attention. The fused feature can be defineds as:

$$f_i = (\mathbf{X}^T \tilde{\mathbf{U}})_i^T A(\mathbf{Y}^T \tilde{\mathbf{V}})_i \qquad (3)$$

where $\tilde{\mathbf{U}} \in \mathbb{R}^{m \times k}$, $\tilde{\mathbf{V}} \in \mathbb{R}^{n \times k}$, $\mathbf{X} \in \mathbb{R}^{m \times \theta}$, $\mathbf{Y} \in \mathbb{R}^{n \times \gamma}$, and $A \in \mathbb{R}^{\theta \times \gamma}$ is the bilinear attention map that sums to 1 as follows:

$$A = softmax((\mathbb{I} \cdot p^T) \circ X^T \mathbf{U})\mathbf{V}^T Y) \qquad (4)$$

where $\mathbb{I} \in \mathbb{R}^\theta$ is a vector with all elements ones, $p \in \mathbb{R}^k$, and $softmax$ is applied element-wisely. Then the fused feature f can be used for further classification.

MFB and BAN represent popular attempts in *uni-attention* and *co-attention* directions, respectively. A thorough analysis for both methods is also expected to shed light on similar limitations of other approaches with attention mechanisms.

4 Deep Study

In this section, we will present detailed analysis for our key observation results. As shown above, we investigate MFB [15] and BAN [5] to make a thorough study. All experiments are conducted on VQA2.0 benchmark, where we train on *train* split with 82,783 images and 443,757 questions, and evaluate on *val* split with 40,503 images and 214,354 questions totally. Each question is annotated with 10 answers by crowdsourcing. In order to give an intuitive demonstration, we report visualizations of image attention vectors α^y in MFB and the bilinear attention maps A in BAN.

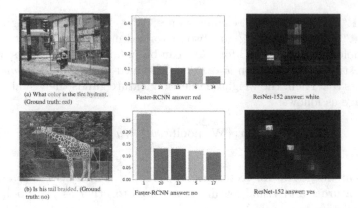

(a) What color is the fire hydrant. (Ground truth: red)   Faster-RCNN answer: red   ResNet-152 answer: white

(b) Is his tail braided. (Ground truth: no)   Faster-RCNN answer: no   ResNet-152 answer: yes

Fig. 1. Visualization of MFB with different visual features. From left to right are the original images, the MFB attention weights of Faster-RCNN proposals and the MFB attention map of the ResNet-152 feature map. The most salient boxes (numbered in the top-left corner of each bounding box and x-axis of the grids) are visualized in both images.

4.1 Object Feature and Image Feature

Visual object features have been proven effective in VQA task [5,13] compared with image-level features. However, the reason behind the performance gain has not been well investigated. In this work, we delve deeper into this from the attention perspective.

In our experiments, we select top-36 Faster-RCNN proposals [11] and ResNet-152 last feature map before *pool5* [3] as object features ($36 \times 2{,}048$) and image features ($196 \times 2{,}048$), respectively. We set the batch size to 64 and the dimension of hidden states to 1024 in BAN. To simplify experiments, we do not integrate counting module [17]. Unlike the original implementation, we augment 300-dimensional random initialized word embedding instead of 300-dimensional computed word embedding to each 300-dimensional Glove word embedding. The performance comparison on the VQA 2.0 validation set is shown in Table 1. Unsurprisingly, we achieve better performance with object features for both methods compared with image-level features. In addition, we found that a more accurate attention distribution can be obtained for object features compared with image features. For example in Fig. 1, given a question about fire hydrant, we can see that MFB with object proposals focuses on the correct entity while image-level representation directs attentions to snow regions. Due to the inaccurate attention distribution, the model with image features predicts a wrong answer, *white*. Similarly when **"Is his tail braided?"** is asked, the tail proposal is highlighted for the method with object-level representations as opposed to arbitrary emphasis with a single feature map.

Although it is difficult to measure the negative effect of features quantitatively on attention maps over the entire dataset, we hypothesize that inaccurate attention maps take a large amount of responsibility for decline in performance.

Table 1. Detailed performance comparison on VQA 2.0 validation set

Feature type	Methods	Overall	Other	Number	Yes/No
ResNet-152 feature map	MFB [15]	60.94	52.93	38.48	79.28
	BAN [5]	59.52	51.19	38.92	77.64
Faster-RCNN proposals	MFB [15]	65.19	57.17	44.37	82.98
	BAN [5]	64.3	55.7	45.45	82.16

We analyse that object proposals have much more specific semantic meanings compared with feature maps and thus the corresponding relations between words and visual features are easier to learn, which leads to a more accurate attention distribution and further performance boost.

4.2 Single Object and Multiple Objects

Based on how many objects are necessary to infer final answers, questions in VQA2.0 can be roughly divided into single object, e.g., "what is the color of the dog?" and multiple objects, e.g.,"what color is the book on the desk?". In our experiment, we conduct the comparison for both kinds of questions. The observation shows that the attention distribution is much more inaccurate for questions related to multiple objects. For example in Fig. 2, both models incorrectly focus on the laptop used by the woman in (a), which implies that the relation between the woman and the laptop are not well captured and modeled. Additionally, relative positions are not well integrated by both models. We can see in Fig. 2, both models make predictions (*white* and *yellow*) based on the person on the left and the person on the middle respectively in (b). In a word, the estimated attention maps cannot learn relative positions. Moreover, spatial locations are crucial to infer the *what* question in (c). Both models concentrate on the wrong objects in other positions, e.g., sink and toilet.

It is worth noting that current attention mechanisms learn attention distributions by only comparing visual and question representations and object features ignore their own locations in images.

However, without well-captured object relations or position information, models are unable to set these visually or semantically similar objects apart when the questions are related to multiple objects or multiple instances exist in an image. The confusion causes an inaccurate attention distribution which leads to a significant accuracy drop between single-object questions and those with multiple objects, which constitutes the main hurdle for current VQA systems.

In order to reduce the performance gap, it could be a crucial step to explicitly consider object relation and position. In particular, graph-based neural networks might be an effective way to handle unstructured object correlations [8,14]. Object relations modeling is still an open question and worth further explorations.

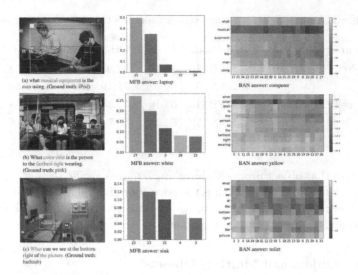

Fig. 2. Visualization of MFB and BAN on questions related to multiple objects. From left to right are the original images, MFB attention vectors and BAN bilinear attention maps. The most salient boxes (numbered in the top-left corner of each bounding box and x-axis of the grids) are visualized in both images. (Color figure online)

4.3   Counting Problem

Counting problem is a special case of questions related to multiple objects. As mentioned in [17], due to that soft-attention mechanism normalizes the attention weights, which leads to the loss of counting-related information. Soft attention is replaced by the gate strategy in [17] and then overlapping object proposals are processed in a differentiable manner.

In this work, we show that poor results can also be obtained even with an accurate attention distribution. For example in Fig. 3, both models focus their attention on multiple detected objects, namely, motorcycles in (a), vehicles in (b) and clocks in (c). However, detected objects are obviously visually similar and thus the weighted average of these visual features is probably similar to one of them, which means cues for counting are lost during soft attention process regardless of attention distributions. The limitations probably exist in a large amount of VQA systems. Therefore, in order to improve the counting performance essentially, additional structures or more flexible attention mechanisms might be needed.

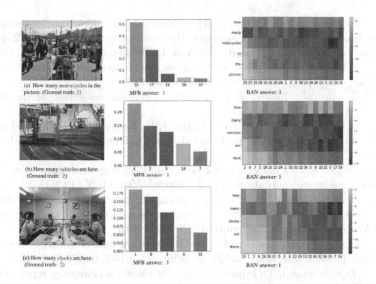

Fig. 3. Visualization of MFB and BAN on counting problems. From left to right are the original images, MFB attention vectors and BAN bilinear attention maps. The most salient boxes (numbered in the top-left corner of each bounding box and x-axis of the grids) are visualized in both images. Both models give the wrong answer, 1.

5 Conclusions

To facilitate further research on the VQA task, we delve into two state-of-the-art methods MFB [15] and BAN [5] on VQA 2.0 dataset by visualizing and analysing their estimated attention maps. We form three main observations. Firstly, the performance improvement with Faster-RCNN proposals is probably related to a more accurate attention distribution. Second, the attention distribution is much more inaccurate for questions related to multiple objects. Finally, counting problem is not well solved by soft attention mechanism due to the attention weight normalization. We believe that these observation results can help future VQA research and analysing attention maps will also assist researchers to debug their own VQA systems.

References

1. Fukui, A., Park, D.H., Yang, D., Rohrbach, A., Darrell, T., Rohrbach, M.: Multi-modal compact bilinear pooling for visual question answering and visual grounding. In: Conference on Empirical Methods in Natural Language Processing (EMNLP) (2016)
2. Goyal, Y., Khot, T., Summers-Stay, D., Batra, D., Parikh, D.: Making the V in VQA matter: elevating the role of image understanding in visual question answering. In: Conference on Computer Vision and Pattern Recognition (CVPR) (2017)

3. He, K., Zhang, X., Ren, S., Sun, J.: Deep residual learning for image recognition. In: Conference on Computer Vision and Pattern Recognition (CVPR) (2016)
4. Johnson, J., Hariharan, B., van der Maaten, L., Fei-Fei, L., Zitnick, C.L., Girshick, R.: CLEVR: a diagnostic dataset for compositional language and elementary visual reasoning. arXiv preprint arXiv:1612.06890 (2016)
5. Kim, J.H., Jun, J., Zhang, B.T.: Bilinear attention networks. arXiv preprint arXiv:1805.07932 (2018)
6. Kim, J.H., On, K.W., Lim, W., Kim, J., Ha, J.W., Zhang, B.T.: Hadamard product for low-rank bilinear pooling. In: International Conference on Learning Representations (ICLR) (2017)
7. Krishna, R., et al.: Visual genome: connecting language and vision using crowd-sourced dense image annotations. Int. J. Comput. Vis. (IJCV) **123**(1), 32–73 (2017)
8. Liu, Y., Wang, R., Shan, S., Chen, X.: Structure inference net: object detection using scene-level context and instance-level relationships. In: Conference on Computer Vision and Pattern Recognition (CVPR) (2018)
9. Lu, J., Yang, J., Batra, D., Parikh, D.: Hierarchical question-image co-attention for visual question answering. arXiv preprint arXiv:1606.00061 (2016)
10. Nguyen, D.K., Okatani, T.: Improved fusion of visual and language representations by dense symmetric co-attention for visual question answering. In: Conference on Computer Vision and Pattern Recognition (CVPR) (2018)
11. Ren, S., He, K., Girshick, R., Sun, J.: Faster R-CNN: towards real-time object detection with region proposal networks. In: Advances in Neural Information Processing Systems (NIPS) (2015)
12. Tenenbaum, J.B., Freeman, W.T.: Separating style and content. In: Advances in Neural Information Processing Systems (NIPS) (1997)
13. Teney, D., Anderson, P., He, X., van den Hengel, A.: Tips and tricks for visual question answering: learnings from the 2017 challenge. In: Conference on Computer Vision and Pattern Recognition (CVPR) (2018)
14. Xu, D., Zhu, Y., Choy, C., Fei-Fei, L.: Scene graph generation by iterative message passing. In: Conference on Computer Vision and Pattern Recognition (CVPR) (2017)
15. Yu, Z., Yu, J., Xiang, C., Fan, J., Tao, D.: Beyond bilinear: generalized multimodal factorized high-order pooling for visual question answering. IEEE Trans. Neural Netw. Learn. Syst. **99**, 1–13 (2018)
16. Zhang, P., Goyal, Y., Summers-Stay, D., Batra, D., Parikh, D.: Yin and Yang: balancing and answering binary visual questions. In: Conference on Computer Vision and Pattern Recognition (CVPR) (2016)
17. Zhang, Y., Hare, J., Prügel-Bennett, A.: Learning to count objects in natural images for visual question answering. In: International Conference on Learning Representations (ICLR) (2018)
18. Zhou, B., Tian, Y., Sukhbaatar, S., Szlam, A., Fergus, R.: Simple baseline for visual question answering. arXiv preprint arXiv:1512.02167 (2015)

Knowing When to Look for What and Where: Evaluating Generation of Spatial Descriptions with Adaptive Attention

Mehdi Ghanimifard$^{(\boxtimes)}$ and Simon Dobnik

Centre for Linguistic Theory and Studies in Probability (CLASP),
Department of Philosophy, Linguistics and Theory of Science,
University of Gothenburg, Box 200, 405 30 Gothenburg, Sweden
{mehdi.ghanimifard,simon.dobnik}@gu.se

Abstract. We examine and evaluate adaptive attention [17] (which balances the focus on visual features and focus on textual features) in generating image captions in end-to-end neural networks, in particular how adaptive attention is informative for generating spatial relations. We show that the model generates spatial relations more on the basis of textual rather than visual features and therefore confirm the previous observations that the learned visual features are missing information about geometric relations between objects.

Keywords: Image descriptions · Grounded neural language model
Attention model · Spatial descriptions

1 Introduction

End-to-end neural networks are commonly used in image description tasks [17,28,29]. Typically, a pre-trained convolutional neural network is used as an encoder which produces visual features, and a neural language model is used as a decoder that generates descriptions of scenes. The underlying idea in this *representation learning* scenario [5] is that hidden features are learned from the observable data with minimum engineering effort of background knowledge. For example in word sequence generation only some general properties of a sequence structure [26] are given to the learner while the learner learns from the observed data what word to choose in a sequence together with a representation of features. Recent models such as [17,29] also add to the neural language model a model of visual attention over visual features which is inspired by the attention mechanism for alignment in neural machine translation [4]. It may be argued

Electronic supplementary material The online version of this chapter (https:// doi.org/10.1007/978-3-030-11018-5_14) contains supplementary material, which is available to authorized users.

L. Leal-Taixé and S. Roth (Eds.): ECCV 2018 Workshops, LNCS 11132, pp. 153–161, 2019.
https://doi.org/10.1007/978-3-030-11018-5_14

that the attention mechanism introduces modularity to representation learning in the sense of *inception modules* [27] and *neural module networks* [2]. The visual attention is intended to detect the salient features of the image and align them with words predicted by the decoder. In particular, it creates a sum of the weighted final visual features at different regions of an image:

$$c_t = \sum_{i=1}^{k} \alpha_{ti} v_i \tag{1}$$

where at time t, c_t represents the pooled visual features, i corresponds to k different regions of image, v_i is the visual representation of a particular region, and α_{ti} represent the amount of attention on the specific region of the image. This representation provides the features for grounding the prediction of next word:

$$logPr(w_{t+1} = y_{t+1}|w_{1:t} = y_{1:t}, I = v_{1:k}) \approx f(y_{1:t}, c_t) \tag{2}$$

where f represents the end-to-end neural network for approximating the prediction of the next word in sentence.

However, not all words in natural language descriptions are directly grounded in visual features which leads [17] to extend the attention model [29] with an adaptive attention mechanism which learns to balance between the contribution of the visual signal and the language signal when generating a sequence of words.

$$\hat{c}_t = \beta_t s_t + (1 - \beta_t) c_t \tag{3}$$

where at time t, $\hat{c}_t$ is a combined representation of language features and visual features in addition to c_t of the visual features from Eq. 2. s_t is obtained from the memory state of the language model, and β_t ranging between $[0, 1]$ is the adaptive attention balancing the combination of vision and language features.

The performance of the image captioning systems when evaluated on the acceptability of the generated descriptions is impressive. However, in order to evaluate the success of learning we also need to understand better what the system has learned especially because good overall results may be due to the dataset artefacts or the system is simply learning from one modality only, ignoring the other [1]. Understanding the representations that have been learned also gives us an insight into building better systems for image captioning, especially since we do not have a clear understanding of the features in the domain. An example of work in this area is [15] which evaluates visual attention on objects localisation. [25] developed the FOIL dataset as a diagnostic tool to investigate if models look at images in caption generation. In [24] they examine the FOIL diagnostic for different parts-of-speech and conclude that the state of the art models can locate objects but their language models do not perform well on other parts-of-speech.

The current paper focuses on generation of spatial descriptions, in particular locative expressions such as "the chair to the left of the sofa" or "people close to the statue in the square". Spatial relations relate a target ("people") and landmark objects ("the statue") with a spatial relation ("close to"). They depend on several contextual sources of information such as scene geometry ("where" objects are in relation to each other), properties or function of objects and their interaction ("what" is related) as well as the interaction between conversational participants [8,10,11,13,21]. The features that are relevant in computational modelling of spatial language are difficult to determine simply by manually considering individual examples and they are normally identified through experimental work. The representation learning models are therefore particularly suited for their computational modelling.

However, the end-to-end vision and language models with attention are implemented in a way to recognise objects and localise their area in an image [3,18]. To generate spatial relations, [20] propose a combination of visual representations from convolutional neural networks and manually designed geometric representation of targets and landmarks. On quick examination, the representation of attention over images as in [29] gives an impression that attention captures both "what" and "where", especially because the attention graphs resemble *spatial templates* [16]. However, [12] argue that due to the design properties of image captioning networks, attention does not capture "where" as these models are built to identify objects but not geometric relations between them which they examine at the level of qualitative evaluation of attention on spatial relations.

In this paper we quantitatively evaluate the model of adaptive attention of [17] in predicting spatial relations in image descriptions. The resources used in our evaluation are described in Sect. 2. In Sect. 3 we examine the grounding of different parts-of-speech in visual and textual part of attention. Furthermore, in Sect. 4 we investigate the attention on spatial relations, targets and landmarks. We conclude by providing the possible directions for future studies and improvements.

2   Datasets and Pre-trained Models

As a part of their implementation [17] provide two different pre-trained image captioning models: Flickr30K [30] and MS-COCO [14].[1] We base our experiments on spatial descriptions of 40,736 images in the MS-COCO test corpus.

3   Visual Attention and Word Categories

Hypothesis. Our hypothesis is that visual attention in the end-to-end image captioning systems works as an object detector similar to [3,18]. Therefore, we expect the adaptive attention to prefer to attend to visual features rather than the language model features when predicting categories of words found in noun phrases that refer to objects, in particular head nouns. We expect that both scores will be reversed: more predictable words by the language model in the blind test receive less visual attention.

---

[1] https://filebox.ece.vt.edu/~jiasenlu/codeRelease/AdaptiveAttention.

Method. We use the pre-trained model of adaptive attention[2] to generate a description for each of the 40,736 images in the MS-COCO-2014 test. All the attention values are logged (α, β). We apply universal part-of-speech tagger from NLTK [6] on the generated sentences and report the average visual attentions on each part-of-speech. We match our results with results on the degree of predictability of each part-of-speech from the language model without looking at the image from the blind test of [24]. Note that we do not investigate the overall quality of the model on the test set (this has already been evaluated by its authors) but what kind of attention this model gives to vision and language features used to generate a word of each category. The evaluation code: https:// github.com/GU-CLASP/eccv18-sivl-attention.

Results. Table 1 indicates that the highest degree of visual attentions is on numbers (NUM), nouns (NOUN), adjectives (ADJ) and determiners (DET) respectively. Pronouns (PRON) and particles (PRT) receive the lowest degree of visual attention. Verbs (VERB) and adverbs (ADV) are placed in the middle of this sorted list. Spatial relations which are mainly annotated as prepositions/adpositions (ADP) receive the second lowest visual attention, higher only than pronouns (PRON) and particles (PRT). Our results are different from the accuracy scores of detecting mismatch descriptions in the FOIL classification task [24]. For example, the model assigns predicts the mismatch on ADJ easier than mismatch on ADV. As hypothesised, the part-of-speech that make up noun phrases receive the highest visual attention (and the lowest language model attention). The results also indicate that the text is never generated by a single attention alone but a combination of visual and language model attentions. Since some spatial relations are often annotated as adjectives (e.g. "front"), a more detailed comparison on spatial terms is required.

4   Visual Attention When Grounding Spatial Descriptions

In generation of a sequence of words that make up a spatial description, which type of features or evidence is taken into consideration by the model as the description unfolds?

Hypothesis. In Sect. 3, we argued that the generation of spatial relations (prepositions/adpositions) is less dependent on visual features compared to noun phrases due to the fact that the learned visual features are used for object recognition and not recognition of geometric spatial relations between objects. Moreover, the visual clues that would predict the choice of spatial relation are not in one specific region of an image; this is dependent on the location of the target, the landmark and the configuration of the environment as a whole. Therefore, our hypothesis is that when generating spatial relations the visual attention is more spread over possible regions rather than being focused on a specific object.

---

[2] https://filebox.ece.vt.edu/~jiasenlu/codeRelease/AdaptiveAttention/model/ COCO/coco_challenge/model_id1_34.t7.

Table 1. The average visual attention $(1 - \beta)$ for predicting words on each part-of-speech. The scores from the blind test indicate the accuracy of detecting a mismatch description in the FOIL-classification task [24].

POS	Count	Mean $\pm$ std	Blind test
NUM	1882	0.81 ± 0.08	-
NOUN	134332	0.78 ± 0.12	0.23
ADJ	23670	0.77 ± 0.14	0.76
DET	96641	0.73 ± 0.12	-
VERB	38381	0.70 ± 0.11	0.57
CONJ	6755	0.70 ± 0.13	-
ADV	184	0.69 ± 0.12	0.18
ADP	64332	0.62 ± 0.15	0.54
PRON	2347	0.53 ± 0.14	-
PRT	6462	0.52 ± 0.21	-

Method. The corpus tagged with POS from the previous section was used. In order to examine the attention on spatial relations, a list of keywords from [11,13] was used to identify them, provided that they have a sufficient frequency in the corpus. The average adaptive visual attention for each word can be compared with the scores in Table 1 for different parts-of-speech. In each sentence, the nouns before the spatial relation and the nouns after the spatial relations are taken as the most likely targets and landmarks respectively. The average adaptive visual attention on targets, landmarks and spatial relations is recorded.

Results. In Table 2 we report for each spatial relation and its targets and landmarks the average adaptive visual attention. The adaptive attentions for triplets are comparable with the figures for each part-of-speech in Table 1. In the current table, the variance of visual attentions is reported with the $max - min$ measure which is the difference between maximum and minimum attentions on a 7×7 plane representing the visual regions in the model. Lower values indicate either a low attention or a wider spread of attended area, hence less visual focus. Higher values indicate that there is more visual focus. For each spatial relation, the triplets must be compared with each other. In all cases, our hypothesis is confirmed: (1) the adaptive visual attention is lower on predicting spatial relations which means that they receive overall less visual attention, (2) with the exception of "under", the difference between maximum and minimum visual attentions are lower with spatial relations which means that the attention is spread more over the 7×7 plane. Figure 1 shows a visualisation of these results for "under" and "over". The results also show that landmarks in most cases receive less visual attention in comparison to targets. This indicates that after providing a target and a spatial relation, the landmark is more predictable from the language model (for a similar observation see [9]).

Table 2. The average score of adaptive visual attention for target (TRG) relation (REL) landmark (LND) triplets per each relation in the first column and the average difference between the highest and the lowest value of visual attention for the same items in the second column.

Descriptions Spatial relations	Average $(1 - \beta_t)$ TRG, REL, LND	Average $(max(\hat{\alpha}_t) - min(\hat{\alpha}_t))$ TRG, REL, LND
Under	0.84, **0.73**, 0.79	0.0252, 0.0151, **0.0139**
Front	0.83, **0.70**, 0.82	0.0230, **0.0136**, 0.0154
Next	0.82, **0.68**, 0.78	0.0224, **0.0136**, 0.0138
Back	0.85, **0.68**, 0.84	0.0332, **0.0186**, 0.0272
In	0.82, **0.68**, 0.77	0.0250, **0.0149**, 0.0164
On	0.81, **0.68**, 0.75	0.0249, **0.0154**, 0.0175
Near	0.80, **0.67**, 0.76	0.0221, **0.0133**, 0.0169
Over	0.77, **0.62**, 0.75	0.0205, **0.0133**, 0.0193
Above	0.73, **0.64**, 0.77	0.0167, **0.0134**, 0.0231

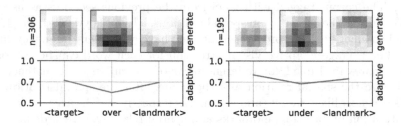

Fig. 1. Each square in a box in the first row represents an averaged attention for a location in the 7×7 grid over all n generated samples ($\hat{\alpha}$). The colours fade to white with lower values. The bottom graphs show their average over the entire plane, indicating the degree of adaptive visual attention $(1 - \beta)$, also reported in Table 2.

5   Discussion and Conclusion

In this paper we explored to what degree adaptive attention is grounding spatial relations. We have shown that adaptive visual attention is more important for grounding objects but less important for grounding spatial relations which are not directly represented with visual features. As a result the visual attention is diffused over a larger space. The cause for a wider attended area can be due to high degree of noise in visual features or lack of evidence for visual grounding.

This is a clear shortcoming of the image captioning model, as it is not able to discriminate spatial relations on the basis of geometric relations between the objects, for example between relations such as "left" and "right". The future work on generating image descriptions therefore requires models where visual geometry between objects is explicitly represented as in [7]. The study also shows that when generating spatial relations, a significant part of the information is predicted by the language model. This is not necessarily a disadvantage. The success of distributional semantics shows that language models with word embeddings can learn a surprising amount of semantic information without access to visual grounding. As mentioned in the introduction, spatial relations do not depend only on geometric arrangement of objects but also functional properties of objects. For example, [9] demonstrate that neural language models encode such functional information about objects when predicting spatial relations. Since, each spatial relation has different degree of functional and geometric bias [8], the adaptive attention considering visual features and textual features is also reflective of this aspect.

Models for explaining language model predictions such as [19] are also related to this study and its future work.

Our study focused on the adaptive attention in [17] which explicitly models attention as a focus on visual and language features. However, further investigations of other types of models of attention could be made and this will be the focus of our future work. We expect that different models of attention will behave similarly in terms of attending visual features on spatial relations because the way visual features are represented: they favour detection of objects and not their relative geometric arrangement. Our future work we will therefore focus on how to formulate a model to be able to learn such geometric information in an end-to-end fashion. Methodologies such as [22] and [23] which investigate the degree of effectiveness of features without attention are also possible directions of the future studies.

Acknowledgements. We are also grateful to the anonymous reviewers for their helpful comments on our earlier draft. The research reported in this paper was supported by a grant from the Swedish Research Council (VR project 2014-39) for the establishment of the Centre for Linguistic Theory and Studies in Probability (CLASP) at the University of Gothenburg.

References

1. Agrawal, A., Batra, D., Parikh, D., Kembhavi, A.: Don't just assume; look and answer: overcoming priors for visual question answering. In: Proceedings of the IEEE Conference on Computer Vision and Pattern Recognition, pp. 4971–4980 (2018)
2. Andreas, J., Rohrbach, M., Darrell, T., Klein, D.: Neural module networks. In: Proceedings of the IEEE Conference on Computer Vision and Pattern Recognition, pp. 39–48 (2016)
3. Ba, J., Mnih, V., Kavukcuoglu, K.: Multiple object recognition with visual attention. arXiv preprint arXiv:1412.7755 (2014)
4. Bahdanau, D., Cho, K., Bengio, Y.: Neural machine translation by jointly learning to align and translate. arXiv preprint arXiv:1409.0473 (2014)
5. Bengio, Y., Courville, A., Vincent, P.: Representation learning: a review and new perspectives. IEEE Trans. Pattern Anal. Mach. Intell. **35**(8), 1798–1828 (2013)

6. Bird, S., Klein, E., Loper, E.: Natural Language Processing with Python: Analyzing Text with the Natural Language Toolkit. O'Reilly Media Inc., Sebastopol (2009)
7. Coventry, K.R., et al.: Spatial prepositions and vague quantifiers: implementing the functional geometric framework. In: Freksa, C., Knauff, M., Krieg-Brückner, B., Nebel, B., Barkowsky, T. (eds.) Spatial Cognition 2004. LNCS (LNAI), vol. 3343, pp. 98–110. Springer, Heidelberg (2005). https://doi.org/10.1007/978-3-540-32255-9_6
8. Coventry, K.R., Garrod, S.C.: Saying, Seeing, and Acting: The Psychological Semantics of Spatial Prepositions. Psychology Press, Hove (2004)
9. Dobnik, S., Ghanimifard, M., Kelleher, J.D.: Exploring the functional and geometric bias of spatial relations using neural language models. In: Proceedings of the First International Workshop on Spatial Language Understanding (SpLU 2018) at NAACL-HLT 2018, pp. 1–11. Association for Computational Linguistics, New Orleans, 6 June 2018
10. Dobnik, S., Kelleher, J.D.: Modular networks: an approach to the top-down versus bottom-up dilemma in natural language processing. In: Forthcoming in Post-proceedings of the Conference on Logic and Machine Learning in Natural Language (LaML), vol. 1, no. 1, pp. 1–8, 12–14 June 2017
11. Herskovits, A.: Language and Spatial Cognition: An Interdisciplinary Study of the Prepositions in English. Cambridge University Press, Cambridge (1986)
12. Kelleher, J.D., Dobnik, S.: What is not where: the challenge of integrating spatial representations into deep learning architectures. CLASP Papers in Computational Linguistics, p. 41 (2017)
13. Landau, B., Jackendoff, R.: "what" and "where" in spatial language and spatial cognition. Behav. Brain Sci. **16**(2), 217–238, 255–265 (1993)
14. Lin, T.-Y., et al.: Microsoft COCO: common objects in context. In: Fleet, D., Pajdla, T., Schiele, B., Tuytelaars, T. (eds.) ECCV 2014. LNCS, vol. 8693, pp. 740–755. Springer, Cham (2014). https://doi.org/10.1007/978-3-319-10602-1_48
15. Liu, C., Mao, J., Sha, F., Yuille, A.L.: Attention correctness in neural image captioning. In: AAAI, pp. 4176–4182 (2017)
16. Logan, G.D., Sadler, D.D.: A computational analysis of the apprehension of spatial relations. In: Bloom, P., Peterson, M.A., Nadel, L., Garrett, M.F. (eds.) Language and Space, pp. 493–530. MIT Press, Cambridge (1996)
17. Lu, J., Xiong, C., Parikh, D., Socher, R.: Knowing when to look: adaptive attention via a visual sentinel for image captioning. In: Proceedings of the IEEE Conference on Computer Vision and Pattern Recognition (CVPR), vol. 6 (2017)
18. Mnih, V., Heess, N., Graves, A., et al.: Recurrent models of visual attention. In: Advances in Neural Information Processing Systems, pp. 2204–2212 (2014)
19. Park, D.H., Hendricks, L.A., Akata, Z., Schiele, B., Darrell, T., Rohrbach, M.: Attentive explanations: justifying decisions and pointing to the evidence. arXiv preprint arXiv:1612.04757 (2016)
20. Ramisa, A., Wang, J., Lu, Y., Dellandrea, E., Moreno-Noguer, F., Gaizauskas, R.: Combining geometric, textual and visual features for predicting prepositions in image descriptions. In: Proceedings of the 2015 Conference on Empirical Methods in Natural Language Processing, pp. 214–220 (2015)
21. Regier, T.: The Human Semantic Potential: Spatial Language and Constrained Connectionism. MIT Press, Cambridge (1996)
22. Ribeiro, M.T., Singh, S., Guestrin, C.: Why should i trust you?: explaining the predictions of any classifier. In: Proceedings of the 22nd ACM SIGKDD International Conference on Knowledge Discovery and Data Mining, pp. 1135–1144. ACM (2016)

23. Selvaraju, R.R., Cogswell, M., Das, A., Vedantam, R., Parikh, D., Batra, D., et al.: Grad-CAM: visual explanations from deep networks via gradient-based localization. In: ICCV, pp. 618–626 (2017)
24. Shekhar, R., Pezzelle, S., Herbelot, A., Nabi, M., Sangineto, E., Bernardi, R.: Vision and language integration: moving beyond objects. In: IWCS 2017–12th International Conference on Computational Semantics–Short papers (2017)
25. Shekhar, R., et al.: FOIL it! find one mismatch between image and language caption. In: Proceedings of the 55th Annual Meeting of the Association for Computational Linguistics (ACL) (Long Papers), vol. 1, pp. 255–265 (2017)
26. Sutskever, I., Vinyals, O., Le, Q.V.: Sequence to sequence learning with neural networks. In: Advances in Neural Information Processing Systems, pp. 3104–3112 (2014)
27. Szegedy, C., et al.: Going deeper with convolutions. In: Proceedings of the IEEE Conference on Computer Vision and Pattern Recognition, pp. 1–9 (2015)
28. Vinyals, O., Toshev, A., Bengio, S., Erhan, D.: Show and tell: a neural image caption generator. In: 2015 IEEE Conference on Computer Vision and Pattern Recognition (CVPR), pp. 3156–3164. IEEE (2015)
29. Xu, K., et al.: Show, attend and tell: neural image caption generation with visual attention. In: International Conference on Machine Learning, pp. 2048–2057 (2015)
30. Young, P., Lai, A., Hodosh, M., Hockenmaier, J.: From image descriptions to visual denotations: new similarity metrics for semantic inference over event descriptions. Trans. Assoc. Comput. Linguist. 2, 67–78 (2014)

How Clever Is the FiLM Model, and How Clever Can it Be?

Alexander Kuhnle[✉][iD], Huiyuan Xie[iD], and Ann Copestake[iD]

Department of Computer Science and Technology, University of Cambridge, Cambridge, UK
{aok25,hx255,aac10}@cam.ac.uk

Abstract. The FiLM model achieves close-to-perfect performance on the diagnostic CLEVR dataset and is distinguished from other such models by having a comparatively simple and easily transferable architecture. In this paper, we investigate in more detail the ability of FiLM to learn various linguistic constructions. Our results indicate that (a) FiLM is not able to learn relational statements straight away except for very simple instances, (b) training on a broader set of instances as well as pretraining on simpler instance types can help alleviate these learning difficulties, (c) mixing is less robust than pretraining and very sensitive to the compositional structure of the dataset. Overall, our results suggest that the approach of big all-encompassing datasets and the paradigm of *"the effectiveness of data"* may have fundamental limitations.

Keywords: VQA · Synthetic data · Evaluation · Deep learning

1 Introduction and Related Work

The task of Visual Question Answering (VQA) lies at the intersection of Computer Vision and Natural Language Processing. It generalizes the vision tasks of object detection and recognition to arbitrary visual-linguistic inferences, limited only by what can be queried by language.

In reaction to various issues that allowed comparatively naive models – for instance, a text-only system ignoring visual information and solely relying on language statistics – to achieve competitive performance on the popular VQA Dataset [1,6,15], abstract and (semi-)automatically generated datasets were introduced [10,12,20,22]. Their motivation is to provide diagnostic tasks, with the aim of analyzing core abilities for visually grounded language understanding, like spatial reasoning or counting. CLEVR [10] is the most widely adopted of these, and several systems have now achieved near-perfect performance on it [8,9,11,14,16,18,19,22].

One of the advantages of CLEVR is that it annotates questions from a set of instance types, like *"count"* or *"compare attribute"*, which makes a more detailed evaluation and model comparison possible. Building on the *"unit-testing"* proposal of [13] and related work for reading comprehension such as the bAbI tasks

© Springer Nature Switzerland AG 2019
L. Leal-Taixé and S. Roth (Eds.): ECCV 2018 Workshops, LNCS 11132, pp. 162–172, 2019.
https://doi.org/10.1007/978-3-030-11018-5_15

[21], which take this idea of targeted evaluation further, we analyzed the FiLM model [16] on the ShapeWorld evaluation framework [12]. In doing so, we aim to investigate whether its close-to-perfect performance on CLEVR translates to ShapeWorld data as expected, and to shed more light on the strengths and weaknesses of FiLM.

Why FiLM? Arguably, it is one of the simplest models on that performance level for CLEVR. In particular, it does not rely on the semantic program trees underlying its instances, as compared to [8,11,14]. The first two strictly require the CLEVR-specific program vocabulary, which is different from the one used by ShapeWorld to generate data. The latter is agnostic to the vocabulary, but still sensitive to the size of the vocabulary, which is bigger for ShapeWorld[1]. Moreover, the code is open-source, and in our experiments we found that the model shows robust learning behavior on ShapeWorld data without any tuning of the CLEVR-based hyperparameters.

While FiLM manages to solve many tasks perfectly, it fails to learn anything on almost all datasets consisting of relational statements. We investigate how two approaches – broader training sets including simpler instances, and a version of curriculum learning [3,5] – can make the difference between no learning at all and perfectly solving these datasets. However, we find that the first approach is very sensitive to details of the dataset structure. These results put into question the common assumption of *"the effectiveness of data"* [7] underlying datasets such as the VQA Dataset [2] (or SQuAD [17] for reading comprehension, or SNLI [4] for language inference): that all necessary abilities for a task can simply be learned from one big all-encompassing dataset, and that more data should lead to improved performance. Curriculum learning, on the other hand, shows promise as a robust approach to solving more complex instances of a task.

2   Experimental Setup

2.1   Task

We look at the task of *image caption agreement*, that is, given a visual scene and a statement, decide whether the latter is true for the former. See Fig. 1 for some examples. The captions here are formal-semantics-style statements and not necessarily good descriptions, which is a vaguer concept and thus not as useful for evaluation. Instead, this task corresponds more to yes/no questions in visual question answering.

2.2   Datasets

We generated various datasets based on existing configurations in the Shape-World repository. The different datasets are defined by the types of captions they contain, see Fig. 1 for more details. Each dataset consists of 500k training instances, plus 10k validation and test instances. Training and validation scenes

---

[1] We ran into memory issues when trying to run this model on ShapeWorld data.

generally contain 1–4, 6–9 or 11–14 non-overlapping (unless mentioned otherwise) objects, further constrained depending on the dataset. Test scenes may in addition exhibit the withheld object numbers 5, 10 and 15, and may also contain withheld object types: *"red square"*, *"green triangle"*, *"blue circle"*, *"yellow rectangle"*, *"magenta cross"*, *"cyan ellipse"*. Consequently, the test data follows a slightly different distribution where models is required to generalize to unseen object numbers and new attribute combinations to achieve a comparable score, similar to the CoGenT version of the CLEVR dataset[2] [10].

Existential: "There is a red square.", "A red shape is a square."
Single-shape: same as above, with only one object present
Logical: two existential statements connected by: and, or, if, if and only if
Numbers: zero to five; with modifiers: less/more than, at most/least, exactly, not
Quantifiers: with modifiers as above: no, half, all, a/two third(s), a/three quarter(s)
Relational: left, right, above, below, closer, farther, darker, lighter, smaller, bigger, same/different shape/color
Simple-spatial: the first four spatial relations, with only two objects per scene
Relational-negation: relational plus negated relations
Implicit-relational: left, right, upper, lower, smaller, bigger, darker, lighter, closer, farther (of two potential objects)
Superlatives: superlative forms of the above, of an arbitrary number of objects.

Examples for visual scenes   Examples for true or false statements

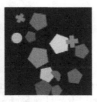

- *"There is a cyan square or a circle is green."*
- *"At least two shapes are green."*
- *"More than half the pentagons are red."*
- *"A red cross is to the left of a yellow shape."*
- *"The left circle is blue."*
- *"The lowermost yellow shape is a circle."*

Fig. 1. *Top*: All basic datasets we experimented with, together with their central words/constructions. *Bottom left*: Two example images. *Bottom right*: Some example captions of different datasets (LOGICAL, NUMBERS, QUANTIFIERS, RELATIONAL, IMPLICIT-RELATIONAL, SUPERLATIVES) (Color figure online)

2.3 Models

We focus on the FiLM model [16] here. The image is processed using a six-layer CNN (stride of two after the third and sixth layer) trained from scratch on the

---

[2] Note, however, that CLEVR CoGenT requires stronger generalization skills, as more shape-color combinations per shape/color are withheld.

task. We found that the common approach of using a pretrained ResNet module did not perform well on our data. The caption as 'question' is processed by a GRU. In four residual blocks, the processed image tensor is linearly modulated conditioned on the caption embedding. Following global max-pooling, the classifier module produces the 'answer', i.e. *"true"* or *"false"* in our case. We train the model for 100k iterations in all experiments, using the default hyperparameters. Training performance is measured on the validation set every 1k iterations for the first 10k iterations and every 5k afterwards. We also compare performance on selected datasets to two common baselines [10]: CNN-LSTM and CNN-LSTM-SA. We will release the ShapeWorld-adapted FiLM repository and the generator configurations to create the datasets on acceptance of the paper.

3   Results

Detailed results are presented in Figs. 2 and 3, unless referred to the appendix.

Initial findings, and what did not work.

(a) In a first experiment, we did not explicitly configure data generation to prevent overlapping objects. This turned out to be a major obstacle for learning in most cases. While FiLM solved EXISTENTIAL (99.7%), performance on NUMBERS stayed at chance level (55.2%) (see Appendix A.1).

(b) We experimented with using a fixed/trainable pretrained ResNet module instead of a custom CNN. Both versions of the model reached an accuracy of 65–70% after 100k iterations on EXISTENTIAL, which is substantially lower than our final result of 100% (see Appendix A.1).

(c) The FiLM model successfully solves many of our datasets. EXISTENTIAL is mastered after only 10k iterations and at the same speed as the trivial SINGLE-SHAPE variant. LOGICAL, NUMBERS and QUANTIFIERS reach close-to-perfect accuracy after around 60k iterations. The learning curves for these three tasks look remarkably alike and thus suggest a similar learning complexity for the model.

(d) The FiLM model successfully generalizes to the test set in most cases. Only for the simplified variants SINGLE-SHAPE and SIMPLE-SPATIAL, test performance is markedly lower, suggesting that there is not enough incentive to learn a compositional representation, presumably because their simplicity makes overfitting a feasible option.

(c) We investigated the performance of two common baselines, CNN-LSTM and CNN-LSTM-SA. While FiLM consistently outperforms both baselines as expected, the supposedly superior CNN-LSTM-SA [10,23] does not always improve upon the results of CNN-LSTM. However, CNN-LSTM-SA in some cases shows stronger generalization to the test distribution, whereas performance always drops for CNN-LSTM (also see Appendix A.2).

166   A. Kuhnle et al.

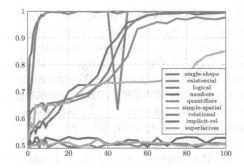

Dataset	CNN-LSTM		CNN-LSTM-SA		FiLM	
single-shape	—		—		100.0	87.2
existential	100.0	81.1	100.0	99.7	100.0	99.9
logical	79.7	62.2	76.5	58.4	99.9	98.9
numbers	75.0	66.4	99.1	98.2	99.6	99.3
quantifiers	72.1	69.1	84.8	80.8	97.7	97.0
simple-spatial	81.4	64.8	81.9	57.7	85.1	61.3
relational	—		—		50.6	51.0
implicit-rel	—		—		52.9	53.2
superlatives	—		—		50.8	50.2

Fig. 2. *Left diagram*: validation performance of the FiLM model trained on various ShapeWorld datasets separately (*x-axis*: iterations in 1000, *y-axis*: accuracy). *Top right table*: final validation (*left*) and test (*right*) accuracy of the trained FiLM models, plus performance of the two baselines on selected datasets (in percent, *green*: ≥95%, *orange*: ≥75%, *red*: <75%) (Color figure online)

Failure to Learn Relational Statements. Surprisingly, we found that, with the exception of SIMPLE-SPATIAL, FiLM struggles to learn anything when trained on the various datasets requiring some form of relational reasoning: RELATIONAL, IMPLICIT-RELATIONAL and SUPERLATIVES (RELATIONAL-LIKE below). We also tried subsets of relations in RELATIONAL (e.g., only spatial relations), with the same result. The only exception is the simplistic two-object SIMPLE-SPATIAL. But even here, learning is comparatively slow and only reaches ~85% after 100k iterations (although the curve indicates that performance is still improving), which further emphasizes the complexity of learning relations for FiLM.

Training on a Broader Set of Instances. Datasets like CLEVR consist of a mix of instances requiring different abilities. Our assumption is that the simpler instances help to stabilize and guide the overall learning process, so that the more complex instances are also learned eventually[3], hence models are able to achieve close-to-perfect performance. We tested this assumption in three setups: First, the FiLM model reaches ~95% accuracy on a dataset augmenting the complex RELATIONAL with the *'pedagogical'* SIMPLE-SPATIAL dataset. Second, when trained on a broader mix of EXISTENTIAL, LOGICAL, NUMBERS, QUANTIFIERS and either of the RELATIONAL-LIKE datasets, instances of the latter dataset are also successfully learned (also see Appendix A.3). Finally, in the failure case of NUMBERS for images with overlapping objects, training on a combination with the EXISTENTIAL dataset helps the model to also solve instances of the former.

Improvements via Augmenting/Mixing are Unstable. Further investigation reveals that this *'synergy effect'* of combining different instances is very sensitive to the composition of the training set. For instance, an unbalanced distribution

---

[3] When referring to "simple" and "complex" or "difficult" instances here, we always mean with respect to the ability of the FiLM model to learn these instances.

of 45% or 60% SIMPLE-SPATIAL and 55% or 40% RELATIONAL shows no improvement above chance level (see Appendix A.5). Similarly, performance stagnates when training on a combination of SIMPLE-SPATIAL and RELATIONAL-NEGATION instead. In the second example above, FiLM sometimes fails to learn mixed datasets with two or more RELATIONAL-LIKE components (see Appendix A.4). Of these, RELATIONAL seems to be the most complex for FiLM.

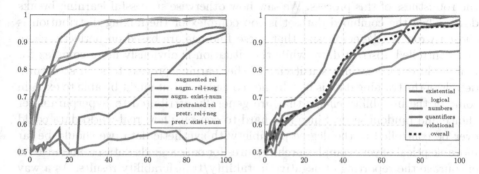

Fig. 3. *Left diagram*: FiLM performance on the RELATIONAL/EXISTENTIAL+NUMBERS (with overlap) dataset, when pretrained on SIMPLE-SPATIAL/EXISTENTIAL instances, or trained on a combination. *Bottom right diagram*: performance per dataset of the FiLM model trained on a broader mix of datasets

The Effectiveness of Pretraining. In another series of experiments, we investigated whether pretraining on simpler instances can bootstrap a successful learning process on more complex datasets, which is the assumption underlying curriculum learning [3,5]. For this, we take the model trained for 100k iterations on SIMPLE-SPATIAL and apply it to other RELATIONAL-LIKE datasets. For both RELATIONAL as well as RELATIONAL-NEGATION we observe a sharp increase in performance at the start, reaching ~95% accuracy after 100k iterations. We particularly want to draw attention to the fact that the pretrained model reaches and eventually surpasses its previous performance level of ~85% after only 20k/40k iterations, despite the more complex instances. Note also that the model trained on RELATIONAL-NEGATION at some point seems to benefit from this dataset's increased complexity. Finally, we also confirmed that, in the case of overlapping objects, the system pretrained on EXISTENTIAL is subsequently also able to learn added NUMBERS instances.

4   Discussion and Conclusion

We have shown how the FiLM model is not able to learn to correctly understand relational statements when trained on a dataset of such statements only. Furthermore, we have investigated two mechanisms which help alleviate these difficulties: augmenting training data with instances that are easier to learn, and pretraining on such simpler instances before moving to more complex ones. The first approach turns out to be very sensitive to the precise composition of the training set, while the second one leads to more reliable improvements.

Augmenting datasets in the limit corresponds to big all-encompassing datasets for general tasks like VQA, where a variety of skills is assumed to be learned implicitly from a lot of input-output pairs. While our results confirm that this is possible (at least for synthetic data), they strongly question the robustness of this process. We saw how otherwise successful learning breaks down when the combined dataset is too complex or the mixing distribution is chosen wrongly. We emphasize that these findings are based on perfectly clean and controlled abstract data, while the situation is obviously more complex for real-world datasets. Such sensitivity of the learning process to such structural details of the training data is usually not considered, but might be able to explain some of the instability effects that are generally attributed to hyperparameter choice and random seeds. Since it is hard to conceive how real-world data could ever be controlled to the degree possible with synthetic data, we should be far more skeptical of very complex architectures for only a single dataset, and instead encourage the reporting of negative instability/transferability results. As a way forward, our findings suggest the potential of curriculum learning as a more robust alternative to bigger monolithic datasets.

Acknowledgments. We thank the anonymous reviewers for their constructive feedback. AK is grateful for being supported by a Qualcomm Research Studentship and an EPSRC Doctoral Training Studentship.

A   Learning Curves for Other Experiments

A.1   Overlapping Objects and Pretrained ResNet Module

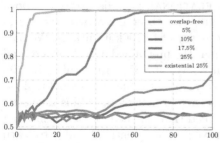

Performance of FiLM on NUMBERS, controlled for max area overlap

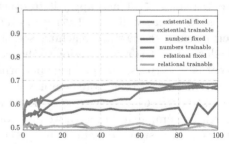

Performance of FiLM using a pretrained ResNet module

A.2   Baselines: CNN-LSTM and CNN-LSTM-SA

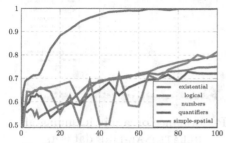
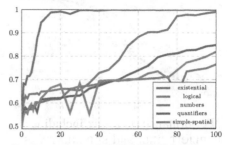

Performance of CNN-LSTM on
various datasets

Performance of CNN-LSTM-SA on
various datasets

A.3   Combinations with Implicit-Relational and Superlatives

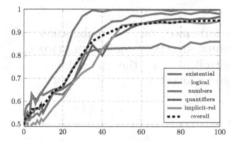
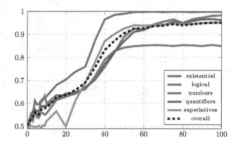

Per-dataset performance on a mix
including IMPLICIT-RELATIONAL

Per-dataset performance on a mix
including SUPERLATIVES

A.4   Combinations with Multiple Relational-Like Datasets

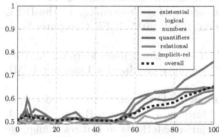
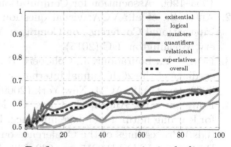

Performance on a mix including
RELATIONAL and IMPLICIT-REL.

Performance on a mix including
RELATIONAL and SUPERLATIVES

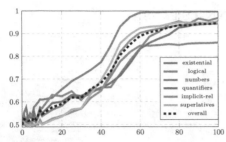
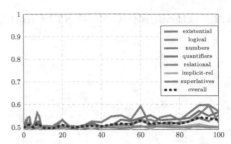

Performance on a mix including
IMPLICIT-REL. and SUPERLATIVES

Performance on a mix including all
RELATIONAL-LIKE datasets

A.5   Mixing Distribution

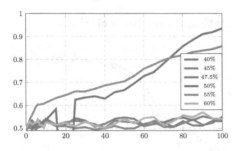

Performance on a combination of
SIMPLE-SPATIAL and RELATIONAL,
controlled for the probability of
SIMPLE-SPATIAL

References

1. Agrawal, A., Batra, D., Parikh, D.: Analyzing the behavior of visual question answering models. In: Su, J., Duh, K., Carreras, X. (eds.) Proceedings of the Conference on Empirical Methods in Natural Language Processing. EMNLP 2016, pp. 1955–1960. Association for Computational Linguistics, Stroudsburg (2016)
2. Antol, S., et al.: VQA: visual question answering. In: Proceedings of the IEEE International Conference on Computer Vision. ICCV 2015. IEEE Computer Society, Washington, DC (2015)
3. Bengio, Y., Louradour, J., Collobert, R., Weston, J.: Curriculum learning. In: Proceedings of the 26th Annual International Conference on Machine Learning. ICML 2009, pp. 41–48. ACM, New York (2009)
4. Bowman, S.R., Angeli, G., Potts, C., Manning, C.D.: A large annotated corpus for learning natural language inference. In: Màrquez, L., Callison-Burch, C., Su, J. (eds.) Proceedings of the Conference on Empirical Methods in Natural Language Processing. EMNLP 2015, pp. 632–642. Association for Computational Linguistics, Stroudsburg (2015)
5. Elman, J.L.: Learning and development in neural networks: the importance of starting small. Cognition **48**(1), 71–99 (1993)
6. Goyal, Y., Khot, T., Summers-Stay, D., Batra, D., Parikh, D.: Making the V in VQA matter: elevating the role of image understanding in visual question answering. In: Proceedings of the IEEE Conference on Computer Vision and Pattern Recognition. CVPR 2017, pp. 6325–6334. IEEE Computer Society, Washington, DC (2017)

7. Halevy, A., Norvig, P., Pereira, F.: The unreasonable effectiveness of data. IEEE Intell. Syst. **24**(2), 8–12 (2009)
8. Hu, R., Andreas, J., Rohrbach, M., Darrell, T., Saenko, K.: Learning to reason: end-to-end module networks for visual question answering. In: Proceedings of the IEEE International Conference on Computer Vision. ICCV 2017. IEEE Computer Society, Washington, DC (2017)
9. Hudson, D.A., Manning, C.D.: Compositional attention networks for machine reasoning. In: Proceedings of the International Conference on Learning Representations. ICLR 2018 (2018)
10. Johnson, J., Hariharan, B., van der Maaten, L., Fei-Fei, L., Zitnick, C.L., Girshick, R.: CLEVR: a diagnostic dataset for compositional language and elementary visual reasoning. In: Proceedings of the IEEE Conference on Computer Vision and Pattern Recognition. CVPR 2017. IEEE Computer Society, Washington, DC (2017)
11. Johnson, J., et al.: Inferring and executing programs for visual reasoning. In: Proceedings of the IEEE International Conference on Computer Vision. ICCV 2017. IEEE Computer Society, Washington, DC (2017)
12. Kuhnle, A., Copestake, A.: ShapeWorld - a new test methodology for multimodal language understanding. arXiv e-prints 1704.04517 (2017)
13. Kuhnle, A., Copestake, A.: Deep learning evaluation using deep linguistic processing. In: Walker, M., Ji, H., Stent, A. (eds.) Proceedings of the Workshop on Generalization in the Age of Deep Learning. NAACL 2018, pp. 17–23. Association for Computational Linguistics, Stroudsburg (2018)
14. Mascharka, D., Tran, P., Soklaski, R., Majumdar, A.: Transparency by design: closing the gap between performance and interpretability in visual reasoning. In: Proceedings of the IEEE Conference on Computer Vision and Pattern Recognition. CVPR 2018. IEEE Computer Society, Washington, DC (2018)
15. Mudrakarta, P.K., Taly, A., Sundararajan, M., Dhamdhere, K.: Did the model understand the question? arXiv e-prints 1805.05492 (2018)
16. Perez, E., Strub, F., de Vries, H., Dumoulin, V., Courville, A.C.: FiLM: visual reasoning with a general conditioning layer. In: AAAI. AAAI Press, Palo Alto (2018)
17. Rajpurkar, P., Zhang, J., Lopyrev, K., Liang, P.: SQuAD: 100,000+ questions for machine comprehension of text. In: Su, J., Duh, K., Carreras, X. (eds.) Proceedings of the Conference on Empirical Methods in Natural Language Processing. EMNLP 2016, pp. 2383–2392. Association for Computational Linguistics, Stroudsburg (2016)
18. Santoro, A., et al.: A simple neural network module for relational reasoning. In: Advances in Neural Information Processing Systems 30: Annual Conference on Neural Information Processing Systems 2017, pp. 4974–4983. Curran Associates Inc., Red Hook (2017)
19. Suarez, J., Johnson, J., Li, F.: DDRprog: a CLEVR differentiable dynamic reasoning programmer. arXiv e-prints 1803.11361 (2018)
20. Suhr, A., Lewis, M., Yeh, J., Artzi, Y.: A corpus of natural language for visual reasoning. In: Barzilay, R., Kan, M.Y. (eds.) Proceedings of the 55th Annual Meeting of the Association for Computational Linguistics. ACL 2017. Association for Computational Linguistics, Stroudsburg (2017)
21. Weston, J., Bordes, A., Chopra, S., Mikolov, T.: Towards AI-complete question answering: a set of prerequisite toy tasks. arXiv e-prints 1502.05698 (2015)

22. Yang, G.R., Ganichev, I., Wang, X.J., Shlens, J., Sussillo, D.: A dataset and architecture for visual reasoning with a working memory. arXiv e-prints 1803.06092 (2018)
23. Yang, Z., He, X., Gao, J., Deng, L., Smola, A.J.: Stacked attention networks for image question answering. In: Proceedings of the IEEE Conference on Computer Vision and Pattern Recognition. CVPR 2016. IEEE Computer Society, Washington, DC (2016)

Image-Sensitive Language Modeling for Automatic Speech Recognition

Kata Naszádi[1(✉)], Youssef Oualil[2], and Dietrich Klakow[2]

[1] Amazon, Aachen, Germany
naszadik@amazon.com
[2] Spoken Language Systems (LSV), Saarland Informatics Campus,
Saarland University, Saarbrücken, Germany
{youalil,dietrich.klakow}@lsv.uni-saarland.de

Abstract. Typically language models in a speech recognizer just use the previous words as a context. Thus they are insensitive to context from the real world. This paper explores the benefits of introducing the visual modality as context information to automatic speech recognition. We use neural multimodal language models to rescore the recognition results of utterances that describe visual scenes. We provide a comprehensive survey of how much the language model improves when adding the image to the conditioning set. The image was introduced to a purely text-based RNN-LM using three different composition methods. Our experiments show that using the visual modality helps the recognition process by a 7.8% relative improvement, but can also hurt the results because of overfitting to the visual input.

Keywords: Multimodal speech recognition
Multimodal language model

1 Introduction

Multimodal neural language models have been widely utilized for image captioning, but their effectiveness for other language modeling tasks is yet to be studied. The language modeling module of an automatic speech recognition pipeline could also benefit from the visual modality if the speaker refers to the visual surroundings. We implemented situated speech recognition by rescoring recognition results using multimodal language models. Natural language generation models, such as image captioning, tend to focus on the more frequent events, typically limiting the vocabulary to be smaller than 10 thousand words. For applications where the language model is used for estimating the likelihood of natural utterances, it is important to have a good probability estimate for rare events. In our language modeling experiments we aimed for high lexical coverage.

This work was done while Kata Naszádi was at the Spoken Language Systems group at Saarland University.

© Springer Nature Switzerland AG 2019
L. Leal-Taixé and S. Roth (Eds.): ECCV 2018 Workshops, LNCS 11132, pp. 173–179, 2019.
https://doi.org/10.1007/978-3-030-11018-5_16

Using three different neural architectures we explore how much information image-conditioned models gain from the image. This is achieved by removing the image as an input while keeping the rest of the architecture as intact as possible. Creating purely text-based baselines also sheds light on the quality of image-captioning datasets with respect to the variability of the language used to describe the images.

2 Models

Two types of neural architectures have been implemented, both of them directly inspired by successful image captioning models. In one of them the image is only presented to the recurrent cell once. The other method only feeds textual data to the recurrent cell, then it uses the image in each time step to rescore the output of the RNN, so the purely text based distribution $P(w|h)$ coming from the RNN becomes conditioned on the image $P(w|h, i)$. We tried two different methods for composing the output RNN-cell with the image feature vector: concatenation and compact bilinear pooling.

We used the Very Deep Convolutional Network with 16 hidden layers [1] for image feature extraction. The hidden activations of the last bottle-neck layer were used to obtain image representations of 4096 dimensions. The image feature vectors were kept fixed during training.

2.1 Text-Based Baseline (NI)

We trained two uni-modal language models to match the multimodal models as closely as possible. Both models are single-layer RNN-LSTM networks with vocabulary-sized softmax output layer. The word embeddings were set to be the same size as the hidden unit. The only difference between the two baseline models is the size of the hidden layer: 400 and 800 nodes. The models containing no image input will be referred to by the acronym NI.

2.2 Feeding the Image to the Recurrent Unit (SaT)

The first architecture we implemented is a slightly adapted version of the Show and Tell (SaT) model [2]. We only changed the hidden size to be 400 units and increased the size of the output layer to match our vocabulary. The architecture builds on a standard recurrent language model with the addition of the image as the input before the start of sentence symbol. The extra parameters introduced by this model compared to a unimodal RNN are the weights of the affine transformation $W_v \in \mathbb{R}^{d \times 4096}$ that maps the image vector v to the input size d. The input of the RNN before the start of sentence symbol x_{t-1} can be computed as:

$$x_{t-1} = W_v x_v \tag{1}$$

This architecture lends itself to being compared to a version without the image. In order to test how much perplexity reduction is due to the image, one simply needs to skip time step $t-1$ and start with the START symbol that denotes the beginning of a sentence.

2.3   Multimodal Composition After the Hidden Unit

Concatenation (Concat). The second group of multimodal architectures compose the image with the output of the recurrent cell in each time step. The first model within this group implements the multimodal composition of the image vector and the RNN as concatenation. The concatenated layer is then directly followed by the softmax output layer. In this case, it is easy to see that the weight matrix following the activations of the concatenated layer can be split into two separate matrices.

$$r = W_v v + W_w h_t \tag{2}$$

The weight matrix is decomposed into two matrices, W_v operates on the image v, while W_w transforms the output of the LSTM unit h_t; $W_{softmax} = [W_v, W_w]$. r contains the scores for each word in the vocabulary before normalization. The final score can be broken down into the contribution of the image and the textual input.

Compact Bilinear Pooling (CBP). In order to exploit more interactions between the two modalities, we also implemented bilinear pooling for the multimodal composition. Bilinear pooling is an unbiased estimator of the outer product. The upper bound of the variance of the estimation is inversely proportional to the size of the lower order estimation d. We implemented two bilinear pooling models, the first has $d = 400$ as the size of the hidden unit and the lower order estimation, the second has d set to 800 in order to decrease the variance. For the details of the algorithm please see [3]. Note that compact bilinear pooling does not add any trainable variables to the model compared to the text-based baseline model.

3   Experiments

For our experiments, we considered two famous image-captioning datasets: MSCOCO [4] and Flickr30k [5]. The vocabulary has been determined independently of the captions; it contains the 100 thousand most frequent words from the 1 Billion Word Language Model Benchmark by Chelba et al. [6].

In order to illustrate the quality of the captions from a language modeling perspective, a 3-gram Kneser-Ney smoothed language model has been trained on the captions. The estimation of the language models was carried out by the KenLM toolkit [7]. All punctuation symbols were removed and pruning was disabled.

3.1   Perplexity Results

The 3-gram baseline perplexities in Table 1 illustrate that the language of the captions is very simplistic. As a comparison, the perplexity on a $25M$-word held-out portion of the Gigaword text corpus [8] is 144.6. The predictability of

Table 1. Perplexity results on different datasets. The number after the name of the model indicates the size of the hidden layer.

Model	Flickr30k	MSCOCO
KN-smoothed 3-gram	63.5	24.7
NI-400	33.2	17
SaT-400	23	12
CBP-400	46.5	16
Concat-400	23.1	11.3
NI-800	32.9	16.8
CBP-800	27.1	14.1
CONCAT-800	23.9	11.2

the language holds especially true for the MSCOCO even though the size of this dataset is more twice than that of the Flickr30k dataset.

The results show that on Flickr30k dataset Compact Bilinear Pooling only reduces perplexity if the size of the lower order estimate is big enough. With 400 hidden units the model without the picture (NI-400) outperforms pooling (CBP-400). We can see the benefit of using the image once the hidden size is large enough as in (CBP-800).

On the MSCOCO dataset there is a slight improvement even when the hidden size is only 400. The reason for this may come down to the fact that there is not a lot of variance in the textual vectors to begin with. It could also be the case that the images only cover a very limited set of visual scenes, but we ran no experiments in order to prove this point.

It is also clear from the results that concatenation always outperforms compact bilinear pooling. We argued for compact bilinear pooling because it is able to exploit interactions between all dimensions of the two modalities, but the method introduces a large estimation error due to the vastly different size of the composed vectors. The results also suggest that such interactions might not play a crucial role. The SaT-400 model performs closely to the Concat-400 model, even though the former is capable of learning non-linear interactions between the modalities.

3.2   Ratio of Loss per Part-of-Speech Tag

The CNN image encoder was trained on an object recognition task, so it would be reasonable to expect that most of the perplexity reduction is due to nouns. Table 2 shows the ratio of the loss between the models SaT-400H and NI-400H broken down to different part of speech categories. The captions were tagged using the Stanford log-linear part-of-speech tagger [9]. For a specific POS-tag each row displays the following ratio:

$$\frac{\sum_{w:POS(w)=pos} -\log(P_{WI}(w|h))}{\sum_{w:POS(w)=pos} -\log(P_{NI}(w|h))} \tag{3}$$

Table 2. Ratio of loss per part of speech tag category between the models with and without the image.

ADVERBS	96%
MODALS	100%
PARTICLES	94%
PREPOSITIONS	92%
NOUNS	94%
TO	97%
PRONOUNS	96%
ADJECTIVES	89%
VERBS	92%
DETERMINERS	96%

$P_{WI}(w|h)$ is the probability of the word according to the model that uses the image, and $P_{NI}(w|h)$ is the same probability estimate without the image. As the results show, the performance is improved across almost all part-of-speech categories. It may only be the content words that get detected from the image, but predicting these words correctly will help the language model to make more accurate predictions for the other word categories too. Given the list of strings, for example *"dog, frisbee"*, there is only a limited way to combine these words into a fully formed sentence. It is also clear to see that the modality of a sentence can not be decided based on visual input.

3.3   Automatic Speech Recognition Rescoring Experiments

The automatic speech recognition experiments were carried out using the MIT Flickr Audio Caption Corpus [10]. 5000 spoken captions were used to tune the acoustic scale and the interpolation weights between the original background language model and the recurrent language models trained on the captions. We report the final results on a test set of 5000 spoken captions.

The first-pass decoding was performed using the HUB4 trigram language model [11]. As a baseline, the 300 best hypotheses were rescored with the neural language model that was only trained on the captions, without using the image (NI-400). This is necessary to account for the effect of the domain-specific language. For image-sensitive rescoring we used the SaT-400 model (Table 3).

Both the image sensitive and the regular language model perform better when linearly interpolated with the 3-gram broadcast news language model that was originally used to generate the 300-best list. The performance of the first-pass language model sets limitations for the final word error-rate. The HUB4 trigram model is trained predominantly on news data, which is not similar enough to the domain of the captions. One could achieve even better performance with a stronger first-pass decoder.

Table 3. Word error rates using the model trained exclusively on the captions (NI-400) and the image-sensitive language model (SaT-400).

	WER	Acoustic-weight	RNN-weight
NI-400	37.04%	0.08	1
SaT-400	36.31%	0.1	1
NI-400	34.80%	0.08	0.9
SaT-400	32.08%	0.1	0.8

Qualitative Analyses of the Decoding Results. Figure 1 shows positive examples where the image-sensitive model seems to have successfully recognized objects from the picture, thus helping the recognition process.

True transcript: Mechanics preparing a plane for departure. **Image-sensitive**: Mechanics preparing a plane for the past. **No image**: Mechanics preparing a clean for the pasture.

True transcript: Two people making their way between rocks. **Image-sensitive**: Two people making their way between rocks. **No image**: Two people making their way between walks.

True transcript: A man fishing under an umbrella. **Image-sensitive**: A man fishing under an umbrella. **No image**: A man fishing under a number.

Fig. 1. Recognizing objects from the images helps the decoding.

On the downside, the image model is prone to overfitting to the image. Figure 2 shows a clear example of this effect. The visual setting depicting a dog gets associated with the word "pizza" during training and rescoring gives too high probability to the sentence containing this word. This effect can be reduced by interpolating with a purely text-based language model that was trained on considerably more data. As illustrated by the optimal interpolation weights, the image model benefits more from the 3-gram language model. Supporting the image-sensitive language model with a richer, text-based model reduces, but does not eliminate this problem.

 A dog is standing in front of a pizza parlor and the man is smiling looking at him. The pizza maker is laughing at the white dog watching him through the window. A small brown and white dog looks in the window of Driggs Pizza. A lost dog trying to find some food in a pizza restaurant. A dog is looking in the window of a pizza parlor .

 **True transcript**: A man on a bench feeds a dog. **Image-sensitive**: A man on a bench pizza. **No image**: A man on a bench feeds a dog.

Fig. 2. The image sensitive language model overfits to the training image.

4 Conclusions

In this paper we set out to explore the possible benefits of introducing the visual modality to language modeling. We showed that adding the image to the conditioning set helps reduce perplexity up to 30% relative to the baseline.

Conditioning on the image helped decrease word error rate from 34.8% to 32.08%. In some cases the image-sensitive model fails to identify the participants and actions in the visual setting and copies training sentences based on superficial visual similarity. One reason for this is that the datasets are not large enough, and the model is not presented with a sufficient variety of scene and description combinations. We also believe that profound image understanding cannot be achieved by using a global image descriptor and optimizing on maximizing the likelihood of the descriptions.

Future work could further explore the benefit of using the visual modality by using a better first-pass decoder and exploring multimodal language models that achieve a more effective grounding in the visual modality.

References

1. Simonyan, K., Zisserman, A.: Very deep convolutional networks for large-scale image recognition. In: International Conference on Learning Representations (2015)
2. Vinyals, O., Toshev, A., Bengio, S., Erhan, D.: Show and tell: a neural image caption generator. In: Proceedings of the IEEE Conference on Computer Vision and Pattern Recognition, pp. 3156–3164 (2015)
3. Pagh, R.: Compressed matrix multiplication. In: Proceedings of the 3rd Innovations in Theoretical Computer Science Conference, pp. 442–451. ACM (2012)
4. Chen, X., et al.: Microsoft coco captions: Data collection and evaluation server (2015). arXiv preprint: arXiv:1504.00325
5. Plummer, B.A., Wang, L., Cervantes, C.M., Caicedo, J.C., Hockenmaier, J., Lazebnik, S.: Flickr30k entities: collecting region-to-phrase correspondences for richer image-to-sentence models. In: Proceedings of the IEEE International Conference on Computer Vision, pp. 2641–2649 (2015)
6. Chelba, C., Mikolov, T., Schuster, M., Ge, Q., Brants, T., Koehn, P.: One billion word benchmark for measuring progress in statistical language modeling. CoRR abs/1312.3005 (2013)
7. Heafield, K., Pouzyrevsky, I., Clark, J.H., Koehn, P.: Scalable modified Kneser-Ney language model estimation. In: Proceedings of the 51st Annual Meeting of the Association for Computational Linguistics, Sofia, Bulgaria, pp. 690–696, August 2013
8. Graff, D., Cieri, C.: English Gigaword, LDC catalog no. LDC2003T05. Linguistic Data Consortium, University of Pennsylvania (2003)
9. Girshick, R., Donahue, J., Darrell, T., Malik, J.: Rich feature hierarchies for accurate object detection and semantic segmentation. In: Proceedings of the IEEE Conference on Computer Vision and Pattern Recognition, pp. 580–587 (2014)
10. Harwath, D., Glass, J.: Deep multimodal semantic embeddings for speech and images (2015). arXiv preprint: arXiv:1511.03690
11. Weng, F., Stolcke, A., Sankar, A.: Hub4 language modeling using domain interpolation and data clustering. In: DARPA Speech Recognition Workshop, p. 147. Citeseer (1997)

Adding Object Detection Skills to Visual Dialogue Agents

Gabriele Bani, Davide Belli, Gautier Dagan, Alexander Geenen, Andrii Skliar,
Aashish Venkatesh, Tim Baumgärtner, Elia Bruni$^{(\boxtimes)}$, and Raquel Fernández

Institute for Logic, Language and Computation, University of Amsterdam,
P.O. Box 94242, 1090 GE Amsterdam, The Netherlands
elia.bruni@gmail.com

Abstract. Our goal is to equip a dialogue agent that asks questions
about a visual scene with object detection skills. We take the first steps
in this direction within the GuessWhat?! game. We use Mask R-CNN
object features as a replacement for ground-truth annotations in the
Guesser module, achieving an accuracy of 57.92%. This proves that our
system is a viable alternative to the original Guesser, which achieves an
accuracy of 62.77% using ground-truth annotations, and thus should be
considered an upper bound for our automated system. Crucially, we show
that our system exploits the Mask R-CNN object features, in contrast to
the original Guesser augmented with global, VGG features. Furthermore,
by automating the object detection in GuessWhat?!, we open up a spec-
trum of opportunities, such as playing the game with new, non-annotated
images and using the more granular visual features to condition the other
modules of the game architecture.

Keywords: Visual dialogue · Object detection

1 Introduction

In recent years, there has been considerable progress in combining natural
language processing and computer vision, with applications that span image
captioning [11], visual question answering [1] and, more recently, visually
grounded dialogue [2]. Despite such advancements, current models achieve a
rather fragile alignment between vision and language—as shown, for example,
by Shekhar et al. [13]—and are thus far from being able to effectively exploit
the two modalities in tandem.

In this work, we make progress in this direction by equipping a visual dialogue
agent that asks natural language questions about an image with automatic object
localisation skills. In particular, we focus on the GuessWhat?! game [3], where
the goal is to identify a target object in an image by asking a series of yes/no
questions to an Oracle agent who is aware of the target.

The model we propose uses as backbone the original architecture by de Vries
et al. [3], but with the crucial difference that the objects in the image are automatically localised. As object detection system, we use Mask R-CNN (MRCNN),

© Springer Nature Switzerland AG 2019
L. Leal-Taixé and S. Roth (Eds.): ECCV 2018 Workshops, LNCS 11132, pp. 180–187, 2019.
https://doi.org/10.1007/978-3-030-11018-5_17

a detection algorithm which has been shown to obtain state-of-the-art performance on standard image detection tasks [8]. We show that an agent equipped with automatic object detection skills performs almost at the level of an agent that has direct access to ground-truth object locations and categories.

2 Guessing in the GuessWhat?! Game

The architectures proposed so far to model agents able to play the GuessWhat?! game [3] split the Questioner agent into two sub-modules: a Question Generator, which poses new questions based on the visual input and the dialogue history (i.e., previous questions and answers), and a Guesser, whose task is to pick an object from a list of candidates once the dialogue is terminated. In this work, we focus on the Guesser component.

In all current GuessWhat?! models, the Guesser relies on ground-truth annotations. In particular, when the guessing phase begins, the Guesser receives a variable number of candidate objects, described by their coordinates and object categories. These annotations (as well as the images of the game) are taken from the MS COCO Dataset [11] (we refer to this as *ground-truth model*). In the present work, we make use of recent advances in object detection to propose a new model for the Guesser that does not require any ground-truth annotations.

Our starting point is the general architecture introduced by de Vries et al. [3]. An LSTM processes the dialogue d into a fixed sized, continuous vector. The objects in the image are represented by an 8-dimensional bounding box feature[1] [9,15] and their categories. The bounding box feature b and a dense embedding of the object category c are concatenated and processed by an MLP with shared weights for all objects producing a representation for each object. A dot product between the dialogue and object representation results in a score for each object o_i. All scores are normalised with a softmax function, as shown in Eq. (1). The model is trained with Cross Entropy Loss.

$$p(o_i) = \text{softmax}\Big(\text{MLP}([b_i, c_i]) \cdot \text{LSTM}(d)\Big) \tag{1}$$

A key limitation of this approach is that it cannot generalise beyond the cases where ground-truth annotations are provided. Furthermore, it exploits a limited part of the information, namely the bounding box and the object category but not the image itself. Although [3] experiment with visual features extracted from the whole image by adding the fully connected layer of VGG16 [14] to the dialogue representation (we refer to this as *global features*), this did not improve results. In our model, we obtain a representation for each object by using different visual features, thus replacing the annotated bounding boxes and object categories. Our aim is to investigate how far we can get in terms of task success with a fully automatic approach, which would make the Guesser able to generalise to new images.

---

[1] This representation consists of the normalised width and height of the bounding box, as well as the lower left and the upper right bounding box coordinates.

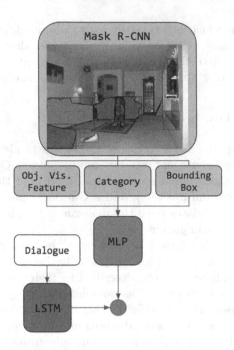

Fig. 1. Proposed guesser architecture with features from MRCNN.

3 Automatic Candidate Localisation

When natural language refers to the outside visual world, it does not only address it holistically, but it also focuses on specific objects and locations. Hence, if we want to ground language in vision, we should provide it with visual features that are at that level of granularity. This is particularly the case for the GuessWhat?! game, where the task is that of localising an object of interest. Previous work on GuessWhat?! relied always on global features instead, such as VGG and Resnet, which provide only a poor representation of the individual objects in the scene and we believe this is the reason why they do not have significant impact on the task [3].

On the other hand, recent advances in object detection allow for precise localisation of multiple objects in a visual scene. We leverage this progress by making use of MRCNN [8], the current state of the art in object detection on MS COCO [11]. We use the Detectron implementation [7] with ResNet-101-FPN [10] as a backbone.

MRCNN performs both object detection and semantic segmentation. It outputs (i) a bounding box for each detected object, (ii) a class probability for each bounding box, and (iii) a class probability for each pixel in the image. Based on the Fast/Faster R-CNN architecture [6,12], MRCNN has a Convolution Neural Network (CNN) at its core, processing the entire image. Given region proposals, the feature maps of the CNN for a region are processed by a pooling and multiple fully connected layers, eventually branching into the three outputs mentioned above. We make use of the last hidden layer as 'visual features' (we refer to this as *object features*).

We explore different types of visual information to obtain object representations for the Guesser model with four different settings:

1. Ground-truth model with manual bounding boxes and object category annotations.
2. Ground-truth model as in 1, but augmented with global features from the first fully connected layer of VGG16 (FC6).
3. The predictions of MRCNN, replacing the ground-truth bounding box and object category.
4. The predictions of MRCNN, replacing the ground-truth bounding box and object category and adding the last hidden layer as visual features representing the object.

Figure 1 sketches the architecture of the last setting, i.e., using the information obtained through MRCNN to represent the object.

4   Training and Evaluation

Performance in object detection is measured by evaluating the Intersection over Union (IoU), which compares two bounding boxes A and B, as shown in Eq. (2). A detection is considered successful if the IoU between the ground-truth and the predicted bounding box is at least 0.5.

$$\text{IoU}(A, B) = \frac{|A \cap B|}{|A \cup B|} \tag{2}$$

4.1   Category Filtering

Since we aim at replacing the manual annotations used in the ground-truth model, we need to label the MRCNN predictions in order to train our model. From the set of bounding boxes and categories, we need to select the prediction which matches the ground-truth annotation best. The simplest option is to select the proposal with the highest IoU ≥ 0.5 as the target. We also experiment with a refined condition where we first filter all proposals by category, i.e., we only consider those proposals where the category prediction matches the ground-truth category. We then select the proposal with the highest IoU as the target.

4.2   Single- vs. Multi-target

The procedure described above makes available one single bounding box as the target, namely the one with the highest IoU. However, since an IoU ≥ 0.5 is considered a correct detection in the object detection literature, we can relax this constraint and consider any prediction with IoU ≥ 0.5 as correct, even if it is not the bounding box with the highest IoU. We evaluate the model trained with the single-target setup, but with the multi-target evaluation procedure.

Table 1. Guessing accuracy with different settings introduced in Sect. 3. Settings 1 and 2 correspond to the ground-truth model without and with added global features. Settings 3 and 4 show results with single-target training using MRCNN bounding box and category predictions. For both settings we report the influence of category filtering. Setting 4 additionally uses object features

Setting	BBox & Cat	Filter	Features	Accuracy
1	Ground-truth	-	-	62.19%
2	Ground-truth	-	Global	62.77%
3	MRCNN	-	-	40.10%
3	MRCNN	Category	-	42.45%
4	MRCNN	-	Object	50.47%
4	MRCNN	Category	Object	53.40%

5   Results and Discussion

5.1   Accuracy Results

We train and evaluate all the models as described in the previous section. Table 1 reports accuracy results on task success when a single target with the highest IoU is considered. The first two rows report results for the two ground-truth models, while the rest of the table shows results for the conditions where the MRCNN object detection pipeline is used.

The first ground-truth model uses the manual bounding box and object category annotations to make a prediction (setting 1) and confirms results originally reported in [3]. Further, we also report results on a ground-truth model with global features added (setting 2). In contrast to [3], adding global features to the model does not decrease performance. This might be due to the lower level features we use in our experiments (first fully connected layer of VGG16, FC6), while [3] use higher level features (last fully connected of VGG16, FC8). However, the usage of these features also does not improve results. We therefore conclude that global features are not helpful enough.

Coming to our proposed model, we first report results on setting 3, which uses the MRCNN predictions of the bounding box and the object category, but not the object features. For this experiment, the performance of setting 1 has to be considered as its exact upper bound, because MRCNN predictions are replacing the ground-truth annotations and there are no added object features. The gap between the models is significant, with a 20% point difference. However, note that also the task becomes inherently harder as the average number of candidate objects jumps from 8.1 objects in the ground truth setting to 15.6 objects in the automated detection setting. Applying the category filter improved the results 2% points.

Next, we look at setting 4, which includes the object features. Remarkably, this leads to a big performance gain. The models obtain about 10% points more on the task than their counterparts without object features.

This result is clearly showing that a more fine-grained visual representation can be exploited by the Guesser in combination with the linguistic input to make its predictions. Again applying the category filter improves results about 3% points.

Table 2 shows accuracy results with the single- and multi-target setup for the best performing model in the single-target setup (MRCNN predictions with object features and category filtering). While the results obtained evaluating on a single-target are promising, when we relax the single-target constraint and allow multi-target evaluation we close the gap on the ground-truth even further, reaching 57.92% accuracy.

Table 2. Guessing accuracy for single- and multi-target evaluation. Results achieved with the best performing model from Table 1

Single-target	53.40%	Multi-target	57.92%

5.2   MS COCO and GuessWhat?! Splits

For all conducted experiments we use MRCNN, which uses the MS COCO train and validation splits. However, these splits do not align with the GuessWhat?! splits. In the GuessWhat?! dataset the training set also contains MS COCO validation images, and vice versa. This could possibly compromise our results, since MRCNN is trained on the original MS COCO training split. Therefore, we reduced the GuessWhat?! splits, keeping only those games which align with the MS COCO split. This results in about 67% of the training data and 32% of validation and test data. The Guesser model with ground-truth information achieves 61.0% on the test set, whereas our proposed model with MRCNN features, category filter, and object features achieves 52.25%. When evaluated on the multi-target setting, the model achieves 56.37%. Since these results do not deviate significantly from using the full GuessWhat?! set, we conclude that performance improvements are not gained form using MS COCO train images in the GuessWhat?! validation and test splits.

5.3   Visualising Predictions During the Dialogue

To gain a qualitative understanding of how the Guesser model behaves, we visualise the predictions incrementally made by the model as the dialogue proceeds.

Figure 2 shows the visualisations for a sample game obtained with the best performing model (setting 4 with category filtering). In general, the Guesser is very accurate in making sense of the dialogue and changing its prediction accordingly, even for complex sentences subordinated to previous questions. The Guesser is especially good at understanding class and position of objects, thanks to the information included in the object features.

Is it a sheep? Yes

Is it standing? Yes

Is it the one on the left? Yes

Fig. 2. Change in object probability over the course of the dialogue. The blue bounding box shows the target object. We colour every bounding box with intensity proportional to the prediction probability of it being the target. (Color figure online)

6   Conclusion and Future Work

We have shown that using features from an object detection network is useful for the task of guessing a referent in the GuessWhat?! game. Our results indicate that the Guesser agent exploits the provided MRCNN visual features, in contrast to the baseline model where adding VGG features does not lead to improvements. This suggests that the MRCNN visual features are more informative than features used for object classification such as VGG. This might be due to the fact that VGG is trained on Imagenet [5], where usually a single object has to be classified. While the task MRCNN is trained on requires the localisation and classification of multiple objects. This setting is much closer to the task faced by the Guesser in the GuessWhat?! game.

With the proposed model, the agent can be scaled to any visual input as no ground-truth annotation of the objects is required. Although we achieve slightly inferior task performance than with annotations, the results are promising, especially considering that the automatically obtained visual information is noisy.

Furthermore, these results also open many new opportunities. Since the object detection is autonomous and end-to-end from the image, the features could also be utilised during the dialogue. For example, the Question Generator can be conditioned on them and maintain a belief state over the candidate objects. This provides more fine-grained grounding of the agent as well as the explicit opportunity to ask more discriminative questions. In future work, we also plan to test the use of MRCNN features for the Oracle agent (which in the model by [3] uses ground-truth annotations) and systematically compare the results to the visual features leveraged by [4].

References

1. Antol, S., et al.: VQA: visual question answering. In: Proceedings of the IEEE International Conference on Computer Vision, pp. 2425–2433 (2015)
2. Das, A., et al.: Visual dialog. In: Proceedings of the IEEE Conference on Computer Vision and Pattern Recognition, vol. 2 (2017)
3. De Vries, H., Strub, F., Chandar, S., Pietquin, O., Larochelle, H., Courville, A.C.: Guesswhat?! visual object discovery through multi-modal dialogue. In: Proceedings of the IEEE Conference on Computer Vision and Pattern Recognition (2017)
4. De Vries, H., Strub, F., Mary, J., Larochelle, H., Pietquin, O., Courville, A.C.: Modulating early visual processing by language. In: Advances in Neural Information Processing Systems, pp. 6594–6604 (2017)
5. Deng, J., Dong, W., Socher, R., Li, L.J., Li, K., Fei-Fei, L.: ImageNet: a large-scale hierarchical image database. In: Proceedings of the IEEE Conference on Computer Vision and Pattern Recognition, pp. 248–255 (2009)
6. Girshick, R.: Fast R-CNN. In: Proceedings of the IEEE International Conference on Computer Vision, pp. 1440–1448 (2015)
7. Girshick, R., Radosavovic, I., Gkioxari, G., Dollár, P., He, K.: Detectron (2018). https://github.com/facebookresearch/detectron
8. He, K., Gkioxari, G., Dollár, P., Girshick, R.: Mask R-CNN. In: Proceedings of the IEEE International Conference on Computer Vision, pp. 2980–2988 (2017)
9. Hu, R., Xu, H., Rohrbach, M., Feng, J., Saenko, K., Darrell, T.: Natural language object retrieval. In: Proceedings of the IEEE Conference on Computer Vision and Pattern Recognition, pp. 4555–4564 (2016)
10. Lin, T.Y., Dollár, P., Girshick, R.B., He, K., Hariharan, B., Belongie, S.J.: Feature pyramid networks for object detection. In: Proceedings of the IEEE Conference on Computer Vision and Pattern Recognition (2017)
11. Lin, T.Y., et al.: Microsoft COCO: common objects in context. In: Fleet, D., Pajdla, T., Schiele, B., Tuytelaars, T. (eds.) ECCV 2014. LNCS, vol. 8693, pp. 740–755. Springer, Cham (2014). https://doi.org/10.1007/978-3-319-10602-1_48
12. Ren, S., He, K., Girshick, R., Sun, J.: Faster R-CNN: towards real-time object detection with region proposal networks. In: Advances in Neural Information Processing Systems, pp. 91–99 (2015)
13. Shekhar, R., et al.: FOIL it! find one mismatch between image and language caption. In: Proceedings of the 55th Annual Meeting of the Association for Computational Linguistics (Volume 1: Long Papers), vol. 1, pp. 255–265 (2017)
14. Simonyan, K., Zisserman, A.: Very deep convolutional networks for large-scale image recognition. arXiv preprint arXiv:1409.1556 (2014)
15. Yu, L., Poirson, P., Yang, S., Berg, A.C., Berg, T.L.: Modeling context in referring expressions. In: Leibe, B., Matas, J., Sebe, N., Welling, M. (eds.) ECCV 2016. LNCS, vol. 9906, pp. 69–85. Springer, Cham (2016). https://doi.org/10.1007/978-3-319-46475-6_5

W22 – 2nd YouTube-8M Large-Scale Video Understanding Workshop

W22 – 2nd YouTube-8M Large-Scale Video Understanding Workshop

The 2nd YouTube-8M Large-Scale Video Understanding Workshop was hosted at ECCV'18 by the Video Understanding Team at Google AI Perception. This workshop is based on the YouTube-8M video classification challenge hosted by Kaggle, composed of 4 invited talks, presentations by top performers at the competition, and a poster session for deeper discussion. We ran two tracks:

- **Classification Challenge Track** was organized as a Kaggle competition for large-scale video classification based on the YouTube-8M dataset. Researchers were invited to participate in the classification challenge by training a model on the public YouTube-8M training and validation sets and submitting video classification results on a blind test set. Top-ranking submissions in the challenge leaderboard were invited to the workshop to present their method.
- **General Paper Track** invited researchers to submit any papers involving research, experimentation, or applications on the YouTube-8M dataset. We encouraged participants to explore any relevant topics of interest using YouTube-8M dataset; for example, large-scale video recommendations, search, and discovery, joining the dataset with other publicly available resources (e.g, video metadata), or data visualization.

Paper submissions were reviewed by the workshop organizers and accepted papers were invited for oral or poster presentations at the workshop. Submissions were evaluated in terms of potential impact (e.g. performance on the classification challenge), technical depth, scalability, novelty, and presentation. At least two reviewers were assigned to review each paper, and two program chairs made the final decision. We did not require blind submissions. We did not restrict submissions of relevant work that is under review or will be published elsewhere. Previously published work was also acceptable as long as it was re-targeted towards YouTube-8M.

We hosted four invited talks:

- **Human action recognition and the Kinetics dataset** by Andrew Zisserman, *Oxford University & Google DeepMind*
- **Segmental Spatio-Temporal Networks for Discovering the Language of Surgery** by Rene Vidal, *Johns Hopkins University*
- **Learning video representations for physical interactions and language-based retrieval** by Josef Sivic, *Inria and Czech Technical University*
- **Towards Video Understanding at Scale** by Manohar Paluri, *Facebook*

We would like to express our gratitude to all our colleagues for submitting papers to the 2nd YouTube-8M Large-Scale Video Understanding Workshop, as well as to the members of the Program Committee for organizing this year's attractive program.

September 2018

Joonseok Lee
George Toderici
Paul Natsev
Rahul Sukthankar

The 2nd YouTube-8M Large-Scale Video Understanding Challenge

Joonseok Lee(✉), Apostol (Paul) Natsev, Walter Reade, Rahul Sukthankar,
and George Toderici

Google Research, Mountain View, USA
joonseok@google.com, natsev@google.com, inversion@google.com,
sukthankar@google.com, gtoderici@google.com

Abstract. We hosted the 2nd YouTube-8M Large-Scale Video Understanding Kaggle Challenge and Workshop at ECCV'18, with the task of classifying videos from frame-level and video-level audio-visual features. In this year's challenge, we restricted the final model size to 1 GB or less, encouraging participants to explore representation learning or better architecture, instead of heavy ensembles of multiple models. In this paper, we briefly introduce the YouTube-8M dataset and challenge task, followed by participants statistics and result analysis. We summarize proposed ideas by participants, including architectures, temporal aggregation methods, ensembling and distillation, data augmentation, and more.

Keywords: YouTube · Video Classification · Video Understanding

1 YouTube-8M Dataset

Many recent breakthroughs in machine learning and machine perception have come from the availability of large labeled datasets, such as ImageNet [8], which has millions of images labeled with thousands of classes. Their availability has significantly accelerated research in image understanding.

Video provides even more information for detecting and recognizing objects, and understanding human actions and interactions with the world. Improving video understanding can lead to better video search, organization, and discovery, for personal memories, enterprise video archives, and public video collections. However, one of the key bottlenecks for further advancements in this area, until recently, has been the lack of labeled video datasets with the same scale and diversity as image datasets.

Recently, Google announced the release of YouTube-8M [1], a dataset of 6.1+ million YouTube video URLs (representing over 350,000 h of video), along with video-level labels from a diverse set of 3,862 Knowledge Graph entities.[1] This represents a significant increase in scale and diversity compared to existing video datasets. For example, Sports-1M [11], the previous largest labeled video dataset

---

[1] This statistics is based on the most recent dataset update on May 14, 2018.

© Springer Nature Switzerland AG 2019
L. Leal-Taixé and S. Roth (Eds.): ECCV 2018 Workshops, LNCS 11132, pp. 193–205, 2019.
https://doi.org/10.1007/978-3-030-11018-5_18

we are aware of, has around 1 million YouTube videos and 500 sports-specific classes–YouTube-8M represents nearly an order of magnitude increase in both number of videos and classes.

YouTube-8M represents a cross-section of our society. It was designed with scale and diversity in mind so that whatever lessons we learn on this dataset can transfer to all areas of our lives, from learning, to communication, and entertainment. It covers over 20 broad domains of video content, including entertainment, sports, commerce, hobbies, science, news, jobs & education, health.

The dataset comes with pre-computed state-of-the-art audio-visual features from billions of frames and audio segments, designed to fit on a single hard disk. This makes it possible to get started on this dataset by training a baseline video model in less than a day on a single machine. Considering the fact that this dataset spans over 450 h of video, training from the raw videos is impractical–it would require 1 petabyte of raw video storage, plus video decoding and training pipelines that run 20,000 times faster than real time video processing in order to do one pass over the data per day. In contrast, by standardizing and pre-extracting the frame-level features, it is possible to fit the dataset on a single commodity hard drive, and train a baseline model to convergence in less than a day on 1 GPU. Also, by standardizing the frame-level vision features, we focus the challenge on video-level temporal modeling and representation learning approaches. The annotations on the training videos are machine-generated from different sources of information and are somewhat noisy and incomplete. A key research angle of the challenge is to design systems that are resilient in presence of noise.

2   Challenge Task

Continuation from the First Google Cloud & YouTube-8M Video Classification Challenge on Kaggle[2] and CVPR'17 Workshop[3], we hosted the challenge on Kaggle[4] with the revised video classification task, described in this section.

Participants are asked to produce up to 20 video-level predictions over the 3,862 classes on the YouTube-8M (blind) test set. The training and validation sets are publicly available, along with 1024-D frame-level and video-level visual features, 128-D audio features, and (on average) 3.0 video-level labels per video. The challenge requires classifying the blind test set of ∼700K videos, labels for which ground truth labels have been withheld. This blind test set is divided into two same-sized partitions, called public and private. For each submission, we evaluate performance on the public portion of the test set and release this score to all participants. Another half is used for final evaluation. Award and final ranking is determined based on this private test set, and this score is visible upon completion of the competition. Participants do not know which examples belong to which set, so they are asked to submit answers to the entire test set.

---

[2] https://www.kaggle.com/c/youtube8m.
[3] https://research.google.com/youtube8m/workshop2017/index.html.
[4] https://www.kaggle.com/c/youtube8m-2018.

Formally, for each video v, we have a set of ground-truth labels G_v. Participants produce up to 20 pairs $(e_{v,k}, f_{v,k})$ for each video v, where $e_{v,k} \in E$ is the class label, and $f_{v,k} \in [0,1]$ is its confidence score. We bucket $f_{v,k}$ with $\tau_j = j/10000$, where $j \in \{0, 1, ...10000\}$, and compute the Global Average Precision (GAP) across all classes as follows:

$$P(\tau) = \frac{\sum_{v \in V} \sum_{k=1}^{20} I(f_{v,k} \geq \tau) I(e_{v,k} \in G_v)}{\sum_{v \in V} \sum_{k=1}^{20} I(f_{v,k} \geq \tau)} \tag{1}$$

$$R(\tau) = \frac{\sum_{v \in V} \sum_{k=1}^{20} I(f_{v,k} \geq \tau) I(e_{v,k} \in G_v)}{\sum_{v \in V} |G_v|} \tag{2}$$

$$GAP = \sum_{j=1}^{10000} P(\tau_j) \left[R(\tau_{j-1}) - R(\tau_j) \right] \tag{3}$$

Performance is measured using this GAP score of all the predictions and the winner and runners-up of the challenge are selected based on this score. Note that this metric is optimized for systems with proper score calibration across videos and across entities.

Table 1. Best performance achieved by top 10 teams from 2017 YouTube-8M Challenge, with number of ensembled models.

Rank	Team name	Best performance (GAP)		# Models in ensemble
		Single model	Ensembled	
1	WILLOW [18]	0.8300	0.8496	25
2	monkeytyping [24]	0.8179	0.8458	74
3	offline [15]	0.8275	0.8454	57
4	FDT [6]	0.8178	0.8419	38
5	You8M [22]	0.8225	0.8418	33
6	Rankyou [25]	0.8246	0.8408	22
7	Yeti [5]	0.8254	0.8396	21
8	SNUVL X SKT [19]	0.8200	0.8389	22
9	Lanzan Ramen	–	0.8372	–
10	Samartian [26]	0.8139	0.8366	36

In addition, we restrict the model size up to 1 GB without compression. This is to discourage participants to try extremely heavy ensemble models, which we observed at the last year's competition (and other Kaggle challenges as well). Table 1 shows the best GAP scores achieved by the top 10 performers, with and without ensembles. We clearly see that most top performers ensembled tens of models and get consistent improvement about 2–3% on GAP. In large-scale applications, it is practical to limit the size of vectors representing videos due to CPU, memory, or storage considerations. We focus our challenge on developing models under a fixed feature size budget, encouraging participants to focus on developing novel single-model architectures, or multi-modal ensembles trained jointly end-to-end, as opposed to training many (in some cases, thousands of) models independently and doing a late-stage model ensemble to squeeze the last 1% of performance. The latter makes the approach infeasible for any real applications, and makes it difficult to compare single-model architectures fairly, as top performance is typically achieved by brute force approaches. This also gives an unfair edge to competitors with large compute resources, as they can afford to train and ensemble the most number of models.

3 Challenge Result

In this section, we review some stats regarding participants, and present the final leaderboard with GAP as well as some other useful metrics to compare performance.

3.1 Participants Overview

This year, total 394 teams participated in the competition, composed of 531 total competitors. For 106 participants among these, the 2nd YouTube-8M competition was their first competition at Kaggle. 61 participants have participated in the First YouTube-8M competition and returned to 2018 competition. Participants come from 40 and more countries, summarized in Table 2. This is based on the IP address where each participant created the account, so this is just an approximate statistics.

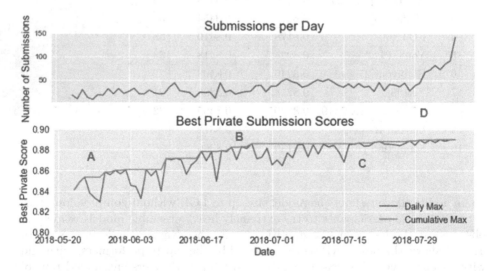

Fig. 1. The number of submissions (top) and best private leaderboard scores on each day and cumulatively (bottom). (Color figure online)

Table 2. Number of participants by country. (*This team is multinational, with a Spanish and an American participant.)

Country	# Competitors	Award winners
United States	136	1st*, 3rd
P. R. China	69	4th
India	56	
Russia	30	2nd
Korea	25	5th
Japan	19	
France	15	
Canada	15	
United Kingdom	14	
Taiwan	10	
Singapore	9	
Hong Kong	9	
Belarus	8	
Ukraine	8	
Germany	7	
Poland	6	
Australia	5	
Greece	4	

In this year's competition, we received total 3,805 submissions. This is about 10 submissions per team on average, which is relatively lower than usual. Median number of competition is 15. Figure 1 shows overall trend of competition progress. We launched the competition on May 22, 2018. Early on in the competition (**A** in Fig. 1), we observe a rapid increase in the best score (green). We also see lots of variability in the best daily scores (blue). This suggests participants were trying a wide variety of different ideas. About mid-way through the competition, around point **B**, the best score starts to plateau, but we still see lots of day-to-day variability, indicating continued exploration of techniques. During the last third of the competition (**C**), the day-to-day variability decreases significantly, suggesting competitors were trying to fine-tune submissions. We observe a sharp increase in model submissions towards the end of the competition (**D**), where participants were trying to get final incremental improvements in their submissions.

Another interesting analysis is about how returning participants performed. Figure 2 shows relative rank change (in percentile) of all returning teams. Red arrows mean moved down, while green ones mean moved up. Group **A**, the teams from lowest ranks last year, showed modest progress up to the 50–70 percentile. Group **B** from the middle last year showed significant improvement to within top 20%. Group **C** slipped a bit from top 10% to 20%. Among the top performers

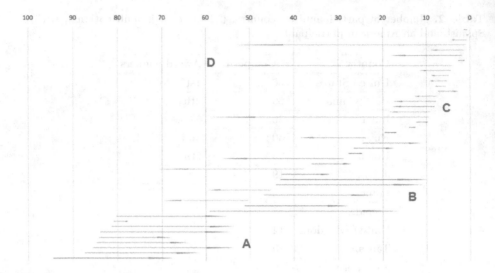

Fig. 2. The number of submissions (top) and best private leaderboard scores on each day and cumulatively (bottom). (Color figure online)

in Group **D**, we observe two patterns. Some of them dropped a lot, probably putting little effort on this year's competition. On the other hand, some teams achieved the top ranks again, including Team Next top GB model from 5th to 1st and Team YT8M-T staying at 4th again.

3.2 Final Leaderboard

Table 3 shows the final leaderboard, sorted by our official evaluation metric, GAP score. We also evaluate submitted final models in terms of the following additional metrics:

– **Mean Average Precision (MAP):** In practice, examples are not uniformly distributed over labels. For some labels, we have a plethora of training examples, while for some other labels, we have just a few of them. This is the case for YouTube-8M as well. Thus, we are also interested in a metric that deals with each label equally. Instead of computing AUC of overall precision-recall curve, MAP computes mean per-class AUC of precision-recall curves. Formally,

$$P_e(\tau) = \frac{\sum_{v \in V} \sum_{k=1}^{20} I(f_{v,k} \geq \tau) I(e_{v,k} \in G_v) I(e_{v,k} = e)}{\sum_{v \in V} \sum_{k=1}^{20} I(f_{v,k} \geq \tau) I(e_{v,k} = e)} \tag{4}$$

$$R(\tau) = \frac{\sum_{v \in V} \sum_{k=1}^{20} I(f_{v,k} \geq \tau) I(e_{v,k} \in G_v) I(e_{v,k} = e)}{|v : e \in G_v|} \tag{5}$$

$$AP_e = \sum_{j=1}^{10000} P_e(\tau_j) \left[R_e(\tau_{j-1}) - R_e(\tau_j) \right] \tag{6}$$

$$MAP = \frac{1}{|E|} \sum_{e \in E} AP_e \tag{7}$$

- **Hit@k** is the fraction of test samples that contain at least one of the ground truth labels in the top k predictions. We measure and report Hit@1 of the top performers.
- **Precision at Equal Recall Rate (PERR)** is similar to MAP, but instead of using a fixed $k = 20$, we compute the mean precision up to the number of ground truth labels in each class. Formally,

$$PERR = \frac{1}{|V|} \sum_{v \in V} \left[\frac{1}{|G_v|} \sum_{k \in G_v} I(rank_{v,k} \leq |G_v|) \right], \tag{8}$$

where G_v is the set of ground truth labels for video v and $I(rank_{v,k} < |G_v|)$ counts the number of correct predictions made within the top $|G_v|$.

For all metrics, higher values indicate better performance. We measure these metrics based on the final submission, although other intermediate models might have achieved higher scores in other metrics.

Table 3. Final leaderboard with 20 top performers in GAP, listed with other metrics (MAP, Hit@1, and PERR). The top performers in each metric are marked **bold**.

Rank	Team name	GAP	MAP	Hit@1	PERR	Model size
1	Next top GB model [21]	**0.88987**	0.59637	0.9074	**0.8311**	1,010 MB
2	Samsung AI Center Moscow [2]	0.88729	0.58436	**0.9075**	0.8297	943 MB
3	PhoenixLin [16]	0.88722	**0.59682**	0.9074	0.8310	901 MB
4	YT8M-T [23]	0.88704	0.58794	0.9059	0.8283	923 MB
5	KANU [12]	0.88527	0.58300	0.9039	0.8260	964 MB
6	[ods.ai] Evgeny Semyonov	0.88506	0.58476	0.9057	0.8274	982 MB
7	Liu [17]	0.88324	0.58194	0.9030	0.8242	1,020 MB
8	Sergey Zhitansky	0.88113	0.50362	0.8861	0.7977	844 MB
9	404 not found	0.88067	0.49868	0.8842	0.7947	**682 MB**
10	Licio.JL	0.88027	–	–	–	817 MB
11	Weimin Wang	0.88012	0.56076	0.9006	0.8197	1,021 MB
12	IIAI	0.87912	–	–	–	–
13	NPhard	0.87796	0.55979	0.8992	0.8178	753 MB
14	CV_Group	0.87662	0.53946	0.8925	0.8067	964 MB
15	NII	0.87465	0.54857	0.8968	0.8143	938 MB
16	DeepCats	0.87342	0.55275	0.8955	0.8122	970 MB
17	Axon AI [7]	0.87287	0.46735	0.8614	0.7608	971 MB
18	Steeve Huang	0.87216	0.55425	0.8962	0.8133	880 MB
19	Running out of time	0.87190		–	–	992 MB
20	Newers	0.87186	–	–	–	–

Table 3 indicates that Next top GB model team [21] achieved the best GAP as well as PERR scores. Samsung AI Center Moscow team [2] achieved the best Hit@1 score, and PhoenixLin [16] did for MAP score. The smallest model we see from the top 20 is achieved by the team 404 not found, which is 682 MB. Note that the GAP metrics in Table 3 are not compatible to those in Table 1 from 2017 leaderboard, as the a different version of YouTube-8M dataset was used each year.

4   Approaches

In this section, we briefly review commonly used techniques for this year's competition, as well as some interesting ideas proposed by participants.

4.1   Architecture

Many participants [4,13,16,17,20] built their models based on the WILLOW architecture illustrated in Fig. 3, designed by the WILLOW team, the 2017 competition winner [18]. In this work, team WILLOW explored combinations of learnable pooling techniques such as Soft Bag-of-words, Fisher Vectors, NetVLAD, GRU, and LSTM to aggregate video features over time. Also, they introduced a learnable non-linear network unit, called Context Gating, aiming at modeling inter-dependencies between features. For other architectures, Samsung AI Team [2] uses ResNet-based model.

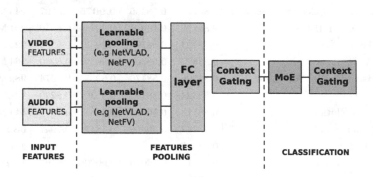

Fig. 3. The WILLOW architecture [18]

4.2   Temporal Aggregation

As the dataset provides frame-level features while the task requires video-level label estimation, a lot of participants propose novel ideas of how to aggregate frame-level features into video-level.

The most widely-used approach within this year's competition is NetVLAD [3] and its variants. Team PhoenixLin [16] substitutes the NetVLAD part with its variant NeXtVLAD. Team Deep Topology [13] applies modified NetVLAD to consider cluster similarity as well. They also try attention-enhanced NetVLAD, with transformer block inserted before and after NetVLAD module. Team YT8M-T [23] proposes non-local NetVLAD, modeling the relations between different local cluster centers. They try variants with early and late fusions of NetVLAD and its variants.

Another popular approach is recurrent neural networks, LSTM and GRU. Samsung AI Moscow Team [2] and Shivam Garg [9] apply uni-directional and bi-directional LSTM to aggregate frame-level features. Team Axon AI [7] uses both LSTM and GRU.

Convolution on temporal axis is another popular way to substitute recurrent neural nets. Shivam Garg [9] proposes ResidualCNN-X, where X is the output size, composed of a fully connected layer and a deep CNN network with several residual modules. Samsung AI team [2] tries time-distributed convolutional layers, containing several layers of convolutions followed by max-pooling for video and audio separately, then concatenating the resulting features.

Team KANU [12] selects informative frames using spatio-temporal attention model; temporal attention on audio guided by image, and temporal attention on image guided by audio.

Lastly, Deep Topology [13] proposes Multi-modal Factorized Bi-linear (MFB) pooling approach. For a video feature $\mathbf{v}$ and an audio feature $\mathbf{a}$, the MFB vector f_i is defined as weighted sum of elements in outer products $\mathbf{v}\mathbf{W}_i\mathbf{a}^\top$, where the weight matrix $\mathbf{W}_i$ is a low-rank bi-linear model. They combine MFB with different video-level features and explore its effectiveness in video classification.

4.3 Ensembles

Top performers are still taking advantage of ensembling, as listed in Table 4. However, the number of combined models has dropped from previous year, with an exception of Samsung team who ensembled 115 (95 video-level and 20 frame-level) models. Most other teams (among those who submitted a paper) ensembled less than 10 models. On average, top performers take advantage of ensembels to improve their final performance by ~2.5%. Most teams ensembled different models or same models with different hyper-parameters. Liu et al. [17] proposed ensembling different checkpoints from the same model with same hyper-parameters.

4.4 Techniques for a Compact Model

Due to the model size limit, many teams propose ideas to make the model compact. The most popular approach among participants is knowledge distillation [10], transferring the generalization ability of a huge teacher model (usually ensembles of multiple models in this competition) to a relatively simpler student network by using prediction from the teacher model as an additional

Table 4. The number of ensembled models by top performers.

Rank	Team name	Best performance (GAP)		# Models in ensemble
		Single model	Ensembled	
1	Next top GB model [21]	0.87237	0.88987	15
2	Samsung AI Center Moscow [2]	0.87417	0.88729	115
3	PhoenixLin [16]	**0.87846**	0.88722	3
4	YT8M-T [23]	0.87030	0.88704	6
5	KANU [12]	0.86078	0.88527	6
7	Liu [17]	0.87440	0.88324	4
17	Axon AI [7]	0.85750	0.87287	7

"soft target" during training. Team PhoenixLin [16] distills from 3 NeXtVLAD models. Samsung AI team [2] distills from ensembles of 95 video-level models and 20 frame-level models. The winner, Next top GB model team, designs two-level distillation on combination of ground truth and predicted labels by teacher models. Axon AI team [7] also applies similar idea to use convex combination of distilling ground truth and teacher model.

Another approach that most teams use is quantization. It is known that full float precision may not be necessary to represent a video [14]. Thus, we can almost preserve the end-to-end accuracy with using less number of bytes to represent values. In other words, increasing the number of dimensions with fewer bytes is more efficient use of space. Most teams use `float16` instead of full precision.

4.5   Other Interesting Ideas

We briefly introduce other interesting approaches proposed by participants. Some of these approaches have not been proved to be superior than the top performing models within the competition, but many of these are indeed novel and worth to explore further.

- **Label Correlation:** Team KANU [12] proposes conditional inference using label dependency for multi-label classification. Assuming $p(y|\mathbf{x})$ can be factorized as $\prod_{i=1}^{q} f_i(\mathbf{x}, y_{<\phi_i})$, they proposed a stage-wise algorithm to find positive labels in a greedy manner. Axon AI [7] proposes an additional regularized term $\mathbf{tr}(\mathbf{W}_{L-1}\Omega^{-1}\mathbf{W}_{L-1}^{\top})$ to guide related labels to have similar estimation, where $\mathbf{W}_{L-1}$ is the last layer's weights. The Ω encodes label relationship, which is driven from the data as well. Team sogang-mm [20] studies imbalance of label distribution, splitting the dataset into two, a fine-grained subset with rare labels and the rest with common labels. They compare training on one and re-training on the other, but conclude that there is no significant difference.

- **Data Augmentation:** Dataset augmentation is an effective way to increase data samples for training, usually by adding noise into existing examples. Team Axon AI [7] proposes generating virtual training data points by interpolating or extrapolating video features from K-nearest neighbors. Training with oversampled dataset in this way shows consistent improvement on performance. Samsung AI [2] also uses similar idea, creating virtual training examples by convex combination of existing ones.
- **Reverse Whitening:** Team PhoenixLin [16] reports that reversing the whitening process, which is applied after dimension reduction by PCA of frame-level features, is beneficial for NeXtVLAD model to generalize better. They argue that whitening after PCA might distort the feature space by eliminating different contributions between feature dimensions with regard to distance measurements, which could be critical for the encoder to find better anchor points and soft assignments for each input feature.
- **Hierarchical Relationship between Frames:** Deep Topology [13] represents a video as a graph with frames as nodes and relationship between frames as edges, and applies Graph Convolutional Networks on it. Their graph is constructed in a hierarchical manner, starting from frame-level, simplified into shot-level, event-level, and final video-level embedding in a row.
- **Circlant Matrix:** Given success of model distillation and compression approaches (Sect. 4.4), Team Alexandre Araujo [4] poses a question if it is possible to devise models that are compact by nature while exhibiting the same generalization properties as large ones. They propose replacing unstructured weight matrices with structured circulant matrices $\mathbf{C} \in R^{n \times n}$, which can be defined with a single vector of size n, and demonstrate to build a compact video classification model based on them.

5   Summary

We hosted the First (2017) and Second (2018) YouTube-8M Large-Scale Video Understanding Kaggle Challenge and Workshop at CVPR'17 and ECCV'18, respectively. With two runs of this competition, researchers indeed proposed interesting working ideas on architecture, temporal aggregation, ensembling, label correlation, data augmentation, and more. Most top performers heavily ensembled tens of models to maximize the Global Average Precision, and distilled it into a smaller model that fits into the size limit (1 GB). Some participants proposed interesting novel ideas to tackle this problem, although they did not outperform the ensembled models. We will continue to host this challenge and workshop to advance research in video understanding, possibly with updated dataset, new features, on diverse metrics or tasks.

References

1. Abu-El-Haija, S., et al.: Youtube-8M: A large-scale video classification benchmark (2016). arXiv preprint: arXiv:1609.08675
2. Alicv, V., et al.: Label denoising with large ensembles of heterogeneous neural networks. In: Proceedings of the 2nd Workshop on YouTube-8M Large-Scale Video Understanding (2018)
3. Arandjelovic, R., Gronat, P., Torii, A., Pajdla, T., Sivic, J.: Netvlad: CNN architecture for weakly supervised place recognition. In: Proceedings of the IEEE Conference on Computer Vision and Pattern Recognition (CVPR) (2016)
4. Araujo, A., Negrevergne, B., Chevaleyre, Y., Atif, J.: Training compact deep learning models for video classification using circulant matrices. In: Proceedings of the 2nd Workshop on YouTube-8M Large-Scale Video Understanding (2018)
5. Bober-Irizar, M., Husain, S., Ong, E.J., Bober, M.: Cultivating DNN diversity for large scale video labelling. In: Proceedings of the CVPR Workshop on YouTube-8M Large-Scale Video Understanding (2017)
6. Chen, S., Wang, X., Tang, Y., Chen, X., Wu, Z., Jiang, Y.G.: Aggregating frame-level features for large-scale video classification. In: Proceedings of the CVPR Workshop on YouTube-8M Large-Scale Video Understanding (2017)
7. Cho, C., et al.: Axon AI's solution to the 2nd Youtube-8M video understanding challenge. In: Proceedings of the 2nd Workshop on YouTube-8M Large-Scale Video Understanding (2018)
8. Deng, J., Dong, W., Socher, R., Li, L.J., Li, K., Fei-Fei, L.: Imagenet: a large-scale hierarchical image database. In: Proceedings of the IEEE Conference on Computer Vision and Pattern Recognition (2009)
9. Garg, S.: Learning video features for multi-label classification. In: Proceedings of the 2nd Workshop on YouTube-8M Large-Scale Video Understanding (2018)
10. Hinton, G., Vinyals, O., Dean, J.: Distilling the knowledge in a neural network (2015). arXiv preprint: arXiv:1503.02531
11. Karpathy, A., Toderici, G., Shetty, S., Leung, T., Sukthankar, R., Fei-Fei, L.: Large-scale video classification with convolutional neural networks. In: Proceedings of the IEEE international conference on Computer Vision and Pattern Recognition (CVPR) (2014)
12. Kim, E.S., et al.: Temporal attention mechanism with conditional inference for large-scale multi-label video classification. In: Proceedings of the 2nd Workshop on YouTube-8M Large-Scale Video Understanding (2018)
13. Kmiec, S., Bae, J.: Learnable pooling methods for video classification. In: Proceedings of the 2nd Workshop on YouTube-8M Large-Scale Video Understanding (2018)
14. Lee, J., Abu-El-Haija, S., Varadarajan, B., Natsev, A.: Collaborative deep metric learning for video understanding. In: Proceedings of the ACM SIGKDD International Conference on Knowledge Discovery and Data Mining (2018)
15. Li, F., et al.: Temporal modeling approaches for large-scale Youtube-8M video understanding. In: Proceedings of the CVPR Workshop on YouTube-8M Large-Scale Video Understanding (2017)
16. Lin, R., Xiao, J., Fan, J.: NeXtVLAD: an efficient neural network to aggregate frame-level features for large-scale video classification. In: Proceedings of the 2nd Workshop on YouTube-8M Large-Scale Video Understanding (2018)
17. Liu, T., Liu, B.: Constrained-size tensorflow models for Youtube-8M video understanding challenge. In: Proceedings of the 2nd Workshop on YouTube-8M Large-Scale Video Understanding (2018)

18. Miech, A., Laptev, I., Sivic, J.: Learnable pooling with context gating for video classification. In: Proceedings of the CVPR Workshop on YouTube-8M Large-Scale Video Understanding (2017)
19. Na, S., Yu, Y., Lee, S., Kim, J., Kim, G.: Encoding video and label priors for multi-label video classification on Youtube-8M dataset. In: Proceedings of the CVPR Workshop on YouTube-8M Large-Scale Video Understanding (2017)
20. Shin, K., Jeon, J., Lee, S.: Approach for video classification with multi-label on Youtube-8M dataset. In: Proceedings of the 2nd Workshop on YouTube-8M Large-Scale Video Understanding (2018)
21. Skalic, M., Austin, D.: Building a size constrained predictive model for video classification. In: Proceedings of the 2nd Workshop on YouTube-8M Large-Scale Video Understanding (2018)
22. Skalic, M., Pekalski, M., Pan, X.E.: Deep learning methods for efficient large scale video labeling. In: Proceedings of the CVPR Workshop on YouTube-8M Large-Scale Video Understanding (2017)
23. Tang, Y., Zhang, X., Wang, J., Chen, S., Ma, L., Jiang, Y.G.: Non-local netVLAD encoding for video classification. In: Proceedings of the 2nd Workshop on YouTube-8M Large-Scale Video Understanding (2018)
24. Wang, H.D., Zhang, T., Wu, J.: The monkeytyping solution to the Youtube-8M video understanding challenge. In: Proceedings of the CVPR Workshop on YouTube-8M Large-Scale Video Understanding (2017)
25. Zhu, L., Liu, Y., Yang, Y.: UTS submission to Google Youtube-8M challenge 2017. In: Proceedings of the CVPR Workshop on YouTube-8M Large-Scale Video Understanding (2017)
26. Zou, H., Xu, K., Li, J., Zhu, J.: The Youtube-8M kaggle competition: challenges and methods. In: Proceedings of the CVPR Workshop on YouTube-8M Large-Scale Video Understanding (2017)

NeXtVLAD: An Efficient Neural Network to Aggregate Frame-Level Features for Large-Scale Video Classification

Rongcheng Lin[✉], Jing Xiao, and Jianping Fan

University of North Carolina at Charlotte, Charlotte, USA
{rlin4,xiao,jpfan}@uncc.edu

Abstract. This paper introduces a fast and efficient network architecture, NeXtVLAD, to aggregate frame-level features into a compact feature vector for large-scale video classification. Briefly speaking, the basic idea is to decompose a high-dimensional feature into a group of relatively low-dimensional vectors with attention before applying NetVLAD aggregation over time. This NeXtVLAD approach turns out to be both effective and parameter efficient in aggregating temporal information. In the 2nd Youtube-8M video understanding challenge, a single NeXtVLAD model with less than 80M parameters achieves a GAP score of 0.87846 in private leaderboard. A mixture of 3 NeXtVLAD models results in 0.88722, which is ranked 3rd over 394 teams. The code is publicly available at https://github.com/linrongc/youtube-8m.

Keywords: Neural network · VLAD · Video classification Youtube8M

1 Introduction

The prevalence of digital cameras and smart phones exponentially increases the number of videos, which are then uploaded, watched and shared through internet. Automatic video content classification has become a critical and challenging problem in many real world applications, including video-based search, recommendation and intelligent robots etc. To accelerate the pace of research in video content analysis, Google AI launched the second Youtube-8M video understanding challenge, aiming to learn more compact video representation under limited budget constraints. Because of both unprecedent scale and diversity of Youtube-8M dataset [1], they also provided the frame-level visual and audio features which are extracted by pre-trained convolutional neural networks (CNNs). The main challenge is how to aggregate such pre-extracted features into a compact video-level representation effectively and efficiently.

NetVLAD, which was developed to aggregate spatial representation for the task of place recognition [2], was found to be more effective and faster than common temporal models, such as LSTM [3] and GRU [4], for the task of temporal aggregation of visual and audio features [5]. One of the main drawbacks

© Springer Nature Switzerland AG 2019
L. Leal-Taixé and S. Roth (Eds.): ECCV 2018 Workshops, LNCS 11132, pp. 206–218, 2019.
https://doi.org/10.1007/978-3-030-11018-5_19

of NetVLAD is that the encoded features are in high dimension. A non-trivial classification model based on those features would need hundreds of millions of parameters. For instance, a NetVLAD network with 128 clusters will encode a feature of 2048 dimension as an vector of 262,144 dimension. A subsequent fully-connected layer with 2048-dimensional outputs will result in about 537M parameters. The parameter inefficiency would make the model harder to be optimized and easier to be overfitting.

To handle the parameter inefficiency problem, inspired by the work of ResNeXt [6], we developed a novel neural network architecture, NeXtVLAD. Different from NetVLAD, the input features are decomposed into a group of relatively lower-dimensional vectors with attention before they are encoded and aggregated over time. The underlying assumption is that one video frame may contain multiple objects and decomposing the frame-level features before encoding would be beneficial for models to produce a more concise video representation. Experimental results on Youtube-8M dataset have demonstrated that our proposed model is more effective and efficient on parameters than the original NetVLAD model. Moreover, the NeXtVLAD model can converge faster and more resistant to overfitting.

2   Related Works

In this section, we provide a brief review of most relevant researches on feature aggregation and video classification.

2.1   Feature Aggregation for Compact Video Representation

Before the era of deep neural networks, researchers have proposed many encoding methods, including BoW (Bag of visual Words) [7], FV (Fisher Vector) [8] and VLAD (Vector of Locally Aggregated Descriptors) [9] etc., to aggregate local image descriptors into a global compact vector, aiming to achieve more compact image representation and improve the performance of large-scale visual recognition. Such aggregation methods are also applied to the researches of large-scale video classification in some early works [10,11]. Recently, [2] proposed a differentiable module, NetVLAD, to integrate VLAD into current neural networks and achieved significant improvement for the task of place recognition. The architecture was then proved to very effective in aggregating spatial and temporal information for compact video representation [5,12].

2.2   Deep Neural Networks for Large-Scale Video Classification

Recently, with the availability of large-scale video datasets [1,13,14] and mass computation power of GPUs, deep neural networks have achieved remarkable advances in the field of large-scale video classification [15–18]. These approaches can be roughly assigned into four categories: (a) **Spatiotemporal Convolutional Networks** [13,17,18], which mainly rely on convolution and pooling to aggregate temporal information along with spatial information. (b) **Two Stream Networks** [16,19–21], which utilize stacked optical flow to recognize human motions in addition to the context frame images. (c) **Recurrent Spatial Networks** [15,22], which applies Recurrent Neural Networks, including LSTM or GRU to model temporal information in videos. (d) **Other approaches** [23–26], which use other solutions to generate compact features for video representation and classification.

3   Network Architecture for NeXtVLAD

We will first review the NetVLAD aggregation model before we dive into the details of our proposed NeXtVLAD model for feature aggregation and video classification.

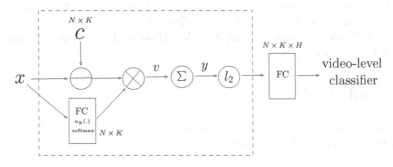

Fig. 1. Schema of NetVLAD model for video classification. Formulas in red denote the number of parameters (ignoring biases or batch normalization). FC means fully-connected layer. (Color figure online)

3.1   NetVLAD Aggregation Network for Video Classification

Considering a video with M frames, N-dimensional frame-level descriptors x are extracted by a pre-trained CNN recursively. In NetVLAD aggregation of K clusters, each frame-level descriptor is firstly encoded to be a feature vector of $N \times K$ dimension using the following equation:

$$v_{ijk} = \alpha_k(x_i)(x_{ij} - c_{kj})$$
$$i \in \{1, \dots, M\}, j \in \{1, \dots, N\}, k \in \{1, \dots, K\} \tag{1}$$

where c_k is the N-dimensional anchor point of cluster k and $\alpha_k(x_i)$ is a soft assignment function of x_i to cluster k, which measures the proximity of x_i and cluster k. The proximity function is modeled using a single fully-connected layer with softmax activation,

$$\alpha_k(x_i) = \frac{e^{w_k^T x_i + b_k}}{\sum_{s=1}^{K} e^{w_s^T x_i + b_s}}. \tag{2}$$

Secondly, a video-level descriptor y can be obtained by aggregating all the frame-level features,

$$y_{jk} = \sum_i^M v_{ijk} \tag{3}$$

and intra-normalization is applied to suppress bursts [27]. Finally, the constructed video-level descriptor y is reduced to an H-dimensional hidden vector via a fully-connected layer before being fed into the final video-level classifier.

As shown in Fig. 1, the parameter number of NetVLAD model before video-level classification is about

$$N \times K \times (H + 2), \tag{4}$$

where the dimension reduction layer (second fully-connected layer) accounts for the majority of total parameters. For instance, a NetVLAD model with $N = 1024$, $K = 128$ and $H = 2048$ contains more than $268M$ parameters.

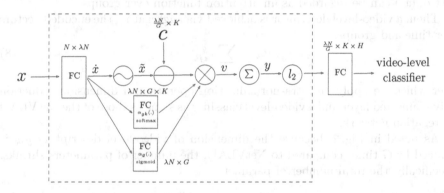

Fig. 2. Schema of our NeXtVLAD network for video classification. Formulas in red denote the number of parameters (ignoring biases or batch normalization). FC represents a fully-connected layer. The wave operation means a reshape transformation. (Color figure online)

3.2 NeXtVLAD Aggregation Network

In our NeXtVLAD aggregation network, the input vector x_i is first expanded as $\dot{x}_i$ with a dimension of λN via a linear fully-connected layer, where λ is a width multiplier and it is set to be 2 in all of our experiments. Then a reshape operation is applied to transform $\dot{x}$ with a shape of $(M, \lambda N)$ to $\tilde{x}$ with a shape of $(M, G, \lambda N/G)$, in which G is the size of groups. The process is equivalent to splitting $\dot{x}_i$ into G lower-dimensional feature vectors $\left\{\tilde{x}_i^g \middle| g \in \{1, \ldots, G\}\right\}$, each of which is subsequently represented as a mixture of residuals from cluster anchor points c_k in the same lower-dimensional space:

$$v_{ijk}^g = \alpha_g(\dot{x}_i)\alpha_{gk}(\dot{x}_i)(\tilde{x}_{ij}^g - c_{kj})$$

$$g \in \{1, \ldots, G\}, i \in \{1, \ldots, M\}, j \in \{1, \ldots, \frac{\lambda N}{G}\}, k \in \{1, \ldots, K\}, \tag{5}$$

where the proximity measurement of the decomposed vector $\tilde{x}_i^g$ consists of two parts for the cluster k:

$$\alpha_{gk}(\dot{x}_i) = \frac{e^{w_{gk}^T \dot{x}_i + b_{gk}}}{\sum_{s=1}^K e^{w_{gs}^T \dot{x}_i + b_{gs}}}, \tag{6}$$

$$\alpha_g(\dot{x}_i) = \sigma(w_g^T \dot{x}_i + b_g), \tag{7}$$

in which $\sigma(.)$ is a sigmoid function with output scale from 0 to 1. The first part $\alpha_{gk}(\dot{x}_i)$ measures the soft assignment of $\tilde{x}_i^g$ to the cluster k, while the second part $\alpha_g(\dot{x}_i)$ can be regarded as an attention function over groups.

Then, a video-level descriptor is achieved via aggregating the encoded vectors over time and groups:

$$y_{jk} = \sum_{i,g} v_{ijk}^g, \tag{8}$$

after which we apply an intra-normalization operation, a dimension reduction fully-connected layer and a video-level classifier as same as those of the NetVLAD aggregation network.

As noted in Fig. 2, because the dimension of video-level descriptors y_{jk} is reduced by G times compared to NetVLAD, the number of parameters shrinks. Specifically, the total number of parameters is:

$$\lambda N(N + G + K(G + \frac{H+1}{G})). \tag{9}$$

Since G is much smaller than H and N, roughly speaking, the number of parameters of NeXtVLAD is about $\frac{G}{\lambda}$ times smaller than that of NetVLAD. For instance, a NeXtVLAD network with $\lambda = 2$, $G = 8$, $N = 1024$, $K = 128$ and $H = 2048$ only contains $71M+$ parameters, which is about 4 times smaller than that of NetVLAD, $268M+$ (Fig. 3).

3.3   NeXtVLAD Model and SE Context Gating

The basic model we used for 2nd Youtube-8M challenge has the similar architecture with the winner solution [5] for the first Youtube-8M challenge. Video and audio features are encoded and aggregated separately with a two-stream architecture. The aggregated representation is enhanced by a SE Context Gating module, aiming to modeling the dependency among labels. At last, a logistic classifier with sigmoid activation is adopted for video-level multi-label classification.

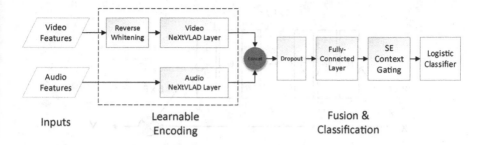

Fig. 3. Overview of our NeXtVLAD model designed for Youtube-8M video classification.

Inspired by the work of Squeeze-and-Excitation networks [28], as shown in Fig. 4, the SE Context Gating consists of 2 fully-connected layers with less parameters than the original Context Gating introduced in [5]. The total number of parameters is:

$$\frac{2F^2}{r} \tag{10}$$

where r denotes the reduction ratio that is set to be 8 or 16 in our experiments. During the competition, we find that reversing the whitening process, which is applied after performing PCA dimensionality reduction of frame-level features, is beneficial for the generalization performance of NeXtVLAD model. The possible reason is that whitening after PCA will distort the feature space by eliminating different contributions between feature dimensions with regard to distance measurements, which could be critical for the encoder to find better anchor points and soft assignments for each input feature. Since the Eigen values $\{e_j | j \in \{1, \ldots, N\}\}$ of PCA transformation is released by the Google team, we are able to reverse the whitening process by:

$$\hat{x}_j = x_j * \sqrt{e_j} \tag{11}$$

where x and $\hat{x}$ are the input and reversed vector respectively.

3.4 Knowledge Distillation with On-the-Fly Naive Ensemble

Knowledge distillation [29–31] was designed to transfer the generalization ability of the cumbersome teacher model to a relatively simpler student network by using prediction from teacher model as an additional "soft target" during training. During the competition, we tried the network architecture introduced in [32] to distill knowledge from a on-the-fly mixture prediction to each sub-model.

As shown in Fig. 5, the logits of the mixture predictions z^e is a weighted sum of logits $\{z^m | m \in \{1, 2, 3\}\}$ from the 3 corresponding sub-models:

$$z^e = \sum_{m=1}^{3} a_m(\bar{x}) * z^m \tag{12}$$

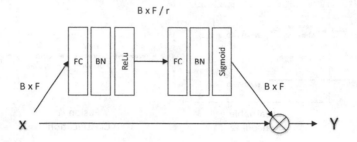

Fig. 4. The schema of the SE Context Gating. FC denotes fully-connected and BN denotes batch normalization. B represents the batch size and F means the feature size of x.

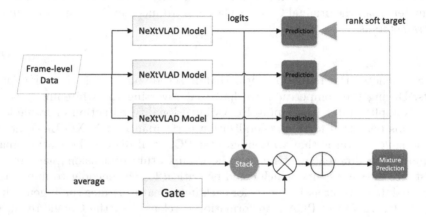

Fig. 5. Overview of a mixture of 3 NeXtVLAD models with on-the-fly knowledge distillation. The orange arrows indicate the distillation of knowledge from mixture predictions to the sub-models. (Color figure online)

where $a_m(.)$ represents the gating network,

$$a_m(\bar{x}) = \frac{e^{w_m^T \bar{x} + b_m}}{\sum_s^3 e^{w_s^T \bar{x} + b_s}} \qquad (13)$$

and $\bar{x}$ represents the frame mean of input features x. The knowledge of the mixture prediction is distilled to each sub-model through minimizing the KL divergence written as:

$$\mathcal{L}_{kl}^{m,e} = \sum_{c=1}^{C} p^e(c) \log \frac{p^e(c)}{p^m(c)}, \qquad (14)$$

where C is the total number of class labels and $p(.)$ represents the rank soft prediction:

$$p^m(c) = \frac{exp(z_c^m/T)}{\sum_{s=1}^{C} exp(z_s^m/T)}, \quad p^e(c) = \frac{exp(z_c^e/T)}{\sum_{s=1}^{C} exp(z_s^e/T)}. \tag{15}$$

where T is a temperature which can adjust the relative importance of logits. As suggested in [29], larger T will increase the importance of logits with smaller values and encourage models to share more knowledge about the learned similarity measurements of the task space. The final loss of the model is:

$$\mathcal{L} = \sum_{m=1}^{3} \mathcal{L}_{bce}^m + \mathcal{L}_{bce}^e + T^2 * \sum_{m=1}^{3} \mathcal{L}_{kl}^{m,e} \tag{16}$$

where $\mathcal{L}_{bce}^m$ ($\mathcal{L}_{bce}^e$) means the binary cross entropy between the ground truth labels and prediction from model m (mixture prediction).

4 Experimental Results

This section provides the implementation details and presents our experimental results on the Youtube-8M dataset [1].

4.1 Youtube-8M Dataset

Youtube-8M dataset (2018) consists of about 6.1M videos from Youtube.com, each of which has at least 1000 views with video time ranging from 120 to 300 s and is labeled with one or multiple tags (labels) from a vocabulary of 3862 visual entities. These videos further split into 3 partitions: train (70%), validate (20%) and test (10%). Along with the video ids and labels, visual and audio features are provided for every second of the videos, which are referred as frame-level features. The visual features consists of hidden representations immediately prior to the classification layer in Inception [33], which is pre-trained on Imagenet [34]. The audio features are extracted from a audio classification CNN [35]. PCA and whitening are then applied to reduce the dimension of visual and audio feature to 1024 and 128 respectively.

In the 2nd Youtube-8M video understanding challenge, submissions are evaluated using Global Average Precision (GAP) at 20. For each video, the predictions are sorted by confidence and the GAP score is calculated as:

$$GAP = \sum_{i=1}^{20} p(i) * r(i) \tag{17}$$

in which $p(i)$ is the precision and $r(i)$ is the recall given the top i predictions.

4.2 Implementation Details

Our implementation is based on the TensorFlow [36] starter code[1]. All of the models are trained using the Adam optimizer [37] with an initial learning rate of 0.0002 on two Nvidia 1080 TI GPUs. The batch size is set to be 160 (80 on each GPU). We apply a l_2(1e-5) regularizer to the parameters of the video-level classifier and use a dropout ratio of 0.5 aiming to avoid overfitting. No data augmentation is used in training NeXtVLAD models and the padding frames are masked out during the aggregation process via:

$$v^g_{ijk} = mask(i)\alpha_g(\dot{x}_i)\alpha_{gk}(\dot{x}_i)(\tilde{x}^g_{ij} - c_{kj}) \qquad (18)$$

where

$$mask(i) = \begin{cases} 1 & \text{if } i \leq M \\ 0 & \text{else} \end{cases} \qquad (19)$$

In all the local experiments, models are trained for 5 epochs (about 120k steps) using only the training partition and the learning rate is exponentially decreased by a factor of 0.8 every 2M samples. Then the model is evaluated using only about $\frac{1}{10}$ of the evaluation partition, which is consistently about 0.002 smaller than the score at public leaderboard[2] for the same models. As for the final submission model, it is trained for 15 epochs (about 460k steps) using both training and validation partitions and the learning rate is exponentially decreased by a factor of 0.9 every 2.5M samples. More details can be found at https://github.com/linrongc/youtube-8m.

4.3 Model Evaluation

We evaluate the performance and parameter efficiency of individual aggregation models in Table 1. For fair comparison, we apply a reverse whitening layer for video features, a dropout layer after concatenation of video and audio features and a logistic model as the video-level classifier in all the presented models. Except for NetVLAD_random which sampled 300 random frames for each video, all the other models didn't use any data augmentation techniques. NetVLAD_small use a linear fully-connected layer to reduce the dimension of inputs to $\frac{1}{4}$ of the original size for visual and audio features, so that the number of parameters are much comparable to other NeXtVLAD models.

From Table 1, one can observe that our proposed NeXtVLAD neural networks are more effective and efficient on parameters than the original NetVLAD model by a significantly large margin. With only about 30% of the size of NetVLAD_random model [5], NeXtVLAD increase the GAP score by about 0.02, which is a significant improvement considering the large size of Youtube-8M dataset. Furthermore, as shown in Fig. 6, the NeXtVLAD model is converging faster, which reaches a training GAP score of about 0.85 in just 1 epoch.

---

[1] https://github.com/google/youtube-8m.
[2] https://www.kaggle.com/c/youtube8m-2018/leaderboard.

Table 1. Performance (on local validation partition) comparison for single aggregation models. The parameters inside parenthesis represents (group number G, dropout ratio, cluster number K, hidden size H)

Model	Parameter	GAP
NetVLAD (-, 0.5drop, 128K, 2048H)	297M	0.8474
NetVLAD_random (-, 0.5drop, 256K, 1024H)	274M	0.8507
NetVLAD_small (-, 0.5drop, 128K, 2048H)	88M	0.8582
NeXtVLAD (32G, 0.2drop, 128K, 2048H)	55M	0.8681
NeXtVLAD (16G, 0.2drop, 128K, 2048H)	58M	0.8685
NeXtVLAD (16G, 0.5drop, 128K, 2048H)	58M	0.8697
NeXtVLAD (8G, 0.5drop, 128K, 2048H)	89M	0.8723

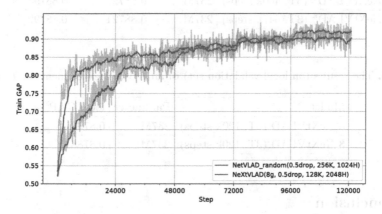

Fig. 6. Training GAP on Youtube-8M dataset. The ticks of x axis are near the end of each epoch.

Surprisingly, the NetVLAD model performs even worse than the NetVLAD_small model, which indicates NetVLAD models tend to overfit the training dataset. Another interesting observation in Fig. 6 is that the most of GAP score gains happens around the beginning of a new epoch for NetVLAD model. The observation implies that the NetVLAD model are more prone to remember the data instead of find useful feature patterns for generalization.

To meet the competition requirements, we use an ensemble of 3 NeXtVLAD models with parameters (0.5drop, 112K, 2048H), whose size is about 944M bytes. As shown in Table 2, training longer can always lead to better performance of NeXtVLAD models. Our best submission is trained about 15 epochs, which takes about 3 days on two 1080 TI GPUs. If we only retain one branch from the mixture model, a single NeXtVLAD model with only 79M parameters will achieve a GAP score of 0.87846, which could be ranked 15/394 in the final leaderboard.

Due to time and resource limit, we set the parameters $T = 3$, which is the temperature in on-the-fly knowledge distillation, as suggested in [32]. We ran an AB test experiments after the competition, as shown in Table 3, somehow indicates $T = 3$ is not optimal. Further tuning of the parameter could result in a better GAP score.

Table 2. The GAP scores of submissions during the competition. All the other parameters used are (0.5drop, 112K, 2048H). The final submissions are tagged with *

Model	Parameter	Private GAP	Public GAP
single NeXtVLAD(460k steps)	79M	0.87846	0.87910
3 NeXtVLAD (3T, 250k steps)	237M	0.88583	0.88657
3 NeXtVLAD (3T, 346k steps)	237M	0.88681	0.88749
3 NeXtVLAD* (3T, 460k steps)	237M	0.88722	0.88794
3 NeXtVLAD* (3T, 647k steps)	237M	0.88721	0.88792

Table 3. The results (on local validation set) of an AB test experiment for T tuning.

Model	Parameter	local GAP
3 NeXtVLAD (0T, 120k steps)	237M	0.8798
3 NeXtVLAD (3T, 120k steps)	237M	0.8788

5   Conclusion

In this paper, a novel NeXtVLAD model is developed to support large-scale video classification under budget constraints. Our NeXtVLAD model has provided a fast and efficient network architecture to aggregate frame-level features into a compact feature vector for video classification. The experimental results on Youtube-8M dataset have demonstrated that our proposed NeXtVLAD model is more effective and efficient on parameters than the previous NetVLAD model, which is the winner of the first Youtube-8M video understanding challenge.

Acknowledgement. The authors would like to thank Kaggle and the Google team for hosting the Youtube-8M video understanding challenge and providing the Youtube-8M Tensorflow Starter Code.

References

1. Abu-El-Haija, S., et al.: Youtube-8m: a large-scale video classification benchmark. arXiv:1609.08675 (2016)
2. Arandjelović, R., Gronat, P., Torii, A., Pajdla, T., Sivic, J.: NetVLAD: CNN architecture for weakly supervised place recognition. In: IEEE Conference on Computer Vision and Pattern Recognition (2016)
3. Hochreiter, S., Schmidhuber, J.: Long short-term memory. Neural Comput. **9**, 1735–1780 (1997)
4. Cho, K., et al.: Learning phrase representations using RNN encoder-decoder for statistical machine translation. In: Moschitti, A., Pang, B., Daelemans, W. (eds.) EMNLP, ACL, pp. 1724–1734 (2014)
5. Miech, A., Laptev, I., Sivic, J.: Learnable pooling with context gating for video classification. CoRR (2017)
6. Xie, S., Girshick, R.B., Dollár, P., Tu, Z., He, K.: Aggregated residual transformations for deep neural networks. CoRR (2016)
7. Sivic, J., Zisserman, A.: Video Google: a text retrieval approach to object matching in videos. In: IEEE International Conference on Computer Vision, vol. 2, pp. 1470–1477 (2003)
8. Perronnin, F., Dance, C.R.: Fisher kernels on visual vocabularies for image categorization. In: CVPR IEEE Computer Society (2007)
9. Jegou, H., Douze, M., Schmid, C., Pérez, P.: Aggregating local descriptors into a compact image representation. In: CVPR IEEE Computer Society, pp. 3304–3311 (2010)
10. Laptev, I., Marszałek, M., Schmid, C., Rozenfeld, B.: Learning realistic human actions from movies. In: CVPR (2008)
11. Schuldt, C., Laptev, I., Caputo, B.: Recognizing human actions: a local SVM approach. In: 17th International Conference on Proceedings of the Pattern Recognition, (ICPR 2004) Volume 3 - Volume 03. ICPR 2004, IEEE Computer Society, pp. 32–36 (2004)
12. Girdhar, R., Ramanan, D., Gupta, A., Sivic, J., Russell, B.: ActionVLAD: learning spatio-temporal aggregation for action classification. In: CVPR (2017)
13. Karpathy, A., Toderici, G., Shetty, S., Leung, T., Sukthankar, R., Fei-Fei, L.: Large-scale video classification with convolutional neural networks. In: CVPR (2014)
14. Caba Heilbron, F., Escorcia, V., Ghanem, B., Carlos Niebles, J.: ActivityNet: a large-scale video benchmark for human activity understanding. In: The IEEE Conference on Computer Vision and Pattern Recognition (CVPR), June 2015
15. Baccouche, M., Mamalet, F., Wolf, C., Garcia, C., Baskurt, A.: Sequential deep learning for human action recognition. In: Salah, A.A., Lepri, B. (eds.) HBU 2011. LNCS, vol. 7065, pp. 29–39. Springer, Heidelberg (2011). https://doi.org/10.1007/978-3-642-25446-8_4
16. Simonyan, K., Zisserman, A.: Two-stream convolutional networks for action recognition in videos. In: Proceedings of the 27th International Conference on Neural Information Processing Systems - Volume 1. NIPS 2014, pp. 568–576. MIT Press (2014)
17. Ji, S., Xu, W., Yang, M., Yu, K.: 3D convolutional neural networks for human action recognition. IEEE Trans. Pattern Anal. Mach. Intell. **35**, 221–231 (2013)
18. Tran, D., Bourdev, L., Fergus, R., Torresani, L., Paluri, M.: Learning spatiotemporal features with 3D convolutional networks. In: Proceedings of the 2015 IEEE International Conference on Computer Vision (ICCV). ICCV 2015, IEEE Computer Society, pp. 4489–4497 (2015)

19. Feichtenhofer, C., Pinz, A., Zisserman, A.: Convolutional two-stream network fusion for video action recognition. CoRR (2016)
20. Wu, Z., Jiang, Y., Wang, X., Ye, H., Xue, X., Wang, J.: Fusing multi-stream deep networks for video classification. CoRR (2015)
21. Ng, J.Y.H., Hausknecht, M., Vijayanarasimhan, S., Vinyals, O., Monga, R., Toderici, G.: Beyond short snippets: deep networks for video classification. In: Computer Vision and Pattern Recognition (2015)
22. Ballas, N., Yao, L., Pal, C., Courville, A.C.: Delving deeper into convolutional networks for learning video representations. CoRR (2015)
23. Fernando, B., Gavves, E., Oramas, J.M., Ghodrati, A., Tuytelaars, T.: Modeling video evolution for action recognition. In: The IEEE Conference on Computer Vision and Pattern Recognition (CVPR), June 2015
24. Wang, X., Farhadi, A., Gupta, A.: Actions transformations. In: CVPR (2016)
25. Bilen, H., Fernando, B., Gavves, E., Vedaldi, A.: Action recognition with dynamic image networks. CoRR (2016)
26. Wang, L., Li, W., Li, W., Gool, L.V.: Appearance-and-relation networks for video classification. Technical report, arXiv (2017)
27. Arandjelovic, R., Zisserman, A.: All about VLAD. In: Proceedings of the 2013 IEEE Conference on Computer Vision and Pattern Recognition, IEEE Computer Society, pp. 1578–1585 (2013)
28. Hu, J., Shen, L., Sun, G.: Squeeze-and-excitation networks. In: CVPR (2018)
29. Hinton, G., Vinyals, O., Dean, J.: Distilling the knowledge in a neural network. In: NIPS Deep Learning and Representation Learning Workshop (2015)
30. Zhang, Y., Xiang, T., Hospedales, T.M., Lu, H.: Deep mutual learning. CoRR (2017)
31. Li, Z., Hoiem, D.: Learning without forgetting. CoRR (2016)
32. Lan, X., Zhu, X., Gong, S.: Knowledge distillation by on-the-fly native ensemble. arXiv:1806.04606 (2018)
33. Ioffe, S., Szegedy, C.: Batch normalization: accelerating deep network training by reducing internal covariate shift. In: Proceedings of the 32nd International Conference on International Conference on Machine Learning - Volume 37. ICML 2015, pp. 448–456. JMLR.org (2015)
34. Deng, J., Dong, W., Socher, R., Li-jia, L., Li, K., Fei-fei, L.: ImageNet: a large-scale hierarchical image database. In: CVPR (2009)
35. Hershey, S., et al.: CNN architectures for large-scale audio classification. CoRR (2016)
36. Abadi, M., et al.: TensorFlow: a system for large-scale machine learning. In: Proceedings of the 12th USENIX Conference on Operating Systems Design and Implementation. OSDI 2016, USENIX Association, pp. 265–283 (2016)
37. Kingma, D.P., Ba, J.: Adam: a method for stochastic optimization. CoRR (2014)

Non-local NetVLAD Encoding for Video Classification

Yongyi Tang[1]([⊠]), Xing Zhang[2], Jingwen Wang[1], Shaoxiang Chen[2], Lin Ma[1], and Yu-Gang Jiang[2]

[1] Tencent AI Lab, Shenzhen, China
yongyi.tang92@gmail.com, jaywongjaywong@gmail.com, forest.linma@gmail.com
[2] Fudan University, Shanghai, China
skyezx2018@gmail.com, forwchen@gmail.com, ygj@fudan.edu.cn

Abstract. This paper describes our solution for the 2nd YouTube-8M video understanding challenge organized by Google AI. Unlike the video recognition benchmarks, such as Kinetics and Moments, the YouTube-8M challenge provides pre-extracted visual and audio features instead of raw videos. In this challenge, the submitted model is restricted to 1 GB, which encourages participants focus on constructing one powerful single model rather than incorporating of the results from a bunch of models. Our system fuses six different sub-models into one single computational graph, which are categorized into three families. More specifically, the most effective family is the model with non-local operations following the NetVLAD encoding. The other two family models are Soft-BoF and GRU, respectively. In order to further boost single models performance, the model parameters of different checkpoints are averaged. Experimental results demonstrate that our proposed system can effectively perform the video classification task, achieving 0.88763 on the public test set and 0.88704 on the private set in terms of GAP@20, respectively. We finally ranked at the fourth place in the YouTube-8M video understanding challenge.

1 Introduction

Understanding video content is a major challenge for numeric applications including video classification [24], video captioning [28,30], video localization [6,11], video attractiveness analysis [8], and so on. Especially with the exponential increment of online videos, video tagging, video retrieval and recommendation is of great demand. Therefore, developing reliable video understanding algorithms and systems has received extensive attentions in the area of computer vision and machine learning.

In order to recognize video content, convolutional neural networks (CNNs) [5,23,24,27] and/or recurrent neural networks based methods [10,26] have achieved state-of-the-arts results. Those methods [24] take the advantages of deep learning methods on static image content as well as the video motion containing temporal information to perform video analysis. However, prior works only perform on those video benchmarks with limited number of videos for model

© Springer Nature Switzerland AG 2019
L. Leal-Taixé and S. Roth (Eds.): ECCV 2018 Workshops, LNCS 11132, pp. 219–228, 2019.
https://doi.org/10.1007/978-3-030-11018-5_20

evaluations such as UCF-101 [25], HMDB-51 [15], and ActivityNet [4] datasets. Recently, several large-scale video datasets are constructed, including the Kinetics dataset [17] developed by DeepMind and the Moments in Time dataset developed by MIT-IBM [21] with about a million of videos. However, for practical video applications such as YouTube and Netflix, such number of videos is still relatively small and not suitable for large-scale video understanding. Nowadays, Google AI releases a large-scale video dataset named YouTube-8M [2], which contains about 8 million YouTube videos with multiple class tags.

For the 1st Youtube-8M video understanding challenge, several techniques including context gating [20], multi-stage training [29], temporal modeling [19], and feature aggregation [7] have been proposed for video classification. However, the excellent performances of prior works mainly attribute to ensemble the results from a bunch of models, which is not practical in real-world applications due to the heavy computational expense. Therefore, the 2nd YouTube-8M video understanding challenge focus on learning video representation under budget constraints. More specifically, the model size of submission is restricted to 1 GB, which encourages the participants to explore compact video understanding models based on the pre-extracted visual and audio features.

In this report, we propose a compact system that meets the requirements and achieves superior results in the challenge. We summarize the contributions as follows. First, we stack the non-local block with the NetVLAD to improve the video feature encoding. Experimental results demonstrate that the proposed non-local NetVLAD pooling method outperforms the vanilla NetVLAD pooling. Second, several techniques are employed for building the large-scale video classification system with limited number of parameters including weight averaging strategy of different checkpoints, model ensemble, and compact encoding of floating point number. Lastly, we show that the selected single models are complementary to each other which makes the whole system achieves a competitive result on the 2nd YouTube-8M video understanding challenge, ranked at the forth position.

2   Approach

The framework of our proposed system is shown in Fig. 1. In this work, we use three different families of video descriptor pooling methods for the video classification task, specifically the non-local NetVLAD, Soft-Bag-of-Feature (Soft-BoF), and GRU. In Sect. 2.1, we introduce the details of the proposed NetVLAD incorporated with the non-local block with its variants introduced in Sect. 2.2. The other two family models, namely the Soft-BoF and GRU, are introduced in Sects. 2.3 and 2.4, respectively. The model ensemble is described in Sect. 2.5.

2.1   Non-local NetVLAD

Vector of Locally Aggregated Descriptors (VLAD). VLAD [14] is a popular descriptor pooling method for instance level retrieval [14] and image classification [12], as it captures the statistic information about the local

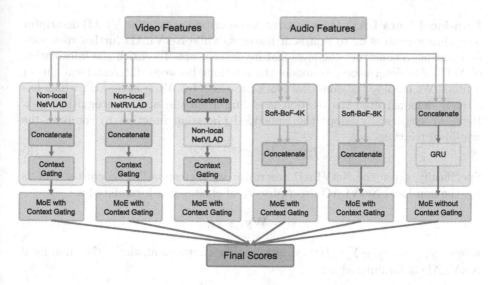

Fig. 1. The framework of our proposed system for video classification.

descriptors aggregated over the image. Specifically, the VLAD summarizes the residuals of descriptors and its corresponding cluster center. Formally, given N D-dimensional descriptors $\{\mathbf{x}_i\}$ as input, and K cluster centers $\{\mathbf{c}_k\}$ as VLAD parameters, the pooling output of VLAD is $K \times D$-dimensional representation V. Writing V as a $K \times D$ matrix, the (j, k) element of V can be computed as follows:

$$V(j,k) = \sum_{i=1}^{N} a_k(\mathbf{x}_i)(x_i(j) - c_k(j)), \tag{1}$$

where the $a_k(\mathbf{x}_i)$ indicates the hard assignment of the descriptor $\mathbf{x}_i$ to k-th visual word $\mathbf{c}_k$. Thus, each column of matrix V records the sum of residuals of the descriptors. Intra-normalization and inter-normalization are performed after VLAD pooling.

NetVLAD Descriptor. However, the VLAD algorithm involves a hard cluster assignment that is non-differentiable. Thus the vanilla VLAD encoding is not appropriate for deep neural network that requires computing gradients for back-propagation. To address this problem, Arandjelovic *et al.* proposed the NetVLAD [3] with soft assignment $\bar{a}_k(\mathbf{x}_i)$ of descriptors $\mathbf{x}_i$ to multiple clusters centers $\mathbf{c}_k$, *i.e.*,

$$\bar{a}_k(\mathbf{x}_i) = \frac{e^{\mathbf{w}_k^T \mathbf{x}_i + b_k}}{\sum_{k'} e^{\mathbf{w}_{k'}^T \mathbf{x}_i + b_{k'}}}, \tag{2}$$

where $\{\mathbf{w}_k\}$, $\{b\}$ and $\{\mathbf{c}_k\}$ are the learnable parameters of the NetVLAD descriptor.

Non-local NetVLAD Descriptor. As described above, the VLAD descriptor uses cluster centers $\mathbf{c}_k$ to represent features, while NetVLAD further uses soft-assignment to construct the local feature descriptors. To enrich the information of NetVLAD descriptors, we model the relations between different local cluster centers. We employ the non-local block proposed by Wang et al. [31], which has already demonstrated the relation modeling ability in action recognition task. Here, we empirically adopt the embedded Gaussian function to compute the non-local relations:

$$f(\mathbf{v}_i, \mathbf{v}_j) = e^{\theta(\mathbf{v}_i)^T \phi(\mathbf{v}_j)}. \tag{3}$$

Specifically, given the NetVLAD descriptor $\mathbf{v}_k$ corresponding to cluster centers $\mathbf{c}_k$, the non-local NetVLAD descriptor $\hat{\mathbf{v}}_k$ of cluster k is formulated as:

$$\hat{\mathbf{v}}_i = \mathbf{W}\mathbf{y}_i + \mathbf{v}_i, \tag{4}$$

where $\mathbf{y}_i = \frac{1}{Z(\mathbf{v})} \sum_{\forall j} f(\mathbf{v}_i, \mathbf{v}_j) g(\mathbf{v}_j)$. For implementation, the non-local NetVLAD is formulated as:

$$\mathbf{y} = \mathrm{softmax}(\mathbf{v}^T \mathbf{W}_\theta^T \mathbf{W}_\phi \mathbf{v}) g(\mathbf{v}), \tag{5}$$

where $g(\mathbf{v})$ is a linear transformation.

2.2 Non-local NetVLAD Model and Its Variants

Note that in our system, we use three variant non-local NetVLAD methods, which are demonstrated to be complementary with each other.

Late-Fused Non-local NetVLAD (LFNL-NetVLAD). The first model is the late-fused non-local NetVLAD (LFNL-NetVLAD). The pre-extracted visual feature and audio feature are encode independently by the non-local NetVLAD pooling method. Afterwards, these two non-local NetVLAD features, encoding visual and audio modalities, are concatenated into a vector, which is followed by the context gating module.

Please note that context gating is introduced by Miech et al. [20], which transforms the input feature into a new representation and captures feature dependencies and prior structure of output space. Context gating is defined as:

$$\mathbf{z} = sigmoid(\mathbf{W}\mathbf{y}) \odot \mathbf{y}, \tag{6}$$

where $\odot$ indicates elements-wise multiplication.

As shown in Fig. 1, the mixture of experts (MoE) model [16] equipped with video level context gating is used for the multi-label video classification.

Late-Fused Non-local NetRVLAD (LFNL-NetRVLAD). In addition, the NetRVLAD that drops the computation of cluster centers is proposed in [20], which can be considered as self-attended local feature representation. Formally, the NetRVLAD can be defined as:

$$V'(j,k) = \sum_{i=1}^{N} \bar{a}_k(\mathbf{x}_i)x_i(j), \qquad (7)$$

where the soft assignment $\{\bar{a}_k\}$ are computed by Eq. 2. Similarly, the video and audio features pass through non-local NetRVLAD pooling and perform concatenation, followed by one context gating module and the MoE equipped with video level context gating.

Early-Fused Non-local NetVLAD (EFNL-NetVLAD). Early fusion that concatenates the video and audio feature before non-local NetVLAD pooling is used to build another model. The early-fused feature lies in different feature space resulting in different expressive ability compared with the late-fused representation. The frame level context gating and video level MoE with context gating are also used in this model.

2.3 Soft-Bag-of-Feature Pooling

For bag-of-feature encoding, we utilize soft-assignment of descriptors to feature clusters [22] to obtain the distinguishable representation. Also, we perform late fusion of Soft-BoF with 4K and 8K clusters, which are named as Soft-BoF-4K and Soft-BoF-8K, respectively. Those outputs only followed by the video level MoE with context gating.

2.4 Gated Recurrent Unit

Recurrent neural networks, especially the Gated Recurrent Unit (GRU) [9], have been investigated for video understanding [7,10,19,20]. We stacked two layers of GRU of 1024 hidden neurons for each layer. The experimental results demonstrate that the GRU model is complementary with the non-local NetVLAD and Soft-BoF families resulting a significant improvement after model ensemble.

2.5 Model Ensemble

Model ensemble is a common way for boosting final results in different challenges [7,19,20,29,32]. The superior improvement may attribute to the various feature expressions of different models. Thus, model ensemble helps to finalize a robust result and relief over-fitting. We perform model ensemble based on the six different models as mentioned. Experimental results along with implementation details will be introduced in the following.

3 Experiments

3.1 YouTube-8M Dataset

The YouTube-8M dataset [2] adopted in the 2nd YouTube-8M Video Understanding Challenge is the 2018 version with higher-quality, more topical annotations, and a cleaner annotation vocabulary. It contains about 6.1 million videos,
3862 class labels and 3 labels per video on average. Because of the large scale of
the dataset, the video information is provided as pre-extracted visual and audio
features at 1 FPS.

Table 1. Single model performances on our split validation set.

Model	LFNL-NetVLAD	EFNL-NetVLAD	LFNL-NetRVLAD
GAP@20	0.8703	0.8674	0.8687
Model size	593M	427M	478M
Model	Soft-BoF-4K	Soft-BoF-8K	GRU
GAP@20	0.8525	0.8512	0.8568
Model size	109M	143M	243M

Table 2. Single averaged model performances on our split validation set.

Averaged model	LFNL-NetVLAD	LFNL-NetRVLAD	EFNL-NetVLAD
GAP@20	0.8716	0.8704	0.8704
Averaged model	Soft-BoF-4K	Soft-BoF-8K	GRU
GAP@20	0.8574	0.8563	0.8612

3.2 Implementation Details

The provided dataset is divided into training, validation and test subsets with
around 70%, 12% and 18% of videos. But in our work, we keep around 100K
videos for validation, and the remaining videos of training and validation subset
are used for training due to the observation of improvement. We found that the
performance on our validation set was 0.02–0.03 lower than the test set on the
public leader board. We report the Global Average Precision (GAP) metric at
top 20 with our split validation subset and the public test set shown on the
leader board.

For most of the models, we empirically used 1024 hidden states except for the
GRU model which adopted 1200 hidden states. We trained every single model
independently with our training split on Tensorflow [1]. The Adam optimizer
[18] with 0.0002 as the initial learning rate was employed throughout our experiments. Training procedures converged around 300k. After finishing the training

procedure, we built a large computational graph of model ensemble, and the parameters within this graph were imported from the independent models. The averaged score of each sub-model was the final score of our system. Further fine-tuning for the system may improve the final score. In the submission, we simply used model-wise averaging due to the lack of time.

3.3   Single Model Evaluation

In this section, we evaluate the six single models used in our system as shown in Table 1. For the LFNL-NetVLAD model, we deployed 64 clusters with 8 MoE in video level model achieving 0.8702 GAP@20 in our validation set, while the vanilla NetVLAD achieves 0.8698 under the same settings. Also, 64 clusters were adopted in the EFNL-NetVLAD and the LFNL-NetRVLAD since we found this setting keeps the balance between model size and performance. And the MoE of these two models were 2 and 4, respectively. The model size of non-local NetVLAD models are around 500M, which takes a large portion of the parameters in our system.

We also adopted the GRU model with model size as 243M and two smaller Soft-BoF models with 4K and 8K clusters, respectively, since we found that those models are complementary to the non-local NetVLAD models. The MoE of these three models were set to 2.

In order to further boost the single model performance, we employed linear model averaging that utilizing the average of multiple checkpoint to improve single model performance inspired by Stochastic Weight Averaging method [13]. The final GAP@20 of each model is shown in Table 2, which shows that linear model averaging can significantly improve single model performance especially for the GRU and Soft-BoF models with over 0.005 improvements.

3.4   Tricks for Compact Model Ensemble

Recall that the challenge requires less than 1 GB model for final submission. We thus adopted several techniques for improving model abilities under the limited parameters including using 'bfloat16' format of parameters and repeatedly random sampling.

At first, we trained the network with float32 in Tensorflow [1], which means that it takes 4 bytes for every parameter. To make our model meet the model size requirement, we used a tensorflow-specific format, 'bfloat16', in the ensemble stage, which is different from IEEE's float16 format. The bfloat16 is a compact 16-bit encoding of floating point number with 8 bits for exponent and 7 bits for mantissa. We found that using 'bfloat16' format can accelerate the process without significant performance decrease, with its benefits on halving the model size which makes ensembling multiple models become possible. As results, we performed ensemble with the models mentioned in Table 2 into one computational graph as our final model as shown in Table 3.

Table 3. Ensemble model performances on our split validation set. M1–M6 denote LFNL-NetVLAD, LFNL-NetRVLAD, EFNL-NetVLAD, Soft-BoF-4k, Soft-BoF-8k and GRU, respectively.

Ensemble model	Validation GAP@20	Public-Test GAP@20
M1 & M4	0.8752	-
M1 & M2	0.8778	-
M1 & M6	0.8782	0.8790
M1 & M4 & M6	0.8800	-
M1 & M2 & M4 & M6	0.8820	-
M1 & M2 & M3 & M4 & M6	0.8839	0.88678
M1 & M2 & M3 & M4 & M5 & M6	0.8842	-

Further, since feature sub-sampling were used in our sub-models for better generalization, we performed multiple running with different feature sub-sampling in the same system to produce the final classification result. By averaging the 10 times repeated results, the final performance gained about 0.0005 improvement on our validation set as shown in Table 4. In practice, we repeated the input feature several times, and averaged the results for each video. The final model size of our submission is 995M.

Table 4. Performances of our model with different times of random averaging.

Ensemble model	Validation GAP@20	Public-Test GAP@20
Our model run once	0.8842	-
Our model run 5 times	0.8846	0.88756
Our model run 10 times (final submission)	0.8847	0.88763

4   Conclusions

In this report, we proposed a compact large-scale video understanding system that effectively performs multi-label classification on the YouTube-8M video dataset with limited model size under 1 GB. A non-local NetVLAD pooling method is proposed for constructing more representative video descriptors. Several models including LFNL-NetVLAD, LFNL-NetRVLAD, EFNL-NetVLAD, GRU, Soft-BoF-4K, and Soft-BoF-8K are incorporated in our system for model ensemble. To halve model size, bfloat16 format is adopted in our final system. Averaging multiple outputs after random sampling is also used in our system for further boosting the performance. Experimental results on the 2nd YouTube-8M video understanding challenge show that the proposed system outperforms most of the competitors, ranking the fourth place in the final result.

References

1. Abadi, M., et al.: Tensorflow: a system for large-scale machine learning (2016)
2. Abu-El-Haija, S., et al.: Youtube-8m: a large-scale video classification benchmark. arXiv preprint arXiv:1609.08675 (2016)
3. Arandjelovic, R., Gronat, P., Torii, A., Pajdla, T., Sivic, J.: NetVLAD: CNN architecture for weakly supervised place recognition. In: Proceedings of the IEEE Conference on Computer Vision and Pattern Recognition, pp. 5297–5307 (2016)
4. Caba Heilbron, F., Escorcia, V., Ghanem, B., Carlos Niebles, J.: Activitynet: a large-scale video benchmark for human activity understanding. In: Proceedings of the IEEE Conference on Computer Vision and Pattern Recognition, pp. 961–970 (2015)
5. Carreira, J., Zisserman, A.: Quo vadis, action recognition? A new model and the kinetics dataset. In: 2017 IEEE Conference on Computer Vision and Pattern Recognition (CVPR), pp. 4724–4733. IEEE (2017)
6. Chen, J., Chen, X., Ma, L., Jie, Z., Chua, T.S.: Temporally grounding natural sentence in video. In: EMNLP (2018)
7. Chen, S., Wang, X., Tang, Y., Chen, X., Wu, Z., Jiang, Y.G.: Aggregating frame-level features for large-scale video classification. arXiv preprint arXiv:1707.00803 (2017)
8. Chen, X., et al.: Fine-grained video attractiveness prediction using multimodal deep learning on a large real-world dataset. In: WWW (2018)
9. Cho, K., Van Merriënboer, B., Bahdanau, D., Bengio, Y.: On the properties of neural machine translation: encoder-decoder approaches. arXiv preprint arXiv:1409.1259 (2014)
10. Donahue, J., et al.: Long-term recurrent convolutional networks for visual recognition and description. In: Proceedings of the IEEE Conference on Computer Vision and Pattern Recognition, pp. 2625–2634 (2015)
11. Feng, Y., Ma, L., Liu, W., Zhang, T., Luo, J.: Video Re-localization. In: Ferrari, V., Hebert, M., Sminchisescu, C., Weiss, Y. (eds.) Computer Vision – ECCV 2018. LNCS, vol. 11218, pp. 55–70. Springer, Cham (2018). https://doi.org/10.1007/978-3-030-01264-9_4
12. Gong, Y., Wang, L., Guo, R., Lazebnik, S.: Multi-scale orderless pooling of deep convolutional activation features. In: Fleet, D., Pajdla, T., Schiele, B., Tuytelaars, T. (eds.) ECCV 2014. LNCS, vol. 8695, pp. 392–407. Springer, Cham (2014). https://doi.org/10.1007/978-3-319-10584-0_26
13. Izmailov, P., Podoprikhin, D., Garipov, T., Vetrov, D., Wilson, A.G.: Averaging weights leads to wider optima and better generalization. arXiv preprint arXiv:1803.05407 (2018)
14. Jégou, H., Douze, M., Schmid, C., Pérez, P.: Aggregating local descriptors into a compact image representation. In: 2010 IEEE Conference on Computer Vision and Pattern Recognition (CVPR), pp. 3304–3311. IEEE (2010)
15. Jhuang, H., Garrote, H., Poggio, E., Serre, T., Hmdb, T.: A large video database for human motion recognition. In: Proceedings of IEEE International Conference on Computer Vision (2011)
16. Jordan, M.I., Jacobs, R.A.: Hierarchical mixtures of experts and the EM algorithm. Neural Comput. 6(?), 181–214 (1994)
17. Kay, W., et al.: The kinetics human action video dataset. arXiv preprint arXiv:1705.06950 (2017)

18. Kingma, D.P., Ba, J.: Adam: a method for stochastic optimization. arXiv preprint arXiv:1412.6980 (2014)
19. Li, F., et al.: Temporal modeling approaches for large-scale youtube-8m video understanding. arXiv preprint arXiv:1707.04555 (2017)
20. Miech, A., Laptev, I., Sivic, J.: Learnable pooling with context gating for video classification. arXiv preprint arXiv:1706.06905 (2017)
21. Monfort, M., et al.: Moments in time dataset: one million videos for event understanding. arXiv preprint arXiv:1801.03150 (2018)
22. Philbin, J., Chum, O., Isard, M., Sivic, J., Zisserman, A.: Lost in quantization: improving particular object retrieval in large scale image databases (2008)
23. Qiu, Z., Yao, T., Mei, T.: Learning spatio-temporal representation with pseudo-3D residual networks. In: 2017 IEEE International Conference on Computer Vision (ICCV), pp. 5534–5542. IEEE (2017)
24. Simonyan, K., Zisserman, A.: Two-stream convolutional networks for action recognition in videos. In: NIPS (2014)
25. Soomro, K., Zamir, A.R., Shah, M.: UCF101: a dataset of 101 human actions classes from videos in the wild. arXiv preprint arXiv:1212.0402 (2012)
26. Tang, Y., Zhang, P., Hu, J.F., Zheng, W.S.: Latent embeddings for collective activity recognition. In: 2017 14th IEEE International Conference on Advanced Video and Signal Based Surveillance (AVSS), pp. 1–6. IEEE (2017)
27. Tran, D., Bourdev, L., Fergus, R., Torresani, L., Paluri, M.: Learning spatiotemporal features with 3D convolutional networks. In: Proceedings of the IEEE International Conference on Computer Vision, pp. 4489–4497 (2015)
28. Wang, B., Ma, L., Zhang, W., Liu, W.: Reconstruction network for video captioning. In: CVPR (2018)
29. Wang, H.D., Zhang, T., Wu, J.: The monkeytyping solution to the youtube-8m video understanding challenge. arXiv preprint arXiv:1706.05150 (2017)
30. Wang, J., Jiang, W., Ma, L., Liu, W., Xu, Y.: Bidirectional attentive fusion with context gating for dense video captioning. In: CVPR (2018)
31. Wang, X., Girshick, R., Gupta, A., He, K.: Non-local neural networks. In: The IEEE Conference on Computer Vision and Pattern Recognition (CVPR), June 2018
32. Xiaoteng, Z., et al.: Qiniu submission to activitynet challenge 2018. arXiv preprint arXiv:1806.04391 (2018)

Learnable Pooling Methods for Video Classification

Sebastian Kmiec$^{(\boxtimes)}$ ⓘ, Juhan Bae$^{(\boxtimes)}$ ⓘ, and Ruijian An$^{(\boxtimes)}$ ⓘ

University of Toronto, Toronto, Canada
{sebastian.kmiec,juhan.bae,ruijian.an}@mail.utoronto.ca

Abstract. We introduce modifications to state-of-the-art approaches to aggregating local video descriptors by using attention mechanisms and function approximations. Rather than using ensembles of existing architectures, we provide an insight on creating new architectures. We demonstrate our solutions in the "The 2nd YouTube-8M Video Understanding Challenge", by using frame-level video and audio descriptors. We obtain testing accuracy similar to the state of the art, while meeting budget constraints, and touch upon strategies to improve the state of the art. Model implementations are available in https://github.com/pomonam/LearnablePoolingMethods.

Keywords: Video classification · Youtube-8M · NetVLAD
Attention · Pooling · Aggregation

1 Introduction

The problem of summarizing local descriptors is highly investigated and encompasses many domains in machine learning such as image retrieval. The goal of aggregating local descriptors is to construct a single global descriptor that encodes useful information. Although progress exists in the context of local video descriptor aggregation [2,12], few works adequately provide solutions for differentiable descriptor aggregation, such as NetBoW [12] and SMK [14,16].

Aggregation of local descriptors extends to the task of video classification. Many existing models focus on learning temporal relations within a video. In particular, recurrent neural networks (RNN) with the help of Long Short Term Memory (LSTM) or gated rectified units (GRU) can capture the long-term temporal patterns in between frames. In this paper, however, we question the usefulness of learning temporal relationships in video classification. This is also largely motivated by the work of NetVLAD [2] and attention clusters [11], producing a dominant result compared to recurrent methods [3,18].

Despite the success of NetVLAD for the task of video understanding [12], many design choices are left unexplained. For example, the individual contribution of cluster center residuals to the global representation is unclear. The model also exhibits several weaknesses. For instance, the global representation generated by NetVLAD is projected to a significantly lower dimensional space

© Springer Nature Switzerland AG 2019
L. Leal-Taixé and S. Roth (Eds.): ECCV 2018 Workshops, LNCS 11132, pp. 229–238, 2019.
https://doi.org/10.1007/978-3-030-11018-5_21

for classification, which we suspect is difficult for a single layer to manipulate. To accommodate these issues, inspired by [5,17], we propose a model capable of learning inter-feature relationships before and after the NetVLAD layer.

2   Related Work

In this section, we outline previous works that heavily influenced the creation of our learnable pooling architectures.

2.1   Attention Mechanisms

Our work is largely inspired by [11], where for a given set of local descriptors, an attention representation is created via a simple weighted sum of local descriptors. These weights are computed as a function of the local descriptors to exclusively obtain information from useful descriptors in the attention representation. This attention representation is termed an attention cluster, and multiple clusters are concatenated to form a final global representation. A novel shifting operation, as in Eq. (1), enables each attention cluster to diverge from each other, while keeping scale invariance. Below is the output of a single attention cluster; $\mathbf{X}$ is a matrix of local descriptors, $\mathbf{a}$ is a vector of attention weights, computed via a simple two layer, feed-forward network.

$$\psi_k(X) = \frac{\alpha \cdot \mathbf{a}\mathbf{X} + \beta}{\sqrt{N}\,\|\alpha \cdot \mathbf{a}\mathbf{X} + \beta\|_2} \tag{1}$$

Although the above mechanism has the capacity to learn the training data, the model heavily overfits, and fails to generalize well. We hypothesize that as you are computing a weighted sum of input descriptors, slight changes in the distribution of inputs will have a large negative impact on performance. Intuitively, to avoid this problem, internal embeddings should be summed instead, and these internal embeddings should be a function of the inputs, to improve generalization.

Following the above logic is the work by Vaswani et al. [17], whom achieved state-of-the-art performance for machine translation tasks, using a novel attention mechanism termed Transformer. In the context of their work, local embeddings are projected to query, key and value spaces. The similarity of keys ($\mathbf{K}$) to queries ($\mathbf{Q}$) is then used to provide weights to the internal embedding vectors (as in Eq. (2)) that are passed to feed forward networks. Both [11] and [17] use dot product attention for attention-based representations. However, attention clusters intend to provide a straight-forward global representation, whereas a Transformer creates a new attention-based encoding of equal dimensionality. Our use of Transformers is covered in detail within Sect. 3.

$$\text{Attention}(Q, K, V) = \text{softmax}(\frac{\mathbf{Q}\mathbf{K}^T}{\alpha})\mathbf{V} \tag{2}$$

2.2 Differentiable Pooling

The work of [12] provides a useful baseline for a video classification model, as it provides the highest known accuracy of any single architecture, as of the "Google Cloud & YouTube-8M Video Understanding Challenge". The authors utilized NetVLAD [2], along with a novel network block that is comparable to residual blocks [7], known as gating. Gating has the effect of re-weighting the importance of features detected, and decisions made based on these features.

VLAD itself summarizes a set of local descriptors by presenting these descriptors via a distribution [8]. This distribution is encoded in the sum of distances to cluster centres. Specifically, looking at Eq. (3), a_j refers to the cluster soft similarity of descriptor x_k to the jth cluster center, introduced by NetVLAD to avoid non-differentiable hard assignments. Here, $x_k - c_j$ refers to a single distance of a local descriptor to a cluster centre. This is a sound technique that is used in many areas [6,20], while achieving state of the art performance in the benchmarks such as [15].

$$VLAD(i, j) = \sum_{k=1}^{N} a_j(x_k)\,(x_k(i) - c_j(i)) \tag{3}$$

Despite the success and prominence of VLAD, numerous design choices in [12] are left unexplained. For instance, the cluster similarities, a_j, are computed via a simple linear transformation, where each local video descriptor is compared via dot product with a key per cluster centre, followed by a softmax layer. It is a straightforward idea to consider multiple keys per cluster centre, or to use multiple temporally close local descriptors per cluster similarity prediction.

Further on the notion of design choices, another weakness arises in the architecture after the NetVLAD block. Aside from the use of gating, all outputs of the NetVLAD module are simply squeezed and/or projected to a low dimensional space for classification, this is too demanding of a task for a single layer to perform optimally. A final criticism is that this model does not attempt to leverage inter-feature relationships prior to the use of the NetVLAD module.

2.3 Regularized Aggregation

Following the success of VLAD is the work of [9]. The authors split the problem of local descriptor pooling into problems of local descriptor embedding and aggregation. We specifically utilize the ideas for local descriptor embeddings. The work of [9] creates a new embedding technique by focusing on overcoming pitfalls when using NetVLAD, by L2 normalizing the distances from cluster centers (residuals) before summing to help give an equal contribution to each residual. These embeddings are known as Triangulation embeddings, or T-embeddings. Further, the authors suggest whitening the residuals by removing a bias and de-correlating the residuals per cluster center, for a given local descriptor, before summing.

We do utilize the above two ideas. However, the suggestion of using democratic weights before summing [9] is avoided. The use of democratic weights is intended to give each local descriptor an equal contribution to the similarity of the class they belong to. Nevertheless, it is not clear how to make an easily parallelizable implementation of the Sinkhorn scaling algorithm to obtain a solution for these weights. The use of weights is described in Eq. (4), where X is the set of local descriptors belonging to a given class, and ϕ_i is an embedding per local descriptor, as displayed in Eq. (5). In Eq. (6), Σ is the covariance matrix of $R(X)$, where $R(X)$ is a random variable representing $R(x_i)$ in the set of X, per class. A single $R(x_i)$ is the concatenation of normalized residuals to K cluster centers for a single local descriptor, as in (6).

$$\psi(X) = \sum_{i=1}^{N} \lambda_i \phi_i \tag{4}$$

$$\phi_i(x_i) = \Sigma^{-1/2}(R(x_i) - E[R(X)]) \tag{5}$$

$$R(x_i) = [r_1(x_i), \ldots, r_K(x_i)] \tag{6}$$

2.4   Function Approximations

The work of [5] builds upon [19], which intends to provide an encoding per image, for the sake of image classification, using a weighted sum of local tangents at anchor points. Despite the dissimilarity of use cases for VLAD and tangent encoding, the authors of [5] provide a mathematical formulation, to describe how given a certain set of cluster similarity weights, tangent encoding is a generalization of VLAD.

As tangent encoding is a technique to linearly approximate a high dimensional function [5], the authors naturally extend VLAD to a second order approximation to obtain a unique local descriptor embedding, while incorporating ideas from other methods such as [9] for aggregation. An embedding per local descriptor is described in Eq. (7), where $\phi_i(x_i)$ is the concatenation of three vectors, per cluster center j. The $a_j(x_i)$ can be thought of as cluster similarities, as in Eq (3).

What is newly introduced to VLAD is the flattened vector of $a_j(x_i) \cdot F(v_{i,j}v_{i,j}^T)$ (in this equation $F(\cdot)$ is the flattening operation), this provides the second order approximation of our hypothetical function, derived from a Taylor expansion [5]. In addition, objective functions are provided to help regularize the learning of weights, so as to ensure a valid function approximation, this is further discussed in Sect. 3.3.

$$\phi_i(x_i) = [a_j(x_i); a_j(x_i) \cdot v_{i,j}; a_j(x_i) \cdot F(v_{i,j}v_{i,j}^T)]_{j=1}^{K} \tag{7}$$

$$v_{i,j} = (x_i - c_j) \tag{8}$$

3   Learnable Pooling Architectures

In this section, we describe the architecture of our proposed learnable, pooling methods, for the purpose of video classification. As inputs to our pooling methods, we have audio and video features already extracted at the frame level per second of video, from the "YouTube-8M Dataset" [1]. Our pooling methods aggregate all local descriptors per frame into a single global representation that describes a video, with possible post-processing afterwards. The final global video descriptor is then passed to a Mixture-of-Experts (MoE) [13] for classification, where probabilities are output across possible video labels.

3.1   Attention Enhanced NetVLAD

Our first approach is to use a transformer encoder before and after a NetVLAD module, as in Fig. 1. Our local descriptor pooling is based largely on the work of [12]. As motivated in Sect. 2.2, NetVLAD with context gating is the current (completely differentiable) state of the art for video pooling, as per benchmarks [15], and the result of the "Google Cloud & YouTube-8M Video Understanding Challenge". Similarly, we have already motivated the use of Transformers in Sect. 2.1.

The first block is a mapping of $f_1 : \mathbb{R}^{N \times F} \to \mathbb{R}^{N \times F}$, where N is the number of frame features sampled, and F is the feature size. The first transformer operates on the level of frames. As we uniformly sample frames per video as input, information relating to the relative positions of local descriptors inherently exists within the attention mechanism.

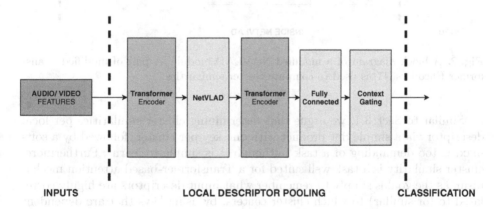

Fig. 1. A block diagram of an attention enhanced NetVLAD model. A modified Transformer Encoder [17] is placed before and after the NetVLAD module.

The second block is a mapping $f_2 : \mathbb{R}^{C \times F} \to \mathbb{R}^{C \times F}$, where C is the number of NetVLAD cluster centers. The second block operates on the level of clusters. Our belief is that using separate query/key/value projection per cluster (as per the Transformer encoder), should be easier to learn than a single fully connected layer, that must perform the function of attention, decision making and dimensionality reduction all at once. We effectively spread the responsibility of these crucial functions across multiple layers, increasing the capacity of the initial work of [12].

The Transformer Encoder in Fig. 1 refers to the work of [17], with batch normalization added to inner layers within the Multi-Head Attention block, to make learning a simpler process.

3.2 NetVLAD with Attention Based Cluster Similarities

Along with the aforementioned Transformer based model, we propose the following model, using modified NetVLAD modules. As in Fig. 2, the first Transformer encoder is a mapping of $g_1 : \mathbb{R}^{N \times F} \to \mathbb{R}^{N \times F}$, whereas the second encoder is modified to be a mapping from $g_2 : \mathbb{R}^{N \times F} \to \mathbb{R}^{C \times F}$.

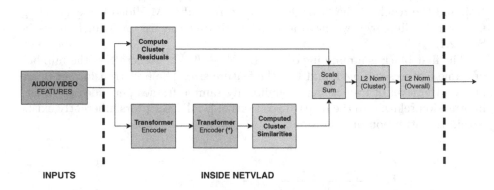

Fig. 2. A block diagram of a modified NetVLAD module. A pair of modified Transformer Encoders [17] is used to compute cluster similarities.

Similar to Sect. 3.1, we argue that determining cluster similarities per local descriptor via a simple dot product with one key per cluster, followed by a softmax, is too demanding of a task (although it is simple to learn). Furthermore, cluster similarity is a task well suited for a Transformer-based attention mechanism, as the goal is simply to remember what input descriptors are highly correlated to (or similar) to which cluster centers, by using keys that are dependent on the inputs themselves. In addition, by using a Transformer, our prediction of input descriptor similarity to a cluster now receives information from other input descriptors, further improving the capacity of the initial work of [12].

The Transformer Encoder (*) in Fig. 2 is similar to the Transformer encoder discussed in Sect. 3.1, however, the final feed forward layer projects to a dimension of size C instead of F, and hence, the final residual connection is removed.

3.3 Regularized Function Approximation Approach

Given our heavy reliance on NetVLAD [2] in our previous two models, our final model attempts to address issues that lie within NetVLAD and adaptations.

The work of [9] already provides useful suggestions regarding possible pitfalls when using NetVLAD, by L2 normalizing the distances from cluster centers (residuals) before summing, as well as whitening these residuals. Unfortunately, we do not make use of democratic weights for aggregation of intermediate T-embeddings, as proposed in [9], as even simplified versions of the Sinkhorn scaling algorithm (with assumptions made) are slow to train with.

To account for the discriminative power lost by missing democratic weights, we unite the works of [5,9,19], as illustrated in Fig. 3. By adding second order terms, we now introduce more useful information in our global representation by adding multiplicative residual terms. To the point, these multiplicative terms cannot be computed by a simple linear transformation that follows our global representation, as is the case in [12].

Notice that for the second order terms, we first project the inputs to a lower space, as the second order cluster residuals are elements of $\mathbb{R}^{B \times N \times C \times F \times F}$, where B is the batch size, N is the number of local descriptors per video, C is the number of clusters and F is the input feature size. This is too large to fit even on multiple high-end commercial GPUs, given a feature size of 1024 (video features). Also note that as we perform a simple linear projection, as well as separate cluster centre and similarity computations for these squeezed features, it is expected that performance is to be lost.

Furthermore, we do not utilize the suggested regularizer terms within cost functions, as in [5]. The reason being that regularization requires tuning in order to provide a valid contribution. Given the large amount of time required to train this model, we avoid additional regularization terms. Although regularizer terms such as in [5], or in [4] (for the sake of cluster center sparsity), may be necessary to overcome generalization issues discussed in Sect. 4.

4   Experiments

Herein, we provide implementation details for experiments performed on models found in Sect. 3. All of the aforementioned models can be found in https://github. com/pomonam/LearnablePoolingMethods, with complete documentation and easily usable modules.

4.1   Training Details

The Youtube-8M dataset is split into training (70%), validation (20%) and testing (10%). For the sake of accuracy, we utilize both training and validation portions of the Youtube-8M dataset for training, while leaving out a random 2% of data for the sake of local validation testing.

All transformer related experiments are trained using the Adam optimizer [10] with an initial learning rate of 0.0003 and a batch size of 32 (64 in all) on two NVIDIA P100 GPUs. All function approximation related experiments are performed using a batch size of 4 (32 in all) on eight NVIDIA K80 GPUs. For each video, we utilized uniform sampling of 256 frames, to be able evenly

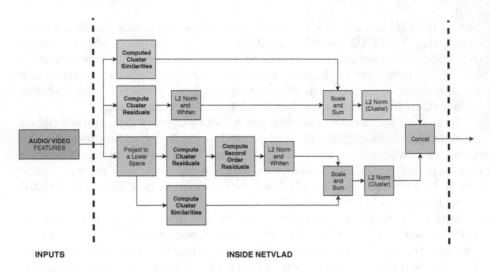

Fig. 3. A block diagram of the second order, function approximation based model. In addition to the usual NetVLAD implementation, we add residual normalization and whitening, along with second order terms based on projected input features.

select features consistently, while maintaining temporal consistency, for the sake of attention-based models.

We did not train many of our models exhaustively due to time and resource constraints while participating in this competition. We stop training early after roughly 3 epochs (270 k steps). For complete implementation details, visit our GitHub repository.

4.2 Testing Results

In the "The 2nd YouTube-8M Video Understanding Challenge", models are evaluated using the Global Average Precision (GAP) metric. In Eq. (9), p(i) and r(i) refer to the precision and recall of the top i predictions, respectively.

$$GAP = \sum_{k=1}^{20} p(i) * r(i) \tag{9}$$

Our results are encouraging, but currently, do not improve the state of the art. Our largest issue for the models listed in Table 1, as well as other models that exist in our GitHub repository, is the problem of generalization and/or overfitting, which is a relatively poorly understood topic. During training, we clearly have the capacity to learn training regularities, however, we inevitably overfit, even when experimenting with common techniques such as dropout and early stop.

Despite our misfortune, it is possible to extend our second order models by creating a parallelizable Sinkhorn scaling algorithm to make use of crucial

Table 1. A collection of the highest testing scores, as determined by Global Average Precision (**GAP**). Second Order refers to Sect. 3.3, Attention Enhanced refers to Sect. 3.1 and Attention NetVLAD refers to Sect. 3.2

Name	Training steps	Batch size	Public test **GAP**
Baseline NetVLAD	270 k	80	**0.870**
Second Order	270 k	32	0.865
Attention Enhanced	270 k	64	0.856
Attention NetVLAD	220 k	64	**0.867**

democratic weights, or by avoiding the stage of projecting input features into a low dimensional space (given hardware resources for such a model). In addition, exploration of other regularization techniques, such as regularizer cost functions from Sect. 3.3 are promising.

5 Conclusions

In this paper, we made modifications to the state-of-the-art approaches for aggregating local video descriptors. We drew a connection between NetVLAD and Transformers to learn cluster similarities per local descriptors. In addition, we had some encouraging results using a function approximation approach. These techniques increased model capacity compared to the state of the art. Experimental results demonstrate that the testing accuracy is similar to that of the state of the art. Due to the time constraints of the competition, we did not fully investigate parameter tuning or overfitting issues. We plan to explore regularization costs, as well as other avenues discussed for accuracy improvement.

References

1. Abu-El-Haija, S., et al.: Youtube-8m: a large-scale video classification benchmark. arXiv:1609.08675 (2016). https://arxiv.org/pdf/1609.08675v1.pdf
2. Arandjelović, R., Gronat, P., Torii, A., Pajdla, T., Sivic, J.: Netvlad: CNN architecture for weakly supervised place recognition. IEEE Trans. Pattern Anal. Mach. Intell. **40**(6), 1437–1451 (2018). https://doi.org/10.1109/TPAMI.2017.2711011
3. Bian, Y., et al.: Revisiting the effectiveness of off-the-shelf temporal modeling approaches for large-scale video classification. arXiv preprint arXiv:1708.03805 (2017)
4. Brock, A., Lim, T., Ritchie, J.M., Weston, N.: Neural photo editing with introspective adversarial networks. CoRR abs/1609.07093 (2016). http://arxiv.org/abs/1609.07093
5. Do, T., Tran, Q.D., Cheung, N.: Faemb: a function approximation-based embedding method for image retrieval. In: IEEE Conference on Computer Vision and Pattern Recognition, CVPR 2015, Boston, MA, USA, 7–12 June 2015, pp. 3556–3564 (2015). https://doi.org/10.1109/CVPR.2015.7298978

6. Girdhar, R., Ramanan, D., Gupta, A., Sivic, J., Russell, B.: Actionvlad: Learning spatio-temporal aggregation for action classification
7. He, K., Zhang, X., Ren, S., Sun, J.: Deep residual learning for image recognition. CoRR abs/1512.03385 (2015). http://arxiv.org/abs/1512.03385
8. Jégou, H., Perronnin, F., Douze, M., Sánchez, J., Pérez, P., Schmid, C.: Aggregating local image descriptors into compact codes. IEEE Trans. Pattern Anal. Mach. Intell. **34**(9), 1704–1716 (2012). https://doi.org/10.1109/TPAMI.2011.235
9. Jégou, H., Zisserman, A.: Triangulation embedding and democratic aggregation for image search. In: 2014 IEEE Conference on Computer Vision and Pattern Recognition, CVPR 2014, Columbus, OH, USA, 23–28 June 2014, pp. 3310–3317 (2014). https://doi.org/10.1109/CVPR.2014.417
10. Kingma, D.P., Ba, J.: Adam: a method for stochastic optimization. CoRR abs/1412.6980 (2014). http://arxiv.org/abs/1412.6980
11. Long, X., Gan, C., de Melo, G., Wu, J., Liu, X., Wen, S.: Attention clusters: purely attention based local feature integration for video classification. CoRR abs/1711.09550 (2017). http://arxiv.org/abs/1711.09550
12. Miech, A., Laptev, I., Sivic, J.: Learnable pooling with context gating for video classification. CoRR abs/1706.06905 (2017). http://arxiv.org/abs/1706.06905
13. Jordan, M.I., Jacobs, R.A.: Hierarchical mixtures of experts and the EM algorithm. Neural Comput. **6**(2), 181–214 (1994). https://doi.org/10.1162/neco.1994.6.2.181
14. Radenovic, F., Iscen, A., Tolias, G., Avrithis, Y., Chum, O.: Revisiting oxford and paris: large-scale image retrieval benchmarking. In: IEEE Computer Vision and Pattern Recognition Conference (2018)
15. Radenovic, F., Iscen, A., Tolias, G., Avrithis, Y.S., Chum, O.: Revisiting oxford and paris: large-scale image retrieval benchmarking. CoRR abs/1803.11285 (2018). http://arxiv.org/abs/1803.11285
16. Tolias, G., Avrithis, Y., Jégou, H.: Image search with selective match kernels: aggregation across single and multiple images. Int. J. Comput. Vis. **116**(3), 247–261 (2016)
17. Vaswani, A., et al.: Attention is all you need. In: Advances in Neural Information Processing Systems 30: Annual Conference on Neural Information Processing Systems 2017, Long Beach, CA, USA, 4–9 December 2017, pp. 6000–6010 (2017). http://papers.nips.cc/paper/7181-attention-is-all-you-need
18. Xie, S., Sun, C., Huang, J., Tu, Z., Murphy, K.: Rethinking spatiotemporal feature learning for video understanding. arXiv preprint arXiv:1712.04851 (2017)
19. Yu, K., Zhang, T.: Improved local coordinate coding using local tangents. In: Proceedings of the 27th International Conference on Machine Learning (ICML 2010), Haifa, Israel, 21–24 June 2010, pp. 1215–1222 (2010). http://www.icml2010.org/papers/454.pdf
20. Zhu, Y., Wang, J., Xie, L., Zheng, L.: Attention-based pyramid aggregation network for visual place recognition. arXiv preprint arXiv:1808.00288 (2018)

Constrained-Size Tensorflow Models for YouTube-8M Video Understanding Challenge

Tianqi Liu[1(✉)] and Bo Liu[2]

[1] Google, New York, USA
`tianqiliu@google.com`
[2] Kensho Technologies, Cambridge, USA
`bo.liu@kensho.com`

Abstract. This paper presents our 7th place solution to the second YouTube-8M video understanding competition which challenges participates to build a constrained-size model to classify millions of YouTube videos into thousands of classes. Our final model consists of four single models aggregated into one Tensorflow graph. For each single model, we use the same network architecture as in the winning solution of the first YouTube-8M video understanding competition, namely Gated NetVLAD. We train the single models separately in Tensorflow's default float32 precision, then replace weights with float16 precision and ensemble them in the evaluation and inference stages, achieving 48.5% compression rate without loss of precision. Our best model achieved 88.324% GAP on private leaderboard. The code is publicly available at https://github.com/boliu61/youtube-8m.

Keywords: Computer vision · Video analysis · Deep learning Tensorflow

1 Introduction

Enormous amount of video content is generated all over the world every day. As an important research topic in computer vision, video analysis has many applications such as recommendation, search, and ranking. Recently, video classification problem gained interest with broad range of applications such as emotion recognition [8], human activity understanding [4], and event detection [28].

YouTube-8M dataset [1] released by Google AI consists of over 6 million YouTube videos of 2.6 billion audio and visual features with 3,700+ of associated visual entities on average of 3.0 labels per video. Each video was decoded at 1 frame-per-second up to the first 360 s, after which features were extracted via pretrained model. PCA and quantization were further applied to reduce dimensions and data size. Visual features of 1024 dimensions and audio features of 128 dimensions were extracted on each frame as input for downstream classifiers.

T. Liu and B. Liu are equally contributed.

© Springer Nature Switzerland AG 2019
L. Leal-Taixé and S. Roth (Eds.): ECCV 2018 Workshops, LNCS 11132, pp. 239–249, 2019.
https://doi.org/10.1007/978-3-030-11018-5_22

Following the first YouTube8M Kaggle competition, the second one is focused on developing compact models no greater than 1 GB uncompressed so that it can be applicable on user's personal mobile phones for personalized and privacy-preserving computation. Challenges in such competition include modeling correlations between labels, handling multiple sequential frame-level features, and efficient model compression.

In the competition, Global Average Precision (GAP) at 20 is used as metric. For each video, the model should predict 20 most confident labels with associated confidence (probability). The list of N tuples $\{video, label, confidence\}$ is sorted by confidence levels in descending order. GAP is then computed as:

$$GAP = \sum_{i=1}^{N} p(i) \Delta r(i) \tag{1}$$

where $p(i)$ is the precision, and $r(i)$ is the recall.

Common approach for video analysis typically extract features from consecutive features followed by feature aggregation. Frame-level feature extraction can be achieved by applying pre-trained Convolutional Neural Networks (CNN) [12,17,23,26]. Common methods for temporal frame feature aggregation include Bag-of-visual-words [6,24], Fisher Vectors [21], Convolutional Neural Networks (CNN) [15], Gated Recurrent Unit (GRU) [3], Long Short-Term Memory (LSTM) [29], and Generalized Vector of Locally Aggregated Descriptors (NetVLAD) [2].

It is well-known that neural networks are memory intensive and deploying such models on mobile devices is difficult for its limited hardware resources. Several approaches were proposed to tackle such difficulty. A straight forward way is to apply tensor decomposition techniques [16,19,30] to a pretrained CNN model [7]. Network Pruning removes low-weight connections on pretrained models [11], or gradually trains binary masks and weights until target sparsity is reached [31]. Network quantization compresses network by reducing number of bits required to represent each weight via weight sharing [10], or vector quantization [9]. Another way to get better performance for limited-size model is to use knowledge distillation [13,22]. The idea behind it is to train student network (small size) to imitate the soft output of a larger teacher network or ensembles of networks.

In Google cloud & YouTube-8M video understanding challenge Kaggle competition, top participates [5,18,20,25,27] trained models such as Gated NetVLAD, GRU, and LSTM with Attention. To leverage the predictability of single models, they averaged checkpoints at different training steps and ensembled predicted probability scores by weighted average, bagging, or boosting.

Our contribution in this paper is threefold: First, we explore size and performance of Gated NetVLAD under different sets of hyper-parameters (cluster size and hidden size). Second, we develop ensemble approach of multiple models in one tensorflow graph which avoids in-place change of graph. Third, we cast trained weights tensors from float32 to float16 data type in evaluation and inference stage which reduces approximately half the model size without sacrificing performance.

The rest of the paper is organized as follows. Section 2 presents our model architecture with compression and ensemble approaches. Section 3 reports experimental results, followed by conclusions in Sect. 4.

2   Approach

In this section, we first introduce Gated NetVLAD model architecture, then describe model compression approaches we have tried, followed by ensemble approaches we developed.

2.1   Frame Level Models

Our architecture for video classification is illustrated in Fig. 1.

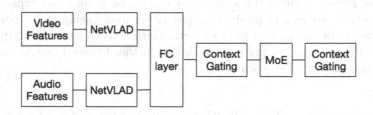

Fig. 1. Overview of our model architecture. FC denotes Fully Connected layer. MoE denotes Mixture of Experts.

NetVLAD

The NetVLAD [2] is a trainable generalized VLAD layer that captures information about the statistics of local descriptors over the image, i.e., the sum of residuals for each visual word. More specifically, let descriptor (video or audio feature) of video i be x_i, which can be assign to one of K clusters with centroid c_k for $k \in [1, K]$. The NetVLAD can be written as summation of residuals with soft assignment

$$V(j, k) = \sum_{i=1}^{N} \frac{e^{\mathbf{w}_k^T \mathbf{x}_i + b_k}}{\sum_{k'} e^{\mathbf{w}_{k'}^T \mathbf{x}_i + b_{k'}}} (x_i(j) - c_k(j)) \tag{2}$$

where $\{\mathbf{w}_k\}$, $\{b_k\}$ and $\{\mathbf{c}_k\}$ are sets of trainable parameters for each cluster k. Number of clusters (referred as cluster size) K is a hyper-parameter we varies across different models.

Fully Connected Layer

Our FC layer consists of two layers. First layer get input of concatenated video and audio VLAD layer, multiplied by weight matrix resulting in hidden size H, followed by batch normalization and ReLU activation. Second layer takes output of first layer as input, multiplied by weight matrix of shape $H \times 2H$ and added by a bias term.

Context Gating

Context Gating (CG) [20] is a learnable non-linear unit aiming to model inter-dependencies among network activations by gating. Concretely, CG transform input vector $X \in \mathbb{R}^p$ to output vector $Y \in \mathbb{R}^p$ of same dimension via

$$Y = \sigma(WX + b) \circ X \tag{3}$$

where $W \in \mathbb{R}^{n \times n}$ and $b \in \mathbb{R}^n$ are trainable parameters. σ is element-wise sigmoid activation and $\circ$ is the element-wise multiplication. CG is known for being able to capture dependencies among features.

Mixture of Experts

Mixture of Experts (MoE) [14] consists of two parts, gating and experts. The final predictions are sum of products of last layers from gating and experts. We use 5 mixtures of one hidden layer experts. Gate activations are multiplied to each expert for probability prediction. MoE is further followed by CG modeling dependencies among video vocabulary labels.

Training

We use two local GPUs, Nvidia 1080Ti and Nvidia 1060, and two Google Cloud Platform accounts with Tesla K80 GPUs to train single models. The training time is two to three days per model for 200k steps with batch size between 80 and 160.

The YouTube-8M Dataset is partitioned into three parts: Train, Validate and Test. Both Train and Validate data come with labels so they are effectively exchangeable. In order to maximize the number of training samples as well as to speed up the evaluation step, we randomly chose 60 out of the 3844 validate files as our validate set, and combine the other validate files with the official train dataset as our training set. We observe constant delta between our validate set and public leaderboard.

2.2   Compression

Float16 Compression

Of the compression methods we have attempted, this is the only one that worked. The idea is to train all the models in the default float32 precision to achieve maximum score, then at evaluation/inference stage, cast all the inference weight tensors to float16 precision to cut model size in half while preserving prediction accuracy.

In actual implementation, we only cast 4 out of the 32 weight tensors in our model architecture. This is because the largest 4 tensors (

`'tower/experts/weights'`,
`'tower/gates/weights'`,
`'tower/gating_prob_weights'`,
`'tower/hidden1_weights/hidden1_weights'`

) make up about 98% of total model size. Modifying the other 28 small weight tensors does not worth the effort in our opinion, since float32 is the default data type in many tensorflow modules and functions, and we had to extend tensorflow's `core.Dense` class and `layers.fully_connected` function to support float16 precision in order to cast those 4 tensors.

The average compression rate is 48.5% across models, as shown in Table 1. Compared to the original float32 models, the float16 compression version perform equally well, with GAPs differing less than 0.0001, which is the level of randomness between different evaluation runs for the same float32 model.

Gradual Binary Mask Pruning

We tried method introduced by [31] as the tensorflow implementation is available on tensorflow's github repo. For every layer chosen to be pruned, the authors added a binary mask variable of the same shape to determine which elements participate in forward execution of the graph. They introduced gradual pruning algorithm updating binary weight masks along with weight in network training. They claimed to achieve high compression rate without losing significant accuracy.

However, we found two main difficulties of the method in our experiments:

1. The sparsity is not identical to compression rate. In the article, sparsity was referred as the ratio between number of non-zero elements of the pruned network and the original network, while after compression the sparse tensor has indices that takes additional storage. Although the authors considered bitmask and CSR(C) sparse matrix representation, there are still two problems we could not solve easily: First, Tensorflow boolean variable takes one byte (not one bit) thus in real implementation the compression rate will be much lower. Second, for large tensors with huge indices range, row and column indices should have each element of type 32 or 64 bit integers, which takes a huge storage.

   For example, if we use float32 to store a tensor of 1024x100000 and set sparsity as 75%. To make use of SparseTensor object in Tensorflow, for each non-zero element, we need to associate it with two 32 bit integers (row and column index). This results in only 25% compression rate though sparsity is set to be 75%. Furthermore, it losses 75% of non-zero elements and sacrifices accuracy with only 25% compression rate. This is not as appealing as float16 compression approach.

2. At the time of competition deadline, the github repo[1] for model pruning only contained the training part that associates tensor to be pruned with binary masks. The sparse tensor representation and bit mask were not implemented at the moment. We implemented it ourselves and found the compression rate not satisfiable.

After some trials and errors and comparison with float16 compression procedure, we decided not to pursue pruning for model compression.

Quantization

Quantization [10] can achieve 75% compression rate by representing element in tensor as 8 bits unsigned integers rather than 32 bits float value. Tensorflow provides useful tools to quantize a pretrained graph. However, we found the output of graph to be frozen graph of pb format. We were able to convert meta, index, and checkpoint files to pb file, but not vice versa. Yet the competition requires that the submitted model must be loadable as a TensorFlow MetaGraph. We did not overcome this technical difficulty and went with our float16 compression method for its easy and elegant usage.

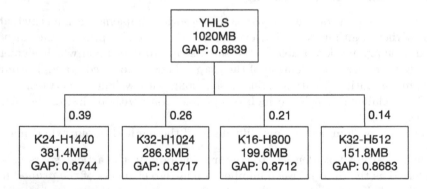

Fig. 2. Illustration of our best ensemble model YHLS, where each letter represents a single model. Kx-Hy in each cell denotes the single model with cluster size $K = x$ and first hidden layer size $H = y$. GAP reported was evaluated on local validate set and adjusted to be Kaggle public leaderboard equivalent. Model size is reported in each cell. (0.39, 0.26, 0.21, 0.14) are the ensemble weights of each model, respectively.

2.3   Ensemble

Checkpoint Average

For each single model, we first evaluate validation set using single checkpoints at some interval (say, every 10k steps) in order to know the approximate range of steps corresponding to higher scores for a particular model. Then we select a few

---

[1] https://github.com/tensorflow/tensorflow/tree/aa15692e54390cf3967d51bc60acf5f7 83df9c08/tensorflow/contrib/model_pruning.

Table 1. The 18 single models, sorted by decreasing size and score. The two numbers in model name refer to the cluster size and hidden size. The letter in parenthesis is our model code name. Model sizes are in MB. The GAPs are evaluated on our validate set but adjusted by the constant delta to represent public leaderboard equivalent GAP.

Model	Float32 model size	Float16 model size	Compression rate	Best avg ckpt GAP	Best single ckpt GAP
K24-H1440 (Y)	714.93	381.40	46.7%	0.8744	0.8682
K32-H1280 (G)	679.73	358.85	47.2%	0.8731	0.8669
K100-H800 (F)	663.87	339.76	48.8%	0.8721	0.8677
K16-H1280 (X)	594.59	316.21	46.8%	0.8718	0.8665
K32-H1024 (H)	549.24	286.85	47.8%	0.8717	0.8665
K20-H960 (K)	469.18	245.31	47.7%	0.8717	0.8661
K16-H800 (L)	384.27	199.61	48.1%	0.8712	0.8666
K64-H512 (J)	365.53	186.11	49.1%	0.8702	0.8664
K100-H400 (A)	357.21	180.93	49.3%	0.8685	0.8647
K32-H600 (N)	339.72	174.20	48.7%	0.8684	0.8648
K32-H512 (S)	297.27	151.85	48.9%	0.8683	0.8647
K16-H512 (O)	263.13	134.71	48.8%	0.8665	0.8641
K8-H512 (T)	246.07	126.15	48.7%	0.8660	0.8627
K16-H400 (Q)	217.05	110.50	49.1%	0.8658	0.8619
K10-H400 (E)	207.04	105.47	49.1%	0.8644	0.8626
K32-H256 (R)	175.78	88.85	49.5%	0.8616	0.8593
K10-H300 (M)	168.87	85.58	49.3%	0.8605	0.8589
K16-H256 (P)	158.65	80.21	49.4%	0.8594	0.8576

ranges with varying starting and ending steps, and average all the checkpoints in that range. Finally we evaluate using these average points and pick the best one to represent this single model in the ensemble. On average, the averaged checkpoint gives a 0.0039 GAP boost over the best single checkpoint that we evaluated, as shown in Table 1.

Ensemble Single Models into One Graph

As the competition requires the final model to be in a single tensorflow graph, it is not viable to ensemble single models' outputs. Instead, we build *ensemble graph* at the evaluation/inference stage, and overwrite the (untrained) float16 weights tensor with previously trained float32 single model weights tensors.

Code snippet to build ensemble graph

```
with tf.variable_scope("tower"):
  result = model_[0].create_model(
      model_input,
      ...,
      cluster_size = FLAGS.netvlad_cluster_size if \
                     type(FLAGS.netvlad_cluster_size) is int \
                     else FLAGS.netvlad_cluster_size[0],
      hidden_size = FLAGS.netvlad_hidden_size if \
                    type(FLAGS.netvlad_hidden_size) is int \
                    else FLAGS.netvlad_hidden_size[0])
  if FLAGS.ensemble_num> 1:
      predictions_lst = [result["predictions"]]
      for ensemble_idx in range(1,FLAGS.ensemble_num):
          with (tf.variable_scope("model"+str(ensemble_idx))):
              result2 = model[ensemble_idx].create_model(
                  model_input,
                  ...,
                  cluster_size = FLAGS.netvlad_cluster_size[ensemble_idx],
                  hidden_size = FLAGS.netvlad_hidden_size[ensemble_idx])
              predictions_lst.append(result2["predictions"])

  if FLAGS.ensemble_num==1:
    predictions = result["predictions"]
  else:
    predictions = 0
    for ensemble_idx in range(FLAGS.ensemble_num):
      predictions += predictions_lst[ensemble_idx] *
                     FLAGS.ensemble_wts[ensemble_idx]
```

To sum up our steps:

1. Train all single models in default float32 precision and average checkpoints.
2. For each potential ensemble model combination, build ensemble graph as above in float16 precision without training.
3. Populate ensemble graph's float16 weight tensors with single model's float32 trained weights.
4. Tune ensemble combinations and coefficients based on validate GAP.

3   Experiment

We trained and evaluated 28 models with same architecture but different cluster size K and hidden size H mentioned in Sect. 2.1. We use the convention Kx-Hy to denote model with cluster size $K = x$ and hidden size $H = y$. If a model has larger size but same or worse score than another model, we mark it an inferior model and eliminate it from the candidate list for later ensemble. There are 18

Table 2. Our best ensemble models. The letters refer to the single models in Table 1. Model sizes are in MB. Public/private delta is public/private leaderboard GAP minus local GAP. The YHLS model is our 7th place model. Some LB scores are left blank because we did not do inference on test set with those models.

Ensemble	Model size	Local GAP	Public LB GAP	Private LB GAP	Public delta	Private delta
YHLS	1019.7	0.8821	0.8839	0.8832	0.0018	0.0011
YFH	1008.0	0.8819				
GHLS	997.2	0.8818	0.8838	0.8832	0.0020	0.0014
YGLP	1020.1	0.8814				
YLSQRP	1012.4	0.8811				
GHLRP	1015.0	0.8811	0.8832	0.8825	0.0021	0.0014
GFX	1014.8	0.8810				
FJSOQR	1012.5	0.8810	0.8828	0.8822	0.0018	0.0012
GFAB	1004.0	0.8808	0.8826	0.8821	0.0018	0.0013
FJSO	812.4	0.8808				
LNSOTQP	977.2	0.8803				
GF	698.9	0.8785				

models left on the list, which is detailed in Table 1. The 10 eliminated models are K20-H1600, K64-H1024, K150-H600, K128-H512, K16-H1024, K32-H400, K128-H1024, K8-H1024, K32-H800 and K8-H800.

We then tried out different combinations of single models, subject to the model size constraint of 1 GB uncompressed. Details of ensemble models are shown in Table 2. Our final selected 7th place model is the YHLS ensemble with ensemble weights $= (0.39, 0.26, 0.21, 0.14)$, see Fig. 2.

4   Conclusions

In this paper we summarized our 7th place solution to the 2nd YouTube-8M Video Understanding Challenge. We chose the same Gated NetVLAD model architecture and trained 28 models with different hyperparameters and varying sizes. We applied three techniques to ensemble single models into a constrained-size tensorflow graph: averaging checkpoints, float16 compression, and building ensemble graph.

In our experiments, we found that in the Gated NetVLAD model, hidden size H can create a bottleneck for information representation. Sacrificing cluster size K in exchange for hidden size H can achieve better results for constrained-size models. In ensemble, we noticed that more smaller size single models do not always beat fewer larger size single models. The optimal number of models in the ensemble is 3 to 4 in our framework. We believe this is due to the boosting effect of ensemble diminishing when we add too many models. For example, even if the ensemble of two smaller models α, β show better GAP score than a single model γ with the same total size, after further ensembling with more models $\eta\theta$, the ensemble $\gamma\eta\theta$ may beat ensemble $\alpha\beta\eta\theta$—the boosting effect between $\alpha\beta$ and $\eta\theta$ is not as good as between γ and $\eta\theta$ as some of the model variety boost is already "used" between α and β.

Had we had more time, we would explore other models and techniques since we had already done a fairly thorough search in gated NetVLAD model's hyperparameter space and tried nearly all the ensemble combinations. Given more time, we would further experiment 8-bit quantization. Should it work out, we would train models with different architectures such as LSTM, Bag-of-visualwords and Fischer Vector and fit them in the gained extra space in the model. In parallel, we could have tried distillation technique since it gives a boost in performance without needing extra model size.

References

1. Abu-El-Haija, S., et al.: Youtube-8M: a large-scale video classification benchmark. arXiv preprint arXiv:1609.08675 (2016)
2. Arandjelovic, R., Gronat, P., Torii, A., Pajdla, T., Sivic, J.: NetVLAD: CNN architecture for weakly supervised place recognition. In: Proceedings of the IEEE Conference on Computer Vision and Pattern Recognition, pp. 5297–5307 (2016)
3. Ballas, N., Yao, L., Pal, C., Courville, A.: Delving deeper into convolutional networks for learning video representations. arXiv preprint arXiv:1511.06432 (2015)
4. Heilbron, F.C., Escorcia, V., Ghanem, B., Niebles, J.C.: Activitynet: a large-scale video benchmark for human activity understanding. In: Proceedings of the IEEE Conference on Computer Vision and Pattern Recognition, pp. 961–970 (2015)
5. Chen, S., Wang, X., Tang, Y., Chen, X., Wu, Z., Jiang, Y.G.: Aggregating frame-level features for large-scale video classification. arXiv preprint arXiv:1707.00803 (2017)
6. Csurka, G., Dance, C., Fan, L., Willamowski, J., Bray, C.: Visual categorization with bags of keypoints. In: Workshop on Statistical Learning in Computer Vision, ECCV, vol. 1, pp. 1–2, Prague (2004)
7. Denton, E.L., Zaremba, W., Bruna, J., LeCun, Y., Fergus, R.: Exploiting linear structure within convolutional networks for efficient evaluation. In: Advances in Neural Information Processing Systems, pp. 1269–1277 (2014)
8. Kahou, S.E., Michalski, V., Konda, K., Memisevic, R., Pal, C.: Recurrent neural networks for emotion recognition in video. In: Proceedings of the 2015 ACM on International Conference on Multimodal Interaction, pp. 467–474. ACM (2015)
9. Gong, Y., Liu, L., Yang, M., Bourdev, L.: Compressing deep convolutional networks using vector quantization. arXiv preprint arXiv:1412.6115 (2014)
10. Han, S., Mao, H., Dally, W.J.: Deep compression: compressing deep neural networks with pruning, trained quantization and huffman coding. arXiv preprint arXiv:1510.00149 (2015)
11. Han, S., Pool, J., Tran, J., Dally, W.: Learning both weights and connections for efficient neural network. In: Advances in Neural Information Processing Systems, pp. 1135–1143 (2015)
12. He, K., Zhang, X., Ren, S., Sun, J.: Deep residual learning for image recognition. In: Proceedings of the IEEE Conference on Computer Vision and Pattern Recognition, pp. 770–778 (2016)

13. Hinton, G., Vinyals, O., Dean, J.: Distilling the knowledge in a neural network. arXiv preprint arXiv:1503.02531 (2015)
14. Jacobs, R.A., Jordan, M.I., Nowlan, S.J., Hinton, G.E.: Adaptive mixtures of local experts. Neural Comput. **3**(1), 79–87 (1991)
15. Karpathy, A., Toderici, G., Shetty, S., Leung, T., Sukthankar, R., Fei-Fei, L.: Large-scale video classification with convolutional neural networks. In: The IEEE Conference on Computer Vision and Pattern Recognition (CVPR), June 2014
16. Kolda, T.G., Bader, B.W.: Tensor decompositions and applications. SIAM Rev. **51**(3), 455–500 (2009)
17. Krizhevsky, A., Sutskever, I., Hinton, G.E.: Imagenet classification with deep convolutional neural networks. In: Advances in Neural Information Processing Systems, pp. 1097–1105 (2012)
18. Li, F., et al.: Temporal modeling approaches for large-scale Youtube-8M video understanding. arXiv preprint arXiv:1707.04555 (2017)
19. Liu, T., Yuan, M., Zhao, H.: Characterizing spatiotemporal transcriptome of human brain via low rank tensor decomposition. arXiv preprint arXiv:1702.07449 (2017)
20. Miech, A., Laptev, I., Sivic, J.: Learnable pooling with context gating for video classification. arXiv preprint arXiv:1706.06905 (2017)
21. Perronnin, F., Dance, C.: Fisher kernels on visual vocabularies for image categorization. In: 2007 IEEE Conference on Computer Vision and Pattern Recognition, pp. 1–8. IEEE (2007)
22. Romero, A., Ballas, N., Kahou, S.E., Chassang, A., Gatta, C., Bengio, Y.: Fitnets: hints for thin deep nets. arXiv preprint arXiv:1412.6550 (2014)
23. Simonyan, K., Zisserman, A.: Very deep convolutional networks for large-scale image recognition. arXiv preprint arXiv:1409.1556 (2014)
24. Sivic, J., Zisserman, A.: Video Google: a text retrieval approach to object matching in videos. In: null, p. 1470. IEEE (2003)
25. Skalic, M., Pekalski, M., Pan, X.E.: Deep learning methods for efficient large scale video labeling. arXiv preprint arXiv:1706.04572 (2017)
26. Szegedy, C., Ioffe, S., Vanhoucke, V., Alemi, A.A.: Inception-v4, inception-resnet and the impact of residual connections on learning. In: AAAI, vol. 4, p. 12 (2017)
27. Wang, H.D., Zhang, T., Wu, J.: The monkey typing solution to the Youtube-8M video understanding challenge. arXiv preprint arXiv:1706.05150 (2017)
28. Xu, Z., Yang, Y., Hauptmann, A.G.: A discriminative CNN video representation for event detection. In: Proceedings of the IEEE Conference on Computer Vision and Pattern Recognition, pp. 1798–1807 (2015)
29. Yue-Hei Ng, J., Hausknecht, M., Vijayanarasimhan, S., Vinyals, O., Monga, R., Toderici, G.: Beyond short snippets: deep networks for video classification. In: Proceedings of the IEEE Conference on Computer Vision and Pattern Recognition, pp. 4694–4702 (2015)
30. Zhang, T., Golub, G.H.: Rank-one approximation to high order tensors. SIAM J. Matrix Anal. Appl. **23**(2), 534–550 (2001)
31. Zhu, M., Gupta, S.: To prune, or not to prune: exploring the efficacy of pruning for model compression. arXiv preprint arXiv:1710.01878 (2017)

Label Denoising with Large Ensembles
of Heterogeneous Neural Networks

Pavel Ostyakov$^{(\boxtimes)}$, Elizaveta Logacheva$^{(\boxtimes)}$, Roman Suvorov$^{(\boxtimes)}$,
Vladimir Aliev$^{(\boxtimes)}$, Gleb Sterkin$^{(\boxtimes)}$, Oleg Khomenko$^{(\boxtimes)}$,
and Sergey I. Nikolenko$^{(\boxtimes)}$

Samsung AI Center, Moscow, Russia
{p.ostyakov,e.logacheva,r.suvorov,v.aliev,g.sterkin,
o.khomenko,s.nikolenko}@samsung.com

Abstract. Despite recent advances in computer vision based on various convolutional architectures, video understanding remains an important challenge. In this work, we present and discuss a top solution for the large-scale video classification (labeling) problem introduced as a Kaggle competition based on the YouTube-8M dataset. We show and compare different approaches to preprocessing, data augmentation, model architectures, and model combination. Our final model is based on a large ensemble of video- and frame-level models but fits into rather limiting hardware constraints. We apply an approach based on knowledge distillation to deal with noisy labels in the original dataset and the recently developed mixup technique to improve the basic models.

Keywords: Video processing · Learning from noisy labels
Attention-based models · Recurrent neural networks · Deep learning

1 Introduction

Video understanding and learning high-quality latent representations for videos is an important problem which largely remains open and needs more advances in computer vision, including video processing and scene understanding, audio processing and speech recognition, and natural language processing. One of the first steps towards true video understanding is video classification/labeling, where the problem is to apply labels from a predefined set to a video. While, e.g., text classifiers achieve very high results despite the fact that general language understanding remains a hard problem, for video data even classification is relatively underexplored.

In this work, we concentrate on video classification task presented in the second YouTube-8M Challenge, where the problem is to automatically annotate YouTube videos with a large number of predefined labels based on video-level and frame-level features. While we have introduced several novel modifications to existing deep learning models and performed a large-scale experimental comparison of convolutional, recurrent, and attention-based architectures, we believe

© Springer Nature Switzerland AG 2019
L. Leal-Taixé and S. Roth (Eds.): ECCV 2018 Workshops, LNCS 11132, pp. 250–261, 2019.
https://doi.org/10.1007/978-3-030-11018-5_23

that our main contribution lies in dealing with noisy labels. One of the main challenges in the YouTube-8M dataset and other large-scale datasets is that the labels, while relatively high-quality, are not completely reliable. In fact, according to the authors of the dataset, precision and recall of YouTube-8M labels is 78.8% and 14.5% respectively compared to the gold standard of human raters [1]. In this work, we deal with this problem with the recently developed knowledge distillation approach which we base on a large ensemble of a wide variety of video- and frame-level models. The ensemble, however, is used only for preparing soft labels, and the final model trained on these soft labels is relatively simple and fits into rather limiting hardware requirements imposed in the challenge. Our final resulting model achieved very high results in video classification and placed 4th in the second YouTube-8M Challenge.

The paper is organized as follows. In Sect. 2, we describe the dataset, introduce the primary evaluation metric that we use throughout the paper, and discuss different data representation methods that we compared for frame-level data. Section 3 describes the main neural architectures used in this work and presents the ensemble-based distillation that we used to alleviate the problem of noisy labels. Section 4 presents an extensive evaluation study of the proposed models and a detailed error analysis, and Sect. 5 concludes the paper.

2 Data and Evaluation

Dataset. The YouTube-8M dataset contains 5.6M videos encoded as a hidden representation produced by Deep CNN pretrained on the ImageNet dataset [2] for both audio spectrogram and video frames taken at rate of 1 Hz (once per second). The dataset also contains aggregated *video-level features* extracted as averaged frame-level features. Each video was automatically annotated with 3862 classes by the YouTube video annotation system. To ensure high quality of the videos in the dataset, videos were preselected to meet the following requirements: each video must be public, have at least 1000 views, be between 120 and 500 s long, and also be associated with at least one entity from the target vocabulary; adult and sensitive content has been removed based on automated classifiers. The dataset is an improved version of the initially released YouTube-8M [1], with some noisy and rare labels filtered out, but the labeling still remains rather noisy.

Evaluation. The primary evaluation metric for our experiments and the competition itself is the *global average precision* (GAP), defined as GAP@$n = \sum_{i=1}^{N} p(i)r(i)$, where N is the total number of final predictions, $p(i)$ is the precision score at rank i, and $r(i)$ denotes the relevance of prediction i: it's 1 if the i-th prediction is correct, and 0 otherwise. For every video top n predicted labels are scored, so $N = nV$, where V is the number of videos.

Frame-Level Augmentation. Alongside with video-level features, the YouTube-8M dataset contains frame-level features: one preprocessed frame per second for every video. To use frame-level data in our models, we have tested several augmentation strategies. First, we computed and used as features various frame-level statistics, including the mean, standard deviation, median, minimum, maximum, mode, and video length (number of frames). These statistics were concatenated and used as input for our network architectures.

To use frame-level features in the models, we computed the above statistics for different frames in the video. There are too many frames in a video, and neighboring frames are generally very similar, so it is detrimental to use all frame-level data and preferable to include only a few representative frames. We have tried several subsampling strategies to choose which frames to include as input:

(1) subsample a subsequence of frames at random or at regular intervals;
(2) assuming that not all frames are equally important for training, we decided to take one frame per "scene" in the video; for this purpose, we cut the video into "scenes" by thresholding cosine distances between neighbouring frames (Fig. 1 shows sample correlations between the frames in a video; the scene structure is usually rather clear) and take one frame per scene;
(3) apart from "scenes" specific for each video, we also found global centroids of frame-level features using large-scale k-means clustering for all frames in the dataset, and then used frame statistics from unique nearest centroids for the frames in a given video; with 10,000 centroids, this approach yielded a GAP score of 0.79 (row 14 of Table 1).

Another approach we tried for frame-level information was to try to capture just the *dynamics* in a video sequence. The intuition behind this approach is that the main information about the video may be captured in what is changing between frames and not in the static component. To this end, we have tried several different techniques:

(1) subtracting per-video average from every frame in the video;
(2) applying a high-pass filter using the *db3* wavelet [3];
(3) computing sparse component with Principal Components Pursuit [4].

However, none of these techniques yielded a GAP score greater than 0.5.

Finally, the best technique that helped us incorporate frame-level information into video-level vectors in the best possible way is as follows. We have taken a number of linear combinations of frames with trainable coefficients (coefficients are linked to frame position) and then applied a ResNet-like model (see Sect. 3) to the concatenated vectors. This approach yielded a GAP score of 0.855 for 5 linear combinations.

3 Models

General Approach. In this section, we define and discuss the models that we have tried in our experiments. In the YouTube-8M competition, one of the requirements for the final model was to fit it into 1Gb of memory. This is a rather limiting constraint for modern state of the art neural networks, so the objective was to both achieve the best possible results in terms of GAP and do it in limited space (and hence also limited inference time). To achieve both, we propose the following approach, illustrated on Fig. 2.

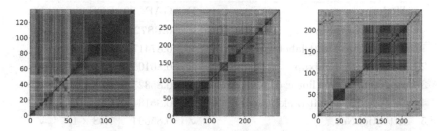

Fig. 1. Cosine distance between subsequent frames in three sample videos; we took abrupt changes in neighboring frames as evidence of a new "scene" beginning.

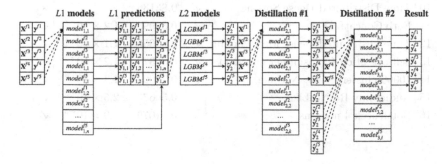

Fig. 2. General flowchart of our approach.

First, we train various models on the video-level and frame-level features provided in the dataset, usually optimizing binary cross-entropy (BCE) with respect to the original hard labels; we call them *first-level* models. The final first-level model is an ensemble based on different other first-level models.

Denoised *soft labels* are then extracted from out-of-fold predictions of the ensemble: we take these predictions (in the form of $[0, 1]$ confidence values) as soft labels. Then, we split the training set into five folds again and train simple fully-connected models with different depth, width, and activation functions.

Finally, we make out-of-fold predictions again, take each model's features on the penultimate layer (before final softmax), concatenate, and feed them into a new trainable classification layer. The feature extractors are frozen during training. This procedure yielded the final metric GAP = 0.88729.

Throughout this section, we refer to evaluation results summarized in Table 1, which shows whether the model uses frame-level features, its GAP@20 and BCE scores, and whether it became part of the final ensemble.

Table 1. Evaluation results for basic models, ordered from best to worst.

	Model	Fr.	GAP@20	BCE	Ens.
	Final ensemble	✓	**0.88729**	–	✓
1	ResNetLike + soft labels	✗	0.87417	9.2×10^{-4}	✓
2	ResNetLike + mixup	✗	0.86105	9.7×10^{-4}	✓
3	ResNetLike over linear combinations	✓	0.85325	1.02×10^{-3}	✓
4	ResNetLike + soft ranking loss	✗	0.85184	–	✓
5	AttentionNet	✓	0.85094	1.08×10^{-3}	✓
6	LSTM-Bi-Attention	✓	0.84645	1.04×10^{-3}	✓
7	Time Distributed Convolutions	✓	0.84144	1.0×10^{-3}	✓
8	VLAD-BOW + learnable power	✓	0.83959	1.1×10^{-3}	✓
9	Video only ResNetLike	✗	0.83212	1.1×10^{-3}	✓
10	Time Distributed Dense Sorting	✓	0.83136	–	✗
11	EarlyConcatLSTM	✓	0.82998	1.2×10^{-3}	✓
12	Time Distributed Dense Max Pooling	✓	0.82656	1.1×10^{-3}	✓
13	Self-attention (transformer encoder)	✓	0.8237	1.2×10^{-3}	✓
14	10000 clusters + ResNetLike	✓	0.7900	1.3×10^{-3}	✓
15	Audio only ResNetLike	✗	0.50676	2.5×10^{-3}	✓
16	Bottleneck 4 neurons	✗	0.41079	2.9×10^{-3}	✓

Video-Level Models. Our main first-level model is based on a ResNet-like architecture previously introduced for this problem in [5]; this architecture is shown on Fig. 3. The model takes three hyperparameters as input: inner_size, av_id_block_num, concat_id_block_num, and dropout. By default we used inner_size=2048, av_id_block_num=1, concat_id_block_num=1, dropout=0.5.

We have not found any strong correlation between network depth and final GAP value during our tests, yet our best first-level validation score GAP = 0.86105 was achieved by a ResNet-like model with parameters $(4, 4, 0.4)$ and mixup $\alpha = 0.3$, trained with binary cross-entropy as the loss function (row 3 of Table 1).

Mixup. One important idea that helped improve first level models was *mixup*, a recently developed new regularization technique [6]. Mixup has been empirically shown to deliver better accuracy on the validation set than original labels. The mixup method produces "virtual" training samples as linear combinations of existing training samples and their targets:

$$x = \lambda x_i + (1 - \lambda)x_j, \quad y = \lambda y_i + (1 - \lambda)y_j,$$

where (x_i, y_i) and (x_j, y_j) are feature-target vectors sampled from training data, and $\lambda \in [0, 1]$ is drawn from a beta distribution, $\lambda \sim \text{Beta}(\alpha, \alpha)$, where α is the main parameter of mixup; in our experiments we set the mixup α parameter to 0.4. Most of our first level models use mixup, and it improves results significantly; e.g., the basic ResNetLike architecture with mixup has GAP = 0.86105 (row 2 of Table 1) compared to GAP = 0.85846 without it.

Recurrent Frame-Level Models. Along with aggregated video-level features, the dataset also provides temporal frame-level representation of the videos. We have conducted multiple experiments with recurrent neural networks based on LSTM and GRU units to incorporate temporal features into the model. We have tried both unidirectional and bidirectional LSTM-based networks with 2 hidden layers size of 1024 followed by fully-connected layer size of 2048; we call this basic RNN model *EarlyConcatLSTM* because it receives as input concatenated audio and video features (row 11 of Table 1).

Another approach was to use a learnable bag-of-words representation. We used the *VLADBoW* model proposed in [7]. One major difference was to introduce a learnable power coefficient, that is, we learned it as

$$\text{BOW}(k) = \sum_{i=1}^{N} a_k(y_i) \text{ with } y_i = [Wx_i + b]_+^p \text{ and } a_k = \frac{e^{y_{ik}}}{\sum_{j=1}^{k} e^{y_{ij}}}$$

with trainable p, getting as a result $p = 0.628$. This model achieved GAP = 0.83959 (row 8 of Table 1).

Attention-Based Frame-Level Models. Recent research indicates that attention-based networks often outperform classical RNNs in similar tasks [8]. We have tried several attention-based architectures:

(1) encoder architectures similar to the ones from the *Transformer* model [9] yielded GAP = 0.8237 (row 13 of Table 1); we used stacked multihead self-attention mechanism with and without position coding, and Transformer without position coding was much more successful; this may indicate that most labels could be detected by taking into account individual frames and disregarding relations between frames and their mutual temporal positions;

(2) *stacked attention* model, which contains multiple layers, each computing a single attention vector for a sequence, concatenates them to obtain the feature vector at every time step, and then performs global average pooling, reaching a very high GAP = 0.85094 (row 5 of Table 1).

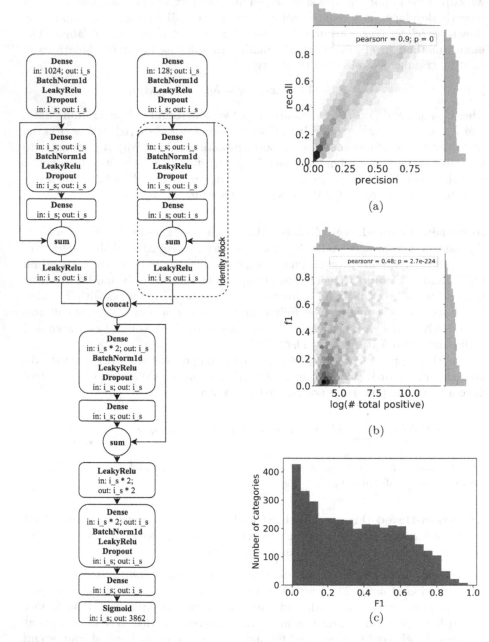

Fig. 3. ResNet-like architecture. i_s, inner size, denotes the size of hidden layers.

Fig. 4. Error analysis: (a) precision-recall heatmap; (b) F1-score as a function of the number of available training samples; (c) distribution of labels according to their final F1-score.

Time-Distributed Models. One more group of approaches is to use time-distributed dense layers with different poolings to finally convert them to a single vector; we have used three different approaches with time-distributed layers. Our simplest model uses a single fully connected layer and frame-wise max pooling afterwards. This approach yields GAP = 0.82656 (row 12 of Table 1). The second approach is to apply a ResNet-like model to every frame in a video with additional two dense layers on the cumulative output of every per-frame model sorted by confidence; this gave us GAP = 0.83136 (row 10 of Table 1). Finally, we tried time-distributed convolutional layers; the best convolutional model contains several layers of convolutions followed by max-pooling for video and audio separately, then concatenating the resulting features. This approach yields GAP = 0.84144 (row 7 of Table 1).

Loss Function Selection. As the main loss function we used the binary cross-entropy (BCE). However, since the primary objective was in terms of a ranking metric, some models were trained using the soft ranking loss; in our experiments, for equivalent models this loss has led to slightly worse GAP scores than BCE. Reweighting BCE using weights derived from mispredicted examples did not show any significant improvements in validation score.

The global average precision metric is based on the ranking among predictions rather than their specific scores. Thus, we applied batch-wise ranking in the following way. First we extract top 30 scores corresponding to negative labels for every sample in the batch. Then we extract all scores corresponding to positive labels in the batch. Finally, we apply the following pairwise ranking loss: $L(p_i, n_j) = \log(1 + \exp(n_j - p_i + 1))$, averaging it across all pairs of scores in the batch. This approach led to, e.g., GAP = 0.85184 (row 4 in Table 1) for ResNetLike compared to GAP = 0.85325 without the ranking loss (row 3), but ranking-based models were still useful for the final ensemble.

We also experimented with standard hinge ranking loss function, but found that hard thresholding is harmful for model convergence and the GAP metric. We have also tried the following related ideas with no strong positive effect (we believe that in this case it is important to report negative results as well):

(1) penalizing predicted confidence for a label by cross-validation classification accuracy for that label (the smaller the accuracy, the stronger the penalty); the intuition here is that noisier labels must receive marginally less confident scores;
(2) inducing noise by flipping labels at random (with higher probability for labels with smaller cross-validation accuracy);
(3) loss function correction as proposed in [10];
(4) dropout technique from [11];
(5) test time dropout with averaging the predictions.

Final Ensemble and Distillation. Our general approach, as shown in the beginning of this section, implies a general ensemble model which is then used to obtain soft labels (similar to the knowledge distillation approach as shown in [12]) used instead of noisy ones to improve the final model's quality.

We used an ensemble of 115 first level models to prepare the final model. On the first level, we used 95 video-level and 20 frame-level models; all of them are neural networks due to the origin and nature of the data provided. However, the ensemble itself was done with a gradient boosting model, namely LightGBM [13]. Distilled soft labels produced by this ensemble allowed us to achieve GAP = 0.88729 with the final compressed model.

4   Experimental Evaluation

In this section we present our experimental results on the YouTube-8M dataset.

Data Preparation and Augmentation. To make the resulting models more robust, we initially shuffled all data and split it into 5 cross-validation folds to train and validate all our models. Throughout the paper, we estimate the validation score as GAP measured on the hold-out fold, and the final GAP scores shown in Table 1 are calculated as an average of 5 folds.

The effectiveness of data augmentation in various tasks, especially related to computer vision, has been known and empirically validated for a long time [14–16]. Despite the fact that the initially provided features were preprocessed embeddings rather than images of frames, we performed several experiments with data augmentation techniques. In particular, we tested statistical bootstrap, using a weighted average for a random subset of frames and mixup [6]. Some models were trained on random subsets of available features.

Compact Representations and Single Modality Experiments. We have conducted experiments to see how performance (in terms of the validation metric) of the model degrades depending on the size of the inner representation within our model. Using only 4 neurons in hidden layers has allowed us to achieve GAP equal to 0.41079.

We have also trained separate audio-only and video-only video-level models based on a single modality only, achieving the best GAP scores of 0.83493 and 0.50676 respectively. These models were included into the final ensemble of first-level models for the sake of diversity.

Training Parameters. All models in our comparison were trained and validated with multiple NVIDIA P40 GPUs. In our experiments, we have attempted to tune the mini-batch size and learning rate. The experiments have shown the following tradeoff: lower mini-batch size increases the convergence rate but the final quality of the model can deteriorate slightly. At the same time, lower batch sizes mean that an experiment takes up significantly less GPU memory (the memory footprint is basically linear in the batch size), which is an important argument for lower batch sizes in practice. Note that larger mini-batch sizes require warmup which does not let one use high learning rates right away [17].

Results. The main results of evaluating our models are summarized in Table 1. We have already discussed our models in detail in Sect. 3. One general result that can be seen from Table 1 is that, rather surprisingly, video-level models on the first level consistently outperform frame-level models despite the fact that they receive far less information about a given video. This probably means that there is still a lot of work to be done to improve recurrent and/or attention-based approaches to video understanding—after all, our final ensemble does use frame-level models and hence this information. Moreover, frame-level models have high importance in the gradient boosting model, which shows that they add a lot of diversity and new information to the ensemble.

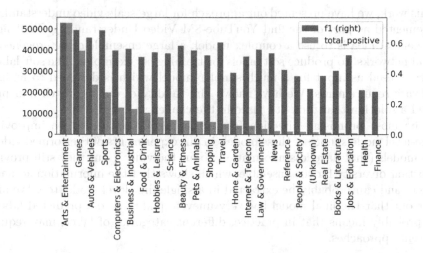

Fig. 5. Classification accuracy across verticals.

Error Analysis. To analyze the quality and characteristic features of our final model, we performed error analysis according to the following methodology. We take top 20 predicted labels for a video and classify these labels into true positive, false positive, and false negative classes. A label is true positive if it is positive and it has predicted score higher than all negative labels for that video; a label is false positive if it is negative and has predicted score higher than at least one positive label for that video; finally, a label is false negative if it is positive and has predicted score less than at least one negative label for that video.

Figure 4 shows the error analysis for our ResNet-like model distilled against the ensemble. Figure 4a shows that false positives are marginally more probable than false negatives, but not by much, which shows that the model is well balanced. Figure 4b illustrated an expected effect: the more training examples we have, the higher is the accuracy; note, however, that the final model can also accurately predict many rare labels. Nevertheless, Fig. 4c shows that vice versa, there are many categories that the model cannot predict accurately; these are mostly rare categories, but for some the reasons might be different and might require further study. Finally, Fig. 5 shows classification accuracy across verticals (coarse-grained labels) in comparison to the number of positive examples in the corresponding training subset (one fold). Again, we see that generally more popular categories are easier to predict, but the effect varies significantly.

5   Conclusion

In this work, we have presented our approach for large-scale video understanding implemented as part of the 2nd YouTube-8M Video Understanding Challenge. Our general idea is to use a complex model, a large ensemble of heterogeneous neural networks, to produce soft labels for training set examples. The soft labels are then used as input for a much simpler model which is designed to fit into hardware requirements. We have shown the validity of our approach and presented a solution that took 4th place in the challenge.

The most promising direction for further work appears to be improving frame-level models: none of these models in our experiments outperformed video-level models (that have less information about the video), but they still provide important diversity for the ensemble, which shows that the information actually is there and can probably be extracted in a single first level model too. We also point out that the final model has very uneven quality across predicted labels; this probably means that in practice, different categories of labels may require different approaches.

References

1. Abu-El-Haija, S., et al.: Youtube-8M: a large-scale video classification benchmark. CoRR abs/1609.08675 (2016)
2. Deng, J., Dong, W., Socher, R., Li, L.J., Li, K., Fei-Fei, L.: ImageNet: a large-scale hierarchical image database. In: CVPR 2009 (2009)
3. Daubechies, I.: Ten lectures on wavelets. In: CBMS-NSF Regional Conference Series in Applied Mathematics, vol. 61 (1992)
4. Candès, E.J., Li, X., Ma, Y., Wright, J.: Robust principal component analysis? J. ACM (JACM) **58**(3), 11 (2011)
5. n01z3: Solution for Google Cloud & Youtube-8M video understanding challenge (2017). https://github.com/n01z3/kaggle_yt8m
6. Zhang, H., Cisse, M., Dauphin, Y.N., Lopez-Paz, D.: mixup: beyond empirical risk minimization. In: International Conference on Learning Representations (2018)

7. Miech, A., Laptev, I., Sivic, J.: Learnable pooling with context gating for video classification. arXiv preprint arXiv:1706.06905 (2017)
8. Vaswani, A., et al.: Attention is all you need. In: Guyon, I., Luxburg, U.V., et al. (eds.) Advances in Neural Information Processing Systems, vol. 30, pp. 5998–6008. Curran Associates, Inc. (2017)
9. Vaswani, A., et al.: Attention is all you need. In: Advances in Neural Information Processing Systems, pp. 5998–6008 (2017)
10. Natarajan, N., Dhillon, I.S., Ravikumar, P.K., Tewari, A.: Learning with noisy labels. In: Burges, C.J.C., Bottou, L., Welling, M., Ghahramani, Z., Weinberger, K.Q. (eds.) Advances in Neural Information Processing Systems, vol. 26, pp. 1196–1204. Curran Associates, Inc. (2013)
11. Jindal, I., Nokleby, M.S., Chen, X.: Learning deep networks from noisy labels with dropout regularization. CoRR abs/1705.03419 (2017)
12. Hinton, G., Vinyals, O., Dean, J.: Distilling the knowledge in a neural network. arXiv preprint arXiv:1503.02531 (2015)
13. Ke, G., et al.: LightGBM: a highly efficient gradient boosting decision tree. In: Guyon, I., et al. (eds.) Advances in Neural Information Processing Systems, vol. 30, pp. 3146–3154. Curran Associates, Inc. (2017)
14. Ciresan, D.C., Meier, U., Gambardella, L.M., Schmidhuber, J.: Deep big simple neural nets excel on handwritten digit recognition. CoRR abs/1003.0358 (2010)
15. Perez, L., Wang, J.: The effectiveness of data augmentation in image classification using deep learning. CoRR abs/1712.04621 (2017)
16. Taylor, L., Nitschke, G.: Improving deep learning using generic data augmentation. CoRR abs/1708.06020 (2017)
17. Goyal, P., et al.: Accurate, large minibatch SGD: training imagenet in 1 hour. CoRR abs/1706.02677 (2017)

Hierarchical Video Frame Sequence Representation with Deep Convolutional Graph Network

Feng Mao$^{(\boxtimes)}$ (iD), Xiang Wu (iD), Hui Xue, and Rong Zhang

Alibaba Group, Hangzhou, China
{maofeng.mf,weiyi.wx}@alibaba-inc.com

Abstract. High accuracy video label prediction (classification) models are attributed to large scale data. These data could be frame feature sequences extracted by a pre-trained convolutional-neural-network, which promote the efficiency for creating models. Unsupervised solutions such as feature average pooling, as a simple label-independent parameter-free based method, has limited ability to represent the video. While the supervised methods, like RNN, can greatly improve the recognition accuracy. However, the video length is usually long, and there are hierarchical relationships between frames across events in the video, the performance of RNN based models are decreased. In this paper, we proposes a novel video classification method based on a deep convolutional graph neural network (DCGN). The proposed method utilize the characteristics of the hierarchical structure of the video, and performed multi-level feature extraction on the video frame sequence through the graph network, obtained a video representation reflecting the event semantics hierarchically. We test our model on YouTube-8M Large-Scale Video Understanding dataset, and the result outperforms RNN based benchmarks.

Keywords: Video classification · Sequence representation
Graph neural network · Deep convolutional neural network

1 Introduction

Nearly 80% of the data on the Internet are images and videos. Research on analyzing, understanding and mining these multimedia data has drawn a significant amount of attention from both academia and industry. Labeling or classifying videos is one of the most important requirements, and challenges remained to be solved. Google's YouTube-8M team introduced a large multi-label video classification dataset which composed of nearly 8 million videos-500K hours of video-annotated with a vocabulary of 4800 visual entities [1]. They used the state-of-the-art Inception-v3 network [2] pre-trained on ImageNet to extract frame features at one-frame-per-second, providing reliable data supporting for large-scale video understanding. The key task is modeling the long sequence of frame features. The popular methods are LSTM (Long Short-Term Memory Networks) [3], GRU (Gated recurrent units) [4], DBoF (Deep Bag of Frame Pooling) [1], etc.

© Springer Nature Switzerland AG 2019
L. Leal-Taixé and S. Roth (Eds.): ECCV 2018 Workshops, LNCS 11132, pp. 262–270, 2019.
https://doi.org/10.1007/978-3-030-11018-5_24

In this work, a novel deep convolutional graph based frame feature sequence modeling method is proposed, which aims to mine the complex relationship between video frames and shots, and perform hierarchical semantic abstraction across video. Evaluations are made based on the YouTube8M-2018 dataset, which containing about 5 million videos and 3862 labels. We use the provided frame level Inception-v3 features to training the model, the results show that our model out-performs the RNN based methods.

2   Related Works

Video feature sequence classification is essentially the task of aggregating video features, that is, to aggregate N D-dimensional features into one D'-dimensional feature by mining statistical relationships between these N features. The aggregated D'-dimensional feature is a highly concentrated embedding, making the classifier easy to mapping the visual embedding space into the label semantic space. It is common using recurrent neural networks, such as LSTM (Long Short-Term Memory Networks) [3,5,6] and GRU (Gated recurrent units) [4,7], both are the state-of-the-art approaches for many sequence modeling tasks. However, the hidden state of RNN is dependent on previous steps, which prevent parallel computations. Moreover, LSTM or GRU use gate to solve RNN gradient vanish problem, but the sigmoid in the gates still cause gradient decay over layers in depth. It has been shown that LSTM has difficulties in converging when sequence length increase [8]. There also exist end-to-end trainable order-less aggregation methods, such as DBoF(Deep Bag of Frame Pooling) [1].

3   Proposed Method

In this paper, we propose a convolutional graph based video representation method for a sequence of video frame features. The main idea is that video is a hierarchical data structure, composed of events, scenes, shots, super-frames and frames. Additionally, the relations between frames, and the relations between shots are more complex than the order of a sequence. Consider an example sequence of "cooking show" as shown in Fig. 1, frames containing same targets are not continuous, and distributed in various timestamps, as well as the events and shots. We model the video frame sequence, shot, and event hierarchically by a deep convolution graph Network (DCGN). It gradually abstracts information from frame level to video level by convolution and information propagating through graph, and finally generates a global representation for further classification. The method is shown in Fig. 2.

3.1   Graph Network with Deep Convolution

We use $\mathrm{F} = \{f_i^D, 0 \leqslant i \leqslant N\}$ to denote video frame feature sequence, where D is the dimension of the frame feature and N is the number of video frames.

Fig. 1. "cooking show" video frame sequence. Frames with same color border contain similar targets.

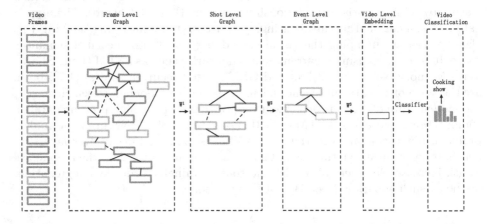

Fig. 2. High-level illustration of our proposed method DCGN. This is an example with label of "cooking show", containing shots of chef cooking, host chatting, food, audience, etc. Rectangle with different color represent different shots or events. We use graph network to represent the relations between frames, shots, or events, that similar ones (nodes) have edge connected. The graph is gradually aggregated that represent frame, shot, event and video hierarchically.

We treat each frame, shot or event as a node of a graph, and the graph is densely connected (each pair of the nodes has an edge). Two nodes are connected weighted by their feature vector similarity. Let A be the adjacency matrix of F, and the elements is calculated by cosine similarity:

$$A(i, j) = \frac{\sum_{d=0}^{D-1}(f[i][d] \times f[j][d])}{\sqrt{\sum_{d=0}^{D-1} f[i][d]^2} \times \sqrt{\sum_{d=0}^{D-1} f[j][d]^2}} \tag{1}$$

Graph neural network uses a differentiable aggregation function 2 to perform "message passing". It is an end-to-end learning model, which can learn node and edge representations simultaneously.

$$h^l = G(A, h^{l-1}, W^l) \tag{2}$$

where h^l is the node representation (messages) after l-th iteration, W^l is the parameters for the l-th iteration. G is the message propagation function. GCN [9] is a popular graph model whose G is:

$$G = \sigma(\sqrt{\overline{D}}A\sqrt{\overline{D}}h^{l-1}W^l) \tag{3}$$

where $\overline{D}$ is the diagonal node degree matrix that normalizing A such that all rows sum to one.

Graph Pooling. In the Eq. 3 the adjacency matrix A is unchanged during iteration, so the topology of the graph is static. However, video frame sequence is a hierarchical structure, hence the graph topology should be abstracted to higher level gradually. We use two pooling methods to aggregate graph.

Average Pooling. This method applies the center of K consecutive nodes as the node of the next level graph:

$$p^l[i][d] = \frac{\sum_{k=0}^{K-1} h^{l-1}[i \times K + k][d]}{K}, d \in [0, D] \tag{4}$$

where K is the pooling kernel size, p^l is the l-th pooled graph node feature vector. After l-th iteration, the graph size is $\frac{1}{K^l}$ of the original.

Self-attention Based Pooling. This method performs a local self-attention to obtain a weight α for each feature of the local consecutive sequence, thereby obtaining a locally weighted and fused output of the feature sequence. Comparing to average pooling, it can better obtain the topology of the next layer graph, which is beneficial to the propagation of feature information. We formulate it as:

$$p_{att}^l[i] = \alpha^l[i] \otimes h^{l-1}[i \times K : (i+1) \times K],$$
$$\alpha^l[i] = softmax(h^{l-1}[i \times K : (i+1) \times K]W_{att}^l + b^l) \tag{5}$$

where K is the number of local features to perform self-attention, and W_{att} and b are the parameters to learn.

Nodes Convolution. Different from GCN [9] which use fully connected layers to represent the nodes, in order to represent frame sequence hierarchically and maintain the local sequence order, we represent the nodes by convolution as follows:

$$c^l[i] = h^{l-1}[i \times K : (i+1) \times K]W^l \tag{6}$$

where c^l is the l-th graph node embedding, and W^l is the convolution kernel weights with size of $K \times D$.

Pooling and convolution are shown in Fig. 3.

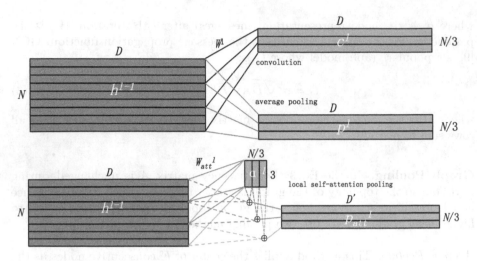

Fig. 3. Convolution and pooling ($K = 3$) of N nodes with D-dimension, outputs new $\frac{N}{3}$ nodes with D-dimension.

Node Feature Propagation. Now, we have obtained a new graph topology and new feature vector for each node. In order to obtain a more complete representation in higher level, we perform the "message passing" across the entire graph, so that the fused feature of each node is generated from the global perspective. We use the similar form as Eq. 3:

$$h^l = \sigma(\sqrt{\overline{D}^{l-1}}A^{l-1}\sqrt{\overline{D}^{l-1}}c^{l-1}W^l) \tag{7}$$

where A^{l-1} is calculated using Eq. 1 in which f is replaced with p^{l-1}. Figure 4 shows the network described above.

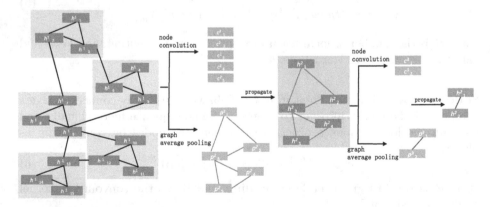

Fig. 4. Illustration of two layer convolutional graph network. 15 input feature vectors are aggregated to 2 output feature vectors.

3.2 Shot Segmentation Aided Graph Pooling

Shot is a basic temporal unit, which is a series of interrelated consecutive pictures taken contiguously by a single camera and representing a continuous action in time and space. It is independent over video category, and can be obtained by unsupervised nonparametric way. Inspired by the kernel temporal segmentation (KTS) algorithm [10], the proposed method applies the deep convolutional neural network features to calculate the matrix of frame-to-frame similarities. The algorithm uses dynamic programming to minimize within segment kernel variances, and get the best shot boundaries under given number of shots, the object function is:

$$\min_{m;t_0,\ldots,t_{m-1}} J_{m,n} := L_{m,n} + Cg(m,n) \tag{8}$$

where

$$L_{m,n} = \sum_{i=0}^{m} v_{t_{i-1},t_i}, g(m,n) = m(log(\frac{n}{m})+1),$$

$$v_{t_{i-1},t_i} = \sum_{t=t_i}^{t_{i=1}-1} \|f_t - \mu_i\|^2, u_i = \frac{\sum_{t=t_{t_i}}^{t_{i+1}-1} f_t}{t_{i+1} - t_i} \tag{9}$$

where m is the number of shots and $g(m,n)$ is a penalty term. Figure 5 shows the segmented shots together with their positions in frame-to-frame similarity matrix.

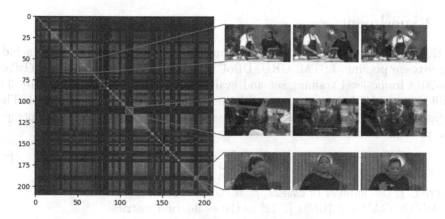

Fig. 5. The left is a matrix of frame-to-frame similarities, which brighter (larger value) points indicate more similar frames. Local bright squares are treated as a shot.

We apply this shot segmentation algorithm to the frame level graph modeling, and the formulation becomes:

$$p^1[t][d] = \frac{\sum_{k=s_t}^{s_{t+1}} f[k][d]}{s_{t+1} - s_t}, d \in [0, D] \tag{10}$$

$$c^1[t] = f[s_t : s_{t+1}]W^1 \qquad (11)$$

where t is the shot number, s_t is frame index of the t-th shot boundary.

Figure 6 shows the network aided with shot segmentation: first, a fixed number m of shots are segmented, and a frame level convolution graph network is applied to get the shot level features H^1. Then deep convolution graph network is applied to modeling higher-level features. Finally, the last level feature vectors are concatenated and inputted to a mixture of experts (MoE) [11] model to get the classification score. The model is trained end-to-end.

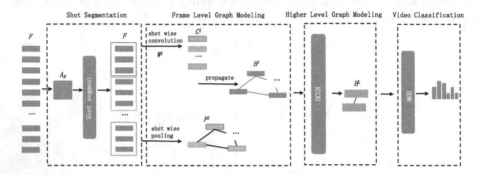

Fig. 6. Overall architecture. Shot-wise convolution and pooling performs at the frame level. The subsequent levels perform DCGN and obtain a video level feature H^L. MoE classifier use H^L as the input to provide the final label predictions.

4   Experiment

In this section, we evaluate the proposed method with other alternatives, including average pooling, LSTM, GRU, DBoF. We train these models on YouTube-8m-2018 frame-level training set and evaluate on validation set. There are 3.9 million videos in the training set and 1.1 million videos in the validation set. The dataset is a multi-class task with 3862 classes in total, and we use cross entropy loss to train the model:

$$Loss = -\sum_{c=1}^{C} y_c log(p_c) \qquad (12)$$

where C is the number of classes, p_c is the prediction for class c.

We use GAP and Hit@1 [1, 12] as the evaluation metrics:

$$GAP = \sum_{i=1}^{N} p(i)\Delta r(i) \qquad (13)$$

where N is the number of final predictions, we set $N = 20$ here, $p(i)$ is the precision, and $r(i)$ is the recall.

$$Hit@1 = \frac{1}{|V|} \sum_{v \in V} \vee_{e \in G_v} \mathbb{I}(rank_{v,e} \leqslant 1) \qquad (14)$$

where G_v is the set of ground-truth entities for v. This is the fraction of test samples that contain at least one of the ground truth labels in the best prediction.

The network architecture parameters and hyper-parameters for training these models are given in Table 1.

Table 1. Training settings

	Ours	Average Pooling	LSTM	GRU	DBoF
network parameters	layers: 5, filter size: 1024 (same for each layer)		cells: 1024, layers: 2	cells: 1024, layers: 2	cluster size: 8192, hidden size: 1024, pooling method: max
base learning rate	0.001				
learning rate decay	0.8				
learning rate decay examples	4M				
mini batch size	1024				
number of epochs	5				
number of mixtures in MoE	2				

Table 2 shows results for all methods. Simple averaging of features across all frames, perform poorly on this dataset. The order-less aggregation methods DBoF perform worse than the RNN based models. Our model outperforms all other models, and the self-attention based graph pooling got the best result.

Table 2. Evaluation results. All values in this table are averaged results and reported in percentage(%). Top-2 of each metrics are bolded.

Methods	GAP	Hit@1	Loss
Average pooling	76.5	83.5	5.49
LSTM	83.6	87.2	4.12
GRU	83.9	**87.9**	4.03
DBoF	81.1	86.2	6.02
ours + average graph pooling	**84.1**	87.4	**4.01**
ours + self-attention graph pooling	**84.5**	**87.7**	**3.98**

5   Conclusions

In this work, we propose a novel sequence representation method DCGN for video classification. One layer in DCGN is composed of graph pooling, nodes convolution and nodes feature propagation. The problem of representing complex relationships between frames or shots is addressed by applying this graph based network hierarchically across the frame sequence. Based on the quantitative results in Sect. 4, the proposed method DCGN outperform the other alternatives such as LSTM and GRU.

References

1. Abu-El-Haija, S., et al.: Youtube-8m: a large-scale video classification benchmark. CoRR abs/1609.08675 (2016)
2. Szegedy, C., Vanhoucke, V., Ioffe, S., Shlens, J., Wojna, Z.: Rethinking the inception architecture for computer vision. CoRR abs/1512.00567 (2015)
3. Hochreiter, S., Schmidhuber, J.: Long short-term memory. Neural Comput. **9**(9), 1735–1780 (1997)
4. Cho, K., van Merrienboer, B., Gülçehre, Ç., Bougares, F., Schwenk, H., Bengio, Y.: Learning phrase representations using RNN encoder-decoder for statistical machine translation. CoRR abs/1406.1078 (2014)
5. Srivastava, N., Mansimov, E., Salakhudinov, R.: Unsupervised learning of video representations using LSTMs. In: International Conference on Machine Learning, pp. 843–852 (2015)
6. Yue-Hei Ng, J., Hausknecht, M., Vijayanarasimhan, S., Vinyals, O., Monga, R., Toderici, G.: Beyond short snippets: deep networks for video classification. In: Proceedings of the IEEE Conference on Computer Vision and Pattern Recognition, pp. 4694–4702 (2015)
7. Ballas, N., Yao, L., Pal, C., Courville, A.: Delving deeper into convolutional networks for learning video representations. arXiv preprint arXiv:1511.06432 (2015)
8. Li, S., Li, W., Cook, C., Zhu, C., Gao, Y.: Independently recurrent neural network (IndRNN): building a longer and deeper RNN. CoRR abs/1803.04831 (2018)
9. Kipf, T.N., Welling, M.: Semi-supervised classification with graph convolutional networks. CoRR abs/1609.02907 (2016)
10. Potapov, D., Douze, M., Harchaoui, Z., Schmid, C.: Category-specific video summarization. In: Fleet, D., Pajdla, T., Schiele, B., Tuytelaars, T. (eds.) ECCV 2014. LNCS, vol. 8694, pp. 540–555. Springer, Cham (2014). https://doi.org/10.1007/978-3-319-10599-4_35
11. Jordan, M.I., Jacobs, R.A.: Hierarchical mixtures of experts and the EM algorithm. Neural Comput. **6**(2), 181–214 (1994)
12. Google: Youtube-8m starter code (2018). https://github.com/google/youtube-8m

Training Compact Deep Learning
Models for Video Classification
Using Circulant Matrices

Alexandre Araujo[1,2]([⊠]), Benjamin Negrevergne[1]([⊠]), Yann Chevaleyre[1]([⊠]),
and Jamal Atif[1]([⊠])

[1] PSL, Université Paris-Dauphine, LAMSADE, CNRS, UMR 7243, Paris, France
alexandre.araujo@dauphine.eu, benjamin.negrevergne@dauphine.fr,
{yann.chevaleyre,jamal.atif}@lamsade.dauphine.fr
[2] Wavestone, Paris, France

Abstract. In real world scenarios, model accuracy is hardly the only factor to consider. Large models consume more memory and are computationally more intensive, which make them difficult to train and to deploy, especially on mobile devices. In this paper, we build on recent results at the crossroads of Linear Algebra and Deep Learning which demonstrate how imposing a structure on large weight matrices can be used to reduce the size of the model. Building on these results, we propose very compact models for video classification based on state-of-the-art network architectures such as *Deep Bag-of-Frames*, *NetVLAD* and *NetFisherVectors*. We then conduct thorough experiments using the large *YouTube-8M* video classification dataset. As we will show, the circulant DBoF embedding achieves an excellent trade-off between size and accuracy.

Keywords: Deep learning · Computer vision · Structured matrices
Circulant matrices

1 Introduction

The top-3 most accurate approaches proposed during the first *YouTube-8M*[1] video classification challenge were all ensembles models. The ensembles typically combined models based on a variety of deep learning architectures such as *NetVLAD*, *Deep Bag-of-Frames* (DBoF), *NetFisherVectors* (NetFV) and *Long-Short Term Memory* (LSTM), leading a large aggregation of models (25 distinct models have been used by the first contestant [24], 74 by the second [33] and 57 by the third [20]). Ensembles are accurate, but they are not ideal: their size make them difficult to maintain and deploy, especially on mobile devices.

A common approach to compress large models into smaller ones is to use *model distillation* [13]. Model distillation is a two steps training procedure: first, a large model (or an ensemble model) is trained to be as accurate as possible. Then, a second compact model is trained to approximate the first one,

---

[1] https://www.kaggle.com/c/youtube8m

© Springer Nature Switzerland AG 2019
L. Leal-Taixé and S. Roth (Eds.): ECCV 2018 Workshops, LNCS 11132, pp. 271–286, 2019.
https://doi.org/10.1007/978-3-030-11018-5_25

while satisfying the given size constraints. The success of model distillation and other model compression techniques begs an important question: is it possible to devise models that are compact by nature while exhibiting the same generalization properties as large ones?

In linear algebra, it is common to exploit structural properties of matrices to reduce the memory footprint of an algorithm. Cheng et al. [6] have used this principle in the context of deep neural networks to design compact network architectures by imposing a structure on weight matrices of fully connected layers. They were able to replace large, unstructured weight matrices with structured *circulant matrices* without significantly impacting the accuracy. And because a n-by-n circulant matrix is fully determined by a vector of dimension n, they were able to train a neural network using only a fraction of the memory required to train the original network.

Inspired by this result, we designed several compact neural network architectures for video classification based on standard video architectures such as NetVLAD, DBoF, NetFV and we evaluated them on the large *YouTube-8M* dataset. However, instead of adopting the structure used by [6] (initially proposed by [32]), we decomposed weight matrices into products of diagonal and circulant matrices (as in [29]). In contrast with [32] which has been proved to approximate distance preserving projections, this structure can approximate *any* transformation (at the cost of a larger number of weights). As we will show, this approach exhibit good results on the video classification task at hand.

In this paper, we bring the following contributions:

– We define a compact architecture for video classification based on circulant matrices. As a side contribution, we also propose a new pooling technique which improves the Deep Bag-of-Frames embedding.
– We conduct thorough experimentations to identify the layers that are less impacted by the use of circulant matrices and we fine-tune our architectures to achieve the best trade-off between size and accuracy.
– We combine several architectures into a single model to achieve new model trained-end-to-end that can benefit from architectural diversity (as in ensembles).
– We train all our models on the Youtube-8M dataset with the 1 GB model size constraint imposed by the *2nd YouTube-8M Video Understanding Challenge*[2], and compares the different models in terms of size vs. accuracy ratio. Our experiments demonstrate that the best trade-off between size and accuracy is obtained using circulant DBoF embedding layer.

2   Related Works

Classification of unlabeled videos streams is one of the challenging tasks for machine learning algorithms. Research in this field has been stimulated by the recent release of several large annotated video datasets such as *Sports-1M* [19], *FCVID* [17] or the *YouTube-8M* [2] dataset.

---

[2] https://www.kaggle.com/c/youtube8m-2018.

The naive approach to achieve video classification is to perform frame-by-frame image recognition, and to average the results before the classification step. However, it has been shown in [2,24] that better results can be obtained by building features across different frames and several deep learning architectures have been designed to learn embeddings for sets of frames (and not single frames). For example Deep Bag-of-Frames (DBoF) [2], NetVLAD [3] or architectures based on Fisher Vectors [27].

The DBoF embedding layer, proposed in [2] processes videos in two steps. First, a learned transformation projects all the frames together into a high dimensional space. Then, a max (or average) pooling operation aggregates all the embedded frames into a single discriminative vector representation of the video. The NetVLAD [3] embedding layer is built on *VLAD* [16], a technique that aggregates a large number of local frame descriptors into a compact representation using a codebook of visual words. In NetVlad, the codebook is directly learned end-to-end during training. Finally, NetFisherVector (NetFV) is inspired by [27] and uses first and second-order statistics as video descriptors also gathered in a codebook. The technique can benefit from deep learning by using a deep neural network to learn the codebook [24].

All the architectures mentioned above can be used to build video features in the sense of features that span across several frames, but they are not designed to exploit the sequential nature of videos and capture motion. In order to learn truly spatio-temporal features and account for motion in videos, several researchers have looked into recurrent neural networks (e.g. LSTM [20,36]) and 3D convolutions [19] (in space and time). However, these approaches do not outperform non-sequential models, and the single best model proposed in [24] (winner of the first *YouTube-8M* competition) is based on NetVLAD [3].

The *2nd YouTube-8M Video Understanding Challenge* includes a constraint on the model size and many competitors have been looking into building efficient memory models with high accuracy. There are two kinds of techniques to reduce the memory required for training and/or inference in neural networks. The first kind aims at *compressing* an existing neural network into a smaller one, (thus it only impacts the size of the model at inference time). The second one aims at *constructing models that are compact* by design.

To compress an existing network several researchers have investigated techniques to prune parameters that are redundant (e.g. [9,12,21]). Redundant parameters can be omitted from the model without significantly changing the accuracy. It is also possible to use sparsity regularizers during training, to be able to compress the model after the training using efficient sparse matrix representations (e.g. [7,9,22]). Building on the observation that weight matrices are often redundant, another line of research has proposed to use matrix factorization [10,15,35] in order to decompose large weight matrices into factors of smaller matrices before inference.

An important idea in model compression, proposed by Buciluă et al. ([4]), is based on the observation that the model used for training is not required to be the same as the one used for inference. First, a large complex model is trained using all the available data and resources to be as accurate as possible, then a smaller and more compact model is trained to approximate the first model. The technique which was later specialized for deep learning models by [13] (a.k.a. model distillation) is often used to compress large ensemble models into compact single deep learning models.

Instead of compressing the model after the training step, one can try to design models that are compact by nature (without compromising the generalization properties of the network). The benefit of this approach is that it reduces memory usage required during both training and inference. As a consequence, users can train models that are virtually larger using less time and less computing resources. They also save the trouble of training two models instead of one as it is done with distillation. These techniques generally work by constraining the weight representation, either at the level of individual weights (e.g. using floating variable with limited precision [11], quantization [8,23,28]) or at the level of the whole matrix, (e.g. using weight hashing techniques [5]) which can achieve better compression ratio. However in practice, hashing techniques are difficult to use because of their irregular memory access patterns which make them inadequate for GPU-execution.

Another way of constraining the weight representation is to impose a structure on weight matrices (e.g. using circulant matrices [6,30], Vandermonde [30] or Fastfood transforms [34]). In this domain, [6] have proposed to replace two fully connected layers of AlexNet by circulant and diagonal matrices where the circulant matrix is learned by a gradient based optimization algorithm and the diagonal matrix entries are sampled at random in $\{-1, 1\}$. The size of the model is reduced by a factor of 10 without loss in accuracy[3]. Most of the time the resulting algorithms are easy to execute on GPU-devices.

3 Preliminaries on Circulant Matrices

In this paper, we use *circulant matrices* to build compact deep neural networks. A n-by-n circulant matrix C is a matrix where each row is a cyclic right shift of the previous one as illustrated below.

$$
C = circ(c) = \begin{bmatrix}
c_0 & c_{n-1} & c_{n-2} & \cdots & c_1 \\
c_1 & c_0 & c_{n-1} & & c_2 \\
c_2 & c_1 & c_0 & & c_3 \\
\vdots & & & \ddots & \vdots \\
c_{n-1} & c_{n-2} & c_{n-3} & & c_0
\end{bmatrix}
$$

Because the circulant matrix $C \in \mathbb{R}^{n \times n}$ is fully determined by the vector $c \in \mathbb{R}^n$, the matrix C can be compactly represented in memory using only n real values instead of n^2.

---

[3] In network such as AlexNet, the last 3 fully connected layers use 58M out of the 62M total trainable parameters (>90% of the total number of parameters).

An additional benefit of circulant matrices, is that they are computationally efficient, especially on GPU devices. Multiplying a circulant matrix C by a vector x is equivalent to a circular convolution between c and x (denoted $c \star x$). Furthermore, the circular convolution can be computed in the Fourier domain as follows.

$$Cx = c \star x = \mathcal{F}^{-1}\left(\mathcal{F}(c) \times \mathcal{F}(x)\right)$$

where $\mathcal{F}$ is the Fourier transform. Because this operation can be simplified to a simple element wise vector multiplication, the matrix multiplication Cx can be computed in $O(n \log n)$ instead of $O(n^2)$.

Among the many applications of circulant matrices, matrix decomposition is one of the interest. In particular, Schmid et al. have shown in [26,29], that any complex matrix $A \in \mathbb{C}^{n \times n}$ can be decomposed into the product of diagonal and circulant matrices, as follows:

$$A = D^{(1)}C^{(1)}D^{(2)}C^{(2)} \dots D^m C^m = \prod_{i=1}^{m} D^{(i)} C^{(i)} \tag{1}$$

Later in [14], Huhtanen and Perämäki have demonstrated that choosing $m = n$ is sufficient to decompose any complex matrix $A \in \mathbb{C}^{n \times n}$. By [29], the result in Eq. 1 also holds for a real matrix $A \in \mathbb{R}^{n \times n}$, but the proof yields a much bigger value of m. However, the construction of [29] is far from optimal and it is likely that most real matrices can be decomposed into a reasonable number of factors. The authors of [25], made this conjecture, and they have leveraged the decomposition described in Eq. 1 in order to implement compact fully connected layers.

4 Compact Video Classification Architecture Using Circulant Matrices

Building on the decomposition presented in the previous section and the previous results obtained in [25], we now introduce a compact neural network architecture for video classification where dense matrices have been replaced by products of circulant and diagonal matrices.

4.1 Base Model

We demonstrate the benefit of circulant matrices using a base model which has been proposed by [24]. This architecture can be decomposed into three blocks of layers, as illustrated in Fig. 1. The first block of layers, composed of the Deep Bag-of-Frames embedding, is meant to process audio and video frames independently. The DBoF layer computes two embeddings: one for the audio and one for the video. In the next paragraph, we will only focus on describing the video embedding. (The audio embedding is computed in a very similar way.)

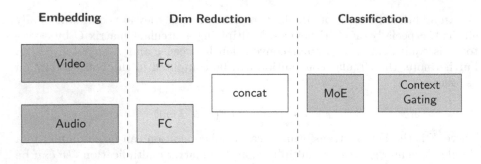

Fig. 1. This figure shows the architecture used for the experiences. The network samples at random video and audio frames from the input. The sample goes through an embedding layer and is reduced with a Fully Connected layer. The results are then concatenated and classified with a Mixture-of-Experts and Context Gating layer.

We represent a video V as a set of m frames $\{v_1, \ldots, v_m\}$ where each frame $v_i \in \mathbb{R}^k$ is a vector of visual features extracted from the frame image. In the context of the *YouTube-8M* competition, each v_i is a vector of 1024 visual features extracted using the last fully connected layer of an Inception network trained on ImageNet. The DBoF embedding layer then embed a video V into a vector v' drawn from a p dimensional vector space as follows.

$$v' = \max\{Wv_i \mid v_i \in V\}$$

where W is a matrix in $\mathbb{R}^{p \times k}$ (learned) and max is the element-wise maximum operator. We typically choose $p > k$, (e.g. $p = 8192$). Note that because this formulation is based on set, it can process videos of different lengths (i.e., a different value of m).

A second block of layers reduces the dimensionality each embedding layer (audio and video), and merges the result into a single vector with using a simple concatenation operation. We chose to reduce the dimensionality of each embedding layer separately *before* the concatenation operation to avoid the concatenation of two high dimensional vectors.

Finally, the classification block uses a combination of Mixtures-of-Experts (MoE) and Context Gating to calculate the final probabilities. The Mixtures-of-Experts layer introduced in [18] and proposed for video classification in [2] are used to predict each label independently. It consists of a gating and experts networks which are concurrently learned. The gating network learns which experts to use for each label and the experts layers learn how to classify each label. The context gating operation was introduced in [24] and captures dependencies among features and re-weight probabilities based on the correlation of the labels. For example, it can capture the correlation of the labels *ski* and *snow* and re-adjust the probabilities accordingly.

Table 1 shows the shapes of the layers as well as the shapes of the weight matrices.

Table 1. This table shows the architecture of our base model with a DBoF Embedding and 150 frames sampled from the input. For more clarity, weights from batch normalization layers have been ignored. The -1 in the activation shapes corresponds to the batch size. The size of the MoE layers corresponds to the number of mixtures used.

Layer	Layer size	Activation shape	Weight matrix shape	#Weights
Video DBoF	8192	$(-1, 150, 1024)$	$(1024, 8192)$	8 388 608
Audio DBoF	4096	$(-1, 150, 128)$	$(128, 4096)$	524 288
Video FC	512	$(-1, 8192)$	$(8192, 512)$	4 194 304
Audio FC	512	$(-1, 4096)$	$(4096, 512)$	2 097 152
Concat	-	$(-1, 1024)$	-	-
MoE gating	3	$(-1, 1024)$	$(1024, 19310)$	19 773 440
MoE experts	2	$(-1, 1024)$	$(1024, 15448)$	15 818 752
Context gating	-	$(-1, 3862)$	$(3862, 3862)$	14 915 044

4.2   Robust Deep Bag-of-Frames Pooling Method

We propose a technique to extract more performance from the base model with DBoF embedding. The maximum pooling is sensitive to outliers and noise whereas the average pooling is more robust. We propose a method which consists in taking several samples of frames, applying the upsampling followed by the maximum pooling to these samples, and then averaging over all samples. More formally, assume a video contains m frames $v_1, \ldots, v_m \in \mathbb{R}^{1024}$. We first draw n random samples $S_1 \ldots S_n$ of size k from the set $\{v_1, \ldots, v_m\}$. The output of the robust-DBoF layer is:

$$\frac{1}{n} \sum_{i=1}^{n} \max \{v \times W : v \in S_i\}$$

Depending on n and k, this pooling method is a tradeoff between the max pooling and the average pooling. Thus, it is more robust to noise, as will be shown in the experiments section.

4.3   Compact Representation of the Base Model

In order to train this model in a compact form we build upon the work of [6] and use a more general framework presented by Eq. 1. The fully connected layers are then represented as follows:

$$h(x) = \phi \left(\left[\prod_{i=1}^{m} D^{(i)} C^{(i)} \right] x + b \right)$$

where the parameters of each matrix $D^{(i)}$ and $C^{(i)}$ are trained using a gradient based optimization algorithm, and m defines the number of factors. Increasing the value of m increases the number of trainable parameters and therefore the modeling capabilities of the layer. In our experiments, we chose the number of factors m empirically to achieve the best trade-off between model size and accuracy.

To measure the impact of the size of the model and its accuracy, we represent layers in their compact form independently. Given that circulant and diagonal matrices are square, we use concatenation and slicing to achieve the desired dimension. As such, with $m = 1$, the weight matrix (1024, 8192) of the video embedding is represented by a concatenation of 8 DC matrices and the weight matrix of size (8192, 512) is represented by a single DC matrix with shape (8192, 8192) and the resulting output is sliced at the 512 dimension. We denote layers in their classic form as *"Dense"* and layers represented with circulant and diagonal factors as *"Compact"*.

4.4 Leveraging Architectural Diversity

In order to benefit from architectural diversity, we also devise a single model architecture that combines different types of embedding layers. As we can see in Fig. 2, video and audio frames are processed by several embedding layers before being reduced by a series of compact fully connected layers. The output of the compact fc layers are then averaged, concatenated and fed into the final classification block. Figure 7 shows the result of different models given the number of parameters. The use of circulant matrices make us able to fit this model in gpu memory. For example, the diversity model with a NetVLAD embedding (cluster size of 256) and NetFV embedding (cluster size of 128) has 160 millions parameters (600 Mo) in the compact version and 728M (2.7 Go) in the dense version.

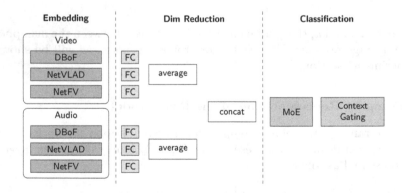

Fig. 2. This figure shows an evolution of the first architecture from Fig. 1 with several embeddings. This architecture is made to leverage the diversity of an Ensemble in a single model.

5   Experiments

In this section, we first evaluate the pooling technique proposed in Sect. 4.2. Then, we conduct experiments to evaluate the accuracy of our compact models. In particular, we investigate which layer benefits the most from a circulant representation and show that the decomposition presented in Sect. 3 performs better than the approach from [6] for the video classification problem. Finally, we compare all our models on a two dimensional size vs. accuracy scale in order to evaluate the trade-off between size and accuracy of each one of our models.

5.1   Experimental Setup

Dataset. All the experiments of this paper have been done in the context of the *2nd YouTube-8M Video Understanding Challenge* with the *YouTube-8M* dataset. We trained our models with the training set and 70% of the validation set which correspond to a total of 4 822 555 examples. We used the data augmentation technique proposed by [31] to virtually double the number of inputs. The method consists in splitting the videos into two equal parts. This approach is motivated by the observation that a human could easily label the video by watching either the beginning or the ending of the video.

All the code used in this experimental section is available online.[4]

Hyper-parameters. All our experiments are developed with TensorFlow Framework [1]. We trained our models with the CrossEntropy loss and used Adam optimizer with a 0.0002 learning rate and a 0.8 exponential decay every 4 million examples. All fully connected layers are composed of 512 units. DBoF, NetVLAD and NetFV are respectively 8192, 64 and 64 of cluster size for video frames and 4096, 32, 32 for audio frames. We used 4 mixtures for the MoE Layer. We used all 150 frames available and robust max pooling introduced in 4.2 for the DBoF embedding. In order to stabilize and accelerate the training, we used batch normalization before each non linear activation and gradient clipping.

Evaluation Metric. We used the GAP (Global Average Precision), as used in the *2nd YouTube-8M Video Understanding Challenge*, to compare our experiments. The GAP metric is defined as follows:

$$GAP = \sum_{i=1}^{P} p(i) \Delta r(i)$$

where N is the number of final predictions, $p(i)$ the precision, and $r(i)$ the recall. We limit our evaluation to 20 predictions for each video.

Hardware. All experiments have been realized on a cluster of 12 nodes. Each node has 160 POWER8 processor, 128 Go of RAM and 4 Nividia Titan P100.

---

[4] https://github.com/araujoalexandre/youtube8m-circulant.

5.2   Robust Deep Bag-of-Frames Pooling Method

We evaluate the performance of our Robust DBoF embedding. In accordance with the work from [2], we find that average pooling performs better than maximum pooling. Figure 3 shows that the proposed robust maximum pooling method outperforms both maximum and average pooling.

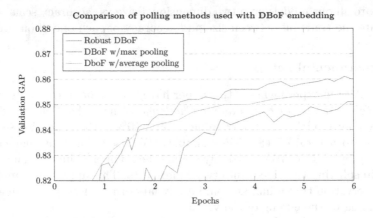

Fig. 3. This graphic shows the impact of *robust DBoF* (i.e. red line) with $n = 10$ and $k = 15$ on the Deep Bag-of-Frames embedding compared to max and average pooling. (Color figure online)

5.3   Impact of Circulant Matrices on Different Layers

This series of experiments aims at understanding the effect on compactness over different layers. Table 2 shows the result in terms of number of weights, size of the model (MB) and GAP. We also compute the compression ratio with respect to the dense model. The compact fully connected layer achieves a compression rate of 9.5 while having a very similar performance, whereas the compact DBoF and MoE achieve a higher compression rate at the expense of accuracy. Figure 4 shows that the model with a compact FC converges faster than the dense model. The model with a compact DBoF shows a big variance over the validation GAP which can be associated with a difficulty to train. The model with a compact MoE is more stable but at the expense of its performance. Another series of experiments investigates the effect of adding factors of the compact matrix DC (i.e. the parameters m specified in Sect. 4.3). Table 3 shows that there is no gain in accuracy even if the number of weights increases. It also shows that adding factors has an important effect on the speed of training. On the basis of this result, i.e. given the performance and compression ratio, we can consider that representing the fully connected layer of the base model in a compact fashion can be a good trade-off.

Table 2. This table shows the effect of the compactness of different layers. In these experiments, for speeding-up the training phase, we did not use the audio features and exploited only the video information.

Baseline model	#Weights	Size (MB)	Compress. Rate (%)	GAP@20	Diff.
Dense model	45 359 764	173	-	**0.846**	-
Compact DBoF	36 987 540	141	18.4	0.838	−0.008
Compact FC	41 181 844	157	9.2	0.845	**−0.001**
Compact MoE	12 668 504	48	72.0	0.805	−0.041

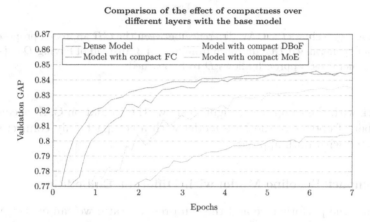

Fig. 4. Validation GAP according to the number of epochs for different compact models.

Table 3. This table shows the evolution of the number of parameters and the accuracy according to the number of factors. Despite the addition of degrees of freedom for the weight matrix of the fully connected layer, the model does not improve in performance. The column *#Examples/sec* shows the evolution of images per sec processed during the training of the model with a compact FC according to the number of factors.

#Factors	#Examples/sec	#Parameters in FC layer	Compress. Rate of FC layer (%)	GAP@20
1	1 052	12 288	99.8	0.861
3	858	73 728	98.8	0.861
6	568	147 456	97.6	0.859
Dense FC	1 007	6 291 456	-	0.861

5.4   Comparison with Related Works

Circulant matrices have been used in neural networks in [6]. They proposed to replace fully connected layers by a circulant and diagonal matrices where the circulant matrix is learned by a gradient based optimization algorithm and the diagonal matrix is random with values in $\{-1, 1\}$. We compare our more general

GAP given the pooling method used with DBoF embedding

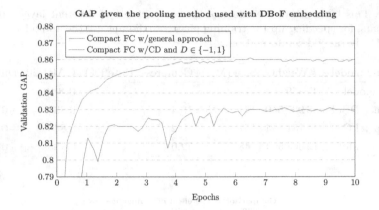

Fig. 5. This figure shows the GAP difference between the CD approach proposed in [6] and the more generalized DC approach from Sect. 4.3. Instead of having $D \in \{-1, +1\}$ fixed, the generalized approach allows D to be learned.

framework with their approach. Figure 5 shows the validation GAP according to the number of epochs of the base model with a compact fully connected layer implemented with both approach.

5.5   Compact Baseline Model with Different Embeddings

To compare the performance and the compression ratio we can expect, we consider different settings where the compact fully connected layer is used together with different embeddings. Figure 6 and Table 4 show the performance of the base model with DBoF, NetVLAD and NetFV embeddings with a *Dense* and *Compact* fully connected layer. Notice that we can get a bigger compression rate with NetVLAD and NetFV due to the fact that the output of the embedding is in a higher dimensional space which implies a larger weight matrix for the fully connected layer. Although the compression rate is higher, it is at the expense of the accuracy.

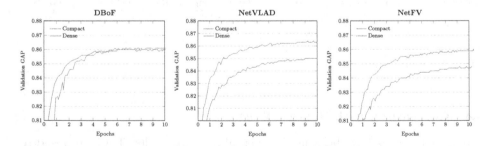

Fig. 6. The figures above show the validation GAP of compact and *Dense* fully connected layer with different embeddings according to the number of epochs.

Table 4. This table shows the impact of the compression of the fully connected layer of the model architecture shown in Fig. 1 with Audio and Video features vector and different types of embeddings. The variable compression rate is due to the different width of the output of the embedding.

Method	#Parameters	Size (MB)	Compress. Rate (%)	GAP@20
DBoF				
FC dense	65 795 732	251	-	0.861
FC circulant	59 528 852	227	9.56	0.861
NetVLAD				
FC dense	86 333 460	330	-	0.864
FC circulant	50 821 140	194	41.1	0.851
NetFisher				
FC dense	122 054 676	466	-	0.860
FC circulant	51 030 036	195	58.1	0.848

5.6   Model Size vs. Accuracy

To conclude our experimental evaluation, we compare all our models in terms of size and accuracy. The results are presented in Fig. 7.

As we can see in this figure, the most compact models are obtained with the circulant NetVLAD and NetFV. We can also see that the complex architectures described in Sect. 4.4 (DBoF + NetVLAD) achieve top performance but at the cost of a large number of weights. Finally, the best trade-off between size and accuracy is obtained using the DBoF embedding layer and achieves a GAP of 0.861 for only 60 millions weights.

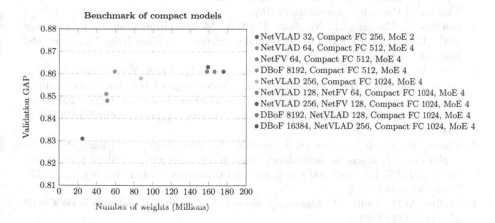

Fig. 7. Comparison between different models with compact fully connected layers.

6   Conclusion

In this paper, we demonstrated that circulant matrices can be a great tool to design compact neural network architectures for video classification tasks. We proposed a more general framework which improves the state of the art and conducted a series of experiments aiming at understanding the effect of compactness on different layers. Our experiments demonstrate that the best trade-off between size and accuracy is obtained using circulant DBoF embedding layers. We investigated a model with multiple embeddings to leverage the performance of an Ensemble but found it ineffective. The good performance of Ensemble models, i.e. why aggregating different distinct models performs better that incorporating all the diversity in a single architecture is still an open problem. Our future work will be devoted to address this challenging question and to pursue our effort to devise compact models achieving the same accuracy as larger one, and to study their theoretical properties.

Acknowledgement. This work was granted access to the OpenPOWER prototype from GENCI-IDRIS under the Preparatory Access AP010610510 made by GENCI. We would like to thank the staff of IDRIS who was really available for the duration of this work, Abdelmalek Lamine and Tahar Nguira, interns at Wavestone for their work on circulant matrices. Finally, we would also like to thank Wavestone to support this research.

References

1. Abadi, M., et al.: TensorFlow: large-scale machine learning on heterogeneous systems (2015). https://www.tensorflow.org/. Software available from tensorflow.org
2. Abu-El-Haija, S., et al.: YouTube-8M: a large-scale video classification benchmark. arXiv:1609.08675 (2016). https://arxiv.org/pdf/1609.08675v1.pdf
3. Arandjelović, R., Gronat, P., Torii, A., Pajdla, T., Sivic, J.: NetVLAD: CNN architecture for weakly supervised place recognition. In: IEEE Conference on Computer Vision and Pattern Recognition (2016)
4. Buciluă, C., Caruana, R., Niculescu-Mizil, A.: Model compression. In: Proceedings of the 12th ACM SIGKDD International Conference on Knowledge Discovery and Data Mining, pp. 535–541. ACM (2006)
5. Chen, W., Wilson, J.T., Tyree, S., Weinberger, K.Q., Chen, Y.: Compressing neural networks with the hashing trick. In: Proceedings of the 32nd International Conference on International Conference on Machine Learning, ICML 2015, vol. 37, pp. 2285–2294. JMLR.org (2015). http://dl.acm.org/citation.cfm?id=3045118.3045361
6. Cheng, Y., Yu, F.X., Feris, R.S., Kumar, S., Choudhary, A., Chang, S.F.: An exploration of parameter redundancy in deep networks with circulant projections. In: 2015 IEEE International Conference on Computer Vision (ICCV), pp. 2857–2865, December 2015
7. Collins, M.D., Kohli, P.: Memory bounded deep convolutional networks. CoRR abs/1412.1442 (2014)

8. Courbariaux, M., Bengio, Y., David, J.P.: BinaryConnect: training deep neural networks with binary weights during propagations. In: Proceedings of the 28th International Conference on Neural Information Processing Systems, NIPS 2015, vol. 2, pp. 3123–3131. MIT Press, Cambridge (2015). http://dl.acm.org/citation.cfm?id=2969442.2969588

9. Dai, B., Zhu, C., Guo, B., Wipf, D.: Compressing neural networks using the variational information bottleneck. In: Dy, J., Krause, A. (eds.) Proceedings of the 35th International Conference on Machine Learning, Proceedings of Machine Learning Research, vol. 80, pp. 1143–1152. PMLR, Stockholmsmässan, Stockholm, Sweden, 10–15 July 2018. http://proceedings.mlr.press/v80/dai18d.html

10. Denil, M., Shakibi, B., Dinh, L., Ranzato, M.A., de Freitas, N.: Predicting parameters in deep learning. In: Burges, C.J.C., Bottou, L., Welling, M., Ghahramani, Z., Weinberger, K.Q. (eds.) Advances in Neural Information Processing Systems 26, pp. 2148–2156. Curran Associates, Inc. (2013). http://papers.nips.cc/paper/5025-predicting-parameters-in-deep-learning.pdf

11. Gupta, S., Agrawal, A., Gopalakrishnan, K., Narayanan, P.: Deep learning with limited numerical precision. In: Proceedings of the 32nd International Conference on International Conference on Machine Learning, ICML 2015, vol. 37, pp. 1737–1746. JMLR.org (2015). http://dl.acm.org/citation.cfm?id=3045118.3045303

12. Han, S., Mao, H., Dally, W.J.: Deep compression: compressing deep neural networks with pruning, trained quantization and Huffman coding. In: International Conference on Learning Representations (ICLR) (2016)

13. Hinton, G., Vinyals, O., Dean, J.: Distilling the knowledge in a neural network. In: NIPS Deep Learning and Representation Learning Workshop (2015). http://arxiv.org/abs/1503.02531

14. Huhtanen, M., Perämäki, A.: Factoring matrices into the product of circulant and diagonal matrices. J. Fourier Anal. Appl. $21(5)$, 1018–1033 (2015). https://doi.org/10.1007/s00041-015-9395-0

15. Jaderberg, M., Vedaldi, A., Zisserman, A.: Speeding up convolutional neural networks with low rank expansions. CoRR abs/1405.3866 (2014)

16. Jégou, H., Douze, M., Schmid, C., Pérez, P.: Aggregating local descriptors into a compact image representation. In: CVPR 2010 - 23rd IEEE Conference on Computer Vision and Pattern Recognition, pp. 3304–3311. IEEE Computer Society, San Francisco, June 2010. https://doi.org/10.1109/CVPR.2010.5540039. https://hal.inria.fr/inria-00548637

17. Jiang, Y.G., Wu, Z., Wang, J., Xue, X., Chang, S.F.: Exploiting feature and class relationships in video categorization with regularized deep neural networks. IEEE Trans. Patt. Anal. Mach. Intell. $40(2)$, 352–364 (2018). https://doi.org/10.1109/TPAMI.2017.2670560

18. Jordan, M.I., Jacobs, R.A.: Hierarchical mixtures of experts and the EM algorithm. In: Proceedings of 1993 International Conference on Neural Networks (IJCNN-93-Nagoya, Japan), vol. 2, pp. 1339–1344, October 1993. https://doi.org/10.1109/IJCNN.1993.716791

19. Karpathy, A., Toderici, G., Shetty, S., Leung, T., Sukthankar, R., Fei-Fei, L.: Large-scale video classification with convolutional neural networks. In: Proceedings of the IEEE Conference on Computer Vision and Pattern Recognition, pp. 1725–1732 (2014)

20. Li, F., et al.: Temporal modeling approaches for large-scale YouTube-8M video understanding. CoRR abs/1707.04555 (2017)

21. Lin, J., Rao, Y., Lu, J., Zhou, J.: Runtime neural pruning. In: Guyon, I., et al. (eds.) Advances in Neural Information Processing Systems 30, pp. 2181–2191. Curran Associates, Inc. (2017). http://papers.nips.cc/paper/6813-runtime-neural-pruning.pdf
22. Liu, B., Wang, M., Foroosh, H., Tappen, M., Penksy, M.: Sparse convolutional neural networks. In: 2015 IEEE Conference on Computer Vision and Pattern Recognition (CVPR), pp. 806–814, June 2015. https://doi.org/10.1109/CVPR.2015.7298681
23. Mellempudi, N., Kundu, A., Mudigere, D., Das, D., Kaul, B., Dubey, P.: Ternary neural networks with fine-grained quantization. CoRR abs/1705.01462 (2017)
24. Miech, A., Laptev, I., Sivic, J.: Learnable pooling with context gating for video classification. CoRR abs/1706.06905 (2017)
25. Moczulski, M., Denil, M., Appleyard, J., de Freitas, N.: ACDC: a structured efficient linear layer. arXiv preprint arXiv:1511.05946 (2015)
26. Müller-Quade, J., Aagedal, H., Beth, T., Schmid, M.: Algorithmic design of diffractive optical systems for information processing. Phys. D Nonlinear Phenom. **120**(1–2), 196–205 (1998)
27. Perronnin, F., Dance, C.: Fisher kernels on visual vocabularies for image categorization. In: 2007 IEEE Conference on Computer Vision and Pattern Recognition, pp. 1–8, June 2007. https://doi.org/10.1109/CVPR.2007.383266
28. Rastegari, M., Ordonez, V., Redmon, J., Farhadi, A.: XNOR-net: ImageNet classification using binary convolutional neural networks. In: Leibe, B., Matas, J., Sebe, N., Welling, M. (eds.) ECCV 2016, Part IV. LNCS, vol. 9908, pp. 525–542. Springer, Cham (2016). https://doi.org/10.1007/978-3-319-46493-0_32
29. Schmid, M., Steinwandt, R., Müller-Quade, J., Rötteler, M., Beth, T.: Decomposing a matrix into circulant and diagonal factors. Linear Algebra Appl. **306**(1–3), 131–143 (2000)
30. Sindhwani, V., Sainath, T., Kumar, S.: Structured transforms for small-footprint deep learning. In: Cortes, C., Lawrence, N.D., Lee, D.D., Sugiyama, M., Garnett, R. (eds.) Advances in Neural Information Processing Systems 28, pp. 3088–3096. Curran Associates, Inc. (2015). http://papers.nips.cc/paper/5869-structured-transforms-for-small-footprint-deep-learning.pdf
31. Skalic, M., Pekalski, M., Pan, X.E.: Deep learning methods for efficient large scale video labeling. arXiv preprint arXiv:1706.04572 (2017)
32. Vybíral, J.: A variant of the johnson-lindenstrauss lemma for circulant matrices. J. Funct. Anal. **260**(4), 1096–1105 (2011). https://doi.org/10.1016/j.jfa.2010.11.014. http://www.sciencedirect.com/science/article/pii/S0022123610004507
33. Wang, H., Zhang, T., Wu, J.: The monkeytyping solution to the YouTube-8M video understanding challenge. CoRR abs/1706.05150 (2017)
34. Yang, Z., et al.: Deep fried convnets. In: 2015 IEEE International Conference on Computer Vision (ICCV), pp. 1476–1483, December 2015. https://doi.org/10.1109/ICCV.2015.173
35. Yu, X., Liu, T., Wang, X., Tao, D.: On compressing deep models by low rank and sparse decomposition. In: 2017 IEEE Conference on Computer Vision and Pattern Recognition (CVPR), pp. 67–76, July 2017. https://doi.org/10.1109/CVPR.2017.15
36. Yue-Hei Ng, J., Hausknecht, M., Vijayanarasimhan, S., Vinyals, O., Monga, R., Toderici, G.: Beyond short snippets: deep networks for video classification. In: Proceedings of the IEEE Conference on Computer Vision and Pattern Recognition, pp. 4694–4702 (2015)

Towards Good Practices for Multi-modal Fusion in Large-Scale Video Classification

Jinlai Liu, Zehuan Yuan[✉], and Changhu Wang

Bytedance AI Lab, Beijing, China
{liujinlai.licio,yuanzehuan,wangchanghu}@bytedance.com

Abstract. Leveraging both visual frames and audio has been experimentally proven effective to improve large-scale video classification. Previous research on video classification mainly focuses on the analysis of visual content among extracted video frames and their temporal feature aggregation. In contrast, multimodal data fusion is achieved by simple operators like average and concatenation. Inspired by the success of bilinear pooling in the visual and language fusion, we introduce multi-modal factorized bilinear pooling (MFB) to fuse visual and audio representations. We combine MFB with different video-level features and explore its effectiveness in video classification. Experimental results on the challenging Youtube-8M v2 dataset demonstrate that MFB significantly outperforms simple fusion methods in large-scale video classification.

Keywords: Video classification · Multi-modal learning
Bilinear model

1 Introduction

Along with the dramatic increase in video applications and production, better video understanding techniques are urgently needed. As one of the fundamental video understanding tasks, multi-label video classification has attracted increasing attentions in both computer vision and machine learning communities. Video classification requires a system to recognize all involved objects, actions and even events in any video based on its available multimodal data such as visual frames and audio.

As deep learning has obtained a remarkable success in image classification [1–3], action recognition [4–6] and speech recognition [7,8], video classification also benefit a lot from these powerful image, snippet, and audio representations. Since videos are composed of continuous frames, aggregating frame or snippet features into video-level representation also plays an important role during recognition process. Besides the direct aggregations such as temporal average or maxpooling, a few sophisticated temporal aggregation techniques are also proposed. For example, Abu-El-Haija *et al.* [9] proposes deep Bag-of-Frames pooling (DBoF) to sparsely aggregate frame features by ReLU activation. On the other hand, recurrent neural networks such as long short-term memory (LSTM) [10]

© Springer Nature Switzerland AG 2019
L. Leal-Taixé and S. Roth (Eds.): ECCV 2018 Workshops, LNCS 11132, pp. 287–296, 2019.
https://doi.org/10.1007/978-3-030-11018-5_26

and gated recurrent unit (GRU) [11]) are applied to model temporal dynamics along frames.

Although much progress has been made in generating video-level visual representations, few work lies on integrating multimodal data which can supplement with each other and further reduce the ambiguity of visual information. Therefore, developing deep and fine-grained multimodal fusion techniques could be a key ingredient towards practical video classification systems. In this paper, we take the first step by introducing multi-modal bilinear factorized pooling into video classification, which has been extensively adopted in visual question answering [12–14]. We select three popular video-level representations, i.e, Average pooling, NetVLAD [15] and DBoF [9], to validate its effectiveness. Experimental results indicate that video classification can achieve a significant performance boost by leveraging the new pooling mechanism over video and audio features. In summary, our contributions are twofold:

- We first introduce multi-modal factorized bilinear pooling to integrate visual information and audio in large-scale video classification.
- We experimentally demonstrate that multi-modal factorized pooling significantly outperforms simple fusion methods over several video-level features.

2 Related Work

2.1 Video Classification

Large-scale datasets [16,17] play a crucial role for deep neural network learning. In terms of video classification, Google recently releases the updated Youtube-8M dataset [9] with 8 millions videos totally. For each video, only visual and audio representations of multiple frames are made public. The approaches for video classification roughly follow two main branches. On the one hand, several architectures are introduced to extract powerful frame or snippet representations similar to image classification. Simonyan and Zisserman et al. first introduces deep convolutional neural networks to video action classification by performing frame-level classification [4]. In order to include more temporal information, 3D convolutional neural network and several variants [18–20] are proposed to generate representations of short snippets. The final video predictions can be estimated by late fusion or early fusion. On the other hand, researchers also direct their eyes to how to model long-term temporal dynamics when frame-level or snippet-level representation available.

Commonly used methods to model long-term temporal dynamics are various variants of Bag of Visual Words (BoVW) including Vector of Locally Aggregated Descriptors (VLAD) [21], Fisher Vector (FV) [22] and so on. But these handcrafted descriptors cannot be finetuned for the target task. Therefore, an end-to-end trainable NetVLAD [15] was proposed where a novel VLAD layer was plugged into a backbone convolutional neural network. Girdhar et al. proposed ActionVLAD that performs spatio-temporal learnable aggregation for video action classification. On the other hand, temporal models such as LSTM

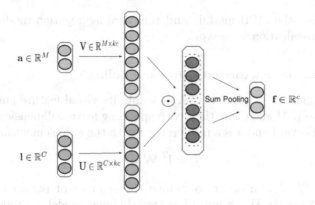

Fig. 1. The architecture of multi-modal factorized bilinear pooling.

and GRU, are also widely used to aggregate frame-level features into a single representation due to its capability of capturing the temporal structures of videos.

2.2   Multimodal Learning

A simple attempt to integrate multimodal data is performing average or concatenation before input to final predictions. However, more fine-grained multimodal fusion models like bilinear pooling operations have been extensively explored and validated in visual and language multimodal learning. Lots of work has focused on addressing the huge number of model parameters and high computation cost in bilinear pooling. Multi-modal compact bilinear (MCB) [12] was proposed to employ tensor sketch algorithm to reduce the computation cost and the amount of parameters. Later, to overcome the high memory usage in MCB, multi-modal low-rank bilinear pooling (MLB) [13] adopted Hadamard product to combine cross-modal feature vectors. Furthermore, multimodal tucker fusion (Mutan) [23] and multi-modal bilinear factorized bilinear pooling (MFB) [14] were proposed to address rather huge dimensionality and boost training.

In the paper, inspired by the success of MFB in visual and language fusion, we apply MFB [14] into the video classification task by combining available visual and audio representations. The most related work to us is probably [24] which tried multi-modal compact bilinear pooling approach [12] in large-video video classification but failed to fit training data.

3   Multi-modal Bilinear Fusion

We apply multi-modal factorized bilinear pooling over video-level visual and audio features. However in practice, only frame-level or snippet-level representations are available. Therefore as mentioned above, three methods are exploited to aggregate frame-level features into a single video feature. In this section, we firstly review the MFB module and temporal aggregation models and then present our classification framework.

3.1 Multi-modal Factorized Bilinear Pooling

For any video, let $l \in \mathbb{R}^C$ and $\mathbf{a} \in \mathbb{R}^M$ denote its visual feature and audio feature, respectively. M and C are their corresponding feature dimensions. Then the output of MFB over l and $\mathbf{a}$ is a new vector $\mathbf{f}$ with the i-th element formulated as

$$f_i = l^T \mathbf{W}_i \mathbf{a}, \tag{1}$$

where $\mathbf{W}_i \in \mathbb{R}^{C \times M}$. In order to reduce the number of parameters and the rank of weight matrix $\mathbf{W}_i$, a novel low-rank bilinear model is proposed in [25]. Specifically, $\mathbf{W}_i$ is decomposed as the multiplication of two low-rank matrices $\mathbf{U}_i$ and $\mathbf{V}_i$, where $\mathbf{U}_i \in \mathbb{R}^{C \times k}$ and $\mathbf{V}_i \in \mathbb{R}^{M \times k}$. k is a predefined constant to control rank. Therefore,

$$\mathbf{f}_i = l^T \mathbf{W}_i \mathbf{a} = l^T \mathbf{U}_i \mathbf{V}_i^T \mathbf{a} = \mathbb{1}^T (\mathbf{U}_i^T l) \odot (\mathbf{V}_i^T \mathbf{a}), \tag{2}$$

where $\mathbb{1} \in \mathbb{R}^k$ is an all-one vector and $\odot$ denotes Hadamard product. It is worthy noting that $\mathbb{1}$ is essentially a sum pooling operator as shown in Fig. 1. We follow the same normalization mechanism as in [25] except that the power normalization layer is replaced with a ReLU layer in our MFB module implementation.

3.2 Temporal Aggregation Model

In order to validate the general effectiveness of MFB in video classification, we experiment with video-level visual and audio features of three kinds obtained by average pooling, DBoF and NetVLAD over respective frame-level features. Let $\mathbf{L} \in \mathbb{R}^{N \times C}$ and $\mathbf{A} \in \mathbb{R}^{N \times M}$ denote frame-level visual and audio features for a given video with N frames, respectively. In our experiment, $C = 1024$ and $M = 128$. $\mathbf{L}$ and $\mathbf{A}$ are processed separately for each pooling mechanism.

Average Pooling (Avgpooling): The average pooling layer is simply averaging features across N frames, that is,

$$1 = \frac{1}{N} \sum_{i=1}^{n} \mathbf{L}_i, \mathbf{a} = \frac{1}{N} \sum_{i=1}^{n} \mathbf{A}_i. \tag{3}$$

DBoF: Deep Bag-of-Frames pooling extends the popular bag-of-words representations for video classification [26,27] and is firstly proposed in [9]. Specifically, the feature of each frame is first fed into a fully connected layer(fc) to increase dimension, Max pooling is then used to aggregate these high-dimensional frame-level features into a fixed-length representation. Following [9], a rectified linear unit (RELU) and batch normalization layer (BN) is used to increase non-linearity and keep training stable.

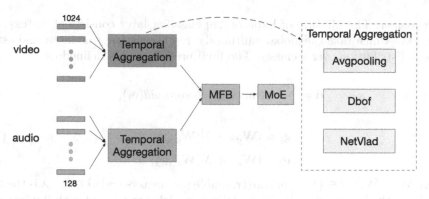

Fig. 2. The overall architecture of our MFB augmented video classification system.

NetVLAD: The NetVLAD [6,15] employed the VLAD encoding [21] in deep convolutional neural networks. The whole architecture can be trained in an end-to-end way. Compared to VLAD encoding, the parameters of clusters are learned by backpropagation instead of k-means clustering. Assuming K clusters are used during training, NetVLAD assigns any descriptor $\mathbf{h}_i$ in $\mathbf{L}$ or $\mathbf{A}$ to the cluster k by a soft assignment weight

$$\alpha_k(\mathbf{h}_i) = \frac{\mathbf{w}_k^T \mathbf{h}_i + b_k}{\sum_{k'=1}^{K} e^{\mathbf{w}_{k'}^T \mathbf{h}_i + b_{k'}}}, \tag{4}$$

where $\mathbf{w}_{k'}$ and $\mathbf{b}_{k'}$ are trainable cluster weights. Compared to the hard assignment, $\alpha_k(\cdot)$ measures the distance between descriptors with the cluster k and thus maintains more information. With all assignments for descriptors, the final NetVLAD representation is a weighted sum of residuals relative to each cluster. For the cluster k:

$$VLAD[k] = \sum_{i=1}^{N} \alpha_k(\mathbf{h}_i)(\mathbf{h}_i - \mathbf{c}_k), \tag{5}$$

where $\mathbf{c}_k$ corresponds to the learnable center of the k-th cluster.

3.3 Video-Level Multi-modal Fusion

In this section we will illustrate that MFB module can be a plug-and-play layer to fuse aggregated visual and audio features. Figure 2 shows the overall video-level fusion architecture. It mainly contains three parts. Firstly, the pre-extracted visual features $\mathbf{L}$ and audio features $\mathbf{A}$ are fed into two temporal aggregation modules separately. Each module outputs a single compact video-level representation and can be any one of the mentioned three aggregating mechanisms shown in the right side of figure. Next, MFB module fuse aggregated visual and audio features into a fixed-length representation. Finally, the classification module takes the resulting compact representation as input and outputs confidence scores of each semantic label. Following [9], we adopt Mixture-of-Experts [28] as our classifier. The Mixture of Experts [28] classifier layer consists of m "expert networks" which take the global multimodal representation f as input and estimate a distribution over c classes. The final prediction $\mathbf{d}$ is defined as

$$\mathbf{d} = \sum_{i=1}^{m} \text{softmax}(\mathbf{g}_i) \odot sigmoid(\mathbf{e}_i), \tag{6}$$

$$\mathbf{g}_i = \mathbf{fW}_{g,i} + \lambda ||\mathbf{W}_{g,i}||_2, \tag{7}$$

$$\mathbf{e}_i = \mathbf{fW}_{e,i} + \lambda ||\mathbf{W}_{e,i}||_2, \tag{8}$$

where $\mathbf{W}_{g,i}, \mathbf{W}_{e,i}, i \in \{1, ..., m\}$ are trainable parameters and $O \in \mathbb{R}^c$. λ is the L2 penalty with the default value 1e-6. All our models are trained with 2-mixtures MoE.

4   Experiments

4.1   Implementation Details

We implement our model based on Google starter code[1]. Each training is performed on a single V100 (16 Gb) GPU. All our models are trained using Adam optimizer [29] with an initial learning rate set to 0.0002. The mini-batch size is set to 128. We found that cross entropy classification loss works well for maximizing the Global Average Precision (GAP). All model are trained with 250 000 steps. In order to observe timely model prediction, we evaluate the model on a subset of validate set every 10 000 training steps. For the cluster-based pooling, the cluster size K is set to 8 for NetVLAD and 2000 for DBoF. To have a fair comparison, 300 frames are sampled before aggregation. In addition, the dropout rate of MFB module is set to 0.1 in all our experiments.

4.2   Datasets and Evaluation Metrics

We conduct experiments on the recently updated Youtube-8M v2 dataset with improved machine-generated labels and higher-quality videos. It contains a total of 6.1 million videos, 3862 classes, 3 labels per video averagely. Visual and audio features are pre-extracted per frame. Visual features are obtained by Google Inception convolutional neural network pretrained on ImageNet [16], followed by PCA-compression to generate a vector with 1024 dimensions. The audio features are extracted from a VGG-inspired acoustic model described in [8]. In the official split, training, validation and test have equal 3844 tfrecord shards. In practice, we use 3844 training shards and 3000 validation shards for training. We randomly select 200 shards from the rest of 844 validation shards (around 243 337 videos) to evaluate our model every 10 000 training steps. Results are evaluated using the Global Average Precision (GAP) metric at top 20 as used in the Youtube-8M Kaggle competition.

---

[1] https://github.com/google/youtube-8m.

Table 1. Comparison study on Avgpooling feature

Model	GAP
Avgpooling + Audio Only	38.1
Avgpooling + Video Only	69.6
Avgpooling + Concatenation	74.2
Avgpooling + FC + Concatenation	81.8
Avgpooling + MFB	**83.3**

Table 2. Comparison study on NetVLAD feature

Model	GAP
NetVLAD + Audio Only	50.7
NetVLAD + Video Only	82.3
NetVLAD + Concatenation	85.0
NetVLAD + FC + Concatenation	84.6
NetVLAD + MFB	**85.5**

4.3 Results

In this section, we verify the effectiveness of MFB module by comparing its performance on the validation set with the simple concatenation fusion. We also conduct two comparative tests with single-modality input (only video or audio). To prove that the improvement of performance does not come from increasing parameters, we add another comparison with the same number of parameters as MFB. Specifically, the temporal aggregated video and audio representations are first projected using a fully connected layer respectively and then the projected video and audio vectors are concatenated to feed into the MoE classifier (For convenience, we call it FC Concatenation module later). The fully connected layers have the same parameter settings with those in MFB module. The superior GAP performance of MFB module on three temporal aggregation models is shown as follows (Table 3).

Table 3. Comparison study on DBoF feature

Model	GAP
DBoF + Audio Only	48.9
DBoF + Video Only	81.8
DBoF + Concatenation	84.0
DBoF + FC + Concatenation	84.1
DBoF + MFB	**85.9**

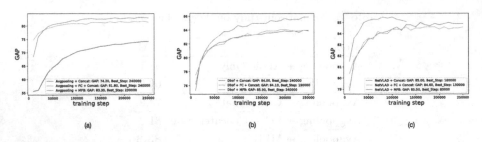

(a)   (b)   (c)

Fig. 3. (a) The GAP Performance of Avgpooling feature with different fusion modules (Concantenation, FC Concantenation, MFB). (b) The GAP Performance of DBoF feature. (c) The GAP Performance of NetVLAD feature.

The detailed results of MFB with Avgpooling features are shown in Table 1. Firstly, the GAP performance of two modal fusion is far superior to single modality input (Video Only or Audio Only). In the NetVLAD and DBof video features, we can draw the same conclusion. Secondly, we can observe a significant increase in performance with the MFB module, which achieves a 9.1% higher GAP compared with the concatenation fusion baseline. Even if the concatenation is augmented with the same number of parameters as MFB, there is still a 1.5% gap. The main reason is probably that the simple fusion can not leverage high-order information across modalities.

In terms of NetVLAD video features, the MFB module improves the GAP from 85.0% to 85.5% compared to the concatenation module as shown in Table 2. However surprisingly, adding fully connected layers performs worse, indicating that NetVLAD has been a quite good temporal model for single modal data aggregation. In some sense, increasing parameters will lead to overfitting. Therefore, it also proves that MFB contributes to the performance boost. For DBoF, the results are consistent with Avgpooling and NetVLAD, MFB module achieves the best GAP of 85.9%, around 1.8% higher than another two methods. We conclude that MFB encourages abundant cross-modal interactions and thus reduce the ambiguity of each modal data.

In order to give an intuitive observation on the advantage of MFB over simple fusion baselines, we illustrate the training processes of three fusion modules in Fig. 3, which shows the GAP performance on validation dataset as the training iteration increases. It is worthy noting that the experiment with the MFB module and NetVLAD features is early stopped at around 13 000 steps due to overfitting. Obviously, MFB module can not only increase the capability of video and audio fusion but also speed-up training.

5   Conclusions

In this paper, we first apply the multimodal factorized bilinear pooling into large-scale video classification task. To validate its effectiveness and robustness, we experiment on three kinds of video-level features obtained by Avgpooling,

NetVLAD and DBoF. We conduct experiments on large-scale video classification benchmark Youtube-8M. Experimental results demonstrate that the carefully designed multimodal factorized bilinear pooling can achieve significantly better results than the popular fusion concatenation operator. Our future work mainly lies on directly combining multimodal factorized bilinear pooling with multimodal frame-level data.

References

1. Krizhevsky, A., Sutskever, I., Hinton, G.E.: Imagenet classification with deep convolutional neural networks. In: International Conference on Neural Information Processing Systems, pp. 1097–1105 (2012)
2. He, K., Zhang, X., Ren, S., Sun, J.: Deep residual learning for image recognition. In: IEEE Conference on Computer Vision and Pattern Recognition, pp. 770–778 (2016)
3. Szegedy, C., Vanhoucke, V., Ioffe, S., Shlens, J., Wojna, Z.: Rethinking the inception architecture for computer vision. In: IEEE Conference on Computer Vision and Pattern Recognition, pp. 2818–2826 (2016)
4. Simonyan, K., Zisserman, A.: Two-stream convolutional networks for action recognition in videos. In: Advances in Neural Information Processing Systems, pp. 568–576 (2014)
5. Wang, L., et al.: Temporal segment networks: towards good practices for deep action recognition. In: Leibe, B., Matas, J., Sebe, N., Welling, M. (eds.) ECCV 2016, Part VIII. LNCS, vol. 9912, pp. 20–36. Springer, Cham (2016). https://doi.org/10.1007/978-3-319-46484-8_2
6. Girdhar, R., Ramanan, D., Gupta, A., Sivic, J., Russell, B.: ActionVLAD: Learning spatio-temporal aggregation for action classification. In: CVPR, pp. 3165–3174 (2017)
7. Hinton, G., et al.: Deep neural networks for acoustic modeling in speech recognition: the shared views of four research groups. IEEE Signal Process. Mag. 29(6), 82–97 (2012)
8. Hershey, S., et al.: CNN architectures for large-scale audio classification. In: International Conference on Acoustics, Speech and Signal Processing (ICASSP), pp. 131–135 (2017)
9. Abu-El-Haija, S., et al.: Youtube-8m: A Large-scale Video Classification Benchmark (2016)
10. Hochreiter, S., Schmidhuber, J.: Long short-term memory. Neural Comput. 9(8), 1735–1780 (1997)
11. Cho, K., Van Merriënboer, B., Bahdanau, D., Bengio, Y.: On the properties of neural machine translation: Encoder-decoder approaches. arXiv preprint arXiv:1409.1259 (2014)
12. Gao, Y., Beijbom, O., Zhang, N., Darrell, T.: Compact bilinear pooling. In: Proceedings of the IEEE Conference on Computer Vision and Pattern Recognition, pp. 317–326 (2015)
13. Kim, J.H., On, K.W., Lim, W., Kim, J., Ha, J.W., Zhang, B.T.: Hadamard product for low-rank bilinear pooling. arXiv preprint arXiv:1610.04325 (2016)
14. Yu, Z., Yu, J., Fan, J., Tao, D.: Multi-modal factorized bilinear pooling with co-attention learning for visual question answering. In: IEEE International Conference on Computer Vision (ICCV), pp. 1839–1848 (2017)

15. Arandjelovic, R., Gronat, P., Torii, A., Pajdla, T., Sivic, J.: NetVLAD: CNN architecture for weakly supervised place recognition. In: Proceedings of the IEEE Conference on Computer Vision and Pattern Recognition, pp. 5297–5307 (2016)

16. Deng, J., Dong, W., Socher, R., Li, L.J., Li, K., Fei-Fei, L.: Imagenet: a large-scale hierarchical image database. In: IEEE Conference on Computer Vision and Pattern Recognition, CVPR 2009, pp. 248–255. IEEE (2009)

17. Caba Heilbron, F., Escorcia, V., Ghanem, B., Carlos Niebles, J.: Activitynet: a large-scale video benchmark for human activity understanding. In: Proceedings of the IEEE Conference on Computer Vision and Pattern Recognition, pp. 961–970 (2015)

18. Tran, D., Wang, H., Torresani, L., Ray, J., LeCun, Y., Paluri, M.: A closer look at spatiotemporal convolutions for action recognition. In: Proceedings of the IEEE Conference on Computer Vision and Pattern Recognition, pp. 6450–6459 (2018)

19. Qiu, Z., Yao, T., Mei, T.: Learning spatio-temporal representation with pseudo-3d residual networks. In: ICCV, pp. 5534–5542 (2017)

20. Carreira, J., Zisserman, A.: Quo vadis, action recognition? A new model and the kinetics dataset. In: IEEE Conference on Computer Vision and Pattern Recognition (CVPR), pp. 4724–4733. IEEE (2017)

21. Jégou, H., Douze, M., Schmid, C., Pérez, P.: Aggregating local descriptors into a compact image representation. In: Computer Vision and Pattern Recognition, pp. 3304–3311 (2010)

22. Perronnin, F., Dance, C.: Fisher kernels on visual vocabularies for image categorization. In: IEEE Conference on Computer Vision and Pattern Recognition, pp. 1–8 (2007)

23. Ben-Younes, H., Cadene, R., Cord, M., Thome, N.: Mutan: multimodal tucker fusion for visual question answering. In: Proceedings of the IEEE International Conference on Computer Vision, vol. 3 (2017)

24. Miech, A., Laptev, I., Sivic, J.: Learnable Pooling with Context Gating for Video Classification, arXiv preprint arXiv:1706.06905 (2017)

25. Pirsiavash, H., Ramanan, D., Fowlkes, C.: Bilinear classifiers for visual recognition. In: International Conference on Neural Information Processing Systems, pp. 1482–1490 (2009)

26. Ng, Y.H., Hausknecht, M., Vijayanarasimhan, S., Vinyals, O., Monga, R., Toderici, G.: Beyond short snippets. Deep Netw. Video Classif. 16(4), 4694–4702 (2015)

27. Wang, H., Ullah, M.M., Kläser, A., Laptev, I., Schmid, C.: Evaluation of local spatio-temporal features for action recognition. In: Proceedings of the British Machine Vision Conference, BMVC 2009, London, UK, 7–10 September 2009 (2009)

28. Jordan, M.I., Jacobs, R.A.: Hierarchical Mixtures of Experts and the EM Algorithm. Springer, London (1994). https://doi.org/10.1007/978-1-4471-2097-1_113

29. Kingma, D.P., Ba, J.: Adam: a method for stochastic optimization. arXiv preprint arXiv:1412.6980 (2014)

Building A Size Constrained Predictive Models for Video Classification

Miha Skalic[1(✉)] and David Austin[2]

[1] University Pompeu Fabra, Barcelona, Spain
miha.skalic@upf.edu
[2] Intel Corporation, Chandler, AZ, USA

Abstract. Herein we present the solution to the 2nd YouTube-8M video understanding challenge which placed 1st. Competition participants were tasked with building a size constrained video labeling model with a model size of less than 1 GB. Our final solution consists of several submodels belonging to Fisher vectors, NetVlad, Deep Bag of Frames and Recurrent neural networks model families. To make the classifier efficient under size constraints we introduced model distillation, partial weights quantization and training with exponential moving average.

Keywords: Deep learning · Multi-label classification
Video processing

1 Introduction

Accelerated by the increase of internet bandwidth, storage space and usage of mobile devices, generation and consumption of video data is on the rise. Paired with recent advances in deep learning [1], specifically image [2] and audio [3] processing the combination opens up new opportunities for better understanding of video content which can then be leveraged for online advertising, video retrieval, video surveillance, etc.

However, usage of deep learning for video processing can be computationally expensive if the model learning starts from raw video and audio [4]. To tackle these limitations YouTube-8M Dataset [5] was generated. In the dataset, samples are represented as a sequence of vectors where each vector, is an embedded representation of a frame and an audio snippet.

Similarly, best performing classifiers are usually computationally expensive meta-predictors that combine several end-to-end classifiers. Meta-predictors or also called ensembles were the best performing models in the first YouTube-8M Video Understanding Challenge[1] [6–10]. Since the ensembles are computationally expensive, in this second iteration of YouTube-8M challenge[2] the participants were asked to build a single Tensorflow [11] model of size less than 1 GB.

M. Skalic and D. Austin—Authors contributed equally to this work.
[1] https://www.kaggle.com/c/youtube8m
[2] https://www.kaggle.com/c/youtube8m-2018

© Springer Nature Switzerland AG 2019
L. Leal-Taixé and S. Roth (Eds.): ECCV 2018 Workshops, LNCS 11132, pp. 297–305, 2019.
https://doi.org/10.1007/978-3-030-11018-5_27

1.1 Data

This work is based on the second iteration of YouTube-8M Dataset [5]. Over 6 million samples were split into 3 partitions: training, validation and test set, following approximately 70%, 20%, 10% split. The videos are labeled with 3862 unique tags with an average of 3 tags per video. The dataset does not provide raw videos, instead each frame representation consists of 1024 image and 128 audio features. The image features are extracted from the last ReLU activated layer prior to classification later of the Inception-v3 network [12]. The extracted features are reduced in size using PCA dimensionality reduction and finally quantized for reduced storage cost. Frames are sampled every second and up to 360 frames are included for each video.

1.2 Evaluation

Model predictions were evaluated based on Global Average precision (GAP) score:

$$GAP = \sum_{i=1}^{N} p(i)\Delta r(i), \tag{1}$$

where N is the number of final predictions, $p(i)$ is the precision, and $r(i)$ is the recall. In the evaluation $N = 20 \times (number\ of\ videos)$ was used.

2 Related Work

2.1 Model Architectures

As the dataset is given as a sequence of vectors corresponding to frames, the main goal of a successful model is to efficiently aggregate the frames. To this end one can use recurrent neural networks, such as long short-term memory (LSTM) [13] or gated recurrent unit (GRU) [14]. Recurrent neural networks can capture the video in temporal fashion, however previous work [15,16] indicates that methods that capture distribution of features and not necessarily temporal ordering can have on a par performance. This group of models includes bag-of-visual-words [15,17], Vector of Locally aggregated Descriptors (VLAD) [18] or Fisher Vector (FV) [19] encoding.

One shortcoming of VLAD and FV methods is that they are not differentiable and thus cannot be trained with backpropagation as part of neural networks. NetVLAD [20] has been proposed as a alternative to VLAD that uses differentiable soft assignments of descriptors to clusters. Similarly, Miech et al. [6]. extended this idea to FV resulting in an approach named FVnet.

This work also includes Deep Bag of Frames (DBoF) network variants originally proposed in [5] and inspired by the success of various classic bag of words representations for video classification.

2.2 Previous Solutions

As this works is based on second iteration of YouTube-8M dataset and challenge we drew inspirations from the first challenge. The first year winner [6] in addition to using NetVLAD and FVnet introduced context gating that allows for capturing of dependencies between features as well as capturing prior structure of the output space. The second placed solution [7] proposed a solution they called chaining to capture label interactions, used boosting and more importantly for this work introduced the concept of model distillation [21]. Other competitors [8,9] used various, but mostly recurrent neural network based, aggregation techniques. Our solution also includes in model weight averaging through exponential moving average [22] similar as has been done in [10].

3   Methods for Improved Performance

3.1   Model Distillation

Model distillation [21] is a method for model compression. Initially a bigger teacher network or multiple networks are trained and then a smaller student network is trained to replicate labels predicted by teacher networks(s). Typically, student networks perform better if they are trained to reproduce teacher values than if they were trained on labels directly. Here we applied so called soft-label distillation, similar to [7], where we optimize for a combination of ground truth and predicted labels, minimizing the combination sum of two binary cross entropies:

$$\mathcal{L}\left(\boldsymbol{y}, \hat{\boldsymbol{y}}, \hat{\boldsymbol{y}}_t\right) = \lambda \frac{1}{l} \sum_{i=1}^{l} -y_i \log\left(\hat{y}_i\right) + \left(1 - y_i\right) \log\left(1 - \hat{y}_i\right)$$

$$+ \left(1 - \lambda\right) \frac{1}{l} \sum_{i=1}^{l} -\hat{\boldsymbol{y}}_{t,i} \log\left(\hat{y}_i\right) + \left(1 - y_{t,i}\right) \log\left(1 - \hat{y}_i\right), \tag{2}$$

where $\boldsymbol{y}$, $\hat{\boldsymbol{y}}_t$ and $\hat{\boldsymbol{y}}$ are vectors of ground truth labels, teacher network prediction and student network predictions, respectively. Factor λ determines how much weight is put on minimizing student predicted labels divergence from ground truth labels versus teacher predicted values. In our experiments we have set $\lambda = 0.5$. Lowering λ to 0.4 or raising to 0.6 did not improve performance.

3.2   Partial Weights Quantization

Previously it has been shown that generally bigger models with larger clusters and hidden layers perform better. For example NetVlad and Fisher vector solutions from Miech et al. [6] were one of the best performing. However, they were individually bigger than 1 GB, making them inadequate for the task at hand. On the other hand, model quantization [23] can significantly reduce the model size at the cost of reduced performance. To minimize drop of accuracy we used partial weights quantization, where only variables with more than 17,000 elements were quantized. In practice this means that fully-connected layer weights were quantized, while batch normalization factors were not.

We used 8 bits quantization for large variables and left default float32 values for variables with less than 17,000 elements. At inference time the 8 bit variables were cast back to float32 values based on stored centroid value. The 256 centroid values were assigned based on min-max uniform quantization.

4 Experiments

4.1 Training Details

Models were trained according to the structure in Fig. 1. The dataset used for training consisted of the prepared training set for the competition, plus all but 800 randomly selected tfrecord files from the validation set. The resulting dataset used was a training set of 4,769,202 training samples and 232,072 validation samples. We observed a very consistent offset of 0.002 GAP between local validation and the public leaderboard score from the test set which made our validation set large enough to avoid overfitting. Our implementation relied on the Tensorflow based starter code published by the competition sponsors for training, validation, and inference[3].

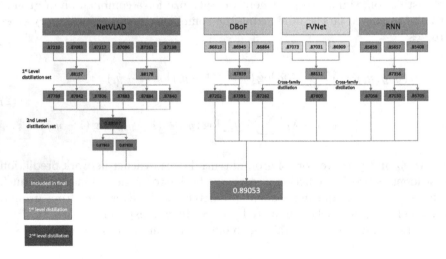

Fig. 1. Overview of our solution.

Each of the four families of models was first trained using hard targets as labels, and the difference between the models was the result of batch size, cluster, and number of hidden layers. Each model was trained using the Adam

---

[3] https://github.com/google/youtube-8m

algorithm with a batch size between 80–256 frames. We did not notice a difference in training time or accuracy between single and multi-GPU training so we limited training to single GPU. For the non-RNN models we sampled 300 frames with replacement during training. Each model combination was evaluated for its ensemble score relative to other model combinations in the same family in order to select the models which would proceed to a distillation round of training. The result of the ensemble selection was a sample of models that had high, mid, and low number of clusters and hidden layers. Batch size did not have a meaningful effect on model performance.

Training of each model consisted of a two step process: first training by the method described thus far, and then secondly by performing an exponential decay average of the weights stored in checkpoint files. Averaging of weights was performed by decreasing the learning rate of a model by a factor of five, and then training the model while storing a shadow copy of the weights that was used for moving averaging.

4.2   Results

The results of averaging weights are summarized in Table 1. For DBoF and RNN architectures the gains from averaging were significant and included for each model, but for bigger models: FVNet and NetVLAD, the gains were either negative or negligible and therefore not used.

Table 1. Weights averaging results

Model family	GAP change post weight averaging
RNN	0.00339
FVNet	−0.00186
DBoF	0.00216
NetVLAD	0.00072

After training was performed we performed partial weights quantization as detailed in Sect. 3.2 in order to reduce model size without compromising accuracy. Table 2 shows the impact of the quantization scheme on a FVNet based architecture during validation inference of 232,073 samples. For a negligible impact on overall GAP score we were able to reduce model size by a factor of 0.75 while incurring a 6.5% inference time penalty. The reason for the longer inference time with the quantized model is due to the implementation of casting quantized variables back to float32 during inference.

Once the initial round of training for each model family was complete, the best combination of three models for a given family were selected to ensemble by equal weighting and the predictions of those models were used to generate soft targets for a distillation dataset. Our implementation resulted in a new training

Table 2. Quantization performance for post distillation FVNet model.

GAP	time (s)	Model size (MB)
0.87236	476.96	467.5
0.87237	507.79	117

Table 3. Distillation performance gain

Model	Post Distillation	No Distillation	Average Gain	Family Avg Gain
RNN1	0.87058	0.85859	0.01199	0.01290
RNN2	0.8703	0.85657	0.01373	
RNN3	0.86705	0.85408	0.01297	
FVNet1	0.87803	0.87031	0.00772	0.00772
DBoF1	0.87202	0.86819	0.00383	0.00409
DBoF2	0.87391	0.86945	0.00446	
DboF3	0.87262	0.86864	0.00398	
NetVLAD1	0.87789	0.8721	0.00579	0.00675
NetVLAD2	0.87842	0.87083	0.00759	
NetVLAD3	0.87806	0.87237	0.00569	
NetVLAD4	0.87833	0.87096	0.00737	
NetVLAD5	0.87884	0.87163	0.00721	
NetVLAD6	0.8784	0.87156	0.00684	

dataset for each family containing the new combination of hard and soft targets as described in Sect. 3.1.

After the distillation dataset was created for each family, we retrained the same model architectures as in the first level of training (pre-distillation). The gains as a result of distillation are summarized in Table 3. The net gain for a given architecture family ranged from 0.00409 for DBoF up to 0.01290 for RNN's. The net gain for a specific given architecture within a given family was consistent and ranged between 0.001–0.002.

Because overall GAP score post distillation was highest for the NetVLAD architecture, we chose to perform a second level distillation which was accomplished by ensembling with equal weight the six models from the first level of NetVLAD distillation, and then performing another round of distillation using the same procedure as in the first round.

Results from the second round of distillation were statistically matched to the first round of distillation results, indicating that the ability of each model to learn from it's teacher had been saturated. However we observed that the diversity of the second level distillation models were increased relative to the other models in the final overall ensemble and for this reason we chose to keep the second level distillation results. The smallest NetVLAD architectures that could retain the GAP score from the first level distillation were chosen.

Thirteen out of fifteen models trained using distillation were performed by using a distillation dataset created from within the same family of architecture. For example, DboF's distillation models were created as a result of combining models from three DBoF teacher models. For 2 of our 15 models, we trained a model using a distillation set trained from another family. Our rationale for training most models within the same architectural family is that it would be more likely for the student models to learn from the same architectural teachers that generated them. The two models that were trained from another family had nearly identical gains in GAP score to models trained from within the same family. We chose to keep these two models in the final ensemble for purely empirical reasons as measured by the overall ensemble scores.

For all models we made sure that all frames were sampled during inferencing. This resulted in an average GAP improvement of 0.001–0.0014 GAP for most models vs using a random subset for sampling.

4.3   Ensembling

In order to achieve the best overall ensemble, we used our validation hold out set to try various combinations of weighting factors between the models. We used random search to test weighting factors, and noticed a range of 0.00050 in GAP score that could be achieved between the best combination found by random search versus taking a flat or weighted average of models.

Final model sizes and weighted contributions of each model are reported in Table 4.

Table 4. Final ensemble matrix

Model family	Model size (MB)	% of overall model size	Weight fraction in final ensemble
RNN1	54	5.13%	0.0063
RNN2	19	1.81%	0.0442
RNN3	19	1.81%	0.1244
FVNet1	369	35.08%	0.202
DBoF1	59	5.61%	0.0956
DBoF2	37	3.52%	0.1088
DBoF3	33	3.14%	0.0951
NetVLAD1	242	23.00%	0.1685
NetVLAD2	220	20.91%	0.1551

5   Conclusions

We have addressed the problem of large-scale video tagging under model size constrains. Models from four different families were used and for all them we have shown that they benefit from distillation in addition to classical ensembling and in model weights averaging. Additionally it was demonstrated that partial weight quantization is an efficient method to reduce model size down to almost a quarter the original size without significant drop in performance. Code used in this challenge, as well as full models architectures and learning parameters, are available at http://github.com/miha-skalic/youtube8mchallange, released under Apache License 2.0.

References

1. LeCun, Y.A., Bengio, Y., Hinton, G.E.: Deep learning. Nature **521**, 436–444 (2015)
2. Krizhevsky, A., Sutskever, I., Hinton, G.E.: ImageNet classification with deep convolutional neural networks. In: Advances in Neural Information Processing Systems (2012)
3. Graves, A., Mohamed, A., Hinton, G.: Speech recognition with deep recurrent neural networks. In: Icassp, pp. 6645–6649 (2013)
4. Ng, J.Y.H., Hausknecht, M., Vijayanarasimhan, S., Vinyals, O., Monga, R., Toderici, G.: Beyond short snippets: deep networks for video classification. In: Proceedings of the IEEE Computer Society Conference on Computer Vision and Pattern Recognition (2015)
5. Abu-El-Haija, S., et al.: YouTube-8m: A large-scale video classification benchmark. CoRR abs/1609.08675 (2016)
6. Miech, A., Laptev, I., Sivic, J.: Learnable pooling with context gating for video classification. CoRR abs/1706.06905 (2017)
7. Wang, H., Zhang, T., Wu, J.: The monkeytyping solution to the Youtube-8m video understanding challenge. CoRR abs/1706.05150 (2017)
8. Li, F., et al.: Temporal modeling approaches for large-scale youtube-8m video understanding. CoRR abs/1707.04555 (2017)
9. Chen, S., Wang, X., Tang, Y., Chen, X., Wu, Z., Jiang, Y.: Aggregating frame-level features for large-scale video classification. CoRR abs/1707.00803 (2017)
10. Skalic, M., Pekalski, M., Pan, X.E.: Deep learning methods for efficient large scale video labeling. CoRR abs/1706.04572 (2017)
11. Abadi, M., et al.: TensorFlow: Large-scale machine learning on heterogeneous systems (2015). Software available from http://tensorflow.org
12. Szegedy, C., Vanhoucke, V., Ioffe, S., Shlens, J., Wojna, Z.: Rethinking the inception architecture for computer vision. In: The IEEE Conference on Computer Vision and Pattern Recognition (CVPR), June 2016
13. Hochreiter, S., Schmidhuber, J.: Long short-term memory. Neural Comput. **9**(8), 1735–1780 (1997)
14. Cho, K., van Merrienboer, B., Gülçehre, Ç., Bougares, F., Schwenk, H., Bengio, Y.: Learning phrase representations using RNN encoder-decoder for statistical machine translation. CoRR abs/1406.1078 (2014)
15. Laptev, I., Marszałek, M., Schmid, C., Rozenfeld, B.: Learning realistic human actions from movies. In: 26th IEEE Conference on Computer Vision and Pattern Recognition, CVPR (2008)
16. Wang, H., Schmid, C.: Action recognition with improved trajectories. In: Proceedings of the IEEE International Conference on Computer Vision, pp. 3551–3558 (2013)

17. Wang, H., Ullah, M.M., Klaser, A., Laptev, I., Schmid, C.: Evaluation of local spatio-temporal features for action recognition. In: BMVC 2009 – British Machine Vision Conference (2009)
18. Jégou, H., Douze, M., Schmid, C., Pérez, P.: Aggregating local descriptors into a compact image representation. In: Proceedings of the IEEE Computer Society Conference on Computer Vision and Pattern Recognition, pp. 3304–3311 (2010)
19. Perronnin, F., Dance, C.: Fisher kernels on visual vocabularies for image categorization. In: Proceedings of the IEEE Computer Society Conference on Computer Vision and Pattern Recognition, pp. 1–8 (2007)
20. Arandjelovic, R., Gronat, P., Torii, A., Pajdla, T., Sivic, J.: NetVLAD: CNN architecture for weakly supervised place recognition. In: IEEE Transactions on Pattern Analysis and Machine Intelligence, pp. 5297–5307 (2018)
21. Hinton, G., Vinyals, O., Dean, J.: Distilling the knowledge in a neural network. In: NIPS Deep Learning and Representation Learning Workshop (2015)
22. Ruppert, D.: Efficient estimations from a slowly convergent robbins-monro process. Technical report, Cornell University Operations Research and Industrial Engineering (2018)
23. Han, S., Mao, H., Dally, W.J.: Deep compression: compressing deep neural network with pruning, trained quantization and huffman coding. CoRR abs/1510.00149 (2015)

Temporal Attention Mechanism with Conditional Inference for Large-Scale Multi-label Video Classification

Eun-Sol Kim[1]([⊠]), Kyoung-Woon On[2], Jongseok Kim[1], Yu-Jung Heo[2],
Seong-Ho Choi[2], Hyun-Dong Lee[2], and Byoung-Tak Zhang[2]

[1] Kakao Brain, Seongnam 13494, South Korea
{epsilon,ozmig}@kakaobrain.com
[2] Seoul National University, Seoul 08826, South Korea
{kwon,yjheo,shchoi,hdlee,btzhang}@bi.snu.ac.kr

Abstract. Here we show neural network based methods, which combine multimodal sequential inputs effectively and classify the inputs into multiple categories. Two key ideas are (1) to select informative frames among a sequence using attention mechanism and (2) to utilize correlation information between labels to solve multi-label classification problems. The attention mechanism is used in both modality (spatio) and sequential (temporal) dimensions to ignore noisy and meaningless frames. Furthermore, to tackle fundamental problems induced by independently predicting each label in conventional multi-label classification methods, the proposed method considers the dependencies among the labels by decomposing joint probability of labels into conditional terms. From the experimental results (5th in the Kaggle competition), we discuss how the suggested methods operate in the YouTube-8M Classification Task, what insights they have, and why they succeed or fail.

Keywords: Multimodal sequential learning · Attention
Multi-label classification · Video understanding

1 Introduction

We focus on finding neural network based methods capable of learning large-scale multimodal sequential data, which are videos collected from YouTube, and classifying the data into multiple categories. To tackle this challenging goal, we postulate three subproblems as follows: (1) combining multimodal inputs effectively, (2) modeling temporal inputs, and (3) using correlation information between labels to resolve multi-label classification problem. Specifically, only two modalities, e.g., image and audio, are considered as the multimodal inputs in this work.

In this work we make the following two contributions. First, we explore spatio-temporal aggregation of visual and auditory features by designing new gate modules. Compared to existing methods for learning spatio-temporal

© Springer Nature Switzerland AG 2019
L. Leal-Taixé and S. Roth (Eds.): ECCV 2018 Workshops, LNCS 11132, pp. 306–316, 2019.
https://doi.org/10.1007/978-3-030-11018-5_28

inputs, such as NetVLAD [2], GRU [6] and LSTM [10], the suggested method can find different importance weight between the temporally neighboring frames. Second, we use correlation information between labels to resolve multi-label classification problem. While the simple binary relevance (BR) method approaches this problem by treating multiple targets independently, the suggested method focuses on exploiting the underlying label structure or inherent relationships.

We evaluate our method on the YoutTube-8M dataset containing about 6.1 M videos and 3862 labels. The proposed method shows significant performance improvement over the baseline models, and finally our ensemble model is ranked 5th out of about 400 teams in the 2nd YouTube-8M Video Understanding Challenge [1].

The remainder of the paper is organized as follows. In the next section, we summarize previous research, including papers from the 1st YouTube-8M workshop related to multimodal, sequential learning and multi-label classification. Then, suggested methods and modules are shown in Sect. 3. In Sect., 4, YouTube-8M dataset is described and the experimental results are shown. In Sect. 5, we show the ensemble model submitted to the Kaggle competition. Finally, we conclude with a discussion about why the methods are successful or not.

2 Related Work

We summarize previous research related to this work in terms of the following topics: multimodal learning, temporal aggregation and large-scale multi-label classification.

2.1 Multimodal Learning

Multimodal learning has been widely used to define representations of multimodal inputs to project unimodal features together into a multimodal space. The simplest method is concatenation of individual unimodal features (Fig. 1(a)). As neural networks has become a popular method for learning unimodal features, it has been considered more popular to concatenate the unimodal features learned from each neural network (Fig. 1(b)). Instead of naive concatenation, each unimodal feature from neural networks projects into a joint representation space with additional networks (Fig. 1(c)).

For the Kaggle competition, preprocessed visual and audio features for each frame are distributed to participants. Visual features are extracted using Inception-V3 image annotation model [20] and audio features are extracted using a VGG-inspired acoustic model [9].

In the last YouTube-8M competition, almost all of the participants tried to concatenate these visual and audio feature vectors via either (1) early fusion or (2) late fusion. The early fusion method concatenates two feature vectors before being fed into a frame level model which deals with both modalities. On the

---

[1] https://www.kaggle.com/c/youtube8m-2018/leaderboard.

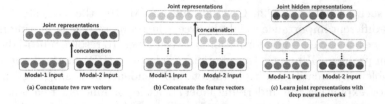

Fig. 1. Multimodal learning with joint representations

other hand, late fusion means that visual and audio features are concatenated after having been processed by two frame level models which deal with each modality. Na et al. [14] tried to learn multimodal joint representation using multimodal compact bilinear pooling [8]. However, they reported that their newly joint features performed significantly worse than simple feature concatenation.

2.2 Temporal Aggregation

In terms of neural network architectures, many problems with sequential inputs are resolved by using Recurrent Neural Networks (RNNs) and their variants as it naturally takes sequential inputs frame by frame. However, as RNN-based methods take frames in (incremental) order, the parameters of the methods are trained to capture patterns in transitions between successive frames, making it hard to find long-term temporal dependencies through overall frames. For this reason, their variants, such as Long Short-Term Memory (LSTM, [10]) and Gated Recurrent Units (GRU, [4,6]), have made the suggestion of ignoring noisy (unnecessary) frames and maintaining the semantic flow by turning switches on and off.

Recently, a number of researches shed new light on Bag-of-Visual-Words (BoVW) techniques [16,19] in order to construct a set of visual descriptors from image data, such as VLAD [3] and DBoF methods [1]. BoVW-based methods have been expanded to the temporal domain, that is, the visual descriptors are extracted from not only an image, but from a sequence of images [2]. After constructing a set of spatio-temporal visual descriptors, a representative vector of a sequence is constructed by applying pooling methods over the set (averaging operations over the descriptors).

2.3 Multi-label Classification

Multi-label classification is a supervised learning problem where each instance has two or more labels. It is more challenging than single-label classification since combinations of labels grow exponentially.

The most common approach to multi-label classification is Binary Relevance (BR), which decomposes the multi-label learning task into a number of independent binary learning tasks. This approach can reduce the search space from $O(2^n)$ as combinations of labels to $O(n)$ as the number of labels n. However, this decomposition makes BR models incapable of exploiting dependencies and correlations between labels.

Classifier Chain (CC) overcomes such disadvantages of basic BR models by passing label information between each BR classifier along a chain [17]. CC treats multi-label classification as a sequential prediction problem, which resembles following a single path in a binary tree in a greedy manner. Probabilistic Classifier Chains (PCC) is an extension of CC and probability theory. PCC estimates the entire joint distribution of the labels and constructs a perfect binary tree required to find the optimal path [7]. Nam et al. [15] applied Recurrent Neural Networks (RNNs) to model the sequential prediction problem. The key idea of the approach is to model the joint probability of positive labels, not the entire joint distribution.

3   The Model

In this section, several methods used for the YouTube-8M competition are introduced. Basically, we tried to find better representations of the multimodal inputs using attention mechanisms, which can capture the correlations between modalities. Furthermore, we suggest a new multi-label classification method that reflects our investigation of the statistics of the label set.

3.1   Multimodal Representation Learning with Attention

Here, we show three multimodal representation learning methods. Before feeding visual vectors $\mathbf{x}_v$ and audio vectors $\mathbf{x}_a$ into temporal aggregation methods, a new vector $\mathbf{x}_f$ is learned using the following methods.

1. Element-wise summation after a linear transformation

$$\mathbf{x}_{a_{exp}} = \mathbf{W}_{va}\mathbf{x}_a + \mathbf{b}_{va} \tag{1}$$
$$\mathbf{x}_f = \mathbf{x}_v + \mathbf{x}_{a_{exp}} \tag{2}$$

2. Temporal attention on $\mathbf{x}_a$ guided by $\mathbf{x}_v$

$$\mathbf{x}_f = \mathbf{x}_v + softmax\left(\mathbf{x}_v^\top \mathbf{W}_a^{att} \mathbf{X}_{a_{exp}}^{t-\frac{w}{2}:t+\frac{w}{2}}\right) \mathbf{X}_{a_{exp}}^{t-\frac{w}{2}:t+\frac{w}{2}} \tag{3}$$

3. Temporal attention on $\mathbf{x}_v$ guided by $\mathbf{x}_a$

$$\mathbf{x}_f = \mathbf{x}_{a_{exp}} + softmax\left(\mathbf{x}_{a_{exp}}^\top \mathbf{W}_v^{att} \mathbf{X}_v^{t-\frac{w}{2}:t+\frac{w}{2}}\right) \mathbf{X}_v^{t-\frac{w}{2}:t+\frac{w}{2}} \tag{4}$$

Method 1 is a simple element-wise summation. Since $\mathbf{x}_v$ and $\mathbf{x}_a$ have different feature vector sizes, a linear transformation is applied to $\mathbf{x}_a$ to match the size.

With method 2, temporal correlations between a visual vector $\mathbf{x}_v$ and neighboring w audio inputs $\mathbf{X}_a^{t-\frac{w}{2}:t+\frac{w}{2}}$ are trained by learning an attention matrix W_a^{att}. By using the temporal attention methods, the latter aggregation methods can focus on a subset of sequential inputs which are relevant to each other and ignore irrelevant and noisy parts of the input sequence. Furthermore, the temporal attention method, which gives different importance weights to the temporally neighboring audio inputs, summarizes the audio inputs based on the weights and assigns a new vector to the corresponding vector, can be interpreted as an aligning method. Although the distributed dataset is already aligned, the sequences of each modality may involve different semantic streams. Applying temporal attention to those sequences can be helpful in resolving the disentanglement in the semantic flows, as it could give a chance to be matched with the neighboring frames.

Similarly, temporal correlations between an audio vector and neighboring visual vectors are trained with method 3.

These three methods are summarized in Fig. 2.

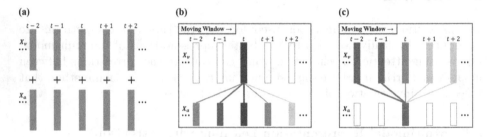

Fig. 2. (a): Element-wize summation after a linear transformation (b): Image guided attention mechanism (c): Audio guided attention mechanism

3.2   Conditional Inference Using Label Dependency for Multi-Label Classification

The objective of the multi-label classification is to maximize likelihood of conditional probability $p(\mathbf{y}|x)$ where $x \in \mathbf{X}$ and $\mathbf{y} \in \{y_1, y_2, \ldots, y_q\}$ with $y_i \in \{0, 1\}$:

$$\mathcal{L}(\theta; \mathbf{y}|x) = \prod_{x \in \mathbf{X}} p(y_1, y_2, ..., y_q | x; \theta) \tag{5}$$

As discussed in Sect. 2.3, The BR method simply hypothesizes that the probabilities of each labels are independent given x:

$$p(\mathbf{y}|x) = \prod_{i=1}^{q} p(y_i|x) \tag{6}$$

The BR method is simple and shows a reasonable performance, but it cannot reflect correlation between labels due to its independence assumption. To avoid losing information of dependencies between labels, the joint probability can be factorized and obtained in a chaining manner.

$$p(\mathbf{y}|x) = \prod_{i=1}^{q} p(y_i|x, y_{<i}) \tag{7}$$

Most of the chaining approaches model the chaining property via building q-classifier for each term of RHS in Eq. 7 [7,15,18]. More specifically, the function f_i is learned on an augmented input space $\mathbf{X} \times \{0, 1\}^{i-1}$ which is taking $y_{<i}$ as additional attributes to determine the probability of y_i. Then the $p(\mathbf{y}|x)$ can be obtained as follows:

$$p(\mathbf{y}|x) = \prod_{i=1}^{q} f_i(x, y_{<i}) \tag{8}$$

However, to estimate the above probability, 2^q-combinations of labels need to be searched or specific order of labels must be pre-defined. Instead, we learn a single function f to map from a given x and an additional label information l to y ($f : \mathbf{X} \times L \rightarrow \mathbf{y}$), where the l is a vector $\{0, 1\}^q$ and represents previously observed labels with 1 values.

In detail, at first, conditional probabilities over all labels $\mathbf{y}$ given x are predicted by function f, and then a label which is the most probable to 1 is chosen as a first observed label. Next, given the same x and previously predicted labels l, conditional probabilities are again predicted and the second observed label is chosen in a same manner. This procedure is iteratively performed and the number of iterative step is selected based on empirical performances. Figure 3(a) illustrates the mechanism with five labels and two iterative steps.

For function f, the neural network architecture is designed to capture the dependencies among x, observed y, and predicted y. It provides a richer representation with low-rank bilinear pooling [11] followed by context gate mechanism [13] which is shown in Fig. 3(b).

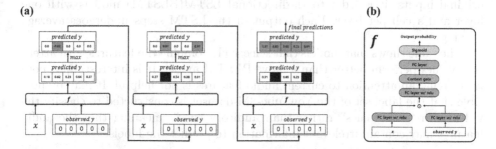

Fig. 3. (a): An illustration of the conditional inference procedure on 5-labels and 2-steps situation. (b): Core neural network architecture of conditional inference.

4   Experiments

4.1   Youtube-8M Dataset

The YouTube-8M dataset consists of 6.1 M video clips collected from YouTube. The average length of the clips is 230.2 s and the maximum/minimum lengths are 303, 1 s respectively (statistics of the 3.9 M training clips). From each clip, image sequences and audio signals are extracted. Visual features are extracted using Inception-V3 image annotation model [20] and audio features are extracted using a VGG-inspired acoustic model [9]. After preprocessing steps including PCA-ed and quantization, a 1024-dimensional image vector and a 128-dimensional audio vector are obtained for every second.

Each clip of the dataset is annotated with multiple labels. The average number of labels annotated for a clip is 3.0, and the maximum and the minimum are 23 and 1 respectively, out of 3862 possible labels. In the YouFurthermore, the number of examples per label is not uniformly distributed. As a specific example, 788,288 clips are annotated with GAME, while only 123 clips are annotated with Cylinder. More than half of the total labels (2086 of 3862 labels) contain less than 500 clips.

4.2   Training Details

Adam optimizer [12] with two parameters, i.e., a learning rate of 0.001 and a learning rate decay of 0.95, is utilized to train models. We also find it helpful to set the gradient clipping value to 5.0 for Bi-directional LSTM models and to 1.0 for NetVLAD models.

4.3   Experimental Results

Effects of Spatio-Temporal Attention. First of all, the effectiveness of the suggested attention methods in Sect. 3.1 is verified. The quantitative results are summarized in Table 1. After applying the temporal attention methods to the original inputs, it is fed into Bi-directional LSTM(BLSTM) models with one layer and a cell per layer. Each output of the LSTM steps undergoes average pooling.

The table shows that models that selectively combine the features with attention values perform better than a naive BLSTM model. It is interesting to note that giving an attention to current audio features is not helpful. It may be possible that the label set of the YouTube-8M dataset is constructed to classify the video with "visual cues" rather than "auditory cues", meaning that the audio features may contain irrelevant information to predict the labels.

Effects of Conditional Inference. To evaluate the effect of conditional inference mechanism for multi-label classification, comparative experiments are conducted with baseline models using video-level features. As shown in Table 2, the

Table 1. Validation Accuracy with Various Attention Methods with BLSTM

Attention method	Window size w	Accuracy (GAP)
None	None	0.858
Image Guided Attention	5	0.86071
Image Guided Attention	9	0.86078
Image Guided Attention	13	0.85920
Image Guided Attention	all	0.86129
Audio Guided Attention	5	0.85670

Table 2. Experimental results of conditional inference modules with video-level features

Attention method	Accuracy (GAP)
Logistic model	0.7942
Mixture of expert (# of expert: 2)	0.8282
Mixture of expert (# of expert: 3)	0.8296
Mixture of expert (# of expert: 4)	0.8305
Mixture of expert (# of expert: 6)	0.8324
Conditional Inference (# of steps: 1)	0.8385
Conditional Inference (# of steps: 2)	0.8398
Conditional Inference (# of steps: 3)	0.8407
Conditional Inference (# of steps: 4)	0.8410
Conditional Inference (# of steps: 5)	0.8403

proposed mechanism outperforms other variant baseline models. In addition, the GAP score increases as the number of steps increases, and it begins to decrease after the fourth step. It can be interpreted as the number of step hyper-parameter can be derived by average number of labels in a instance.

5 The Final Ensemble Model

Unfortunately, it was hard to find the optimal combination of the suggested methods described in Sect. 3. In this section, the final model that ranked 5th in the final leaderboard of the Kaggle competition is described, which may not be directly related to the methods in Sect. 3.

Based on the three criteria (Fig. 4), we designed basic modules. As basic modules for temporal aggregation, vanilla RNN, GRU, LSTM, BLSTM, hierarchical RNN [5] and NetVLAD are tested with various methods on multimodal learning and MLC methods suggested in Sect. 3. Various number of layers, hidden states, and well-known techniques such as dropout, zoneout and skip-connection

Criteria	Methods
Multimodal Inputs	Concatenate, Element-wise summation, Attention, Differential Features, Bilinear Pooling
Temporal Aggregation	LSTM, GRU, Bidirectional LSTM, Hierarchical RNN, NetVLAD, CBHG
Classification Modules	Logistic Regression, Mixture of Experts, Class Chaining, Conditional Inference
Additional Modules	Layer Normalization, Skip Connection, Dropout, Gradient Clipping

Fig. 4. Various methods with three criteria which are postulated to solve this competition and additional options for the methods.

are tested with the temporal aggregation models. Among more than 100 experimental results with the possible combinations of those techniques, six of the experiments were selected for the final ensemble model by using a beam search method with a validation dataset.

The final six models selected for the final ensemble model are as follows:

1. MC-BLSTM-MoE2
2. MA-BLSTM-MoE2
3. MC-BLSTM-CG-MoE2
4. MC-NetVLAD-diff-C64-MoE4
5. MS-NetVLAD-C64-MoE4
6. MC-NetVLAD-C128-MoE4

where *MC, MA, MS* represent the methods to construct multimodal representation. *MC* represents an early fusion with a concatenation, *MA* and *MS* represent method 3 and 2 in Sect. 3.1 respectively. For the attention methods, we set the window size to 5 based on the empirical performance. *CG* represents the context gating method [13], *C* stands for cluster size, and *MoE* is the number of experts.

diff means that the differential feature is concatenated. As the NetVLAD model could lose the temporal relationship between successive frames, the differences $\mathbf{x}_{diff}^{t}$ between the frames are concatenated to original inputs.

$$\mathbf{x}_{diff}^{t} = \left[\mathbf{x}^{t} : \frac{2 \times \mathbf{x}^{t} - \mathbf{x}^{t-1} - \mathbf{x}^{t+1}}{2}\right] \qquad (9)$$

The logits of the six models are combined with different weight values(ensemble weights), which are learned by a single-layer neural network, and the exact values are 0.21867326, 0.22206327, 0.13936463, 0.16840834, 0.14120385, and 0.11028661.

The final test accuracy of the ensemble model is 0.88527, which is ranked at 5th in the final leader board.

We should note that there was a strict constraint on the final model size with 1GB, so the models are searched with this constraints, and the sizes of the selected models are 162 M, 163 M, 168 M, 138 M, 136 M, and 200 M.

6   Conclusion

Even though the suggested methods in Sect. 3 could not be selected for the final ensemble model, we think that the newly suggested attention and MLC method might be helpful to improve the performance if we can find more suitable model architectures with more intensive exploring. From the competition point of view, we observe that the ensemble method dramatically improves the performance. Performances of NetVLAD models alone were not better than those of BLSTM models. But the ensemble of NetVLAD and BLSTM outperformed the ensemble of BLSTM models alone.

Acknowledgement. This work was partly supported by the Institute for Information & Communications Technology Promotion (R0126-16-1072-SW.StarLab, 2017-0-01772-VTT , 2018-0-00622-RMI) and Korea Evaluation Institute of Industrial Technology (10060086-RISF) grant funded by the Korea government (MSIP, DAPA).

References

1. Abu-El-Haija, S., Kothari, N., Lee, J., Natsev, P., Toderici, G., Varadarajan, B., Vijayanarasimhan, S.: Youtube-8m: a large-scale video classification benchmark. arXiv preprint arXiv:1609.08675 (2016)
2. Arandjelovic, R., Gronat, P., Torii, A., Pajdla, T., Sivic, J.: Netvlad: CNN architecture for weakly supervised place recognition. In: Proceedings of the IEEE Conference on Computer Vision and Pattern Recognition, pp. 5297–5307 (2016)
3. Arandjelovic, R., Zisserman, A.: All about VLAD. In: Proceedings of the IEEE conference on Computer Vision and Pattern Recognition, pp. 1578–1585 (2013)
4. Cho, K., et al.: Learning phrase representations using RNN encoder-decoder for statistical machine translation. arXiv preprint arXiv:1406.1078 (2014)
5. Chung, J., Ahn, S., Bengio, Y.: Hierarchical multiscale recurrent neural networks. arXiv preprint arXiv:1609.01704 (2016)
6. Chung, J., Gulcehre, C., Cho, K., Bengio, Y.: Empirical evaluation of gated recurrent neural networks on sequence modeling. arXiv preprint arXiv:1412.3555 (2014)
7. Dembczynski, K., Cheng, W., Hüllermeier, E.: Bayes optimal multilabel classification via probabilistic classifier chains. ICML. **10**, 279–286 (2010)
8. Fukui, A., Park, D.H., Yang, D., Rohrbach, A., Darrell, T., Rohrbach, M.: Multimodal compact bilinear pooling for visual question answering and visual grounding. arXiv preprint arXiv:1606.01847 (2016)
9. Hershey, S., et al.: CNN architectures for large-scale audio classification. In: International Conference on Acoustics, Speech and Signal Processing (ICASSP) (2017). https://arxiv.org/abs/1609.09430
10. Hochreiter, S., Schmidhuber, J.: Long short-term memory. Neural Comput. **9**(8), 1735–1780 (1997)
11. Kim, J.H., On, K.W., Lim, W., Kim, J., Ha, J.W., Zhang, B.T.: Hadamard product for low-rank bilinear pooling. arXiv preprint arXiv:1610.04325 (2016)
12. Kingma, D.P., Ba, J.: Adam: a method for stochastic optimization. arXiv preprint arXiv:1412.6980 (2014)
13. Miech, A., Laptev, I., Sivic, J.: Learnable pooling with context gating for video classification. arXiv preprint arXiv:1706.06905 (2017)

14. Na, S., Yu, Y., Lee, S., Kim, J., Kim, G.: Encoding video and label priors for multi-label video classification on youtube-8m dataset. arXiv preprint arXiv:1706.07960 (2017)
15. Nam, J., Mencía, E.L., Kim, H.J., Fürnkranz, J.: Maximizing subset accuracy with recurrent neural networks in multi-label classification. In: Advances in Neural Information Processing Systems, pp. 5413–5423 (2017)
16. Philbin, J., Chum, O., Isard, M., Sivic, J., Zisserman, A.: Object retrieval with large vocabularies and fast spatial matching. In: IEEE Conference on Computer Vision and Pattern Recognition, CVPR 2007, pp. 1–8. IEEE (2007)
17. Read, J., Pfahringer, B., Holmes, G., Frank, E.: Classifier chains for multi-label classification. In: Buntine, W., Grobelnik, M., Mladenić, D., Shawe-Taylor, J. (eds.) ECML PKDD 2009, Part II. LNCS (LNAI), vol. 5782, pp. 254–269. Springer, Heidelberg (2009). https://doi.org/10.1007/978-3-642-04174-7_17
18. Read, J., Pfahringer, B., Holmes, G., Frank, E.: Classifier chains for multi-label classification. Mach. Learn. **85**(3), 333 (2011)
19. Sivic, J., Zisserman, A.: Video Google: a text retrieval approach to object matching in videos. In: null, p. 1470. IEEE (2003)
20. Tensorflow: Tensorflow: image recognition. https://www.tensorflow.org/tutorials/images/image_recognition

Approach for Video Classification with Multi-label on YouTube-8M Dataset

Kwangsoo Shin$^{(\boxtimes)}$ ⓘ, Junhyeong Jeon ⓘ, Seungbin Lee ⓘ, Boyoung Lim, Minsoo Jeong, and Jongho Nang

Department of Computer Science and Engineering,
Sogang University, Seoul, South Korea
{ksshin,junhyeong.jeon,mercileesb,bylim,msjeong,jhnang}@sogang.ac.kr
http://mmlab.sogang.ac.kr

Abstract. Video traffic is increasing at a considerable rate due to the spread of personal media and advancements in media technology. Accordingly, there is a growing need for techniques to automatically classify moving images. This paper use NetVLAD and NetFV models and the Huber loss function for video classification problem and YouTube-8M dataset to verify the experiment. We tried various attempts according to the dataset and optimize hyperparameters, ultimately obtain a GAP score of 0.8668.

Keywords: Video classification · Large-scale video · Multi-label

1 Introduction

Video traffic from video sites such as YouTube has increased in recent years. The growth of personal media through technological development is particularly remarkable. With the development of smartphones, media is now brought to the consumer's hand, and individuals are no longer only consumers of multimedia but are now producers as well. This trend may be confirmed by internet traffic statistics and other global data. As a result, it is becoming increasingly difficult for consumers to identify desirable media. Accordingly, there is a growing need for techniques to recommend videos or automatically classify subjects. Much effort has been made to process video. Many recent advancements in artificial neural networks have been applied to video processing in an attempt to understand each frame of the video using a convolutional neural network (CNN) [7]. Other methods used include VLAD [6] for processing time series data, recurrent neural network (RNN) series and long short-term memory (LSTM) [4] or GRU [3] for processing time series data. The skipLSTM and skipGRU [2],

---

K. Shin and J. Jeon—Contributed equally.

Electronic supplementary material The online version of this chapter (https://doi.org/10.1007/978-3-030-11018-5_29) contains supplementary material, which is available to authorized users.

© Springer Nature Switzerland AG 2019
L. Leal-Taixé and S. Roth (Eds.): ECCV 2018 Workshops, LNCS 11132, pp. 317–324, 2019.
https://doi.org/10.1007/978-3-030-11018-5_29

which add a skip connection to the RNN network, have been proven effective ways to process time series data. The present paper uses NetVLAD and NetFV, which are known as effective methods for video processing, to find the optimal network by adjusting various hyperparameters used in the network. A single model was sought to solve the problem rather than an ensemble technique. In this process, YouTube-8M dataset was used, and a GAP rating of 0.8668 was obtained for the test set.

2   Methods and Materials

2.1   Dataset

The total number of video in YouTube-8M dataset is 6.1 million. The training set consists of 3.9 million videos. The test and validation sets are each 1.1 million. All video has an average of three labels, and each label is composed of 3,862 multi-labels. Every video is between 120 and 500 seconds in length. This paper use frame-level and audio features. The frame-level features are 1,024-dimensional vectors in which selects one frame per second in video and extracts through Inception V3 model. The audio features are extracted with 128-dimensional vectors drawn through a VGG-inspired acoustic model.

2.2   Models

This paper used NetVLAD [1] and NetFV [10], which were the most successful models used by Willow, the first place–winning team of the YouTube-8M video understanding challenge [8]. A hyperparameter was identified to match the 2nd YouTube-8M video understanding challenge limit (model size < 1 GB). NetVLAD and NetFV model uses integrated frame-level features and audio features.

2.3   Loss Function

This paper used the Huber loss function [5], which was used by SNUVL X SKT when the team earned 8th place in the YouTube-8M video understanding challenge [9]. The Huber loss combines L2 loss and L1 loss as shown in Eq. 1. As the YouTube-8M dataset is substantially imbalanced by a label, the Huber loss function was used to somewhat reduce the noise.

$$L_\delta(a) = \delta^2 \left(\sqrt{1 + (a/\delta)^2} - 1 \right) \tag{1}$$

2.4   Evaluation Metric

In this paper, the global average precision (GAP) is used as an evaluation method. The GAP is calculated with the top N predictions sorted by confidence score as shown in Eq. 2.

$$GAP = \sum_{i=1}^{N} p(i)\Delta r(i) \tag{2}$$

In Eq. 2, $p(i)$ is the precision and $r(i)$ is the recall. In the 2nd YouTube-8M video understanding challenge, N is set to 20 and this paper is calculated accordingly also.

3   Experiments

The following experiments were performed: performance comparison of epoch, performance comparison by learning rate, performance comparison of modified dataset preprocessing.

3.1   Epoch

Of particular interest is the evaluation performed of each validation dataset for each epoch. Usually, dozens of epochs are trained in the image training process. However, that was not necessary for the YouTube-8M dataset. The validation results for each epoch are shown in Fig. 1. In the case of the YouTube-8M dataset, the training of one epoch was performed in approximately 25,000 steps when setting the batch size was 80 and used 2-GPU (total 160-batch). Although the GAP difference was slight, it was possible to observe an optimal training performance between approximately 2.5 and 3 epochs. In addition, the GAP for the training set increased in the additional training, but for the validation set decreased. Similar trends were found for various parameters of various models. In this way, it was discovered that not many epochs were needed in the training process of this dataset, thus training was completed after 2.5 epochs.

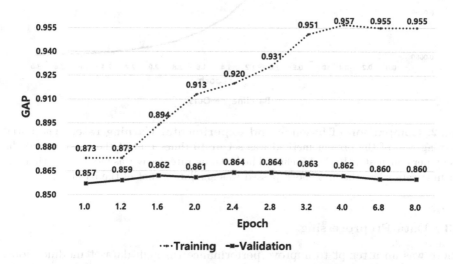

Fig. 1. GAP per epoch curve. The dotted line represents GAP per epoch in the training set, the solid line is GAP per epoch in the validation dataset. As the epoch increases, the training GAP curve also increases. However, the validation GAP curve shows a trend of declining after about 2.5 epochs.

3.2 Learning Rate

The epoch experiment revealed that overfitting of the training set occurs when the model continues to train more than 3 epochs. This paper resolves this problem by adjusting the learning rate to be more effective. In the early part of training, it is good to provide a relatively high learning rate to ensure quick training. Conversely, at the end of the training, the learning rate should be decreased. Thus, the experiment began with a high learning rate, which was set to diminish over time. The learning rate decay per epoch was set to 1/10 of the baseline. It also increased the initial learning rate by 10 times that of the baseline. These ways have helped reduce overfitting. The learning rate decay was 0.8, for the purpose of keeping the learning rate of the two methods similar when the first epoch is complete. So that the learning rate was greater than the baseline even if the training data is in the latter half. This ensured training about these data. The learning rate change at this method is shown in Fig. 2. The resulting performance improvement is shown in Table 1.

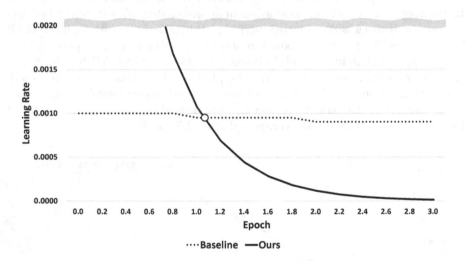

Fig. 2. Comparison of baseline and experimental learning rates. The initial learning rate of the present method was set at 10 times that of the baseline and the decay per epoch at 1/10 the baseline. The learning rate decay was modified so that the learning rate when the first epoch passed was similar to that of the baseline.

3.3 Data Preprocessing

There was an attempt to improve performance through dataset modifications. First, the imbalance of the dataset was identified and addressed. Second, the false values of the results obtained were analyzed by validating the data trained with the default training set.

Table 1. Hyperparameters and its GAP score. Hyperparameters were modified. GAP increased by 0.002.

Hyperparameter	Baseline	Ours
Initial learning rate	0.001	0.01
Learning rate decay	0.95	0.80
Learning rate decay per epoch	1.0	0.1
GAP	**0.864**	**0.866**

Overfit to Non-dominant Pattern. Figure 3 illustrates that the top 900 labels in the training set accounted for 89% of the multi-label video data, or 10,445,267 of the 11,711,620 total labels for video data. The remaining 2,962 labels represent only 10% of 1,266,353 individuals. To solve this data imbalance, a small training set was constructed with a label index > 977. In this small training set, one epoch of training is performed at 7,300 steps with 2-GPU and each 80-batch (160-batch in total). This small training set was used in two ways. The first method was to train the small training set when the train GAP converged to 1.0 and retrain it as the existing default training set. However, this performance was lower than that of the existing GAP of 0.86 (see Fig. 4). In the second method, 2.5 epochs were trained with the default training set and retrained with a small training set (see Fig. 5). But, performance dropped when trained with a small training set.

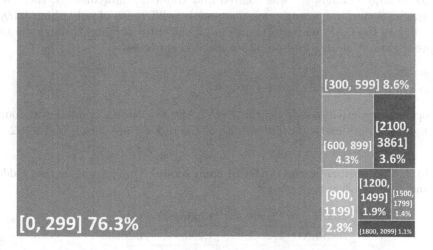

Fig. 3. Visualization of training set imbalance. The top 300 labels represent 76% of the total multi-labels. Expanding the range to the top 900 labels takes up 89% of the total.

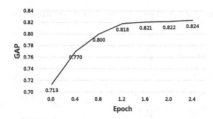

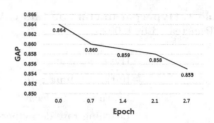

Fig. 4. GAP curve about validation set: Training with a small training set and retraining with the default training set. 0.0 Epoch means when overfitted with the small training set.

Fig. 5. GAP curve about validation set: Training with the default training set and retraining with the small training set. 0.0 Epoch is when 2.5 epochs were trained with the default training set.

Analysis of Validation Results and Additional Experiment. The correct answer was compared to the top 20 prediction results of the model. The model validation GAP is 0.86. The analysis showed that 117,410 in a total of 1,112,357 validation set did not include some or all of the correct answers in the top 20 predictions. Of these, 21,828 were single-label, and 55,470 had more than 4 labels. Those with 1 label involved a unique feature of the video label, and those with 4 or more labels had overlapping label features and did not train well. So, training data was selected with only 1 or 4-plus labels. These data were added to the training data by tripling them from other data. In all, about 8,500,000 large training set was created and trained. Unfortunately, there was no significant performance improvement; with a difference of only about 0.0001 according to the GAP, no performance improvement was found through dataset preprocessing. A clearer interpretation method is needed.

3.4 Final Submission Model

An optimal hyperparameter for the NetVLAD and NetFV models was found through the above methods. The results of the test set are shown in Table 2.

Table 2. The performance (GAP) of each model. Optimal cluster size, hidden size and GAP are shown.

Model	Cluster size	Hidden size	GAP
NetVLAD	192	1,200	0.86668
NetFV	120	1,024	0.86633
Result			**0.86668**

In the end, a GAP score of 0.8668 was obtained at the 2nd YouTube-8M video understanding challenge.

4 Conclusions

This paper used video classification of the YouTube-8M dataset, applying the NetVLAD and NetFV models with reference to previous research data and using the Huber loss function. Experimental verification is effective for improving performance by adjusting the training epoch, learning rate, and training set. Unlike in conventional training for classification problem, the performance of 2.5 epochs is found to be optimal, as the training set is sufficiently large. The learning rate was also adjusted for optimal training. Even though no performance improvement was found, an attempt was made to train with the set that emphasized frequently-wrong patterns.

Acknowledgement. This work was partly supported by Institute for Information & communications Technology Promotion (IITP) grant funded by the Korea government (MSIT) (2017-0-01772, Development of QA system for video story understanding to pass Video Turing Test), Information & communications Technology Promotion (IITP) grant funded by the Korea government (MSIT) (2017-0-01781, Data Collection and Automatic Tuning System Development for the Video Understanding), and Institute for Information & communications Technology Promotion (IITP) grant funded by the Korea government (MSIT) (No. 2017-0-00271, Development of Archive Solution and Content Management Platform).

References

1. Arandjelovic, R., Gronat, P., Torii, A., Pajdla, T., Sivic, J.: NetVLAD: CNN architecture for weakly supervised place recognition. In: Proceedings of the IEEE Conference on Computer Vision and Pattern Recognition, pp. 5297–5307 (2016)
2. Campos Camunez, V., Jou, B., Giró Nieto, X., Torres Viñals, J., Chang, S.F.: Skip RNN: learning to skip state updates in recurrent neural networks. In: Proceedings of the Sixth International Conference on Learning Representations, Monday April 30–Thursday 3 May 2018, Vancouver Convention Center, Vancouver, pp. 1–17 (2018)
3. Cho, K., Van Merriënboer, B., Bahdanau, D., Bengio, Y.: On the properties of neural machine translation: Encoder-decoder approaches (2014). arXiv preprint: arXiv:1409.1259
4. Hochreiter, S., Schmidhuber, J.: Long short-term memory. Neural Comput. **9**(8), 1735–1780 (1997)
5. Huber, P.J.: Robust statistics. In: Lovric, M. (ed.) International Encyclopedia of Statistical Science, pp. 1248–1251. Springer, Heidelberg (2011)
6. Jégou, H., Douze, M., Schmid, C., Pérez, P.: Aggregating local descriptors into a compact image representation. In: 2010 IEEE Conference on Computer Vision and Pattern Recognition (CVPR), pp. 3304–3311. IEEE (2010)
7. Kim, Y.: Convolutional neural networks for sentence classification (2014). arXiv preprint: arXiv:1408.5882

8. Miech, A., Laptev, I., Sivic, J.: Learnable pooling with Context Gating for video classification. ArXiv e-prints (2017)
9. Na, S., Yu, Y., Lee, S., Kim, J., Kim, G.: Encoding Video and Label Priors for Multi-label Video Classification on YouTube-8M dataset. ArXiv e-prints (2017)
10. Perronnin, F., Dance, C.: Fisher kernels on visual vocabularies for image categorization. In: 2007 IEEE Conference on Computer Vision and Pattern Recognition, pp. 1–8. IEEE (2007)

Learning Video Features for Multi-label Classification

Shivam Garg[✉] ⓘ

Samsung Research Seoul R&D Campus, Seoul, South Korea
shivgarg@live.com

Abstract. This paper studies some approaches to learn representation of videos. This work was done as a part of Youtube-8M Video Understanding Challenge. The main focus is to analyze various approaches used to model temporal data and evaluate the performance of such approaches on this problem. Also, a model is proposed which reduces the size of feature vector by 70% but does not compromise on accuracy.

The first approach is to use recurrent neural network architectures to learn a single video level feature from frame level features and then use this aggregated feature to do multi-label classification. The second approach is to use video level features and deep neural networks to assign the labels.

Keywords: RNN · LSTM · MoE · ResidualCNN

1 Introduction

Video classification is one of the most important problem in computer vision. Video content consists of temporally related images. This temporal dimension adds a new level of complexity to the image classification problem. In recent years, with the advent of faster computational platforms alongwith high quality large datasets like Imagenet [4], MS COCO [14], Pascal VOC [5], robust image classification and detection algorithms have been developed. Human level performance on Imagenet was surpassed in 2015 by ResNet [8]. Many object detection approaches use some of the highly performant approaches on imagenet as a backbone network for eg. Faster RCNN [19], Yolo [18], SSD [15]. This approach of transfer learning aids the object detection a lot. Similarly development of good video classification models would lead to improvement in a lot of tasks like tracking object movement in videos, detecting suspicious activity, video captioning, summarisation , robotic vision, affective computing, HCI etc.

Understanding a video involves two parts, understanding what is happening in a single frame and correlating the information present in various frames. The harder part lies in the correlation of information in different frames. LSTM's [24] have shown promising results in natural language modelling problems which exhibit similar difficulties. Thus a similar approach is used here.

L. Leal-Taixé and S. Roth (Eds.): ECCV 2018 Workshops, LNCS 11132, pp. 325–337, 2019.
https://doi.org/10.1007/978-3-030-11018-5_30

For the former part of extracting features from a single frame, approaches based on deep convolution networks [8,20,21] are good at capturing salient features outperforming many hand crafted techniques [2,3,16,17] on various computer vision tasks.

The paper is divided into the following sections: Sect. 2 describes the dataset, Sect. 3 describes the evaluation criteria, Sect. 4 describes the models, Sect. 5 presents the experimental results and Sect. 6 concludes the work.

2   Dataset

The dataset used for analysis is the Youtube-8M [1]. This is by far the largest dataset for video classification available to date. Other video datasets include Sports-1M [12] and ActivityNet [6]. These datasets are limited to sports videos and human activity recognition tasks respectively.

Youtube-8M contains 6.1 million videos, which have been roughly partitioned in 3.84 million examples for training and 1.13 million each for validation and test set. The total number of labels is 3862 across 24 top level entities in knowledge graph. The average number of labels per video is 3.

The dataset is divided into two parts, frame-level and video-level.The frame-level features contain features of upto 360 frames per video. The frames are processed at 1 fps and a maximum of first 6 min of each video is processed. Each frame has a 1024 length vector containing rgb features and 128 length vector containing audio features. The visual features have been extracted from Inception V3 [22]. The features are extracted just after the last global pooling layer. The audio features have been extracted using a model similar to VGG as described in Hershey et al. [9]. The visual features extracted from the inception network are further processed. The extracted feature length is 2048 which is reduced to 1024 by PCA. Both audio and visual features are quantized to 8bits to reduce the size of the features. The data is presented in 3844 shards of equal sizes for each of the train,test and validation split. The total size of frame-level features is 1.53 TB.

The video-level dataset is similar. The rgb and audio features are mean aggregated frame level features. The feature values are not quantized in contrast to frame level features. The dataset is formatted in tfrecord format. Similar to frame level, it is provided in 3844 equally sized shards for each train, validation and test split.The total size of video-level features is 31 GB.

The data has a lot of challenging aspects which are listed here under:-

1. Scale:- As mentioned above, there are approx. 5 million videos in the train + validation set of the dataset. Processing all the videos for some frame-level models takes a lot of time (in order of days). So GPUs with large amount of memory, alongwith high speed storage device is essential for quick experimentation and hyperparameter tuning.
2. Noisy labels: The dataset is annotated by youtube annotation system which results in missing labels. This makes training even harder with model getting contradictory signals for similar inputs.

3. Imbalance: The data is highly imbalanced with a small number of label entities having a majority of videos. The log log plot of number of videos for
each entity follows a zipf (Fig. 1) distribution, depicting the imbalance in the
data distribution. This imbalance in the dataset makes it difficult to learn
about rare classes, leading to poor performance over those classes. This fact
is supported by low MAP values obtained by the models.

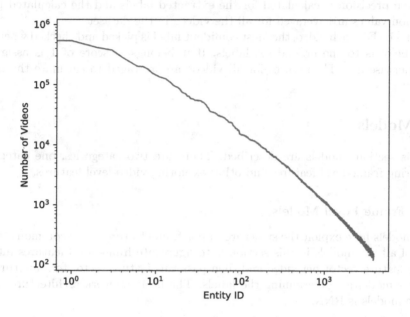

Fig. 1. Log-Log plot of number of videos for a single entity

As the rgb and audio information is provided in encoded form, the focus of the
problem shifts to analysis of temporal modeling approaches for given features.

3 Evaluation

The following metrics have been used to evaluate the performance of a model.

1. GAP@20:- Global Average Precision is the primary evaluation metric used
in the paper. For each video, a list of labels and the confidence scores is
calculated. Then top 20 labels and the confidence scores are picked and added
as individual data points to a global pool. Then this pool of label-confidence
pairs is sorted and the average precision is calculated over this pool.

$$GAP = \sum_{i=0}^{T} [p(i)\{r(i+1) - r(i)\}] \tag{1}$$

where p(i) denotes the precision of the first i examples, and r(i) denotes the recall till the first i examples.
2. MAP:- Mean Average Precision is the mean of average precision of each class. For each class, average precision of the predictions for that class is calculated. The mean of these values for all classes is MAP.
3. PERR:- Precision at Equal Recall Rate. To calculate this metric, top k labels for each video are extracted where k is number of labels in the ground truth. Then precision is calculated for the extracted labels and the calculated precision values are averaged for all the videos in the dataset.
4. Hit@1:- For each video, the most confident label is picked and checked whether it belongs to the ground set labels. If it belongs, a score of 1 is assigned otherwise a 0. Then scores for all videos are averaged to calculate the final score.

4   Models

In this section, models are described. There are two categories, one category exploring frame-level features and other exploring video-level features.

4.1   Frame Level Models

The models here exploit the structure in per frame features. The common structure of all the models in this section is to aggregate frame level features into a single feature vector per video and then pass this feature vector to a mixture of experts model for determining the labels. The basic network architecture used in the models is RNN.

LSTM. Recurrent Neural Networks are designed to handle temporal data. In this work, LSTM [24] cell is used in all RNN's. Long Short Term Memory is one of the most successful tool in solving various NLP problems. They have been used in a variety of problems like machine translation, image captioning, text to speech, speech to text, etc. LSTMs are designed to learn long term dependencies. LSTM cell maintains a cell state, which helps the cell to remember relevant information from all the preceding steps. A basic LSTM cell operation can be summarized in four steps:

1. Calculate the forget_gate which determines the part of the cell state that should be remembered and the part that should be forgotten.

$$f_t = \sigma\left[W_f.(h_{t-1}\|x_t) + b_f\right] \qquad (2)$$

2. Filter out relevant information from input at step t, which is used to update the cell state.(input_gate).

$$i_t = \sigma\left[W_i.(h_{t-1}\|x_t) + b_i\right] \qquad (3)$$

$$\hat{c}_t = tanh\left[W_c.(h_{t-1}\|x_t) + b_c\right] \qquad (4)$$

3. Update the cell state by using the forget_gate and input_gate

$$c_t = \sigma \left[f_t * c_{t-1} + i_t * \hat{c}_t \right] \tag{5}$$

4. Determine the parts of the cell state which should be given as output of the cell(output_gate).

$$o_t = \sigma \left[W_o.(h_{t-1} \| x_t) + b_o \right] \tag{6}$$

$$h_t = o_t * tanh(c_t) \tag{7}$$

In the above equations, $\|$ denotes concatenation operation, $*$ denotes elementwise multiplication.

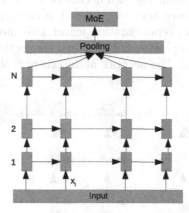

Fig. 2. N layer LSTM model with a pooling module and a final mixture of experts layer to produce outputs.

The first set of models use N layer LSTM architecture which is followed by a pooling layer to pool the outputs of each lstm cell. The pooled feature is then passed into a MoE model to determine the labels (Fig. 2). Three different pooling mechanisms are used:-

1. Choosing the last state of lstm.
2. Maxpooling all the feature vectors.
3. Applying attention weighting to input feature vectors.

All frames in a video are not equally important for determining the semantic content in the video. For eg., the starting and ending frames do not contain much information, dark frames in a video do not convey much or in a talk show most of the frames are similar, it is the audio content that describes the genre of video. Attention module can help to solve this problem which weighs the feature vectors at all time steps according to the importance of the feature vector for classification task. Then a weighted sum of these feature vectors is used as an input for the MoE model. The method of calculating weighted vector (F) is described here under:-

$$I = tanh\ (H) \tag{8}$$
$$w = softmax\ [I.W_a] \tag{9}$$
$$F = tanh(reduce\_sum(w.H)) \tag{10}$$

H is the output of lstm network at all time steps. W_a is a learnable column vector, which weighs the vectors.

Deeper LSTM models are harder to optimise due to introduction of a lot of non-linearities, and they might suffer from vanishing or exploding gradient problems. Residual connections introduced in ResNet [8] come handy to solve some of the problems in optimizing such networks. The residual connections force a part of the network to learn h(x) −x , where h is the hypothesis function to be learnt and x is the interim representation learnt.This modeling trick facilitates the flow of gradients in deep networks. Residual connections are utilized in lstm network with a depth of 3. The network architecture is shown in Fig. 3.

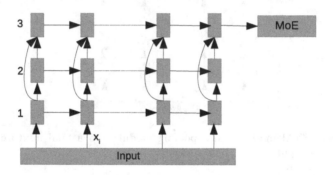

Fig. 3. 3 layer LSTM model with residual connections.

BiLSTM. BiLSTM is similar to LSTM, with the difference being BiLSTM contains two LSTM chains, one of which processes the data in forward direction and the other processes the data in backward direction. BiLSTMs try to learn representations by considering temporal relations in both directions. A lot of times, context from future frames is helpful in understanding the present frame, which BiLSTMs model efficiently.The basic architecture is depicted in Fig. 4. The outputs of both the forward and backward lstms is concatenated to produce the output for BiLSTM. Other approaches like mean, max aggregation, attention weighting can be applied to produce the output vector.

A variant of BiLSTM is also proposed here. Currently, the forward and backward lstms do not interact with each other throughout the depth of BiLSTM.This limits the ability of network to capture various dependencies for

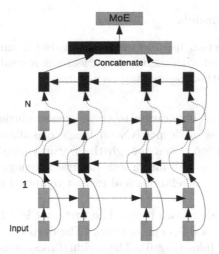

Fig. 4. N layer BiLSTM model

eg. when a state depends on both past and future states. In this N layer network, the forward and backwards outputs at each time step of every layer are pooled before passing them as input to upper layers. It can be thought of as N single BiLSTM layers stacked over one another, where the input to the nth layer will be the pooled output of $n-1^{th}$ layer at each time step. Since the network contains N single BiLSTM stacked over one another, it would be referred to as Stacked BiLSTM in this paper.

Multi-modal Approaches. The data contains rgb and audio features for each frame. Therefore, various multi-modal techniques can be adopted to model rgb and audio features separately. The audio and rgb features may have different distributions and independent models for each data stream can help to capture such relations efficiently. A simple framework as shown in Fig. 5 was adopted to judge the effectiveness of such techniques. The details of the model used is given in the experiments section.

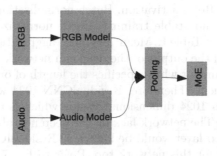

Fig. 5. Multi modal architecture

4.2 Video-Level Models

The models is this section use the mean aggregated frame level features. The models were approached with the motive of learning a smaller representation of video-level features without sacrificing on accuracy.

ResidualCNN-X. The inspiration to try deep convolutional neural networks comes from the success of deep CNN on image classification tasks especially on Imagenet Competition. Even though the features here lack explicit spatial relations, CNN's perform well for various natural language problems where the inputs lack explicit spatial relations and exhibit temporal relations as shown in Kim et al. [13].

The network is made of two parts. The first part is a fully connected layer and the second part is a deep cnn network. The deep cnn network is made up of several residual modules (Fig. 6). The residual module is made up of dilated convolution layers with kernel size (9,1) and stride $= 1$. The dilation of conv layer depends on the position in residual module where the conv layer is located. The ith layer of residual module has a dilation of $2 * i + 1$ with index starting from 0. Dilation helps the cnn to cover large parts of input length. Each convolution layer has same padding, which keeps the output dimension equal to input dimension. The number of channels in convolution layers of residual modules varies with each instance of module.

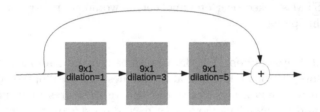

Fig. 6. A 3 layer residual module

The depth of residual modules used in ResidualCNN-X is atmost 3. All the convolution layers use ReLu activation. Batch normalisation [11] has been used which helps in faster and stable training. Batch normalization layer is added after layers specified in Table 1. Mean and max aggregation pooling methods have been used to pool the output of the deep cnn network. X in ResidualCNN-X denotes a hyperparameter which specifies the length of output vector used by MoE for label assignment. Therefore, ResidualCNN-1024 would mean that the output of network is a 1024 dimensional vector which is then passed to MoE for label classification. The network lacking the deep neural network, containing only the fully connected layer would be known as ResidualCNN-FC-X. X would carry similar meaning for this network too. Refer to Fig. 7 and Table 1 for full details of ResidualCNN-X architecture.

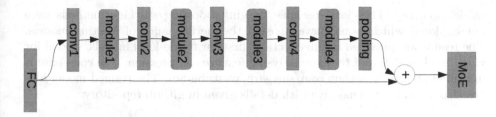

Fig. 7. ResidualCNN-X architecture

Table 1. ResidualCNN-X architecture details

Layer	Kernel size	Depth[a]	Output size	9×1,dil=1	9×1,dil=3	9×1,dil=5	Batch norm
FC			X×1×1				
conv1	49×1	64	X×1×64				y
module1		3	X×1×64	128	192	64	y
conv2	1×1	128	X×1×128				y
module2		3	X×1×128	256	512	128	y
conv3	1×1	256	X×1×256				y
module3		2	X×1×256	512	256		y
conv4	1×1	X	X×1×X				y
module4		2	X×1×X	512	X		y
pooling			X×1×1				

[a]num. of channels for conv layer, num. of conv layer for residual module.

5 Experiments and Results

This section contains details of experiments and the results obtained. The details common to all experiments are:-

- The input to the models was the concatenation of rgb and audio features resulting in 1152 length feature vector except multi-modal approaches.
- Adam optimizer was used to optimize the models, with learning rate decay rate of 0.95 every epoch.
- Cross entropy loss was used as the loss function for model optimization.
- All the models were trained on the train split of the dataset and validation set was used to evaluate the performance of models.

The accuracy measures on validation set followed closely (within 0.2%) the results on test dataset as reported by the kaggle leaderboard. Since test labels were not available, to compute all performance measures, validation set is used. The compute platform was Nvidia GTX 1080Ti graphic card, Ubuntu 16.04 OS, 8 GB RAM and a 2 TB external storage. Due to limitation of computational resources, the experiments were limited to maximize single model accuracy. Therefore ensemble/bagging/boosting/stacking methods were not explored which would have boosted the performance of existing models. The results are provided in three sections,first for frame-level models, second for video-level models and the last analysing feature compression. The code base is uploaded at https://github.com/shivgarg/youtube-8m. The trained model files are also uploaded to Onedrive with details given in github repository.

5.1   Frame-Level-Models

The models have been described in Sect. 4.1. All the models were trained for 2 epochs. Learning rate of 0.001 was used for all models. The training time ranged from 1 day for smaller models to about 3 days for large models. The details of models, their hyperparameters and accuracy values is given in Table 2. (LSTM 3 layer, res, 1024) model and (Stacked BiLSTM 2 layer, 2048) perform the best, beating all other models in three metrics. It is closely followed by (LSTM 3 layer, 1024) and (BiLSTM 1 layer,2048). Some general trends observed:-

Table 2. Frame-level model hyperparameters and results

Model	Batch size	Hit@1	PERR	MAP	GAP
LSTM 1 layer, 1024[a]	256	0.848	0.741	0.334	0.805
LSTM 2 layer, 1024	256	0.859	0.754	0.354	0.816
LSTM 2 layer, 1280,640[b]	256	0.862	0.759	0.357	0.820
LSTM 3 layer, 1024	128	0.874	0.776	0.399	0.837
LSTM 3 layer, res[c], 1024	128	**0.877**	**0.780**	0.422	**0.842**
LSTM 1 layer, 1024, max-pooling	256	0.844	0.735	0.341	0.795
LSTM 1 layer, 1024, att-pooling[d]	256	0.863	0.761	0.378	0.822
BiLSTM 1 layer, 2048	256	0.874	0.778	**0.437**	0.839
BiLSTM 2 layer, 2048	128	0.869	0.771	0.409	0.833
Stacked BiLSTM 2 layer, 2048	128	**0.876**	**0.780**	0.427	**0.841**
BiLSTM 3 layer, 1024	128	0.866	0.763	0.359	0.824
Stacked BiLSTM 3 layer, res[c], 1024	128	0.866	0.752	0.358	0.828
Multi-modal, DBoF, DBoF	512	0.854	0.747	0.353	0.800
Multi-modal, (LSTM 2,1024), (LSTM 2,1024)	128	0.856	0.752	0.358	0.814

[a] LSTM output feature size
[b] LSTM 2 layer with hidden state sizes of 1280 and 640
[c] Residual connections as in Fig. 3
[d] Attention mechanism as defined in Eqs. 8, 9 and 10

– Deeper networks lead to better accuracy.
– Residual connections help to optimize deeper networks.

- Stacked BiLSTM perform better than simple BiLSTM.
- Attention pooling boosts the performance of LSTM.

The performance of each of the above models can be increased by training for larger number of iterations.

5.2 Video-Level Models

The models have been described in 4.2. Learning rate for MoE model was 0.01, and ResidualCNN-X was 0.0001. Batch size was 1024 for MoE, and 256 for ResidualCNN-X models. The main aim of these models was to learn condensed representation without compromising with accuracy. The details of experiments, model hyperparameters are given in Table 3.

ResidualCNN-1024 performs the best in video-level models, beating the baseline by about 1.4%. ResidualCNN-X models tend to perform better than baseline demonstrating the effectiveness of deeper neural networks. Also, max-pooled variants performed consistently better than their mean pooled counterparts.

Table 3. Video-level model hyperparameters and results

Model	Batch size	Hit@1	PERR	MAP	GAP
MoE	1024	0.854	0.759	**0.466**	0.817
ResidualCNN-FC-320	1024	0.832	0.726	0.348	0.782
ResidualCNN-FC-1024	1024	0.840	0.735	0.374	0.795
ResidualCNN-320, Mean-pooling	256	0.851	0.724	0.304	0.796
ResidualCNN-320, Max-pooling	256	0.862	0.764	0.418	0.822
ResidualCNN-512, Mean-pooling	256	0.857	0.758	0.408	0.818
ResidualCNN-512, Max-pooling	256	0.864	0.766	0.428	0.827
ResidualCNN-1024, Mean-pooling	256	0.861	0.764	0.425	0.825
ResidualCNN-1024, Max-pooling	256	**0.863**	**0.768**	0.427	**0.831**

5.3 Feature Compression

This section highlights some models, which learnt video representations significantly smaller than the one presented and still achieved better accuracy numbers than the baseline (MoE). ResidualCNN-320, MaxPool reduces the feature size by 72% without losing on the performance metrics. This network can be used to further encode the features, which can be used by other models to predict labels.

Another direction for reducing the feature size is to explore the autoencoder category of models which perform well on the task of reducing the size of input representation and capturing salient features in the input [4].

Table 4. Feature Compression Results

Model	Feature size	GAP	Δ GAP (in%)[a]	Δ Feature size[b]
LSTM 2 layer, (1280,640)	640	0.820	0.3%	0.44
ResidualCNN-512, Max Pooling	512	0.827	1%	0.55
ResidualCNN-320, Max Polling	320	0.822	0.5%	0.72

[a] (GAP(Model) - GAP(MoE))
[b] (1152 - Feature_size)/1152

6   Conclusion

In this paper, a lot of techniques were used to learn features of video for classification task. LSTM and it variations were used to model the video features for the classification task. A deep convolution neural network architecture is also proposed which helps in reducing the feature size. Deeper neural networks, both LSTM's and CNN's can give improved results. Transformer [23] based approaches may perform good as they show promising results on machine translation task. Ensemble methods can improve the accuracy of the approaches mentioned in this paper. Techniques such as model distillation [10] can be used to transfer the knowledge from large models to smaller models to increase the accuracy of smaller models which are more scalable and efficient. Various network structure optmisiation strategies like weights quantization, pruning networks [7] etc. can be used to reduce the size and complexity of large models.

References

1. Abu-El-Haija, S., et al.: Youtube-8m: a large-scale video classification benchmark. CoRR abs/1609.08675 (2016), arXiv:1609.08675
2. Chandrasekhar, V., Takacs, G., Chen, D., Tsai, S., Grzeszczuk, R., Girod, B.: Chog: compressed histogram of gradients a low bit-rate feature descriptor. In: IEEE Conference on Computer Vision and Pattern Recognition, 2009. CVPR 2009, pp. 2504–2511. IEEE (2009)
3. Dalal, N., Triggs, B.: Histograms of oriented gradients for human detection. In: IEEE Computer Society Conference on Computer Vision and Pattern Recognition, CVPR 2005, vol. 1, pp. 886–893. IEEE (2005)
4. Deng, J., Dong, W., Socher, R., Li, L. J., Li, K., Fei-Fei, L.: Imagenet: a large-scale hierarchical image database. In: IEEE Conference on Computer Vision and Pattern Recognition, 2009. CVPR 2009, pp. 248–255. IEEE (2009)
5. Everingham, M., Eslami, S.M.A., Van Gool, L., Williams, C.K.I., Winn, J., Zisserman, A.: The pascal visual object classes challenge: a retrospective. Int. J. Comput. Vis. 111(1), 98–136 (2015)
6. Caba Heilbron, F., Escorcia, V., Ghanem, B., Niebles, J.C.: Activitynet: a large-scale video benchmark for human activity understanding. In: Proceedings of the IEEE Conference on Computer Vision and Pattern Recognition, pp. 961–970 (2015)

7. Han, S., Mao, H., Dally, W.J.: Deep compression: compressing deep neural networks with pruning, trained quantization and huffman coding. arXiv preprint arXiv:1510.00149 (2015)
8. He, K., Zhang, X., Ren, S., Sun, J.: Delving deep into rectifiers: surpassing human-level performance on imagenet classification. CoRR abs/1502.01852 (2015). http://arxiv.org/abs/1502.01852
9. Hershey, S., et al.: CNN architectures for large-scale audio classification. In: International Conference on Acoustics, Speech and Signal Processing (ICASSP) (2017). https://arxiv.org/abs/1609.09430
10. Hinton, G., Vinyals, O., Dean, J.: Distilling the knowledge in a neural network. arXiv preprint arXiv:1503.02531 (2015)
11. Ioffe, S., Szegedy, C.: Batch normalization: accelerating deep network training by reducing internal covariate shift. arXiv preprint. arXiv:1502.03167 (2015)
12. Karpathy, A., Toderici, G., Shetty, S., Leung, T., Sukthankar, R., Fei-Fei, L.: Large-scale video classification with convolutional neural networks. In: CVPR (2014)
13. Kim, Y.: Convolutional neural networks for sentence classification. arXiv preprint. arXiv:1408.5882 (2014)
14. Lin, T., et al.: Microsoft COCO: common objects in context. CoRR abs/1405.0312 (2014)
15. Liu, W., et al.: SSD: single shot multibox detector. In: Leibe, B., Matas, J., Sebe, N., Welling, M. (eds.) ECCV 2016, Part I. LNCS, vol. 9905, pp. 21–37. Springer, Cham (2016). https://doi.org/10.1007/978-3-319-46448-0_2
16. Lowe, D.G.: Distinctive image features from scale-invariant keypoints. Int. J. Comput. Vis. **60**(2), 91–110 (2004)
17. Mikolajczyk, K., Schmid, C.: Indexing based on scale invariant interest points. In: Proceedings of the Eighth IEEE International Conference on Computer Vision, ICCV 2001, vol. 1, pp. 525–531. IEEE (2001)
18. Redmon, J., Divvala, S., Girshick, R., Farhadi, A.: You only look once: unified, real-time object detection. In: The IEEE Conference on Computer Vision and Pattern Recognition (CVPR), June 2016
19. Ren, S., He, K., Girshick, R.B., Sun, J.: Faster R-CNN: towards real-time object detection with region proposal networks. CoRR abs/1506.01497 (2015). http://arxiv.org/abs/1506.01497
20. Simonyan, K., Zisserman, A.: Very deep convolutional networks for large-scale image recognition. arXiv preprint arXiv:1409.1556 (2014)
21. Szegedy, C., Ioffe, S., Vanhoucke, V.: Inception-v4, inception-resnet and the impact of residual connections on learning. corr abs/1602.07261. http://arxiv.org/abs/1602.07261 (2016)
22. Szegedy, C., Vanhoucke, V., Ioffe, S., Shlens, J., Wojna, Z.: Rethinking the inception architecture for computer vision. In: IEEE Conference on Computer Vision and Pattern Recognition (CVPR), pp. 2818–2826 (2016)
23. Vaswani, A., et al.: Attention is all you need. CoRR abs/1706.03762 (2017). http://arxiv.org/abs/1706.03762
24. Zaremba, W., Sutskever, I., Vinyals, O.: Recurrent neural network regularization. arXiv preprint arXiv:1409.2329 (2014)

Large-Scale Video Classification with Feature Space Augmentation Coupled with Learned Label Relations and Ensembling

Choongyeun Cho[1]([✉]), Benjamin Antin[1,2], Sanchit Arora[3], Shwan Ashrafi[1],
Peilin Duan[1], Dang The Huynh[1], Lee James[1], Hang Tuan Nguyen[1],
Mojtaba Solgi[1], and Cuong Van Than[1]

[1] Axon, 1100 Olive Way, Seattle, WA 98004, USA
{cycho,sashrafi,pduan,dhuynh,ljames,hnguyen,msolgi,cthan}@axon.com
[2] Stanford University, 450 Serra Mall, Stanford, CA 94305, USA
bantin@stanford.edu
[3] Upenn/Possible Finance, 1929 3rd Ave #300, Seattle, WA 98101, USA
sanchitarora13@gmail.com

Abstract. This paper presents the Axon AI's solution to the 2nd YouTube-8M Video Understanding Challenge, achieving the final global average precision (GAP) of 88.733% on the private test set (ranked 3rd among 394 teams, not considering the model size constraint), and 87.287% using a model that meets size requirement. Two sets of 7 individual models belonging to 3 different families were trained separately. Then, the inference results on a training data were aggregated from these multiple models and fed to train a compact model that meets the model size requirement. In order to further improve performance we explored and employed data over/sub-sampling in feature space, an additional regularization term during training exploiting label relationship, and learned weights for ensembling different individual models.

Keywords: Video classification · YouTube-8M dataset

1 Introduction

Video classification and understanding is an emerging and active area of research as a video domain may be the fastest growing data source in the last decade. Yet the video classification problem is still largely unsolved and far behind human capability. One of the reasons for this has been a lack of realistic, large-scale video dataset. YouTube-8M is such a large-scale video dataset with high-quality machine-annotated labels. It provides pre-extracted audio and visual features computed from millions of YouTube videos for faster data access and training. The goal of this YouTube-8M Video Understanding Challenge was to develop a machine learning model that accurately predicts labels associated with each unseen test video.

© Springer Nature Switzerland AG 2019
L. Leal-Taixé and S. Roth (Eds.): ECCV 2018 Workshops, LNCS 11132, pp. 338–346, 2019.
https://doi.org/10.1007/978-3-030-11018-5_31

2   Challenge Strategy

Our overall plan for the Challenge was as follows: (1) designing or identifying a set of efficient and strong submodels; (2) ensembling predictions from all the submodels; (3) distilling into a model that satisfies the model size constraint (i.e. less than 1 GB when uncompressed); and (4) exploring and implementing various improvement ideas during individual model training or knowledge-distillation training, namely (a) data augmentation, (b) exploiting label relationship, and (c) trying different ensembling methods.

Early in the competition stage, we started to identify powerful and efficient baseline models regardless of their model sizes. We explored approaches and models from top-performing participants in the last year's Kaggle Challenge [5], and the model architectures from the 1st place winner [9] turned out to be excellent references as they present high performance (in terms of GAP) and quick training and inference time. We also observed train, validate and supposedly test datasets are well randomized and balanced so that GAP on the validate set is representative of GAP on the test set, and even very small subset of labeled data can reliably serve as a new "validate" data. In order to increase data samples for training, we used all training data (i.e. `train????.tfrecord` files in a wildcard notation) and about 90% of the validate data (i.e. `validate???[0-4,6-9].tfrecord`) for all the training of single models. Only one tenth of the validate data (i.e. `validate???5.tfrecord`) was set aside for training monitoring, model and hyper-parameter selection, and ensemble weight learning.

The predictions from multiple models were aggregated and ensembled in order to enhance the GAP performance. In a nutshell, all the information about a single model is represented as predictions on a training dataset. In this way, many single models can be effectively combined without having to run inference of multiple models concurrently. For ensembling schemes, we implemented (1) simple averaging with equal weights, (2) per-model linearly weighted average, and (3) per-model and per-class linearly weighted average. Among these ensembling schemes, the per-model weights provided the best performance improvement.

In order to meet the model size requirement for the Challenge, knowledge distillation was performed based on the implementation from the original paper [6] using only the soft targets from a "teacher" model (an ensemble of multiple submodels), and not the ground truth (hard targets).

We experimented other improvement ideas which will be described in the subsequent subsections.

2.1   Single Baseline Models

We took advantage of three model families depending on the pooling strategy to aggregate frame-level representations into a global, video-level representation, namely: learnable pooling (LP), bag of words (BoW), and recurrent neural network (RNN) models from the last year's winning method [9].

LP method encodes the frame-level features using Fisher vectors (FV) or some of its simplified variants including vector of locally aggregated descriptors (VLAD), residual-less VLAD (RVLAD). For all these variations of LP method, the cluster centers and soft assignments are learned in an end-to-end fashion.

"Gated" version of each model utilizes context gating, the learned element-wise multiplications (gates) at the last layer of a model:

$$y = \sigma(W \cdot x + b) \circ x \tag{1}$$

where x and y are input and output feature vectors respectively, σ is an element-wise sigmoid function, and $\circ$ means element-wise multiplication.

Table 1. A set of 7 single baseline models before ensembling

Model family	Brief description of individual models
LP	Gated NetVLAD with 256 clusters
LP	Gated NetFV with 128 clusters
BoW	Gated soft-DBoW with 4096 clusters
BoW	Soft-DBoW with 8000 clusters
LP	Gated NetRVLAD with 256 clusters
RNN	Gated recurrent unit (GRU) with 2 layers and 1024 cells per layer
RNN	LSTM with 2 layers and 1024 cells per layer

Table 1 lists a brief description of a set of 7 submodels later used in an ensembled model, roughly in the order of decreasing GAP accuracy (hence, Gated NetVLAD being the most powerful and LSTM being the least). As in the original approach of Willow team, we utilized all 7 models as they represent diverse model architecture families and are known to perform very competitively. In the end, we used two sets of these 7 models, totaling 14 single models.

All the single models are trained with the cross-entropy loss as it is known to work well for the performance metric of choice, GAP. The source code for these models was publicly available [8].

3   Experiments

Table 2 shows progressive improvements of classification accuracy in terms of GAP (all evaluated on a test set unless stated otherwise).

The strongest single model was gated NetVLAD achieving 85.75%. This model was combined (simple averaging) with video-level 16-expert MoE model trained with augmented dataset to achieve 0.23% gain (see Subsect. 3.1).

From this trained model, another 40,000 iterations were trained with additional regularized term that exploits label relationship (see Subsect. 3.2), to reach 87.88%.

Simple averaging of one or two sets of 7 models offered 88.27% and 88.62% respectively (see Subsect. 3.3). Learned weights per model instead of equal weights for all models, provided additional 0.11% improvement.

After teacher-student knowledge distillation (see Subsect. 3.4) we achieved 87.32%.

Table 2. GAP performance per experiment

Experiment	Test GAP (%)
Single baseline model (gated NetVLAD)	85.75 (Val GAP)
Single gated NetVLAD model + video-level MoE model trained with augmented dataset in feature space	85.98 (Val GAP)
Single gated NetVLAD model + regularized DNN exploiting label relationship	87.88 (Val GAP)
A simple average ensembling of all of the 7 models	88.27
A simple average ensembling of two sets of all of the 7 models (14 models in total)	88.62
Ensembled using learned weights	**88.73**
Distilled model	**87.32**

3.1 Data Over- and Sub-sampling

Train dataset augmentation is an effective way to increase data samples for training, hence potentially improving generalizability and performance of a classifier, without having to explicitly annotate additional data. A common practice is to apply a small perturbation in the original data domain (cropping, mirroring, color jittering in the case of image domain, for example).

Figure 1 shows TSNE visualization of visual features for several selected classes. Note that data examples belonging to only single label have been plotted in this figure for the sake of easier visualization. It is observed that examples (videos) associated with a same semantic concept (label) form a cluster while videos belonging to different concepts are separated to some degree.

The label frequencies (counts) are plotted in log-log scale Fig. 2. It is clear that the plot follows a Zipf distribution: relatively few classes dominate the number of examples, and the tail distribution is very "fat." In order to cope with this distribution both over- and sub-sampling were employed. With data augmentation (over-sampling) we hoped to fill in the gap inside a cluster of same label especially for those classes with fewer examples. In addition to over-sampling, sub-sampling (random sampling) for classes with more than enough examples will make training set more balanced and expedite the training time.

In YouTube-8M dataset we are provided with pre-extracted features. As for the video-level visual features, PCA, whitening and quantization have been performed on a Inception-model deep feature (DNN output) per frame, and all the frame-level features are averaged.

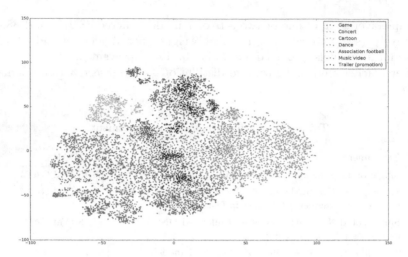

Fig. 1. A TSNE plot of visual features for a few selected classes (best viewed in color) (Color figure online)

Data augmentation was performed inspired by [4] on the video-level visual features due to memory and computation limitations. The simplest transform is to simply add small noise to the feature vector.

$$x'_i = x_i + \gamma Z, Z \sim \mathcal{N}(0, \sigma^2) \tag{2}$$

For each sample in the dataset, we find its K nearest neighbors in feature space (in L2 sense) which share its class label. For each pair of neighboring feature vectors, a new feature vector can then be generated using interpolation:

$$x'_i = x_i + \lambda_i(x_j - x_i) \tag{3}$$

where x'_i is the synthesized feature vector, x_j is a neighboring feature vector to x_i and λ_i is a parameter in the range of 0 to 1 which dictates the degree of interpolation.

In a similar fashion, extrapolation can also be applied to the feature vectors:

$$x'_i = x_i + \lambda_e(x_i - x_j) \tag{4}$$

We used 0.5 for both λ's and σ value of 0.03 for the additive Gaussian noise.

The label frequencies (before and after over- and sub-sampling) are plotted in log-log scale Fig. 2, both of which exhibit a Zipf-like distribution.

There were some implementation considerations because of limited memory and storage resources: Instead of finding "global" nearest neighbors over all examples for a given label (scanning all tfrecord files), we limited a number of tfrecord files to search within, to 256 files at a time, effectively processing data augmentation in 256 tfrecord chunks. Also, since YouTube8M dataset is inherently multi-labeled, the decision of whether and how much over-sampling and

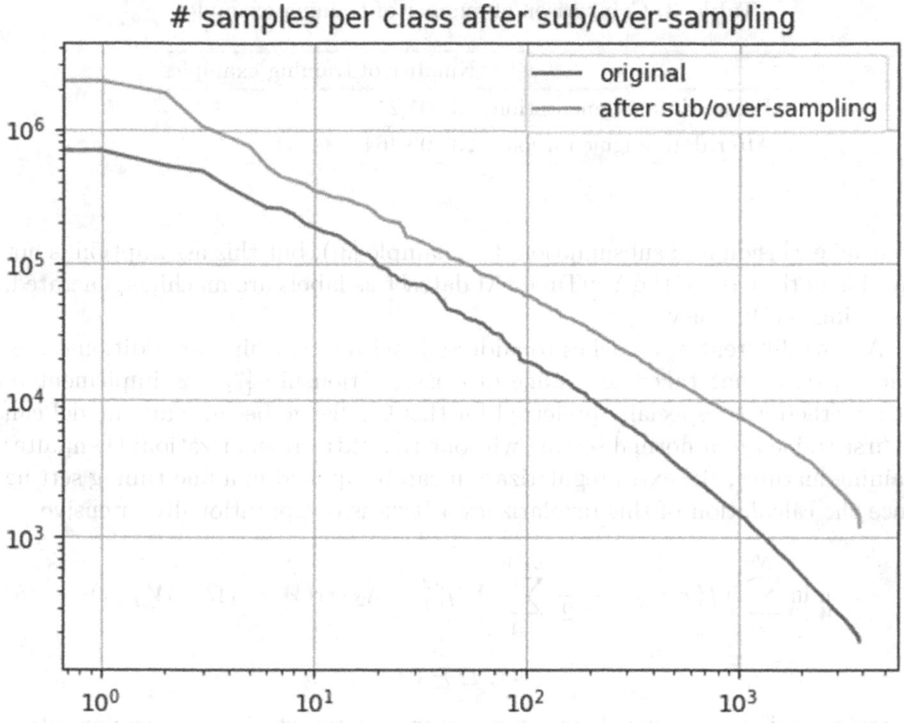

samples per class after sub/over-sampling

Fig. 2. Label counts before and after data augmentation in feature space

sub-sampling will be done given an example is based on a single label which is least frequently occurring over all labels. That is, if a video is associated with a single label which is in a sub-sampling regime (i.e. having more than 10^4 examples which is likely to be more than enough), this video will be subject to random **sub-sampling**. If a video is associated with a single label which is in a over-sampling regime (having less than 10^4 examples), this video will be **over-sampled** using aforementioned augmentation schemes. Number of nearest neighbors are selected heuristically based on label frequencies (more nearest neighbors for the labels with fewer examples). If a video is associated with multiple labels, then the label with the least examples will dictate the over- and sub-sampling decision.

Table 3 shows number of training examples before and after data augmentation. Data augmentation more than quadrupled the number of samples.

3.2   Label Relationship

Utilizing label relationship in multi-label classification setting is actively investigated. Many of the approaches involve modification of the existing model architecture and explicitly calculating and incorporating co-occurrence matrix [1,10]. Some have explored strict hierarchical relationships among different classes

Table 3. Comparison of number of training examples

	Number of training examples
Before data augmentation	5,001,275
After data augmentation	23,590,464

(mutual exclusion and subsumption, for example [3]), but this assumption is not suitable in the case of the YouTube-8M dataset as labels are machine-generated, hence inherently noisy.

Among different approaches to address label relationship, an additional regularized term that takes advantage of class relationship [7] was implemented. This method was especially preferred for this Challenge because any model can be first trained in a normal setting without this extra regularization; then, after training matures, the extra regularization can be applied in a fine-tuning setting since the calculation of this regularization term is computationally intensive.

$$\min_{W,\Omega} \sum_{i=1}^{N} l(f(x_i), y_i) + \frac{\lambda_1}{2} \sum_{l=1}^{L-1} \|W_l\|_F^2 + \lambda_2 \cdot \mathrm{tr}(W_{L-1}\Omega^{-1}W_{L-1}^T) \qquad (5)$$

$$\text{s.t. } \Omega \succeq 0$$

where x_i and y_i are an i-th input example and target, λ's are regularization coefficients, and W_l is a l-th layer model weights (hence, W_{L-1} being the last layer's weights), and $\Omega \in \mathbb{R}^{C \times C}$ encodes label relationship.

The first part in the above cost function measures the empirical loss on the training data, which summarizes the discrepancy between the outputs of the network and the ground-truth labels. The second part is a regularization term to mitigate overfitting.

The last part imposes a trace norm regularization term over the coefficients of the output layer W_{L-1} with the class relationships augmented as a matrix variable Ω. The positive semidefinite constraint, $\Omega \succeq 0$ indicates that the class relationship matrix is viewed as the similarity measure of the semantic classes. The original paper [7] suggests using alternating optimization algorithm to solve for both W and Ω. After updating W using backpropagation, Ω can be updated as:

$$\Omega = \frac{(W_{L-1}^T W_{L-1})^{\frac{1}{2}}}{\mathrm{tr}((W_{L-1}^T W_{L-1})^{\frac{1}{2}})}. \qquad (6)$$

3.3   Ensembling

For training of individual baseline models, we stopped training when a model starts to overfit slightly by monitoring validation GAP in the spirit of the finding from [2] and our own observations. For ensembles, we implemented (1) simple averaging (equal weights for all models), (2) per-model linearly-weighted average,

(3) per-model and per-class linearly-weighted average. Among these ensembling methods, per-model weights provided the best performance improvement.

To learn the per-model weights for ensembling, a dataset was made that comprised of each model's inference results on our validation set (one tenth of the original validation set as described in Sect. 2). Stochastic gradient descent (SGD) with the Adam optimizer was then used to minimize the mean-square-error (MSE) loss between a linear combination of the models' inferences and the ground truth. A custom initializer was used to make the model converge, typically in less than 10 epochs, on useful weights. The initializer used a normal distribution with a mean of $1/(\#\text{model})$ and standard deviation of 0.05 to approximate weights for MSE. Learned per-model weights (Table 4) look reasonable as (1) Gated NetVLAD was the strongest model in terms of GAP performance, and as (2) weights are roughly in a decreasing order from most powerful (Gated NetVLAD) to least powerful model (LSTM).

Table 4. Learned weights for 7 baseline models

Model	Weight
Gated NetVLAD	0.2367
Gated NetFV	0.1508
Gated soft-DBoW	0.1590
Soft-DBoW	0.1000
Gated NetRVLAD	0.1968
GRU	0.1306
LSTM	0.0621

3.4 Knowledge Distillation

We used the predictions of the ensemble model $\tilde{p}$ as soft targets along with the ground truth targets q for training a student model. The loss function can be written as the weighted sum of two cross-entropy losses $(CE(\cdot, \cdot))$ as

$$L = \lambda \cdot CE(p, \tilde{p}) + (1 - \lambda) \cdot CE(p, q), \tag{7}$$

where p is the predictions of the student model. We trained the student model using different values of λ's, and the best GAP result was achieved with $\lambda = 1$, i.e. pure distillation without using the ground truth targets.

The choice of the student model was based on two factors (1) the 1 GB constraint on the size of the final model and (2) the best GAP number one could expect from the candidate single models. As such we chose to use the gated NetVLAD model for it had the best performance amongst the single models as reported by [9]. However, the NetVLAD with 1024 hidden weights in the last fully connected layer results in a model size greater that the 1 GB limit. Therefore, the number of hidden weights was reduced to 800 which yielded in a model size slightly less that the limit.

3.5 Training Details

We kept training details unchanged from the original implementation of these models [9]. All models are trained using the Adam optimizer. The learning rate is initialized to 0.0002 and is exponentially decreased with the factor of 0.8 for every 4M examples. For all the clustering-based pooling methods (NetVLAD, NetRVLAD, NETFV, and Soft-DBoW), 300 frames were randomly sampled with replacement.

4 Conclusions

We approached this YouTube-8M Video Understanding Challenge with a clear and methodical planning and strategy, and achieved 88.733% final GAP (ranked the 3rd place, not considering the model size constraint), and 87.287% using a valid model that meets size requirement. In addition to identifying and employing strong baseline classifiers, we implemented data augmentation in feature space, an extra regularization term that exploits label relationship, and learned weights for the ensembling.

Acknowledgement. The authors would like to thank Youtube-8M Challenge organizers for hosting this exciting competition and for providing the excellent starter code, and the Axon team to support this project.

References

1. Bengio, S., et al.: Using web co-occurrence statistics for improving image categorization. In: Computer Vision and Pattern Recognition (CVPR) (2013)
2. Bober-Irizar, M., Husain, S., Ong, E.J., Bober, M.: Cultivating DNN diversity for large scale video labelling. In: Computer Vision and Pattern Recognition (CVPR) Youtube-8M Workshop (2017)
3. Deng, J., et al.: Large-scale object classification using label relation graphs. In: Fleet, D., Pajdla, T., Schiele, B., Tuytelaars, T. (eds.) ECCV 2014, Part I. LNCS, vol. 8689, pp. 48–64. Springer, Cham (2014). https://doi.org/10.1007/978-3-319-10590-1_4
4. DeVries, T., Taylor, G.W.: Dataset augmentation in feature space (2017). https://arxiv.org/abs/1702.05538
5. Google: Google cloud & youtube-7m video understanding challenge (2017). https://www.kaggle.com/c/youtube8m
6. Hinton, G., Vinyals, O., Dean, J.: Distilling the knowledge in a neural network. In: NIPS 2014 Deep Learning Workshop (2014)
7. Jiang, Y.G., Wu, Z., Wang, J., Xue, X., Chang, S.F.: Exploiting feature and class relationships in video categorization with regularized deep neural networks. IEEE TPAMI **40**(2), 352–364 (2018)
8. Miech, A., Laptev, I., Sivic, J.: https://github.com/antoine77340/loupe
9. Miech, A., Laptev, I., Sivic, J.: Learnable pooling with context gating for video classification. In: Computer Vision and Pattern Recognition (CVPR) Youtube-8M Workshop (2017)
10. Rabinovich, A., Vedaldi, A., Galleguillos, C., Wiewiora, E., Belongie, S.: Objects in context. In: IEEE ICCV (2007)

W23 – 2nd International Workshop on Compact and Efficient Feature Representation and Learning in Computer Vision

W23 – 2nd International Workshop on Compact and Efficient Feature Representation and Learning in Computer Vision

Welcome to the Proceedings for the 2nd International Workshop on Compact and Efficient Feature Representation and Learning in Computer Vision, held in conjunction with the European Conference on Computer Vision on September 9th 2018.

Feature representation is at the core of many computer vision problems. In the past two decades, we have witnessed remarkable progress in feature representation and learning, from hand-crafted features to deep learning based ones. Nowadays, featuring the exponentially increasing number of images and videos, the emerging phenomenon of high dimensionality renders the inadequacies of existing approaches. There is thus a pressing need for new scalable and efficient methods that can cope with this explosion of dimensionality. In addition, with the prevalence of social media networks and portable devices which have limited computational capabilities and storage space, the demand for sophisticated real-time applications in handling large-scale visual data is rising. Therefore, there is a growing need for feature descriptors that are fast to compute, memory efficient, and yet exhibiting good discriminability and robustness. This workshop aims to stimulate researchers to present high-quality work and to provide a cross-fertilization ground for stimulating discussions on the next steps in this important research area.

In total, we received 32 full-paper submissions, each of which was sent to at least two independent reviewers in the related area. Based on the reviewers' suggestions, 19 papers were accepted to the workshop, eight of which were accepted as oral presentations and the rest as poster presentations. We had three keynote speakers in our workshop, *i.e.* Prof. Shih-Fu Chang from Columbia University, Dr. Julien Mairal from Inria, and Dr. Boqing Gong from Tencent AI Lab. They delivered three insightful speeches, covering different research directions regarding our topic. The 2nd CEFRL workshop, for the first time, announced two Best Paper Awards, *i.e.* Best Paper and Best Paper Honorable Mention. We acknowledge the financial support from the Inception Institute of Artificial Intelligence.

We sincerely thank the authors, the invited speakers, and the program committee for the valuable involvement and the active attendance at our workshop. Their participation has made the 2nd CEFRL workshop a very successful event.

September 2018

Jie Qin
Li Liu
Li Liu
Fan Zhu
Matti Pietikäinen
Luc Van Gool

Multi-style Generative Network
for Real-Time Transfer

Hang Zhang[1,2]($\boxtimes$) and Kristin Dana[2]

[1] Amazon AI, East Palo Alto, USA
hzaws@amazon.com
[2] Rutgers University, New Brunswick, USA
kdana@ece.rutgers.edu

Abstract. Despite the rapid progress in style transfer, existing approaches using feed-forward generative network for multi-style or arbitrary-style transfer are usually compromised of image quality and model flexibility. We find it is fundamentally difficult to achieve comprehensive style modeling using 1-dimensional style embedding. Motivated by this, we introduce CoMatch Layer that learns to match the second order feature statistics with the target styles. With the CoMatch Layer, we build a Multi-style Generative Network (MSG-Net), which achieves real-time performance. In addition, we employ an specific strategy of upsampled convolution which avoids checkerboard artifacts caused by fractionally-strided convolution. Our method has achieved superior image quality comparing to state-of-the-art approaches. The proposed MSG-Net as a general approach for real-time style transfer is compatible with most existing techniques including content-style interpolation, color-preserving, spatial control and brush stroke size control. MSG-Net is the first to achieve real-time brush-size control in a purely feed-forward manner for style transfer. Our implementations and pre-trained models for Torch, PyTorch and MXNet frameworks will be publicly available (Links can be found at http://hangzhang.org/).

1 Introduction

Style transfer can be approached as reconstructing or synthesizing texture based on the target image semantic content [1]. Many pioneering works have achieved success in classic texture synthesis starting with methods that resample pixels [2–5] or match multi-scale feature statistics [6–8]. These methods employ traditional image pyramids obtained by handcrafted multi-scale linear filter banks [9,10] and perform texture synthesis by matching the feature statistics to the target style. In recent years, the concepts of texture synthesis and style transfer have been revisited within the context of deep learning. Gatys *et al.* [11] shows that using

---

Electronic supplementary material The online version of this chapter (https://doi.org/10.1007/978-3-030-11018-5_32) contains supplementary material, which is available to authorized users.

L. Leal-Taixé and S. Roth (Eds.): ECCV 2018 Workshops, LNCS 11132, pp. 349–365, 2019.
https://doi.org/10.1007/978-3-030-11018-5_32

Fig. 1. Examples of transferred images and the corresponding styles using the proposed MSG-Net.

feature correlations (*i.e.* Gram Matrix) of convolutional neural nets (CNN) successfully captures the image styles. This framework has brought a surge of interest in texture synthesis and style transfer using iterative optimization [1,11,12] or training feed-forward networks [13–16]. Recent work extends style flexibility using feed-forward networks and achieves multistyle or arbitrary style transfer [17–20]. These approaches typically encode image styles into 1-dimensional space, *i.e.* tuning the featuremap mean and variance (bias and scale) for different styles. However, the comprehensive appearance of image style is fundamentally difficult to represent in 1D embedding space. Figure 3 shows style transfer results using the optimization-based approach [12] and we can see Gram matrix representation produces more appealing image quality comparing to mean and variance of CNN featuremap.

In addition to the image quality, concerns about the flexibility of current feed-forward generative models have been raised in Jing *et al.* [21], and they point out that no generative methods can adjust the brush stroke size in real-time. Feeding the generative network with high-resolution content image usually results in unsatisfying images as shown in Fig. 6. The generative network as a fully convolutional network (FCN) can accept arbitrary input image sizes. Resizing the style image changes the relative brush size and the multistyle generative network matching the image style at run-time should naturally enable brush-size control by changing the input style image size. *What limits the current generative model from being aware of the brush size?* The 1D style embedding (featuremap mean and variance) fundamentally limits the potential of exploring finer behavior for style representations. Therefore, a 2D method is desired for finer representation of image styles.

As the **first contribution** of the paper, we introduce an *CoMatch Layer* which embeds style with a 2D representation and learns to match the second-order feature statistics (Gram Matrix) of the style targets inherently during the training. The CoMatch Layer is differentiable and end-to-end learnable

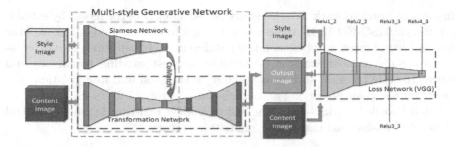

Fig. 2. An overview of MSG-Net, Multi-style Generative Network. The transformation network explicitly matches the features statistics of the style targets captured by a Siamese network using the proposed CoMatch Layer (introduced in Sect. 3). A pretrained loss network provides the supervision of MSG-Net learning by minimizing the content and style differences with the targets as discussed in Sect. 4.2.

| (a) Input | (b) Mean & Var | (c) Gram Matrix |

Fig. 3. Comparing 1D and 2D style representation using an optimization-based approach [12]. (a) Input image and style. (b) Style transfer result minimizing difference of CNN featuremap mean and variance. (c) Style transfer result minimizing the difference in Gram matrix representation.

with existing generative network architectures without additional supervision. The proposed CoMatch Layer enables multi-style generation from a single feed-forward network (Fig. 2).

The **second contribution** of this paper is building *Multi-style Generative Network (MSG-Net)* with the proposed CoMatch Layer and a novel *Upsample Convolution*. The MSG-Net as a feed-forward network runs in real-time after training. Generative networks typically have a decoder part recovering the image details from downsampled representations. Learning fractionally-strided convolution [22] typically brings checkerboard artifacts. For improving the image quality, we employ a strategy we call *upsampled convolution*, which successfully avoids the checkerboard artifacts by applying an integer stride convolution and outputs an upsampled featuremap (details in Sect. 4.1). In addition, we extend the Bottleneck architecture [23] to an *Upsampling Residual Block*, which reduces computational complexity without losing style versatility by preserving larger number of channels. Passing identity all the way through the generative network enables the network to extend deeper and converge faster. The experimental results show that MSG-Net has achieved superior image fidelity and test speed compared to previous work. We also study the scalability of the model by extending 100-style MSG-Net to 1K styles using a larger model size and longer training time, and we observe no obvious quality differences. In addition, MSG-Net as a general multi-style strategy is compatible to most existing techniques and progress in style transfer, such as content style trade-off and interpolation [17], spatial control, color preserving and brush-size control [24,25].

To our knowledge, MSG-Net is the first to achieve real-time brush-size control in a purely feed-forward manner for multistyle transfer.

1.1 Related Work

Relation to Pyramid Matching. Early methods for texture synthesis were developed using multi-scale image pyramids [4,6–8]. The discovery in these earlier methods was that realistic texture images could be synthesized from manipulating a white noise image so that its feature statistics were matched with the target at each pyramid level. Our approach is inspired by classic methods, which match feature statistics within the feed-forward network, but it leverages the advantages of deep learning networks while placing the computational costs into the training process (feed-forward vs. optimization-based).

Relation to Fusion Layers. Our proposed CoMatch Layer is a kind of fusion layer that takes two inputs (content and style representations). Current work in fusion layers with CNNs include feature map concatenation and element-wise sum [26–28]. However, these approaches are not directly applicable, since there is no separation of style from content. For style transfer, the generated images should not carry semantic information of the style target nor styles of the content image.

Relation to Generative Adversarial Training. The Generative Adversarial Network (GAN) [29], which jointly trains an adversarial generator and discriminator simultaneously, has catalyzed a surge of interest in the study of image generation [26,27,30–39]. Recent work on image-to-image GAN [26] adopts a conditional GAN to provide a general solution for some image-to-image generation problems. For those problems, it was previously hard to define a loss function. However, the style transfer problem cannot be tackled using the conditional GAN framework, due to missing ground-truth image pairs. Instead, we follow the work [13,14] to adopt a discriminator/loss network that minimizes the perceptual difference of synthesized images with content and style targets and provides the supervision of the generative network learning. The initial idea of employing Gram Matrix to trigger style synthesis is inspired by a recent work [30] that suggests using an encoder instead of random vector in GAN framework.

Recent Work in Multiple or Arbitrary Style Transfer. Recent/concurrent work explores multiple or arbitrary style transfer [17,18,20]. A style swap layer is proposed in [20], but gets lower quality and slower speed (compared to existing feed-forward approaches). An adaptive instance normalization is introduced

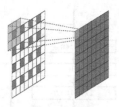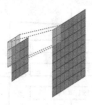

Fig. 4. Left: fractionally-strided convolution. Right: Upsampled convolution, which reduces the checkerboard artifacts by applying an integer stride convolution and outputting an upsampled featuremaps.

in [18] to match the mean and variance of the feature maps with the style target. Instead, our CoMatch Layer matches the second order statistics of Gram Matrices for the feature maps. We also explore the scalability of our approach in the Experiment Sect. 5.

2 Content and Style Representation

CNNs pre-trained on a very large dataset such as ImageNet can be regarded as descriptive representations of image statistics containing both semantic content and style information. Gatys *et al.* [12] provides explicit representations that independently model the image content and style from CNNs, which we briefly describe in this section for completeness.

The semantic content of the image can be represented as the activations of the descriptive network at i-th scale $\mathcal{F}^i(x) \in \mathbb{R}^{C_i \times H_i \times W_i}$ with a given the input image x, where the C_i, H_i and W_i are the number of feature map channels, feature map height and width. The texture or style of the image can be represented as the distribution of the features using Gram Matrix $\mathcal{G}(\mathcal{F}^i(x)) \in \mathbb{R}^{C_i \times C_i}$ given by

$$\mathcal{G}\left(\mathcal{F}^i(x)\right) = \sum_{h=1}^{H_i} \sum_{w=1}^{W_i} \mathcal{F}^i_{h,w}(x) \mathcal{F}^i_{h,w}(x)^T. \tag{1}$$

The Gram Matrix is orderless and describes the feature distributions. For zero-centered data, the Gram Matrix is the same as the covariance matrix scaled by the number of elements $C_i \times H_i \times W_i$. It can be calculated efficiently by first reshaping the feature map $\Phi\left(\mathcal{F}^i(x)\right) \in \mathbb{R}^{C_i \times (H_i W_i)}$, where $\Phi()$ is a reshaping operation. Then the Gram Matrix can be written as $\mathcal{G}\left(\mathcal{F}^i(x)\right) = \Phi\left(\mathcal{F}^i(x)\right) \Phi\left(\mathcal{F}^i(x)\right)^T$.

3 CoMatch Layer

In this section, we introduce *CoMatch Layer*, which explicitly matches second order feature statistics based on the given styles. For a given content target x_c and a style target x_s, the content and style representations at the i-th scale using

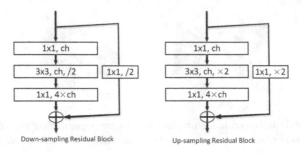

Fig. 5. We extend the original down-sampling residual architecture (left) to an up-sampling version (right). We use a 1×1 fractionally-strided convolution as a shortcut and adopt reflectance padding.

(a) input   (b) MSG-Net (ours)   (c) baseline

Fig. 6. Comparing Brush-size control. (a) High-resolution input image and dense styles. (b) Style transfer results using MSG-Net with brush-size control. (c) Standard generative network [14] without brush-size control. See also Fig. 8

the descriptive network can be written as $\mathcal{F}^i(x_c)$ and $\mathcal{G}(\mathcal{F}^i(x_s))$, respectively. A direct solution $\hat{\mathcal{Y}}^i$ is desirable which preserves the semantic content of input image and matches the target style feature statistics:

$$
\hat{\mathcal{Y}}^i = \underset{\mathcal{Y}^i}{\mathrm{argmin}} \{ \|\mathcal{Y}^i - \mathcal{F}^i(x_c)\|_F^2 \\
+ \alpha \|\mathcal{G}(\mathcal{Y}^i) - \mathcal{G}\left(\mathcal{F}^i(x_s)\right)\|_F^2 \}.
\tag{2}
$$

where α is a trade-off parameter that balancing the contribution of the content and style targets.

The minimization of the above problem is solvable by using an iterative approach, but it is infeasible to achieve it in real-time or make the model differentiable. However, we can still approximate the solution and put the computational burden to the training stage. We introduce an approximation which tunes the feature map based on the target style:

$$\hat{y}^i = \Phi^{-1} \left[\Phi\left(\mathcal{F}^i(x_c)\right)^T W \mathcal{G}\left(\mathcal{F}^i(x_s)\right) \right]^T, \tag{3}$$

where $W \in \mathbb{R}^{C_i \times C_i}$ is a learnable weight matrix and $\Phi()$ is a reshaping operation to match the dimension, so that $\Phi\left(\mathcal{F}^i(x_c)\right) \in \mathbb{R}^{C_i \times (H_i W_i)}$. For intuition on the functionality of W, suppose $W = \mathcal{G}\left(\mathcal{F}^i(x_s)\right)^{-1}$, then the first term in Eq. 2 (content term) is minimized. Now let $W = \Phi\left(\mathcal{F}^i(x_c)\right)^{-T} \mathcal{L}(\mathcal{F}^i(x_s))^{-1}$, where $\mathcal{L}\left(\mathcal{F}^i(x_s)\right)$ is obtained by the Cholesky Decomposition of $\mathcal{G}\left(\mathcal{F}^i(x_s)\right) = \mathcal{L}\left(\mathcal{F}^i(x_s)\right)\mathcal{L}\left(\mathcal{F}^i(x_s)\right)^T$, then the second term of Eq. 2 (style term) is minimized. We let W be learned directly from the loss function to dynamically balance the trade-off. The CoMatch Layer is differentiable and can be inserted in the existing generative network and directly learned from the loss function without any additional supervision.

4 Multi-style Generative Network

4.1 Network Architecture

Prior feed-forward based single-style transfer work learns a generator network that takes only the content image as the input and outputs the transferred image, i.e. the generator network can be expressed as $G(x_c)$, which implicitly learns the feature statistics of the style image from the loss function. We introduce a *Multi-style Generative Network* which takes both content and style target as inputs. i.e. $G(x_c, x_s)$. The proposed network explicitly matches the feature statistics of the style targets at runtime.

As part of the Generator Network, we adopt a Siamese network sharing weights with the encoder part of transformation network, which captures the feature statistics of the style image x_s at different scales, and outputs the Gram Matrices $\{\mathcal{G}(\mathcal{F}^i(x_s))\}(i = 1, ...K)$ where K is the total number of scales. Then a transformation network takes the content image x_c and matches the feature statistics of the style image at multiple scales with CoMatch Layers.

Upsampled Convolution. Standard CNN for image-to-image tasks typically adopts an encoder-decoder framework, because it is efficient to put heavy operations (style switching) in smaller featuremaps and also important to keep a larger receptive field for preserving semantic coherence. The decoder part learns a fractionally-strided convolution to recover the detail information from downsampled featuremaps. However, the fractionally strided convolution [22] typically introduces checkerboard artifacts [40]. Prior work suggests using upsampling followed by convolution to replace the standard fractionally-strided convolution [40]. However, this strategy will decrease the receptive field and it is inefficient to apply convolution on an upsampled area. For this, we use *upsampled*

Fig. 7. Content and style trade-off and interpolation.

convolution, which has an integer stride, and outputs upsampled featuremaps. For an upsampling factor of 2, the upsampled convolution will produce a 2×2 outputs for each convolutional window as visualized in Fig. 4. Comparing to fractionally-strided convolution, this method has the same computation complexity and 4 times parameters. This strategy successfully avoid upsampling artifacts in the network decoder.

Upsample Residual Block. Deep residual learning has achieved great success in visual recognition [23,41]. Residual block architecture plays an important role by reducing the computational complexity without losing diversity by preserving the large number of feature map channels. We extend the original architecture with an upsampling version as shown in Fig. 5 (right), which has a fractionally-strided convolution [22] as the shortcut and adopts reflectance padding to avoid artifacts of the generative process. This upsampling residual architecture allows us to pass identity all the way through the network, so that the network converges faster and extends deeper.

Fig. 8. Brush-size control using MSG-Net. Top left: High-resolution input image and dense style. Others: Style transfer results using MSG-Net with brush-size control.

Brush Stroke Size Control. Feeding the generative model with high-resolution image usually results in unsatisfying style transfer outputs, as shown in Fig. 6(c). Controlling brush stroke size can be achieved using optimization-based approach [25]. Resizing the style image changes the brush-size, and feed-forward generative model matches the feature statistics at runtime should naturally achieve brush stoke size control. However, prior work is mainly limited by the 1D style embedding, because this finer style behavior cannot be captured using merely featuremap mean and variance. With MSG-Net, the CoMatch Layer matching the second order statistics elegantly solves the brush-size control. During training, we train the network with different style image sizes to learn from different brush stroke sizes. After training, the brush stroke size can be an option to the user by changing style input image size. Note that the MSG-Net can accept different input sizes for style and content images. Example results are shown in Fig. 8.

Other Details. We only use in-network down-sample (convolutional) and up-sample (upsampled convolution) in the transformation network. We use reflectance padding to avoid artifacts at the border. Instance normalization [16] and ReLU are used after weight layers (convolution, fractionally-strided convolution and the CoMatch Layer), which improves the generated image quality and is robust to the image contrast changes.

4.2 Network Learning

Style transfer is an open problem, since there is no gold-standard ground-truth to follow. We follow previous work to minimize a weighted combination of the style and content differences of the generator network outputs and the targets for a given pre-trained loss network $\mathcal{F}$ [13,14]. Let the generator network be

| input | Dumoulin *et al.* [17] | MSG-Net (ours) | Gatys *et al.* [12] | Huang *et al.* [18] | Chen & Schmidt [20] |

Fig. 9. The tradeoff between style-flexibility and output-image quality is challenging for generative models. Our approach enables multi-style transfer and has minimal difference in quality compared to the optimization-based Gatys approach [12].

denoted by $G(x_c, x_s)$ parameterized by weights W_G. Learning proceeds by sampling content images $x_c \sim X_c$ and style images $x_s \sim X_s$ and then adjusting the parameters W_G of the generator $G(x_c, x_s)$ in order to minimize the loss:

$$
\begin{aligned}
\hat{W}_G = \operatorname*{argmin}_{W_G} E_{x_c, x_s} \{ & \\
\lambda_c \| \mathcal{F}^c \left(G(x_c, x_s) \right) - \mathcal{F}^c(x_c) \|_F^2 & \\
+ \lambda_s \sum_{i=1}^{K} \| \mathcal{G} \left(\mathcal{F}^i(G(x_c, x_s)) \right) - \mathcal{G}(\mathcal{F}^i(x_s)) \|_F^2 & \\
+ \lambda_{TV} \ell_{TV} \left(G(x_c, x_s) \right) \}, &
\end{aligned}
\tag{4}
$$

where λ_c and λ_s are the balancing weights for content and style losses. We consider image content at scale c and image style at scales $i \in \{1, ..K\}$. $\ell_{TV}()$ is the total variation regularization as used prior work for encouraging the smoothness of the generated images [14,42,43].

Table 1. Comparing model size on disk and inference/test speed fps (frames/sec) of images with the size of 256×256 and 512×512 on a NVIDIA Titan Xp GPU average over 50 samples. MSG-Net-100 and MSG-Net-1K have 2.3M and 8.9M parameters respectively.

	Model-size	Speed (256)	Speed (512)
Gatys et al. [12]	N/A	0.07	0.02
Johnson et al. [14]	6.7 MB	91.7	26.3
Dumoulin et al. [17]	6.8 MB	88.3	24.7
Chen et al. [20]	574 MB	5.84	0.31
Huang et al. [18]	28.1 MB	37.0	10.2
MSG-Net-100 (ours)	9.6 MB	92.7	29.2
MSG-Net-1K (ours)	40.3 MB	47.2	14.3

5   Experimental Results

5.1   Style Transfer

Baselines. We use the implementation of the work of Gatys et al. [12] as a gold standard baseline for style transfer approach (technical details will be included in the supplementary material). We also compare our approach with state-of-the-art multistyle or arbitrary style transfer methods, including patch-based approach [20] and 1D style embedding [17,18]. The implementations from original authors are used in this experiments.

Method Details. We adapt 16-layer VGG network [44] pre-trained on ImageNet as the loss network in Eq. 4, because the network features learned from a diverse set of images are likely to be generic and informative. We consider the style representation at 4 different scales using the layers ReLU1_2, ReLU2_2, ReLU3_3 and ReLU4_3, and use the content representation at the layer ReLU2_2. The Microsoft COCO dataset [45] is used as the content image image set X_c, which has around 80,000 natural images. We collect 100 style images, choosing from previous work in style transfer. Additionally 900 real paintings are selected from the open-source artistic dataset wikiart.org [46] as additional style images for training MSG-Net-1K. We follow the work [13,14] and adopt Adam [47] to train the network with a learning rate of 1×10^{-3}. We use the loss function as described in Eq. 4 with the balancing weights $\lambda_c = 1, \lambda_s = 5, \lambda_{TV} = 1 \times 10^{-6}$ for content, style and total regularization. We resize the content images $x_c \sim X_c$ to 256×256 and learn the network with a batch size of 4 for 80,000 iterations. We iteratively update the style image x_s every iteration with size from $\{256, 512, 768\}$ for runtime brush-size control. After training, the MSG-Net as a fully convolutional network [22] can accept arbitrary input image size. For comparing the style transfer approaches, we use the same content image size, by resizing the image to 512 along the long side. Our implementations are based on Torch [48], PyTorch [49] and MXNet [50]. It takes roughly 8 h for training MSG-Net-100 model on a Titan Xp GPU.

Fig. 10. Color control using MSG-Net, (left) content and style images, (right) color-preserved transfer result. (Color figure online)

Fig. 11. Spatial control using MSG-Net. Left: input image, middle: foreground and background styles, right: style transfer result. (Input image and segmentation mask from Shen *et al.* [51,52].)

Model Size and Speed Analysis. For mobile applications or cloud services, the model size and test speed are crucial. We compare the model size and inference/test speed of style transfer approaches in Table 1. Our proposed MSG-Net-100 has a comparable model size and speed with single style network [13,14]. The MSG-Net is faster than Arbitrary Style Transfer work [18], because of using a learned compact encoder instead of pre-trained VGG network.

Qualitative Comparison. Our proposed MSG-Net achieves superior performance comparing to state-of-the-art generative network approaches as shown in Fig. 9. One may argue that the arbitrary style work has better scalability/capacity [18,20]. The style flexibility and image quality are always hard trade-off for generative model, and we particularly focus on the image quality in this work. More examples of the transfered images using MSG-Net are shown in Fig. 12.

Model Scalability. Prior work using 1D style embedding has achieved success in the scalability of style transfer towards the goal of arbitrary style transfer [18].

Fig. 12. Diverse images that are generated using a single MSG-Net-100 (2.3M parameters). First row shows the input content images and the other rows are generated images with different style targets (first column).

To test the scalability of MSG-Net, we augment the style set to 1K images, by adding 900 extra images from the wikiart.org [46]. We also build a larger model MSG-Net-1K with larger model capacity by increasing the width/channels of the model at mid stage (64×64) by a factor of 2, resulting in 8.9M parameters. We also increase the training iterations by 4 times (320K) and follow the same training procedure as MSG-Net-100. We observe no quality degradation when increasing the number of styles (examples shown in the supplementary material).

5.2   Runtime Manipulation

MSG-Net as a general approach for real-time style transfer is compatible with existing recent progress for both feed-forward and optimization methods, including but not limited to: content-style trade-off and interpolation (Fig. 7), color-preserving transfer (Fig. 10), spatial manipulation (Fig. 11) and brush stroke size control (Figs. 6 and 8). For style interpolation, we use an affine interpolation of our style embedding following the prior work [17,18]. For color pre-serving, we match the color of style image with the content image as Gatys et. al. [24]. Brush-size control has been discussed in the Sect. 4.1. We use the segmentation mask provided by Shen et al. [51] for spatial control. The source code and technical detail of runtime manipulation will be included in our PyTorch implementation.

6   Conclusion and Discussion

To improve the quality and flexibility of generative models in style transfer, we introduce a novel CoMatch Layer that learns to match the second order statistics as image style representation. Multi-style Generative Network has achieved superior image quality comparing to state-of-the-art approaches. In addition, the proposed MSG-Net is compatible with most existing techniques and recent progress of stye transfer including style interpolation, color-preserving and spatial control. Moreover, MSG-Net first enables real-time brush-size control in a fully feed-forward manor. The compact MSG-Net-100 model has only 2.3M parameters and runs at more than 90 fps (frame/sec) on NVIDIA Titan Xp for the input image of size 256×256 and at 15 fps on a laptop GPU (GTX 750M-2GB).

References

1. Li, C., Wand, M.: Combining Markov random fields and convolutional neural networks for image synthesis. In: The IEEE Conference on Computer Vision and Pattern Recognition (CVPR), June 2016
2. Efros, A.A., Leung, T.K.: Texture synthesis by non-parametric sampling. In: The Proceedings of the Seventh IEEE International Conference on Computer Vision, vol. 2, pp. 1033–1038. IEEE (1999)
3. Efros, A.A., Freeman, W.T.: Image quilting for texture synthesis and transfer. In: Proceedings of the 28th Annual Conference on Computer Graphics and Interactive Techniques, pp. 341–346. ACM (2001)
4. Wei, L.Y., Levoy, M.: Fast texture synthesis using tree-structured vector quantization. In: Proceedings of the 27th Annual Conference on Computer Graphics and Interactive Techniques, pp. 479–488. ACM Press/Addison-Wesley Publishing Co. (2000)

5. Kwatra, V., Schödl, A., Essa, I., Turk, G., Bobick, A.: Graphcut textures: image and video synthesis using graph cuts. ACM Trans. Graph. (ToG) **22**, 277–286 (2003)
6. De Bonet, J.S.: Multiresolution sampling procedure for analysis and synthesis of texture images. In: Proceedings of the 24th Annual Conference on Computer Graphics and Interactive Techniques, pp. 361–368. ACM Press/Addison-Wesley Publishing Co. (1997)
7. Heeger, D.J., Bergen, J.R.: Pyramid-based texture analysis/synthesis. In: Proceedings of the 22nd Annual Conference on Computer Graphics and Interactive Techniques, pp. 229–238. ACM (1995)
8. Portilla, J., Simoncelli, E.P.: A parametric texture model based on joint statistics of complex wavelet coefficients. Int. J. Comput. Vis. **40**(1), 49–70 (2000)
9. Simoncelli, E.P., Freeman, W.T.: The steerable pyramid: a flexible architecture for multi-scale derivative computation. In: Proceedings of the International Conference on Image Processing, vol. 3, pp. 444–447. IEEE (1995)
10. Burt, P., Adelson, E.: The laplacian pyramid as a compact image code. IEEE Trans. Commun. **31**(4), 532–540 (1983)
11. Gatys, L., Ecker, A.S., Bethge, M.: Texture synthesis using convolutional neural networks. In: Advances in Neural Information Processing Systems, pp. 262–270 (2015)
12. Gatys, L.A., Ecker, A.S., Bethge, M.: Image style transfer using convolutional neural networks. In: Proceedings of the IEEE Conference on Computer Vision and Pattern Recognition, pp. 2414–2423 (2016)
13. Ulyanov, D., Lebedev, V., Vedaldi, A., Lempitsky, V.: Texture networks: feed-forward synthesis of textures and stylized images. In: International Conference on Machine Learning (ICML) (2016)
14. Johnson, J., Alahi, A., Fei-Fei, L.: Perceptual losses for real-time style transfer and super-resolution. In: Leibe, B., Matas, J., Sebe, N., Welling, M. (eds.) ECCV 2016, Part II. LNCS, vol. 9906, pp. 694–711. Springer, Cham (2016). https://doi.org/10.1007/978-3-319-46475-6_43
15. Li, C., Wand, M.: Precomputed real-time texture synthesis with Markovian generative adversarial networks. In: Leibe, B., Matas, J., Sebe, N., Welling, M. (eds.) ECCV 2016, Part III. LNCS, vol. 9907, pp. 702–716. Springer, Cham (2016). https://doi.org/10.1007/978-3-319-46487-9_43
16. Ulyanov, D., Vedaldi, A., Lempitsky, V.: Improved texture networks: maximizing quality and diversity in feed-forward stylization and texture synthesis (2017). arXiv preprint: arXiv:1701.02096
17. Dumoulin, V., Shlens, J., Kudlur, M.: A learned representation for artistic style (2016)
18. Huang, X., Belongie, S.: Arbitrary style transfer in real-time with adaptive instance normalization (2017). arXiv preprint: arXiv:1703.06868
19. Chen, D., Yuan, L., Liao, J., Yu, N., Hua, G.: Stylebank: an explicit representation for neural image style transfer. In: IEEE Conference on Computer Vision and Pattern Recognition (CVPR) (2017)
20. Chen, T.Q., Schmidt, M.: Fast patch-based style transfer of arbitrary style (2016). arXiv preprint: arXiv:1612.04337
21. Jing, Y., Yang, Y., Feng, Z., Ye, J., Song, M.: Neural style transfer: A review (2017). arXiv preprint: arXiv:1705.04058
22. Long, J., Shelhamer, E., Darrell, T.: Fully convolutional networks for semantic segmentation. In: Proceedings of the IEEE Conference on Computer Vision and Pattern Recognition, pp. 3431–3440 (2015)

23. He, K., Zhang, X., Ren, S., Sun, J.: Deep residual learning for image recognition. In: Proceedings of the IEEE Conference on Computer Vision and Pattern Recognition, pp. 770–778 (2016)
24. Gatys, L.A., Bethge, M., Hertzmann, A., Shechtman, E.: Preserving color in neural artistic style transfer (2016). arXiv preprint: arXiv:1606.05897
25. Gatys, L.A., Ecker, A.S., Bethge, M., Hertzmann, A., Shechtman, E.: Controlling perceptual factors in neural style transfer (2016). arXiv preprint: arXiv:1611.07865
26. Isola, P., Zhu, J.Y., Zhou, T., Efros, A.A.: Image-to-image translation with conditional adversarial networks (2016). arXiv preprint: arXiv:1611.07004
27. Zhang, H., et al.: StackGAN: Text to photo-realistic image synthesis with stacked generative adversarial networks (2016). arXiv preprint: arXiv:1612.03242
28. Feichtenhofer, C., Pinz, A., Zisserman, A.: Convolutional two-stream network fusion for video action recognition. In: Proceedings of the IEEE Conference on Computer Vision and Pattern Recognition, pp. 1933–1941 (2016)
29. Goodfellow, I., et al.: Generative adversarial nets. In: Advances in Neural Information Processing Systems, pp. 2672–2680 (2014)
30. Che, T., Li, Y., Jacob, A.P., Bengio, Y., Li, W.: Mode regularized generative adversarial networks (2016). arXiv preprint: arXiv:1612.02136
31. Radford, A., Metz, L., Chintala, S.: Unsupervised representation learning with deep convolutional generative adversarial networks (2015). arXiv preprint: arXiv:1511.06434
32. Huang, X., Li, Y., Poursaeed, O., Hopcroft, J., Belongie, S.: Stacked generative adversarial networks. arXiv (2016)
33. Sindagi, V.A., Patel, V.M.: Generating high-quality crowd density maps using contextual pyramid CNNs. In: 2017 IEEE International Conference on Computer Vision (ICCV). IEEE (2017)
34. Zhang, H., Sindagi, V., Patel, V.M.: Image de-raining using a conditional generative adversarial network (2017). arXiv preprint: arXiv:1701.05957
35. Xian, W., Sangkloy, P., Lu, J., Fang, C., Yu, F., Hays, J.: TextureGAN: Controlling deep image synthesis with texture patches. arXiv preprint (2018)
36. Zhang, Z., Xie, Y., Yang, L.: Photographic text-to-image synthesis with a hierarchically-nested adversarial network. In: The IEEE Conference on Computer Vision and Pattern Recognition (CVPR) (2018)
37. Zhang, H., Patel, V.M.: Density-aware single image de-raining using a multi-stream dense network (2018). arXiv preprint: arXiv:1802.07412
38. Zhang, H., Patel, V.M.: Densely connected pyramid dehazing network. In: The IEEE Conference on Computer Vision and Pattern Recognition (CVPR) (2018)
39. Xu, T., et al.: AttnGAN: Fine-grained text to image generation with attentional generative adversarial networks. arXiv preprint (2017)
40. Odena, A., Dumoulin, V., Olah, C.: Deconvolution and checkerboard artifacts. Distill (2016)
41. He, K., Zhang, X., Ren, S., Sun, J.: Identity mappings in deep residual networks. In: Leibe, B., Matas, J., Sebe, N., Welling, M. (eds.) ECCV 2016, Part IV. LNCS, vol. 9908, pp. 630–645. Springer, Cham (2016). https://doi.org/10.1007/978-3-319-46493-0_38
42. Mahendran, A., Vedaldi, A.: Understanding deep image representations by inverting them. In: Proceedings of the IEEE Conference on Computer Vision and Pattern Recognition, pp. 5188–5196 (2015)

43. Zhang, H., Yang, J., Zhang, Y., Huang, T.S.: Non-local kernel regression for image and video restoration. In: Daniilidis, K., Maragos, P., Paragios, N. (eds.) ECCV 2010, Part III. LNCS, vol. 6313, pp. 566–579. Springer, Heidelberg (2010). https://doi.org/10.1007/978-3-642-15558-1_41

44. Simonyan, K., Zisserman, A.: Very deep convolutional networks for large-scale image recognition (2014). arXiv preprint: arXiv:1409.1556

45. Lin, T.-Y., et al.: Microsoft COCO: common objects in context. In: Fleet, D., Pajdla, T., Schiele, B., Tuytelaars, T. (eds.) ECCV 2014, Part V. LNCS, vol. 8693, pp. 740–755. Springer, Cham (2014). https://doi.org/10.1007/978-3-319-10602-1_48

46. Duck, S.Y.: Painter by numbers (2016). https://www.kaggle.com/c/painter-by-numbers

47. Kingma, D., Ba, J.: Adam: A method for stochastic optimization (2014). arXiv preprint: arXiv:1412.6980

48. Collobert, R., Kavukcuoglu, K., Farabet, C.: Torch7: a matlab-like environment for machine learning. In: BigLearn, NIPS Workshop, Number EPFL-CONF-192376 (2011)

49. Paszke, A., et al.: Automatic differentiation in PyTorch (2017)

50. Chen, T., et al.: MXNet: A flexible and efficient machine learning library for heterogeneous distributed systems (2015). arXiv preprint: arXiv:1512.01274

51. Shen, X., et al.: Automatic portrait segmentation for image stylization. In: Computer Graphics Forum, vol. 35, pp. 93–102. Wiley Online Library (2016)

52. Zhang, H., et al.: Context encoding for semantic segmentation. In: The IEEE Conference on Computer Vision and Pattern Recognition (CVPR), June 2018

Frustratingly Easy Trade-off Optimization Between Single-Stage and Two-Stage Deep Object Detectors

Petru Soviany[1] and Radu Tudor Ionescu[1,2(✉)]

[1] University of Bucharest, 14 Academiei, Bucharest, Romania
petru.soviany@yahoo.com, raducu.ionescu@gmail.com
[2] Inception Institute of Artificial Intelligence (IIAI), Abu Dhabi, UAE

Abstract. There are mainly two types of state-of-the-art object detectors. On one hand, we have two-stage detectors, such as Faster R-CNN (Region-based Convolutional Neural Networks) or Mask R-CNN, that (*i*) use a Region Proposal Network to generate regions of interests in the first stage and (*ii*) send the region proposals down the pipeline for object classification and bounding-box regression. Such models reach the highest accuracy rates, but are typically slower. On the other hand, we have single-stage detectors, such as YOLO (You Only Look Once) and SSD (Singe Shot MultiBox Detector), that treat object detection as a simple regression problem, by taking an input image and learning the class probabilities and bounding box coordinates. Such models reach lower accuracy rates, but are much faster than two-stage object detectors. In this paper, we propose and evaluate four simple and straightforward approaches to achieve an optimal trade-off between accuracy and speed in object detection. All the approaches are based on separating the test images in two batches, an *easy* batch that is fed to a faster single-stage detector and a *difficult* batch that is fed to a more accurate two-stage detector. The difference between the four approaches is the criterion used for splitting the images in two batches. The criteria are the image difficulty score (easier images go into the easy batch), the number of detected objects (images with less objects go into the easy batch), the average size of the detected objects (images with bigger objects go into the easy batch), and the number of detected objects divided by their average size (images with less and bigger objects go into the easy batch). The first approach is based on an image difficulty predictor, while the other three approaches employ a faster single-stage detector to determine the approximate number of objects and their sizes. Our experiments on PASCAL VOC 2007 show that using image difficulty compares favorably to a random split of the images. However, splitting the images based on the number objects divided by their size, an approach that is frustratingly easy to implement, produces even better results. Remarkably, it shortens the processing time nearly by half, while reducing the mean Average Precision of Faster R-CNN by only 0.5%.

Keywords: Object detection · Deep neural networks
Single-shot multibox detector · Faster R-CNN

© Springer Nature Switzerland AG 2019
L. Leal-Taixé and S. Roth (Eds.): ECCV 2018 Workshops, LNCS 11132, pp. 366–378, 2019.
https://doi.org/10.1007/978-3-030-11018-5_33

1   Introduction

Object detection, the task of predicting the location of an object along with its class in an image, is perhaps one of the most important problems in computer vision. Nowadays, there are mainly two types of state-of-the-art object detectors. On one hand, we have two-stage detectors, such as Faster R-CNN (Region-based Convolutional Neural Networks) [17] or Mask R-CNN [10], that (*i*) use a Region Proposal Network (RPN) to generate regions of interests in the first stage and (*ii*) send the region proposals down the pipeline for object classification and bounding-box regression. Such models reach the highest accuracy rates, but are typically slower. On the other hand, we have single-stage detectors, such as YOLO (You Only Look Once) [16] and SSD (Singe Shot MultiBox Detector) [15], that treat object detection as a simple regression problem in which class probabilities and bounding box coordinates are learned directly from the input images. Such models reach lower accuracy rates, but are much faster than two-stage object detectors. In this context, finding a model that provides the optimal trade-off between accuracy and speed does not seem to be a straightforward task, at first hand. Based on the principles of curriculum learning [1], we hypothesize that using more complex (two-stage) object detectors for *difficult* images and less complex (single-stage) detectors for *easy* images will provide an optimal trade-off between accuracy and speed, without ever having to change anything about the object detectors. The only problem that prevents us from testing our hypothesis in practice is finding an approach to classify the images into easy or hard. In order to be useful in practice, the approach also has to work fast enough, e.g. at least as fast as a single-stage detector. To this end, we propose and evaluate four simple and straightforward approaches to achieve an optimal trade-off between accuracy and speed in object detection. All the approaches are based on separating the test images in two batches, an *easy* batch that is fed to the faster single-stage detector and a *hard* (or *difficult*) batch that is fed to the more accurate two-stage detector. The difference between the four approaches is the criterion used for splitting the images in two batches. The first approach assigns a test image to the easy or the hard batch based on the image difficulty score, as also described in [20]. The difficulty score is estimated using a recent approach for image difficulty prediction introduced by Ionescu et al. [13]. The image difficulty predictor is obtained by training a deep neural network to regress on the difficulty scores produced by human annotators. The other three approaches used for splitting the test images (into easy or hard) employ a faster single-stage detector, namely MobileNet-SSD [11], in order estimate the number of objects and each of their sizes. The second and the third approaches independently consider the number of detected objects (images with less objects go into the easy batch) and the average size of the objects (images with bigger objects go into the easy batch), while the fourth approach is based on the number of objects divided by their average size (images with less and bigger objects go into the easy batch). If one of the latter three approaches classifies an image as easy, there is nothing left to do (we can use the detections provided by MobileNet-SSD), unless we want to use a different (slower, but more accurate) single-stage detector, e.g. SSD300 [15], for the easy images. Our experiments on PASCAL VOC 2007 [4] show that using image difficulty as a primary cue for splitting the test images compares favorably to a random split of the images. However, the other three approaches, which are frustratingly easy to implement, can produce even better results. Among the four proposed methods, the best results are obtained by splitting the images based on the number objects divided by their average size. This approach shortens the processing time nearly by half, while slightly reducing the mean Average Precision of Faster R-CNN from 0.7837 to no less than 0.7779. Moreover, all our methods are simple and have the advantage that they allow us to choose the desired trade-off on a continuous scale.

The rest of this paper is organized as follows. Recent related works on object detection are presented in Sect. 2. Our methodology is described in Sect. 3. The object detection experiments are presented in Sect. 4. Finally, we draw our conclusions in Sect. 5.

2   Related Work

Although there are quite a few models for the object detection task available in the recent literature [10,11,15–17], it is difficult to pick one as the best model in terms of both accuracy and speed. Some [10,17] are more accurate and require a higher computational time, while others [11,15,16] are much faster, but provide less accurate results. Hence, finding the optimal trade-off between accuracy and speed is not a trivial task. To our knowledge, the only work that studied the trade-off between accuracy and speed for deep object detection models is [12]. Huang et al. [12] have tested different configurations of deep object detection frameworks by changing various components and parameters in order to find optimal configurations for specific scenarios, e.g. deployment on mobile devices. Different from their approach, we treat the various object detection frameworks as black boxes. Instead of looking for certain configurations, we propose a framework that allows to set the trade-off between accuracy and speed on a continuous scale, by specifying the point of splitting the test images into easy versus hard, as desired. It is important to note that a different line of research is to build models for tasks such as object detection [22] or semantic segmentation [14], that offer an optimal trade-off between accuracy and speed.

In the rest of this section, we provide a brief description of the most recent object detectors, in chronological order. Faster R-CNN [17] is a very accurate region-based deep detection model which improves Fast R-CNN [8] by introducing the Region Proposal Networks (RPN). It uses a fully convolutional network that can predict object bounds at every location in order to solve the challenge of selecting the right regions. In the second stage, the regions proposed by the RPN are used as an input for the Fast R-CNN model, which will provide the final object detection results. On the other hand, SSD [15] is a single-shot detection method which uses a set of predefined boxes of different aspect ratios and scales in order to predict the presence of an object in a certain image. SSD does not include the traditional proposal generation and resampling stages, common for two-stage detectors such as Faster R-CNN, but it encapsulates all computations in a single network, thus being faster than the two-stage models. YOLO [16] is another fast model, which treats the detection task as a regression problem. It uses a single neural network to predict the bounding boxes and the corresponding classes, taking the full image as an input. The fact that it does not use sliding window or region proposal techniques provides more contextual information about classes. YOLO works by dividing each image into a fixed grid, and for each grid location, it predicts a number of bounding boxes and a confidence for each bounding box. The confidence reflects the accuracy of the bounding box and whether the bounding box actually contains an object (regardless of class). YOLO also predicts the classification score for each box for every class in training. MobileNets [11] are a set of lightweight models that can be used for classification, detection and segmentation tasks. Although their accuracy is not as high as that of the state-of-the-art very deep models, they have the great advantage of being very fast and low on computational requirements, thus being suitable for mobile devices. MobileNets are built on depth-wise separable convolutions with a total of 28 layers, and can be further parameterized in order to work even faster. Mask R-CNN [10] is yet another model used in image detection and segmentation tasks, which extends the Faster R-CNN architecture. If Faster R-CNN has only two outputs, the bounding boxes and the corresponding classes, Mask R-CNN also provides, in parallel, the segmentation masks. An important missing piece of the Faster R-CNN model is a pixel alignment method. To address this problem, He et al. [10] propose a new layer (RoIAlign) that can correct the misalignments between the regions of interest and the extracted features.

3 Methodology

Humans learn much better when the examples are not randomly presented, but organized in a meaningful order which gradually illustrates more complex concepts. This is essentially reflected in all the curricula taught in schooling systems around the world. Bengio et al. [1] have explored easy-to-hard strategies to train machine learning models, showing that machines can also benefit from learning by gradually adding more difficult examples. They introduced a general formulation of the easy-to-hard training strategies known as *curriculum learning*. However, we can hypothesize that an *easy-versus-hard* strategy can also be applied at test time in order to obtain an optimal trade-off between accuracy and processing speed. For example, if we have two types of machines (one that is simple and fast but less accurate, and one that is complex and slow but more accurate), we can devise a strategy in which the fast machine is fed with the easy test samples and the complex machine is fed with the difficult test samples. This kind of strategy will work as desired especially when the fast machine can reach an accuracy level that is close to the accuracy level of the complex machine for the easy test samples. Thus, the complex and slow machine will be used only when it really matters, i.e. when the examples are too difficult for the fast machine. The only question that remains is how to determine if an example is

---

Algorithm 1. Easy-versus-Hard Object Detection

---

1 **Input:**
2 I – an input test image;
3 D_{fast} – a fast (single-stage) object detector;
4 D_{slow} – a slow (two-stage) object detector;
5 C – a criterion function used for dividing the images;
6 t – a threshold for dividing images into easy or hard;

7 **Computation:**
8 **if** $C(I) \leq t$ **then**
9 $\quad \lfloor B \leftarrow D_{fast}(I);$
10 **else**
11 $\quad \lfloor B \leftarrow D_{slow}(I);$

12 **Output:**
13 B – the set of predicted bounding boxes.

---

easy or hard in the first place. If we focus our interest on image data, the answer to this question is provided by the recent work of Ionescu et al. [13], which shows that the difficulty level of an image (with respect to a visual search task) can be automatically predicted. With an image difficulty predictor at our disposal, we have a first way to test our hypothesis in the context of object detection from images. However, if we further focus our interest on the specific task of object detection in images, we can devise additional criteria for splitting the images into easy or hard, by considering the output of a very fast single-stage detector, e.g. MobileNet-SSD [11]. These criteria are the number of detected objects in the image, the average size of the detected objects, and the number of detected objects divided by their average size.

To obtain an optimal trade-off between accuracy and speed in object detection, we propose to employ a more complex (two-stage) object detector, e.g. Faster R-CNN [17], for difficult test images and a less complex (single-stage) detector, e.g. SSD [15], for easy test images. Our simple easy-versus-hard strategy is formally described in Algorithm 1. Since we apply this strategy at test time, the object detectors as well as the image difficulty predictor can be independently trained beforehand. This allows us to directly apply state-of-the-art pre-trained object detectors [11,15,17], essentially as black boxes. It is important to note that we propose to use one of the following four options as the criterion function C in Algorithm 1:

1. an image difficulty predictor that estimates the difficulty of the input image;
2. a fast single-stage object detector that returns the number of objects detected in the input image (*less objects* is easier);
3. a fast single-stage object detector that returns the average size of the objects detected in the input image (*bigger objects* is easier);
4. a fast single-stage object detector that returns the number of detected objects divided by their average size (*less and bigger objects* is easier).

We note that if either one of the last three criteria are employed in Algorithm 1, and if the single-stage object detector used in the criterion function C is the same as D_{fast}, we can slightly optimize Algorithm 1 by applying the single-stage object detector only once, when the input image I turns out to be easy. Another important note is that, for the last three criteria, we consider an image to be *difficult* if the single-stage detector does not detect any object. Our algorithm has only one parameter, namely the threshold t used for dividing images into easy or hard. This parameter depends on the criterion function and it needs to be tuned on a validation set in order to achieve a desired trade-off between accuracy and time. While the last three splitting criteria are frustratingly easy to implement when a pre-trained single stage object detector is available, we have to train our own image difficulty predictor as described below.

Image Difficulty Predictor. We build our image difficulty prediction model based on CNN features and linear regression with ν-Support Vector Regression (ν-SVR) [2]. For a faster processing time, we consider a rather shallow pre-trained CNN architecture, namely VGG-f [3]. The CNN model is trained on the ILSVRC benchmark [18]. We remove the last layer of the CNN model and use it to extract deep features from the fully-connected layer known as $fc7$. The 4096 CNN features extracted from each image are normalized using the L_2-norm. The normalized feature vectors are then used to train a ν-SVR model to regress to the ground-truth difficulty scores provided by Ionescu et al. [13] for the PASCAL VOC 2012 data set [5]. We use the learned model as a continuous measure to automatically predict image difficulty. Our predictor attains a Kendall's τ correlation coefficient [21] of 0.441 on the test set of Ionescu et al. [13]. We note that Ionescu et al. [13] obtain a higher Kendall's τ score (0.472) using a deeper CNN architecture [19] along with VGG-f. However, we are interested in using an image difficulty predictor that is faster than all object detectors, even faster than MobileNet-SSD [11], so we stick with the shallower VGG-f architecture, which reduces the computational overhead at test time.

4 Experiments

4.1 Data Set

We perform object detection experiments on the PASCAL VOC 2007 data set [4], which consists of 9963 images that contain 20 object classes. The training and validation sets have roughly 2500 images each, while the test set contains about 5000 images.

4.2 Evaluation Details

Evaluation Measure. The performance of object detectors is typically evaluated using the mean Average Precision (mAP) over classes, which is based on the ranking of detection scores for each class [7]. For each object class, the Average Precision is given by the area under the precision-recall (PR) curve for the detected objects. The PR curve is constructed by first mapping each detected bounding box to the most-overlapping ground-truth bounding box, according to the Intersection over Union (IoU) measure, but only if the IoU is higher than 50% [6]. Then, the detections are sorted in decreasing order of their scores. Precision and recall values are computed each time a new positive sample is recalled. The PR curve is given by plotting the precision and recall pairs as lower scored detections are progressively included.

Models and Baselines. We choose Faster R-CNN [17] based on the ResNet-101 [9] architecture as our two-stage object detector that provides accurate bounding boxes. We set its confidence threshold to 0.6. In the experiments, we use the pre-trained Faster R-CNN model from https://github. com/endernewton/tf-faster-rcnn. We experiment with two single-shot detectors able to provide fast object detections, namely MobileNet-SSD [11] and SSD300 [15]. We use the pre-trained MobileNet-SSD model from https://github. com/chuanqi305/MobileNet-SSD. We use the model provided at https://github. com/weiliu89/caffe/tree/ssd for SSD300, which is based on the VGG-16 [19] architecture. SSD300 takes input images of 300 × 300 pixels and performs the detection task in a single step. We also tried the SSD512 detector, but we did not find it interesting for our experiments, since its speed is a bit too high for a fast object detector (1.57 s per image).

The main goal of the experiments is to compare our four different strategies for splitting the images between the single-stage detector (MobileNet-SSD or SSD300) and the two-stage detector (Faster R-CNN) with a baseline strategy that splits the images randomly. To reduce the accuracy variation introduced by the random selection of the baseline strategy, we repeat the experiments for 5 times and average the resulted mAP scores. We note that all standard deviations are lower than 0.5%. We consider various splitting points starting with a 100%–0% split (applying the single-stage detector only), going through three intermediate splits (75%–25%, 50%–50%, 25%–75%) and ending with a 0%–100% split (applying the two-stage detector only). To obtain these splitting points, we individually tune the parameter t of Algorithm 1 on the PASCAL VOC 2007 validation set, for each splitting criterion.

4.3   Results and Discussion

Table 1 presents the mAP scores and the processing times of MobileNet-SSD [11], Faster R-CNN [17] and several combinations of the two object detectors, on the PASCAL VOC 2007 data set. Different model combinations are obtained by varying the percentage of images processed by each detector. The table includes results starting with a 100%–0% split (equivalent with MobileNet-SSD [11] only), going through three intermediate splits (75%–25%, 50%–50%, 25%–75%) and ending with a 0%–100% split (equivalent with Faster R-CNN [11] only). In the

Table 1. Mean Average Precision (mAP) and time comparison between MobileNet-SSD [11], Faster R-CNN [17] and various combinations of the two object detectors on PASCAL VOC 2007. The test data is partitioned based on a random split (baseline) or four easy-versus-hard splits given by: the image difficulty score, the number of objects (n), the average size of the objects (avg), and the number of objects divided by their average size (n/avg). For the random split, we report the mAP over 5 runs to reduce bias. The reported times are measured on a computer with Intel Core i7 2.5 GHz CPU and 16 GB of RAM.

| | MobileNet-SSD (left) to Faster-RCNN (right) | | | | |
	100%–0%	75%–25%	50%–50%	25%–75%	0%–100%
Splitting criterion	Mean Average Precision (mAP)				
(1) Random (baseline)	0.6668	0.6895	0.7131	0.7450	0.7837
(2) Image difficulty	0.6668	0.6981	0.7431	0.7640	0.7837
(3) Number of objects (n)	0.6668	0.7091	0.7382	0.7551	0.7837
(4) Average object size (avg)	0.6668	0.7202	0.7503	0.7680	0.7837
(5) n/avg	0.6668	0.7336	0.7574	0.7775	0.7837
Component	Time (seconds)				
(2) Image difficulty	-	0.05	0.05	0.05	-
(3, 4, 5) Estimation of n, avg	-	0.07	0.07	0.07	-
Object detection	0.07	2.38	4.08	6.07	7.74
Object detection + (2)	0.07	2.43	4.13	6.12	7.74
Object detection + (3, 4, 5)	0.07	2.40	4.12	6.12	7.74

same manner, Table 2 shows the results for similar combinations of SSD300 [15] and Faster R-CNN [17]. While the results of various model combinations are listed on different columns in Tables 1 and 2, the results of various splitting strategies are listed on separate rows.

We first analyze the mAP scores and the processing time of the three individual object detectors, namely Faster R-CNN [17], MobileNet-SSD [11] and SSD300 [15]. Faster R-CNN reaches a mAP score of 0.7837 in about 7.74 s per image, while SSD300 reaches a mAP score of 0.69 in 0.56 s per image. MobileNet-SDD is even faster, attaining a mAP score of 0.6668 in just 0.07 s per image. We hereby note that we also considered the SSD512 object detector, but its results (a mAP score of 0.7046 in 1.57 s per image) did not convince us to include it in the evaluation.

We next analyze the average object detection times per image of the various model combinations. As expected, the time improves by about 21% when running MobileNet-SSD on 25% of the test set and Faster R-CNN on the rest of 75%. On the 50%–50% split, the processing time is nearly 47% shorter than the time required for processing the entire test set with Faster R-CNN only (0%–100% split). On the 75%–25% split, the processing time further improves by 69%. As SSD300 is slower than MobileNet-SSD, the time improvements are close, but not as high. The improvements in terms of time are 20% for the 25%–75% split, 44% for the 50%–50% split, and 68% for the 75%–25% split. We note that unlike the random splitting strategy, the easy-versus-hard splitting strategies require additional processing time, either for computing the difficulty scores or for estimating the number of objects and their average size. The image difficulty predictor runs in about 0.05 s per image, while the MobileNet-SSD detector (used for estimating the number of objects and their average size) runs in about 0.07 s per image. Hence, the extra time required by our easy-versus-hard splitting strategies is almost insignificant with respect to the total time required by the various combinations of object detectors. For instance, in the 50%–50% split with MobileNet-SSD and Faster R-CNN, the difficulty predictor accounts for roughly 1% of the total processing time (0.05 out of 4.13 s per image).

Table 2. Mean Average Precision (mAP) and time comparison between SSD300 [15], Faster R-CNN [17] and various combinations of the two object detectors on PASCAL VOC 2007. The test data is partitioned based on a random split (baseline) or four easy-versus-hard splits given by: the image difficulty score, the number of objects (n), the average size of the objects (avg), and the number of objects divided by their average size (n/avg). For the random split, we report the average mAP over 5 runs to reduce bias. The reported times are measured on a computer with Intel Core i7 2.5 GHz CPU and 16 GB of RAM.

| | SSD300 (left) to Faster-RCNN (right) | | | | |
	100%–0%	75%–25%	50%–50%	25%–75%	0%–100%
Splitting criterion	Mean Average Precision (mAP)				
(1) Random (baseline)	0.6900	0.7003	0.7178	0.7561	0.7837
(2) Image difficulty	0.6900	0.7117	0.7513	0.7732	0.7837
(3) Number of objects (n)	0.6900	0.7386	0.7619	0.7725	0.7837
(4) Average object size (avg)	0.6900	0.7078	0.7413	0.7664	0.7837
(5) n/avg	0.6900	0.7464	0.7779	0.7840	0.7837
Component	Time (seconds)				
(2) Image difficulty	-	0.05	0.05	0.05	-
(3, 4, 5) Estimation of n, avg	-	0.07	0.07	0.07	-
Object detection	0.56	2.46	4.33	6.12	7.74
Object detection + (2)	0.56	2.51	4.38	6.17	7.74
Object detection + (3, 4, 5)	0.56	2.53	4.40	6.19	7.74

Regarding our four easy-versus-hard strategies for combining object detectors, the empirical results indicate that all the proposed splitting strategies give better performance than the random splitting strategy, for all model combinations. For the splitting strategy based on image difficulty, the highest improvements over the random strategy can be observed for the 50%–50% split. When using MobileNet-SSD for the easy images (Table 1), our strategy based on image

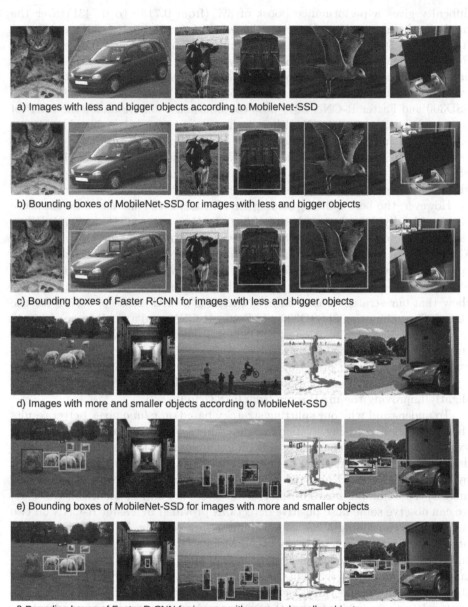

a) Images with less and bigger objects according to MobileNet-SSD

b) Bounding boxes of MobileNet-SSD for images with less and bigger objects

c) Bounding boxes of Faster R-CNN for images with less and bigger objects

d) Images with more and smaller objects according to MobileNet-SSD

e) Bounding boxes of MobileNet-SSD for images with more and smaller objects

f) Bounding boxes of Faster R-CNN for images with more and smaller objects

Fig. 1. Examples of easy (top three rows) and hard images (bottom three rows) from PASCAL VOC 2007 according to the number of objects divided by their average size. For each set of images, the bounding boxes predicted by the MobileNet-SSD [11] and the Faster R-CNN [17] detectors are also presented. The correctly predicted bounding boxes are shown in green, while the wrongly predicted bounding boxes are shown in red. Best viewed in color. (Color figure online)

difficulty gives a performance boost of 3% (from 0.7131 to 0.7431) over the random splitting strategy. However, the mAP of the MobileNet-SSD and Faster R-CNN 50%–50% combination is 4.06% under the mAP of the standalone Faster R-CNN. When using SSD300 for the easy images (Table 2), our strategy based on image difficulty gives a performance boost of 3.35% (from 0.7178 to 0.7513) over the baseline strategy, for the 50%–50% split. This time, the mAP of the SSD300 and Faster R-CNN 50%–50% combination is 3.24% under the mAP of the standalone Faster R-CNN, although the processing time is reduced by almost half. While using the average size of the objects as splitting criterion gives better results than using the image difficulty scores when the fast detector is MobileNet-SSD (Table 1), it seems that using the number of objects as splitting criterion gives better results when the fast detector is SSD300 (Table 2).

However, the best splitting strategy in all cases is the one based on the score obtained by dividing the number of objects by their average size (n/avg). When the fast detector is MobileNet-SSD (Table 1), our strategy based on n/avg gives a performance boost of more than 4% (from 0.7131 to 0.7574) over the random splitting strategy for the 50%–50% split, but the results are even better when SSD300 is used as the fast detector. Indeed, the results presented in Table 2 show that our strategy based on n/avg attains a mAP score of 0.7779 for the 50%–50% combination of SSD300 and Faster R-CNN, and a mAP score of 0.7840 for the 25%–75% combination of SSD300 and Faster R-CNN. Remarkably, for the 50%–50% split, the n/avg strategy reduces the time by almost half with a very small reduction in performance (from 0.7837 to 0.7779). Moreover, the n/avg strategy slashes about 1.55 s from the Faster R-CNN execution time, while slightly improving the mAP score from 0.7837 to 0.7840.

To understand why our splitting strategy based on n/avg gives better results than the random splitting strategy, we randomly select a few easy examples (with less and bigger objects) and a few difficult examples from the PASCAL VOC 2007 data set, and we display them in Fig. 1 along with the bounding boxes predicted by the MobileNet-SSD and the Faster R-CNN object detectors. On the easy images, the bounding boxes of the two detectors are almost identical. However, we can observe some false positive detections provided by Faster R-CNN on two easy images containing a car and a monitor, respectively. Nevertheless, we can perceive a lot more differences between MobileNet-SSD and Faster R-CNN on the hard images. In the left-most hard image, MobileNet-SSD wrongly detects a large rock as an object, while in the second image MobileNet-SSD fails to detect the motorbike. In the third and fifth images, MobileNet-SSD provides some wrong detections, while Faster R-CNN provides accurate detections (without any false positives). In the fourth image, Faster R-CNN is able to detect more people in the background, but it also detects the surfboard and wrongly labels it as a boat. We thus conclude that the difference between MobileNet-SSD and Faster R-CNN is less noticeable on the easy images than on the hard images. This could explain why our splitting strategy based on n/avg is effective in choosing an optimal trade-off between accuracy and speed.

5   Conclusion

In this paper, we have presented four easy-versus-hard strategies to obtain an optimal trade-off between accuracy and speed in object detection from images. Our strategies are based on dispatching each test image either to a fast and less accurate single-shot detector or to a slow and more accurate two-stage detector, according to the image difficulty score, the number of objects contained in the image, the average size of the objects, or the number of objects divided by their average size. We have conducted experiments using state-of-the-art object detectors such as SSD300 [15] or Faster R-CNN [17] on the PASCAL VOC 2007 [4] data set. The empirical results indicate that using the strategy based on dividing the number of objects by their average size for splitting the test images compares favorably to a random split of the images, and perhaps surprisingly, it also provides better results than splitting the images according to their difficulty score. Since our best splitting strategy is simple and easy to implement, it can be immediately adopted by anyone that needs a continuous accuracy versus speed trade-off optimization strategy in object detection. In future work, we aim to investigate whether training object detectors to specifically deal with easy or hard image samples can help to further improve our results.

Acknowledgments. The work of Petru Soviany was supported through project grant PN-III-P2-2.1-PED-2016-1842. The work of Radu Tudor Ionescu was supported through project grant PN-III-P1-1.1-PD-2016-0787.

References

1. Bengio, Y., Louradour, J., Collobert, R., Weston, J.: Curriculum learning. In: Proceedings of ICML, pp. 41–48 (2009)
2. Chang, C.C., Lin, C.J.: Training ν-support vector regression: theory and algorithms. Neural Comput. **14**, 1959–1977 (2002)
3. Chatfield, K., Simonyan, K., Vedaldi, A., Zisserman, A.: Return of the devil in the details: delving deep into convolutional nets. In: Proceedings of BMVC (2014)
4. Everingham, M., Van Gool, L., Williams, C., Winn, J., Zisserman, A.: The PASCAL Visual Object Classes Challenge 2007 Results (2007)
5. Everingham, M., Van Gool, L., Williams, C., Winn, J., Zisserman, A.: The PASCAL Visual Object Classes Challenge 2012 Results (2012)
6. Everingham, M., Eslami, S.M., Gool, L., Williams, C.K., Winn, J., Zisserman, A.: The PASCAL visual object classes challenge: a retrospective. Int. J. Comput. Vis. **111**(1), 98–136 (2015)
7. Everingham, M., van Gool, L., Williams, C.K., Winn, J., Zisserman, A.: The PASCAL visual object classes (VOC) challenge. Int. J. Comput. Vis. **88**(2), 303–338 (2010)
8. Girshick, R.: Fast R-CNN. In: Proceedings of ICCV, pp. 1440–1448 (2015)
9. He, K., Zhang, X., Ren, S., Sun, J.: Deep residual learning for image recognition. In: Proceedings of CVPR, pp. 770–778 (2016)
10. He, K., Gkioxari, G., Dollár, P., Girshick, R.: Mask R-CNN. In: Proceedings of ICCV, pp. 2961–2969 (2017)

11. Howard, A.G., et al.: MobileNets: efficient convolutional neural networks for mobile vision applications. arXiv preprint http://arxiv.org/abs/1704.04861arXiv:1704.04861 (2017)
12. Huang, J., et al.: Speed/accuracy trade-offs for modern convolutional object detectors. In: Proceedings of CVPR, pp. 7310–7319 (2017)
13. Ionescu, R., Alexe, B., Leordeanu, M., Popescu, M., Papadopoulos, D.P., Ferrari, V.: How hard can it be? Estimating the difficulty of visual search in an image. In: Proceedings of CVPR, pp. 2157–2166 (2016)
14. Li, X., Liu, Z., Luo, P., Loy, C.C., Tang, X.: Not all pixels are equal: difficulty-aware semantic segmentation via deep layer cascade. In: Proceedings of CVPR, pp. 3193–3202 (2017)
15. Liu, W., et al.: SSD: single shot multibox detector. In: Proceedings of ECCV, pp. 21–37 (2016)
16. Redmon, J., Divvala, S., Girshick, R., Farhadi, A.: You only look once: unified, real-time object detection. In: Proceedings of CVPR, pp. 779–788 (2016)
17. Ren, S., He, K., Girshick, R., Sun, J.: Faster R-CNN: towards real-time object detection with region proposal networks. In: Proceedings of NIPS, pp. 91–99 (2015)
18. Russakovsky, O., et al.: ImageNet large scale visual recognition challenge. Int. J. Comput. Vis. **115**, 211–252 (2015)
19. Simonyan, K., Zisserman, A.: Very deep convolutional networks for large-scale image recognition. In: Proceedings of ICLR (2014)
20. Soviany, P., Ionescu, R.T.: Optimizing the trade-off between single-stage and two-stage deep object detectors using image difficulty prediction. In: Proceedings of SYNASC (2018)
21. Upton, G., Cook, I.: A Dictionary of Statistics. Oxford University Press, Oxford (2004)
22. Zhou, P., Ni, B., Geng, C., Hu, J., Xu, Y.: Scale-transferrable object detection. In: Proceedings of CVPR, pp. 528–538 (2018)

Targeted Kernel Networks: Faster Convolutions with Attentive Regularization

Kashyap Chitta[✉]

The Robotics Institute, Carnegie Mellon University, Pittsburgh, USA
kchitta@andrew.cmu.edu

Abstract. We propose Attentive Regularization (AR), a method to constrain the activation maps of kernels in Convolutional Neural Networks (CNNs) to specific regions of interest (ROIs). Each kernel learns a location of specialization along with its weights through standard backpropagation. A differentiable attention mechanism requiring no additional supervision is used to optimize the ROIs. Traditional CNNs of different types and structures can be modified with this idea into equivalent Targeted Kernel Networks (TKNs), while keeping the network size nearly identical. By restricting kernel ROIs, we reduce the number of sliding convolutional operations performed throughout the network in its forward pass, speeding up both training and inference. We evaluate our proposed architecture on both synthetic and natural tasks across multiple domains. TKNs obtain significant improvements over baselines, requiring less computation (around an order of magnitude) while achieving superior performance.

Keywords: Soft attention · Region of interest · Network acceleration

1 Introduction

Convolutional Neural Networks (CNNs) have been largely responsible for the significant progress achieved on visual recognition tasks in recent years [23,27,33]. By sharing weights to be used by convolutional kernels across the entire spatial area of their input activations, CNNs use translated replicas of learned feature detectors, allowing them to translate knowledge about good weight values acquired at one position in an image to all other positions. This leads to translational equivariance– a translated input to a convolutional layer will end up producing an identically translated activation after passing through it.

Though it works well in nearly all situations, it is possible for this 'knowledge translation' to be a double-edged sword. By sharing weights across the whole input, we bias the network to prioritize learning representations that would be useful over the entire image area. Due to this, it may have to compromise on learning some weights that are critical to the network's final objective, simply

L. Leal-Taixé and S. Roth (Eds.): ECCV 2018 Workshops, LNCS 11132, pp. 379–397, 2019.
https://doi.org/10.1007/978-3-030-11018-5_34

because these weights were useful only in a small area of the whole image. The possibility of this happening increases if the inputs possess a uniform spatial layout.

Assuming that the network inputs are captured or preprocessed in a way that provides some spatial structure, certain objects are more likely to be in particular locations than others. For example, if the inputs are all upright faces cropped with a face detector, it is far more likely to find an eye in one of the top quadrants of the input than in the bottom ones. In images of outdoor scenes, it is more likely to see blue skies at the top than the bottom. More often than not, there is some such spatial structure associated with the inputs to any visual recognition task. This means that based on what a kernel is supposed to look for, independently learning weights at different spatial locations can potentially generate better representations.

A locally connected layer takes this idea to the extreme– its forward pass involves convolutions with no weight sharing at all, with a different kernel for every spatial location in the input. By perfectly aligning facial images and then learning representations using locally connected layers, human-level accuracy was first achieved in face recognition [64]. Unfortunately, the feasibility of this approach is limited due to the heavy dependence on perfect alignment of inputs and drastic increase in parameter count, leading to a requirement of far more training data (since there is no longer any 'knowledge translation').

Only sharing weights over selected Regions of Interest (ROIs) is another possibility that has been explored, implemented by training separate CNNs on different ROIs and merging their representations at a point deeper in the network [38,39,60,73]. The kernels are now specialized to their input ROIs, and the parameter count increase is controlled by architectural choices. Finding the right ROIs to use, however, is a tedious step usually requiring domain-specific knowledge to be done effectively. Any manual selection, even by the best domain experts, would almost certainly not lead to the most optimal choice of ROIs for the given task and network topology.

An alternative approach would be to learn the most optimal ROI for each kernel directly from the data, by end-to-end training. Trying to do this as a tuple of the ROI center and spatial size results in models that are not differentiable and require complex learning procedures [3]. We propose Attentive Regularization (AR), a method to achieve this using a differentiable attention mechanism [21], allowing our models to be trained end-to-end with simple backpropagation. The key idea behind AR is to associate each rectangular ROI with the parameters of a smooth differentiable attention function. The attention function helps generate gradients of the loss with respect to the location and size of the ROI. Figure 1 illustrates the effect of AR, comparing it with a standard convolution and a fixed ROI based approach. For the purpose of illustration, we use a 'layer' operating on an RGB image with only four kernels, each looking for a semantically meaningful part.

An attractive consequence of having ROIs for each kernel is computational efficiency– computing convolutions over small ROIs for every kernel in a layer

Fig. 1. (a) Input (b) Activations after a standard convolution with four kernels (actually correlation filters). These kernels are optimized to be activated by the left eye, right eye, nose and mouth respectively. However, they give large, unpredictable responses across the image. (c) Manual ROI selection and activations after convolutions on these selected ROIs. (d) The proposed approach, attention functions learned from data, and activations after AR. We observe that through spatial specialization, even crude features can become powerful, as they become independent of other spatial locations.

greatly reduces redundant operations in the network, speeding up both training and evaluation.

Our contribution is three-fold: First, we propose and describe AR and its incorporation into existing CNN architectures, resulting in Targeted Kernel Networks (TKNs). Second, we evaluate TKNs on digit recognition benchmarks with coarse alignment in the form of digit centering, as well as synthetic settings with more alignment, significantly outperforming CNN baselines. Finally, we demonstrate their application for network acceleration on more complicated structured data, like faces and road traffic signs.

2 Related Work

Regularizing CNNs. Deep CNNs have a vast potential to overfit data when they have to be trained from scratch. Conventional machine learning approaches to handle this like weight decay, data augmentation, and model ensembles alleviate the problem only to an extent. Dropout [57] was one of the most successful methods for regularizing layers with very large parameter counts in CNNs [33,55].

Most recent models have substituted this with some constraint on the activations [31], the most popular of which is batch normalization [28]. This uses other images in the mini-batch along with learned scaling parameters to constrain the activations using computed statistics. We force the network to find good weights without giving the kernels free access to all spatial locations in the image during training, with a similar approach of applying constraints through learned parameters.

Spatially Specialized CNNs. Several approaches look into architectures that operate on ROIs, specifically in object detection [19,20,48]. However, these methods typically propose ROI based object candidates for each input image, and not for the network kernels. Additional bounding box supervision is also necessary to learn these proposals. Unlike these methods, ROIs at a kernel level have been used in facial action unit detection [14], but the regions are hand-crafted [38,39,73].

Attention. One of the most promising trends in research is the emergence of attention based models. Early work in this area [10,34,51] was inspired by the process of sequential recognition used by the biological vision system in humans. Recent adaptations have leveraged the representational power of deep neural networks with visual attention for a variety of tasks, some of which were image classification [4,17,59,66], image generation [21], image captioning [5,25,42,68], visual question answering [44,53,67,69], action recognition [18] and one-shot learning [54]. More closely related approaches to AR are attempts at multi-layer [52] and multi-channel [5] attention. Our main advantage over existing soft attention methods is that we systematically remove computational processing throughout the network while maintaining the fully differentiable property. Other approaches require hard attention with reinforcement learning for network acceleration.

Efficient CNNs. Cheng et al. [8] summarize model compression and acceleration approaches into four categories– parameter pruning and sharing [7,22,35, 46,56], low-rank factorization [11,30,63], transferred or compact convolutional filters [12,62,65], and knowledge distillation [6,26,49,70]. One of the primary goals of early attention models was increasing efficiency [3]. This has resurfaced recently in the form of various architectures for spatially restricting computation.

Spatial Computation Restriction in CNNs. Dynamic Capacity Networks [2] define attention maps to apply sub-networks to only specific input patches for fine representations, which they later combine with the representations of a coarse network. Similarly, SBNet [47] uses a low resolution sub-network to obtain a computation mask for the main deep network. A more recent idea uses a learnable application of channel-wise sparsity to completely eliminate certain kernels dynamically [13]. All these techniques restrict computation to the uncertain regions of the current image, whereas in our work, we restrict computation to certain (learnable) regions for all images. The two ideas are orthogonal and computational gains could be observed by combining them.

PerforatedCNNs [16] study strategies for skipping calculation of convolutions tied to certain spatial locations in a convolutional layer. These strategies are loosely based on using grid-like lattices, where computations at the intermediate points are approximated with interpolation. Our work removes computation in a similar fashion, but no interpolation is required since we do not have any intermediate values to recover.

3 Attentive Regularization

In its simplest form, AR can be considered an additional layer operating on the activation of a convolutional layer using an attention window. We begin by explaining the one-dimensional implementation in this form before moving on to the generalized version and higher dimensional inputs.

3.1 AR in One Dimension

Consider the activation tensor $\mathbf{A} \in \mathbb{R}^{D \times L}$ resulting from a one dimensional convolution of a sequence of length L with D different kernels. Let $\mathbf{a}^C \in \mathbb{R}^L$ denote the row of this tensor corresponding to the Cth kernel in the layer. The objective of AR is to constrain each one of these activation vectors using a differentiable attention function f_{att}. The window for attention is constructed as this function drops off numerically from 1 to 0. By sampling $f_{att}(x)$ at L equally spaced points, we obtain an equivalent attention vector representing our function, $\mathbf{f}_{att} \in \mathbb{R}^L$. Element-wise multiplication can now be used to weigh the original activation vector using its corresponding attention vector:

$$\mathbf{a}^C_{att} = \mathbf{a}^C \odot \mathbf{f}^C_{att} \tag{1}$$

where $\mathbf{a}^C_{att}$ is the attentively regularized activation along the channel C, and $\odot$ denotes the element-wise product.

The key to optimizing the area of specialization of the kernels is now a problem of learning the right parameters to define the function f_{att}.

3.2 Differentiable Functions for Attention

The most obvious choice of f_{att} to create a smooth attention window is the Gaussian function:

$$f_{att}(x; \mu, \sigma) = e^{-(x-\mu)^2/2\sigma^2} \tag{2}$$

This is completely parametrized by two variables, its mean μ and variance σ^2. Every time an update is applied to the convolutional layer weights during backpropagation, we can also update these two parameters in the AR layer. By varying μ, the attention can translate to the optimal location in the sequence, and varying σ^2 allows the layer to learn the optimal scale, i.e., the amount of focus to pay at the chosen location.

We also experimented with Cauchy functions, which have distinctively heavier tails than the corresponding Gaussians as shown in Fig. 2. We premised that this property would improve the gradient flow and help speed up the training of our layers, following [54]. The Cauchy function with mean μ and scale parameter σ is given by:

$$f_{att}(x; \mu, \sigma) = \frac{1}{\left[1 + \left(\frac{x-\mu}{\sigma}\right)^2\right]} \tag{3}$$

Fig. 2. Left: Gaussian (blue) and Cauchy (orange) attention functions and the equivalent bivariate functions (Gaussian on top). The Cauchy function has more weight in the tail of the distribution. Right: One slice of $\mathbf{F}_x$, $\mathbf{F}_y$ and $\mathbf{F}_{att}$ associated with a single 2D kernel at initialization, using the Gaussian function as f_{att}. Due to linear separability, AR can be trained extremely efficiently. (Color figure online)

3.3 AR in Two Dimensions

The same logic used for one dimension can be generalized to images by considering two-dimensional attention maps associated with each kernel, instead of the attention vectors used for sequences. The input tensor $\mathbf{A} \in \mathbb{R}^{C \times H \times W}$ has slices $\mathbf{A}^C \in \mathbb{R}^{H \times W}$. We build the attention map by sampling $\mathbf{F}_{att}^C$ from a bivariate $\mathcal{F}_{att}(x, y)$ along both dimensions. While using the Gaussian function, this now takes the form:

$$\mathcal{F}_{att}(x, y; \mu_x, \mu_y, \sigma_x, \sigma_y, \rho) = e^{-\alpha(x,y)} \tag{4}$$

where

$$\alpha(x, y) = (f(x))^2 - 2\rho f(x)f(y) + (f(y))^2 \tag{5}$$

$$f(x) = \frac{x - \mu_x}{\sigma_x} \tag{6}$$

$$f(y) = \frac{y - \mu_y}{\sigma_y} \tag{7}$$

The attentively regularized activation $\mathbf{A}_{att}^C$ is now obtained by the same procedure of element-wise multiplication as in Eq. (1).

In our experiments, we found that the correlation parameter ρ introduces an unnecessary degree of freedom to the attention map, as all scales and translations can be achieved by learning only μ_x, μ_y, σ_x and σ_y. Setting $\rho = 0$ allows for more efficiency through a linearly separable implementation. Let the ith row of $\mathbf{A}^C$ be denoted by $\mathbf{a}^{(C,i,:)}$. We initially compute an intermediate activation $\mathbf{A}_{int}^C$ by performing the following operation on all i rows of $\mathbf{A}^C$:

$$\mathbf{a}_{int}^{(C,i,:)} = \mathbf{a}^{(C,i,:)} \odot \mathbf{f}_x^C \tag{8}$$

and then follow up with an operation on each of the j columns of $\mathbf{A}_{int}^C$ to get our final activation $\mathbf{A}_{att}^C$:

$$\mathbf{a}_{att}^{(C,:,j)} = \mathbf{a}_{int}^{(C,:,j)} \odot \mathbf{f}_y^C. \tag{9}$$

Here $\mathbf{f}_x \in \mathbb{R}^H$ and $\mathbf{f}_y \in \mathbb{R}^W$ are simply two separate one-dimensional attention vectors sampled from:

$$f_x(x; \mu_x, \sigma_x) = e^{-(x-\mu_x)^2/2\sigma_x^2} \tag{10}$$

$$f_y(y; \mu_y, \sigma_y) = e^{-(x-\mu_y)^2/2\sigma_y^2} \tag{11}$$

when using the Gaussian function.

3.4   Tensor-Based Implementation

While working with batch-sized tensors, it is more efficient to pre-compute the entire tensor $\mathbf{F}_{att} \in \mathbb{R}^{C \times H \times W}$ directly from the parameter vector of means $\mathbf{m} \in \mathbb{R}^C$ and the vector of scale parameters $\mathbf{s} \in \mathbb{R}^C$ after using tile operations to broadcast them to the required dimensions. The combined tensor of all C attention vectors $\mathbf{f}_{att} \in \mathbb{R}^{C \times H}$ (or $\mathbb{R}^{C \times W}$) can be computed as:

$$\mathbf{f}_{att}(\mathbf{x}; \mathbf{m}, \mathbf{s}) = e^{-(\mathbf{x}-\mathbf{m})^2/2\mathbf{s}^2} \tag{12}$$

Where $\mathbf{x}$ is a range vector (0 to H or 0 to W) scaled to lie in $[0, 1]$. $\mathbf{m}$ is initialized to a vector with each entry 0.5 so the window is initially centered. $\mathbf{s}$ is initialized to a vector of ones, such that the window tapers off from a value of 1 at the center to $f(\sigma = 1)$ at the image boundaries. For the two-dimensional case, $\mathbf{f}_x \in \mathbb{R}^{C \times H}$ and $\mathbf{f}_y \in \mathbb{R}^{C \times W}$ are computed as in Eq. (12), broadcasted into three dimensions ($\mathbb{R}^{C \times H \times W}$), and $\mathbf{F}_{att}$ is computed as

$$\mathbf{F}_{att} = \mathbf{F}_x \odot \mathbf{F}_y \tag{13}$$

This is illustrated in Fig. 2. Every forward pass, an AR layer computes the element-wise product of its input and this attention function. After the backward pass, the function shifts slightly based on the updates to the vectors $\mathbf{m}$ and $\mathbf{s}$. The forward pass layer function is defined as:

$$\mathbf{A}_{att} = \mathbf{A} \odot \mathbf{F}_{att}. \tag{14}$$

In this work, we limit ourselves to AR in two dimensions. Its extension to higher dimensions is trivial, using linearly separable one-dimensional attention windows along each input dimension.

3.5   Efficient Convolutions with Targeting

$\mathbf{F}_{att}$ multiplicatively scales $\mathbf{A}$ in the forward pass. Over training, as the values in $\mathbf{m}$ and $\mathbf{s}$ change, a portion of the activation far enough away from the mean on the attention window gets scaled down to very small values. This effect is magnified when AR is used repeatedly, leading to a large number of near-zero activations through the network.

We exploit the fact that these activations are all located far from the mean, by performing the convolution operation for each kernel in only a rectangular ROI around the mean. This is mathematically equivalent to using an approximation to $\mathbf{F}_{att}$ for AR, with values below a certain threshold clipped down to zero. We determine this ROI, given by its top-left and bottom-right coordinates:

$$\mathbf{roi}^C = [(\mathbf{m}_x - \frac{\mathbf{s}_x}{\sqrt{2}}) \times W; (\mathbf{m}_y - \frac{\mathbf{s}_y}{\sqrt{2}}) \times H; \tag{15}$$
$$(\mathbf{m}_x + \frac{\mathbf{s}_x}{\sqrt{2}}) \times W; (\mathbf{m}_y + \frac{\mathbf{s}_y}{\sqrt{2}}) \times H].$$

This sliced ROI is used by a *target* layer that efficiently performs the composite operation of both convolution and AR.

$$\mathbf{A}_{tar}^C[\mathbf{roi}^C] = \mathbf{A}^C[\mathbf{roi}^C] * \mathbf{K}^C. \tag{16}$$

$$\mathbf{A}_{att} = \mathbf{A}_{tar} \odot \mathbf{F}_{att} \tag{17}$$

where $\mathbf{K}^C$ is the Cth kernel in the target layer, $\mathbf{A}$ is the input activation, $\mathbf{A}_{tar}$ is the intermediate result after the sliced convolution and $\mathbf{A}_{att}$ is the layer output. * denotes the single channel 2D convolution operation.

During training, the values of $\mathbf{m}$ and $\mathbf{s}$ are clipped such that the size of the ROI never collapses to a value smaller than the kernel width. In addition, the overall ROI values are clipped so as to not exceed the boundaries of the input activation. At initialization, the ROI for all kernels is the entire input activation.

In all our experiments, convolutions are done after the required amount of padding at the input boundaries so as to maintain constant spatial dimensions. We do not use an additive bias term in any convolutional layer. Our models were implemented with TensorFlow [1] and Keras [9].

4   Experiments

We empirically demonstrate the effectiveness of TKNs on four tasks: digit recognition on the MNIST [36] and SVHN [45] datasets, traffic sign recognition on the German Traffic Sign Recognition Benchmark [58], and facial analysis on the UNBC-McMaster Pain Archive [43]. We also generate the tlMNIST dataset as a sanity check for TKNs, which aids us in understanding the visualizations of the learned attention mechanism.

4.1   Datasets

MNIST. The MNIST dataset contains 28×28 grayscale images of handwritten numerical digits (0–9). The dataset is divided into 60,000 images for training and 10,000 for testing. The number of images per digit is not uniformly distributed. We perform no data augmentation or preprocessing except division of pixel values by 255 to place them in the range $[0, 1]$.

tlMNIST. The tlMNIST dataset, short for top-left MNIST, is a set of 56×56 grayscale images generated directly from MNIST. The 60,000 training images are created by placing each digit from the training partition of MNIST into the top-left 28×28 quadrant of the images, and selecting 3 other digits from the same partition randomly to place in the other 3 image quadrants. The 10,000 image test set is similarly generated using only the test partition of MNIST. We use identical settings for both MNIST and tlMNIST experiments. The idea behind this task is to introduce a known synthetic 'alignment' to the data, so that it can be used as a sanity check for TKNs (kernels should focus on the top-left). Figure 3 shows some image samples from this dataset.

Fig. 3. tlMNIST data. The label assigned to each sample is that of the number in the top-left quadrant. The other three numbers serve as distractors to vanilla CNNs.

SVHN. The SVHN dataset contains 32×32 RGB digit images, cropped from pictures of house numbers. There are 73,257 images in the training set, 26,032 images in the test set, and 531,131 images for additional training. The digit of interest is centered in the cropped images, but nearby digits and other distractors are kept in the image. We train on only the 73,257 images in the training set, and report performances on the test set. Following [71], we do no preprocessing except pixel intensity scaling.

GTSRB. GTSRB contains RGB images of road traffic signs taken in Germany, with bounding boxes provided for 43 different classes of signs. The main challenges of this dataset are low resolution and contrast. We follow the standard split for evaluation, involving 39,209 training images and a test set of 12,630 images. We preprocess each cropped bounding box by resizing it to 32×32, followed by pixel intensity scaling.

Pain. The Pain Archive is a major publicly available test bed for research in facial analysis of induced pain expression. It consists of 200 video sequences of 25 subjects with 48,398 frames in total, each annotated with 66 facial landmarks and pain intensity levels (on a scale of 0–16). We split off around 30% of the data (sequences of 7 of the subjects) for validation and use the remaining 70% for training. This is a challenging task, which is also well suited to TKNs as we can preprocess the frames to create scale and viewpoint invariance. This is done by using the 66 landmark annotations to warp the faces to a frontal upright reference position before cropping and scaling to 48×48. We perform data augmentation by adding a small Gaussian noise to the landmarks before warping, and also randomly flipping the faces horizontally after warping.

4.2　Training

Our networks on the digit recognition tasks are trained using stochastic gradient descent (SGD). On MNIST and tlMNIST we train using batch size 128 for 20 epochs. The initial learning rate is set to 0.1, and is divided by 10 at the epochs 10 and 15. On SVHN, we train our models for 40 epochs with a batch size of 64. The learning rate is set to 0.1 initially, and is lowered by a factor of 10 after 20 epochs. Following [27], we use a weight decay of 10^{-4} and a Nesterov momentum [61] of 0.9 without dampening.

Table 1. CNN baselines. Convolutional layers replaced in TKNs are marked in **bold**. θ is the compression factor used to reduce the number of channels using a 1×1 convolution at the transition blocks. The activation depths are reduced from C to $(1 - \theta)C$ at these layers. LocNet is a small localization network used to perform a learnable affine transform on the input. The final regression or classification layer is an FC layer with dimensions based on the task (10 for MNIST/SVHN, 43 for GTSRB, and 1 for Pain). The softmax cross entropy loss is used for classification, and a Euclidean loss is used for regression.

Layers	Output	CNN6	DN10	DN40	STN
Convolution (1)	$n \times n$	**5 × 5 conv**	3×3 conv		LocNet
			$[3 \times 3$ **conv**$] \times 2$	$\begin{bmatrix} 1 \times 1\,\text{conv} \\ 3 \times 3\,\text{conv} \end{bmatrix} \times 6$	**7 × 7 conv**
Transition (1)	$\frac{n}{2} \times \frac{n}{2}$	2 × 2 max pool	1×1 conv	1×1 conv, $\theta = 0.5$	2 × 2 max pool
			2 × 2 avg pool		
Convolution (2)		**5 × 5 conv**	$[3 \times 3$ **conv**$] \times 2$	$\begin{bmatrix} 1 \times 1\,\text{conv} \\ 3 \times 3\,\text{conv} \end{bmatrix} \times 6$	**5 × 5 conv**
Transition (2)	$\frac{n}{4} \times \frac{n}{4}$	2 × 2 max pool	1×1 conv	1×1 conv, $\theta = 0.5$	2 × 2 max pool
			2 × 2 avg pool		
Convolution (3)		**5 × 5 conv**	$[3 \times 3$ **conv**$] \times 2$	$\begin{bmatrix} 1 \times 1\,\text{conv} \\ 3 \times 3\,\text{conv} \end{bmatrix} \times 6$	**3 × 3 conv**
Flatten	1×1	328D FC 192D FC	$\frac{n}{4} \times \frac{n}{4}$ global avg pool		2 × 2 max pool 96D FC

On GTSRB and Pain, we use the Adam optimizer [32] with a learning rate of 0.001, and train for a total of 100 epochs with a batch size of 64. For GTSRB, we use a higher weight decay of 0.05. We adopt the weight initialization introduced by He et al. [24]. We checkpoint the models after every epoch of training and report the error rates of the best single model. Test errors were only evaluated once for each task and model setting.

4.3　Network Architectures

To show that the benefits of AR are model-agnostic, we use four different CNN baselines across experiments. They are summarized in Table 1. The first is a vanilla 6-layer CNN network with 3 convolutional layers (with 256, 256 and 128 kernels respectively) and 3 fully connected (FC) layers. The last layer is

Table 2. Error rates (%) on the MNIST dataset. Our best results in **bold**. AR improves both performance and efficiency.

Network	Params	FLOPs	Error
Network in network [41]	-	-	0.47
Deeply-supervised nets [37]	-	-	0.39
Competitive multi-scale convolution [40]	4.48M	632M	0.33
CapsNet [50]	8.21M	202M	0.25
CNN6	4.59M	368M	0.42
TKN6 (Gaussian, $L_2 = 10^{-4}, \beta = 2$)	4.59M	52.9M	0.48
TKN6 (Cauchy, $L_2 = 10^{-4}, \beta = 4$)	4.59M	28.6M	0.43
DN10	44.7K	11.3M	0.48
TDN10 (Gaussian, $L_2 = 10^{-4}, \beta = 2$)	45.0K	6.93M	0.42
TDN10 (Cauchy, $L_2 = 10^{-4}, \beta = 4$)	45.0K	**6.26M**	**0.38**

regularized with a dropout [57] of 0.5, and the ReLU non-linearity is used for all intermediate layers.

The second is a DenseNet [27] with 3 densely connected blocks of 2 layers each. We use a growth rate of 12 and do not perform compression at the transition layers between blocks. We denote this model as DN10. Note that all convolutions in DenseNets are actually performed as the composite function, Batch Normalization [28] – ReLU – convolution.

We use a single baseline for our SVHN and Pain Archive experiments, a DenseNet-BC architecture with 3 blocks of 12 layers each. There are 21 connections in each block. We use a growth rate of 36, dropout with probability 0.2 after each convolution, and a compression factor of 0.5 at the 2 transition layers. We denote this model as DN40.

The final baseline is a Spatial Transformer Network (STN) [29] for GTSRB. This network learns how to warp the inputs with an affine transformation such that they are ideally aligned for the task. This meshes well with TKNs which are designed for aligned data. The main network we use is a 5-layer CNN with 3 convolutional layers (with 128, 128 and 256 kernels respectively) and 2 FC layers. We use batch normalization between all intermediate layers, and a dropout of 0.6 for the final FC layer. The localization network that computes warp parameters is a smaller version of the same network, with 3 convolutional layers of the same kernel size (with 16, 32 and 64 kernels respectively) and 3 FC layers (128, 64 and 6 units).

Given a CNN baseline, converting it to an equivalent TKN involves replacing convolutional layers with target layers. For the CNN6 and STN baselines, we simply replace all the convolutional layers in the main network, giving TKN6 and TSTN. For the DenseNet baselines, we replace the 3×3 convolutional layers within the dense blocks, assuming that the bulk of the representation learning

Table 3. Error rates (%) on the tlMNIST dataset. Our best results in **bold**. With AR, performance on tlMNIST becomes equivalent to the standard MNIST task.

Network	Params	FLOPs	Error
CNN6	10.76M	1470M	0.83
TKN6 (Gaussian, $L_2 = 10^{-4}, \beta = 2$)	10.76M	145M	0.48
TKN6 (Cauchy, $L_2 = 10^{-4}, \beta = 2$)	10.76M	125M	0.48
TKN6 (Cauchy, $L_2 = 10^{-4}, \beta = 4$)	10.76M	68.3M	0.53
DN10	44.7K	45.2M	0.50
TDN10 (Gaussian, $L_2 = 10^{-4}, \beta = 2$)	45.0K	29.7M	0.41
TDN10 (Cauchy, $L_2 = 10^{-4}, \beta = 2$)	45.0K	**25.6M**	**0.38**

Table 4. Error rates (%) on the SVHN dataset. Our best results in **bold**. We obtain state-of-the-art results on this reduced SVHN training set.

Network	Params	FLOPs	Error
CapsNet [50]	1.00M	41.3M	4.25
DN40	0.83M	357M	3.17
TDN40 (Cauchy, $L_2 = 10^{-4}, \beta = 2$)	0.83M	**205M**	3.11

happens in these layers. We keep the initial, transitional and bottleneck 1×1 convolutions as they are. We call these Targeted DenseNets (TDN10 and TDN40).

Further, there are three design choices within a target layer which we vary– the choice of attention function (Gaussian or Cauchy); an L_2 weight penalty on scale parameters $\mathbf{s}_x$ and $\mathbf{s}_y$ to encourage more 'targeted' or 'focused' representations; and a multiplicative factor β we build up the L_2 penalty by as we go deeper into the network, based on the intuition that deeper layers benefit less from weight sharing than shallow ones. This build up factor is applied by scaling the L_2 penalty by a factor of β for all layers in the Convolution (2) block, and β^2 for all layers in the Convolution (3) block of the network.

4.4   Results

We compare our results on MNIST to other approaches that use single models with no data augmentation in Table 2. Our best model does better than all previous CNN based methods on MNIST except a competitive multi-scale convolutional approach [40]. We are also outperformed by CapsNets [50], a new kind of neural network and not a drop in modification like AR. Both these network types have far more parameters and computational expenses than ours.

The TKNs corresponding to the CNN6 baseline (TKN6) match its performance, coupled with a huge boost in efficiency (**13× less floating point operations** in the forward pass). Introducing target layers benefits both the efficiency and performance when used with the DN10 models (**21% reduced error rate**).

Table 5. Error rates (%) on the GTSRB dataset. We achieve comparable performance with nearly a 3× reduction in #FLOPS.

Network	Params	FLOPs	Error
STN	1.18M	145M	1.52
TSTN (Cauchy, $L_2 = 0.001, \beta = 2$)	1.18M	55.7M	1.53

Table 6. Regression errors (on a scale of 0–16) on the UNBC-McMaster Pain Archive. Here, we achive a 2× reduction in #FLOPS without loss in performance.

Network	Params	FLOPs	MSE	MAE
DN40	0.83M	802M	1.67	0.51
TDN40 (Cauchy, $L_2 = 10^{-4}, \beta = 4$)	0.83M	391M	1.67	0.50

The results on tlMNIST are shown in Table 3. Since the input data is highly 'aligned', we see significant improvement in results for both baselines. Another interesting observation is that the performance of the best networks on tlMNIST matches the MNIST results, showing that the effect of additional distractors has been completely negated by AR.

The results on SVHN are shown in Table 4. Since models with the Gaussian attention function were far more difficult to tune in experiments on MNIST, we fix the Cauchy attention function for the remaining experiments. We obtain the best reported results (to our knowledge) on the reduced SVHN dataset where the extra training images are not used.

The classification errors on the GTSRB test set are shown in Table 5. We also report the mean squared error (MSE) and mean average error (MAE) for regression on the validation partition of the Pain Archive in Table 6. On both tasks, we see distinctive benefits in terms of efficiency without loss in performance, showing the applicability of AR to network acceleration on practical tasks. Because we adopted hyper-parameter settings optimized for the CNN baselines in our study, we believe that further gains in accuracy of TKNs may be obtained by more detailed tuning of hyper-parameters and learning rate schedules.

5 Discussion

Figure 4 shows the attention maps $\mathbf{F}_{att}$ learned by the TDN10 models corresponding to each of the six target layers. Our experimental results combined with these visualizations give us some insight into the role of attention in CNN architectures.

Implicit Attention in CNNs. A surprising observation is the near-identical error rate of the DN10 baseline on both MNIST (0.48%) and tlMNIST (0.50%). The network has no explicit way to pay more attention to any part of the input

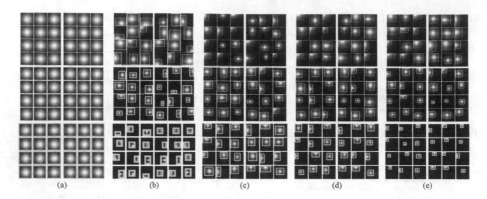

Fig. 4. Attention maps using the *Cauchy* function. (a) Initialization. (b) After training on MNIST, $L_2 = 10^{-4}, \beta = 4$. We notice large portions of the attention maps are vacant, particularly in the deeper layers. (c) After training on tlMNIST, $L_2 = 2 \times 10^{-4}, \beta = 1$. (d) tlMNIST, $L_2 = 10^{-4}, \beta = 2$. Though (c) and (d) have similar computational costs, (d) obtains slightly better performance. (e) tlMNIST, $L_2 = 10^{-4}, \beta = 4$. Slightly better gains in efficiency can be obtained by scaling β instead of L_2.

images, since it has no max pooling or FC layers. This means that for the tlM-NIST task, the convolutional architecture itself learns to 'attend' to only the top-left portion of the image. This is possible because of the large convolutional receptive fields of the deeper layers. Each unit in the final convolutional layer has an effective receptive field larger than the entire input image. For tlMNIST, these units can learn locations associated with a given handwritten digit by simply looking for not just the digit, but a formation of the digit and a pattern associated with its location, such as the empty space to its bottom right and some portion of the three random digits around it. This is still an inconvenient task, which is why TKNs significantly improve the baseline (24% reduction in error rate). The size of the receptive fields explains why the attention maps of the deeper layers in Fig. 4(c), (d) and (e) are not all on the extreme top-left portion of the image.

Fully Convolutional TKNs. Each TKN kernel location is parametrized by $\mathbf{m}_x$, $\mathbf{m}_y$, $\mathbf{s}_x$ and $\mathbf{s}_y$, which are all relative values with respect to the absolute height and width of the image. Spatial structure in terms of layout is the crucial ingredient in the performance of TKNs, and if this remains similar, they can be applied to images of varying sizes and aspect ratios by using the same relative learned parameters scaled as per the new input resolution. To apply a TKN in a fully convolutional manner over a large image (for example, as a face detector), we first convert the relative parameters to absolute parameters by choosing a scaling for the attention layers in our fully convolutional TKN. This means a TKN learned at any resolution can be specialized to any other resolution by adjusting the chosen parameter scaling.

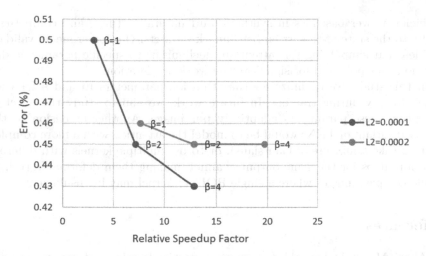

Fig. 5. Effect of L_2 and β on performance and efficiency. Relative speedup factor is the ratio of #FLOPs between the network and the CNN6 baseline. Better speed-performance tradeoffs are achieved through larger values of β.

Network Interpretability. In traditional CNNs, we have seen how a deeper convolutional kernel may represent a mixture of patterns using its implicit attention and large receptive field. For example, when dealing with facial images, a kernel may learn to be activated by a certain combination of the eyes and mouth. Such complex knowledge representations greatly decrease the interpretability of the network [72]. By introducing attention explicitly, kernels in TKNs can be encouraged to look at tiny areas in the inputs by increasing L_2. This makes them much more likely to be associated with single objects or parts, increasing the network interpretability. This is of great value when we need humans to trust a network's predictions.

Network Acceleration. Figure 5 shows the performance of TKN6 on MNIST as the L_2 penalty is varied. We see that a trade-off between speed and accuracy can be tuned by adjusting this penalty term while training. We also see that building up the L_2 penalty gradually over depth using β improves performance in comparison to having a fixed penalty throughout the network. This validates our assumption that deeper, more abstract features require less weight sharing.

6 Conclusion

We proposed a new regularization method for CNNs called Attentive Regularization. It constrains the activation maps throughout the network to lie within specific ROIs associated with each kernel. This is done through a simple yet powerful modification of the convolutional layers, retaining end-to-end trainability with backpropagation. In our experiments, TKNs give a consistent improvement in efficiency over baselines in synthetic and natural settings, and competitive results to the state-of-the-art on benchmark datasets. Our experiments validate the idea that simplifying soft attention mechanisms to specific parametric distributions has potential for significant network acceleration.

In this study, we optimize for the attention parameters $\mathbf{m}$ and $\mathbf{s}$ for each kernel directly during training. In future work, we aim to study the effect of generating these parameters adaptively per image. Another extension to the proposed variant of TKNs would be to model the attention with a more complex function (like a mixture of Gaussians), or to use multiple kernels with different attention maps for the same output channel, making them deformable [15]; to handle complex images where a single ROI per kernel may be insufficient.

References

1. Abadi, M., et al.: TensorFlow: large-scale machine learning on heterogeneous distributed systems. CoRR abs/1603.04467 (2016)
2. Almahairi, A., Ballas, N., Cooijmans, T., Zheng, Y., Larochelle, H., Courville, A.C.: Dynamic capacity networks. CoRR abs/1511.07838 (2015)
3. Ba, J., Mnih, V., Kavukcuoglu, K.: Multiple object recognition with visual attention. CoRR abs/1412.7755 (2014)
4. Cao, C., et al.: Look and think twice: capturing top-down visual attention with feedback convolutional neural networks. In: ICCV (2015)
5. Chen, L., et al.: SCA-CNN: spatial and channel-wise attention in convolutional networks for image captioning. In: CVPR (2017)
6. Chen, T., Goodfellow, I.J., Shlens, J.: Net2Net: accelerating learning via knowledge transfer. CoRR abs/1511.05641 (2015)
7. Chen, W., Wilson, J.T., Tyree, S., Weinberger, K.Q., Chen, Y.: Compressing neural networks with the hashing trick. CoRR abs/1504.04788 (2015)
8. Cheng, Y., Wang, D., Zhou, P., Zhang, T.: A survey of model compression and acceleration for deep neural networks. ArXiv e-prints (2017)
9. Chollet, F.: Keras (2015). https://github.com/fchollet/keras
10. Denil, M., Bazzani, L., Larochelle, H., de Freitas, N.: Learning where to attend with deep architectures for image tracking. Neural Comput. **24**, 2151–2184 (2012)
11. Denton, E., Zaremba, W., Bruna, J., LeCun, Y., Fergus, R.: Exploiting linear structure within convolutional networks for efficient evaluation. CoRR abs/1404.0736 (2014)
12. Dieleman, S., Fauw, J.D., Kavukcuoglu, K.: Exploiting cyclic symmetry in convolutional neural networks. CoRR abs/1602.02660 (2016)
13. Dong, X., Huang, J., Yang, Y., Yan, S.: More is less: a more complicated network with less inference complexity. CoRR abs/1703.08651 (2017). http://arxiv.org/abs/1703.08651
14. Ekman, P., Friesen, W., Hager, J.: Facs manual. In: A Human Face (2002). https://www.scirp.org/(S(i43dyn45teexjx455qlt3d2q))/reference/ReferencesPapers.aspx?ReferenceID=1850657
15. Felzenszwalb, P.F., Girshick, R.B., McAllester, D., Ramanan, D.: Object detection with discriminatively trained part-based models. IEEE Trans. Pattern Anal. Mach. Intell. **32**, 1627–1645 (2010)

16. Figurnov, M., Vetrov, D.P., Kohli, P.: PerforatedCNNs: acceleration through elimination of redundant convolutions. CoRR abs/1504.08362 (2015). http://arxiv.org/abs/1504.08362

17. Fu, J., Zheng, H., Mei, T.: Look closer to see better: recurrent attention convolutional neural network for fine-grained image recognition. In: CVPR (2017)

18. Girdhar, R., Ramanan, D.: Attentional pooling for action recognition. In: NIPS (2017)

19. Girshick, R.B.: Fast R-CNN. CoRR abs/1504.08083 (2015)

20. Girshick, R.B., Donahue, J., Darrell, T., Malik, J.: Rich feature hierarchies for accurate object detection and semantic segmentation. CoRR abs/1311.2524 (2013)

21. Gregor, K., Danihelka, I., Graves, A., Rezende, D.J., Wierstra, D.: DRAW: a recurrent neural network for image generation. In: ICML (2015)

22. Han, S., Mao, H., Dally, W.J.: Deep compression: compressing deep neural network with pruning, trained quantization and huffman coding. CoRR abs/1510.00149 (2015)

23. He, K., Zhang, X., Ren, S., Sun, J.: Deep residual learning for image recognition. arXiv preprint arXiv:1512.03385 (2015)

24. He, K., Zhang, X., Ren, S., Sun, J.: Delving deep into rectifiers: surpassing human-level performance on imagenet classification. CoRR abs/1502.01852 (2015)

25. Hendricks, L.A., Venugopalan, S., Rohrbach, M., Mooney, R.J., Saenko, K., Darrell, T.: Deep compositional captioning: describing novel object categories without paired training data. CoRR abs/1511.05284 (2015)

26. Hinton, G., Vinyals, O., Dean, J.: Distilling the knowledge in a neural network. ArXiv e-prints (2015)

27. Huang, G., Liu, Z., van der Maaten, L., Weinberger, K.Q.: Densely connected convolutional networks. In: CVPR, July 2017

28. Ioffe, S., Szegedy, C.: Batch normalization: accelerating deep network training by reducing internal covariate shift. CoRR abs/1502.03167 (2015)

29. Jaderberg, M., Simonyan, K., Zisserman, A., Kavukcuoglu, K.: Spatial transformer networks. CoRR abs/1506.02025 (2015)

30. Jaderberg, M., Vedaldi, A., Zisserman, A.: Speeding up convolutional neural networks with low rank expansions. CoRR abs/1405.3866 (2014)

31. Kawaguchi, K., Kaelbling, L.P., Bengio, Y.: Generalization in deep learning. ArXiv e-prints (2017)

32. Kingma, D.P., Ba, J.: Adam: a method for stochastic optimization. CoRR abs/1412.6980 (2014)

33. Krizhevsky, A., Sutskever, I., Hinton, G.: Imagenet classification with deep convolutional neural networks. In: NIPS (2012)

34. Larochelle, H., Hinton, G.E.: Learning to combine foveal glimpses with a third-order Boltzmann machine. In: NIPS (2010)

35. Lebedev, V., Lempitsky, V.S.: Fast ConvNets using group-wise brain damage. CoRR abs/1506.02515 (2015)

36. Lecun, Y., Bottou, L., Bengio, Y., Haffner, P.: Gradient-based learning applied to document recognition. Proc. IEEE **86**, 2278–2324 (1998)

37. Lee, C.Y., Xie, S., Gallagher, P., Zhang, Z., Tu, Z.: Deeply-supervised nets. ArXiv e-prints (2014)

38. Li, W., Abtahi, F., Zhu, Z.: Action unit detection with region adaptation, multi-labeling learning and optimal temporal fusing. CoRR abs/1704.03067 (2017)

39. Li, W., Abtahi, F., Zhu, Z., Yin, L.: EAC-NET: a region-based deep enhancing and cropping approach for facial action unit detection. CoRR abs/1702.02925 (2017)

40. Liao, Z., Carneiro, G.: Competitive multi-scale convolution. CoRR abs/1511.05635 (2015)
41. Lin, M., Chen, Q., Yan, S.: Network in network. CoRR abs/1312.4400 (2013)
42. Lu, J., Xiong, C., Parikh, D., Socher, R.: Knowing when to look: adaptive attention via a visual sentinel for image captioning. In: CVPR (2017)
43. Lucey, P., Cohn, J.F., Prkachin, K.M., Solomon, P.E., Matthews, I.: Painful data: the UNBC-McMaster shoulder pain expression archive database. In: Face and Gesture 2011 (2011)
44. Nam, H., Ha, J.W., Kim, J.: Dual attention networks for multimodal reasoning and matching. In: CVPR (2017)
45. Netzer, Y., Wang, T., Coates, A., Bissacco, A., Wu, B., Ng, A.Y.: Reading digits in natural images with unsupervised feature learning (2011)
46. Rastegari, M., Ordonez, V., Redmon, J., Farhadi, A.: XNOR-Net: imagenet classification using binary convolutional neural networks. CoRR abs/1603.05279 (2016)
47. Ren, M., Pokrovsky, A., Yang, B., Urtasun, R.: SBNet: sparse blocks network for fast inference. CoRR abs/1801.02108 (2018). http://arxiv.org/abs/1801.02108
48. Ren, S., He, K., Girshick, R.B., Sun, J.: Faster R-CNN: towards real-time object detection with region proposal networks. CoRR abs/1506.01497 (2015)
49. Romero, A., Ballas, N., Kahou, S.E., Chassang, A., Gatta, C., Bengio, Y.: FitNets: hints for thin deep nets. CoRR abs/1412.6550 (2014)
50. Sabour, S., Frosst, N., Hinton, G.E.: Dynamic routing between capsules. ArXiv e-prints (2017)
51. Schmidhuber, J., Huber, R.: Learning to generate artificial fovea trajectories for target detection. Int. J. Neural Syst. 2, 125–134 (1991)
52. Seo, P.H., Lin, Z., Cohen, S., Shen, X., Han, B.: Hierarchical attention networks. CoRR abs/1606.02393 (2016)
53. Shih, K.J., Singh, S., Hoiem, D.: Where to look: focus regions for visual question answering. CoRR abs/1511.07394 (2015)
54. Shyam, P., Gupta, S., Dukkipati, A.: Attentive recurrent comparators. In: ICML (2017)
55. Simonyan, K., Zisserman, A.: Very deep convolutional networks for large-scale image recognition. CoRR abs/1409.1556 (2014)
56. Srinivas, S., Babu, R.V.: Data-free parameter pruning for deep neural networks. CoRR abs/1507.06149 (2015)
57. Srivastava, N., Hinton, G., Krizhevsky, A., Sutskever, I., Salakhutdinov, R.: Dropout: a simple way to prevent neural networks from overfitting. J. Mach. Learn. Res. 15, 1929–1958 (2014)
58. Stallkamp, J., Schlipsing, M., Salmen, J., Igel, C.: The German traffic sign recognition Benchmark: a multi-class classification competition. In: IEEE International Joint Conference on Neural Networks (2011)
59. Stollenga, M.F., Masci, J., Gomez, F.J., Schmidhuber, J.: Deep networks with internal selective attention through feedback connections. CoRR abs/1407.3068 (2014)
60. Sun, Y., Wang, X., Tang, X.: Deep learning face representation from predicting 10,000 classes. In: CVPR (2014)
61. Sutskever, I., Martens, J., Dahl, G., Hinton, G.: On the importance of initialization and momentum in deep learning. In: ICML (2013)
62. Szegedy, C., Ioffe, S., Vanhoucke, V.: Inception-v4, inception-resnet and the impact of residual connections on learning. CoRR abs/1602.07261 (2016)
63. Tai, C., Xiao, T., Wang, X., E, W.: Convolutional neural networks with low-rank regularization. CoRR abs/1511.06067 (2015)

64. Taigman, Y., Yang, M., Ranzato, M., Wolf, L.: DeepFace: closing the gap to human-level performance in face verification. In: CVPR (2014)
65. Wu, B., Iandola, F.N., Jin, P.H., Keutzer, K.: SqueezeDet: unified, small, low power fully convolutional neural networks for real-time object detection for autonomous driving. CoRR abs/1612.01051 (2016)
66. Xiao, T., Xu, Y., Yang, K., Zhang, J., Peng, Y., Zhang, Z.: The application of two-level attention models in deep convolutional neural network for fine-grained image classification. CoRR abs/1411.6447 (2014)
67. Xiong, C., Merity, S., Socher, R.: Dynamic memory networks for visual and textual question answering. CoRR abs/1603.01417 (2016)
68. Xu, K., et al.: Show, attend and tell: neural image caption generation with visual attention. CoRR abs/1502.03044 (2015)
69. Yang, Z., He, X., Gao, J., Deng, L., Smola, A.: Stacked attention networks for image question answering. In: CVPR (2016)
70. Zagoruyko, S., Komodakis, N.: Paying more attention to attention: improving the performance of convolutional neural networks via attention transfer. CoRR abs/1612.03928 (2016)
71. Zagoruyko, S., Komodakis, N.: Wide residual networks. CoRR abs/1605.07146 (2016)
72. Zhang, Q., Wu, Y.N., Zhu, S.: Interpretable convolutional neural networks. CoRR abs/1710.00935 (2017)
73. Zhao, K., Chu, W.S., Zhang, H.: Deep region and multi-label learning for facial action unit detection. In: CVPR (2016)

Small Defect Detection Using Convolutional Neural Network Features and Random Forests

Xinghui Dong[✉], Chris J. Taylor, and Tim F. Cootes

Centre for Imaging Sciences, The University of Manchester,
Manchester M13 9PT, UK
{xinghui.dong,chris.taylor,timothy.f.cootes}@manchester.ac.uk

Abstract. We address the problem of identifying small abnormalities in an imaged region, important in applications such as industrial inspection. The goal is to label the pixels corresponding to a defect with a minimum of false positives. A common approach is to run a sliding-window classifier over the image. Recent Fully Convolutional Networks (FCNs), such as U-Net, can be trained to identify pixels corresponding to abnormalities given a suitable training set. However in many application domains it is hard to collect large numbers of defect examples (by their nature they are rare). Although U-Net can work in this scenario, we show that better results can be obtained by replacing the final softmax layer of the network with a Random Forest (RF) using features sampled from the earlier network layers. We also demonstrate that rather than just thresholding the resulting probability image to identify defects it is better to compute Maximally Stable Extremal Regions (MSERs). We apply the approach to the challenging problem of identifying defects in radiographs of aerospace welds.

Keywords: Defect detection · Non-destructive evaluation · CNN Local features · Random Forests

1 Introduction

Inspection tasks, where one is looking for small defects in large regions, can be challenging because (1) any useful system must have a very low false positive rate and (2) since defects are rare it is not always easy to obtain large numbers of examples to train a classifier or a region-based object detector. Given their success in other areas [16], it is natural to try Fully Convolutional Networks such as U-Net [21] to label each pixel in a region to indicate those that belong to abnormalities of interest. In this paper we show that when only small numbers of training examples are available, such techniques perform poorly. However, we go on to show that the features that are learnt in the different U-Net layers are useful for discriminating good from bad, and that a Random Forest, trained to

© Springer Nature Switzerland AG 2019
L. Leal-Taixé and S. Roth (Eds.): ECCV 2018 Workshops, LNCS 11132, pp. 398–412, 2019.
https://doi.org/10.1007/978-3-030-11018-5_35

classify each pixel based on such features, achieves a much better result than the usual final softmax layer in the U-Net.

The output of such an approach is a label image, giving the probability that each pixel belongs to a defect. A natural approach to identifying defects using such an image is to apply a threshold, then select the connected regions passing this threshold. This approach is prone to false positives. We show that better results can be obtained by computing Maximally Stable Extremal Regions (MSERs) [18] in the probability image, then identifying which are likely to be true defects by examining the distribution of probabilities across the region.

We demonstrate the system on the task of identifying defects in radiographs of welds in aerospace components - a safety critical application where currently visual inspection by a human expert is the norm. Figure 1 shows an example of a region extracted along a typical weld [7], and an example of a defect that should be detected. Note that this is a particularly obvious defect - many are much more subtle.

(a) Image covering region around a weld, with an example of a defect

(b) Patch

Fig. 1. Examples of a radiograph along a weld [7].

To inspect large regions, we first normalise them and then break them down into patches. Each patch is fed to a U-Net [21]. The U-Net is trained only on patches sampled around the defects in the training set to avoid the system being overwhelmed with normal (non-defect) pixels which are in the vast majority.

The contributions of the work are (1) we describe a system for identifying small defect regions in large images; (2) we show that using a Random Forest at the end of the process significantly improves on the performance of U-Net in this domain; and (3) false positives can be reduced by using MSER to identify candidate regions, rather than a simple thresholding.

The rest of this paper is organised as follows. In the next section, we review some existing work. Our methodology is introduced in Sect. 3. The experiments are re-ported in Sect. 4. Our conclusions are drawn in Sect. 5.

2   Related Work

2.1   Defect Detection Using Images

Non-destructive evaluation (NDE) of manufactured components [1,7,14] is critical in many industries such as aerospace. Even small defects can significantly reduce the life of a component, potentially leading to failure and accidents. Human inspection by trained experts is still the norm in the industry, but can be inconsistent, subjective, tedious and time-consuming [14]. There is a need to develop of automatic inspection systems to reduce the workload of inspectors and provide more consistent, objective and efficient decisions.

Kehoe and Parker [11] applied a thresholding method to the statistics of pixels for defect detection. Wang and Liao [25] detected defect candidates using the background subtraction and histogram thresholding approaches. The two-stage method that Wang et al. [26] introduced for line defect detection includes defect detection and defect refinement. Yazid et al. [27] used the inverse surface thresholding technique for defect detection. Using grayscale arranging pairs (GAP) features, Zhao et al. [29] first constructed a model based on the pixel pairs which own the stable intensity relationship. Defect detection was performed by thresholding the difference in the intensity-difference signs between the novel image and the model. A series of basic image processing operations were used by Boaretto and Centeno [1]. Recently, Dong et al. [7] developed a weld defect detection method using Haar-like features [24] and Random Forests [2]. Although this method produced promising results, some defects were still missed.

2.2   CNN-Based Image Segmentation

The above approaches were normally implemented using either basic image processing methods, or traditional features and classifiers. In contrast, Convolutional Neural Network (CNN) techniques [13] have shown state-of-the-art performance in many computer vision tasks. Training a CNN requires a large number of labelled examples. Alternatively, the fully-connected (FC) layer of a pre-trained CNN can be used as a generic feature extractor [19]. Ren et al. [20] used the FC features extracted from a set of image patches to train a classifier. The classifier can be used to predict as to whether or not a patch contains defects. However, extraction of FC features from patches is time-consuming. This issue limits the practicability of the method in the real industrial inspection. Using a large image patch set, Chen and Jahanshahi [3] trained a CNN classifier from scratch for detecting cracks. Naïve Bayes decision making was used to remove false positives. However, where only few images are available for training, the system will not work so well.

Using a sliding-window CNN classifier, Ciresan et al. [5] segmented the neuronal membranes contained in electron microscopy images. Girshick et al. [8] applied a region classifier to semantic segmentation. The FC features extracted from a set of regions that were produced by region proposal were first fed into a regressor. Then, the regressor was used to predict the quality score of each region in terms of a class. Hariharan et al. [10] proposed the hypercolumn features that were extracted at multiple CNN layers in order to exploit both the localisation and semantic data. Instead of using a pre-trained CNN as the feature extractor, Long et al. [16] adapted it into a Fully Convolutional Network (FCN) and transferred its representations to semantic segmentation by fine-tuning this CNN using a large domain-specific dataset.

However, such a large dataset may be unavailable in some fields, e.g. medical image processing. To address this problem, Ronneberger et al. [21] developed a novel CNN architecture, U-Net. It comprises a contracting path encoding the context information and a symmetric expanding path that captures the localisation data (see Fig. 2). Using even a small dataset, U-Net can be trained end-to-end from scratch and outperformed the method that Ciresan et al. [5] proposed. For segmentation of neuronal cells in confocal microscopy images, it is challenging to label the pixel-wise ground-truth. When only a relatively small set of instance-wise ground-truth images are available, the direct training of FCNs becomes impractical. Chen et al. [4] proposed a method to train pixel-wise Complete Bipartite Networks (CB-Net) using these data. Zhang et al. [28] applied a Deep Adversarial Network (DAN) model to biomedical image segmentation in which the annotated or unannotated images were available.

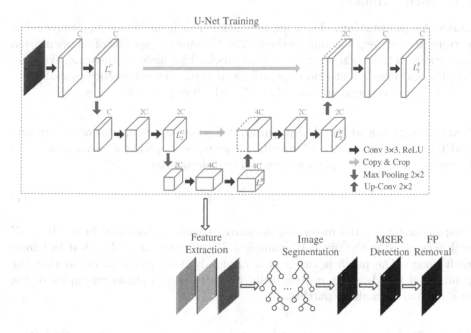

Fig. 2. The flowchart of the proposed small defect detection approach.

3 Methodology

We assume that we have a training set containing example images each containing typical defects, together with binary label images indicating the pixels belonging to each defect. Since defects are small and rare, the defect pixels are a tiny minority of all pixels, making training difficult. To train a U-Net [21], each image is first augmented with rotations, reflections and distortions, and is then normalised by applying a linear transformation to zero the mean and arrange for the variance to be unity. Patches are further extracted around each defect. We train a U-Net to predict the binary pixel labels using this set. We then train a Random Forest to use features extracted at each pixel position in the U-Net to predict the pixel label - essentially replacing the final softmax layer of U-Net with a Random Forest classifier. Random Forests are known to generalise well from small numbers of samples [6,15], so are suitable for this application.

Figure 2 shows the flowchart of the proposed approach to process a new image. The output of the U-Net + RF is a probability image. We compute Maximally Stable Extremal Regions (MSERs) in this probability image, and analyse each to discard false positives. In the following we describe the steps of the training and processing in detail, and show the results of experiments evaluating the performance of the different parts of the system.

3.1   U-Net Training

Data Augmentation. Data augmentation has been shown to improve the performance of deep learning methods [23]. We apply a pipeline of augmentation operations to the images and associated labels. This includes shearing, skewing, flipping and elastic distortion operations in turn. The occurrence probabilities for the four operations are 0.5, 0.5, 0.75 and 1.0 respectively.

Normalisation and Patch Sampling. We enhance the contrast of each image, and improve invariance to illumination effects, by applying z-normalisation [9] to each image. At each pixel we apply a transformation.

$$p' = \frac{p - \mu}{\sigma}, \tag{1}$$

where μ and σ are the mean and standard deviation computed in the $W \times W$ region centered at the pixel. We sample a $P \times P$ patch around each defect from each image. The patch is taken at a randomly displaced position so that the position of the defect is not centrally biased. Figure 3 shows examples of the original and normalised patches.

Model Training. We use the Adam [12] approach for parameter optimisation in U-Net [21], training on the pre-processed patches.

3.2   Feature Extraction Using the Pre-trained U-Net

Using the pre-trained U-Net [21], one can extract features from an image at different convolutional layers. We use the second convolutional layer at each level on one path for feature extraction (see Fig. 2 for more details). Given the U-Net contains L levels, the second convolutional layer at the bottom level (i.e. the L-th level) is denoted as L^B. In terms of the contracting (left) and expanding (right) paths at the j-th ($j \in \{1, \cdots, L - 1\}$) level, we denote the second convolutional

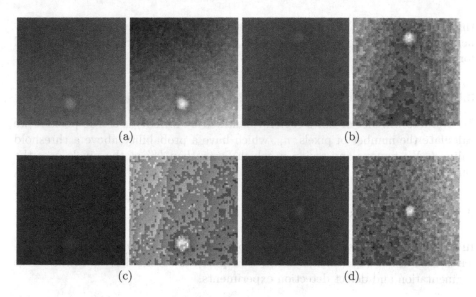

Fig. 3. Examples of z-normalisation ($W = 71$). (Left: Original, Right: Normalised). For display purposes, the image patches have been enlarged.

layer as: L_j^C and L_j^E respectively. For an $M \times N$ image, a series of $M' \times N' \times C$ (C is the number of filters) feature maps can be computed at one of the L^B, L_j^C and L_j^E layers. Each feature map is individually resized to the size of $M \times N$ using bilinear interpolation. In this context, each pixel is represented by C features. Motivated by the use of hypercolumn features [10], we also extracted features at multiple layers and concatenate these along the feature channel axis. The feature vectors at each pixel are independently L_2 normalised.

3.3 Image Segmentation Using a Random Forest

We apply the U-Net [21] to the (un-augmented) training set and obtain feature vectors for each pixel. We create a training set of feature vectors by extracting the vectors associated with every positive (defect) pixel and an equal number of (randomly sampled) negative pixels. These samples are used to train a random forest to estimate the pixel label based from the feature vector.

Given a new image, an output probability image is created by applying U-Net, then using the random forest to estimate the defect probability at every pixel.

3.4 Defect Candidate Detection Using the MSER Detector

We use the Maximally Stable Extremal Region (MSER) detector [18] to identify defect candidates from each probability image. The image is first linearly stretched to the range $[0, 255]$. Compared with applying a threshold to the image, this method exploits the higher level characteristics encoded in connected components. After MSER detection is complete, a set of defect candidates are obtained for each test image.

3.5 False Positive Removal

To evaluate whether or not a region (identified by MSER) is a true positive we calculate the number of pixels, n_p, which have a probability above a threshold value, t. We remove any region in which fewer than $k\%$ of the pixels pass the threshold.

4 Experiments

In this section, we first introduce the experimental setup and performance measures used in our experiments. Then, we report the results derived in the image segmentation and defect detection experiments.

4.1 Setup

We used a set of 43 X-ray images and associated label images collected by Dong et al. [7] from an aerospace manufacturing company. Each image had at least one defect. Defects are rare in aerospace components, making it difficult to obtain a large dataset. We used a 10-fold cross validation scheme for all experiments reported. For each split, data augmentation leads to 10 extra images for each training image. 64×64 patches sampled from the original and augmented images were used for training a single U-Net [21]; while only the original images were used for training an individual random forest classifier [2]. When testing, only the original images were used for both U-Net and random forests. All images (including those used for sampling patches) were processed using z-normalisation with $W = 71$.

U-Net [21] was trained using different levels and numbers of filters (batch size = 8, 100 epochs and 32 iterations per epoch). To train the random forest, feature vectors were extracted from one or more U-Net layers and concatenated. All images or patches were padded with zeros in order to generate the probability map with the same size as the input. Given an F dimensional feature vector, a subset of $\lceil \sqrt{F} \rceil$ features were randomly selected using the random forest classifier. The Gini impurity measure [2] was used to choose the feature and threshold at each node. The minimum number of samples at each terminal node was set to 0.01% of the training set size.

4.2 Performance Measures

We measure the per-pixel classification performance using the Receiver Operating Characteristic (ROC) curve, plotting the true positive against false positive fraction for each of a choice of probability threshold values, t. In order to derive a single quantitative measure, we computed the Area under the Curve (AUC) from a ROC curve. Since defect detection focuses on identifying defects rather than single pixels we use an object level measure, i.e. Free Response Operating Characteristic (FROC), plotting the proportion of defects detected against the number of false positives per image. We consider a defect detected if more than half of its area is included in a positive detection region. We used a threshold of $k = 59$ (chosen empirically using pilot experiments) when discarding false positive MSERs.

4.3   Image Segmentation

We first tested the impact of different experimental parameters on image segmentation. Then, we compared the proposed feature set with other image feature sets.

Impact of the Number of Levels. We first trained U-Net [21] using between 1 and 4 levels. Figure 4 shows the ROC curves and AUC values derived using L ($L \in \{1, \cdots, 4\}$) levels U-Net alone. The best result for this data (AUC: 0.9825) was obtained using three levels.

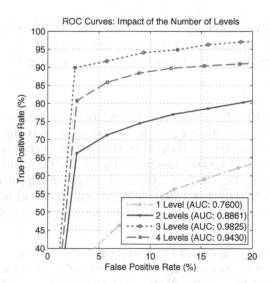

Fig. 4. ROC curves plotted using the results of different numbers of U-Net [21] levels for weld image segmentation. (Only the top-left part of each curve is shown. See main text for details).

Impact of the Number of Filters. We trained 3-level U-Nets using C ($C \in \{32, 64, 128\}$) filters - see Fig. 5. The highest AUC value: 0.9825 was produced using 64 filters.

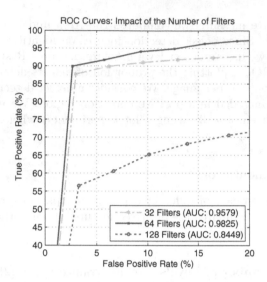

Fig. 5. ROC curves plotted using the results of the 3-level U-Net [21] with different numbers of filters for weld image segmentation. (Only the top-left part of each curve is shown. See main text for details).

Impact of Z-Normalisation. We trained the U-Net with and without z-normalisation [9] on the input patches. As shown in Fig. 6, the use of z-normalisation greatly boosted the performance, increasing the AUC from 0.88 to 0.98.

Softmax vs. Random Forests. Since the softmax layer is immediately placed behind the convolutional layer: L_1^E in U-Net, we examined the performance of the random forest classifier [2] along with the features extracted at this layer. We used 25 and 200 trees for the classifier individually. The results are compared with that generated by the softmax layer in Fig. 7. Although softmax yielded the slightly higher AUC value than those obtained using random forests, the latter produced higher true positive rates when false positive rates were below 11%.

Impact of Different Layers of the Pre-trained U-Net. Given three levels were used for U-Net we tested features from five different convolutional layers, L_1^C, L_2^C, L^B, L_2^E and L_1^E (see Fig. 2). For each layer, features were extracted and used to train a single random forest classifier. The results are displayed in Fig. 8. Features from the bottom convolutional layer, L^B, produced the best results.

Single-layer vs. Multi-layer of the Pre-trained U-Net. Inspired by the application of hypercolumn features [10], we extracted features at multiple layers of U-Net. Table 1 reports the AUC values obtained using the convolutional layer: L^B and nine different combinations of U-Net layers. As can be seen, the

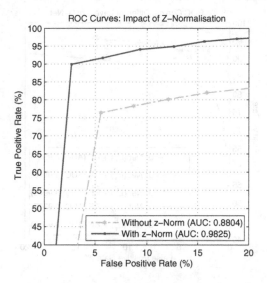

Fig. 6. ROC curves plotted using the results of the end-to-end trained U-Nets [21] with and without z-normalisation for weld image segmentation. (Only the top-left part of each curve is shown. See main text for details).

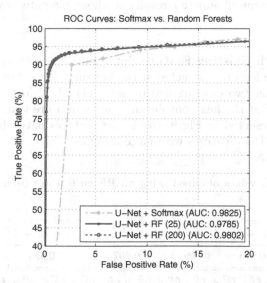

Fig. 7. ROC curves plotted using the results of the end-to-end trained U-Net [21] and the features extracted using this U-Net and random forests for weld image segmentation. (Only the top-left part of each curve is shown. See main text for details).

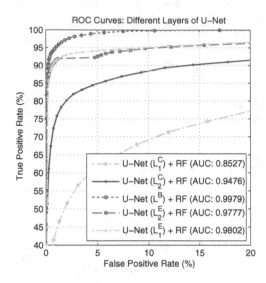

Fig. 8. ROC curves plotted using the results of the different layers of a pre-trained 3-level U-Net [21] for weld image segmentation. (Only the top-left part of each curve is shown. See main text for details).

single layer L^B produced superior results to those generated by its multi-layer counterparts.

Comparison with Existing Feature Sets. Finally, we compared the results obtained using the features extracted at the bottom layer L^B of U-Net [21] with those derived using two existing feature sets, (1) SIFT features [17] and (2) features extracted at the last convolutional layer of a pre-trained VGG-VD-16 [22] model. As presented in Fig. 9, the U-Net features outperformed both the SIFT and VGG-VD-16 features with large margins.

Table 1. The AUC values obtained using an RF on features from various layers of U-Net [21]

Layers	L^B	$L_1^E + L_2^E$	$L^B + L_1^E$	$L_1^C + L^B + L_1^E$	$L_2^C + L^B + L_2^E$	$L_1^C + L_2^C + L^B$
AUC	**0.998**	0.973	0.996	0.997	0.995	0.997

Layers	$L^B + L_2^E$	$L_1^C + L^B$	$L^B + L_2^E + L_1^E$	$L_1^C + L_2^C + L^B + L_2^E + L_1^E$
AUC	0.995	0.997	0.994	0.994

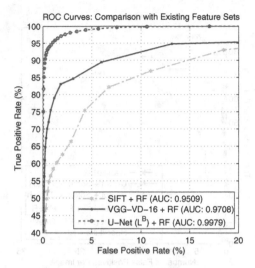

Fig. 9. ROC curves plotted using the results of random forests [2] and the SIFT [17] features, the local convolutional features extracted from the pre-trained VGG-VD-16 [22] and the features extracted from the pre-trained 3-level U-Net [21] for weld image segmentation. (Only the top-left part of each curve is shown. See main text for details).

4.4   Defect Detection

Figure 10 shows the FROC curves (proportion of defects detected vs. number of false positives per image) obtained using a hand-crafted method [25], the end-to-end trained U-Net with softmax, the U-Net features plus random forests, and the Haar-like features [24] plus random forests. We also compared the proposed MSER [18] based defect detection method with that implemented by thresholding the probability image for the two U-Net approaches. It can be seen that (1) the MSER-based defect detection performed better than the thresholding method; and (2) our approach (U-Net + RF) produced superior results to the other methods. Specifically, 84.5% of defects were detected when in average 2.4 false positives were detected per image. In contrast, the two digits are 83% and 2.7 for the Haar-like features plus random forests that Dong et al. [7] used. On the other hand, 72.4% of defects were detected using our approach with in average 0.5 false positives were obtained per image; while only 65.5% of defects were detected by the Haar-like features plus random forests. A more traditional image processing technique proposed by Wang and Liao [25] achieves much worse results; 34.5% of defects were detected when in average 31.2 false positives per image were generated.

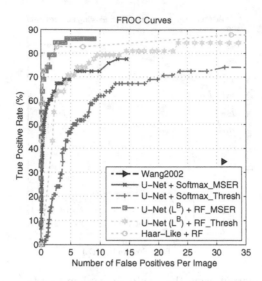

Fig. 10. The FROC curves obtained using four methods: a hand-crafted method [25], the end-to-end trained U-Net with softmax [21], the features extracted from the pre-trained U-Net plus random forests [2], and the Haar-like features [24] plus random forests. (See main text for details).

5   Conclusions

We described an approach for detecting rare, small abnormalities in imaging data, with a focus on defects visible in X-ray images of welds. The method augments U-Net with a Random Forest (RF), with the RF being trained to classify each pixel using features extracted from the U-Net. End-to-end training of U-Net leads to useful features, but the RF can make better use of them when only relatively small numbers of training examples are available. Instead of thresholding the probability map produced by the classifier, we identify defect candidates using the Maximally Stable Extremal Region (MSER) detector. This uses the higher level characteristics contained in connected components rather than simple pixel-wise thresholding. Some false positive regions can be removed by studying the pixel probabilities across the regions. The best performance obtained using our approach was superior to a variety of alternatives tested.

Although our approach was restricted by the limited number of training data, it still produced promising results. While all the learning based methods explored are likely to benefit from larger training sets, it is useful to identify techniques which will work well when few examples are available.

Acknowledgement. This work is supported by the Engineering and Physical Sciences Research Council (EPSRC) (No. EP/L022125/1). The Titan Xp used for this research was donated by the NVIDIA Corporation.

References

1. Boaretto, N., Centeno, T.: Automated detection of welding defects in pipelines from radiographic images DWDI. NDT & E Int. **86**, 7–13 (2017)
2. Breiman, L.: Random forests. Mach Learn. **45**(1), 5–32 (2001)
3. Chen, F., Jahanshahi, M.R.: NB-CNN: deep learning-based crack detection using convolutional neural network and Naïve Bayes data fusion. IEEE Trans. Industr. Electron. **65**(5), 4392–4400 (2018)
4. Chen, J., Banerjee, S., Grama, A., Scheirer, W.J., Chen, D.Z.: Neuron segmentation using deep complete bipartite networks. In: Descoteaux, M., Maier-Hein, L., Franz, A., Jannin, P., Collins, D.L., Duchesne, S. (eds.) MICCAI 2017, Part II. LNCS, vol. 10434, pp. 21–29. Springer, Cham (2017). https://doi.org/10.1007/978-3-319-66185-8_3
5. Ciresan, D., Gambardella, L., Giusti, A., Schmidhuber, J.: Deep neural networks segment neuronal membranes in electron microscopy images. In: Proceedings of NIPS, pp. 2852–2860 (2012)
6. Dong, X., Dong, J., Zhou, H., Sun, J., Tao, D.: Automatic chinese postal address block location using proximity descriptors and cooperative profit random forests. IEEE Trans. Industr. Electron. **65**(5), 4401–4412 (2018)
7. Dong, X., Taylor, C.J., Cootes, T.F.: Automatic inspection of aerospace welds using x-ray images. In: Proceedings of International Conference on Pattern Recognition (2018)
8. Girshick, R., Donahue, J., Darrell, T., Malik, J.: Rich feature hierarchies for accurate object detection and semantic segmentation. In: Proceedings of IEEE Conference on Computer Vision and Pattern Recognition (2014)
9. Goldin, D.Q., Kanellakis, P.C.: On similarity queries for time-series data: constraint specification and implementation. In: Montanari, U., Rossi, F. (eds.) CP 1995. LNCS, vol. 976, pp. 137–153. Springer, Heidelberg (1995). https://doi.org/10.1007/3-540-60299-2_9
10. Hariharan, B., Arbelez, P., Girshick, R., Malik, J.: Hypercolumns for object segmentation and fine-grained localization. In: Proceedings of IEEE Conference on Computer Vision and Pattern Recognition (2015)
11. Kehoe, A., Parker, G.: An intelligent knowledge based approach for the automated radiographic inspection of castings. NDT & E Int. **25**(1), 23–36 (1992)
12. Kingma, D., Adam, J.: A method for stochastic optimization (2017). arXiv:1412.6980
13. LeCun, Y., Bengio, Y., Hinton, G.: Deep learning. Nature **521**, 436–444 (2015)
14. Liao, T., Li, Y.: An automated radiographic ndt system for weld inspection: Part ll - flaw detection. NDT & E Int. **31**(3), 183–192 (1998)
15. Lindner, C., Bromiley, P., Ionita, M., Cootes, T.: Robust and accurate shape model matching using random forest regression-voting. IEEE Trans. PAMI **37**(9), 862–1874 (2015)
16. Long, J., Shelhamer, E., Darrell, T.: Fully convolutional networks for semantic segmentation. In: Proceedings of IEEE Conference on Computer Vision and Pattern Recognition, pp. 3431–3440 (2015)
17. Lowe, D.: Distinctive image features from scale-invariant keypoints. Int. J. Comput. Vis. **60**(2), 91–110 (2004)
18. Matas, J., Chum, O., Urban, M., Pajdla, T.: Robust wide baseline stereo from maximally stable extremal regions. In: Proceedings of British Machine Vision Conference, pp. 384–396 (2002)

19. Razavian, A., Azizpour, H., Sullivan, J., Carlsson, S.: CNN features off-the-shelf: an astounding baseline for recognition. In: Proceedings of IEEE Conference on Computer Vision and Pattern Recognition Workshops, pp. 512–519 (2014)
20. Ren, R., Hung, T., Tan, K.: A generic deep-learning-based approach for automated surface inspection. IEEE Trans. Cybern. **48**(3), 929–940 (2018)
21. Ronneberger, O., Fischer, P., Brox, T.: U-Net: convolutional networks for biomedical image segmentation. In: Navab, N., Hornegger, J., Wells, W.M., Frangi, A.F. (eds.) MICCAI 2015, Part III. LNCS, vol. 9351, pp. 234–241. Springer, Cham (2015). https://doi.org/10.1007/978-3-319-24574-4_28
22. Simonyan, K., Zisserman, A.: Very deep convolutional networks for large-scale visual recognition. In: Proceedings of International Conference on Learning Representations (2015)
23. Taylor, L., Nitschke, G.: Improving deep learning using generic data augmentation (2017). arXiv:1708.06020
24. Viola, P., Jones, M.: Rapid object detection using a boosted cascade of simple features. In: Proceedings of CVPR, pp. 511–518 (2001)
25. Wang, G., Liao, T.: Automatic identification of different types of welding defects in radiographic images. NDT & E Int. **35**, 519–528 (2002)
26. Wang, Y., Sun, Y., Lv, P., Wang, H.: Detection of line weld defects based on multiple thresholds and support vector machine. NDT & E Int. **41**, 517–524 (2008)
27. Yazid, H., Arof, H., Yazid, H., Ahmad, S., Mohamed, A., Ahmad, F.: Discontinuities detection in welded joints based on inverse surface thresholding. NDT & E Int. **44**, 563–570 (2011)
28. Zhang, Y., Yang, L., Chen, J., Fredericksen, M., Hughes, D.P., Chen, D.Z.: Deep adversarial networks for biomedical image segmentation utilizing unannotated images. In: Descoteaux, M., Maier-Hein, L., Franz, A., Jannin, P., Collins, D.L., Duchesne, S. (eds.) MICCAI 2017, Part III. LNCS, vol. 10435, pp. 408–416. Springer, Cham (2017). https://doi.org/10.1007/978-3-319-66179-7_47
29. Zhao, X., He, Z., Zhang, S.: Defect detection of castings in radiography images using a robust statistical feature. J. Opt. Soc. Am. A **31**(1), 196–205 (2014)

Compact Deep Aggregation
for Set Retrieval

Yujie Zhong[1](✉), Relja Arandjelović[2](✉), and Andrew Zisserman[1](✉)

[1] Visual Geometry Group, Department of Engineering Science,
University of Oxford, Oxford, UK
{yujie,az}@robots.ox.ac.uk
[2] DeepMind, London, UK
relja@google.com

Abstract. The objective of this work is to learn a compact embedding of a set of descriptors that is suitable for efficient retrieval and ranking, whilst maintaining discriminability of the individual descriptors. We focus on a specific example of this general problem – that of retrieving images containing multiple faces from a large scale dataset of images. Here the set consists of the face descriptors in each image, and given a query for multiple identities, the goal is then to retrieve, in order, images which contain all the identities, all but one, etc.

To this end, we make the following contributions: first, we propose a CNN architecture – *SetNet* – to achieve the objective: it learns face descriptors and their aggregation over a set to produce a compact fixed length descriptor designed for set retrieval, and the score of an image is a count of the number of identities that match the query; second, we show that this compact descriptor has minimal loss of discriminability up to two faces per image, and degrades slowly after that – far exceeding a number of baselines; third, we explore the speed vs. retrieval quality trade-off for set retrieval using this compact descriptor; and, finally, we collect and annotate a large dataset of images containing various number of celebrities, which we use for evaluation and will be publicly released.

1   Introduction

Suppose we wish to retrieve all images in a very large collection of personal photos that contain a particular set of people, such as a group of friends or a family. Then we would like the retrieved images that contain all of the set to be ranked first, followed by images containing subsets, e.g. if there are three friends in the query, then first would be images containing all three friends, then images containing two of the three, followed by images containing only one of them. We would also like this retrieval to happen in real time.

Electronic supplementary material The online version of this chapter (https://doi.org/10.1007/978-3-030-11018-5_36) contains supplementary material, which is available to authorized users.

© Springer Nature Switzerland AG 2019
L. Leal-Taixé and S. Roth (Eds.): ECCV 2018 Workshops, LNCS 11132, pp. 413–430, 2019.
https://doi.org/10.1007/978-3-030-11018-5_36

Fig. 1. Images ranked using set retrieval for two example queries. The query faces are given on the left of each example column, together with their names (only for reference). Left: a query for two identities; right: a query for three identities. The first ranked image in each case contains all the faces in the query. Lower ranked images partially satisfy the query, and contain progressively fewer faces of the query. The results are obtained using the compact set retrieval descriptor generated by the SetNet architecture, by searching over 200k images of the *Celebrity Together* dataset introduced in this paper.

This is an example of a *set retrieval problem*: each image contains a set of elements (faces in this case), and we wish to order the images according to a query (on multiple identities) such that those images satisfying the query completely are ranked first (i.e. those images that contain all the identities of the query), followed by images that satisfy all but one of the query identities, etc. An example of this ranking is shown in Fig. 1 for two queries.

We can operationalize this by scoring each face in each photo of the collection as to whether they are one of the identities in the query. Each face is represented by a fixed length vector, and identities are scored by logistic regression classifiers. But, consider the situation where the dataset is very large, containing millions or billions of images each containing multiple faces. In this situation two aspects are crucial for real time retrieval: first, that all operations take place in memory (not reading from disk), and second that an efficient algorithm is used when searching for images that satisfy the query. The problem is that storing a fixed length vector for each *face* in memory is prohibitively expensive at this scale, but this cost can be significantly reduced if a fixed length vector is only stored for each *set of faces* in an image (since there are far fewer images than faces). As well as reducing the memory cost this also reduces the run time cost of the search since fewer vectors need to be scored.

So, the question we investigate in this paper is the following: can we aggregate the *set of vectors* representing the multiple faces in an image into a *single vector* with little loss of set-retrieval performance? If so, then the cost of both memory and retrieval can be significantly reduced as only one vector per *image* (rather than one per *face*) have to be stored and scored.

Although we have motivated this question by face retrieval it is quite general: there is a set of elements, each element is represented by a vector of dimension D, and we wish to represent this set by a single vector of dimension D', where $D' = D$ in practice, without losing information essential for the task. Of course, if the total number of elements in all sets, N, is such that $N \leq D$ then this certainly can be achieved provided that the set of vectors are orthogonal. However, we will consider the situation commonly found in practice where $N \gg D$, e.g. D is small, typically 128 (to keep the memory footprint low), and N is in the thousands.

We make the following contributions: first, we introduce a trainable CNN architecture for the set-retrieval task that is able to learn to aggregate face vectors into a fixed length descriptor in order to minimize interference, and also is able to rank the face sets according to how many identities are in common with the query using this descriptor. To do this, we propose a paradigm shift where we draw motivation from image retrieval based on local descriptors. In image retrieval, it is common practice to aggregate all local descriptors of an image into a fixed-size image-level vector representation, such as bag-of-words [25] and VLAD [12]; this brings both memory and speed improvements over storing all local descriptors individually. We generalize this concept to set retrieval, where instead of aggregating local interest point descriptors, set element descriptors are pooled into a single fixed-size set-level representation. For the particular case of face set retrieval, this corresponds to aggregating face descriptors into a set representation. The novel aggregation procedure is described in Sect. 2 where compact set-level descriptors are trained in an end-to-end manner using a ResNet-50 [8] as the base CNN.

Our second contribution is to introduce a dataset annotated with multiple faces per images. In Sect. 3 we describe a pipeline for automatically generating a labelled dataset of pairs (or more) of celebrities per image. This *Celebrity Together* dataset contains around 200k images with more than half a million faces in total. It will be publicly released.

The performance of the set-level descriptors is evaluated in Sect. 4. We first 'stress test' the descriptors by progressively increasing the number of faces in each set, and monitoring their retrieval performance. We also evaluate retrieval on the *Celebrity Together* dataset, where images contain a variable number of faces, with many not corresponding to the queries, and explore efficient algorithms that can achieve immediate (real-time) retrieval on very large scale datasets.

Note, although we have grounded the set retrieval problem as faces, the treatment is quite general: it only assumes that dataset elements are represented by vectors and the scoring function is a scalar product. We return to this point in the conclusion.

1.1 Related Work

To the best of our knowledge, this paper is the first to consider the set retrieval problem. However, the general area of image retrieval has an extensive literature that we build on here.

One of the central problems that has been studied in large scale image instance retrieval is how to condense the information stored in multiple local descriptors such as SIFT [16], into a single compact vector to represent the image. This problem has been driven by the need to keep the memory footprint low for very large image datasets. An early approach is to cluster descriptors into visual words and represent the image as a histogram of word occurrences – bag-of-visual-words [25]. Performance can be improved by aggregating local descriptors within each cluster, in representations such as Fisher Vectors [13,20] and VLAD [12]. In particular, VLAD – 'Vector of Locally Aggregated Descriptors' by Jégou et al. [12] and its improvements [2,5,14] was used to obtain very compact descriptions via dimensionality reduction by PCA, considerably reducing the memory requirements compared to earlier bag-of-words based methods [18,22,25]. VLAD has superior ability in maintaining the information about individual local descriptors while performing aggressive dimensionality reduction.

VLAD has recently been adapted into a differentiable CNN layer, NetVLAD [1], making it end-to-end trainable. We incorporate a modified form of the NetVLAD layer in our SetNet architecture. An alternative, but related, very recent approach is the memory vector formulation of [10], but we have not employed it here as it has not been made differentiable yet.

Another strand of research we build on is category level retrieval, where in our case the category is a face. This is another classical area of interest with many related works [4,21,28,30,32]. For the case of faces, the feature vector is produced from the face region using a CNN trained to classify or embed faces [19,24,27].

Also relevant are works that explicitly deal with sets of vectors. Kondor and Jebara [15] developed a kernel between vector sets by characterising each set as a Gaussian in some Hilbert space. However, their set representation cannot currently be combined with CNNs and trained in an end-to-end fashion. Recently, Zaheer et al. [31] investigate permutation-invariant objective functions for operating on sets, although their method boils down to average pooling of input vectors, which we compare to as a baseline. Rezatofighi et al. [7] consider the problem of predicting sets, i.e. having a network which outputs sets, rather than our case where a set of elements is an input to be processed and described with a single vector.

2 SetNet – A CNN for Set Retrieval

As described in the previous section, using a single fixed-size vector to represent a set of vectors is a highly appealing approach due to its superior speed and memory footprint over storing a descriptor-per-element. In this section, we propose a CNN architecture, *SetNet*, for the end-task of set retrieval. There are two objectives:

1. To learn the element descriptors together with the aggregation in order to minimise the loss in face classification performance between using individual descriptors for each face, and an aggregated descriptor for the set of faces. This is achieved by training the network for this task, using an architecture combining ResNet for the individual descriptors together with NetVLAD for the aggregation.
2. To be able to rank the images using the aggregated descriptor in order of the number of faces in each image that correspond to the identities in the query. This is achieved by scoring each face using a logistic regression classifier. Since the score of each classifier lies between 0 and 1, the score for the image can simply be computed as the sum of the individual scores, and this summed score determines the ranking function.

As an example of the scoring function, if the search is for two identities and an image contains faces of both of them (and maybe other faces as well), then the ideal score for each relevant face would be one, and the sum of scores for the image would be two. If an image only contains one of the identities, then the sum of the scores would be one. The images with higher summed scores are then ranked higher and this naturally orders the images by the number of faces it contains that satisfy the query.

To deploy the set level descriptor for retrieval in a large scale dataset, there are two stages:

Offline: SetNet is used to compute face descriptors for each face in an image, and aggregate them to generate a set-vector representing the image. This procedure is carried out for every image in the dataset, so that each image is represented by a single vector.

At **run-time**, to search for an identity, a face descriptor is computed for the query face using SetNet, and a logistic regression classifier used to score each image based on the scalar product between its set-vector and the query face descriptor. Searching with a set of identities amounts to summing up the image scores of each query identity.

2.1 SetNet Architecture

In this section we introduce our CNN architecture, designed to aggregate multiple element (face) descriptors into a single fixed-size set representation. The *SetNet* architecture (Fig. 2) conceptually has two parts: (i) each face is passed through a feature extractor network separately, producing one descriptor per face; (ii) the multiple face descriptors are aggregated into a single compact vector using a modified NetVLAD layer, followed by a trained dimensionality reduction. At training time, we add a third part which emulates the run-time use of logistic regression classifiers. All three parts of the architecture are described in more detail next.

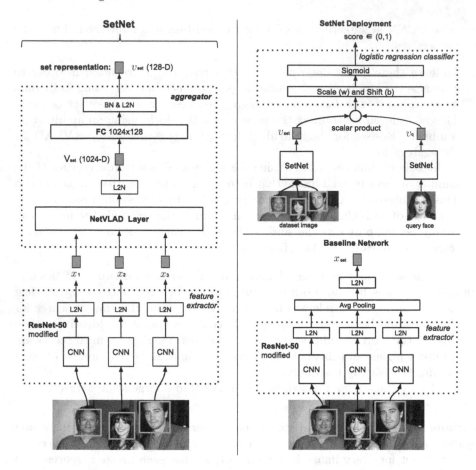

Fig. 2. SetNet architecture and training. Left: SetNet – features are extracted from each face in an image using a modified ResNet-50. They are aggregated using a modified NetVLAD layer into a single 1024-D vector which is then reduced to 128-D via a fully connected dimensionality reduction layer, and L2-normalized to obtain the final image-level compact representation. **Right (top)**: at test time, a query descriptor, v_q, is obtained for each query face using SetNet (the face is considered as a single-element set), and the dataset image is scored by a logistic regression classifier on the scalar product between the query descriptor v_q and image set descriptor v_{set}. The final score of an image is then obtained by summing the scores of all the query identities. **Right (bottom)**: the baseline network has the same feature extractor as SetNet, but the feature aggregator uses an average-pooling layer, rather than NetVLAD.

Feature Extraction. The first part is a modified ResNet-50 [8] chopped after the global average pooling layer. The ResNet-50 is modified to produce 128-D vectors in order to keep the dimensionality of our feature vectors relatively low (we have not observed a significant drop in face recognition performance from the original 2048-D descriptors). The modification is implemented by adding a

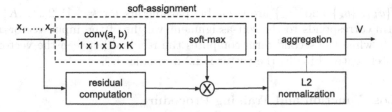

Fig. 3. NetVLAD layer. Illustration of the NetVLAD layer [1], corresponding to Eq. (1), and slightly modified to perform L2-normalization before aggregation; see Sect. 2.2 for details.

fully-connected (FC) layer of size 2048×128 after the global average pooling layer in the original ResNet, in order to obtain a lower dimensional face descriptor (full details of the architecture are given in the supplementary material). In this part, individual element descriptors $(x_1, \ldots, x_F)$ are obtained from ResNet, where F is the number of faces in an image.

Feature Aggregation. Face features are aggregated into a single vector V using a NetVLAD layer (illustrated in Fig. 3, and described below in Sect. 2.2). The NetVLAD layer is slightly modified by adding an additional L2-normalization step – the total contribution of each face descriptor to the aggregated sum (i.e. its weighted residuals) is L2-normalized in order for each face descriptor to contribute equally to the final vector; this procedure is an adaptation of residual normalization [5] of the vanilla VLAD to NetVLAD. The NetVLAD-pooled features are reduced back to 128-D by means of a fully-connected layer followed by batch-normalization [9], and L2-normalized to produce the final set representation v_{set}.

Training Block. At training time, an additional logistic regression loss layer is added to mimic the run-time scenario where a logistic regression classifier is used to score each image based on the scalar product between its set-vector and the query face descriptor. Note, SetNet is used to generate both the set-vector and the face descriptor. Section 2.3 describes the appropriate loss and training procedure in more detail.

2.2 NetVLAD Trainable Pooling

NetVLAD has been shown to outperform sum and max pooling for the same vector dimensionality, which makes it perfectly suited for our task. Here we provide a brief overview of NetVLAD, for full details please refer to [1].

For F D-dimensional input descriptors $\{x_i\}$ and a chosen number of clusters K, NetVLAD pooling produces a single $D \times K$ vector V (for convenience written as a $D \times K$ matrix) according to the following equation:

$$V(j,k) = \sum_{i=1}^{F} \frac{e^{a_k^T x_i + b_k}}{\sum_{k'} e^{a_{k'}^T x_i + b_{k'}}} (x_i(j) - c_k(j)) \qquad (1)$$

where $\{a_k\}$, $\{b_k\}$ and $\{c_k\}$ are trainable parameters for $k \in [1, 2, \ldots, K]$. The first term corresponds to the soft-assignment weight of the input vector x_i for cluster k, while the second term computes the residual between the vector and the cluster centre. Finally, the vector is L2-normalized.

2.3   Loss Function and Training Procedure

In order to achieve the two objectives outlined at the beginning of Sect. 2, a Multi-label logistic regression loss is used. Suppose a particular training image contains F faces, and the mini-batch consists of faces for P identities. Then in a forward pass at training time, the descriptors for the F faces are aggregated into a single feature vector, v_{set}, using the SetNet architecture, and a face descriptor, v_f, is computed using SetNet for each of the faces of the P identities. The training image is then scored for each face f by applying a logistic regressor classifier to the scalar product $v_{set}^T v_f$, and the score should ideally be one for each of the F identities in the image, and zero for the other $P - F$ faces. The loss measures the deviation from this ideal score, and the network learns to achieve this by maintaining the discriminability for individual face descriptors after aggregation.

In detail, incorporating the loss is achieved by adding an additional layer at training time which contains a logistic regression loss for each of the P training identities, and is trained together with the rest of the network.

Multi-label Logistic Regression Loss. For each training image (set of faces), the value of the loss is:

$$-\sum_{f=1}^{P} y_f \log(\sigma(w(v_f^T v_{set}) + b)) + (1 - y_f)\log(1 - \sigma(w(v_f^T v_{set}) + b)) \quad (2)$$

where $\sigma(s) = 1/(1 + \exp(-s))$ is a logistic function, P is the number of face descriptors (the size of the mini-batches at training), and w and b are the scaling factor and shifting bias respectively of the logistic regression classifier, and y_f is a binary indicator whether face f is in the image or not. Note that multiple y_f's are equal to 1 if there are multiple faces which correspond to the identities in the image.

2.4   Implementation Details

This section gives full details of the training procedure, including how the network is used at run-time to rank the dataset images given query examples.

Training Data. The network is trained using faces from the training partition of the VGGFace2 dataset [3]. This consists of 8631 identities, with on average 360 face samples for each identity.

Balancing Positives and Negatives. For each training image (face set) there are many more negatives (the $P - F$ identities outside of the image set) than positives (identities in the set), i.e. most y_f's in Eq. (2) are equal to 0 with only a few 1's. To restore balance, the contributions of the positives and negatives to the loss function is down-weighted by their respective counts.

Initialization and Pre-training. A good (and necessary) initialization for the network is obtained as follows. The face feature extraction block is pretrained for single face classification on the VGGFace2 Dataset [3] using softmax loss. The NetVLAD layer, with $K = 8$ clusters, is initialized using k-means as in [1]. The fully-connected layer, used to reduce the NetVLAD dimensionality to 128-D, is initialized by PCA, i.e. by arranging the first 128 principal components into the weight matrix. Finally, the entire SetNet is trained for face aggregation using the Multi-label logistic regression loss (Sect. 2.3).

Training Details. Training requires face set descriptors computed for each image, and query faces (which may or may not occur in the image). The network is trained on synthetic face sets which are built by randomly sampling identities (e.g. two identities per image). For each identity in a synthetic set, two faces are randomly sampled (from the average of 360 for each identity): one contributes to the set descriptor (by combining it with samples of the other identities), the other is used as a query face, and its scalar product is computed with all the set descriptors in the same mini-batch. In our experiments, each mini-batch contains 84 faces. Stochastic gradient descent is used to train the network (implemented in MatConvNet [29]), with weight decay 0.001, momentum 0.9, and an initial learning rate of 0.001 for pre-training and 0.0001 for fine-tuning; the learning rates are divided by 10 in later epochs.

Training faces are resized such that the smallest dimension is 256 and random 224×224 crops are used as inputs to the network. To further augment the training faces, random horizontal flipping and up to $10°$ rotation is performed. At test time, faces are resized so that the smallest dimension is 224 and the central crop is taken.

Dataset Retrieval. Suppose we wish to retrieve images containing multiple query faces (or a subset of these). First, a face descriptor is produced by *SetNet* for each query face. The face descriptors are then used to score a dataset image for each query identity, followed by summing the individual logistic regression scores to produce the final image score. A ranked list is obtained by sorting the dataset images in non-increasing score order. In the case where multiple face examples are available for a query identity, the multiple descriptors produced by *SetNet* are simply averaged and L2-normalized to form a richer descriptor for that query identity.

3 'Celebrity Together' Dataset

A new dataset, *Celebrity Together*, is collected and annotated. It contains images that portray multiple celebrities simultaneously (Fig. 4 shows a sample), making it ideal for testing set retrieval methods. Unlike the other face datasets, which exclusively contain individual face crops, *Celebrity Together* is made of full images with multiple labelled faces. It contains 194k images and 546k faces

Fig. 4. Example images of the Celebrity Together Dataset. Note that only those celebrities who appear in the VGG Face Dataset are listed, as the rest are labelled as 'unknown'. (a) Amy Poehler, Anne Hathaway, Kristen Wiig, Maya Rudolph. (b) Bingbing Fan, Blake Lively. (c) Kat Dennings, Natalie Portman, Tom Hiddleston. (d) Kathrine Narducci, Naturi Naughton, Omari Hardwick, Sinqua Walls. Additional examples of the dataset images are given in the supplementary material.

in total, averaging 2.8 faces per image. The image collection and annotation procedures are explained next.

The dataset is created with the aim of containing multiple people per image, which makes the image collection procedure much more complex than when building a single-face-per-image dataset, such as [19]. The straightforward strategy of [19], which involves simply searching for celebrities on an online image search engine, is inappropriate: consider an example of searching for Natalie Portman on Google Image Search – *all* top ranked images contain only her and no other person. Here we explain how to overcome this barrier to collect images with multiple celebrities in them.

Search String Selection. We use the list of 2622 celebrities from the VGG Face Dataset [19] and aim to download images containing at least two celebrities each. Since it is inappropriate to query internet image search engines for single celebrities, here we explain how to obtain sets of celebrities to search for. A straightforward approach would be to query for all pairs of celebrities; assuming top 100 images are downloaded for each query, this would result in 300 million images, which is clearly prohibitively time-consuming to download and exhaustively annotate. We use the fact that only a small portion of the name pairs is actually useful as not all pairs of celebrities have photos taken together. To obtain a list of plausible celebrity pairs, we consider each celebrity as a "seed" in turn. For each seed-celebrity, a search is performed for '`seed-celebrity and`' to obtain a list of images of the seed-celebrity together with another person. The meta information associated with these images (image caption in Google Image Search) is then scanned for other celebrity names, producing a list of (seed-celebrity, celebrity-friend) pairs.

Image Download and Filtering. The list of celebrity pairs is used to query Google Image Search and download the images, which are then filtered using the meta information to contain both queried celebrities, and a face detector [17] is used to filter out images which contain fewer than two faces. De-duplication is performed using the method of [19], and images in common with the VGG Face Dataset [19] are removed as well.

Table 1. Distribution of faces/image.

No. faces/image	2	3	4	5	>5
No. images	113k	43k	19k	9k	10k

Table 2. Distribution of annotations/image.

No. celeb/image	1	2	3	4	5	>5
No. images	88k	89k	12k	3k	0.7k	0.3k

Image Annotation. Since the same list of celebrities is used as in the VGG Face Dataset [19], we use the pre-trained Deep Face CNN [19] to aid with annotation. Combining the very confident CNN classifications with our prior belief of who is depicted in the image (i.e. the query terms), results in many good quality automatic annotations which further decreases the manual annotation effort and costs. Remaining images are annotated manually using Mechanical Turk. Full details of the annotation procedure are provided in the supplementary material. Note that not all faces in the dataset correspond to the 2622 queried celebrities, and these are labelled as "unknown" people, but are kept in the dataset as distractors; 41% of all faces are distractors. Table 1 shows the breakdown of the total number of faces appearing in each image, while Table 2 shows the same breakdown but for celebrities (i.e. people with known identities).

4   Experiments and Results

In this section we investigate three aspects: first, in Sect. 4.1 we study the performance of different models (SetNet and baselines) as the number of faces per image in the dataset is increased. Second, we compare the performance of Set-Net and the best baseline model on the real-world *Celebrity Together* dataset in Sect. 4.2. Third, the trade-off between time complexity and set retrieval quality is investigated in Sect. 4.3.

Note, in all the experiments, there is no overlap between the query identities used for testing and the identities used for training the network, as the VGG Face Dataset [19] (used for testing, e.g. for forming the *Celebrity Together* dataset) and the VGGFace2 Dataset [3] (used for training) share no common identities.

Evaluation Protocol. We use Normalized Discounted Cumulative Gain (nDCG) to evaluate set retrieval performance, as it can measure how well images containing *all* the query identities and also *subsets* of the queries are retrieved. For this measurement, images have different relevance, not just a binary positive/negative label; the relevance of an image is equal to the number of query identities it contains. We report nDCG@10 and nDCG@30, where nDCG@N is the nDCG for the ranked list cropped at the top N retrievals. nDCGs are written as percentages, so the scores range between 0 and 100.

4.1   Stress Test

In this test, we aim to investigate how different models perform with increasing number of faces per set (image) in the test dataset. The effects of varying the number of faces per set used for training are also studied.

Test Dataset Synthesis. To this end, a base dataset with 64k face sets of 2 faces each is synthesized, using only the face images of labelled identities in the *Celebrity Together* dataset. A random sample of 100 sets of 2 identities are used as queries, taking care that the two queried celebrities do appear together in some dataset face sets. To obtain four datasets of varying difficulty, 0, 1, 2 and 3 distractor faces per set are sampled from the unlabelled face images in *Celebrity Together* Dataset, taking care to include only true distractor people, i.e. people who are not in the list of labelled identities in the *Celebrity Together* dataset. Therefore, all four datasets contain the same number of face sets (64k) but have a different number of faces per set, ranging from 2 to 5. Importantly, by construction, the relevance of each set to each query is the same across all four datasets, which makes the performance numbers comparable across them.

Methods. The *SetNet* models are trained as described in Sect. 2.4, where the suffix '*-2*' or '*-3*' denotes whether 2- or 3-element sets are used during training. For baselines, the optional suffix '*+W*' indicates whether the face descriptors have been whitened and L2-normalized before aggregation; whereas for SetNet, '*+W*' means that the set descriptors are whitened. For example, *SetNet-2+*W is a model trained with 2-element sets and whitening. Baselines follow the same naming convention, and use ResNet-50 with average-pooling (i.e. the same feature extractor network, data augmentation, optional whitening, etc.), where the architectural difference from the SetNet is that the aggregator block is replaced with average-pooling followed by L2-normalization (as shown in Fig. 2). The baselines are trained in the same manner as SetNet. The exceptions are *Baseline* and *Baseline+W*, which simply use ResNet-50 with average-pooling, but no training. For reference, an upper bound performance (*Descriptor-per-element*, see Sect. 4.3 for details) is also reported, where no aggregation is performed and all descriptors for all elements are stored. In this test, one randomly sampled face example per query identity is used to query the dataset. The experiment is repeated 10 times using different face examples, and the nDCG scores are averaged.

Results. From the results in Fig. 5 it is clear that *SetNet-2+W* and *SetNet-3+W* outperform all baselines. A similar trend also happens for nDCG@30; results for this are included in the supplementary material. As expected, the performance of all models decreases as the number of elements per set increases due to larger cross-element interference. However, *SetNet+W* deteriorates more gracefully (the margin between it and the baselines increases), demonstrating that our training makes SetNet learn representations which minimise the interference between elements. The set training is beneficial for all architectures, as *Baseline-2+W* and *Baseline-3+W* achieve better results than *Baseline+W* which is not trained for set retrieval.

Whitening improves the performance for all architectures when there are more than 2 elements per set, which is a somewhat surprising result since adding whitening only happens after the network is trained. However, using whitening is common in the retrieval community as it is usually found to be very helpful

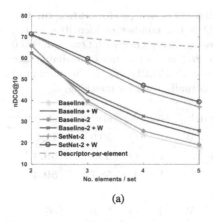

Scoring model	2/set	3/set	4/set	5/set
Baseline	66.3	38.8	23.7	17.5
Baseline-2	65.8	39.7	25.6	19.0
Baseline-3	65.9	39.4	24.8	18.4
SetNet-2	71.0	57.7	44.6	36.9
SetNet-3	71.9	57.9	44.7	37.0
Baseline + W	62.3	42.3	30.8	23.3
Baseline-2 + W	62.3	44.1	32.6	25.7
Baseline-3 + W	62.1	44.0	32.3	25.6
SetNet-2 + W	71.3	59.5	47.0	39.3
SetNet-3 + W	71.8	59.8	47.1	39.3
Desc-per-element	72.4	69.4	67.1	65.3

(a)   (b)

Fig. 5. Stress test comparison of different models. There are 100 query sets, each with two identities. (a) nDCG@10 for different number of elements (faces) per set (image) in the test dataset. (b) Table of nDCG@10 of stress test. Columns corresponds to the four different test datasets defined by the number of elements (faces) per set.

[2,11], but has also been used recently to improve CNN representations [23, 26]. It is likely that whitening before aggregation is beneficial also because it makes descriptors more orthogonal to each other, which helps to reduce the amount of information lost by aggregation. However, *SetNet* gains much less from whitening, which may indicate that it learns to produce more orthogonal face descriptors. In the supplementary material we investigate the orthogonality of descriptors further by analysing the Gram matrix computed on the identities in the VGG Face Dataset. We observe that SetNet produces even more orthogonal descriptors than the whitened baselines.

It is also important to note that, as illustrated by Fig. 5b, the cardinality of the sets used for training does not affect the performance much, regardless of the architecture. Therefore, training with a set size of 2 or 3 is sufficient to learn good set representations which generalize to larger sets.

4.2   Evaluating on the Celebrity Together Dataset

Here we evaluate the SetNet performance on the full *Celebrity Together* dataset.

Test Dataset. The dataset is described in Sect. 3. To increase the retrieval difficulty, random 355k distractor images are sampled from the MS-Celeb-1M Dataset [6], as before taking care to include only true distractor people. The sampled distractor sets are constructed such that the number of faces per set follows the same distribution as in the *Celebrity Together* dataset. The statistics of the resultant test dataset are shown in Table 3. There are 1000 test queries, formed by randomly sampling 500 queries containing two celebrities and 500 queries containing three celebrities, under the restriction that the queried celebrities do appear together in some dataset images.

Table 3. Number of images and faces in the test dataset. The test dataset consists of the *Celebrity Together* dataset and distractor images from the MS-Celeb-1M dataset [6].

	Celebrity Together	Dist. from MS1M	Total
Images	194k	355k	549k
Faces	546k	1M	1546k

Table 4. Set retrieval performance on the test set. Q is the number of identities in the query. There are 500 queries with $Q = 2$, and 500 with $Q = 3$. N_{ex} is the number of available face examples for each identity. N_{qd} is the number of descriptors actually used for querying.

Scoring model	N_{ex}	N_{qd}	nDCG@10	nDCG@30
Baseline-2 + W	1	Q	50.0	49.4
SetNet-3 + W	1	Q	**59.1**	**59.4**
SetNet-3 + W w/ query avg.	1	1	58.7	**59.4**
Baseline-2 + W	3	Q	56.6	56.0
SetNet-3 + W	3	Q	**63.8**	**64.1**
SetNet-3 + W w/ query avg.	3	1	62.9	**64.1**

Experimental Setup and Baseline. In this test we consider two scenarios: first, where only one face example is available for each query identity, and second, where three face examples per query identity are available. In the second scenario, for each query identity, three extracted face descriptors are averaged and L2-normalized to form a single enhanced descriptor which is then used to query the dataset. In both scenarios the experiment is repeated 10 times using different face examples for each query identity, and the nDCG score is averaged. The best baseline from the stress test (Sect. 4.1) *Baseline-2+W*, is used as the main comparison method.

Results. Table 4 shows that *SetNet-3+W* outperforms the best baseline for all performance measures by a large margin. Particularly impressive is the boost when only one face example is available for each query identity, where *Baseline-2+W* is beaten by 9.1% and 10.0% at nDCG@10 and nDCG@30 respectively. The results demonstrate that our trained aggregation method is indeed beneficial since it is designed and trained end-to-end exactly for the task in hand. The improvement is also significant for the second scenario where three face examples are available for each query identity, namely an improvement of 7.2% and 8.1% over the baseline. Figure 1 shows the top 3 retrieved images out of 549k images for two examples queries using SetNet (images are cropped for better viewing). The supplementary material contains many more examples.

Query Averaging. We also investigate a more efficient method to query the database for multiple identities. Namely, we average the descriptors of all the query identities to produce a single descriptor which represents all query identities, and query with this single descriptor. In the second scenario, when three face examples are available for each query identity, all of the descriptors are simply averaged to a single descriptor. With this query representation we obtain a slightly lower nDCG@10 compared to the original method shown in Table 4 (62.9 vs 63.8), and the same nDCG@30 (64.1). However, as will be seen in the next section, this drop can be nullified by re-ranking, making *query averaging* an attractive method due to its efficiency.

4.3 Efficient Set Retrieval

Our SetNet approach stores a single descriptor-per-set making it very fast though with potentially sacrificed accuracy. This section introduces alternatives and evaluates trade-offs between set retrieval quality and retrieval speed. To evaluate computational efficiency formally with the big-O notation, let Q, F and N be the number of query identities, average number of faces per dataset image, and the number of dataset images, respectively, and let the face descriptor be D-dimensional. Recall that our SetNet produces a compact set representation which is also D-dimensional, and $D = 128$ throughout.

Descriptor-per-set (SetNet). Storing a single descriptor per set is very computationally efficient as ranking only requires computing a scalar product between Q query D-dimensional descriptors and each of the N dataset descriptors, passing them through a logistic function, followed by scoring the images by the sum of similarity scores, making this step $O(NQD)$. For the more efficient *query averaging* where only one query descriptor is used to represent all the query identities, this step is even faster with $O(ND)$. Sorting the scores is $O(N \log N)$. Total memory requirements are $O(ND)$.

Descriptor-per-element. Set retrieval can also be performed by storing all element descriptors, requiring $O(NFD)$ memory. An image can be scored by obtaining all $Q \times F$ pairs of (query-identity, image-face) scores and finding the optimal assignment by considering it as a maximal weighted matching problem in a bipartite graph. Instead of solving the problem using the Hungarian algorithm which has computational complexity that is cubic in the number of faces and is thus prohibitively slow, we use a greedy matching approach which is $O(QF \log(QF))$ per image. Therefore, the total computational complexity is $O(NQFD + NQF \log(QF) + N \log N)$. For our problem, we do not find any loss in retrieval performance compared to optimal matching, while being 7× faster.

Combinations by Re-ranking. Borrowing ideas again from image retrieval [22,25], it is possible to combine the speed benefits of the faster methods with the accuracy of the slow descriptor-per-element method by using the former for initial ranking, and the latter to re-rank the top N_r results. The computational complexity is then equal to that of the fast method of choice, plus $O(N_r QFD + N_r QF \log(QF) + N_r \log N_r)$.

Experimental Setup. The performance is evaluated on the 1000 test queries and on the same full dataset with distractors as in Sect. 4.2. N_r is varied in this experiment to demonstrate the trade-off between accuracy and retrieval speed. For the descriptor-per-element method, we use the Baseline + W features. In

Table 5. Retrieval speed vs quality trade-off with varied number of re-ranking images. Retrieval performance, average time required to execute a set query and speedup over *Desc-per-element* are shown for each method. 'Re.' denotes re-ranking. The evaluation is on the 1000 test queries and on the same full dataset with distractors as in Sect. 4.2.

Scoring method	N_r	Without query averaging				With query averaging			
		nDCG@10	nDCG@30	Timing	Speedup	nDCG@10	nDCG@30	Timing	Speedup
Desc-per-set	-	59.1	59.4	0.11 s	57.5×	58.7	59.4	0.01s	635×
Desc-per-set + Re.	100	76.5	70.1	0.13 s	48.8×	76.4	70.1	0.03s	212×
Desc-per-set + Re.	1000	84.2	80.0	0.20 s	31.8×	84.1	80.0	0.10s	63.5×
Desc-per-set + Re.	2000	85.3	81.4	0.28 s	22.7×	85.3	81.4	0.18s	35.3×
Desc-per-element	-	85.4	81.7	6.35 s	-	-	-	-	-

the supplementary material we also discuss a naive approach of pre-tagging the dataset with a list of identities.

Results. Table 5 shows set retrieval results for the various methods together with the time it takes to execute a set query. The full descriptor-per-element approach is the most accurate one, but also prohibitively slow for most uses, taking more than 6 s to execute a query. The descriptor-per-set (i.e. SetNet) approach with query averaging is blazingly fast with only 0.01s per query using one descriptor to represent all query identities, but sacrifices retrieval quality to achieve this speed. However, using SetNet for initial ranking followed by re-ranking achieves good results without a significant speed hit – the accuracy almost reaches that of the full slow descriptor-per-element, while being more than 35× faster. Furthermore, by combining *desc-per-set* and *desc-per-element* it is possible to choose the trade-off between speed and retrieval quality, as appropriate for specific use cases. For a task where speed is crucial, *desc-per-set* can be used with few re-ranking images (e.g. 100) to obtain a 212× speedup over the most accurate method (*desc-per-element*). For an accuracy-critical task, it is possible to re-rank more images while maintaining a reasonable speed.

5 Conclusion

We have considered a new problem of set retrieval, discussed multiple different approaches to tackle it, and evaluated them on a specific case of searching for sets of faces. Our learnt compact set representation, produced using the SetNet architecture and trained in a novel manner directly for the set retrieval task, beats all baselines convincingly. Furthermore, due to its high speed it can be used for fast set retrieval in large image datasets. The set retrieval problem has applications beyond multiple faces in an image. For example, a similar situation would also apply for the task of video retrieval when the elements themselves are images (frames), and the set is a video clip or shot.

We have also introduced a new dataset, *Celebrity Together*, which can be used to evaluate set retrieval performance and to facilitate research on this new topic. The dataset will be released publicly.

Acknowledgements. This work was funded by an EPSRC studentship and EPSRC Programme Grant Seebibyte EP/M013774/1.

References

1. Arandjelović, R., Gronat, P., Torii, A., Pajdla, T., Sivic, J.: NetVLAD: CNN architecture for weakly supervised place recognition. In: Proceedings of CVPR (2016)
2. Arandjelović, R., Zisserman, A.: All about VLAD. In: Proceedings of CVPR (2013)
3. Cao, Q., Shen, L., Xie, W., Parkhi, O.M., Zisserman, A.: VGGFace2: a dataset for recognising faces across pose and age. In: Proceedings of International Conference on Automatic Face and Gesture Recognition (2018)
4. Chatfield, K., Lempitsky, V., Vedaldi, A., Zisserman, A.: The devil is in the details: an evaluation of recent feature encoding methods. In: Proceedings of BMVC (2011)
5. Delhumeau, J., Gosselin, P.H., Jégou, H., Pérez, P.: Revisiting the VLAD image representation. In: Proceedings of ACMM (2013)
6. Guo, Y., Zhang, L., Hu, Y., He, X., Gao, J.: MS-Celeb-1M: a dataset and benchmark for large-scale face recognition. In: Leibe, B., Matas, J., Sebe, N., Welling, M. (eds.) ECCV 2016, Part III. LNCS, vol. 9907, pp. 87–102. Springer, Cham (2016). https://doi.org/10.1007/978-3-319-46487-9_6
7. Rezatofighi, S.H., Kumar, B., Milan, A., Abbasnejad, E., Dick, A., Reid, I.: DeepSetNet: predicting sets with deep neural networks. In: Proceedings of CVPR (2017)
8. He, K., Zhang, X., Ren, S., Sun, J.: Deep residual learning for image recognition. In: Proceedings of CVPR (2016)
9. Ioffe, S., Szegedy, C.: Batch normalization: accelerating deep network training by reducing internal covariate shift. In: Proceedings of ICML (2015)
10. Iscen, A., Furon, T., Gripon, V., Rabbat, M., Jégou, H.: Memory vectors for similarity search in high-dimensional spaces. IEEE Trans. Big Data **4**, 65–77 (2017)
11. Jégou, H., Chum, O.: Negative evidences and co-occurences in image retrieval: the benefit of PCA and whitening. In: Fitzgibbon, A., Lazebnik, S., Perona, P., Sato, Y., Schmid, C. (eds.) ECCV 2012, Part II. LNCS, pp. 774–787. Springer, Heidelberg (2012). https://doi.org/10.1007/978-3-642-33709-3_55
12. Jégou, H., Douze, M., Schmid, C., Pérez, P.: Aggregating local descriptors into a compact image representation. In: Proceedings of CVPR (2010)
13. Jégou, H., Perronnin, F., Douze, M., Sánchez, J., Pérez, P., Schmid, C.: Aggregating local image descriptors into compact codes. IEEE PAMI **34**, 1704–1716 (2011)
14. Jégou, H., Zisserman, A.: Triangulation embedding and democratic aggregation for image search. In: Proceedings of CVPR (2014)
15. Kondor, R., Jebara, T.: A kernel between sets of vectors. In: Proceedings of ICML. AAAI Press (2003)
16. Lowe, D.: Distinctive image features from scale invariant keypoints. IJCV **00**(2), 91–110 (2004)

17. Mathias, M., Benenson, R., Pedersoli, M., Van Gool, L.: Face detection without bells and whistles. In: Fleet, D., Pajdla, T., Schiele, B., Tuytelaars, T. (eds.) ECCV 2014, Part IV. LNCS, vol. 8692, pp. 720–735. Springer, Cham (2014). https://doi.org/10.1007/978-3-319-10593-2_47
18. Nister, D., Stewenius, H.: Scalable recognition with a vocabulary tree. In: Proceedings of CVPR, pp. 2161–2168 (2006)
19. Parkhi, O.M., Vedaldi, A., Zisserman, A.: Deep face recognition. In: Proceedings of BMVC (2015)
20. Perronnin, F., Liu, Y., Sánchez, J., Poirier, H.: Large-scale image retrieval with compressed fisher vectors. In: Proceedings of CVPR (2010)
21. Perronnin, F., Sánchez, J., Mensink, T.: Improving the fisher kernel for large-scale image classification. In: Daniilidis, K., Maragos, P., Paragios, N. (eds.) ECCV 2010, Part IV. LNCS, vol. 6314, pp. 143–156. Springer, Heidelberg (2010). https://doi.org/10.1007/978-3-642-15561-1_11
22. Philbin, J., Chum, O., Isard, M., Sivic, J., Zisserman, A.: Object retrieval with large vocabularies and fast spatial matching. In: Proceedings of CVPR (2007)
23. Radenović, F., Tolias, G., Chum, O.: CNN image retrieval learns from BoW: unsupervised fine-tuning with hard examples. In: Leibe, B., Matas, J., Sebe, N., Welling, M. (eds.) ECCV 2016, Part I. LNCS, vol. 9905, pp. 3–20. Springer, Cham (2016). https://doi.org/10.1007/978-3-319-46448-0_1
24. Schroff, F., Kalenichenko, D., Philbin, J.: FaceNet: a unified embedding for face recognition and clustering. In: Proceedings of CVPR (2015)
25. Sivic, J., Zisserman, A.: Video google: a text retrieval approach to object matching in videos. In: Proceedings of ICCV, vol. 2, pp. 1470–1477 (2003)
26. Sun, Y., Zheng, L., Deng, W., Wang, S.: SVDNet for pedestrian retrieval. In: Proceedings of ICCV (2017)
27. Taigman, Y., Yang, M., Ranzato, M., Wolf, L.: Deep-face: closing the gap to human-level performance in face verification. In: IEEE CVPR (2014)
28. Torresani, L., Szummer, M., Fitzgibbon, A.: Efficient object category recognition using classemes. In: Daniilidis, K., Maragos, P., Paragios, N. (eds.) ECCV 2010, Part I. LNCS, vol. 6311, pp. 776–789. Springer, Heidelberg (2010). https://doi.org/10.1007/978-3-642-15549-9_56
29. Vedaldi, A., Lenc, K.: MatConvNet: convolutional neural networks for MATLAB. In: Proceedings of ACMM (2015)
30. Wang, J., Yang, J., Yu, K., Lv, F., Huang, T., Gong, Y.: Locality-constrained linear coding for image classification. In: Proceedings of CVPR (2010)
31. Zaheer, M., Kottur, S., Ravanbakhsh, S., Poczos, B., Salakhutdinov, R., Smola, A.: Deep sets. In: NIPS, pp. 3391–3401 (2017)
32. Zhou, X., Yu, K., Zhang, T., Huang, T.S.: Image classification using super-vector coding of local image descriptors. In: Daniilidis, K., Maragos, P., Paragios, N. (eds.) ECCV 2010, Part V. LNCS, vol. 6315, pp. 141–154. Springer, Heidelberg (2010). https://doi.org/10.1007/978-3-642-15555-0_11

Adversarial Network Compression

Vasileios Belagiannis[1]([✉]), Azade Farshad[1,2], and Fabio Galasso[1]

[1] Innovation OSRAM GmbH, Garching b. München, Germany
v.belagiannis@osram.com
[2] Technische Universität München, Garching b. München, Germany

Abstract. Neural network compression has recently received much attention due to the computational requirements of modern deep models. In this work, our objective is to transfer knowledge from a deep and accurate model to a smaller one. Our contributions are threefold: (i) we propose an adversarial network compression approach to train the small student network to mimic the large teacher, without the need for labels during training; (ii) we introduce a regularization scheme to prevent a trivially-strong discriminator without reducing the network capacity and (iii) our approach generalizes on different teacher-student models.

In an extensive evaluation on five standard datasets, we show that our student has small accuracy drop, achieves better performance than other knowledge transfer approaches and it surpasses the performance of the same network trained with labels. In addition, we demonstrate state-of-the-art results compared to other compression strategies.

1 Introduction

Deep learning approaches dominate on most recognition tasks nowadays. Convolutional Neural Networks (ConvNets) rank highest on classification [56], object detection [35], image segmentation [6] and pose estimation [38], just to name a few examples. However, the superior performance comes at the cost of model complexity and large hardware requirements. Consequently, deep models often struggle to achieve real-time inference and cannot generally be deployed on resource-constrained devices, such as mobile phones.

In this work, our objective is to compress a large and complex deep network to smaller one. Network compression is a solution that only recently attracted more attention because of the deep neural networks. One can train a deep model with quantized or binarized parameters [41,48,54], factorize it, prune network connections [16,26] or transfer knowledge to a small network [2,4,20]. In the latter case, the *student* network is trained with the aid of the *teacher*.

We present a network compression algorithm whereby we complement the knowledge transfer, in the teacher-student paradigm, with adversarial training. In our method, a large and accurate *teacher* ConvNet is trained in advance. Then, a small *student* ConvNet is trained to mimic the *teacher*, i.e. to obtain the

---

V. Belagiannis and A. Farshad—Equal contribution.

© Springer Nature Switzerland AG 2019
L. Leal-Taixé and S. Roth (Eds.): ECCV 2018 Workshops, LNCS 11132, pp. 431–449, 2019.
https://doi.org/10.1007/978-3-030-11018-5_37

same output. Our novelty lies in drawing inspiration from Generative Adversarial Networks (GANs) [14] to align the teacher-student distributions. We propose a two-player game, where the discriminator distinguishes whether the input comes from the teacher or student, thus effectively pushing the two distributions close to each other. In addition, we come up with a regularization scheme to help the student in competing with the discriminator. Our method does not require labels, only the discriminator's objectives and an L2 loss between the teacher and student output. We name our new algorithm *adversarial network compression*.

An extensive evaluation on CIFAR-10 [27], CIFAR-100 [27], SVHN [37], Fashion-MNIST [55] and ImageNet [10] shows that our student network has small accuracy drop and achieves better performance than the related approaches on knowledge transfer. In addition, we constantly observe that our student achieves better accuracy than the same network trained with supervision (i.e. labels). In our comparisons, we demonstrate superior performance next to other compression approaches. Finally, we employ three teacher and three student architectures to support our claim for generalization.

We make the following contributions: (i) a knowledge transfer method based on adversarial learning to bridge the performance of a large model with a smaller one with limited capacity, without requiring labels during learning; (ii) a regularization scheme to prevent a trivially-strong discriminator and (iii) generalization on different teacher-student architectures.

2 Related Work

Neural network compression has been known since the early work of [17,49], but recently received much attention due to the combined growth of performance and computational requirements in modern deep models. Our work mostly relates to model compression [2,4] and network distillation [20]. We review the related approaches on neural network compression by defining five main categories and then discuss adversarial training.

I. Quantization and Binarization. The standard way to reduce the size and accelerate the inference is to use weights with discrete values [48,54]. The Trained Ternary Quantization [65] reduces the precision of the network weights to ternary values. In incremental network quantization [64], the goal is to convert progressively a pre-trained full-precision ConvNet to a low-precision. Based on the same idea, Gong *et al.* [13] have clustered the weights using k-means and then performed quantization. The quantization can be efficiently reduced up to binary level as in XNOR-Net [41], where the weight values are -1 and 1, and in BinaryConnect [9], which binarizes the weights during the forward and backward passes but not during the parameters' update. Similar to binary approaches, ternary weights $(-1,0,1)$ have been employed as well [31].

II. Pruning. Reducing the model size (memory and storage) is also the goal of pruning by removing network connections [5,51,60]. At the same time, it prevents over-fitting. In [16], the unimportant connections of the network are pruned and the remaining network is fine-tuned. Han *et al.* [15] have combined the idea of quantization with pruning to further reduce the storage requirements and network computations. In HashedNets [7], the network connections have been randomly grouped into hash buckets where all connections of the same bucket share the weight. However, the sparse connections do not necessarily accelerate the inference when employing ConvNets. For this reason, Li *et al.* [32] have pruned complete filters instead of individual connections. Consequently, the pruned network still operates with dense matrix multiplications and it does not require sparse convolution libraries. Parameter sharing has also contributed to reduce the network parameters in neural networks with repetitive patterns [3,46].

III. Decomposition / Factorization. In this case, the main idea is to construct low rank basis of filters. For instance, Jaderberg *et al.* [26] have proposed an agnostic approach to have rank-1 filters in the spatial domain. Related approaches have also explored the same principle of finding a low-rank approximation for the convolutional layers [11,29,43,58]. More recently, it has been proposed to use depthwise separable convolutions, as well as, pointwise convolutions to reduce the parameters of the network. For example, MobileNets are based on depthwise separable convolutions, followed by pointwise convolutions [21]. In a similar way, ShuffleNet is based on depthwise convolutions and pointwise group convolutions, but it shuffles feature channels for increased robustness [63].

IV. Efficient Network Design. The most widely employed deep models, AlexNet [28] and VGG16 [47], demand large computational resources. This has motivated more efficient architectures such as the Residual Networks (ResNets) [18] and their variants [23,61], which reduced the parameters, but maintained (or improved) the performance. SqueezeNet [24] trims the parameters further by replacing 3×3 filters with 1×1 filters and decreasing the number of channels for 3×3 filters. Other recent architectures such as Inception [50], Xception [8], CondenseNet [22] and ResNeXt [56] have also been efficiently designed to allow deeper and wider networks without introducing more parameters than AlexNet and VGG16. Among the recent architectures, we pick ResNet as the standard model to build the *teacher* and *student*. The reason is the model simplicity where our approach applies to ResNet variations as well as other architectures.

Network compression categories **I–IV** address the problem by reducing the network parameters, changing the network structure or designing computationally efficient components. By contrast, we focus on knowledge transfer from a complex to a simpler network without interventions on the architecture. Our knowledge transfer approach is closer to network distillation, but it has important differences that we discuss below.

V. Distillation. Knowledge transfer has been successfully accomplished in the past [2,33], but it has been popularized by Hinton *et al.* [20]. The goal is to transfer knowledge from the *teacher* to the *student* by using the output before the softmax function (logits) or after it (soft targets). This task is known as network compression [2,4] and distillation [20,40]. In our work, we explore the problem for recent ConvNet architectures for the *teacher* and *student* roles. We demonstrate that network compression performs well with deep models, similar to the findings of Urban *et al.* [53]. Differently from the earlier works, we introduce adversarial learning into compression for the first time, as a tool for transferring knowledge from the teacher to the student by their cooperative exploration. Also differently from the original idea of Hinton *et al.* [20] and the recent one from Xu *et al.* [57], we do not require labels for the *student* training during compression. In the experiments, our results are constantly better than network distillation.

VI. Adversarial Learning. Our work is related to the Generative Adversarial Networks (GAN) [14] where a network learns to generate images with adversarial learning, i.e. learning to generate images which cannot be distinguished by a discriminator network. We take inspiration from GANs and introduce adversarial learning in model compression by challenging the student's output to become identical to the teacher. Closer to our objective is the work from Isola *et al.* [25] to map an image to another modality with a conditional Generative Adversarial Network (cGAN) [36]. Although, we do not have a generator in our model, we aim to map the *student* to *teacher* output given the same input image. However, compared to the *teacher*, the *student* is a model with limited capacity. This motivates a number of novel contributions, needed for the successful adversarial training.

3 Method

We propose the adversarial network compression, a new approach to transfer knowledge between two networks. In this section, we define the problem and discuss our approach.

3.1 Knowledge Transfer

We define a deep and accurate network as *teacher* $f_t(x; w_t)$ and a small network as *student* $f_s(x; w_s)$. The *teacher* has very large capacity and is trained on labeled data. The *student* is a shallower network with significant less parameters. Both networks perform the same task, given an input image x. Our objective is to train the *student* to mimic the *teacher* by predicting the same output. To achieve it, we introduce the discriminator D, another network that learns to detect the *teacher* / *student* output based on adversarial training. We train the *student* together with D by using the knowledge of the *teacher* for supervision.

In this work, we address the problem of classification. For transferring knowledge, we consider the unscaled log-probability values (i.e. logits) before the softmax activation function, as well as, features from earlier layers. Bellow, we simplify the notation to $f_t(x)$ for the teacher and $f_s(x)$ for the student network output (logits). In addition, the feature representation of the *teacher* at $k - th$ layer is defined as $f_t^k(x)$ and for the *student* at $l - th$ layer is denoted as $f_s^l(x)$. In practice, $f_t^k(x)$ and $f_s^l(x)$ are the last layers before the logits. An overview of our method is illustrated in Fig. 1.

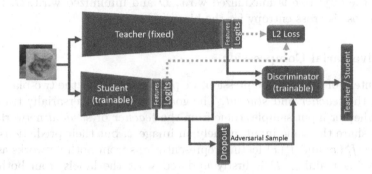

Fig. 1. Adversarial Network Compression: Our method consists of the *teacher*, *student* and discriminator networks. The teacher is trained in advance and used for supervision during adversarial learning, while the *student* and discriminator are both trainable. The discriminator takes as input the features from the *teacher* and *student*, as well as, the adversarial sample (i.e. student labeled as teacher). For the adversarial sample, we empirically found that dropout is beneficial. In addition, there is a L2 loss to force the *student* to mimic the output of the *teacher*. (Color figure online)

3.2 Generative Adversarial Networks

We shortly discuss the Generative Adversarial Networks (GANs) [14] to illustrate the connection with our approach. In GANs, the main idea is to simultaneously train two networks (two-player game) that compete with each other in order to improve their objectives. The first network, the generator G, takes random noise (i.e. latent variables) input z to generate images. In addition to the noise, the input can be conditioned on images or labels [36]. In both cases, the goal is to learn generating images that look real by aligning the real data and model distributions. The second network, the discriminator D, takes as input an image from the data distribution and the generator's output; and the objective is to classify whether the image is real or fake. Overall, G tries to fool D, while D tries to detect input from G. Isola *et al.* [25] have shown that a conditional

Generative Adversarial Network (cGAN) successfully transforms an input image to another modality y using the adversarial learning. The objective of cGAN can be written as:

$$\mathcal{L}_{cGAN}(G, D) = \mathbb{E}_{x,y \sim p_{data}(x,y)}[\log(D(x,y))]$$
$$+ \mathbb{E}_{x \sim p_{data}(x), z \sim p_z(z)}[\log(1 - D(x, G(x,z)))], \qquad (1)$$

where $p_{data}(x, y)$ corresponds to the real data distribution over the input image x and label y; and $p_z(z)$ to the prior distribution over the input noise z. During training, the objective is maximized w.r.t. D and minimized w.r.t. G. In both cases, the loss is cross entropy for the binary D output.

3.3   Adversarial Compression

In the context of network compression, we propose to adapt the two-player game based on the *teacher* and *student*. The goal now is to adversarially train D to classify whether input samples come from the *teacher* or *student* network. Both networks share the same input, namely an image x, but their predictions differ. We choose $f_t^k(x)$ and $f_s^l(x)$ feature representations from both networks as input to D. During training, D is firstly updated w.r.t the labels from both input samples (blue lines, Fig. 1). Next, the *student* network is updated by inverting the labels for the *student* samples (calling them *teacher*). The reason for changing the labels is to back-propagate gradients that guide the *student* to produce output as the *teacher* for the same input image (red line, Fig. 1). The *teacher* network has been trained in advance with labels and it is not updated during training. Eventually, fooling the discriminator translates in predicting the same output for *teacher* and *student* networks. This is the same objective as in network distillation. After reformulating Eq. (1), we define our objective as:

$$\mathcal{L}_{Adv}(f_s, D) = \mathbb{E}_{f_t^k(x) \sim p_{teacher}(x)}[\log(D(f_t^k(x)))]$$
$$+ \mathbb{E}_{f_s^l(x) \sim p_{student}(x), z \sim p_z(z)}[\log(1 - D(f_s^l(x)))]. \qquad (2)$$

where $p_{teacher}(x)$ and $p_{student}(x)$ correspond to the *teacher* and *student* feature distribution. We provide the noise input in the form of dropout applied on the *student*, similar to [25]. However, the dropout is active only during the student update (red arrow in Fig. 1). We experimentally found that using the dropout only for the *student* update gives more stable results for our problem. We omit z in $f_s^l(x)$ to keep the notation simple.

   The reason for using the features $f_t^k(x)$ and $f_s^l(x)$ as input to D, instead of the logits $f_t(x)$ and $f_s(x)$, is their dimensionality. The features usually have higher dimensions, which makes the judgment of the discriminator more challenging. We evaluate this statement later in the experimental section. Training D with input from intermediate output ($f_t^k(x)$ and $f_s^l(x)$) from *teacher* and *student* works fine for updating the parameters of D and partially for the *student*. In *student*, there is a number of parameters until the final output $f_s(x)$ (logits) which also has to be updated. To address this problem, we seek to minimize the difference between the two networks output, namely $f_t(x)$ and $f_s(x)$. This is the data objective in our formulation that is given by:

$$\mathcal{L}_{Data}(f_s) = \mathbb{E}_{f_s(x) \sim p_{student}(x)} \left[\| f_t(x) - f_s(x) \|_2^2 \right]. \tag{3}$$

The data term contributes to the update of all *student* parameters. We found it very important for the *student* network convergence (green dashed lines, Fig. 1) since our final goal is to match the output between the *teacher* and *student*. The final objective with both terms is expressed as:

$$\arg\min_{f_s} \max_{D} \mathcal{L}_{Adv}(f_s, D) + \lambda \mathcal{L}_{Data}(f_s). \tag{4}$$

where λ is a tuning constant between the two terms.

The data term of our model is the same with the compression objective of Ba and Caruana [2] and in accordance with the work of Isola *et al.* [25]. In addition, we aim for the exact output between *teacher - student* and thus using only the adversarial objective does not force the *student* to be as close as possible to the *teacher*. Note also that the role of G is implicitly assigned to the *student*, but it is not explicitly required in our approach. For the adversarial part, we share the label inversion idea for the adversarial samples from ADDA [52] and reversal gradient [12]. Below, we discuss the network architectures for exploring the idea of adversarial learning in network compression.

3.4   Network Architectures

Our model is composed of three networks: the *teacher*, *student* and discriminator D. Here, we present all three architectures.

Teacher. We choose the latest version of ResNet [19] for this role, since it is currently the standard architecture for recognition tasks. The network has adaptive capacity based on the number of bottlenecks and number of feature per bottleneck. We select ResNet-164 for our experiments. To examine the generalization of our approach on small-scale experiments, the Network in Network (NiN) [34] is also selected as *teacher*. The *teacher* is trained in advance with labeled data using cross-entropy.

Student. We found it meaningful to choose ResNet architecture for the *student* too. Although, the student is based on the same architecture, it has limited capacity. We perform our experiments with ResNet-18 and ResNet-20. For small-scale experiments, we employ LeNet-4 [30] for the *student* role. It is a shallow network and we experimentally found that it can be easily paired with NiN. The *student* network parameters are not trained on the labeled data. Furthermore, the labels are not used in the adversarial compression.

Discriminator. This discriminator D plays the most important role among the others. It can be interpreted as a loss function with parameters. The discriminator has to strike a balance between simplicity and network capacity to avoid being trivially fooled. We choose empirically a relative architecture. Our network is composed of three fully-connected (FC) layers (128 - 256 -128) where the network input comes from the *teacher* $f_t^k(x)$ and *student* $f_s^l(x)$. The intermediate activations are non-linearities (ReLUs). The output is a binary prediction, given by a sigmoid function. The network is trained with cross entropy where the objective is to predict between *teacher* or *student*. This architecture has been chosen among others, which we present in the experimental part (Sect. 4.1). Similar architectures are also maintained by [52,62] for adversarial learning.

3.5   Discriminator Regularization

The input to the discriminator has significantly lower dimensions in our problem compared to GANs for image generation [25,45]. As a result, it is simpler for the discriminator to understand the source of input. In particular, it can easily distinguish *teacher* from *student* samples from the early training stages (as also maintained in [14]). To address this limitation, we explore different ways of regularizing the discriminator. Our goal is to prevent the discriminator from dominating the training, while retaining the network capacity. We consider therefore three types of regularization, which we examine in our experiments.

L2 Regularization. This is the standard way of regularizing a neural network [39]. At first, we try the L2 regularization to force the weights of the discriminator not to grow. The term is given by:

$$\mathcal{L}_{regul}(D) = -\mu \sum_{i=1}^{n} \|w_{D,i}\|_2^2 \qquad (5)$$

where n is the number of network parameters and μ controls the contribution of the regularizer to the optimization. The parameters of D correspond to $w_{D,i}$.

L1 Regularization. Additionally, we try L1 regularization which supports sparse weights. This is formalized as:

$$\mathcal{L}_{regul}(D) = -\mu \sum_{i=1}^{n} |w_{D,i}|. \qquad (6)$$

In both Eqs. (5) and (6) there is negative sign, because the term is updated during the maximization step of Eq. (4).

Adversarial Samples for D. In the above cases, there is no guarantee that the discriminator will become weaker w.r.t *student*. We propose to achieve it by updating D with adversarial samples. According to the objective in Eq. (4), the discriminator is updated only with correct labels. Here, we additionally update D with *student* samples that are labeled as *teacher*. This means that we use the same adversarial samples to update both *student* and D. The new regularizer is defined as:

$$\mathcal{L}_{regul}(D) = \mathbb{E}_{f_s^l(x) \sim p_{student}(x)}[\log D(f_s^l(x))]. \qquad (7)$$

The motivation behind the regularizer is to prolong the game between the *student* and discriminator. Eventually, the discriminator manages to distinguish *teacher* and *student* samples, as we have observed. However, the longer it takes the discriminator to win the game, the more valuable gradient updates the *student* receives. The same principle has been also explored for text synthesis [42]. Applying the same idea on the teacher samples does not hold, since it is fixed and thus a reference in training. Our objective now becomes:

$$\arg\min_{f_s}\max_{D} \mathcal{L}_{Adv}(f_s, D) + \lambda\mathcal{L}_{Data}(f_s) + \mathcal{L}_{regul}(D) \tag{8}$$

where the regularization $\mathcal{L}_{regul}(D)$ corresponds to one of the above approaches. In the experimental section, we show that our method requires the regularization in order to achieve good results. In addition, we observed that the introduced regularization had the most significant influence in fooling D, since it is conditioned on the *student*.

3.6 Learning and Optimization

The network compression occurs in two phases. First, the *teacher* is trained from scratch on labeled data. Second, the *student* is trained together with D. The *student* is randomly initialized, as well as, D. All models are trained using Stochastic Gradient Descent (SGD) with momentum. The learning rate is 0.001 for the first $80k$ training iterations and then it is decreased by one magnitude. The weight decay is set to 0.0002. The min-batch size is to 128 samples. Furthermore, the dropout is set to 0.5 for the adversarial sample input to D. To further regularize the data, data augmentation (random crop and flip) is also included in training. In all experiments, the mean of the training set images is subtracted and they are divided by the standard deviation. Lastly, different weighting factors λ have been examined, but we concluded that equal weighting is a good compromise for all evaluations. In the L1/L2 regularization, the value of μ is set to 0.99. The same protocol is followed for all datasets, unless it is differently stated.

4 Evaluation

In this section, we evaluate our approach on five standard classification datasets: CIFAR-10 [27], CIFAR-100 [27], SVHN [37], Fashion-MNIST [55] and ImageNet 2012 [10]. In total, we examine three *teacher* and three *student* architectures.

Our ultimate goal is to train the shallower and faster *student* network to perform, at the level of accuracy, as close as possible to the deeper and complex *teacher*. Secondly, we aim to outperform the *student* trained with supervision by transferring knowledge from the teacher. We report therefore for each experiment the error, numbers of parameters and floating point operations (FLOPs). The last two metrics are reported in M-Million or B-Billion scale.

Once we choose the discriminator D and regularization in Sect. 4.1, we perform a set of baseline evaluations and comparisons with related approaches for all datasets in Sects. 4.2 and 4.3.

Implementation Details. Our implementation is based on TensorFlow [1]. We also rely on our own implementation for the approach of Ba and Caruana [2] and Hinton *et al.* [20]. The results of the other approaches are obtained from the respective publications. Regarding the network architectures, we rely on the official TF code for all ResNet variants, while we implement by ourselves the Network in Network (NiN) and LeNet-4 models.

Table 1. Discriminator Evaluation. We choose the discriminator which enables the best student performance on CIFAR-100, when integrated in the proposed adversarial compression framework. Fully connected (fc) and convolutional (conv) layers are examined. We report the *student* classification error. The best performing model (128fc - 256fc - 128fc) is used in all other evaluations.

Architecture	Error [%]	Architecture	Error [%]
128fc - 256fc - 128fc	**32.45**	500fc - 500fc	33.28
64fc - 128fc - 256fc	32.78	256fc - 256fc - 64fc	33.46
256fc - 256fc	32.82	64fc - 64fc	33.51
256fc - 128fc - 64fc	33.05	128conv - 256conv	33.68
64fc - 128fc - 128fc - 64fc	33.09	128fc - 128fc - 128fc	33.72

4.1   Discriminator Model

We discuss the choice of the discriminator D architecture and the impact of the regularization on D.

Architecture. We examine which D architecture should be considered for adversarial compression. To this end, we consider CIFAR-100 dataset as the most representative among the small-scale datasets and train our student with adversarial compression. Since the role of the discriminator would be to ensure the best student training, we explore several architectures and select the one that is providing the minimum classification error of the trained student. The discriminator models, except one, are fully connected (fc) with (ReLU) activation, other than the last layer. We explore two to four fc-layer models with different capacity. We also made experiments with a convolutional (conv) discriminator which has lower performance than fc discriminators. The results for the discriminator trials are in Table 1. The best architecture is given by 3 fc-layers of depth 128-256-128. Notice that our best architecture is similar to the D models for adversarial domain adaption [52] and perceptual similarity [62].

Regularization. Here we experiment on the three regularization techniques, described in Sect. 3.5, on four datasets. We rely on our best performing model, i.e. the one with features provided as input to D and dropout on the *student*. The results are summarized in Table 2. The lack of regularization leads to poorer performance since it is more difficult to fool the discriminator based on our observations. In particular, the performance without regularization is worse than training the *student* architecture on supervised learning as we show in Sect. 4.2. Adding the L1 or L2 regularizer indicates an important error drop (L1 and L2 column in Table 2). However, our proposed regularization introduces the most difficulties in the discriminator that leads to better performance. We use the adversarial samples for D regularization for the rest evaluations.

4.2   Component Evaluation

Initially, the *teacher* is trained with labels (i.e. supervised *teacher* in Tables 3, 4, 5 and 6). Next, the adversarial compression is performed under different configurations. The input to D is either the logits or features. In both cases, we also examine the effect of the dropout on the student. In all experiments, we train the student only based on teacher supervision and without labels. The results for every experiment are reported in Tables 3, 4, 5 and 6. In all baselines, there is the $L2$ loss on the logits from the *teacher* and *student* (i.e. $f_t(x)$ and $f_s(x)$). We also provide the results of the same network as the *student* trained with labels (i.e. supervised *student* in Tables 3, 4, 5 and 6).

Table 2. Regularization Evaluation. We evaluate three different ways of regularizing the discriminator D. We also show the performance without regularization. The error is in percentage. Our adversarial sample in D regularization is presented in the last column. All experiments have been accomplished with our complete model, namely features input to D and dropout on the *student*.

Dataset	Teacher	Student	W/o Regul.	L1	L2	Ours
CIFAR-10	ResNet-164	ResNet-20	10.07	8.19	8.16	8.08
CIFAR-100	ResNet-164	ResNet-20	34.10	33.36	33.02	32.45
SVHN	ResNet-164	ResNet-20	3.73	3.67	3.68	3.66
F-MNIST	NiN	LeNet-4	9.62	8.91	8.75	8.64

On CIFAR-10, CIFAR-100 and SVHN experiments, the input to D from ResNet-164 and ResNet-20 is the features of the *average pool* layer, which are used for *teacher* $f_t^k(x)$ and *student* $f_s^l(x)$. On Fashion-MNIST, it is the output of the last fully connected layer before the logits both for NiN (teacher) and LeNet-4 (student). The model training runs for 260 epochs in CIFAR 10, CIFAR-100 and SVHN, while for 120 epochs in Fashion-MNIST. Below, the results are individually discussed for each dataset.

Table 3. CIFAR-10 Evaluation. We evaluate the components of our approach. ResNet-164 Parameters: **2.6M**, FLOPs: **97.49B**. ResNet-20 Parameters: **0.27M**, FLOPs: **10.52B**. Our *student*, ResNet-20, has around 10x less parameters.

Model	Error [%]
Supervised *teacher* ResNet-164	6.57
Supervised *student* ResNet-20	8.58
Our *student* (*D* with logits)	8.31
+ dropout on *student*	8.10
Our *student* (*D* with features)	8.10
+ dropout on *student*	8.08

Table 4. CIFAR-100 Evaluation. The component evaluation is presented. We use the same *teacher* and *student* models as in CIFAR-10. ResNet-164 Parameters: **2.6M**, FLOPs: **97.49B**. ResNet-20 Parameters: **0.27M**, FLOPs: **10.52B**.

Model	Error [%]
Supervised *teacher* ResNet-164	27.76
Supervised *student* ResNet-20	33.36
Our *student* (*D* with logits)	33.96
+ dropout on *student*	33.41
Our *student* (*D* with features)	33.40
+ dropout on *student*	32.45

CIFAR-10, Table 3. All compression baselines, based on *student* with ResNet-20, have only around 1.5% drop in performance compared to the *teacher* (ResNet-164). Moreover, they are all better than the *student* network, trained with supervision (i.e. labels), which is 2% behind the *teacher*. Our complete model benefits from the dropout on the adversarial samples and achieves the best performance using feature input to *D*.

Table 5. SVHN Evaluation. We evaluate the components of our approach. ResNet-164 Parameters: **2.6M**, FLOPs: **97.49B**. ResNet-20 Parameters: **0.27M**, FLOPs: **10.52B**. The *teacher* and *student* model are similar to CIFAR evaluation.

Model	Error [%]
Supervised *teacher* ResNet-164	3.98
Supervised *student* ResNet-20	4.20
Our *student* (*D* with logits)	3.74
+ dropout on *student*	3.81
Our *student* (*D* with features)	3.74
+ dropout on *student*	3.66

Table 6. Fashion-MNIST Evaluation. We evaluate the components with different *teacher* and *student*. NiN Parameters: **10.6M**, FLOPs: **60.23B**. LeNet-4 Parameters: **2.3M**, FLOPs: **7.06B**. Our *student*, LeNet-4, has around 5x less parameters.

Model	Error [%]
Supervised *teacher* NiN	7.98
Supervised *student* LeNet-4	8.77
Our *student* (*D* with logits)	8.90
+ dropout on *student*	8.84
Our *student* (*D* with features)	8.86
+ dropout on *student*	8.61

Table 7. CIFAR-10 and CIFAR-100 Comparisons. We compare our results and number of network parameters with related methods on similar architectures. We use ResNet-20 for our *student* and our complete model.

CIFAR-10	Error [%]	Param.	CIFAR-100	Error [%]	Param.
L2 - Ba *et al.* [2]	9.07	0.27M	Yim *et al.* [59]	36.67	-
Hinton *et al.* [20]	8.88	0.27M	FitNets [44]	35.04	2.50M
Quantization [65]	8.87	0.27M	Hinton *et al.* [20]	33.34	0.27M
FitNets [44]	8.39	2.50M	L2 - Ba *et al.* [2]	32.79	0.27M
Binary Connect [9]	8.27	15.20M	Our *student*	**32.45**	0.27M
Yim *et al.* [59]	11.30	-			
Our *student*	**8.08**	0.27M			

CIFAR-100, Table 4. We also use Resnet-164 for *teacher* and ResNet-20 for *student* to have 10x less parameters as in CIFAR-10. In this evaluation, the performance drop between the *teacher* and the compressed models is slightly larger. The overall behavior is similar to CIFAR-10. However, the error is reduced by 1% after adding the dropout to the *student* using features as input to D. Here, we had the biggest improvement after using dropout.

SVHN, Table 5. In this experiment, the *teacher* and *student* architectures are still the same. Although, we tried the Network in Network (NiN) and LeNet-4 as teacher and *student*, the pair did not perform as well as ResNet. Unlike in the previous experiments, here the Adam optimizer was used, as it improved across all ablation results. Notice that our *student* achieves better performance not only from the same network trained with labels, the supervised *student*, but from the teacher too. This is a known positive side product of the distillation [2].

Fashion-MNIST, Table 6. We select Network in Network (NiN) as *teacher* and LeNet-4 as *student*. The dataset is relative simple and thus a ResNet architecture is not necessary. All approaches are close to each other.It is clear that the features input to D and the dropout are important to obtain the best performance in comparison to the other baselines. For instance, the *student* network trained with supervision (error 8.77%) is better than our baselines other than our complete model (error 8.61%). Finally the Adam optimizer has been used.

Common Conclusions. There is a number of common outcomes for all evaluations: 1. the adversarial compression reaches the lowest error when using features as input to D; 2. our *student* performs always better than training the same network with labels (i.e. supervised student) and 3. we achieve good generalization on different *teacher* - *student* architectures.

Comparisons to State-of-the-Art. In Tables 7 and 8, we compare our *student* with other compression strategies on CIFAR-10 and CIFAR-100. We choose four distillation [2,20,44,59] and two quantization [9,65] approaches for CIFAR-10. We examine the same four distillation methods for a comparison on CIFAR-100.

Table 8. SVHN and F-MNIST Comparisons. We compare our results and number of network parameters with related methods on the same *student* architecture that is ResNet-20 for SVHN and LeNet-4 for Fashion-MNIST.

SVHN	Error [%]	Param.	F-MNIST	Error [%]	Param.
L2 - Ba *et al.* [2]	3.75	0.27M	L2 - Ba *et al.* [2]	8.89	2.3M
Hinton *et al.* [20]	3.66	0.27M	Hinton *et al.* [20]	8.71	2.3M
Our *student*	**3.66**	0.27M	Our *student*	**8.64**	2.3M

The work of Ba and Caruana [2] is closer to our approach, because it relies on L2 minimization, though it is on the logits (see Table 7). The Knowledge Distillation (KD) [20] is also related to our idea, but it relies on labels. Both evaluations demonstrate that we achieve the lowest error and our *student* has the smallest number of parameters. In addition, we compare our results on SVHN and Fashion-MNIST with two distillation approaches (see Table 8). The error here is much lower for methods, but we are consistently better than the other approaches. Next, We demonstrate the same findings on large-scale experiments.

4.3   ImageNet Evaluation

We perform an evaluation on ImageNet to examine whether the distillation is possible on a large-scale dataset with class number set to 1000. The *teacher* is a pre-trained ResNet-152, while we try two different *student* architectures. At first, we choose ResNet-18 to train our *student* using features as input to D and adding the dropout on the adversarial samples. Regarding the experimental settings, we have set the batch size to 256, while the rest hyper-parameters remain the same. All networks use the average pool layer to output features for D. We evaluate on the validation dataset. The results are presented in Table 9.

Our findings are consistent with the earlier evaluations. Our best performing model (features input to D and dropout on *student*) perform at best and better than the student trained with supervision. Secondly, we examine a stronger

Table 9. ImageNet Baselines. We evaluate the components of our approach. ResNet-152 Parameters: **58.21M**, FLOPs: **5587B**. ResNet-18 Parameters: **13.95M**, FLOPs: **883.73B**. Our *student* has around 4x less parameters. Our model has features as input to D and dropout on the adversarial samples.

Model	Top-1 Error [%]	Top-5 Error [%]
Supervised *teacher* (ResNet-152)	27.63	5.90
Supervised *student* (ResNet-18)	43.33	20.11
Our *student* (D with features)	33.31	11.96
+ dropout on *student*	**32.89**	**11.72**

Table 10. ImageNet Evaluation. We evaluate two versions of our *student* and compare with related methods. ResNet-152 Parameters: **58.21M**, FLOPs: **5587B**. ResNet-50 Parameters: **37.49M**, FLOPs: **2667B**. Our *student*, ResNet-50, has around 2x less parameters. We also include the *student* ResNet-18 from the evaluation in Table 9. Our *student* is trained with features as input to D and dropout on the *student*.

Model	Top-1 Error [%]	Top-5 Error [%]	Parameters
Supervised *teacher* (ResNet-152)	27.63	5.90	58.21M
Supervised *student* (ResNet-50)	30.30	10.61	37.49M
XNOR [41] (ResNet-18)	48.80	26.80	13.95M
Binary-Weight [41] (ResNet-18)	39.20	17.00	13.95M
L2 - Ba *et al.* [2] (ResNet-18)	33.28	11.86	13.95M
MobileNets [21]	29.27	10.51	4.20M
L2 - Ba *et al.* [2] (ResNet-50)	27.99	9.46	37.49M
Our *student* (ResNet-18)	32.89	11.72	13.95M
Our *student* (ResNet-50)	**27.48**	**8.75**	37.49M

student where we employ ResNet-50 for training our model. We present our results in Table 10 where we also compare with binarization, distillation and factorization methods. Although we achieve the best results, MobileNets has fewer parameters. We see the adversarial network compression on MobileNets as future work.

5   Conclusion

We have presented the adversarial network compression for knowledge transfer between a large model and a smaller one with limited capacity. We have empirically shown that regularization helps the student to compete with the discriminator. Finally, we show state-of-the-art performance without using labels in an extensive evaluation of five datasets, three teacher and three student architectures. As future work, we aim to explore adversarial schemes with more discriminators that use intermediate feature representations, as well as, transferring our approach to different tasks such as object detection and segmentation.

Acknowledgements. This research was partially supported by BMWi - Federal Ministry for Economic Affairs and Energy (MEC-View Project).

References

1. Abadi, M., et al.: TensorFlow: a system for large-scale machine learning. In: OSDI, vol. 16, pp. 265–283 (2016)
2. Ba, J., Caruana, R.: Do deep nets really need to be deep? In: Advances in Neural Information Processing Systems, pp. 2654–2662 (2014)

3. Belagiannis, V., Zisserman, A.: Recurrent human pose estimation. In: 2017 12th IEEE International Conference on Automatic Face and Gesture Recognition (FG 2017), pp. 468–475. IEEE (2017)
4. Buciluâ, C., Caruana, R., Niculescu-Mizil, A.: Model compression. In: Proceedings of the 12th ACM SIGKDD International Conference on Knowledge Discovery and Data Mining, pp. 535–541. ACM (2006)
5. Carreira-Perpinán, M.A., Idelbayev, Y.: "learning-compression" algorithms for neural net pruning. In: Proceedings of the IEEE Conference on Computer Vision and Pattern Recognition, pp. 8532–8541 (2018)
6. Chen, L.C., Papandreou, G., Kokkinos, I., Murphy, K., Yuille, A.L.: DeepLab: semantic image segmentation with deep convolutional nets, atrous convolution, and fully connected CRFs. arXiv preprint arXiv:1606.00915 (2016)
7. Chen, W., Wilson, J., Tyree, S., Weinberger, K., Chen, Y.: Compressing neural networks with the hashing trick. In: International Conference on Machine Learning, pp. 2285–2294 (2015)
8. Chollet, F.: Xception: deep learning with depthwise separable convolutions. arXiv preprint arXiv:1610.02357 (2016)
9. Courbariaux, M., Bengio, Y., David, J.P.: BinaryConnect: training deep neural networks with binary weights during propagations. In: Advances in Neural Information Processing Systems, pp. 3123–3131 (2015)
10. Deng, J., Dong, W., Socher, R., Li, L.J., Li, K., Fei-Fei, L.: ImageNet: a large-scale hierarchical image database. In: 2009 IEEE Conference on Computer Vision and Pattern Recognition, CVPR 2009, pp. 248–255. IEEE (2009)
11. Denton, E.L., Zaremba, W., Bruna, J., LeCun, Y., Fergus, R.: Exploiting linear structure within convolutional networks for efficient evaluation. In: Advances in Neural Information Processing Systems, pp. 1269–1277 (2014)
12. Ganin, Y., Lempitsky, V.: Unsupervised domain adaptation by backpropagation. In: International Conference on Machine Learning, pp. 1180–1189 (2015)
13. Gong, Y., Liu, L., Yang, M., Bourdev, L.: Compressing deep convolutional networks using vector quantization. arXiv preprint arXiv:1412.6115 (2014)
14. Goodfellow, I., et al.: Generative adversarial nets. In: Advances in Neural Information Processing Systems, pp. 2672–2680 (2014)
15. Han, S., Mao, H., Dally, W.J.: Deep compression: compressing deep neural networks with pruning, trained quantization and Huffman coding. arXiv preprint arXiv:1510.00149 (2015)
16. Han, S., Pool, J., Tran, J., Dally, W.: Learning both weights and connections for efficient neural network. In: Advances in Neural Information Processing Systems, pp. 1135–1143 (2015)
17. Hassibi, B., Stork, D.G.: Second order derivatives for network pruning: optimal brain surgeon. In: Advances in Neural Information Processing Systems, pp. 164–171 (1993)
18. He, K., Zhang, X., Ren, S., Sun, J.: Deep residual learning for image recognition. In: Proceedings of the IEEE Conference on Computer Vision and Pattern Recognition, pp. 770–778 (2016)
19. He, K., Zhang, X., Ren, S., Sun, J.: Identity mappings in deep residual networks. In: Leibe, B., Matas, J., Sebe, N., Welling, M. (eds.) ECCV 2016, Part IV. LNCS, vol. 9908, pp. 630–645. Springer, Cham (2016). https://doi.org/10.1007/978-3-319-46493-0_38
20. Hinton, G., Vinyals, O., Dean, J.: Distilling the knowledge in a neural network. arXiv preprint arXiv:1503.02531 (2015)

21. Howard, A.G., et al.: MobileNets: efficient convolutional neural networks for mobile vision applications. arXiv preprint arXiv:1704.04861 (2017)
22. Huang, G., Liu, S., van der Maaten, L., Weinberger, K.Q.: CondenseNet: an efficient DenseNet using learned group convolutions. Group **3**(12), 11 (2017)
23. Huang, G., Sun, Y., Liu, Z., Sedra, D., Weinberger, K.Q.: Deep networks with stochastic depth. In: Leibe, B., Matas, J., Sebe, N., Welling, M. (eds.) ECCV 2016, Part IV. LNCS, vol. 9908, pp. 646–661. Springer, Cham (2016). https://doi.org/10.1007/978-3-319-46493-0_39
24. Iandola, F.N., Han, S., Moskewicz, M.W., Ashraf, K., Dally, W.J., Keutzer, K.: SqueezeNet: alexnet-level accuracy with 50X fewer parameters and <0.5 MB model size. arXiv preprint arXiv:1602.07360 (2016)
25. Isola, P., Zhu, J.Y., Zhou, T., Efros, A.A.: Image-to-image translation with conditional adversarial networks. arXiv preprint arXiv:1611.07004 (2016)
26. Jaderberg, M., Vedaldi, A., Zisserman, A.: Speeding up convolutional neural networks with low rank expansions. arXiv preprint arXiv:1405.3866 (2014)
27. Krizhevsky, A., Hinton, G.: Learning multiple layers of features from tiny images (2009)
28. Krizhevsky, A., Sutskever, I., Hinton, G.E.: ImageNet classification with deep convolutional neural networks. In: Advances in Neural Information Processing Systems, pp. 1097–1105 (2012)
29. Lebedev, V., Ganin, Y., Rakhuba, M., Oseledets, I., Lempitsky, V.: Speeding-up convolutional neural networks using fine-tuned CP-decomposition. arXiv preprint arXiv:1412.6553 (2014)
30. LeCun, Y., et al.: Handwritten digit recognition with a back-propagation network. In: Advances in Neural Information Processing Systems, pp. 396–404 (1990)
31. Li, F., Zhang, B., Liu, B.: Ternary weight networks. arXiv preprint arXiv:1605.04711 (2016)
32. Li, H., Kadav, A., Durdanovic, I., Samet, H., Graf, H.P.: Pruning filters for efficient ConvNets. arXiv preprint arXiv:1608.08710 (2016)
33. Li, J., Zhao, R., Huang, J.T., Gong, Y.: Learning small-size DNN with output-distribution-based criteria. In: Fifteenth Annual Conference of the International Speech Communication Association (2014)
34. Lin, M., Chen, Q., Yan, S.: Network in network. arXiv preprint arXiv:1312.4400 (2013)
35. Lin, T.Y., Goyal, P., Girshick, R., He, K., Dollár, P.: Focal loss for dense object detection. In: Proceedings of the IEEE International Conference on Computer Vision (2017)
36. Mirza, M., Osindero, S.: Conditional generative adversarial nets (2014)
37. Netzer, Y., Wang, T., Coates, A., Bissacco, A., Wu, B., Ng, A.Y.: Reading digits in natural images with unsupervised feature learning. In: NIPS Workshop on Deep Learning and Unsupervised Feature Learning 2011 (2011)
38. Newell, A., Yang, K., Deng, J.: Stacked hourglass networks for human pose estimation. In: Leibe, B., Matas, J., Sebe, N., Welling, M. (eds.) ECCV 2016, Part VIII. LNCS, vol. 9912, pp. 483–499. Springer, Cham (2016). https://doi.org/10.1007/978-3-319-46484-8_29
39. Ng, A.Y.: Feature selection, L 1 vs. L 2 regularization, and rotational invariance. In: Proceedings of the Twenty-First International Conference on Machine Learning, p. 78. ACM (2004)
40. Polino, A., Pascanu, R., Alistarh, D.: Model compression via distillation and quantization. arXiv preprint arXiv:1802.05668 (2018)

41. Rastegari, M., Ordonez, V., Redmon, J., Farhadi, A.: XNOR-Net: ImageNet classification using binary convolutional neural networks. In: Leibe, B., Matas, J., Sebe, N., Welling, M. (eds.) ECCV 2016, Part IV. LNCS, vol. 9908, pp. 525–542. Springer, Cham (2016). https://doi.org/10.1007/978-3-319-46493-0_32

42. Reed, S., Akata, Z., Yan, X., Logeswaran, L., Schiele, B., Lee, H.: Generative adversarial text to image synthesis. arXiv preprint arXiv:1605.05396 (2016)

43. Rigamonti, R., Sironi, A., Lepetit, V., Fua, P.: Learning separable filters. In: Proceedings of the IEEE Conference on Computer Vision and Pattern Recognition, pp. 2754–2761 (2013)

44. Romero, A., Ballas, N., Kahou, S.E., Chassang, A., Gatta, C., Bengio, Y.: FitNets: hints for thin deep nets. arXiv preprint arXiv:1412.6550 (2014)

45. Salimans, T., Goodfellow, I., Zaremba, W., Cheung, V., Radford, A., Chen, X.: Improved techniques for training GANs. In: Advances in Neural Information Processing Systems, pp. 2234–2242 (2016)

46. Schmidhuber, J.: Learning complex, extended sequences using the principle of history compression. Neural Comput. **4**(2), 234–242 (1992)

47. Simonyan, K., Zisserman, A.: Very deep convolutional networks for large-scale image recognition. arXiv preprint arXiv:1409.1556 (2014)

48. Soudry, D., Hubara, I., Meir, R.: Expectation backpropagation: parameter-free training of multilayer neural networks with continuous or discrete weights. In: Advances in Neural Information Processing Systems, pp. 963–971 (2014)

49. Ström, N.: Phoneme probability estimation with dynamic sparsely connected artificial neural networks. Free Speech J. **5**, 1–41 (1997)

50. Szegedy, C., Vanhoucke, V., Ioffe, S., Shlens, J., Wojna, Z.: Rethinking the inception architecture for computer vision. In: Proceedings of the IEEE Conference on Computer Vision and Pattern Recognition, pp. 2818–2826 (2016)

51. Tung, F., Mori, G.: CLIP-Q: deep network compression learning by in-parallel pruning-quantization. In: Proceedings of the IEEE Conference on Computer Vision and Pattern Recognition, pp. 7873–7882 (2018)

52. Tzeng, E., Hoffman, J., Saenko, K., Darrell, T.: Adversarial discriminative domain adaptation. arXiv preprint arXiv:1702.05464 (2017)

53. Urban, G., et al.: Do deep convolutional nets really need to be deep and convolutional? arXiv preprint arXiv:1603.05691 (2016)

54. Wu, J., Leng, C., Wang, Y., Hu, Q., Cheng, J.: Quantized convolutional neural networks for mobile devices. In: Proceedings of the IEEE Conference on Computer Vision and Pattern Recognition, pp. 4820–4828 (2016)

55. Xiao, H., Rasul, K., Vollgraf, R.: Fashion-MNIST: a novel image dataset for benchmarking machine learning algorithms. arXiv preprint arXiv:1708.07747 (2017)

56. Xie, S., Girshick, R., Dollár, P., Tu, Z., He, K.: Aggregated residual transformations for deep neural networks. arXiv preprint arXiv:1611.05431 (2016)

57. Xu, Z., Hsu, Y.C., Huang, J.: Training student networks for acceleration with conditional adversarial networks. In: BMVC. British Machine Vision Association (2018)

58. Yang, Z., et al.: Deep fried ConvNets. In: Proceedings of the IEEE International Conference on Computer Vision, pp. 1476–1483 (2015)

59. Yim, J., Joo, D., Bae, J., Kim, J.: A gift from knowledge distillation: fast optimization, network minimization and transfer learning. In: The IEEE Conference on Computer Vision and Pattern Recognition (CVPR) (2017)

60. Yu, R., et al.: NISP: pruning networks using neuron importance score propagation. Preprint at https://arxiv.org/abs/1711.05908 (2017)

61. Zagoruyko, S., Komodakis, N.: Wide residual networks. arXiv preprint arXiv:1605.07146 (2016)
62. Zhang, R., Isola, P., Efros, A.A., Shechtman, E., Wang, O.: The unreasonable effectiveness of deep features as a perceptual metric. arXiv preprint arXiv:1801.03924 (2018)
63. Zhang, X., Zhou, X., Lin, M., Sun, J.: ShuffleNet: an extremely efficient convolutional neural network for mobile devices. arXiv preprint arXiv:1707.01083 (2017)
64. Zhou, A., Yao, A., Guo, Y., Xu, L., Chen, Y.: Incremental network quantization: Towards lossless CNNs with low-precision weights (2017)
65. Zhu, C., Han, S., Mao, H., Dally, W.J.: Trained ternary quantization. arXiv preprint arXiv:1612.01064 (2016)

Target Aware Network Adaptation
for Efficient Representation Learning

Yang Zhong[1(✉)], Vladimir Li[1], Ryuzo Okada[2], and Atsuto Maki[1]

[1] KTH Royal Institute of Technology, Stockholm, Sweden
{yzhong,vlali,atsuto}@kth.se
[2] Toshiba Corporate Research and Development Center, Kawasaki, Japan
ryuzo.okada@toshiba.co.jp

Abstract. This paper presents an automatic network adaptation method that finds a ConvNet structure well-suited to a given target task, e.g. image classification, for efficiency as well as accuracy in transfer learning. We call the concept target-aware transfer learning. Given only small-scale labeled data, and starting from an ImageNet pre-trained network, we exploit a scheme of removing its potential redundancy for the target task through iterative operations of filter-wise pruning and network optimization. The basic motivation is that compact networks are on one hand more efficient and should also be more tolerant, being less complex, against the risk of overfitting which would hinder the generalization of learned representations in the context of transfer learning. Further, unlike existing methods involving network simplification, we also let the scheme identify redundant portions across the entire network, which automatically results in a network structure adapted to the task at hand. We achieve this with a few novel ideas: (i) cumulative sum of activation statistics for each layer, and (ii) a priority evaluation of pruning across multiple layers. Experimental results by the method on five datasets (Flower102, CUB200-2011, Dog120, MIT67, and Stanford40) show favorable accuracies over the related state-of-the-art techniques while enhancing the computational and storage efficiency of the transferred model.

Keywords: Target-aware · Network Adaptation · Model compaction
Transfer learning

1 Introduction

The methodology of constructing feature representations has been recently advanced from a well-known hand-crafted manner to a learning-based one. Conventional hand-crafted features are typically designed by leveraging the domain knowledge of human experts [1,4,21]. The learning based approaches often generate discriminative image representations using large-scale labeled datasets, such as ImageNet [6], Places [38], MS COCO [18], and CelebA [19], with deep and

© Springer Nature Switzerland AG 2019
L. Leal-Taixé and S. Roth (Eds.): ECCV 2018 Workshops, LNCS 11132, pp. 450–467, 2019.
https://doi.org/10.1007/978-3-030-11018-5_38

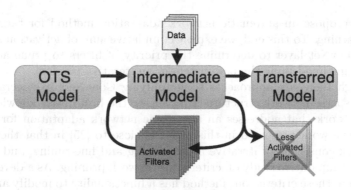

Fig. 1. A schematic of network adaptation proposed in this paper. An off-the-shelf (OTS) model is iteratively structured during the process of transfer learning where in each iteration, less significant filters in terms of activation statistics are discarded while the rest of the filters are reused in the next iteration.

complex convolutional neural networks (ConvNets). Thanks to the generic transferability, these learned deep representations from the ConvNets can also be utilized for other unseen tasks by means of transfer learning [3,7,27,35,36]: one way is to directly use the pre-trained ConvNet to map images to the learned feature space with or without selecting more discriminative features [37]; a more common practice, however, is to transfer a large off-the-shelf (OTS) model to a target task by mildly tuning the ConvNet parameters to make it more specific to a new target task [3,19,35] (Fig. 1).

Despite the successful applications of ConvNets along the scenario of transfer learning, a basic question with respect to the model structure is still unaddressed: a question about whether the off-the-shelf network is sufficiently complex or more than ample to model the target task. That is, most of the existing approaches to ConvNet transfer learning take a predefined network architecture as given and optimize the parameters therein, without seeking for a better suited network structure even though the given task can be much simpler and therefore requiring a less complex model. Indeed, it has been shown that a model built for a source task could be less activated on target tasks [23]. This suggests that ConvNets can be made more compact to derive discriminative feature representations more efficiently in transfer learning scenarios. Moreover, learning representations by reusing a model designed for a very large-scale problem (such as ImageNet classification [6]) for smaller target tasks would risk models to get overfitted to the target domain. Tailoring a network suitable for a target task helps to enhance regularization when learning the target task representations.

As a natural progression for the transferred model to be more effectively adapted to target task, which we call *target-aware transfer learning*, an intuitive next step is to automatically remove possible redundancy from the transferred off-the-shelf model. Besides an obvious benefit in improving computational efficiency, one could expect increased accuracy on a target task if it were possible to find a less complex model that is better structured to target data. Thus, in this paper, we propose an automatic network adaptation method for target-aware transfer learning. To this end, we exploit cumulative sum of activation statistics for each ConvNet layer to determine the priority of filters to prune across the network while fine-tuning the parameters in an iterative pipeline.

Although there are approaches to simplifying ConvNets in general [16] or learning a sparse network structure [2,33,39], to the best of our knowledge this is the first work that addresses an automatic network adaptation for transfer learning. The work presented in this paper is close to [25] in that they deploy a framework consisting of iterative filter pruning and fine-tuning, and [25] also provides a comparative study on criteria for network pruning. As a development orthogonal to those criteria, our method has a functionality to modify and adapt the network structure according to the target task while also avoiding a greedy search to select parts of the network to be removed. The contributions of this paper are summarized as follows:

- We propose a target-aware feature learning framework, *Network Adaptation*, which efficiently generates useful image representations.
- The Network Adaptation automatically tailors an off-the-shelf network (the weights and architecture) to the target task data at hand, so that the learned representations are more favorable and more efficient on the target tasks than the ones from simply fine-tuned off-the-shelf models.
- The results highlight that the generalization of the features gets enhanced through the model compaction by our Network Adaptation for transferring given models to new target tasks.

In Sect. 2, we introduce recent related work. The Network Adaptation method is described in detail in Sect. 3. Comparative experimental results are demonstrated in Sects. 4.2 and 4.3 with ablation studies of different pruning strategies in Sect. 4.4. Section 5 concludes the paper.

2   Related Work

Transfer learning with deep ConvNets addresses a question of how to exploit a trained network for the sake of another task that has some commonality (to some unknown extent) to the source problem which the model has been trained on. For instance, one may use an ImageNet trained model and further train it to classify a subset of ImageNet classes, or even perform a rather different task [13] which has less abundant data. The goal of transfer learning is to construct feature representations for a target task.

A commonly adopted way of transferring a ConvNet is to fine-tune a source task model for a target task. A small learning rate is often used to optimize the target-task orientated objective function so that the learned representations still preserve the generalization learned from the data in the source domain. Feature selection could also be performed before fine-tuning, as different levels of features have different utility for the target task [7,27,36]. One can see feature selection in this context as a plain data-dependent network compaction approach since some high-level layers may be skipped in a transferred network. In our work, network compaction is considered and applied on all across the network based on the activation statistics.

Although ConvNets transfer learning has demonstrated higher performance than the conventional approaches in solving many computer vision problems [3], the enormous computational cost and memory footprint for using ConvNets have hindered applications in some practical scenarios. To alleviate demanding hardware requirements, attentions have been paid to network compaction [9, 12, 22, 23, 25]. Most of the existing compaction methods consider pruning models through coding [9], sparsity [10, 33], matrix decomposition [23], or norm of filter weights [16].

Although it is known that small-scale target data often provides a poor sampling of the target domain, which causes overfitting with complex models, it is still very seldom that network compaction is explicitly employed to counteract overfitting to further help transfer learning. Very recently, Pavlo et al. [25] proposed an iterative pruning method to optimize a fine-tuned networks for a target task. In every iteration, all the filters in the network are evaluated and one filter is pruned at a time based on saliency. The iterative loop needs to be carried out until a reasonable trade-off between accuracy and efficiency is reached. In our method, it is sufficient to perform the network adaptation for much fewer iterations and it prunes many insignificant filters along the network in every single iteration.

On another aspect, to improve regularization for fine-tuning, it has been found that optimizing multiple helpful objectives leads to better model effectiveness compared to plain fine-tuning which only utilizes a cross-entropy loss [8, 17]. One can attempt to reduce the domain variance through certain metrics (i.e. perform domain adaptation) as in [20, 31]. It is also viable to perform multitask learning explicitly. In [8], a data selection approach was developed to select (source-domain) data similar in low-level features to perform multi-task learning. Rather than relying on the availability of foreign data as in the aforementioned work, in [17], the predictions of target domain images given by the source model were recorded before training. They were used later as replacements of extra training data. Then, the current predictions were compared to the recorded ones to compose an additional objective in the loss function. In this way, the network was able to be optimized on the target tasks, but at the same time be able to "remember" how to perform well on the source task. In this work, our approach also achieved better regularization without dependence on the availability of any extra data other than the target task at hand.

3   Target-Aware Network Adaptation

As the intermediate representations along the network are likely to be redundant (over-completed) for a target task, it is reasonable to question if an off-the-shelf architecture is unnecessarily over-structured when being transferred to a target task. By rethinking this commonly adopted fine-tuning procedure, in this section, we propose a network adaptation method to prune and structure an off-the-shelf network for a given target task in Sect. 3.1.

3.1 Network Adaptation

The details of our network adaptation procedure are described in Algorithm 1. First, it takes an off-the-shelf network as a starting point and performs fine-tuning on the target task. After that, in Step 1, it first collects activation statistics and prunes the trained network. Specifically, in Step 1(a), the average intensity of the activation maps is calculated on every layer after feeding in the entire training set.

Algorithm 1. Iterative Network Adaptation process.

Source: (1) An off-the-shelf network, (2) Labeled data in target domain.

1 **Step 0**: Fine-tuning the off-the-shelf network on the target task.

2 **for** *iteration i* **do**

3   Break from the loop when *i* reaches a certain value.

4   **Step 1:** Prune filters in the network optimized in the previous step according to the activation statistics for the training data:
    (a) On each layer, identify less significant filters in terms of cumulative sum of average activations;
    (b) Among all the network layers, prioritize the need for pruning identified filters by the global priority.

    Step 2: Fine-tune the pruned network on the target task, with the same objective function as in **Step 0**.

Let us assume a convolutional layer which has an output activation tensor A, with a size of $H \times W \times K$ (where K represents the number of output channels, and H and W stand for the height and width of feature maps, respectively). The channel-wise activation, $\mathbf{a}^{(k)}(k = 1, ..., K)$, is simply calculated as:

$$\mathbf{a}^{(k)} = \frac{1}{W \times H} \sum_{w=1}^{W} \sum_{h=1}^{H} A_{w,h}^{(k)}. \tag{1}$$

After feeding N training images, $\mathbf{a}^{(k)}$ is averaged over N instances:

$$\bar{\mathbf{a}} = \{\bar{a}_k\}_1^K, \bar{a}_k = \sum_{n=1}^{N} (a_n^{(k)})/N. \tag{2}$$

The channel-wise mean activation is then normalized by its $L1$ norm:

$$\hat{\mathbf{a}} = \frac{\bar{\mathbf{a}}}{\|\bar{\mathbf{a}}\|_1}. \tag{3}$$

Then, we compute the cumulative sum of descendingly sorted normalized mean activation $\hat{a}$, which is denoted by

$$c = cumsum(\hat{a}') \mid \hat{a}' = sort(\hat{a}). \tag{4}$$

Figure 2 illustrates the curve c. Based on the cumulative sum, the filters corresponding to a cumulative sum value higher than a threshold r can be identified, i.e.,

$$h = \arg\min_k \mid c_k - r \mid, \tag{5}$$

$$\mathbf{m}'_p = \{m'_k\}_1^K, \quad m'_k = \begin{cases} 1, k \leq h \\ 0, k > h \end{cases}, \tag{6}$$

$$\mathbf{m}_p = sort^{-1}(\mathbf{m}'_p), \tag{7}$$

where c_k is an individual element in c and $\mathbf{m}_p$ is a binary vector that indicates the indexes of potential filters to keep on a certain layer. The ratio between h and K is illustrated in Fig. 2 as the vertical broken line. The filters corresponding to the right side of that line are considered for pruning.

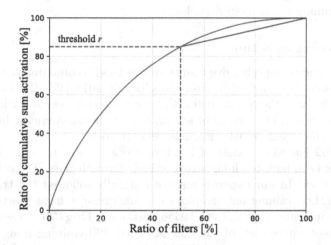

Fig. 2. Cumulative sum of activations: an example from FC6 layer of the VGG-16 network based on the Flower102 dataset. The horizontal red broken line indicates the cumulative threshold ratio r, which is 85% in this case. Filters corresponding to the right side of the vertical broken line are considered for pruning. The slope of the brown line represents the priority in Eq. 8.

Next, in Step 1 (b), in order to further encourage the nature of data-dependent network adaptation, we additionally develop a way to calculate the priority. It helps us to decide whether to perform pruning or not to potential filters on a certain layer. The priority s for layer l is:

$$s^{(l)} = \frac{1 - r}{1 - h^{(l)}/K^{(l)}} \tag{8}$$

Finally, the filters are pruned on the layers that have a priority lower than the mean of priority of all layers guided by $\mathbf{m}_p$; pruning is therefore dynamically performed on the layers that are globally less important. The pruned network is thereafter optimized in Step 2 and the network adaptation is performed iteratively. The network adaptation can be terminated after a number of iterations when the validation accuracy starts to drop or the model size falls below a certain ratio.

4   Experiments

In this section, we first describe the datasets we used for the experiments and the details of how we trained the networks in Sect. 4.1. We then demonstrate the improvement brought about by our method in both accuracy and efficiency by comparing to the recent work addressing transfer learning and network compaction in an identical or a similar context in Sect. 4.2. Sections 4.3 and 4.4 reveal how the Network Adaptation impacts the network structure and computational efficiency. In addition, we also performed an ablation study which demonstrates the significance of activation-based network adaptation versus random filter pruning methods in Sect. 4.5.

4.1   Experimental Setup

In order to provide comprehensive results, our method is comparatively evaluated on five datasets: the Flower102 [26], the CUB200-2011 [32], the Dog120 [14], the MIT67 [28], and the Stanford40 [34], which represent classification tasks in different scenarios. These datasets are among the most common benchmarks employed by the recent transfer learning related work.

Flower102 has 8189 images of 102 flower classes. The training set and the validation set both have ten images respectively for each class. The other images form the test set. In our experiments, we faithfully followed the training and test protocol, i.e. training only employs the 1020 images from the training set without any mixture with the validation instances. **Dog120** dataset contains 120 dog classes where each of the dog class has 100 training images and the test set contains 8580 images. **CUB200-2011** (denoted by "CUB200" in the following) dataset has 6000 training images and 5700 test images of 200 bird species. **MIT67** has 80 training images and 20 test images per indoor scene class. **Stanford40** dataset contains images of human actions of 40 classes, each of which contains 180 to 300 images. On the Dog120, CUB200, MIT67, and Stanford40, 10% training images were separated to form the validation set for model training.

To augment the training images, we employed random jittering and subtle scaling and rotation perturbations to the training images. We resized images of all involved datasets to 250 × 250 and the aspect ratio of the images was retained by applying zero padding all the time. During test time, we averaged over the network responses from the target-task classifiers over ten crops which were sampled from the corners and the centers of originals and the flipped counterparts.

There are a few well-known off-the-shelf networks that can be used in this study such as the AlexNet [15], the InceptionNet [30], the ResNet [11], and the VGGNet [29]. We choose the VGG-16 architecture in our experiments as it is a well studied and widely utilized structure for different kinds of computer vision problems. More importantly, it facilitates comparisons to be as fair as possible since the VGG-16 performs neutrally comparing to the "main-stream" architectures. The off-the-shelf VGG-16 model used in our experiments was pre-trained on the ImageNet [6] and is publicly accessible [24].

For training networks, we used a batch size of 32 with a conservative learning rate of 10^{-4}, which was helpful to achieve stable convergence, on all the datasets. The learning rate was dropped by a factor of 10 once the validation loss stopped decreasing. On most of the datasets, the learning rate was reduced to 10^{-5} within 20 epochs. The model training was terminated when the validation loss stopped decreasing. The model snapshots which performed best on the validation sets during the training were used for performance evaluation on the corresponding test sets. We set weight decay to 0.0005 and Dropout ratio to 0.5.

4.2   Comparative Performance Evaluations

Our experiments in this section focus on comparing our Network Adaptation approach with the standard fine-tuning on the selected target tasks. One straightforward way to apply the Network Adaptation to an off-the-shelf architecture is to perform filter-wise pruning along the entire network, i.e. pruning filters from Conv1_1 until FC7 in the VGG-16 architecture. Considering the "blessing of dimensionality" [5], however, another rational choice is to apply the Network Adaptation excluding the FC7 layer. In this case, the dimensionality of the high-level feature is maintained, which could be helpful to ensure the discrimination power, although at a cost of marginal computational overhead. In the following experiments, we evaluate both options by running independent Network Adaptation processes from the same fine-tuned starting point (i.e. from an identical model at "Step 0" in Algorithm 1 on each dataset).

Specifically, in our experiments, we first performed fine-tuning on each dataset and then performed Network Adaptation iteratively. At each iteration, we used the best performing model on the validation set for performance evaluations. It was then used as the starting model standpoint for the next step. For the Network Adaptation, it is easy to see that the validation accuracy could fluctuate in the first few iterations and decrease eventually. With this regard, we ran 20 Network Adaptation iterations and selected the best performing model (on the validation sets) for the performance evaluation and compared them to the corresponding fine-tuning baselines.

Table 1 shows how the Network Adaptation performs over the standard fine-tuning. First, it can be seen that by keeping the dimensionality of FC7 (NwA w/o FC), it outperforms the standard fine-tuning except on Flower102 and Dog120 dataset. When the dimensionality of the FC7 layer is reduced, Network Adaptation outperforms the standard fine-tuning on all the datasets by an error rate reduction of 3.72% on CUB200, 0.52% on Dog120, 1.20% on Flower102, 3.50%

Table 1. Comparing the test accuracy of fine-tuning with Network Adaptation (NwA) of different design options. The test accuracy of Network Adaptation given here was determined by the best validation accuracy on the corresponding dataset. The Network Adaptation iteration (shortened to "Iter.") number when the best validation accuracy occurred is listed in the parenthesis after test accuracy. Threshold ratio r was set to 2%.

	Fine-tune	NwA w/FC7	NwA w/o FC7
CUB200	75.84%	76.74% (@Iter. 1)	**77.49%** (@Iter. 2)
Dog120	82.79%	**82.88%** (@Iter. 1)	82.73% (@Iter. 2)
Flower102	84.96%	**85.14%** (@Iter. 1)	83.51% (@Iter. 9)
MIT67	70.30%	**71.34%** (@Iter. 5)	71.34% (@Iter. 4)
Stanford40	76.23%	**77.19%** (@Iter. 5)	77.01% (@Iter. 5)

on MIT67, and 4.03% on Stanford40. Remember that such a performance gain was achieved by using more compact networks and only the target task training data. It suggests that how to restructure the network structure to achieve better model effectiveness could also be taken into consideration when transferring an off-the-shelf model to a new target task.

Second, by applying the Network Adaptation along the entire VGG-16 architecture, even better test accuracy can be achieved on almost all datasets except CUB200. This means that restructuring the entire network not only results in even lower computational cost but also promises better performance margin on average. In other words, keeping the dimensionality of the high-level abstractions may not be as important in general. In the following experiments, we perform the Network Adaptation along the entire network unless otherwise stated.

To comprehensively evaluate the Network Adaptation, we focus on the recent approaches which employed network compaction based methods (but brought about accuracy gains) to address transfer learning problems. Given that regularization may be improved by building compact networks for target tasks, a recent state-of-the-art method [17] that explicitly enhanced regularization through multi-task learning is also compared to our approach. These approaches may not employ exactly the same network architecture and other experimental setups (e.g. [23] used a deeper VGG-19 network) as ours, which consequently resulted in slightly different fine-tuning baseline accuracy. To handle the discrepancies, a reasonable comparative evaluation is to compare the relative accuracy gain of these methods, as shown in Table 2.

On the effectiveness of the learned representations, it is clear that the Network Adaptation contributed to superior accuracy than other methods except for the case when it was not applied to the FC7 layer of a VGG-16 network on Flower102. We argue that this is an obvious advantage to some existing network pruning methods which have to make compromises to the performance on target tasks. The accuracy gain, in general, is attributed to the improved regularization (which was achieved in different ways in these methods). It can be seen that making networks more compact is potentially a useful means to

Table 2. Comparing the gain of the test accuracy on various datasets with the recent related approaches. Each entry is the accuracy gain compared to the corresponding fine-tuning baseline. Threshold ratio r set to 2% in our Network Adaptation.

	CUB200	Dog120	Flower102	MIT67	Stanford40
Best of deep compression [23]	0.12%	—	0.1%	—	0.79%
Best of efficient inference [25]	0.5%	—	—	—	—
LwF [17]	−0.6%	—	—	0.3%	—
Ours, w/o FC7	1.65%	−0.04%	−1.45%	1.04%	0.78%
Ours, w/ FC7	0.9%	0.09%	0.18%	1.04%	0.96%

Note that our total compression ratio is on-par with that in [23], see Fig. 4.
The best gain on CUB200 from [25] was manually retrieved from Fig. 4 in [25].

improve regularization owing to the positive gains. Our Network Adaptation indeed achieved better regularization than others given the more favorable performance improvements. In addition, we noticed that the network compaction process is quite efficient with the Network Adaptation approach as it does not depend on exhaustive search as in [25]; the compaction is also more effective for reducing the computational cost than in [23] as filters across the entire network were simultaneously considered for pruning. The network compaction effects of our approach are demonstrated with details in the following sections.

4.3   Evolution of Network Size During Network Adaptation

The Network Adaptation, on the one hand, can be used to improve the model effectiveness on the target tasks, on the other hand, it also enforces target data-driven model compaction which effectively reduces the size of ConvNets. In this way, one can make a trade-off between the network size and the model accuracy on the target task with our Network Adaptation.

To demonstrate how the discriminability of the learned representations varies on the target tasks along the Network Adaptation process, we show the validation accuracy and the test accuracy along 20 Network Adaptation iterations in Fig. 3. One can find that after fine-tuning on the target tasks (Iteration 0) the Network Adaptation is able to boost the discrimination power of the learned representations, which was reflected on the validation and test accuracy in the first few iterations. It is clear that the improvement in the test accuracy is data dependent. We can expect around or more than 1% accuracy increment on MIT67, CUB200, and Stanford40, which have moderately large training sets. But the improvement was less significant when training data was too sparse or much too large. As on the Flower102, it had only 10 training images per class, while on Dog120 each class had around 100 images for training for each class, which was 2 to 3 times larger than other datasets. The accuracies dropped at later iterations when the networks lost more capacity. As our threshold r was only 2%, the test accuracies were not significantly decreased even at Iteration 20.

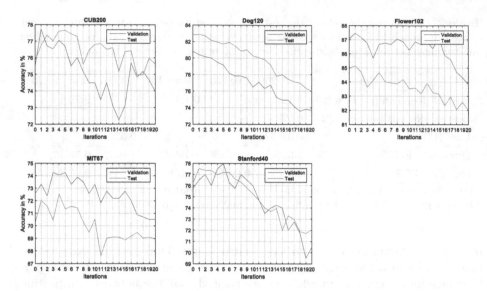

Fig. 3. Validation accuracy versus test accuracy on the datasets during 20 iterations of Network Adaptation.

The reduction of the total number of parameters and the corresponding computational costs at each Network Adaptation iteration are shown in Fig. 4. First, it can be seen that the total number of network coefficient was reduced in an exponential trend. The network size can be halved in the first five iterations on all the tasks even with an insignificant threshold value. The network size got linearly reduced after Iteration 8. Second, the Network Adaptation resulted in roughly a linear decrementing trend in the computational cost in terms of Floating-point Operation (FLOP). For both of the decreasing curves of network size and FLOP, a similar data-dependent character can be observed; on the tasks with more abundant data, they shared a common tendency which was deviated on the task with the least data.

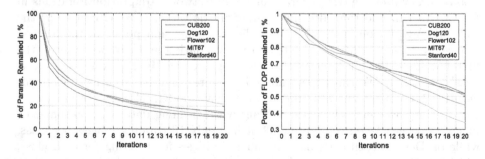

Fig. 4. Normalized reduction of the number of network coefficients (left) and the corresponding normalized reduction of FLOP (right) with a VGG-16 architecture achieved by the Network Adaptation on different datasets.

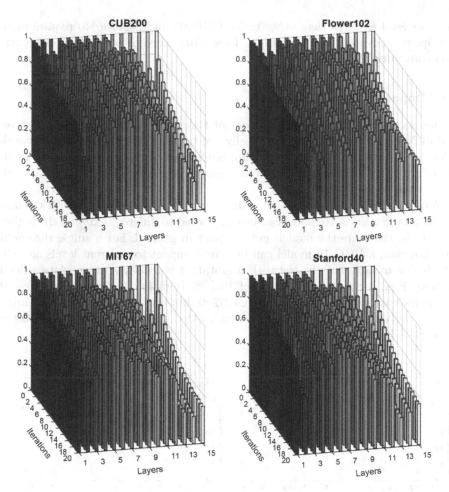

Fig. 5. Relative change of layer width at each Network Adaptation iteration. The "Layers" scale, from 1 to 15, represents the learnable layers from "Conv1_1" till "FC7" in a VGG-16 structure.

The detailed sizes of each layer width (number of filters) for the 20 Network Adaptation iterations on the selected datasets are visualized in Fig. 5. It is easy to see that a VGG-16 architecture was (re-)shaped differently by our Network Adaptation on different tasks. An interesting phenomenon is that the lower level filters in the vicinity of Conv2_1 layer were pruned relatively more than other layers, but on MIT67 the pruning rate was not as large as on the others. This suggests a large but task-specific redundancy in the lower layers of the off-the-shelf model. The same situation can be observed on higher-level convolutional layers. It can, therefore, be inferred that the learned high-level image representation at the FC7 layer indeed depends on different combinations of the convolutional features: the indoor scene classification MIT67 relies more on lower level features than other tasks; CUB200 and Stanford40 require more descriptive mid-level representations; Flower102 more or less relies on higher-level convolutional features.

4.4 Impact of Threshold Ratio

In this section, we evaluate the impact of threshold ratio (r) to the effectiveness of Network Adaptation. Specifically, we perform ten iterations of Network Adaptation with 2%, 5%, and 10% threshold ratios and evaluate the best models indicated by the validation sets to explore the performance of the Network Adaptation with different setups.

As shown in Fig. 6, by employing different threshold ratios in Network Adaptation, a target VGG-16 model can be compacted to different extents; the higher the rate is, the more the models get compact in general. For a single threshold rate, however, a VGG-16 model can become compact to different levels as well. This is due to fact that the Network Adaptation is totally a target data guided method. E.g., for a threshold ratio of 10% at Iteration 10, more than 10% of the coefficients were retained on the CUB200, but on the MIT67 the remaining portion was only around 6%. MIT67 data yielded stronger pruning effect in the Network Adaptation process.

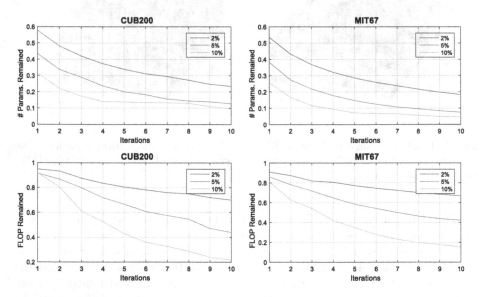

Fig. 6. Comparing pruning effects by using different threshold ratios in Network Adaptation. The x-axis represents the iterations of the Network Adaptation from 1 to 10, and the relative residual portion of network parameters and computational costs of a VGG-16 architecture is shown in y-axis.

Table 3. Test accuracy on the CUB200 and the MIT67 with different threshold ratios. The Network Adaptation iteration which gave the best performing model (on validation set) are given in parenthesis.

	Threshold ratios		
	2%	5%	10%
CUB200	77.49% (@Iter. 2)	76.19% (@Iter. 4)	76.64% (@Iter. 1)
MIT67	71.34% (@Iter. 4)	71.49% (@Iter. 2)	69.48% (@Iter. 2)

Table 3 lists the test accuracy values on the CUB200 and the MIT67 under three threshold ratios. It reveals a rough relation between the number of iterations and the threshold ratios with respect to the best test accuracy; a mild pruning rate may require more steps to achieve the best accuracy and vice versa. From these results, we may infer that a threshold ratio between 5% and 10% would be a practical choice which balances between the training speed and the model accuracy.

4.5 Significance of Least Activation Pruning

In our Network Adaptation, we prune filters which correspond to the least activations of a given dataset. As shown in Fig. 5, it shapes the model architecture based on the target data in a way that it removes different numbers of filters on different layers. To highlight the importance of this pruning strategy, we evaluate two alternative filter pruning methods which can be potentially used by our Network Adaptation framework in two stages.

In the first experiment, we compared the performance discrepancy between removing a random 10% of filters versus pruning 10% of the least activated filters in each layer along the whole network. In both ways, the models were uniformly pruned along the structure but these pruning strategies cannot (re-)shape the model structure. Due to the randomness, we ran five independent experiments for one iteration with both strategies and compared the average accuracy.

The second experiment intended to further verify that randomly pruning filters performs less effectively than filters selected based on activation. This is done by directly comparing random pruning versus activation based pruning in the Network Adaptation procedure, where random pruning removes an equal amount of filters as by the Network Adaptation in each layer in each iteration (we also ran 20 iterations with the threshold ratio r set to 2%). The same starting models at "Step 0" as in the previous experiments were used in these experiments but the Network Adaptation iterations were run independently for the comparative studies here. The results are listed in Table 4.

The results of Experiment 1 show that uniformly pruning a network performs inferior to the Network Adaptation. Comparing the accuracy of the random pruning strategy in both experiments to that of the Network Adaptation, one can see that in general random filter pruning performs less effectively than

Table 4. Comparing other pruning strategies to the activation based approach we used in the Network Adaptation. "Least Act." indicates "Least Activation". "Random" is short for random pruning strategies for each experiment.

	Experiment 1		Experiment 2	
	Random 10%	Least Act., 10%	Random	NwA
CUB200	76.02%	**76.46%**	75.96% (@Iter. 1)	**77.03%** (@Iter. 7)
MIT67	65.33%	**67.60%**	68.73% (@Iter. 4)	**71.34%** (@Iter. 5)

activation based as used in our method, i.e. activation based methods offer a more reasonable pruning.

5   Conclusions

We proposed an iterative network adaptation approach to learn useful representations for transfer learning problems which have access to only small-scale target data. Our approach automatically structures model architecture by pruning less important filters, in which a data dependent method is developed to identify less important filters. Being adapted in the proposed pipeline, the transferred models are shown to be more computationally efficient and demonstrate at least comparable performance to the widely used "fine-tuning" practice and even the related state-of-the-art approaches.

In addition to the experimental results, the current development of our Network Adaptation approach left us some interesting open questions. First, for transfer learning, how to enhance regularization with limited labeled data is not fully studied yet; we demonstrated that model compaction would be a promising candidate, but it will be also interesting to evaluate other alternatives. Second, for network adaptation, it is ideal to have equally favorable performance to all target tasks but the classification accuracies by our approach slightly decreased in some situations. This hints us that it is also helpful to consider partly expanding the network architecture according to data to complement the capacity of the transferred model.

Acknowledgements. We acknowledge fruitful discussions and comments to this work from colleagues of Toshiba Corporate Research and Development Center. We thank NVIDIA Corporation for their generous donation of NVIDIA GPUs.

References

1. Ahonen, T., Hadid, A., Pietikäinen, M.: Face recognition with local binary patterns. In: Pajdla, T., Matas, J. (eds.) ECCV 2004, Part I. LNCS, vol. 3021, pp. 469–481. Springer, Heidelberg (2004). https://doi.org/10.1007/978-3-540-24670-1_36

2. Alvarez, J.M., Salzmann, M.: Learning the number of neurons in deep networks. Adv. Neural Inf. Process. Syst. **29**, 2270–2278 (2016)
3. Azizpour, H., Razavian, A., Sullivan, J., Maki, A., Carlsson, S.: Factors of transferability for a generic convnet representation. IEEE Trans. Patt. Anal. Mach. Intell. **38**(9), 1790–1802 (2016)
4. Bay, H., Tuytelaars, T., Van Gool, L.: SURF: speeded up robust features. In: Leonardis, A., Bischof, H., Pinz, A. (eds.) ECCV 2006, Part I. LNCS, vol. 3951, pp. 404–417. Springer, Heidelberg (2006). https://doi.org/10.1007/11744023_32
5. Chen, D., Cao, X., Wen, F., Sun, J.: Blessing of dimensionality: high-dimensional feature and its efficient compression for face verification. In: 2013 IEEE Conference on Computer Vision and Pattern Recognition, pp. 3025–3032 (2013). https://doi.org/10.1109/CVPR.2013.389
6. Deng, J., Dong, W., Socher, R., Li, L.J., Li, K., Fei-Fei, L.: ImageNet: a large-scale hierarchical image database. In: The IEEE Conference on Computer Vision and Pattern Recognition (CVPR), June 2009
7. Donahue, J., et al.: DeCAF: a deep convolutional activation feature for generic visual recognition. In: Proceedings of the 31st International Conference on Machine Learning, vol. 32, pp. 647–655 (2014)
8. Ge, W., Yu, Y.: Borrowing treasures from the wealthy: deep transfer learning through selective joint fine-tuning. In: The IEEE Conference on Computer Vision and Pattern Recognition (CVPR), July 2017
9. Han, S., Mao, H., Dally, W.J.: Deep compression: compressing deep neural network with pruning, trained quantization and Huffman coding. CoRR abs/1510.00149 (2015). http://arxiv.org/abs/1510.00149
10. Han, S., Pool, J., Tran, J., Dally, W.: Learning both weights and connections for efficient neural network. Adv. Neural Inf. Process. Syst. **28**, 1135–1143 (2015)
11. He, K., Zhang, X., Ren, S., Sun, J.: Deep residual learning for image recognition. In: The IEEE Conference on Computer Vision and Pattern Recognition (CVPR), June 2016
12. Hinton, G.E., Vinyals, O., Dean, J.: Distilling the knowledge in a neural network
13. Kendall, A., Grimes, M., Cipolla, R.: PoseNet: a convolutional network for real-time 6-DOF camera relocalization. In: Proceedings of the International Conference on Computer Vision (ICCV) (2015)
14. Khosla, A., Jayadevaprakash, N., Yao, B., Fei-Fei, L.: Novel dataset for fine-grained image categorization. In: IEEE Conference on Computer Vision and Pattern Recognition First Workshop on Fine-Grained Visual Categorization, June 2011
15. Krizhevsky, A., Sutskever, I., Hinton, G.E.: Imagenet classification with deep convolutional neural networks. Adv. Neural Inf. Process. Syst. **25**, 1097–1105 (2012)
16. Li, H., Kadav, A., Durdanovic, I., Samet, H., Peter Graf, H.: Pruning filters for efficient ConvNets. In: Proceedings of the International Conference on Learning Representations (ICLR), April 2017
17. Li, Z., Hoiem, D.: Learning without forgetting. In: Leibe, B., Matas, J., Sebe, N., Welling, M. (eds.) ECCV 2016, Part IV. LNCS, vol. 9908, pp. 614–629. Springer, Cham (2016). https://doi.org/10.1007/978-3-319-46493-0_37
18. Lin, T.-Y., et al.: Microsoft COCO: common objects in context. In: Fleet, D., Pajdla, T., Schiele, B., Tuytelaars, T. (eds.) ECCV 2014, Part V. LNCS, vol. 8693, pp. 740–755. Springer, Cham (2014). https://doi.org/10.1007/978-3-319-10602-1_48
19. Liu, Z., Luo, P., Wang, X., Tang, X.: Deep learning face attributes in the wild. In: The IEEE International Conference on Computer Vision (ICCV), pp. 3730–3738 (2015)

20. Long, M., Cao, Y., Wang, J., Jordan, M.: Learning transferable features with deep adaptation networks. In: Proceedings of the 32nd International Conference on Machine Learning, vol. 37, pp. 97–105 (2015)
21. Lowe, D.G.: Object recognition from local scale-invariant features. In: Proceedings of the Seventh IEEE International Conference on Computer Vision, vol. 2, pp. 1150–1157 (1999)
22. Luo, J., Wu, J., Lin, W.: ThiNet: a filter level pruning method for deep neural network compression. CoRR abs/1707.06342 (2017). http://arxiv.org/abs/1707.06342
23. Masana, M., van de Weijer, J., Herranz, L., Bagdanov, A.D., Alvarez, J.M.: Domain-adaptive deep network compression. In: The IEEE International Conference on Computer Vision (ICCV), October 2017
24. ModelZoo: Pretrained VGG-16 model for TensorFlow. http://download.tensorflow.org/models/vgg_16_2016_08_28.tar.gz. Accessed Aug 2017
25. Molchanov, P., Tyree, S., Karras, T., Aila, T., Kautz, J.: Pruning convolutional neural networks for resource efficient inference. In: Proceedings of the International Conference on Learning Representations (ICLR), April 2017
26. Nilsback, M.E., Zisserman, A.: Automated flower classification over a large number of classes. In: Proceedings of the Indian Conference on Computer Vision, Graphics and Image Processing, December 2008
27. Oquab, M., Bottou, L., Laptev, I., Sivic, J.: Learning and transferring mid-level image representations using convolutional neural networks. In: The IEEE Conference on Computer Vision and Pattern Recognition (CVPR) (2014)
28. Quattoni, A., Torralba, A.: Recognizing indoor scenes. In: 2009 IEEE Computer Society Conference on Computer Vision and Pattern Recognition Workshops (CVPR Workshops), pp. 413–420 (2009)
29. Simonyan, K., Zisserman, A.: Very deep convolutional networks for large-scale image recognition. CoRR abs/1409.1556 (2014)
30. Szegedy, C., et al.: Going deeper with convolutions. In: The IEEE International Conference on Computer Vision (ICCV) (2014)
31. Tzeng, E., Hoffman, J., Darrell, T., Saenko, K.: Simultaneous deep transfer across domains and tasks. In: The IEEE International Conference on Computer Vision (ICCV), December 2015
32. Wah, C., Branson, S., Welinder, P., Perona, P., Belongie, S.: The Caltech-UCSD Birds-200-2011 Dataset. Technical report (2011)
33. Wen, W., Wu, C., Wang, Y., Chen, Y., Li, H.: Learning structured sparsity in deep neural networks. Adv. Neural Inf. Process. Syst. **29**, 2074–2082 (2016)
34. Yao, B., Jiang, X., Khosla, A., Lin, A.L., Guibas, L., Fei-Fei, L.: Human action recognition by learning bases of action attributes and parts. In: The IEEE International Conference on Computer Vision (ICCV), pp. 1331–1338 (2011)
35. Yosinski, J., Clune, J., Bengio, Y., Lipson, H.: How transferable are features in deep neural networks? Adv. Neural Inf. Process. Syst. **27**, 3320–3328 (2014)
36. Zeiler, M.D., Fergus, R.: Visualizing and understanding convolutional networks. In: Fleet, D., Pajdla, T., Schiele, B., Tuytelaars, T. (eds.) ECCV 2014, Part I. LNCS, vol. 8689, pp. 818–833. Springer, Cham (2014). https://doi.org/10.1007/978-3-319-10590-1_53
37. Zhong, Y., Sullivan, J., Li, H.: Transferring from face recognition to face attribute prediction through adaptive selection of off-the-shelf CNN representations. In: 23rd International Conference on Pattern Recognition (ICPR), pp. 2264–2269 (2016)

38. Zhou, B., Lapedriza, A., Xiao, J., Torralba, A., Oliva, A.: Learning deep features for scene recognition using places database. Adv. Neural Inf. Process. Syst. **27**, 487–495 (2014)
39. Zhou, H., Alvarez, J.M., Porikli, F.: Less is more: towards compact CNNs. In: Leibe, B., Matas, J., Sebe, N., Welling, M. (eds.) ECCV 2016, Part IV. LNCS, vol. 9908, pp. 662–677. Springer, Cham (2016). https://doi.org/10.1007/978-3-319-46493-0_40

Learning CCA Representations
for Misaligned Data

Hichem Sahbi$^{(\boxtimes)}$

CNRS, Sorbonne University, Paris, France
hichem.sahbi@sorbonne-universite.fr

Abstract. Canonical correlation analysis (CCA) is a statistical learning method that seeks to build view-independent latent representations from multi-view data. This method has been successfully applied to several pattern analysis tasks such as image-to-text mapping and view-invariant object/action recognition. However, this success is highly dependent on the quality of data pairing (i.e., alignments) and mispairing adversely affects the generalization ability of the learned CCA representations.

In this paper, we address the issue of alignment errors using a new variant of canonical correlation analysis referred to as alignment-agnostic (AA) CCA. Starting from erroneously paired data taken from different views, this CCA finds transformation matrices by optimizing a constrained maximization problem that mixes a data correlation term with context regularization; the particular design of these two terms mitigates the effect of alignment errors when learning the CCA transformations. Experiments conducted on multi-view tasks, including multi-temporal satellite image change detection, show that our AA CCA method is highly effective and resilient to mispairing errors.

Keywords: Canonical correlation analysis
Learning compact representations · Misalignment resilience
Change detection

1 Introduction

Several tasks in computer vision and neighboring fields require *labeled* datasets in order to build effective statistical learning models. It is widely agreed that the accuracy of these models relies substantially on the availability of large labeled training sets. These sets require a tremendous human annotation effort and are thereby very expensive for many large scale classification problems including image/video-to-text (a.k.a captioning) [1–4], multi-modal information retrieval [5], multi-temporal change detection [6,7], object recognition and segmentation [8,9], etc. The current trend in machine learning, mainly with the data-hungry deep models [1,2,10–12], is to bypass supervision, by making the training of these models totally unsupervised [13], or at least weakly-supervised using: fine-tuning [14], self-supervision [15], data augmentation and game-based models

© Springer Nature Switzerland AG 2019
L. Leal-Taixé and S. Roth (Eds.): ECCV 2018 Workshops, LNCS 11132, pp. 468–485, 2019.
https://doi.org/10.1007/978-3-030-11018-5_39

[16]. However, the hardness of collecting annotated datasets does not *only* stem from assigning accurate labels to these data, but also from aligning them; for instance, in the neighboring field of machine translation, successful training models require accurately aligned bi-texts (parallel bilingual training sets), while in satellite image change detection, these models require accurately georeferenced and registered satellite images. This level of requirement, *both* on the accuracy of labels and *their alignments*, is clearly hard-to-reach; alternative models, that skip the sticky alignment requirement, should be preferred.

Canonical correlation analysis (CCA) [17–20] is one of the statistical learning models that require accurately aligned (paired) multi-view data[1]; CCA finds – for each view – a transformation matrix that maps data from that view to a view-independent (latent) representation such that aligned data obtain highly correlated latent representations. Several extensions of CCA have been introduced in the literature including nonlinear (kernel) CCA [21], sparse CCA [22–24], multiple CCA [25], locality preserving and instance-specific CCA [26,27], time-dependent CCA [28] and other unified variants (see for instance [29,30]); these methods have been applied to several pattern analysis tasks such as image-to-text [31], pose estimation [21,26] and object recognition [32], multi-camera activity correlation [33,34] and motion alignment [35,36] as well as heterogeneous sensor data classification [37].

The success of all the aforementioned CCA approaches is highly *dependent* on the accuracy of alignments between multi-view data. In practice, data are subject to misalignments (such as registration errors in satellite imagery) and sometimes completely unaligned (as in muti-lingual documents) and this skews the learning of CCA. Excepting a few attempts – to handle temporal deformations in monotonic sequence datasets [38] using canonical time warping [36] (and its deep extension [39]) – none of these existing CCA variants address alignment errors for non-monotonic datasets[2]. Besides CCA, the issue of data alignment has been approached, in general, using manifold alignment [40–42], Procrustes analysis [43] and source-target domain adaption [44] but none of these methods consider resilience to misalignments as a part of CCA design (which is the main purpose of our contribution in this paper). Furthermore, these data alignment solutions rely on a strong "apples-to-apples" comparison hypothesis (*that data taken from different views have similar structures*) which does not always hold especially when handling datasets with heterogeneous views (as text/image data and multi-temporal or multi-sensor satellite images). Moreover, even when data are globally well (re)aligned, some *residual* alignment errors are difficult to handle (such as parallax in multi-temporal satellite imagery) and harm CCA (as shown in our experiments).

In this paper, we introduce a novel CCA approach that handles misaligned data; i.e., it does not require any preliminary step of accurate data alignment.

---

[1] Multi-view data stands for input data described with multiple modalities such as documents described with text and images.

[2] Non-monotonic stands for datasets without a "unique" order (such as patches in images).

This is again very useful for different applications where aligning data is very time demanding or when data are taken from multiple sources (sensors, modalities, etc.) which are intrinsically misaligned[3]. The benefit of our approach is twofold; on the one hand, it models the uncertainty of alignments using a new data correlation term and on the other hand, modeling alignment uncertainty allows us to use not only decently aligned data (if available) when learning CCA, but also the unaligned ones. In sum, this approach can be seen as an extension of CCA on unaligned sets compared to standard CCA (and its variants) that operate only on accurately aligned data. Furthermore, the proposed method is as efficient as standard CCA and its computationally complexity grows w.r.t the dimensionality (and not the cardinality) of data, and this makes it very suitable for large datasets.

Our CCA formulation is based on the optimization of a constrained objective function that combines two terms; a correlation criterion and a context-based regularizer. The former maximizes a weighted correlation between data with a high cross-view similarity while the latter makes this weighted correlation high for data whose neighbors have high correlations too (and vice-versa). We will show that optimizing this constrained maximization problem is equivalent to solving an iterative generalized eigenvalue/eigenvector decomposition; we will also show that the solution of this iterative process converges to a fixed-point. Finally, we will illustrate the validity of our CCA formulation on different challenging problems including change detection both on *residually and strongly* misaligned multi-temporal satellite images; indeed, these images are subject to alignment errors due to the hardness of image registration under challenging conditions, such as occlusion and parallax.

The rest of this paper is organized as follows; Sect. 2 briefly reminds the preliminaries in canonical correlation analysis, followed by our main contribution: a novel alignment-agnostic CCA, as well as some theoretical results about the convergence of the learned CCA transformation to a fixed-point (under some constraints on the parameter that weights our regularization term). Section 3 shows the validity of our method both on synthetic toy data as well as real-world problems namely satellite image change detection. Finally, we conclude the paper in Sect. 4 while providing possible extensions for a future work.

2   Canonical Correlation Analysis

Considering the input spaces $\mathcal{X}_r$ and $\mathcal{X}_t$ as two sets of images taken from two modalities; in satellite imagery, these modalities could be two different sensors, or the same sensor at two different instants, etc. Denote $\mathcal{I}_r = \{\mathbf{u}_i\}_i$, $\mathcal{I}_t = \{\mathbf{v}_j\}_j$ as two subsets of $\mathcal{X}_r$ and $\mathcal{X}_t$ respectively; our goal is learn a transformation between $\mathcal{X}_r$ and $\mathcal{X}_t$ that assigns, for a given $\mathbf{u} \in \mathcal{X}_r$, a sample $\mathbf{v} \in \mathcal{X}_t$. The learning of this transformation usually requires accurately *paired* data in $\mathcal{X}_r \times \mathcal{X}_t$ as in CCA.

---

[3] Satellite images – georeferenced with the Global Positioning System (GPS) – have localization errors that may reach 15 m in some geographic areas. On high resolution satellite images (sub-metric resolution) this corresponds to alignment errors/drifts that may reach 30 pixels.

2.1   Standard CCA

Assuming centered data in $\mathcal{I}_r$, $\mathcal{I}_t$, standard CCA (see for instance [19]) finds two projection matrices that map aligned data in $\mathcal{I}_r \times \mathcal{I}_t$ into a latent space while maximizing their correlation. Let $\mathbf{P}_r$, $\mathbf{P}_t$ denote these projection matrices which respectively correspond to reference and test images. CCA finds these matrices as $(\mathbf{P}_r, \mathbf{P}_t) = \arg\max_{\mathbf{A},\mathbf{B}} \text{tr}(\mathbf{A}'\mathbf{C}_{rt}\mathbf{B})$, subject to $\mathbf{A}'\mathbf{C}_{rr}\mathbf{A} = \mathbf{I}_u$, $\mathbf{B}'\mathbf{C}_{tt}\mathbf{B} = \mathbf{I}_v$; here $\mathbf{I}_u$ (resp. $\mathbf{I}_v$) is the $d_u \times d_u$ (resp. $d_v \times d_v$) identity matrix, d_u (resp. d_v) is the dimensionality of data in $\mathcal{X}_r$ (resp. $\mathcal{X}_t$), $\mathbf{A}'$ stands for transpose of $\mathbf{A}$, tr is the trace, $\mathbf{C}_{rt}$ (resp. $\mathbf{C}_{rr}$, $\mathbf{C}_{tt}$) correspond to inter-class (resp. intra-class) covariance matrices of data in $\mathcal{I}_r$, $\mathcal{I}_t$, and equality constraints control the effect of scaling on the solution. One can show that problem above is equivalent to solving the eigenproblem $\mathbf{C}_{rt}\mathbf{C}_{tt}^{-1}\mathbf{C}_{tr}\mathbf{P}_r = \gamma^2 \mathbf{C}_{rr}\mathbf{P}_r$ with $\mathbf{P}_t = \frac{1}{\gamma}\mathbf{C}_{tt}^{-1}\mathbf{C}_{tr}\mathbf{P}_r$. In practice, learning these two transformations requires "paired" data in $\mathcal{I}_r \times \mathcal{I}_t$, i.e., aligned data. However, and as will be shown through this paper, accurately paired data are not always available (and also expensive), furthermore the cardinality of $\mathcal{I}_r$ and $\mathcal{I}_t$ can also be different, so one should adapt CCA in order to learn transformation between data in $\mathcal{I}_r$ and $\mathcal{I}_t$ as shown subsequently.

2.2   Alignment Agnostic CCA

We introduce our main contribution: a novel alignment agnostic CCA approach. Considering $\{(\mathbf{u}_i, \mathbf{v}_j)\}_{ij}$ as a subset of $\mathcal{I}_r \times \mathcal{I}_t$ (cardinalities of $\mathcal{I}_r$, $\mathcal{I}_t$ are not necessarily equal), we propose to find the transformation matrices $\mathbf{P}_r$, $\mathbf{P}_t$ as

$$\max_{\mathbf{P}_r, \mathbf{P}_t} \text{tr}(\mathbf{U}'\mathbf{P}_r\mathbf{P}_t'\mathbf{V}\mathbf{D})$$
$$\text{s.t.} \quad \mathbf{P}_r'\mathbf{C}_{rr}\mathbf{P}_r = \mathbf{I}_u \ \text{ and } \ \mathbf{P}_t'\mathbf{C}_{tt}\mathbf{P}_t = \mathbf{I}_v, \tag{1}$$

the non-matrix form of this objective function is given subsequently. In this constrained maximization problem, $\mathbf{U}$, $\mathbf{V}$ are two matrices of data in $\mathcal{I}_r$, $\mathcal{I}_t$ respectively, and $\mathbf{D}$ is an (application-dependent) matrix with its given entry $\mathbf{D}_{ij}$ set to the cross affinity or the likelihood that a given data $\mathbf{u}_i \in \mathcal{I}_r$ aligns with $\mathbf{v}_j \in \mathcal{I}_t$ (see Sect. 3.2 about different setting of this matrix). This definition of $\mathbf{D}$, together with objective function (1), make CCA *alignment agnostic*; indeed, this objective function (equivalent to $\sum_{i,j}\langle \mathbf{P}_r'\mathbf{u}_i, \mathbf{P}_t'\mathbf{v}_j \rangle \mathbf{D}_{ij}$) aims to maximize the correlation between pairs (with a high cross affinity of alignment) while it also minimizes the correlation between pairs with small cross affinity. For a particular setting of $\mathbf{D}$, the following proposition provides a *special case*.

Proposition 1. Provided that $|\mathcal{I}_r| = |\mathcal{I}_t|$ and $\forall \mathbf{u}_i \in \mathcal{I}_r$, $\exists! \mathbf{v}_j \in \mathcal{I}_t$ such that $\mathbf{D}_{ij} = 1$; the constrained maximization problem (1) implements standard CCA.

Proof. Considering the non-matrix form of (1), we obtain

$$\text{tr}(\mathbf{U}'\mathbf{P}_r\mathbf{P}_t'\mathbf{V}\mathbf{D}) = \sum_{i,j}\langle \mathbf{P}_r'\mathbf{u}_i, \mathbf{P}_t'\mathbf{v}_j \rangle \mathbf{D}_{ij}, \tag{2}$$

considering a particular order of $\mathcal{I}_t$ such that each sample $\mathbf{u}_i$ in $\mathcal{I}_r$ aligns with a unique $\mathbf{v}_i$ in $\mathcal{I}_t$ we obtain

$$
\begin{aligned}
\text{tr}(\mathbf{U}'\mathbf{P}_r\mathbf{P}_t'\mathbf{V}\mathbf{D}) &= \sum_{i,j}\langle\mathbf{P}_r'\mathbf{u}_i,\mathbf{P}_t'\mathbf{v}_j\rangle\mathbb{1}_{\{i=j\}} \\
&= \sum_i\langle\mathbf{P}_r'\mathbf{u}_i,\mathbf{P}_t'\mathbf{v}_i\rangle \\
&= \text{tr}(\mathbf{P}_r'(\sum_i\mathbf{u}_i\mathbf{v}_i')\mathbf{P}_t) \\
&= \text{tr}(\mathbf{P}_r'\mathbf{C}_{rt}\mathbf{P}_t),
\end{aligned}
\tag{3}
$$

with $\mathbf{C}_{rt}$ being the inter-class covariance matrix and $\mathbb{1}_{\{\}}$ the indicator function. Since the equality constraints (shown in Sect. 2.1) remain unchanged, the constrained maximization problem (1) is strictly equivalent to standard CCA for this particular $\mathbf{D}$ □

This particular setting of $\mathbf{D}$ is relevant only when data are accurately paired and also when $\mathcal{I}_r$, $\mathcal{I}_t$ have the same cardinality. In practice, many problems involve unpaired/mispaired datasets with different cardinalities; that's why $\mathbf{D}$ should be relaxed using affinity between multiple pairs (as discussed earlier in this section) instead of using strict alignments. With this new CCA setting, the learned transformations $\mathbf{P}_t$, and $\mathbf{P}_r$ generate latent data representations $\phi_t(\mathbf{v}_i) = \mathbf{P}_t'\mathbf{v}_i$, $\phi_r(\mathbf{u}_j) = \mathbf{P}_r'\mathbf{u}_j$ which align according to $\mathbf{D}$ (i.e., $\|\phi_r(\mathbf{v}_i) - \phi_t(\mathbf{u}_j)\|_2$ decreases if $\mathbf{D}_{ij}$ is high and vice-versa). However, when multiple entries $\{\mathbf{D}_{ij}\}_j$ are high for a given i, this may produce noisy correlations between the learned latent representations and may impact their discrimination power (see also experiments). In order to mitigate this effect, we also consider context regularization.

2.3   Context-Based Regularization

For each data $\mathbf{u}_i \in \mathcal{I}_r$, we define a (typed) neighborhood system $\{\mathcal{N}_c(i)\}_{c=1}^C$ which corresponds to the typed neighbors of $\mathbf{u}_i$ (see Sect. 3.2 for an example). Using $\{\mathcal{N}_c(.)\}_{c=1}^C$, we consider for each c an intrinsic adjacency matrix $\mathbf{W}_u^c$ whose $(i,k)^{\text{th}}$ entry is set as $\mathbf{W}_{u,i,k}^c \propto \mathbb{1}_{\{k\in\mathcal{N}_c(i)\}}$. Similarly, we define the matrices $\{\mathbf{W}_v^c\}_c$ for data $\{\mathbf{v}_j\}_j \in \mathcal{I}_t$; extra details about the setting of these matrices are again given in experiments.

Using the above definition of $\{\mathbf{W}_u^c\}_c$, $\{\mathbf{W}_v^c\}_c$, we add an extra-term in the objective function (1) as

$$
\max_{\mathbf{P}_r,\mathbf{P}_t} \text{tr}(\mathbf{U}'\mathbf{P}_r\mathbf{P}_t'\mathbf{V}\mathbf{D}) + \beta\sum_{c=1}^C\text{tr}\big(\mathbf{U}'\mathbf{P}_r\mathbf{P}_t'\mathbf{V}\mathbf{W}_v^c\mathbf{V}'\mathbf{P}_t\mathbf{P}_r'\mathbf{U}\mathbf{W}_u^{c'}\big)
\tag{4}
$$
$$
\text{s.t.}\quad \mathbf{P}_r'\mathbf{C}_{rr}\mathbf{P}_r = \mathbf{I}_u \quad\text{and}\quad \mathbf{P}_t'\mathbf{C}_{tt}\mathbf{P}_t = \mathbf{I}_v.
$$

The above right-hand side term is equivalent to

$$
\beta\sum_c\sum_{i,j}\langle\mathbf{P}_r'\mathbf{u}_i,\mathbf{P}_t'\mathbf{v}_j\rangle\sum_{k,\ell}\langle\mathbf{P}_r'\mathbf{u}_k,\mathbf{P}_t'\mathbf{v}_\ell\rangle\mathbf{W}_{u,i,k}^c\mathbf{W}_{v,j,\ell}^c
$$

the latter corresponds to a neighborhood (or context) criterion which considers that a high value of the correlation $\langle \mathbf{P}'_r \mathbf{u}_i, \mathbf{P}'_t \mathbf{v}_j \rangle$, in the learned latent space, should imply high correlation values in the neighborhoods $\{\mathcal{N}_c(i) \times \mathcal{N}_c(j)\}_c$. This term (via β) controls the sharpness of the correlations (and also the discrimination power) of the learned latent representations (see example in Fig. 2). Put differently, if a given $(\mathbf{u}_i, \mathbf{v}_j)$ is surrounded by highly correlated pairs, then the correlation between $(\mathbf{u}_i, \mathbf{v}_j)$ should be maximized and vice-versa [45, 46].

2.4 Optimization

Considering Lagrange multipliers for the equality constraints in Eq. (4), one may show that optimality conditions (related to the gradient of Eq. (4) w.r.t $\mathbf{P}_r$, $\mathbf{P}_t$ and the Lagrange multipliers) lead to the following generalized eigenproblem

$$\mathbf{K}_{rt}\mathbf{C}_{tt}^{-1}\mathbf{K}_{tr}\mathbf{P}_r = \gamma^2 \mathbf{C}_{rr}\mathbf{P}_r \\ \text{with} \quad \mathbf{P}_t = \frac{1}{\gamma}\,\mathbf{C}_{tt}^{-1}\mathbf{K}_{tr}\mathbf{P}_r, \tag{5}$$

here $\mathbf{K}_{tr} = \mathbf{K}'_{rt}$ and

$$\mathbf{K}_{tr} = \mathbf{V}\mathbf{D}\mathbf{U}' + \beta \sum_c \mathbf{V}\mathbf{W}_v^c \mathbf{V}' \mathbf{P}_t \mathbf{P}'_r \mathbf{U}\mathbf{W}_u^{c'} \mathbf{U}'$$
$$+ \beta \sum_c \mathbf{V}\mathbf{W}_v^{c'} \mathbf{V}' \mathbf{P}_t \mathbf{P}'_r \mathbf{U}\mathbf{W}_u^c \mathbf{U}'. \tag{6}$$

In practice, we solve the above eigenproblem iteratively. For each iteration τ, we fix $\mathbf{P}_r^{(\tau)}$, $\mathbf{P}_t^{(\tau)}$ (in $\mathbf{K}_{tr}$, $\mathbf{K}_{rt}$) and we find the subsequent projection matrices $\mathbf{P}_r^{(\tau+1)}$, $\mathbf{P}_t^{(\tau+1)}$ by solving Eq. (5); initially, $\mathbf{P}_r^{(0)}$, $\mathbf{P}_t^{(0)}$ are set using projection matrices of standard CCA. This process continues till a fixed-point is reached. In practice, convergence to a fixed-point is observed in less than five iterations.

Proposition 2. Let $\|.\|_1$ denote the entry-wise L_1-norm and $\mathbf{1}_{vu}$ a $d_v \times d_u$ matrix of ones. Provided that the following inequality holds

$$\beta < \gamma_{\min} \times \left(\sum_c \|\mathbf{E}_c\, \mathbf{1}_{vu}\, \mathbf{F}'_c\|_1 + \sum_c \|\mathbf{G}_c\, \mathbf{1}_{vu}\, \mathbf{H}'_c\|_1 \right)^{-1} \tag{7}$$

with $\gamma_{\min}$ being a lower bound of the positive eigenvalues of (5), $\mathbf{E}_c = \mathbf{V}\mathbf{W}_v^c \mathbf{V}' \mathbf{C}_{tt}^{-1}$, $\mathbf{F}_c = \mathbf{U}\mathbf{W}_u^c \mathbf{U}' \mathbf{C}_{rr}^{-1}$, $\mathbf{G}_c = \mathbf{V}\mathbf{W}_v^{c'} \mathbf{V}' \mathbf{C}_{tt}^{-1}$ and $\mathbf{H}_c = \mathbf{U}\mathbf{W}_u^{c'} \mathbf{U}' \mathbf{C}_{rr}^{-1}$; the problem in (5), (6) admits a unique solution $\tilde{\mathbf{P}}_r$, $\tilde{\mathbf{P}}_t$ as the eigenvectors of

$$\tilde{\mathbf{K}}_{rt}\mathbf{C}_{tt}^{-1}\tilde{\mathbf{K}}_{tr}\mathbf{P}_r = \gamma^2 \mathbf{C}_{rr}\mathbf{P}_r \\ \mathbf{P}_t = \frac{1}{\gamma}\,\mathbf{C}_{tt}^{-1}\tilde{\mathbf{K}}_{tr}\mathbf{P}_r, \tag{8}$$

with $\tilde{\mathbf{K}}_{tr}$ being the limit of

$$\mathbf{K}_{tr}^{(\tau+1)} = \Psi\big(\mathbf{K}_{tr}^{(\tau)}\big), \tag{9}$$

and $\Psi : \mathbb{R}^{d_v \times d_u} \rightarrow \mathbb{R}^{d_v \times d_u}$ is given as

$$\Psi(\mathbf{K}_{tr}) = \mathbf{V}\mathbf{D}\mathbf{U}' + \beta \sum_c \mathbf{V}\mathbf{W}_v^c \mathbf{V}'\mathbf{P}_t\mathbf{P}_r'\mathbf{U}\mathbf{W}_u^c \mathbf{U}'$$
$$+ \beta \sum_c \mathbf{V}\mathbf{W}_v^{c'} \mathbf{V}'\mathbf{P}_t\mathbf{P}_r'\mathbf{U}\mathbf{W}_u^c \mathbf{U}', \tag{10}$$

with $\mathbf{P}_t$, $\mathbf{P}_r$, in (10), being functions of $\mathbf{K}_{tr}$ using (5). Furthermore, the matrices $\mathbf{K}_{tr}^{(\tau+1)}$ in (9) satisfy the convergence property

$$\left\| \mathbf{K}_{tr}^{(\tau+1)} - \tilde{\mathbf{K}}_{tr} \right\|_1 \leq L^\tau \left\| \mathbf{K}_{tr}^{(\tau+1)} - \mathbf{K}_{tr}^{(0)} \right\|_1, \tag{11}$$

with $L = \frac{\beta}{\gamma_{\min}} \left(\sum_c \left\| \mathbf{E}_c \mathbf{1}_{vu} \mathbf{F}_c' \right\|_1 + \sum_c \left\| \mathbf{G}_c \mathbf{1}_{vu} \mathbf{H}_c' \right\|_1 \right).$

Proof. See appendix

Note that resulting from the extreme sparsity of the *typed* adjacency matrices $\{\mathbf{W}_u^c\}_c$, $\{\mathbf{W}_v^c\}_c$, the upper bound about β (shown in the sufficient condition in Eq. 7) is loose, and easy to satisfy; in practice, we observed convergence for all the values of β that were tried in our experiments (see the x-axis of Fig. 2).

3 Experiments

In this section, we show the performance of our method both on synthetic and real datasets. The goal is to show the extra gain brought when using our alignment agnostic (AA) CCA approach against standard CCA and other variants.

3.1 Synthetic Toy Example

In order to show the strength of our AA CCA method, we first illustrate its performance on a 2D toy example. We consider 2D data sampled from an "arc" as shown in Fig. 1(a); each sample is endowed with an RGB color feature vector which depends on its curvilinear coordinates in that "arc". We duplicate this dataset using a 2D rotation (with an angle of 180°) and we add a random perturbation field (noise) both to the color features and the 2D coordinates (see Fig. 1). Note that accurate ground-truth pairing is available but, of course, not used in our experiments.

We apply our AA CCA (as well as standard CCA) to these data, and we show alignment results; this 2D toy example is very similar to the subsequent real data task as the goal is to find for each sample in the original set, its correlations and its realignment with the second set. From Fig. 1, it is clear that standard CCA fails to produce accurate results when data is contaminated with random perturbations and alignment errors, while our AA CCA approach successfully realigns the two sets (see again details in Fig. 1).

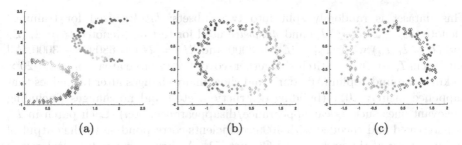

(a)   (b)   (c)

Fig. 1. This figure shows the realignment results of CCA; (a) we consider 100 examples sampled from an "arc", each sample is endowed with an RGB feature vector. We duplicate this dataset using a 2D rotation (with an angle of $180°$) and we add a random perturbation field both to the color features and 2D coordinates. (b) realignment results obtained using standard CCA; note that original data are not aligned, so in order to apply standard CCA, each sample in the first arc-set is paired with its nearest (color descriptor) neighbor in the second arc-set. (c) realignment results obtained using our AA CCA approach; again data are not paired, so we consider a fully dense matrix $\mathbf{D}$ that measures the cross-similarity (using an RBF kernel) between the colors of the first and the second arc-sets. In these toy experiments, β (weight of context regularizer) is set to 0.01 and we use an isotropic neighborhood system in order to fill the context matrices $\{\mathbf{W}_u^c\}_{c=1}^C$, $\{\mathbf{W}_v^c\}_{c=1}^C$ (with $C = 1$) and a given entry $\mathbf{W}_{u,i,k}^c$ is set to 1 iff $\mathbf{u}_k$ is among the 10 spatial neighbors of $\mathbf{u}_i$. Similarly, we set the entries of $\{\mathbf{W}_v^c\}_c^C$. **For a better visualization of these results, better to view/zoom the PDF of this paper.**

3.2 Satellite Image Change Detection

We also evaluate and compare the performance of our proposed AA CCA method on the challenging task of satellite image change detection (see for instance [6, 47–50]). The goal is to find instances of relevant changes into a given scene acquired at instance t_1 with respect to the same scene taken at instant $t_0 < t_1$; these acquisitions (at instants t_0, t_1) are referred to as reference and test images respectively. This task is known to be very challenging due to the difficulty to characterize relevant changes (appearance or disappearance of objects[4]) from irrelevant ones such as the presence of cars, clouds, as well as *registration errors*. This task is also practically important; indeed, in the particular important scenario of damage assessment after natural hazards (such as tornadoes, earth quakes, etc.), it is crucial to achieve automatic change detection accurately in order to organize and prioritize rescue operations.

JOPLIN-TORNADOES11 Dataset. This dataset includes 680928 non overlapping image patches (of 30 × 30 pixels in RGB) taken from six pairs of (reference and test) GeoEye-1 satellite images (of 9850 × 10400 pixels each).

---

[4] This can be any object so there is no a priori knowledge about what object may appear or disappear into a given scene.

This dataset is randomly split into two subsets: *labeled* used for training[5] (denoted $\mathcal{L}_r \subset \mathcal{I}_r$, $\mathcal{L}_t \subset \mathcal{I}_t$) and *unlabeled* used for testing (denoted $\mathcal{U}_r = \mathcal{I}_r \backslash \mathcal{L}_r$ and $\mathcal{U}_t = \mathcal{I}_t \backslash \mathcal{L}_t$) with $|\mathcal{L}_r| = |\mathcal{L}_t| = 3000$ and $|\mathcal{U}_r| = |\mathcal{U}_t| = 680928 - 3000$. All patches in $\mathcal{I}_r$ (or in $\mathcal{I}_t$), stitched together, cover a very large area – of about 20×20 km^2 – around Joplin (Missouri) and show many changes after tornadoes that happened in may 2011 (building destruction, etc.) and no-changes (including irrelevant ones such as car appearance/disappearance, etc.). Each patch in $\mathcal{I}_r$, $\mathcal{I}_t$ is rescaled and encoded with 4096 coefficients corresponding to the output of an inner layer of the pretrained VGG-net [51]. A given test patch is declared as a "change" or "no-change" depending on the score of SVMs trained on top of the learned CCA latent representations.

In order to evaluate the performances of change detection, we report the equal error rate (EER). The latter is a balanced generalization error that equally weights errors in "change" and "no-change" classes. Smaller EER implies better performance.

Data Pairing and Context Regularization. In order to study the impact of AA CCA on the performances of change detection – both with residual and relatively stronger misalignments – we consider the following settings for comparison (see also Table 1).

- **Standard CCA:** patches are *strictly* paired by assigning each patch, in the reference image, to a unique patch in the test image (in the same location), so it assumes that satellite images are correctly registered. CCA learning is *supervised* (only labeled patches are used for training) and *no-context* regularization is used (i.e, $\beta = 0$). In order to implement this setting, we consider $\mathbf{D}$ as a diagonal matrix with $\mathbf{D}_{ii} = \pm 1$ depending on whether $\mathbf{v}_i \in \mathcal{L}_t$ is labeled as "no-change" (or "change") in the ground-truth, and $\mathbf{D}_{ii} = 0$ otherwise.
- **Sup+CA CCA:** this is similar to "standard CCA" with the only difference being β which is set to its "optimal" value (0.01) on the validation set (see Fig. 2).
- **SemiSup CCA:** this setting is similar to "standard CCA" with the only difference being the unlabeled patches which are now added when learning the CCA transformations, and $\mathbf{D}_{ii}$ (on the unlabeled patches) is set to $2\kappa(\mathbf{v}_i, \mathbf{u}_i) - 1$ (score between -1 and $+1$); here $\kappa(.,.) \in [0, 1]$ is the RBF similarity whose scale is set to the 0.1 quantile of pairwise distances in $\mathcal{L}_t \times \mathcal{L}_r$.
- **SemiSup+CA CCA:** this setting is similar to "SemiSup CCA" but context regularization is used (with again β set to 0.01).
- **Res CCA:** this is similar to "standard CCA", but strict data pairing is *relaxed*, i.e., each patch in the reference image is assigned to multiple patches in the test image; hence, $\mathbf{D}$ is no longer diagonal, and set as $\mathbf{D}_{ij} = \kappa(\mathbf{v}_i, \mathbf{u}_j) \in [0, 1]$ iff $(\mathbf{v}_i, \mathbf{u}_j) \in \mathcal{L}_t \times \mathcal{L}_r$ is labeled as "no-change" in the ground-truth, $\mathbf{D}_{ij} = \kappa(\mathbf{v}_i, \mathbf{u}_j) - 1 \in [-1, 0]$ iff $(\mathbf{v}_i, \mathbf{u}_j) \in \mathcal{L}_t \times \mathcal{L}_r$ is labeled as "change" and $\mathbf{D}_{ij} = 0$ otherwise.

---

[5] From which a subset of 1000 is used for validation (as a dev set).

- **Res+Sup+CA CCA:** this is similar to "Res CCA" with the only difference being β which is again set to 0.01.
- **Res+SemiSup CCA:** this setting is similar to "Res CCA" with the only difference being the unlabeled patches which are now added when learning the CCA transformations; on these unlabeled patches $D_{ij} = 2\kappa(\mathbf{v}_i, \mathbf{u}_j) - 1$.
- **Res+SemiSup+CA CCA:** this setting is similar to "Res+SemiSup CCA" but context regularization is used (i.e., $\beta = 0.01$).

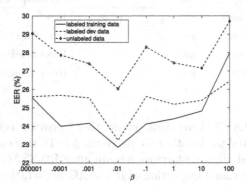

Fig. 2. This figure shows the evolution of change detection performances w.r.t β on labeled training/dev data as well as the unlabeled data. These results correspond to the baseline Sup+CA CCA (under the regime of strong misalignments); we observe from these curves that $\beta = 0.01$ is the best setting which is kept in all our experiments.

Context setting: in order to build the adjacency matrices of the context (see Sect. 2.3), we define for each patch $\mathbf{u}_i \in \mathcal{I}_r$ (in the reference image) an anisotropic (typed) neighborhood system $\{\mathcal{N}_c(i)\}_{c=1}^C$ (with $C = 8$) which corresponds to the eight spatial neighbors of $\mathbf{u}_i$ in a regular grid [52]; for instance when $c = 1$, $\mathcal{N}_1(i)$ corresponds to the top-left neighbor of $\mathbf{u}_i$. Using $\{\mathcal{N}_c(.)\}_{c=1}^8$, we build for each c an intrinsic adjacency matrix $\mathbf{W}_u^c$ whose $(i, k)^{\text{th}}$ entry is set as $\mathbf{W}_{u,i,k}^c \propto \mathbb{1}_{\{k \in \mathcal{N}_c(i)\}}$; here $\mathbb{1}_{\{\}}$ is the indicator function equal to 1 iff (i) the patch $\mathbf{u}_k$ is neighbor to $\mathbf{u}_i$ and (ii) its relative position is typed as c ($c = 1$ for top-left, $c = 2$ for left, etc. following an anticlockwise rotation), and 0 otherwise. Similarly, we define the matrices $\{\mathbf{W}_v^c\}_c$ for data $\{\mathbf{v}_j\}_j \in \mathcal{I}_t$.

Impact of AA CCA and Comparison. Table 2 shows a comparison of different versions of AA CCA against other CCA variants under the regime of small residual alignment errors. In this regime, reference and test images are first registered using RANSAC [53]; an exhaustive visual inspection of the overlapping (reference and test) images (after RANSAC registration) shows sharp boundaries in most of the areas covered by these images, but some areas still include residual misalignments due to the presence of changes, occlusions (clouds, etc.) as well as parallax. Note that, in spite of the relative success of RANSAC in registering

Table 1. This table shows different configurations of CCA resulting from different instances of our model. In this table, "Sup" stands for supervised, "SemiSup" for semi-supervised, "CA" for context aware and "Res" for resilient.

Pairing	CCA learning	Context regularization	Designation
strict	supervised	no	Standard CCA
strict	supervised	yes	Sup+CA CCA
strict	semi-sup	no	SemiSup CCA
strict	semi-sup	yes	SemiSup+CA CCA
relaxed	supervised	no	Res CCA
relaxed	supervised	yes	Res+Sup+CA CCA
relaxed	semi-sup	no	Res+SemiSup CCA
relaxed	semi-sup	yes	Res+SemiSup+CA CCA

these images, our AA CCA versions (rows #5–8) provide better performances (see Table 2) compared to the other CCAs (rows #1–4); this clearly corroborates the fact that residual alignment errors remain after RANSAC (re)alignment (as also observed during visual inspection of RANSAC registration). Put differently, our AA CCA method is not an opponent to RANSAC but complementary.

These results also show that when reference and test images are globally well aligned (with some residual errors; see Table 2), the gain in performance is dominated by the positive impact of alignment resilience; indeed, the impact of the unlabeled data is not always consistent (#5,6 vs. #7,8 resp.) in spite of being positive (in #1,2 vs. #3,4 resp.) while the impact of context regularization is globally positive (#1,3,5,7 vs. #2,4,6,8 resp.). This clearly shows that, under the regime of small residual errors, the use of labeled data is already enough in order to enhance the performance of change detection; the gain comes essentially

Table 2. This table shows change detection EER (in %) on labeled (training and validation) and unlabeled sets under the residual error regime. When context regularization (referred to as CA in this table) is used, β is set to 10^{-2}.

#	Configurations	Labeled (train)	Labeled (dev)	Unlabeled
1	Standard CCA	14.91	15.18	12.81
2	Sup+CA CCA	12.95	14.90	11.44
3	SemiSup CCA	11.26	12.80	11.18
4	SemiSup+CA CCA	12.57	11.82	09.96
5	Res CCA	05.81	04.97	**05.38**
6	Res+Sup+CA CCA	06.35	05.53	**05.55**
7	Res+SemiSup CCA	08.60	08.74	08.33
8	Res+SemiSup+CA CCA	08.77	08.60	06.94

Table 3. This table shows change detection EER (in %) on labeled (training and validation) and unlabeled sets under the strong error regime. When context regularization (referred to as CA in this table) is used, β is set to 10^{-2}.

#	Configurations	Labeled (train)	Labeled (dev)	Unlabeled
1	Standard CCA	25.63	25.61	28.44
2	Sup+CA CCA	22.85	23.23	26.03
3	SemiSup CCA	22.31	23.58	24.99
4	SemiSup+CA CCA	25.74	25.40	25.47
5	Res CCA	16.42	14.34	**19.67**
6	Res+Sup+CA CCA	16.55	16.80	**19.90**
7	Res+SemiSup CCA	19.01	19.24	**19.55**
8	Res+SemiSup+CA CCA	23.71	21.55	26.76

from alignment resilience with a marginal (but clear) positive impact of context regularization.

In order to study the impact of AA CCA w.r.t stronger alignment errors (i.e. w.r.t a more challenging setting), we apply a relatively strong motion field to all the pixels in the reference image; precisely, each pixel is shifted along a direction whose x–y coordinates are randomly set to values between 15 and 30 pixels. These shifts are sufficient in order to make the quality of alignments used for CCA very weak so the different versions of CCA, mentioned earlier, become more sensitive to alignment errors (EERs increase by more than 100% in Table 3 compared to EERs with residual alignment errors in Table 2). With this setting, AA CCA is clearly more resilient and shows a substantial relative gain compared to the other CCA versions.

3.3 Discussion

Invariance: resulting from its misalignment resilience, it is easy to see that our AA CCA is *de facto* robust to local deformations as these deformations are strictly equivalent to local misalignments. It is also easy to see that our AA CCA may achieve invariance to similarity transformations; indeed, the matrices used to define the spatial context are translation invariant, and can also be made rotation and scale invariant by measuring a "characteristic" scale and orientation of patches in a given satellite image. For that purpose, dense SIFT can be used to recover (or at least approximate) the field of orientations and scales, and hence adapt the spatial support (extent and orientation) of context using the characteristic scale, in order to make context invariant to similarity transformations.

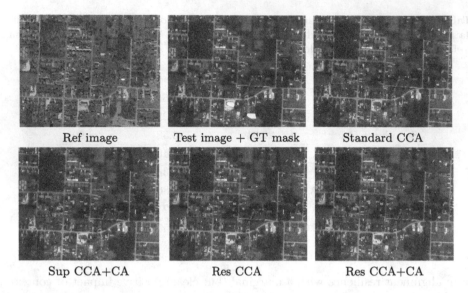

Fig. 3. These examples show the evolution of detections (in red) for four different settings of CCA; as we go from top-right to bottom-right, change detection results get better. CCA acronyms shown below pictures are already defined in Table 1. (Color figure online)

Computational Complexity: provided that VGG-features are extracted (offline) on all the patches of the reference/test images, and provided that the adjacency matrices of context are precomputed[6], and since the adjacency matrices $\{\mathbf{W}_u^c\}_c$, $\{\mathbf{W}_v^c\}_c$ are very sparse, the computational complexity of evaluating Eq. (6) and solving the generalized eigenproblem in Eq. (5) both reduce to $O(\min(d_u^2 d_v, d_v^2 d_u))$, here d_u, d_v are again the dimensions of data in $\mathbf{U}$, $\mathbf{V}$ respectively; hence, this complexity is very equivalent to standard CCA which also requires solving a generalized eigenproblem. Therefore, the gain in the accuracy of our AA CCA is obtained without any overhead in the computational complexity that remains dependent on dimensionality of data (which is, in practice, smaller compared to the cardinality of our datasets) (see also Fig. 3).

4   Conclusion

We introduced in this paper a new canonical correlation analysis method that learns projection matrices which map data from input spaces to a latent common space where unaligned data become strongly or weakly correlated depending on their cross-view similarity and their context. This is achieved by optimizing a

---

[6] Note that the adjacency matrices of the spatial neighborhood system can be computed offline once and reused.

criterion that mixes two terms: the first one aims at maximizing the correlations between data which are likely to be paired while the second term acts as a regularizer and makes correlations spatially smooth and provides us with robust context-aware latent representations. Our method considers both labeled and unlabeled data when learning the CCA projections while being resilient to alignment errors. Extensive experiments show the substantial gain of our CCA method under the regimes of residual and strong alignment errors.

As a future work, our CCA method can be extended to many other tasks where alignments are error-prone and when context can be exploited in order to recover from these alignment errors. These tasks include "text-to-text" alignment in multilingual machine translation, as well as "image-to-image" matching in multi-view object tracking.

A   Appendix (Proof of Proposition 2)

We will prove that Ψ is L-Lipschitzian, with $L = \frac{\beta}{\gamma_{\min}}(\sum_c \|\mathbf{E}_c \mathbf{1}_{vu} \mathbf{F}'_c\|_1 + \sum_c \|\mathbf{G}_c \mathbf{1}_{vu} \mathbf{H}'_c\|_1)$. For ease of writing, we omit in this proof the subscripts t, r in $\mathbf{K}_{tr}$ (unless explicitly required and mentioned).

Given two matrices $\mathbf{K}^{(2)}$, $\mathbf{K}^{(1)}$, we have $\|\mathbf{K}^{(2)} - \mathbf{K}^{(1)}\|_1 = (*)$ with

$$(*) = \beta \left\| \sum_c \mathbf{V}\mathbf{W}_v^c\mathbf{V}'(\mathbf{P}_t^{(1)}\mathbf{P}_r'^{(1)} - \mathbf{P}_t^{(0)}\mathbf{P}_r'^{(0)})\mathbf{U}\mathbf{W}_u^{c'}\mathbf{U}' \right.$$
$$\left. + \sum_c \mathbf{V}\mathbf{W}_v^{c'}\mathbf{V}'(\mathbf{P}_t^{(1)}\mathbf{P}_r'^{(1)} - \mathbf{P}_t^{(0)}\mathbf{P}_r'^{(0)})\mathbf{U}\mathbf{W}_u^c\mathbf{U}' \right\|_1. \qquad (12)$$

Using Eq. (5), one may write

$$\mathbf{P}_t\mathbf{P}_r' = \frac{1}{\gamma}\mathbf{C}_{tt}^{-1}\mathbf{K}_{tr}\mathbf{C}_{rr}^{-1}, \qquad (13)$$

which also results from the fact that $\mathbf{K}_{rt}\mathbf{C}_{tt}^{-1}\mathbf{K}_{tr}$ is Hermitian and $\mathbf{C}_{rr}$ is positive semi-definite. By adding the superscript τ in $\mathbf{P}_t$, $\mathbf{P}_r$, γ, $\mathbf{K}_{tr}$ (with $\tau = 0, 1$), omitting again the subscripts t, r in $\mathbf{K}_{tr}$ and then plugging (13) into (12) we obtain

$$(*) = \beta \left\| \sum_c \mathbf{E}_c (\frac{1}{\gamma^{(1)}}\mathbf{K}^{(1)} - \frac{1}{\gamma^{(0)}}\mathbf{K}^{(0)}) \mathbf{F}'_c + \sum_c \mathbf{G}_c (\frac{1}{\gamma^{(1)}}\mathbf{K}^{(1)} - \frac{1}{\gamma^{(0)}}\mathbf{K}^{(0)}) \mathbf{H}'_c \right\|_1$$
$$\leq \frac{\beta}{\gamma_{\min}} \left\| \sum_c \mathbf{E}_c (\mathbf{K}^{(1)} - \mathbf{K}^{(0)}) \mathbf{F}'_c \right\|_1 + \frac{\beta}{\gamma_{\min}} \left\| \sum_c \mathbf{G}_c (\mathbf{K}^{(1)} - \mathbf{K}^{(0)}) \mathbf{H}'_c \right\|_1, \qquad (14)$$

here $\gamma_{\min}$ is the lower bound of the eigenvalues of (5) which can be derived (see for instance [54]). Considering $\mathbf{K}_{k,\ell}$ as the $(k, \ell)^{\text{th}}$ entry of $\mathbf{K}$, we have

$$(*) \leq \frac{\beta}{\gamma_{\min}} \sum_{i,j} \left| \sum_{k,\ell} (\mathbf{K}_{k,\ell}^{(1)} - \mathbf{K}_{k,\ell}^{(0)}) \sum_c \mathbf{E}_{c,i,k} \ \mathbf{F}_{c,j,\ell} \right|$$

$$+ \frac{\beta}{\gamma_{\min}} \sum_{i,j} \left| \sum_{k,\ell} (\mathbf{K}_{k,\ell}^{(1)} - \mathbf{K}_{k,\ell}^{(0)}) \sum_c \mathbf{G}_{c,i,k} \ \mathbf{H}_{c,j,\ell} \right|$$

$$\leq \frac{\beta}{\gamma_{\min}} \sum_{i,j} \sum_{k,\ell} |\mathbf{K}_{k,\ell}^{(1)} - \mathbf{K}_{k,\ell}^{(0)}| \sum_c |\mathbf{E}_{c,i,k} \ \mathbf{F}_{c,j,\ell}|$$

$$+ \frac{\beta}{\gamma_{\min}} \sum_{i,j} \sum_{k,\ell} |\mathbf{K}_{k,\ell}^{(1)} - \mathbf{K}_{k,\ell}^{(0)}| \sum_c |\mathbf{G}_{c,i,k} \ \mathbf{H}_{c,j,\ell}|$$

$$\leq \frac{\beta}{\gamma_{\min}} \sum_{k,\ell} |\mathbf{K}_{k,\ell}^{(1)} - \mathbf{K}_{k,\ell}^{(0)}|$$

$$\times \left(\sum_{i,j} \sum_{k,\ell,c} |\mathbf{E}_{c,i,k} \ \mathbf{F}_{c,j,\ell}| + \sum_{i,j} \sum_{k,\ell,c} |\mathbf{G}_{c,i,k} \ \mathbf{H}_{c,j,\ell}| \right)$$

$$(\text{as } \sum_i |a_i|.|b_i| \leq \sum_{i,j} |a_i|.|b_j|, \ \forall \ \{a_i\}_i, \{b_j\}_i \subset \mathbb{R})$$

$$= L \ \|\mathbf{K}^{(1)} - \mathbf{K}^{(0)}\|_1,$$

$$\text{with} \quad L = \frac{\beta}{\gamma_{\min}} \left(\sum_c \|\mathbf{E}_c \ \mathbf{1}_{vu} \ \mathbf{F}_c'\|_1 + \sum_c \|\mathbf{G}_c \ \mathbf{1}_{vu} \ \mathbf{H}_c'\|_1 \right) \qquad \square$$

References

1. Krizhevsky, A., Sutskever, I., Hinton, G.E.: ImageNet classification with deep convolutional neural networks. In: Advances in Neural Information Processing Systems, pp. 1097–1105 (2012)
2. Russakovsky, O., et al.: ImageNet large scale visual recognition challenge. Int. J. Comput. Vis. **115**(3), 211–252 (2015)
3. Boujemaa, N., Fleuret, F., Gouet, V., Sahbi, H.: Visual content extraction for automatic semantic annotation of video news. In: The proceedings of the SPIE Conference, San Jose, CA, vol. 6 (2004)
4. Wang, L., Sahbi, H.: Directed acyclic graph kernels for action recognition. In: Proceedings of the IEEE International Conference on Computer Vision, pp. 3168–3175 (2013)
5. Tollari, S., et al.: A comparative study of diversity methods for hybrid text and image retrieval approaches. In: Peters, C., et al. (eds.) CLEF 2008. LNCS, vol. 5706, pp. 585–592. Springer, Heidelberg (2009). https://doi.org/10.1007/978-3-642-04447-2_72
6. Hussain, M., Chen, D., Cheng, A., Wei, H., Stanley, D.: Change detection from remotely sensed images: from pixel-based to object-based approaches. ISPRS J. Photogrammetry Remote Sens. **80**, 91–106 (2013)
7. Bourdis, N., Marraud, D., Sahbi, H.: Spatio-temporal interaction for aerial video change detection. In: 2012 IEEE International Geoscience and Remote Sensing Symposium (IGARSS), pp. 2253–2256. IEEE (2012)
8. Sahbi, H., Boujemaa, N.: Coarse-to-fine support vector classifiers for face detection. In: null, p. 30359. IEEE (2002)

9. Li, X., Sahbi, H.: Superpixel-based object class segmentation using conditional random fields. In: 2011 IEEE International Conference on Acoustics, Speech and Signal Processing (ICASSP), pp. 1101–1104. IEEE (2011)

10. He, K., Zhang, X., Ren, S., Sun, J.: Deep residual learning for image recognition. In: Proceedings of the IEEE Conference on Computer Vision and Pattern Recognition, pp. 770–778 (2016)

11. Goodfellow, I., Bengio, Y., Courville, A.: Deep learning. Book in preparation for MIT Press (2016). http://www.deeplearningbook.org

12. Jiu, M., Sahbi, H.: Nonlinear deep kernel learning for image annotation. IEEE Trans. Image Process. 26(4), 1820–1832 (2017)

13. Erhan, D., Bengio, Y., Courville, A., Manzagol, P.A., Vincent, P., Bengio, S.: Why does unsupervised pre-training help deep learning? J. Mach. Learn. Res. 11, 625–660 (2010)

14. Yosinski, J., Clune, J., Bengio, Y., Lipson, H.: How transferable are features in deep neural networks? In: Advances in Neural Information Processing Systems, pp. 3320–3328 (2014)

15. Doersch, C., Zisserman, A.: Multi-task self-supervised visual learning. arXiv preprint arXiv:1708.07860 (2017)

16. Richter, S.R., Vineet, V., Roth, S., Koltun, V.: Playing for data: ground truth from computer games. In: Leibe, B., Matas, J., Sebe, N., Welling, M. (eds.) ECCV 2016, Part II. LNCS, vol. 9906, pp. 102–118. Springer, Cham (2016). https://doi.org/10.1007/978-3-319-46475-6_7

17. Hotelling, H.: Relations between two sets of variates. Biometrika 28(3/4), 321–377 (1936)

18. Anderson, T.W.: An Introduction to Multivariate Statistical Analysis, vol. 2. Wiley, New York (1958)

19. Hardoon, D.R., Szedmak, S., Shawe-Taylor, J.: Canonical correlation analysis: an overview with application to learning methods. Neural Comput. 16(12), 2639–2664 (2004)

20. Sahbi, H.: Interactive satellite image change detection with context-aware canonical correlation analysis. IEEE Geosci. Remote Sens. Lett. 14(5), 607–611 (2017)

21. Melzer, T., Reiter, M., Bischof, H.: Appearance models based on kernel canonical correlation analysis. Patt. Recogn. 36(9), 1961–1971 (2003)

22. Hardoon, D.R., Shawe-Taylor, J.: Sparse canonical correlation analysis. Mach. Learn. 83(3), 331–353 (2011)

23. Witten, D.M., Tibshirani, R.J.: Extensions of sparse canonical correlation analysis with applications to genomic data. Stat. Appl. Genet. Mol. Biol. 8(1), 1–27 (2009)

24. Zhang, Z., Zhao, M., Chow, T.W.: Binary-and multi-class group sparse canonical correlation analysis for feature extraction and classification. IEEE Trans. Knowl. Data Eng. 25(10), 2192–2205 (2013)

25. Vía, J., Santamaría, I., Pérez, J.: A learning algorithm for adaptive canonical correlation analysis of several data sets. Neural Netw. 20(1), 139–152 (2007)

26. Sun, T., Chen, S.: Locality preserving cca with applications to data visualization and pose estimation. Image Vis. Comput. 25(5), 531–543 (2007)

27. Zhai, D., Zhang, Y., Yeung, D.Y., Chang, H., Chen, X., Gao, W.: Instance-specific canonical correlation analysis. Neurocomputing 155, 205–218 (2015)

28. Yger, F., Berar, M., Gasso, G., Rakotomamonjy, A.: Adaptive canonical correlation analysis based on matrix manifolds. arXiv preprint arXiv:1206.6453 (2012)

29. De la Torre, F.: A unification of component analysis methods. In: Handbook of Pattern Recognition and Computer Vision, pp. 3–22 (2009)

30. Sun, J., Keates, S.: Canonical correlation analysis on data with censoring and error information. IEEE Trans. Neural Netw. Learn. Syst. **24**(12), 1909–1919 (2013)
31. Sun, L., Ji, S., Ye, J.: Canonical correlation analysis for multilabel classification: a least-squares formulation, extensions, and analysis. IEEE Trans. Patt. Anal. Mach. Intell. **33**(1), 194–200 (2011)
32. Haghighat, M., Abdel-Mottaleb, M.: Low resolution face recognition in surveillance systems using discriminant correlation analysis. In: 2017 12th IEEE International Conference on Automatic Face and Gesture Recognition (FG 2017), pp. 912–917. IEEE (2017)
33. Ferecatu, M., Sahbi, H.: Multi-view object matching and tracking using canonical correlation analysis. In: 2009 16th IEEE International Conference on Image Processing (ICIP), pp. 2109–2112. IEEE (2009)
34. Loy, C.C., Xiang, T., Gong, S.: Multi-camera activity correlation analysis. In: 2009 IEEE Conference on Computer Vision and Pattern Recognition, CVPR 2009, pp. 1988–1995. IEEE (2009)
35. Zhou, F., Torre, F.: Canonical time warping for alignment of human behavior. In: Advances in Neural Information Processing Systems, pp. 2286–2294 (2009)
36. Zhou, F., De la Torre, F.: Generalized canonical time warping. IEEE Trans. Patt. Anal. Mach. Intell. **38**(2), 279–294 (2016)
37. Kim, T.K., Cipolla, R.: Canonical correlation analysis of video volume tensors for action categorization and detection. IEEE Trans. Patt. Anal. Mach. Intell. **31**(8), 1415–1428 (2009)
38. Fischer, B., Roth, V., Buhmann, J.M.: Time-series alignment by non-negative multiple generalized canonical correlation analysis. BMC Bioinform. **8**(10), S4 (2007)
39. Trigeorgis, G., Nicolaou, M., Zafeiriou, S., Schuller, B.: Deep canonical time warping for simultaneous alignment and representation learning of sequences. IEEE Trans. Patt. Anal. Mach. Intell. **40**(5), 1128–1138 (2017)
40. Ham, J., Lee, D.D., Saul, L.K.: Semisupervised alignment of manifolds. In: AISTATS, pp. 120–127 (2005)
41. Lafon, S., Keller, Y., Coifman, R.R.: Data fusion and multicue data matching by diffusion maps. IEEE Trans. Patt. Anal. Mach. Intell. **28**(11), 1784–1797 (2006)
42. Wang, C., Mahadevan, S.: Manifold alignment using procrustes analysis. In: Proceedings of the 25th International Conference on Machine Learning, pp. 1120–1127. ACM (2008)
43. Luo, B., Hancock, E.R.: Iterative procrustes alignment with the EM algorithm. Image Vis. Comput. **20**(5), 377–396 (2002)
44. Feuz, K.D., Cook, D.J.: Collegial activity learning between heterogeneous sensors. Knowl. Inf. Syst. 1–28 (2017)
45. Sahbi, H., Li, X.: Context-based support vector machines for interconnected image annotation. In: Kimmel, R., Klette, R., Sugimoto, A. (eds.) ACCV 2010, Part I. LNCS, vol. 6492, pp. 214–227. Springer, Heidelberg (2011). https://doi.org/10.1007/978-3-642-19315-6_17
46. Sahbi, H.: CNRS-TELECOM ParisTech at imageCLEF 2013 scalable concept image annotation task: winning annotations with context dependent SVMs. In: CLEF (Working Notes) (2013)
47. Sahbi, H.: Discriminant canonical correlation analysis for interactive satellite image change detection. In: IGARSS, pp. 2789–2792 (2015)
48. Bourdis, N., Denis, M., Sahbi, H.: Constrained optical flow for aerial image change detection. In: 2011 IEEE International Geoscience and Remote Sensing Symposium (IGARSS), pp. 4176–4179 (2011)

49. Bourdis, N., Denis, M., Sahbi, H.: Camera pose estimation using visual servoing for aerial video change detection. In: 2012 IEEE International Geoscience and Remote Sensing Symposium (IGARSS), pp. 3459–3462 (2012)
50. Sahbi, H.: Relevance feedback for satellite image change detection. In: 2013 IEEE International Conference on Acoustics, Speech and Signal Processing (ICASSP), pp. 1503–1507. IEEE (2013)
51. Simonyan, K., Zisserman, A.: Very deep convolutional networks for large-scale image recognition. CoRR abs/1409.1556 (2014)
52. Thiemert, S., Sahbi, H., Steinebach, M.: Applying interest operators in semi-fragile video watermarking. In: Security, Steganography, and Watermarking of Multimedia Contents VII, vol. 5681, International Society for Optics and Photonics, pp. 353–363 (2005)
53. Kim, T., Im, Y.J.: Automatic satellite image registration by combination of matching and random sample consensus. IEEE Trans. Geosci. Remote Sens. **41**(5), 1111–1117 (2003)
54. Lu, L.Z., Pearce, C.E.M.: Some new bounds for singular values and eigenvalues of matrix products. Ann. Oper. Res. **98**(1), 141–148 (2000)

Learning Relationship-Aware Visual Features

Nicola Messina[✉], Giuseppe Amato, Fabio Carrara, Fabrizio Falchi,
and Claudio Gennaro

ISTI-CNR, via G. Moruzzi 1, 56124 Pisa, Italy
{nicola.messina,giuseppe.amato,fabio.carrara,fabrizio.falchi,
claudio.gennaro}@isti.cnr.it

Abstract. Relational reasoning in Computer Vision has recently shown impressive results on visual question answering tasks. On the challenging dataset called CLEVR, the recently proposed Relation Network (RN), a simple plug-and-play module and one of the state-of-the-art approaches, has obtained a very good accuracy (95.5%) answering relational questions. In this paper, we define a sub-field of Content-Based Image Retrieval (CBIR) called Relational-CBIR (R-CBIR), in which we are interested in retrieving images with given relationships among objects. To this aim, we employ the RN architecture in order to extract relation-aware features from CLEVR images. To prove the effectiveness of these features, we extended both CLEVR and Sort-of-CLEVR datasets generating a ground-truth for R-CBIR by exploiting relational data embedded into scene-graphs. Furthermore, we propose a modification of the RN module – a two-stage Relation Network (2S-RN) – that enabled us to extract relation-aware features by using a preprocessing stage able to focus on the image content, leaving the question apart. Experiments show that our RN features, especially the 2S-RN ones, outperform the RMAC state-of-the-art features on this new challenging task.

Keywords: CLEVR · Content-based image retrieval · Deep learning
Relational reasoning · Relation networks · Deep features

1 Introduction

Relational reasoning refers to a particular kind of reasoning process that is able to understand and process relations among multiple entities. In this regard, Krawczyk et al. [1] characterize relational reasoning as the human brain "unique capacity to reason about abstract relationships among items in our environment". Biological intelligence developed such reasoning capabilities during thousands of years of evolution: comparing objects is indeed a critical task since it triggers decisions that could influence the safety of the individual, hence the survival of the species.

In Computer Vision (CV), deep architectures obtain great performance at tasks such as classifying or recognizing objects; however, latest studies demonstrated the difficulties of such architectures to understand a complex scene, where

© Springer Nature Switzerland AG 2019
L. Leal-Taixé and S. Roth (Eds.): ECCV 2018 Workshops, LNCS 11132, pp. 486–501, 2019.
https://doi.org/10.1007/978-3-030-11018-5_40

understand means catching relations among objects to compare them in a spatial and temporal dimension, exactly as the biological intelligence would operate. In other words, differently from biological intelligence, as of now deep architectures can *perceive* with quite a good accuracy the world that surrounds us, but still cannot *understand* it very well.

Starting from [2], VQA has been a very active task in the recent CV literature. Given an image and a natural language question about the image, the task is to provide an accurate natural language answer. Recently, a great interest has grown around the possibility to ask relational questions. In this scenario, questions regard the spatial arrangement of objects inside the image and the task is called Relation-oriented VQA (R-VQA). The most relevant works in this area have used CLEVR [3] for both training and testing.

The contribution of this paper is many-fold:

- we introduce the novel task of relation-oriented content-based image retrieval (R-CBIR);
- we extend the CLEVR diagnostic dataset with a benchmark intended to verify to what extent a CBIR system is able to retrieve similar images in terms of objects spatial arrangement;
- we propose a novel two-stage Relation Network that is able to produce state-of-the-art features on the newly defined task.

The rest of the paper is organized as follows. In Sect. 2, we review some of the related work. In Sect. 3, we define the novel Relational-CBIR task. In Sect. 4, we extend the CLEVR dataset in order to generate a R-CBIR ground-truth. Details about features extraction from RN and from our novel two-stage RN are presented in Sect. 5. In Sect. 6, we report the results of the experiments conducted using features extracted both from the original RN architecture and our proposed two-stage network solution. We make concluding remarks in Sect. 7. In the Appendix, we leave some in-depth details about the two-stage network setup.

2   Related Work

Visual Relationship Detection. Recent work has addressed the problem of visual relationships detection (VRD) in images in the form of triplets (*subject, predicate, object*), where *subject* and *object* are common objects present in an image, and *predicate* indicates a relationship between them out of a set of possible relationships containing verbs, prepositions, comparatives, etc.

Several datasets comprised of a large set of visual relations [4–6] have opened the way to approaches aimed to detect those kinds of relationships in images. In [7], a CRF model is used to ground relationships given in the form of a scene graphs to test images for image retrieval purposes. In [8], a spatial feature map is extracted from images through a CNN and then combined with an embedded natural language expression in order to produce a pixel-wise segmentation output relevant to the relational textual query.

In [5], each pair of (*subject, object*) proposals is scored using a visual appearance module and a language module; two CNNs are used respectively to identify the entities into play and to predict the presence of relationships between them, and a language prior is exploited to refine predictions using pre-trained word embeddings. In [6], authors presented strong yet flexible visual features that encode not only the appearance of the objects, but also explicitly encode their spatial configuration in terms of bounding box relative translation, overlap, size, and aspect ratio. This representation is then used together with language priors to assign a score to every relationship triplet.

Differently from objects-relationship concatenation carried out in previous works, [9] exploits statistical relations between objects and relationship predicates, all in a deep neural network framework.

Notwithstanding approaches that solve VRD are able to detect relationships, they usually do not encode information about the relationships within an image in a compact representation; instead, all possible relationships are combinatorially tested on prediction time. Recently, [10] implemented a large scale image retrieval system able to map textual triplets into visual ones (object-subject-relation inferred from the image) projecting them into a common space learned through a modified version of triplet-loss. Unlike our work, however, this system is unable to produce a compact relational descriptor for the entire image, since it only encodes relations under the form of triplets.

Visual Question Answering. In contrast to VRD, in visual question answering (VQA) relationships among objects are often implicit, making it a more challenging task. However, the potentiality of deep learning approaches has led to various successful approaches that tackle VQA with a learnable end-to-end solution.

Early proposals simply concatenated question embeddings and visual features. This method constitutes the main building block behind solutions like CNN+BoW or CNN+LSTM [11]. Both methods use a CNN to analyze the image and produce visual features.

Stacked Attention (SA) layers [12] replace the raw embeddings concatenation with a simple but quite effective reasoning module, built by exploiting two cascaded attention layers.

In [13,14] authors propose a novel architecture specialized to think in a relational way. They introduced a particular layer called Relation Network (RN), which is specialized in comparing pairs of objects. Objects representations are learned by means of a four-layer CNN and the question embedding is generated through an LSTM. The overall architecture composed of CNN, LSTM and the RN can be trained fully end-to-end, and it is able to reach superhuman performances.

Other solutions [15,16] introduce compositional approaches, able to explicitly model the reasoning process by dynamically building a reasoning graph.

Latest proposals [17,18] used conditioning approaches: they injected question related features into the visual pipeline. They reached the current state-of-the-art on R-VQA.

Work related to VQA is often far off from approaching CBIR tasks, with respect to works developed around VRD. Unlike experimental setups in [4–6,10], whose focus concentrates on the retrieval of specific relationships, our work aims at evaluating a relational descriptor defined for the full scene. [19] uses a very similar experimental setup to the one we introduced. It exploits the graph data associated with every image in order to produce a ranking goodness metric (nDCG) for evaluating the quality of the ranking produced for a given query.

3   Relational-CBIR

In this paper, we define a sub-field of Content-Based Image Retrieval (CBIR) in which we are interested in retrieving images with given relationships among objects. We call this task Relational-CBIR (R-CBIR).

Typically, CBIR is performed extracting a compact descriptor from an image, namely *feature*, that is able to characterize the image. When exploiting relational deep-learning architectures, information about relationships among objects is internally encoded during the learning process. These stored relational concepts could be extracted under the form of *features*, like the ones used in classical CBIR systems. But, unlike classical CBIR features, R-CBIR ones are asked not to encode shapes, corners, regions or even objects; instead, they should be able to embed complex relational patterns. For example, two city skylines should be compared not by matching singularly each architectonic element or finding a similar building; instead, the exploited information should reside in the three-dimensional arrangement of buildings and skyscrapers that uniquely identifies that particular city.

In this work, our attention is focused on spatial relations. Hence, R-CBIR consists in the following: given a query image, find all images in a database containing elements spatially arranged in a similar way to respect the ones present in the query.

4   A Relational-CBIR Ground-Truth

Our major contribution consists in the introduction of a novel benchmark for the R-CBIR task, for the purpose of evaluating architectures on this novel challenge. In order to evaluate the quality of any relational feature extracted from a relation-aware system, we compute a specific ground-truth, built by exploiting relational knowledge embedded into graphs (*scene-graphs*). The generation of the ground-truth, in fact, must rely on a formal and objective *a-priori* relational knowledge of the scene.

By carefully choosing a distance function between graphs, we are able to give a good estimation of the relational similarity between scenes. In order to accomplish this task, we need some datasets that include a formal and precise description of relations occurring inside the scene, so that a precise scene-graph can be derived. Synthetic datasets CLEVR and Sort-of-CLEVR perfectly fit these needs, since they come with rendered images automatically generated using a-priori built scene-graphs.

Besides the native availability of graph-structured data, we target synthetic datasets since evaluating a new retrieval method on a simpler and controlled environment is often a preferable choice than moving directly to bigger and more challenging datasets.

4.1   CLEVR

CLEVR [3] is a synthetic dataset composed of 3D rendered scenes. There are 100k rendered images, subdivided among training (70k), validation (15k) and test (15k) sets. The total number of questions is ∼865k, again split among training (∼700k), validation (∼150k) and test (∼15k).

The main concept behind CLEVR is the *scene*. A *scene* contains different simple shaped objects, with mixtures of colors, materials and sizes. There are cubes, spheres, cylinders, each one of which can have a color chosen among eight; they can be big or small, and they can be made of one of two different materials, metal or rubber. The *scene* is fully and uniquely described by a *scene graph*. The scene graph describes in a formal way all the relationships between objects.

The question is formulated under the form of a *functional program*. The answer to a question represented by its functional program on a scene is simply calculated by executing the functional program on the scene graph. Scene graphs are rendered to photo-realistic 3D scenes by using Blender, a free 3D software; instead, functional programs are converted to natural language expressions compiling some *templates* embedded in the dataset and written in English.

CLEVR dataset gives us way more control on the learning phase than other datasets present in literature. Information in each sample of the dataset is *complete* and *exclusive*. This means that no common-sense awareness is needed in order to correctly answer the questions. Answers can be given simply understanding the question and reasoning exclusively on the image, without needing external concepts.

4.2   Sort-of-CLEVR

Sort-of-CLEVR consists in a simplification of the original CLEVR dataset. It is created mainly for testing and debugging architectures that are designed to work with CLEVR. Thus, this dataset is composed of simpler building blocks with respect to the full CLEVR. Images, in fact, are simpler than 3D renders provided with the original dataset; they instead carry simple 2D scenes, consisting of a certain number of 2D shapes. Shapes can be circles or squares and come in different colors. Every object, however, is uniquely identified by its color.

Differently from the CLEVR dataset, this one splits the questions into two different subsets:

– **relational questions**, asking for the color or shape of the farthest or the nearest object with respect to the given one; example: *What is the shape of the object that is farthest from the gray object?*

- **non-relational questions**, involving specific attributes that characterize a single object, in particular the shape, or the absolute position of the object with respect to the overall scene; example: *What is the shape of the gray object?*

Questions are directly encoded into 11-dimensional vectors, so there is no need for LSTM modules processing natural language.

Even if this dataset seems extremely simple, it can help to spot out some architectural problems that inhibit the network to think in a relational way.

4.3 Scene Graphs

The best way to formally describe relations inside a scene is by making use of *scene graphs*, already available both in CLEVR and Sort-of-CLEVR. More in details, a scene graph contains *nodes*, that account for objects occupying the scene and *edges*, that describe relations occurring among them. Every node or edge can be assigned a set of attributes that fully describe them.

For Sort-of-CLEVR, nodes carry information regarding objects *color*, *shape* together with their absolute positions (*left/right* or *up/down* with respect to the scene). An edge, instead, carries information about the kind of relation it is describing. In Sort-of-CLEVR, an edge can refer to *farthest* and *nearest* relations.

Unlike the Sort-of-CLEVR case, CLEVR object attributes do not include absolute positions, since CLEVR deals uniquely with relational questions. Instead, possible attributes are the *color*, the *shape*, the *material* and the *size*.

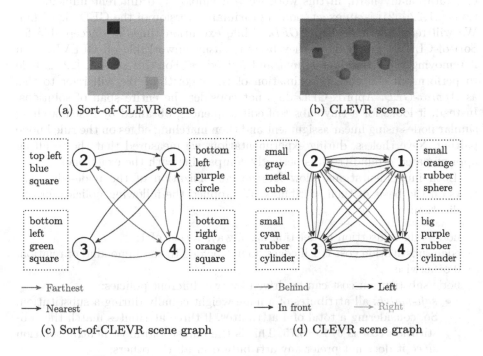

(a) Sort-of-CLEVR scene   (b) CLEVR scene

(c) Sort-of-CLEVR scene graph   (d) CLEVR scene graph

Fig. 1. Example of scenes with associated scene-graphs

CLEVR also includes an higher number and more detailed spatial relations: *to the left of, to the right of, in front of, behind.*

In Fig. 1, we report an example image for each dataset together with the associated scene-graphs. Note that, although CLEVR graph is complete, half of the edges can be removed without losing information, since *to the right of* implies an opposite edge *to the left of* and *in front of* implies an opposite edge *behind.*

4.4   Ground-Truth Generation

We define a ground-truth for retrieving images with similar relations among objects relying on the similarity between scene graphs. Two scene graphs should be similar if they can depict almost the same relations between the same objects. However, evaluating the similarity between two graphs is not trivial; it is often a subjective task, since there are aspects of the graph (e.g., the attributes associated to nodes) that weight differently, depending on the specific application.

Although many solutions have been proposed in literature for defining distances between graph-structured data [20], concerning this particular use-case, we decided to employ the *graph edit-distance* (GED), that is an extension of the well-known edit-distance working on strings.

Differently from strings, edit operations on graphs include *delete, insert, substitute* for both nodes and edges, for a total of 6 edit operations. The problem is faced as an optimization problem. Since the GED problem is known to be computationally hard, in this work we will employ two different implementations [21,22]. [21] is an exact, non-approximated version of the GED algorithm. We will reference it as *Exact-GED*. While execution times are acceptable for Sort-of-CLEVR graph data, they become easily unworkable on CLEVR, even if removing the redundant *behind* and *left* edges. For this reason, [22] is able to perform an efficient approximation of the algorithm. We will refer to this as *Approx-GED*. Approx-GED does not consider the entire span of solutions. Instead, it looks for a tiny subset of edit sequences, obtained by first matching similar nodes using linear assignment and then matching edges on the ruled node pairing. Nevertheless, during experimentation, we measured that the resulting approximated ground-truth is perfectly comparable with the exact one.

Both implementations allow for the customization of the node-edge edit costs on the basis of their attributes. We applied the following policies for our application:

- nodes-edges insertion or deletion has always a cost of 1;
- edge substitution cost is 1 if edges do not belong to the same kind of relation, 0 otherwise;
- node substitution cost can be driven by two different policies:
    - *soft-match*: all attributes of a node weight equally during a substitution. So, considering a total of 4 attributes, if three attributes match the substitution cost is $3/4 = 0.75$. This is the fairest and most neutral solution since it does not prefer any attribute over all the others;

- *hard-match*: the cost is 1 if at least one attribute value differs. It is 0 only if all attributes match.

To clarify GED algorithm functioning using our cost policies, we report below an example on CLEVR with *soft-match*. This instance of GED computation transforming the upper image into the below one will return a cost of 1.5.

	Steps	Cost
	1. Substitute node **small-cyan-metal-cylinder** with **big-cyan-metal-sphere** (change 2 attributes)	0.5
	2. Substitute edge **small-cyan-metal-cylinder behind small-blue-rubber-cylinder** with **big-cyan-metal-sphere in front of small-blue-rubber-cylinder**	1.0

In the light of this, given a query, we compute the ground-truth ranking of the dataset by sorting all scenes using computed GED distances between scene graph of the query image and graphs from all the others.

Given an image ranking produced by an arbitrary relation-aware system, a rank correlation metric is computed against the ground-truth ranking. In this work we will use the *Spearman-Rho* correlation index, that is a common ranking similarity measure often employed in information retrieval scenarios [23].

5   R-CBIR Features from Relation Network

5.1   RN Overview

We build upon the Relation Network (RN) module proposed in [13] in order to extract state-of-the-art features for the newly defined R-CBIR task.

RN obtained impressive results on relational tasks and in particular on CLEVR. RN modules combine input objects forming all possible pairs and applies a common transformation to them, producing activations aimed to store information about possible relationships among input objects.

For the specific task of VQA, authors used a four-layer CNN to learn visual object representations, that are then fed to the RN module and combined with the textual embedding of the question produced by an LSTM, conditioning the relationship information on the textual modality. The core of the RN module is given by the following:

$$r = \sum_{i,j} g_\theta(o_i, o_j, q) \tag{1}$$

where g_θ is a parametric functions whose parameters θ can be learned during the training phase. Specifically, it is a multi-layer perceptrons (MLP) network. o_i and o_j are the objects forming the pair under consideration and q is the question embedding vector obtained from the LSTM module.

The overall architecture composed of CNN, LSTM and the RN can be trained fully end-to-end and it is able to reach superhuman performances.

Relation-aware features useful for R-CBIR should be extracted from a stage inside the network still not conditioned to the question. Hence, valid CBIR features can be extracted from the original RN module only at the output of the convolutional layer, since, after that, questions condition entirely the remaining pipeline. Inspired by the state-of-the-art works on CBIR [24,25], we obtain an overall description for the image aggregating all object pair features in output from the CNN.

More in details, we considered extracting $H_{i,j}([o_i, o_j])$, where o_i is a vector extracted from the i-*th* position of the last flattened convolutional layer, $[\cdot, \cdot]$ denotes concatenation and $H_{i,j}(\cdot)$ is an arbitrary aggregation function over all object pairs. However, in this paper, we aim at producing an R-CBIR baseline for the introduced benchmark by exploiting only two simple aggregations, namely $max_{i,j}(\cdot)$ and $avg_{i,j}(\cdot)$. It can be noticed that for these aggregations the following property holds: $H_{i,j}([o_i, o_j]) = [H_i(o_i), H_j(o_j)]$. This reveals that the resulting vector is constructed by concatenating two identical aggregated representations. This is mainly because these simple aggregation functions process each single object descriptor component independently. Hence, in this scenario, we can simply discard half of the vector and consider only the aggregation $H_i(o_i)$. This, in the end, consists in simply taking the global max/avg pooling from the last layer of the convolutional module.

We will show in Sect. 6 that these features already embed relational knowledge able to defeat state-of-the-art CBIR solutions on this task. Also, we will use these features as baseline for evaluating the novel two-stage approach we are introducing.

5.2 Two-Stage RN (2S-RN)

The two-stage pipeline is aimed at decoupling visual relationships processing (*first-stage*) from the question elaboration (*second-stage*) so that activations from a layer in the first stage can be employed as visual relation-aware features.

Our contribution consists in the following: first, we consider all possible relations between objects $g_\theta(o_i, o_j)$ in the image. This is what we denoted as *first-stage*. The output from this stage is a representation of the relationships between objects in the image not conditioned on the question. Then, we combine the obtained relational representations $r_{i,j} = g_\theta(o_i, o_j)$ with the query embedding q as follows:

$$r = \sum_{i,j} h_\psi(r_{i,j}, q) = \sum_{i,j} h_\psi(g_\theta(o_i, o_j), q) \tag{2}$$

where h_ψ is the *second-stage*. It is a multi-layer perceptron network with parameters ψ. Using this solution, we constrained the network to learn relational concepts without considering the questions, at least during the first stage, before the $h_\psi(\cdot)$ function evaluation. Hence, relation-aware features for the images can potentially be extracted from the output of any layer of the $g_\theta(\cdot)$ function.

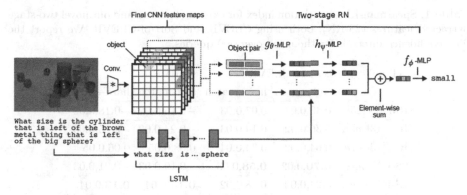

Fig. 2. The proposed two-stage Relation Network module and the whole architecture. This figure show the difference with respect to the original architecture shown in [13].

The overall new architecture, named 2S-RN, is shown in Fig. 2. For training, we stick to the procedure reported in [13]. Detailed configurations for 2S-RN on both CLEVR and Sort-of-CLEVR are reported in Appendix A. With the proposed architecture, we obtain a representation $r_{i,j}$ for each pair of objects i, j. In Sect. 6, we report the results we obtained with *max* and *average* aggregations approaches, obtained by computing respectively $avg_{i,j}(r_{i,j})$ and $max_{i,j}(r_{i,j})$.

6   Experiments

We evaluate both convolutional and 2S-RN features against the generated ground-truth. In our experiments, features from 2S-RN are extracted from the last layer of $g_\theta(\cdot)$. We generate image rankings from relational features by calculating the Euclidean distance between the query feature and all the others, and then sorting the entire dataset by using this distance as score. Spearman-Rho is used to give a score to the obtained ranking, as explained in Sect. 4.4.

As a baseline for convolutional features from the original RN, we choose the ranking obtained with one of the state-of-the-art non-relational image descriptors for image instance retrieval, namely the RMAC descriptor [24]. This descriptor encodes and aggregates several regions of the image in a dense and compact global image representation exploiting a pre-trained fully convolutional network for feature map extraction. The aggregated descriptor is obtained by max-pooling the feature map over different regions and scales, and summing them together, followed by an $l2$-normalization. A similarity score between two images is obtained by computing the cosine similarity between their RMAC descriptors. In our experiments, we adopted the RMAC descriptor extracted from the trained model proposed in [25].

We employ features extracted from the convolutional layer of the original RN as baseline for evaluating features from the first-stage of our novel two-stage approach. Table 1 reports values of Spearman-Rho for the two considered datasets.

Table 1. Spearman-Rho correlation index for existing features and our novel two-stage extracted features (2S-RN), both using CLEVR and Sort-of-CLEVR. We report the 95% confidence intervals for the mean over 500 queries.

GT policy	Sort-of-CLEVR		CLEVR	
	soft-match	hard-match	soft-match	hard-match
RMAC [25]	0.49,0.03	0.07,0.03	−0.15,0.02	−0.18,0.02
RN [13] *max*	0.36,0.02	0.14,0.03	−0.24,0.02	−0.25,0.03
RN [13] *avg*	0.64,0.02	0.34,0.04	0.08,0.05	0.06,0.05
2S-RN *max*	**0.70**,0.02	**0.58**,0.03	−0.19,0.03	−0.21,0.03
2S-RN *avg*	0.24,0.02	0.18,0.02	**0.15**,0.04	**0.13**,0.04

CLEVR results can be reproduced using the code publicly available on GitHub[1]. Spearman-Rho correlations are relative to the two generated ground-truths, *soft-match* and *hard-match* obtained by ranking images using Approx-GED. Exact-GED could have been employed only for Sort-of-CLEVR, due to unacceptable computational times if applied on CLEVR graphs. Spearman-Rho correlation between rankings obtained with exact and approximated versions on Sort-of-CLEVR dataset over 500 queries gives a value of 0.89, using the *soft-match* policy. Hence, we can empirically claim that this approximation is legitimate in this particular scenario. In light of this, we decided to use Approx-GED for both datasets in order to produce a fair comparison.

Correlation index has been evaluated over multiple rankings, generated using 500 query images, in order to produce statistically meaningful results. As it can be noticed, with a 95% confidence interval on the mean, convolutional relational features definitely defeat RMAC features on this relational task. Furthermore, relational features extracted from the two-stage RN are noticeably better than convolutional relational features. These results are reasonable since the original RN presents problems reasoning on the image alone, while RMAC tends to retrieve images containing the very same objects present in the query disregarding relative size, order or position.

Depending on the dataset, different aggregation methods can produce diverse optimal results. In particular, *max* aggregation seems working better on Sort-of-CLEVR dataset, while *average* obtain the best results on CLEVR. The *average* aggregation keeps into consideration the number of identical relations happening inside the scene; and number of relations involved among objects having same attributes is quite important when considering CLEVR, since, unlike Sort-of-CLEVR, in CLEVR there is a better overall randomness and multiple instances of the same relationship could emerge (multiple relations insisting on similar objects). Hence, discriminating them by their cardinality becomes a must for an overall better ranking. Moreover, the *max* aggregation becomes unstable and sensible to outliers when the number of samples increases; a single huge activation

---

[1] https://github.com/mesnico/learning-relationship-aware-visual-features.

in one of the 4,096 features in CLEVR can significantly affect the aggregation results. This is in line with findings in aggregation techniques for CNN features [24,25], where sum (and similarly avg) aggregation is preferred. Relations in Sort-of-CLEVR are significantly less and easily encoded in the feature space.

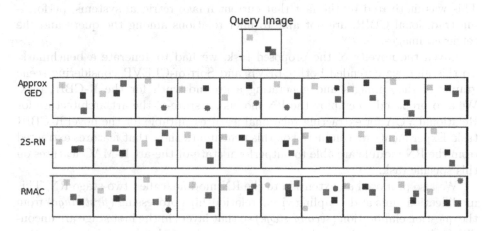

Fig. 3. Top 10 Sort-of-CLEVR images using our solution (2S-RN) and RMAC against our ground-truth for a given query (on top).

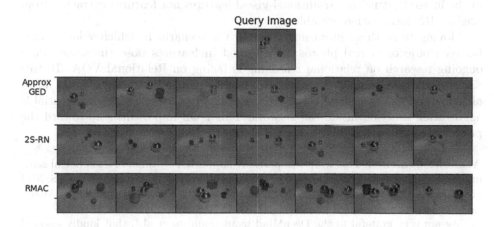

Fig. 4. Top 7 CLEVR images using our solution (2S-RN) and RMAC against our ground-truth for a given query (on top).

Even if it is quite difficult to give an objective evaluation of RN features and RMAC ones by only looking at the first 10 more relevant images, visual evaluation reported in Figs. 3 and 4 are useful for giving an intuition beyond statistics. On our paper website rcbir.org you can find an interactive browsing system for viewing R-CBIR results for different query images.

7   Conclusions and Future Work

State-of-the-art methods for relational reasoning evaluate their capabilities on VQA tasks. In this work, we defined the sub-task of R-CBIR in which retrieved images should be similar to the query in terms of relationships among objects. This was motivated by the fact that current image retrieval systems, performing traditional CBIR, are not able to infer relations among the query and the retrieved images.

Given the novelty of the proposed task, we had to generate a benchmark. To this aim, we extended both CLEVR and Sort-of-CLEVR considering scene graphs of their images and generating a ground-truth for the R-CBIR task. We also proposed to employ the RN module, a state-of-the-art architecture for Relational VQA for extracting relational features suitable for the novel R-CBIR task. Experiments we conducted on this benchmark show that features extracted from the RN module are able to outperform state-of-the-art R-MAC features on this specific task.

We also proposed an extension to the RN module, called two-stage RN. This modification aims at decoupling visual relationships processing (*first-stage*) from the question elaboration (*second-stage*) so that layers in the first stage are unconditioned to the question and can be consequently used as candidate extraction points for obtaining good visual relation-aware features. We proved that features from our two-stage RN are able to encode relationships between objects in the image that neither traditional visual features nor features extracted from original RN formulation are able to detect.

Moving from these promising results to a scenario in which relationships between objects in real photos are encoded in features pose the same issues ongoing research on relational reasoning is facing on Relational VQA. To this aim, we will have to move from artificial images (CLEVR) to photos (e.g., VisualGenome). Also, we plan to learn the aggregation by placing a differentiable aggregation function inside the network. This is an important step toward the production of a compact yet powerful feature.

Acknowledgments. This work was partially supported by Smart News, Social sensing for breaking news, co-founded by the Tuscany region under the FAR-FAS 2014 program, CUP CIPE D58C15000270008, and Automatic Data and documents Analysis to enhance human-based processes (ADA), CUP CIPE D55F17000290009.

We are very grateful to the DeepMind team (Santoro et al.), that kindly assisted us during the replication of their work on Relation Networks.

We also gratefully acknowledge the support of NVIDIA Corporation with the donation of the Tesla K40 GPU used for this research.

A   Detailed Configuration

Hyper-parameters for the 2S-RN architecture have been tuned starting from the configurations given in [13]. We first replicated experiments from [13], so that we were able to get a solid starting point. Training with these configurations we

obtained an overall accuracy of 93.6% on CLEVR and 94.0% on Sort-of-CLEVR, quite enough to use the learned weights from the first stage as a feature. Code for training CLEVR architecture is made publicly available here:
https://github.com/mesnico/RelationNetworks-CLEVR.

A.1   2S-RN on CLEVR

Hyper-parameters for 2S-RN architecture working on CLEVR are the following:

- CNN is composed of 4 convolutional layers each with 24 kernels, ReLU non-linearities and batch normalization;
- g_θ, h_ψ and f_ϕ are multilayer perceptrons each composed of 2 fully-connected layers, 256 neurons each and ReLU non-linearities;
- a final linear layer with 29 units produces logits for a softmax layer over the answers vocabulary;
- dropout with 50% dropping probability is inserted after the penultimate layer of f_ϕ;
- the gradient norm is clipped to 50;
- the learning rate follows an exponential step increasing policy, that doubles it every 20 epochs, from 5e-6 up to 5e-4.

A.2   2S-RN on Sort-of-CLEVR

Hyper-parameters for 2S-RN architecture working on Sort-of-CLEVR are the following:

- CNN is composed of 4 convolutional layers each with 24 kernels, ReLU non-linearities and batch normalization;
- g_θ is a multi-layer perceptron composed of 4 fully-connected layers, containing respectively 2048, 1024, 512, and 256 neurons with ReLU non-linearities;
- h_ψ is a single-layer perceptron with 256 neurons and ReLU non-linearities;
- f_ϕ is a multi-layer perceptron composed of 2 fully-connected layers, 256 neurons each and ReLU non-linearities;
- a final linear layer with 10 units produces logits for a softmax layer over the answers vocabulary;
- a dropout with 50% dropping probability is inserted after the penultimate layer of f_ϕ;
- the learning rate is set to 1e-4.

References

1. Krawczyk, D.C., McClelland, M.M., Donovan, C.M.: A hierarchy for relational reasoning in the prefrontal cortex. Cortex **47**, 588–597 (2011)
2. Antol, S., et al.: VQA: visual question answering. In: Proceedings of the IEEE International Conference on Computer Vision, pp. 2425–2433 (2015)

3. Johnson, J., Hariharan, B., van der Maaten, L., Fei-Fei, L., Zitnick, C.L., Girshick, R.: CLEVR: a diagnostic dataset for compositional language and elementary visual reasoning (2017)
4. Krishna, R., et al.: Visual genome: connecting language and vision using crowd-sourced dense image annotations (2016)
5. Lu, C., Krishna, R., Bernstein, M., Fei-Fei, L.: Visual relationship detection with language priors. In: Leibe, B., Matas, J., Sebe, N., Welling, M. (eds.) ECCV 2016, Part I. LNCS, vol. 9905, pp. 852–869. Springer, Cham (2016). https://doi.org/10.1007/978-3-319-46448-0_51
6. Peyre, J., Laptev, I., Schmid, C., Sivic, J.: Weakly-supervised learning of visual relations. In: ICCV 2017 - International Conference on Computer Vision 2017, Venice, Italy, October 2017
7. Johnson, J., et al.: Image retrieval using scene graphs. In: Proceedings of the IEEE Conference on Computer Vision and Pattern Recognition, pp. 3668–3678 (2015)
8. Hu, R., Rohrbach, M., Darrell, T.: Segmentation from natural language expressions. In: Leibe, B., Matas, J., Sebe, N., Welling, M. (eds.) ECCV 2016, Part I. LNCS, vol. 9905, pp. 108–124. Springer, Cham (2016). https://doi.org/10.1007/978-3-319-46448-0_7
9. Dai, B., Zhang, Y., Lin, D.: Detecting visual relationships with deep relational networks. In: 2017 IEEE Conference on Computer Vision and Pattern Recognition (CVPR), pp. 3298–3308. IEEE (2017)
10. Zhang, J., Kalantidis, Y., Rohrbach, M., Paluri, M., Elgammal, A.M., Elhoseiny, M.: Large-scale visual relationship understanding. CoRR abs/1804.10660 (2018)
11. Zhou, B., Tian, Y., Sukhbaatar, S., Szlam, A., Fergus, R.: Simple baseline for visual question answering. CoRR abs/1512.02167 (2015)
12. Yang, Z., He, X., Gao, J., Deng, L., Smola, A.J.: Stacked attention networks for image question answering. CoRR abs/1511.02274 (2015)
13. Santoro, A., et al.: A simple neural network module for relational reasoning. CoRR abs/1706.01427 (2017)
14. Raposo, D., Santoro, A., Barrett, D.G.T., Pascanu, R., Lillicrap, T.P., Battaglia, P.W.: Discovering objects and their relations from entangled scene representations. CoRR abs/1702.05068 (2017)
15. Hu, R., Andreas, J., Rohrbach, M., Darrell, T., Saenko, K.: Learning to reason: end-to-end module networks for visual question answering. CoRR abs/1704.05526 (2017)
16. Johnson, J., et al.: Inferring and executing programs for visual reasoning. CoRR abs/1705.03633 (2017)
17. Perez, E., de Vries, H., Strub, F., Dumoulin, V., Courville, A.C.: Learning visual reasoning without strong priors. CoRR abs/1707.03017 (2017)
18. Perez, E., Strub, F., de Vries, H., Dumoulin, V., Courville, A.C.: FiLM: visual reasoning with a general conditioning layer. CoRR abs/1709.07871 (2017)
19. Belilovsky, E., Blaschko, M.B., Kiros, J.R., Urtasun, R., Zemel, R.: Joint embeddings of scene graphs and images. In: ICLR (2017)
20. Cai, H., Zheng, V.W., Chang, K.C.: A comprehensive survey of graph embedding: problems, techniques and applications. CoRR abs/1709.07604 (2017)
21. Abu-Aisheh, Z., Raveaux, R., Ramel, J.Y., Martineau, P.: An exact graph edit distance algorithm for solving pattern recognition problems 1 (2015)
22. Riesen, K., Bunke, H.: Approximate graph edit distance computation by means of bipartite graph matching. Image Vis. Comput. **27**(7), 950–959 (2009). 7th IAPR-TC15 Workshop on Graph-based Representations (GbR 2007)

23. Melucci, M.: On rank correlation in information retrieval evaluation. SIGIR Forum **41**(1), 18–33 (2007)
24. Tolias, G., Sicre, R., Jégou, H.: Particular object retrieval with integral max-pooling of CNN activations. arXiv preprint arXiv:1511.05879 (2015)
25. Gordo, A., Almazan, J., Revaud, J., Larlus, D.: End-to-end learning of deep visual representations for image retrieval. arXiv preprint arXiv:1610.07940 (2016)

DNN Feature Map Compression Using Learned Representation over GF(2)

Denis Gudovskiy$^{(\boxtimes)}$ (ID), Alec Hodgkinson (ID), and Luca Rigazio

Panasonic Beta Research Lab, Mountain View, CA 94043, USA
{denis.gudovskiy,alec.hodgkinson,luca.rigazio}@us.panasonic.com

Abstract. In this paper, we introduce a method to compress intermediate feature maps of deep neural networks (DNNs) to decrease memory
storage and bandwidth requirements during inference. Unlike previous
works, the proposed method is based on converting fixed-point activations into vectors over the smallest GF(2) finite field followed by nonlinear dimensionality reduction (NDR) layers embedded into a DNN. Such
an end-to-end learned representation finds more compact feature maps by
exploiting quantization redundancies within the fixed-point activations
along the channel or spatial dimensions. We apply the proposed network architectures derived from modified SqueezeNet and MobileNetV2
to the tasks of ImageNet classification and PASCAL VOC object detection. Compared to prior approaches, the conducted experiments show a
factor of 2 decrease in memory requirements with minor degradation in
accuracy while adding only bitwise computations.

Keywords: Feature map compression · Dimensionality reduction
Network quantization · Memory-efficient inference

1 Introduction

Recent achievements of deep neural networks (DNNs) make them an attractive
choice in many computer vision applications including image classification [7]
and object detection [10]. The memory and computations required for DNNs
can be excessive for low-power deployments. In this paper, we explore the task
of minimizing the memory footprint of DNN feature maps during inference and,
more specifically, finding a network architecture that uses minimal storage without introducing a considerable amount of additional computations or on-the-fly
heuristic encoding-decoding schemes. In general, the task of feature map compression is tightly connected to input sparsity. The input sparsity can determine
several different usage scenarios. This may lead to substantial decrease in memory requirements and overall inference complexity. First, pen sketches are spatially sparse and can be processed efficiently by recently introduced submanifold
sparse CNNs [5]. Second, surveillance cameras with mostly static input contain
temporal sparsity that can be addressed by Sigma-Delta networks [16]. A more
general scenario presumes a dense input e.g. video frames from a high-resolution

© Springer Nature Switzerland AG 2019
L. Leal-Taixé and S. Roth (Eds.): ECCV 2018 Workshops, LNCS 11132, pp. 502–516, 2019.
https://doi.org/10.1007/978-3-030-11018-5_41

camera mounted on a moving autonomous car. In this work, we address the latter scenario and concentrate on feature map compression in order to minimize memory footprint and bandwidth during DNN inference which might be prohibitive for high-resolution cameras.

We propose a method to convert intermediate fixed-point feature map activations into vectors over the smallest finite field called the Galois field of two elements (GF(2)) or, simply, binary vectors followed by compression convolutional layers using a nonlinear dimensionality reduction (NDR) technique embedded into DNN architecture. The compressed feature maps can then be projected back to a higher cardinality representation over a fixed-point (integer) field using decompression convolutional layers. A layer fusion method allows to keep only the compressed feature maps for inference while adding only computationally inexpensive bitwise operations. Compression and decompression layers over GF(2) can be repeated within the proposed network architecture and trained in an end-to-end fashion. In brief, the proposed method resembles autoencoder-type [8] structures embedded into a base network that work over GF(2). Binary conversion and compression-decompression layers are implemented in the Caffe [13] framework and are publicly available[1].

The rest of the paper is organized as follows. Section 2 reviews related work. Section 3 gives notation for convolutional layers, describes conventional fusion and NDR methods, and explains the proposed method including details about network training and the derived architectures from SqueezeNet [12] and MobileNetV2 [20]. Section 4 presents experimental results on ImageNet classification and PASCAL VOC object detection using SSD [14], memory requirements, and obtained compression rates.

2   Related Work

Feature Map Compression Using Quantization. Unlike weight compression, surprisingly few papers consider feature map compression. This can most likely be explained by the fact that feature maps have to be compressed for every network input as opposed to offline weight compression. Previous feature map compression methods are primarily developed around the idea of representation *approximation* using a certain quantization scheme: fixed-point quantization [3,6], binary quantization [11,18,21,22], and power-of-two quantization [15]. The base floating-point network is converted to the approximate quantized representation and, then, the quantized network is retrained to restore accuracy. Such methods are inherently limited in finding more compact representations since the base architecture remains unchanged. For example, the dynamic fixed-point scheme typically requires around 8-bits of resolution to achieve baseline accuracy for state-of-the-art network architectures. At the same time, binary networks experience significant accuracy drops for large-scale datasets or compact (not over-parametrized) network architectures. Instead, our method can be considered in a narrow sense as a learned quantization using binary representation.

---

[1] https://github.com/gudovskiy/fmap_compression.

Embedded NDR and Linear Layers. Another interesting approach is implicitly proposed by Iandola et al. [12]. Although the authors emphasized weight compression rather than feature map compression, they introduced NDR-type layers into network architecture that allowed to decrease not only the number of weights but also feature map sizes by a factor of 8, if one keeps only the outputs of so-called *squeeze* layers. The latter is possible because such network architecture does not introduce any additional convolution *recomputations* since *squeeze* layer computations with a 1×1 kernel can be fused with the preceding *expand* layers.

Recently, a similar method was proposed for MobileNet architecture [20] with embedded *bottleneck* compression layers, which are, unlike SqueezeNet, linear. Authors view the task of compression aside from the rest of the network and argue that linear layers are more suitable for compression because no information is lost. While a small accuracy gain achieved for such layers compared to NDR layers in floating-point according to their experiments, we believe that it is due to a larger set of numbers ($\mathbb{R}$ vs. $\mathbb{R}_{\geq 0}$ for NDR with rectified linear unit (ReLU)). This is justified by our experiments using quantized models with limited set of available values. We consider the linear compression approach as a subset of nonlinear. Our work goes beyond previous approaches [12,20] by extending compression layers to work over GF(2) to find a more compact feature map representation.

Hardware Accelerator Architectures. Horowitz [9] estimated that off-chip DRAM access requires approximately $100\times$ more power than local on-chip cache access. Therefore, currently proposed DNN accelerator architectures propose various schemes to decrease memory footprint and bandwidth. One obvious solution is to keep only a subset of intermediate feature maps at the expense of recomputing convolutions [1]. The presented fusion approach seems to be oversimplified but effective due to high memory access cost. Our approach is complementary to this work but proposes to keep only compressed feature maps with minimum additional computations.

Another recent work [17] exploits weight and feature map sparsity using a more efficient encoding for zeros. While this approach targets similar goals, it requires having high sparsity, which is often unavailable in the first and the largest feature maps. In addition, a special control and encoding-decoding logic decrease the benefits of this approach. In our work, compressed feature maps are stored in a dense form without the need of special control and enconding-decoding logic.

3   Feature Map Compression Methods

3.1   Model and Notation

The input feature map of lth convolutional layer in commonly used DNNs can be represented by a tensor $\mathbf{X}^{l-1} \in \mathbb{R}^{\acute{C} \times H \times W}$, where $\acute{C}$, H and W are the number of input channels, the height and the width, respectively. The input $\mathbf{X}^{l-1}$ is convolved with a weight tensor $\mathbf{W}^l \in \mathbb{R}^{C \times \check{C} \times H_f \times W_f}$, where C is the number of output channels, H_f and W_f are the height and the width of filter kernel, respectively. A bias vector $\boldsymbol{b} \in \mathbb{R}^C$ is added to the result of convolution operation. Once all C channels are computed, an element-wise nonlinear function is applied to the result of the convolution operations. Then, the cth channel of the output tensor $\mathbf{X}^l \in \mathbb{R}^{C \times H \times W}$ can be computed as

$$\mathbf{X}_c^l = g\left(\mathbf{W}_c^l * \mathbf{X}^{l-1} + b_c\right), \tag{1}$$

where $*$ denotes convolution and $g()$ is some nonlinear function. In this paper, we assume $g()$ is the most commonly used ReLU defined as $g(x) = \max(0, x)$ such that all activations are non-negative.

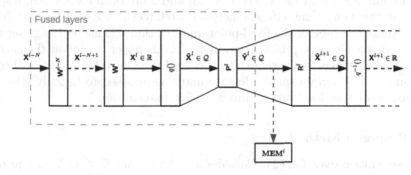

Fig. 1. The unified model of conventional methods: fusion allows to keep only *bottleneck* feature maps and quantization compresses each activation.

3.2 Conventional Methods

We formally describe previously proposed methods briefly reviewed in Sect. 2 using the unified model illustrated in Fig. 1. To simplify notation, biases are not shown. Consider a network built using multiple convolutional layers and processed according to (1). Similar to Alwani et al. [1], calculation of N sequential layers can be fused together without storing intermediate feature maps $\mathbf{X}^{l-N+1}, \ldots, \mathbf{X}^{l-1}$. For example, fusion can be done in a channel-wise fashion using memory buffers which are much smaller than the whole feature map. Then, feature map $\mathbf{X}^l \in \mathbb{R}$ can be quantized into $\hat{\mathbf{X}}^l \in \mathcal{Q}$ using a nonlinear quantization function $q()$ where $\mathcal{Q}$ is a finite field over integers. The quantization step may introduce a drop in accuracy due to imperfect approximation. The network can be further finetuned to restore some of the original accuracy [3,6]. The network architecture is not changed after quantization and feature maps can be compressed only up to a certain suboptimal bitwidth resolution.

The next step implicitly introduced by SqueezeNet [12] is to perform NDR using an additional convolutional layer. A mapping $\hat{\mathbf{X}}^l \in \mathcal{Q}^{C \times H \times W} \to \hat{\mathbf{Y}}^l \in$

$Q^{\tilde{C} \times H \times W}$ can be performed using projection weights $\mathbf{P}^l \in \mathbb{R}^{\tilde{C} \times C \times H_f \times W_f}$, where the output channel dimension $\tilde{C} < C$. Then, only the compressed *bottleneck* feature map $\hat{\mathbf{Y}}^l$ needs to be stored in the memory buffer. During the inverse steps, the compressed feature map can be projected back onto the higher-dimensional tensor $\hat{\mathbf{X}}^{l+1} \in Q$ using weights $\mathbf{R}^l \in \mathbb{R}^{C \times \tilde{C} \times H_f \times W_f}$ and, lastly, converted back to $\mathbf{X}^{l+1} \in \mathbb{R}$ using an inverse quantization function $q^{-1}()$. In the case of a fully quantized network, the inverse quantization can be omitted.

In practice, the number of bits for the feature map quantization step depends on the dataset, network architecture and desired accuracy. For example, over-parameterized architectures like AlexNet may require only 1 or 2 bits for small-scale datasets (CIFAR-10, MNIST, SVHN), but experience significant accuracy drops for large-scale datasets like ImageNet. In particular, the modified AlexNet (with the first and last layers kept in full-precision) top-1 accuracy is degraded by 12.4% and 6.8% for 1-bit XNOR-Net [18] and 2-bit DoReFa-Net [22], respectively. At the same time, efficient network architectures e.g. [12] using NDR layers require 6–8 bits for the fixed-point quantization scheme on ImageNet and fail to work with lower precision activations. In this paper, we follow the path to select an efficient base network architecture and then introduce additional compression layers to obtain smaller feature maps as opposed to initially selecting an over-parametrized network architecture for quantization.

3.3   Proposed Method

Representation over GF(2). Consider a scalar x from $\mathbf{X}^l \in \mathbb{R}$. A conventional feature map quantization step can be represented as a scalar-to-scalar mapping or a nonlinear function $\hat{x} = q(x)$ such that

$$x \in \mathbb{R}^{1 \times 1} \xrightarrow{q()} \hat{x} \in Q^{1 \times 1} : \min \|x - \hat{x}\|_2, \tag{2}$$

where $\hat{x}$ is the quantized scalar, Q is the $GF(2^B)$ finite field for fixed-point representation and B is the number of bits.

We can introduce a new $\hat{x}$ representation by a linear binarization function $b()$ defined by

$$\hat{x} \in Q^{1 \times 1} \xrightarrow{b()} \tilde{x} \in \mathcal{B}^{B \times 1} : \tilde{x} = \boldsymbol{b} \otimes \hat{x}, \tag{3}$$

where $\otimes$ is a bitwise AND operation, vector $\boldsymbol{b} = [2^0, 2^1, \dots, 2^{B-1}]^T$ and $\mathcal{B}$ is $GF(2)$ finite field.

An inverse linear function $b^{-1}()$ can be written as

$$\tilde{x} \in \mathcal{B}^{B \times 1} \xrightarrow{b^{-1}()} \hat{x} \in Q^{1 \times 1} : \hat{x} = \boldsymbol{b}^T \tilde{x} = \boldsymbol{b}^T \boldsymbol{b} \otimes \hat{x} = (2^B - 1) \otimes \hat{x}. \tag{4}$$

Equations (3)–(4) show that a scalar over a higher cardinality finite field can be linearly converted to and from a vector over a finite field with two elements. Based on these derivations, we propose a feature map compression method shown in Fig. 2. Similar to [3], we quantize activations to obtain $\hat{\mathbf{X}}^l$

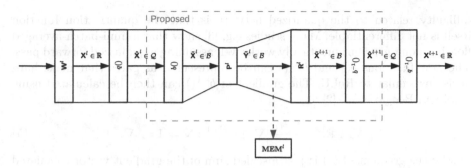

Fig. 2. Scheme of the proposed method: binarization is added and compression happens in GF(2) followed by inverse operations.

and, then, apply transformation (3). The resulting feature map can be represented as $\tilde{\mathbf{X}}^l \in \mathcal{B}^{B \times C \times H \times W}$. For implementation convenience, a new bit dimension can be concatenated along channel dimension resulting in the feature map $\tilde{\mathbf{X}}^l \in \mathcal{B}^{BC \times H \times W}$. Next, a single convolutional layer using weights $\mathbf{P}^l$ or a sequence of layers with $\mathbf{P}^l_i$ weights can be applied to obtain a compressed representation over GF(2). Using the fusion technique, only the compressed feature maps $\tilde{\mathbf{Y}}^l \in \mathcal{B}$ need to be stored in memory during inference. Non-compressed feature maps can be processed using small buffers e.g. in a sequential channel-wise fashion. Lastly, the inverse function $b^{-1}()$ from (4) using convolutional layers $\mathbf{R}^l_i$ and inverse of quantization $q^{-1}()$ undo the compression and quantization steps.

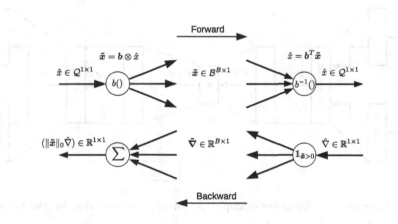

Fig. 3. Forward and backward passes during inference and backpropagation.

Learning over GF(2). The graph model shown in Fig. 3 explains details about the inference (forward pass) and backpropagation (backward pass) phases of the newly introduced functions. The inference pass represents (3)–(4) as explained above. The backpropagation pass may seem non-obvious at first glance. One difficulty related to the quantized network is that the quantization function itself is not differentiable. Many studies e.g. [3] show that a mini-batch-averaged floating-point gradient practically works well assuming a quantized forward pass. The new functions $b()$ and $b^{-1}()$ can be represented as gates that make hard decisions similar to ReLU. The gradient of $b^{-1}()$ can then be calculated using results of Bengio et al. [2] as

$$\hat{\nabla} \in \mathbb{R}^{1\times 1} \xrightarrow{b^{-1}()} \tilde{\nabla} \in \mathbb{R}^{B\times 1} : \tilde{\nabla} = \mathbb{1}_{\tilde{x}>0}\nabla. \tag{5}$$

Lastly, the gradient of $b()$ is just a scaled sum of the gradient vector calculated by

$$\tilde{\nabla} \in \mathbb{R}^{B\times 1} \xrightarrow{b()} \hat{\nabla} \in \mathbb{R}^{1\times 1} : \hat{\nabla} = \mathbb{1}^T\tilde{\nabla} = \mathbb{1}^T\mathbb{1}_{\tilde{x}>0}\nabla = \|\tilde{x}\|_0\nabla, \tag{6}$$

where $\|\tilde{x}\|_0$ is a gradient scaling factor that represents the number of nonzero elements in $\tilde{x}$. Practically, the scaling factor can be calculated based on statistical information only once and used as a static hyperparameter for gradient normalization.

Since the purpose of the network is to learn and keep only the smallest $\tilde{Y}^l$, the choice of $\mathbf{P}^l$ and $\mathbf{R}^l$ initialization is important. Therefore, we can initialize these weight tensors by an identity function that maps the non-compressed feature map to a truncated compressed feature map and vice versa. That provides a good starting point for training. At the same time, other initializations are possible e.g. noise sampled from some distribution studied by [2] can be added as well.

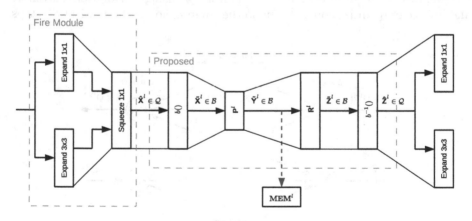

Fig. 4. SqueezeNet architecture example: *fire* module is extended by the proposed method.

Network Architecture. A base network architecture can be selected among existing networks with the embedded *bottleneck* layers e.g. SqueezeNet [12] or MobileNetV2 [20]. We explain how a base network architecture can be modified according to Sect. 3.3 using SqueezeNet example.

The latter network architecture consists of a sequence of *fire* modules where each module contains two concatenated *expand* layers and a *squeeze* layer illustrated in Fig. 4. The *squeeze* layers perform NDR over the field of real or, in case of the quantized model, integer numbers. Specifically, the size of the concatenated *expand 1×1* and *expand 3×3* layers is compressed by a factor of 8 along channel dimension by *squeeze 1×1* layer. Activations of only the latter one can be stored during inference using the fusion method. According to the analysis presented in Gysel et al. [6], activations quantized to 8-bit integers do not experience significant accuracy drop.

The quantized *squeeze* layer feature map can be converted to its binary representation following Fig. 2. Then, the additional compression rate is defined by selecting parameters of $\mathbf{P}_i^l$. In the simplest case, only a single NDR layer needs to be introduced with the weights $\mathbf{P}^l$. In general, a number of NDR layers can be added with 1×1, 3×3 and other kernels with or without pooling at the expense of increased computational cost. For example, 1×1 kernels allow to learn optimal quantization and to compensate redundancies along channel dimension only. But 3×3 kernels can address spatial redundancies and, while being implemented with stride 2 using convolutional-deconvolutional layers, decrease feature map size along spatial dimensions.

MobileNetV2 architecture can be modified using the proposed method with few remarks. First, its *bottleneck* layers compress feature maps by a 1×1 kernel with variable compression factor from 2 to 6 unlike fixed factor in SqueezeNet. Second, linear compression layers either have to be turned into NDR layers by adding ReLUs or implementation of compression-decompression layers needs to support negative integers. In practice, the former approach might be less cumbersome.

4   Experiments

4.1   ImageNet Classification

We implemented the new binarization layers from Sect. 3 as well as quantization layers using modified [6] code in the Caffe [13] framework. The latter code is modified to accurately support binary quantization during inference and training. SqueezeNetV1.1 and MobilenetV2 are selected as a base floating-point network architectures, and their pretrained weights were downloaded from the publicly available sources[2,3].

SqueezeNet Architecture. We compress the *fire2/squeeze* and *fire3/squeeze* layers which consume 80% of total network memory footprint when fusion is applied due to high spatial dimensions. The input to the network has a resolution of 227×227, and the weights are all floating-point.

---

[2] https://github.com/DeepScale/SqueezeNet.
[3] https://github.com/shicai/MobileNet-Caffe.

Table 1. SqueezeNet ImageNet accuracy: A - *fire2,3/squeeze* feature maps and W - weights.

Model	W size, MB	A size, KB	Top-1 accuracy, %	Top-5 accuracy, %
fp32	4.7	392.0	58.4	81.0
Quantized				
uint8	4.7	98.0	58.6(58.3)	81.1(81.0)
uint6	4.7	73.5	57.8(55.5)	80.7(78.7)
uint4	4.7	49.0	54.9(18.0)	78.3(34.2)
Proposed: $b() \to 1 \times 1 \to 1 \times 1 \to b^{-1}()$				
uint6	5.0	73.5	58.8	81.3
uint4	4.9	49.0	57.3	80.0
Proposed: $b() \to 3 \times 3/2 \to 3 \times 3 * 2 \to b^{-1}()$				
uint8	7.6	24.5	54.1	77.4
uint6	6.9	18.4	53.8	77.2

The quantized and compressed models are retrained for 100,000 iterations with a mini-batch size of 1024 on the ImageNet [19] (ILSVRC2012) training dataset, and SGD solver with a step-policy learning rate starting from 1e-3 divided by 10 every 20,000 iterations. Although this large mini-batch size was used by the original model, it helps the quantized and compressed models to estimate gradients as well. The compressed models were derived and retrained iteratively from the 8-bit quantized model. Table 1 reports top-1 and top-5 inference accuracies of 50,000 images from ImageNet validation dataset.

According to Table 1, the retrained quantized models experience -0.2%, 0.6% and 3.5% top-1 accuracy drops for 8-bit, 6-bit and 4-bit quantization, respectively. For comparison, the quantized models without retraining are shown in parentheses. The proposed compression method using 1×1 kernels allows us to restore corresponding top-1 accuracy by 1.0% and 2.4% for 6-bit and 4-bit versions at the expense of a small increase in the number of weights and bitwise convolutions. Moreover, we evaluated a model with a convolutional layer followed by a deconvolutional layer both with a 3×3 stride 2 kernel at the expense of a 47% increase in weight size for 6-bit activations. That allowed us to decrease feature maps in spatial dimensions by exploiting local spatial quantization redundancies. Then, the feature map size is further reduced by a factor of 4, while top-1 accuracy dropped by 4.3% and 4.6% for 8-bit and 6-bit activations, respectively. A comprehensive comparison for fully quantized models with the state-of-the-art binary and ternary networks is given below.

MobileNetV2 Architecture. We compress the *conv2_1/linear* feature map which is nearly $3 \times$ larger than any other *bottleneck* layer feature map. The same training hyperparameters are used as in previous experiment setup with few differences. The number of iterations is 50,000 with proportional change in

Table 2. MobileNetV2 ImageNet accuracy: A - *conv2_1/linear* feature maps and W - weights.

Model	W size, MB	A size, KB	Top-1 accuracy, %	Top-5 accuracy, %
fp32	13.5	784.0	71.2	90.2
Quantized				
int9	13.5	220.5	71.5(71.2)	89.9(90.2)
int7	13.5	171.5	71.5(68.5)	89.8(88.4)
int5	13.5	122.5	70.9(7.3)	89.4(17.8)
Modified: ReLU nonlinearity added				
uint8	13.5	196.0	71.6	90.0
Proposed: $b() \rightarrow 1 \times 1 \rightarrow 1 \times 1 \rightarrow b^{-1}()$				
uint6	13.7	147.0	70.9	89.4
uint4	13.6	98.0	69.5	88.5
Proposed: $b() \rightarrow 2 \times 2/2 \rightarrow 2 \times 2 * 2 \rightarrow b^{-1}()$				
uint8	14.2	49.0	66.6	86.9
uint6	14.0	36.8	66.7	86.9

learning rate policy. Second, we add a ReLU layer after *conv2_1/linear* to be compatible with the current implementation of the compression method. Hence, the *conv2_1/linear* feature map contains signed integers in the original model and unsigned integers in the modified one. Lastly, we found that batch normalization layers cause some instability to training process. Therefore, normalization and scaling parameters are fixed and merged into weights and biases of convolutional layers. Then, the modified model was retrained from the original one.

According to Table 2, the original (without ReLU) quantized models after retraining experience -0.3%, -0.3% and 0.3% top-1 accuracy drops for 9-bit, 7-bit and 5-bit quantization, respectively. For comparison, the quantized models without retraining are shown in parentheses. Surprisingly, quantized MobileNetV2 is resilient to smaller bitwidths with only 0.6% degradation for 5-bit model compared to 9-bit one. The modified (with ReLU nonlinearity) 8-bit model outperforms all the original quantized model by 0.1%, even the one with more bits, unlike results reported by [20] for floating-point models. Hence, the conclusions about advantages of linear compression layers could be reconsidered in finite (integer) field. Accuracies of the proposed models using 1×1 kernels are on par with the conventional quantization approaches. Most likely, lack of batch normalization layers does not allow to increase accuracy which should be investigated. The proposed models with a convolutional-deconvolutional layers and 2×2 stride 2 kernel compress feature maps by another factor of 2 with around 4.5% accuracy degradation and 5% increase in weight size. A comparison in the object detection section further compares 2×2 and 3×3 stride 2 kernels and concludes that the former one is preferable due to accuracy and size.

Table 3. ImageNet accuracy: W - weights, A - feature maps, F - fusion, Q - quantization, C - compression.

Model	Base network	W, bits	W size, MB	A, bits	A size, KB	Top-1 Acc., %	Top-5 Acc., %
AlexNet	-	32	232	32	3053.7	56.6	79.8
AlexNet	-	32	232	6	572.6	55.8	79.2
XNOR-Net	AlexNet	1^a	22.6	1	344.4^b	44.2	69.2
XNOR-Net	ResNet-18	1^a	3.34	1	1033.0^b	51.2	73.2
DoReFa-Net	AlexNet	1^a	22.6	1	95.4	43.6	-
DoReFa-Net	AlexNet	1^a	22.6	2	190.9	49.8	-
DoReFa-Net	AlexNet	1^a	22.6	4	381.7	53.0	-
Tang'17	AlexNet	1^c	7.43	2	190.9	46.6	71.1
Tang'17	NIN-Net	1^c	1.23	2	498.6	51.4	75.6
The proposed models							
SqueezeNet	-	32	4.7	32	12165.4	58.4	81.0
F+Q	SqueezeNet	8	1.2	8	189.9	58.3	80.8
F+Q+C(1 × 1)	SqueezeNet	8	1.2	$6(8)^d$	165.4	$58.3(58.8)^e$	$81.0(81.3)^e$
F+Q+C(1 × 1)	SqueezeNet	8	1.2	$4(8)^d$	140.9	$56.6(57.3)^e$	$79.7(80.0)^e$
F+Q+C(3 × 3s2)	SqueezeNet	8	1.9	$8(8)^d$	116.4	$53.5(54.1)^e$	$76.7(77.4)^e$
F+Q+C(3 × 3s2)	SqueezeNet	8	1.7	$6(8)^d$	110.3	$53.0(53.8)^e$	$76.8(77.2)^e$

[a] Weights are not binarized for the first and the last layer.
[b] Activation size estimates are based on 8-bit assumption since it is not clear from [18] whether the activations were binarized or not for the first and the last layer.
[c] Weights are not binarized for the first layer.
[d] Number of bits for the compressed *fire2,3/squeeze* layers and, in parentheses, for the rest of layers.
[e] For comparison, accuracy in parentheses represents result for the corresponding model in Table 1.

Comparison with Binary and Ternary State-of-the-Art. We compare recently reported ImageNet results for low-precision networks as well as several configurations of the proposed approach for which, unlike previous experiments, all weights and activations are quantized. Most of the works use the over-parametrized AlexNet architecture while ours is based on the SqueezeNet architecture in this comparison. Table 3 shows accuracy results for base networks as well as their quantized versions. Binary XNOR-Net [18] estimates based on AlexNet as well as ResNet-18. DoReFa-Net [22] is more flexible and can adjust the number of bits for weights and activations. Since its accuracy is limited by the number of activation bits, we present three cases with 1-bit, 2-bit, and 4-bit activations. The most recent work [21] solves the problem of binarizing the last layer weights, but weights of the first layer are full-precision. Overall, AlexNet-based low-precision networks achieve 43.6%, 49.8%, 53.0% top-1 accuracy for 1-bit, 2-bit and 4-bit activations, respectively. Around 70% of the memory footprint is defined by the first two layers of AlexNet. The fusion technique is difficult in such architectures due to large kernel sizes (11 × 11 and 5×5 for AlexNet) which can cause extra recomputations. Thus, activations require 95.4 KB, 190.0 KB and 381.7 KB of memory for 1-bit, 2-bit and 4-bit models, respectively. The NIN-based network from [21] with 2-bit activations achieves 51.4% top-1 accuracy, but its activation memory is larger than AlexNet due to late pooling layers.

The SqueezeNet-based models in Table 3 are finetuned from the corresponding models in Table 1 for 40,000 iterations with a mini-batch size of 1024, and SGD solver with a step-policy learning rate starting from 1e-4 divided by 10 every

10,000 iterations. The model with fusion and 8-bit quantized weights and activations, while having an accuracy similar to floating-point model, outperforms the state-of-the-art networks in terms of weight and activation memory. The proposed four models from Table 1 further decrease activation memory by adding compression-decompression layers to *fire2,3* modules. This step allowed us to shrink memory from 189.9 KB to 165.4 KB, 140.9 KB, 116.4 KB and 110.3 KB depending on the compression configuration. More compression is possible, if the proposed approach is applied to other *squeeze* layers.

4.2   PASCAL VOC Object Detection Using SSD

Accuracy Experiments. We evaluate object detection using the Pascal VOC [4] dataset which is a more realistic application for autonomous cars where the high-resolution cameras emphasize feature map compression benefits. The VOC2007 test dataset contains 4,952 images and a training dataset of 16,551 images is a union of VOC2007 and VOC2012. We adopted the SSD512 model [14] for the proposed architecture. SqueezeNet pretrained on ImageNet is used as a feature extractor instead of the original VGG-16 network. This reduces number of parameters and overall inference time by a factor of 4 and 3, respectively. The original VOC images are rescaled to 512×512 resolution. As with ImageNet experiments, we generated several models for comparisons: a base floating-point model, quantized models, and compressed models. We apply quantization and compression to the *fire2/squeeze* and *fire3/squeeze* layers which represent, if the fusion technique is applied, more than 80% of total feature map memory due to their large spatial dimensions. Typically, spatial dimensions decrease quadratically because of max pooling layers compared to linear growth in the depth dimension. The compressed models are derived from the 8-bit quantized model, and both are retrained for 10,000 iterations with a mini-batch size of 256 using SGD solver with a step-policy learning rate starting from 1e-3 divided by 10 every 2,500 iterations.

Table 4 presents mean average precision (mAP) results for SqueezeNet-based models as well as size of the weights and feature maps to compress. The 8-bit quantized model with retraining drops accuracy by less than 0.04%, while 6-bit, 4-bit and 2-bit models decrease accuracy by 0.5%, 2.2% and 12.3%, respectively. For reference, mAPs for the quantized models without retraining are shown in parentheses. Using the proposed compression-decompression layers with a 1×1 kernel, mAP for the 6-bit model is increased by 0.5% and mAP for the 4-bit is decreased by 0.5%. We conclude that compression along channel dimension is not beneficial for SSD unlike ImageNet classification either due to low quantization redundancy in that dimension or the choice of hyperparameters e.g. mini-batch size. Then, we evaluate the models with spatial-dimension compression which is intuitively appealing for high-resolution images. Empirically, we found that a 2×2 kernel with stride 2 performs better than a corresponding 3×3 kernel

Table 4. VOC2007 SSD512 accuracy: A - *fire2,3/squeeze* feature maps and W - weights.

Model	W size, MB	A size, KB	mAP, %
fp32	23.7	2048	68.12
Quantized			
uint8	23.7	512	68.08(68.04)
uint6	23.7	384	67.66(67.14)
uint4	23.7	256	65.92(44.13)
uint2	23.7	128	55.86(0.0)
Proposed $b() \rightarrow 1 \times 1 \rightarrow 1 \times 1 \rightarrow b^{-1}()$			
uint6	23.9	384	68.17
uint4	23.8	256	65.42
Proposed: $b() \rightarrow 3 \times 3/2 \rightarrow 3 \times 3 * 2 \rightarrow b^{-1}()$			
uint8	26.5	128	63.53
uint6	25.9	96	62.22
Proposed: $b() \rightarrow 2 \times 2/2 \rightarrow 2 \times 2 * 2 \rightarrow b^{-1}()$			
uint8	24.9	128	64.39
uint6	24.6	96	62.09

Table 5. SSD512 memory requirements: A - feature map, F - fusion, Q - quantization, C - compression ($2 \times 2s2$).

A size, KB	Base, fp32	F, fp32	F+Q, uint8	F+Q, uint4	F+Q+C, uint8
input (int8)	768	768	768	768	768
conv1	16384	0	0	0	0
mpool1	4096	0	0	0	0
fire2,3/squeeze	2048	2048	512	256	128
fire2,3/expand	16384	0	0	0	0
Total	38912	2048	512	256	128
mAP, %	68.12	68.12	68.08	65.92	64.39
Compression	-	$19 \times$	$76\times$	$152 \times$	$304\times$

while requiring less parameters and computations. According to Table 4, an 8-bit model with 2×2 kernel and downsampling-upsampling layers achieves 1% higher mAP than a model with 3×3 kernel and only 3.7% lower than the base floating-point model.

Memory Requirements. Table 5 summarizes memory footprint benefits for the evaluated SSD models. Similar to the previous section, we consider only the largest feature maps that represent more than 80% of total activation memory.

Assuming that the input frame is stored separately, the fusion technique allows to compress feature maps by a factor of 19. Note that no additional recomputations are needed. Second, conventional 8-bit and 4-bit fixed-point models decrease the size of feature maps by a factor of 4 and 8, respectively. Third, the proposed model with 2×2 stride 2 kernel gains another factor of 2 compression compared to 4-bit fixed-point model with only 1.5% degradation in mAP. This result is similar to ImageNet experiments which showed relatively limited compression gain along channel dimension only. At the same time, learned quantization along combined channel and spatial dimensions pushes further compression gain. In total, the memory footprint for this feature extractor is reduced by two orders of magnitude.

5 Conclusions

We introduced a method to decrease memory storage and bandwidth requirements for DNNs. Complementary to conventional approaches that use layer fusion and quantization, we presented an end-to-end method for learning feature map representations over GF(2) within DNNs. Such a binary representation allowed us to compress network feature maps in a higher-dimensional space using autoencoder-inspired layers embedded into a DNN along channel and spatial dimensions. These compression-decompression layers can be implemented using conventional convolutional layers with bitwise operations. To be more precise, the proposed representation traded cardinality of the finite field with the dimensionality of the vector space which makes possible to learn features at the binary level. The evaluated compression strategy for inference can be adopted for GPUs, CPUs or custom accelerators. Alternatively, existing binary networks can be extended to achieve higher accuracy for emerging applications such as object detection and others.

References

1. Alwani, M., Chen, H., Ferdman, M., Milder, P.A.: Fused-layer CNN accelerators. In: MICRO, pp. 1–12, October 2016
2. Bengio, Y., Léonard, N., Courville, A.: Estimating or propagating gradients through stochastic neurons for conditional computation. arXiv preprint arXiv:1308.3432 (2013)
3. Courbariaux, M., Bengio, Y., David, J.: Training deep neural networks with low precision multiplications. In: ICLR, May 2015
4. Everingham, M., Van Gool, L., Williams, C.K.I., Winn, J., Zisserman, A.: The pascal visual object classes (VOC) challenge. IJCV 88(2), 303–338 (2010)
5. Graham, B., van der Maaten, L.: Submanifold sparse convolutional networks. arXiv preprint arXiv:1706.01307 (2017)
6. Gysel, P., Motamedi, M , Ghiasi, S : Hardware-oriented approximation of convolutional neural networks. In: ICLR, May 2016
7. He, K., Zhang, X., Ren, S., Sun, J.: Deep residual learning for image recognition. arXiv preprint arXiv:1512.03385 (2015)

8. Hinton, G., Salakhutdinov, R.: Reducing the dimensionality of data with neural networks. Science **313**(5786), 504–507 (2006)
9. Horowitz, M.: Computing's energy problem (and what we can do about it). In: ISSCC, pp. 10–14, February 2014
10. Huang, J., et al.: Speed/accuracy trade-offs for modern convolutional object detectors. In: CVPR, July 2017
11. Hubara, I., Courbariaux, M., Soudry, D., El-Yaniv, R., Bengio, Y.: Binarized neural networks. In: NIPS, pp. 4107–4115 (2016)
12. Iandola, F.N., Han, S., Moskewicz, M.W., Ashraf, K., Dally, W.J., Keutzer, K.: Squeezenet: alexnet-level accuracy with 50x fewer parameters and <0.5MB model size. arXiv preprint arXiv:1602.07360 (2016)
13. Jia, Y., et al.: Caffe: convolutional architecture for fast feature embedding. arXiv preprint arXiv:1408.5093 (2014)
14. Liu, W., et al.: SSD: single shot multibox detector. In: Leibe, B., Matas, J., Sebe, N., Welling, M. (eds.) ECCV 2016. LNCS, vol. 9905, pp. 21–37. Springer, Cham (2016). https://doi.org/10.1007/978-3-319-46448-0_2
15. Miyashita, D., Lee, E.H., Murmann, B.: Convolutional neural networks using logarithmic data representation. arXiv preprint arXiv:1603.01025 (2016)
16. O'Connor, P., Welling, M.: Sigma delta quantized networks. In: ICLR, April 2017
17. Parashar, A., et al.: SCNN: an accelerator for compressed-sparse convolutional neural networks. In: ISCA, pp. 27–40 (2017)
18. Rastegari, M., Ordonez, V., Redmon, J., Farhadi, A.: XNOR-Net: imagenet classification using binary convolutional neural networks. arXiv preprint arXiv:1603.05279 (2016)
19. Russakovsky, O., et al.: ImageNet large scale visual recognition challenge. IJCV **115**(3), 211–252 (2015)
20. Sandler, M., Howard, A., Zhu, M., Zhmoginov, A., Chen, L.C.: MobileNetv 2: inverted residuals and linear bottlenecks. In: CVPR, June 2018
21. Tang, W., Hua, G., Wang, L.: How to train a compact binary neural network with high accuracy? In: AAAI (2017)
22. Zhou, S., Wu, Y., Ni, Z., Zhou, X., Wen, H., Zou, Y.: DoReFa-Net: training low bitwidth convolutional neural networks with low bitwidth gradients. arXiv preprint arXiv:1606.06160 (2016)

LBP-Motivated Colour Texture Classification

Raquel Bello-Cerezo[1(✉)], Paul Fieguth[2], and Francesco Bianconi[1]

[1] Department of Engineering, Università degli Studi di Perugia,
Via Goffredo Duranti 93, 06125 Perugia, Italy
bellocerezo@gmail.com, bianco@ieee.org
[2] Systems Design Engineering, University of Waterloo,
200 University Avenue West, N2L 3G1 Waterloo, ON, Canada
pfieguth@uwaterloo.ca

Abstract. In this paper we investigate extensions of Local Binary Patterns (LBP), Improved Local Binary Patterns (ILBP) and Extended Local Binary Patterns (ELBP) to colour textures via two different strategies: intra-/inter-channel features and colour orderings. We experimentally evaluate the proposed methods over 15 datasets of general and biomedical colour textures. Intra- and inter-channel features from the RGB space emerged as the best descriptors and we found that the best accuracy was achieved by combining multi-resolution intra-channel features with single-resolution inter-channel features.

Keywords: Colour · Texture · Local Binary Patterns

1 Introduction

Colour and texture, along with transparency and gloss, are among the most important visual features of objects, materials and scenes. As a consequence, colour and texture analysis plays a fundamental role in many computer vision applications such as surface inspection [1–3], medical image analysis [4–7] and object recognition [8–10]. It is generally believed that combining colour and texture improves accuracy (at least under steady imaging conditions [11,12]), though it is not quite clear which is the best way to do it. Indeed this has been subject of debate since early on, both in computer vision [11,12] and perception science [13].

Approaches to colour texture analysis can be roughly categorised into three groups: *parallel*, *sequential* and *integrative* [14], though more involved taxonomies have been proposed too [15]. In this paper we investigate the problem of representing colour texture features starting from three LBP variants as grey-scale texture descriptors. Even in the era of Deep Learning, there are good reasons

R. Bello-Cerezo—Performed part of this work as a visiting graduate student in the Systems Design Engineering department at the University of Waterloo, Canada.

© Springer Nature Switzerland AG 2019
L. Leal-Taixé and S. Roth (Eds.): ECCV 2018 Workshops, LNCS 11132, pp. 517–533, 2019.
https://doi.org/10.1007/978-3-030-11018-5_42

why Local Binary Patterns and related variations are worth investigating: they are conceptually simple, compact, easy to implement, computationally cheap – yet very accurate. We consider two strategies to extend LBP variants to colour textures: the combination of inter- and intra-channel features, and colour orderings. We also evaluate the effect of the colour space used (RGB, HSV, YUV and YIQ) and of the spatial resolution(s) of the local neighbourhood.

2   Background: Grey-Scale LBP Variants

Local Binary Patterns variants [16–22] (also referred to as *Histograms of Equivalent Patterns* [23]) are a well-known class of grey-scale texture descriptors. They are particularly appreciated for their conceptual ease, low computational demand yet high discrimination capability. Nonetheless, extensions to colour images have received much less attention than the original, grey-scale descriptors. In this paper we investigate extensions to the colour domain of Local Binary Patterns [16], Improved Local Binary Patterns [24] and Extended Local Binary Patterns [25], though the same methods could be easily extended to other descriptors of the same class (see [22] for an up-to-date review).

The three methods are all based on comparing the grey-levels of the pixels in a neighbourhood of given shape and size, but the comparison scheme is different in the three cases (see [16, 24, 25] for details). In general, any such comparison scheme can be regarded as a hand-designed function (also referred to as the *kernel function* [23]), which maps a local image pattern to one visual word among a set of pre-defined ones (dictionary). In formulas, denoted with $\mathcal{N}$ the neighbourhood, $\mathcal{P}$ a local image pattern (set of grey-scale values over that neighbourhood) and f the kernel function we can write:

$$\mathcal{P} : \xrightarrow{f} w; \; w \in \{w_1, \ldots, w_K\}, \tag{1}$$

where $\{w_1, \ldots, w_K\}$ is the dictionary. Consequently, any LBP variant identifies with its kernel function and vice-versa, as clearly shown in [26]. The dimension of the dictionary depends on the kernel function and the number of pixels in the neighbourhood: standard LBP [16, 18, 19] for instance generates a dictionary of 2^{n-1} words, being n the number of pixels in the neighbourhood. Image features are the one-dimensional, orderless distribution of the visual words over the dictionary (bag of visual words model).

Rotation-invariant versions of LBP and variants are computed by grouping together the visual words that can be obtained from one another via a discrete rotation of the peripheral pixels (also usually referred to as the '*ri*' configuration [16]). In this case the dimension of the (reduced) dictionary can be computed through standard combinatorial methods [27].

3 Extensions to Colour Images

3.1 Intra- and Inter-channel Analysis

Intra- and/or inter-channel analysis are classic tools for extending texture descriptors to colour images [28–30]. Intra-channel features are computed from each colour channel separately, inter-channel features from pairs of channels. In both cases the resulting features are concatenated into a single vector. As for inter-channel features, if we consider three-channel images and indicate with i, j and k the colour channels, there are six possible combinations: ij, ik, jk, ji, ki and kj. However, to avoid redundancy and reduce the overall number of features, it is customary to retain only the first three [29,30]. Figures 1 and 2 show how to compute intra- and inter-channel features in the RGB space.

Intra- and inter-channel analysis applies to grey-scale LBP variants by replacing the comparison between the grey levels with that between the intensity levels within each colour channel and/or pairs of them, respectively. Therefore, both intra- and inter-channel analysis multiply by three the dimension of the original descriptor (by six when used together). Intra- and inter-channel analysis extends LBP, ILBP and ELBP seamlessly to the colour domain. In the remainder we refer to these colour extensions respectively as Opponent Colour LBP (OCLBP) [29], Improved Opponent Colour LBP (IOCLBP) [30] and Extended Opponent Colour LBP (EOCLBP).

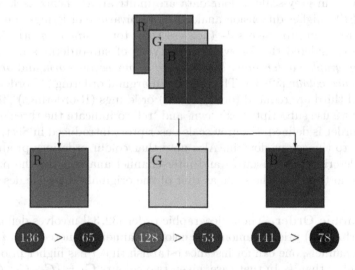

Fig. 1. Computing intra-channel features in the RGB space: the intensity values (circles in the figure) are compared within each of the R, G and B channels separately (squares in the figure) (Color figure online)

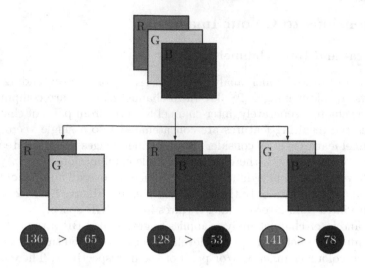

Fig. 2. Computing inter-channel features in the RGB space: the intensity values (circles in the figure) are compared between each of the R/G, R/B and G/B pairs of colour channels (squares in the figure) (Color figure online)

3.2   Colour Orderings

Differently from grey-scale, colour data are multivariate, hence lack a natural ordering. Still, higher-dimension analogues of univariate orderings can be introduced by recurring to some *sub-* (i.e. less than total) *ordering* principles [31]. Herein we considered the following three types of sub-orderings in the colour space: *lexicographic order, order based on the colour vector norm* and *order based on a reference colour* [32–37]. The first is a marginal ordering (M-ordering), the second and third are reduced (or aggregate) orderings (R-orderings) [31]. In the remainder we use subscripts 'lex', 'cvn' and 'rcl' to indicate the three orderings. Once the order is defined, the grey-scale descriptors introduced in Sect. 2 extend seamlessly to the colour domain. Also note that colour orderings produce more compact descriptors than intra- and inter-channel analysis, for the number of features is, in this case, the same as that of the original grey-scale descriptor.

Lexicographic Order. The lexicographic order [32,34] involves defining some kind of (arbitrary) priority among the colour channels. Denoted with i, j and k the three channels, one can for instance establish that i has higher priority than j and j higher than k. In that case, given two colours $\mathbf{C}_1 = \{C_{1i}, C_{1j}, C_{1k}\}$ and $\mathbf{C}_2 = \{C_{2i}, C_{2j}, C_{2k}\}$, we shall write:

$$\mathbf{C}_1 \geq \mathbf{C}_2 \iff (C_{1i} > C_{2i}) \vee [(C_{1i} = C_{2i}) \wedge (C_{1j} > C_{2j})] \vee \qquad (2)$$
$$[(C_{1i} = C_{2i}) \wedge (C_{1j} = C_{2j}) \wedge (C_{1k} \geq C_{2k})].$$

For three-dimensional colour data there are $3! = 6$ priority rules, and, consequently, as many lexicographic orders.

Aggregate Order Based on the Colour Vector Norm. This is based on comparing the vector norm [33] of the two colours:

$$\mathbf{C}_1 \geq \mathbf{C}_2 \iff \|\mathbf{C}_1\| \geq \|\mathbf{C}_2\|, \tag{3}$$

where '$\|\cdot\|$' indicates the vector norm. In the remainder we shall assume that this be the L_2 norm, although other types of distance can be used as well.

Aggregate Order Based on a Reference Colour. In this case the comparison is based on the distance from a given (and again arbitrary) reference colour $\mathbf{C}_{\text{ref}}$ [35]:

$$\mathbf{C}_1 \geq \mathbf{C}_2 \iff \|\mathbf{C}_1 - \mathbf{C}_{ref}\| \geq \|\mathbf{C}_2 - \mathbf{C}_{ref}\|. \tag{4}$$

Clearly this case reduces to the order based on the colour vector norm when $\mathbf{C}_{\text{ref}} = \{0, 0, 0\}$.

4   Experiments

Different strategies have been proposed to extend LBP (and variants) to colour textures. In order to evaluate the effectiveness of the approaches described in Sect. 3 and to explore which one works better in the case of colour images, we carried out a set of supervised image classification experiments using 15 colour texture datasets (more details on this in Sect. 5). We first run a group of three experiments to determine the optimal settings regarding the colour space used (Experiment 1), the colour orderings (Experiment 2) and the combination of resolutions for intra- and inter-channel features (Experiment 3). To reduce the overall computational burden we only used datasets #1 to #5 for this first group of experiments. Finally, in the last experiment we selected the best settings and carried out a comprehensive evaluation using all the datasets.

We computed rotation-invariant ('ri') features from non-interpolated pixel neighbourhoods of radius 1px, 2px and 3px (Fig. 3) and concatenated them.

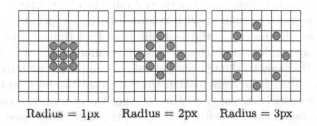

Radius = 1px   Radius = 2px   Radius = 3px

Fig. 3. Pixel neighbourhoods corresponding to resolutions 1, 2 and 3, respectively

In the remainder, symbol '&' will indicate concatenation; therefore we shall write, for instance, '1&2&3' to signal concatenation of the feature vectors computed at resolution 1, 2 and 3.

The accuracy was estimated via split sample validation with stratified sampling using a train ratio of $1/2$, i.e.: half of the samples of each class (train set) were used to train the classifier and the remaining half (test set) to compute the figure of merit. This was the fraction of samples of the test set classified correctly. Classification was based on the nearest neighbour rule with L_1 ('city-block') distance.

4.1   Experiment 1: Selecting the Best Colour Space for Intra- and Inter-channel Features

This experiment aimed to determine the best colour space among RGB, HSV, YUV and YIQ (conversion formulae from RGB available in [38]). Since HSV separates colour into heterogeneous components (hue, saturation and value), we also used a normalized version of this space (HSV_{norm} in the remainder):

$$H_{norm} = \frac{H - \mu_H}{\sigma_H},$$
$$S_{norm} = \frac{S - \mu_S}{\sigma_S}, \tag{5}$$
$$V_{norm} = \frac{V - \mu_V}{\sigma_V}.$$

where μ and σ indicate the average values over the input image. Normalized versions of YUV and YIQ were also considered, but not reported in the results owing to their poor performance. We computed both intra- and inter-channel features at resolutions 1, 2 and 3, and concatenated the results ('1&2&3'). We considered the following combinations of colour spaces respectively for the intra- and inter-channel features: RGB-RGB, HSV-HSV, HSV-RGB, HSV-HSV$_{norm}$, HSV-YUV and HSV-YIQ (see Table 3, boldface figures).

4.2   Experiment 2: Colour Orderings Vs. Intra- and Inter-channel Features

The objective of this experiment was to evaluate the effectiveness of intra- and inter-channel features compared with colour orderings (Sect. 3.2) in the RGB colour space, which emerged as the best one from Experiment 1. For the lexicographic order we considered all the six possible combinations of priority among the R, G and B channels, though for the sake of simplicity we only report (see Table 4) the results of the combination that attained the best accuracy in the majority of the cases (this was $G \succ R \succ B$). For the order based on a reference colour we considered three possible references, the same three used in [36] since they were the best among the eight vertices of the RGB colour cube: white $(1,1,1)$, green $(0,1,0)$ and magenta $(1,0,1)$, and the first gave the best results (see Table 4).

Table 1. Summary table of the generic colour texture datasets used in the experiments

ID	Name	No. of classes	No. of samples per class	Size (px×px)	Sample images
1	KTH-TIPS	10	81	200×200	
2	KTH-TIPS2b	11	432	200×200	
3	Outex-00013	68	20	128×128	
4	Outex-00014	68	60	128×128	
5	PlantLeaves	20	60	128×128	
6	CUReT	61	92	128×128	
7	ForestSpecies	112	20	768×768	
8	NewBarkTex	6	272	64×64	

As in Experiment 1, the image features were computed at resolution 1, 2 and 3 and the resulting vectors concatenated ('1&2&3').

4.3   Experiment 3: Selecting Optimal Resolutions for Intra- and Inter-channel Features

Since the use of intra- and inter-channel analysis increased by six the number of features of grey-scale descriptors, in this experiment we investigated how to reduce the overall number of features – this way generating reasonably compact descriptors – by selecting appropriate resolutions for intra- and inter-channel features. Specifically, we used three concatenated resolutions ('1&2&3') for intra-channel features and one ('1', '2' or '3') or two concatenated resolutions ('1&2', '1&3' or '2&3') for inter-channel features.

4.4   Experiment 4: Overall Evaluation with Optimised Settings

In this last experiment we computed the classification accuracy over all the 15 datasets described in Sect. 5 using the settings that emerged as optimal from the previous experiments. For calibration purposes we also included five pre-trained convolutional neural network models – specifically: three residual networks (ResNet-50, ResNet-101 and ResNet-152 [39]) and two VGG 'very deep' models (VGG-VeryDeep-16 and VGG-VeryDeep-19 [40]). Image features in this case were the L_1 normalised output of the last fully-connected layer (usually referred to as the 'FC' configuration [41,42]). The results are reported in Tables 6–7.

Table 2. Summary table of the biomedical textures used in the experiments

ID	Name	No. of classes	No. of samples per class	Size (px×px)	Sample images
9	BioMediTechRPE	4	150–949	480×480	
10	BreakHis 40×	2	625–1370	460×460	
11	BreakHis 100×	2	644–1437	460×460	
12	BreakHis 200×	2	623–1390	460×460	
13	BreakHis 400×	2	588–1232	460×460	
14	Epistroma	2	551–825	Variable	
15	Kather	8	625	150×150	

Table 3 summarises the results of Experiment 1. As can be seen, the RGB-RGB combination for intra- and inter-channel features emerged as the best option in seven datasets, followed by HSV-HSV (five datasets) and HSV-RGB (four datasets).

5   Datasets

For the experimental evaluation we considered eight datasets of generic colour textures and seven of biomedical textures as detailed in Sects. 5.1–5.2. The main characteristics of each dataset are also summarised in Tables 1–2.

5.1   Generic Colour Textures

#1 – #2: KTH-TIPS [43,44] and KTH-TIPS2b [44,45]. Generic materials as *bread, cotton, cracker, linen, orange peel, sandpaper, sponge* or *styrofoam*, acquired at nine scales, three viewpoints and three different illuminants.

#3 – #4: Outex-00013 [16,46] and Outex-00014 [16,46]. Generic materials such as *carpet, chips, flakes, granite, paper, pasta* or *wallpaper*. Images from Outex-00013 were acquired under invariable imaging conditions and those from Outex-00014 under three different illumination conditions.

#5, #7 – #8: PlantLeaves [47], ForestSpecies [48,49] and NewBarkTex [50,51]. Images from different species of plants, trees and bark acquired under controlled and steady imaging conditions.

Table 3. Results of Experiment 1: selecting the best colour space for intra- and inter-channel features. Boldface text indicates the best combination descriptor + colour spaces; framed text the overall best accuracy by dataset. Although the KTH-TIPS and KTH-TIPS2b datasets saw improvements with HSV, all other datasets performed best by remaining in RGB space. Classifier was 1-NN (L_1)

Descriptor-[1&2&3]	Colour space	Datasets				
	Intra-Inter	#1	#2	#3	#4	#5
OCLBP	RGB-RGB	95.2	97.8	90.9	**91.5**	**76.9**
OCLBP	HSV-HSV	**96.6**	97.5	91.9	86.7	71.0
OCLBP	HSV-RGB	96.0	**98.4**	90.4	90.3	73.7
OCLBP	HSV-HSV$_{norm}$	96.0	97.8	84.9	84.5	73.8
OCLBP	HSV-YUV	92.5	96.2	86.5	84.8	72.6
OCLBP	HSV-YIQ	92.4	96.3	86.6	85.5	74.0
IOCLBP	RGB-RGB	96.2	98.5	91.0	**91.9**	**77.7**
IOCLBP	HSV-HSV	97.4	98.2	**91.5**	87.4	71.9
IOCLBP	HSV-RGB	96.6	98.7	89.4	89.8	73.2
IOCLBP	HSV-HSV$_{norm}$	96.4	98.1	84.5	85.2	74.0
IOCLBP	HSV-YUV	94.2	97.5	87.9	85.9	73.0
IOCLBP	HSV-YIQ	94.2	97.4	87.8	86.8	74.8
EOCLBP	RGB-RGB	95.3	98.2	**91.5**	92.0	**77.0**
EOCLBP	HSV-HSV	**97.2**	98.5	90.9	87.0	70.7
EOCLBP	HSV-RGB	**97.2**	98.7	90.4	89.2	70.6
EOCLBP	HSV-HSV$_{norm}$	96.9	98.2	85.6	85.0	71.7
EOCLBP	HSV-YUV	96.4	98.1	87.3	85.6	71.0
EOCLBP	HSV-YIQ	96.0	98.0	87.2	85.9	71.7
Baseline						
LBP	GREY	94.2	93.5	80.9	83.7	73.8
ILBP	GREY	95.4	95.1	85.5	88.6	76.9
ELBP	GREY	94.5	94.5	84.6	87.4	78.3

#6: CUReT [52]. A reduced version of the Columbia-Utrecht Reflectance and Texture database maintained by the Visual Geometry Group, University of Oxford, United Kingdom [53], containing samples of generic materials.

5.2 Biomedical Textures

The following databases were acquired through digital microscopy under fixed and reproducible conditions, and are therefore intrinsically different from those presented in the preceding section.

#9: BioMediTechRPE [54,55]. Retinal pigment epithelium (RPE) cells from different stages of maturation.

#10 – #13: BreakHis [56,57]. Histological images from benign/malignant breast cancer tissue. Each image was taken under four magnification factors (40×, 100×, 200× and 400×), and we considered each factor as making up a different dataset (see Table 2).

#14 – #15: Epistroma [5,58] and Kather [59–61]. Histological images from colorectal cancer tissue representing different tissue sub-types.

6   Results and Discussion

The results of Experiment 2 (Table 4) show that in most cases intra- and inter-channel features from the RGB space improved the accuracy of the original, grey-scale descriptors by a good margin. By contrast, no clear advantage emerged from using colour orderings as an alternative to grey-scale values.

Table 4. Results of Experiment 2: colour orderings vs. intra- and inter-channel features. Boldface text indicates, for each dataset, the best accuracy by descriptor + colour ordering; framed text the overall best accuracy by dataset. Colour priority for lexicographic order ('lex') was $G \succ R \succ B$, distance for colour vector norm ('cvn') was L_2 and reference colour for 'rcl' was white $(1,1,1)$. The features were computed on the RGB space. The significant reduction in dimensionality offered by the colour orderings does not lead to any improvement

Descriptor-[1&2&3]	Datasets					No. of features
	#1	#2	#3	#4	#5	
LBP$_{lex}$	**94.3**	**92.3**	**79.8**	**82.9**	65.2	108
LBP$_{cvn}$	**94.3**	**92.3**	78.5	81.3	69.9	108
LBP$_{rcl}$	94.0	92.1	78.6	80.2	**71.9**	108
ILBP$_{lex}$	**95.0**	**95.7**	**84.6**	87.8	67.6	213
ILBP$_{cvn}$	94.9	95.5	83.6	87.5	70.3	213
ILBP$_{rcl}$	94.7	95.3	83.9	**88.2**	**73.4**	213
ELBP$_{lex}$	94.3	**94.2**	84.5	86.1	66.7	215
ELBP$_{cvn}$	**94.7**	94.1	**85.6**	**86.3**	73.7	215
ELBP$_{rcl}$	94.6	93.8	84.6	86.0	**77.3**	215
Baseline						
LBP	94.2	93.5	80.9	83.7	73.8	108
ILBP	95.4	95.1	85.5	88.6	76.9	213
ELBP	94.5	94.5	84.6	87.4	78.3	215
OCLBP	95.2	97.8	90.9	91.5	76.9	648
IOCLBP	96.2	98.5	91.0	91.9	77.7	1287
EOCLBP	95.3	98.2	91.5	92.0	77.0	1299

Experiment 3 indicated that the best accuracy was achieved by concatenating multi-resolution intra-channel features and single-resolution inter-channel features. In fact, adding more than one inter-channel resolution degraded the performance in the majority of cases, as clearly shown in Table 5. The results were however inconclusive as to which resolution ('1', '2' or '3') should be used.

Table 5. Experiment 3: best combination of resolutions for intra- and inter-channel features. Boldface text indicates, for each dataset, the best combination descriptor + resolutions used for computing the inter-channel features; framed text the overall accuracy by dataset. The features were computed on the RGB space. In general, strongest performance is realized by limiting the number of resolutions associated with inter-channel features. That is, the added information present in multiple inter-channels is more than offset by the decrease in classification performance due to the increase in feature dimensionality

Descriptor-[1&2&3]$_{intra}$	Datasets					No. of features
	#1	#2	#3	#4	#5	
OCLBP-[1]$_{inter}$	**96.6**	**98.3**	91.3	91.6	78.2	432
OCLBP-[2]$_{inter}$	96.2	98.1	91.7	92.1	78.6	432
OCLBP-[3]$_{inter}$	95.9	98.1	**91.9**	**92.5**	**78.8**	432
OCLBP-[1&2]$_{inter}$	96.1	98.1	91.3	91.7	77.2	540
OCLBP-[1&3]$_{inter}$	96.0	98.1	91.6	92.3	77.4	540
OCLBP-[2&3]$_{inter}$	95.8	98.0	91.7	92.4	77.2	540
IOCLBP-[1]$_{inter}$	**97.1**	**98.7**	92.2	92.5	**80.2**	855
IOCLBP-[2]$_{inter}$	**97.1**	**98.7**	92.3	92.6	79.7	855
IOCLBP-[3]$_{inter}$	96.8	98.6	**92.9**	**93.0**	79.4	855
IOCLBP-[1&2]$_{inter}$	96.8	98.6	91.4	92.0	78.7	1071
IOCLBP-[1&3]$_{inter}$	96.6	98.6	91.9	92.3	78.6	1071
IOCLBP-[2&3]$_{inter}$	96.4	98.5	91.7	92.2	78.5	1071
EOCLBP-[1]$_{inter}$	**96.8**	98.4	91.7	91.4	**79.5**	759
EOCLBP-[2]$_{inter}$	96.7	98.4	91.8	91.5	**79.5**	759
EOCLBP-[3]$_{inter}$	96.6	98.4	**91.9**	91.5	79.4	759
EOCLBP-[1&2]$_{inter}$	96.5	**98.5**	91.7	91.3	78.8	867
EOCLBP-[1&3]$_{inter}$	96.5	**98.5**	91.8	91.4	78.8	867
EOCLBP-[2&3]$_{inter}$	96.5	**98.5**	**91.9**	91.5	78.8	867
Baseline						
LBP	94.2	93.5	80.9	83.7	73.8	108
ILBP	95.4	95.1	85.5	88.6	76.9	213
ELBP	94.5	94.5	84.6	87.4	78.3	215
OCLBP	95.2	97.8	90.9	91.5	76.9	648
IOCLBP	96.2	98.5	91.0	91.9	77.7	1287
EOCLBP	95.3	98.2	91.5	92.0	77.0	1299

The comparison between LBP variants and pre-trained convolutional networks (Experiment 4, Tables 6 and 7) showed nearly perfectly split results, with the former achieving the best performance in seven datasets out of 15 and the reverse occurring in the other eight. Convolutional models seemed better at classifying textures with higher intra-class variability (as a consequence of texture non-stationariness and/or changes in the imaging conditions), as for instance in datasets #1, #2 and #7 (see Sect. 5.1). Conversely, homogeneous textures acquired under steady imaging conditions (most of the biomedical datasets) were still better classified by LBP variants. This finding generally agrees with those obtained in previous studies [62]. Pre-trained convolutional networks, however, achieved this result by employing at least twice as many features than LBP variants.

Table 6. Results of Experiment 4: overall evaluation with optimised settings (datasets #1 to #8). Boldface text indicates, for each dataset, the best combination descriptor + resolutions used for computing the inter-channel features; framed text the overall best accuracy by dataset

Descriptor-$[1\&2\&3]_{intra}$	Generic textures								No. of features
	1	2	3	4	5	6	7	8	
OCLBP-$[1]_{inter}$	**96.6**	**98.3**	91.3	91.6	78.2	97.5	76.0	82.9	432
OCLBP-$[2]_{inter}$	96.2	98.1	91.7	92.1	78.6	97.5	76.1	82.7	432
OCLBP-$[3]_{inter}$	95.9	98.1	**91.9**	**92.5**	**78.8**	**97.7**	**76.4**	**83.0**	432
IOCLBP-$[1]_{inter}$	**97.1**	**98.7**	92.2	92.5	**80.2**	**98.2**	81.9	**84.5**	855
IOCLBP-$[2]_{inter}$	**97.1**	**98.7**	92.3	92.6	79.7	98.0	**82.1**	83.8	855
IOCLBP-$[3]_{inter}$	96.8	98.6	**92.9**	**93.0**	79.4	98.1	**82.1**	83.2	855
EOCLBP-$[1]_{inter}$	96.8	**98.4**	91.7	91.4	**79.5**	**98.1**	83.0	**84.8**	759
EOCLBP-$[2]_{inter}$	96.7	**98.4**	91.8	91.5	**79.5**	**98.1**	**83.1**	**84.8**	759
EOCLBP-$[3]_{inter}$	96.6	**98.4**	**91.9**	91.5	79.4	98.0	**83.1**	84.4	759
Baseline									
OCLBP	95.2	97.8	90.9	91.5	76.9	97.4	74.8	79.9	648
IOCLBP	96.2	98.5	91.0	91.9	77.7	97.7	79.9	80.2	1287
EOCLBP	95.3	98.2	91.5	**92.0**	77.0	97.6	77.3	79.1	1299
CNNs									
VGG-VD-16-FC	99.4	99.5	84.3	83.5	77.4	97.0	85.6	79.1	4096
VGG-VD-19-FC	99.4	99.4	83.8	82.8	78.0	96.9	82.8	81.6	4096
ResNet-50-FC	99.6	99.7	**87.2**	**86.0**	86.6	98.5	93.0	90.7	2048
ResNet-101-FC	99.9	99.7	86.4	85.5	82.1	98.6	92.8	90.5	2048
ResNet-152-FC	99.8	99.8	84.8	84.7	83.9	98.5	91.8	90.9	2048

Table 7. Results of Experiment 4: overall evaluation with optimised settings (datasets #9 to #15). Boldface text indicates, for each dataset, the best combination descriptor + resolutions used for computing the inter-channel features; framed text the overall best accuracy by dataset

Descriptor-[1&2&3]$_{intra}$	Biomedical textures							No. of features
	9	10	11	12	13	14	15	
OCLBP-[1]$_{inter}$	**85.4**	**92.6**	**91.8**	92.2	91.1	92.3	91.5	432
OCLBP-[2]$_{inter}$	**85.4**	92.5	91.6	**92.4**	91.4	92.5	91.6	432
OCLBP-[3]$_{inter}$	85.3	92.4	91.3	92.3	**91.5**	**92.6**	**92.0**	432
IOCLBP-[1]$_{inter}$	**85.5**	93.6	92.9	93.2	91.7	92.0	92.9	855
IOCLBP-[2]$_{inter}$	85.4	93.7	92.8	93.3	91.8	92.2	**93.1**	855
IOCLBP-[3]$_{inter}$	85.4	94.0	**93.0**	93.4	92.1	**92.8**	**93.1**	855
EOCLBP-[1]$_{inter}$	85.9	**93.7**	93.2	93.2	90.7	96.0	93.2	759
EOCLBP-[2]$_{inter}$	**86.0**	**93.7**	93.3	93.3	90.8	**96.1**	93.2	759
EOCLBP-[3]$_{inter}$	**86.0**	**93.7**	93.1	93.4	90.9	**96.1**	93.3	759
Baseline								
OCLBP	85.2	91.5	91.2	92.1	90.5	91.8	91.0	648
IOCLBP	85.4	93.1	92.2	92.7	91.0	91.8	92.2	1287
EOCLBP	85.8	92.5	91.6	92.4	90.6	93.1	91.6	1299
CNNs								
VGG-VD-16-FC	86.3	89.7	87.0	87.0	83.4	95.3	86.0	4096
VGG-VD-19-FC	86.5	88.8	86.4	85.6	83.4	94.5	84.1	4096
ResNet-50-FC	87.5	93.4	**90.9**	**91.6**	**89.8**	97.3	**89.6**	2048
ResNet-101-FC	87.7	**93.5**	90.6	91.0	88.8	96.6	89.1	2048
ResNet-152-FC	87.6	93.3	90.7	91.2	88.3	96.7	89.4	2048

7   Conclusions

In this work we have investigated two strategies for extending LBP variants to the colour domain: intra- and inter-channel features on the one hand and colour orderings on the other. Colour orderings did not prove particularly effective; however, intra- and inter-channel features improved the accuracy of the original, grey-scale descriptors in virtually all the cases. The best results were obtained by combining multi-resolution intra-channel features with single-resolution inter-channel features, and this represents a novel finding. In future works we plan expand the study to consider more LBP variants [22] and different strategies for compacting the feature vectors [63].

Acknowledgments. R. Bello-Cerezo wants to thank the colleagues at Systems Design Engineering, University of Waterloo, Canada, for the assistance received during her research visit from Sep. 2017 to Feb. 2018. F. Bianconi wishes to acknowledge support from the Italian Ministry of University and Research (MIUR) under the Individual Funding Scheme for Fundamental Research ('FFABR' 2017) and from the Department of Engineering at the Università degli Studi di Perugia, Italy, under the Fundamental Research Grants Scheme 2018.

References

1. Weszka, J.S., Rosenfeld, A.: An application of texture analysis to materials inspection. Pattern Recognit. **8**(4), 195–200 (1976)
2. Tsai, D.M., Huang, T.Y.: Automated surface inspection for statistical textures. Image Vis. Comput. **21**(4), 307–323 (2003)
3. Koch, C., Georgieva, K., Kasireddy, V., Akinci, B., Fieguth, P.: A review on computer vision based defect detection and condition assessment of concrete and asphalt civil infrastructure. Adv. Eng. Inform. **29**(2), 196–210 (2015)
4. Meijer, G.A., Beliën, J.A.M., Van Diest, P.J., Baak, J.P.A.: Image analysis in clinical pathology. J. Clin. Pathol. **50**(5), 365–370 (1997)
5. Linder, N., et al.: Identification of tumor epithelium and stroma in tissue microarrays using texture analysis. Diagn. Pathol. **7**(22), 1–11 (2012)
6. Nanni, L., Lumini, A., Brahnam, S.: Local binary patterns variants as texture descriptors for medical image analysis. Artif. Intell. Med. **49**(2), 117–125 (2010)
7. Jalalian, A., Mashohor, S., Mahmud, R., Karasfi, B., Saripan, I., Ramli, A.R.: Computer-assisted diagnosis system for breast cancer in computed tomography laser mammography (CTLM). J. Digit. Imaging **30**(6), 796–811 (2017)
8. Lowe, D.G.: Object recognition from local scale-invariant features. In: Proceedings of Seventh IEEE International Conference on Computer Vision, 1999, vol. 2, pp. 1150–1157 (1999)
9. Serre, T., Wolf, L., Bileschi, S., Riesenhuber, M., Poggio, T.: Robust object recognition with cortex-like mechanisms. IEEE Trans. Pattern Anal. Mach. Intell. **29**(3), 411–426 (2007)
10. Liu, H., Wu, Y., Sun, F., Guo, D.: Recent progress on tactile object recognition. Int. J. Adv. Robot. Syst. **14**(4) (2017)
11. Drimbarean, A., Whelan, P.: Experiments in colour texture analysis. Pattern Recognit. Lett. **22**(10), 1161–1167 (2001)
12. Mäenpää, T., Pietikäinen, M.: Classification with color and texture: jointly or separately? Pattern Recognit. Lett. **37**(8), 1629–1640 (2004)
13. Cavina-Pratesi, C., Kentridge, R.W., Heywood, C., Milner, A.: Separate channels for processing form, texture, and color: evidence from FMRI adaptation and visual object agnosia. Cereb. Cortex **20**(10), 2319–32 (2010)
14. Palm, C.: Color texture classification by integrative co-occurrence matrices. Pattern Recognit. **37**(5), 965–976 (2004)
15. Bianconi, F., Harvey, R., Southam, P., Fernández, A.: Theoretical and experimental comparison of different approaches for color texture classification. J. Electron. Imaging **20**(4) (2011). Article number 043006
16. Ojala, T., Pietikäinen, M., Mäenpää, T.: Multiresolution gray-scale and rotation invariant texture classification with local binary patterns. IEEE Trans. Pattern Anal. Mach. Intell. **24**(7), 971–987 (2002)
17. Huang, D., Shan, C., Ardabilian, M., Wang, Y., Chen, L.: Local binary patterns and its application to facial image analysis: a survey. IEEE Trans. Syst. Man Cybern. Part C **41**(6), 765–781 (2017)
18. Pietikäinen, M., Hadid, A., Zhao, G., Ahonen, T.: Computer Vision Using Local Binary Patterns. Computational Imaging and Vision, vol. 40. Springer, Heidelberg (2011). https://doi.org/10.1007/978-0-85729-748-8

19. Brahnam, S., Jain, L., Nanni, L., Lumini, A.: Local Binary Patterns: New Variants and Applications. Studies in Computational Intelligence, vol. 506. Springer, Heidelberg (2014). https://doi.org/10.1007/978-3-642-39289-4
20. Pietikäinen, M., Zhao, G.: Two decades of local binary patterns: a survey. In: Bingham, E., Kaski, S., Laaksonen, J., Lampinen, J. (eds.) Advances in Independent Component Analysis and Learning Machines, pp. 175–210. Academic Press, London (2015)
21. Liu, L., Lao, S., Fieguth, P., Guo, Y., Wang, X., Pietikäinen, M.: Median robust extended local binary pattern for texture classification. IEEE Trans. Image Process. **25**(3), 1368–1381 (2016)
22. Liu, L., Fieguth, P., Guo, Y., Wang, X., Pietikäinen, M.: Local binary features for texture classification: taxonomy and experimental study. Pattern Recognit. **62**, 135–160 (2017)
23. Fernández, A., Álvarez, M.X., Bianconi, F.: Texture description through histograms of equivalent patterns. J. Math. Imaging Vis. **45**(1), 76–102 (2013)
24. Jin, H., Liu, Q., Lu, H., Tong, X.: Face detection using improved LBP under Bayesian framework. In: Proceedings of the 3rd International Conference on Image and Graphics, Hong Kong, China, pp. 306–309, December 2004
25. Liu, L., Zhao, L., Long, Y., Kuang, G., Fieguth, P.: Extended local binary patterns for texture classification. Image Vis. Comput. **30**(2), 86–99 (2012)
26. Bianconi, F., Fernández, A.: A unifying framework for LBP and related methods. In: Brahnam, S., Jain, L.C., Nanni, L., Lumini, A. (eds.) Local Binary Patterns: New Variants and Applications. Studies in Computational Intelligence, vol. 506, pp. 17–46. Springer, Heidelberg (2014). https://doi.org/10.1007/978-3-642-39289-4_2
27. Charalambides, C.A.: Enumerative Combinatorics. Discrete Mathematics and Its Applications. Chapman and Hall/CRC, Boca Raton (2002)
28. Jain, A., Healey, G.: A multiscale representation including opponent color features for texture recognition. IEEE Trans. Image Process. **7**(1), 124–128 (1998)
29. Mäenpää, T., Pietikäinen, M.: Texture analysis with local binary patterns. In: Chen, C.H., Wang, P.S.P. (eds.) Handbook of Pattern Recognition and Computer Vision, 3rd edn, pp. 197–216. World Scientific Publishing, London (2005)
30. Bianconi, F., Bello-Cerezo, R., Napoletano, P.: Improved opponent colour local binary patterns: an effective local image descriptor for colour texture classification. J. Electron. Imaging **27**(1) (2017)
31. Barnett, V.: The ordering of multivariate data. J. R. Stat. Soc. Ser. A (Gen.) **139**(3), 318–355 (1976)
32. Aptoula, E., Lefèvre, S.: A comparative study ion multivariate mathematical morphology. Pattern Recognit. **40**(11), 2914–2929 (2007)
33. Porebski, A., Vandenbroucke, N., Macaire, L.: Haralick feature extraction from LBP images for colour texture classification. In: Proceedings of the International Workshops on Image Processing Theory, Tools and Applications (IPTA 2008), Sousse, Tunisie, pp. 1–8 (2008)
34. Barra, V.: Expanding the local binary pattern to multispectral images using total orderings. In: Richard, P., Braz, J. (eds.) VISIGRAPP 2010. CCIS, vol. 229, pp. 67–80. Springer, Heidelberg (2011). https://doi.org/10.1007/978-3-642-25382-9_5
35. Ledoux, A., Richard, N., Capelle-Laizé, A.-S., Fernandez-Maloigne, C.: Toward a complete inclusion of the vector information in morphological computation of texture features for color images. In: Elmoataz, A., Lezoray, O., Nouboud, F., Mammass, D. (eds.) ICISP 2014. LNCS, vol. 8509, pp. 222–229. Springer, Cham (2014). https://doi.org/10.1007/978-3-319-07998-1_25

36. Ledoux, A., Losson, O., Macaire, L.: Color local binary patterns: compact descriptors for texture classification. J. Electron. Imaging **25**(6) (2016)
37. Fernández, A., Lima, D., Bianconi, F., Smeraldi, F.: Compact colour texture descriptor based on rank transform and product ordering in the RGB color space. In: Proceedings of the 2017 IEEE International Conference on Computer Vision Workshops (ICCVW) (2017)
38. Palus, H.: Representations of colour images in different colour spaces. In: Sangwine, S.J., Horne, R.E.N. (eds.) The Colour Image Processing Handbook, pp. 67–90. Springer, Boston (1998). https://doi.org/10.1007/978-1-4615-5779-1_4
39. He, K., Zhang, X., Ren, S., Sun, J.: Deep residual learning for image recognition. In: 2016 IEEE Conference on Computer Vision and Pattern Recognition (2016)
40. Simonyan, K., Zisserman, A.: Very deep convolutional networks for large-scale image recognition. In: Proceedings of the 5th International Conference on Learning Representations, San Diego, USA, May 2015
41. Cimpoi, M., Maji, S., Kokkinos, I., Vedaldi, A.: Deep filter banks for texture recognition, description, and segmentation. Int. J. Comput. Vis. **118**(1), 65–94 (2016)
42. Cusano, C., Napoletano, P., Schettini, R.: Evaluating color texture descriptors under large variations of controlled lighting conditions. J. Opt. Soc. Am. A **33**(1), 17–30 (2016)
43. Hayman, E., Caputo, B., Fritz, M., Eklundh, J.-O.: On the significance of real-world conditions for material classification. In: Pajdla, T., Matas, J. (eds.) ECCV 2004. LNCS, vol. 3024, pp. 253–266. Springer, Heidelberg (2004). https://doi.org/10.1007/978-3-540-24673-2_21
44. The kth-tips and kth-tips2 image databases. http://www.nada.kth.se/cvap/databases/kth-tips/download.html. Accessed 11 Jan 2017
45. Caputo, B., Hayman, E., Mallikarjuna, P.: Class-specific material categorisation. In: Proceedings of the Tenth IEEE International Conference on Computer Vision (ICCV 2005), vol. 2, pp. 1597–1604 (2005)
46. Outex texture database. http://www.outex.oulu.fi/. Accessed 12 Jan 2017
47. Casanova, D., Sá, J.J., Bruno, O.: Plant leaf identification using Gabor wavelets. Int. J. Imaging Syst. Technol. **19**(3), 236–246 (2009)
48. Forest species database. http://web.inf.ufpr.br/vri/image-and-videos-databases/forest-species-database. Accessed 11 Jan 2017
49. Martins, J., Oliveira, L.S., Nigkoski, S., Sabourin, R.: A database for automatic classification of forest species. Mach. Vis. Appl. **24**(3), 567–578 (2013)
50. New BarkTex benchmark image test suite for evaluating color texture classification schemes. https://www-lisic.univ-littoral.fr/~porebski/BarkTex_image_test_suite.html. Accessed 12 Jan 2017
51. Porebski, A., Vandenbroucke, N., Macaire, L., Hamad, D.: A new benchmark image test suite for evaluating color texture classification schemes. Multimed. Tools Appl. J. **70**(1), 543–556 (2014)
52. CUReT: columbia-utrecht reflectance and texture database. http://www.cs.columbia.edu/CAVE/software/curet/index.php. Accessed 25 Jan 2017
53. Visual geometry group: CUReT: columbia-utrecht reflectance and texture database. http://www.robots.ox.ac.uk/~vgg/research/texclass/setup.html. Accessed 26 Jan 2017
54. BioMediTechRPE database (2016). https://figshare.com/articles/BioMediTech_RPE_dataset/2070109. Accessed 16 May 2017
55. Nanni, L., Paci, M., Santos, F.L.C., Skottman, H., Juuti-Uusitalo, K., Hyttinen, J.: Texture descriptors ensembles enable image-based classification of maturation of human stem cell-derived retinal pigmented epithelium. Plos One **11**(2) (2016)

56. Breast cancer histopathological database (breakhis) (2015). http://web.inf.ufpr. br/vri/breast-cancer-database. Accessed 16 May 2017

57. Spanhol, F., Oliveira, L.S., Petitjean, C., Heutte, L.: Breast cancer histopathological image classification using convolutional neural networks. In: International Joint Conference on Neural Networks (IJCNN 2016), Vancouver, Canada (2016)

58. Webmicroscope. EGFR colon TMA stroma LBP classification (2012). http://fimm. webmicroscope.net/Research/Supplements/epistroma. Accessed 16 May 2017

59. Collection of texture in colorectal cancer histology (2016). https://zenodo.org/ record/53169#.WRsdEPmGN0w. Accessed 16 May 2017

60. Kather, J.N., Marx, A., Reyes-Aldasoro, C.C., Schad, L.R., Zöllner, F.G., Weis, C.A.: Continuous representation of tumor microvessel density and detection of angiogenic hotspots in histological whole-side images. Oncotarget **6**(22), 19163– 19176 (2015)

61. Kather, J.N., et al.: Multi-class texture analysis in colorectal cancer histology. Sci. Rep. **6** (2016). 27988

62. Bello-Cerezo, R., Bianconi, F., Cascianelli, S., Fravolini, M.L., di Maria, F., Smeraldi, F.: Hand-designed local image descriptors vs. off-the-shelf CNN-based features for texture classification: an experimental comparison. In: De Pietro, G., Gallo, L., Howlett, R.J., Jain, L.C. (eds.) KES-IIMSS 2017. SIST, vol. 76, pp. 1–10. Springer, Cham (2018). https://doi.org/10.1007/978-3-319-59480-4_1

63. Orjuela, S., Quinones, R., Ortiz-Jaramillo, B., Rooms, F., De Keyser, R., Philips, W.: Improving textures discrimination in the local binary patterns technique by using symmetry & group theory. In: Proceedings of the 17th International Conference on Digital Signal Processing, Corfu, Greece, July 2011. Article no. 6004978

Discriminative Feature Selection by Optimal Manifold Search for Neoplastic Image Recognition

Hayato Itoh[1]($\boxtimes$), Yuichi Mori[2], Masashi Misawa[2], Masahiro Oda[1],
Shin-Ei Kudo[2], and Kensaku Mori[1,3,4]

[1] Graduate School of Informatics, Nagoya University, Nagoya, Japan
hitoh@mori.m.is.nagoya-u.ac.jp
[2] Digestive Disease Center, Showa University Northern Yokohama Hospital,
Yokohama, Japan
[3] Information Technology Center, Nagoya University, Nagoya, Japan
[4] Research Center for Medical Bigdata, National Institute of Informatics,
Tokyo, Japan

Abstract. An endocytoscope provides ultramagnified observation that enables physicians to achieve minimally invasive and real-time diagnosis in colonoscopy. However, great pathological knowledge and clinical experiences are required for this diagnosis. The computer-aided diagnosis (CAD) system is required that decreases the chances of overlooking neoplastic polyps in endocytoscopy. Towards the construction of a CAD system, we have developed texture-feature-based classification between neoplastic and non-neoplastic images of polyps. We propose a feature-selection method that selects discriminative features from texture features for such two-category classification by searching for an optimal manifold. With an optimal manifold, where selected features are distributed, the distance between two linear subspaces is maximised. We experimentally evaluated the proposed method by comparing the classification accuracy before and after the feature selection for texture features and deep-learning features. Furthermore, we clarified the characteristics of an optimal manifold by exploring the relation between the classification accuracy and the output probability of a support vector machine (SVM). The classification with our feature-selection method achieved 84.7% accuracy, which is 7.2% higher than the direct application of Haralick features and SVM.

Keywords: Feature selection · Manifold learning · Texture feature
Convolutional neural network · Endocytoscopic images
Automated pathological diagnosis

1 Introduction

An endocytoscope was recently developed as a new endoscopic imaging modality for minimally-invasive diagnosis. Endocytoscopy enables direct observation

© Springer Nature Switzerland AG 2019
L. Leal-Taixé and S. Roth (Eds.): ECCV 2018 Workshops, LNCS 11132, pp. 534–549, 2019.
https://doi.org/10.1007/978-3-030-11018-5_43

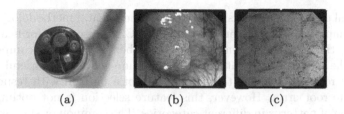

Fig. 1. (a) Endocytoscopy (CF-H290ECI, Olympus, Tokyo). (b) Conventional endoscope observation of a polyp by an endocytoscope. (c) Ultramagnified view by an endocytoscope. Small blue spots represent cell nuclei. In (b) and (c), a polyp's surface is stained by methylene blue. (Color figure online)

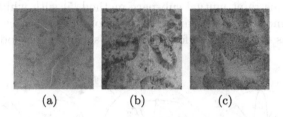

Fig. 2. Typical examples of endocytoscopic images for neoplastic- and non-neoplastic polyps. (a), (b), and (c) are categorised to neoplastic and non-neoplastic polyps.

of the cells and their nuclei on the colon wall at a 500-time-maximum ultramagnification as shown in Fig. 1. However, great pathological knowledge and clinical experiences are necessary to achieve accurate endocytoscopy. Automated pathological diagnosis is required to prevent overlooking neoplastic lesions to support physicians [12,18,19]. This automated pathological diagnosis is achieved by robust two-category image classification. Figure 2 shows typical examples of neoplastic and non-neoplastic endocytoscopic images. The differences between the two categories are observed as differences of textures as shown in Fig. 2.

Robust two-category classification is a fundamental problem in pattern recognition, since multi-category classification is also based on a two-category classification concept. A robust classification can be achieved by an optimal pipeline of feature extraction, feature selection, and the classification of the selected features. A recent approach in image pattern recognition adopt deep learning architectures [15,16,23] as a full pipeline from feature extraction to the classification of extracted features. This deep learning approach can achieve robust multi-category classification with sufficiently large training dataset. However, deep learning fails to find optimal parameters with a small dataset. In medical image classification, collecting a large amount of training data with sufficient patient cases is difficult. Therefore, we have to tackle this problem with medical image classification, especially for a new medical modality, using a handcraft feature and a robust classifier. Previous works [12,18,19,25,26] adopted texture-based feature extraction and support-vector-machine classification without feature selection.

Principal component analysis (PCA) is a fundamental methodology for analysis and compression in data processing [14]. PCA is also used for feature selection [2,20], through which finds a small number of principal components to represent the patterns in a category. This feature selection is useful and optimal for the representation of the distribution of a pattern with respect to the mean square root error. However, this feature selection is not optimal for the classification of patterns in different categories. The common or similar principal components among patterns in different categories can lead to incorrect classification. Fukunaga and Koontz proposed feature selection methods using PCA for clustering [7]. Their method removes the features shared by two categories from the features. The validity of their method is experimentally presented with phantom data, where the means of each category patterns are known. Fukui et al. proposed a constraint mutual subspace method [5] with which they tried to remove the common subspace among patterns of different categories. However, this methods was only designed for the mutual subspace method [17].

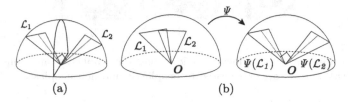

(a)   (b)

Fig. 3. Interpretation of relation between category subspace by canonical angles between them: (a) Linear separation by hyper plane for ideal features; (b) Before and after feature selection.

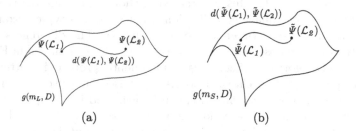

(a)   (b)

Fig. 4. Grassmann distance between two category subspaces. (a) and (b) show Grassmann distance between category subspaces in D-dimensional space for different feature selections ψ and $\tilde{\psi}$. In (a), Grassmann distance for m_L-dimensional subspace is longer than the one for m_S-dimensional subspace in (b). An optimal manifold gives largest distance between two-category subspaces for classification.

We propose a new feature-selection method for the linear classification of neoplastic and non-neoplastic lesions on endocytoscopic images. This selection method is achieved by searching for an optimal manifold for classification.

Figure 3 summarises the concept of our feature-selection method. Triangles $\mathcal{L}_1$ and $\mathcal{L}_2$ represent the linear category subspaces spanned by the features of each category. The ideal discriminative feature gives a hyper-plane between the features of the two categories, as shown in Fig. 3(a). This ideal feature extraction gives robust classification by a linear classifier. The difference between the two category subspaces can be represented by the canonical angle between two subspaces. If a feature contains worthless elements, it gives a common subspace for two categories with small canonical angles. These worthless elements can lead to classification errors. The overlap region of the triangles in Fig. 3(b) shows the common subspace between two categories. For feature selection, we have to find a map Ψ that maximises the canonical angles between two-category subspaces on a manifold as shown in Fig. 3(b). By projection with Ψ, we obtained a discriminative features as shown in Fig. 3(a). To find linear map Ψ, we used feature normalisation [7] and the Grassmann distance [4, 8, 10, 22].

Feature normalisation clarifies the importance of each eigenvector for category representations in PCA [7]. The Grassmann distance represents the difference of two linear subspaces by canonical angles [1, 4, 8, 10, 22, 24]. We obtained discriminative features by selecting the eigenvectors of the normalised features, which give the maximum Grassmann distance between two category subspaces as shown in Fig. 4. Our proposed method can analyse the extracted features and improve the classification accuracy. Furthermore, we integrated our proposed method to the processing flow of the classification shown in Fig. 5 that output the probabilities of each category for practical applications. In such practical applications as computer-aided diagnosis, accurate probabilities for each category are helpful information for physicians during a diagnosis. We evaluated the proposed method and its classification procedure to the classify neoplastic and non-neoplastic colorectal endocytoscopic images in numerical experiments.

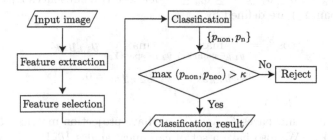

Fig. 5. Processing flow of classification of an endocytoscopic image. We use texture features for feature extraction. Classification is achieved by linear support vector machine with probability estimation. In the classification, we utilise rejection option with estimated probabilities. To selection the discriminative features, we propose a new selection method.

2   Mathematical Preliminaries

2.1   Linear Subspace of a Pattern

We have a set $\{x_i\}_i^N$ of N extracted D-dimensional features from observed patterns $\{\mathcal{X}_i\}_{i=1}^N$ of a category with the condition $d \ll N$. These extracted features span $\mathcal{L} = \mathrm{span}(x_1, \ldots, x_N)$ for a category. We call this linear subspace a category subspace, which is approximated by

$$\mathcal{L} \approx \mathrm{span}(y_1, \ldots, y_m), \tag{1}$$

where $m \leq D$. In such standard approaches as subspace methods [11,17,20,28], we obtain bases $y_i, i = 1, 2, \ldots, m$ from the following eigendecomposition

$$My = \eta y, \quad M = \frac{1}{N} \sum_{i=1}^N x_i x_i^\top. \tag{2}$$

For this eigendecomposition, an eigenvector y_i correspond to an eigenvalue η_i with conditions $\eta_1 \geq \eta_2 \geq \ldots \eta_D$ and $\eta_i \geq 0$. We project an input feature vector x to a linear subspace $\mathrm{span}(y_1, \ldots, y_m)$ by $Y^\top x$, where $Y = [y_1, y_2, \ldots, y_m]$.

2.2   Grassmannian and Canonical Angle

The Grassmannian manifold (Grassmannian) $\mathcal{G}(m, D)$ is the set of m-dimensional linear subspaces of $\mathbb{R}^D$ [8]. An element of $\mathcal{G}(m, D)$ can be represented by an orthogonal matrix Y of size D by m, where Y is comprised of the m basis vectors for a set of patterns in $\mathbb{R}^D$.

Let Y_1 and Y_2 be the orthogonal matrices of size $D \times m$. Canonical angles (principal angles) $0 \leq \theta_1 \leq \cdots \leq \theta_m \leq \frac{\pi}{2}$ between two subspaces $\mathcal{L}_1 = \mathrm{span}(Y_1)$ and $\mathcal{L}_2 = \mathrm{span}(Y_2)$ are defined by

$$\cos \theta_k = \max_{y_{1,k} \in \mathrm{span}(Y_1)} \max_{y_{2,k} \in \mathrm{span}(Y_2)} y_{1,k}^\top y_{2,k}, \tag{3}$$
$$\text{s.t. } y_{1,k}^\top y_{1,i} = 0, \ y_{2,k}^\top y_{2,i} = 0,$$

where $i = 1, 2, \ldots, k - 1$.

For two linear subspaces $\mathcal{L}_1$ and $\mathcal{L}_2$, we have projection matrices $P = Y_1 Y_1^\top$ and $Q = Y_2 Y_2^\top$. We also have a set of canonical angles $\{\theta_k\}_{i=1}^m$ between these two linear subspaces with conditions $\theta_1 \leq \theta_2 \leq \ldots \theta_K$. We obtain the canonical angles from the solution of the eigendecomposition problem

$$PQPu = \lambda u \text{ or } QPQu = \lambda u. \tag{4}$$

The solutions of these eigendecomposition problems are coincident [17]. For the practical computation of canonical angles, we have singular value decomposition

$$Y_1^\top Y_2 = U \Sigma V^\top, \tag{5}$$

where $\boldsymbol{\Sigma} = \operatorname{diag}(\cos\theta_1, \cos\theta_2, \ldots, \cos\theta_m)$ is the diagonal matrix, and $\boldsymbol{U}, \boldsymbol{V} \in \mathbb{R}^{m \times m}$ are the orthogonal matrices. Note that we have the following relation,

$$\lambda_i = \cos^2\theta_i \tag{6}$$

for eigenvalues λ_k, $i = 1, 2, \ldots m$ in the eigendecomposition in Eq. (4). Canonical angles are used to define the geodesic distance on a Grassmannian.

2.3   Grassmannian Distances

For the two points represented by $\boldsymbol{Y}_1$ and $\boldsymbol{Y}_2$ on a Grassmann manifold, we have the following seven distances on the Grassmannian,

1. $d_p(\boldsymbol{Y}_1, \boldsymbol{Y}_2)$: projection metric
2. $d_\mu(\boldsymbol{Y}_1, \boldsymbol{Y}_2)$: mean distance
3. $d_{\min}(\boldsymbol{Y}_1, \boldsymbol{Y}_2)$: minimum canonical angle
4. $d_{\max}(\boldsymbol{Y}_1, \boldsymbol{Y}_2)$: maximum canonical angle
5. $d_{BC}(\boldsymbol{Y}_1, \boldsymbol{Y}_2)$: Binet-Caucy metric
6. $d_g(\boldsymbol{Y}_1, \boldsymbol{Y}_2)$: geodesic distance
7. $d_c(\boldsymbol{Y}_1, \boldsymbol{Y}_2)$: Procrustes (chordal) distance

These seven distances are defined using the canonical angles between two linear subspaces. The projection metric and mean distance are defined by

$$d_p(\boldsymbol{Y}_1, \boldsymbol{Y}_2) = \left(\sum_{i=1}^{m} \sin^2\theta_i\right)^{1/2} = \left(m - \sum_{i=1}^{m} \lambda_i\right)^{1/2} \tag{7}$$

and

$$d_\mu(\boldsymbol{Y}_1, \boldsymbol{Y}_2) = \frac{1}{m}\sum_{i=1}^{m} \sin^2\theta_i = 1 - \frac{1}{m}\sum_{i=1}^{m} \lambda_i. \tag{8}$$

Furthermore, the sines of the maximum and minimum canonical angles

$$d_{\min}(\boldsymbol{Y}_1, \boldsymbol{Y}_2) = \sin\theta_1 = (1 - \lambda_1)^{1/2}, \tag{9}$$

$$d_{\max}(\boldsymbol{Y}_1, \boldsymbol{Y}_2) = \sin\theta_m = (1 - \lambda_m)^{1/2}, \tag{10}$$

are also used as distances on a Grassmannian. Moreover, the Binet-Caucy distance is defined by

$$d_{BQ}(\boldsymbol{Y}_1, \boldsymbol{Y}_2) = \left(1 - \Pi_{i=1}^{m}\cos^2\theta_i\right) = \left(1 - \Pi_{i=1}^{m}\lambda_i\right), \tag{11}$$

where the product of $\cos\theta_i$ represents the similarity between two linear subspaces. Using canonical angles, we have geodesic distance

$$d_g(\boldsymbol{Y}_1, \boldsymbol{Y}_2) = \left(\sum_{i=1}^{m} \theta_i^2\right)^{1/2} = \left(\sum_{i=1}^{m} \left(\arccos\lambda_i^{1/2}\right)^2\right)^{1/2} \tag{12}$$

on a Grassmann manifold. We have two definitions of the Procrustes (chordal) distance,

$$d_C(\boldsymbol{Y_1}, \boldsymbol{Y_2}) = \min_{\boldsymbol{R_1}, \boldsymbol{R_2} \in O(m)} \|\boldsymbol{Y_1 R_1} - \boldsymbol{Y_2 R_2}\|_F = 2 \left(\sum_{i=1}^{m} \sin^2(\theta_i/2) \right)^{1/2}, \quad (13)$$

where $\| \cdot \|_F$ is the Frobenius norm.

2.4   Normalisation of Features

We project the extracted features onto the discriminative feature space for accurate classification. We extract a set of features $\{\boldsymbol{x}_i \in \mathbb{R}^D\}_{i=1}^{N}$ from a set of images with condition $D \ll N$. Let $\boldsymbol{\mu} = \mathrm{E}(\boldsymbol{x}_i)$ be the mean of the features. By setting $\bar{\boldsymbol{x}}_i = \boldsymbol{x}_i - \boldsymbol{\mu}$, we obtain a set of centred features $\{\bar{\boldsymbol{x}}_i\}_{i=1}^{N}$. We assume each image belongs to either category $\mathcal{C}_1$ or $\mathcal{C}_2$. Therefore, set $\{\bar{\boldsymbol{x}}_i\}_{i=1}^{N}$ is divided into two sets $\{\boldsymbol{x}_i^{(1)}\}_{i=1}^{N_1}$ and $\{\boldsymbol{x}_i^{(2)}\}_{i=1}^{N_2}$, where N_1 and N_2, respectively, represent the number of images in the first and second categories.

We define the autocorrelation matrices in the centred feature space as

$$\boldsymbol{A_1} = \frac{1}{N_1} \boldsymbol{X_1 X_1^\top}, \ \boldsymbol{A_2} = \frac{1}{N_2} \boldsymbol{X_2 X_2^\top}, \quad (14)$$

where $\boldsymbol{X_1} = [\boldsymbol{x}_1^{(1)}, \boldsymbol{x}_2^{(1)}, \dots, \boldsymbol{x}_{N_1}^{(1)}]$ and $\boldsymbol{X_2} = [\boldsymbol{x}_1^{(2)}, \boldsymbol{x}_2^{(2)}, \dots, \boldsymbol{x}_{N_2}^{(2)}]$, for the two categories. We define the covariance matrix of all the features as

$$\boldsymbol{C} = P(\mathcal{C}_1) \boldsymbol{A_1} + P(\mathcal{C}_2) \boldsymbol{A_2}, \quad (15)$$

where we set $P(\mathcal{C})_1 = \frac{N_1}{N_1 + N_2}$ and $P(\mathcal{C})_2 = \frac{N_2}{N_1 + N_2}$. Fukunaga [7] used the autocorrelation matrix of all the features instead of $\boldsymbol{C}$ in Eq. (15). Fukunaga [6] used covariance matrices $\boldsymbol{C_1}$ and $\boldsymbol{C_2}$ for the two categories instead of $\boldsymbol{A_1}$ and $\boldsymbol{A_2}$ in Eq. (15). In this manuscript, we adopt covariance matrix $\boldsymbol{C}$ for all features to remove the common features of the two categories. Here, autocorrelation matrices $\boldsymbol{A_1}$ and $\boldsymbol{A_2}$ include the gaps of the means between all the features and each category. The covariance matrix gives the following eigendecomposition problem $\boldsymbol{CV} = \boldsymbol{V\Xi}$, where $\boldsymbol{\Xi} = \mathrm{diag}(\xi_1, \xi_2, \dots, \xi_D)$ consists of eigenvalues ξ_i for $i = 1, 2, \dots, D$ the condition $\xi_1 \geq \xi_2 \geq \dots \geq \xi_D$. The eigendecomposition results derive a whitening matrix $\boldsymbol{W} = \boldsymbol{\Xi}^{-\frac{1}{2}} \boldsymbol{V}^\top$.

Using this whitening matrix and Eq. (15), we obtain the following relation

$$\boldsymbol{WCW}^\top = \boldsymbol{W} P(\mathcal{C}_1) \boldsymbol{A_1 W}^\top + \boldsymbol{W} P(\mathcal{C}_2) \boldsymbol{A_2 W}^\top = \tilde{\boldsymbol{A}}_1 + \tilde{\boldsymbol{A}}_2 = \boldsymbol{I}, \quad (16)$$

where $\boldsymbol{I}$ is an identity matrix. The solutions of the eigenvalue problems

$$\tilde{\boldsymbol{A}}_j \phi_i^{(j)} = \lambda_i^{(j)} \phi_i^{(j)}, \quad (17)$$

where we set $j = 1, 2$, give the bases of two category subspaces. From Eqs. (16) and (17), we have

$$\tilde{\boldsymbol{A}}_2 \phi_i^{(2)} = (\boldsymbol{I} - \tilde{\boldsymbol{A}}_1) \lambda_i \phi_i^{(2)}. \quad (18)$$

This leads $\tilde{A}_1\phi_i^{(2)} = (1 - \lambda_i^{(2)})\phi_i^{(2)}$. These relation give the following relations

$$\phi_i^{(2)} = \phi_{D-i+1}^{(1)} \tag{19}$$

and

$$\lambda_i^{(2)} = 1 - \lambda_{D-i+1}^{(1)}. \tag{20}$$

Equations (19) and (20) show that both eigenvalue problems give the same set of eigenvectors, and corresponding eigenvalues. Note that the two sets of eigenvalues are reversely ordered. The eigenvalue orders in Eq. (20) satisfy

$$1 \geq \lambda_1^{(1)} \geq \lambda_2^{(1)} \geq \cdots \geq \lambda_D^{(1)} \geq 0, \tag{21}$$

$$0 \leq 1 - \lambda_1^{(1)} \leq 1 - \lambda_2^{(1)} \leq \cdots \leq 1 - \lambda_D^{(1)} \leq 1. \tag{22}$$

These relations imply that the eigenvectors corresponding to the large eigenvalues of $\tilde{A}_1$ contribute to represent the subspace for C_1, although they only make minor contribution to the representation for C_2. Therefore, we obtained discriminative features by projecting the features to a linear subspace given by span($\phi_1^{(1)}, \phi_1^{(2)}, \phi_2^{(1)}, \phi_2^{(2)}, \ldots, \phi_d^{(1)}, \phi_d^{(2)}$). We discuss how to decide number d in the next section.

2.5   Linear Classification with Rejection Option

We use a linear support vector machine (SVM) as a classifier. SVM classifies an input feature vector $x \in \mathbb{R}^D$ by sing($f(x)$), where $f(\cdot)$ is a decision function. The parameters and the hyperparameters of this decision function are optimised by a training procedure with training data. We can estimate the probability of belonging to each category with the optimised decision function. For two categories with label $\mathcal{L} \in \{0, 1\}$, we can approximately estimate the probabilities

$$P(\mathcal{L} = 1|x) \approx P(A, B, f(x)) = \frac{1}{1 + \exp(Af(x) + B)}, \tag{23}$$

where A, B are the parameters in Platt's method [21] for category i. $P(\mathcal{L} = 0|x)$ is obtained by $1 - P(\mathcal{L} = 1|x)$. After the training for decision function, we obtain A, B by maximum likelihood estimation with the training dataset. In our method, we represent the non-neoplastic and neoplastic categories by 0 and 1. SVM can output the probabilities [21] p_{non} and p_{nneo} that satisfy $p_{\text{non}} + p_{\text{neo}} = 1$ and $p_{\text{non}}, p_{\text{non}} \in [0, 1]$, for non-neoplastic and neoplastic images. We adopt the rejection option to remove low confident classification [2]. The rejection option discards classifications with low probabilities such that max $(p_{\text{non}}, p_{\text{neo}}) < \kappa$, where criteria κ was decided from preliminary experiments.

3   Feature-Selection Method

We have a set $\{\mathcal{X}_i\}_{i=1}^N$ of three-channel images. We extract a feature vector $x_i \in \mathbb{R}^D$ from each image $\mathcal{X}_i$. As in the same manner of Sect. 2.4, we divide

---

Algorithm 1. Feature-selection method for training data

Input: Two sets of feature vectors $\{x_i^{(1)}\}_{i=1}^{N_1}$ and $\{x_i^{(2)}\}_{i=1}^{N_2}$,
    criteria $\tau_k = 1.0 - 0.01 * k$, $k = 1, 2, \ldots, 50$, a small value ε.
Output: Projected features $\{\check{x}_i^{(1)}\}_{i=1}^{N_1}$ and $\{\check{x}_i^{(2)}\}_{i=1}^{N_2}$, matrices P^* and W.
1. Compute two sets of eigenvectors $\{\phi_i^{(1)}\}_{i=1}^d$ and $\{\phi_i^{(2)}\}_{i=1}^d$.
2. For all τ_k:
    2-1. Select eigenvectors $\{\phi_i^{(1)}\}_{i=1}^{m_k}$ and $\{\phi_i^{(2)}\}_{i=1}^{m_k}$ that
        correspond to eigenvalues larger than τ_k.
    2-2. Construct a matrix $P^{(k)} = [\phi_1^{(1)}, \phi_1^{(2)}, \ldots, \phi_{m_k}^{(1)}, \phi_{m_k}^{(2)}]^\top$.
    2-3. Project all features by $\check{x}_i^{(j)} = P^{(k)} x_i^{(j)}$, where $i = 1, 2, \ldots, N_j$, $j = 1, 2$.
    2-4. Compute eigenvectors $Y_1^{(k)}$ and $Y_2^{(k)}$ for two
        categories by solving the eigenproblem in Eq. (2).
    2-5. Compute Grassmann distance $d(Y_1^{(k)}, Y_2^{(k)})$ between two category subspaces.
    2-6. If $|d(Y_1^{(k)}, Y_2^{(k)}) - d(Y_1^{(k-1)}, Y_2^{(k-1)})| < \varepsilon$, set $P^* = P^{(k)}$, and iteration break.
3. Return projected feature vectors $\{\check{x}_i^{(j)} | \check{x}_i^{(j)} = P^* W x_i^{(j)} \forall i, j\}$, and P^* and W.

$\{x_i\}_{i=1}^N$ to two sets $\{x_i^{(1)}\}_{i=1}^{N_1}$ and $\{x_i^{(2)}\}_{i=1}^{N_2}$, where N_1 and N_2 represent the number of images in the first and second categories.

We find a linear map $\Psi(x) = P^* W(x - \mu)$ by solving

$$\arg \min_P(\text{rank}(P P^\top)) \quad \text{s.t.} \quad \max_P(d(\Psi(Y_1), \Psi(Y_2))) \tag{24}$$

where $d(\cdot, \cdot)$ represents one of the seven Grassmann distances. In this equation, $\max(\cdot)$ returns one or more matrices that give the maximum distance, and $\min(\cdot)$ selects one matrix with the minimum rank from the matrices. The solution is an orthogonal matrix $P^* = [\phi_1^{(1)}, \phi_1^{(2)}, \phi_2^{(1)}, \phi_2^{(2)}, \ldots, \phi_m^{(1)}, \phi_m^{(2)}]^\top$, which is comprised of $2m$ eigenvectors. Algorithm 1, which summarises a procedure to find the P^* using the training data, also returns the selected features for the training data.

4   Numerical Experiments

We evaluated our feature-selection method by applying the image classification of neoplastic and non-neoplastic images of a colon polyp. We used images of the magnified surfaces of polyps captured by an endocytoscope (CF-H290ECI, Olympus, Tokyo) with IRB approval. The neoplastic and non-neoplastic labels of the images ware annotated by expert physicians. The number of images of neoplastic and non-neoplastic polyps is summarised in Table 1. We extracted two kinds of features from these images: the Haralick features [9] and the convolutional neural network (CNN) features [15]. In this section, we first compare the classification accuracy before and after the feature selection for the Haralick features and next compare the classification accuracy before and after the feature selection of the combined Haralick and CNN features. We finally analysed the

Table 1. Dataset details: 14,840 training and 4,126 test images.

Category	♯ training	♯ test	♯ total
Neoplasia	7,800	1,925	9,725
Non-neoplasia	7,040	2,201	9,241

Table 2. Dimension and classification accuracy for extracted features with SVM.

	Haralick	CNN	Haralick+CNN
Dimension	312	576	888
Accuracy [%]	77.3	75.6	78.3

Table 3. Dimension and classification accuracy of selected features of Haralick feature for each Grassmann distance.

	d_g, d_p, d_c	d_{BC}, d_{max}, d_{min}	d_μ
Dimension	312	60	96
	($\tau = 0.5$)	($\tau = 0.99$)	($\tau = 0.77$)
Accuracy [%]	77.5	76.4	78.0

Table 4. Dimension and classification accuracy of selected features of combination of Haralick and CNN features for each Grassmann distance.

	d_g, d_p, d_c	d_{BC}, d_{max}	d_{min}, d_μ
Dimension	888	74	102
	($\tau = 0.5$)	($\tau = 0.99$)	($\tau = 0.97$)
Accuracy [%]	79.7	78.4	77.7

relation between the output probability and the accuracy with rejection option. The relation clarifies the validity of our feature-selection method as a manifold optimisation. In the final analysis, we also show the performance of two-category classification with a rejection option.

In these evaluations, we used a SVM [27] for the classifications and trained it by the training data and the best hyperparameters. We obtained the best hyperparameters of the SVM by five-fold cross validation with the training data. For a practical computation of SVM, we used libsvm [3]. We note that kernel SVM with a radius basis function gives less classification accuracy than the linear SVM for the endocytoscopic images in our preliminary experiments. The classification accuracy of the original Haralick, CNN and their combined features without feature selection is summarised in Table 2.

4.1   Haralick Feature

The Haralick feature represents the texture information measured by fourteen statistical categories of a gray-level co-occurrence matrix. In this case, we used thirteen categories for eight directions with three scales. To compute the statistics, we used contrast normalisation for each local region for the achievement of robustness against illumination changes. We then extracted 312-dimensional Haralick feature vector for an image, each element of which is normalised to a range of $[0, 1]$. We applied the proposed feature-selection method to the normalised Haralick features.

Figures 7(a), and (b) and (c) show the eigenvalues of the whitened autocorrelation matrices for two categories, and the Grassmann distances. Table 3 summarises the dimensions and classification accuracy for each feature selection with respect to seven Grassmann distances.

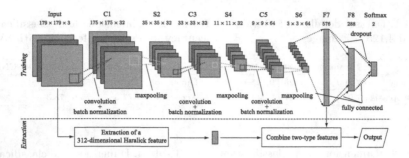

Fig. 6. Architecture of convolutional neural network for feature extraction.

4.2 Combination of Haralick and CNN Features

We combined the Haralick and CNN features into a single feature vector. Figure 6 illustrates the architecture of our CNN. Its settings were decided by preliminary experiments [12], where we compared the several parameter settings with AlexNet [15], VGG Net [23], and their modified versions. Our shallow architecture gave the best classification accuracy among them. Before the extraction of the CNN features, we trained the CNN with training data from scratch. We applied batch normalisation and drop out to convolutional layers and full connected layers for the training. We used the values in full connection layer F7 in Fig. 6 for the feature extraction. Each element of the extracted CNN feature was normalised to a range of $[0, 1]$. For the CNN implementation, we used the Caffe platform [13] and combined the normalised Haralick and normalised CNN features as 888-dimensional column vectors.

We applied the proposed method to these normalised combined features. Figures 7(d), and (e) and (f) show the eigenvalues of the whitened autocorrelation matrices for two categories, and the Grassmann distances. Table 4 summarises the dimensions of the selected feature and classification accuracy for the selection with respect to seven Grassmann distances.

4.3 Analysis of an Optimal Manifold

We evaluated the classification accuracy with respect to the divided range of the output probabilities. The relation between the classification accuracy and the output probability represents the characteristics of the optimal manifold given by our feature selection. Figure 8(a) illustrates the distributions of the output probabilities for the original Haralick features and the selected features. Table 5 summarises the accuracy for each range of the output probabilities for the original Haralick features and the selected features. We also evaluated the classification accuracy with the rejection option of $\kappa \in \{0.50, 0.55, \ldots, 0.90\}$. The rejection rate is the ratio of the rejected images in the test data. The classification results with the rejection option are summarised in Fig. 8(b). We respectively obtained classification accuracy of 82.1%, 82.9% and 84.7% for the original Haralick feature, the selected features of the Haralick and the combined features

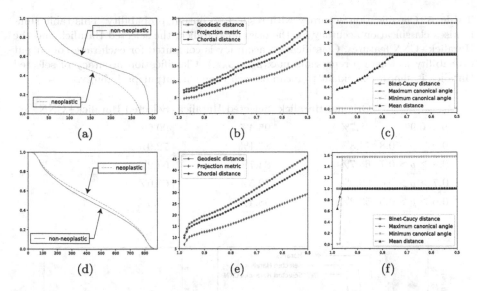

Fig. 7. Eigenvalues and Grassmann distance in feature selection: upper and lower rows represent results for Haralick features and combined features, respectively. (a) and (d) show eigenvalues of $\tilde{A}_1$ and $\tilde{A}_1$ for non-neoplastic and neoplastic images. Horizontal and vertical axes represent indices of eigenvalues and eigenvalues. (b), (c), (e) and (f) summarise Grassmann distance after projection with respect to P given by a criteria τ. Horizontal and vertical axes represent τ and Grassmann distance.

with the same rejection rate of about 20%. Note that the percentage of inappropriate images in practical diagnosis is close to 20–30%. In these cases, we set κ to 0.70, 0.60 and 0.72 for them. Figure 9 shows examples of rejected images in the classification.

5   Discussion

The curves shown in Fig. 7(a) imply that a small number of eigenvectors is discriminative for classification, since almost all the eigenvalues are close to 0.5. Figures 7(b) and (c) imply that d_μ gives the largest distance with the fewest selected eigenvectors. The accuracy is improved after the selection based on d_μ as shown in Table 3. The dimension of the selected features is 30% of the dimension of an original Haralick feature.

The curves shown in Fig. 7(d) imply that there are no particular discriminative eigenvectors, since they are distributed almost uniformly from zero to one. In Table 4, d_g, d_p, and d_c give the largest distance with all the eigenvectors. In this case, features are just whitened and used for classification. In both the cases of the Haralick and the combined features, our proposed method found discriminative features and improved the classification accuracy.

Table 5. Classification accuracy with respect to output probability. This table summarises classification accuracy for the original Haralick, the selected Haralick and the Haralick+CNN features. Classification accuracy is computed for each range of output probability p, where p represents $\max(p_{non}, p_{neo})$. Classification accuracy of selected Haralick is almost coincident to mean of each range of output probability.

	Original Haralick	Selected Haralick	Selected Haralick+CNN
$p > 0.9$	88.7%	95.4%	90.0%
$0.9 \geq p > 0.8$	74.3%	87.1%	72.0%
$0.8 \geq p > 0.7$	68.7%	84.7%	64.2%
$0.7 \geq p > 0.6$	60.5%	72.5%	61.0%
$0.6 \geq p > 0.5$	53.2%	58.4%	50.0%

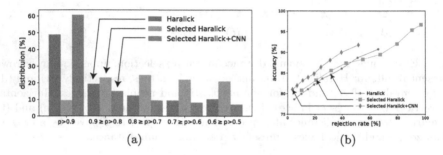

(a)   (b)

Fig. 8. Analysis of optimal manifold. (a) Distributions of output probabilities for original and selected features: Figure illustrates probability distributions of the original Haralick, the selected Haralick and the Haralick+CNN features. Vertical axis represents percentage of output probabilities for each range. Horizontal axis represent divided rages. In this figure, p is given as $\max(p_{non}, p_{neo})$. (b) Receiver operating characteristic (ORC) curves for classification accuracy and rejection rate: Vertical and horizontal axes represent classification accuracy and rejection rate for original Haralick, selected Haralick and Haralick+CNN features.

The results summarised in Fig. 8(b) indicate that the rejection option improved the classification accuracy. The rejection option correctly removed the low-confident classification in both the cases of the Haralick and the combined features. Table 5 also supports the validity of the rejection option. We can observe low classification accuracy for low output probabilities. Figure 9 shows that the rejected images are inappropriate due to bad observation conditions: over staining, bad illumination, and a lack of discriminative texture.

The mean distance gives the best feature selection for the Haralick feature. In this case, the distributions of the output probabilities were characteristic. We have low distribution for $p > 0.9$ and medium distribution for $0.6 \geq p > 0.5$. The highest distribution is given for $0.8 \geq p > 0.7$. For these distributions, the output probability approximated the classification accuracy well, as shown gray

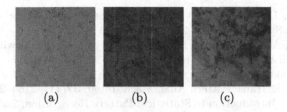

(a)   (b)   (c)

Fig. 9. Examples of rejected endocytoscopic images in classification: (a) insufficient texture for classification; (b) bad (too dark) illumination; (c) over staining of a polyp. These images were labelled as inappropriate for practical diagnosis. In practice, medical doctors also recognised them as inappropriate.

in Table 5. This characteristic of the relation between classification accuracy and output probability suggests the validity of the obtained manifold. In the case of the combined features, we did not observe the same characteristic even though the selected combined features achieved the highest classification accuracy.

6   Conclusions

We proposed a feature-selection method that improves the classification accuracy of two categories by an optimal manifold search for classification. We experimentally evaluated the proposed method by comparing the classification accuracy before and after feature selection for about 19,000 endocytoscopic images. The experimental results showed the validity of our proposed method with the improvement of classification accuracy. Furthermore, we experimentally demonstrated the validity of the obtained optimal manifold by exploring the relation between output probability and classification accuracy. The output probability is helpful information for practical diagnosis. Moreover, we achieved robust classification with our feature-selection method and a linear classifier with a rejection option. The classification accuracy was 84.7% with a rejection rate of 20%, in which the classification accuracy was 7.2% higher than the classification with the original Haralick feature and SVM.

Acknowledgements. Parts of this research were supported by the Research on Development of New Medical Devices from the Japan Agency for Medical Research and Development (No. 18hk0102034h0103), and MEXT KAKENHI (No. 26108006, No. 17H00867).

References

1. Absil, P.A., Mahony, R., Sepulchre, R.: Optimization Algorithms on Matrix Manifolds. Princeton University Press, Princeton (2009)
2. Bishop, C.M.: Pattern Recognition and Machine Learning. Springer, New York (2006)

3. Chang, C.C., Lin, C.J.: LIBSVM: a library for support vector machines. ACM Trans. Intell. Syst. Technol. **2**, 27:1–27:27 (2011)
4. Edelman, A., Arias, T., Smith, S.: The geometry of algorithms with orthogonality constraints. SIAM J. Matrix Anal. Appl. **20**(2), 303–353 (1998)
5. Fukui, K., Maki, A.: Difference subspace and its generalization for subspace-based methods. IEEE Trans. Pattern Anal. Mach. Intell. **37**(11), 2164–2177 (2015)
6. Fukunaga, K.: Introduction to Statistical Pattern Recognition, 2nd edn. Academic Press, London (1990)
7. Fukunaga, K., Koontz, W.L.G.: Application of the Karhunen-Loéve expansion to feature selection and ordering. IEEE Trans. Comput. **C–19**(4), 311–318 (1970)
8. Hamm, J., Lee, D.: Grassmann discriminant analysis: a unifying view on subspace-based learning. In: Proceedings of International Conference on Machine Learning, pp. 376–383 (2008)
9. Haralick, R.M., Shanmugam, K., Dinstein, I.: Textural features for image classification. IEEE Trans. Syst., Man, Cybern. **3**(6), 610–621 (1973). https://doi.org/10.1109/TSMC.1973.4309314
10. Harandi, M., Sanderson, C., Shen, C., Lovell, B.: Dictionary learning and sparse coding on Grassmann manifolds: an extrinsic solution. In: Proceedings of The IEEE International Conference on Computer Vision, pp. 3120–3127 (2013)
11. Iijima, T.: Theory of pattern recognition. In: Electronics and Communications in Japan, pp. 123–134 (1963)
12. Itoh, H., Mori, Y., Misawa, M., Oda, M., Kudo, S.E., Mori, K.: Cascade classification of endocytoscopic images of colorectal lesions for automated pathological diagnosis. In: Proceedings of SPIE Medical Imaging (2018, in Press)
13. Jia, Y., et al.: Caffe: convolutional architecture for fast feature embedding. arXiv preprint arXiv:1408.5093 (2014)
14. Jollife, I.T.: Principal Component Analysis. Springer, New York (2002). https://doi.org/10.1007/b98835
15. Krizhevsky, A., Sutskever, I., Hinton, G.: ImageNet classification with deep convolutional neural networks. In: Proceedings of International Conference on Neural Information Processing Systems, vol. 1, pp. 1097–1105 (2012)
16. Lecun, Y., et al.: Gradient-based learning applied to document recognition. Proc. IEEE **86**(11), 2278–2324 (1998)
17. Maeda, K.: From the subspace methods to the mutual subspace method. In: Cipolla, R., Battiato, S., Farinella, G.M. (eds.) Computer Vision. SCI, vol. 285, pp. 135–156. Springer, Berlin (2010). https://doi.org/10.1007/978-3-642-12848-6_5
18. Mori, Y., et al.: Impact of an automated system for endocytoscopic diagnosis of small colorectal lesions: an international web-based study. Endoscopy **48**, 1110–1118 (2016)
19. Mori, Y., et al.: Novel computer-aided diagnostic system for colorectal lesions by using endocytoscopy. Gastrointest. Endosc. **81**, 621–629 (2015)
20. Oja, E.: Subspace Methods of Pattern Recognition. Research Studies Press, Boston (1983)
21. Platt, J.C.: Probabilistic outputs for support vector machines and comparisons to regularized likelihood methods. Adv. Large Margin Classif. **10**, 61–74 (1999). MIT Press
22. Shigenaka, R., Raytchev, B., Tamaki, T., Kaneda, K.: Face sequence recognition using Grassmann distances and Gassmann kernels. In: Proceedings of International Joint Conference on Neural Networks, pp. 1–7 (2012)

23. Simonyan, K., Zisserman, A.: Very deep convolutional networks for large-scale image recognition. In: Proceedings of International Conference on Learning Representations (2015)
24. Slama, R., Wannous, H., Daoudi, M., Srivastava, A.: Accurate 3D action recognition using learning on the Grassmann manifold. Pattern Recognit. **48**(2), 556–567 (2015)
25. Tamaki, T., et al.: Computer-aided colorectal tumor classification in NBI endoscopy using CNN features. In: Proceedings of Korea-Japan Joint Workshop on Frontiers of Computer Vision (2016)
26. Tamaki, T., et al.: Computer-aided colorectal tumor classification in NBI endoscopy using local features. Mediacal Image Anal. **17**, 78–100 (2013)
27. Vapnik, V.N.: Statistical Learning Theory. Wiley, New York (1998)
28. Watanabe, S., Pakvasa, N.: Subspace method of pattern recognition. In: Proceedings of of the 1st International Joint Conference of Pattern Recognition (1973)

Fast, Visual and Interactive Semi-supervised Dimensionality Reduction

Dimitris Spathis[1,2], Nikolaos Passalis[1(✉)], and Anastasios Tefas[1]

[1] Aristotle University of Thessaloniki, Thessaloniki, Greece
passalis@csd.auth.gr
[2] University of Cambridge, Cambridge, UK

Abstract. Recent advances in machine learning allow us to analyze and describe the content of high-dimensional data ranging from images and video to text and audio data. In order to visualize that data in 2D or 3D, usually Dimensionality Reduction (DR) techniques are employed. Most of these techniques produce static projections without taking into account corrections from humans or other data exploration scenarios. In this work, we propose a novel interactive DR framework that is able to learn the optimal projection by exploiting the user interactions with the projected data. We evaluate the proposed method under a widely used interaction scenario in multidimensional projection literature, i.e., project a subset of the data, rearrange them better in classes, and then project the rest of the dataset, and we show that it greatly outperforms competitive baseline and state-of-the-art techniques, while also being able to readily adapt to the computational requirements of different applications.

Keywords: Interactive dimensionality reduction
Similarity-embeddings

1 Introduction

Recent advances in statistical machine learning allow us to tackle hard real-world problems such as machine translation, speech recognition, image captioning and developing self-driving cars [1]. In order to train machine learning models for the aforementioned tasks huge amounts of data are required. However, the process of data collection and processing is costly since human annotators must validate the *ground truth* of each dataset. This issue is further aggravated by the limited involvement of domain experts, who are also potential users of such systems, in the training process [2].

Interactive systems that learn by users have been proposed during the last decade for applications like image segmentation [3]. While these systems allowed to manipulate the input or some parameters of the model, they rarely offered

© Springer Nature Switzerland AG 2019
L. Leal-Taixé and S. Roth (Eds.): ECCV 2018 Workshops, LNCS 11132, pp. 550–563, 2019.
https://doi.org/10.1007/978-3-030-11018-5_44

ways to interact with the data points *per se*. To further increase the involvement of end-users in training machine learning systems, we also have to think about the interface and cognitive load we provide them with. In this work we research on dimensionality reduction techniques, which provide ways of projecting high-dimensional data in 2D. While dimensionality reduction is used for many purposes, such as to reduce storage space and preprocessing time, we focus on its usage for interactive visualization. By visualizing the data in a two-dimensional (2D) or three-dimensional (3D) space, we make it easier for humans to understand the structure of data in a manner that feels natural.

For a dataset that consists of N n-dimensional points $\mathbf{p}_i \in \mathbb{R}^n$, dimensionality reduction (DR) can be defined as a function which maps each point $\mathbf{p}_i \in \mathbb{R}^n$ to a low-dimensional point $\mathbf{q}_i \in \mathbb{R}^m$:

$$f_{\mathbf{W}} : \mathbb{R}^n \to \mathbb{R}^m. \tag{1}$$

Here, n is typically large (from tens to thousands of dimensions), m represents number of dimensions in the low-dimensional space, typically 2 or 3, while $\mathbf{W}$ denotes the parameters of the function used to perform the projection.

Even though many dimensionality reduction techniques leverage different concepts, most of them share a common property: the objective function used to optimize the final projection is a linear combination of pairwise distances between the data points. However, this renders most of the existing dimensionality reduction techniques prone to outliers, while increases the difficulty of interacting with the data since it is not always straightforward to manipulate the distance between different points (there is no universally small or large distance). The aforementioned limitations highlights the need for methods that use bounded similarity metrics instead of unbounded distance metrics. An illustrative example is the recent success of t-SNE [4], which transforms distances to probabilities using a non-linearity (Gaussian kernel). That way it effectively addresses the so-called *crowding problem* [4]. In this work, another recently proposed powerful similarity-based dimensionality method, the Similarity Embedding Framework (SEF) [5], is adapted towards interactive visualization tasks.

The main contribution of this paper is the extension of the Similarity Embedding Framework (SEF) towards efficiently handing interactive visualization tasks for semi-supervised learning. To this end, we adopt a common interaction scenario in multidimensional projection literature. First, a subset of the data, called control points, is projected, then the user rearrange them better in classes or clusters, and finally the rest of the dataset is projected based on that manipulation. The proposed method is evaluated on four datasets from a diverse range of domains and it is demonstrated that it outperforms the other evaluated baseline and state-of-the-art methods. The proposed approach can be combined with any differentiable projection function, ranging from fast and lightweight linear projection functions to more powerful kernel projections and deep neural networks. This allows the proposed method to readily adapt to different use cases, e.g., a linear projection function can be used for providing lightweight interactive projections on mobile devices with limited computing power or used on the client-side of a web application, while a more powerful and complex neural network can be used for scientific visualization tasks, e.g., visualizing and interacting with genome data [6,7], when more powerful infrastructure is available.

The rest of the paper is structured as follows. First, the related work is briefly discussed and compared to the proposed approach in Sect. 2. Then the proposed approach is presented in detail (Sect. 3) and evaluated (Sect. 4). Finally, conclusions are drawn and future work is discussed in Sect. 5.

2   Related Work

Popular dimensionality reduction techniques include linear methods, such as Principal Components Analysis (PCA) and Linear Discriminant Analysis (LDA) [8], and non-linear ones, such as Multidimensional Scaling (MDS) [9], t-Distributed Stochastic Neighbor Embedding (t-SNE) [4], and Uniform Manifold Approximation and Projection (UMAP) [10].

A group of literature (*multidimensional projection*) focuses on observation-level interaction [11] and uses some seeding direct manipulation points (also called *"control points"*), which are a subset of original data points. The intuition goes that by manipulating a subset of data points, a mapping function is (implicitly or explicitly) learned. Then, this function is used (or approximated) to project the rest of the dataset. Numerous approaches related to control-point manipulation have been suggested. The *Local Affine Multidimensional Projection* (LAMP) starts by projecting a subset of control points and then interpolates the remaining points through orthogonal affine mappings, using the Singular Value Decomposition (SVD) method [12]. The *Part-Linear Multidimensional Projection* (PLMP) [13] allows for scaling to big datasets by first constructing a linear map of the control points using *Force Scheme* [14]. Next, this mapping is used to project the remaining points. Finally, the *Kernel-based Linear Projection* (KELP) [15], which is a recent state-of-the-art interactive visualization method, allows for visualizing how *kernel functions* project the data in high-dimensional spaces, while allowing for interacting with the learned projection.

To the best of our knowledge the proposed method is the first interactive visualization method that uses similarity measures to extract information for users' interactions with the data and then learns a projection function by exploiting this information. Building upon the SEF allows for better handling possible outliers and provides an intuitive way for users to perform direct manipulation of data points. Furthermore, the proposed method can be used with fast linear projection functions, that can be readily implemented on mobile devices or other systems with limited computational power, while at the same time providing high-quality and responsive interactive projections. Finally, the proposed method can be initialized by cloning any of the existing visualization or DR methods for providing the initial control points, significantly increasing its flexibility (note that even methods that do not provide out-of-sample extensions, such as t-SNE, can be readily used for the initialization).

3 Proposed Method

First we briefly review the Similarity Embedding Framework [5], upon which the proposed method is built. Then, we derive and discuss the proposed fast interactive data visualization method.

Let $S(\mathbf{x}_i, \mathbf{x}_j)$ be the pairwise similarity between the data points $\mathbf{x}_i$ and $\mathbf{x}_j$. Note that a similarity metric S is a bounded function that ranges between 0 and 1 and expresses the proximity between two points. Then, the similarity matrix of the projected data is defined as $[\mathbf{P}]_{i,j} = S(f_{DR}(\mathbf{x}_i), f_{DR}(\mathbf{x}_j))$, where i is a row and j is a column of this matrix and f_{DR} is the projection function.

SEF's main goal is to learn a projection in which the similarities in the low-dimensional space, i.e., in our case the visual space, are as close as possible to a selected "target". The target similarity matrix $\mathbf{T}$ is a square matrix that can be the result of many methods, such as direct manipulation of data points (as in out case), or other DR techniques (if we want to mimic them), such as PCA, LDA, t-SNE, etc. In order to learn the projection function $f_{DR}(\mathbf{x})$ we optimize the following objective function:

$$J_s = \frac{1}{2 \parallel \mathbf{M} \parallel_1} \sum_{i \neq j}^{N} [\mathbf{M}]_{i,j}([\mathbf{P}]_{i,j} - [\mathbf{T}]_{i,j})^2, \tag{2}$$

where $\mathbf{M}$ is a matrix acting as a weighting mask defining the importance of attaining the target similarity of the data and $\parallel \mathbf{M} \parallel_1$ is the l_1 norm of matrix $\mathbf{M}$. When each data point pair achieves its target similarity, the objective function (2) is minimized, while when a pair has different similarity from its target, it is getting penalized.

Although $\mathbf{T}$ can be any target that we want to achieve during the projection, we use the Gaussian kernel (also known as Heat kernel) to define the similarity between the projected points, i.e.:

$$S(\mathbf{x}_i, \mathbf{x}_j) = exp(- \parallel \mathbf{x}_i - \mathbf{x}_j \parallel_2^2 / \sigma_p), \tag{3}$$

where σ_p acts a scaling factor. Therefore, the final similarity matrix $\mathbf{P}$ is defined as:

$$[\mathbf{P}]_{i,j} = exp(- \parallel f_{DR}(\mathbf{x}_i) - f_{DR}(\mathbf{x}_j) \parallel_2^2 / \sigma_p), \tag{4}$$

Note that among the options that the SEF provides, is to clone existing DR techniques. Let $c(\mathbf{x})$ be a technique to be cloned. Then, SEF can mimic $c(\mathbf{x})$ by setting the target matrix as:

$$[\mathbf{T}]_{i,j} = exp(-\frac{\parallel c(\mathbf{x}_i) - c(\mathbf{x}_j) \parallel_2^2}{\sigma_{copy}}), \tag{5}$$

where σ_{copy} is the scaling factor used to calculate the similarities between the low-dimensional points, as projected using the techniques that is to be cloned. This approach can be used to initialize the employed projection function for providing the initial control points. Note the great flexibility of the proposed method that can clone virtually any visualization or DR method, including methods that do not provide out-of-sample-extensions, such as t-SNE.

The projection function f_{DR} could be defined in multiple ways, ranging from simple fast linear transformations to non-linear methods, such as kernel projections and deep neural networks. In order to minimize the loss in objective function (2), gradient descent is used. Therefore, it is required to calculate the derivative of the objective function J_s with respect to the parameters of each projection.

One of the simplest projection methods is the linear transformation of the input space, such that $f_{DR}(\mathbf{x}) = \mathbf{W}^T\mathbf{x}$, where $\mathbf{W}$ is the projection matrix. Let the relationship between the original data $\mathbf{X}$ and the projected $\mathbf{Y}$ be that of $\mathbf{y}_i = f_{DR}(\mathbf{x}_i)$. The derivative of the objective function J_s when a linear transformation is used is calculated as:

$$\frac{\partial J_s}{\partial [\mathbf{W}]_{kt}} = \frac{1}{\parallel \mathbf{M} \parallel_1} \sum_{i=1}^{N} \sum_{j=1}^{N} [\mathbf{M}]_{i,j}([\mathbf{P}]_{i,j} - [\mathbf{T}]_{i,j}) \frac{\partial [\mathbf{P}]_{i,j}}{\partial [\mathbf{W}]_{kt}}, \tag{6}$$

where

$$\frac{\partial [\mathbf{P}]_{i,j}}{\partial [\mathbf{W}]_{kt}} = -\frac{2}{\sigma_p}[\mathbf{P}]_{i,j}([\mathbf{Y}]_{it} - [\mathbf{Y}]_{jt})([\mathbf{X}]_{ik} - [\mathbf{X}]_{jk}). \tag{7}$$

The objective function (2) is optimized using gradient descent:

$$\Delta \mathbf{W} = -\eta \frac{\partial J}{\partial \mathbf{W}}, \tag{8}$$

where η is the learning rate. In this work the Adam algorithm is used for the optimization [16], since it has been proved to be fast and reliable.

On the other hand, kernel methods are known to provide superior solutions, since they transform the input space into a higher dimensional one in order to solve the problem in a linear manner there. Let $\boldsymbol{\Phi} = \phi(\mathbf{X})$ be the matrix of data in the high dimensional space (also known as Hilbert space), where $\phi(\mathbf{x})$ is a function that projects the data in a higher dimensional space. In a similar way with the linear version, we seek to learn a linear mapping from the Hilbert space into the visual space. We use the Representer theorem to express the matrix $\mathbf{W}$ as a linear combination of the training data $\mathbf{X}$:

$$\mathbf{W} = \phi(\mathbf{X})^T = \boldsymbol{\Phi}^T \mathbf{A}, \tag{9}$$

where $\mathbf{A}$ is the coefficient matrix of the linear combination. Therefore, the final projection is derived as:

$$\mathbf{Y}^T = \mathbf{W}^T \boldsymbol{\Phi}^T = \mathbf{A}^T \boldsymbol{\Phi}\boldsymbol{\Phi}^T = \mathbf{A}^T \mathbf{K}, \tag{10}$$

where $\mathbf{K} = \boldsymbol{\Phi}\boldsymbol{\Phi}^T$ is the kernel matrix, i.e., it contains the inner products of data in the high-dimensional space. Similar to most kernel techniques, we exploit the so-called *kernel trick*, meaning that we can calculate the matrix $\mathbf{K}$ without explicitly calculating the inner products in Hilbert space. In this work, we use the popular RBF kernel:

$$[\mathbf{K}]_{i,j} = exp(\| \mathbf{x}_i - \mathbf{x}_j \|_2^2 / \gamma^2). \tag{11}$$

Compared to the linear version we have to learn the matrix $\mathbf{A}$ instead of the matrix $\mathbf{W}$. Regarding the optimization, the derivative $\frac{\partial[\mathbf{P}]_{i,j}}{\partial[\mathbf{A}]_{kt}}$ is similarly calculated:

$$\frac{\partial J}{\partial[\mathbf{A}]_{kt}} = \frac{1}{\|\mathbf{M}\|_1} \sum_{i=1}^{N} \sum_{j=1}^{N} [\mathbf{M}]_{ij}([\mathbf{P}]_{ij} - [\mathbf{T}]_{ij}) \frac{\partial[\mathbf{P}]_{ij}}{\partial[\mathbf{A}]_{kt}}, \tag{12}$$

where

$$\frac{\partial[\mathbf{P}]_{ij}}{\partial[\mathbf{A}]_{kt}} = -\frac{2}{\sigma_P}[\mathbf{P}]_{ij}([\mathbf{Y}]_{it} - [\mathbf{Y}]_{jt})([\mathbf{K}]_{ik} - [\mathbf{K}]_{jk}).$$

Algorithm 1. Interactive Similarity-based Dimensionality Reduction Learning Algorithm

---

Input: A matrix $\mathbf{X} = [\mathbf{x}_i, ..., \mathbf{x}_N]$ of N data points, the subset of the control points
$\quad \mathbf{X}_s$, and a technique $s(\mathbf{x})$ that can be used for initializing the projection
Output: Projected dataset $\widetilde{\mathbf{Y}}$.
1: **procedure** INTERACTIVEDRLEARNING
2: $\quad T \leftarrow$ clone $(s(\mathbf{X}_s))$ $\quad \triangleright$ Clone Force Scheme, t-SNE, or any other DR technique
$\quad$ using (5).
3: $\quad \mathbf{W} \, or \, \mathbf{A} \leftarrow$ SimilarityEmbeddingLearning$(\mathbf{X}_s, T)$ $\triangleright$ Learn projection using (6).
4: $\quad \mathbf{Y}_s \leftarrow$ project $(\mathbf{X}_s)$ $\triangleright$ Project control points using projection matrix $\mathbf{W}$ or $\mathbf{A}$.
5: $\quad \widetilde{\mathbf{Y}}_s \leftarrow$ manipulate $(\mathbf{Y}_s)$ $\quad \triangleright$ Adjust control points on interactive scatter plot.
6: $\quad \widetilde{T} \leftarrow$ clone $(\widetilde{\mathbf{Y}}_s)$ $\qquad\qquad\qquad\qquad\qquad \triangleright$ Clone control points using (5).
7: $\quad \widetilde{\mathbf{W}} \, or \, \widetilde{\mathbf{A}} \leftarrow$ SimilarityEmbeddingLearning$(\widetilde{\mathbf{Y}}_s, \widetilde{T})$ $\triangleright$ Learn projection using (6).
8: $\quad \widetilde{\mathbf{Y}} \leftarrow$ project $(\mathbf{X})$ $\triangleright$ Project original dataset using projection matrix $\widetilde{\mathbf{W}}$ or $\widetilde{\mathbf{A}}$.
9: **return** the projected dataset $\widetilde{\mathbf{Y}}$

The complete proposed interactive dimensionality reduction learning algorithm is summarized in Algorithm 1. More formally, let $\mathbf{X} = [\mathbf{x}_i, \dots, \mathbf{x}_N]$ be the data matrix (in the original feature space) and $\mathbf{X}_s = [\mathbf{x}_{s_i}, \dots, \mathbf{x}_{s_{N_i}}]$ a subset of the data that is used as control points. Let $\mathbf{Y}_s$ be the projection of control points $\mathbf{X}_s$ in the visual space and $\mathbf{Y}$ the final projection of $\mathbf{X}$ in the visual space. First, the projection is initialized by cloning an existing technique (lines 2–3). The user interacts and manipulates the control points $\mathbf{Y}_s$ and their respective coordinates producing $\widetilde{\mathbf{Y}}_s$ (lines 4–5). Finally, the previous projection is optimized according to the user's interaction (lines 6–7) and the whole dataset is visualized by calculating $\widetilde{\mathbf{Y}}$ (line 8). Note that tilde'd characters are used to denote the results after the manipulation.

It worth noting the great flexibility of the proposed approach. The method can be initialized by cloning any of the existing visualization or DR methods, e.g., t-SNE, UMAP, etc. Then, any differentiable projection function can be used to project the data into the lower dimensional space. The complexity of the projection function can be adapted to the needs of each application, as it was already mentioned before. For example, a linear projection function can be used for mobile devices, while more powerful non-linear projection functions can be used when more computational resources are available. Note that the complexity of kernel methods can be also readily reduced using various methods, such as using low-rank Nyström approximations [17]. Furthermore, the optimization can be adapted to the available memory by using small batches that fit in memory instead of computing the whole similarity matrix described in (4). Note that in this case the samples must be appropriately shuffled before each optimization epoch to ensure that different data pairs are used for the optimization.

4   Experiments

For evaluating the proposed techniques, the following datasets from a wide range of domains are used: a handwritten digit recognition dataset (MNIST) [18], an outdoor image segmentation dataset (Segmentation) [19], a breast cancer diagnosis dataset (Cancer) [19] and a chemical–wine recognition dataset (Wine) [19]. The used datasets are summarized in Table 1.

Table 1. Description of the datasets used for the conducted experiments.

Dataset	Size	Dimensions
MNIST	60000	784
Segmentation	2100	19
Cancer	569	30
Wine	178	13

To ensure a fair comparison with other techniques proposed in the literature we use the same control points and the same manipulations for all the evaluated methods. That is, the same control points after the user's manipulations are fed into the proposed technique and the other evaluated techniques, i.e., the LAMP, the PLMP and the KELP. The public available implementation of each of these techniques was used in the conducted experiments, while the default parameter selection procedure was used. Also, the number of iterations of our optimization is fixed to 500. By inspecting the loss minimization curve during the experiments though, we saw that it converges way before the 500th iteration most of the times. With that in mind, our computation time could be even lower.

In the conducted experiments we estimate the class separation, clustering assignment, and neighbor error. The class separation is evaluated with the nearest centroid algorithm. Clustering assignment is measured with the Silhouette coefficient [20], that measures the cohesion and separation between grouped data. In order to visualize the neighbor error per data point, we calculate the 10 neighbors of each point in the visual space and we sum their Euclidean distance in the high-dimensional space. This score is then normalized to [0,1], so that a point that its 2D neighbors are far in the feature space, gets a high error close to 1.

Table 2. Mean classification precision of projected datasets after manipulation of control points. Best results marked bold. Standard deviation of 10 runs in parenthesis.

Data	Initialization	Nearest Centroid			Proposed	
		KELP	LAMP	PLMP	Linear	Kernel
Wine	PCA	66.11 (6.71)	59.86 (10.42)	58.79 (9.93)	**81.98 (7.23)**	71.56 (4.09)
	tSNE	61.42 (4.95)	63.52 (7.23)	52.63 (8.92)	62.50 (13.04)	**70.19 (4.44)**
	Force	62.76 (11.07)	61.10 (11.45)	52.45 (9.30)	57.97 (7.03)	**63.95 (6.33)**
Cncr	PCA	89.84 (2.21)	83.38 (3.22)	63.04 (6.12)	71.77 (7.83)	**90.68 (0.75)**
	tSNE	87.91 (5.01)	82.87 (2.54)	61.74 (5.35)	72.17 (4.94)	**90.95 (1.80)**
	Force	86.99 (5.31)	83.97 (1.78)	59.91 (4.89)	74.37 (5.34)	**87.84 (8.14)**
Segm.	PCA	58.37 (6.01)	50.32 (6.33)	44.20 (8.84)	50.45 (11.05)	**60.98 (5.52)**
	tSNE	62.43 (4.79)	53.91 (4.11)	44.24 (6.96)	55.59 (11.72)	**64.77 (3.50)**
	Force	59.70 (5.60)	53.44 (4.95)	39.43 (8.79)	54.71 (6.06)	**63.40 (4.22)**
MNIST	PCA	63.12 (5.59)	72.79 (5.84)	29.67 (4.30)	36.04 (3.10)	**77.92 (4.53)**
	tSNE	59.85 (11.84)	**74.00 (3.43)**	29.72 (3.62)	39.11 (4.06)	68.57 (5.73)
	Force	60.87 (10.52)	72.20 (5.32)	31.76 (2.31)	45.40 (6.32)	**75.52 (5.90)**

The class separation evaluation results are shown in Table 2. For the MNIST dataset 1240 digits that belongs in four classes (2, 4, 7 and 9) were used. As proposed in the literature [13], $\sqrt{n}$ control points are used, where n is the dataset size. The proposed technique, especially when used with a kernel-based projection function, almost always outperforms all the other compared techniques, regardless the used initialization scheme and dataset.

Figure 1 illustrates the projected points along with their classes for all the evaluated techniques using the Segmentation dataset (the kernel variant is used for the proposed method), while in Fig. 2 the Cancer dataset is visualized (again the kernel variant of the proposed method is used). The proposed method always leads to better class separation compared to the proposed methods, as well as it provides more stable behavior on previously unseen data (note that the PLMP and the KELP methods collapses in some cases).

Next, we evaluate the proposed method using a clustering setup (the number of clusters equals the number of classes) using the silhouette coefficient which attempts to count how tightly grouped all the data in each cluster are. Note that the silhouette coefficient normally ranges from -1 to 1. However, to improve the readability of results, values have been scaled to [-100, 100]. The results are reported in Table 3. The proposed technique achieves the highest score in every dataset, while the kernel version of the proposed technique still greatly outperforms the linear variant.

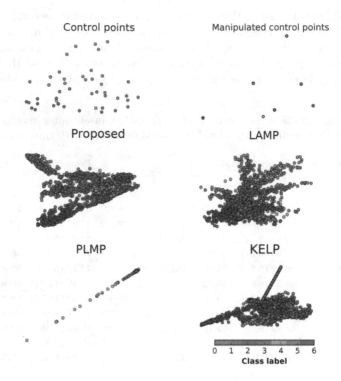

Fig. 1. Visualizing the image segmentation dataset. Classes correspond to the following labels: green – sky, orange – cement, purple – window, bordeaux – brickface, yellow – foliage, mustard – path, gray – grass. (figure best viewed in color) (Color figure online)

Table 3. Average silhouette coefficient after manipulation of control points. Best results marked bold. Standard deviation of 10 runs in parenthesis.

Data	Initialization	Silhouette coefficient			Proposed	
		KELP	LAMP	PLMP	Linear	Kernel
Wine	PCA	12.52 (7.00)	−9.28 (3.69)	0.55 (4.63)	**28.13 (12.22)**	19.18 (4.23)
	tSNE	11.95 (6.58)	−14.70 (4.56)	−0.76 (6.05)	8.23 (8.58)	**14.49 (8.72)**
	Force	**15.96 (7.47)**	−11.41 (5.29)	1.60 (4.44)	4.71 (4.75)	12.11 (9.35)
Cncr	PCA	55.15 (13.60)	34.14 (4.26)	12.22 (5.49)	19.26 (7.63)	**57.93 (4.75)**
	tSNE	53.75 (13.78)	36.07 (4.22)	10.89 (3.13)	21.64 (5.60)	**60.35 (5.04)**
	Force	52.34 (15.51)	36.01 (5.09)	9.08 (3.56)	22.74 (6.93)	**56.15 (10.45)**
Segm.	PCA	6.02 (5.87)	−0.61 (5.26)	−11.66 (10.09)	−0.74 (10.87)	**16.00 (5.07)**
	tSNE	7.11 (2.95)	0.02 (3.52)	−10.58 (7.63)	5.54 (10.53)	**18.56 (4.49)**
	Force	6.35 (4.39)	−0.70 (3.68)	−15.48 (5.60)	1.55 (7.16)	**17.12 (3.54)**
MNIST	PCA	−24.39 (5.28)	17.28 (4.71)	−6.78 (0.93)	−6.38 (1.31)	**25.14 (4.65)**
	tSNE	−22.09 (9.28)	**19.26 (3.43)**	−6.05 (1.75)	−4.85 (2.00)	13.42 (6.81)
	Force	−28.30 (7.97)	17.65 (4.68)	−6.13 (0.95)	−3.02 (2.85)	**22.07 (6.98)**

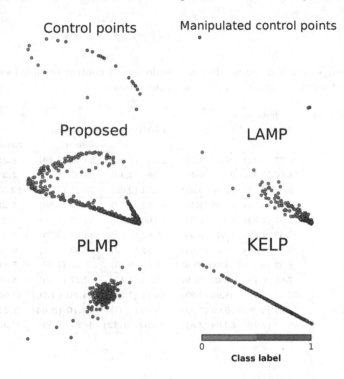

Fig. 2. Visualizing the cancer dataset. (best viewed in color) (Color figure online)

Table 4 shows the neighbor error, which evaluates how far the 10 neighbors of each point in the visual space are in the original high-dimensional space. As an error metric, lower-values indicate better projections. For the neighbor error metric, the results are more diverse than the previous two metrics. While the proposed kernel version performs considerably better than the linear and baselines in first two datasets (Wine and Cancer), it presents similar results with the linear and baselines in the other two datasets (Segmentation and MNIST). The neighbor error for the Cancer dataset (same setup as before) is visualized in Fig. 3. Note that the proposed method better captures the manifold structure of the data, creating smooth low neighbor error regions.

Finally, we evaluate the effect of the number of used control points on the quality of the learned projection. The results are shown in Fig. 4 using the proposed method and a linear projection function (PCA is used for the initialization). Even when a small number of control points is used, the proposed method outperforms the other methods. Qualitatively similar results were obtained using different initializations (e.g., tSNE or Force), as well as for other metrics and datasets.

Table 4. Average Neighbor error after manipulation of control points. Best results marked bold. Standard deviation of 10 runs in parenthesis.

Data	Initialization	Neighbor error				
		KELP	LAMP	PLMP	Proposed	
					Linear	Kernel
Wine	PCA	20.77 (5.84)	26.24 (3.74)	27.73 (4.01)	24.63 (2.19)	**8.33 (4.87)**
	tSNE	18.56 (3.41)	27.75 (6.46)	27.86 (4.42)	25.92 (6.49)	**7.27 (2.34)**
	Force	19.03 (4.28)	26.36 (5.39)	25.34 (2.68)	25.81 (3.72)	**12.52 (5.60)**
Cncr	PCA	12.37 (3.56)	13.48 (1.48)	15.52 (2.30)	13.40 (2.90)	**5.23 (1.44)**
	tSNE	11.51 (2.39)	13.58 (2.31)	15.69 (2.47)	14.48 (2.15)	**8.44 (1.78)**
	Force	12.43 (2.66)	12.04 (1.66)	13.62 (0.84)	14.04 (2.23)	**7.49 (1.95)**
Segm.	PCA	8.19 (1.38)	7.00 (0.83)	9.11 (1.12)	8.83 (1.74)	**6.00 (0.83)**
	tSNE	8.52 (0.64)	**4.90 (0.65)**	8.02 (0.95)	7.51 (1.20)	5.84 (0.77)
	Force	7.69 (0.79)	**5.01 (0.90)**	7.83 (1.47)	7.27 (1.50)	5.57 (0.97)
MNIST	PCA	50.19 (2.72)	48.96 (3.20)	46.31 (3.23)	**44.50 (4.10)**	47.66 (2.88)
	tSNE	51.97 (3.20)	50.60 (1.63)	45.16 (4.94)	**45.10 (3.04)**	48.03 (2.40)
	Force	50.15 (3.76)	50.09 (3.34)	**46.57 (3.32)**	46.87 (2.55)	47.91 (2.54)

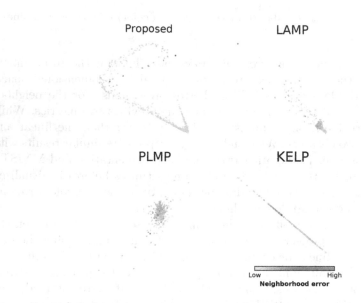

Fig. 3. Visualizing the neighbor error for the Cancer dataset. (best viewed in color) (Color figure online)

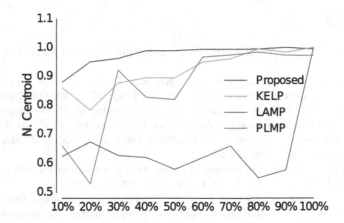

Fig. 4. Nearest Centroid precision in relation to control point increase (over the baseline proposed in the literature, i.e., $\sqrt{(n)}$) on the Wine dataset.

5   Conclusions

In this work, a novel interactive DR framework that is able to learn the optimal projection by exploiting the user interactions with the projected data was proposed. The proposed method can be combined with a number of different projection functions to readily adapt to the needs of each application, ranging from fast, lightweight linear projection functions to powerful deep neural networks. The user interaction was modeled as a target similarity matrix that was used to learn either a fast linear or a non-linear kernel projection using gradient descent. The proposed method was evaluated using a common interaction scenario in multidimensional projection literature, i.e., a subset of the data was projected, the data were rearranged in classes or clusters, and then a new projection function was learned based on that manipulation. The proposed method outperforms competitive baseline and state-of-the-art methods in the used benchmark datasets, while also being able to provide fast lightweight interactive projections. Namely, our methods improve the classification precision in Wine dataset by 16–29%, in Cancer by 1–31%, in Segmentation by 2–25% and in MNIST by 4–48%. Similarly, our methods improve the clustering coefficient in Wine dataset by 12–43, in Cancer by 5–51, in Segmentation by 11–30 and in MNIST by 6–53. There are several interesting future work directions. First, the target similarity matrix can be enriched with high-dimensional neighbor information using the rest of the dataset. Preliminary experiments using image and text datasets show promising results. It can be also used for interactive end-to-end-learning for manifold exploration [21,22], domain adaptation [23] and transfer learning [24], as well as to interact with multimodal data [25,26].

References

1. LeCun, Y., Bengio, Y., Hinton, G.: Deep learning. Nature **521**(7553), 436–444 (2015)
2. Amershi, S., Cakmak, M., Knox, W.B., Kulesza, T.: Power to the people: the role of humans in interactive machine learning. AI Mag. **35**(4), 105–120 (2014)
3. Fails, J.A., Olsen Jr, D.R.: Interactive machine learning. In: Proceedings of the 8th International Conference on Intelligent User Interfaces, pp. 39–45. ACM (2003)
4. van der Maaten, L., Hinton, G.: Visualizing data using t-SNE. J. Mach. Learn. Res. **Nov**(10), 2579–2605 (2008)
5. Passalis, N., Tefas, A.: Dimensionality reduction using similarity-induced embeddings. IEEE Trans. Neural Netw. Learn. Syst. **99**, 1–13 (2017)
6. Derrien, T., André, C., Galibert, F., Hitte, C.: Autograph: an interactive web server for automating and visualizing comparative genome maps. Bioinformatics **23**(4), 498–499 (2006)
7. Wang, Y., et al.: The 3D genome browser: a web-based browser for visualizing 3D genome organization and long-range chromatin interactions. BioRxiv 112268 (2017)
8. Jolliffe, I.: Principal component analysis. Wiley Online Library (2002)
9. Kruskal, J.B., Wish, M.: Multidimensional scaling, vol. 11 (1978)
10. McInnes, L., Healy, J.: UMAP: Uniform Manifold Approximation and Projection for Dimension Reduction. ArXiv e-prints arXiv:1802.03426, February 2018
11. Endert, A., Han, C., Maiti, D., House, L., North, C.: Observation-level interaction with statistical models for visual analytics. In: 2011 IEEE Conference on Visual Analytics Science and Technology (VAST), pp. 121–130. IEEE (2011)
12. Joia, P., Coimbra, D., Cuminato, J.A., Paulovich, F.V., Nonato, L.G.: Local affine multidimensional projection. IEEE Trans. Vis. Comput. Graph. **17**(12), 2563–2571 (2011)
13. Paulovich, F.V., Silva, C.T., Nonato, L.G.: Two-phase mapping for projecting massive data sets. IEEE Trans. Vis. Comput. Graph. **16**(6), 1281–1290 (2010)
14. Tejada, E., Minghim, R., Nonato, L.G.: On improved projection techniques to support visual exploration of multi-dimensional data sets. Inf. Vis. **2**(4), 218–231 (2003)
15. Barbosa, A., Paulovich, F.V., Paiva, A., Goldenstein, S., Petronetto, F., Nonato, L.G.: Visualizing and interacting with kernelized data. IEEE Trans. Vis. Comput. Graph. **22**(3), 1314–1325 (2016)
16. Kingma, D., Ba, J.: Adam: A method for stochastic optimization. arXiv preprint arXiv:1412.6980 (2014)
17. Drineas, P., Mahoney, M.W.: On the nyström method for approximating a gram matrix for improved kernel-based learning. J. Mach. Learn. Res. **6**(Dec), 2153–2175 (2005)
18. LeCun, Y.: The mnist database of handwritten digits (1998). http://yann.lecun.com/exdb/mnist/
19. Lichman, M.: UCI machine learning repository (2013)
20. Rousseeuw, P.J.: Silhouettes: a graphical aid to the interpretation and validation of cluster analysis. J. Comput. Appl. Math. **20**, 53–65 (1987)
21. Belkin, M., Niyogi, P., Sindhwani, V.: Manifold regularization: a geometric framework for learning from labeled and unlabeled examples. J. Mach. Learn. Res. **7**, 2399–2434 (2006)

22. Zhang, Y., Zhang, Z., Qin, J., Zhang, L., Li, B., Li, F.: Semi-supervised local multi-manifold isomap by linear embedding for feature extraction. Pattern Recognit. **76**, 662–678 (2018)

23. Glorot, X., Bordes, A., Bengio, Y.: Domain adaptation for large-scale sentiment classification: a deep learning approach. In: Proceedings of the International Conference on Machine Learning, pp. 513–520 (2011)

24. Pan, S.J., Yang, Q., et al.: A survey on transfer learning. IEEE Trans. Knowl. Data Eng. **22**(10), 1345–1359 (2010)

25. Kim, J., Chung, H.J., Park, C.H., Park, W.Y., Kim, J.H.: Chromoviz: multimodal visualization of gene expression data onto chromosomes using scalable vector graphics. Bioinformatics **20**(7), 1191–1192 (2004)

26. Liu, Y., Liu, L., Guo, Y., Lew, M.S.: Learning visual and textual representations for multimodal matching and classification. Pattern Recognit. **84**, 51–67 (2018)

Efficient Texture Retrieval
Using Multiscale Local Extrema
Descriptors and Covariance Embedding

Minh-Tan Pham[(⊠)] [iD]

IRISA - University of Southern Brittany, 56000 Vannes, France
minh-tan.pham@irisa.fr

Abstract. We present an efficient method for texture retrieval using multiscale feature extraction and embedding based on the local extrema keypoints. The idea is to first represent each texture image by its local maximum and local minimum pixels. The image is then divided into regular overlapping blocks and each one is characterized by a feature vector constructed from the radiometric, geometric and structural information of its local extrema. All feature vectors are finally embedded into a covariance matrix which will be exploited for dissimilarity measurement within retrieval task. Thanks to the method's simplicity, multiscale scheme can be easily implemented to improve its scale-space representation capacity. We argue that our handcrafted features are easy to implement, fast to run but can provide very competitive performance compared to handcrafted and CNN-based learned descriptors from the literature. In particular, the proposed framework provides highly competitive retrieval rate for several texture databases including 94.95% for MIT Vistex, 79.87% for Stex, 76.15% for Outex TC-00013 and 89.74% for USPtex.

Keywords: Texture retrieval · Handcrafted features · Local extrema
Feature covariance matrix

1 Introduction

Content-based image retrieval (CBIR) has been always drawing attention from researchers working on image analysis and pattern recognition within computer vision field. Texture, i.e. a powerful image feature involving repeated patterns which can be recognized by human vision, plays a significant role in most of CBIR systems. Constructing efficient texture descriptors to characterize the image becomes one of the key components which have been focused in most research works related to texture image retrieval [4, 35, 41].

From the literature, a great number of multiscale texture analysis methods using probabilistic approach have been developed to tackle retrieval task. In [8], the authors proposed to model the spatial dependence of pyramidal discrete wavelet transform (DWT) coefficients using the generalized Gaussian distributions (GGD) and the dissimilarity measure between images was derived based

© Springer Nature Switzerland AG 2019
L. Leal-Taixé and S. Roth (Eds.): ECCV 2018 Workshops, LNCS 11132, pp. 564–579, 2019.
https://doi.org/10.1007/978-3-030-11018-5_45

on the Kullback-Leibler divergences (KLD) between GGD models. Sharing the similar principle, multiscale coefficients yielded by the discrete cosine transform (DCT), the dual-tree complex wavelet transform (DT-CWT), the Gabor Wavelet (GW), etc. were modeled by different statistical models such as GGD, the multivariate Gaussian mixture models (MGMM), Gaussian copula (GC), Student-t copula (StC), or other distributions like Gamma, Rayleigh, Weibull, Laplace, etc. to perform texture-based image retrieval [5,17–19,21,43,47]. However, one of the main drawbacks of these techniques is the their expensive computational time which has been observed an discussed in several papers [17,19,21].

Other systems which have provided effective CBIR performance include the local pattern-based framework and the block truncation coding (BTC)-based approach. The local binary patterns (LBP) were first embedded in a multiresolution and rotation invariant scheme for texture classification in [25]. Inspired from this work, many studies have been developed for texture retrieval such as the local maximum edge binary patterns (LMEBP) [39], local ternary patterns (LTP) [40], local tetra patterns (LTrP) [22], local tri-directional patterns (LTriDP) [44], local neighborhood difference pattern (LNDP) [45], etc. These descriptors, in particular LTrP and LTRiDP, can provide good retrieval rate. However, due to the fact that they work on grayscale images, their performance on natural textures is limited without using color information. To overcome this issue, recent schemes have proposed to incorporate these local patterns with color features. Some techniques can be mentioned here are the joint histogram of color and local extrema patterns (LEP+colorhist) [23], the local oppugnant color texture pattern (LOCTP) [14], the local extrema co-occurrence pattern (LECoP) [46], LBPC for color images [38]. Beside that, many studies have also developed different BTC-based frameworks, e.g. the ordered-dither BTC (ODBTC) [10,12], the error diffusion BTC (EDBTC) [11] and the dot-diffused BTC (DDBTC) [13], which have provided competitive retrieval performance. Within these approaches, an image is divided into multiple non-overlapping blocks and each one is compressed into the so-called color quantizer and bitmap image. Then, a feature descriptor is constructed using the color histogram and color co-occurrence features combined with the bit pattern feature (including edge, shape, texture information) of the image. These features are extracted from the above color quantizer and bitmap image to tackle CBIR task.

Last but not least, not focusing on developing handcrafted descriptors as all above systems, learned descriptors extracted from convolution neural networks (CNNs) have been recently applied to image retrieval task [36,42]. An end-to-end CNN framework can learn and extract multilevel discriminative image features which are extremely effective for various computer vision tasks including recognition and retrieval [36]. In practice, instead of defining and training their own CNNs from scratch, people tend to exploit pre-trained CNNs (on a very large dataset such as ImageNet [7]) as feature extractors. Recent studies have shown the effective performance of CNN learned features w.r.t. traditional handcrafted descriptors applied to image classification and retrieval [6,24].

In this work, we continue the traditional approach of handcrafted feature designing by introducing a powerful retrieval framework using multiscale local extrema descriptors and covariance embedding. Here, we inherit the idea of using local extrema pixels for texture description and retrieval from [28] but provide a simpler and faster feature extraction algorithm which can be easily integrated into a multiscale scheme. Due to the fact that natural images usually involve a variety of local textures and structures which do not appear homogeneous within the entire image, an approach taking into account local features becomes relevant. Also, a multiscale approach could help to provide a better scale-space representation capacity to deal with complex textures. Within our approach, a set of local maximum and local minimum pixels (in terms of intensity) is first detected to represent each texture image. Then, to extract local descriptors, the image is divided into regular overlapping blocks of equal size and each block is characterized by a feature vector constructed using the radiometric (i.e. color), geometric ans structural information of its local extrema. The descriptor of each block is named SLED, i.e. simple local extrema descriptor. Thus, the input image is encoded by a set of SLED vectors which are then embedded into a feature covariance matrix. Moreover, thanks to the simplicity of the approach, we propose to upsample and downsample each image to perform the algorithm at different scales. Finally, we exploit the geometric-based riemannian distance [9] between covariance matrices for dissimilarity measurement within retrieval task. Our experiments show that the proposed framework can provide highly competitive performance for several popular texture databases compared against both state-of-the-art handcrafted and learned descriptors. In the rest of this paper, Sect. 2 describes the proposed retrieval framework including the details of SLED feature extraction, covariance embedding and multiscale scheme. We then present our experiments conducted on four popular texture databases in Sects. 3 and 4 finally concludes the paper with some potential developments.

2   Proposed Texture Retrieval Framework

2.1   Texture Representation Using Local Extrema Pixels

The idea of using the local extrema (i.e. local max and local min pixels) for texture analysis was introduced in [26,27,30] for texture segmentation in very high resolution images and also exploited in [28,29,34] for texture image retrieval. Regarding to this point of view, a texture is formed by a certain spatial distribution of pixels holding some illumination (i.e. intensity) variations. Hence, different textures are reflected by different types of pixel's spatial arrangements and radiometric variations. These meaningful properties can be approximately captured by the local extrema detected from the image. Hence, these local keypoints are relevant for texture representation and description [31–33].

The detection of local extrema from a grayscale image is quite simple and fast. Using a sliding window, the center pixel (at each sliding position) is supposed to be a local maximum (resp. local minimum) if it has the highest (resp. lowest) intensity value. Hence, by only fixing a $w \times w$ window size, the local extrema are detected by scanning the image only once. To deal with color images, there are different ways to detect local extrema (i.e. detecting from the grayscale version, using the union or intersection of extrema subsets detected from each color channel, etc.). For simplicity, we propose to detect local extrema from grayscale version of color images in this paper. To illustrate the capacity of the local extrema of representing and characterizing different texture contents, Fig. 1 shows their spatial apperance within 4 different textures of the MIT Vistex database [3]. Each 128×128 color texture (at the bottom) is first converted to a grayscale image (in the middle). On the top, we display for each one a 3-D surface model using the grayscale image intensity as the surface height. The local maxima (in red) and local minima (in green) are detected using a 5×5 sliding window. Some green points may be unseen since they are obscured by the surface. We observe that these extrema contain rich information that represent each texture content. Therefore, extracting and encoding their radiometric (or color) and geometric features could provide a promising texture description tool.

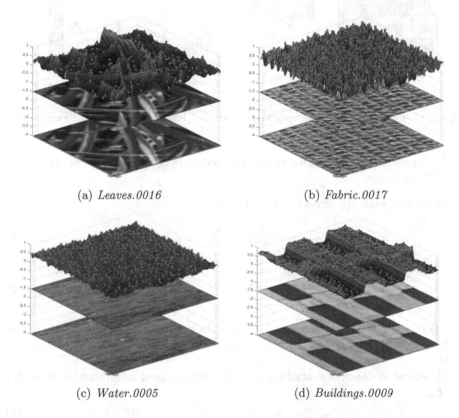

(a) *Leaves.0016*   (b) *Fabric.0017*

(c) *Water.0005*   (d) *Buildings.0009*

Fig. 1. Illustration: spatial distribution and arrangement of local max pixels (red) and local min pixels (green) within 4 different textures from the MIT Vistex database [3]. These local extrema are detected using a 5×5 search window. (Color figure online)

2.2   Simple Local Extrema Descriptor (SLED)

Given an input texture image, after detecting the local extrema using a $w \times w$ sliding window, the next step is to divide the image into N overlapping blocks of size $W \times W$ and then extract the simple local extrema descriptor (SLED) feature vector from each block. The generation of SLED vector is summarized in Fig. 2. From each image block $B_i, i = 1 \ldots N$, we first separate the local maxima set $S_i^{\max}$ and the local minima set $S_i^{\min}$, and then extract the color, spatial and gradient features of local keypoints to form their description vectors.

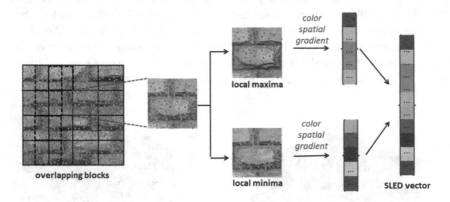

Fig. 2. Generation of SLED feature vector for each image block. (Color figure online)

In details, below are the features extracted from $S_i^{\max}$, the feature generation for $S_i^{\min}$ is similar.

+ Mean and variance of each color channel:

$$\mu_{i,\text{color}}^{\max} = \frac{1}{|S_i^{\max}|} \sum_{(x,y) \in S_i^{\max}} I_{\text{color}}(x,y), \tag{1}$$

$$\sigma_{i,\text{color}}^{2\max} = \frac{1}{|S_i^{\max}|} \sum_{(x,y) \in S_i^{\max}} (I_{\text{color}}(x,y) - \mu_{i,\text{color}}^{\max})^2, \tag{2}$$

where color $\in \{\text{red}, \text{green}, \text{blue}\}$ represents each of the 3 color components; (x,y) is the pixel position on the image grid and $|S_i^{\max}|$ is the cardinality of the set $S_i^{\max}$.

+ Mean and variance of spatial distances from each local maximum to the center of B_i:

$$\mu_{i,\text{spatial}}^{\max} = \frac{1}{|S_i^{\max}|} \sum_{(x,y) \in S_i^{\max}} d_i(x,y), \tag{3}$$

$$\sigma_{i,\text{spatial}}^{2\max} = \frac{1}{|S_i^{\max}|} \sum_{(x,y) \in S_i^{\max}} (d_i(x,y) - \mu_{i,\text{spatial}}^{\max})^2, \tag{4}$$

where $d_i(x, y)$ is the spatial distance from the pixel (x, y) to the center of block B_i on the image plane.

+ Mean and variance of gradient magnitudes:

$$\mu_{i,\text{grad}}^{\max} = \frac{1}{|S_i^{\max}|} \sum_{(x,y) \in S_i^{\max}} \nabla I(x, y), \tag{5}$$

$$\sigma_{i,\text{grad}}^{2\,\max} = \frac{1}{|S_i^{\max}|} \sum_{(x,y) \in S_i^{\max}} (\nabla I(x, y) - \mu_{i,\text{grad}}^{\max})^2, \tag{6}$$

where ∇I is the gradient magnitude image obtained by applying the Sobel filter on the gray-scale version of the image.

All of these features are integrated into the feature vector $f_i^{\max} \in \mathbb{R}^{10}$, which encodes the color (i.e. three channels), spatial and structural features of the local maxima inside the block B_i:

$$f_i^{\max} = \left[\mu_{i,\text{color}}^{\max}, \sigma_{i,\text{color}}^{2\,\max}, \mu_{i,\text{spatial}}^{\max}, \sigma_{i,\text{spatial}}^{2\,\max}, \mu_{i,\text{grad}}^{\max}, \sigma_{i,\text{grad}}^{2\,\max}\right] \in \mathbb{R}^{10}. \tag{7}$$

The generation of $f_i^{\min}$ from the local min set $S_i^{\min}$ is similar. Now, let f_i^{SLED} be the SLED feature vector generated for block B_i, we finally define:

$$f_i^{\text{SLED}} = \left[f_i^{\max}, f_i^{\min}\right] \in \mathbb{R}^{20}. \tag{8}$$

The proposed feature vector f_i^{SLED} enables us to characterize the local textures of each image block B_i by understanding how local maxima and local minima are distributed and arranged, and how they capture color information as well as structural properties (given by gradient features). The extraction of our handcrafted SLED is quite simple and fast. We observe that it is also feasible to add other features to create more complex feature vector as proposed in [28]. However, we argue that by using covariance embedding and performing multiscale framework (described in the next section), the simple and fast SLED already provides very competitive retrieval performance.

2.3   Covariance Embedding and Multiscale Framework

The previous section has described the generation of SLED vector for each block of the image. Once all feature vectors are extracted to characterize all image blocks, they are embedded into a covariance matrix as shown in Fig. 3. Given a set of N SLED feature vectors $f_i^{\text{SLED}}, i = 1 \ldots N$, the embedded covariance matrix is estimated as follow:

$$C^{\text{SLED}} = \frac{1}{N} \sum_{i=1}^{N} (f_i^{\text{SLED}} - \mu^{\text{SLED}})(f_i^{\text{SLED}} - \mu^{\text{SLED}})^T, \tag{9}$$

where $\mu^{\text{SLED}} = \frac{1}{N} \sum_{i=1}^{N} f_i^{\text{SLED}}$ is the estimated mean feature vector.

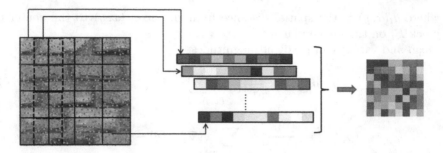

Fig. 3. Proposed method to extract SLED feature vectors from all image overlapping blocks and embed them into a covariance matrix.

Last but not least, thanks to the simplicity of the proposed SLED extraction and embedding strategy, we also propose a multi-scale framework as in Fig. 4. Here, each input image will be upsampled and downsampled with the scale factor of 3/2 and 2/3, respectively, using the bicubic interpolation approach. Then, the proposed scheme in Fig. 3 is applied to these two rescaled images and the original one to generate three covariance matrices. It should be noted that the number of rescaled images as well as scaling factors can be chosen differently. Here, without loss of genarality, we fix the number of scales to 3 and scale factors to 2/3, 1 and 3/2 for all implementations in the paper. To this end, due to the fact that covariance matrices possess a postitive semi-definite structure and do not lie on the Euclidean space, we finally exploit the geometric-based riemannian distance for dissimilarity measurement within retrieval task. This metric has been proved to be relevant and effective for covariance descriptors in the literature [9].

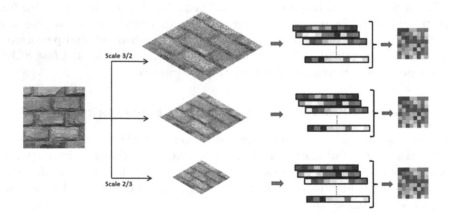

Fig. 4. Proposed multi-scale framework.

3   Experimental Study

3.1   Texture Databases

Four popular texture databases including the MIT Vistex [3], the Salzburg Texture (Stex) [16], the Outex TC-00013 [1] and the USPtex [2] were exploited to conduct our experiments. Vistex is one of the most widely used texture databases for performance evalution and comparative study in the CBIR field. It consists of 640 texture images (i.e. 40 classes × 16 images per class) of size 128 × 128 pixels. Being much larger, the Stex database is a collection of 476 texture classes captured in the area around Salzburg, Austria under real-word conditions. As for Vistex, each class includes 16 images of 128 × 128 pixels, hence the total number of images from the database is 7616. The third dataset, the Outex TC-00013 [1], is a collection of heterogeneous materials such as paper, fabric, wool, stone, etc. It comprises 68 texture classes and each one includes 20 image samples of 128 × 128 pixels. Finally, the USPtex database [2] includes 191 classes of both natural scene (road, vegetation, cloud, etc.) and materials (seeds, rice, tissues, etc.). Each class consists of 12 image samples of 128 × 128 pixels. Figure 5 shows some examples of each texture database and Table 1 provides a summary of their information.

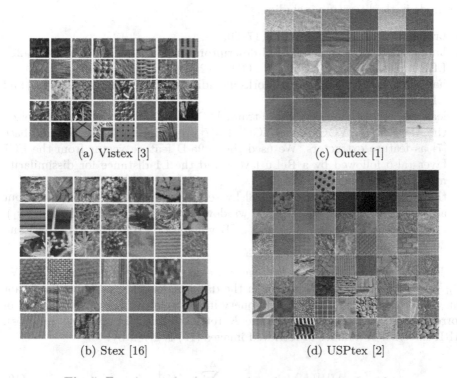

(a) Vistex [3]   (c) Outex [1]

(b) Stex [16]   (d) USPtex [2]

Fig. 5. Four image databases used in the experimental study.

Table 1. Number of total images (N_t), number of classes (N_c) and number of relevant images (N_R) per class within the 4 experimental texture databases.

	Vistex	Stex	Outex	USPtex
N_t	640	7616	1380	2292
N_c	40	476	68	191
N_R	16	16	20	12

3.2   Experimental Setup

To perform our retrieval framework, the local extrema keypoints were detected using a 3×3 search window $(w = 3)$. We recommend this small window size to ensure a dense distribution of local extrema for different texture scenes. Next, each texture image is divided into overlapping blocks of size 32×32 pixels and two consecutive blocks are 50% overlapped. Thus, for each 128×128 image, the number of blocks is $N = 64$. For multiscale framework as in Fig. 4, we set 3 scales of $2/3$, 1 and $3/2$ as previously mentioned. There are no other parameters to be set, which confirms the simplicity of our proposed method.

For comparative evaluation, we compare our results to several state-of-the-art methods in the literature including:

+ probabilistic approaches in [5,8,17–20,43];
+ handcrafted local pattern-based descriptors such as LMEBP [39], LtrP [22], LEP+colorhist [23], LECoP [46], ODII [12];
+ handcrafted BTC-based frameworks including DDBTC [13], ODBTC [10] and EDBTC [11];
+ learned descriptors based on pre-trained CNNs [6,24]. For these, we exploited the AlexNet [15], VGG-16 and VGG-19 [37] pre-trained on ImageNet database [7] as feature extractors. We used the 4096-D feature vector from the FC7 layer (also followed by a ReLu layer) and the L1 distance for dissimilarity measure as recommended in [24].
+ the LED framework proposed [28] by setting equivalent parameters to our algorithm. In details, we set the 3 window sizes for keypoint extraction (ω_1), local extrema detection (ω_2) and LED generation (W) to 9×9, 3×3 and 36×36, respectively.

For evaluation criteria, the average retrieval rate (ARR) is adopted. Let N_t, N_R be the total number of images in the database and the number of relevant images for each query, and for each query image q, let $n_q(K)$ be the number of correctly retrieved images among the K retrieved ones (i.e. K best matches). ARR in terms of number of retrieved images (K) is given by:

$$\text{ARR}(K) = \frac{1}{N_t \times N_R} \sum_{q=1}^{N_t} n_q(K) \Big|_{K \geq N_R} \tag{10}$$

We note that K is generally set to be greater than or equal to N_R. By setting K equal to N_R, ARR becomes the primary benchmark considered by most studies to evaluate and compare the performance of different CBIR systems. All of ARR results shown in this paper were produced by setting $K = N_R$.

3.3   Results and Discussion

Tables 2 and 3 show the ARR performance of the proposed SLED and mutilscale SLED (MS-SLED) on our four texutre databases compared to reference methods. The first observation is that, most local feature-based CBIR schemes (e.g. LtrP [22], LEP+colorhist [23], LECoP [46]) or BTC-based techniques [10,11,13] have achieved better retrieval performance than probabilistic methods which model the entire image using different statistical distributions [5,8,17–19,43]. Also, learned descriptors based on pre-trained CNNs have yielded very competitive retrieval rate compared to handcrafted features which prove the potential of

Table 2. Average retrieval rate (%) on the **Vistex** and **Stex** databases yielded by the proposed method compared to reference methods.

Method	Vistex	Stex
GT+GGD+KLD [8]	76.57	49.30
MGG+Gaussian+KLD [43]	87.40	-
MGG+Laplace+GD [43]	91.70	71.30
Gaussian Copula+Gamma+ML [17]	89.10	69.40
Gaussian Copula+Weibull+ML [17]	89.50	70.60
Student-t Copula+GG+ML [17]	88.90	65.60
Gaussian Copula+Gabor Wavelet [21]	92.40	76.40
LMEBP [39]	87.77	-
LtrP [22]	90.02	-
LEP+colorhist [23]	82.65	59.90
DDBTC [13]	92.65	44.79
ODBTC [10]	90.67	-
EDBTC [11]	92.55	-
LECoP [46]	92.99	74.15
ODII [12]	93.23	-
CNN-AlexNet [24]	91.34	68.84
CNN-VGG16 [24]	92.97	74.92
CNN-VGG19 [24]	93.04	73.93
LED [28]	94.13	76.71
Proposed SLED	**94.31**	**77.78**
Proposed MS-SLED	**94.95**	**79.87**

CNN feature extractor applied to retrieval task [6,24]. Then, more importantly, our proposed SLED and MS-SLED frameworks have outperformed all reference methods for all datasets. We now discuss the results of each database to validate the effectiveness of the proposed strategy.

Table 3. Average retrieval rate (%) on the **Outex** and **USPtex** databases yielded by the proposed method compared to reference methods.

Method	Outex	UPStex
DDBTC (L_1) [13]	61.97	63.19
DDBTC (L_2) [13]	57.51	55.38
DDBTC (χ^2) [13]	65.54	73.41
DDBTC (Canberra) [13]	66.82	74.97
CNN-AlexNet [24]	69.87	83.57
CNN-VGG16 [24]	72.91	85.03
CNN-VGG19 [24]	73.20	84.22
LED [28]	75.14	87.50
Proposed SLED	**75.96**	**88.60**
Proposed MS-SLED	**76.15**	**89.74**

The best ARR of 94.95% and 79.87% was produced for Vistex and Stex by our MS-SLED algorithm. A gain of 0.82% and 3.16% was achieved compared to the second-best method with original LED features in [28]. Within the proposed strategy, the multi-scale scheme has considerable improved the ARR from the single-scale SLED (i.e. 0.62% for Vistex and 2.09% for Stex), which confirms the efficiency of performing multiscale feature extraction and embedding for better texture description, as our motivation in this work. Next, another important remark is that most of the texture classes with strong structures and local features such as buildings, fabric categories, man-made object's surfaces, etc. were perfectly retrieved. Table 4 shows the per-class retrieval rate for each class of the Vistex database. As observed, half of the classes (20/40 classes) were retrieved with 100% accuracy (marked in bold). These classes generally consist of many local textures and structures. Similar behavior was also remarked for Stex data. This issue is encouraging since our motivation is to continue developing hand-designed descriptors which represent and characterize local features better than both handcrafted and learned descriptors from the literature.

Similarly, the proposed MS-SLED framework also provided the best ARR for both Outex (76.15%) and USPtex data (89.74%) (with a gain of 1.01% and 2.24%, respectively), as observed in Table 3. Compared to learned descriptors based on pretrained AlexNet, VGG-16 and VGG-19, an improvement of 2.95% and 4.71% was adopted, which confirms the superior performance of our method over the CNN-based counterparts. To this end, the efficiency of the proposed framework is validated for all tested databases.

Table 4. Per-class retrieval rate (%) on the **Vistex-640** database using the proposed LED+RD method

Class	Rate	Class	Rate	Class	Rate
Bark.0000	75.00	Fabric.0015	**100.00**	Metal.0002	**100.00**
Bark.0006	94.14	Fabric.0017	96.88	Misc.0002	**100.00**
Bark.0008	84.38	Fabric.0018	**100.00**	Sand.0000	**100.00**
Bark.0009	77.73	Flowers.0005	**100.00**	Stone.0001	85.55
Brick.0001	99.61	Food.0000	**100.00**	Stone.0004	93.75
Brick.0004	97.27	Food.0005	99.61	Terrain.0010	94.14
Brick.0005	**100.00**	Food.0008	**100.00**	Tile.0001	90.23
Buildings.0009	**100.00**	Grass.0001	94.53	Tile.0004	**100.00**
Fabric.0000	**100.00**	Leaves.0008	**100.00**	Tile.0007	**100.00**
Fabric.0004	78.13	Leaves.0010	**100.00**	Water.0005	**100.00**
Fabric.0007	99.61	Leaves.0011	**100.00**	Wood.0001	98.44
Fabric.0009	**100.00**	Leaves.0012	60.93	Wood.0002	88.67
Fabric.0011	**100.00**	Leaves.0016	90.23	**ARR**	**94.95**
Fabric.0014	**100.00**	Metal.0000	99.21		

Table 5. Comparison of feature vector length of different methods.

Method	Feature dimension
DT-CWT [8]	$(3 \times 6 + 2) \times 2 = 40$
DT-CWT+DT-RCWT [8]	$2 \times (3 \times 6 + 2) \times 2 = 80$
LBP [25]	256
LTP [40]	$2 \times 256 = 512$
LMEBP [39]	$8 \times 512 = 4096$
Gabor LMEBP [39]	$3 \times 4 \times 512 = 6144$
LEP+colorhist [23]	$16 \times 8 \times 8 \times 8 = 8192$
LECoP($H_{18}S_{10}V_{256}$) [46]	$18 + 10 + 256 = 284$
LECoP($H_{36}S_{20}V_{256}$) [46]	$36 + 20 + 256 = 312$
LECoP($H_{72}S_{20}V_{256}$) [46]	$72 + 20 + 256 = 348$
ODII [12]	$128 + 128 = 256$
CNN-AlexNet [24]	4096
CNN-VGG16 [24]	4096
CNN-VGG19 [24]	4096
LED [28]	$33 \times (33 + 1)/2 = 561$
Proposed SLED	$\mathbf{20 \times (20 + 1)/2 = 210}$
Proposed MS-SLED	$\mathbf{3 \times 210 = 630}$

Last but not least, Table 5 provides the comparison of descriptor dimensions within different methods. We note that our SLED involves a 20×20 covariance matrix estimated as (9). Since the matrix is symmetrical, it is only necessary to store its upper or lower triangular entries. Thus, the SLED feature dimension is calculated as $20 \times (20+1) = 210$. For MS-SLED, we multiply this to the number of scales and hence the length becomes 630 in our implementation. Other feature lengths from the table are illustrated from their related papers. We observe that the proposed SLED has lower dimension than the standard LED in [28] (i.e. 210 compared to 561) but can provide faster and better retrieval performance. To support this remark, we show in Table 6 a comparison of computational time for feature extraction and dissimilarity measurement of LED and SLED. In short, a total amount of 95.17 s is required by our SLED to run on the Vistex data, thus 0.148 s per image, which is very fast. All implementations were carried out using MATLAB 2017a on computer of 3.5 GHz/16 GB RAM.

Table 6. Computation time (in second) of LED and SLED feature extraction (FE) and dissimilarity measurement (DM). Experiments were conducted on the Vistex database.

Version	FE time		DM time (s)		Total time	
	t_{data}	t_{image}	t_{data}	t_{image}	t_{data}	t_{image}
LED [28]	193.77	0.308	21.39	0.033	215.16	0.336
SLED (ours)	86.35	0.135	8.82	0.013	95.17	0.148

t_{data}: time for the total database; t_{image}: time per each image.

4   Conclusions

We have proposed a simple and fast texture image retrieval framework using multiscale local extrema feature extraction and covariance embedding. Without chasing the current trends of deep learning era, we continue the classical way of designing novel handcrafted features in order to achieve highly competitive retrieval performance compared to state-of-the-art methodologies. The detection of local extrema as well as the extraction of their color, spatial and gradient features are quite simple but they are effective for texture description and encoding. We argue that the proposed MS-SLED does not require many parameters for tuning. It is easy to implement, fast to run and feasible to extend or improve. The best retrieval rates obtained for four texture benchmarks shown in our experimental study have confirmed the effectiveness of the proposed strategy. Future work can improve the performance of MS-SLED by exploiting other textural features within its construction. Also, we are now interested in integrating SLED features into an auto-encoder framework in order to automatically learn and encode richer information for better texture representation.

References

1. Outex texture database. University of Oulu, Available online
2. USPtex dataset, Scientific Computing Group (2012). http://fractal.ifsc.usp.br/dataset/USPtex.php
3. Vision texture, MIT Vision and Modeling group. http://vismod.media.mit.edu/pub/VisTex/
4. Alzu'bi, A., Amira, A., Ramzan, N.: Semantic content-based image retrieval: a comprehensive study. J. Vis. Commun. Image Represent. **32**, 20–54 (2015)
5. Choy, S.K., Tong, C.S.: Statistical wavelet subband characterization based on generalized gamma density and its application in texture retrieval. IEEE Trans. Image Process. **19**(2), 281–289 (2010). https://doi.org/10.1109/TIP.2009.2033400
6. Cusano, C., Napoletano, P., Schettini, R.: Evaluating color texture descriptors under large variations of controlled lighting conditions. JOSA A **33**(1), 17–30 (2016)
7. Deng, J., Dong, W., Socher, R., Li, L.J., Li, K., Fei-Fei, L.: Imagenet: a large-scale hierarchical image database. In: CVPR, pp. 248–255. IEEE (2009)
8. Do, M.N., Vetterli, M.: Wavelet-based texture retrieval using generalized gaussian density and Kullback-Leibler distance. IEEE Trans. Image Process. **11**(2), 146–158 (2002). https://doi.org/10.1109/83.982822
9. Förstner, W., Moonen, B.: A metric for covariance matrices. In: Grafarend, E.W., Krumm, F.W., Schwarze, V.S. (eds.) Geodesy-The Challenge of the 3rd Millennium, pp. 299–309. Springer, Heidelberg (2003). https://doi.org/10.1007/978-3-662-05296-9_31
10. Guo, J.M., Prasetyo, H.: Content-based image retrieval using features extracted from halftoning-based block truncation coding. IEEE Trans. Image Process. **24**(3), 1010–1024 (2015). https://doi.org/10.1109/TIP.2014.2372619
11. Guo, J.M., Prasetyo, H., Chen, J.H.: Content-based image retrieval using error diffusion block truncation coding features. IEEE Trans. Circuits Syst. Video Technol. **25**(3), 466–481 (2015). https://doi.org/10.1109/TCSVT.2014.2358011
12. Guo, J.M., Prasetyo, H., Su, H.S.: Image indexing using the color and bit pattern feature fusion. J. Vis. Commun. Image Repres. **24**(8), 1360–1379 (2013). https://doi.org/10.1016/j.jvcir.2013.09.005
13. Guo, J.M., Prasetyo, H., Wang, N.J.: Effective image retrieval system using dot-diffused block truncation coding features. IEEE Trans. Multimedia **17**(9), 1576–1590 (2015). https://doi.org/10.1109/TMM.2015.2449234
14. Jacob, I.J., Srinivasagan, K., Jayapriya, K.: Local oppugnant color texture pattern for image retrieval system. Pattern Recogn. Lett. **42**, 72–78 (2014). https://doi.org/10.1016/j.patrec.2014.01.017
15. Krizhevsky, A., Sutskever, I., Hinton, G.E.: Imagenet classification with deep convolutional neural networks. In: NIPS, pp. 1097–1105 (2012)
16. Kwitt, R., Meerwald, P.: Salzburg texture image database. http://www.wavelab.at/sources/STex/
17. Kwitt, R., Meerwald, P., Uhl, A.: Efficient texture image retrieval using copulas in a Bayesian framework. IEEE Trans. Image Process. **20**(7), 2063–2077 (2011). https://doi.org/10.1109/TIP.2011.2108663
18. Kwitt, R., Uhl, A.: Image similarity measurement by Kullback-Leibler divergences between complex wavelet subband statistics for texture retrieval. In: Proceedings of IEEE International Conference on Image Processing (ICIP), pp. 933–936 (2008). https://doi.org/10.1109/ICIP.2008.4711909

19. Lasmar, N.E., Berthoumieu, Y.: Gaussian copula multivariate modeling for texture image retrieval using wavelet transforms. IEEE Trans. Image Process. **23**(5), 2246–2261 (2014). https://doi.org/10.1109/TIP.2014.2313232

20. Li, C., Duan, G., Zhong, F.: Rotation invariant texture retrieval considering the scale dependence of Gabor wavelet. IEEE Trans. Image Process. **24**(8), 2344–2354 (2015). https://doi.org/10.1109/TIP.2015.2422575

21. Li, C., Huang, Y., Zhu, L.: Color texture image retrieval based on Gaussian copula models of Gabor wavelets. Pattern Recognit. **64**, 118–129 (2017). https://doi.org/10.1016/j.patcog.2016.10.030

22. Murala, S., Maheshwari, R., Balasubramanian, R.: Local tetra patterns: a new feature descriptor for content-based image retrieval. IEEE Trans. Image Process. **21**(5), 2874–2886 (2012). https://doi.org/10.1109/TIP.2012.2188809

23. Murala, S., Wu, Q.J., Balasubramanian, R., Maheshwari, R.: Joint histogram between color and local extrema patterns for object tracking. In: IS&T/SPIE Electronic Imaging, pp. 86630T–86630T-7. International Society for Optics and Photonics (2013). https://doi.org/10.1117/12.2002185

24. Napoletano, P.: Hand-crafted vs learned descriptors for color texture classification. In: Bianco, S., Schettini, R., Trémeau, A., Tominaga, S. (eds.) CCIW 2017. LNCS, vol. 10213, pp. 259–271. Springer, Cham (2017). https://doi.org/10.1007/978-3-319-56010-6_22

25. Ojala, T., Pietikäinen, M., Mäenpää, T.: Multiresolution gray-scale and rotation invariant texture classification with local binary patterns. IEEE Trans. Pattern Anal. Mach. Intell. **24**(7), 971–987 (2002). https://doi.org/10.1109/TPAMI.2002.1017623

26. Pham, M.T., Mercier, G., Michel, J.: Pointwise graph-based local texture characterization for very high resolution multispectral image classification. IEEE J. Sel. Top. Appl. Earth Obs. Remote Sens. **8**(5), 1962–1973 (2015)

27. Pham, M.T.: Pointwise approach for texture analysis and characterization from very high resolution remote sensing images. Ph.D. thesis, Télécom Bretagne (2016)

28. Pham, M.T., Mercier, G., Bombrun, L.: Color texture image retrieval based on local extrema features and riemannian distance. J. Imaging **3**(4), 43 (2017)

29. Pham, M.T., Mercier, G., Bombrun, L., Michel, J.: Texture and color-based image retrieval using the local extrema features and riemannian distance. arXiv preprint arXiv:1611.02102 (2016)

30. Pham, M.T., Mercier, G., Michel, J.: Textural features from wavelets on graphs for very high resolution panchromatic pléiades image classification. Fr. J. Photogram Remote. Sens. **208**, 131–136 (2014)

31. Pham, M.T., Mercier, G., Michel, J.: Change detection between SAR images using a pointwise approach and graph theory. IEEE Trans. Geosci. Remote Sens. **54**(4), 2020–2032 (2016)

32. Pham, M.T., Mercier, G., Michel, J.: PW-COG: an effective texture descriptor for VHR satellite imagery using a pointwise approach on covariance matrix of oriented gradients. IEEE Trans. Geosci. Remote Sens. **54**(6), 3345–3359 (2016)

33. Pham, M.T., Mercier, G., Regniers, O., Michel, J.: Texture retrieval from VHR optical remote sensed images using the local extrema descriptor with application to vineyard parcel detection. Remote Sens. **8**(5), 368 (2016)

34. Pham, M.T., Mercier, G., Regniers, O., Bombrun, L., Michel, J.: Texture retrieval from very high resolution remote sensing images using local extrema-based descriptors. In: Proceedings of IEEE International Geoscience and Remote Sensing Symposium (IGARSS), pp. 1839–1842. IEEE (2016)

35. Raghuwanshi, G., Tyagi, V.: A survey on texture image retrieval. In: Satapathy, S.C., Raju, K.S., Mandal, J.K., Bhateja, V. (eds.) Proceedings of the Second International Conference on Computer and Communication Technologies. AISC, vol. 381, pp. 427–435. Springer, New Delhi (2016). https://doi.org/10.1007/978-81-322-2526-3_44

36. Schmidhuber, J.: Deep learning in neural networks: an overview. Neural Netw. **61**, 85–117 (2015)

37. Simonyan, K., Zisserman, A.: Very deep convolutional networks for large-scale image recognition. arXiv preprint arXiv:1409.1556 (2014)

38. Singh, C., Walia, E., Kaur, K.P.: Color texture description with novel local binary patterns for effective image retrieval. Pattern Recognit. **76**, 50–68 (2018)

39. Subrahmanyam, M., Maheshwari, R., Balasubramanian, R.: Local maximum edge binary patterns: a new descriptor for image retrieval and object tracking. Signal Process. **92**(6), 1467–1479 (2012). https://doi.org/10.1016/j.sigpro.2011.12.005

40. Tan, X., Triggs, B.: Enhanced local texture feature sets for face recognition under difficult lighting conditions. IEEE Trans. Image Process. **19**(6), 1635–1650 (2010). https://doi.org/10.1109/TIP.2010.2042645

41. Tyagi, V.: Content-based image retrieval techniques: a review. Content-Based Image Retrieval, pp. 29–48. Springer, Singapore (2017). https://doi.org/10.1007/978-981-10-6759-4_2

42. Tzelepi, M., Tefas, A.: Deep convolutional learning for content based image retrieval. Neurocomputing **275**, 2467–2478 (2018)

43. Verdoolaege, G., De Backer, S., Scheunders, P.: Multiscale colour texture retrieval using the geodesic distance between multivariate generalized Gaussian models. In: Proceedings of IEEE International Conference on Image Processing (ICIP), pp. 169–172 (2008). https://doi.org/10.1109/ICIP.2008.4711718

44. Verma, M., Raman, B.: Local tri-directional patterns: a new texture feature descriptor for image retrieval. Digit. Signal Process. **51**, 62–72 (2016). https://doi.org/10.1016/j.dsp.2016.02.002

45. Verma, M., Raman, B.: Local neighborhood difference pattern: a new feature descriptor for natural and texture image retrieval. Multimedia Tools Appl. **77**(10), 11843–11866 (2018)

46. Verma, M., Raman, B., Murala, S.: Local extrema co-occurrence pattern for color and texture image retrieval. Neurocomputing **165**, 255–269 (2015). https://doi.org/10.1016/j.neucom.2015.03.015

47. Yang, H.y., Liang, L.l., Zhang, C., Wang, X.b., Niu, P.p., Wang, X.y.: Weibull statistical modeling for textured image retrieval using nonsubsampled contourlet transform. Soft Comput. 1–16 (2018)

Extended Non-local Feature for Visual Saliency Detection in Low Contrast Images

Xin Xu[1,2(⊠)] and Jie Wang[1]

[1] School of Computer Science and Technology,
Wuhan University of Science and Technology, Wuhan 430065, China
xuxin0336@163.com
[2] Hubei Province Key Laboratory of Intelligent Information Processing
and Real-Time Industrial System, Wuhan University of Science and Technology,
Wuhan 430065, China

Abstract. Saliency detection model can substantially facilitate a wide range of applications. Conventional saliency detection models primarily rely on high level features from deep learning and hand-crafted low-level image features. However, they may face great challenges in nighttime scenario, due to the lack of well-defined feature to represent saliency information in low contrast images. This paper proposes a saliency detection model for nighttime scene. This model is capable of extracting non-local feature that is jointly learned with local features under a unified deep learning framework. The key idea of the proposed model is to hierarchically introduce non-local module with local contrast processing blocks, aiming to provide robust representation of saliency information towards low contrast images with low signal-to-noise ratio property. Besides, both nighttime and daytime images are utilized in training to provide complementary information. Extensive experiments have been conducted on five challenging datasets and our nighttime image dataset to evaluate the performance of the proposed model.

Keywords: Deep learning · Non-local feature · Saliency detection
Low contrast images

1 Introduction

The purpose of saliency detection is to highlight significant areas and targets in images. Saliency detection aims to mimic the human visual system, which can naturally separate predominant objects of a scene from the rest of image. As a computer vision preprocessing step, saliency detection has achieved great success in various applications, such as object retargeting [1], photo synthesis [2, 3], visual tracking [4], image retrieval [5, 6], semantic segmentation [7], and etc.

Conventional saliency detection models primarily extract effective information from images based on low-level visual features [8–10]. With the development of deep learning in recent years, high level features extracted from deep learning have demonstrated superior results in saliency detection. Current deep learning based saliency detection models can be generally divided into three categories: 1. Global

© Springer Nature Switzerland AG 2019
L. Leal-Taixé and S. Roth (Eds.): ECCV 2018 Workshops, LNCS 11132, pp. 580–592, 2019.
https://doi.org/10.1007/978-3-030-11018-5_46

features extraction using *convolutional neural network* (CNN); 2. Multi-scale local features extraction; and 3. Constructing non-local neural networks to integrate global and local features. The first type extracts global features containing image objectiveness via a straight forward CNN model [11–13]. The second one extracts local image features incorporating multi-task processing, such as generative object proposals, postprocessing, superpixel smoothing, superpixel segmentation [1, 14–17], and etc. However, either global features or local features can only reflect partial aspect of visual saliency and may cause certain bias. Combination of the information from both global and local features can be accurate and effective. Accordingly, the third category utilizes non-local structure to extract local and global features [18, 19]. The non-local structure has demonstrated its effectiveness efficiency in saliency detection.

However, current non-local based saliency detection models simply perform mean processing or short connection to different feature layers. They are mainly based on patch operation, and may face great challenges in nighttime scenario, due to the lack of well-defined feature to represent saliency information in low contrast images. In this paper, we propose a novel saliency detection model for nighttime scene. This model can extract non-local feature that is jointly learned with local features under a unified deep learning framework.

The rest of the paper is organized as follows. Section 2 provides an overview of saliency detection models. Section 3 describes the theory and practical implementation of our network. Section 4 shows the performance of the proposed model against the state-of-the-art models. Finally, Sect. 5 gives the conclusions.

2 Related Works

Most of current saliency detection models highlight salient object by comparing its difference with backgrounds, and primarily rely on low level features, including color [8], contrast [9], contour [10], objectness [20], focusness [21], backgroundness [22], uniqueness [23], and etc. These methods do not need the training process, and extract saliency feature at pixel level [9], region level [8] and graph [2] respectively. Recently, deep learning models have demonstrated their effectiveness in saliency detection, which can extract high level features directly from image.

Early deep learning based saliency detection models [12, 13] mainly utilize convolutional layer to obtain the global features in images, and use fully connected layers for output. However, this structure only extracts objectiveness features in images, and can only roughly determine the location of salient object with incomplete information. Aiming to address this problem, local neural networks [1] and multi-tasking neural networks [16] are proposed recently. For example, Li *et al.* [1] proposed the *multiscale deep features* (MSDF) neural network, which decomposes input images into a set of non-overlapping blocks and then puts them into the three-scale neural networks to learn the local features, finally outputs with a full connected layer. Li *et al.* [16] proposed the *multi-task* (MT) neural network, which uses convolution to extract global feeble features and combines superpixel segmentation to jointly guide the output of saliency maps.

However, multiple levels of convolutional and pooling layers "blur" the object boundaries, and high level features from the output of the last layer are too coarse spatially for the saliency detection task. Accordingly, the non-local neural networks [18, 19] are proposed to improve the performance. Luo *et al.* [18] proposed the *non-local deep features* (NLDF) network, which uses the convolution to extract local and global features. Then it uses upsampling to connect each local feature. Finally, the local and global features are linearly fused to output the saliency map. In order to get the local depth feature, it subtracts the local mean from the local feature in the contrast layer, so that a simple processing is done on the pixel-wise. Hou *et al.* [19] proposed a *deeply supervised short connections* (DSSC) neural network by upsampling to connect low-level and high-level features shortly, so that high-level features can share the information from the low-level features. Both of these methods increase the receptive fields of convolution, and greatly improve their effectiveness to avoid blurring object boundaries.

However, current non-local based saliency detection models simply perform mean processing or short connection to different feature layers [24]. They are mainly based on patch operation, and may face great challenges in nighttime scenario, due to the lack of well-defined feature to represent saliency information in low contrast images. In this paper, we propose a novel saliency detection model for nighttime scene. As illustrated in Fig. 1, our model differs from current models as it extracts non-local feature which is jointly learned with local features under a unified deep learning framework.

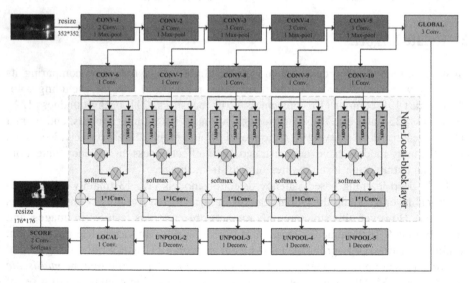

Fig. 1. Architecture of our 4 × 5 grid-CNN network for salient object detection.

The main attributions of the proposed model are in three folds:

1. The model employs non-local blocks with local contrast processing units to learn saliency information from low contrast images;
2. The model introduces an IoU boundary loss to the loss function to make the boundary robust in training process;
3. Both nighttime and daytime images are used in training. Although the proposed model still falls behind the existing deep saliency models on daytime images, it receives the highest performance on nighttime images. Thus, the experimental results show that the non-local block layers efficiently extract local details on low contrast images.

3   Proposed Model

3.1   Network Architecture

As illustrated in Fig. 1, this paper provides a deep convolutional network architecture to learn discriminant saliency features from nighttime scene. Both local and global features are incorporated for salient object detection. In additions, pixel-wise calculating can provide sufficient information from low contrast images. Specifically, we have implemented a novel grid-like CNN network containing 5 columns and 4 rows. Each column extracts features at a given input scale. As illustrated in Fig. 2, the input image (on the left) is a 352×352 image and the output (on the right) is a 176×176 saliency map which was resized to 352×352 via bilinear interpolation.

The first row of our model contains five convolutional blocks derived from VGG-16 [1] (CONV-1 to CONV-5), as shown in Fig. 1. These convolution blocks contain a max pooling operation of stride 2 which downsamples their feature maps $\{A1, \ldots, A5\}$, as shown in Fig. 2. The last and rightmost convolution block of the first row computes features G that are specific to the global context of the image.

The second and third row is a set of ten convolutional blocks, CONV-6 to CONV-10 for row 2 and non-local layer for row 3 (see in Fig. 1). The aim of these blocks is to compute the similarity of any two pixels by self-attention to each resolution. The non-local layer capture the difference of each feature against its local neighborhood favoring regions that are either brighter or darker than their neighbors.

The last row is a set of deconvolution layers used to upscale the features maps from 11×11 (bottom right) all the way to 176×176 (bottom left). These UNPOOL layers are a means of combining the feature maps (Ci, Ui) computed at each scale. The lower left block constructs the final local feature map L. The SCORE block has 2 convolution layers and a softmax to compute the saliency probability by fusing the local (L) and global (G) features. Further details of our model are given in Fig. 2.

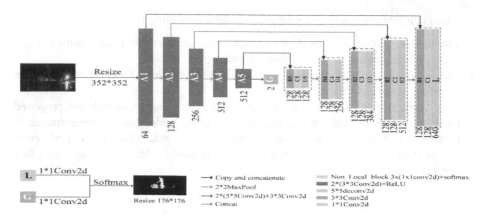

Fig. 2. Network: as an input, we have RGB channels image. A1-A5 feature maps are obtained by the first layer with five convolutional blocks. The global (G) feature map is acquired after A5. B1-B5 are computed by the second layer with five convolutional blocks that change the channels to 128. C1-C5 are calculated by the third layer with five non-local blocks that obtain more useful features from low contrast images. We perform upsampling on last layer which generated U2-U5, followed by the series of the deconvolution layers. A 1×1 convolution is added after C1 to sum the number of channels to 640, and then local feature map L is gained. Finally, G and L are liner-fused by a 1×1 convolution to generate the saliency map.

3.2   Non-local Feature Extraction

First, the size of input images is resized to 352×352, and then the feature maps of the first layer in the network are extracted by VGG-16 (Conv-1 to Conv-5), denoted as Ai, $i = 1, \ldots, 5$. Finally, the feature maps outputted by VGG-16 are connected by the convolutional blocks CONV-6 to CONV-10 each of which has a kernel with size 3×3 and 128 channels. The feature maps after the convolution are denoted as Bi, $i = 1, \ldots, 5$.

In the architecture of NLDF, the contrast features layer adopts a simple mean layer, which cannot obtain a larger receptive field in local features. Differently, in this layer, we use the architecture of non-local block to generate three feature maps by 1×1 convolution of the input value Bi. Next, the similarity of any two pixels in the feature map is determined by Gaussian filter, which makes up for the lack of local computing information of a single mean layer. At last, the weight of each pixel in the feature map is updated by residual network, so that the salient object in the feature map is more prominent to achieve the purpose of noise reduction, and acquire more useful features from low contrast images, and make the edge of the salient object clearer.

In order to learn more useful information from low contrast images, we are motivated by non-local mean [25] and bilateral filters [26], and then take advantage of the matrix multiplication to calculate the similarity of any two pixels and make the feature map embedded into Gaussian after 1×1 convolution, which is defined as:

$$f(x_i, x_j) = e^{(W_\theta x_i)^T W_\phi x_j}, \tag{1}$$

where x_i, x_j represent any two pixels of Bi. W_θ and W_ϕ represent the weight of convolution. After the convolution, the number of channels becomes half as many as it was before.

The similarity calculated above is stored in feature maps by means of self-attention, which is defined by $y_i = soft\max(Bi^T W_\theta^T W_\phi Bi)g(Bi)$. After that, the feature map Ci, $i = 1, \ldots, 5$ is obtained through a process of residual operation by y_i and Bi via:

$$Ci = W_B y_i + Bi, \tag{2}$$

where W_B is a weighting parameter to restore the same number of channels y_i same as Bi. Therefore, the size of the Ci feature map is the same as before after the process of the non-local network layer Bi.

The last layer is the deconvolution layer, which is designed to connect the pre-computed local features of the five branches of network inversely one by one. At the same time, each size of the feature map is increased by a ratio of $\{2, 4, 8, 16\}$. By doing so, the information expressed by the feature map becomes richer. Different from the NLDF [18], we replaced the mean layer with a non-local module layer, the output of which is connected by upsampling. The feature map deconvolved is defined as $Ui = UNPOOL(Ci, U(i+1))$, where the Ui, $i = 2, \ldots, 5$ is the resulting unpooled feature map. After that, the local feature map (denoted as L) is acquired by.

$$L = CONV(C1, U2) \tag{3}$$

3.3 Cross Entropy Loss

We adopt the method of linear combination to combine the local features L and global features G.

$$\hat{y}(v) = p(y(v) = c) = \frac{e^{W_L^c L(v) + b_L^c + W_G^c G + b_G^c}}{\sum_{c' \in \{0,1\}} e^{W_L^{c'} L(v) + b_L^{c'} + W_G^{c'} G + b_G^{c'}}}, \tag{4}$$

The formula uses two linear operators (W_L, b_L) and (W_G, b_G). The $y(v)$ represents ground truth. The final saliency map is predicted as $\hat{y}(v_i)$.

The cross-entropy loss function is defined as:

$$H_j(y(v), \hat{y}(v)) = -\frac{1}{N} \sum_{i=1}^{N} \sum_{c \in \{0,1\}} (y(v_i) = c)(\log(\hat{y}(v_i) = c)). \tag{5}$$

What's more, we make great use of the IoU boundary loss of NLDF [18] to make the boundary robust.

$$IoU(C_j, \hat{C}_j) = 1 - \frac{2|C_j \cap \hat{C}_j|}{|C_j| + |\hat{C}_j|}. \tag{6}$$

Finally, the final loss function is obtained by a combination of the cross-entropy loss function and the IoU boundary loss,

$$Total\,Loss \approx \sum_j \lambda_i \int H_j(y(v), \hat{y}(v)) + \sum_j \gamma_i \int (1 - IoU(C_j, \hat{C}_j)). \tag{7}$$

Our whole loss computation procedure is end-to-end train, and an example is shown in Fig. 3.

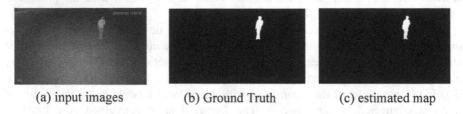

    (a) input images   (b) Ground Truth   (c) estimated map

Fig. 3. A single input image. (a) together with its ground truth saliency; (b) the estimated boundary; (c) after training for 17 epochs is in good agreement with the true bound.

4   Experiments

4.1   Datasets

In order to evaluate the performance of the proposed approach, we conduct a set of qualitative and quantitative experiments on six benchmark datasets annotated with pixelwise ground-truth labeling, including MSRA-B [27], HKU-IS [1], DUT-OMRON [28], PASCAL-S [29], and ECSSD [30]. Besides, we built a nighttime images (NTI) dataset with 478 nighttime natural scene images to facilitate this study.

MSRA-B: contains 5000 images, most of which have one salient object and corresponding pixel ground truth [31].

HKU-IS: contains 4447 images, most of which are used for multiple salient objects.

DUT-OMRON: contains 5168 images, each of which contains one or more new salient objects with a complex background.

PASCAL-S: contains 850 images. This dataset contains both pixel-wise saliency ground truth and eye fixation ground truth labeled by 12 subjects.

ECSSD: contains 1000 images with complicated architecture all of which are collected from the Internet. The ground truth masks were labeled by 5 subjects.

NTI: contains 478 nighttime natural scene images, This dataset contains two degree low contrast images, which consists of 3 subjects, the one about Only a person, the another with many people, others included human and object (such as bicycle, car, and house and etc.). So the model with low contrast features can be learned via the dataset.

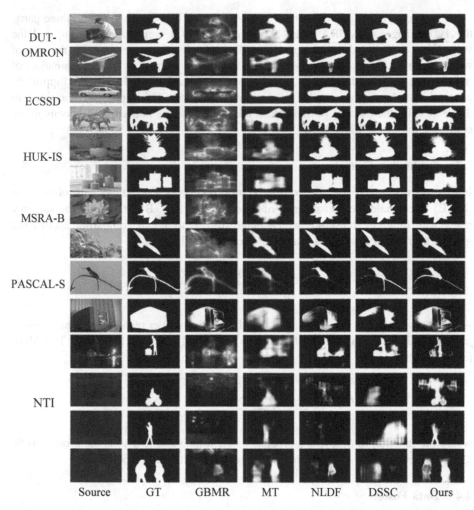

| Source | GT | GBMR | MT | NLDF | DSSC | Ours |

DUT-OMRON

ECSSD

HUK-IS

MSRA-B

PASCAL-S

NTI

Fig. 4. Saliency maps produced by the GBMR [28], MT [16], DSSC [19], NLDF [18] methods compared to our method on six datasets. The Our maps provides clear salient regions and exhibit good uniformity as compared to the saliency maps from the other deep learning methods (MT, NLDF, DSSC) on NTI dataset. Our method is also more robust to background clutter than the non-deep-learning method (GBMR).

4.2 Implementation and Experimental Setup

Our method is accomplished by TensorFlow. The weights of CONV-1 to CONV-5 are initialized with network of VGG-16 [13]. All of the weights added in the network were initialized randomly by a truncated normal ($\sigma = 0.01$). Besides, the biases were initialized to zero. There is an adam optimizer [32] used to train our model with a learning rate of 10^{-6}, $\beta_1 = 0.9$, and $\beta_2 = 0.999$.

In our experiment, the datasets of MSRA-B and NTI were divided into three parts: the 1000 images in MSRA-B and 220 images in NTI were used to train, and the validation set included 500 images in MSRA-B and 100 images in NTI, the rest of which were added to the test set. Our models were trained by the combination of training set and validation set. What's more, the method of horizontal flipping is adopted to achieve the purpose of data augmentation. The inputs were resized to 352×352 for the training of network. It takes about seven hours for 17 epochs in the configuration of NVIDIA 1070.

4.3   Evaluation Criteria

In this paper, we make use of *precision-recall* (PR) curves, F_β and *mean absolute error* (MAE) to evaluate the performance of saliency detection. By binarizing the saliency maps with different thresholds which range from 0 to 1 and comparing against the ground truth, the PR curve is obtained. The F_β is defined as,

$$F_\beta = \frac{(1+\beta^2) \cdot Precision \cdot Recall}{\beta^2 \cdot Precision + Recall}, \qquad (8)$$

where β^2 is valued by 0.3 as usual so that the precision over recall can be emphasized just like [33]. The maximum F-Measure is computed from the PR curve. The MAE [34] is defined as

$$MAE = \frac{1}{W \times H} \sum_{x=1}^{W} \sum_{y=1}^{H} |S(x,y) - L(x,y)|, \qquad (9)$$

where the function of $S(x,y)$ is a predicted salient map and $L(x,y)$ is the ground truth. The parameters of W and H represent the width and height, respectively.

4.4   Data Fusion

There are three models obtained by the progress of training. We call the model trained with only the night images NT-model and the model trained with high contrast images is called the DT-model, Furthermore, the NDT-model was defined by a model trained by combining night images with high contrast images. The performance of the models is shown in Fig. 5. MAE and Max F_β are illustrated in Table 1.

Through the test, we can see from the evaluation indicators that the NDT-model is 13.1% lower than the DT-model in MAE, and a 46.5% increase of Max F_β. In addition, the NDT-model is 11% higher than the NT-model, and the MAE is 1% lower (see Table 1). The model after a data fusion becomes more robust than before (see Fig. 5).

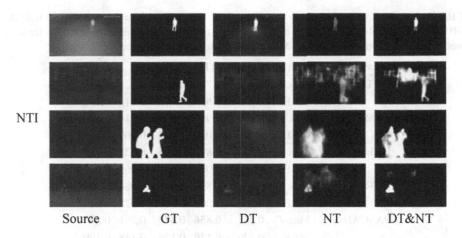

| | Source | GT | DT | NT | DT&NT |

Fig. 5. Daytime datasets to get the model DT and the model NT obtained by the night datasets. Naturally we acquired the model of DT&NT with a fusion of them. It turned out that the DT detected no objects and NT measured objects with relatively blurry edges. After a fusion of them, the performance of the model is greatly improved.

Table 1. MAE and Max F_β performance of NT-model, DT-model, NDT-model.

Dataset	Metric	Daytime (DT)	Nighttime (NT)	DT&NT (NDT)
NTI	Max F_β	0.316	0.631	0.741
	MAE	0.171	0.050	0.040

4.5 Comparison with the State-of-the-Art

Visual comparison of the saliency maps is provided in Fig. 4. All saliency maps of other methods were either provided by the authors or computed using the authors' released code. PR curves are shown in Fig. 6, and the Max F_β and MAE scores are in Table 2.

Our network structure is similar to NLDF. Differently, a non-local block is added into the local module to calculate any two pixels similarity of the feature maps by self-attention. In result, the MAE decreased by 0.2%, Max F_β increased by 7.3% compared with NLDF in NTI dataset.

Although low-level and high-level features are combined by short connections to make the feature map more informative in DSSC, it is difficult to learn some useful features for the night scene. Thus, more useful features are obtained via non-local block for low contrast images in our method.

Moreover, the MT adopted superpixel segmentation to enhance the correlation between pixels in the environment of low SNR, but the convolution model is too simple to learn serviceable features. We took great advantage of the non-local network to compute the similarity of any two pixels for a better effect in NTI dataset.

Table 2. Quantitative performance of our model on six benchmark datasets compared with the GBMR [28], MT [16], DSSC [19], and NLDF [18] models. The latter three are deep learning methods and the former is not. The Max and MAE metrics are defined in the text.

Dataset	Metric	GBMR	MT	NLDF	SC	Ours
DUT-OMRON	Max F_β	0.474	**0.774**	0.753	0.726	0.747
	MAE	0.247	**0.084**	0.080	0.113	0.088
ECSSD	Max F_β	0.549	0.900	0.905	**0.914**	0.896
	MAE	0.297	0.079	**0.063**	0.069	0.066
HKU-IS	Max F_β	0.525	0.871	0.915	**0.928**	0.907
	MAE	0.267	0.084	**0.049**	0.069	0.052
MSRA-B	Max F_β	0.592	0.893	**0.941**	0.884	0.903
	MAE	0.245	0.069	**0.030**	0.075	0.049
PASCAL-S	Max F_β	0.587	**0.856**	0.849	0.851	0.835
	MAE	0.320	**0.140**	0.146	0.148	0.149
NTI	Max F_β	0.271	0.667	0.668	0.423	**0.741**
	MAE	0.080	0.048	0.042	0.135	**0.040**

As for the traditional method GBMR, it is difficult to find an effective feature applying to nighttime scenes. Differently, the proposed model adopted a data-driven approach to gain more effective features to make our method more robust.

Since our method is designed for nighttime scenes, the daytime images can be optionally used for data fusion to improve the performance at nighttime. As illustrated in Fig. 6, the proposed model can achieve the best performance compared to NLDF, MT, DSSC and GBMR.

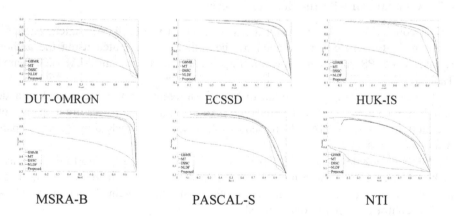

DUT-OMRON ECSSD HUK-IS

MSRA-B PASCAL-S NTI

Fig. 6. PR curves for our model compared to GBMR [28], MT [16], DCSS [19], and NLDF [18]. Our model can deliver state-of-the-art performance on NTI datasets.

5 Conclusion

In this paper, we utilized a unified deep learning framework to integrate local and global features, and introduce non-local module with local contrast processing blocks. This method can provide robust representation of saliency information towards low contrast images with low signal-to-noise ratio property. Moreover, we utilize both nighttime and daytime images in training, which can provide complementary information to enhance performance of saliency detection. Our method has achieved the best performance compared to the state-of the-art methods.

Acknowledgments. This work was supported by the Natural Science Foundation of China (61602349 and 61440016).

References

1. Li, G., Yu, Y.: Visual saliency based on multiscale deep features. In: IEEE Computer Society Conference on Computer Vision and Pattern Recognition, pp. 5455–5463 (2015)
2. Chen, T., Cheng, M.-M., Tan, P., Shamir, A., Hu, S.-M.: Sketch2photo: internet image montage. ACM Trans. Graph. **28**(5), 124:1–124:10 (2009)
3. Hu, S.-M., Chen, T., Xu, K., Cheng, M.-M., Martin, R.-R.: Internet visual media processing: a survey with graphics and vision applications. Vis. Comput. **29**(5), 393–405 (2013)
4. Borji, A., Frintrop, S., Sihite, D.-N., Itti, L.: Adaptive object tracking by learning background context. In: IEEE Conference on Computer Vision and Pattern Recognition Workshops, pp. 23–30 (2012)
5. Gao, Y., Wang, M., Tao, D., Ji, R., Dai, Q.: 3-D object retrieval and recognition with hypergraph analysis. IEEE Trans. Image Process. **21**(9), 4290–4303 (2012)
6. Cheng, M.-M., Hou, Q.-B., Zhang, S.-H., Rosin, P.-L.: Intelligent visual media processing: when graphics meets vision. J. Comput. Sci. Technol. **32**(1), 110–121 (2017)
7. Mehrani, P., Veksler, O.: Saliency segmentation based on learning and graph cut refinement. In: British Machine Vision Conference, pp. 110.1–110.12 (2010)
8. Zhang, J., Wang, M., Zhang, S., Li, X., Wu, X.: Spatiochromatic context modeling for color saliency analysis. IEEE Trans. Neural Netw. Learn. Syst. **27**(6), 1177–1189 (2016)
9. Goferman, S., Zelnik-Manor, L., Tal, A.: Context-aware saliency detection. IEEE Trans. Pattern Anal. Mach. Intell. **34**(10), 1915–1926 (2012)
10. Liu, Q., Hong, X., Zou, B., Chen, J., Chen, Z., Zhao, G.: Hierarchical contour closure-based holistic salient object detection. IEEE Trans. Image Process. **26**(9), 4537–4552 (2017)
11. Mu, N., Xu, X., Zhang, X., Zhang, H.: Salient object detection using a covariance-based CNN model in low-contrast images. Neural Comput. Appl. **29**(8), 181–192 (2018)
12. Pan, J., Sayrol, E., Giro-I-Nieto, X., McGuinness, K., O'Connor, N.-E.: Shallow and deep convolutional networks for saliency prediction. In: IEEE Conference on Computer Vision and Pattern Recognition, pp. 598–606 (2016)
13. Simonyan, K., Zisserman, A.: Very deep convolutional networks for large-scale image recognition. In: IEEE Conference on Computer Vision and Pattern Recognition, pp. 1–14 (2014)
14. Li, G., Yu, Y.: Deep contrast learning for salient object detection. In: IEEE Conference on Computer Vision and Pattern Recognition, pp. 478–487 (2016)

15. Liu, N., Han, J., Zhang, D., Wen, S., Liu, T.: Predicting eye fixations using convolutional neural networks. In: IEEE Conference on Computer Vision and Pattern Recognition, pp. 362–370 (2015)
16. Li, X., et al.: DeepSaliency: multi-task deep neural network model for salient object detection. IEEE Trans. Image Process. **25**(8), 3919–3930 (2016)
17. Zhao, R., Ouyang, W., Li, H., Wang, X.: Saliency detection by multi-context deep learning. In: IEEE Conference on Computer Vision and Pattern Recognition, pp. 1265–1274 (2015)
18. Luo, Z., Mishra, A., Achkar, A., Eichel, J., Li, S., Jodoin, P.-M.: Non-local deep features for salient object detection. In: IEEE Conference on Computer Vision and Pattern Recognition, pp. 6593–6601 (2017)
19. Hou, Q., Cheng, M.-M., Hu, X., Borji, A., Tu, Z., Torr, P.: Deeply supervised salient object detection with short connections. In: IEEE Conference on Computer Vision and Pattern Recognition, pp. 5300–5309 (2017)
20. Jiang, P., Ling, H., Yu, J., Peng, J.: Salient region detection by UFO: uniqueness, focusness and objectness. In: IEEE International Conference on Computer Vision, pp. 1976–1983 (2013)
21. Wei, Y., Wen, F., Zhu, W., Sun, J.: Geodesic saliency using background priors. In: Fitzgibbon, A., Lazebnik, S., Perona, P., Sato, Y., Schmid, C. (eds.) ECCV 2012. LNCS, vol. 7574, pp. 29–42. Springer, Heidelberg (2012). https://doi.org/10.1007/978-3-642-33712-3_3
22. Chang, K.-Y., Liu, T.-L., Chen, H.-T., Lai, S.-H.: Fusing generic objectness and visual saliency for salient object detection. In: IEEE International Conference on Computer Vision, pp. 914–921 (2011)
23. Perazzi, F., Krahenbuhl, P., Pritch, Y., Hornung, A.: Saliency filters: contrast based filtering for salient region detection. In: IEEE International Conference on Computer Vision, pp. 733–740 (2012)
24. Wang, X., Girshick, R., Gupta, A., He, K.: Non-local neural networks. In: IEEE Conference on Computer Vision and Pattern Recognition, pp. 7794–7803 (2018)
25. Buades, A., Coll, B., Morel, J.-M.: A non-local algorithm for image denoising. In: IEEE Computer Society Conference on Computer Vision and Pattern Recognition, pp. 60–65 (2005)
26. Tomasi, C., Manduchi, R.: Bilateral filtering for gray and color images. In: IEEE International Conference on Computer Vision, pp. 839–846 (1998)
27. Liu, T., et al.: Learning to detect a salient object. IEEE Trans. Pattern Anal. Mach. Intell. **33**(2), 353–367 (2011)
28. Yang, C., Zhang, L., Lu, H., Ruan, X., Yang, M.: Saliency detection via graph-based manifold ranking. In: IEEE Conference on Computer Vision and Pattern Recognition, pp. 3166–3173 (2013)
29. Li, Y., Hou, X., Koch, C., Rehg, J., Yuille, A.: The secrets of salient object segmentation. In: IEEE Conference on Computer Vision and Pattern Recognition. CVPR, pp. 280–287 (2014)
30. Yan, Q., Xu, L., Shi, J., Jia, J.: Hierarchical saliency detection. In: IEEE Conference on Computer Vision and Pattern Recognition, pp. 1155–1162 (2013)
31. Jiang, H., Wang, J., Yuan, Z., Wu, Y., Zheng, N., Li, S.: Salient object detection: a discriminative regional feature integration approach. In: IEEE Conference on Computer Vision and Pattern Recognition, pp. 2083–2090 (2013)
32. Kingma, D.P., Ba, J.: Adam: a method for stochastic optimization. In: International Conference for Learning Representations, pp. 1–15 (2014)
33. Achanta, R., Hemami, S., Estrada, F., Susstrunk, S.: Frequency-tuned salient region detection. In: IEEE Conference on Computer Vision and Pattern Recognition, pp. 1597–1604 (2009)
34. Perazzi, F., Krahenbuhl, P., Pritch, Y., Hornung, A.: Saliency filters: contrast based filtering for salient region detection. In: IEEE Conference on Computer Vision and Pattern Recognition, pp. 733–740 (2012)

Incomplete Multi-view Clustering via Graph Regularized Matrix Factorization

Jie Wen[1], Zheng Zhang[1,2], Yong Xu[1(✉)], and Zuofeng Zhong[1]

[1] Bio-Computing Research Center, Harbin Institute of Technology, Shenzhen,
Shenzhen 518055, Guangdong, China
wenjie@hrbeu.edu.cn, darrenzz219@gmail.com, yongxu@ymail.com,
zfzhong2010@gmail.com
[2] The University of Queensland, Brisbane, Australia

Abstract. Clustering with incomplete views is a challenge in multi-view clustering. In this paper, we provide a novel and simple method to address this issue. Specially, the proposed method simultaneously exploits the local information of each view and the complementary information among views to learn the common latent representation for all samples, which can greatly improve the compactness and discriminability of the obtained representation. Compared with the conventional graph embedding methods, the proposed method does not introduce any extra regularization term and corresponding penalty parameter to preserve the local structure of data, and thus does not increase the burden of extra parameter selection. By imposing the orthogonal constraint on the basis matrix of each view, the proposed method is able to handle the out-of-sample. Moreover, the proposed method can be viewed as a unified framework for multi-view learning since it can handle both incomplete and complete multi-view clustering and classification tasks. Extensive experiments conducted on several multi-view datasets prove that the proposed method can significantly improve the clustering performance.

Keywords: Multi-view clustering · Incomplete view
Common latent representation · Out-of-sample

1 Introduction

Multi-view clustering has been achieved great development and has been successfully applied in many applications, such as image retrieval [9], webpage classification [1,25], and speech recognition [12]. Recently, many methods have been proposed, such as multi-view k-means clustering [2], multi-view spectral clustering via bipartite graph [10], and co-regularized multi-view spectral clustering [8], etc. Compared with the single-view clustering, multi-view clustering can exploit the complementary information among multiple views, and thus has the potential to achieve a better performance [29].

J. Wen and Z. Zhang—Equally contributed.

© Springer Nature Switzerland AG 2019
L. Leal-Taixé and S. Roth (Eds.): ECCV 2018 Workshops, LNCS 11132, pp. 593–608, 2019.
https://doi.org/10.1007/978-3-030-11018-5_47

For the conventional multi-view clustering, they commonly require that the available samples should have all of the views. However, it always happens that some views are missing for parts of samples in real world applications [18]. For example, the data obtained by the blood test and images scanned by the magnetic resonance can be regarded as two necessary views for diagnosing the disease. However, it is often the case that we only have the results of one view for some individuals since they would like to take only one of the two tests. In this case, the conventional methods fail. In this paper, we refer to the clustering task with incomplete views as incomplete multi-view clustering (IMC).

For IMC, a few methods have been proposed, which can be commonly categorized into two groups. The one group is based on completing the incomplete views. For example, Trivedi et al. proposed a kernel CCA based method, which tries to recover the kernel matrix of the incomplete view and then learns two projections for the two views, respectively [18]. However, it requires at least one complete view for reference. In other words, it is not applicable to the case that all views are incomplete. To address this issue, Gao et al. proposed a two-step approach, which first fills in the missing views with the corresponding average of all samples, and then learns the common representation for the two views based on the spectral graph theory [5]. The shortcoming of this approach is that it introduces some useless even noisy information to the data. For data with small incomplete percentages, this approach may be effective. However, for the data with large incomplete percentages, this approach is harmful to find the common representation since these useless information may dominate the representation learning [17]. The other group focuses on directly learning the common latent subspace or representation for all views, in which the most representative works are the partial multi-view clustering (PVC) [30], multi-incomplete-view clustering (MIC) [17], and incomplete multi-modality grouping (IMG) [28]. Based on the non-negative matrix factorization (NMF), PVC directly learns a common latent representation for two views by simply regularizing different views of the same sample to have the same representation [30]. MIC jointly learns the latent representation of each view and the consensus representation by utilizing the weighted NMF algorithm, in which the missing views are constrained with the small weight even 0 during learning [17]. IMG can be viewed as an extension of PVC, which further embeds an adaptively learned graph on the latent representation [28].

Although some methods have been proposed to address the IMC problem, several problems still exist which limit their performances. For example, these methods all ignore the geometric structure of data. This indicates that the intrinsic geometric structure of data may be destroyed in the representation space, which may lead to a bad performance. The second shortcoming of these methods, especially MIC and IMG, is that there are many penalty parameters (more than three) to be set. These tunable parameters directly influence the clustering performance and limit its real applications because it is still an open problem to adaptively select the optimal parameter for different datasets. The third shortcoming is that these methods all cannot handle the out-of-sample problem. In this paper, we propose a novel and simple IMC method, named incomplete multi-view clustering via graph regularized matrix factorization (IMC_GRMF), to solve the above problems and improve the performance. Similar to PVC, the matrix factorization technique is exploited to learn the common latent representation, in which the representation corresponding to those samples with all views are regularized to be consistent. In addition, a nearest neighbor graph is neatly imposed on the reconstruction errors of the matrix factorization to exploit the local geometric structure of data, which enables the method to learn a more compact and discriminative representation for clustering. Compared with the other methods, our approach does not introduce any extra regularization term and corresponding penalty parameter to preserve the locality structure of data. Extensive experimental results prove the effectiveness of the proposed method for incomplete multi-view clustering.

2 Notations and Related Work

2.1 Notations

Let $X^{(k)} = [X_c^{(k)T}; \bar{X}^{(k)T}]^T \in R^{(n_c+n_k) \times m_k}$ be the kth view of data, where each sample in the corresponding view is represented by a row vector with m_k features, n_c is the number of paired samples (*i.e.*, there are no missing views for these samples). $x_i^{(k)}$ denotes the features of the kth view of the ith sample. We refer to the kth view as $Vi(k)$. $\bar{X}^{(k)} \in R^{n_k \times m_k}$ represents that n_k samples only contain the features of $Vi(k)$ while the features of the other views are missing. The total samples of the data is $n = n_c + \sum_{k=1}^{v} n_k$. For a matrix $A \in R^{m \times n}$, its l_F norm and l_1 norm are defined as $\|A\|_F = \sqrt{\sum_{j=1}^{n} \sum_{i=1}^{m} a_{i,j}^2}$ and $\|A\|_1 = \sum_{j=1}^{n} \sum_{i=1}^{m} |a_{i,j}|$, respectively, where $a_{i,j}$ denotes the ith row and jth column element of matrix A [14,23]. $Tr(\cdot)$ is the trace operation. We use A^T to denote the transposition of matrix A [15]. I is the identity matrix. $A \geq 0$ means that all elements of matrix A are not less than zero.

2.2 Partial Multi-View Clustering (PVC)

For data with two incomplete views, PVC seeks to learn a common latent subspace for both two views, where different views of the same sample should have the same representation [14]. The learning model of PVC is formulated as follows:

$$\min_{P_c, \bar{P}^{(1)}, \bar{P}^{(2)}, U^{(1)}, U^{(2)}} \left\| \begin{bmatrix} X_c^{(1)} \\ \bar{X}^{(1)} \end{bmatrix} - \begin{bmatrix} P_c \\ \bar{P}^{(1)} \end{bmatrix} U^{(1)} \right\|_F^2 + \lambda \left\| \begin{bmatrix} P_c \\ \bar{P}^{(1)} \end{bmatrix} \right\|_1$$
$$+ \left\| \begin{bmatrix} X_c^{(2)} \\ \bar{X}^{(2)} \end{bmatrix} - \begin{bmatrix} P_c \\ \bar{P}^{(2)} \end{bmatrix} U^{(2)} \right\|_F^2 + \lambda \left\| \begin{bmatrix} P_c \\ \bar{P}^{(2)} \end{bmatrix} \right\|_1 \quad (1)$$
$$s.t.\ U^{(1)} \geq 0, U^{(2)} \geq 0, P_c \geq 0, \bar{P}^{(1)} \geq 0, \bar{P}^{(2)} \geq 0,$$

where λ is the penalty parameter. $U^{(1)} \in R^{K \times m_1}$ and $U^{(2)} \in R^{K \times m_2}$ are the latent space basis matrices for the two views, $P_c \in R^{n_c \times K}$, $\bar{P}^{(1)} \in R^{n_1 \times K}$, and $\bar{P}^{(2)} \in R^{n_2 \times K}$ are the latent representations of the original data, K is the feature dimension in the latent space.

For PVC, the new representation corresponding to all samples can be expressed as $P = \begin{bmatrix} P_c \\ \bar{P}^{(1)} \\ \bar{P}^{(2)} \end{bmatrix} \in R^{n \times K}$. Then the conventional k-means can be performed on it to obtain the final clustering result.

3   The Proposed Method

For multi-view data, learning a common latent representation for all views is one of the most favorite approaches in the field of multi-view clustering. However, how to learn a compact and discriminative common representation for the incomplete multi-view data is a challenge task. In this section, a novel multi-view clustering framework shown in Fig. 1 is provided to address this issue, in which the local information of each view and the complementary information across different views are jointly integrated.

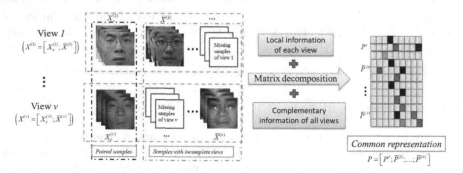

Fig. 1. The description of IMC_GRMF. In this work, we suppose that there are only n_c samples (paired samples) have features of all views.

3.1   Learning Model of the Proposed Method

In past years, exploiting the locality geometric structure of data has been proved an effective approach for representation learning, which not only can improve the discriminability and compactness of the learned representation, but also avoids overfitting [3,13,16,20,22,26,27]. For example, in [13,16], a nearest neighbor graph is introduced to constrain the new representation or basis for incomplete multi-view clustering. Although the purpose is realized, the complexity is also increased because they commonly introduce at least one tunable penalty parameter to the model. Since some basic models already have two or more tuned parameters, introducing any extra tuned parameter to the model will greatly increase the burden in parameter selection. So the conventional graph embedding approaches are not a good choice to guide the representation learning. In this section, we propose a novel and simple approach to solve this challenge, in which the local information of each view are embedded into the learning model based on the following Lemma [21].

Lemma 1: For three samples $\{x_1, x_2, x_3\} \in R^m$, suppose x_1 and x_2 are the nearest neighbor to each other, x_3 is not the nearest neighbor to samples x_1 and x_2. If there is a complete dictionary $U \in R^{k \times m}$ that satisfies $x_i = p_i U$ ($i = \{1, 2, 3\}$), where $p_i \in R^k$ can be viewed as the reconstruction coefficient. Then we have the following conclusion: the reconstructed sample $p_2 U$ ($p_1 U$) is also the nearest neighbor to the original sample x_1 (x_2) and is still not the nearest neighbor to sample x_3.

The proof to Lemma 1 is very simple and thus we omit it here. From Lemma 1, we know that the reconstruction operation does not destroy the local geometric structure of the original data. Inspired by this motivation, we design the following objective function to exploit the local information of data for common representation learning:

$$\min_{P^{(k)}, U^{(k)}} \sum_{k=1}^{v} \sum_{j=1}^{n_c+n_k} \sum_{i=1}^{n_c+n_k} \left\| x_i^{(k)} - p_j^{(k)} U^{(k)} \right\|_2^2 w_{i,j}^{(k)} + \lambda_2 \sum_{k=1}^{v} \left\| P^{(k)} \right\|_1 \qquad (2)$$
$$s.t. U^{(k)} U^{(k)T} = I,$$

where λ_2 is a penalty parameter. $p_j^{(k)}$ is the new representation of the jth sample in the kth view. $w_{i,j}^{(k)}$ is a binary value which is simply pre-defined as follows:

$$w_{i,j}^{(k)} = \begin{cases} 1, & if \ x_i^{(k)} \in \Phi\left(x_j^{(k)}\right) \ or \ x_j^{(k)} \in \Phi\left(x_i^{(k)}\right) \\ 0, & otherwise, \end{cases} \qquad (3)$$

where $\Phi\left(x_j^{(k)}\right)$ denotes the sample set of nearest neighbors to sample $x_j^{(k)}$.

By introducing the binary weight to regularize the data reconstruction, the locality structure of the original data in each view can be well preserved. Meanwhile, from (2), we can find that the proposed method does not introduce any extra regularization term and corresponding tuned parameter to preserve such locality property, which greatly reduces the complexity of penalty parameter selection in comparison with the other graph regularized IMC methods, such as DCNMF [13] and GPMVC [16] which all commonly introduce at least an extra tuned penalty parameter to preserve such locality property. For the paired samples across different views, their new representation should be consensus. To this end, we further add a regularization term based on the paired information of different views as follows:

$$\min_{P^{(k)}, P^c, U^{(k)}} \sum_{k=1}^{v} \sum_{j=1}^{n_c+n_k} \sum_{i=1}^{n_c+n_k} \left\| x_i^{(k)} - p_j^{(k)} U^{(k)} \right\|_2^2 w_{i,j}^{(k)}$$
$$+ \lambda_1 \sum_{k=1}^{v} \left\| G^{(k)} P^{(k)} - P^c \right\|_F^2 + \lambda_2 \sum_{k=1}^{v} \left\| P^{(k)} \right\|_1 \qquad (4)$$
$$s.t. U^{(k)} U^{(k)T} = I,$$

where λ_1 is a penalty parameter. $P^c \in R^{c \times K}$ is the common latent representation for the paired samples of different views. $G^{(k)} \in R^{n_c \times (n_c + n_k)}$ can be viewed as an index matrix used to remove the unpaired representation $\bar{P}^{(k)}$ from $P^{(k)} = \begin{bmatrix} P_c^{(k)} \\ \bar{P}^{(k)} \end{bmatrix}$. Since the first n_c samples of each view are regarded as the paired samples, matrix $G^{(k)}$ can be simply defined as follows:

$$G_{i,j}^{(k)} = \begin{cases} 1, & if\ i = j \\ 0, & otherwise. \end{cases} \tag{5}$$

For model (4), $P = [P^{cT}, \bar{P}^{(1)T}, \ldots, \bar{P}^{(v)T}]^T$ can be viewed as the new representations for all samples. After obtaining the new representations, we use k-means algorithm to partition those samples into their respective groups. Several good properties of the proposed model (4) are summarized as follows.

Remark 1: The proposed method is not only a clustering algorithm, but also an unsupervised classification algorithm because it can handle the out-of-sample. In essence, for any sample $x_i^{(k)}$ in the kth view, its new representation is obtained by the matrix factorization $x_i^{(k)} = p_i^{(k)} U^{(k)}$, which is equivalent to $x_i^{(k)} U^{(k)T} = p_i^{(k)}$ since $U^{(k)} U^{(k)T} = I$. Therefore, when the basis matrix $U^{(k)}$ is obtained, we can first achieve the discriminative representation for any new coming sample $y^{(k)}$ by projecting it onto the basis matrix as $p_y^{(k)} = y^{(k)} U^{(k)T}$, and then use the conventional unsupervised classification methods like k-nearest neighbor classify to predict its label.

Remark 2: The proposed model (4) is a unified multi-view learning framework, which can be applied to the incomplete and complete cases by defining different index matrices $G^{(k)}$.

Remark 3: The proposed method simultaneously exploits the local information of each view and the complementary information across different views, which is beneficial to learn a more compact and discriminative representation for clustering, and thus has the potential to perform better. Moreover, embedding the local information into the model can avoid the overfitting in handing the new sample.

Remark 4: Most importantly, we do not introduce any extra regularization term to preserve the local geometric structure of data. In other words, compared with the conventional graph embedding methods, the proposed method does not increase the burden of parameter tuning.

Remark 5: The proposed method has the potential to recover the missing views. Specifically, for a sample with only the kth view $x^{(k)}$, when its new representation $p_{x^{(k)}}$ is obtained via the proposed method, we can recover its fth missing view via $x^{(f)} = p_{x^{(k)}} U^{(f)}$.

3.2   Solution to IMC_GRMF

For the first term of (4), we can rewrite it into the following equivalent formula

$$
\sum_{k=1}^{v} \sum_{j=1}^{n_c+n_k} \sum_{i=1}^{n_c+n_k} \left\| x_i^{(k)} - p_j^{(k)} U^{(k)} \right\|_2^2 w_{i,j}^{(k)}
$$
$$
= \sum_{k=1}^{v} \left(\begin{array}{l} Tr\left(X^{(k)T} D^{(k)} X^{(k)} \right) + Tr\left(U^{(k)T} P^{(k)T} D^{(k)} P^{(k)} U^{(k)} \right) \\ -2Tr\left(X^{(k)T} W^{(k)} P^{(k)} U^{(k)} \right) \end{array} \right), \qquad (6)
$$

where $D^{(k)}$ is a diagonal matrix with each diagonal element $D_{i,i}^{(k)} = \sum_{j=1}^{n_c+n_k} W_{i,j}^{(k)}$.

Considering that the first term of (6) is constant and condition $U^{(k)} U^{(k)T} = I$, we can simplify (4) as follows according to (6):

$$
L\left(P^{(k)}, P^c, U^{(k)} \right) = \lambda_1 \sum_{k=1}^{v} \left\| G^{(k)} P^{(k)} - P^c \right\|_F^2 + \lambda_2 \sum_{k=1}^{v} \left\| P^{(k)} \right\|_1
$$
$$
+ \sum_{k=1}^{v} \left(Tr\left(P^{(k)T} D^{(k)} P^{(k)} \right) - 2Tr\left(X^{(k)T} W^{(k)} P^{(k)} U^{(k)} \right) \right). \qquad (7)
$$

Then all variables can be calculated alternatively as follows.

Step 1: Calculate $U^{(k)}$. The basis matrix $U^{(k)}$ for each view can be calculated by optimizing the following problem:

$$
\min_{U^{(k)} U^{(k)T} = I} -2Tr\left(X^{(k)T} W^{(k)} P^{(k)} U^{(k)} \right). \qquad (8)
$$

Then we can obtain the optimum value of $U^{(k)}$ as [19,31]:

$$
U^{(k)} = J^{(k)} B^{(k)T}, \qquad (9)
$$

where $J^{(k)}$ and $B^{(k)}$ are the right and left singular matrices of $(X^{(k)T} W^{(k)} P^{(k)})$, i.e., $X^{(k)T} W^{(k)} P^{(k)} = B^{(k)} \Sigma^{(k)} J^{(k)T}$.

Step 2: Calculate $P^{(k)}$. Fixing the other variables, variable $P^{(k)}$ can be calculated by minimizing the following problem:

$$
\min_{P^{(k)}} \lambda_1 \left\| G^{(k)} P^{(k)} - P^c \right\|_F^2 + \lambda_2 \left\| P^{(k)} \right\|_1
$$
$$
+ Tr\left(P^{(k)T} D^{(k)} P^{(k)} \right) - 2Tr\left(X^{(k)T} W^{(k)} P^{(k)} U^{(k)} \right). \qquad (10)
$$

Define $A^{(k)} = U^{(k)} X^{(k)T} W^{(k)} + \lambda_1 P^{cT} G^{(k)}$, $M^{(k)} = D^{(k)} + \lambda_1 G^{(k)T} G^{(k)}$. Obviously, $M^{(k)}$ is still a diagonal matrix with all diagonal elements $M_{i,i}^{(k)} > 0$. Thus, (10) can be rewritten into the following equivalent problem:

$$
\min_{P^{(k)}} \left\| \left(M^{(k)} \right)^{\frac{1}{2}} P^{(k)} - \left(A^{(k)} \left(M^{(k)} \right)^{-\frac{1}{2}} \right)^T \right\|_F^2 + \lambda_2 \left\| P^{(k)} \right\|_1. \qquad (11)
$$

Define $C^{(k)} = (A^{(k)}(M^{(k)})^{-\frac{1}{2}})^T$, problem (11) can be rewritten as follows

$$\min_{P^{(k)}} \sum_{i=1}^{n_c+n_k} M_{i,i}^{(k)} \left\| P_{i,:}^{(k)} - C_{i,:}^{(k)} \Big/ \sqrt{M_{i,i}^{(k)}} \right\|_2^2 + \lambda_2 \left\| P_{i,:}^{(k)} \right\|_1. \qquad (12)$$

where $P_{i,:}^{(k)}$ and $C_{i,:}^{(k)}$ denote the ith row vector of matrices $P^{(k)}$ and $C^{(k)}$, respectively. For problem (12), its solution can be computed independently to each row by the conventional shrinkage operation as follows [19]:

$$P_{i,:}^{(k)} = \Theta_{\lambda_2 \big/ 2M_{i,i}^{(k)}} \left(C_{i,:}^{(k)} \Big/ \sqrt{M_{i,i}^{(k)}} \right), \qquad (13)$$

where Θ denotes the shrinkage operator.

Step 3: Calculate P^c. Fixing the other variables, the common latent representation P^c can be calculated by solving the following minimization problem:

$$\min_{P^c} \sum_{k=1}^{v} \left\| G^{(k)} P^{(k)} - P^c \right\|_F^2. \qquad (14)$$

Problem (14) has the following closed form solution:

$$P^c = \sum_{k=1}^{v} G^{(k)} P^{(k)} / v. \qquad (15)$$

Algorithm 1 summarizes the computing procedures of IMC_GRMF.

Algorithm 1. IMC_GRMF (solving problem (4))

Input: Multi-view $X^{(k)}$, index matrix $G^{(k)}$, $k \in [1, v]$, parameters λ_1, λ_2.
Initialization: Initialize $P^{(k)}$ and $U^{(k)}$ with random values, construct the nearest
neighbor graph $W^{(k)}$, $P^c = \sum_{k=1}^{v} G^{(k)} P^{(k)} \Big/ v$.
while not converged **do**
   for k from 1 to v
      Update $U^{(k)}$ using (9).
      Update $P^{(k)}$ using (13).
   end
   Update P^c using (15).
end while
Output: $P^c, P^{(k)}, U^{(k)}$

3.3   Computational Complexity and Convergence Property

For Algorithm 1, it is obvious that the biggest computational cost is the singular value decomposition (SVD) in Step 1. Note that the computational complexities of matrix multiplication and addition are ignored since their computational costs are far less than SVD. Thus, we only take into account the computational complexity of Step 1. Generally, the computational complexity of SVD is $O(mn^2)$ for a $m \times n$ matrix [11]. Therefore, the computational complexity of Step 1 is about $O\left(vmK^2\right)$. v is the number of views, K is the reduced dimension or the number of clusters. Therefore, the computation complexity of the proposed method listed in Algorithm 1 is about $O\left(\tau vmK^2\right)$, where τ is the iteration number.

From the above presentations, it is obvious to see that the proposed optimization problem (7) is convex with respect to variables $P^{(k)}, P^c, U^{(k)}$, respectively. Then we have the following Theorem 1.

Theorem 1: The objective function value of problem (4) is monotonically decreasing during the iteration.

Proof. Suppose $\Upsilon\left(P_t^{(k)}, P_t^c, U_t^{(k)}\right)$ denotes the objective function value at the tth iteration. Since all sub-problems with respect to variables $P^{(k)}, P^c, U^{(k)}$ are convex and have the closed form solution, the following inequations are satisfied:

$$\Upsilon\left(P_t^{(k)}, P_t^c, U_t^{(k)}\right) \geq \Upsilon\left(P_t^{(k)}, P_t^c, U_{t+1}^{(k)}\right)$$
$$\geq \Upsilon\left(P_{t+1}^{(k)}, P_t^c, U_{t+1}^{(k)}\right) \geq \Upsilon\left(P_{t+1}^{(k)}, P_{t+1}^c, U_{t+1}^{(k)}\right). \tag{16}$$

This inequation illustrates that the objective function value of problem (4) is monotonically decreasing during the iteration. Thus we complete the proof.

Meanwhile, we can find that problem (4) is lower bounded because it at least satisfies the condition $\Upsilon\left(P_t^{(k)}, P_t^c, U_t^{(k)}\right) \geq 0$, thus Theorem 1 guarantees that the proposed method will finally converge to the local optimal solution after a few iterations.

4   Experiments and Analysis

4.1   Experimental Settings

Dataset: (1) ***Handwritten digit*** dataset [2]: The used handwritten digit is composed of 2000 samples from 10 digits, *i.e.*, 0–9. Each sample is represented by two views, in which the one is represented by a feature vector with 240 features obtained by the average of pixels in 2×3 windows, and the other one is represented by the Fourier coefficient vector with 76 features. (2) ***BUAA-visnir face dataset (BUAA)*** [7]: Following the experimental settings in [28], we evaluate different methods on the first 10 persons with 90 visual images and 90 near infrared images. Each image was pre-resized to a 10×10 matrix and then transformed into the vector. (3) **Cornell** dataset [1,6]: This dataset contains 195 webpages collected from the Cornell University. Webpages in the dataset are partitioned into five classes and each webpage is represented by two views, *i.e.*, the content view and citation view. (4) **Caltech101** dataset [4]: The original Caltech101 dataset contains 8677 images from 101 objects. In the experiments, a subset named **Caltech7** [10], which is composed of 1474 images from 7 classes, is used to compare different methods. The popular two types of features, *i.e.*, GIST and LBP, are extracted from each image as the two views. The above used datasets are briefly summarized in Table 1.

Evaluation: Three well-known matrices, *i.e.*, clustering accuracy (ACC), normalized mutual information (NMI), and purity are chosen to evaluate the performance of different methods [2]. For the above datasets, we randomly select the percentage of 10, 30, 50, 70, and 90 samples as the paired samples with all views, and treat the remaining samples as incomplete samples, in which half of samples only have one of the views. All methods are repeatedly performed 5 times and their average values (%) are reported for comparison.

Compared Methods: Following the experimental settings in [17,28], we compare the proposed method with the following baselines. (1) **BSV** (Best Single View): BSV first fills in the missing views with the average of samples in the corresponding view, and then performs k-means on each view separately. Finally, the best clustering result of the two views is reported. (2) **Concat**: It first fills in all missing views with the average of samples of the corresponding view, and then concatenates all views of each sample into one feature vector, followed by performing k-means to obtain the clustering result. (3) **PVC** [30]. PVC uses the non-negative matrix factorization technique to learn a common latent representation for incomplete multi-view clustering. (4) **IMG** [28]: IMG extends the PVC by embedding the adaptively learned Laplacian graph. (5) Double constrained NMF (**DCNMF**) [13]: DCNMF is an extension of PVC, which further introduces a Laplacian graph regularizer into PVC. (6) Graph regularized partial multi-view clustering (**GPMVC**) [16]: GPMVC can be viewed as an improved method to DCNMF, which exploits a scale normalization technique in the consensus representation learning term. *The code of the proposed method is available at:* http://www.yongxu.org/lunwen.html.

Table 1. Description of the used benchmark datasets.

Database	Class No.	No. of view	No. of samples	Feature No. of $Vi(1)/Vi(2)$
Handwritten digit	10	2	2000	240/76
BUAA	10	2	90	100/100
Cornell	5	2	195	195/1703
Caltech7	7	2	1474	512/928

4.2   Experimental Results and Analyses

The clustering results of different methods on the above four datasets are enumerated in Tables 2, 3, 4, 5 and Fig. 2. It is obvious to see that the proposed method can significantly improve the ACC, NMI, and purity. In particular, the proposed method archives nearly 8% higher than those of the related methods in terms of the ACC on the BUAA dataset. The good performance strongly validates the effectiveness of the proposed method in handling the IMC tasks. Besides, we can obtain the following observations from the experimental results.

(1) Generally, with the ratio of missing views decreases, the clustering performances of all methods improve obviously. This proves that the complementary information of different views is very useful in multi-view learning.

(2) In most cases, BSV and Concat perform much worse than the other methods. This proves that filling in the missing views with the average of samples of the corresponding view is not a useful approach.

(3) DCNMF, GPMVC and the proposed method perform better than PVC in most cases. Compared with PVC, the other two methods and the proposed method all exploit the local geometric structure of each view to guide the representation learning. Thus, the experimental results prove that the local information of each view contain very useful information, which is beneficial to learn a more compact and discriminative representation. Meanwhile, we can find that our method achieves better performance than DCNMF and GPMVC, which further proves the effectiveness of the proposed novel graph regularization term.

Table 2. ACCs/NMIs (%) of different methods on the handwritten digit dataset.

Method/Rate	0.1	0.3	0.5	0.7	0.9
BSV	43.08/37.04	50.46/44.48	57.39/51.50	64.44/58.61	69.29/66.26
Concat	46.01/47.71	57.46/54.43	66.45/61.12	78.64/70.30	86.63/79.34
PVC	63.81/55.13	70.90/60.85	73.44/64.88	75.20/68.54	77.82/72.83
IMG	69.22/58.04	75.41/62.38	76.36/64.91	77.54/68.21	81.78/73.57
DCNMF	51.21/54.23	76.63/65.56	80.61/74.41	86.16/78.14	89.16/80.90
GPMVC	65.60/60.99	74.04/63.99	76.94/72.23	79.06/73.68	81.08/75.24
Ours	**72.70/66.48**	**79.67/71.28**	**86.22/77.27**	**88.98/80.48**	**90.77/83.55**

Table 3. ACCs/NMIs (%) of different methods on the BUAA dataset.

Method/Rate	0.1	0.3	0.5	0.7	0.9
BSV	48.33/43.10	56.96/53.03	64.26/61.78	70.81/69.91	80.16/82.56
Concat	45.62/51.22	46.61/51.95	47.46/52.43	52.34/56.51	57.58/62.66
PVC	57.41/61.35	66.46/67.07	70.01/71.97	75.92/78.70	80.73/84.22
IMG	53.95/54.72	67.39/67.53	76.14/76.74	79.36/82.83	80.78/85.90
DCNMF	58.36/61.78	67.58/68.75	72.15/72.05	76.58/79.66	82.42/86.42
GPMVC	58.98/62.12	68.75/70.25	74.28/74.33	78.28/81.63	84.24/86.78
Ours	**63.82/64.64**	**76.72/76.04**	**82.76/81.35**	**86.20/85.77**	**92.62/91.20**

Table 4. ACCs/NMIs (%) of different methods on the cornell dataset.

Method/Rate	0.1	0.3	0.5	0.7	0.9
BSV	42.41/8.66	43.93/8.19	44.84/8.89	46.32/12.69	47.66/19.34
Concat	38.80/8.07	38.06/7.56	36.96/8.30	36.79/10.21	38.48/13.47
PVC	42.56/15.76	42.56/16.00	43.79/18.21	42.56/19.76	43.03/21.03
IMG	45.13/12.56	45.79/16.62	47.08/19.24	45.51/20.89	44.76/22.98
DCNMF	39.94/13.59	43.29/17.72	43.18/19.17	45.74/21.69	45.52/23.98
GPMVC	40.39/13.90	43.86/16.07	46.53/18.99	44.56/15.03	44.35/17.07
Ours	**46.99/17.23**	**47.40/18.36**	**49.03/21.01**	**48.78/22.11**	**49.20/25.02**

Table 5. ACCs/NMIs (%) of different methods on the Caltech7 dataset.

Method/Rate	0.1	0.3	0.5	0.7	0.9
BSV	42.66/29.04	40.97/32.11	39.83/35.13	42.92/38.83	46.99/44.16
Concat	36.83/33.82	31.74/34.44	36.36/34.56	43.38/38.15	47.08/45.44
PVC	43.46/38.99	43.96/40.26	44.46/40.17	44.76/41.60	44.34/41.94
IMG	42.05/32.38	42.36/33.29	42.23/35.05	41.17/35.96	43.23/37.64
DCNMF	40.63/33.86	44.53/38.19	45.62/41.40	48.50/41.24	50.74/44.04
GPMVC	45.57/40.05	47.19/40.96	46.99/41.83	46.99/42.61	49.10/46.02
Ours	**50.88/41.01**	**51.15/42.74**	**51.40/45.69**	**51.79/46.78**	**51.88/48.28**

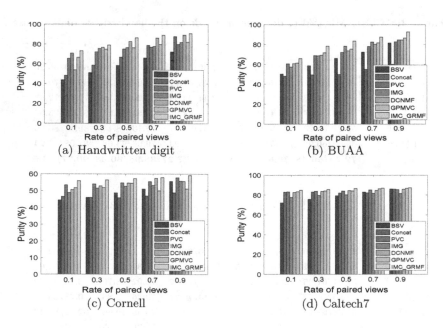

Fig. 2. Purity (%) of different methods on the above four datasets.

4.3   Parameter Analysis

Figure 3 shows the ACC versus the parameters λ_1 and λ_2 on the handwritten digit and BUAA datasets with 70% paired samples. It is obvious that the ACC of the proposed method is relatively stable in some local areas, which indicates that the proposed method is insensitive to the selection of parameters to some extent. Moreover, we can find that when the two parameters are selected with proper values from the candidate range of $([10^0, 10^2], [10^{-5}, 10^{-1}])$, the proposed method can achieve the satisfactory performance. This indicates that a relative larger value of parameter λ_1 encourages a better performance. In our work, we use the grid searching approach to find the optimal combinations of the two parameters from the two dimensional grid formed by $([10^0, 10^2], [10^{-5}, 10^{-1}])$ [24].

Figure 4 plots the relationships of ACC and the number of nearest neighbors of the proposed method on the handwritten digit and BUAA datasets. From the figures, we have the following conclusions: (1) The clustering performance is insensitive to the selection of nearest neighbor number to some extent when the nearest neighbor number is located in the proper range, such as $[8, 18]$ for the handwritten digit dataset and $[2, 6]$ for the BUAA dataset. (2) Generally, the number of nearest neighbors should better be less than the number of sample of each class. For example, from Fig. 3(b), we can find that when the number of nearest neighbors is larger than the number of sample per class, i.e., $N > 10$, the ACC decreases dramatically. However, in the real world applications, it is impossible to obtain the real number of sample per class. In this work, we use the following criterion to select the number of the nearest neighbors. Suppose we try to partition the available multi-view data with n samples into c groups, $m = n/c$. If $m \gg 10$, then we empirically select 10 as the number of nearest neighbors, otherwise we select $min(m - 4, 2)$ as the nearest neighbor number.

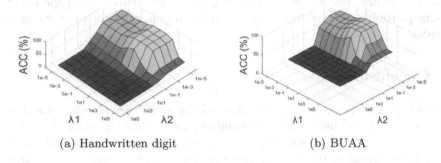

(a) Handwritten digit   (b) BUAA

Fig. 3. ACC (%) versus parameters λ_1 and λ_2 of the proposed method on (a) handwritten digit and (b) BUAA datasets with 70% paired samples.

4.4   Experimental Convergence Study

Figure 5 shows the objective function value and ACC at each iteration step on the handwritten digit and BUAA datasets with 70% paired samples. From the

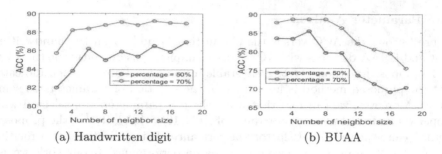

Fig. 4. ACC (%) versus the number of nearest neighbors of our method on (a) handwritten digit and (b) BUAA datasets with 50% and 70% paired samples.

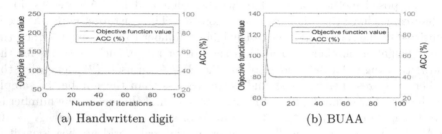

Fig. 5. The objective function value and ACC (%) versus the iteration step of the proposed method on (a) handwritten digit and (b) BUAA datasets with 70% paired samples.

figures, it is obvious to see that the objective function value decreases dramatically in the first few iteration steps (within 20 iterations). The experimental results plotted in the two figures prove the good convergence property of our method.

5   Conclusions

In this paper, we propose a novel framework for multi-view learning, which not only can handle the incomplete and complete multi-view clustering, but also is able to deal with the out-of-sample. Moreover, the proposed method has the potential to complete the missing views for any sample. Besides, we provide a novel approach to exploit the local information of data without introducing any extra regularization term and penalty parameter, which does not increase the complexity and computational burden. Extensive experimental results prove the effectiveness of the proposed method.

Acknowledgments. This work is supported in part by Economic, Trade and information Commission of Shenzhen Municipality (Grant no. 20170504160426188).

References

1. Blum, A., Mitchell, T.: Combining labeled and unlabeled data with co-training. In: COLT, pp. 92–100. ACM (1998)
2. Cai, X., Nie, F., Huang, H.: Multi-view k-means clustering on big data. In: IJCAI, pp. 2598–2604 (2013)
3. Fei, L., Xu, Y., Zhang, B., Fang, X., Wen, J.: Low-rank representation integrated with principal line distance for contactless palmprint recognition. Neurocomputing **218**, 264–275 (2016)
4. Fei-Fei, L., Fergus, R., Perona, P.: Learning generative visual models from few training examples: an incremental bayesian approach tested on 101 object categories. Comput. Vis. Image Underst. **106**(1), 59–70 (2007)
5. Gao, H., Peng, Y., Jian, S.: Incomplete multi-view clustering. In: Shi, Z., Vadera, S., Li, G. (eds.) IIP 2016. IAICT, vol. 486, pp. 245–255. Springer, Cham (2016). https://doi.org/10.1007/978-3-319-48390-0_25
6. Guo, Y.: Convex subspace representation learning from multi-view data. In: AAAI, vol. 1, pp. 387–393 (2013)
7. Huang, D., Sun, J., Wang, Y.: The buaa-visnir face database instructions. Technical report IRIP-TR-12-FR-001, School of Computational Science and Engineering, Beihang University, Beijing, China (2012)
8. Kumar, A., Rai, P., Daume, H.: Co-regularized multi-view spectral clustering. In: NIPS, pp. 1413–1421 (2011)
9. Li, M., Xue, X.B., Zhou, Z.H.: Exploiting multi-modal interactions: a unified framework. In: IJCAI, pp. 1120–1125 (2009)
10. Li, Y., Nie, F., Huang, H., Huang, J.: Large-scale multi-view spectral clustering via bipartite graph. In: AAAI, pp. 2750–2756 (2015)
11. Liu, G., Lin, Z., Yan, S., Sun, J., Yu, Y., Ma, Y.: Robust recovery of subspace structures by low-rank representation. IEEE TPAMI **35**(1), 171–184 (2013)
12. Ngiam, J., Khosla, A., Kim, M., Nam, J., Lee, H., Ng, A.Y.: Multimodal deep learning. In: ICML, pp. 689–696 (2011)
13. Qian, B., Shen, X., Gu, Y., Tang, Z., Ding, Y.: Double constrained NMF for partial multi-view clustering. In: DICTA, pp. 1–7. IEEE (2016)
14. Qin, J., et al.: Binary coding for partial action analysis with limited observation ratios. In: CVPR, pp. 146–155 (2017)
15. Qin, J., et al.: Zero-shot action recognition with error-correcting output codes. In: CVPR, pp. 2833–2842 (2017)
16. Rai, N., Negi, S., Chaudhury, S., Deshmukh, O.: Partial multi-view clustering using graph regularized NMF. In: ICPR, pp. 2192–2197. IEEE (2016)
17. Shao, W., He, L., Yu, P.S.: Multiple incomplete views clustering via weighted non-negative matrix factorization with $L_{2,1}$ regularization. In: Appice, A., Rodrigues, P.P., Santos Costa, V., Soares, C., Gama, J., Jorge, A. (eds.) ECML PKDD 2015. LNCS (LNAI), vol. 9284, pp. 318–334. Springer, Cham (2015). https://doi.org/10.1007/978-3-319-23528-8_20
18. Trivedi, A., Rai, P., Daumé III, H., DuVall, S.L.: Multiview clustering with incomplete views. In: NIPSW, pp. 1–7 (2010)
19. Wen, J., et al.: Robust sparse linear discriminant analysis. In: IEEE TCSVT (2018). https://doi.org/10.1109/TCSVT.2018.2799214
20. Wen, J., Fang, X., Xu, Y., Tian, C., Fei, L.: Low-rank representation with adaptive graph regularization. Neural Netw. **108**, 83–96 (2018)

21. Wen, J., Han, N., Fang, X., Fei, L., Yan, K., Zhan, S.: Low-rank preserving projection via graph regularized reconstruction. In: IEEE TCYB, vol. 99, pp. 1–13 (2018). https://doi.org/10.1109/TCYB.2018.2799862

22. Zhang, Y., Zhang, Z., Qin, J., Zhang, L., Li, B., Li, F.: Semi-supervised local multi-manifold isomap by linear embedding for feature extraction. Pattern Recogn. **76**, 662–678 (2018)

23. Zhang, Z.; Zhao, M., Chow, T.W.: Binary-and multi-class group sparse canonical correlation analysis for feature extraction and classification. IEEE TKDE **25**(10), 2192–2205 (2013)

24. Zhang, Z., Lai, Z., Xu, Y., Shao, L., Wu, J., Xie, G.S.: Discriminative elastic-net regularized linear regression. IEEE TIP **26**(3), 1466–1481 (2017)

25. Zhang, Z., et al.: Highly-economized multi-view binary compression for scalable image clustering. In: Ferrari, V., Hebert, M., Sminchisescu, C., Weiss, Y. (eds.) ECCV 2018, Part XII. LNCS, vol. 11216, pp. 731–748. Springer, Cham (2018). https://doi.org/10.1007/978-3-030-01258-8_44

26. Zhang, Z., Shao, L., Xu, Y., Liu, L., Yang, J.: Marginal representation learning with graph structure self-adaptation. IEEE TNNLS (2017). https://doi.org/10.1109/TNNLS.2017.2772264

27. Zhang, Z., Xu, Y., Shao, L., Yang, J.: Discriminative block-diagonal representation learning for image recognition. IEEE TNNLS **29**(7), 3111–3125 (2018)

28. Zhao, H., Liu, H., Fu, Y.: Incomplete multi-modal visual data grouping. In: IJCAI, pp. 2392–2398 (2016)

29. Zhao, J., Xie, X., Xu, X., Sun, S.: Multi-view learning overview: recent progress and new challenges. Inf. Fusion **38**, 43–54 (2017)

30. Zhi, S.Y., Zhou, H.: Partial multi-view clustering. In: AAAI, pp. 1968–1974 (2014)

31. Zou, H., Hastie, T., Tibshirani, R.: Sparse principal component analysis. J. Comput. Graph. Stat. **15**(2), 265–286 (2006)

GA-Based Filter Selection
for Representation in Convolutional
Neural Networks

Junbong Kim[1], Minki Lee[1], Jongeun Choi[2], and Kisung Seo[1($\boxtimes$)]

[1] Department of Electronic Engineering, Seokyeong University, Seoul, Korea
[2] School of Mechanical Engineering, Yonsei University, Seoul, Korea
{tpeprrwq,perpetmon,ksseo}@skuniv.ac.kr, jongeunchoi@yonsei.ac.kr

Abstract. One of the deep learning models, a convolutional neural network (CNN) has been very successful in a variety of computer vision tasks. Features of a CNN are automatically generated, however, they can be further optimized since they often require large scale parallel operations and there exist the possibility of overlapping redundant features. The aim of this paper is to use feature selection via evolutionary algorithms to remove the irrelevant deep features. This will minimize the computational complexity and the amount of overfitting while maintaining a good quality of representation. We demonstrate the improvement of the filter representation by performing experiments on three data sets of CIFAR10, metal surface defects, and variation of MNIST and by analyzing the classification performance as well as the variance of the filter.

Keywords: CNN · Feature representation · Filter optimization

1 Introduction

Recent years, the deep learning technique such as convolutional neural networks (CNNs) is widely utilized for image recognition [8]. In general, a CNN [9] is known to be powerful in automatic feature extraction and it does not require manual feature engineering. The manual design of the feature representation is not adaptive to the data and is dependent on the specific design choices. Deep convolutional neural networks (DCNN) [4,7,14,16] has a hierarchical structure that attempts to learn representations of input data with multiple levels of abstraction automatically. As the deep learning network grows deeper, the importance of feature representation in the computer vision is increasing [1]. CNN based features often rely on computationally expensive deep models, which requires high computational complexity for numerous applications. There is a strong need for new scalable and efficient approaches that can cope with this explosion of dimensionality [17]. Therefore, there is a growing need for feature descriptors that are fast to compute, memory efficient, and yet exhibiting good discriminability and robustness with respect to the input feature space.

© Springer Nature Switzerland AG 2019
L. Leal-Taixé and S. Roth (Eds.): ECCV 2018 Workshops, LNCS 11132, pp. 609–618, 2019.
https://doi.org/10.1007/978-3-030-11018-5_48

In this paper, we propose an approach to refine the filter expression as well as computational expense. In particular, an evolutionary algorithm (e.g., a genetic algorithm (GA) [2]) will make a selection of the filters that are automatically designed by a CNN. Because a CNN has a large number of filters, instead of expressing the selected filters as genes, we try to improve the efficiency of genetic computation by expressing the filters as genes to be deleted in order to reduce the size of the genes. We represent genotypes and phenotypes differently and implement them through transformations. We use enough data to train the CNN network that consists of six layers (three convolutional layers and three pooling layers), and reconstruct the filters of each layer of the learned network through evolutionary computation. We then optimize the reconstruction by calculating the fitness using the test data. The reduction rate of the filters is set to 15.6% and 31.3% of the total filters, and the classification accuracy performance, (ACC) is used for performing evolutionary calculation of a generation. In addition, we observe the improvement of the performance by performing additional learning on the reduced CNN obtained from the final generation. We demonstrate the quality of the filter representation by performing experiments on CIFAR10, MNIST variations, and surface defect data and by analyzing the variance of the filters as well as the classification accuracy performance.

2   Literature Survey

Convolutional Feature representations and/or selections are closely related to CNN network quantization and efficient CNN architectures. A number of efforts have been made in this direction, such as feature selection [1], compact binary features [11], CNN network compressions [3,6], and optimization of CNN architectures [13,15,18]. Following works adopt fine-tuned strategies to further improve the discriminative power of the descriptors. First, various masking schemes are applied to select a representative subset of local convolutional features and remove a large number of redundant features from a feature map to achieve competitive retrieval performance [1]. Quantized CNN is proposed to simultaneously speed-up the computation and reduce the storage and memory overhead of CNN models. Both filter kernels in convolutional layers and weighting matrices in fully-connected layers are quantized, aiming at minimizing the estimation error of each layer's response [17].

Compression techniques to reduce the network size without affecting their accuracy are another popular approaches. Deep compression, a three stage pipeline: pruning, trained quantization and Huffman coding that work together to reduce the storage requirement of neural networks by 35 to 49x without affecting their accuracy, is introduced [3]. In a similar way, SqueezeNet [6] achieves AlexNet-level accuracy on ImageNet with 50x fewer parameters. Additionally, with model compression techniques, they are able to compress SqueezeNet to less than 0.5 MB.

Designing CNN architectures automatically is also coupled with feature representations. Recently, some meta-heuristic algorithms, such as genetic algorithm (GA) and genetic programming (GP), have been used to optimize CNNs.

GA based optimization of CNN structures with the number and size of filters, connection between consecutive layers, and activation functions of each layer is introduced [13]. Long length of chromosome is adopted to cover above variables and showed not much improved performance results. The other GA based approach is a new encoding method to represent complex convolutional layers in a fixed-length binary string. Many popular network structures can be represented using the proposed encoding scheme. Examples include VGGNet [14], ResNet [4], and a modified variant of DenseNet [5]. However, a large fraction of network structures are still unexplored and the currently available main results are at the averaged levels and so they still require to be improved.

A Cartesian genetic programming (CGP) [12] based method is adopted for a CNN structure optimization with highly functional modules, such as convolutional blocks and tensor concatenation, as the node functions in CGP [15]. The CNN structure and connectivity represented by the CGP encoding method are optimized to maximize the validation accuracy. The proposed method can be used to automatically find the competitive CNN architecture compared with state-of-the-art models.

Evolutionary algorithm based approaches on CNN design have the emphasis that is on optimizing the external structure of the network, which is far from the expression of the filter.

3   Optimization of CNN Representation

3.1   CNN and Representation Problems

One of the most related variables to the CNN representation are convolution filter weights. Filters that are automatically generated through learning include various types of filters and are responsible for feature extraction across multiple stages through the hierarchical forward network. Nevertheless, the filters used in previous studies may contain redundant filters. In this study, we select the filters that significantly contribute to the image recognition through the evolutionary computation of the fully learned CNN filters. This reduces the overall number of filters and refines the filter group. The methodology differs from the existing pruning technique [10] in that it chooses the appropriate filters for the situation (or environment) using evolutionary optimization, rather than simply choosing the importance of the filter based on weight values. In other words, our evolutionary approach is more focused on relational combination set of filters among convolutional layers rather than separated operations in each layer.

3.2   Evolutionary Algorithm

Evolutionary computation consists of gene expression, gene generation, fitness evaluation, selection, and genetic computation. The process of GA is as follows. Firstly, each chromosome composed of strings is randomly generated. Then, the candidate solution obtained by interpreting each object is evaluated by a fitness function. Then, the entities to participate in the genetic operation are selected by the given selection method. Perform genetic calculations (mating, mutation) on selected entities. The entire process is repeated until the termination condition is satisfied. The mating operator in GA is performed by replacing a portion of the parent's string at an arbitrary point.

Unlike optimization by general evolutionary computation, the optimization of CNN requires a long computation time for repetition of generations because the evaluation process of an object includes the CNN test. That is, several hundred epochs of test process should be performed to evaluate one entity. In this study, we choose a method to reduce the computation volume by applying only the test procedure to the evaluation of the changed object first by separating the learning and the test. The overall GA structure for removing redundant filters in a CNN is summarized as shown in Algorithm 1.

Algorithm 1. Evolutionary optimization algorithm for CNN filters

1: CNN training for train dataset
2: $t \leftarrow 0$
3: initialize $P(t)$ ▷ individuals for filter selection
4: **procedure** EVALUATE $P(t)$
5:     CNN test for test dataset
6:     calculate accuracy
7: **while** not termination-condition **do**
8:     $t \leftarrow t + 1$
9:     select $P(t)$ from $P(t-1)$
10:    crossover and mutation $P(t)$
11:    **procedure** EVALUATE $P(t)$
12:        CNN test for test dataset
13:        calculate accuracy

3.3 Evolutionary Selection of CNN Filters

Including all filters in the genes for selection is very inefficient for genetic calculations because small CNNs consist of dozens of filters per layer. Therefore, we set a certain percentage (15.6% and 31.3%) to be deleted from the whole filter, and then represent filters to be deleted as genes since their size is relatively small. This is illustrated in Fig. 1. The gene number in genotype means the filter number to be deleted from the layer and the gray filters are shown to be deleted. Duplicate numbers are treated as a single one, and 0 represents a filter not to be deleted. The phenotype is remaining (or selected) filters which are used for evaluations.

In order to verify the proposed scheme, a filter selection procedure is performed on a basic network with a relatively simple CNN structure as shown in Fig. 2. The corresponding parameters are listed in Table 1. We have trained enough a network consisting of 6 layers (3 convolutional layers, 3 pooling layers) by using CIFAR10, surface defect data, MNIST Variations. We then apply the GA evolutionary selection to the automatically generated filters of each convolution layer.

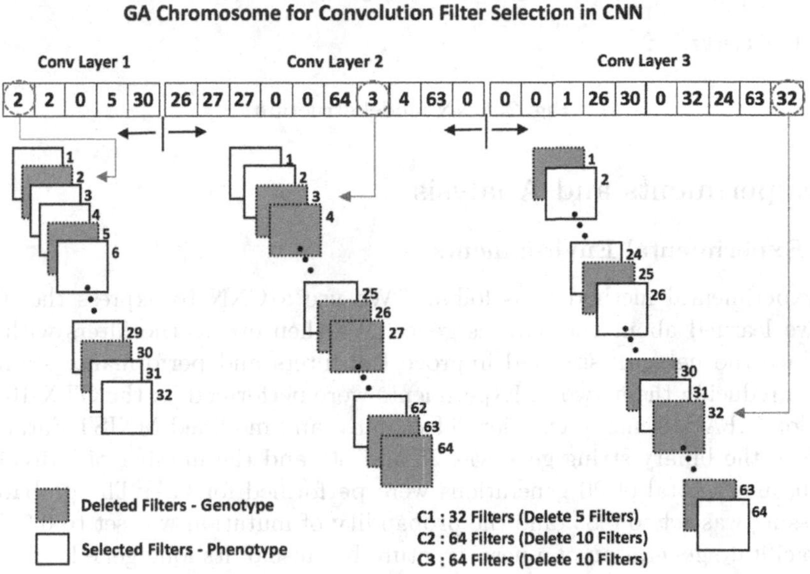

GA Chromosome for Convolution Filter Selection in CNN

Fig. 1. GA for deleting redundant filters in a CNN a case of 15.6% deletion.

Table 1. Parameters of CNN model.

Layer	Filters	Filter size	Stride	Pad
Conv1	32	2×2×32	1	0
Pool1		2×2	2	0
Conv2	64	2×2×64	1	0
Pool2		2×2	2	0
Conv3	64	2×2×64	1	0
Pool3		2×2	2	0
Fc	128	1×1×128	1	0

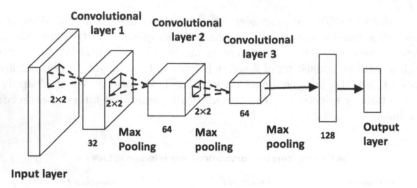

Fig. 2. CNN model structure

4   Experiments and Analysis

4.1   Experimental Environments

The experimental method is as follows. We use a CNN to express the filters that we learned about the data as genes. We then evolve the filters with GA to reduce the network size and improve the filters and performance similarly prior to reducing the network. Experiments were performed on the GTX-1080Ti GPU for CIFAR10, metal exterior defect data, and modified MNIST data. The length of the binary string gene was 25 and 50, and the number of individuals was 50, and a total of 20 generations were performed for GA. The probability of crossing was set to 0.85, and the probability of mutation was set to 0.2. This is to facilitate generation of a new structure because of its long gene length. For CIFAR10, learning time per a candidate(or individual) solution took 3–4 min, and the total GA evolution process took about 48 h. The learning time per a candidate for the metal exterior defects data took about 2–3 min, and the whole GA evolution process took about 36 h. For MNIST variations, the learning time per a candidate took 3–4 min, and the entire GA evolution process took about 48 h. The specific gene expression is as follows. The first group is the convolution C1, the second group is the three convolutions in C3, and the third group is the collection of filter numbers to be removed in C3. Gene length consists of gene 25 (5 + 10 + 10) and gene 50 (10 + 20 + 20) as shownbelow. The specific procedure is shown in Algorithm 2. The GA parameters are listed in Table 2.

Algorithm 2

1: Store network parameters after training a CNN
2: Input learned network parameters to GA
3: Select the filter on each candidate according to the GA performance
4: Fitness calculation (i.e., ACC by net CNN propagation using only reduced filters)
5: Re-train the CNN by lowering the learning rate of reduced networks by GA

Table 2. GA parameters

Number of generations	20
Population size	50
Selection	Tournament (size = 7)
Crossover	0.85
Mutation	0.2

4.2 Experimental Results

Results for Reduction Rate of 15.6%. Table 3 shows the results of experiments with a reduction ratio of 15.6% ((5 + 10 + 10)/(32+64+64)). For the CIFAR-10, the ACC performance that was learned and tested with CNN shown in Fig. 2 was 64.6%, and the result after randomly selecting and removing the filters of each layer within 15.6% was down to 54.57%.

Table 3. GA-based filtering reduction (15.6% reduction rate)

ACC	Original	GA filter selection (initial gen)	GA filter selection (final gen)	Retrain after GA filter selection (epoch 100)	Retrain after GA filter selection (epoch 500)
CIFAR-10	64.60%	54.57%	57.94%	62.90%	63.55% (98.3%)
Surface defect	86.91%	84.00%	85.19%	86.40%	86.85% (99.9%)
MNIST variations	94.13%	92.75%	92.78%	93.45%	93.48% (99.3%)

Through the GA evolution calculation, the best performance after 20th generation is 57.94%. The performance of the re-learning of the evolved network with this reduced number of filters was very close to 98.3% of the original network ACC performance, from 500 epochs to ACC of 63.55%, while the network filter was reduced to 15.6% of the reduction rate. As for the surface defect data, the re-learning result after filter reduction is 86.85% ACC, which is equivalent to 99.9% of the original network performance of 86.91%. For the MNIST variation data, the ACC performance of the reduced network is 93.48%, 99.3% of the original ACC performance 94.13%. Our successful results show that the number of network filters is reduced by 15.6% while the performance is maintained at 98%–99% of the original deep learning network. In addition, the proposed approach is meaningful in the sense that it is a process of selecting filters that are efficient for representation rather than simple compression.

Results for Reduction Rate of 31.3%. The results of the second experiment with a reduction of 31.3%((10 + 20 + 20)/(32+64+64)) are shown in Table 4. For the CIFAR-10, the ACC performance that we learned and tested with CNN shown in Fig. 2 is 64.6%, where the results are reduced to 47.33% after randomly selecting and removing the filters of each layer by 31.3%.

Table 4. GA-based filtering reduction (31.3% reduction rate)

ACC	Original	GA filter selection (initial gen)	GA filter selection (final gen)	Retrain after GA filter selection (epoch 100)	Retrain after GA filter selection (epoch 500)
CIFAR-10	64.60%	47.33%	53.74%	59.65%	60.33% (93.4%)
Surface defect	86.91%	73.02%	78.37%	85.73%	85.74% (98.7%)
MNIST variations	94.13%	87.94%	90.49%	92.12%	92.55% (98.3%)

Through the GA evolution computation, the performance of the best after 20th generation is 53.74%. The ACC performance of the re-learning of the evolved network with the reduced number of filters was 60.33% at 500 epochs, which was 93.4% of the original network performance, which was somewhat lower than 15.6% at the reduction rate. Instead, the number of filters in the network has been reduced to 31.3%. As for the surface defect data, 85.74% of the re-learning result after filter reduction is almost equal to 98.7% of the original network performance 86.91%. For MNIST variation data, the performance of the reduced network is 92.55%, which is 98.3% of the original 94.13%. The successful results show that the number of network filters is reduced by 31.3% while the performance is maintained at 93%–98% of the original network performance.

Tables 5 and 6 show the comparisons of the spatial re-learning of CNNs and GA evolution (15.6% reduction) for CIFAR-10 and surface defect data, respectively, in each activation map of the first convolution layer. The large variance of the each pixel means that the recognition of the object in the activation map is more pronounced. For the 10 classes of CIFAR-10, we can clearly see that the

Table 5. Variance of the activation map on the first convolutional layer CIFAR-10

Average deviations	Original	Retrain after GA filter selection (epoch 100)	Retrain after GA filter selection (epoch 500)
CIFAR-10 class			
Airplane	816.6	919.2 (12.6%)	918.2 (12.4%)
Automobile	1166.3	1313.6 (12.6%)	1312.0 (12.5%)
Bird	717.8	809.2 (12.7%)	808.3 (12.6%)
Cat	1042.1	1178.5 (13%)	1176.8 (13%)
Deer	626.9	707.1 (12.8%)	707.1 (12.8%)
Dog	1090.4	1234.1 (13.1%)	1232.4 (13%)
Frog	713.0	805.4 (13%)	804.4 (12.8%)
Horse	1076.6	1217.4 (13%)	1215.8 (12.9%)
Ship	965.5	1088.7 (12.8%)	1087.3 (12.6%)
Truck	1225.5	1381.1 (12.7%)	1379.4 (12.6%)

Table 6. Variance of the activation map on the first convolutional layer Surface Defect

Average deviations	Original	Retrain after GA filter selection (epoch 100)	Retrain after GA filter selection (epoch 500)
Surface Defect class			
Stain	1555.7	1653.2 (6.3%)	1733.6 (11.4%)
Normal	380.8	404.8 (6.3%)	424.1 (11.4%)
Scratch	554.4	589.3 (6.3%)	616.6 (11.2%)
Stamped	510.3	542.3 (6.3%)	568.4 (11.4%)

variance values after GA evolution and re-learning, increased by an average of 12%–13%. In CIFAR-10, there is little difference between epoch 100 and epoch 500. Surface defects are classified into four types of defects: an average increase of 6.3% in the epoch 100 and an increase of 11% in the epoch 500. In summary, we observed the mechanism of our approach that is the GA-based filter reduction for complexity and overfitting reduction, has been well compensated by re-training and resulted in the increased spatial variance of the activation map in the remaining filters.

5   Conclusions

In this paper, we have proposed a procedure to remove the existing filters in order to reduce the computational complexity while maintaining the ACC performance by utilizing a carefully designed GA. In particular, we formulate our problem as selecting filters to be removed to reduce the complexity in GA. Our results of three different data sets (CIFAR10, metal surface defects, and variation of MNIST) show that we have successfully remove filters with weak representation and retain filters with strong representation. Our approach can be applied to different deep leaning architectures in order to suppress the detrimental effect of overfitting and computational complexity. Further study will aim at refinement of feature selection for better representation using advanced evolutionary algorithm and improvement of computation costs by integrating compression techniques.

Acknowledgement. This work was supported by National Research Foundation of Korea Grant funded by the Korea government (NRF-2016R1D1A1A09919650). This work was also funded by the Korea Meteorological Administration Research and Develop- ment Program under Grant KMIPA(KMI2018-06710).

References

1. Do, T.T., Hoang, T., Tan, D.K.L., Cheung, N.M.: From selective deep convolutional features to compact binary representations for image retrieval. arXiv preprint arXiv:1802.02899 (2018)

2. Goldberg, D.: Genetic Algorithms in Search, Optimization, and Machine Learning. Addison-Wesley, Reading (1989). Google Scholar (2014)
3. Han, S., Mao, H., Dally, W.J.: Deep compression: compressing deep neural networks with pruning, trained quantization and huffman coding. arXiv preprint arXiv:1510.00149 (2015)
4. He, K., Zhang, X., Ren, S., Sun, J.: Deep residual learning for image recognition. In: Proceedings of the IEEE Conference on Computer Vision and Pattern Recognition, pp. 770–778 (2016)
5. Huang, G., Liu, Z., Van Der Maaten, L., Weinberger, K.Q.: Densely connected convolutional networks. In: CVPR, vol. 1, p. 3 (2017)
6. Iandola, F.N., Han, S., Moskewicz, M.W., Ashraf, K., Dally, W.J., Keutzer, K.: Squeezenet: Alexnet-level accuracy with 50x fewer parameters and < 0.5 mb model size. arXiv preprint arXiv:1602.07360 (2016)
7. Krizhevsky, A., Sutskever, I., Hinton, G.E.: ImageNet classification with deep convolutional neural networks. In: Advances in Neural Information Processing Systems, pp. 1097–1105 (2012)
8. LeCun, Y., Bengio, Y., Hinton, G.: Deep learning. Nature **521**(7553), 436 (2015)
9. LeCun, Y., Bottou, L., Bengio, Y., Haffner, P.: Gradient-based learning applied to document recognition. Proc. IEEE **86**(11), 2278–2324 (1998)
10. Li, H., Kadav, A., Durdanovic, I., Samet, H., Graf, H.P.: Pruning filters for efficient convnets. arXiv preprint arXiv:1608.08710 (2016)
11. Lin, K., Lu, J., Chen, C.S., Zhou, J.: Learning compact binary descriptors with unsupervised deep neural networks. In: Proceedings of the IEEE Conference on Computer Vision and Pattern Recognition, pp. 1183–1192 (2016)
12. Miller, J.F., Thomson, P.: Cartesian genetic programming. In: Poli, R., Banzhaf, W., Langdon, W.B., Miller, J., Nordin, P., Fogarty, T.C. (eds.) EuroGP 2000. LNCS, vol. 1802, pp. 121–132. Springer, Heidelberg (2000). https://doi.org/10.1007/978-3-540-46239-2_9
13. Rikhtegar, A., Pooyan, M., Manzuri-Shalmani, M.T.: Genetic algorithm-optimised structure of convolutional neural network for face recognition applications. IET Comput. Vis. **10**(6), 559–566 (2016)
14. Simonyan, K., Zisserman, A.: Very deep convolutional networks for large-scale image recognition. arXiv preprint arXiv:1409.1556 (2014)
15. Suganuma, M., Shirakawa, S., Nagao, T.: A genetic programming approach to designing convolutional neural network architectures. In: Proceedings of the Genetic and Evolutionary Computation Conference, pp. 497–504. ACM (2017)
16. Szegedy, C., et al.: Going deeper with convolutions. In: Proceedings of the IEEE Conference on Computer Vision and Pattern Recognition, pp. 1–9 (2015)
17. Wu, J., Leng, C., Wang, Y., Hu, Q., Cheng, J.: Quantized convolutional neural networks for mobile devices. In: Proceedings of the IEEE Conference on Computer Vision and Pattern Recognition, pp. 4820–4828 (2016)
18. Xie, L., Yuille, A.L.: Genetic CNN. In: ICCV, pp. 1388–1397 (2017)

Active Descriptor Learning for Feature Matching

Aziz Koçanaoğulları[1] and Esra Ataer-Cansızoğlu[2](✉)

[1] Northeastern University, Boston, MA, USA
akocanaogullari@ece.neu.edu
[2] Mitsubishi Electric Research Labs (MERL), Cambridge, MA, USA
cansizoglu@ieee.org

Abstract. Feature descriptor extraction lies at the core of many computer vision tasks including image retrieval and registration. In this paper, we present an active learning method for extracting efficient features to be used in matching image patches. We train a Siamese deep neural network by optimizing a triplet loss function. We develop a more efficient and faster training procedure compared to the state-of-the-art methods by increasing difficulty during batch training. We achieve this by adjusting the margin in the loss and picking harder samples over time. The experiments are carried out on Photo Tourism dataset. The results show a significant improvement on matching performance and faster convergence in training.

Keywords: Feature matching · Active learning · Curriculum learning

1 Introduction

Extraction of feature descriptors lies at the core of many computer vision tasks. There exists a tremendous amount of work to represent image patches and match them across images. Initial studies included hand-crafted features such as SIFT [8], SURF [3] and ORB [9]. Recently, with the rise in deep neural network methods, learned features are developed and introduced as a more efficient alternative to the hand-crafted features.

Recent work on learned feature representation focus on formulating the loss function or designing neural network architectures. However, training for feature learning is challenging since it heavily depends on the selected matching/non-matching pairs and the initialization. In this paper, we present an active learning procedure that increases the difficulty of batch training over time. We achieve this by (i) increasing the margin between the similarities of matched and non-matched pairs in the loss function and (ii) picking harder sample pairs over time. Similar to a kid learning pattern matching starting from easier primitive shapes, we start batch training by feeding samples with low loss values that are easily detected as matching or non-matching with our current model. Gradually we increase the difficulty of patterns presented while expecting to see a better

© Springer Nature Switzerland AG 2019
L. Leal-Taixé and S. Roth (Eds.): ECCV 2018 Workshops, LNCS 11132, pp. 619–630, 2019.
https://doi.org/10.1007/978-3-030-11018-5_49

separation between examples. Thus, over time we add harder samples with higher loss values, while increasing the margin between distances of matching and non-matching pairs in our loss function. We demonstrate the use of our technique for matching image patches in Photo Tourism dataset [16]. The experiments show a significant improvement in performance and a faster convergence rate compared to the state-of-the-art learning-based features. Our method provides more robust features with a significant speed up in training.

1.1   Existing Work

In deep feature learning, final performance of the feature matching is highly dependent on sample selection. In order to increase performance of the model, learning should be supervised. As an obvious example, a feature representation that is learned by training with matching samples only ends up having a constant function, in contrast a representation coming from a training with non-matching samples only has a scattered range.

The importance of selecting a 1 : 1 match and non-match ratio during training was emphasized in [7,17]. Zeng et al. [19] stated that they accumulate training samples in a reservoir and generate batches online without violating 1 : 1 ratio constraint. Similarly, Balntas et al. [2] presented triplet-loss as a way of enabling a totally randomized batch sampling. Since triplets consist of two matching samples and a non-matching sample, it already satisfies 1 : 1 ratio between matching and non matching pairs. However, these approaches suffer from incorrect gradient estimates due to batches being dominated by samples close to zero loss. In order to tackle this problem, authors in [10,14] proposed to discard training samples with zero loss. This approach suffers from low sample noise assumption. Discarding such samples causes overestimated gradients, making the training sensitive to outliers. Hence it slows down the training and prevents convergence to a local minimum. In order to solve this issue, instead of discarding training samples directly, it is more convenient to select samples actively to ensure convergence. Simo et al. [10] used more matching pairs in the beginning of training and increase the number of non-matches in each batch as the training progress. Therefore, their method learns boundaries after determining cluster centers. Increasing difficulty was structured further by authors in [1]. Their technique involved selecting samples based on their discriminative scores on a state-of-the-art model. Although these methods aim to increase difficulty in training by actively selecting samples, they ignore the effect of the loss function in learning the feature space. The non-match distance, namely margin, for both pairwise and triplet loss in all these scenarios is a constant that is cross-validated across random trials. In this approach, after certain number of iterations learned features do not change since most of the training samples already satisfy the condition. Hence, a better separation between clusters is omitted. In this work we propose to use an active objective that adjusts the margin (correlated with the intra-class distance) gradually to ensure convergence to better local optimum.

In order to address these drawbacks we propose an active training procedure for feature learning. We aim to achieve better local minimum with the following contributions (i) by actively increasing difficulty of the training with a sequence of loss functions that converge to a local optimum and (ii) by an active sample batch selection based on descriptive scores to increase difficulty of the training over time. We build a deep descriptor map that finds an embedding in a lower dimensional Euclidean space where clusters are separable. We evaluate the performance of our model by using a publicly available dataset to compare with the literature.

2   Method

We propose a curriculum for the training session and increase difficulty of the training over time. We increase difficulty by adjusting the loss function and picking batches during training. Before discussing our contributions, we first present the problem formulation and notation:

Preliminaries/Notation

Given a set of clusters $\{\mathcal{D}_1, \mathcal{D}_2, \cdots, \mathcal{D}_k\} = \mathcal{D}$, with corresponding distributions $p^{\mathcal{D}_i}$, in feature learning the aim is to learn a mapping f that has a range where each cluster is separable in the range space. Let $f_\theta : \mathbb{R}^{N \times N} \to \mathbb{R}^M$ be the mapping from image domain to the feature domain parameterized by θ with $N^2 >> M$ and d be a distance metric in range. Feature map tries to achieve the following:

$$d(f_\theta(a), f_\theta(p)) < d(f_\theta(a), f_\theta(n))$$
$$\forall i, j \neq i \text{ and } \forall a, p \sim p^{\mathcal{D}_i}, n \sim p^{\mathcal{D}_j} \tag{1}$$

We follow a, p, n notation for 'anchor', 'pair', 'non-pair' respectively, which is a conventional naming in the field. In many applications cluster information is not accessible or number of clusters is arbitrarily large, e.g. patch matching, thus maximum likelihood over the indicator defined in (1) is not possible. Hence, the problem is approximately solved with pairwise loss [6] or triplet loss [15] efficiently where only match or non-match information is used. In this paper we focus on the triplet loss, which enforces that the distance between non-matching samples should be at least a margin m larger than the distance between matching pairs. The loss $\mathcal{L}$ is defined as,

$$\mathcal{L}_m(a, p, n, f_\theta) = d(f_\theta(a), f_\theta(p)) - d(f_\theta(a), f_\theta(n)) + m \tag{2}$$

Conventionally, distance metric d is selected as the Euclidean distance to have a Euclidean similarity space. Deep feature maps are learned back-propagating the triplet loss through the network. The parameters are optimized with the following optimization:

$$\hat{\theta} = \arg \min_\theta \sum_{\mathcal{T}} \mathcal{L}_m(a, p, n, f_\theta) \tag{3}$$

Here $\mathcal{T} = \{(a, p, n) | \forall a, p \in \mathcal{D}_i, n \in \mathcal{D}_j, j \neq i\}$ denotes set of sampled triplets. Triplets are usually pre-generated before training and fed through the network as batches to stochastically solve (3), thus the local minimum is biased to the batches at step i of epoch e as $\mathcal{T}_e^i \subset \mathcal{T}$. Additionally based on m, training triplets that satisfy the constraint may yield to incorrect gradient estimate and hence increase training time and may yield bad local minimum.

2.1   Loss Function Sequence

In feature learning, margin as a hyperparameter is selected based on best convention of the dataset and such convention is learned with multiple trials. We propose to approximate margin empirically based on the trajectory of the error during training. Let $\hat{m}$ denote the true margin for a particular local minimum $\hat{\theta}$. Without loss of generality let us assume $\mathcal{L} \to 0$ then $\mathcal{L}_{\hat{m}+\varepsilon}(\hat{\theta}) > 0 \ \forall \varepsilon > 0$. Let $\mathcal{L}_{m_e}$ be a sequence of functions that converge to the correct estimate of the loss $\mathcal{L}_{\hat{m}}(\hat{\theta})$ and hence allowing us to approximately find solution during training:

$$\lim_{e \to \infty} \mathcal{L}_{m_e}(a, p, n, f_\theta) \to \mathcal{L}_{\hat{m}}(a, p, n, f_{\hat{\theta}}) \quad \forall a, p, n \tag{4}$$

Analysis of deep learning error trajectory is difficult, hence this is not trivial to find such sequence of margins that satisfy such convergence. Without loss of generality, we assume loss in training is non-increasing epoch-wise $\mathcal{L}_m(\theta_e) \geq \mathcal{L}_m(\theta_{e+1})$ where θ_e denotes model parameters at epoch e. One possible approach would be starting from a margin of $m_0 = 0$ and increasing the margin by a constant when an error bound is reached in the training loss. Thus, we can make the following proposition:

Proposition 1. *Given a separable set, $m_0 = 0$, and let $\bar{\mathcal{L}} = \sum_{(a,p,n)} \mathcal{L}$ and $\mathbb{1}(.)$ be indicator function; $\exists c_e \in \mathbb{R}$ s.t. $m_{e+1} = m_e + c_e \times \mathbb{1}(\bar{\mathcal{L}}_{m_e} \leq \varepsilon)$ satisfies (4) for an arbitrary θ with $\varepsilon \leq \mathcal{L}_{\hat{m}}(\hat{\theta}) \approx 0$.*

Proof. $\mathcal{L}_m$ is a convex function of m for a fixed θ. $\mathcal{L}_m = 0 \ \forall m \in [0, \hat{m}]$ and $\mathcal{L}$ is monotonically increasing $\forall m \in [\hat{m}, \infty]$, hence $\exists \hat{m}$ the unique solution.

By definition for fixed m $\mathcal{L}(\theta_e)$ is non increasing wrt. e and converges to a point. Hence, if $\exists \varepsilon = \mathcal{L}_{\hat{m}}(\hat{\theta})$, the network converges to minimum loss and $\hat{\theta}, \hat{m}$ are found in order.

We can observe that the proposition works in the case of noiseless samples. We propose to pick an empirical ε, due to incorrect gradient estimates and the sample observation noise. Here the selection of ε will affect the final convergence of training as it is indirectly enforced as the minimum loss expected from the learned feature space.

The following corollary states that instead of putting a threshold on the total loss as a condition for increasing margin, we can consider the number of samples with a zero loss and hence instead of a loss threshold we can put a threshold on the size of the set of zero loss samples.

Corollary 1. $m_{e+1} = m_e + c_e \times \mathbb{1}(|A_e| = 0)$ *where* $A_e = \{(a, p, n) | \mathcal{L}_{m_e}(a, p, n, \theta_e) > 0 \ \forall (a, p, n) \in \mathcal{T}\}$ *satisfies* (4).

The corollary follows the proposition by considering the number of samples in A_e, which contain the samples with nonzero loss in epoch e. However, due to noise in samples, having an empty set of samples with nonzero loss is not achievable. Considering noise and outliers in the dataset, we propose to update m_e with a single scalar if the number of samples in A_e is smaller than a threshold. This threshold can be selected based on a proportion of samples in the training set. The details of the margin update method can be seen in Algorithm 1. At the first line, margin m, constant margin update factor c and proportion k of samples to be used as a threshold for number of nonzero loss samples are initialized. Each epoch starts with an empty set A_e (Line 3). Lines 5 and 6 receive the training batch and updates model parameters respectively. In line 7, the number of samples with loss values close to 0 are added to the set A_e. Finally, in line 8 we test whether the number of samples in A_e is greater than a certain proportion of total training samples. If so, the margin is updated by c.

Algorithm 1. Margin Update: training procedure given all samples T consisting of batches T_e^i for ith batch of epoch e.

1: $m \in \mathbb{R}^+, c \in \mathbb{R}^+, k \in \mathbb{N}^+$
2: **procedure** TRAINING($e \to$ num-epoch)
3:     $A_e \leftarrow \{\}$
4:     **for** $i \to$ num-batch **do**
5:         $(a, p, n) \leftarrow T_e^i$
6:         $\theta \leftarrow \theta - \gamma \nabla_\theta \mathcal{L}_m(a, p, n, m)$
7:         $A_e \leftarrow A_e \cup \{(a, p, n) | \mathcal{L}_m(a, p, n, f_\theta) = 0, \forall (a, p, n) \in T_e^i\}$
8:         **if** $|A_e|/|T| > k$ **then** $m \leftarrow m + c$
9: **return** θ

2.2 Active Batch Sampling

Going from easy to hard during training can be satisfied feeding triplets with smaller/larger loss value at a current epoch. For a particular dataset D with k clusters, number of triplets is approximately $\binom{k}{2}|D_i|\binom{|D_i|}{2}$ where D_i is taken as average number of samples in a cluster. Hence determining all triplets might slow down training. Therefore, we propose a stochastic approximate of sample selection for practical reasons. For a fixed batch size b we randomly sample $2 \times b$ triplets from T and pick a subset of b samples of our interest. Such selection might vary due to the interest and in order to have a curriculum with increasing difficulty we propose two selection methods.

First few epochs of the deep learning is biased to the random initialization of the network parameters. Therefore first few epochs form the baseline of the similarity range by putting samples onto space. In order to have descriptive cluster centers, we propose to use samples that are easy to be separated and hence we pick samples with low triplet loss. However, observe that, if we choose triplets with close to zero loss only, we end up having incorrect gradient estimates. Therefore before selection we limit sampled triplets to the ones without zero loss. Let us denote such subset of triplets with $\bar{\mathcal{T}}_e^i = \{(a, p, n) | \mathcal{L}_m(a, p, n, f_\theta) \neq 0, \forall (a, p, n) \in \mathcal{T}_e^i\}$, the batch for training with easy samples is formed as the following,

$$\hat{\mathcal{T}}_e^i = \arg\min_{\mathcal{T} \subset \bar{\mathcal{T}}_e^i} \sum_{(a,p,n) \in \mathcal{T}} \mathcal{L}_m(a, p, n, f_\theta) \quad \text{s.t. } |\mathcal{T}| = b \tag{5}$$

As training moves forward it is expected that the cluster centers are well structured and hence we propose to fine tune the similarity map by using the hard samples. Since aim in training is to fit the data, in contrast to the initial step we do not discard the triplets with zero loss. Otherwise we will be prune to the dataset noise and outliers. Discarding triplets with zero loss results in an overestimated gradient and cause possible divergence in the long run, conversely keeping samples will saturate the gradient and avoid changes in the parameter domain. Our hard sample selection policy is as the following:

$$\hat{\mathcal{T}}_e^i = \arg\max_{\mathcal{T} \subset \bar{\mathcal{T}}_e^i} \sum_{(a,p,n) \in \mathcal{T}} \mathcal{L}_m(a, p, n, f_\theta) \quad \text{s.t. } |\mathcal{T}| = b \tag{6}$$

The details of our active sampling policy are given in Algorithm 2. Given number of epochs f, the algorithm generate batches by easy sampling until epoch f (Line 4) and by hard sampling after epoch f (Line 5). Lines 6 and 7 receives the batch and updates the model parameters respectively.

Algorithm 2. Active sampling: shows the steps of active sampling during batch training given number of epochs f. The algorithm selects the batches with easy sampling until epoch f and switches to hard sampling afterwards.

1: $f \in \mathbb{N}^+$
2: **procedure** TRAINING($e \rightarrow$ num-epoch)
3:     **for** $i \rightarrow$ num-batch **do**
4:         **if** $e < f$ **then** $\mathcal{T}_e^i \leftarrow$ (5)
5:         **else** $\mathcal{T}_e^i \leftarrow$ (6)
6:         $(a, p, n) \leftarrow \mathcal{T}_e^i$
7:         $\theta \leftarrow \theta - \gamma \nabla_\theta \mathcal{L}_m(a, p, n, m)$
8: **return** θ

In the next section we propose the implementation details of active similarity learning and how we put loss updates and sampling together.

3   Implementation Details

Margin update and active sampling procedures are decoupled in training. Namely, sampling is called at each batch state and margin update is called after each epoch. Therefore we simply use both methods without any further

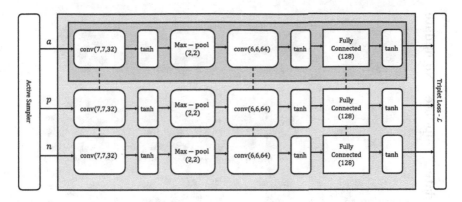

Fig. 1. Network architecture used for descriptor learning. Active sampler provides a, p, n as anchors, positives and negatives respectively for training. As denoted with dashed lines, convolutional and fully connected layers share parameters. During inference (after training) only one of the Siamese networks is used.

adjustments. Initial margin value is set as $m = 1$ for most of the experiments and c is selected from the range $[0, 1]$ empirically in margin update algorithm. The proportion of samples is set as $k = 0.7$ which is used to decide whether to do a margin update or not. Our batch size is $b = 128$, thus we performed sampling from 256 triplets. For active sampling algorithm, we switched from easy to hard sampling after $f = 2$ epochs.

In order to better evaluate the affect of the proposed active learning method, we use the same shallow network architecture defined in [2]. The architecture consists of Conv(7, 7)-Tanh-MaxPool(2, 2)-Conv(6, 6)-Tanh-FullyConnected(128) as seen in Fig. 1. The system is implemented in Tensorflow. During training we use stochastic gradient descent with momentum [12] with a fixed learning rate of 10^{-4} and a momentum of 0.9.

4   Experiments

The goal of this work is to improve the performance of feature matching by following an active learning procedure. In addition to sample selection during batch training, we increase the difficulty of objective function. We carry out two sets of experiments. First we demonstrate the use of margin update for feature learning on MNIST dataset. Second we carry out experiments on the image patch benchmarks of Photo Tourism dataset in order to demonstrate the performance of our technique in local descriptor matching problem.

Feature Learning on MNIST Dataset
In order to show how active adjustment of objective affects feature learning, we used MNIST hand written digits dataset and apply sequence of loss function idea on training. MNIST is a good example to better observe descriptor difference,

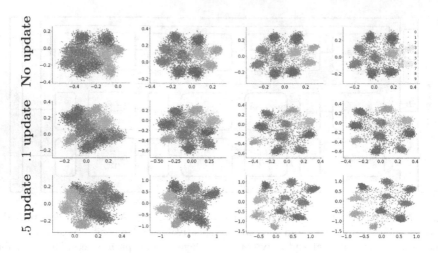

Fig. 2. Descriptor learning on MNIST dataset. Initial margin is selected as .2. Rows represent no-margin update, margin update with .1 and .5 in order. Each column is a snapshot of test images through training in ascending order.

since it has a small number of clusters (i.e. 10 clusters for 10 digits). We set initial margin as $m = 0.2$ and we do not limit output of the network into an interval (e.g. $[0, 1]$) in order to visualize the separation. The learned features on MNIST dataset can be seen in Fig. 2 in various times during training. Rows represent no-margin update, margin update with $c = 0.1$ and margin update with $c = 0.5$ respectively. Each column is a snapshot of learned features in ascending epoch indexes. As can be seen gradual increase of margin during training increases class separation without scattering the descriptors through space. Moreover, a more aggressive margin update step (i.e. $c = 0.5$) can give a larger separation between classes as expected.

Patch Pair Classification

We evaluate the performance of the model in local descriptor learning, where the aim is to determine whether two provided patches are different images of the same point in the world. Performance in patch pair similarity is conventionally reported using receiver operation characteristics (ROC) curve [16]. ROC curve is formed using pairs where matches have label 1 and non matches are 0 and calculation of the curve using a scalar threshold is obvious. We report false positive rate at .95 recall (true positive rate). Hence this measure tells us how likely a model is to put matching pairs together and non-matching pairs apart. In our experiments we use the UBC patches taken from Photo Tourism dataset presented in [16]. This dataset contains three different patch sets extracted using SIFT detector and each set includes pre-defined pairs for the dataset. We compare our method with hand SIFT as a hand crafted feature baseline with other learned descriptors [4,13,18]. We also compare the method with other deep learning techniques [5,10,18]. Specifically; Han et al. [7] propose a network with con-

Table 1. False positive rate at .95 recall for the Photo Tourism dataset. Proposed method is on the bottom of the table in italics. Better results are indicated with bold-font. Models trained using one training set and tested on the test-set. If a row has 3 numbers, that indicates model is trained using both training dataset.

Train-set		Notredame Liberty		Notredame Yosemite		Yosemite Liberty	
Test-set		Yosemite		Liberty		Notredame	
Method	Dim						
SIFT	128	27.29		29.84		22.53	
[13]	64	15.86	19.63	18.05	21.03	13.73	14.15
[4]	29	13.55	–	16.85	18.27	11.98	–
[11]	64	10.54	11.63	12.88	14.82	7.11	7.52
[5]	128	30.22		14.26		9.64	
[10]	128	16.19		8.82		4.54	
[18]	256	15.89	19.91	13.24	17.25	8.38	6.01
[7]	128	12.17	14.40	9.48	15.40	8.27	5.18
[7]	256	11.00	13.58	8.84	13.08	5.67	3.87
[2]	128	7.08	7.82	7.22	9.79	**3.85**	**3.12**
active	128	**6.64**	**5.16**	**6.28**	**4.83**	4.44	**3.12**

trastive loss which is specifically optimized for matching. Furthermore, Balantas et al. [2] propose anchor swapping for training a shallow descriptor network with triplet loss. Since Balantas proposes the best performing model, through the experiments we refer this model as "conventional".

In order to compare proposed method with previous work we also use the same pre-defined pairs and generate our triplets randomly based on provided information. We generate $1,28M$ triplets prior to the training which is a lot smaller than the number of training samples in other methods. Even with less number of training samples, we observed that active learned descriptors perform better in matching. We report the results in Table 1. Compared to the other variants with similar dimensionality (e.g we omitted 4096 dimensional representation presented in [7]) we achieve lower error rates. For implementation we set both $m = 1$ and number of initialization epochs to $f = 1$ by default. However, we observed that, subset Yosemite includes the most number of triplets with 0 loss with $m = 1$ and random initialization. In order to prevent over-fitting we initialized training with $m = 3$ and used $f = 2$ initialization epochs. We cross validated across different margin increments $c \in [0, 1]$ and reported the best. Empirically we observed that $c = 0.5$ improves performance over all scenarios. For our comparison with performance we directly use reported values of each proposed method. For evaluating the gradual performance increase to indicate the impact of the active learning, we use the same baseline (e.g. same training data size, learning rate etc.) for the conventional method and proposed method.

In order to show increase in performance during training we compare proposed method with its components only and conventional triplet based training. We train the same architecture using Notredame dataset and validate on Liberty dataset. We visualize our findings in Fig. 3. Observe that, propose method

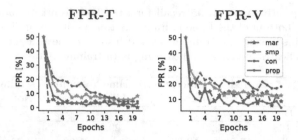

Fig. 3. Training on Notredame, validating on liberty dataset. Figure divided columns of false positive rate (FPR) for [V], [T] which denote validation and training respectively. Compares proposed method (prop) to active sampling only (smp), active margin only (mar) and conventional method (con) in model performance.

outperforms other approaches. Margin increases causes faster convergence in training dataset, unfortunately causes over fitting if samples are not correctly selected. Active sampling results a smoother training and validation error trajectory compared to other methods. We conclude that by stating, proposed method achieves better performance and hence using both margin updates and active sample selection together is crucial.

We also compare our method's performance to the conventional methods for both where training set has 1.28M and 5M training samples. We visualize our findings in Fig. 4. The impact of the proposed active learning procedure is

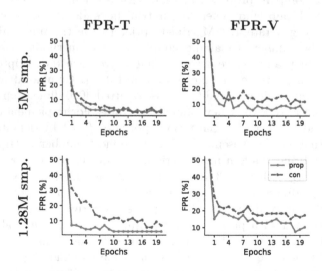

Fig. 4. Training on Liberty, validating on Notredame dataset. Figure divided columns of false positive rate (FPR) for [V], [T] which denote validation and training respectively. First row visualizes results for 5M pre-sampled triplets, second row visualizes results for 1.28M pre-sampled triplets. **act** and **con** denotes active and conventional training respectively.

more clear when number of samples are smaller. False positive rates in both training and validation for 1.28M triplet case has a marginal difference than conventional training and hence we conclude that carefully selecting samples increase the performance. We also note that, although loss functions for both cases are different, the loss values during training are close to each other for 5M triplet case and increasing margin did not increase the loss in 1.28M case. Hence, we state that initial margin is underestimated for such scenario which is later compensated by the proposed method. But, it is observable that as number of samples increase, active sampling increases performance less. Therefore we state that active sampling is useful for small training data set applications. In Fig. 4 we only demonstrate first 20 epochs of the training, at further iterations performance margin between the conventional method and the proposed method decreases.

5 Conclusion

We presented an active feature learning method. Our method actively increase the difficulty of training by adjusting th emarging between matching and non-matching pairs and picking harder samples over time during batch training. We demonstrates the use of our algorithm on the problem of feature matching. The experiments were carried out on Photo Tourism dataset. The presented technique outperforms existing methods in matching performance while speeding up training time significantly. We additionally consider using statistical and/or nearest neighborhood based outlier rejection methods during training to further increase the performance of active sampling. Additionally, proposed margin updates can be designed as a gradient update based on the loss function directly and hence we also consider incorporating a generalized margin update with faster convergence guarantees. Future work will focus on the use of geometric information such as depth of the patch and camera view-point in feature learning.

Acknowledgements. We thank Alan Sullivan, Radu Corcodel and Anoop Cherian for their helpful comments. This work was supported by and done at MERL.

References

1. Appalaraju, S., Chaoji, V.: Image similarity using deep CNN and curriculum learning. arXiv preprint arXiv:1709.08761 (2017)
2. Balntas, V., Riba, E., Ponsa, D., Mikolajczyk, K.: Learning local feature descriptors with triplets and shallow convolutional neural networks. In: BMVC, vol. 1, p. 3 (2016)
3. Bay, H., Tuytelaars, T., Van Gool, L.: SURF: speeded up robust features. In: Leonardis, A., Bischof, H., Pinz, A. (eds.) ECCV 2006. LNCS, vol. 3951, pp. 404–417. Springer, Heidelberg (2006). https://doi.org/10.1007/11744023_32
4. Brown, M., Hua, G., Winder, S.: Discriminative learning of local image descriptors. IEEE Trans. Pattern Anal. Mach. Intell. **33**(1), 43–57 (2011)

5. Fischer, P., Dosovitskiy, A., Brox, T.: Descriptor matching with convolutional neural networks: a comparison to SIFT. arXiv preprint arXiv:1405.5769 (2014)
6. Hadsell, R., Chopra, S., LeCun, Y.: Dimensionality reduction by learning an invariant mapping. In: 2006 IEEE Computer Society Conference on Computer Vision and Pattern Recognition, vol. 2, pp. 1735–1742. IEEE (2006)
7. Han, X., Leung, T., Jia, Y., Sukthankar, R., Berg, A.C.: MatchNet: unifying feature and metric learning for patch-based matching. In: Proceedings of the IEEE Conference on Computer Vision and Pattern Recognition, pp. 3279–3286 (2015)
8. Lowe, D.G.: Object recognition from local scale-invariant features. In: 1999 the Proceedings of the Seventh IEEE International Conference on Computer vision, vol. 2, pp. 1150–1157. IEEE (1999)
9. Rublee, E., Rabaud, V., Konolige, K., Bradski, G.: ORB: an efficient alternative to SIFT or SURF. In: 2011 IEEE International Conference on Computer Vision (ICCV), pp. 2564–2571. IEEE (2011)
10. Simo-Serra, E., Trulls, E., Ferraz, L., Kokkinos, I., Fua, P., Moreno-Noguer, F.: Discriminative learning of deep convolutional feature point descriptors. In: Proceedings of the IEEE International Conference on Computer Vision, pp. 118–126 (2015)
11. Simonyan, K., Vedaldi, A., Zisserman, A.: Learning local feature descriptors using convex optimisation. IEEE Trans. Pattern Anal. Mach. Intell. 36(8), 1573–1585 (2014)
12. Sutskever, I., Martens, J., Dahl, G., Hinton, G.: On the importance of initialization and momentum in deep learning. In: International Conference on Machine Learning, pp. 1139–1147 (2013)
13. Trzcinski, T., Christoudias, M., Lepetit, V., Fua, P.: Learning image descriptors with the boosting-trick. In: Advances in Neural Information Processing Systems, pp. 269–277 (2012)
14. Wang, J., et al.: Learning fine-grained image similarity with deep ranking. In: Proceedings of the IEEE Conference on Computer Vision and Pattern Recognition, pp. 1386–1393 (2014)
15. Weinberger, K.Q., Saul, L.K.: Distance metric learning for large margin nearest neighbor classification. J. Mach. Learn. Res. 10(Feb), 207–244 (2009)
16. Winder, S.A., Brown, M.: Learning local image descriptors. In: 2007 IEEE Conference on Computer Vision and Pattern Recognition, CVPR 2007, pp. 1–8. IEEE (2007)
17. Yi, K.M., Trulls, E., Lepetit, V., Fua, P.: LIFT: learned invariant feature transform. In: Leibe, B., Matas, J., Sebe, N., Welling, M. (eds.) ECCV 2016. LNCS, vol. 9910, pp. 467–483. Springer, Cham (2016). https://doi.org/10.1007/978-3-319-46466-4_28
18. Zagoruyko, S., Komodakis, N.: Learning to compare image patches via convolutional neural networks. In: Proceedings of the IEEE Conference on Computer Vision and Pattern Recognition, pp. 4353–4361 (2015)
19. Zeng, A., Song, S., Nießner, M., Fisher, M., Xiao, J., Funkhouser, T.: 3Dmatch: learning local geometric descriptors from RGB-D reconstructions. In: 2017 IEEE Conference on Computer Vision and Pattern Recognition (CVPR), pp. 199–208. IEEE (2017)

A Joint Generative Model for Zero-Shot Learning

Rui Gao[1], Xingsong Hou[1,5]([✉]), Jie Qin[2], Li Liu[3], Fan Zhu[3], and Zhao Zhang[4]

[1] School of Electronic and Information Engineering,
Xi'an Jiaotong University, Xi'an, China
houxs-xjtu@qq.com
[2] Computer Vision Laboratory, ETH Zurich, Zürich, Switzerland
[3] Inception Institute of Artificial Intelligence, Abu Dhabi, UAE
[4] Soochow University, Suzhou, China
[5] Guangdong Xi'an Jiaotong University Academy, Guangdong, China

Abstract. Zero-shot learning (ZSL) is a challenging task due to the lack of data from unseen classes during training. Existing methods tend to have the strong bias towards seen classes, which is also known as the domain shift problem. To mitigate the gap between seen and unseen class data, we propose a joint generative model to synthesize features as the replacement for unseen data. Based on the generated features, the conventional ZSL problem can be tackled in a supervised way. Specifically, our framework integrates Variational Autoencoders (VAE) and Generative Adversarial Networks (GAN) conditioned on class-level semantic attributes for feature generation based on element-wise and holistic reconstruction. A categorization network acts as the additional guide to generate features beneficial for the subsequent classification task. Moreover, we propose a perceptual reconstruction loss to preserve semantic similarities. Experimental results on five benchmarks show the superiority of our framework over the state-of-the-art approaches in terms of both conventional ZSL and generalized ZSL settings.

Keywords: Zero-shot learning · Variational autoencoder
Generative adversarial network · Perceptual reconstruction

1 Introduction

Deep learning contributes significantly to the rapid progress in computer vision owing to its strong capabilities of data representation. However, there exists a non-negligible issue that training deep neural networks requires a huge amount of annotated data, which is usually unavailable in realistic scenarios due to labor-intensive data annotations. Meanwhile, with the explosive growth of new categories (*e.g.* of objects), it is even impossible to get any training data from certain classes. To deal with this, zero-shot learning (ZSL) has recently emerged as an

© Springer Nature Switzerland AG 2019
L. Leal-Taixé and S. Roth (Eds.): ECCV 2018 Workshops, LNCS 11132, pp. 631–646, 2019.
https://doi.org/10.1007/978-3-030-11018-5_50

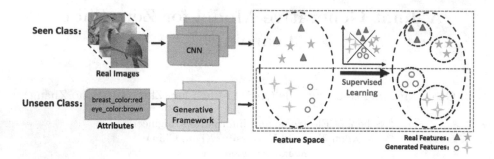

Fig. 1. The flow chart of the proposed approach. We address the zero-shot learning (ZSL) problem in a supervised way, by generating features for unseen classes via our generative framework. The red dotted box denotes the conventional ZSL task, and the blue dotted box denotes the generalized ZSL (GZSL) task. (Color figure online)

effective solution [17–19,28]. ZSL considers a more challenging case that training (seen) and test (unseen) classes are disjoint, *i.e.* the data of unseen classes is totally missing during the training process.

Specific intermediate representations (*e.g.* semantic attributes [8,11,18] and word vectors [10,27,37,48]) have been widely used by ZSL methods to bridge the gap between seen and unseen classes. However, an inherent problem, known as 'domain shift' [12], still remains challenging for conventional ZSL methods. In other words, classifiers trained on seen classes are not suitable for unseen ones due to their different underlying distributions. Consequently, most existing methods have the strong bias towards seen data and their performance is unacceptable for conventional ZSL settings, let alone the recently proposed more realistic generalized ZSL (GZSL) settings [7,42] where both seen and unseen classes are present at test time. Therefore, it is highly desirable to develop a generalized framework that could mitigate the domain shift and provide a universal classifier for both seen and unseen classes. As shown in Fig. 1, in this work, we aim to address the above issues from a new perspective, *i.e.* converting ZSL to supervised learning, by hallucinating unseen class features based on deep generative models.

Deep generative models, such as Generative Adversarial Networks (GAN) and Variational Autoencoders (VAE), have been extensively studied in the recent few years. GAN [13] is appealing to generate realistic images, especially conditioned on additional information [26,33]. VAE [15], especially the conditional VAE (CVAE) [38], has great potential to generate data through element-wise similarity metrics. In a similar spirit to our work, Xian *et al.* [43] proposed a ZSL framework to generate features for unseen classes based on conditional GAN (CGAN). However, GAN generally concentrates on more abstract and global data structure. In our problem, element-wise reconstruction is also essential for hallucinating unseen classes. Thus, we propose a joint framework by taking the advantages of CGAN and CVAE for more delicate data generation. Note that existing works [4,21] have already shown the effectiveness of this kind of generative model in image synthesis. In contrast, we aim at generating features instead of images for unseen classes since the generated images are typically of insufficient quality to train deep networks for the final classification [43]. We add an additional categorization network to ensure the discriminability of the synthesized features. Different from [43], the categorizer and the generator in our framework compete in a two-player minimax game. That is, the generator tries to generate features that belong to the classes of real features, and the categorizer tries to distinguish the generated features from the real ones in the category level simultaneously. Through the competition, the generated features will be well suited for training the final discriminative classifier. Moreover, we propose a perceptual reconstruction loss to preserve class-wise semantics based on the intermediate outputs of the discriminator and the categorizer.

The main contributions of this paper are summarized as follows:

- We propose a novel generative framework for zero-shot learning, which addresses conventional ZSL problems in a supervised manner. The framework takes the advantages of CGAN and CVAE to generate features conditioned on semantic attributes with the additional help of a categorization network. As a result, the generated features are not only similar to the real ones but also discriminative for the subsequent classification task.
- We leverage the intermediate outputs of the networks for perceptual reconstruction so that the generated features have the pixel-wise similarity as well as the semantic similarity to the real features.
- Extensive experimental results on five standard ZSL benchmarks demonstrate that the proposed method achieves notable improvement over the state-of-the-art approaches in not only the conventional ZSL but also the more challenging GZSL tasks.

The remainder of the paper is organized as follows. In Sect. 2, we give a brief review of existing ZSL methods and generative models. In Sect. 3, we introduce the proposed joint generative framework, which includes several networks to synthesize high-quality features of unseen classes for the subsequent classification task. Section 4 first introduces the datasets and experimental setup and then provides the demonstration of the experimental results. We finally draw our conclusion in Sect. 5.

2 Related Work

2.1 Zero-Shot Learning

Zero-shot learning is a challenging task because of the lack of training data. Many attempts [1,8,17–19,27,28,30,31,34,45,48] have been made to exploit the relationships between seen and unseen classes. Semantic representations, such as semantic attributes [8,9,11,17,18] and word vectors [10,27,37,48], are employed as the intermediate embedding to bridge the gap between the visual space and class space. Typically, a mapping from the visual space to semantic space is learned and then leveraged for the following classification task.

Recently, there were some works that learned the inverse mapping from the semantic space to visual space [5,23,24,43,46], which was shown effective for mitigating the domain shift problem. For instance, Zhang et al. [46] proposed an end-to-end architecture to embed the semantic representation into the visual space. Different from the above works, we choose not to learn the inverse mapping directly but generate synthesized features of unseen classes conditioned on class-level semantic attributes. Recently, some works focused on data generation using generative models, which are similar to our work. For instance, Bucher et al. [5] generated features via GMMN [22]. Xian et al. [43] proposed a framework combining WGAN [3] and a categorization network to generate features. Our framework differs from them by exploiting two generative models (i.e. CVAE and CGAN) for realistic feature generation. Moreover, we propose both categorization and perceptual losses to generate discriminative features.

In comparison to the conventional ZSL, the generalized zero-shot learning (GZSL) is a more realistic and difficult task, where both seen and unseen classes are available at test time [7,42]. Despite that the conventional ZSL has gained a lot of attention, few studies [7,37] concentrated on solving GZSL problems. It is more desirable to design robust ZSL methods that could eliminate the bias towards the seen data for more realistic scenarios.

2.2 Deep Generative Models

Deep generative models [13,15] have shown the great potential in data generation. There have been a variety of deep generative models [13,15,20,21,32,38]. Among these models, Variational Autoencoder (VAE) [15] and Generative Adversarial Network (GAN) [13] play the indispensable roles. VAE models the relationship directly through element-wise reconstruction, while GAN captures the global relationship indirectly [21]. However, VAE has a disadvantage of often generating blurry images as reported in [4] because element-wise distance cannot describe the complex data structure. GAN can obtain more abstract information, but the training process is not stable [36].

Due to the above shortcomings, some recent works attempted to combine these two generative models for better data generation, such as VAE/GAN [21], adversarial autoencoder [25], and CVAE-GAN [4]. Our work is thus motivated by the above approaches; however, we utilize conditioned generative models to synthesize features instead of images as the quality of generated images are too low to achieve satisfactory performance in ZSL problems [43]. Specifically, our model is conditioned on semantic attributes instead of category-level labels, so that more delicate description can be used for feature generation. Moreover, we add a categorization network to ensure that the generated features are helpful for the following classification task. We also take advantage of the intermediate outputs of the networks for perceptual reconstruction to form a richer semantic similarity metric for feature generation.

3   Approach

This work aims to synthesize high-quality features for unseen classes by establishing a joint generative model, based on which conventional ZSL can be

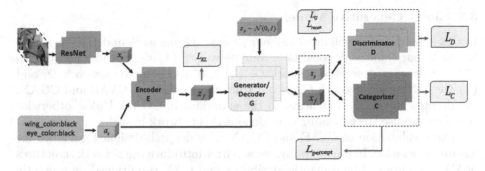

Fig. 2. The illustration of our generative framework. Particularly, our framework consists of four networks: the Encoder E, the Generator G, the Discriminator D, and the Categorizer C. Given real features and the corresponding semantic attributes as the input, our framework will synthesize high-quality features after generative learning.

transformed into supervised learning. Specifically, our proposed model generates semantically expressive features for unseen classes conditioned on the class-level semantic attributes. Subsequently, we train classifiers based on the generated features of unseen classes w.r.t. conventional ZSL settings and on both the generated features of unseen classes and real features of seen classes w.r.t. GZSL settings. As a result, the domain shift between seen and unseen classes will be mitigated significantly as classifiers are learned on both seen and unseen features.

In the following, we will first introduce the problem settings for ZSL and GZSL, and then present our joint generative model in detail. Finally, how to perform zero-shot recognition in a supervised manner is elaborated.

3.1 Problem Settings

In zero-shot learning, the training set S consists of image features, attributes, and class labels of seen classes, *i.e.* $S = \{(x_s, a_s, y_s) | x_s \in X, a_s \in A, y_s \in Y_s\}$. $x_s \in R^{d_x}$ denotes the features of seen data, where d_x denotes the feature dimension. $Y_s = \{y_s^1, ..., y_s^{C_s}\}$ represents the labels of C_s seen classes. $a_s \in \mathbb{R}^{d_a}$ denotes the class-level attributes of seen classes, where d_a indicates the dimension of semantic attributes. In terms of unseen classes, no features are available during training and we can only employ some class-level information, *e.g.* semantic attributes in our case. Specifically, the unseen set is denoted by $U = \{(a_u, y_u) | a_u \in A, y_u \in Y_u\}$, where $Y_u = \{y_u^1, ..., y_u^{C_u}\}$ represents the labels of C_u unseen classes and $a_u \in \mathbb{R}^{d_a}$ denotes the class-level attributes of unseen classes.

It should be noted that the seen and unseen classes are disjoint, namely $Y_s \cap Y_u = \emptyset$. Given S and U, the conventional zero-shot learning task is to learn a classifier $f_{ZSL} : X \to Y_u$, and the generalized zero-shot learning aims to learn a universal classifier $f_{GZSL} : X \to Y_s \cup Y_u$, which is a more challenging task.

3.2   Joint Generative Model

In this subsection, we will introduce our proposed framework in detail. As shown in Fig. 2, our framework consists of four networks: (1) the encoder network E, (2) the decoder/generator network G, (3) the discriminator network D, and (4) the categorizer network C. As our framework combines CVAE and CGAN, the decoder in CVAE is identical to the generator in CGAN. Unless otherwise specified, we use the generator G to denote this network branch.

The combination of CVAE and CGAN provides well-designed guidance for feature generation. In the following, we will first introduce the network structures of VAE conditioned on semantic attributes and GAN conditioned on semantic attributes and category labels, respectively. An additional categorization network will also be introduced along with the conditional GAN. Subsequently, we will present our perceptual reconstruction loss and the overall objective for training in detail. Finally, we will introduce the procedure for zero-shot recognition at test time.

VAE Conditioned on Semantic Attributes. VAE consists of an encoder network and a generator network. In our architecture, VAE is conditioned on class-level semantic attributes. In other words, attributes act as a part of the input to both encoder and generator for the purpose of providing class-level semantic information for feature generation.

As for the encoder network E with parameters θ_E, we aim to encode the real features x_s into a latent representation

$$z_f \sim p_E(z|x_s, a_s), \tag{1}$$

where $x_s \sim p(x)$ and $a_s \sim p(a)$, and $p(x)$ and $p(a)$ denote the prior distributions of real features and semantic attributes, respectively. The encoder learns the inherent structure of features and then imposes this prior over the distribution $p(z)$, which is usually $z_p \sim \mathcal{N}(0, I)$. The generator G with parameters θ_G decodes the latent representation into the feature space to generate synthesized features

$$x_f \sim p_G(x|z_f, a_s). \tag{2}$$

The overall loss function of CVAE is a combination of the reconstruction loss and the Kullback-Leibler divergence loss:

$$L_{CVAE}(\theta_E, \theta_G) = L_{KL} + L_{recon}, \tag{3}$$

where

$$L_{KL}(\theta_E, \theta_G) = KL(p_E(z|x_s, a_s)||p(z)), \tag{4}$$

$$L_{recon}(\theta_E, \theta_G) = -E[\log(p_G(x|z_f, a_s))]. \tag{5}$$

By minimizing Eq. (3), we can reduce the reconstruction error and the difference between the distribution of latent representation and the prior distribution. As a consequence, the encoder is capable of capturing the inherent structure of data and the generator will generate features with similar structures as the real ones.

GAN Conditioned on Attributes and Categories. In the conventional generative adversarial network, the generator and the discriminator try to make a balance in a two-player minimax competition. In our framework, the generator is conditioned on the semantic attributes. In addition, the category-wise information (*i.e.* labels), exploited by a categorizer, works as another clue to help the generator obtain discriminative features. We define the discriminator with parameters θ_D and the categorizer with parameters θ_C. Concretely, the generator tries to minimize the following loss:

$$
\begin{aligned}
L_G(\theta_G, \theta_D, \theta_C) = &- E[\log(p_D(G(z_p, a_s)))] - E[\log(p_D(G(z_f, a_s)))] \\
&- E[\log(p_C(y_s|x_p)] - E[\log(p_C(y_s|x_f)],
\end{aligned}
\tag{6}
$$

where

$$
x_p = G(z_p, a_s) \sim p_G(x|z_p, a_s), x_f = G(z_f, a_s) \sim p_G(x|z_f, a_s).
$$

In the meantime, the discriminator tries to minimize

$$
L_D(\theta_G, \theta_D, \theta_C) = -E[\log(p_D(x_s))] - E[\log(1 - p_D(x_f))] - E[\log(1 - p_D(x_p))] \tag{7}
$$

Given z_p and z_f along with the semantic attributes as the input, the generator aims to synthesize features that are similar to the real features and belong to the same class as the real ones at the same time. The discriminator tries to distinguish real features from synthesized ones. After iterative training, the network will generate high-quality features with the guidance from semantic attributes as well as from category-wise information.

As mentioned above, the categorizer helps to promote the discriminability of the generated features, which has the similar spirit with the classification network in [43]. However, we find that this additional regularization is not enough for the subsequent classification task. To this end, we make the categorizer as the other 'discriminator', which plays a minimax competition with the generator in the category level. Concretely, the real features x_s, and synthesized features x_f and x_p, are fed into the categorizer, which tries to minimize the softmax based categorization loss:

$$
L_C(\theta_C) = -E[\log(p_C(y_s|x_s)] - E[\log(p_C(y_f|x_p)] - E[\log(p_C(y_f|x_f)], \tag{8}
$$

where y_f denotes the label of the 'fake' class that is disjoint from the seen and unseen classes. In this way, the categorizer not only needs to classify the real features into the right classes but also regards the synthesized features as another 'fake' class. Through the competition, the generator is encouraged to generate features from the same classes as the real features.

Perceptual Reconstruction. In addition to the superior characteristics of CVAE and CGAN, we try to find a richer similarity metric to achieve more delicate generation results. As we mentioned above, element/pixel-wise information and holistic structures can be preserved by using VAE and GAN respectively, yet the semantic information may not be enough. Thus, we incorporate a perceptual reconstruction loss into our framework. The perceptual loss has been explored in the field of image style transfer and super-resolution [14], and could encourage the generated features to be semantically similar to real ones.

Specifically, we take advantage of the intermediate output of the discriminator and categorizer for perceptual reconstruction:

$$L_{percept}(\theta_D, \theta_C) = \|f_D(x_s) - f_D(x_f)\|_2^2 + \|f_C(x_s) - f_C(x_f)\|_2^2, \qquad (9)$$

where f_D and f_C are the outputs of the last hidden layers of the discriminator and categorizer, respectively.

Overall Objective. The ultimate goal of our framework is to minimize the following overall loss function:

$$L = L_{KL} + L_{recon} + L_D + L_C + \alpha L_G + \beta L_{percept}. \qquad (10)$$

In particular, we alternatively optimize every network branch in our framework as follows:

$$Encoder(\theta_E) \leftarrow L_{KL} + L_{recon} + \beta L_{percept}; \qquad (11)$$

$$Generator(\theta_G) \leftarrow L_{recon} + \alpha L_G + \beta L_{percept}; \qquad (12)$$

$$Discriminator(\theta_D) \leftarrow L_D; \qquad (13)$$

$$Categorizer(\theta_C) \leftarrow L_C. \qquad (14)$$

L_{KL} only appears in Eq. (11) because it is only related to the encoder. Similarly, L_C and L_D are the objectives of the categorizer and discriminator respectively. The generator is shared between the CVAE and CGAN so its loss can be divided into two parts: i.e. L_{recon} and $L_{percept}$ form the loss w.r.t. CVAE and L_G is the loss w.r.t. CGAN. All the objectives are complementary to each other, while the joint training process could result in superior performance.

3.3   Zero-Shot Recognition

After finishing the training process, the synthesized features of unseen classes can be obtained through our generator network. In particular, given an arbitrary latent representation drawn from the Gaussian distribution $z_t \sim \mathcal{N}(0, I)$ and the semantic attributes a_u of the corresponding unseen class as the input, the generator will output the synthesized features as follows:

$$x_{gen} = G(z_t, a_u) \sim p_G(x|z_t, a_u). \qquad (15)$$

Based on the generated features, zero-shot recognition can be transformed into the conventional supervised learning problem. As we previously mentioned, there exist two settings for zero-shot recognition, i.e. the conventional ZSL and the more challenging GZSL. In conventional ZSL settings, we train the softmax classifier based on x_{gen} and then test on the real features of unseen classes,

---

Algorithm 1. The training process of our proposed framework

Input:

   Training features of seen classes: x_s; semantic attributes of seen classes: a_s; initial parameters of Encoder E, Generator G, Discriminator D, and Categorizer C: θ_E, θ_G, θ_D, and θ_C; total training epoch: T.

Output:

   The learned parameters of each network: θ_E, θ_G, θ_D, and θ_C.

1: **while** epoch < T **do**
2:     Sample a batch of real features $\{x_s, a_s\} \subseteq S$;
3:     The Encoder E maps the real features into a latent representation: z_f;
4:     Compute KL loss using Eq. (4);
5:     Get synthesized features x_f through the Generator G;
6:     Compute reconstruction loss using Eq. (5);
7:     Sample z_p from the Gaussian distribution: $z_p \sim \mathcal{N}(0, I)$;
8:     Get synthesized features x_p through the Generator G;
9:     Compute the generator loss using Eq. (6);
10:     Compute the discriminator loss using Eq. (7);
11:     Classify x_s and synthesized features x_f, x_p through the Categorizer C;
12:     Compute the categorization loss using Eq. (8);
13:     Compute the perceptual reconstruction loss using Eq. (9);
14:     Optimizing the parameters of each network using Eq. (11) - (14), respectively;
15: **end while**

---

i.e. x_u. As for GZSL settings, the original data of seen classes x_s will be divided into two parts, *i.e.* x_s^{tr} for training and x_s^{ts} for test. During training, we employ x_{gen} together with x_s^{tr} as the training samples to learn the softmax classifier. At test time, we evaluate on x_u and x_s^{ts} to obtain the final recognition accuracy.

4 Experimental Results

In this section, we evaluate the proposed method on five ZSL benchmark datasets. First, we make a brief introduction of the datasets, implementation details of our framework and evaluation protocols. In order to show the effectiveness of our framework, we then present our experimental results on both conventional ZSL and GZSL tasks by comparing with several state-of-the-art ZSL methods and baseline methods. Finally, we show the high quality of the generated features quantitatively and qualitatively.

4.1 Datasets

Five classic datasets for ZSL are adopted in our experiments, *i.e.* AWA1 [18], AWA2 [42], CUB [40], SUN [29], and aPY [8]. AWA1 [18] is the original Animals with Attributes dataset, which has 30475 images in 50 classes, and each class is annotated with 85 attributes. However, the images of AWA1 are not publicly available. The AWA2 [42] dataset, containing 37322 images, is a good replacement for AWA1. These two datasets share the same classes and class-level

Table 1. Statistics of datasets in term of number of images, attributes, and seen/unseen classes, and the training/test split.

Dataset	Image	Attribute	Seen/Unseen	Training		Test	
				Seen	Unseen	Seen	Unseen
CUB [40]	11788	312	150/50	7057	0	1764	2967
AWA1 [18]	30475	85	40/10	19832	0	4958	5685
AWA2 [42]	37322	85	40/10	23527	0	5882	7913
SUN [29]	14340	102	645/72	10320	0	2580	1440
aPY [8]	15539	64	20/12	5932	0	1483	7924

attributes. Caltech-UCSD Birds 200-2011 (CUB) [40] is a fine-grained dataset with 11788 images of birds of 200 different types annotated with 312 attributes. SUN [29] is also a fine-grained dataset that contains 14340 images from 717 types of scenes annotated with 102 attributes. Attribute Pascal and Yahoo (aPY) [8] is a small-scale dataset with 15339 images from 32 classes annotated with 64 attributes. The details of the five datasets are summarized in Table 1.

As for image features, we employ the ResNet features proposed in [42]. Regarding class embeddings, we use the class-level continuous attributes for all datasets because using continuous attributes could achieve better performance than binary ones, as pointed out in [1]. As for data splits, in early standard splits [18] for each dataset, some of the test classes are among the 1 K classes of ImageNet, which are used to pre-train the ResNet. This will lead to biased results. Therefore, we follow the recently proposed split in [42] to avoid this. The detailed seen/unseen splits are also shown in Table 1.

4.2   Implementation Details and Parameter Settings

In our framework, all the networks are Multi-Layer Perceptrons (MLP) with LeakyReLU activations [44]. The encoder, generator, and discriminator consist of a single hidden layer with 1000 units, and the categorizer contains a single hidden layer with 1024 units. As each dataset has different attribute annotations, we set the dimension d_z of z_f and z_p according to the number of class-level attributes respectively. Specifically, we set $d_z = 256$ for AWA1, AWA2, SUN, and aPY, and $d_z = 512$ for CUB as CUB dataset has much more attributes.

For network training, we first pre-train the categorizer branch using the seen data for fast convergence. In terms of the parameters, we empirically set $\alpha = 0.01$, and $\beta = 0.1$ across all the datasets. The number of the generated features are chosen to make a trade-off between the computational efficiency and classification accuracy. Specifically, in the conventional ZSL task, we set the number of generated features as eight times the number of ground-truth unseen features on CUB, SUN and aPY, and twice on AWA1 and AWA2. As for GZSL, we set the number of generated features as eight times the number of ground-truth unseen features on SUN and aPY, and six times on CUB, AWA1, and AWA2.

Table 2. Comparison results with the state-of-the-art methods in terms of both ZSL and GZSL settings. T1 = top-1 accuracy, u = top-1 accuracy on unseen data, s = top-1 accuracy on seen data, and H = harmonic mean. We report top-1 accuracies in %.

Method	Zero-Shot Learning					Generalized Zero-Shot Learning														
	CUB	AWA1	AWA2	SUN	aPY	CUB			AWA1			AWA2			SUN			aPY		
	T1	T1	T1	T1	T1	u	s	H	u	s	H	u	s	H	u	s	H	u	s	H
DAP[18]	40.0	44.1	46.1	39.9	33.8	1.7	67.9	3.3	0.0	88.7	0.0	0.0	84.7	0.0	4.2	25.1	7.2	4.8	78.3	9.0
IAP[18]	24.0	35.9	35.9	19.4	36.6	0.2	72.8	0.4	2.1	78.2	4.1	0.9	87.6	1.8	1.0	37.8	1.8	5.7	65.6	10.4
CONSE[27]	34.3	45.6	44.5	38.8	26.9	1.6	72.2	3.1	0.4	88.6	0.8	0.5	90.6	1.0	6.8	39.9	11.6	0.0	91.2	0.0
CMT[37]	34.6	39.5	37.9	39.9	28.0	7.2	49.8	12.6	0.9	87.6	1.8	0.5	90.0	1.0	8.1	21.8	11.8	1.4	85.2	2.8
SSE[47]	43.9	60.1	61.0	51.5	34.0	8.5	46.9	14.4	7.0	80.5	12.9	8.1	82.5	14.8	2.1	36.4	4.0	0.2	78.9	0.4
LATEM[41]	49.3	55.1	55.8	55.3	35.2	15.2	57.3	24.0	7.3	71.7	13.3	11.5	77.3	20.0	14.7	28.8	19.5	0.1	73.0	0.2
ALE[1]	54.9	59.9	62.5	58.1	39.7	23.7	62.8	34.4	16.8	76.1	27.5	14.0	81.8	23.9	21.8	33.1	26.3	4.6	73.7	8.7
DEVISE[10]	52.0	54.2	59.7	56.5	39.8	23.8	53.0	32.8	13.4	68.7	22.4	17.1	74.7	27.8	16.9	27.4	20.9	4.9	76.9	9.2
SJE[2]	53.9	65.6	61.9	53.7	32.9	23.5	59.2	33.6	11.3	74.6	19.6	8.0	73.9	14.4	14.7	30.5	19.8	3.7	55.7	6.9
ESZSL[35]	53.9	58.2	58.6	54.5	38.3	12.6	63.8	21.0	6.6	75.6	12.1	5.9	77.8	11.0	11.0	27.9	15.8	2.4	70.1	4.6
SYNC[6]	55.6	54.0	46.6	56.3	23.9	11.5	70.9	19.8	8.9	87.3	16.2	10.0	90.5	18.0	7.9	43.3	13.4	0.2	78.9	0.4
SAE[16]	33.3	53.0	54.1	40.3	8.3	7.8	54.0	13.6	1.8	77.1	3.5	1.1	82.2	2.2	8.8	18.0	11.8	0.4	80.9	0.9
f-CLSWGAN[43]	57.3	68.2	-	60.8	-	**43.7**	57.7	**49.7**	57.9	61.4	59.6	-	-	-	42.6	36.6	**39.4**	-	-	-
SE-GZSL[39]	**59.6**	69.5	69.2	**63.4**	-	41.5	53.3	46.7	56.3	67.8	61.5	**58.3**	68.1	62.8	40.9	30.5	34.9	-	-	-
Proposed	54.9	**69.9**	**69.5**	59.0	36.3	42.7	45.6	44.1	**62.7**	60.6	**61.6**	56.2	71.7	**63.0**	44.4	30.9	36.5	**31.1**	43.3	**36.2**

4.3 Evaluation Protocol

As mentioned above, in conventional ZSL settings, we aim to classify the unseen features x_u into the corresponding unseen classes Y_u. In GZSL settings, the class space is $Y_s \cup Y_u$ and we need to assign class labels to both unseen features and some of the seen features. Here we follow the unified evaluation protocol in [42].

In the conventional ZSL setting, we compute the average top-1 accuracy for each class and then average the per-class top-1 accuracy to mitigate the imbalance among the classes. The evaluation metric is defined as follows:

$$acc = \frac{1}{\|C\|} \sum_{c=1}^{\|C\|} \frac{n_{cp}}{n_c}, \tag{16}$$

where $\|C\|$ denotes the number of classes, n_c denotes the number of data in each class, and n_{cp} is the number of correct predictions in each class. Regarding GZSL, we use the harmonic mean, which can be computed as follows:

$$H = \frac{2 * s * u}{s + u} \tag{17}$$

where s and u represent the average per-class top-1 accuracies of seen classes and unseen classes respectively. A higher harmonic mean indicates the high accuracies on both seen and unseen classes.

4.4 Comparison with the State-of-the-Art Methods

Table 2 shows the conventional ZSL results of our framework and the state-of-the-art methods. In this setting, the search space is restricted to unseen classes at test time. From the table, we can observe that our method achieves better zero-shot recognition accuracies than the traditional ZSL methods. The overall

Table 3. Comparison results with the baseline models in terms of both ZSL and GZSL settings. T1 = top-1 accuracy, u = top-1 accuracy on unseen data, s = top-1 accuracy on seen data, and H = harmonic mean. We report top-1 accuracies in %.

Method	Zero-Shot Learning					Generalized Zero-Shot Learning														
	CUB	AWA1	AWA2	SUN	aPY	CUB			AWA1			AWA2			SUN			aPY		
	T1	T1	T1	T1	T1	u	s	H	u	s	H	u	s	H	u	s	H	u	s	H
CVAE+CAT	48.7	65.0	65.2	54.4	32.0	33.3	**54.0**	41.2	39.3	75.9	55.7	34.7	**83.3**	49.0	45.1	25.5	32.6	20.4	48.5	28.7
CGAN+CAT	41.2	59.6	56.6	42.3	17.3	0.0	41.8	0.0	10.8	**76.9**	19.0	12.0	82.8	20.9	0.0	**41.1**	0.0	10.3	89.6	18.5
CVAE+CGAN	48.6	65.4	59.8	56.3	33.7	38.4	42.6	40.4	46.5	70.5	56.0	41.8	77.0	54.1	38.8	29.2	33.3	22.0	**96.7**	33.4
Proposed (w/o $L_{percept}$)	51.1	68.4	66.2	58.5	34.9	40.5	7.8	43.9	50.5	67.8	57.9	51.7	74.8	61.1	**49.0**	26.0	34.0	30.8	37.5	33.8
Proposed	54.9	69.9	69.5	59.0	36.3	**42.7**	45.6	**44.1**	**62.7**	60.6	**61.6**	**56.2**	71.7	**63.0**	44.4	30.9	**36.5**	31.1	43.3	**36.2**

improvement is especially obvious on AWA1 and AWA2, with 6.6% and 11.2% higher accuracies than the second best ones in traditional ZSL methods, respectively. Compared with the generative models in ZSL tasks, our method have better performance on AWA1 and AWA2 datasets, with 0.6% higher accuracies on both of the datasets. Concerning CUB, SUN and aPY datasets, our method performs competitively with the best ones, *i.e.* SE-GZSL [39] and DEVISE [10] methods, respectively. The results clearly demonstrate that our framework is capable of generating useful and expressive features of unseen classes, which are beneficial for ZSL tasks.

In terms of the GZSL task, as illustrated in Table 2, our framework shows the superiority over the traditional ZSL methods on all the five datasets. For example, significant improvements w.r.t. harmonic mean are observed, with 172.2%, 123.7%, 122.2%, 32.7%, and 28.2% higher than the second best ones on aPY, AWA2, AWA1, SUN, and CUB, respectively. It is noteworthy that most traditional ZSL methods achieve high accuracies on seen classes but much worse performance on unseen classes, which indicates that those methods have strong biases towards seen classes. Our model can mitigate the bias to a large extent as shown in Table 2. Compared with the ZSL methods based on the generative models, our model shows the superiorities on AWA1 and AWA2 datasets. Moreover, our model has the highest accuracy for unseen classes on AWA1, SUN and aPY datasets, indicating that our model has the capability of balancing the accuracy between seen and unseen classes. Therefore, our generative framework is very useful and competitive in this realistic and challenging task.

4.5   Comparison with the Baseline Models

As our framework contains several networks together with the perceptual reconstruction, we compare the proposed framework with four baseline models by omitting each of them, in order to verify the importance of each branch. For example, as shown in Table 3, 'CVAE+CAT' indicates the framework only containing the CVAE and categorizer, and 'Proposed (w/o $L_{percept}$)' denotes the whole network without the perceptual reconstruction.

The results w.r.t. conventional ZSL settings are shown in Table 3. From the results of 'CVAE+CAT' and 'CGAN+CAT', we can conclude that integrating the CVAE and CGAN are beneficial for the ZSL task, and the improvement is more

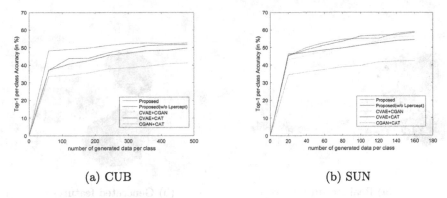

(a) CUB   (b) SUN

Fig. 3. Top-1 accuracy with different numbers of generated features on the CUB and SUN datasets.

significant by incorporating the CVAE. This shows that element-wise reconstruction is essential for our task. The results of 'CVAE+CGAN' also demonstrate the necessity of the categorizer branch. For example, the accuracy is improved by 7.7% on aPY by adding the categorizer. Finally, we can see that our framework with perceptual reconstruction outperforms the one without $L_{percept}$.

As for GZSL, compared with the above baselines, the proposed model has higher accuracies on unseen classes and higher harmonic mean since it can balance the seen and unseen classes. Overall, 'CGAN+CAT' achieves the worst performance probably because CGAN captures the holistic data structure, which is not enough for feature generation. After combining the CVAE, the performance is enhanced significantly. All the above results in ZSL and GZSL settings clearly demonstrate the indispensability of each part in our whole framework.

4.6   Analysis of the Generated Features

In this section, we present some further analyses of the synthesized features of unseen classes. Figure 3 shows the classification accuracies for the unseen classes with the increasing numbers of the generated features. In general, the accuracy increases when generating more unseen features. We also observe that the satisfactory accuracies can be achieved when the numbers of the generated features are relatively small, which indicates that our model can generate high-quality features for the classification task. The generated features can be used as the excellent replacement of the missing unseen features. Taking some unseen classes on the AWA1 dataset as an example, we can see from Fig. 4 that the generated feature distribution is even more discriminative compared with the real feature distribution. This further indicates that our generative model can synthesize high-quality features that are beneficial for the classification task.

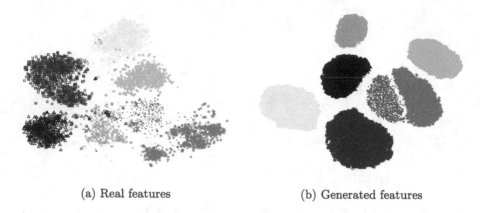

(a) Real features   (b) Generated features

Fig. 4. t-SNE visualization of the real/generated features of some unseen classes on the AWA1 dataset.

5   Conclusion

In this work, we proposed an effective joint generative framework for feature generation in the context of zero-shot learning. Specifically, our model combined two popular generative models, *i.e.* VAE and GAN, to capture the element-wise and holistic data structures at the same time. We took advantage of the class-level semantic attributes as the conditional information. An additional categorization network worked as the guidance for generating discriminative features. Importantly, we incorporated the perceptual reconstruction into the framework to preserve semantic similarities. We showed the superiority of the proposed generative framework by conducting experiments on five standard datasets in terms of the conventional ZSL task as well as the more challenging GZSL task. The extensive experimental results indicated that our model could generate high-quality features to mitigate the domain gap in ZSL due to the lack of unseen data.

Acknowledgements. This work was supported in part by the NSFC under Grant 61872286, u1531141, 61732008, 61772407 and 61701391, the National Key R&D Program of China under Grant 2017YFF0107700, the National Science Foundation of Shaanxi Province under Grant 2018JM6092, and Guangdong Provincial Science and Technology Plan Project under Grant 2017A010101006 and 2016A010101005.

References

1. Akata, Z., Perronnin, F., Harchaoui, Z., Schmid, C.: Label-embedding for attribute-based classification. In: CVPR (2013)
2. Akata, Z., Reed, S., Walter, D., Lee, H., Schiele, B.: Evaluation of output embeddings for fine-grained image classification. In: CVPR (2015)
3. Arjovsky, M., Chintala, S., Bottou, L.: Wasserstein gan. In: ICML (2017)

4. Bao, J., Chen, D., Wen, F., Li, H., Hua, G.: CVAE-GAN: fine-grained image generation through asymmetric training. In: ICCV (2017)
5. Bucher, M., Herbin, S., Jurie, F.: Generating visual representations for zero-shot classification. In: ICCV Workshop (2017)
6. Changpinyo, S., Chao, W.L., Gong, B., Sha, F.: Synthesized classifiers for zero-shot learning. In: CVPR (2016)
7. Chao, W.-L., Changpinyo, S., Gong, B., Sha, F.: An empirical study and analysis of generalized zero-shot learning for object recognition in the wild. In: Leibe, B., Matas, J., Sebe, N., Welling, M. (eds.) ECCV 2016, Part II. LNCS, vol. 9906, pp. 52–68. Springer, Cham (2016). https://doi.org/10.1007/978-3-319-46475-6_4
8. Farhadi, A., Endres, I., Hoiem, D., Forsyth, D.: Describing objects by their attributes. In: CVPR (2009)
9. Ferrari, V., Zisserman, A.: Learning visual attributes. In: NIPS (2008)
10. Frome, A., et al.: Devise: A deep visual-semantic embedding model. In: NIPS (2013)
11. Fu, Y., Hospedales, T.M., Xiang, T., Gong, S.: Attribute learning for understanding unstructured social activity. In: Fitzgibbon, A., Lazebnik, S., Perona, P., Sato, Y., Schmid, C. (eds.) ECCV 2012, Part IV. LNCS, vol. 7575, pp. 530–543. Springer, Heidelberg (2012). https://doi.org/10.1007/978-3-642-33765-9_38
12. Fu, Y., Hospedales, T.M., Xiang, T., Gong, S.: Transductive multi-view zero-shot learning. IEEE Trans. Pattern Anal. Mach. Intell. **37**(11), 2332–2345 (2015)
13. Goodfellow, I., et al.: Generative adversarial nets. In: NIPS (2014)
14. Johnson, J., Alahi, A., Fei-Fei, L.: Perceptual losses for real-time style transfer and super-resolution. In: Leibe, B., Matas, J., Sebe, N., Welling, M. (eds.) ECCV 2016, Part II. LNCS, vol. 9906, pp. 694–711. Springer, Cham (2016). https://doi.org/10.1007/978-3-319-46475-6_43
15. Kingma, D.P., Welling, M.: Auto-encoding variational bayes. In: ICLR (2014)
16. Kodirov, E., Xiang, T., Gong, S.: Semantic autoencoder for zero-shot learning. In: CVPR (2017)
17. Lampert, C.H., Nickisch, H., Harmeling, S.: Learning to detect unseen object classes by between-class attribute transfer. In: CVPR (2009)
18. Lampert, C.H., Nickisch, H., Harmeling, S.: Attribute-based classification for zero-shot visual object categorization. IEEE Trans. Pattern Anal. Mach. Intell. **36**(3), 453–465 (2014)
19. Larochelle, H., Erhan, D., Bengio, Y.: Zero-data learning of new tasks. In: AAAI (2008)
20. Larochelle, H., Murray, I.: The neural autoregressive distribution estimator. In: Proceedings of the Fourteenth International Conference on Artificial Intelligence and Statistics (2011)
21. Larsen, A.B.L., Sønderby, S.K., Larochelle, H., Winther, O.: Autoencoding beyond pixels using a learned similarity metric. In: ICML (2016)
22. Li, Y., Swersky, K., Zemel, R.: Generative moment matching networks. In: ICML (2015)
23. Long, Y., Liu, L., Shao, L.: Towards fine-grained open zero-shot learning: inferring unseen visual features from attributes. In: WACV (2017)
24. Long, Y., Liu, L., Shao, L., Shen, F., Ding, G., Han, J.: From zero-shot learning to conventional supervised classification: unseen visual data synthesis. In: CVPR (2017)
25. Makhzani, A., Shlens, J., Jaitly, N., Goodfellow, I., Frey, B.: Adversarial autoencoders. arXiv preprint arXiv:1511.05644 (2015)
26. Mirza, M., Osindero, S.: Conditional generative adversarial nets. In: Computer Science, pp. 2672–2680 (2014)

27. Norouzi, M., et al.: Zero-shot learning by convex combination of semantic embeddings. In: ICLR (2014)
28. Palatucci, M., Pomerleau, D., Hinton, G.E., Mitchell, T.M.: Zero-shot learning with semantic output codes. In: NIPS (2009)
29. Patterson, G., Hays, J.: Sun attribute database: Discovering, annotating, and recognizing scene attributes. In: CVPR (2012)
30. Qin, J., et al.: Zero-shot action recognition with error-correcting output codes. In: CVPR (2017)
31. Qin, J., Wang, Y., Liu, L., Chen, J., Shao, L.: Beyond semantic attributes: discrete latent attributes learning for zero-shot recognition. IEEE Signal Process. Lett. 23(11), 1667–1671 (2016)
32. Radford, A., Metz, L., Chintala, S.: Unsupervised representation learning with deep convolutional generative adversarial networks. Computer Science (2015)
33. Reed, S., Akata, Z., Yan, X., Logeswaran, L., Schiele, B., Lee, H.: Generative adversarial text to image synthesis. In: ICML (2016)
34. Rohrbach, M., Stark, M., Schiele, B.: Evaluating knowledge transfer and zero-shot learning in a large-scale setting. In: CVPR (2011)
35. Romera-Paredes, B., Torr, P.: An embarrassingly simple approach to zero-shot learning. In: ICML (2015)
36. Salimans, T., Goodfellow, I., Zaremba, W., Cheung, V., Radford, A., Chen, X.: Improved techniques for training gans. In: NIPS (2016)
37. Socher, R., Ganjoo, M., Manning, C.D., Ng, A.: Zero-shot learning through cross-modal transfer. In: NIPS (2013)
38. Sohn, K., Lee, H., Yan, X.: Learning structured output representation using deep conditional generative models. In: NIPS (2015)
39. Verma, V.K., Arora, G., Mishra, A.: Generalized zero-shot learning via synthesized examples. In: CVPR (2018)
40. Welinder, P., et al.: Caltech-ucsd birds 200. California Institute of Technology (2010)
41. Xian, Y., Akata, Z., Sharma, G., Nguyen, Q., Hein, M., Schiele, B.: Latent embeddings for zero-shot classification. In: CVPR (2016)
42. Xian, Y., Lampert, C.H., Schiele, B., Akata, Z.: Zero-shot learning-a comprehensive evaluation of the good, the bad and the ugly. In: CVPR (2017)
43. Xian, Y., Lorenz, T., Schiele, B., Akata, Z.: Feature generating networks for zero-shot learning. In: CVPR (2018)
44. Xu, B., Wang, N., Chen, T., Li, M.: Empirical evaluation of rectified activations in convolutional network. Computer Science (2015)
45. Yu, X., Aloimonos, Y.: Attribute-based transfer learning for object categorization with zero/one training example. In: Daniilidis, K., Maragos, P., Paragios, N. (eds.) ECCV 2010, Part V. LNCS, vol. 6315, pp. 127–140. Springer, Heidelberg (2010). https://doi.org/10.1007/978-3-642-15555-0_10
46. Zhang, L., et al.: Learning a deep embedding model for zero-shot learning. In: CVPR (2017)
47. Zhang, Z., Saligrama, V.: Zero-shot learning via semantic similarity embedding. In: ICCV (2015)
48. Zhang, Z., Saligrama, V.: Zero-shot recognition via structured prediction. In: Leibe, B., Matas, J., Sebe, N., Welling, M. (eds.) ECCV 2016, Part VII. LNCS, vol. 9911, pp. 533–548. Springer, Cham (2016). https://doi.org/10.1007/978-3-319-46478-7_33

W24 – Women in Computer Vision Workshop

W24 – Women in Computer Vision Workshop

We present Women in Computer Vision Workshop (WiCV) in conjunction with ECCV 2018 to increase the visibility and inclusion of female researchers in the field of computer vision. Computer vision and machine learning have made incredible progress over the past years, yet the number of female researchers is still low both in academia and industry. WiCV is organized to raise the visibility of female researchers, to increase collaboration, and to provide mentorship and opportunities to female-identifying junior researchers in the field.

The fifth WiCV workshop was organized for the first time in Europe, in conjunction with ECCV, unlike previous editions which were held at CVPR. The workshop attracted unprecedented attendance, i.e the number of attendees exceeded the room capacity of 100. We had 50 high quality submissions from a diverse range of topics and institutions. The most popular topics were object recognition and detection, applications of computer vision, and machine learning approaches. Each 4-page extended abstract received 2 single-blind reviews from 42 reviewers. 40 papers were accepted (5 of them oral) for poster presentations. Among the accepted posters, and 16 papers appeared in proceedings. The workshop discussion paper from the organizers was not peer-reviewed.

The program included 3 keynotes (Prof. Dr. Tamara Berg, Prof. Dr. Svetlana Lazebnik, and Prof. Dr. Kate Saenko), 5 oral presentations, 40 poster presentations, and a panel discussion on diversity (Prof. Dr. Tamara Berg, Prof. Dr. Svetlana Lazebnik, and Prof. Dr. Kate Saenko, Andrew Fitzgibbon, and Prof. Dr. Jitendra Malik). The workshop was followed by a mentoring dinner, where senior researchers were matched with mentees. The dinner included 3 talks by Megan Maher, Prof. Dr. Tinne Tuytelaars, and Prof. Dr. Raquel Urtasun.

We believe that future sessions of WiCV at ECCV would be a great venue for a more connected community in Europe to overcome the ongoing imbalance in the workforce and its negative side effects for all the participants.

Acknowledgments. We want to thank the computer vision community for their support over many years. We would like to specifically thank the sponsors (banquet: Apple, platinum: DeepMind, gold: Amazon, Argo AI, Facebook, Microsoft, Siemens, IBM Research, Uber, silver: Adobe Research, Disney Research, Google, Lyft, Naver Labs Europe, Nvidia, Snap Inc, Zalando, start-up: Aquifi, media: RSIP vision), the keynote speakers, the panelists, the reviewers, the participants, and the previous organizers.

September 2018

Zeynep Akata
Dena Bazazian
Yana Hasson
Angjoo Kanazawa
Hildegard Kuehne
Gül Varol

WiCV at ECCV2018: The Fifth Women in Computer Vision Workshop

Zeynep Akata[1,2], Dena Bazazian[3(✉)], Yana Hasson[4], Angjoo Kanazawa[5], Hildegard Kuehne[6], and Gül Varol[4]

[1] University of Amsterdam, Amsterdam, Netherlands
[2] Max Planck Institute, Saarbrücken, Germany
[3] Computer Vision Center (CVC), Barcelona, Spain
dena.bazazian@cvc.uab.es
[4] Inria, Paris, France
[5] UC Berkeley, Berkeley, USA
[6] University of Bonn, Bonn, Germany
https://wicvworkshop.github.io/ECCV2018

Abstract. We report a summary of the Women in Computer Vision Workshop (WiCV) at ECCV 2018. WiCV focuses on creating a more inclusive environment for women researchers, a minority in the currently male dominated field of Computer Vision. In fact, despite the incredible progress of computer vision and machine learning and the growing interest towards these topics, the amount of female researchers is still limited both in academia and industry. The workshop is therefore an opportunity to promote collaborations, increase visibility and inclusion, and provide mentoring. Moreover the workshop offers a venue to discuss gender related biases still present throughout the work environments and are often not discussed with the due importance. This was the fifth WiCV workshop in its fourth year, and also the first WiCV held in Europe, in conjunction with ECCV. We have made changes in our program according to lessons learned from previous workshops and were able to obtain an unprecedented attendance exceeding the room capacity. We report a summary of statistics for presenters and attendees, followed by expectations for future iterations of the workshop.

1 Introduction

The fifth 'Women in Computer Vision' workshop was organized for the first time in conjunction with ECCV, extending the successful 'Women in Computer Vision' series at CVPR. The idea behind bringing WiCV to ECCV was to make it easier for female researchers from Europe, Asia and Middle east to attend the event.

Whereas themes like female inclusion in work environments and equal opportunities beyond gender are getting increasing attention, certain fields are still poorly populated by females. This also holds for the field of computer science and in particular of computer vision and machine learning, which has become

L. Leal-Taixé and S. Roth (Eds.): ECCV 2018 Workshops, LNCS 11132, pp. 649–653, 2019.
https://doi.org/10.1007/978-3-030-11018-5_51

one of its largest research communities. Not even the tremendous progress in the past years over a broad range of areas such as object recognition, video analysis, 3D reconstruction and autonomous driving has helped to reduce the disparity between males and females in the field, both in academia and industry. This leads to isolation of many female computer vision researchers, who end up working in an unbalanced work environment.

While this problem is commonly experienced by females, most of the community is not even aware of it. Yet issues are not limited to this. In the previous editions of the workshop [1], important topics have been raised such as *unconscious bias*, where men unwillingly tend to undervalue females i.e. in grading or job interviews. For this reason, the workshop on Women in Computer Vision is a gathering for both men and women working in computer vision, targeting a broad and diverse audience of researchers in academia and industry, including graduate students pursuing doctoral studies, masters or undergraduates.

This workshop is envisioned as a unique opportunity to raise awareness on the problems of the female community and help inclusion and visibility of female computer vision researchers at all levels, seeking to serve women from universities, research programs and backgrounds from all around the world.

To reach the goals of inclusion and opportunity for female researchers, a series of events has been organized throughout the workshop. First of all, female researchers were encouraged to submit a contribution to be presented in the conference venue and therefore spread their work with the community. The papers were peer reviewed and a selection of the best papers was presented in an oral session. All accepted papers were further presented in a poster session. Paper submission required a four page manuscript on a novel or recently published work authored by at least one researcher identifying as female. In particular, works from junior graduates students were encouraged in order to allow them to get acquainted with the community and look for career opportunities such as collaborations or internships while gathering feedback and suggestions about their work. As workshop is not focused on any specific computer vision topic and, on the contrary, strives for diversity, the selected papers give a cross-sectional overview of current research topics.

Moreover, female presenters of accepted papers were encouraged to apply for a travel award in order to ease and encourage their participation and, following the trend of the previous edition, choose whether or not to appear in the workshop proceedings. Along the travel awards, an additional prize has been awarded, by donating two Nvidia GPUs to randomly selected female participants.

In addition to the presentations, the workshop features a series of keynotes from well-known female computer vision researchers. The most important aspect of these lectures is to showcase work of senior female researchers in general, but also as potential role-models and as a form of inspiration for young researchers. Newcomers can find a neutral ground to collaborate and follow the steps of the speakers in their career paths. The workshop also included a panel, where the topics of inclusion and diversity were discussed in an open and friendly environment between female and male colleagues.

Another high-level goal of the workshop is to maintain and grow the WiCV network, where female students and professionals share experiences and career advice. A mentoring banquet has been organized to provide a safe and casual environment for those relationships to be seeded in the workshop and possibly become ongoing mentorships or collaborations in the future. The dinner sets an informal environment in which junior women can meet, exchange ideas, and form beneficial relationships with senior faculty and researchers of all genders in the field.

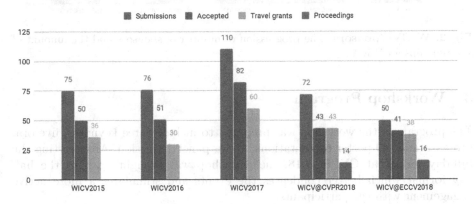

Fig. 1. WiCV Submissions. The number of submissions over the past years of WiCV.

2   Workshop Statistics

In comparison with the previous edition of WiCV [1], for this workshop we had 50 high quality submissions from a diverse range of topics and institutions. The most popular topics were object recognition and detection, applications of computer vision, and machine learning approaches. The comparison with previous years is presented in Fig. 1. Overall the number of submission was a bit lower than for previous CVPR events. One of the reasons here might be that ECCV in general hosts less attendees than CVPR and that the workshop was the first in context of this conference series.

As in the previous WiCV edition at CVPR 2018, the workshop organization has been able to provide travel grants for all the authors of accepted submissions who applied for a travel stipend. This was possible thanks to sponsor donations that have been used to cover the grants and the expenses for the mentorship banquet, workshop bags and promotional materials, in addition to some travel support for keynotes and organizers. Sponsorship amounts are depicted in Fig. 2.

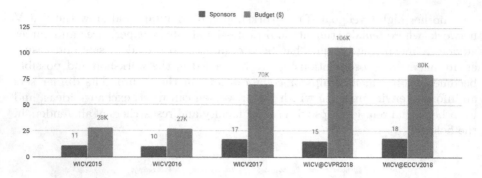

Fig. 2. WiCV Sponsors. The progression of number of sponsors and the amount of sponsorships for WiCV.

3   Workshop Program

The program of the workshop was prepared to include three keynotes, five oral presentations, 40 poster presentations, and a panel discussion. After testing the full-day format at CVPR 2018, the workshop was brought back to the half day format which better condenses the events and stimulates a more active engagement with the participants.

Overall, the WiCV workshop at ECCV 2018 offered three tracks, consisting of three keynotes, two oral sessions featuring five high quality publications and a poster session providing a platform for young researchers to show their work to a broader audience.

For this edition of the workshop, three high profile researchers have been invited as keynote speakers:

- Tamara Berg (UNC Chapel Hill, Shopagon): *Vision and Language*
- Svetlana Lazebnik (University of Illinois at Urbana-Champaign): *Adapting Neural Networks to New Tasks*
- Kate Saenko (Boston University): *Explainable AI Models and Why We Need Them*

The speakers were selected to offer a diverse variety of expertise over different computer vision topics and for their important impact in their research fields. By diversifying the set of speakers, junior researchers are provided with potential role models with whom they can identify and who can help them envision their own career paths.

The workshop concluded with a one hour panel discussion on diversity. The panel was made up of the three female keynote speakers as well as two male researchers, Andrew Fitzgibbon (Microsoft HoloLens) and Jitendra Malik (UC Berkeley). A diverse range of subjects was addressed during the panel discussion with anonymous questions from the audience. Questions ranged from suggestions for specific situations, such as how one can encourage their male coworkers in providing a safe working environment, to personal questions addressed to the panel about their biggest research mistakes in life. An important point arose following CVPR's publication of a code of conduct, as well as naming a conference ombud for reports about violations. The recommendation for ECCV to follow this example has been forwarded to ECCV 2020 organizers.

The workshop was followed by the WiCV banquet, where senior researchers were able to meet as mentors with mentees in a casual environment and gave them advice about career paths in research. The banquet begun with three talks by Megan Maher, Tinne Tuytelaars and Raquel Urtasun sharing their stories and experiences and giving constructive advice to young female researchers.

4   Conclusions

WiCV at ECCV 2018 has continued to increase awareness concerning the gender imbalance in the computer vision community, with the aim to overcome issues tied to exclusive workspaces or unfair impediments in female careers. To this end, the collective effort is tuned towards building an increasingly big and connected community of female researchers capable of providing the necessary support.

Given the high number of attendees (more than 100), with an elevated number of male participants of 40%, we believe that the workshop is making important steps in the right direction. To further increase the pace towards reaching the desired goals, the organizing committee of the workshop is also attempting to convert the structure of WiCV to a non-profit organization to be an autonomous entity for all related events and gatherings.

Acknowledgments. We want to thank the computer vision community for their support over many years. We would like to specifically thank the sponsors (banquet: Apple, platinum: DeepMind, gold: Amazon, Argo AI, Facebook, Microsoft, Siemens, IBM Research, Uber, silver: Adobe Research, Disney Research, Google, Lyft, Naver Labs Europe, Nvidia, Snap Inc, Zalando, start-up: Aquifi, media: RSIP vision), the keynote speakers, the panelists, the reviewers, the participants, and the previous organizers.

References

1. Demir, I., Bazazian, D., Romero, A., Sharmanska, V., Tchapmi, L.: WiCV 2018: the fourth women in computer vision workshop. In: Proceedings of the IEEE Conference on Computer Vision and Pattern Recognition Workshops 2018, pp. 1860–1862 (2018)

Gait Energy Image Reconstruction from Degraded Gait Cycle Using Deep Learning

Maryam Babaee[✉], Linwei Li, and Gerhard Rigoll

Chair of Human-Machine Communication, Technical University of Munich,
Theresienstrasse 90, Munich, Germany
maryam.babaee@tum.de

Abstract. Gait energy image (GEI) is considered as an effective gait representation for gait-based human identification. In gait recognition, normally, GEI is computed from one full gait cycle. However in many circumstances, such a full gait cycle might not be available due to occlusion. Thus, the GEI is not complete, giving a rise to degrading gait identification rate. In this paper, we address this issue by proposing a novel method to reconstruct a complete GEI from a few frames of gait cycle. To do so, we propose a deep learning-based approach to transform incomplete GEI to the corresponding complete GEI obtained from a full gait cycle. More precisely, this transformation is done gradually by training several fully convolutional networks independently and then combining these as a uniform model. Experimental results on a large public gait dataset, namely OULP demonstrate the validity of the proposed method for gait identification when dealing with very incomplete gait cycles.

Keywords: Gait energy image · Gait recognition · Deep learning

1 Introduction

Gait (the style of natural walking) [2] can be used to identify individuals at a distance, when other biometric features such as face and fingerprint might not be available. Here, a sequence of images showing a person walking is analyzed as input data. Since the natural walking of a person is periodic, it is sufficient to consider only one period (gait cycle) from the whole sequence. The gait cycle is defined as the time interval between the exact same repetitive events of walking (any position of the foot during walking can be regarded as the starting point of the gait cycle).

The main assumption in many gait-based human identification techniques [1, 5] is that a full gait cycle of individuals is available, which is a strong assumption in video surveillance applications, where occlusion occurs a lot and a person might be observed in only a few frames. From a full gait cycle, a simple and effective gait representation, namely gait energy image (GEI) [4] can be computed, which is the average of silhouette images of a walking person (see Fig. 1).

© Springer Nature Switzerland AG 2019
L. Leal-Taixé and S. Roth (Eds.): ECCV 2018 Workshops, LNCS 11132, pp. 654–658, 2019.
https://doi.org/10.1007/978-3-030-11018-5_52

This standard gait feature has been widely used alone or in combination with other features for gait recognition.

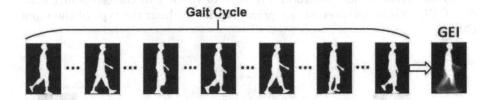

Fig. 1. GEI is computed by averaging gait silhouettes over one gait cycle.

We propose a deep-based method to reconstruct a GEI from a few frames, i.e., incomplete gait cycle. More specifically, having only a few frames of a full gait cycle, we first generate an incomplete GEI. Next, we train a uniform fully convolutional neural network (FCN) which gets the computed incomplete GEI (average of a few frames) as input and outputs the reconstructed complete GEI. The conducted experiments confirm that this network can successfully reconstruct a complete GEI.

2   Method

In our method, the complete GEI reconstruction is done in a progressive way (i.e. various types of incomplete GEIs are gradually converted to the complete GEI). To this end, we propose an incremental GEI reconstruction approach using ten FCNs that each single FCN enhances the quality of input incomplete GEI (IC-GEI). Since the gait cycle length depends on the frame rate and is different from a dataset to another dataset, we consider the partial transformations every 10% of the gait cycle length. The first FCN transforms a GEI generated from one frame to the GEI corresponds to the consecutive 10% of the gait cycle. Similarly, the other FCNs enhance their incomplete GEI by predicting the information of the following 10% of gait cycle. The structures of the all FCNs are the same, but they are trained on different types of GEI in terms of the number of frames and the starting frame in a gait cycle. Each FCN like an auto-encoder consists of two parts; the encoder (convolutional) and the decoder (deconvolutional) part.

After training the ten FCNs, their last convolutional hidden layers are combined to have one uniform model named ITCNet (see Fig. 2). The input of the ITCNet could be any type of IC-GEI, and the target is the corresponding complete GEI. The convolutional hidden layer i maps an mf-GEI (composed of m frames) to the corresponding nf-GEI, where $n - m = 0.1 * T$, and T is the gait cycle length. For example, if the aim is to transform a 1f-GEI to the complete

GEI and the full gait cycle is 30 frames long, the input is first mapped to 3f-GEI, then to 6f-GEI by passing through the first two hidden layers, and so on. All generated incomplete GEIs are used to fine tune the ITCNet. In this way, this end-to-end network can transform any type of IC-GEI to corresponding complete GEI, without the need of any prior knowledge about the type of the input IC-GEI.

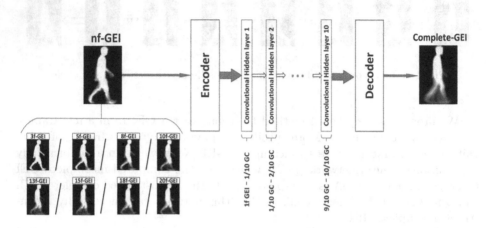

Fig. 2. ITCNet structure for reconstructing a complete GEI from an incomplete GEI.

3   Results

Figure 3 shows some samples of the reconstructed GEIs from only 3 frames for 10 different subjects in the OULP dataset [3]. It can be seen that the reconstructed GEIs recovered by our end-to-end ITCNet are almost similar to the ground truth. Regarding the gait recognition performance, Table 1 presents the rank-1 and rank-5 identification rates for incomplete GEIs and reconstructed GEIs. This experiment was performed on 500 subjects of the OULP dataset. Clearly, the end-to-end ITCNet has greatly improved the identification performance, especially for IC-GEIs generated from smaller partial gait cycle. As the number of frames increases (larger partial gait cycle), the rank-1 and rank-5 identification rates get closer to that of ground truth complete GEI.

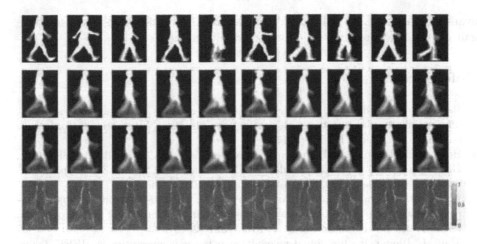

Fig. 3. Best viewed in color. Qualitative results of our GEI reconstruction method; Incomplete GEI generated from 3 frames for different subjects (first row), ground truth GEIs (second row), the corresponding reconstructed GEIs (third row), and the difference images of reconstructed and ground truth GEIs in color scale (last row).

Table 1. Comparison of rank-1 and rank-5 identification rates between incomplete GEIs and reconstructed GEIs from different portion of gait cycle. Note that rank-1 and rank-5 for ground truth complete GEI are **86.30%** and **94.24%**, respectively.

Partial gait cycle (%)	Rank-1 [%]		Rank-5 [%]	
	Reconst. GEI	Incomp. GEI	Reconst. GEI	Incomp. GEI
10	53.40	8.42	73.35	12.81
20	65.11	12.70	82.57	17.76
30	71.19	17.09	86.39	24.24
40	77.53	26.50	89.95	35.62
50	80.46	34.63	91.67	47.83
60	82.59	61.96	93.06	77.31
70	84.22	72.40	93.02	85.53
80	85.76	72.94	93.75	86.98
90	86.00	73.06	94.10	86.40

4 Conclusions

We have proposed a fully convolutional neural network for gait energy image (GEI) reconstruction from an incomplete gait cycle. The model could reconstruct a GEI, given an incomplete-GEI which is composed of only a few frames of a gait cycle. Experimental results show that the proposed model can improve recognition rate greatly, particularity when there is only 10% of a gait cycle is available. In future, we will extend this model to an end-to-end model for both gait energy image reconstruction and recognition.

References

1. Babaee, M., Rigoll, G.: View-invariant gait representation using joint Bayesian regularized non-negative matrix factorization. In: The IEEE International Conference on Computer Vision (ICCV) (2017)
2. Boyd, J.E., Little, J.J.: Biometric gait recognition. In: Tistarelli, M., Bigun, J., Grosso, E. (eds.) Advanced Studies in Biometrics. LNCS, vol. 3161, pp. 19–42. Springer, Heidelberg (2005). https://doi.org/10.1007/11493648_2
3. Iwama, H., Okumura, M., Makihara, Y., Yagi, Y.: The OU-ISIR gait database comprising the large population dataset and performance evaluation of gait recognition. IEEE Trans. Inf. Forensics Secur. **7**, 1511–1521 (2012)
4. Man, J., Bhanu, B.: Individual recognition using gait energy image. IEEE Trans. Pattern Anal. Mach. Intell. **28**, 316–322 (2006)
5. Wolf, T., Babaee, M., Rigoll, G.: Multi-view gait recognition using 3D convolutional neural networks. In: Proceedings of the International Conference on Image Processing (ICIP), pp. 4165–4169. IEEE (2016)

Hierarchical Video Understanding

Farzaneh Mahdisoltani[1]([✉]), Roland Memisevic[2], and David Fleet[1]

[1] University of Toronto, Toronto, Canada
{farzaneh,fleet}@cs.toronto.edu
[2] Twenty Billion Neurons, Toronto, Canada
roland.memisevic@twentybn.com

Abstract. We introduce a hierarchical architecture for video understanding that exploits the structure of real world actions by capturing targets at different levels of granularity. We design the model such that it first learns simpler coarse-grained tasks, and then moves on to learn more fine-grained targets. The model is trained with a joint loss on different granularity levels. We demonstrate empirical results on the recent release of Something-Something (Second release of Something-Something is used throughout this paper) dataset, which provides a hierarchy of targets, namely coarse-grained action groups, fine-grained action categories, and captions. Experiments suggest that models that exploit targets at different levels of granularity achieve better performance on all levels.

Keywords: Video understanding · Hierarchical models
Fine-grained targets · Video classification · Video captioning
Something-Something Dataset

1 Introduction

Actions in the real world are structured, as are objects. We design an architecture that exploits some semantics of this structure through a target hierarchy. In particular, we show that works extract better features by learning targets at different levels of granularity, yielding better performance at all levels. We use Something-Something [3] dataset for our experiments. It comprises over 220,000 videos and a hierarchy of targets, namely, 50 coarse-grained action groups, 174 fine-grained action categories, and video captions with information about the actions, the objects, and their properties. Our contribution is two-fold:

1. We present a hierarchical architecture that makes use of different levels of task granularity by jointly learning fine-grained and coarse-grained targets, as well as captions.
2. We show that such model perform better than networks trained solely on one level of target labels.

L. Leal-Taixé and S. Roth (Eds.): ECCV 2018 Workshops, LNCS 11132, pp. 659–663, 2019.
https://doi.org/10.1007/978-3-030-11018-5_53

2 Related Work

The literature on action recognition is vast (e.g. [1,6,7]), as is the growing literature on video captioning [2,5,8], this paper focuses on architecture to learn a common encoding for both recognition and captioning, leveraging different levels of granularity in video targets, which is not studied extensively to date.

3 Approach

Our deep neural network leverages information at different levels of granularity. It simultaneously performs coarse-grained classification of action groups, fine-grained classification of action categories, and video captioning. It is trained end-to-end with a joint loss on all aforementioned targets.

The overall architecture is depicted in Fig. 2. Video frames are fed into the video encoder, resulting in encoding vector V, which is then passed to processing modules (classifiers or captioners) for targets with different granularity. Let i denote the ith level of target granularity, with higher values of i representing more fine-grained targets. Let T_i be the set of targets at level i. In order to capture the structure between actions, the concatenation of probability distribution over T_i and V is passed to $(i + 1)^{th}$ processing module. The model then tries to estimate the probability over T_{i+1}. In our model, $\forall c \in T_{i+1} : P(c|V) = \Sigma_{g \in T_i} P(c|g, V) P(g|V)$. In other words, at level $i + 1$, given $p(g|V)$, instead of estimating the posterior $p(c|V)$ directly, we implicitly estimate $P(c|g, V)$, integrating out g. Decomposing the posterior in this way is expected to simplify learning, as it provides some hints from coarse- to fine-grained classification. The total loss being optimized, is sum of losses of different levels: $loss = \Sigma_i w_i * loss_i$.

As mentioned before, Something-Something has 3 levels of targets. In the first step (yellow box in Fig. 2), the model infers the action group, e.g. "Putting", vs. "Taking". In the second step (orange box in Fig. 2), the output distribution over coarse-grained groups (grey boxes in Fig. 2) is used along with video features to infer the fine-grained action category, e.g. if the model has figured out the group "Putting" in the previous step, here it needs to distinguish between "Putting on top", "Putting behind", and "Putting next to". We move one step further with more details, where the model needs to generate a caption (red box in Fig. 2), and describe what is happening in the video. At this step, the output distribution over fine-grained classes is passed to the caption decoder. For an accurate caption, the model needs to recognize and explain objects and their properties as well as the action. The rest of the section explains each component of our architecture in more details.

Video Encoder. We use a minimal video encoder with 6 layers of 3D-CNN [4] with $3 \times 3 \times 3$ filters, and 4 spatial max pooling layers (see Fig. 1). For temporal aggregation we use a bidirectional LSTM. We then average the outputs over different time steps, yielding the final video encoding V.

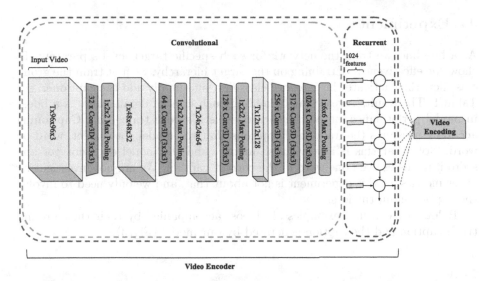

Fig. 1. Our video encoder architecture includes 6 layers of 3DCNN, and 4 layers of spatial max-pooling followed by an LSTM layer. T denotes the number of frames across time.

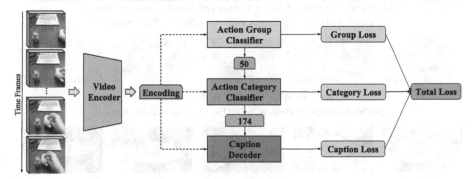

Fig. 2. Our hierarchical architecture for targets with different levels of granularity, along with the loss functions on different levels. (Color figure online)

Video Classification. For classification at level i, we pass V to a fully connected layer of size $|V| \times |T_i|$ followed by a softmax layer, T_i being the set of targets at level i. Note that the dimensions of this layer varies for different levels i. We train classifiers using the usual cross-entropy loss over classes at the intended target level.

Video Captioning. We use a two-layer LSTM for decoding captions. At each time-step, we use a softmax over the vocabulary words, conditioned on previously generated words. The captioning loss is the negative log-probability of the word sequence.

4 Experiments

As a baseline, we train the network for each specific target level separately. To show the effectiveness of training on the target hierarchy, we first train the group classifier, then activate the category classifier, and finally add the captioner, see Table 1. The results reveal that by adding each level of detail, there is a boost in model performance, on all the target levels it's been trained on. Captioning accuracy measures the fraction of captions that the model got correct, word by word. Note that this is a very harsh metric, and the model does not get any score if it misses even one word of the correct caption. We are not investigating other metrics, as this experiment is not about that, and we only need to involve the captioning in the loss.

Below you can find examples of videos, accompanied by their their ground truth caption and the caption generated by our model (Fig. 3).

Ground Truth: Letting a bottle roll along a flat surface.
Model output: Letting a can roll along a flat surface.

Ground Truth: Tipping Water bottle over.
Model output: Poking a bottle so that it falls over.

Ground Truth: Lifting plate with cutlery on it.
Model output: Lifting plate with spoon on it.

Ground Truth: Putting pen on a surface.
Model output: Putting pen that cant roll onto a slanted surface, so it stays.

Fig. 3. Ground truth captions and model outputs for video examples of Something-Something dataset.

Training Settings. We use frame rate of 12 fps, and randomly pick 48 consecutive frames. Videos with less than 48 frames are padded by replicating first and last frames. We re-size frames to 128×128, and then use random cropping of size 96×96. For validation and testing, we use center cropping with same size.

Table 1. Comparing models trained with different weight vectors for joint loss. W shows weights on different level's losses, with the rightmost weight denoting the weight for captioning loss.

Loss weight vector	Coarse-grained accuracy	Fine-grained accuracy	Captioning accuracy
$W = [0, 1, 0]$	0	48.40	0
$W = [0, 0, 1]$	0	0	3.13
$W = [1, 0, 0]$	58.04	0	0
$W = [1, 1, 0]$	61.17	48.94	0
$W = [1, 1, 1]$	61.65	50.28	3.34

We optimize all models using Adam, with an initial learning rate of 0.001. Each step is finished after 20 epochs of training over the full dataset.

5 Conclusions

We present a new architecture that leverages information from hierarchy of targets, at different levels of granularity. To train the architecture we use a joint loss on the different target levels. This makes it possible to simultaneously classify the input video in different levels and produce a caption. Our experiments show that the architecture achieves a performance boost over models that aim to solve the tasks individually.

References

1. Carreira, J., Zisserman, A.: Quo vadis, action recognition? A new model and the kinetics dataset (2017). arXiv preprint: arXiv:1705.07750
2. Donahue, J., et al.: Long-term recurrent convolutional networks for visual recognition and description. In: CVPR 2015 (2015)
3. Goyal, R., et al.: The "something something" video database for learning and evaluating visual common sense. In: ICCV 2017 (2017)
4. Ji, S., et al.: 3d convolutional neural networks for human action recognition. TPAMI **35**, 221–231 (2013)
5. Kaufman, D., et al.: Temporal tessellation for video annotation and summarization (2016). arXiv preprint: arXiv:1612.06950
6. Laptev, I., et al.: Learning realistic human actions from movies. In: CVPR 2008 (2008)
7. Tran, D., et al.: Learning spatiotemporal features with 3d convolutional networks. In: ICCV 2015 (2015)
8. Venugopalan, S., et al.: Translating videos to natural language using deep recurrent neural networks (2014). arXiv preprint: arXiv:1412.4729

Fine-Grained Vehicle Classification with Unsupervised Parts Co-occurrence Learning

Sara Elkerdawy[✉], Nilanjan Ray, and Hong Zhang

Computing Science Department, Alberta University, Edmonton, Canada
{elkerdaw,nray1,hzhang}@ualberta.edu

Abstract. Vehicle fine-grained classification is a challenging research problem with little attention in the field. In this paper, we propose a deep network architecture for vehicles fine-grained classification without the need of parts or 3D bounding boxes annotation. Co-occurrence layer (COOC) layer is exploited for unsupervised parts discovery. In addition, a two-step procedure with transfer learning and fine-tuning is utilized. This enables us to better fine-tune models with pre-trained weights on ImageNet in some layers while having random initialization in some others. Our model achieves 86.5% accuracy outperforming the state of the art methods in BoxCars116K by 4%. In addition, we achieve 95.5% and 93.19% on CompCars on both train-test splits, 70-30 and 50-50, outperforming the other methods by 4.5% and 8% respectively.

1 Introduction

Vehicle fine-grained classification is a challenging problem in computer vision for multiple reasons. First, in contrast to the classification problem as in ImageNet [1], fine-grained classification deals with different classes within the same category. Secondly, fine-grained classification suffers from scarcity of datasets. Few public datasets for vehicle fine-grained classification exist, such as Cars [2], BoxCars116K [3], and CompCars [4]. Lastly, class hierarchy can be illustrated in three different levels: make, model, and year. Difficulty increases with deeper class definition as the number of samples per class becomes smaller and the visual cues become more challenging to detect.

Multiple methods rely on extra annotation either parts annotation or 3D CAD models such as [2,5]. These annotations require extensive laborious work and not feasible for large datasets. Shih et al. [6] proposed a co-occurrence layer evaluated on fine-grained bird-species recognition. COOC layer makes use of the semantic learned features in CNN models that jointly co-occur for a class. On the other hand, Sochor et al. [3] proposed an unpacking algorithm for vehicle view normalization based on 3D bounding box estimation. They used two networks as a preprocessing for 3D bounding box estimation. Then, they apply fine grained recognition with a third classification network on the unpacked images. Not to mention the unpacking distortion (Fig. 2), the use of three deep networks is

© Springer Nature Switzerland AG 2019
L. Leal-Taixé and S. Roth (Eds.): ECCV 2018 Workshops, LNCS 11132, pp. 664–670, 2019.
https://doi.org/10.1007/978-3-030-11018-5_54

computationally expensive for real-time applications such as traffic monitoring and surveillance.

2 Our Approach

In this section, we provide a detailed description of the architecture and the two-step fine-tuning procedure.

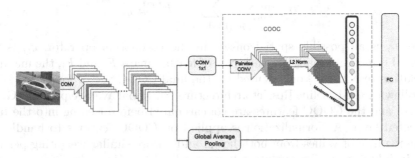

Fig. 1. Overall architecture. Applying Co-occurrence (COOC) layer [6] on the last convolution layers concatenated with global average pooling (GAP).

2.1 Two-Step Fine-Tuning

Fine-tuning ImageNet pre-trained models as widely shown in practice has better initial weights for the task at hand than random initialization. The network up to the last convolution layers is initialized with the weights trained on a large dataset (e.g. ImageNet). Subsequently, the whole network is fine-tuned including the new randomly initialized last fully connected layers for the new classification problem. However, recent work [7] highlighted that the two-step fine-tuning achieves better results than one-step fine-tuning. The reason for this is that these random weights have high gradient in the first few epochs and it is possible to wreck up the last few learned convolution features. In our paper, a transfer learning first is trained by freezing all the pre-trained initialized weights and updating only the newly added layers for few epochs. This step prevents the high gradient to back-prob into the already learned initial features. Then, after converging, a proper fine-tuning with good initial weights is applied on the whole network.

2.2 Co-occurrence Layer

In fine-grained categorization, the collection of parts detected and recognized is what count to decide on the final categorization. To make use of the part localization learned by deep CNN networks, we exploit co-occurrence (COOC) layer [6]. Co-occurrence (COOC) layer is a trainable end-to-end layer without additional learned weights into the network. It encodes the relationship between the parts learned by the network instead of only a small set of pre-specified manually annotated parts. Full architecture is shown in Fig. 1 where only one COOC block is added after the last convolution layer. In general, COOC layer treats each feature map $F_i \in \mathbb{R}^{m \times m}$ as a filter and calculates the correlation between the feature map F_i and each other feature map F_j. This implicitly enforces learning the co-occurrence of the different visual parts detected by the ith filter and the jth filter, i.e.

$$c_{ij} = \max_{o_{ij}} \sum_{p \in [1,m] \times [1,m]} F_p^i F_{p+o_{ij}}^j \qquad (1)$$

where o_{ij} is all possible spatial offsets in the correlation operator, c_{ij} is the maximal response. Finally, for each pair of feature maps F_i and F_j, the maximal correlation response c_{ij} only is used for the final COOC vector for F_i.

Following the baseline ResNet architecture [8], global average pooling (GAP) features and the COOC features are concatenated before feeding into the fully connected layer. A Normalization is applied on COOC features to handle the different range of values from both layers and ensure similar weighting per feature. In addition, 1×1 convolution layer is added to reduce the dimensionality of the COOC layer and also increase correlation between the features. Given an input with N channels, COOC layer output has a size of N^2. Without the 1×1 convolution layer, the high dimensional COOC vector is highly sparse with weak relations between neurons and thus performing useless additional computations.

3 Experimental Results

We did our experiments on BoxCars116k [3] and CompCars [4] datasets. None of these datasets have parts annotation, so we compare only with methods that rely on labels and/or 3D bounding boxes annotation if available. BoxCars116k is a surveillance only fine-grained classification while CompCars has both web-based collected and surveillance nature images. However, the surveillance data in CompCars is far less in size compared to BoxCars116k and contain frontal data only. For this reason, we evaluate on BoxCars116k and the web-collected images in CompCars to show the model in both scenarios with different views. On the training side, we apply data transformation at each epoch to introduce diversity to all images. We use transformations such as color alternation, image drop, random cuts and image flip. We used the same setup for all the models with Adam optimizer, initial learning rate 0.001, batch size 8 for BoxCars116k and 32 for CompCars. In two-step fine-tuning setup, layers initialized with random weights are first trained for 10 epochs before training the whole network for 30 epochs.

3.1 Evaluation

BoxCars116k: The dataset is divided into easy, medium, and hard subsets, based on the fine categorization in the make-model-year hierarchy. Evaluation is done

Table 1. Classification accuracy in percentage on BoxCars116K. The best accuracy is shown in bold for each split.

Method	Medium	Hard
VGG19 [3]	75.40	76.74
VGG19 + UNPACK [3]	83.98	84.12
ResNet50 [3]	75.07	75.48
ResNet50 + UNPACK [3]	82.28	82.27
ResNet152 [3]	78.44	76.46
ResNet152 + UNPACK [3]	83.80	83.74
ResNet50 + two-step	78.50	79.94
ResNet152 + two-step	81.43	79.76
ResNet50 (Ours)	86.00	**86.38**
ResNet152 (Ours)	**86.57**	85.31

Table 2. Classification accuracy in percentage on CompCars. The best accuracy in 70-30 split (top section) and 50-50 split (bottom section) is shown in bold.

Method	Top-1	Top-5
AlexNet [4]	81.9	94.0
GoogLeNet [4]	91.2	98.1
Overfeat [4]	87.9	96.9
ResNet50 (Ours)	**95.58**	**99.23**
Overfeat [4]	76.7	91.7
BoxCars [9]	84.8	95.4
ResNet50 [4]	90.80	98.16
ResNet50 + two-step	92.42	98.43
ResNet50 (Ours)	**93.19**	**98.98**

on the medium and hard subset of the dataset containing 79 and 107 class respectively. We use the provided training-test splits in both datasets for fair comparison with the other methods. Table 1 summarizes the results on BoxCars116k with different architectures compared with [3], baseline CNN models and our method's additional experiments. As can be seen, two-step fine-tuning achieves better results by up to 3.4% in accuracy than one shot fine-tuning. Still models with unpacking outperform two-step fine-tuned baseline models in accuracy by around 3%. However, this is achieved without the 3D estimation and contour finding preprocessing needed for the unpack. In addition, adding the relationship between the last feature maps via cooc layer boosts the performance further by 4% compared to the unpacking method. Also, our network with ResNet50 outperforms deeper networks like ResNet152 with unpacking by 2.2%.

CompCars: There is two training-test split provided in CompCars, one is 50-50 split and the other is 70-30 split respectively. We evaluated on both splits for further comparisons consistency. Results summary are shown in Table 2. Our model outperforms GoogLeNet, the best model, by 4.5% margin. It is also worth noting, that even with less data used in training our 50-50 model outperforms the best 70-30 achieved model by 2%. In addition, outperforming BoxCars that is using the same split by more than 8%. The accuracy gain (1.5%) holds in CompCars as well when applying two-step fine-tuning compared with its counterpart model with one-step fine-tuning.

3.2   Explanatory Analysis

Two-Step Tuning Analysis: To show the effect of the two step fine-tuning on vehicle categorization, visualization with class-activation map (CAM) [10] is performed on the last learned features. In CAM, the last layer in the network should be a global average pooling layer (GAP) after the last convolution. This GAP layer is then connected with the fully connected layers and the weights are learned. By doing this, we can know the weight of each feature map j before the GAP layer for each class i by examining the weight W_{ij}. In Fig. 2, the heat map for BoxCars [3], one-step fine-tuning, and two-step fine-tuning are shown. BoxCars method, due to 3D unboxing, attends mostly to the side view parts only regardless the category. On the extreme side, the one step fine-tuning with random weights initialization in the last layers gives a heat map that is scattered all over the image. The network did not learn to attend to particular parts of the image although there can be some negatively attended parts (blue). However in the two-step fine-tuning, the network's heat map is more similar to unboxing output with focused attention on certain parts of the vehicle for each category. It is worth noting that the network attends to the same areas/parts for vehicles of the same category even with slight rotations.

Fig. 2. CAM visualization for the ResNet50 networks trained on BoxCars116. The three rows shows heat map for 3D unboxing [3], one-step fine-tuning, and two-step fine-tuning from top to bottom respectively. Each pair of columns belong to the same vehicle with slight camera rotation but has similar heat maps in two-step fine-tuning. (color figure online)

Co-occurrence Analysis: As CompCars has finer high resolution, we visualize the learned features in COOC layer. Figure 3 shows three different categories defined by their make and model. Visualization is done by inspecting the pair of features corresponding to the most activated COOC neuron in a category and displaying the corresponding F_i and F_j maps. As can be seen, the most activated pair of features that jointly occur are recurring within the category. This highlights the importance of COOC layer to capture the relations between the detected features.

Fig. 3. Co-occurence heat map. Each row is a different vehicle class where each triplet of images represent the two highly jointly activated features and the input image respectively. The pair of features are consistently activated within the same category.

4   Conclusion

We have proposed an architecture for fine-grained vehicle classification without part annotation or 3D information. Our approach achieves the best results compared to the state-of-the art methods by a margin 4% on BoxCars116K and CompCars datasets. We utilize the learned high-level features in deep networks with co-occurrence layer to obtain unsupervised part information. In addition, we fine-tune with two steps (1) transfer, and (2) fine-tune for better weights transfer with existent random weights.

References

1. Deng, J., Dong, W., Socher, R., Li, L.J., Li, K., Fei-Fei, L.: ImageNet: a large-scale hierarchical image database. In: CVPR09 (2009)
2. Krause, J., Stark, M., Deng, J., Fei-Fei, L.: 3D object representations for fine-grained categorization. In: 4th International IEEE Workshop on 3D Representation and Recognition (3dRR-13), Sydney, Australia (2013)
3. Sochor, J., Špaňhel, J., Herout, A.: Boxcars: improving vehicle fine-grained recognition using 3D bounding boxes in traffic surveillance. arXiv preprint arXiv:1703.00686 (2017)
4. Yang, L., Luo, P., Change Loy, C., Tang, X.: A large-scale car dataset for fine-grained categorization and verification. In: Proceedings of the IEEE Conference on Computer Vision and Pattern Recognition, pp. 3973–3981 (2015)
5. Lin, Y.-L., Morariu, V.I., Hsu, W., Davis, L.S.: Jointly optimizing 3D model fitting and fine-grained classification. In: Fleet, D., Pajdla, T., Schiele, B., Tuytelaars, T. (eds.) ECCV 2014. LNCS, vol. 8692, pp. 466–480. Springer, Cham (2014). https://doi.org/10.1007/978-3-319-10593-2_31
6. Shih, Y.F., Yeh, Y.M., Lin, Y.Y., Weng, M.F., Lu, Y.C., Chuang, Y.Y.: Deep co-occurrence feature learning for visual object recognition. In: Proceedings of Conference on Computer Vision and Pattern Recognition (2017)
7. Branson, S., Van Horn, G., Belongie, S., Perona, P.: Bird species categorization using pose normalized deep convolutional nets. arXiv preprint arXiv:1406.2952 (2014)

8. He, K., Zhang, X., Ren, S., Sun, J.: Deep residual learning for image recognition. In: Proceedings of the IEEE Conference on Computer Vision and Pattern Recognition, pp. 770–778 (2016)
9. Sochor, J., Herout, A., Havel, J.: Boxcars: 3D boxes as CNN input for improved fine-grained vehicle recognition. In: Proceedings of the IEEE Conference on Computer Vision and Pattern Recognition, pp. 3006–3015 (2016)
10. Zhou, B., Khosla, A., Lapedriza, A., Oliva, A., Torralba, A.: Learning deep features for discriminative localization. In: Proceedings of the IEEE Conference on Computer Vision and Pattern Recognition, pp. 2921–2929 (2016)

Multiple Wavelet Pooling for CNNs

Aina Ferrà[1]([envelope]) [iD], Eduardo Aguilar[1,2] [iD], and Petia Radeva[1,2] [iD]

[1] Universitat de Barcelona, Barcelona, Spain
aferrama10@alumnes.ub.edu, {eduardo.aguilar,petia.ivanova}@ub.edu
[2] Computer Vision Center, Barcelona, Spain

Abstract. Pooling layers are an essential part of any Convolutional Neural Network. The most popular pooling methods, as max pooling or average pooling, are based on a neighborhood approach that can be too simple and easily introduce visual distortion. To tackle these problems, recently a pooling method based on Haar wavelet transform was proposed. Following the same line of research, in this work, we explore the use of more sophisticated wavelet transforms (Coiflet, Daubechies) to perform the pooling. Additionally, considering that wavelets work similarly to filters, we propose a new pooling method for Convolutional Neural Network that combines multiple wavelet transforms. The results achieved demonstrate the benefits of our approach, improving the performance on different public object recognition datasets.

Keywords: Wavelet · CNN · Pooling functions · Object recognition

1 Introduction

Neural networks, the main tool of deep learning, are a *before-and-after* in the history of computer science. Pooling layers are one of the main components of Convolutional Neural Networks (CNNs). They are designed to compact information, i.e. reduce data dimensions and parameters, thus increasing computational efficiency. Since CNNs work with the whole image, the number of neurons increases and so does the computational cost. For this reason, some kind of control over the size of our data and parameters is needed. However, this is not the only reason to use pooling methods, as they are also very important to perform a multi-level analysis. This means that rather than the exact pixel where the activation happened, we look for the region where it is located. Pooling methods vary from deterministic simple ones, such as max pooling, to probabilistic more sophisticated ones, like stochastic pooling. All of these methods have in common that they use a neighborhood approach that, although fast, introduce edge halos, blurring and aliasing. Specifically, max pooling is a basic technique that usually works, but perhaps too simple since it neglects substantial information applying just the max operation on the activation map. On the other hand, average pooling is more resistant to overfitting, but it can create blurring effects to certain datasets. Choosing the right pooling method is key to obtain good results.

L. Leal-Taixé and S. Roth (Eds.): ECCV 2018 Workshops, LNCS 11132, pp. 671–675, 2019.
https://doi.org/10.1007/978-3-030-11018-5_55

Recently, wavelets have been incorporated in deep learning frameworks for different purposes [3,4,8], among them as pooling function [8]. In [8], the authors propose a pooling function that consists in performing a 2nd order decomposition in the wavelet domain according to the fast wavelet transform (FWT). The authors demonstrate that their proposed method outperforms or performs comparatively with traditional pooling methods.

In this article, inspired by [8], we explore the application of different wavelet transforms as pooling methods, and then, we propose a new pooling method based on the best combination of them. Our work differs with [8] mainly in three aspects: 1. We perform 1st order decomposition in the wavelet domain according to the discrete wavelet transform (DWT), and therefore, we can extract directly the images from the low-low (LL) sub-band, 2. We explore different wavelets transforms instead of using only Haar wavelet, and 3. We propose a new pooling method based on the combination of different wavelet transforms.

The organization of the article is as follows. In Sect. 2, we present the Multiple Wavelet Pooling methodology and in Sect. 3, we present the datasets, the experimental setup, discuss the results and describe the conclusion.

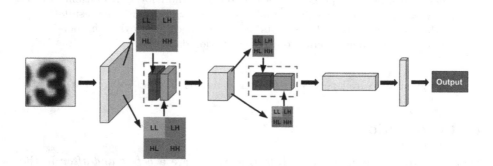

Fig. 1. Overview of multiple wavelet pooling

2   Multiple Wavelet Pooling

Wavelet transform is a representation of the data, similar to the Fourier transform, that allows us to compact information. Given a smooth function $f(t)$, the continuous case is defined as

$$CWT_{(s,l)}f = s^{-1/2} \int f(t)\psi\left(\frac{t-l}{s}\right) dt.$$

where $\psi(t)$ is a mother wavelet and $s \in \mathbb{Z}$ is the *scale index* and $l \in \mathbb{Z}$ is the location index. Given an image A of size (n, n, m), the finite Discrete Wavelet Transform (DWT) can be achieved building a matrix, as explained in [2]:

$$W = \left(\frac{H}{G}\right), H = \begin{pmatrix} h_0 & h_1 & \cdots & h_{n-2} & h_{n-1} \\ h_{n-2} & h_{n-1} & \cdots & h_{n-4} & h_{n-3} \\ \vdots & \vdots & \ddots & \vdots & \vdots \\ h_2 & h_3 & \cdots & h_0 & h_1 \end{pmatrix}, G = \begin{pmatrix} g_0 & g_1 & \cdots & g_{n-2} & g_{n-1} \\ g_{n-2} & g_{n-1} & \cdots & g_{n-4} & g_{n-3} \\ \vdots & \vdots & \ddots & \vdots & \vdots \\ g_2 & g_3 & \cdots & g_0 & g_1 \end{pmatrix}$$

Note that H and G are submatrices of size $(\frac{n}{2}, n, m)$ and $WAW^T = \left(\begin{array}{c|c} LL & HL \\ \hline LH & HH \end{array}\right)$.

The original image A is transformed into 4 *subbands*: the LL subband is the low resolution residual which consists of low frequency components, which means that it is an approximation of our original image; and thee subbands HL, LH and HH give horizontal, vertical and diagonal details, respectively.

In this article, we propose to form the pooling layer by combining different wavelets: Haar, Daubechie and the Coiflet [1] one. Haar basis is formed by $h = (1/\sqrt{2}, 1/\sqrt{2})$ and $g = (1/\sqrt{2}, -1/\sqrt{2})$; the Daubechies basis is formed by $h = ((1 + \sqrt{3})/4\sqrt{2}, (3 + \sqrt{3})/4\sqrt{2}, (3 - \sqrt{3})/4\sqrt{2}, (1 - \sqrt{3})/4\sqrt{2})$ and $g = ((1 - \sqrt{3})/4\sqrt{2}, (-3+\sqrt{3})/4\sqrt{2}, (3+\sqrt{3})/4\sqrt{2}, (-1-\sqrt{3})/4\sqrt{2})$; and finally the Coiflet basis is formed by $h = (-0.0157, -0.0727, 0.3849, 0.8526, 0.3379, -0.0727)$ and $g = (-0.0727, -0.3379, 0.8526, -0.3849, -0.0727, -0.0157)$. From these, you can populate the wavelet matrix following the Lemma 3.3 and Theorem 3.8 in [2].

The algorithm for multiple wavelet pooling is as follows:

1. Choose two different wavelet bases and compute their associated matrices, W_1 and W_2.
2. Present the image feature F and perform, in parallel, the two associated discrete wavelet transforms $W_1 F W_1^T$ and $W_2 F W_2^T$.
3. Discard HL, LH, HH from every matrix, thus only tacking into account the approximated image LL_1 and LL_2 by the two different basis.
4. Concatenate both results and pass on to the next layer.

In Fig. 1, we can see an example of how this pooling method works within a CNN architecture.

3   Results and Conclusions

We used three different datasets for our testing: MNIST [6], CIFAR-10 [5] and SVHN [7]. In order to compare the convergence, we use the categorical entropy loss function; as a metric, we use the accuracy. For the MNIST dataset, we used a batch size of 600, we performed 20 epochs and we used a learning rate of 0.01. For the CIFAR-10 dataset, we performed two different experiments: one without dropout, with 45 epochs and one with dropout, with 75 epochs. For both cases, we used a dynamic learning rate. For the SVHN dataset, we performed a set of experiments with 45 epochs and a dynamic learning rate. All CNN structures are taken from [8] for the respective datasets. In this case, we test algorithms without dropout to observe the pooling method's resistance to overfit. Only in the case of CIFAR-10, we take into account both performances with and without dropout.

Table 1 shows the accuracies obtained for each pooling method together with their position on the ranking; additionally, we highlight in bold the best performance for each dataset. We will denote "d" the case when we perform the model training with dropout. For the MNIST data-set, the choice of the Daubechie basis improves the accuracy, compared to the Haar basis. For CIFAR-10 and SVHN, we can see that the multiple wavelet pooling performed evenly or better than max and average pooling. Specially, for the case with dropout, the multiple wavelet pooling algorithm outperformed all other pooling algorithms.

Table 1. Accuracy obtained for each pooling method together with the ranking position. We highlight with boldface the three best results for each dataset. The last column represents the mean rank of each pooling method across all datasets

	MNIST	CIFAR-10	CIFAR-10 (d)	SVHN	Rank
Max	**98.93% (1)**	73.35% (8)	70.50% (8)	88.51% (6)	5th
Average	**98.36% (3)**	**76.40% (1)**	78.49% (5)	88.27% (8)	3rd
Haar	98.15% (5)	74.79% (7)	77.89% (6)	89.23% (4)	4th
Daubechie	98.29% (4)	**76.12% (2)**	**78.45% (3)**	88.29% (7)	2nd
Coiflet	98.08% (7)	74.94% (6)	77.36% (7)	89.20% (5)	6th
Haar + Daubechie	**98.41% (2)**	75.39% (4)	**79.33% (1)**	**91.01% (1)**	1st
Haar + Coiflet	98.18% (6)	**75.43% (3)**	78.80% (4)	**90.61% (3)**	2nd
Daubechie + Coiflet	97.80% (8)	75.13% (5)	**79.19% (2)**	**90.88% (2)**	3rd

In Fig. 2 (left), we present an example of the convergence of every pooling method compared. In general lines, the multiple wavelet algorithm always converges faster or comparatively to max and average pooling. Simple wavelet pooling, for any of its variants, is always the second fastest convergence method.

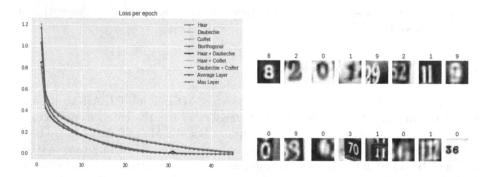

Fig. 2. SVHN loss function (left) and Multiple wavelet Haar + Daubechie results (right)

In Fig. 2 (right), we show an example of predictions for the SVHN dataset with Haar and Daubechie basis. The first row represents correct predictions, the second row represents wrong predictions. The network has trouble distinguishing images where more than one digit appears. Still, it is very consistent: the first, second, third and fifth images could be considered to be correct.

In conclusion, we proved that multiple wavelet pooling are capable of competing and outperforming the well-known max and average pooling: yielding better results and at the same time converging faster.

Acknowledgements. This work was partially funded by TIN2015-66951-C2-1-R, 2017 SGR 1742, Nestore, 20141510 (La MaratoTV3) and CERCA Programme/Generalitat de Catalunya. E. Aguilar acknowledges the support of CONICYT Becas Chile. P. Radeva is partially supported by ICREA Academia 2014. We acknowledge the support of NVIDIA Corporation with the donation of Titan Xp GPUs.

References

1. Daubechies, I.: Ten Lectures on Wavelets, vol. 61. Siam, Philadelphia (1992)
2. Frazier, M.W.: An Introduction to Wavelets Through Linear Algebra. Springer, Heidelberg (2006)
3. Fujieda, S., Takayama, K., Hachisuka, T.: Wavelet convolutional neural networks. arXiv preprint arXiv:1805.08620 (2018)
4. Huang, H., He, R., Sun, Z., Tan, T.: Wavelet-SRNet: a wavelet-based CNN for multi-scale face super resolution. In: CVPR, pp. 1689–1697 (2017)
5. Krizhevsky, A., Hinton, G.: Learning multiple layers of features from tiny images. Technical report, Citeseer (2009)
6. LeCun, Y.: The MNIST database of handwritten digits (1998). http://yann.lecun.com/exdb/mnist/
7. Netzer, Y., Wang, T., Coates, A., Bissacco, A., Wu, B., Ng, A.Y.: Reading digits in natural images with unsupervised feature learning. In: NIPS Workshop on Deep Learning and Unsupervised Feature Learning, vol. 2011, p. 5 (2011)
8. Williams, T., Li, R.: Wavelet pooling for convolutional neural networks. In: International Conference on Learning Representations (2018). https://openreview.net/forum?id=rkhlb8lCZ

Automated Facial Wrinkles Annotator

Moi Hoon Yap[1]([⊠])[ID], Jhan Alarifi[1], Choon-Ching Ng[2], Nazre Batool[3], and Kevin Walker[4]

[1] Manchester Metropolitan University, Manchester M1 5GD, UK
M.Yap@mmu.ac.uk
[2] Panasonic R&D Center Singapore, Singapore, Singapore
[3] Scania CV AB, Södertälje, Sweden
[4] Image Metrics Ltd., Manchester, UK

Abstract. This paper presents an automated facial wrinkles annotator for coarse wrinkles, fine wrinkles and wrinkle depth map extraction. First we extended Hybrid Hessian Filter by introducing a multi-scale filter to isolate the coarse wrinkles from fine wrinkles. Then we generate a wrinkle probabilistic map. When evaluated on 20 high resolution full face images (10 from our in-house dataset and 10 from FERET dataset), we achieved good accuracy when the result of coarse wrinkles was validated with manual annotation. Furthermore, we visually illustrate the ability of the annotator in detecting fine wrinkles. This paper advances the field by automate the localisation of the fine wrinkles, which might not be possible to annotate manually. Our automated facial wrinkles annotator will be beneficial to large-scale data annotation and cosmetic applications.

Keywords: Wrinkles annotator · Hessian filter · Wrinkles depth

1 Introduction

The appearance of wrinkle is affected by many factors. Even though wrinkles are highly associated with ageing, it is observed that some individuals have less wrinkles than others. Wrinkle growing pattern and its rates are still not well understood. Wrinkles detection has gained popularity recently and many automated computerised methods were proposed [3–5,8,9] to localise wrinkles. Although the research reported a good reliability of the wrinkle detection algorithms [3,6,8,9], there are still a few limitations of current work:

- The majority of previous research was only validated on forehead datasets.
- Due to the majority of the wrinkles orientation are horizontal [2], some algorithms [8,9] focused on the horizontal wrinkles only.
- The evaluation methods for wrinkle detection were based on wrinkle lines (line segment after thinning process), not wrinkle regions.
- The existing algorithms were not able to separate coarse wrinkles and fine wrinkles.

ⓒ Springer Nature Switzerland AG 2019
L. Leal-Taixé and S. Roth (Eds.): ECCV 2018 Workshops, LNCS 11132, pp. 676–680, 2019.
https://doi.org/10.1007/978-3-030-11018-5_56

- The existing algorithms were not able to provide clear definition of wrinkles depth.

To address the issues above and the limitations of human annotation, we propose an automated facial wrinkles annotator for full face high resolution images, represent wrinkle as region (not line) and we demonstrate that our annotator is able to separate fine wrinkles from coarse wrinkles. Our key contributions are:

- Automated annotation of coarse and fine wrinkles regions on high resolution face images.
- Generation of Probabilistic Wrinkle Map alongside with the wrinkles regions to provide wrinkle depth information.
- Demonstration of the robustness of our facial wrinkles annotator across two datasets.

2   Proposed Method

The focus of this work is to demonstrate the ability of our proposed wrinkles annotator in extracting coarse and fine wrinkles, including the width and depth information. Hence, only high resolution images are used to demonstrate the capability of proposed method, particularly in detecting fine wrinkles. To generate the ground truth from human annotation, we are not able to use large-scale dataset due to it is a time consuming and arduous process. Therefore, we have selected 20 full face images, 10 images from our in-house social habit dataset [1,10] and 10 images from FERET dataset [11]. Similar to the state-of-the-art research, we have generated ground truth based on manual annotation.

Given an input image I, the directional gradient $\left(\frac{\partial I}{\partial x}, \frac{\partial I}{\partial y}\right)$ of I is computed. $\frac{\partial I}{\partial y}$ (denoted as $\mathcal{I}$) emphasizes a horizontal variation, which was proposed by [7,8] to detect horizontal wrinkles. $\frac{\partial I}{\partial x}$ (denoted as $\mathcal{V}$) emphasizes a vertical variation, where we used it to detect vertical wrinkles regions. Both are used as the input for Hessian filter $\mathcal{H}$ calculation [7] at location (x, y) denoted by

$$\mathcal{H}_\sigma\left(x, y\right) = \begin{bmatrix} \mathcal{H}_{a,\sigma}\left(x, y\right) & \mathcal{H}_{b,\sigma}\left(x, y\right) \\ \mathcal{H}_{b,\sigma}\left(x, y\right) & \mathcal{H}_{c,\sigma}\left(x, y\right) \end{bmatrix} \tag{1}$$

where σ is the filter scale; $H_{a,\sigma}$, $H_{b,\sigma}$ and $H_{c,\sigma}$ are the second derivatives of $\mathcal{I}$ along horizontal, diagonal and vertical directions, respectively. In this work, we use the parameter σ as multi-scale filter to differentiate coarse and fine wrinkles.

For both the horizontal and vertical wrinkles detection, our proposed wrinkles annotator focuses on two filter scale (σ). One scale is for coarse wrinkles (σ_c) and one scale is for fine wrinkles (σ_f). The size of FERET dataset is 512×768 and the size of our in-house dataset is 1000×1300. From our empirical experiment, the best settings for FERET dataset: $\sigma_f = 2$ for fine wrinkles and $\sigma_c = 4$ for coarse wrinkles; and for our in-house high resolution dataset: $\sigma_f = 3$ for fine wrinkles and $\sigma_c = 6$ for coarse wrinkle. This is due to different resolution requires different filter scale for wrinkles extraction. When applying the filter σ_f,

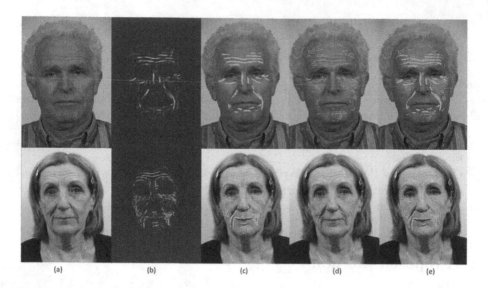

Fig. 1. Visual illustration of automated extraction of coarse wrinkles and fine wrinkles regions: (a) Original image, (b) Probabilistic wrinkles map, (c) Coarse wrinkles, (d) fine wrinkles, and (e) Combined wrinkles regions.

the location of coarse wrinkles were also detected. To separate the fine wrinkle from coarse wrinkles, we perform a post-processing stage. Let R_f be the regions detected as fine wrinkles and R_c be the regions detected as coarse wrinkles, the updated R'_f is defined as $R'_f = \{\forall x \in R_f \mid x \notin R_c\}$. We generated probabilistic wrinkle map as in Fig. 2. This map is generated alongside with the annotator to provide wrinkles depth information. The high value indicates deep wrinkle and vice versa.

3   Results and Discussion

Figure 1 illustrates the step by step results of our proposed method on coarse and fine wrinkles annotation. Figure 1(a) shows the input image from FERET dataset (first row) and in-house social habit dataset (second row). Figure 1(b) illustrates the probabilistic map (depth information) for the images. Figure 1(c) and (d) display the results of coarse wrinkles and fine wrinkles, respectively. Then, Fig. 1(e) illustrates the combined annotated wrinkles. When validate the coarse wrinkles detection results with ground truth label in terms of *Jaccard Similarity Index (JSI)*, the annotator achieved accuracy of 80%. When overlay the manual annotated wrinkles onto the probabilistic map, we observed the majority of the annotated lines overlay on high probability regions, as in Fig. 2(d), which we defined it as coarse wrinkles. This is due to the difficulties for human to annotate the detailed and fine wrinkles. Thus, this proposed automated annotator will be useful to annotate fine wrinkles.

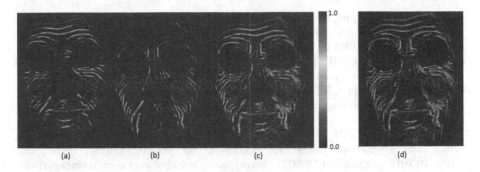

Fig. 2. Probabilistic map on: (a) Horizontal wrinkles; (b) Vertical wrinkles; (c) Probabilistic map by our proposed method; and (d) Manual annotation of Wrinkle lines (RED) overlay on our probabilistic map. (Color figure online)

4   Conclusion

We proposed a new fully automated wrinkles annotator for coarse wrinkle and fine wrinkle labeling. With the rapid growth of the use of deep learning in computer vision, automated annotator for data labeling play an important role for ground truth preparation. Since it is impossible to manually annotate the fine wrinkles, our proposed method will benefit data driven approaches. In addition, it can be used to assess the skin quality in terms of fine lines.

As in many areas of computer vision, we illustrated that images captured from different devices and settings are the main challenges in dataset acquisition. Whilst this method required adjustment on filter scale based on empirical experiment, future work with machine intelligence will be able to overcome the problem.

Acknowledgment. This work was supported by the Royal Society Industry Fellowship (IF160006). The authors would like to thanks Phillips et al. [11] for the FERET dataset.

References

1. Alarifi, J.S., Goyal, M., Davison, A.K., Dancey, D., Khan, R., Yap, M.H.: Facial skin classification using convolutional neural networks. In: Karray, F., Campilho, A., Cheriet, F. (eds.) ICIAR 2017. LNCS, vol. 10317, pp. 479–485. Springer, Cham (2017). https://doi.org/10.1007/978-3-319-59876-5_53
2. Albert, A., Ricanek, K., Patterson, E.: A review of the literature on the aging adult skull and face: implications for forensic science research and applications. Forensic Sci. Int. **172**(1), 1–9 (2007)
3. Batool, N., Chellappa, R.: A Markov point process model for wrinkles in human faces. In: 2012 19th IEEE International Conference on Image Processing, pp. 1809–1812. IEEE (2012)

4. Batool, N., Chellappa, R.: Detection and inpainting of facial wrinkles using texture orientation fields and Markov random field modeling. IEEE Trans. Image Process. **23**(9), 3773–3788 (2014)

5. Cula, G.O., Bargo, P.R., Nkengne, A., Kollias, N.: Assessing facial wrinkles: automatic detection and quantification. Skin Res. Technol. **19**(1), e243–e251 (2013)

6. Batool, N., Chellappa, R.: Fast detection of facial wrinkles based on Gabor features using image morphology and geometric constraints. Pattern Recogn. **48**(3), 642–658 (2015)

7. Ng, C.C., Yap, M.H., Cheng, Y.T., Hsu, G.S.: Hybrid ageing patterns for face age estimation. Image Vis. Comput. **69**, 92–102 (2018). https://doi.org/10.1016/j.imavis.2017.08.005, http://www.sciencedirect.com/science/article/pii/S026288561730121X

8. Ng, C.-C., Yap, M.H., Costen, N., Li, B.: Automatic wrinkle detection using hybrid Hessian filter. In: Cremers, D., Reid, I., Saito, H., Yang, M.-H. (eds.) ACCV 2014. LNCS, vol. 9005, pp. 609–622. Springer, Cham (2015). https://doi.org/10.1007/978-3-319-16811-1_40

9. Ng, C.C., Yap, M.H., Costen, N., Li, B.: Wrinkle detection using Hessian line tracking. IEEE Access **3**, 1079–1088 (2015)

10. Osman, O.F., Elbashir, R.M.I., Abbass, I.E., Kendrick, C., Goyal, M., Yap, M.H.: Automated assessment of facial wrinkling: a case study on the effect of smoking. In: 2017 IEEE International Conference on Systems, Man, and Cybernetics (SMC), pp. 1081–1086, October 2017. https://doi.org/10.1109/SMC.2017.8122755

11. Phillips, P., Moon, H., Rizvi, S., Rauss, P.: The FERET evaluation methodology for face-recognition algorithms. IEEE Trans. Pattern Anal. Mach. Intell. **22**(10), 1090–1104 (2000)

Deep Learning of Appearance Models for Online Object Tracking

Mengyao Zhai[1]($\boxtimes$), Lei Chen[1], Greg Mori[1], and Mehrsan Javan Roshtkhari[2]

[1] Simon Fraser University, Burnaby, Canada
mzhai@sfu.ca
[2] SPORTLOGiQ, Montreal, Canada

Abstract. This paper introduces a deep learning based approach for vision based single target tracking. We address this problem by proposing a network architecture which takes the input video frames and directly computes the tracking score for any candidate target location by estimating the probability distributions of the positive and negative examples. An online fine-tuning step is carried out at every frame to learn the appearance of the target. The tracker has been tested on the standard tracking benchmark and the results indicate that the proposed solution achieves state-of-the-art tracking results.

1 Introduction

Visual target tracking is a fundamental task in computer vision and vision based analysis. In general, single target tracking algorithms consider a bounding box around the object in the first frame and automatically track the trajectory of the object over the subsequent frames. Readers may refer to [13] and [12] for a review of the state-of-the-art in object tracking and a detailed analysis and comparison of representative methods.

In this paper, we propose a new deep learning based tracking architecture (Fig. 1 shows the overall architecture of the proposed tracking system) that can effectively track a target given a single observation. The main contribution of this paper is a unified deep network architecture for object tracking in which the probability distributions of the observations are learnt and the target is identified using a set of weak classifiers (Bayesian classifiers) which are considered as one of the hidden layers. In addition, we fine-tune the CNN tracking system to adaptively learn the appearance of the target in successive frames. Experimental results indicate the effectiveness of the proposed tracking system.

2 Proposed Approach

This section presents the algorithmic description and the network architecture for the proposed tracking system. The system consists of a two stage training process, an *offline fine-tuning* procedure and an *online target specific fine-tuning* step.

L. Leal-Taixé and S. Roth (Eds.): ECCV 2018 Workshops, LNCS 11132, pp. 681–686, 2019.
https://doi.org/10.1007/978-3-030-11018-5_57

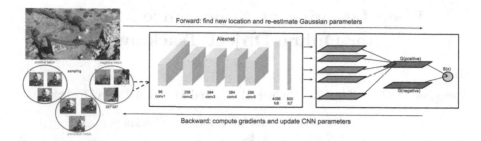

Fig. 1. Overview of our approach: given one frame, we sample three batches: positive batch, negative batch, and prediction batch. In the forward procedure, given CNN parameters, we use the positive batch and negative batch to re-estimate Gaussian parameters. Then we search in the prediction batch for the new location with maximum score. In the backward procedure, given Gaussian parameters, we compute gradients with respect to feature nodes and update CNN parameters.

Offline Fine-Tuning. The fine-tuning of the pre-trained network is carried out through two phases: *obj-general* as phase 1 and *obj-specific* as phase 2. The first step is carried out by taking a pre-trained CNN which is already trained for large-scale image classification tasks, and then is fine-tuned for the generic object detection task which is referred to as *objectness* [1]. In order to learn generic features for objects and be able to distinguish objects from the background, we sampled 100k auxiliary image patches from the ImageNet 2014 detection dataset[1]. For each annotated bounding box, we randomly generate negative examples from the images in such a way that they have low intersection of union with the annotated bounding box. During this phase, all CNN layers are fine-tuned. The fine-tuned CNN can now be considered as a generic feature descriptor of objects, but it still cannot be used for tracking because it cannot discriminate a specific target from other objects in the scene. In other words, this network is equally activated for any object in the scene.

Another phase of fine-tuning is conducted given the bounding box around the target in the first frame. In order to generate a sufficient number of samples to fine-tune the network, we randomly sample bounding boxes around the original one. Those bounding boxes have to have a very high overlap ratio with the original bounding box. For the negative bounding boxes we sampled bounding boxes whose centers are far from the original one. During this phase, only fully connected layers are fine-tuned.

Online Target Specific Fine-Tuning. When a new frame comes, our model would take the features from the network and compute scores for all candidate bounding boxes as described below. Given a single bounding box representing the target of interest in the current frame of a video sequence (which can be initialized by either running an object detector or using manual labeling), first

---

[1] http://image-net.org/challenges/LSVRC/2014/.

we use a sampling scheme to sample some positive patches around it and some negative patches whose centers are far from positive ones. Then, the probability density functions of the positive and negative examples are computed using (1). This process is repeated when a new frame comes.

Similar to [2,14], we assume that the distributions of the positive and negative examples' features can be represented by Gaussian distributions. Therefore, the posterior probability of the positive examples $P(\mathbf{x}|pos)$ is:

$$\mathcal{G}_{pos} = P(\mathbf{x}|pos)$$

$$= \prod_{i=1}^{N} \frac{1}{\sqrt{2\pi}\sigma_{pos_i}} e^{-\frac{(x_i - \mu_{pos_i})^2}{2\sigma_{pos_i}^2}} \tag{1}$$

where μ_{pos_i} and σ_{pos_i} are the mean and variance of the Gaussian distribution of the ith attribute of the positive feature vector, x_i, respectively. Similarly, we can get distribution $\mathcal{G}_{neg}$ for negative examples.

Then the tracking score $\mathcal{S}(\mathbf{x})$ given an observation $\mathbf{x}$ is computed as:

$$\mathcal{S}(\mathbf{x}_i) = log\left(\prod_{i=1}^{n} \frac{P(x_i|pos)}{P(x_i|neg)}\right) = \log(\mathcal{G}_{pos}(\mathbf{x}_i)) - \log(\mathcal{G}_{neg}(\mathbf{x}_i)) \tag{2}$$

The candidate bounding box which has the highest tracking score is then taken to be the new *true* location of the target:

$$\mathbf{x}^* = \arg \max_{\mathbf{x}_i \in \mathbf{X}} \mathcal{S}(\mathbf{x}_i) \tag{3}$$

Once the *true* target bounding box is determined in the following frame, the whole model shall be fine-tuned again in order to adapt itself to the new target appearance. We consider updating Gaussian parameters first, and then updating the network weights.

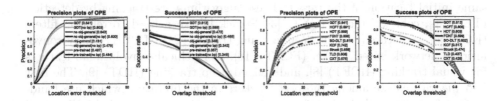

Fig. 2. Ablation study   **Fig. 3.** Comparision with state-of-the-arts

3 Experiments

In order to evaluate the performance of our deep learning based tracker, we have carried out extensive experiments using the CVPR13 "Visual Tracker Benchmark" dataset [12]. We follow the "Visual Tracker Benchmark" protocol introduced in [12] in order to compare the tracking accuracy to the state-of-the-art approaches.

In our experiments, Opencv[2] and Caffe[3] libraries are used for the CNN-based tracking system. The CNN is fine-tuned for $100k$ iterations for objectness and the maximum number of iterations for the specific target fine-tuning in the first frame is set to be equal to 500. During online tracking, the CNN is backpropagated 1 iteration per frame. The aspect ratio is fixed as the same as the initialization given in the first frame of each sequence. The learning rate for Gaussian parameters is set to 0.95. The current prototype of the proposed algorithm runs at approximately 1 fps on a PC with an Intel i7-4790 CPU and a Nvidia Titan X GPU.

Ablation Study. For ablation study, we have conducted multiple experiments with three pairs of baselines. The first pair of baseline, which we refer to it as the "pre-trained" is to take the pre-trained model [7] as the feature extractor (without fine-tuning for objectness and target appearance) and use the same tracker as GDT to track every target in each sequence. By "no bp" we mean that during tracking process only Gaussian parameters are updated and CNNs are not fine-tuned. The second pair of baselines, which we call them the "obj-general", is to take the CNN model we trained for objectness as the feature extractor. To show the importance of fine-tuning for objectness, we add third pair of baselines, which we refer to as the "no obj-general". For this baseline, we remove the objectness step and CNNs are fine-tuned directly from the pre-trained model. All results listed in this section adopt same tracker, the only difference is the CNN models that are used. We summarize comparisons with all baselines in Fig. 2. From Fig. 2, it is clear that each step of our algorithm boosts the tracking results.

Comparison with State-of-the-art. Our tracking results are quantitatively compared with the eight state state-of-the-art tracking algorithms with the same initial location of the target. These algorithms are tracking-by-detection (TLD) [6], context tracker (CXT) [3], Struck [4], kernelized correlation filters (KCF) [5], structured output deep learning tracker (SO-DLT) [11], fully convolutional network based tracker (FCNT) [10], hierarchical convolutional features for visual tracking (HCFT) [8], and hedged deep tracking (HDT) [9]. The first four algorithms are among the best trackers in the literature which use hand-crafted features, and the last four are among best approaches for CNN-based tracking. **GDT** represents our proposed approach.

Figure 3 shows the success and precision plots for the whole 50 videos in the dataset. Overall, the proposed tracking algorithm performs favorably against the other state-of-the-art algorithms on all tested sequences. It outperforms all of the state-of-the-art approaches given success plot and produces favourable results compared to other deep learning-based trackers given precision plot, specifically for low location error threshold values. We show some visualizations of detection results of all approaches in Fig. 4.

---

[2] http://opencv.org.
[3] http://caffe.berkeleyvision.org.

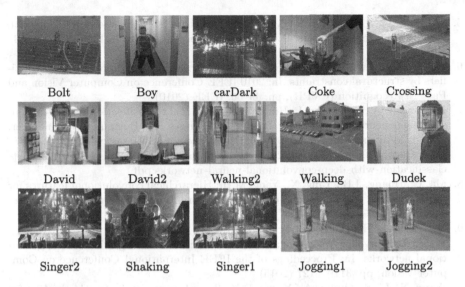

Bolt	Boy	carDark	Coke	Crossing
David	David2	Walking2	Walking	Dudek
Singer2	Shaking	Singer1	Jogging1	Jogging2

Fig. 4. Visualizations of all tracking algorithms on challenging sequences. Ground Truth: red, GDT(ours): yellow, FCNT: gray, HDT: dark green, HCFT: blue, SO-DLT: green, KCF: black, Struck: orange, TLD: magenta, CXT: cyan. (Color figure online)

4   Conclusion

We proposed a novel tracking algorithm in this paper. The CNN for tracking is trained in a simple but very effective way and the CNN provides good features for object tracking. First stage fine-tuning using auxiliary data largely alleviates the problem of a lack of labelled training instances. A second stage of fine-tuning, though used only with a few hundred instances and trained for tens of iterations, greatly boosts the performance of the tracker. On top of CNN features, a classifier is learnt. The experimental results show that our deep, appearance model learning tracker produces results comparable to state-of-the-art approaches and can generate accurate tracking results.

References

1. Alexe, B., Deselaers, T., Ferrari, V.: What is an object? In: 2010 IEEE Conference on Computer Vision and Pattern Recognition (CVPR), pp. 73–80. IEEE (2010)
2. Babenko, B., Yang, M.H., Belongie, S.: Robust object tracking with online multiple instance learning. IEEE Trans. Pattern Anal. Mach. Intell. **33**(8), 1619–1632 (2011)
3. Dinh, T.B., Vo, N., Medioni, G.: Context tracker: exploring supporters and distracters in unconstrained environments. In: 2011 IEEE Conference on Computer Vision and Pattern Recognition (CVPR), pp. 1177–1184. IEEE (2011)
4. Hare, S., Saffari, A., Torr, P.: Struck: structured output tracking with kernels. In: 2011 IEEE International Conference on Computer Vision (ICCV), pp. 263–270, November 2011. https://doi.org/10.1109/ICCV.2011.6126251

5. Henriques, J.F., Caseiro, R., Martins, P., Batista, J.: High-speed tracking with kernelized correlation filters. IEEE Trans. Pattern Anal. Mach. Intell. **37**(3), 583–596 (2015)
6. Kalal, Z., Matas, J., Mikolajczyk, K.: P-N learning: bootstrapping binary classifiers by structural constraints. In: 2010 IEEE Conference on Computer Vision and Pattern Recognition (CVPR), pp. 49–56. IEEE (2010)
7. Krizhevsky, A., Sutskever, I., Hinton, G.E.: Imagenet classification with deep convolutional neural networks. In: Pereira, F., Burges, C., Bottou, L., Weinberger, K. (eds.) Advances in Neural Information Processing Systems, vol. 25, pp. 1097–1105. Curran Associates, Inc. (2012). http://papers.nips.cc/paper/4824-imagenet-classification-with-deep-convolutional-neural-networks.pdf
8. Ma, C., Huang, J.B., Yang, X., Yang, M.H.: Hierarchical convolutional features for visual tracking. In: Proceedings of the IEEE International Conference on Computer Vision, pp. 3074–3082 (2015)
9. Qi, Y., et al.: Hedged deep tracking (2016)
10. Wang, L., Ouyang, W., Wang, X., Lu, H.: Visual tracking with fully convolutional networks. In: Proceedings of the IEEE International Conference on Computer Vision, pp. 3119–3127 (2015)
11. Wang, N., Li, S., Gupta, A., Yeung, D.Y.: Transferring rich feature hierarchies for robust visual tracking. arXiv preprint arXiv:1501.04587 (2015)
12. Wu, Y., Lim, J., Yang, M.H.: Online object tracking: a Benchmark. In: IEEE Conference on Computer Vision and Pattern Recognition (CVPR) (2013)
13. Yang, H., Shao, L., Zheng, F., Wang, L., Song, Z.: Recent advances and trends in visual tracking: a review. Neurocomputing **74**(18), 3823–3831 (2011)
14. Zhang, K., Zhang, L., Yang, M.H.: Real-time object tracking via online discriminative feature selection. IEEE Trans. Image Process. **22**(12), 4664–4677 (2013)

Towards Cycle-Consistent Models
for Text and Image Retrieval

Marcella Cornia[1]([✉]), Lorenzo Baraldi[1], Hamed R. Tavakoli[2],
and Rita Cucchiara[1]

[1] University of Modena and Reggio Emilia, Modena, Italy
{marcella.cornia,lorenzo.baraldi,rita.cucchiara}@unimore.it
[2] Aalto University, Espoo, Finland
hamed.r-tavakoli@aalto.fi

Abstract. Cross-modal retrieval has been recently becoming an hot-spot research, thanks to the development of deeply-learnable architectures. Such architectures generally learn a joint multi-modal embedding space in which text and images could be projected and compared. Here we investigate a different approach, and reformulate the problem of cross-modal retrieval as that of learning a translation between the textual and visual domain. In particular, we propose an end-to-end trainable model which can translate text into image features and vice versa, and regularizes this mapping with a cycle-consistency criterion. Preliminary experimental evaluations show promising results with respect to ordinary visual-semantic models.

Keywords: Cross-modal retrieval · Cycle consistency
Visual-semantic models

1 Introduction

Matching visual data and natural language is an important challenge for multimedia as it enables a large variety of different applications ranging from retrieval, visual question answering, image and video captioning [1,3,7,12,13]. One of the core challenges in this scenario is that of enabling a cross-modal retrieval, *i.e.* the retrieval of visual items given textual queries, and vice versa.

Current cross-modal retrieval methods often rely on the construction of a common multi-modal embedding space in which project data from the two modalities (*i.e.* images and text) [4,9,14]. The retrieval, in this case, is then carried out by measuring distances in the joint space, which should be low for matching text-image pairs and higher for non-matching pairs. While this approach leads to very good results, it is not the only possible solution.

Here, we foresee a different approach and address the problem of retrieving images and captions as a translation from the image domain to the textual domain and vice versa. In the first direction, an image i (usually, represented with a feature vector x) is converted to a textual representation $\tilde{s}$ of its content;

L. Leal-Taixé and S. Roth (Eds.): ECCV 2018 Workshops, LNCS 11132, pp. 687–691, 2019.
https://doi.org/10.1007/978-3-030-11018-5_58

in the latter direction, a sentence s is converted into an image feature $\tilde{x}$ which reflects its meaning.

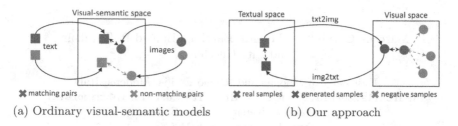

(a) Ordinary visual-semantic models   (b) Our approach

Fig. 1. Instead of relying on a joint embedding space, we address the problem of cross-modal retrieval as that of learning a translation between the textual and visual domain, with a reconstruction objective which keeps the overall process cycle-consistent

Figure 1 visually describes the idea: a learnable architecture translates textual data to a suitable representation in a visual domain, and visual features back to the textual domain. The overall architecture is trainable end-to-end: generated visual features are required to be realistic with respect to positive and negative image samples, and a cyclic constraint is imposed to guarantee that the forward and backward translation are feasible at the same time and consistent.

2   Cycle-Consistent Retrieval

We introduce a cycle-consistent text and image retrieval network which operates a translation between the textual and the visual domains. Under the model, input captions can be translated to proper image features, and image vectors can be translated back to the textual domain. Exploiting this translation capability, a reconstruction constraint makes sure that the reconstructed text is similar to the original one. The overall architecture is shown in Fig. 2.

From Text to Image (txt2img). The first part of the architecture consists of a visual-semantic model which can transform a sentence s in a meaningful vector in the image feature space, $\tilde{x}$. Words are represented with one-hot vectors that are embedded with a linear embedding, which can be either learned end-to-end together with the model, or pre-trained using another word embedding model, like Word2Vec [10], GloVe [11] or FastText [2]. Under the model, words are consumed by a GRU layer.

We train this model with a cost function which encourages the generated image vector to be close to the one of an image which has been described by the same caption. To this aim, we define a similarity function inside the image feature space (*e.g.* the cosine similarity), and apply a hinge-based triplet ranking loss commonly used in image-text retrieval [4, 9].

From Image to Text (img2txt). While sentences can be projected into an image feature space, the second component of the model translates image vectors

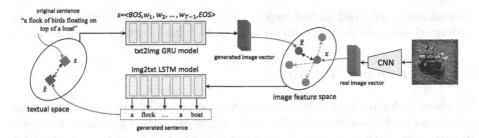

Fig. 2. Architecture of our model

x into the textual space by generating a textual description $\tilde{s}$. This roughly corresponds to an image captioning model in which the image is treated as the first input of an LSTM-based recurrent model.

At each iteration, the hidden state is linearly projected to the dimensionality of the vocabulary, and a softmax activation is then used to produce a probability distribution over the vocabulary. For each input image vector, the model generates the corresponding textual representation $\tilde{s}$ composed by the words produced at each time-step of the LSTM.

Closing the Loop. The `txt2img` and `img2txt` models defined above realize the forward and backward translations between the image and the textual domain. Due to the diversity and high dimension of raw images, directly translating to and from the image domain would be intractable, therefore both models operate in the space of image feature vectors extracted from a CNN.

The mapping between the two spaces is regularized with a cycle-consistency criterion, in which we require the feasibility of the forward and backward translation at the same time. In practice, we require that the projection of a generated image vector into the textual space should be similar to the text from which the vector originated, *i.e.*

$$\texttt{img2txt}(\texttt{txt2img}(s)) \approx s. \tag{1}$$

The similarity constraint imposed by Eq. 1 could be realized by taking into account the semantics of both sentences, either by evaluating a machine translation metric or by defining a network in charge of learning the similarity between two sentences. To keep the model simple and concentrate on the evaluation of the regularization power of the proposal, we realize Eq. 1 by computing the negative log-likelihood of generated words with respect to the words in s.

Implementation Details. To encode input images, we extract feature vectors from the average pooling layer of a ResNet-152 [5], thus obtaining an image dimensionality of 2048. For encoding image captions, since we do not project images and corresponding captions in a joint embedding space, we set the output size of the GRU to the same size of image embeddings (*i.e.* 2048). The dimensionality of word embeddings is set to 300. All experiments have been performed using the Adam optimizer [8] with an initial learning rate of 2×10^{-4}.

3   Experimental Results

We show preliminary evaluation results for the proposed approach, employing rank-based performance metrics $R@K$ ($K = 1, 5, 10$) for text and image retrieval. In particular, $R@K$ computes the percentage of test images or test sentences for which at least one correct result is found among the top-K retrieved sentences, in the case of text retrieval, or the top-K retrieved images, in the case of image retrieval.

As a baseline, we consider the txt2img model, which removes the cycle-consistency regularizer and is therefore well suited to evaluate the claims of the proposal regarding the role of the cycle-consistent constraint. This, also, is practically equivalent to a visual-semantic embedding model in which the visual projector is the identity function.

Table 1. Experimental results of our model on the Flickr8K and Flickr30k dataset using different word embeddings

Model	Word Emb.	Flickr8K						Flickr30K					
		Text retrieval			Image retrieval			Text retrieval			Image retrieval		
		R@1	R@5	R@10	R@1	R@5	R@10	R@1	R@5	R@10	R@1	R@5	R@10
txt2img	-	25.7	54.8	69.0	15.8	41.6	56.0	36.9	67.0	78.2	22.8	50.0	63.3
Ours	-	**28.2**	**57.4**	**71.1**	**17.5**	**44.6**	**59.0**	**41.7**	**68.9**	**78.9**	**23.8**	**51.3**	**64.0**
txt2img	GloVe	29.2	60.2	74.5	19.2	46.7	61.7	36.4	67.4	78.4	22.8	50.7	64.2
Ours	GloVe	**32.2**	**62.7**	**76.2**	**19.9**	**48.8**	**62.8**	**41.1**	**68.9**	**79.0**	**23.0**	**51.3**	**64.6**
txt2img	FastText	29.8	58.7	73.4	17.9	45.8	60.3	37.7	66.0	77.8	22.1	49.8	63.4
Ours	FastText	**32.2**	**61.4**	**74.1**	**19.2**	**47.5**	**62.0**	**40.8**	**68.5**	**79.1**	**23.5**	**51.3**	**63.8**
txt2img	Word2Vec	28.1	58.0	71.3	17.1	44.1	58.7	35.9	66.4	76.9	**22.3**	49.7	62.9
Ours	Word2Vec	**30.9**	**59.4**	**72.7**	**18.9**	**46.8**	**61.2**	**41.2**	**68.2**	**79.3**	22.3	**50.7**	**63.7**

Table 1 reports the results of our model on the Flickr8K [6] and Flickr30K [15] datasets using different word embedding strategies, together with that of the txt2img model alone. It can been observed that the performance of the complete model is always superior to that of the baseline, thus confirming the importance of translating backwards to the textual space and demonstrating the effectiveness of our promising solution.

Acknowledgments. We gratefully acknowledge the support of Facebook AI Research and NVIDIA Corporation with the donation of the GPUs used for this research.

References

1. Baraldi, L., Cornia, M., Grana, C., Cucchiara, R.: Aligning text and document illustrations: towards visually explainable digital humanities. In: International Conference on Pattern Recognition (2018)
2. Bojanowski, P., Grave, E., Joulin, A., Mikolov, T.: Enriching word vectors with subword information. arXiv preprint arXiv:1607.04606 (2016)
3. Cornia, M., Baraldi, L., Serra, G., Cucchiara, R.: Paying more attention to saliency: image captioning with saliency and context attention. ACM Trans. Multimedia Comput. Commun. Appl. **14**(2), 48:1–48:21 (2018)
4. Faghri, F., Fleet, D.J., Kiros, J.R., Fidler, S.: VSE++: improving visual-semantic embeddings with hard negatives. In: British Machine Vision Conference (2018)
5. He, K., Zhang, X., Ren, S., Sun, J.: Deep residual learning for image recognition. In: IEEE International Conference on Computer Vision and Pattern Recognition (2016)
6. Hodosh, M., Young, P., Hockenmaier, J.: Framing image description as a ranking task: data, models and evaluation metrics. J. Artif. Intell. Res. **47**, 853–899 (2013)
7. Karpathy, A., Fei-Fei, L.: Deep visual-semantic alignments for generating image descriptions. In: IEEE International Conference on Computer Vision and Pattern Recognition (2015)
8. Kingma, D., Ba, J.: Adam: a method for stochastic optimization. arXiv preprint arXiv:1412.6980 (2014)
9. Kiros, R., Salakhutdinov, R., Zemel, R.S.: Unifying visual-semantic embeddings with multimodal neural language models. arXiv preprint arXiv:1411.2539 (2014)
10. Mikolov, T., Sutskever, I., Chen, K., Corrado, G.S., Dean, J.: Distributed representations of words and phrases and their compositionality. In: Advances in Neural Information Processing Systems (2013)
11. Pennington, J., Socher, R., Manning, C.D.: GloVe: global vectors for word representation. In: Conference on Empirical Methods in Natural Language Processing (2014)
12. Shetty, R., Tavakoli, H.R., Laaksonen, J.: Image and video captioning with augmented neural architectures. IEEE MultiMedia **25**, 34–46 (2018)
13. Tavakoli, H.R., Shetty, R., Borji, A., Laaksonen, J.: Paying attention to descriptions generated by image captioning models. In: IEEE International Conference on Computer Vision (2017)
14. Wang, L., Li, Y., Lazebnik, S.: Learning two-branch neural networks for image-text matching tasks. IEEE Trans. Pattern Anal. Mach. Intell. (2018)
15. Young, P., Lai, A., Hodosh, M., Hockenmaier, J.: From image descriptions to visual denotations: new similarity metrics for semantic inference over event descriptions. Trans. Assoc. Comput. Linguist. **2**, 67–78 (2014)

From Attribute-Labels to Faces: Face Generation Using a Conditional Generative Adversarial Network

Yaohui Wang[1,2]([⊠]), Antitza Dantcheva[1,2], and Francois Bremond[1,2]

[1] Inria, Sophia Antipolis, Valbonne, France
{yaohui.wang,antitza.dantcheva,francois.bremond}@inria.fr
[2] Université Côte d'Azur, Nice, France

Abstract. Facial attributes are instrumental in semantically character-izing faces. Automated classification of such attributes (i.e., age, gen-der, ethnicity) has been a well studied topic. We here seek to explore the inverse problem, namely given attribute-labels the *generation of attribute-associated faces*. The interest in this topic is fueled by related applications in law enforcement and entertainment. In this work, we propose two models for attribute-label based facial image and video gen-eration incorporating 2D and 3D deep conditional generative adversarial networks (DCGAN). The attribute-labels serve as a tool to determine the specific representations of generated images and videos. While these are early results, our findings indicate the methods' ability to generate realistic faces from attribute labels.

Keywords: Attributes · Generative adversarial network
Face generation

1 Introduction

While attribute extraction and classification [3–5] is a well studied topic, the inverse problem, namely face generation, given attribute-labels is a novel area of high interest, due to related applications in law enforcement and entertain-ment. One specific application relates to the generation of realistic faces in cases of witness description, where the descriptions are the only available evidence (*e.g.*, in the absence of facial images). Particularly, law enforcement utilizes facial hand-drawn sketches or composites, which seek to support the process of suspect-identification. Such methods for face synthesis are slow, tedious, rel-atively unrealistic, as well as impeding efficient face recognition (*i.e.*, match-ing sketches or composites with existing mugshot databases maintained by law enforcement agencies poses a heterogeneous face recognition problem, which is highly challenging). Thus, reliable and automated label-based face generation constitutes beneficial in this context.

© Springer Nature Switzerland AG 2019
L. Leal-Taixé and S. Roth (Eds.): ECCV 2018 Workshops, LNCS 11132, pp. 692–698, 2019.
https://doi.org/10.1007/978-3-030-11018-5_59

In spite of the aforementioned applications of interest, limited research concerns attribute-based face generation.

Motivated by the above, in this work we propose to generate faces based on attribute-labels. This incorporates two steps: (i) the learning of a text feature representation that captures the important visual details, as well as (ii) given the features, the generation of compelling realistic images. We propose two approaches based on deep conditional convolutional generative adversarial network (DCGAN) [11], which was introduced to *modify* images based on attributes (image-to-image translation). We train the proposed 2D GAN with the dataset CelebA and generate faces pertained to the attribute-set *glasses*, *gender*, *hair color*, *smile* and *age*. We selected these set of attributes for the associated high descriptiveness, *e.g.*, such attributes are commonly used by humans to describe their peers. For the experiment we generate facial images, which we evaluate by 2 common GAN-quality-scores, as well as by well established face detectors and an attribute classifier. More analysis of the 2D model is presented in Wang et al. [13]. In addition we propose a 3D GAN model, trained with the UvA-NEMO[1], generating facial smiling videos pertained to the attributes *gender* and *age*. Results indicate the method's ability to generate realistic faces from attribute labels.

2   Proposed Methods

2D Model. The proposed conditional GAN aims to fit the conditional probability $P(x|z, y)$, as depicted in Fig. 1. We let z be the noise vector sampled from $\mathcal{N}(0, 1)$ with dimension $N = 100$, y be the vector representing attribute-labels (with $y_i \in \pm 1$, where i corresponds to the i_{th} attribute). We train a GAN, adding attribute-labels in both, generator and discriminator. While the generator accepts as input the combination of prior noise $p(z)$ and attributes vector y, the discriminator accepts both, real or generated images, as well as the attribute-labels. We have the objective function of our model be (Tables 1 and 2):

$$\min_G \max_D V(D, G) = \mathbb{E}_{x,y \sim p_{data}}[\log D(x, y)] + \mathbb{E}_{z \sim p_z, y \sim p_y}[\log(1 - D(G(z, y), y))].$$
(1)

Table 1. Architecture of 2D generator

Operation	Kernel	Stride	Filters	Norm	Activation
Concatenation	Concatenate z and y on 1st dimension				
ConvTranspose	4 × 4	2 × 2	512	BN	ReLU
ConvTranspose	4 × 4	2 × 2	256	BN	ReLU
ConvTranspose	4 × 4	2 × 2	128	BN	ReLU
ConvTranspose	4 × 4	2 × 2	64	BN	ReLU
ConvTranspose	4 × 4	2 × 2	3	No	Tahn

Table 2. Architecture of 2D discriminator

Operation	Kernel	Stride	Filters	Norm	Activation
Conv	4 × 4	2 × 2	64	No	LeakyReLU
Concatenation	Replicate y and concatenate to 1st conv. layer				
Conv	4 × 4	2 × 2	128	SN	LeakyReLU
Conv	4 × 4	2 × 2	256	SN	LeakyReLU
Conv	4 × 4	2 × 2	512	SN	LeakyReLU
Conv	4 × 4	1 × 1	1	No	Sigmoid

---

[1] http://www.uva-nemo.org/.

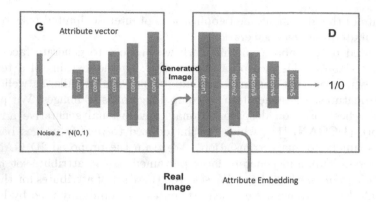

Fig. 1. Architecture of proposed 2D method consisting of two modules, a discriminator D and a generator G. While D learns to distinguish between real and fake images, classifying based on attribute-labels, G accepts as input both, noise and attribute-labels in order to generate realistic face images.

3D Model. We expand the above presented 2D model onto 3D, in order to create a conditional 3DGAN (Fig. 2), generating videos. In both, generator and discriminator, the convolutional kernels have been expanded onto three dimensions (H, W, T), where H, W and T represent the height, the width and the temporal step of the receptive fields in each kernel.

We feed the attribute vectors into 3D model in a similar manner as the 2D model. Specifically, in the generator we concatenate the attribute vector with the noise vector. In the discriminator, the feature map after the first layer has the dimension of (H, W, C, T), each $(H, W, C, t), t \in T$ containing spatial-temporal features of a certain time period. Our goal is to generate face videos based on attributes, so we proceed to provide each spatial-temporal feature map with the same attribute embedding. Based on this, we insert an attribute embedding onto the spatial-temporal feature map from the first layer of the discriminator, creating a new feature map with the dimension $(H, W, C + y, T)$, where y is the dimension of the attribute vector (Tables 3 and 4).

Table 3. Architecture of 3D generator

Operation	Kernel	Stride	Filters	Norm	Activation
Concatenation	Concatenate z and y on 1st dimension				
Conv Transpose3D	$2 \times 4 \times 4$	$2 \times 4 \times 4$	512	BN	ReLU
Conv Transpose3D	$4 \times 4 \times 4$	$2 \times 2 \times 2$	256	BN	ReLU
Conv Transpose3D	$4 \times 4 \times 4$	$2 \times 2 \times 2$	128	BN	ReLU
Conv Transpose3D	$4 \times 4 \times 4$	$2 \times 2 \times 2$	64	BN	ReLU
Conv Transpose3D	$4 \times 4 \times 4$	$2 \times 2 \times 2$	3	No	Tahn

Table 4. Architecture of 3D discriminator

Operation	Kernel	Stride	Filters	Norm	Activation
Conv3D	$4 \times 4 \times 4$	$2 \times 2 \times 2$	64	No	LeakyReLU
Concatenation	Replicate y and concatenate to 1st conv. layer				
Conv3D	$4 \times 4 \times 4$	$2 \times 2 \times 2$	128	SN	LeakyReLU
Conv3D	$4 \times 4 \times 4$	$2 \times 2 \times 2$	256	SN	LeakyReLU
Conv3D	$4 \times 4 \times 4$	$2 \times 2 \times 2$	512	SN	LeakyReLU
Conv3D	$2 \times 4 \times 4$	$1 \times 1 \times 1$	1	No	Sigmoid

3   Experiments

2D Model. We train our network with the benchmark dataset CelebA [10] comprising of 202, 599 face images annotated with 40 *binary* attribute labels. We generate images given five attributes glasses, gender, hair color, smile and age), in total 2048 images.

Figure 3 illustrates generated samples of the proposed approach. We observe that the model succeeds specifically in generation of local-attribute-labels based faces (*e.g.*, glasses, smile). The generated glasses appear to be similar, which is a limitation associated to DCGAN and the related loss function we use.

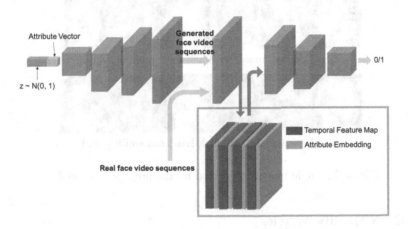

Fig. 2. Architecture of proposed 3D model for face video generation

3D Model. To train our 3DGAN model, we use the UvA-NEMO dataset [7]. It contains 1240 smile videos (597 spontaneous and 643 posed) from 400 subjects. Each subject has two attributes, gender and age. We label the subjects into two categories, adolescent (under 25 years old) and adults (above 25 years old). The generated smile video samples are portrayed in Fig. 4.

4   Evaluation

To evaluate how realistic our generated images are, in this section, we report the results based on the pre-trained face and attribute classification models. Then we proceed to present evaluation results of two quality metrics, namely Inception Score (IS) [12] and Fréchet Inception Distance (FID) [9], which have been widely used in image quality evaluation for GANs.

We obtain face detection results of up to 96% by DFace [6]) and gender true classification rate of up to 81.8% by the attribute classifier Face++ [8]. For age, note a shift in estimated age for the old/young labels, but the shift is not profound

(a) no glasses, female, black hair, smiling, young

(b) glasses, female, black hair, not smiling, old

(c) no glasses, male, no black hair, smiling, young

(d) glasses, male, no black hair, not smiling, old

Fig. 3. Example images generated by the proposed 2D model.

4.1 GAN Quality Metrics

We proceed to compute two commonly used GAN - quality measures, namely the Inception Score and the Fréchet Inception Distance, that we firstly proceed to describe. *Inception Score (IS)* is a metric for automated quality evaluation of images originated from generative models. The score is computed by an Inception V3 Network pre-trained on ImageNet and calculates a statistic of the network's outputs, when applied to generated images. *Fréchet Inception Distance (FID)* is an improvement of Inception Score. *IS* has the limitation of not utilizing statistics of real world samples are not used, and compared to the statistics of synthetic samples. Overcoming that, the Frćhet distance measures the distance between a generated image set and a source dataset.

We obtain $IS = 2.2$ and $FID = 43.8$. For IS, higher values indicate a higher quality, while for FID the opposite is the case. As a comparison Wasserstein GAN (WGAN) [1] reportedly achieves an $IS = 8.42$ and $FID = 55.2$; the Boundary Equilibrium Generative Adversarial Network BEGAN [2] obtains an $IS = 5.62$ and $FID = 71.4$.

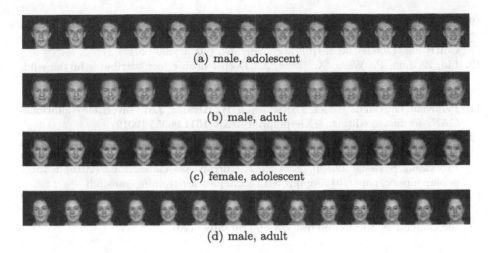

(a) male, adolescent

(b) male, adult

(c) female, adolescent

(d) male, adult

Fig. 4. Chosen output samples from 3DGAN

5   Conclusions

In this work we presented 2D and 3D models for attribute based facial images and video generation, both based on DCGAN. Results, evaluated by a face detector, an attribute estimator and benchmark quality scores, suggest the models' ability to generate realistic faces from attribute labels. The presented approaches can be instrumental in the visualization of witness descriptions. Future work will involve experiments related to matching of generated faces with existing faces.

References

1. Arjovsky, M., Chintala, S., Bottou, L.: Wasserstein gan. arXiv preprint arXiv:1701.07875 (2017)
2. Berthelot, D., Schumm, T., Metz, L.: BEGAN: boundary equilibrium generative adversarial networks. arXiv preprint arXiv:1703.10717 (2017)
3. Chen, C., Dantcheva, A., Ross, A.: Impact of facial cosmetics on automatic gender and age estimation algorithms. In: 2014 International Conference on Computer Vision Theory and Applications (VISAPP) (2014)
4. Dantcheva, A., Elia, P., Ross, A.: What else does your biometric data reveal? a survey on soft biometrics. IEEE Trans. Inf. Forensics Secur., pp. 1–26 (2015)
5. Dantcheva, A., Velardo, C., D'Angelo, A., Dugelay, J.L.: Bag of soft biometrics for person identification. Multimed. tools Appl. **51**(2), 739–777 (2011)
6. DFace: Deeplearning face. (2018) https://github.com/kuaikuaikim/DFace
7. Dibeklioğlu, H., Salah, A.A., Gevers, T.: Are you really smiling at me? Spontaneous versus posed enjoyment smiles. In: Fitzgibbon, A., Lazebnik, S., Perona, P., Sato, Y., Schmid, C. (eds.) ECCV 2012. LNCS, vol. 7574, pp. 525–538. Springer, Heidelberg (2012). https://doi.org/10.1007/978-3-642-33712-3_38
8. Face++: Face++ API. (2018) https://www.faceplusplus.com.cn/

9. Heusel, M., Ramsauer, H., Unterthiner, T., Nessler, B., Klambauer, G., Hochreiter, S.: Gans trained by a two time-scale update rule converge to a nash equilibrium. CoRR abs/1706.08500, http://arxiv.org/abs/1706.08500 (2017)
10. Liu, Z., Luo, P., Wang, X., Tang, X.: Deep learning face attributes in the wild. In: Proceedings of the IEEE International Conference on Computer Vision, pp. 3730–3738 (2015)
11. Perarnau, G., van de Weijer, J., Raducanu, B., Álvarez, J.M.: Invertible conditional GANs for image editing. arXiv preprint arXiv:1611.06355 (2016)
12. Salimans, T., et al.: Improved techniques for training gans. In: Lee, D.D., Sugiyama, M., Luxburg, U.V., Guyon, I., Garnett, R. (eds.) Advances in Neural Information Processing Systems 29, pp. 2234–2242. Curran Associates, Inc., (2016) http://papers.nips.cc/paper/6125-improved-techniques-for-training-gans.pdf
13. Wang, Y., Dantcheva, A., Bremond, F.: From attributes to faces: a conditional generative adversarial network for face generation. In: International Conference of the Biometrics Special Interest Group (BIOSIG) (2017)

Optimizing Body Region Classification with Deep Convolutional Activation Features

Obioma Pelka[1,2(✉)] [ID], Felix Nensa[3] [ID], and Christoph M. Friedrich[1,4] [ID]

[1] Department of Computer Science, University of Applied Sciences
and Arts Dortmund (FHDO), Dortmund, NRW, Germany
{obioma.pelka,christoph.friedrich}@fh-dortmund.de
[2] Faculty of Medicine, University of Duisburg-Essen, Essen, NRW, Germany
[3] Department of Diagnostic and Interventional Radiology and Neuroradiology,
University Hospital Essen, Essen, NRW, Germany
felix.nensa@uk-essen.de
[4] Institute for Medical Informatics, Biometry and Epidemiology (IMIBE),
University Hospital Essen, Essen, NRW, Germany

Abstract. The goal of this work is to automatically apply generated image keywords as text representations, to optimize medical image classification accuracies of body regions. To create a keyword generative model, a Long Short-Term Memory (LSTM) based Recurrent Neural Network (RNN) is adopted, which is trained with preprocessed biomedical image captions as text representation and visual features extracted using Convolutional Neural Networks (CNN). For image representation, deep convolutional activation features and Bag-of-Keypoints (BoK) features are extracted for each radiograph and combined with the automatically generated keywords. Random Forest models and Support Vector Machines are trained with these multimodal image representations, as well as just visual representation, to predict body regions. Adopting multimodal image features proves to be the better approach, as the prediction accuracy for body regions is increased.

Keywords: Bag-of-Keypoints · DeCaf · Deep learning
Multimodal representation · Natural language processing · Radiographs

1 Introduction

To build classification systems capable of reliable performance, adequate image representation is necessary. Adopting multimodal image features presented in [10,12,13], proves to achieve higher classification accuracies for biomedical images, as this contributes towards sufficient image representation. However, some classification tasks such as ImageCLEF 2015 Medical Clustering Task [8], as well as real clinical cases, lack corresponding text representations.

Hence, this paper utilizes automatic generated keywords proposed in [14] to substitute as text representation for the classification of radiographs into body

© Springer Nature Switzerland AG 2019
L. Leal-Taixé and S. Roth (Eds.): ECCV 2018 Workshops, LNCS 11132, pp. 699–704, 2019.
https://doi.org/10.1007/978-3-030-11018-5_60

regions, focusing on a different feature extraction method. The obtained keywords are combined with visual features for multi modal image representation.
The generated text information can also be further applied for semantic tagging
and image retrieval purposes.

We show that by adopting a multi-modal image representation and classification method described in Subsects. 2.2 and 2.3, the overall prediction accuracy is
increased as shown in Sect. 3, by evaluating the model performance on a dataset
presented in Subsect. 2.1.

2   Materials and Methods

2.1   Dataset

The Medical Clustering Task was held at ImageCLEF 2015, an evaluation cam-
paign organized by the CLEF Initiative[1]. For this task, 750 high resolution x-ray
images collected from a hospital in Dhaka, Bangladesh [1] were distributed. The
training set included 500 images and test set 250 images, with annotations of the
following classes: 'Body', 'Head-Neck', 'Upper-Limb', 'Lower-Limb' and 'True-
Negative'. An excerpt of the x-rays is displayed in Fig. 1.

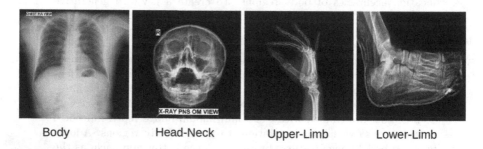

| Body | Head-Neck | Upper-Limb | Lower-Limb |

Fig. 1. An excerpt of images from the CVC digital x-ray dataset, Medical Clustering
task, ImageCLEF 2015. Original data is available from www.cvcrbd.org.

For the creation of the keyword generative model, the dataset distributed
for the ImageCLEF Caption Prediction Task [7] was applied and is presented
in [14].

2.2   Image Representation

For visual representation, two methods are applied for comparison purposes:
Deep convolutional activation features (DeCaf) [6] and Bag-of-Keypoints [5]
computed with dense SIFT descriptors [11]. The deep visual features are the

---

[1] http://www.clef-initiative.eu/.

average pool layer of the deep learning system Inception_V3 [18], which is pre-trained on ImageNet [15]. The activation features were extracted using the neural network API Keras 2.2.0 [4]. The Bag-of Keypoints visual features were created using the *VLFEAT* library [19].

To obtain multi-modal image representation, text information was created. The keyword generative model proposed in [14] was used to automatically create keywords for all 750 images, belonging to training and test sets. Furthermore, a compact text representation was achieved by applying vector quantization on a Bag-of-Words [17] codebook and Term Frequency-Inverse Document Frequency (Tf-IDF) [16].

2.3   Classification Models

Random forest (RF) [2] models with 1,000 trees were created as image classifi-cation models. These RF-models were trained using either visual or multi-modal image representations. Principal Component Analysis (PCA) [9] was applied to reduce computational time, feature dimension and noise. The vector size for visual features was reduced from 2,048 to 50, and from 150 to 50 for the text features. For comparison, multi-class Support Vector Machines (SVM) [3] using the same multi-modal image representations as the RF models, were modeled with the following parameters: kernel = radial basis function, cost parameter = 10 and gamma = 1/num_of_features.

3   Results

The achieved prediction accuracies using either visual or multi-modal image rep-resentation are listed in Table 1. For comparison purposes, the different classifier setups used for training are shown in the first column.

Table 1. Prediction accuracies obtained using the different visual and text repre-sentations, as well as classifier setup. Evaluation was done on ImageCLEF Medical Clustering test set with 250 x-rays.

Classifier setup	Accuracy	Image representation
Random Forest + BoK	65.60%	Visual
Support Vector Machines + BoK	66.40%	Visual
Random Forest + DeCaf	74.00%	Visual
Support Vector Machines + DeCaf	72.89%	Visual
Random Forest + BoK + BoW (TF-IDF)	71.09%	Visual + Text
Support Vector Machines + BoK + BoW (TF-IDF)	69.13%	Visual + Text
Random Forest + DeCaf + BoW (TF-IDF)	**77.20%**	Visual + Text
Support Vector Machines + DeCaf + BoW (TF-IDF)	76.35%	Visual + Text
Best group ImageCLEF 2015 Med Clustering Task [1]	75.20%	Visual

Figure 2 displays a word cloud created with the automatically generated key-words from the ImageCLEF Medical Clustering Training Set.

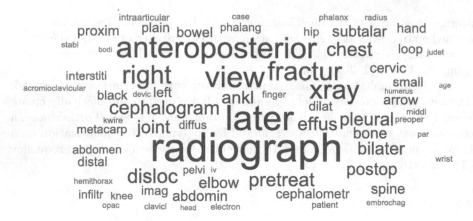

Fig. 2. Word cloud of automatically generated keywords for images in the ImageCLEF 2015 Medical Clustering Training Set.

4   Discussion

Adopting multi-modal representations for classification task proves to obtain higher prediction accuracies, as listed in Table 1. This is the case for both Random Forest and Support Vector Machines classification models. The prediction rate is optimized by applying DeCaf as visual representation, in comparison to the traditional Bag-of-Keypoints features. It can be seen from Fig. 2, that the generated keywords contribute to a more adequate representation, as information on body regions achieved.

5   Conclusions

An approach for optimizing prediction accuracies using deep convolutional activation features combined with automatically generated keywords was presented. Following the results shown in Table 1, using multimodal image representations achieves higher classification accuracies than just visual features. This is observed for the different classification models and visual feature extraction method. As the prediction models trained with deep convolutional activation features outperform those trained with traditional Bag-of-Keypoints, continuous work can be based on evaluating several image enhancement techniques.

Acknowledgements. The work of Obioma Pelka was partially funded by a PhD grant from the University of Applied Sciences and Arts Dortmund (FHDO), Germany.

References

1. Amin, M.A., Mohammed, M.K.: Overview of the ImageCLEF 2015 medical clustering task. In: Working Notes of CLEF 2015 - Conference and Labs of the Evaluation forum, Toulouse, France, 8–11 September 2015. (2015). http://ceur-ws.org/Vol-1391/inv-pap1-CR.pdf
2. Breiman, L.: Random forests. Mach. Learn. **45**(1), 5–32 (2001). https://doi.org/10.1023/A:1010933404324
3. Burges, C.J.C.: A tutorial on support vector machines for pattern recognition. Data Min. Knowl. Discovery **2**(2), 121–167 (1998). https://doi.org/10.1023/A:1009715923555
4. Chollet, F., et al.: Keras (2015). https://keras.io
5. Csurka, G., Dance, C.R., Fan, L., Willamowski, J., Bray, C.: Visual categorization with bags of keypoints. In: Workshop on Statistical Learning in Computer Vision, European Conference on Computer Vision ECCV, Prague, Czech Republic, 11–14 May 2004, pp. 1–22 (2004)
6. Donahue, J., et al.: DeCAF: a deep convolutional activation feature for generic visual recognition. In: Proceedings of the 31th International Conference on Machine Learning, ICML 2014, Beijing, China, 21–26 June 2014, pp. 647–655 (2014). http://jmlr.org/proceedings/papers/v32/donahue14.html
7. Eickhoff, C., Schwall, I., de Herrera, A.G.S., Müller, H.: Overview of ImageCLEFcaption 2017 - image caption prediction and concept detection for biomedical images. In: Working Notes of CLEF 2017 - Conference and Labs of the Evaluation Forum, Dublin, Ireland, 11–14 September 2017
8. de Herrera, A.G.S., Schaer, R., Bromuri, S., Müller, H.: Overview of the ImageCLEF 2016 medical task. In: Working Notes of CLEF 2016 - Conference and Labs of the Evaluation forum, Évora, Portugal, 5–8 September, 2016. CEUR-WS Proceedings Notes, vol. 1609, pp. 219–232 (2016). http://ceur-ws.org/Vol-1609/16090219.pdf
9. Jolliffe, I.T.: Principal component analysis. In: International Encyclopedia of Statistical Science, pp. 1094–1096 (2011)
10. Kalpathy-Cramer, J., de Herrera, A.G.S., Demner-Fushman, D., Antani, S.K., Bedrick, S., Müller, H.: Evaluating performance of biomedical image retrieval systems - an overview of the medical image retrieval task at ImageCLEF 2004–2013. Comput. Med. Imaging Graph. **39**, 55–61 (2015). https://doi.org/10.1016/j.compmedimag.2014.03.004
11. Lowe, D.G.: Distinctive image features from scale-invariant keypoints. Int. J. Comput. Vis. **60**, 91–110 (2004)
12. Pelka, O., Friedrich, C.M.: FHDO biomedical computer science group at medical classification task of ImageCLEF 2015. In: Working Notes of CLEF 2015 - Conference and Labs of the Evaluation forum, Toulouse, France, 8–11 September 2015. http://ceur-ws.org/Vol-1391/14-CR.pdf
13. Pelka, O., Friedrich, C.M.: Modality prediction of biomedical literature images using multimodal feature representation. GMS Med. Inform. Biom. Epidemiol. **12**(2), 1345–1359 (2016). https://doi.org/10.3205/mibe000166
14. Pelka, O., Nensa, F., Friedrich, C.M.: Adopting semantic information of grayscale radiographs for image classification and retrieval. In: Proceedings of the 11th International Joint Conference on Biomedical Engineering Systems and Technologies (BIOSTEC 2018), BIOIMAGING, Funchal, 19–21 January 2018, vol. 2, pp. 179–187 (2018). https://doi.org/10.5220/0006732301790187

15. Russakovsky, O., et al.: ImageNet large scale visual recognition challenge. Int. J. Comput. Vis. (IJCV) **115**(3), 211–252 (2015). https://doi.org/10.1007/s11263-015-0816-y
16. Salton, G., Buckley, C.: Term-weighting approaches in automatic text retrieval. Inf. Process. Manag. **24**(5), 513–523 (1988). https://doi.org/10.1016/0306-4573(88)90021-0
17. Salton, G., McGill, M.J.: Introduction to Modern Information Retrieval. McGraw-Hill Computer Science Series. McGraw-Hill, New York (1983)
18. Szegedy, C., Vanhoucke, V., Ioffe, S., Shlens, J., Wojna, Z.: Rethinking the inception architecture for computer vision. In: 2016 IEEE Conference on Computer Vision and Pattern Recognition, CVPR 2016, Las Vegas, NV, USA, 27–30 June 2016, pp. 2818–2826 (2016). https://doi.org/10.1109/CVPR.2016.308
19. Vedaldi, A., Fulkerson, B.: VLFEAT: an open and portable library of computer vision algorithms. In: Proceedings of the 18th International Conference on Multimedia 2010, Firenze, Italy, 25–29 October 2010, pp. 1469–1472 (2010). https://doi.org/10.1145/1873951.1874249

Efficient Interactive Multi-object Segmentation in Medical Images

Leissi Margarita Castañeda Leon[✉] and Paulo André Vechiatto de Miranda

Institute of Mathematics and Statistics, University of São Paulo, São Paulo, Brazil
leissicl@ime.usp.br, pmiranda@vision.ime.usp.br

Abstract. In medical image segmentation, it is common to have several complex objects that are difficult to detect with simple models without user interaction. Hence, interactive graph-based methods are commonly used in this task, where the image is modeled as a connected graph, since graphs can naturally represent the objects and their relationships. In this work, we propose an efficient method for the multiple object segmentation of medical images. For each object, the method constructs an associated weighted digraph of superpixels, attending its individual high-level priors. Then, all individual digraphs are integrated into a hierarchical graph, considering structural relations of inclusion and exclusion. Finally, a *single* energy optimization is performed in the hierarchical weighted digraph satisfying all the constraints and leading to globally optimal results. The experimental evaluation on 2D medical images indicates promising results comparable to the state-of-the-art methods, with low computational complexity.

Keywords: Medical image segmentation · Interactive segmentation · Graph-based image segmentation · Superpixels segmentation

1 Introduction

Although automatic segmentation is attractive in real applications, user intervention is inevitable in many practical scenarios [15]. Interactive graph-based methods are commonly used in medical image segmentation tasks, where the image and the object's relationships are modeled as graphs, while the segmentation is obtained by a graph partitioning algorithm subject to hard constraints, such as scribble pixels (*seeds*) selected in the image domain for the foreground objects and background [4].

In the context of multiple object segmentation, each object has its own distinctive features, such as shape constraints [9,14] and boundary polarity [11,12], which are advantageous to explore together with the structural relations between the different objects in the image, in order to incorporate prior knowledge to guide the segmentation process. Most such methods are based on graph-cut optimization and are performed by a min-cut/max-flow algorithm [3,13], using geometric priors based on inclusion or exclusion interactions.

© Springer Nature Switzerland AG 2019
L. Leal-Taixé and S. Roth (Eds.): ECCV 2018 Workshops, LNCS 11132, pp. 705–710, 2019.
https://doi.org/10.1007/978-3-030-11018-5_61

However, their globally optimal results are restricted only to some particular cases and even their approximate solutions have a high computational cost.

We propose a hierarchical graph-based approach for the multiple object segmentation in medical images with a low computational cost, overcoming the mentioned limitations from previous works. A similar idea of this method was firstly introduced in [7] and a formal extended version in [6] under the name of *Hierarchical Layered Image Foresting Transform* (HLOIFT). In this paper, a superpixel-based adaptation of the method is presented, leading to a more efficient and adequate solution for large medical images.

2   Main Framework

In this section, we briefly describe our proposed method working with super-pixels. Figure 1 shows an overview of our framework using a synthetic phantom image, inspired by [5], where its layout tries to simulate the configuration of thoracic and abdominal organs in a coronal cross-section of a CT scan. The framework receives as input a given image, the seeds for some objects, the tree of relations between objects and their individual priors. Three steps are then performed to produce a labeled image as result.

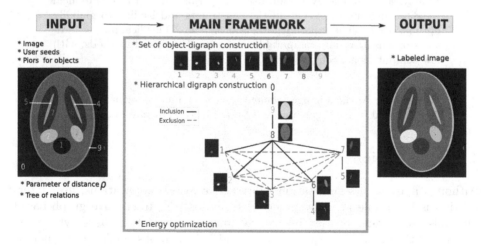

Fig. 1. Overview of our framework. Given the input parameters, a hierarchical weighted digraph of layers (digraphs of superpixels) is constructed and a graph-cut measure is optimized by our algorithm. Finally, we have a labeled image as output.

Set of Object-Digraph Construction. We first create a set of m weighted digraphs of superpixels $\mathcal{H}_i$, $i = 1, \ldots, m$, where each digraph corresponds to a single object O_i of an (*n-dimensional*) image $\mathcal{I}$. Each graph $\mathcal{H}_i = (\mathcal{N}_i, \mathcal{A}_i, \omega_i)$ is a triple consisting of a vertex set $\mathcal{N}_i$, a directed edge set $\mathcal{A}_i$ and a weight function ω_i. Each pair $(\mathcal{N}_i, \mathcal{A}_i)$ is an isomorphic copy of a Region Adjacency Graph (RAG) of the given image $\mathcal{I}$ segmented in superpixels by IFT-SLIC [1], while ω_i is a defined weight function for every $(s,t) \in \mathcal{A}_i$, where s and t are superpixels. For example, we may consider $\omega_i(s,t) = \mid I(s) - I(t) \mid$, where $I(t)$ is the mean intensity inside superpixel t. Of course, ω_i should also highlight the priors for each O_i whenever it is appropriate. For this purpose, we consider the same modification scheme of the weight assignment that was adopted by the regular OIFT method [11] for *boundary polarity* priors, where the polarity of each O_i is defined to highlight boundary transitions from *bright to dark* superpixels or from *dark to bright*. Also, we use the *geodesic star convexity prior*, prioritizing the segmentation of the object with more regular shape. This prior is obtained by setting the weights of some arcs to $-\infty$, according to the scheme proposed in [8]. Moreover, it is still possible to simultaneously handle boundary polarity and shape priors [9].

Hierarchical Digraph Construction. In this step, we generate a *hierarchical weighted digraph* $\mathcal{H} = (\mathcal{N}, \mathcal{A}, \omega)$ as the union of all object-digraphs of superpixels $\mathcal{H}_i$, $i = 1, \ldots, m$, with additional arcs connecting only some of the distinct object-digraphs, based on the priors given by the parent *tree h* and the parameter $\rho \geq 0$ representing the minimal distance between the boundaries of objects. The hierarchy prior (h) between any pair $\langle O_i, O_j \rangle$ of objects is understood as an *exclusion case* when $O_i \cap O_j = \emptyset$, or as an *inclusion case* when one of them is properly contained in the other. For convenience, object 0 is the root of the tree representing the image domain. The notation $h(i) = j$ indicates that $O_i \subset O_j$, being O_j the *parent* of O_i and we say that two objects O_i and O_j are *siblings* if $h(i) = h(j)$, meaning that both have the same parent. For the exclusion case we consider $\|p - q\| > \rho$ for every pixels $p \in O_i$ and $q \in O_j$. Therefore, the weights of the arcs for the *inclusion case* are given by $\omega(s,t) = -\infty$ and $\omega(t,s) = \infty$ for $h(i) = j$, $s \in \mathcal{N}_i$ and $t \in \mathcal{N}_j$, whenever the superpixels s and t have pixels with a distance smaller than ρ. For the *exclusion case*, we have special arcs to avoid overlapping between sibling objects, defining $\omega(s,t) = \omega(t,s) = -\infty$. Under this scheme, it is possible to have many different and sophisticated cases of hierarchical constraints which cannot be easily modeled with graph cuts [3].

Energy Optimization. Finally, we execute our proposed method using an algorithm similar to the one presented in [6], but running on the hierarchical weighted digraph of superpixels $\mathcal{H}$ as constructed above. Its output maximizes a single energy defined to ensure that the output satisfies all the constraints, including the constraints imposed by h and ρ, according to the theoretical result presented in [6].

3 Experimental Evaluation

This section presents an experimental evaluation of our method to assess its performance. In our first experiment, presented in Table 1, we show the execution time gains of the proposed approach in comparison to Image Foresting Transform

(IFT) [10] and the multiple object segmentation by HLOIFT [6] without super-pixels, for different image resolutions and superpixel sizes, for the segmentation of three objects in a CT image of the knee with inclusion and exclusion relations. The proposed method significantly reduced the size of the graph, resulting in a great saving of memory and computation time, thus compensating the additional cost of the three object-digraphs (layers) of HLOIFT in relation to IFT that has a single layer. Moreover, the segmentation results for different superpixel sizes were similar to those obtained by HLOIFT at pixel level demonstrating the robustness of the proposed method (Fig. 2).

Table 1. Time in ms for the different methods and image resolutions.

	171×193	342×386	684×772	1368×1544
IFT [10]	8.46	29.26	106.61	333.13
HLOIFT [6]	54.55	200.44	724.73	2,878.91
HLOIFT superpixel size 10×10	0.52	1.88	8.08	33.05
HLOIFT superpixel size 5×5	1.61	8.14	24.78	91.29
HLOIFT superpixel size 3×3	4.37	17.25	62.93	260.24

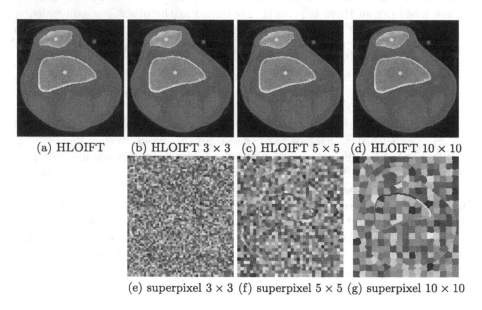

(a) HLOIFT   (b) HLOIFT 3×3 (c) HLOIFT 5×5 (d) HLOIFT 10×10

(e) superpixel 3×3 (f) superpixel 5×5 (g) superpixel 10×10

Fig. 2. The segmentation of a CT image of the knee for different superpixel sizes.

We also compared the running time between our approach and the hierarchical min-cut/max-flow algorithm with the inclusion case from [2]. Our approach has the best running time. For an image composed of two objects with the inclusion relation and size of 1520 × 1280 pixels, our algorithm takes 158.35 ms, 58.06 ms and 20.38 ms for superpixels of size 3 × 3, 5 × 5 and 10 × 10, respectively, while HLOIFT takes 1,823.55 ms and min-cut/max-flow takes 19,021.71 ms, using a laptop Intel Core i3-5005U CPU 2.00 GHz ×4.

Finally, we present visual comparisons between our results and the IFT results on different medical images, such as brain, abdominal region and wrist, in Fig. 3.

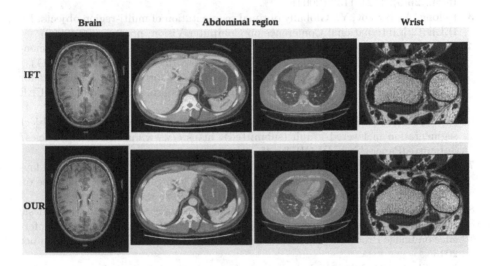

Fig. 3. Segmentation results comparing our method with the IFT method.

4   Conclusions

We proposed a new graph-based method based on superpixels, which computes a globally optimal result for arbitrary hierarchies, optimizing a single energy subject to all individual object priors, as well as their relations, with a low computational cost and being less restrictive. Our experiments show good segmentation results, even when considering a simple measure of dissimilarity for the arc weights. As future work, we are interested in using a machine learning method to estimate the arc weights, exploring other high-level priors, and also to evaluate our method in 3D medical images.

Acknowledgments. This research is part of the FAPESP Thematic Research Project (proc. 2014/12236-1). Also, this work is part of the INCT of the Future Internet for Smart Cities funded by CNPq, proc. 465446/2014-0, CAPES proc. 88887.136422/2017-00, and FAPESP, proc. 2014/50937-1.

References

1. Alexandre, E.B., Chowdhury, A.S., Falcao, A.X., Miranda, P.A.V.: IFT-SLIC: a general framework for superpixel generation based on simple linear iterative clustering and image foresting transform. In: 2015 28th SIBGRAPI Conference on Graphics, Patterns and Images (SIBGRAPI), pp. 337–344 (2015)
2. Boykov, Y., Kolmogorov, V.: An experimental comparison of min-cut/max-flow algorithms for energy minimization in vision. IEEE Trans. Pattern Anal. Mach. Intell. **26**(9), 1124–1137 (2004)
3. Delong, A., Boykov, Y.: Globally optimal segmentation of multi-region objects. In: IEEE 12th International Conference on Computer Vision, pp. 285–292 (2009)
4. Golodetz, S., Voiculescu, I., Cameron, S.: Simpler editing of graph-based segmentation hierarchies using zipping algorithms. Pattern Recognit. **70**, 44–59 (2017)
5. Kéchichian, R., Valette, S., Desvignes, M., Prost, R.: Shortest-path constraints for 3D multiobject semiautomatic segmentation via clustering and graph cut. IEEE Trans. Image Process. **22**(11), 4224–4236 (2013)
6. Leon, L.M.C., Ciesielski, K.C., Miranda, P.A.V.: Efficient hierarchical multi-object segmentation in layered graph (submitted). https://www.math.wvu.edu/~kcies/SubmittedPapers/SS29.HLOIFT.pdf
7. Leon, L.M.C., De Miranda, P.A.V.: Multi-object segmentation by hierarchical layered oriented image foresting transform. In: 2017 30th SIBGRAPI Conference on Graphics, Patterns and Images (SIBGRAPI), pp. 79–86 (2017)
8. Mansilla, L., Jackowski, M., Miranda, P.: Image foresting transform with geodesic star convexity for interactive image segmentation. In: IEEE International Conference on Image Processing (ICIP), Melbourne, Australia, pp. 4054–4058, September 2013
9. Mansilla, L.A.C., Miranda, P.A.V.: Image segmentation by oriented image foresting transform with geodesic star convexity. In: Wilson, R., Hancock, E., Bors, A., Smith, W. (eds.) CAIP 2013. LNCS, vol. 8047, pp. 572–579. Springer, Heidelberg (2013). https://doi.org/10.1007/978-3-642-40261-6_69
10. Miranda, P.A., Falcão, A.X.: Links between image segmentation based on optimum-path forest and minimum cut in graph. J. Math. Imaging Vis. **35**(2), 128–142 (2009)
11. Miranda, P.A., Mansilla, L.A.: Oriented image foresting transform segmentation by seed competition. IEEE Trans. Image Process. **23**(1), 389–398 (2014)
12. Singaraju, D., Grady, L., Vidal, R.: Interactive image segmentation via minimization of quadratic energies on directed graphs. In: IEEE Conference on Image Processing (CVPR), pp. 1–8 (2008)
13. Ulén, J., Strandmark, P., Kahl, F.: An efficient optimization framework for multiregion segmentation based on lagrangian duality. IEEE Trans. Med. Imaging **32**(2), 178–188 (2013)
14. Veksler, O.: Star shape prior for graph-cut image segmentation. In: Forsyth, D., Torr, P., Zisserman, A. (eds.) ECCV 2008. LNCS, vol. 5304, pp. 454–467. Springer, Heidelberg (2008). https://doi.org/10.1007/978-3-540-88690-7_34
15. Zhu, L., Kolesov, I., Gao, Y., Kikinis, R., Tannenbaum, A.: An effective interactive medical image segmentation method using fast growcut. In: MICCAI Workshop on Interactive Medical Image Computing (2014)

Cross-modal Embeddings for Video and Audio Retrieval

Didac Surís[1], Amanda Duarte[1,2]([✉]), Amaia Salvador[1], Jordi Torres[1,2],
and Xavier Giró-i-Nieto[1,2]

[1] Universitat Politécnica de Catalunya - UPC, Barcelona, Spain
{amanda.duarte,amaia.salvador,xavier.giro}@upc.edu
[2] Barcelona Supercomputing Center - BSC, Barcelona, Spain

Abstract. In this work, we explore the multi-modal information provided by the Youtube-8M dataset by projecting the audio and visual features into a common feature space, to obtain joint audio-visual embeddings. These links are used to retrieve audio samples that fit well to a given silent video, and also to retrieve images that match a given query audio. The results in terms of Recall@K obtained over a subset of YouTube-8M videos show the potential of this unsupervised approach for cross-modal feature learning.

Keywords: Cross-modal · Retrieval · YouTube-8M

1 Introduction

Videos have become the next frontier in artificial intelligence. The rich semantics make them a challenging data type posing several challenges in both perceptual, reasoning or even computational level. In addition to that, the popularization of deep neural networks among the computer vision and audio communities has defined a common framework boosting multi-modal research. Tasks like video sonorization, speaker impersonation or self-supervised feature learning have exploited the opportunities offered by artificial neurons to project images, text and audio in a feature space where bridges across modalities can be built.

Videos are used in this work for two main reasons. Firstly, they naturally integrate both visual and audio data, providing a weak labeling of one modality with respect to the other. Secondly, the high volume of both visual and audio data allows training machine learning algorithms whose models are governed by a high amount of parameters. The huge scale video archives available online and the increasing number of video cameras that constantly monitor our world, offer more data than computation power available to process them.

Thus we exploit the relation between the visual and audio contents in a video clip to learn a joint embedding space with deep neural networks. We propose a joint audiovisual space to address a retrieval task formulating a query from any of the two modalities.

© Springer Nature Switzerland AG 2019
L. Leal-Taixé and S. Roth (Eds.): ECCV 2018 Workshops, LNCS 11132, pp. 711–716, 2019.
https://doi.org/10.1007/978-3-030-11018-5_62

2   Related Works

As online music streaming and video sharing websites have become increasingly popular, some research has been done on the relationship between music and album covers [4,5,11,12] and also on music and videos (instead of just images) as the visual modality [2,7,15,17] to explore the multimodal information present in both types of data.

A recent study [10] also explored the cross-modal relations between the two modalities but using images with people talking and speech. It is done through Canonical Correlation Analysis (CCA) and cross-modal factor analysis. Also applying CCA, [18] uses visual and sound features and common subspace features for aiding clustering in image-audio datasets. In a work presented by [13], the key idea was to use greedy layer-wise training with Restricted Boltzmann Machines (RBMs) between vision and sound.

The present work is focused on using the information present in each modality to create a joint embedding space to perform cross-modal retrieval. This idea has been exploited especially using text and image joint embeddings [9,14,16], but also between other kinds of data, for example creating a visual-semantic embedding [6] or using synchronous data to learn discriminative representations shared across vision, sound and text [3].

However, joint representations between the images (frames) of a video and its audio have yet to be fully exploited, being [8] the work that most has explored this option up to the knowledge of the authors. In their paper, they seek for a joint embedding space but only using music videos to obtain the closest and farthest video given a query video, only based on either image or audio.

The main idea of the current work is borrowed from [14], which is the baseline to understand our approach. There, the authors create a joint embedding space for recipes and their images. They can then use it to retrieve recipes from any food image, looking to the recipe that has the closest embedding.

3   Architecture

This research aims to transform two different features representation (image and audio, separately) into a *joint space*.

Our model, depicted in the Fig. 1, consists of two separated sets of different sizes of fully connected layers, one for visual features and a second for audio features. Both are trained to be mapped into the same cross-modal representation. We adopt a self-supervised approach, as we exploit the unsupervised correspondence between the audio and visual tracks in any video clip. In the end, a classification from the two embeddings using a sigmoid as activation function is performed, also using a fully connected layer.

Each hidden layer uses ReLu as activation function, and all the weights in each layer are regularized by the L2 norm.

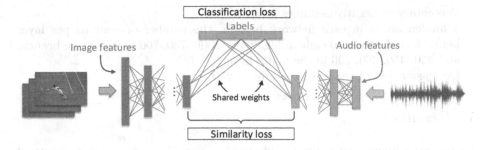

Fig. 1. Schematic of the used architecture.

4 Training

The objective here is to get the two embeddings of the same video (visual and audio) to be as close as possible (ideally, the same), while keeping embeddings from different videos as far as possible. The notion of "similarity" or "closeness" here is mathematically represented by the *cosine similarity* between the embeddings.

In addition to that, inspired by the work presented in [14], we provide additional information to our system by incorporating the video labels (classes) provided by the YouTube-8M dataset. This information is added as a regularization term that seeks to solve the high-level classification problem, both from the audio and the video embeddings, sharing the weights between the two branches. The key idea here is to have the classification weights from the embeddings to the labels shared between the two modalities. To that end, the loss function used for the classification is the well known *cross entropy* loss. This loss is optimized together with the cosine similarity loss, serving as a regularization term. In another words, the system learns to classify the audio and the images of a video (separately) into different classes or labels provided by the dataset. We limit its effect by using a regularization parameter λ.

The features used to train our model are already pre-computed and provided by the YouTube-8M dataset [1]. In particular, we use the *video-level* features, which represent the whole video clip with two vectors: one for the audio and another one for the video. These feature representations are the result of an average pooling of the local audio features computed over windows of one second, and local visual features computed over frames sampled at 1 Hz.

4.1 Parameters and Implementation Details

For our experiments we used the following parameters:

- Batch size of 1024.
- We saw that starting with λ different than zero led to a bad embedding similarity because the classification accuracy was preferred. Thus, we began the training with $\lambda = 0$ and set it to 0.02 at step number 10,000.
- Margin $\alpha = 0.2$.

- Percentage of negative samples $p_{negative} = 0.6$.
- 4 hidden layers in each network branch, the number of neurons per layer being, from features to embedding, 2000, 2000, 700, 700 in the image branch, and 450, 450, 200, 200 in the audio branch.
- Dimensionality of the feature vector $= 250$.

5   Results

All the experiments presented in this section were developed over a subset of 6,000 video clips from the YouTube-8M dataset [1].

5.1   Quantitative Performance Evaluation

To obtain the quantitative results we use the Recall@K metric. We define Recall@K as the recall rate at top K for all the retrieval experiments, this is, the percentage of all the queries where the corresponding video is retrieved in the top K, hence higher is better.

The experiments are performed with different dimensions of the feature vector. The Table 1 shows the results of recall from audio to video, while the Table 2 shows the recall from video to audio.

To have a reference, the random guess result would be k/Number of elements, represented in the first column of each table. The obtained results show a very clear correspondence between the embeddings coming from the audio features and the ones coming from the video features. It is also interesting to notice that the results from audio to video and from video to audio are very similar, because the system has been trained bidirectionally.

Table 1. Evaluation of recall from audio to video

k	Recall@1	Recall@5	Recall@10
256	21.5%	52.0%	63.1%
512	15.2%	39.5%	52.0%
1024	9.8%	30.4%	39.6%

Table 2. Evaluation of recall from video to audio

k	Recall@1	Recall@5	Recall@10
256	22.3%	51.7%	64.4%
512	14.7%	38.0%	51.5%
1024	10.2%	29.1%	40.3%

5.2   Qualitative Performance Evaluation

To obtain the qualitative results, a random video was chosen and from its image embedding, we retrieved the video with the closest audio embedding, and the other way around. In case the closest embedding retrieved corresponded to the same video, we took the second one in the ordered list.

On the left side of Fig. 2 we can see the results given a video query; and on the right the input query is an audio. Examples depicting the real videos and

Video Query	Audio Retrieval	Audio Query	Video Retrieval

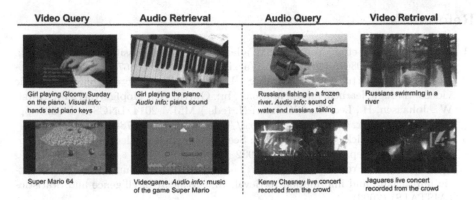

Fig. 2. Qualitative results. On the left we show the results obtained when we gave a video as a query. On the right, the results are based on an audio as a query.

audio are available online[1]. For each result and each query, we also show their YouTube-8M labels.

The results show that when starting from the image features of a video, the retrieved audio represents a very accurate fit for those images.

6   Conclusions and Future Work

We presented an simple but effective method to retrieve audio samples that fit correctly to a given (muted) video. The qualitative results show that the already existing online videos, due to its variety, represent a very good source of audio for new videos, even in the case of only retrieving from a small subset of this large amount of data. Due to the existing difficulty of creating new audio from scratch, we believe that a retrieval approach is the path to follow in order to give audio to videos.

As future work we would be to make use of the temporal information provided by the individual image and audio features of the YouTube-8M dataset to match audio and images, making use of the implicit synchronization that both modalities have, without needing any supervised control. Thus, the next step in our research is introducing a recurrent neural network, which will allow us to create more accurate representations of the video, and also retrieve different audio samples for each image, creating a fully synchronized system.

The source code and trained model used in this paper is publicly available at https://github.com/surisdi/youtube-8m.

Acknowledgements. This work was partially supported by the Spanish Ministry of Economy and Competitivity and the European Regional Development Fund (ERDF) under contract TEC2016-75976-R. Amanda Duarte was funded by the mobility grant of the Severo Ochoa Program at Barcelona Supercomputing Center (BSC-CNS).

---

[1] https://goo.gl/NAcJah.

References

1. Abu-El-Haija, S., et al.: YouTube-8M: a large-scale video classification Benchmark. CoRR abs/1609.08675 (2016). http://arxiv.org/abs/1609.08675
2. Acar, E., Hopfgartner, F., Albayrak, S.: Understanding affective content of music videos through learned representations. In: Gurrin, C., Hopfgartner, F., Hurst, W., Johansen, H., Lee, H., O'Connor, N. (eds.) MMM 2014. LNCS, vol. 8325, pp. 303–314. Springer, Cham (2014). https://doi.org/10.1007/978-3-319-04114-8_26
3. Aytar, Y., Vondrick, C., Torralba, A.: See, hear, and read: deep aligned representations. arXiv preprint arXiv:1706.00932 (2017)
4. Brochu, E., De Freitas, N., Bao, K.: The sound of an album cover: probabilistic multimedia and information retrieval. In: Artificial Intelligence and Statistics (AISTATS) (2003)
5. Chao, J., Wang, H., Zhou, W., Zhang, W., Yu, Y.: TuneSensor: a semantic-driven music recommendation service for digital photo albums. In: 10th International Semantic Web Conference (2011)
6. Frome, A., et al.: DeViSE: a deep visual-semantic embedding model. In: Neural Information Processing Systems (2013)
7. Gillet, O., Essid, S., Richard, G.: On the correlation of automatic audio and visual segmentations of music videos. IEEE Trans. Circuits Syst. Video Technol. 17(3), 347–355 (2007)
8. Hong, S., Im, W., Yang, H.S.: Deep learning for content-based, cross-modal retrieval of videos and music. CoRR abs/1704.06761 (2017)
9. Kiros, R., Salakhutdinov, R., Zemel, R.S.: Unifying visual-semantic embeddings with multimodal neural language models. CoRR abs/1411.2539 (2014)
10. Li, D., Dimitrova, N., Li, M., Sethi, I.K.: Multimedia content processing through cross-modal association. In: Proceedings of the Eleventh ACM International Conference on Multimedia, pp. 604–611. ACM (2003)
11. Libeks, J., Turnbull, D.: You can judge an artist by an album cover: using images for music annotation. IEEE MultiMedia 18(4), 30–37 (2011)
12. Mayer, R.: Analysing the similarity of album art with self-organising maps. In: Laaksonen, J., Honkela, T. (eds.) WSOM 2011. LNCS, vol. 6731, pp. 357–366. Springer, Heidelberg (2011). https://doi.org/10.1007/978-3-642-21566-7_36
13. Ngiam, J., Khosla, A., Kim, M., Nam, J., Lee, H., Ng, A.Y.: Multimodal deep learning. In: Proceedings of the 28th International Conference on Machine Learning, pp. 689–696 (2011)
14. Salvador, A., et al.: Learning cross-modal embeddings for cooking recipes and food images. In: CVPR (2017)
15. Schindler, A., Rauber, A.: An audio-visual approach to music genre classification through affective color features. In: Hanbury, A., Kazai, G., Rauber, A., Fuhr, N. (eds.) ECIR 2015. LNCS, vol. 9022, pp. 61–67. Springer, Cham (2015). https://doi.org/10.1007/978-3-319-16354-3_8
16. Wang, L., Li, Y., Lazebnik, S.: Learning deep structure-preserving image-text embeddings. CoRR abs/1511.06078 (2015). http://arxiv.org/abs/1511.06078
17. Wu, X., Qiao, Y., Wang, X., Tang, X.: Bridging music and image via cross-modal ranking analysis. IEEE Trans. Multimedia 18(7), 1305–1318 (2016)
18. Zhang, H., Zhuang, Y., Wu, F.: Cross-modal correlation learning for clustering on image-audio dataset. In: 15th ACM International Conference on Multimedia, pp. 273–276. ACM (2007)

Understanding Center Loss Based Network for Image Retrieval with Few Training Data

Pallabi Ghosh[✉] and Larry S. Davis

University of Maryland, College Park, USA
pallabig@cs.umd.edu, lsd@umiacs.umd.edu

Abstract. Performance of convolutional neural network based image retrieval depends on the characteristics and statistics of the data being used for training. We show that for training datasets with a large number of classes but small number of images per class, the combination of cross-entropy loss and center loss works better than either of the losses alone. While cross-entropy loss tries to minimize misclassification of data, center loss minimizes the embedding space distance of each point in a class to its center, bringing together data-points belonging to the same class.

Keywords: Center loss · Image retrieval · Small training dataset

1 Introduction

A common approach to identifying features in CBIR is to train a multi-class deep model with a large fully supervised training set, and then use features from various layers of the network as a basis for coding database images (which need not be drawn from the classes used to train the network). Early attempts at retrieval were based on cross-entropy loss. Triplet loss has been used to train networks for image retrieval [4]. However optimizing triplet loss is challenging because the level of relative similarity or dissimilarity in each training triplet determines how fast the network learns.

In this paper we study the use of center loss [14,16] for image retrieval. Center loss reduces the distance of each data point to its class center. It is not as difficult to train as triplet loss and performance is not based on the selection process of the training data points (triplets). Combining it with a softmax loss, prevents embeddings from collapsing.

Experiments will show that for training datasets with few images per class but with a large number of classes, the improvement using center loss for retrieval is significant.

2 Related Works

Some of the classical papers in image retrieval include [3,7,8,13]. Most of the recent work is based on training CNN models [2,5,12]. Both [11] and [17] review these techniques.

© Springer Nature Switzerland AG 2019
L. Leal-Taixé and S. Roth (Eds.): ECCV 2018 Workshops, LNCS 11132, pp. 717–722, 2019.
https://doi.org/10.1007/978-3-030-11018-5_63

Algorithm 1. Resnet18 pre-trained on Imagenet is the base network. L is the output size of the pre-final (512 for Resnet18). The training set contain K classes and B is the batch size. The center for each class is calculated by averaging the pre-final layer output of the network after passing each image in the class through the network.

Input Dataset with K classes and N_k images in k_{th} class. Center matrix $C_{K \times L}$ containing the centers of each class.

Output The recomputed center matrix C'

1: **procedure** CENTER LOSS + CROSS-ENTROPY LOSS BASED NETWORK TRAINING
2:     **while** not converge **do**
3:         Mini-batch of images is passed through the network
            $f^1 \leftarrow$ pre-final layer output
            $f^2 \leftarrow$ final FC layer output
4:         $L_s \leftarrow$ cross-entropy function applied to f^2
5:         $\bar{C} \leftarrow$ normalized $C_{K \times L}$
            $\bar{f}^1 \leftarrow$ normalized $f^1_{B \times L}$
6:         $D_{B \times L} \leftarrow \text{trace}(\bar{f}^1 \bar{f}^{1\,T}) * [1 \cdots 1]_{1 \times K} + \begin{bmatrix} 1 \\ \vdots \\ 1 \end{bmatrix}_{B \times 1} * \text{trace}(\bar{C}\bar{C}^T)^T - 2\bar{f}^1 \bar{C}^T$
7:         $\frac{1}{D} \leftarrow$ element wise inverse of D after adding 1e-4 to prevent division by 0
8:         $L_c \leftarrow$ cross-entropy function applied to $\frac{1}{D}$
9:         Backpropagate loss $L = L_s + L_c$ and update weights of network
10:        Recompute centers C' using updated network. All images in batches are
           passed through the network to get a new f^1.
           $C'_k \leftarrow \frac{1}{N_k} \sum_{y_i = k} f^1_{y_i}(x_i)$ where x are images, y are corresponding labels
           and k is a particular class in K.
           For the next epoch $C = C'$.

---

[2] achieved huge performance improvements by training the network on datasets related to the query. [9] showed that using intermediate layers captures local patterns of objects which performs better than using the final layer output for image retrieval. Similarly [15] uses the regional maximum activations of convolutions, R-MAC, for the same purpose. R-MAC uses a CNN to obtain a local descriptor of the image, which is then max pooled from different regions in a rigid grid, normalized, whitened and sum-aggregated to give a compact output vector. [4] also uses a similar process but with region proposals instead of the rigid grid to define the aggregation regions.

Center Loss was first used for face recognition by [16]. They update centers per mini-batch based on the gradient of center loss, and combines center loss with softmax loss for stability. [14] used a similar idea for few shot learning where they apply softmax over center distances. Instead of updating centers, they recalculate the centers per mini-batch based on the image classes in the support set in the mini-batch using episodic learning.

3   Our Algorithm

Our technique combines center loss with cross-entropy loss on a Resnet18 [6] based network as shown in Fig. 1. Suppose there are K classes and that the kth class has N_k images. Let $f^1_{y_i}(x_i)$ be the pre-final layer output by passing the i_{th} image (x_i) with label y_i through the network. Similarly let $f^2_{y_i}(x_i)$ be the final FC layer output and let B be the number of images per batch.

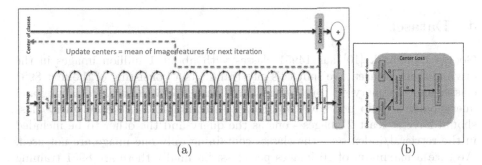

(a)   (b)

Fig. 1. (a) Our Algorithm (Resnet18 image from [1]) (b) The center loss computation block

First the training images are passed through a network pre-trained on Imagenet, giving us $f^1_{y_i}(x_i)$ feature descriptor. Then the center c_k of the kth class is computed as follows:

$$c_k = \frac{1}{N_k} \sum_{y_i=k} f^1_{y_i}(x_i) \tag{1}$$

Also the distance d_{ik} of the feature descriptor for each image to each class center c_k is calculated as follows:

$$d_{ik} = ||f^1_{y_i}(x_i) - c_k||^2_2 \tag{2}$$

Let this matrix be D with each element d_{ik}. Each d_{ik} is inverted to get $\frac{1}{D}$ so that it can be equated to a normal cross-entropy loss model where the input to the loss layer is a scores array. Let each row in $\frac{1}{D}$ be represented as $\frac{1}{d_i}$ and the labels corresponding to each row be y_i. Finally $\frac{1}{D}$ values are passed into a cross-entropy loss function which yields the center loss, L_c. This is combined with a normal cross-entropy loss applied on the final Fully-Connected layer with number of classes as output size, L_s. The total loss L can be expressed as:

$$L = L_s + L_c = -\sum_{i=1}^{B} log \frac{e^{W^T_{y_i} f^2_{y_i}(x_i)+b_{y_i}}}{\sum_{j=1}^{K} e^{W^T_j f^2_{y_i}(x_i)+b_j}} - \sum_{i=1}^{B} log \frac{e^{W^T_{y_i} \frac{1}{d_i}+b_{y_i}}}{\sum_{j=1}^{K} e^{W^T_j \frac{1}{d_i}+b_j}} \tag{3}$$

This is similar to the loss in [16] except that we replace the squared Euclidean center loss with cross entropy function being applied on this distance as in [14]. The difference with [14] is that we use inverse instead of negative distance function. The use of cross-entropy function on the squared Euclidean distance helps to remove the instability of the center loss. At the end of each epoch we use Eq. 1 to recompute the centers globally for the entire dataset. [16] uses an update formula to update the centers whereas [14] recomputes them, but both of them recalculate only at the mini-batch level, and not globally.

4   Dataset

Google Landmark [10] has 14951 classes with about 1 million images in the original train dataset. We split this into training set consisting of the first 8951 classes and the query set containing the remaining 6000 classes, so training and query partitions do not have any classes in common. Since each query class should have at least 2 images - one as the query and the other to be included in the retrieval/index set - the classes containing only one image are not used. We take a maximum of 10 images per class. So finally there are 8951 training classes with 72244 images, 5943 query classes with 1 query image per class and an index set consisting of 42709 images from these 5943 classes.

5   Results

We use Resnet models in Pytorch pre-trained on Imagenet as initialization. The final layer size is modified to suit the number of classes in our training set and it is initialized using Xavier uniform initialization. The output size of the pre-final layer is model dependent (512 for Resnet18), which would be the size of the feature descriptor for the image. For all networks, we used Adam optimization for training with a weight decay of 2e–4. The initial learning rate was set at 0.001 and a stepwise scheduler with drop rate of 0.92 per epoch was used. We ran the experiments with a batch size of 224.

Mean average precision or mAP score was used as the evaluation criterion. For Google Landmark dataset, given a query image all other images from the same class are correct retrieval results and images from other classes are incorrect retrieval results.

From Table 1 when the training datasets have few ($<= 10$) images per class, center loss leads to improvement. To understand the performance of center loss based network, we conducted a t-sne analysis for all the 3 models in Table 1 as seen in Fig. 2.

One main point of difference with previous works is that we are training on a very different data distribution with huge number of classes and few images per class. Unfortunately we do not have any previous results that have been trained on a similar data distribution as the partial Google Landmarks for comparison purposes.

Table 1. Comparative study of mAP scores for different losses using different models. We see that the model fine tuned using both cross-entropy loss and center loss performs better than just using cross-entropy loss

Model	Pre-trained on Imagenet	Fine-tuned using cross-entropy loss	Fine-tuned using cross-entropy and center loss
Resnet18	31.43%	49.54%	56.42%
Resnet101	35.17%	45.165%	61.22%

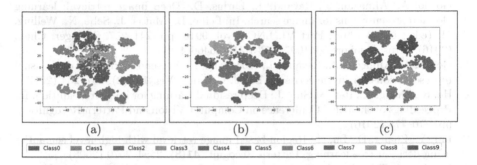

(a)   (b)   (c)

Class0   Class1   Class2   Class3   Class4   Class5   Class6   Class7   Class8   Class9

Fig. 2. We plot the t-SNE scatter plots for 10 random classes with 500 images from each class. The first figure (a) is the scatter plot for model pre-trained on Imagenet, the second (b) for model fine-tuned with cross-entropy loss only and the third figure (c) is for model fine-tuned with cross-entropy loss and center loss. As we can see in the figure, center+ cross-entropy loss performs better clustering than just cross-entropy loss and they both perform better than the model just pre-trained on Imagenet. Specifically between (b) and (c) - in (b) classes 0, 1 and 6 are split into 2 groups with other classes in between. This is not observed in (c)

6   Conclusion

We explored the effect of center loss training on image retrieval applications. A combination of center loss and cross-entropy loss performs better than just using cross-entropy loss or center loss separately. Also using cross-entropy on center distance to compute center loss instead of just the squared Euclidean distance stabilizes the center loss network. Any of the earlier techniques including VLAD encoding of intermediate layers, R-MAC etc can be used on top of this network for better results. Center loss based network is most useful when the training dataset has a large number of classes with few images per class. In the future, we plan to apply the model to other applications such as clustering and few-shot learning.

Acknowledgement. This work was supported by the DARPA MediFor program under cooperative agreement FA87501620191, "Physical and Semantic Integrity Measures for Media Forensics". The authors acknowledge the Maryland Advanced Research Computing Center (MARCC) for providing computing resources.

References

1. https://www.kaggle.com/pytorch/resnet18
2. Babenko, A., Slesarev, A., Chigorin, A., Lempitsky, V.: Neural codes for image retrieval. In: Fleet, D., Pajdla, T., Schiele, B., Tuytelaars, T. (eds.) ECCV 2014, Part I. LNCS, vol. 8689, pp. 584–599. Springer, Cham (2014). https://doi.org/10.1007/978-3-319-10590-1_38
3. Chen, Y., Wang, J.Z., Krovetz, R.: Clue: cluster-based retrieval of images by unsupervised learning. IEEE Trans. Image Process. **14**(8), 1187–1201 (2005)
4. Gordo, A., Almazán, J., Revaud, J., Larlus, D.: Deep image retrieval: learning global representations for image search. In: Leibe, B., Matas, J., Sebe, N., Welling, M. (eds.) ECCV 2016, Part VI. LNCS, vol. 9910, pp. 241–257. Springer, Cham (2016). https://doi.org/10.1007/978-3-319-46466-4_15
5. Gordo, A., Almazan, J., Revaud, J., Larlus, D.: End-to-end learning of deep visual representations for image retrieval. Int. J. Comput. Vis. **124**(2), 237–254 (2017)
6. He, K., Zhang, X., Ren, S., Sun, J.: Deep residual learning for image recognition. In: Proceedings of the IEEE Conference on Computer Vision and Pattern Recognition, pp. 770–778 (2016)
7. Liu, Y., Zhang, D., Lu, G.: Region-based image retrieval with high-level semantics using decision tree learning. Pattern Recognit. **41**(8), 2554–2570 (2008)
8. Manjunath, B.S., Ma, W.Y.: Texture features for browsing and retrieval of image data. IEEE Trans. Pattern Anal. Mach. Intell. **18**(8), 837–842 (1996)
9. Ng, J.Y.H., Yang, F., Davis, L.S.: Exploiting local features from deep networks for image retrieval. arXiv preprint arXiv:1504.05133 (2015)
10. Noh, H., Araujo, A., Sim, J., Weyand, T., Han, B.: Large-scale image retrieval with attentive deep local features. In: Proceedings of the IEEE Conference on Computer Vision and Pattern Recognition, pp. 3456–3465 (2017)
11. Rafiee, G., Dlay, S.S., Woo, W.L.: A review of content-based image retrieval. In: 7th International Symposium on Communication Systems Networks and Digital Signal Processing (CSNDSP), pp. 775–779. IEEE (2010)
12. Salvador, A., Giró-i Nieto, X., Marqués, F., Satoh, S.: Faster r-cnn features for instance search. In: Computer Vision and Pattern Recognition Workshops (CVPRW), 2016 IEEE Conference on. pp. 394–401. IEEE (2016)
13. Schmid, C., Mohr, R.: Local grayvalue invariants for image retrieval. IEEE Trans. Pattern Anal. Mach. Intell. **19**(5), 530–535 (1997)
14. Snell, J., Swersky, K., Zemel, R.: Prototypical networks for few-shot learning. In: Advances in Neural Information Processing Systems, pp. 4080–4090 (2017)
15. Tolias, G., Sicre, R., Jégou, H.: Particular object retrieval with integral max-pooling of CNN activations. arXiv preprint arXiv:1511.05879 (2015)
16. Wen, Y., Zhang, K., Li, Z., Qiao, Y.: A discriminative feature learning approach for deep face recognition. In: Leibe, B., Matas, J., Sebe, N., Welling, M. (eds.) ECCV 2016, Part VII. LNCS, vol. 9911, pp. 499–515. Springer, Cham (2016). https://doi.org/10.1007/978-3-319-46478-7_31
17. Zheng, L., Yang, Y., Tian, Q.: Sift meets CNN: a decade survey of instance retrieval. IEEE Trans. Pattern Anal. Mach. Intell. **40**(5), 1224 (2017)

End-to-End Trained CNN Encoder-Decoder Networks for Image Steganography

Atique ur Rehman$^{(\boxtimes)}$, Rafia Rahim$^{(\boxtimes)}$, Shahroz Nadeem$^{(\boxtimes)}$,
and Sibt ul Hussain$^{(\boxtimes)}$

Reveal (Recognition, Vision and Learning) Lab,
National University of Computer and Emerging Sciences (NUCES-FAST),
Islamabad, Pakistan
{atique.rehman,rafia.rahim,shahroz.nadeem,sibtul.hussain}@nu.edu.pk

Abstract. All the existing image steganography methods use manually crafted features to hide binary payloads into cover images. This leads to small payload capacity and image distortion. Here we propose a convolutional neural network based encoder-decoder architecture for embedding of images as payload. To this end, we make following three major contributions: (i) we propose a deep learning based generic encoder-decoder architecture for image steganography; (ii) we introduce a new loss function that ensures joint end-to-end training of encoder-decoder networks; (iii) we perform extensive empirical evaluation of proposed architecture on a range of challenging publicly available datasets (MNIST, CIFAR10, PASCAL-VOC12, ImageNet, LFW) and report *state-of-the-art* payload capacity at high PSNR and SSIM values.

Keywords: Steganography · CNN · Encoder-decoder
Deep neural networks

1 Introduction

In the field of information security steganography and steganalysis are considered as two important techniques [6,10]. Steganography is used to conceal secret information (*i.e.* a message, a picture or a sound) also known as payload into another non-secret object (that can be an image, a sound or a text message) also known as cover object, such that both the secret message as well as its content remain invisible.

In image steganography, most of the work has been done to hide a specific text message into a cover image. Thus the focus of all the existing techniques has been finding either noisy regions or low-level image features such as edges [7], textures [4], *etc.*, in cover image for embedding maximum amount of secret information without distorting the original image.

© Springer Nature Switzerland AG 2019
L. Leal-Taixé and S. Roth (Eds.): ECCV 2018 Workshops, LNCS 11132, pp. 723–729, 2019.
https://doi.org/10.1007/978-3-030-11018-5_64

In this work, we propose a novel and completely automatic steganography method for hiding one image to another. For this, we design a deep learning network that automatically identifies the best features from both cover and payload images to merge information. The biggest advantage of our this approach is that its generic and can be used with any type of images, to validate this we test our approach on variety of publicly available datasets including ImageNet, MNIST, CIFAR10, LFW and PASCAL-VOC12.

Overall our main contributions are as follows: (i) we propose a deep learning based generic encoder-decoder architecture for image steganography; (ii) we design a new loss function that ensures joint end-to-end training of encoder-decoder networks; (iii) we perform extensive empirical evaluation of proposed architecture on range of challenging publicly available datasets and report *state-of-the-art* payload capacity at high PSNR and SSIM values. Specifically, using our proposed algorithm we can reliably embed a unary channel image ($m \times n$ pixels) into a color image ($m \times n \times 3$ pixels). Our experiments show that we can achieve this payload of 33% (on average 8 bpp) with the average PSNR values of 32.9 db (SSIM = 0.96) for cover and 36.6 db (SSIM = 0.96) for recovered payload image.

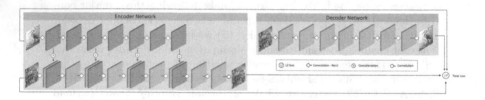

Fig. 1. Pictorial representation of encoder and decoder networks architecture. Top row in encoder network represents the guest branch while bottom row represents host branch.

2   Methodology

We train end-to-end a pair of encoder and decoder Convolutional Neural Networks (CNNs) for creating the hybrid image from pair of input images, and recovering the payload image from input hybrid image – *c.f.* Fig. 1 for architecture details. Here, we make use of observation that CNN layers learns a hierarchy of image features from low-level generic to high-level domain specific features. Thus our encoder identifies specific features from cover image to hide the details from the payload images, while decoder learns to separate those hidden features from the "hybrid" image.

Specifically, the encoder network takes two images (*i.e.* a "host" cover image and a "guest" payload image) as input and produces a single hybrid output image. Thus, the goal of encoder network is to produce a hybrid image, that remains visually identical to the host image but should also contain the guest image content in it. The decoder network takes as input the encoder produced hybrid image and recovers the guest image from it. The goal of decoder network is to recover the guest image from the input hybrid that remains visually similar to input guest image of encoder.

Let I_h and I_g represent input host and guest images to encoder, while O_e and O_d represent the output hybrid image and output decoder image respectively, then the complete loss function for encoder and decoder network can be written as:

$$L(I_g, I_h) = \alpha||I_h - O_e||^2 + \beta||I_g - O_d||^2 + \lambda(||W_e||^2 + ||W_d||^2) \qquad (1)$$

Here W_e and W_d represent the learned weights for the encoder and decoder networks respectively while α and β are controlling parameters for encoder and decoder. The first term in loss function defines encoder loss and the second one decoder loss.

2.1 Encoder Architecture

The encoder network at the input end has two parallel branches named as guest branch and host branch. Guest branch receives the input guest image I_g and uses a sequence of convolution and ReLU layers to decompose the input image into low-level (edges, colors, textures, *etc.*) and high level features. Host branch receives the input host image I_h and uses a sequence of convolution and ReLU layers (except the last layer which does not include ReLU layer) to decompose the input image into a hierarchy of feature representations and merge the extracted representations of guest image into host image.

Precisely, for merging the information from guest image, encoder concatenates the extracted feature maps from each alternating layer of guest branch (starting from input) to the corresponding output features maps of host branch. This procedure is repeated up to a layer of depth k (we found $k = 7$ as the best parameter), at this point we completely merge the guest branch features into host branch and guest branch cease to exist. After merging a further sequence of convolution and ReLU layers are used before the final convolution layer which produces as output hybrid image O_e.

2.2 Decoder Architecture

Our decoder network receives the encoder produced hybrid image O_e as input and runs it through sequence of convolution and ReLU layers (except the last layer which does not include ReLU) to recover the concealed representation O_d of guest image I_g.

We also experimented with other design choices, however in our initial experiments this architecture comes out as the best choice. During training both encoder and decoder are trained end-to-end using the joint loss function – *c.f.* Eq. (1). However during testing both encoder and decoder are used in disjoint manner.

Table 1. Comparison of bpp, PSNR and SSIM values for different runs of our algorithm on different datasets.

No.	Cover image	Payload image	No. of epochs	Avg. bpp	Encoder PSNR (db)	Decoder PSNR (db)	Payload %	SSIM encoder	SSIM decoder
1	CIFAR10	MNIST	50	7	32.9	32.0	29.1	0.87	0.85
2	CIFAR10	CIFAR10	50	8	30.9	29.9	33.3	0.98	0.96
3	ImageNet	ImageNet	50	8	29.6	31.3	33.3	0.88	0.88
4	ImageNet	ImageNet	150	8	32.9	36.6	33.3	0.96	0.96

Table 2. Bpp, PSNR and SSIM values of our ImageNet trained algorithm on different datasets.

No.	Cover image	Payload image	Avg. bpp	Encoder PSNR (db)	Decoder PSNR (db)	Payload %	SSIM encoder	SSIM decoder
1	PASCAL-VOC12	PASCAL-VOC12	8	33.7	35.9	33.3	0.96	0.95
2	LFW	LFW	8	33.7	39.9	33.3	0.95	0.96
3	PASCAL-VOC12	LFW	8	33.8	37.7	33.3	0.96	0.95

3   Experiments and Results

In this section, we report our experimental settings. We also report quantitative and qualitative results of our algorithm on a diverse set of publicly available datasets, that is on ImageNet [1], CIFAR10 [8], MNIST [9], LFW [5] and PASCAL-VOC12 [2].

We randomly divided each dataset sample images into three datasets: training, validation and testing. All the configurations have been done using validation set and we report the final performance on test set.

For payload, we randomly select an image from the corresponding dataset and either convert it to gray-scale or just choose a single channel from the RGB channels. For cover, we randomly select an RGB image from the corresponding dataset.

For all experiments we use the same encoder and decoder architecture as explained in Sect. 2. However each input image is zero-centered. Encoder and decoder weights are randomly initialized using Xavier initialization [3]. For learning these weights we use Adam optimizer with a fixed learning rate of 1E−4 and a batch size of 32 where regularization parameter was set to 0.0001 and $\alpha = \beta = 1$. During each epoch, we disjointly sample images for cover and payload usage from the training set. All the filters in CNN layers are applied with stride of single pixel and using same padding.

We use Peak Signal to Noise Ratio (PSNR), Structural SIMilarity (SSIM) index and bits per pixel (bpp) to report the perceptual quality of images produced and embedding capacity of our algorithm.

For our initial experiment, we used cover images ($32 \times 32 \times 3$) from CIFAR10 while payload images were taken ($28 \times 28 \times 1$) from MNIST dataset. For this experiment, we were able to hide approximately 29.1% payload (*i.e.* 7 bpp) in our cover images with average PSNR of 32.85 db and 32.0 db for encoder and decoder networks produced images respectively – *c.f.* Table 1. These results show that using our algorithm, we can successfully hide a huge payload with reasonably high PSNR and SSIM values. According to our best of knowledge, no one has been able to report such results on this dataset.

However, MNIST is a relatively simple dataset as majority of pixels in each image belong to plain background (white color) class. Thus, we conducted another experiment on CIFAR10 dataset – CIFAR10 being dataset of natural classes contains much larger variation in image foreground and background regions – with identical experimental settings.

In this experiment, both cover ($32 \times 32 \times 3$) and payload images ($32 \times 32 \times 1$) were randomly and disjointly sampled from CIFAR10 training batch. In this experiment we were able to hide a payload of 33.3% (*i.e.* 8 bpp) in our cover images with average PSNR of 30.9 db and 29.9 db for encoder and decoder networks produced images respectively.

From our these experiments, we can conclude that our proposed algorithm is extremely generic and one can, using the same architecture, reliably guarantee huge payloads and acceptable PSNR values for complex images as well – *c.f.* Table 1. For both these experiments we ran our algorithm for 50 epochs.

To further consolidate our findings and to evaluate our algorithm's embedding capacity and reconstruction performance on images of large size, we designed another experiment using ImageNet dataset. A subset of 8,000 images was randomly chosen from one million images. These selected images were then divided into two disjoints sets: training (6,000 images) and testing (2,000 images) – no validation set was used here since we reuse the earlier experiments settings. To allow uniform sized images as cover and payload all of these images were then resized to 300×300 pixels. For our initial version of this experiment and to ensure a fair comparison with other results, we first ran our algorithm for 50 epochs.

For randomly sampled cover ($300 \times 300 \times 3$) and guest images ($300 \times 300 \times 1$) from our ImageNet test dataset, we were able to hide a payload of 33.3% (*i.e.* 8 bpp) in our cover images with average PSNR of 29.6 db and 31.3 db for encoder and decoder networks produced images respectively. As we were able to hide high payload for similar PSNR values to earlier experiments for this complex dataset as well, so we further explored different experimental settings.

Our final model on ImageNet was trained for 150 epochs further improving the PSNR values for encoder and decoder to 32.92 db (SSIM = 0.96) and 36.58 db (SSIM = 0.96) respectively from 29.6 db and 31.3 db while maintaining similar payload capacity of 33.3% (on average 8 bpp) – *c.f.* Table 1.

To further evaluate the generalization capacity of our algorithm, we ran the ImageNet trained algorithm on sample of 1,000 unseen images from PASCAL-VOC12 [2] and Labelled Faces in Wild (LFW) [5] datasets. Table 2 shows the results of our this experiment. Here, even though our algorithm is trained on different dataset, it is still being able to achieve high payload capacity at high

PSNR and SSIM values which shows the generalization capabilities of our proposed algorithm.

Figure 2 shows a sample of result images from LFW, PASCAL-VOC12 and ImageNet datasets. Here once again we can verify using qualitative analysis that our method is being able to conceal and recover unseen complex payload images.

Therefore, given this quantitative and qualitative analysis, we can conclude that our algorithm is generic and robust to complex backgrounds and variations in objects appearance, thus can be reliably used for image steganography.

Fig. 2. Sample results of our algorithm on LFW (top row), PASCAL-VOC12 (middle row) and ImageNet (bottom row) images. In each subfigure, first column represents the cover image I_h, second the payload I_g, third the hybrid image O_e and fourth column represents the recovered guest image O_d.

4   Conclusions

In this paper, we have presented a novel CNN based encoder-decoder architecture for image steganography. In comparison to earlier methods, which only consider binary representation as payload our algorithm directly takes an image as payload and uses a pair of encoder-decoder networks to embed and robustly recover it from the cover image. According to our best of knowledge, no such earlier work exists and we are the first one to introduce this method for image-in-image hiding using deep neural networks. We have performed extensive experiments and empirically proven the superiority of our proposed method by showing excellent results with strong payload capacity on a wide range of wild-image datasets.

References

1. Deng, J., Dong, W., Socher, R., Li, L.J., Li, K., Li, F.-F.: ImageNet: a large-scale hierarchical image database. In: 2009 IEEE Conference on Computer Vision and Pattern Recognition, CVPR 2009, pp. 248–255. IEEE (2009)
2. Everingham, M., Van Gool, L., Williams, C.K., Winn, J., Zisserman, A.: The pascal visual object classes (VOC) challenge. Int. J. Comput. Vis. **88**(2), 303–338 (2010)
3. Glorot, X., Bengio, Y.: Understanding the difficulty of training deep feedforward neural networks. In: AISTATS, vol. 9, pp. 249–256 (2010)
4. Holub, V., Fridrich, J.: Designing steganographic distortion using directional filters. In: 2012 IEEE International Workshop on Information Forensics and Security (WIFS), pp. 234–239. IEEE (2012)
5. Huang, G.B., Mattar, M., Berg, T., Learned-Miller, E.: Labeled faces in the wild: a database for studying face recognition in unconstrained environments. In: Workshop on faces in 'Real-Life' Images: Detection, Alignment, and Recognition (2008)
6. Hussain, M., Hussain, M.: A survey of image steganography techniques (2013)
7. Islam, S., Modi, M.R., Gupta, P.: Edge-based image steganography. EURASIP J. Inf. Secur. **2014**(1), 8 (2014)
8. Krizhevsky, A., Nair, V., Hinton, G.: The CIFAR-10 dataset (2014)
9. LeCun, Y., Cortes, C., Burges, C.J.: The MNIST database of handwritten digits (1998)
10. Subhedar, M.S., Mankar, V.H.: Current status and key issues in image steganography: a survey. Comput. Sci. Rev. **13**, 95–113 (2014)

Cancelable Knuckle Template Generation Based on LBP-CNN

Avantika Singh[1]([✉]), Shreya Hasmukh Patel[2], and Aditya Nigam[1]

[1] Indian Institute of Technology Mandi, Mandi, India
d16027@students.iitmandi.ac.in, aditya@iitmandi.ac.in
[2] Indian Institute of Technology Jodhpur, Jodhpur, India
hasmukh.1@iitj.ac.in

Abstract. Security is a prime issue whenever biometric templates are stored in centralized databases. Templates are highly susceptible to varied security and privacy attacks. Unlike passwords, biometric traits are permanently unrecoverable if lost once. In this paper efforts have been made to generate cancelable knuckle print templates. To the best of our knowledge, this is the first attempt for generating secure template for this biometric-trait. Here for learning feature representation of a biometric sample, local binary pattern based CNN is used. The experimental results are evaluated on PolyU FKP knuckle database and demonstrate high performance. The proposed protected template is resilient to various privacy attacks as well as it satisfies one important criteria of cancelable biometrics i.e. revocability.

Keywords: Cancelable biometrics · Knuckle-print · Bio-hashing

1 Introduction

Among the three major personnel security mechanisms, which are based on either password, token or biometric scheme, appears to be insufficient in addressing the challenges of identity frauds. Passwords and pins are easily forgotten or cracked, whereas biometric traits suffer from the privacy assault and non-revocable issues. It simply means, if a biometric is compromised, it is rendered worthless, just like a password or pin. In such circumstances, replacement of a biometric trait with new template is not reasonable, as a person has only limited set of biometric samples. To address these critical issues, the concept of cancelable biometrics was emerged few years back that replaces the raw biometric template as a mixture of user-defined random values with biometric features [2,7]. Nevertheless, biometric modalities have been proved to carry unique biological information of an individual than any of the conventional passwords or token based methods. Although the use of biometrics is always problem specific but the good performance of finger knuckle print represents a recent trend in this field [3]. The convex shape lines and creases on finger dorsal surface are very distinctive to everyone and easily collectible using low-resolution imaging cameras [6].

© Springer Nature Switzerland AG 2019
L. Leal-Taixé and S. Roth (Eds.): ECCV 2018 Workshops, LNCS 11132, pp. 730–733, 2019.
https://doi.org/10.1007/978-3-030-11018-5_65

Major Concerns and Contribution: The major open issues in knuckle bio-metrics are the lack of robustness against outdoor illumination, low image qual-ity, inconsistent ROI segmentation and poor matching between weaker texture regions. Also, no commercial usage of finger knuckle biometric is available till the date. To the best of our knowledge, this is the first time efforts are made to introduce knuckle modality as cancelable biometric template, where the bio-metric features of a finger knuckle are modified using a well known Bio-hashing technique.

2   Proposed Architecture

Local binary patterns have been widely used in the past in variety of image processing applications and surprisingly have shown tremendous success in the face recognition area. In our work we have used local binary convolution neural networks as proposed by [5] for feature extraction. The main reason for chos-ing this kind of convolution is its ability to reduce large number of learnable parameters in comparison to the standard convolution layer. Thus this kind of convolution can work pretty well if we have limited data set at our disposal as the case with most of the biometric applications. Our proposed architecture is shown in Fig. 1. The detailed description of the LBP based CNN that is used in our work is shown in Table 1. We have used Adam optimizer with learning rate 0.001 and all the implementations has been done on Intel (R) Xenon(R) CPU E5-2630 V4 and NVIDIA Tesla K40C GPU card with 12 GB on card RAM.

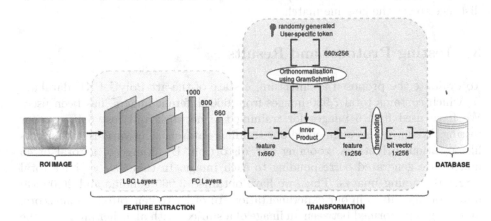

Fig. 1. Proposed architecture framework

2.1   Cancelable Knuckle Template Generation

Once the feature vector corresponding to a particular subject is obtained from LBP-CNN, they are transformed using the biohashing [4] technique to generate

Table 1. LBP based CNN architecture

Layer	No of filters	Size of filters
Conv1	8	3 * 3
Conv2	16	3 * 3
Conv3	32	3 * 3
Conv4	64	3 * 3
Maxpooling (2 * 2)		
Conv5	128	3 * 3
Maxpooling (2 * 2)		
Fully connected-1000		
Fully connected-800		
Fully connected-660		

cancelable knuckle template. Under this technique a user specific key is used to generate pseudo-random vectors, which are further transformed into orthonormal sets by applying Gram-Schmidt process. Then the inner product of the feature vector with the orthonormal set is computed. After that the resultant is further thresholded to generate bit-vector representation which is our cancelable template and stored in database. During authentication phase, the query image is processed through the same architecture to generate bit-vector representation which is compared with the templates stored in the databases using Euclidean distance to get the genuine match.

3   Testing Protocol and Results

To evaluate the proposed architecture, a state-of-the-art PolyU FKP database [1] which contains total 7,920 images from 660 different fingers, has been used. We have used first 6 images for training the network and rest 6 images for testing. We have also augmented our training dataset using various parameters like rotation, brightness, zooming and distortion. By doing so, a total of 46 images are generated corresponding to each image. In this way we have total 1,82,160 training images. Thus, we have obtained 3,960 genuine and 26,09,640 impostor matchings in our experimentation. In order to generate genuine score, matching is performed between an image of a subject with all other images of the same subject. On the other hand imposter score is generated by comparing an image of each subject against the images of all other subjects. The Genuine Vs Impostor score distribution graph is depicted in Fig. 2 that shows genuine and imposters are well separated with each other which is the prime requirement of any biometric based application. In this experiment, the performance comes out to be very superior i.e. FAR = 0.125 and FRR = 0.212.

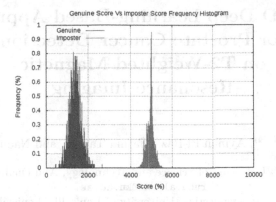

Fig. 2. Genuine vs imposter score graph

4   Conclusion

In this paper, we proposed a cancelable knuckle template which is inspired from LBP-CNN and bio-hashing. Experimental results show exceptional performance on PolyU FKP dataset. Finally, the proposed technique can potentially be extended to other biometric modalities also. Cancelable multi-biometrics is an emerging area. In future we will try to design effective non-invertible transformations for multiple biometric modalities.

References

1. Finger-knuckle-print polyu (2009). http://www.comp.polyu.edu.hk/biometrics
2. Cho, S., Teoh, A.B.J.: Face template protection via random permutation maxout transform. In: Proceedings of the 2017 International Conference on Biometrics Engineering and Application, pp. 21–27. ACM (2017)
3. Jaswal, G., Kaul, A., Nath, R.: Knuckle print biometrics and fusion schemes-overview, challenges, and solutions. ACM Comput. Surv. (CSUR) **49**(2), 34 (2016)
4. Jin, A.T.B., Ling, D.N.C., Goh, A.: Biohashing: two factor authentication featuring fingerprint data and tokenised random number. Pattern Recognit. **37**(11), 2245–2255 (2004)
5. Juefei-Xu, F., Boddeti, V.N., Savvides, M.: Local binary convolutional neural networks. In: 2017 IEEE Conference on Computer Vision and Pattern Recognition, CVPR, pp. 4284–4293 (2017)
6. Kumar, A., Xu, Z.: Personal identification using minor knuckle patterns from palm dorsal surface. IEEE Trans. Inf. Forensics Secur. **11**(10), 2338–2348 (2016)
7. Lai, Y.L., et al.: Cancellable iris template generation based on indexing-first-one hashing. Pattern Recognit. **64**, 105–117 (2017)

A 2.5D Deep Learning-Based Approach for Prostate Cancer Detection on T2-Weighted Magnetic Resonance Imaging

Ruba Alkadi[1(✉)], Ayman El-Baz[2], Fatma Taher[1], and Naoufel Werghi[1]

[1] Khalifa University of Science and Technology, Abu Dhabi, UAE
ruba.alkadi@ku.ac.ae
[2] Department of Bioengineering, University of Louisville, Louisville, KY, USA

Abstract. In this paper, we propose a fully automatic magnetic resonance image (MRI)-based computer aided diagnosis (CAD) system which simultaneously performs both prostate segmentation and prostate cancer diagnosis. The system utilizes a deep-learning approach to extract high-level features from raw T2-weighted MR volumes. Features are then remapped to the original input to assign a predicted label to each pixel. In the same context, we propose a 2.5D approach which exploits 3D spatial information without a compromise in computational cost. The system is evaluated on a public dataset. Preliminary results demonstrate that our approach outperforms current state-of-the-art in both prostate segmentation and cancer diagnosis.

1 Introduction

According to a recent study by the American Cancer Society, prostate cancer (CaP) is the second leading cause of cancer deaths in the United States [1]. Several screening and diagnostic tests are used in daily clinical routines to ensure early detection and treatment. Besides its non-invasive nature, MR screening is favored among other diagnostic tests due to its relatively high potential in CaP detection and diagnosis. However, the exploitation of the full potential of MR images is still limited, due to the fact that analyzing these volumetric images is time consuming, subjective, and requires specialized expertise. These facts fueled the need for developing an accurate automatic MRI-based CaP detection system.

Multiple CAD systems were proposed in the last decade [6,7,10]. Most of the research on these systems used carefully hand-crafted features from a combination of MR modalities. In response to the breakthrough of Convolutional Neural Networks (CNNs) [4], a shift from systems that use hand-crafted low-level features, to those that learn descriptive high-level features has gradually taken place in the area of medical image analysis. To date, the most successful medical image analysis systems rely on CNNs [8].

© Springer Nature Switzerland AG 2019
L. Leal-Taixé and S. Roth (Eds.): ECCV 2018 Workshops, LNCS 11132, pp. 734–739, 2019.
https://doi.org/10.1007/978-3-030-11018-5_66

Surprisingly, a recent comprehensive review [5] of more than 40 prostate MRI CAD systems reports no use of deep-learning-based approaches for this specific application. While a more recent review of deep learning in medical image analysis [8] reports only very few attempts to employ deep architectures for the task of CaP detection and diagnosis.

Lemaitre et al. [6], proposed a multi-stage multi-parametric MRI CAD for CaP system. In their final model, they selected 267 out of 331 features extracted from four modalities and used them to train a random forest classifier. They validated their system on data from 19 patients from a publicly available dataset. On the other hand, Kiraly et al. [3] proposed another approach that uses deep learning for slice-wise detection of CaP in multi-parametric MR images. They reformulated the task as a semantic segmentation problem and use a SegNet-like architecture to detect possible lesions. They achieved an average area under the receiver operating characteristic of 0.834 on data from 202 patients.

In contrast to [3], our work differs from several perspectives. First, we explicitly exploit 3D spatial contextual information to guide the segmentation process which eventually improves the overall system performance. Second, we simultaneously perform anatomical segmentation and lesion detection in MR images. Third, unlike [3] our work relies on input data from only one modality (T_2W). We thus highlight the potential of extracting sufficiently meaningful information from a single modality. In fact, this also has a significant clinical advantage, as it reduces the time and cost of screening and eliminates the need of contrast agent injection. Finally, and most importantly, this work implements a deeper convolutional architecture compared to the one used in [3] and, to the best of our knowledge, is the first to assess CNNs performance on the public dataset of [5].

2   Proposed Method

To address the trade-off between 2D and 3D image processing approaches, we propose a 2.5D method which exploits important 3D features without a compromise in the computational complexity. This is achieved by extending the dimension of the lowest resolution of the input MR volume into the RGB dimension. This fusion approach has several advantages. First, it enables us to exploit the 3D spatial information of the middle slice with no extra computational cost. Second, this technique allows to transform gray-level volumetric images to colored images with embedded 3D information. Finally, this approach copes with the problem of inter- and intra-patient variability which mainly results from variable prostate size and scanner resolution, respectively.

Although, the term 2.5D is previously used in [9] to refer to fusing three orthogonal views of an input image, we use it here to refer to a sub-volume of dimensions $x \times y \times 3$ where x and y are the slice dimensions (see Fig. 1).

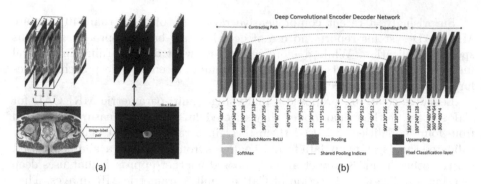

Fig. 1. (a) Illustration of sliding a 3D window across the input volume. (b) The architecture of the deep convolutional encoder-decoder network presented in [2]

2.1 Network Design and Training

We reformulate the problem of CaP detection and diagnosis as a multi-class segmentation problem. We first define four classes from the raw data including: Non-prostatic tissues (background), PZ, CG and CaP. These four classes are well distinguished in the T_2w [5]. We utilize a deep convolutional encoder-decoder network similar to [2]. The network architecture is illustrated in Fig. 1. The encoder part consists of thirteen convolutional layers that are topologically identical to those in vgg16. Each encoder block has a corresponding decoder which mainly consists of deconvolutional layers. Pooling indices are communicated between the encoder and the decoder to perform non-linear upsampling [2]. Finally, a multi-class SoftMax layer is placed at the end of the network followed by a pixel classification layer. To assess the benefit of our 2.5D approach, we trained the same network using gray-level slices. Each slice was replicated three times in order to fit in the input RGB channels. Throughout this paper, we refer to this method as M1, while we refer to our 2.5D method as M2.

Table 1. Results of multi-class segmentation on prostate-contained slices

	Mean BF score		Recall	
	M1	M2	M1	M2
CG	0.783	**0.799**	0.815	**0.836**
PZ	0.825	**0.855**	**0.901**	0.886
Non prostate	0.974	**0.980**	0.980	**0.986**
CaP	0.879	**0.891**	0.916	**0.928**

3   Experiments and Results

We performed our experiments on the public dataset released by [5], which is acquired from a cohort of patients with higher-than-normal level of PSA. All patients were screened using a 3 T whole body MRI scanner (Siemens Magnetom Trio TIM, Erlangen, Germany). The dataset is composed of a total of 19 patients of which 17 have biopsy proven CaP and 2 are healthy with negative biopsies. An experienced radiologist segmented the prostate organ on T_2w-MRI, as well as the prostate zones (i.e. PZ and CG), and CaP. Three-dimensional T_2w fast spin-echo (TR: 3600 ms, TE: 143 ms, ETL: 109, slice thickness:1.25 mm) images are acquired in an oblique axial plane. The nominal matrix and field of view (FOV) of the 3D T_2w fast spin-echo images are 320mm × 256mm and 280mm × 240mm, respectively. The network was trained on 60% of the samples using a GPU. The weights of the encoder were initialized using a pre-trained vgg16. We set a constant learning rate of 0.001, a momentum of 0.9, and a maximum number of ephocs to 100. We evaluated the segmentation performance of each class using the mean boundary F1 (BF) score, and recall. These metrics were calculated for all prostate-contained images. The average of each metric is presented in Table 1. Notably, CaP segmentation performance is significantly improved by the introduced approach with respect to all metrics. Figure 2 compares the heatmaps generated by projecting the activations of the SoftMax layer for the two alternative methods explained above, and the output of the CAD system proposed by [6]. Clearly, better performance is achieved using a deep learning based semantic segmentation architecture compared to the standard handcrafted features-based learning used in [6]. Also, the performance of the same architecture is improved by the employment of the 3D sliding window approach (Fig. 2 (d), (h)). With respect to the prostate segmentation task, Fig. 2 qualitatively demonstrates the gains achieved by using the proposed approach.

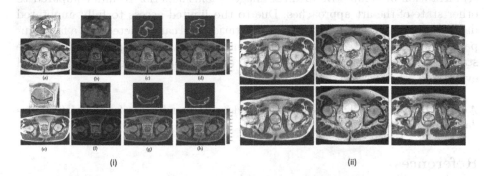

Fig. 2. (i) (a, e) Ground truth of case 1 and 2, respectively. White contour shows the radiologist segmentation of the prostate, while blue contour is the ground truth lesion. Heatmaps generated by [6] (b, f), using M1 (c, g), and using M2 (d, h). (ii) Prostate segmentation results of M1 and M2. The first row shows examples of segmentation performed using M1. The corresponding segmentation of M2 on the same slices is shown in the second row. (Color figure online)

We also quantitatively assess and compare the performance of our system for the detection and diagnosis of malignant lesions against other recently proposed systems, as can be realized in Table 2. Clearly, our approach outperforms the more traditional pattern recognition and machine learning approach presented by Lemaitre et al. [6] method by more that 15% average AUC. The proposed architecture also outperforms [3] by a significant margin. Note that Kiraly et al. [3] used similar but shallower architecture, with only 5 convolutions in each of the decoder and encoder. Expectedly, the system performance is boosted as a result of adding more convolutional layers. Results suggest that our hybrid 2.5D approach outperforms M1 pipeline which uses the same CNN architecture.

Table 2. Comparison of CPM of CaP results with the literature

	Lemaitre et al. [6]	kiraly et al. [3]	M1	M2
Average AUC	0.836	0.834	**0.997**	0.995
Accuracy	-	-	0.876	**0.894**

4   Conclusions

A simple, yet efficient, deep learning-based approach for joint prostate segmentation and CaP diagnosis on MRI was presented in this paper. From our experiments, we draw two general conclusions. First, the incorporation of 3D spatial information through the RGB channels is possible, potentially beneficial, and generally applicable to similar medical images with no extra computational cost. Second, the use of a deep convolutional encoder-decoder network for the segmentation of volumetric medical images yields superior results compared to other state-of-the-art approaches. Due to the limited access to fully annotated datasets for simultaneous prostate segmentation and cancer detection, a fair comparison was thus limited. Accordingly, future work will focus on re-validating the state-of-the-art approaches on the public dataset to guarantee a more rational evaluation.

Acknowledgement. This work is supported by a research grant from Al-Jalila foundation Ref: AJF-201616.

References

1. Key Statistics for Prostate Cancer | Prostate Cancer Facts. American Cancer Society. https://www.cancer.org/cancer/prostate-cancer/about/key-statistics.html. Accessed 24 July 2018
2. Badrinarayanan, V., Kendall, A., Cipolla, R.: SegNet: a deep convolutional encoder-decoder architecture for image segmentation. IEEE Trans. Pattern Anal. Mach. Intell. **39**(12), 2481–2495 (2017)

3. Kiraly, A.P., et al.: Deep convolutional encoder-decoders for prostate cancer detection and classification. In: Descoteaux, M., Maier-Hein, L., Franz, A., Jannin, P., Collins, D.L., Duchesne, S. (eds.) MICCAI 2017. LNCS, vol. 10435, pp. 489–497. Springer, Cham (2017). https://doi.org/10.1007/978-3-319-66179-7_56

4. Krizhevsky, A., Sutskever, I., Hinton, G.E.: ImageNet classification with deep convolutional neural networks. In: Advances in Neural Information Processing Systems, pp. 1097–1105 (2012)

5. Lemaître, G., Martí, R., Freixenet, J., Vilanova, J.C., Walker, P.M., Meriaudeau, F.: Computer-aided detection and diagnosis for prostate cancer based on mono and multi-parametric MRI: a review. Comput. Biol. Med. **60**, 8–31 (2015)

6. Lemaitre, G., Martí, R., Rastgoo, M., Mériaudeau, F.: Computer-aided detection for prostate cancer detection based on multi-parametric magnetic resonance imaging. In: 2017 39th Annual International Conference of the IEEE Engineering in Medicine and Biology Society (EMBC), pp. 3138–3141. IEEE (2017)

7. Litjens, G., Debats, O., Barentsz, J., Karssemeijer, N., Huisman, H.: Computer-aided detection of prostate cancer in MRI. IEEE Trans. Med. Imaging **33**(5), 1083–1092 (2014)

8. Litjens, G., et al.: A survey on deep learning in medical image analysis. Med. Image Anal. **42**, 60–88 (2017)

9. Roth, H.R., et al.: A new 2.5D representation for lymph node detection using random sets of deep convolutional neural network observations. In: Golland, P., Hata, N., Barillot, C., Hornegger, J., Howe, R. (eds.) MICCAI 2014. LNCS, vol. 8673, pp. 520–527. Springer, Cham (2014). https://doi.org/10.1007/978-3-319-10404-1_65

10. Trigui, R., Mitéran, J., Walker, P.M., Sellami, L., Hamida, A.B.: Automatic classification and localization of prostate cancer using multi-parametric MRI/MRS. Biomed. Signal Process. Control. **31**, 189–198 (2017)

GreenWarps: A Two-Stage Warping Model for Stitching Images Using Diffeomorphic Meshes and Green Coordinates

Geethu Miriam Jacob[(✉)] and Sukhendu Das

Visualization and Perception Lab, Department of Computer Science and Engineering,
Indian Institute of Technology, Madras, Chennai, India
geethumj@cse.iitm.ac.in, sdas@iitm.ac.in

Abstract. Image Stitching is a hard task to solve in the presence of large parallax in the images. Specifically, for a sequence of frames from unconstrained videos which are considerably shaky, recent works fail to align such a sequence of images accurately. The proposed method "GreenWarps" aims to accurately align frames/images with large parallax. The method consists of two novel stages, namely, Prewarping and Diffeomorphic Mesh warping. The first stage warps unaligned image to the reference image using Green Coordinates. The second stage of the model refines the alignment by using a demon-based diffeomorphic warping method for mesh deformation termed "DiffeoMeshes". The warping is performed using Green Coordinates in both the stages without the assumption of any motion model. The combination of the two stages provide accurate alignment of the images. Experiments were performed on two standard image stitching datasets and one dataset consisting of images created from unconstrained videos. The results show superior performance of our method compared to the state-of-the-art methods.

Keywords: Green coordinates · Diffeomorphic registration
Content preserving warps · Image stitching

1 Introduction

Image Stitching is a widely studied problem in the field of computer vision and graphics, which generates a single wide field-of-view image from a set of narrow field-of-view images. Several warping models, including homography-based warps [1,2] spatially varying warping models [3–5], hybrid models [6–9], parallax tolerant models [10–12] and image stitching softwares such as Adobe Photoshop and Autostitch, fail to perform well when non-ideal data is provided as input.

Electronic supplementary material The online version of this chapter (https://doi.org/10.1007/978-3-030-11018-5_67) contains supplementary material, which is available to authorized users.

© Springer Nature Switzerland AG 2019
L. Leal-Taixé and S. Roth (Eds.): ECCV 2018 Workshops, LNCS 11132, pp. 740–744, 2019.
https://doi.org/10.1007/978-3-030-11018-5_67

The main challenges of any stitching algorithm are parallax error, occlusions, motion blur and presence of moving objects. Specifically, for stitching frames of an unconstrained video (e.g shaky/jittery videos), the state-of-the-art techniques fail to provide satisfactory results. The reason is that image stitching assume specific underlying motion models, thus making the task highly challenging in presence of large parallax.

Common approaches to the image stitching algorithms follow the pipeline of estimating transformations between the images, aligning the images using a warping model and stitching them using seam techniques or blending techniques. We present a novel mesh-based warping model termed "GreenWarps", utilizing Green coordinates [13] and a demon-based diffeomorphic warping model [14] to align the images. "GreenWarps" warping model consists of two stages, namely, pre-warping and "DiffeoMeshes". The first stage produces a global conformal mapping between the images to be stitched. The conformal mappings induce no shear at all, thereby providing shape-preserving and distortion-free deformations. The second stage of the proposed method, termed "DiffeoMeshes", provides a mesh deformation based on semi-dense correspondences of the two images and refines the alignment obtained from the first stage. Both the stages utilize Green coordinates for warping the deformed meshes, instead of warping the images based on computed transformations as in previous approaches. Since our method does not assume any motion model, it is immune to large parallax error.

2   Proposed Framework

The steps of the proposed "GreenWarps" method are: (i) estimate SIFT correspondences, (ii) pre-warping based on Green coordinates, (iii) mesh deformation based on DiffeoMeshes and warping based on Green coordinates, (iv) blend the images to obtain stitched image. Similar to spatially varying warps, GreenWarps perform a shape preserving deformation of the mesh for aligning images to the reference image. Interestingly, our approach does not compute any transformation matrix during the process of alignment or warping. This ensures that our method does not assume any motion model. Warping in both the stages (Pre-warping and DiffeoMeshes) is performed based on Green coordinates.

Among the images to be stitched, we take one of them as Reference image (R) and the other as Unaligned image (U). The unaligned image is first divided into image grids, where each grid has 4 vertices. The pre-warping stage takes a 2×2 mesh grid of U. Every point X_k of the unaligned image is defined in terms of the Green coordinates [13] of its corresponding mesh grid as $X_k = \phi_k(X_k)^T V_k + \psi_k(X_k)^T N_k$, where $\phi_k(X_k), \psi_k(X_k)$ are the Green coordinate vectors associated with the 4 coordinates and edges of the mesh grid containing the point X_k, V_k is a vector of 4 vertices and $N_k = [n(t_k^1)\ n(t_k^2)\ n(t_k^3)\ n(t_k^4)]$ is a vector of normals of edges t_k^i of the grid containing the point X_k. An as-similar-as-possible mesh deformation [3] is performed generating the deformed vertices $\hat{V}$ based on the corresponding SIFT features. The Green coordinates (for every pixel in the image) are first estimated from the initial mesh as derived in [15]. The warping of the image based on the deformed vertices are performed using the computed Green coordinates. The corresponding position of any point of the unaligned image in the pre-warped image $(\hat{X}_k)$, with the deformed vertices $\hat{V}$ and updated normals $\hat{N}$ is obtained as follows: $\hat{X}_k = \phi_k(X_k)^T \hat{V}_k + \psi_k(X_k)^T m_k \hat{N}_k$. Here, m_k is the normalized edge length [13]. Warping based on Green coordinates, as in [13] provides a conformal mapping, preserving the shape of the structures. Thus, Green coordinates provide a natural transformation of the image for alignment without assuming any motion model. Perspective distortion, a problem in many previous approaches [10,12,16] is absent in our approach.

The second stage of our approach, termed DiffeoMeshes, refines the alignment by obtaining a per-pixel displacement (spatial transformation) of the region of the overlap of the pre-warped and reference images. Let the overlap regions of the pre-warped and reference images be M_U and M_R respectively. A mesh deformation is performed based on the spatial transformation obtained. The demon-based diffeomorphic transformation, s is estimated using the following optimization function [14]:

$$E_{diff}(s) = Sim(M_U, M_R \circ s) + Reg(s) \tag{1}$$

The similarity (correspondence) term is $Sim(M_U, M_R \circ s) = \sum_{p=1}^{L} \|M_U(p) - M_R(p) \circ s(p)\|_2^2$, and the second regularization term is defined as $\sum_{p=1}^{L} \|\nabla s(p)\|_2$, where, $\circ$ indicates the per-pixel spatial warping function and $L = |M_U| = |M_R|$, where $|.|$ is the cardinality function. All the demon-based diffeomorphic registrations [14,17,18] uses Gaussian smoothing for the purpose of regularization. Our proposed method utilizes TV-based regularization [19] and this helps in preserving the edges while updating the transformation. An iterative alternating minimization of the correspondence energy and the regularization energy is performed to obtain the diffeomorphic transformation.

Let the mesh grid vertices at the second stage before and after deformation be V and $\hat{V}$. DiffeoMeshes minimizes the optimization function $E(\hat{V}) = E_d(\hat{V}) + w_s E_s(\hat{V})$ where E_d is the data term and E_s is the smoothness term. The data term minimizes the distance between the measured point and the interpolated location in the mesh using diffeomorphic transformation. The data term of DiffeoMeshes is: $E_d(\hat{V}) = \sum_{p=1}^{N_d} \|s(p)\|_2^2$, where N_d is the number of pixels selected from the overlap region of the pre-warped and reference images and $s(p)$ is the diffeomorphic transformation in pixel p. Only those pixels belonging to the edges, with exact match are taken for obtaining the mesh (semi-dense correspondences). $E_s(\hat{V})$ is the same as that used in [3]. The smoothness term minimizes the deviation of each deformed mesh grid from a similarity transformation of its input mesh. The solution of the problem is obtained using a Jacobi based linear solver. Once the deformed mesh vertices are obtained, the refined alignment is obtained by warping using Green coordinates similar to the first stage. The aligned images are then blended using the multi-band blending method of [20].

Fig. 1. Comparison of our method with (a) SPHP [8], (b) Parallax tolerant [10], (c) APAP [4], (d) SEAGULL [12]. In each example, the first column shows the input images, the second column shows the output of the comparing method and the third column shows the output of the proposed method. (Color figure online)

Table 1. Comparison of the performances for two standard datasets [10,12] for large parallax and one dataset consisting of frames from unconstrained videos.

E_{mg}					E_{corr}				
Average	[4]	[8]	[3]	Ours	Average	[4]	[8]	[3]	Ours
Dataset 1 [10]	4.28	6.44	7.37	**2.31**	Dataset 1 [10]	0.36	0.34	0.35	**0.32**
Dataset 2 [12]	4.74	6.34	6.99	**3.14**	Dataset 2 [12]	0.36	0.33	0.35	**0.32**
Dataset 3	25.49	11.91	11.47	**9.03**	Dataset 3		0.33	0.31	0.32	**0.28**

3   Experimental Results

Experiments were performed on two parallax-tolerant image stitching datasets [10,12] and a new dataset consisting of 2-3 frames of unconstrained videos. Parallax error and presence of moving objects are the main challenges of the images in the dataset. Our method is evaluated with the state-of-the-art methods [3,4,8,21]. The error measures used for determining the alignment quality of the images are mean geometric error (E_{mg}) and correlation error (E_{corr}). E_{mg} measures the average distance between the corresponding feature points after alignment and E_{corr} is defined as the average of one minus Normalized Cross Correlation(NCC) over a neighborhood in the overlapped region. Lower values of the measure indicates better performance. Table 1 shows the average (over the whole dataset) alignment errors of all 3 datasets in comparison to the state-of-the-art methods. As seen in the table, our method outperforms the state-of-the-art methods for every dataset. Some qualitative results are also shown in Fig. 1. The comparison with the methods [4,8,10,12] are shown in the figure. The red boxes indicate the erroneous regions of alignment, whereas the blue boxes shows the corresponding regions accurately aligned. The superiority of the method can be seen from the qualitative and quantitative results.

References

1. Brown, M., Lowe, D.G.: Automatic panoramic image stitching using invariant features. Int. J. Comput. Vis. **74**(1), 59–73 (2007)
2. Szeliski, R., Shum, H.Y.: Creating full view panoramic image mosaics and environment maps. In: SIGGRAPH (1997)
3. Liu, F., Gleicher, M., Jin, H., Agarwala, A.: Content-preserving warps for 3D video stabilization. ACM Trans. Graph. (TOG) **28**(3), 44 (2009)
4. Zaragoza, J., Chin, T.J., Brown, M.S., Suter, D.: As-projective-as-possible image stitching with moving DLT. In: CVPR (2013)
5. Lin, C.C., Pankanti, S.U., Natesan Ramamurthy, K., Aravkin, A.Y.: Adaptive as-natural-as-possible image stitching. In: CVPR (2015)
6. Yan, W., Hou, C., Lei, J., Fang, Y., Gu, Z., Ling, N.: Stereoscopic image stitching based on a hybrid warping model. IEEE Trans. Circuits Syst. Video Technol. **27**(9), 1934–1946 (2017)
7. Gao, J., Kim, S.J., Brown, M.S.: Constructing image panoramas using dual-homography warping. In: CVPR (2011)
8. Chang, C.H., Sato, Y., Chuang, Y.Y.: Shape-preserving half-projective warps for image stitching. In: CVPR (2014)
9. Lin, K., Jiang, N., Liu, S., Cheong, L.F., Lu, M.D.J.: Direct photometric alignment by mesh deformation. In: CVPR (2017)
10. Zhang, F., Liu, F.: Parallax-tolerant image stitching. In: CVPR (2014)
11. Chen, Y.-S., Chuang, Y.-Y.: Natural image stitching with the global similarity prior. In: Leibe, B., Matas, J., Sebe, N., Welling, M. (eds.) ECCV 2016. LNCS, vol. 9909, pp. 186–201. Springer, Cham (2016). https://doi.org/10.1007/978-3-319-46454-1_12
12. Lin, K., Jiang, N., Cheong, L.-F., Do, M., Lu, J.: SEAGULL: seam-guided local alignment for parallax-tolerant image stitching. In: Leibe, B., Matas, J., Sebe, N., Welling, M. (eds.) ECCV 2016. LNCS, vol. 9907, pp. 370–385. Springer, Cham (2016). https://doi.org/10.1007/978-3-319-46487-9_23
13. Lipman, Y., Levin, D., Cohen-Or, D.: Green coordinates. ACM Trans. Graph. (TOG) **27**(3), 78 (2008)
14. Vercauteren, T., Pennec, X., Perchant, A., Ayache, N.: Diffeomorphic demons: efficient non-parametric image registration. NeuroImage **45**(1), S61–S72 (2009)
15. Lipman, Y., Levin, D.: Derivation and analysis of green coordinates. Comput. Methods Funct. Theory **10**(1), 167–188 (2010)
16. Li, J., Wang, Z., Lai, S., Zhai, Y., Zhang, M.: Parallax-tolerant image stitching based on robust elastic warping. IEEE Trans. Multimedia **20**, 1672–1687 (2017)
17. Thirion, J.P.: Image matching as a diffusion process: an analogy with Maxwell's demons. Med. Image Anal. **2**(3), 243–260 (1998)
18. Santos-Ribeiro, A., Nutt, D.J., McGonigle, J.: Inertial demons: a momentum-based diffeomorphic registration framework. In: Ourselin, S., Joskowicz, L., Sabuncu, M.R., Unal, G., Wells, W. (eds.) MICCAI 2016. LNCS, vol. 9902, pp. 37–45. Springer, Cham (2016). https://doi.org/10.1007/978-3-319-46726-9_5
19. Chambolle, A.: An algorithm for total variation minimization and applications. J. Math. Imaging Vis. **20**(1), 89–97 (2004)
20. Burt, P.J., Adelson, E.H.: A multiresolution spline with application to image mosaics. ACM Trans. Graph. (TOG) **2**(4), 217–236 (1983)
21. Li, N., Xu, Y., Wang, C.: Quasi-homography warps in image stitching. arXiv preprint arXiv:1701.08006 (2017)

Author Index

Printed in the United States
By Bookmasters